THE ARCHAEOLOGY OF CANTERBURY
NEW SERIES

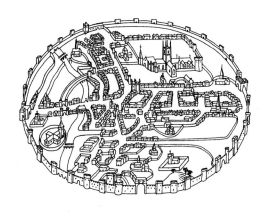

THE ARCHAEOLOGY OF CANTERBURY

New Series

VOLUME VI

BUCKLAND ANGLO-SAXON CEMETERY, DOVER EXCAVATIONS 1994

by

Keith Parfitt and Trevor Anderson[†]

with

John Andrews, Birte Brugmann, Cathy Haith, Ian Riddler and Penelope Walton Rogers

and

Nöel Adams, Barry Ager, Alex Bayliss, Nancy Beavan, Robin Bendrey, Hayley Bullock, Angela Care Evans,
Caroline Cartwright, Jean Cook[†], Barry Corke, Vera Evison, John Hines, Ian Hodgins, Karen Høilund Nielsen,
Axel Kerep, Janet Lang, Gerry McCormac, Susan La Niece, Heidi Leseur, Don Mackreth, Ailsa Mainman,
Sonja Marzinzik, Eric Nordgren, Christopher Scull, Fleur Shearman, Stephanie Spain, Ana Töpf,
Sarah Watkins-Kenney and Gareth Williams

Published by Canterbury Archaeological Trust Ltd
2012

Produced by Canterbury Archaeological Trust Ltd
Printed in Great Britain by Geerings Print Ltd, Ashford, Kent

ISBN 978-1-870545-23-5
British Library Cataloguing-in-Publication Data
A catalogue record for this book is available from the British Library

This publication was funded by English Heritage, the British Museum
and Canterbury Archaeological Trust Ltd

ENGLISH HERITAGE | The British Museum | CANTERBURY ARCHAEOLOGICAL TRUST LTD

The death of Trevor Anderson in June 2005 was a great sadness,
not only to those involved with the Buckland excavations and publication,
but to all who had worked with him in Canterbury over the years.
We hope this volume will stand as a fitting tribute
to his meticulous work both on and off
the Buckland site.

CONTENTS

PART 4: THE GRAVE GOODS

FOREWORD

Sometime in June 1994, I had a phone call from Keith Parfitt. He was directing what had been planned as a small excavation of a few Anglo-Saxon graves at Buckland, Dover, in advance of development by a housing association, Orbit Housing. The site lay just the other side of the railway tracks from the location of an important Anglo-Saxon cemetery excavated in the 1950s, the finds from which had subsequently been acquired by the British Museum. Despite the fierce gradient of the site, graves were turning up in unexpected numbers, densely crammed together on the steeply sloping hillside; and several of them were beginning to yield up contents which might perhaps be worth a look. Would I be interested in coming down to visit? I and other colleagues had been involved with Keith on other sites in Kent, and knew him to be an outstanding excavator with a nice line in laconic understatement. If Keith said that there was something which might be worth seeing, one didn't pass up the invitation. And so it was that on a bright summer's day, a small group of us from the British Museum's Departments of Medieval and Later Antiquities and of Conservation, stood marvelling in the site hut as box after box was opened to reveal some of the first astonishing finds from this excavation – iron weapons, glass vessels, gold pendants and garnet-inlaid brooches, some Kentish-made, others brought from southern Scandinavia and Merovingian Gaul.

The dramatic revelation of the scale and complexity of the burials and their contents made it clear that this project had to be a collaborative venture between several partners. Orbit Housing contributed the excavation funding and generously presented the finds to the British Museum, which in turn agreed to undertake the finds conservation and drawing programme and to provide specialist support in the field and in the post-excavation process. English Heritage contributed funding and support to the post-excavation research and analysis. The direction of the excavation, the coordination of the complex post-excavation project, and the preparation of the ensuing report were carried out by Keith Parfitt and his colleagues at the Canterbury Archaeological Trust. Along with the many specialists who have contributed to these pages, they deserve our thanks and congratulations; the substantial volume that is the result of this collaboration is a most significant achievement. These graves, together with the other part of the fifth- to seventh-century cemetery excavated earlier, represent one of the richest communities in the wealthy Anglo-Saxon kingdom of Kent, and contain a striking number of luxury goods of continental origin, indicative of Kent's close links with its North Sea and cross-Channel neighbours, and of Dover's strategic place in this kingdom and its networks. The publication does this complex story full justice, and will undoubtedly serve as a benchmark for future work on the early history of the Anglo-Saxon kingdom of Kent, and for Anglo-Saxon cemetery studies as a whole.

Leslie Webster
Former Keeper, Department of Prehistory and Europe, British Museum

LIST OF FIGURES

xv

LIST OF TABLES

ACKNOWLEDGEMENTS

Thanks are due to the very significant number of people who assisted with the project in a variety of ways. First and foremost, the contribution of the developer, Orbit Housing, who allowed access and funded the fieldwork must be recorded. Of particular importance to the project were John Ellaway, Orbit's Regional Manager, together with Nigel Hoad (project manager, Playle and Partners) and Keith Hampson (construction manager for Denne Builders). On site every assistance was given by Tony Foreman, as agent for Denne, and a keen interest in the work was taken by the developers throughout the project. The staff of Invicta Security Services maintained a constant presence every night in order to prevent illicit treasure hunting.

At the British Museum, Leslie Webster of the then Department of Medieval and Later Antiquities provided much encouragement and assistance, whilst Cathy Haith produced the preliminary finds catalogue. Dr John Williams, Head of Kent County Council's Heritage Conservation Group, gave significant support throughout the course of the project, as did Professor Vera Evison. In addition, the keen interest of staff from Dover Museum must be gratefully acknowledged here. The Museum is also thanked for allowing us to reproduce the late Michael Copus's imaginative reconstruction of Anglo-Saxon Buckland.

The enthusiasm and dedication of the excavation team has to be mentioned. Of the diggers, the hard work of Tim Allen, Ben Brodie, Alison Deegan, Lynne Harris, Andy Linklater, Dave Lish, Adrian Murphy, Andy Smith and Paul Wheelhouse must be recorded. The full-time team was assisted by a number of local volunteers, including members of the Dover Archaeological Group. Members of the newly formed White Cliffs Metal Detector Club spent many hours searching the site spoilheaps for metallic finds, with some useful results.

The substantial costs of the post-excavation analysis and conservation programme have been met jointly by the British Museum and English Heritage. At the British Museum, post-excavation work was initially championed by Leslie Webster and Cathy Haith, followed by Jonathan Williams and Sonja Marzinzik. At English Heritage, the late Sarah Jennings and Dave Fellows provided helpful guidance and monitored progress throughout the post-excavation and publication programmes.

The detailed work of members of Conservation and Scientific Research at the British Museum formed a key dimension to the study and the authors of the published reports would like to thank the following. At the British Museum, Trevor Springett (photographer); Ruth Goldstraw, Pippa Pearce, Janet Haynes, John Cooper, Heidi Leseur (conservators); Sophie Julien, Catherine Didelot, Ulrike Neuhauser, Eric Nordgren, Rosemarie Heulin (conservation students); Sue Bradley (then Head of Conservation Research) and Andrew Oddy (then Keeper of Conservation). On site thanks go to Mike Halliwell and Pan Garrard (Canterbury Archaeological Trust) and Nicholas Whitehead (Gooch & Wagstaff, Chartered Surveyors).

Ian Riddler co-ordinated the work of the numerous specialists involved. Birte Brugmann, Sonja Marzinzik and Axel Kerep studied the significance of the material from a continental perspective. Birte

Brugmann would like to thank Karen Høilund Nielsen for many useful discussions and helpful suggestions on archaeological matters, in particular weapon grave chronology, and the Scandinavian background of Anglo-Saxon material culture and demography. John Hines would like to thank Pernille Kruse (née Sørensen) and Charlotte Behr for their comments on the report on the bracteates.

Kate Morton and Claire Thorne at the British Museum illustrated all the grave objects and Kate prepared all the figures for publication working closely with Mark Duncan. At Canterbury, Barry Corke drew the overall site plans, individual grave plans and sections, and also prepared all the tables for publication. Will Foster prepared the bead images.

Paul Bennett and Peter Clark, Director and Assistant Director respectively of Canterbury Archaeological Trust, provided support, guidance and advice throughout.

The volume was copy edited and prepared for print by Jane Elder and Mark Duncan who would like to extend special thanks to Kate Morton for her invaluable assistance and patience in tying up the last loose ends during the final stages of the preparation of this monograph.

A personal note

Looking back over the eighteen years that have elapsed since this remarkable site was excavated, the number of richly furnished graves; the astonishing variety and wealth of the grave goods; the implications for our knowledge of Anglo-Saxon Dover and East Kent; the excitement of fieldworkers and visiting specialists, marked this excavation as one of the high points in the career of any archaeologist or in the history of an archaeological organization. We were making history in 1994, and it was a privilege to have been present.

Notwithstanding the time it has taken to bring this volume to press, the excitement generated by the period of discovery has not diminished, nor has its importance for our knowledge of the Golden Age of Anglo-Saxon Kent. In acknowledgement of this Orbit Housing Association generously gifted all finds to the Nation and a partnership was formed between the British Museum, English Heritage and Canterbury Archaeological Trust to bring the discovery to a high level of publication.

We have provided in this introductory section some details of the protracted period of archive, conservation, study and report generation, and of the many hands that have formed this volume. I acknowledge and thank all who have participated in a marathon endeavour, some sadly no longer with us to celebrate the publication.

But I write this to pay tribute to the work of my friend and colleague, Keith Parfitt, excavation Director and principal author, who has worked tirelessly to bring his and others' work on Buckland 1994 to publication. This is one of many achievements for a fellow former Dover Grammar School boy, but in these pages you will find the record of a landmark excavation and publication that will be a standard work of reference for many years to come.

Paul Bennett
January 2012

PREFACE

A combination of factors has caused a significant delay in the final publication of the 1994 excavations conducted on the Anglo-Saxon cemetery at Buckland. The draft report text was returned from English Heritage, after peer review, in July 2007 but ever growing pressure of work and the exhaustion of funds then caused the project to stall. The tragically early death in June 2005 of Trevor Anderson, one of the principal authors, had already come as a major blow to all the report production team and his colleagues further afield.

Continuing fieldwork commitments for various members of the Canterbury Archaeological Trust team unavoidably pushed the post-excavation work onto the back burner for several years. At the British Museum, the successive retirements of Anglo-Saxon specialists, Angela Care Evans and Leslie Webster, further contributed to a loss of momentum. A temporary lull in the pace of work towards the end of 2010, however, allowed the publication project to be restarted with additional funding provided by English Heritage and the British Museum, and a determination to bring the report to fruition before an embarrassing time-lag became completely unacceptable.

In the seventeen years that have elapsed since the excavations were completed, a number of specialists have made reference to the discoveries at the 1994 Buckland site, there being a general policy to provide details ahead of the main publication whenever requested. It has not been possible, however, to fully integrate into the present text, references to every one of these independent studies. Nor have time and resources been available to incorporate information contained in the many more general works recently published, which may have some bearing on the results from Buckland and their interpretation. Clearly, Anglo-Saxon studies are continuing to progress steadily on all fronts. Selective updating of the original draft reports has been undertaken where possible but the basis of much of the text published here remains that as completed by 2006.

Since the conclusion of the 1994 excavations (and in the absence of any clear directive to the contrary) there has been a tendency for scholars to refer to the excavated cemetery areas as 'Buckland I' and 'Buckland II'. From the outset of the work in 1994, the excavation team were keen to emphasise the point that the new graves then being revealed represented a continuation of the cemetery dug further up-slope by Vera Evison in 1951–3, rather than it forming a separate, lower burial ground. For this reason the designation as 'Buckland I' and 'Buckland II' has always very specifically been avoided, with a continuous grave numbering system being employed for the burials on Long Hill, so as to prevent duplication and confusion between excavated graves in the two areas. The designation of parish and Roman numeral for individual Anglo-Saxon burial sites is a well established convention. In Audrey Meaney's (1964) gazetteer of Anglo-Saxon cemeteries, Evison's discoveries on Long Hill, Buckland are entered as Dover II. In Andrew Richardson's (2005) expanded listing the site is similarly recorded, with the 1994 discoveries being entered as subsequent work on the same site. The present writer would therefore much prefer to see the use of 'Buckland I' and 'Buckland II' discontinued; the grave number alone (1951–3, Graves B–F, 1–165; 1994, Graves 201–444) should adequately signify when and in which part of the site a specific grave was located. Where clarity is required in the present report, the separate excavations have generally been referred to as Buckland 1951–3 or Buckland 1994.

Keith Parfitt,
Dover
July 2011

The 1994 excavations in progress.

PART 1: INTRODUCTION AND ARCHAEOLOGICAL BACKGROUND

Keith Parfitt

Background to the 1994 excavations

The beginning of 1994 saw proposals advanced for the construction of a new housing estate at Buckland, near Dover in east Kent. The site (named 'Castle View' by the developer) lay across the lower slopes of Long Hill, a broad chalk spur situated on the north-eastern side of the Dour valley, 1.75km inland from Dover town centre (NGR TR 3087 4291). A short distance above the site, beyond the cutting for the Dover–Deal railway line, excavations by Miss (now Professor) Vera Evison had, in the 1950s, revealed an important early Anglo-Saxon cemetery (Evison 1987; Fig 1.3). In view of this previous discovery, the Heritage Conservation Group of Kent County Council requested that evaluation trenching be carried out across the Castle View site in order to ascertain if any outlying graves associated with the known cemetery were present. The work was undertaken by South-Eastern Archaeological Services in a one-day operation during March 1994.

Eleven machine-cut trenches were dug and these somewhat unexpectedly located a dozen graves. The report concluded that 'It is impossible to accurately predict the number of burials ... it is feasible that in excess of fifty [graves] are present' (Place 1994, 9). Since the entire site was due to be deeply terraced and heavily disturbed during the course of the new building works, a major excavation became necessary in order to locate, record and respectfully remove any further graves. Canterbury Archaeological Trust was engaged by the developer, Orbit Housing Association, to carry out this excavation in June 1994, working to a detailed specification prepared by Kent County Council (Howard

1994). The excavation was completed as scheduled in mid September of the same year after more than 100 days of continuous fieldwork (Parfitt 1994; Parfitt 1995a; Parfitt and Haith 1996).

The original costings for the excavation had assumed a total of no more than fifty graves and allowed for a team of six, including a conservator and an osteo-archaeologist, working on site for a period of up to eight weeks, at a total cost of £30,500. Within a few days of starting, however, it became abundantly clear that the number of graves present was far in excess of fifty. The final total was almost 250, including several graves containing more than one body. The project costs and timetable were rapidly revised to allow for a team of twelve, working on site for fifteen weeks, at an overall cost of £77,000.

The substantial increase in excavation costs exhausted Orbit's available funds for archaeological work and it became obvious to the field staff that further sources of funding would not be forthcoming within the short timeframe available for the excavation. It was only possible to successfully complete the project on time with the help of volunteers and by Trust staff working unpaid in their own time. The British Museum kindly offered help and sent Cathy Haith, an Anglo-Saxon specialist, to assist with the project. Subsequently, it was agreed that the developer would donate the entire artefact and skeletal assemblage to the British Museum to join the 1950s material.

The cemetery site proved to be considerably more extensive and complex than the initial evaluation work had suggested. As a result, both the time and funds available to undertake the investigations were severely stretched. The highly important results obtained, however, fully justify all the effort that was put into the project and have major implications both for our understanding of that part of the cemetery previously excavated in the 1950s (Fig 1.3) and for Anglo-Saxon studies in general. The British Museum and English Heritage have jointly funded the post-excavation analysis of the 1994 excavations and its finds; details are set out in the following chapters.

Anglo-Saxon settlement and cemeteries around Dover

A detailed survey of the known early Anglo-Saxon remains around Dover was undertaken by Evison as part of the first Buckland report (Evison 1987, 168–78) and this identified several other cemetery sites in the area. A number of significant new discoveries may now be added, which help refine our understanding of the local situation (Fig 1.1).

The Roman background

The narrow gap created in the North Downs at Dover, where the valley of the River Dour meets the sea, represents the only significant break in almost 20km of unscaleable chalk cliffs, facing the continent of Europe. A Roman port (*Portus Dubris*) was established at the river mouth probably at the start of the second century AD (Philp 1989, 272–4). This was strategically situated at the narrowest part of the English Channel and provided the shortest sea-crossing to Gaul and the rest of the Roman Empire. The crucial port installations here were guarded by two successive forts (Philp 1981; 1989). The earliest of these was a naval fort occupied between *c* AD 120 and 210 by the *Classis Britannica* (Philp 1981, 91–7). A small town grew up outside its walls but the limitations imposed by the local topography meant that this never grew to any size (Philp 1989, figs 2 and 3).

The later fort was larger than its predecessor and mostly occupied a new site, closer to the waterfront. It was established *c* AD 275 (Philp 1989, 283; Wilkinson 1994, 70–2) and saw extensive archaeological excavation during the 1970s and 1980s. With its thick walls, solid projecting bastions and deep enclosing ditch, this fort has been generally recognised as representing one of the Roman forts of the 'Saxon Shore', as listed in the early fifth-century official register, the *Notitia Dignitatum* (Philp 1981, 11). The *Notitia* records that stationed here, under the overall command of the *Comitis Litoris Saxonici per Britanniam* (the 'Count of the Saxon Shore of Britain') was the *Milites Tungrecani*. This is a little known auxiliary unit, perhaps 500 men strong, originally raised in the Tongres area of *Germania Secunda* (modern Belgium). Quite probably, the unit had been first brought to Britain by Count Theodosius in about AD 369, during the restoration of the province after the Barbarian Conspiracy of AD 367 (Johnson 1976, 68; Hassall 1977, 8; Pearson 2002, 148). If so, it must have replaced an earlier, unrecorded, unit that originally garrisoned the Shore fort at Dover.

Evidence for Roman settlement in the countryside around Dover is quite widespread. There are traces of a series of native settlements and their associated cemeteries in the surrounding area (Philp 1989, fig 2; Parfitt 2002, 394) and no doubt the port and town served as a market and administrative centre for the district. The bulk of the locally known Romano-British settlements and cemeteries date to between the first and third centuries AD. Several appear to have been established before *Portus Dubris* itself and some certainly have pre-Conquest origins (Philp 1981, 11; Parfitt 2002). A light scatter of 'Belgic' and early Roman pottery and tile recovered from the 1994 excavations suggests that there was some activity on Long Hill (*see* pp 173–6) and this is reinforced by the discovery of a small, early Roman pit during the 1951–3 excavations, further up-slope (Evison 1987, 15). Whether the Roman crossbow brooch found in the general fill of Grave 264 (*see* p 173) was originally lost on this hillside or subsequently brought in is less clear.

There is comparatively little definite evidence for fourth-century occupation in the region and the Roman Shore fort at Dover seems to have then been the main centre of activity in this part of south-east Kent. The fort itself was apparently occupied into the earlier fifth century, but exactly for how long remains unclear (*see* pp 367–8).

The early Anglo-Saxon period

Since Evison's study (1987, 168–78) the important evidence for Anglo-Saxon occupation within the former Roman Shore fort at Dover has been published in some detail (Philp 2003). The earliest recognisable Anglo-Saxon finds from inside the fort probably date to the late fifth century, most notably a Class A1.2 button brooch (Willson 1987; Suzuki 2008, 44, 357), but such finds presently appear to be few in number and most of the structural and occupation evidence dates to the sixth century or later (Philp 2003, 123–4). Five sunken-featured buildings (SFB) have been recorded, together with the remains of three surface-built structures that could represent halls. Another large, multi-phased timber building has been interpreted as the historically documented monastic church of St Martin, with a recorded foundation date in the seventh century. Philp (2003, 124) suggests that a number of the seventh-century (and later) buildings excavated might have

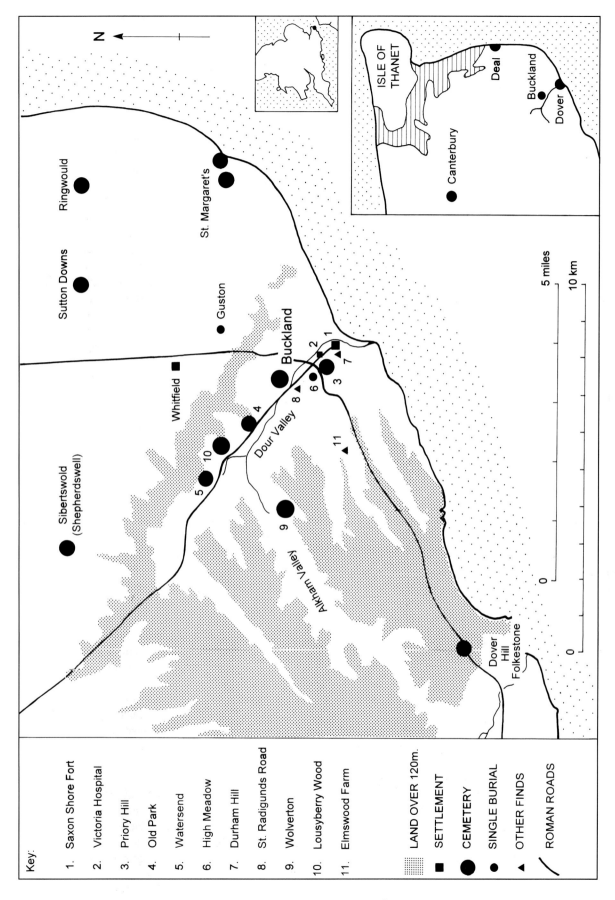

Key:

1. Saxon Shore Fort
2. Victoria Hospital
3. Priory Hill
4. Old Park
5. Watersend
6. High Meadow
7. Durham Hill
8. St. Radigunds Road
9. Wolverton
10. Lousyberry Wood
11. Elmswood Farm

LAND OVER 120m.
■ SETTLEMENT
● CEMETERY
● SINGLE BURIAL
▲ OTHER FINDS
ROMAN ROADS

Ringwould
Sutton Downs
St. Margaret's
Guston
Buckland
Whitfield
Dour Valley
Sibertswold
(Shepherdswell)
Alkham Valley
Dover
Hill
Folkestone

5 miles
10 km

ISLE OF THANET
Canterbury
Deal
Buckland
Dover

Fig 1.1. Map of the Dour valley area showing topography, Roman roads, Anglo-Saxon sites and finds, with inset location maps.

3

been associated with this monastery, which raises the question of the extent to which Anglo-Saxon settlement and the port at Dover (*Dofras*) developed under monastic influence.

A number of other significant discoveries have been made in the surrounding district. Work during 1993–4 at the former Royal Victoria Hospital site in the valley bottom some 500m to the north-west of the Shore fort (Fig 1.1), produced a quantity of pottery of fifth- to seventh-century date (Parfitt 1995b). This material appears to have been dumped as domestic rubbish on low-lying ground adjacent to the River Dour and implies the presence of an Anglo-Saxon occupation site in the immediate area. Overlooking the site, adjacent Priory Hill has long been known to be occupied by a sixth- to seventh-century cemetery (Batcheller 1828, 235; Payne 1889, 205; Rigold and Webster 1970; Richardson 2005, ii, 27). Building work there during the 1980s revealed five new graves (Willson 1988). It now seems likely that both the domestic rubbish at the hospital site and the burials at the hilltop cemetery are associated with a settlement that lay some distance inland of the one established within the defences of the old Roman fort (Fig 1.1; Philp 2003).

On the chalk downlands above Dover, excavations on a new by-pass at Church Whitfield in 1995 revealed the remains of an Anglo-Saxon farmstead or hamlet (Fig 1.1). Lying close to the Dover–Richborough Roman road, some 250m to the south-east of the probably eighth-century parish church, the settlement as excavated comprised two timber-framed hall-houses and four sunken-featured buildings in use during the late sixth and seventh centuries. Other buildings may have existed beyond the excavation limits (Parfitt *et al* 1997; Parfitt forthcoming).

To the west of Dover, modern research on an eighteenth-century find of silver coins made somewhere at Hougham (Boys 1792, 870) has shown that this comprised an eighth-century hoard of *sceattas* contained within a pottery vessel (Blunt 1979). The hoard may have been buried close to a settlement but more probably it was hidden in an isolated spot, well away from any habitation site (see also finds from Elmswood Farm at Hougham, below).

Other new Anglo-Saxon grave finds have been made in addition to those on Priory Hill. Further burials have been discovered at the Old Park cemetery site (Meaney 1964, 117; Evison 1987, 176; KARU 1989; Cross and Parfitt 1999; Richardson 2005, ii, 81–2), the precise location of which can now be firmly placed on the valley-side immediately to the north-east of *Woodside* mansion, about 1.7km north-west of the Buckland cemetery (Fig 1.1; Parfitt and Dickinson 2007). Research indicates that the Anglo-Saxon *tumuli* recorded by Hasted at River (Hasted 1800, 438) were situated here, rather than in Lousyberry Wood above Temple Ewell as previously

suggested by the Ordnance Survey (Phillips 1964). However, a number of Anglo-Saxon graves have recently been discovered at Lousyberry Wood itself, implying another cemetery site there (Richardson 2005, ii, 77–8; Parfitt and Dickinson 2007). Yet another burial ground, with a very similar valley-side position, appears to have been discovered near Waters End, north-west of Temple Ewell in 1843 (Fig 1.1). According to early accounts, there were at least twenty closely spaced graves on this site (Parfitt 1998; Richardson 2005, ii, 78). In the adjoining Alkham Valley, excavations on a spur overlooking Wolverton (Fig 1.1) have revealed a further sixth- to seventh-century cemetery site, focussed on a Bronze Age barrow (Philp 2007; Burrows 2009). Metal-detector finds, including a button brooch, part of a radiate-headed brooch and a sword pommel, found near Elmswood Farm at Hougham, in the Elms Vale valley west of Dover could represent a hillside burial site in another of the Dour's tributary valleys (Richardson 2005, ii, 29; Fig 1.1).

Taken with the new finds from Buckland, the local evidence combines to show that the area around the Dour valley was quite intensively occupied during the early Anglo-Saxon period (Fig 1.1). Significant topographical factors probably influencing the development of this coastal region might include: the close proximity of the Continent; the fertile soils of the local downlands; the sheltered valley and fresh running water provided by the River Dour; and the remains of a major Roman harbour at the mouth of the river, with an adjacent strongly walled fort from which roads led into the Kentish hinterland (Fig 1.1). The influence of, and relationship between, any surviving indigenous Romano-British population (see above) and Anglo-Saxon settlers coming into this region, however, remains rather less clear and is further considered in Part 9 (pp 381–3).

Discoveries on Long Hill

The slopes of Long Hill at Buckland have now seen two major campaigns of archaeological excavation which have revealed parts of an extensive Anglo-Saxon cemetery together with evidence for an earlier Bronze Age round barrow, and also portions of probable Iron Age and medieval field systems (Figs 1.2, 1.3, 2.1). These, and earlier discoveries, may be usefully summarised.

The Dover to Deal railway line

From the overall plan of the Buckland cemetery which has now been compiled (Fig 1.3) it seems certain, even allowing for areas of unused ground between individual burial areas,

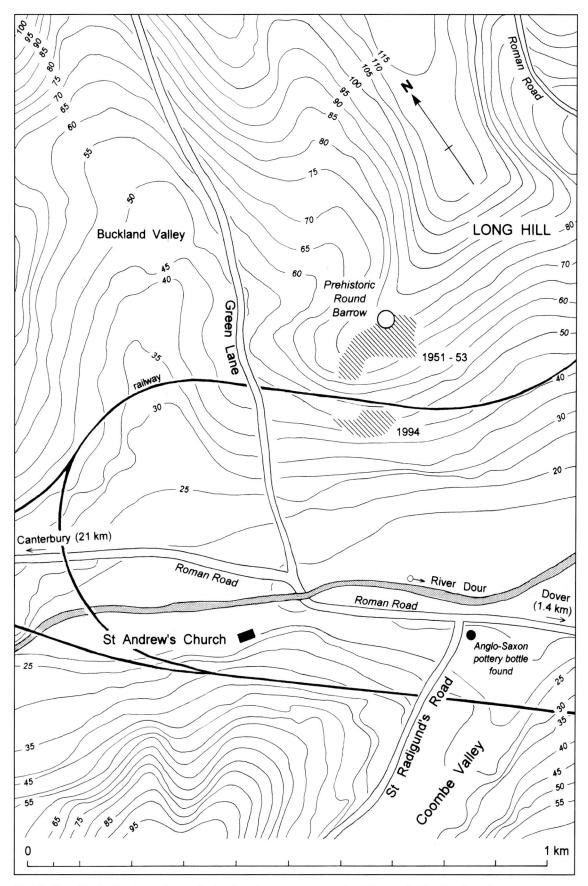

Fig 1.2. Map of the Buckland area, showing the location of excavated cemetery in relation to relief, the River Dour, Roman roads, railways and the medieval parish church (contours in metres).

that Anglo-Saxon graves must have been encountered, probably in some numbers, during the construction of the Dover to Deal railway line in the nineteenth century. The 1950s excavations located several graves that had been rifled in relatively recent times and their excavator believed that this might have happened during the period of the railway construction, as navvies searched for buried treasure in the area immediately beyond the line of the railway (Evison 1987, 15, pl 2a). If this was so, it pre-supposes that the workmen had already found some evidence of the cemetery and presumably had recovered valuable objects during the excavation of the Long Hill cutting itself. Built as a 13km long branch off the London, Chatham and Dover railway between May 1878 and June 1881, there is no definite record within the contemporary archaeological literature of any discoveries on the line at Long Hill, but there are two poorly recorded finds, both made in 1879, that could have been recovered from the workings in this area.

The *Dover Express* for July 4th 1879 records:

A curious discovery is represented to have been made in a cutting of the Dover and Deal Railway. While some men were excavating in No 10 cutting they came across the perfect skeleton of a man buried in what was evidently an antique grave, with a sword, which is in fair preservation, and has the appearance of belonging to the Roman period by his side.

The same account is repeated by Chapman (1921, 124) without stating the source or adding any further details. Given the relative scarcity of Iron Age and Roman warrior burials in southern Britain, it seems much more likely that the remains reported were those of an Anglo-Saxon. There appears to have been no direct archaeological involvement with the find, however, and nothing seems to have been preserved. It has not been possible to ascertain the location of 'No 10 cutting', but apart from those situated at either end of the nearby Guston Tunnel, that through Long Hill represents the only significant cutting on the Deal line. Moreover, the appearance of the report in a Dover newspaper might imply that the find was made at the Dover rather than the Deal end of the new line.

In October 1879, the British Museum purchased from Edward Murden, a Dover jeweller, an ornate Anglo-Saxon composite disc brooch. This had apparently come from a grave and there were a number of beads and other objects with it that may have come from the same burial, but the exact provenance was not recorded (Rigold and Webster 1970, 13–7). Evison (1987, 46) has suggested that these finds came from the Buckland cemetery and certainly the

date of the purchase corresponds with the time of the railway construction. Previously, Rigold and Webster (1970, 10) had inferred that the items more probably came from a grave disturbed by building work on the site of the Priory Hill cemetery (Fig 1.1; see above). Either location remains a possibility but, given the discovery date, the present writer would agree with Evison that Buckland seems the more likely site.

Excavations in 1951–3

Situated across a slight shoulder projecting from the middle slopes of Long Hill, lies the Hobart Crescent/Napier Road housing estate (Figs 1.1–1.3). It was during the early stages of construction work for this estate in 1951 that workmen first discovered human remains and artefacts. An initial site investigation by local archaeologist W P D Stebbing succeeded in locating a rich Anglo-Saxon sword burial (Grave C; Evison 1967; Evison 1987, 11). Subsequently, more extensive excavations were conducted under very difficult conditions by a small team led by Miss Evison on behalf of the Inspectorate of Ancient Monuments. These excavations were completed in 1953. The work revealed the presence of a major early Anglo-Saxon cemetery (Evison 1987) containing at least 171 graves dating to the period *c* AD 475–750 (Evison 1987, text fig 2; Fig 1.3). A large prehistoric ring-ditch was also discovered and from this it seems clear that the area had also once been occupied by a substantial round barrow, presumably of Bronze Age date (Grinsell 1992, Dover 5).

Analysis of the grave goods recovered from the 1951–3 excavations took more than thirty years and eventually resulted in the publication of a detailed report in 1987, as English Heritage Archaeological Report No 3 (Evison 1987). The report represented a major contribution to both Kentish and national Anglo-Saxon studies and clearly provides the basis from which the present account must begin. The general conclusions of that previous report have now to be reconsidered in the light of the more extensive recent discoveries. The reader will thus need to use the present report in close conjunction with that concerning the earlier excavations.

The 1987 report included a detailed description of all the grave good types recovered, together with an in depth consideration of the phasing and layout of the cemetery. A total of fourteen individual burial plots (Plots A–N) was identified and the individuals buried within these were grouped into seven chronological phases (Phases 1–7), according to the dating of the associated grave goods and positioning within the cemetery. Graves assigned to Phase 1 (AD 475–525) occurred at the western end of the excavated

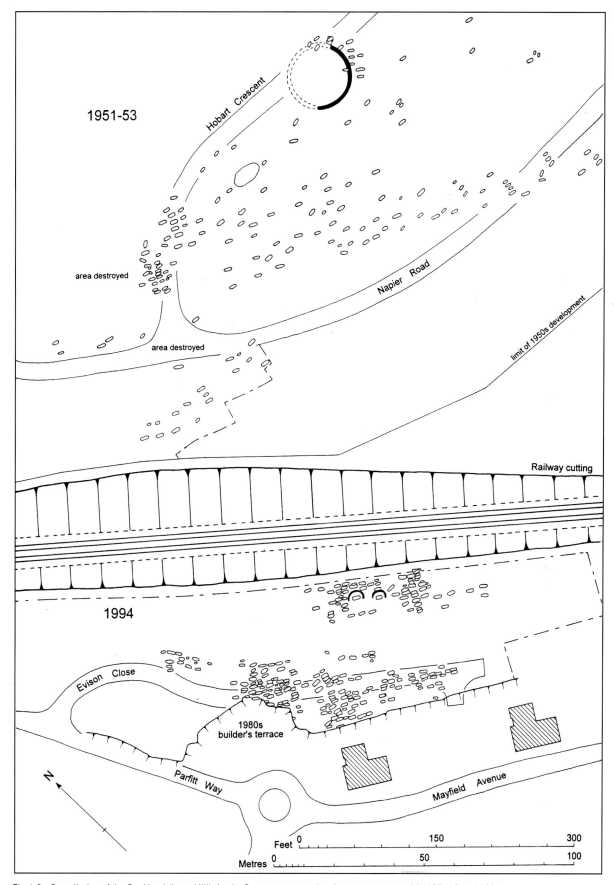

Fig 1.3. Overall plan of the Buckland (Long Hill) Anglo-Saxon cemetery showing areas excavated in 1951–3 and 1994.

area (Evison 1987, fig 101; Fig 9.2), whilst those of Phase 7 (AD 700–750) lay more towards the east (Evison 1987, fig 107). A general, easterly drift along the hillside through time was thus apparent (Evison 1987, figs 101–7).

Excavations in 1994

The Castle View site lay on the steep chalk slope which forms the lower part of Long Hill (Figs 1.2, 1.3, 2.1, 2.5–7). On the Tithe Map of 1842 this land is shown as forming part of *Shatterlock* field (Evison 1987, 145; text fig 28); prior to the excavations it had been allotment gardens for many years.

Machine stripping of the covering soil across 1.3 hectares led to the identification and excavation of 244 individual graves cut into the chalk bedrock (frontispiece). These occupied the south-eastern half of the site and lay between the 42 and 54m contours (Fig 2.1). In addition, the steep hillside (generally with a slope of about 1 in 4 to 1 in 5) was also found to be occupied by a series of cultivation terraces (Fig 2.1a), infilled with substantial deposits of colluvium that contained large quantities of prehistoric lithic material and some pottery of prehistoric and medieval date (see below).

The 1994 excavations were carried out under the overall direction of Keith Parfitt assisted by Barry Corke, Trevor Anderson, Michael Halliwell (conservator) and Cathy Haith (British Museum).

In response to very considerable local interest in the project, it was possible through the good offices of the developers to open the Castle View site for public inspection over the 1994 August Bank Holiday weekend. About 1600 visitors were given guided tours of the excavation (Fig 2.8) and were able to view a small selection of the objects recovered from the graves.

The excavated site has now been fully developed as a housing estate which is served by new roads named Evison Close and Parfitt Way (Fig 1.3).

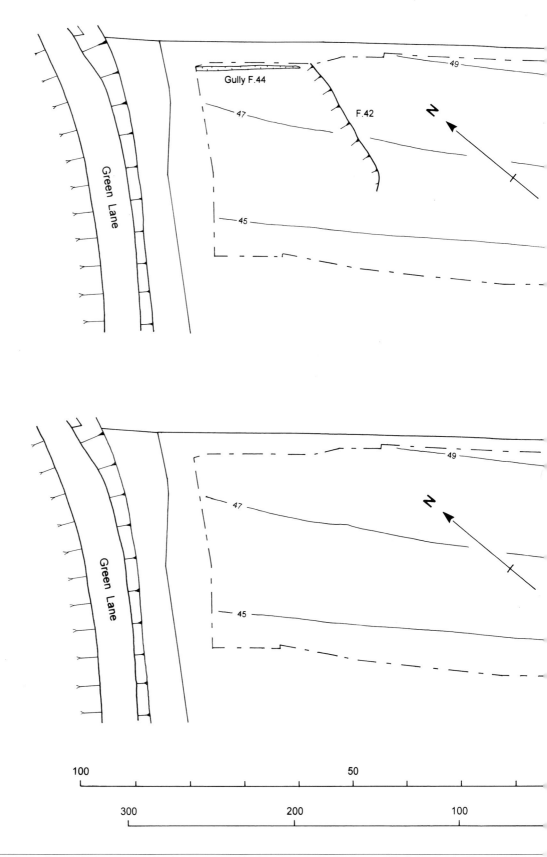

Fig 2.1a (top). Plan of 1994 excavations showing contours, cultivation terraces and other features. Fig 2.1b (above). Plan of 1994 excav

Overleaf: Fig 2.2. General site plan of the 1994 cemetery excavation.

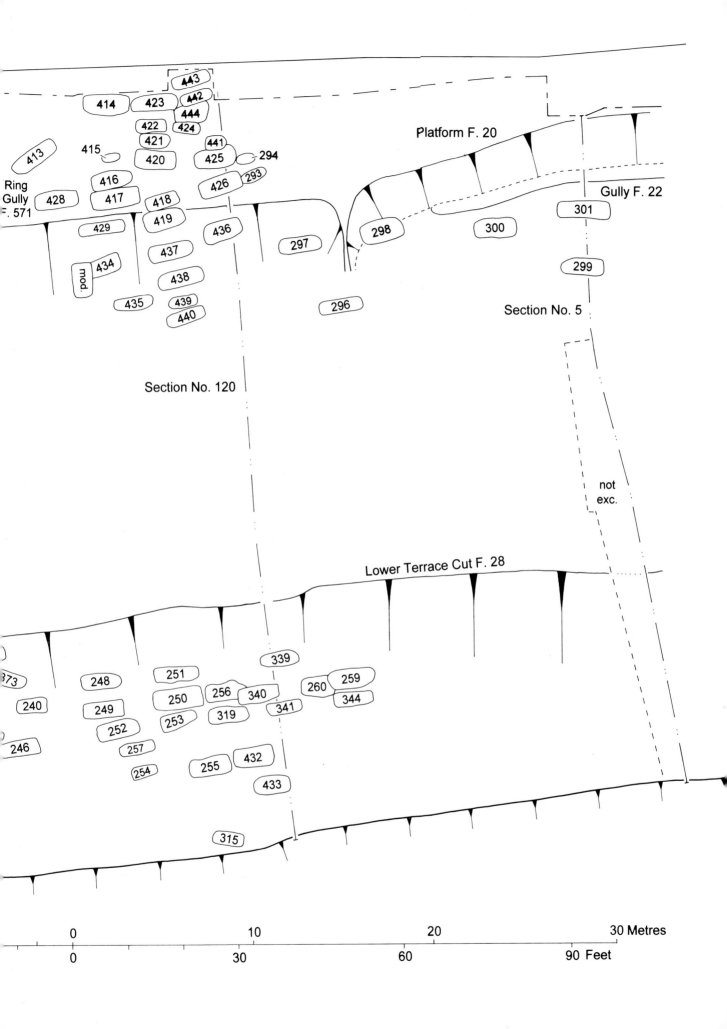

Platform F. 20

Gully F. 22

Ring
Gully
F. 571

443
414   423   442
              444
       422   424
       421
413 415   420   441
              425   294
       416   426   293
428   417   418
       429   419   436
              437   297   298   300   301
434   mod.   299
       435   438   296   Section No. 5
              439
              440

Section No. 120   not
                                   exc.

Lower Terrace Cut F. 28

373   339
       248   251   260   259
240   249   250   256   340   344
       252   253   319   341
246   257   255   432
       254   433
              315

0   10   20   30 Metres
0   30   60   90 Feet

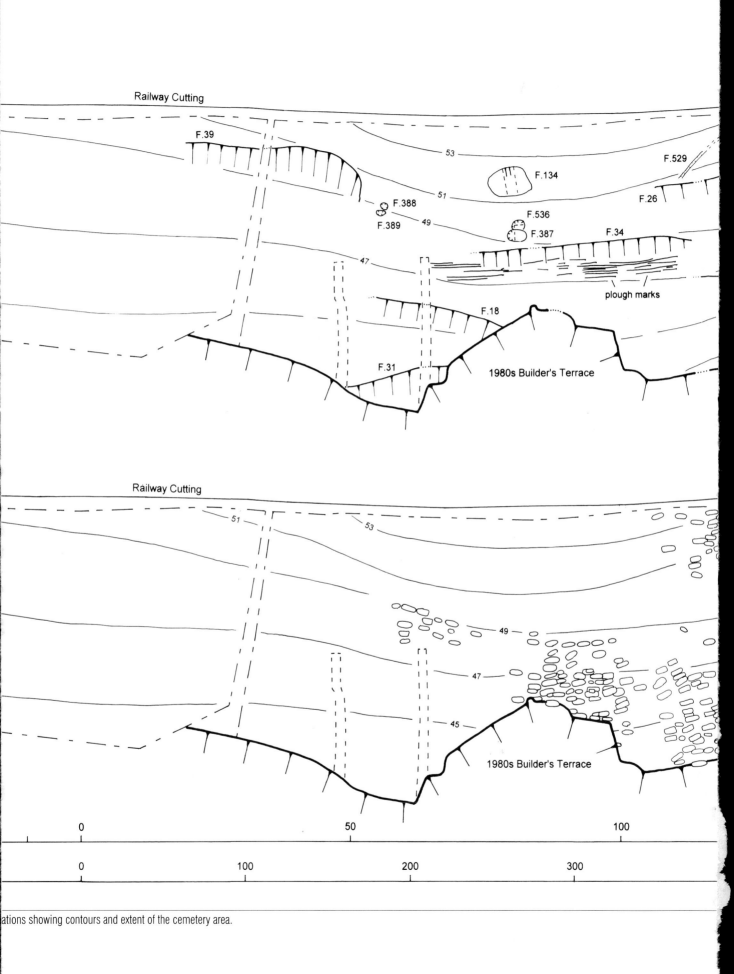

Railway Cutting

F.39

53

F.529

F.134

51

F.26

F.388

F.389

49

F.536

F.387

F.34

47

plough marks

F.18

F.31

1980s Builder's Terrace

Railway Cutting

51

53

49

47

45

1980s Builder's Terrace

0   50   100

0   100   200   300

...ations showing contours and extent of the cemetery area.

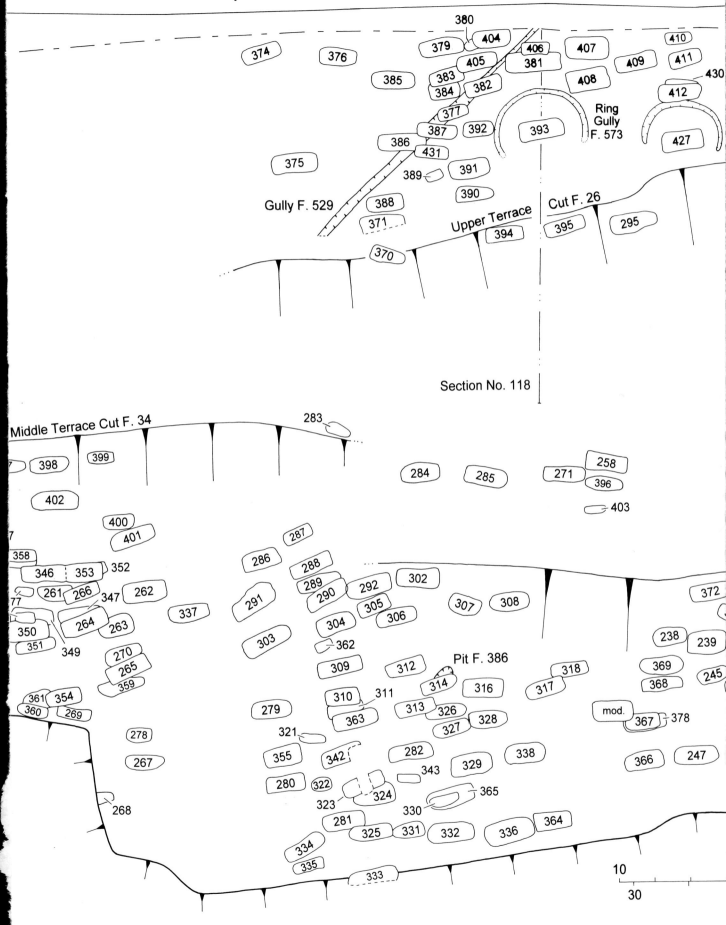

Railway Embankment

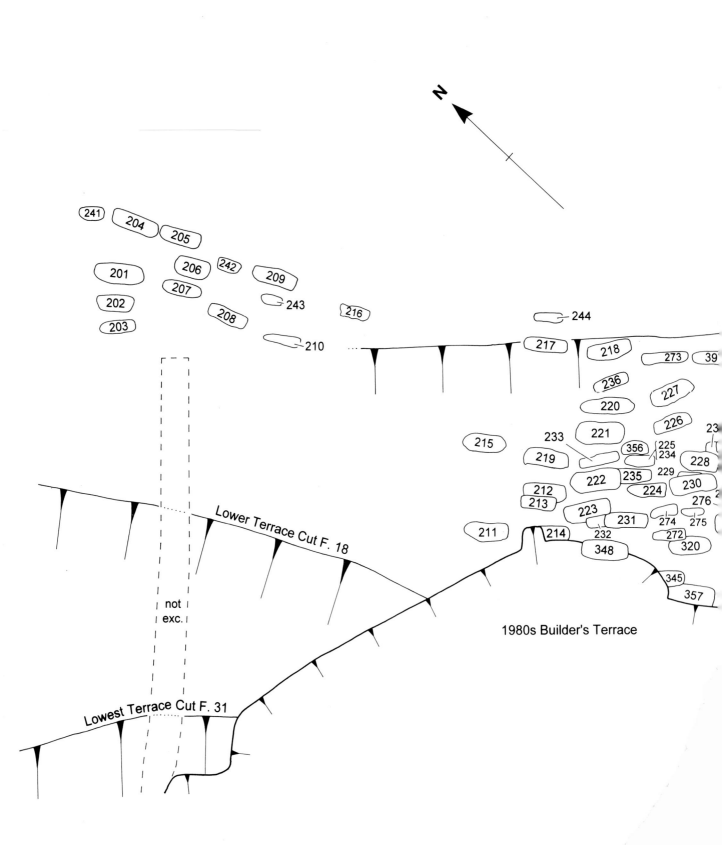

fence line

limit of excavation

N

241   204   205

201   206   242   209
207
202   243
208
203   216   244
210   217   218   273   39
236   227
220
226
215   233   221   23
219   356   225
234   228
212   222   235   229   230
213   224
223   276
211   214   231   274   275
232   272   320
348

Lower Terrace Cut F. 18

not
exc.

345
357

1980s Builder's Terrace

Lowest Terrace Cut F. 31

PART 2: THE 1994 EXCAVATIONS

Keith Parfitt

The 1994 excavations covered an area measuring some 290m (north-west–south-east) by 45m (north-east–south-west) (Figs 2.1 and 2.2). The site was bounded by Green Lane on the north-west side, the broad, deep cutting of the Dover to Deal railway line on the north-east side, Mayfield Gardens to the south-east, with Mayfield Avenue and Maresfield Road to the south-west (Figs 1.2 and 1.3). Running along the side of the adjoining Buckland valley, Green Lane most probably represents an ancient trackway leading up from the bottom of the Dour valley onto the high ground around Whitfield and may once have provided access to the Anglo-Saxon cemetery (Fig 1.2).

Features other than Anglo-Saxon graves

A significant number of archaeological features unrelated to the Anglo-Saxon cemetery were discovered on the site. These provide evidence for prehistoric, Roman and medieval activity on this hillside and serve to demonstrate that the cemetery formed only one part of a more extensive ancient landscape.

The terraces

A series of artificial terraces cut into the hillside was revealed (Fig 2.1a). These terraces were of different dates: the most recent represented shallow builder's trackways and construction terraces cut in the 1980s during adjacent housing development. A deeper terrace, also dug at that time, formed the lower boundary of the Castle View site and this must have destroyed a number of Anglo-Saxon graves without record (Figs 1.3, 2.1 and 2.2; *see* pp 370–1).

Nine other terraces were earlier and certainly of archaeological interest (F18, F20, F26, F28, F31, F34, F39,

F42 and F591). All but one occurred on the steeper slopes of the south-eastern part of the site where the Anglo-Saxon cemetery was also located (Figs 2.1 and 2.2). They were all aligned roughly north-west by south-east, following the contours and clearly constituted the negative elements of field lynchets produced through centuries of ploughing (see Taylor 1975, 28 and 90, for an account of lynchet formation). None was visible on the surface before excavation work started, being infilled by colluvial soils (Fig 2.3) that very probably represented material derived from associated positive lynchets, subsequently slumped and spread. At the extreme north-west end of the site a shallow, isolated terrace (F42) ran roughly north–south, almost parallel with the adjacent Green Lane. Its different axis, still following the contours of the hillside, reflects the changing configuration of the spur as it curves around into the Buckland valley (Fig 2.1b).

Due to their extent and the large amounts of soil which they contained, there was insufficient time to investigate the terrace fillings in any detail and the bulk of the deposits unfortunately had to be stripped away by machine without any detailed examination. A series of reference baulks were, however, preserved and these subsequently provided the opportunity to hand-dig sample areas. This operation produced useful dating evidence which suggested that the cultivation terraces belonged to at least two separate periods; none appeared to be directly related to the Anglo-Saxon burials (Figs 2.1–2.3). The principal terraces are described in chronological order below.

The upper terrace, F26

Lying between the 50 and 51m contours this terrace was quite extensive and seemed to be one of the earliest (Figs 2.1 and 2.2). It was traced for a total distance of about 46m and cut up to 0.50m deep into the hillside. At its south-eastern end it stopped just short of another, slightly deeper, terrace or platform of rather different character (F20, see below). At the north-western end it merged into the natural slope. As surviving, the cut terrace floor was between 6 and 11m in width. On the floor at the south-east end was a shallow, irregular pit (Fig 2.1; F168) which produced a few prehistoric struck flints. This could perhaps represent the truncated remains of a root-hole. A series of Anglo-Saxon graves was also recorded in this area (Fig 2.2).

The terrace was filled by a succession of light brown loam deposits (contexts 27, 407, 408 and 409; Fig 2.3, Sections 118 and 120) containing frequent chalk and flint lumps and very occasional carbon specks. This material must represent soil eroded from further up-slope. A hand-dug sample produced very large quantities of fresh prehistoric flintwork, some calcined flints (pot-boilers) and about seventy potsherds, mostly of early Iron Age date, *c* 550–350 BC, with perhaps a few earlier pieces, including two sherds of possible Beaker. In addition, several late Iron Age sherds, comprising a number of local 'Belgic' grog-tempered wares and a small fragment from an imported Gallo-Belgic butt-beaker, all datable to the period *c* 50 BC to AD 75, came from the uppermost filling.

The ?hut platform, F20

This feature lay immediately beyond the south-eastern end of the upper terrace (F26) and occupied a relatively small area. Quite well defined on three sides, it was distinguished by the presence of a shallow gully at the foot of the rearward slope (F22; Fig 2.1a). A narrow spur of undisturbed chalk separated the platform from the upper terrace (F26, see above), implying that the terrace had been formed sometime after the present feature (Fig 2.1–2.2).

Cut to a maximum depth of 0.75m into the hillside, the floor of the platform sloped gently down to the south-west (Fig 2.3, Section 5). It covered an area subrectangular in shape and measured about 25m (north-west–south-east) by 7.50m (north-east–south-west). Apart from the gully (F22) and four outlying Anglo-Saxon graves, seemingly dug in from a higher level (see below), no other features were noted here.

The flat-bottomed gully (F22) at the foot of the rear slope was presumably for drainage. It varied between 0.65 and 0.85m in width and was 0.05 to 0.20m deep (Fig 2.3, Section 5). The chalk and silt filling (context 23) was carefully excavated by hand and produced a significant quantity of prehistoric lithic material, including many small, fresh flakes. These sometimes occurred in localised clusters suggesting

that knapping had been taking place immediately adjacent. There were also some calcined flints, together with two flint-tempered Iron Age potsherds, broadly datable to the period *c* 600–300 BC and two chalk spindle-whorls (one incomplete).

Another gully (F12), immediately beyond the eastern edge of the platform, further served to delimit the area (Fig 2.1a). Gully F12 ran north-east by south-west and was traced for a total distance of 9m. It appeared to be associated with a series of other gullies located immediately to the south-east (see below). The filling produced a quantity of fresh prehistoric struck flints.

The main cut for the platform itself, was infilled with deposits of cream-brown silty loam (Fig 2.3, Section 5, context 19/21), again seemingly representing down-washed material derived from further up-slope. These deposits produced a significant quantity of prehistoric flintwork and eight more sherds of early Iron Age pottery.

The precise purpose of this feature remains unclear. The fairly small size, moderately well-defined edges and the presence of a gully at the foot of its rearward slope strongly suggests that, unlike the other terraces examined, this platform had been deliberately dug into the hillside, rather than being the product of gradual erosion through ploughing. Although no evidence for post-holes was found, the notion that a building originally stood on the platform remains attractive. The limited dating evidence could suggest that it was constructed during the early Iron Age, if not before. The position of the rear gully and its elongated form, however, shows that this did not form a drip gully surrounding a circular hut, as might have been anticipated; nevertheless, the structure as a whole is very reminiscent of a prehistoric hut platform.

The lowest terrace, F31

This terrace was located along the south-western edge of the site between the 43 and 44m contours (Figs 2.1 and 2.2). A substantial section had already been destroyed by building contractors in the 1980s. As surviving, the terrace was visible for a distance of some 20m. It cut 0.60m into the chalk slope and was filled by two layers of brown loam (context 32, over 33). In a small hand-dug sample, the upper deposit (32) produced moderate amounts of sharp prehistoric flintwork and twenty-six sherds of flint-tempered pottery, once again datable to the early Iron Age period. The lower filling (33) produced a few more struck flints. No Anglo-Saxon graves occurred in the area. The available dating evidence could suggest that this terrace is prehistoric and more or less contemporary with the upper terrace, F26.

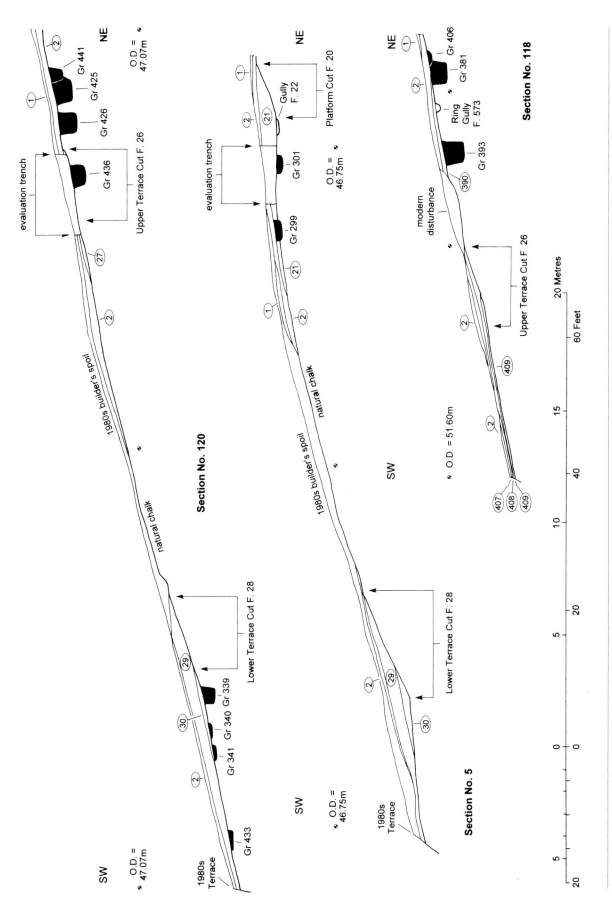

NE

Gr 441

Gr 425

Gr 426

Gr 436

Upper Terrace Cut F. 26

evaluation trench

27

2

1

2

O.D. =
47.07m

Section No. 120

1980s builder's spoil

natural chalk

SW

O.D. =
47.07m

1980s
Terrace

Gr 433

2

Gr 341

Gr 340 Gr 339

30

29

Lower Terrace Cut F. 28

NE

1

Gully
F. 22

Platform Cut F. 20

21

2

Gr 301

Gr 299

21

1

2

O.D. =
46.75m

evaluation trench

Section No. 5

1980s builder's spoil

natural chalk

SW

O.D. =
46.75m

1980s
Terrace

2

29

30

Lower Terrace Cut F. 28

NE

1

Gr 406

Gr 381

Ring
Gully
F. 573

Gr 393

390

2

Section No. 118

modern
disturbance

Upper Terrace Cut F. 26

409

2

O.D. = 51.60m

407
408
409

2

20 Metres

60 Feet

15

40

10

5

20

0

0

5

20

Fig 2.3. Long sections of terraces, 1994 excavation.

11

The lower terrace, F28

Positioned immediately below and roughly parallel to the upper terrace (F26), this was initially assumed to be of a similar date. Running at a slight angle between the 44 and 47m contours, it was traced for a total distance of about 90m across the site and continued beyond the south-eastern limit of the excavated area (Figs 2.1 and 2.2). At the north-western end it merged into the natural hill-slope. Cut up to 0.90m into the chalk slope, the filling comprised two deposits of light cream-brown silty loam (Fig 2.3, Sections 5 and 120, context 29, over 30). A hand-dug sample of these soils produced nineteen sherds of medieval pottery, ranging in date from *c* AD 1175 to 1450, together with a few pieces of post-medieval pottery and several peg-tile fragments. Prehistoric struck flints were comparatively scarce and there was no Iron Age pottery. A substantial number of Anglo-Saxon graves occurred in the area (Figs 2.1b and 2.2; Plots T, V and W).

The middle terrace, F34

This extended from a point roughly mid way between the ends of the upper and lower terraces north-westwards for almost 39m, between the 48 and 49m contours (Figs 2.1 and 2.2). It was up to 0.30m deep and was distinguished by the presence of a series of more than twenty V-shaped grooves cut into its base (Fig 2.1a). Running along the axis of the terrace between 0.30 and 0.50m apart, there can be no doubt that these score-marks were produced by a metal-tipped plough. They could be seen to cut through the tops of seven Anglo-Saxon graves, indicating that this ploughing had occurred sometime after the cemetery had been given up.

The terrace was filled with light brown loam which produced seven sherds of medieval pottery ranging in date from *c* AD 1075 to 1275, together with an iron horseshoe fragment and a few prehistoric struck flints.

Dating and discussion of the terraces

Precise dating of the terraces discovered is difficult and must be based largely upon their relationship to the Anglo-Saxon graves and the date of the material recovered from the colluvial soils infilling them (Fig 2.3). Unfortunately, the relationship of the graves to the terraces was rarely certain on site and the finds recovered from the terrace fills must be treated with caution as they are clearly all derived.

Due to its essentially homogeneous nature, changes in soil colour and texture were virtually impossible to discern and attempts to ascertain the relationship of the Anglo-Saxon grave cuts to the colluvial deposits generally proved

inconclusive. Yet the relationship of the terraces to the Anglo-Saxon graves must, theoretically, provide important evidence for their dating. There are three possibilities: the Anglo-Saxon graves were cut directly into the open terraces and then sealed by the colluvium; they were cut into the colluvium sometime after its deposition within the terraces; the terraces were cut across the graves and became infilled during post-Saxon times. The available evidence suggests that the various terraces are probably of different dates and have different relationships with the graves.

The area of the upper terrace was occupied by fifteen Anglo-Saxon graves, mostly cut into the chalk to only a very shallow depth. The bulk of the graves here cut the steep slope of the terrace side, rather than its more convenient, level floor. Importantly, in several of the graves it was observed that the undisturbed burial deposit (particularly the skull and pelvis) actually projected above the general level of the chalk. This must preclude a later date for the formation of the terrace as the burial deposit would certainly have been damaged or destroyed by any passing plough. It also seems highly unlikely that the Anglo-Saxon graves would have been dug to such a shallow depth on an open terrace that the body was hardly covered. The most likely option is, therefore, that these Anglo-Saxon graves had been cut through colluvial deposits already infilling an earlier terrace. An early date for the terrace filling is also implied by the significant quantities of prehistoric material recovered (see above).

It would thus appear that the upper terrace was partially infilled and perhaps only just visible in Anglo-Saxon times. That some remnant of this terrace still remained, however, is suggested by the presence of two graves (Graves 393 and 427) enclosed by ring-gullies (Fig 2.2; see below). These burials were fairly certainly once marked by small barrows and it is probably significant that they are situated immediately above the top of the terrace, in what would have been a quite prominent position (when viewed from down-slope) all the time some vestige of the terracing remained (*see* p 371; Fig 2.4). Overall then, the available evidence, though limited, suggests that the upper terrace was both created and partially infilled during the prehistoric period and that it was subsequently cut into by the Anglo-Saxon graves, when it was still visible as a slight earthwork.

The lower terrace, F28, appears to be different. Many of the Anglo-Saxon graves located here were also very shallow, but none of the skeletons appeared to project above the surviving level of the chalk surface (Fig 2.3). Again, it may be reasonably assumed that the burials had not originally been laid in extremely shallow grave-pits cut directly into the open terrace side or base. The significant quantity of medieval finds from the terrace filling, together with a corresponding absence

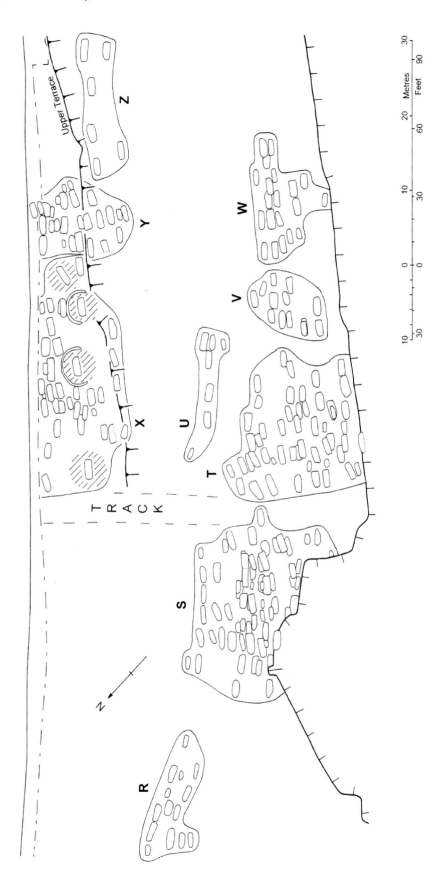

Fig 2.4.　Plan showing hypothetical layout of the 1994 cemetery area, with position of burial plots, prehistoric upper terrace, probable barrows and possible trackway.

of prehistoric material, strongly suggests that this terrace was both formed and subsequently infilled during post-Saxon times. If this is correct, it must follow that the original chalk surface, together with many of the Anglo-Saxon graves, has been truncated by later ploughing (Fig 2.3, Sections 5 and 120). An unknown number of other graves in this area could thus have been destroyed without trace.

Medieval pottery from the filling of the middle terrace (F34) together with the presence of plough grooves scored by metal-tipped implements cutting through the tops of several graves, more positively indicates a post-cemetery date for this terrace.

Apart from the slight terrace at the extreme south-east end of the site (F591), which is quite possibly contemporary with the prehistoric ones, the limited dating evidence from the remaining terraces (F18, F39, F42 and F591; Figs 2.1 and 2.2) suggests that these are all of post-cemetery date, although a prehistoric origin for some is still possible.

Considering the evidence overall, it seems probable that the prehistoric terraces identified represent negative lynchets that actually formed part of a more extensive system of what might be traditionally termed 'Celtic fields', once occupying the south-west facing slopes of Long Hill (*see* pp 369–70). The occurrence of prehistoric flintwork, broadly datable to the Neolithic to Bronze Age (see below), together with pottery of early Iron Age, late Iron Age and early Roman date seems to suggest that cultivation of the hillside occurred over many centuries, although it had probably ceased by late Roman times. Based upon this evidence, it may be suggested that the Anglo-Saxon cemetery was established in this area specifically to take advantage of the slightly more level pieces of ground that an abandoned field system had left on this steep hillside.

Sometime during the medieval period, after the early Anglo-Saxon cemetery had been given up, the land once again came back under the plough. New lynchets were formed on the slope and significant damage and reworking of the earlier field system probably occurred. Post-cemetery ploughing must account for the disappearance of small barrow mounds over graves situated above the upper terrace (see below) and was also probably responsible for the destruction of an unknown number of flat graves too. This is particularly likely to be the case in the central part of the cemetery area (Fig 2.2), where soils forming the positive lynchet associated with the prehistoric upper terrace would have built up. Any subsequent graves wholly cut into this accumulated material above the chalk will have been completely removed as the profile of the hillside was reconfigured.

Metal-detector searches of the site spoilheaps produced a number of Anglo-Saxon objects most probably derived from

such damaged and destroyed graves. These included buckles (Sf nos 305, 409, 923 and 1236), an iron spear ferrule (Sf 1264) and a spiral finger ring (Sf 1235). There is no record of any material of this date ever being found during the course of working the preceding allotments and none of the excavated graves showed any evidence of recent disturbance.

Other features

Several other features unrelated to the Anglo-Saxon cemetery were recorded. A number were situated at the extreme south-east end of the excavated area, beyond ?hut platform (F20). Here a series of parallel gullies (F6, F8, F10, F12, F14 and F16) may well have defined small, rectilinear cultivation plots (Fig 2.1a). On the evidence of their shallow, irregular form and 120 pieces of fresh struck flint recovered from their filling, these are quite probably of prehistoric date. None produced any pottery. Gully F10 appeared to represent a partial recutting of F8, suggesting that the complex was in use for some time.

Elsewhere, an east–west gully (F529) running diagonally across the slope had been cut through by a number of Anglo-Saxon graves above the upper terrace (Fig 2.1a; Plot X). This gully was traced for a minimum distance of 16.45m, although its relationship to the terrace had been destroyed by a modern disturbance. The gully was between 0.14 and 0.65m wide and was 0.20–0.25m deep, with sloping sides and a rounded base. Its brown loam filling produced a few pieces of flintwork, again suggesting a prehistoric date. Another gully at the extreme north-west end of the site (Fig 2.1a; F44) produced a late medieval potsherd dated *c* AD 1425–1525, but the feature itself could be even later and associated with construction of the railway because it runs across the contours, parallel with the railway boundary fence.

A large chalk-filled pit (Fig 2.1a, F134) in the centre of the excavated area was recent but dating evidence from the small number of the other features located is generally inconclusive. Most contained at least a few prehistoric flints and many probably belong to this period. Several shallow, irregular pits (eg Fig 2.1a, F24 and F168) could be interpreted as tree-root holes, created when the hillside was first cleared of vegetation prior to cultivation. A medieval sherd recovered from pit F388 suggests that it is connected with post-Saxon agricultural activity on the site. Evison previously recorded an early Roman pit on the upper part of the cemetery site (Evison 1987, 15).

Almost 3,000 pieces of prehistoric struck flint were recovered from the 1994 excavations. The bulk of this material was contained within the colluvial deposits infilling the terraces (Fig 2.3) and in later features and graves cut through these deposits. A very substantial amount of flintwork was removed from the site during the initial site clearance work but several useful control sample groups were excavated and much material was salvaged from the spoilheaps. The flintwork is not reported in detail here but the bulk of the assemblage appears to belong to a single industry, broadly datable to the late Neolithic to Bronze Age period. Other local scatters of similar later prehistoric lithic material have been recorded on the Dour valley slopes at Lousyberry Wood, Temple Ewell; Old Park Hill, Whitfield and Coombe Hole, Guston (Canterbury Archaeological Trust and Dover Archaeological Group archives; Cross and Parfitt 1999). Taken with the evidence from Long Hill, extensive prehistoric activity along the north-eastern side of the Dour valley thus seems to be implied.

The Anglo-Saxon cemetery

As revealed in the 1994 excavations, Anglo-Saxon graves covered an area measuring some 45m (north-east–south-west) by 110m (north-west–south-east). Their limits on the south-east and north-west sides were fairly certainly located but to the south-west, the downhill margin of the burial area had clearly been destroyed during building work in the 1980s (see above; Fig 2.1b). Along the north-eastern side, graves appeared to be continuing beyond the railway boundary fence onto the narrow strip of undisturbed ground which survives immediately above the deep railway cutting.

Recording techniques, 1994

Each grave was numbered in sequence, from 201 to 444, so as not to duplicate numbers already allocated to graves excavated in the 1950s (Graves B–F, 1–165). Graves 166 to 200 remain unallocated.

The main plan of the cemetery was drawn at a scale of 1:50, grave axes being carefully logged and checked. A one-tenth scale plan and section of each grave and its contents was prepared, with individual grave goods being plotted and given an identifying code-letter (retained in this report). Where required, full-size (1:1) plans of specific groups of items, such as bead clusters, were drawn. The filling of each grave was normally given two context numbers (prefixed by the site code DBC-94), one for its general filling and one for the actual burial deposit. This primary context number is quoted in the grave catalogue (pp 385–453). Every burial was photographed and further details were noted on standardised recording sheets, which included a full list of the associated grave objects. The human bones were recorded *in situ* and lifted by Trevor Anderson.

All the grave goods and human remains from the excavation, together with the field records and post-excavation analysis archive, have been deposited at the British Museum which also houses the 1950s archive. The 1994 field records comprise: 264 measured plans; 235 measured sections; 652 recorded contexts and seventy rolls of photographic film. Some of the more interesting finds from both the 1951–3 and 1994 excavations are currently exhibited in displays at the British Museum and Dover Museum.

The great majority of the graves excavated in 1994 date to between the late fifth and early seventh centuries and most belong to the sixth century. In order to allow cross referencing with the earlier report, Professor Evison's phasing for the 1951–3 part of the cemetery has been broadly retained in the present study, although some slight modifications have been necessary. Of the seven chronological phases originally identified at Buckland (Evison 1987, Phases 1–7), only the first three are represented in any numbers on the 1994 site. Some refinement of the date range of these early phases has been possible in the light of new finds and Evison's Phase 4 now falls into our revised Phase 3. Only three of the 1994 graves may be placed within Evison's phases 5 to 7. A detailed consideration of the chronology of the entire cemetery appears in Part 8 and Table 8.5 (pp 352–5) includes revised phasing for graves excavated in 1951–3.

Cemetery organisation and layout

The distribution of the 244 graves recorded in 1994 was uneven and various discrete geographical groupings could be discerned (Fig 2.4; Table 2.1). The middle slopes of the cemetery area were found to be largely devoid of burials, but it seems possible that their absence here is at least partially due to subsequent plough erosion (see above), rather than to any significant break within the original layout of the cemetery.

Following Evison (1987, fig 98), the various grave groupings identified in 1994 have been arranged to suggest nine individual burial plots. These were lettered R to Z, again to follow labelling initiated in the 1950s when Plots A to N were identified. Plots O, P and Q remain unallocated and available for use in any future excavation. Plots R to Z contained burials of men, women and children (Figs 7.1–7.3), mostly laid out on south-east–north-west axes (*see* p 23). Males equipped with weapons occurred in all plots except R and U (Fig 4.1). The number of burials present within each plot varied (Table 2.1). The largest was Plot S, which contained at least sixty-eight burials; the smallest was Plot Z with just six. It seems possible that in reality the three smallest plots identified actually represent detached portions

Fig 2.5. General view looking south-east across burial Plots X, Y and Z, towards Dover Castle and the English Channel.

Plot	No of graves	Grave goods absent	Sword graves	Barrow graves	Double-stacked graves	Child graves (0–12 years)
R	14	8	-	-	-	3
S	68	28	3	-	3	16
T	51	21	-	-	2	10
U	7	5	-	-	-	2
V	13	3	-	-	1	-
W	20	3	1	-	1	2
X	38	9	1	?4	4	11
Y	27	1	2	-	-	9
Z	6	-	-	?6	-	-
Total	244	78	7	?10	11	53

Table 2.1. Details of grave numbers and types within burial plots.

of adjacent larger plots. Thus Plot U could be part of Plot T, Plot V could be a sub-division of W and Z may be linked with Plot Y (see below and p 378).

The dating evidence (Part 8) shows that the graves within the various plots belong to several chronological phases and each plot seems to have been used over a significant period of time, with no indication that the use of any one plot was confined to one specific phase (see Parts 8 and 9). Burials containing typologically early grave goods occurred in most plots (Fig 9.2). In no case, however, did these early burials lie close to the centre of their respective plots in such a way as to suggest that they might represent founder's graves (see below and pp 377–8 for further discussion; Fig 9.2).

Plot R, with a small group of fourteen poorly furnished graves somewhat isolated from the main cemetery area, marked the north-western limit of the burials (Figs 2.2 and

Fig 2.6. General view across Plot X, looking south-east.

2.4). To the south-east, Plots S, T, V and W formed closely adjacent groups occupying the lower part of the site (Figs 2.2 and 2.4). On the middle slopes, a little uphill of the Plot T burials, was Plot U, a small group of seven mostly unfurnished graves.

Plot S comprised a substantial cluster of nearly seventy densely packed graves (Fig 2.7). Many of these were loosely arranged in rough rows. An unknown number of other graves along the south-western margin of this group must have been destroyed by earlier building work (see above; Fig 2.2). The surviving burials included several rich males and females, with no less than three adjacent sword graves (Graves 264, 265 and 346).

A short distance to the south-east of Plot S was another group of around fifty graves, again roughly set out in rows but not quite so densely packed (Plot T). This plot also included several fairly rich male and female burials but there were no sword graves. The narrow division between Plots S and T was quite well marked with only warrior burial Grave 337 occurring in the gap. This could perhaps suggest that there was originally some sort of path or trackway dividing these

plots (Fig 2.4). Immediately to the south-east of Plot T lay two further small groups of graves. These totalled about thirty and constitute Plots V and W. The graves here included several rich male and female burials, notably a man with a sword in a triple-stacked grave in Plot W (Grave 249; *see* pp 26–7) and, nearby, a rich woman buried with beads, a gold bracteate, weaving batten and three glass vessels (Grave 250; Fig 3.15).

On the upper part of the 1994 site lay three more adjacent groups of graves (Plots X, Y and Z; Figs 2.2, 2.4, 2.5 and 2.6). The burials located within Plots X and Y totalled more than sixty and were quite densely packed, with the north-western group (Plot X) seemingly clustered around two ditched graves that were presumably once covered by small barrow mounds. The spacing suggests that two other small barrow graves might also have originally been present here (see below; Fig 2.4). There were again a number of rich male and female burials and graves containing children were slightly more common here, but whether this is of particular significance remains unclear (see Parts 7 and 9). It seems certain that Plots X and Y must continue beyond the railway boundary fence, up to the edge of the cutting.

Fig 2.7. General view looking south across burial Plot S into the Dour valley.

A possible barrow grave (Grave 375) marked the north-western edge of Plot X (p 24) and contained a male with a sword, assigned to Phase 3b. Close by was the grave of an unequipped male (Grave 385) whose unusual physical features (*see* p 290) and burial rite (see pp 24–5) combine to suggest that his ethnic origins might lie far away from east Kent. As marked by the graves, the north-western boundary of Plot X corresponded closely with that of Plot T further down slope, perhaps providing additional evidence for the existence of a trackway running across the burial area, past the end of the prehistoric upper terrace (F26) and roughly parallel with Green Lane (Fig 2.4; see above). There were apparently no barrow graves in Plot Y and most of the burials here were contained within three closely spaced rows. Two sword graves were present (Graves 414 and 437).

The three latest graves encountered in the 1994 excavations (Graves 376, 391A and 413) were all contained within Plot X. These burials belong to the seventh to eighth century (Phases 5–7) and seem to be significantly later than the other burials on the site. As such, they are contemporary with a larger number of graves located on the upper part of

the cemetery excavated during the 1950s (Evison 1987, figs 105–7). Grave 413 stands out as being on a rather different axis in comparison to its neighbours and may have been aligned on barrow burial Grave 427 (see below). The higher of the two burials discovered in double Grave 391 (Sk A) appeared to have been inserted into a timber-lined grave sometime after the original burial (Sk B) was interred (*see* p 28). Grave 376 lay near the edge of the plot and may have been originally positioned at the foot of a barrow mound covering Grave 375 (see above).

A scatter of six widely spaced graves occurred to the south-east of Plot Y and these marked the south-eastern limit of the burial area; they have been designated as Plot Z (Fig 2.4). They comprised four certain or possible males, buried with weapons (Graves 297 and 299–301), together with two possible females (Graves 296 and 298). The wide spacing of the graves here might suggest that these burials also were originally covered by small barrow mounds (*see* p 371). At the Buckland 1951–3 excavations, further uphill, a change from rows to more widely spaced graves occurred at the end of Phase 3 (Evison 1987, figs

Fig 2.8. Public open-day on site, August 1994.

101–7) but at nearby Mill Hill, Deal, it was earlier, broadly contemporary with Buckland Phase 2. In the present plot, Grave 300 falls within Phase 1b–2a, and Graves 296 and 297 within Phase 2; the others cannot be closely dated. The change at Mill Hill mostly involved males with weapons (Parfitt and Brugmann 1997, 122, figs 7 and 8), so it seems possible that the layout of Plot Z mirrors that of Plot A at Mill Hill more closely than Buckland 1951–3 (*see* p 383 for further discussion).

Barrow burial

Two graves (393 and 427), situated near the centre of the densely occupied Plot X immediately above the prehistoric upper terrace (F26), were partially enclosed by shallow, semi-circular ring-gullies (Figs 2.2 and 2.6; F571 and F573). These features may be readily interpreted as the remains of ditches that originally encircled small round barrows that have subsequently been destroyed, presumably by ploughing. Such structures can be paralleled at a number of other Anglo-Saxon cemeteries in east Kent and beyond

(Parfitt and Brugmann 1997, 121f). Perhaps significantly, both gullies enclosed graves containing double-stacked burials (see below). Grave 427 contained a 20–25 year old of uncertain sex, apparently placed within a coffin (Sk B), overlain by a female assignable to Phase 1b–2 (Sk A). The two male skeletons in Grave 393 could not be dated from the associated grave goods but it seems quite likely that they are contemporary with Grave 427, the two barrow mounds being raised at the same time.

Open on the south-western side, the ring-gully enclosing Grave 393 (F573) was 4.55m in diameter (Fig 3.11). The gully itself was about 0.30m wide and 0.15–0.25m deep, with steep-sloping sides and a rounded base (Fig 2.3, Section 118). Its brown loam filling contained a quantity of prehistoric struck flints and two Roman potsherds.

Also open on the south-western side, the gully enclosing Grave 427 (F571) was slightly smaller, with an internal diameter of 3.95m (Fig 3.12). The gully was about 0.40m wide and 0.15–0.20m deep, with steep-sloping sides and a rounded base. It was again filled with brown loam, which produced a single prehistoric struck flint. On the north-eastern side, the filling of the gully had been cut by a later Anglo-Saxon burial (Grave 412), assigned to Phase 2b–3a.

Beyond these ditched burials, two other graves on the margins of Plot X might also originally have been covered by mounds, for which no ring-gullies survived (Fig 2.4). Immediately to the east of Grave 427 lay Grave 413, containing a moderately well-equipped female aged 22–27 and broadly dated to Phases 5–7. This late east–west grave makes use of a clear area that separated the earlier burials of Plots X and Y, where there was space to erect a small barrow. Similarly, on the north-western edge of Plot X, Grave 375, that of a high status male aged 25–30 buried with a sword and dated to Phase 3b, lay apart from the other graves in such a way as would have allowed it to have been covered by a mound serving to mark the limit of the burial area. On the

eastern side several burials appeared to be arranged around it, including Grave 376 dated to Phase 5–7.

The inferred barrows of Plot X stand in a line along the top of the prehistoric upper terrace and it seems likely that they were deliberately placed here to take advantage, in terms of visibility, of the still-surviving crest that would have been created by the existence of the cultivation terrace earthworks (*see* p 12).

The comparatively wide spacing of the graves within Plot Z would have allowed them to have been covered originally by small mounds (see above and pp 371–2). A few widely spaced graves on the lower slopes of the 1994 excavated area could also once have been covered by small barrows but no clear evidence survived in any instance.

PART 3: DESCRIPTION OF
THE ANGLO-SAXON GRAVES

Keith Parfitt

with Birte Brugmann, Trevor Anderson†, Ian Riddler, Hayley Bullock and Fleur Shearman

The excavations in 1994 revealed a total of 244 inhumation graves. Fifteen of these contained the remains of more than one individual and at least 260 bodies must have originally been present. Typically, for cemetery sites in east Kent, no cremations were discovered. Bone preservation was variable and although a number of moderately complete skeletons was recovered, a substantial group of graves contained only very poorly preserved remains. No bone at all had survived in twenty-seven of the graves. Just over two-thirds of the burials were provided with grave goods, and this included seven high status male graves each with a sword.

The osteological and archaeological data on sex and gender have been compared and this generally shows a reasonably close correlation between these independent sources. The combined evidence allows the identification of eighty-six buried individuals as certainly or probably male and ninety-eight as certainly or probably female. A further seventy-six burials cannot be sexed; just over half of these are probably children, although in the absence of both bones and grave goods this assumption has sometimes been based solely upon the short length of the grave.

Grave form

In plan, most graves were either rectangular or subrectangular with rounded corners; some had rounded ends and others were distinctly ovoid in outline (Fig 10.93). They ranged in overall length from 0.85m (Grave 362) to 3.00m (Grave 381) and in width from 0.41m (Grave 415) to 1.25m (Grave 239). The smallest generally seem to have contained children, while the largest could have originally held a body within a coffin (Fig 3.1). The three graves containing contemporary

double burials interred side by side (see below) all fall well within the range of single grave widths. The range of sizes for graves recorded across the entire cemetery, including the 1951–3 area, is closely comparable. As most graves in the 1994 area date to a phase earlier than the majority of those previously excavated higher up the hill (see Part 8), it would seem that there was no significant variation in excavated grave sizes over time.

Most graves had been quite neatly cut, although a number were more irregular. Variations in the quality of the digging did not seem to be specifically connected with individual plots or phases and any irregularity with particular graves is more probably due to shattered, poor quality chalk bedrock at that particular spot. A number of the graves appear to have been originally dug into the deep colluvial deposits infilling the earlier cultivation terraces, with their bases just touching the surface of the underlying chalk (*see* p 12).

The sides of the individual graves were generally steep or vertical but very occasionally they were slightly under-cut in places. Others had more sloping sides. Bases were normally flat or dished, although a number were quite uneven and poorly finished. The bottoms of several graves sloped down to the south-west, reflecting the natural fall of the ground.

As surviving, the individual grave cuts into the chalk were often very shallow and it seems certain that many had been truncated by later activity on the hillside (see above). Concentrations of deeper graves occurred in Plots X and Y, above the upper terrace (F26), and at the western end of the lower terrace (F28), where erosion seems to have been less severe. In the majority of graves the maximum depth measurement was obtained along the north-eastern, uphill, side due to the fall of the ground. Recorded depths ranged from just 0.05m to 1.10m. Most graves survived between

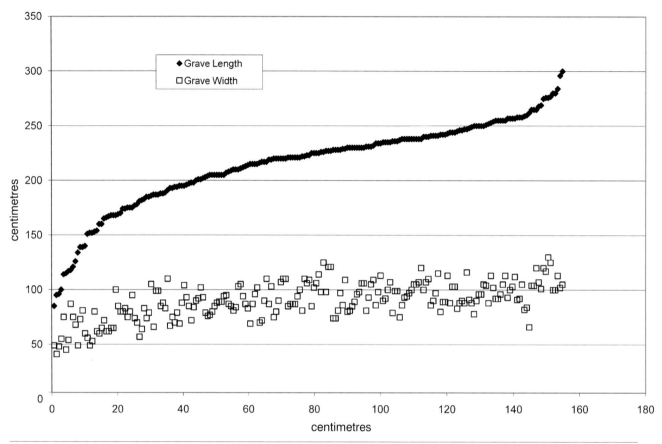

Fig 3.1. Buckland 1994. Grave lengths and widths sorted after length. Double graves excluded.

0.10 and 0.50m deep, with over a quarter between 0.20 and 0.30m. None of the vertical, double-stacked burials identified (see below) could be distinguished by their greater depth in comparison to the single graves. In the 1950s excavations the deepest grave recorded (Grave 19) was 0.76m.

The generally loose, rubbly nature of the natural chalk bedrock across the site meant that only ten graves showed clear evidence of tool-marks on their sides or base (Fig 3.11). These were confined to the north-western end of the cemetery where a band of unusually hard rock occurred. The tool-marks indicate the use of metal mattocks and picks during the original excavation of the graves. In the earlier excavations at Buckland, part of a broken iron mattock blade had been found still embedded in the side of Grave 145 (Evison 1987, 17).

The changes that occur in the choice of grave goods and female fashion in fifth- to seventh-century Kent (see Parts 5 and 9) do not allow any direct comparison between 'wealth'

and grave size. It is, however, possible to observe a tendency to bury juveniles in smaller graves than young adult, adult and mature individuals (Figs 3.3–3.4). In the case of children, this is likely to simply reflect stature as much as age-related status. Comparison of grave lengths used for young adult, adult and mature individuals, does not show a relationship that could suggest an increase of status based on age alone, because the proportion of young adults in large graves is relatively high. Nor is there any clear indication that males were generally buried in larger graves than females, although this may be a reflection of the relatively large number of unsexed individuals.[1] The same applies to a comparison of grave widths and gender.

The graves had been mostly backfilled with layers of cream, cream-brown or brown loam, containing varying amounts of chalk rubble and flints. Deposits of compacted chalk and large flint nodules occurred in a number of burials and these often seemed to represent packing around decayed

---

1.   Sex is used as an indication for gender, a simplification that seems justified in this particular context in view of Stoodley's results on the construction and meaning of gender in the early Anglo-Saxon burial rite (Stoodley 1999).

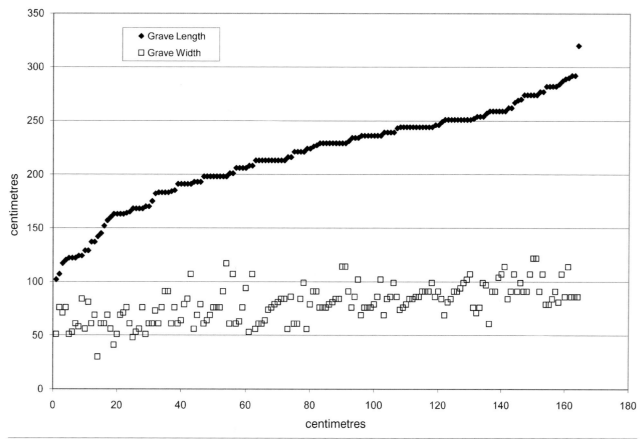

Fig 3.2. Buckland 1951–3. Grave lengths and widths sorted after length. Double graves excluded.

wooden coffin structures (see below). Very few graves showed any evidence to indicate that they had been re-opened or disturbed after the burial had been interred.

The general fill of many graves contained residual prehistoric and Roman material. A late second- to third-century cross-bow brooch was found in Grave 264 (j) (*see* p 173). A few Anglo-Saxon objects were also found in the grave fills, although it generally remains unclear whether these had been thrown into the grave whilst it was being backfilled, or whether they are derived from earlier activity on the site.

Grave orientation (Figs 2.1b and 2.2)

There can be no doubt that the principal factor influencing grave orientation on the 1994 site was the steep slope of the hillside (Fig 2.1b; 2.3), rather than any requirement to align graves on sunrise or some other significant setting (Parfitt and Brugmann 1997, 121). The same practical approach

to grave-digging seems to have occurred at the Bifrons cemetery, similarly situated on the side of the valley of the Little Stour (Chadwick Hawkes 2000, 8). The majority of the graves excavated at Buckland in 1994 were thus broadly aligned south-east by north-west, following the contours of the hill (Fig 2.1b). The graves within Plot R, on the north-western edge of the cemetery, were placed slightly closer to a north–south axis, following the curve of the hillside round into the adjoining Buckland valley.

There were few significant variations within the general range of grave axes represented. Contained within Plots S and T was a scatter of eighteen graves set on a east-south-east–west-north-west axis (Fig 2.2). A third of these graves cut into earlier burials and it initially seemed possible that they might represent a late group, subsequently dug across the two plots. Other graves with this same orientation, however, have subsequently proved to be early, so that there does not seem to be a close correlation between this particular orientation and date (see below and Table 8.7, p 358). Two of the Plot S sword burials (Graves 264 and 265B) were contained within this group. Also of passing

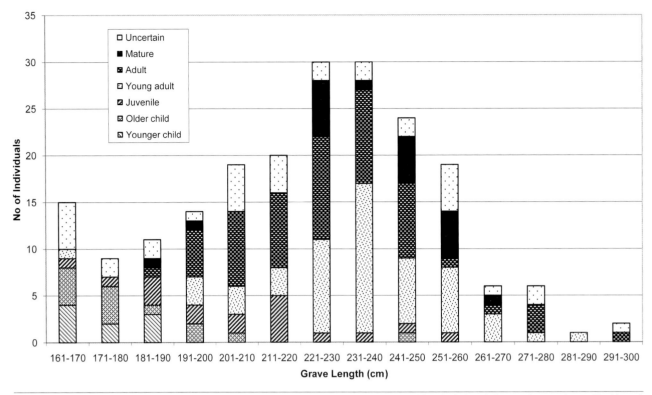

Fig 3.3. Buckland 1994. Osteological evidence on age, in relation to grave lengths of more than 1.60m. Includes skeletons of uncertain age. Double and disturbed graves excluded.

note is Grave 413 in Plot X, containing a late, well-furnished female burial, broadly dated to Phases 5–7, which was unusually aligned almost east–west and appeared to be orientated upon the earlier barrow grave, Grave 427. It may, itself, have been covered by a barrow (see above). Such an orientation is typical of many seventh-century graves in other east Kent cemeteries, although less so at Buckland.

In most cases where sufficient evidence had survived, it could be seen that the head of the deceased had been placed at the western end of the grave. Spread throughout the various plots identified, however, were at least eleven burials (Graves 234, 238, 254, 257, 339, 354, 372, 397, 405, 414 and 444) where the head had been placed towards the eastern end. These included burials of men, women and children. One (Grave 238) was double-stacked, with both female skeletons reversed (*see* p 28). The filling of Grave 234 had subsequently been cut into by Grave 225 containing a skeleton more conventionally laid out with the head at the north-west. A high status male with a sword was found in Grave 414. Other graves were moderately well equipped but several more were only poorly furnished and the upper burial in Grave 238 (Sk A) had nothing. The datable graves fall within Phases 1 to 3a (Table 8.7, p 358). The exact

meaning of these reversed burials remains unclear. Work on the upper part of the cemetery in the 1950s had shown that the majority of the burials there were also placed with their head at the western end of the grave. There was only one certain reversed burial, Grave 21 (Evison 1987, 16).

Skeleton position (Figs 10.71–10.117)

Based upon the surviving skeletal evidence, it would seem that the great majority of graves at Buckland contained a single individual interred in a supine and essentially extended position, although in a significant number of cases, limbs were slightly bent at the knee or elbow. A few bodies had been placed on their sides. During the 1951–3 work this arrangement was only recorded in Grave 146, where a 20–30 year old male had been laid on his right side (Evison 1987, 249). From the 1994 excavations, of particular interest would seem to be Grave 385 in Plot X, where an unaccompanied male, aged 20–25, had been buried in an extended position, lying on his right side with his head to the north-west (Fig 3.15). The osteological evidence would favour an origin for this individual in a region with a cold and dry polar climate, such as might be found in

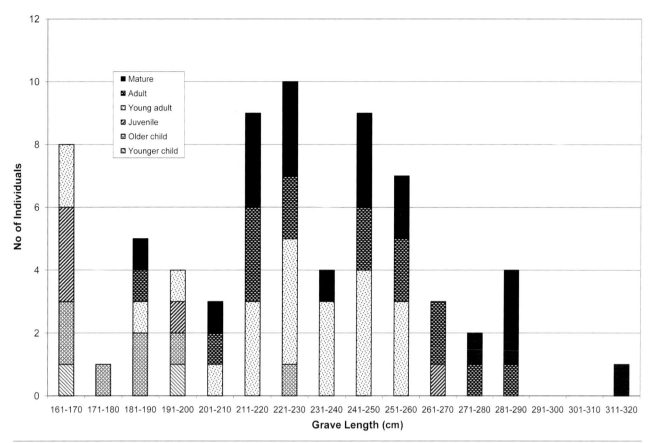

Fig 3.4. Buckland 1951–3. Osteological evidence for age in relation to grave lengths of more than 1.60m. Double and disturbed graves excluded.

northern European or Asian latitudes (p 290). Future scientific analysis by oxygen isotope, or similar, might provide further useful information.

Among the fifteen graves which produced evidence to show that they had originally held more than one body (see below), Grave 228 in Plot S seemingly contained a teenage male and female, laid on their sides facing each other (see below, Fig 7.4). The fragmentary skeletons surviving within Grave 238 (Sk A) and Grave 249 (Sk B) may also have originally been placed on their sides, but too little remained for this to be certain.

In Plot S the upper part of the body in double Grave 263 (Sk A) had been damaged by a subsequent grave (Grave 264) but from the fragmentary pelvis and leg bones remaining, it would seem that this was a fully grown male buried face-down, with his head towards the north-west. Modestly equipped with a knife and belt buckle, there was nothing to suggest that this individual had been buried before death occurred, but it is of interest to note that he constituted the upper body in a 'double-stacked' grave (see below), lying above a moderately well-equipped 25–30 year

old woman. Such prone burials are generally rare in Anglo-Saxon cemeteries (Stoodley 1999, 55), particularly in Kent (Reynolds 2009, 75) and the present example represents the only one from the 1994 Buckland excavations. Vaguely comparable is the curiously contorted burial of a female aged 20–30, previously discovered during 1951–3 (Grave 67). Elements of that skeleton were also front-downwards (Evison 1987, 18, 133–4) and the excavator believed the individual to have been buried alive, in a way similar to that suggested for the female in Sewerby (East Yorks), grave 41 (Hirst 1985, 38–43). Like Grave 263A, the burial at Sewerby also constituted the upper burial in a double grave with a well-equipped female below (Hirst 1985, 38–43; see below).

Both sexes and all ages except foetal, have been found as prone depositions in Anglo-Saxon cemeteries (see Tables 7.9 and 7.10). Overall, females seem to be a little more frequently encountered than males (Lucy 2000, 78–80; Reynolds 2009, 72). There remains some evidence to suggest that certain prone burials might be indicative of live burial or disrespect and punishment after death (Wilson 1992, 77ff; Reynolds 2009, 71) but this does not appear to be the case with most examples.

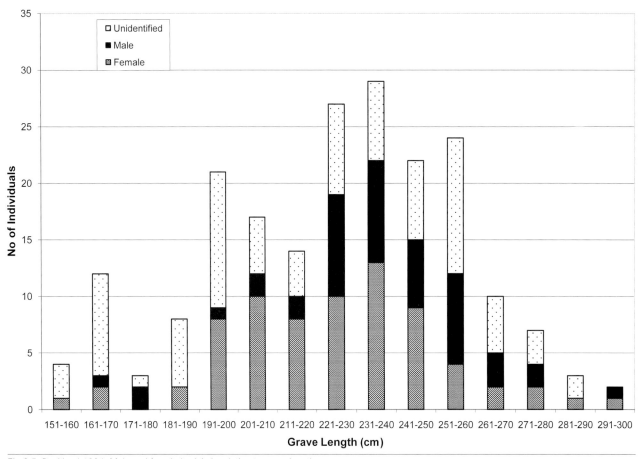

Fig 3.5. Buckland 1994. Male and female burials in relation to grave length.

More often than not in early Anglo-Saxon cemeteries, such burials are associated with grave goods, as Buckland Grave 263A, and provide no clear evidence to suggest that the individuals concerned were considered to be in disgrace (Wilson 1992, 84). Nevertheless, Reynolds' recent research has re-emphasised that this was 'a powerful rite that must have been enacted very consciously by a burial party fully aware of its social meaning' (Reynolds 2009, 69) and that such individuals, for whatever reason, did require this special form of burial. The occurrence of Buckland Grave 263A as the upper interment of a double-stacked burial further highlights this grave as being atypical and in some way special.

Double and triple graves

The fifteen graves that produced evidence to show that they had originally held more than one body were scattered across Plots S, T, V, W and X. Just three of these contained contemporary double burials horizontally laid out, side-by-side (termed on site, '*twinned burials*'; Graves 224, 228, Plot S and Grave 314, Plot T). Another example was recorded in 1951–3, double sword Grave 96 (Evison 1987, 239). The two burials within Grave 228, probably a teenage male and female, had been laid on their sides facing each other (Fig 7.4), perhaps indicating some special relationship between them. Analysis of their skeletons has suggested a possible familial link (*see* p 298), arguing against them representing, say, a pair of young lovers who died together. This is a rare type of burial, which is paralleled at Gunthorpe, Norfolk, where two adult females, including the richest female on site, were buried facing each other (Christine Osborne, unpublished). More common at Buckland 1994 were graves where the burials had been placed vertically, one above the other in a single width grave ('*double-stacked burials*', Graves 238, 263, 265, 282, 303, 350, 351, 386, 391, 393 and 427). Also of this type was Grave 249, which contained elements from three separate individuals, positioned one above the other.

The discovery of these double and triple graves at Buckland once again re-focuses attention on the problem

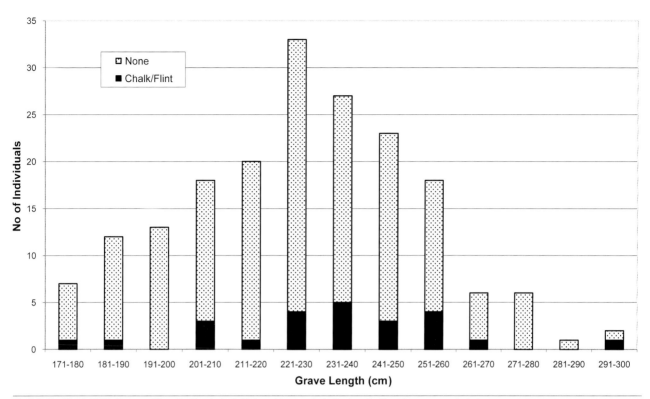

Fig 3.6. Buckland 1994. Graves with and without chalk/flint packings sorted after length. Double graves excluded.

of the interpretation of multiple burials in cemeteries. Individual deaths through natural causes are unlikely to have often occurred sufficiently close in time to allow the ready use of the same grave for more than one body, even if this was acceptable to the bereaved. Compared to many other Kentish cemeteries, including St Peter's, Broadstairs (9.2 per cent; Duhig 1996); Stowting (12 per cent; Brent 1867); Polhill (15.9 per cent; Philp 1973a); Darenth Park (18.2 per cent; Batchelor 1990; Walsh 1981) and Ozengell (23.1 per cent; Meaney 1964, 131), multiple burials are relatively uncommon at Buckland (*c* 4.5 per cent). This is most noticeable in the 1951–3 excavations where only two double graves are reported (Evison 1987, Graves 96 and 110).

The 'double-stacked' graves identified in 1994 merit some further consideration. Four occurred in Plots S and X, two in Plot T and one Plot V, with triple-stacked Grave 249 in Plot W. Two of the graves in Plot X (Graves 393 and 427; Figs 3.9 and 3.10) were enclosed within ring-gullies, suggesting that they had once been covered by small barrows (see above), whilst in Plot S, the only example of a prone burial discovered in 1994 occurred among the double-stacked graves here (Grave 263A, see above). Also in Plot S, Grave 351 (Phase 1–2), had subsequently been cut along its north-eastern side by a later double-stacked grave, Grave

350. The 1950s excavations at Buckland revealed just one double-stacked grave (Grave 94; Evison 1987, 238).

Overall, the surviving depth of these double graves into the chalk varied from 0.22 to 0.81m but two-thirds were less than 0.45m deep. Thus, they do not seem to be distinguishable by their greater depth in comparison with the single burials (see above), although all had clearly been truncated. Preservation of the uppermost body was often poor because it was very close to the surface. Post-cemetery ploughing (*see* p 14) is most probably responsible for most of the damage. Three of the surviving high-level burials were represented by nothing more than one or two long bones. In the remaining graves, however, sufficient groups of articulated bones lying in their anatomically correct positions remained to indicate that these had once been complete skeletons. In every case where the orientation could be determined, the upper body always appeared to have been laid out on the same axis as the lower one. Based on the poor survival of several high-level skeletons it seems possible that an upper body in some other graves could have been completely removed without trace, leaving the 1994 excavators with an apparently single burial.

A deposit of soil and chalk separated the two bodies within the 'stacked' graves, in every instance, its thickness ranging between 0.05 and 0.75m. There was no clear evidence to suggest that any of the corpses had originally been placed directly in contact, one upon the other (see below). As seen during excavation, the soil and rubble filling of these graves generally appeared to represent a single episode, with no clear indication in the outline of the fill to suggest that the original grave had subsequently been re-opened in order to inter the second corpse. Nor did any of the lower burials show any sign of having been disturbed during the insertion of a later one. The stacked individuals buried in Grave 238 were two of the few bodies found in 1994 which had their heads placed, not at the west, but at the eastern end of the grave (*see* p 24). The fact that both skeletons were reversed suggests a close relationship and also implies a detailed knowledge of the arrangement of the first burial by those interring the second body.

From the available evidence, the bodies in these 'stacked graves' mostly appear to have been buried at the same time, and thus stand in contrast to graves where it could be seen that later burials had been dug into the top of earlier ones on the same spot (eg Graves 225, 276, 330, and 367, see below). Possible exceptions to this may be represented by the three double-stacked burials that contained evidence for the former presence of a timber coffin or lining within the grave. Graves 386, 391 and 427 each preserved chalk and flint packing around the lower edges of the grave, which clearly had once been set on the outside of a centrally positioned internal timber structure (see below). Such an arrangement might have readily allowed the existing grave, perhaps initially only covered with a semi-permanent, removable top, to have been re-opened at a subsequent time to receive a second body; alternatively, perhaps these later burials had been laid within the depression created after the collapse of the original timber structure.

In Graves 249, 263, 265, 351 and 391, a comparatively rich or well-equipped lower burial was overlain by an individual less well provided for. The primary interments in Graves 249 and 265 were high status males buried with a sword and spear. The primary burials in the other three graves were all probably or certainly females. The upper burials in Graves 263 and 351 both appeared to be grown males, very modestly equipped, whilst that in Grave 238 was probably a female, buried without any grave goods. Unusually, Grave 249 contained the remains of two subsequent bodies, an adult male and a probable female, both unaccompanied (*see* p 285 and Table 7.4).

The uppermost woman in Grave 391 (Sk A) was only slightly less well equipped than the rich primary female burial below (Sk B; Fig 10.107), even though she seems to

have been interred much later (see below). In Graves 393 and 427, enclosed within barrow ring-gullies (see above), the reverse situation occurred; Grave 393 contained a 25–30 year old male provided with a spear and knife (Sk A), lying above an older male buried without any grave goods (Sk B). Grave 427 held a female aged 30–35 and moderately well equipped (Sk A), overlying a slightly younger adult, of uncertain sex and associated with only a single copper alloy fitting (Sk B).

Both bodies in Graves 238, 282, 303 and 386 were either poorly equipped or buried without grave goods. Grave 238 probably contained two adult females; Grave 282, two adult probable males; and Grave 386, two adults of which one (Sk B) was male. Grave 303 contained a 3 year old child (Sk A) buried above an adult male (Sk B), conceivably its father, whilst Grave 350 held a child about 8 years old (Sk A), perhaps also related to the 20–25 year old female below (Sk B).

Amongst the 'stacked' graves, the earliest datable lower burials range from Phase 1 (Graves 263B and 351B) to Phase 3a (Grave 265B). The earliest upper burials are Graves 263A, 351A and 427A, all assigned to Phase 1–2, with Grave 303A falling in Phase 3b. There is, unfortunately, only one, timber-lined Grave 391, where the two interments contain sufficient items to allow them to be closely dated independently and their phases compared. On the basis of the associated grave goods, the lower body here, Sk B, may be dated to Phase 2, whilst the upper (Sk A) falls rather later, within the collective Phases 5–7 (*see* p 333). This apparent chronological difference has been largely confirmed by two radiocarbon dates, which gave a calibrated result of AD 435–535 for Sk B (UB-4960) and AD 600–660 for the subsequent Sk A (UB-4959). Taken together, the evidence thus seems to indicate that there was a gap of perhaps a century between these two interments. Overall, a broad date range is suggested for the occurrence of stacked graves. The lower burial of the only stacked grave in Buckland 1951–3, Grave 94B, is dated to Phase 2–3.

Double stacked graves have been recorded in several other Kentish cemeteries. Excavations at Finglesham, near Deal revealed three graves of this type (Chadwick Hawkes and Grainger 2006, graves 21, 129 and 211). Grave 21 there had originally been covered by a timber mortuary structure probably supporting a pitched roof (Chadwick Hawkes and Grainger 2006, 44; see below for consideration of the possible significance of this). At sixth-century Sarre on Thanet, a double-stacked burial, grave 39, contained a well-equipped male armed with a sword, two spears and a shield. He was overlain by another male provided with just a spear and a knife (Brent 1864–5, 165–6). In grave 64 at

Bifrons, near Canterbury an unaccompanied burial overlay a rich female provided with beads, brooches and a crystal ball (Godfrey-Faussett 1880, 553; Chadwick Hawkes 2000, 8; *see also* Tables 7.4–7.8).

Discussion of shared graves

Birte Brugmann

Wilson (1992, 71ff) has suggested that family relationships probably account for most communal graves in Anglo-Saxon cemeteries. However, in his survey of multiple burials incorporating the evidence from Buckland, Stoodley (2002) has pointed out that consecutive burials using the same grave pit include a number of cases in which the later burial disturbed the earlier one. He interprets these disturbances as accidental and concludes that this, together with the lack of any clear structure governing the deposition of consecutive burials, argues against the interpretation of such burials as being principally family-related (*ibid*, 114). Contemporary multiple burials are interpreted by him as a practice that dealt with the unusual and threatening situation of individuals in a small rural community dying at the same time. A more recent study has reached some broadly similar conclusions (Reynolds 2009, 67).

An extensive survey of double and multiple burials found in row-grave cemeteries on the Continent by Lüdemann (1994) has shown that there is a wide variety of forms, including burials side-by-side in the same grave pit, variations of 'stacked' burial and 'semi-detached' grave pits with a partition made of wood or stone. Interments on the same level in the same pit were not necessarily contemporary, as is shown by cases in which the remains of the primary interment had been shifted to make space for a second body. Among the 'stacked' graves are two types - interment in the same grave pit with the second body placed directly on the first, in some cases facing in the opposite direction, and the type that occurs at Buckland, with a soil layer between the upper and lower body.

Lüdemann (1994, 516f) argues on the basis of the evidence reviewed by him that early medieval grave-pits were sometimes not just simply backfilled but were often left open, protected by a removable cover. There would be no need for such a covering to be particularly elaborate – wooden planks or branches supporting brushwood, reeds or fur would have been entirely adequate (*ibid*, fig 24). As long as any wood or stone lining and the cover survived reasonably intact, a grave could be easily re-opened to allow the insertion of a secondary burial (Lüdemann 1994, 436). There seem, however, to be cases of graves being re-used

after the wooden structure had already deteriorated and soil had entered the cavity.

At Buckland, both radiocarbon and grave good dates for Grave 391 imply that this timber-lined grave had, indeed, been re-opened much later in order to allow the addition of a second body (*see* p 359). By that time it seems likely that any timberwork associated with the original burial would have been in an advanced state of decay. Indications for a later insertion were also found in double-stacked grave 21 at Finglesham, where there was evidence for an associated timber structure (Chadwick Hawkes and Grainger 2006, 44, with a reference to Ozengell; *see* p 33).

It is suggested by Lüdemann that double burials were used to express a particularly close relationship between the members of a household, especially when space on a burial site was limited. Ancestor worship may have been a specific feature connected with secondary burials (Lüdemann 1994, 522f). The particular relationship between a primary and secondary burial in most cases seems to have spanned no more than one generation, with no clear evidence to suggest the premature death of an individual related to the death of a previously interred body (Lüdemann 1994, 515ff).

In Part 8 it is argued that intercutting graves at Buckland (*see* p 325) are not a specific reflection of the lack of space within the plots but that the digging of 'secondary' graves associated with 'primary' graves was part of the burial rite. Some of the 'stacked' burials found in 1994 can perhaps be interpreted in much the same way, as contemporary secondary burials specifically associated with primary graves. The use of space in Anglo-Saxon burial practice may, in fact, have been as significant for the demonstration of the status of an individual as the choice of grave goods.

Intercutting graves

Despite the density of burials in many parts of the cemetery, there were only about thirty instances of graves intercutting. In most cases this consisted of a single, later burial slightly impinging upon the site of an earlier one. Several cases of three graves cutting each other occurred. There were very few instances, however, where an earlier burial had been substantially destroyed by a subsequent interment (Fig 2.2).

The positioning and general lack of damage caused by later burials clearly implies that the positions of graves within the cemetery had once been marked in some way and that their sites were generally respected by subsequent grave-diggers. However, no definite evidence for grave markers was recorded, apart from the two graves enclosed by ring-

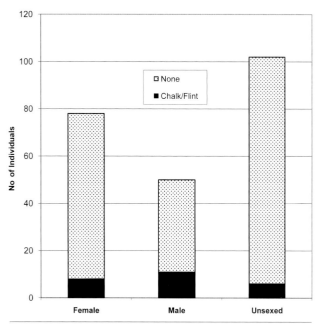

Fig 3.7. Buckland 1994. The graves of males, females and unsexed individuals with or without chalk/flint packing. Double graves excluded.

gullies (Graves 393 and 427, see below) that were probably originally covered by small barrows. In a few cases the cut for a later burial was contained entirely within the filling of an earlier grave (Graves 225, 276, 330, and 367), but in most cases graves overlapped by only a small amount. Overall, the evidence suggests that most of the later graves represent 'secondary burials' carefully placed to fill gaps between a 'primary' series of graves (see above and also pp 325–9 for further discussion).

Similarity of the grave fills sometimes meant that it was impossible to determine with complete certainty which grave cut which, and in one or two instances, subsequent dating of the grave goods has suggested that the recorded site sequence should be revised. In Plot T, Grave 290, now assigned to Phase 1 on the evidence of the associated objects, was recorded as *cutting* Grave 289, which appears to belong to Phase 2b or later, on the evidence of the buckle present (*see* p 129 and p 348). Accepting that the field evidence was misinterpreted, Grave 290 might now be viewed as belonging to a neat row of primary burials (Graves 287, 288, 290 and 304), with Grave 289 representing a secondary insertion, occupying an available gap (see above; Figs 2.2; 10.120, Section 122).

Professor Evison, with the experienced eye of a seasoned Anglo-Saxon cemetery excavator, has suggested a more complex sequence for Graves 352 and 353, in Plot S. As excavated, Grave 353 appeared to be one of the few which

substantially cut across an earlier burial (Grave 352; see Fig 10.80). However, Evison (pers comm) wonders whether Grave 353 might not, in fact, represent parts of two separate burials. The skull and upper body are suggested as forming an initial interment that was subsequently partially cut away by Grave 352, which in turn, was cut through by a later burial on the same axis as the first. Such an interpretation is partly based on the grave goods, where the glass claw beaker (f) at the lower end of Grave 353 appears to be of a later date than the brooch (b/j) at the upper end of the grave. However, Birte Brugmann (*see* p 76) has noted that the brooch was seemingly an old object re-used and on balance the present writers would prefer, in this case, to follow the original field records.

Grave goods and furnishings

Sixty-nine per cent of the burials excavated at Buckland in 1994 had been provided with grave goods and it would seem that the majority of bodies were buried fully clothed and equipped (see Part 5). A significant number were quite richly furnished but forty-one burials contained only a single item, most frequently a knife (sixteen examples), a buckle (twelve examples), sometimes a pottery vessel (five examples), or occasionally a bead necklace (two examples), a glass bowl or some other item. A further seventy-nine burials (30 per cent) contained no recognisable grave goods at all. Unfurnished graves and those provided with just a single item were slightly more frequent in Plots R, S, T and U, although richer graves also occurred in these plots. Graves without any objects included burials of men, women and children in roughly equal proportions. Burials provided with a single item showed a similar range but with an apparent bias towards males. The proportion of unfurnished graves in the upper part of the cemetery excavated in the 1950s seems to have been significantly lower (less than 12 per cent; Evison 1987, 214–52).

On the evidence of the grave goods, a fairly broad social spectrum appears to be represented on the 1994 site, ranging from high status males armed with swords, spears and shields, rich women possessing fine brooches and bead necklaces, through to a substantial number of individuals, perhaps servants or slaves, buried with few or no grave goods. However, there is now also clear evidence to demonstrate that the number and type of grave object found with a burial is partially determined by chronological factors, so that notions of 'rich' and 'poor' graves must be tempered with a consideration of the date of the burial (*see* pp 378–83).

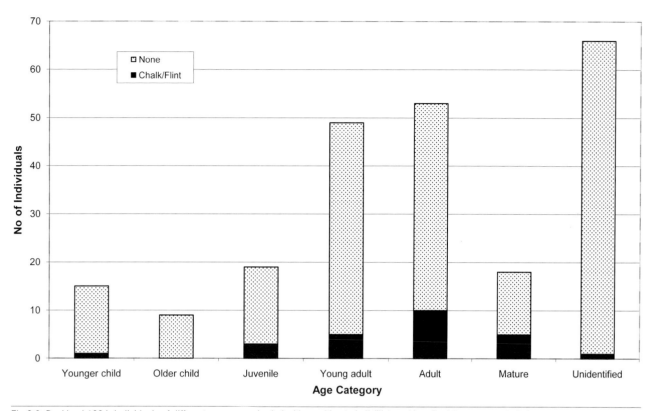

Fig 3.8. Buckland 1994. Individuals of different age groups buried with or without chalk/flint packing. Double graves excluded.

The total grave good assemblage from 1994 includes: twenty-six iron spearheads; seven iron shield bosses with handles; seven pattern-welded swords; over 100 iron knives; gold braids; just over 2,300 amber and glass beads; seventy-four brooches; thirteen glass vessels; nineteen pottery vessels; over ninety buckles and a small bronze-bound wooden bucket, together with a range of other personal equipment. Some grave good types were clearly associated with males and others with females only. Males are principally represented by weapons. Indicators of female gender are considered to be brooches, bracelets, two or more beads, crystal balls, keys and châtelaines, iron lozenges and spindle-whorls. All these classes of object are detailed in Part 4.

Although almost all traces of fur, leather and textile had long-since rotted away, the various metal fittings for belts and fastenings often preserved traces of such decayed organic material amongst the corrosion products. Gold threads from decayed garments were recovered from four female graves (Graves 347, 354, 391B and 420; *see* p 200; Tables 5.6 and 9.3). Sheep bones (a) found over the body in Grave 372 seem most likely to represent a joint of meat and a sheep-skin intended to accompany the deceased to the afterlife (*see* pp 176–8). Inhumation burials at a number of other Anglo-Saxon cemeteries containing animal remains have been recorded and many of these appear to have been food offerings (Lucy 2000, 94). Evidence for the presence of straw and other plant material might well provide evidence for linings within certain graves (see below).

A limpet shell was located by the body in Grave 289 (e). This seems to have been deliberately placed and may represent a symbolic food offering. Limpet shells have also come from Anglo-Saxon graves on Priory Hill, Dover (Payne 1889, 205) and Lousyberry Wood, Temple Ewell (Parfitt and Dickinson 2007, 124). Today, similar edible limpets can be collected from the rocky foreshore at Dover, a short distance away. A single vertebra from the skeleton of a fish was fortuitously discovered in the area of the decayed body of Grave 246 (j). Fairly certainly, this is derived from the gut of the deceased and must represent part of the last meal consumed. The exact fish species has not been identified. It seems possible that similar finds might have been made in some other graves if time and resources had been available to undertake wet sieving of their fills.

Fig 3.9. Grave 393 and its enclosing ring-gully (F 573), looking south-west. Scale 1m.

A number of burials had been interred with odd artefacts which were of pre-Saxon date. The great majority of these objects were Roman coins, with one Iron Age potin coin (*see* p 173). Most items had presumably been collected as amulets or curios (Meaney 1981). The Roman coins from Grave 265B had been used to provide a set of weights for a balance scale (*see* pp 150–2) and may be directly compared with a similar find from Buckland Grave C (Evison 1987, 214). There were Roman or probable Roman glass beads in Graves 222 (a)38, 245 (a), 257(g), 263B (h), 331 (e) and 372 (g). Several broken pieces of Roman glass occurred (Grave 208, Sf 924; Grave 238 (b); Grave 266 (b and c); Grave 350B (i); Grave 367 (c); Grave 377 (b)), together with a small piece of marble in Grave 266 (d), a Roman horse harness pendant in Grave 377 (m), and a late Iron Age toggle in Grave 407 (c). The general fill of Grave 264 produced a Roman crossbow brooch (j). Many of these items could have been collected from amongst the ruins of Roman *Dubris*, only a short distance away. The Iron Age coin is of a type well-known in east Kent, although the Iron Age toggle and Roman horse pendant are scarce finds. Several natural fossils, including a shark's tooth, are also

present. Such miscellaneous items were often found in groups around the pelvis and it would seem that they had frequently been contained within small trinket bags/purses suspended from a belt on the waist. Other oddments, such as loose garnets, spindle-whorls, brooches and beads also occur amongst the contents of these bags.

Random vegetal material in association with iron objects

Fleur Shearman

Straw or other random plant/vegetal material was recorded on iron objects from Grave 218, chain link (d); Grave 240, spearhead (a) and ferrule (b); the spearheads from Graves 249C (c), 259 (a), 264 (a), 300 (q); an arrowhead from Grave 302 (b); a purse-frame from Grave 381 (g) and items from Grave 413, (c)–(f).

Where textile remains have been found in association with objects, associated plant material might be interpreted as stuffing for a mattress, other bedding or possibly a pillow

Fig 3.10. Grave 427 and its enclosing ring-gully (F 571), looking south-west. Scale 1m.

placed within the grave. In the case of the spearhead from Grave 264 (a), in addition to the random plant material, feathers were found in association with textile; this is interpreted as evidence for a pillow (*see* p 203). In the case of Grave 413 (c), one of the textiles has been interpreted as a mattress and it is possible that the associated vegetal material represents the mattress filling (see Table 5.7). In the case of the spearhead and ferrule from Grave 240 and the spearhead from Grave 259, the close conformity of the textile to the spears is more likely to be evidence for a wrapping. The random plant material in these two instances would appear to be independent of the textiles. Random plant material found above a layer of garment textile from the pursemount from Grave 381 (g) may also have an independent origin. The body in Grave 300 appears to have been laid on timber planking, perhaps ship timbers (see below); random vegetal material was found on the spearhead, the point of which was close to the feet with the socket retaining traces of mineral-preserved textile. Both textile and plant remains were found on the chain link from Grave 218 (d) but not enough survives of the latter to interpret it with confidence.

Where no textile is recorded on objects, extensive remains of random plant material may be cautiously interpreted as evidence for a grave lining, or possibly a covering, depending on how the objects were orientated in the grave (orientation was not specifically recorded on site). The possibility that the random vegetal material without associated textile may be intrusive and derive from a source such a grass turves being incorporated in the grave fill might also be considered.

Internal structures

Integral mortuary structures represented by post-holes, ledges and beam slots in and around the individual graves, such as have been recorded at St Peter's on the Isle of Thanet (Hogarth 1973) and Finglesham, near Deal (Chadwick Hawkes and Grainger 2006), are largely absent at Buckland, both in the present excavations and the earlier work (Evison 1987, 17). Evidence for a timber coffin, packed round with large flints, was recorded in Grave 8 during the 1951–3 excavations (*ibid*) and further evidence to suggest that certain graves had

Grave no	Plot	Phase	Gender	Coffin evidence
215	S	-	?M	Two coffin nails
221	S	1b	F	Large grave-pit
222	S	3a	F	Large grave-pit
231	S	-	M	Flint packing at head and foot ends
239	V	1a	F	Large grave-pit
246	V	-	M	Iron nails around coffin
247	W	2a	F	Large grave-pit; iron nail above skull
248	W	-	M	Flint packing along NE side
250	W	3a	F	Large grave-pit
252	W	-	M	One iron nail
256	W	-	M	Two iron nails
260	W	-	M	Two iron nails
261	S	1	?F	Two iron nails
262	S	2–3	M	Flint packing along NE side; large grave-pit
263*	S	1b–2a	?M & ?F	Large grave-pit
265*	S	3a	? & ?M	One iron nail
281	T	1b	F	One iron nail
285	U	-	?F	Large grave-pit
286	T	-	F	Large grave-pit
291	T	-	M	Large grave-pit
292	T	-	M	Large grave-pit
297	Z	2	M	Flint and chalk packing; coffin 2.10 x 0.45-0.65m
298	Z	-	?F	Large grave-pit
300	Z	1b–2a	M	Two rows of clench nails under body
320	S	-	child	Large grave-pit
329	T	-	M	Flint packing - mainly on NE side
336	T	2b	F	Large grave-pit
347	S	2a	?F	Flint packing along NE side
348	S	1b–2a	M	Chalk packing; coffin 1.98 x 0.50m
350*	S	1b–3b	child & ?M	Large grave-pit - 350B; two iron nails
351*	S	1–2	M & F	Large grave-pit

Grave no	Plot	Phase	Gender	Coffin evidence
360	S	3b	F	One iron nail
362	T	-		Two iron nails
365	T	-	?M	Large grave-pit
368	V	-	M	Flint packing along NE side
375	X	3b	M	Large grave-pit
381	X	1b–2a	F	Chalk and flint packing along NE side; three iron nails
386*	X	-	? & M	Flint packing along SW and NW sides
388	X	-	child	Angle-irons at corners; flint packing; coffin 1.50 x 0.40m
390	X	-	?F	Chalk and flint packing along NE side
391*	X	5–7, 2	F & F	Chalk and flint packing; coffin 2.05 x 0.55m; one iron nail (B)
392	X	2	F	One iron nail
393*	X	-	M & M	Large grave-pit
404	X	-	child	Flint packing
407	X	2	F	Large grave-pit
411	X	-	child	Chalk and flint packing
414	Y	2b–3a	M	Flint packing; coffin 2.23 x 0.67m
416	Y	-	M	Chalk and flint packing; coffin 2.10 x 0.60m
417	Y	2a	F	Chalk and flint packing; coffin 2.30 x 0.58m
418	Y	1–2	?F	Chalk and flint packing; coffin 1.46 x 0.46m
419	Y	2a	F	Chalk and flint packing along NE side
420	Y	2–3a	F	Chalk packing along NE side
423	Y	2–3a	M	Flint packing at head end
425	Y	1b–2	F	Chalk and flint packing; coffin 2.00 (min) x 0.60m
426	Y	2	?F	Chalk and flint packing
427*	X	1b–2	? & F	Flint packing; large grave-pit
432	W	1b–2	F	Large grave-pit
443	Y	1b–2	?F	Flint packing at SE end; one iron nail
444	Y	1–2	child	Iron nails along NE side

Table 3.1. Details of graves containing possible evidence for a coffin/timber structure (*denotes double-stacked graves).

originally contained some sort of internal timber structure or coffin was identified during the more recent investigations. Occurring throughout the various plots excavated in 1994 were burials with indications of the former presence of timberwork, although no obvious traces of decayed wood survived in any (see below and Table 3.1). Such evidence occurred mainly with males but also with some females and mostly, but not exclusively, with adults. These were slightly more common in Plots X and Y. There are several children in coffins, most notably the 6–12 month old baby contained within Grave 388. From those burials which can be dated it would seem that the use of internal timber structures was not confined to any particular phase (Table 3.1).

Nineteen graves contained occasional iron nails and other fittings which are probably fixings derived from coffins and other internal wooden structures (detailed below). Nails in Graves 246 and 444 preserved mineralised traces of oak

wood, suggesting the species used in the manufacture of the coffin (*see* p 280; Table 6.12). Of particular interest were eight angle-irons recovered from the corners of infant Grave 388 in Plot X and two horizontal rows of clench nails, again with traces of mineralised oak wood, found under the male body in Grave 300 of Plot Z (see below).

In another twenty-six burials, mostly situated within Plots X and Y and including three double-stacked graves (see below), the former presence of a wooden lining or coffin could be readily inferred from traces of distinctive flint and chalk rubble packing deposits located around the edges of the grave (Table 3.1). Such deposits were generally best preserved on the north-eastern, uphill, side of the grave-pit. The rubble must originally have been packed around a now decayed internal timber structure (Welch 1992, 56). Several further graves with deliberate flint packing around their edges had been recorded in the 1950s excavations

Fig 3.11. Grave 402, detail of tool-marks in base. Scale 10cm.

(Evison 1987, 17–18). The flints used as packing generally took the form of large unworked nodules that had clearly been specifically collected for the purpose. In nine graves (Graves 297, 348, 388, 391, 414, 416, 417, 418 and 425) the approximate dimensions of the internal timber structure had been preserved by the rubble (see Table 3.1).

Although no packing deposits or other features were apparent within their filling, about twenty more graves may perhaps be suggested to have also originally contained some sort of internal coffin structure on the evidence of the substantial dimensions of the grave-pit. Even including these, however, it would seem that less than a quarter of the burials on the 1994 site had originally been provided with any sort of coffin or timber lining. One of the inferred barrow burials (Grave 427) and the sword Grave 414 each included flint rubble packing, implying that they had originally been timber-lined, but many of the other 'richer' burials do not seem to have been similarly provided. Analysis of the grave objects has raised the possibility that some graves may have been furnished with a pillow or mattress, or lined with loose straw (see above) but the majority of the dead

appear to have been placed directly into a simple, unlined, chalk-cut grave.

The bodies contained within Graves 206 and 209 of Plot R both appear to have been laid over large lumps of chalk rubble resting on the base of the grave. The significance of this is unclear; it seems to be a deliberate act and is unlikely simply to represent tumble from the heap of spoil by the graveside. Something similar was previously recorded in Grave 149. Here, the skeleton lay on top of a few inches of fill, with some large flints around and underneath it (Evison 1987, 17). The excavator concluded that the corpse must have originally been placed in the grave on a bed or bier which had stood a few inches above the floor of the grave.

Structural ironwork from graves

Ian Riddler with Hayley Bullock

Comparatively little structural ironwork was recovered from the 1994 excavations, although a number of graves included iron nails (see above). The principal assemblages are the

Fig 3.12. Grave 300, detail of clench nails. Scale 10cm.

group of clench nails from Grave 300 and the set of eight angle-irons from Grave 388. In addition, small numbers of iron nails were found within a series of graves described below (Tables 3.1 and 3.5).

Clench nails

Fourteen clench nails were discovered in Grave 300, arranged in two rows 5–8mm apart, beneath the waist and legs of the deceased (Fig 3.12 and 10.89). All of the clench nails are of a similar size and they fastened wood of 40–45mm in total thickness (Table 3.2). Their arrangement in the grave suggests that they fixed two or three overlapping oak boards together, forming a support for the lower part of the body.

Two clench nails were previously recovered from Buckland Grave 135 and a group of five came from a medieval pit, within which grave goods from one or more burials had been re-interred (Evison 1987, 99). Grave 135 was tentatively assigned to Phase 4 (Evison 1987, 176). Clench nails have also been recovered from other Anglo-Saxon graves in Kent, at Ozengell; Sarre; Thorne

Farm, Monkton; Half Mile Ride, Margate; Mill Hill, Deal; Bekesbourne and Rochester. Details of these graves are provided in Table 3.3. They include burials of both sixth- and seventh-century date.

The practice of using clench nails to secure wooden structures within graves continued into the Middle Saxon period, and examples are known from Barton-on-Humber, North Lincolnshire; Caister-on-Sea, Norfolk; Jarrow; Thorpe-by-Norwich, Norfolk and York (Rodwell and Rodwell 1982, 290–2; Rodwell 1993, 253–5; Rogers 1993, 1410–2; Kjølbye-Biddle 1995, 500–3). They occur also in Viking period graves within Scandinavia. An example has come also from an inhumation burial at Birka in Sweden, whilst others were retrieved from Fyrkat, Denmark (Gräslund 1980, 25 and fig 17; Roesdahl 1977, 14, 83–91, 111 and figs 4, 109, 168). The clench nails in these burials are thought to derive from carts placed in the graves.

The arrangement of clench nails in Grave 300 implies that two or three sections of overlapping oak wood were secured along the centre of the grave, possibly extending for just half of its length. The distribution of clench nails within

Find letter	Total length (mm)	Clenched length (mm)	Shank width (mm)
a			
b			
c			
d	45		
e	50	40	10
f			
g			
h			
i	55		
j	58	48	8
k	55	40	
l	57	45	10
m	62	45	9
n	58	45	

Table 3.2. Clench nails from Grave 300.

graves at Mill Hill, Deal and Sarre is rather different, with one or more rows running down the side of the grave, rather than its centre (Parfitt and Brugmann 1997, 24–5 and fig 62; Brent 1864–5, 159, 178; 1868, 313), recalling the situation with Buckland Grave 135 (Evison 1987, 99). Where this arrangement occurs, it is possible that they secured two overlapping vertical planks placed on one side of the grave (eg Parfitt and Brugmann 1997, 24). The clench nails within Thorne Farm grave 1 at Monkton may have been moved slightly in post-depositional processes, and it is possible to visualise two rows there, lying on either side of the body. The section drawing of that grave indicates that the rows sloped from a position effectively on the surface of the grave at the head, to its base at the feet (Perkins 1985, fig 5). If the body lay on the base of the grave, then it may have been covered

by clenched boards, in the manner of several of the graves from Caister-on-Sea.

A number of the graves from the cemetery at Caister-on-Sea included clench nails (Rodwell 1993). Most have clench nails set high in the grave, over the deceased, but grave 136 included a single row lying below the body (Darling and Gurney 1993, fig 31 and pl XIX). In a similar manner at York, nineteen clench nails were aligned in two rows, 0.20m apart (Kjølbye-Biddle 1995, 500). The suggestion that this is the grave of a Viking, on the basis of the clench nails alone, is extremely tenuous and speculative.

Clench nails have inevitably been associated with ship burials, particularly following the excavations at Sutton Hoo. Prior to that excavation, however, they were thought to have been used for other purposes. John Brent felt that they served to secure textile stretchers to wooden supports at Sarre (Brent 1867, 417–18). Charles Roach Smith, in describing those from Ozengell, confused them with rivets from shields. He did point out, however, that they were also found within graves in northern France (Roach Smith 1854, 17). In effect, the maritime connection goes back to the work of Charles Green at Caister-on-Sea, who described the burials there as 'boat or pseudo-ship burials' shortly after their excavation (Green 1963, 54; Rodwell 1993, 253). In the same vein, Perkins reconstructed the Thorne Farm grave as a pseudo-ship burial (Perkins 1985, 58–9 and fig 5).

It should be emphasised, however, that clench nails were ubiquitous structural fittings of the Anglo-Saxon period, used to fasten overlapping sections of wood. They have been found on numerous settlement sites, extending into the medieval period (Hope-Taylor 1977, 192–3; Evison 1980, 39; Ottaway 1992, 615–8; Parfitt *et al* 2006, 67).

Cemetery	Grave	Quantity	Location	Gender	Category	Age	Dating
Dover, Buckland	135	2	Left side of grave	Male	Adult	25–30	*c* 625–650
Dover, Buckland	300	14	Two rows between legs	Male	Adult	30–40	*c* 500–540/50
Ozengell		20					
Monkton, Thorne Farm	1	18			Juvenile	12–15	*c* 575–650
Deal, Mill Hill	38	31	Two rows, side of grave	Female	Adult	22–29	*c* 500–540
Margate, Half Mile Ride	3			?Female	Juvenile		*c* 600–700
Bekesbourne	37/8	1					
Sarre	7		Down left side				
Sarre	33/4	a few					
Sarre	134		At head & down left side				
Sarre	208						
Sarre	231	16					
Sarre	245						
Sarre	255	80					
Sarre	259	1					
Rochester Cathedral		some					

Table 3.3. Clench nails from Anglo-Saxon graves in east Kent.

Fig 3.13. Grave 250, detail of upper part of body, showing grave goods. Scale 10cm.

No direct connection with ship burials needs to be made, although Brookes (2007) has recently reaffirmed the case for this in Anglo-Saxon Kent. As Rodwell has previously noted, however, the grave covers or supports could simply represent re-used boat timbers, interred without any symbolic connotations (Rodwell 1993, 254). Equally, they could represent re-used wood from buildings. In the absence of the survival of hazelwood plugs from most examples, a feature of maritime vessel construction, it is difficult to differentiate between these alternatives.

Angle-irons

Eight angle-irons were retrieved from Grave 388, (a)–(h). They were arranged towards the four corners of the grave, in four pairs (Fig 10.51). Their location implies that they helped to fasten the ends of a coffin. In each case, one side of the angle-iron is longer than the other. From the recorded evidence, it would seem that the longer faces were fixed to the ends of the coffin, but this cannot be certain. A tentative reconstruction (one of six possible interpretations) of the coffin is shown on Fig 10.107.

Cemetery	Grave	Quantity	Location	Gender	Dating
Dover, Buckland	388	8	At corners of coffin	Child	Unphased
Deal, Mill Hill	92	4	At corners of coffin	Female	Phase III: *c* 530–570
Kingston	146	4		Male	Seventh century
Kingston	176	several		Male	Seventh century
Kingston	301	2		Child	Seventh century
Gilton	87	4		Female	Seventh century
Finglesham	22	4	3 at one end of grave, 1 in disturbed fill	Male	Unphased
Finglesham	204	8	At corners of coffin	Male	*c* 525
Saltwood	200	8	At corners of coffin	Male	Late sixth to early seventh century

Table 3.4. Angle-irons from Anglo-Saxon graves in east Kent.

Fig 3.14. Grave 391A, general view of body with surrounding packing stones. Scale 1m.

Angle-irons have been discovered in a small number of other Anglo-Saxon graves in east Kent (Table 3.4). The angle-irons from Finglesham were not associated with any of the graves excavated by Stebbing, but Chadwick thought that they might have come from graves D3 and G2 (Chadwick 1958, 9, 18 and 27; see now also Chadwick Hawkes and Grainger 2006, graves 22 and 204). As with the clench nails, it is likely that angle-irons occurred in graves of both males and females of sixth- and seventh-century date. Buckland Grave 388 is the burial of an infant, interred with a ceramic feeding bottle (*see* p 134 and p 283). It recalls the situation with Kingston grave 302, where two iron clasps were found in the fill of the grave, above the body of a child (Faussett 1856, 93–4). The shape and size of the accompanying comb from that grave (Faussett 1856, pl XIII.1) suggest that it was a burial of the seventh century.

'Several pieces of iron clasps, and one whole one, much like those we now make use of in order to strengthen and hold together the corners of chest, etc' were found in a grave at Crundale, which appears, however, to be of late Roman date (Faussett 1856, 187). The 'large clasps and riveted pieces of iron' mentioned in relation to grave 205 from

Kingston by Faussett may refer to angle-irons and cleats, but unfortunately the ironwork was not illustrated and it does not survive.

Angle-irons are comparatively rare in early Anglo-Saxon graves outside Kent, but they have also been found at Broomfield, Essex; Garton Slack, Yorkshire, grave 33A and Winkelbury Hill, Wiltshire (Mortimer 1905, fig 717; Pitt Rivers 1898, 257–8). Four angle-irons were noted also at Morken in Germany (Böhner 1959, pl 10, Abb 141.1; Hinz 1969, Taf 11).

Technical data on the investigation of the angle-irons from Grave 388   Hayley Bullock

All the fittings are L-shaped and have a disc-headed rivet at each end. The shanks of the rivets are rectangular in section and taper to a point at the ends. There are mineral-preserved wood remains on the inside of the fittings. By studying the individual grain direction of the wood in combination with the position of the objects in the grave it is clear that the objects are iron coffin fittings and it is possible to begin to reconstruct the coffin complete with fittings (Fig 10.107).

Fig 3.15. Grave 385, general view of body. Scale 1m.

The wood remains were examined at x40 magnification. The coffin was made from radially-cut, ring-porous wood. It appears to be oak (*Quercus* sp; identification Caroline Cartwright). Using the excavator's grave plans the coffin measures approximately 1.13m in length, 0.30m in width at the head and tapers to 0.20m at the feet. The coffin is very small and is clearly that of a child. There was enough mineral-preserved wood present to indicate that the coffin was made from flat planks. By measuring the length of the complete nail shanks that had wood present, eg bracket (e), it was established that the minimum thickness of these planks was 37mm.

The brackets are distinctly placed at the four corners of the grave, occurring at differing depths in the soil. Assuming that there has been limited movement of the brackets since burial and taking into account the positions of the brackets in the grave, including the depth the objects were found and the grain direction of the wood, it is likely that brackets (h), (g), (d) and (f) formed corner brackets and (a), (b), (c) and (e) lid brackets. Based on the grain direction of the wood only it is possible that (a), (b), (c) and (e) formed brackets for the base of the coffin. However, when looking at the positions

of the brackets in the grave it is more likely they are lid brackets. Bracket (h) shows valuable information relating to joint construction of the coffin and may indicate the use of a rebated butt joint (Watson 1993) due to the transverse section of the wood grain present in the corner of the bracket.

Brackets (h) and (a) were excavated from the west corner of the grave, (h) 150mm above the grave base and (a) 250mm above the grave base. The grain of the mineralised wood on the inside of bracket (h) runs vertically along the length of the short end of the bracket showing a radial section. The grain of the wood changes direction and runs horizontally on the long end of the bracket showing a radial section. This bracket may indicate the use of a rebated butt joint due to the transverse section of the wood grain present in the corner of the bracket. The grain of the mineralised wood on the inside of bracket (a) runs vertically along the length of both the short and long ends showing a radial section. Taking into account the positions of the brackets in the grave including the depth the objects were found and the grain direction of the wood, it is likely that these brackets formed part of the west corner of the coffin with (h) forming a corner bracket and (a) a lid bracket.

Grave	Quantity	Location	Gender	Category	Age	Phasing
111	1	Right knee	Male	-	-	-
162	1	Head of grave; in general fill	Male	Juvenile	-	-
163	1	To right of head	-	Juvenile	-	-
215	2	Chest area and general fill	?Male	Adult	25–30	-
246	7	To side of head; one at feet	Male	Adult	30–40	-
247	1	General fill, north corner	Female	Adult	23–28	2a
252	1	By right femur	Male	Adult	30–40	-
256	2	By left foot	Male	Adult	35–45	-
260	2	Inside and under right forearm	?Male	Adult	40–50	-
261	2	Waist area	?Female	Juvenile	15–17	1
265B	1	Under skull	?Male	Adult	25–30	3a
281	1	Beyond left pelvis	Female	Adult	25–30	1b
350B	2	Between femurs	Female	Adult	20–25	-
360	1	Under left pelvis	Female	Adult	30–40	3b
362	2	South-east end of grave	-	Child	-	-
381	3	By right humerus	Male	Adult	30–40	1b–2a
391B	3	Left of left knee	Female	Adult	20–25	2
392	1	Area of right waist	Female	Child	8–10	2
443	1	Above left pelvis	?Female	Adult	30–35	1b–2
444	4	Along side of grave	-	Child	6–8	1–2

NB Does not include Grave 388; see angle-irons

Table 3.5. Iron nails from graves, Buckland 1951–3 and 1994.

Brackets (g) and (b) were excavated from the north corner of the grave, (g) 150mm above the grave base and (b) 220mm above the grave base. The grain of the mineralised wood on the inside of bracket (g) runs vertically along the length of the short end of the bracket showing a radial section. The grain of the wood changes direction and runs horizontally on the long end of the bracket and rivet, showing a radial section. The changing grain direction may indicate a joint on the coffin and may be a corner bracket. The grain of the mineralised wood on the inside of bracket (b) runs vertically along the length of both the short and long ends showing a radial section. Taking into account the positions of the brackets in the grave including the depth the objects were found and the grain direction of the wood, it is likely that these brackets formed part of the north corner of the coffin with (g) representing a corner bracket and (b) a lid bracket.

Brackets (d) and (c) were excavated from the south corner, both 90mm above its base. The grain of the mineralised wood on the inside of bracket (d) runs vertically along the length of the short end of the bracket showing a radial section. The grain of the wood changes direction and runs horizontally on the long end of the bracket showing a radial section. The changing grain direction may indicate a joint on the coffin and may be a corner bracket. The grain of the mineralised wood of bracket (c) runs vertically along the length of both the short and long ends showing a radial section. Taking into

account the positions of the brackets in the grave and the grain direction of the wood, it is likely that these brackets formed part of the south corner of the coffin, with (d) forming a corner bracket and (c) a lid bracket.

Brackets (f) and (e) were excavated from the east corner of the grave, (f) 140mm above the grave base and (e) 120mm above the base. The grain of the mineralised wood on the inside of bracket (f) runs vertically along the length of the short end of the bracket showing a radial section. The grain of the wood changes direction and runs horizontally on the long end of the bracket and rivet showing a radial section around the rivet. The changing grain direction may indicate a joint on the coffin and may be a corner bracket. The grain of the mineralised wood on the inside of bracket (e) runs vertically along the length of both the short and long ends showing a radial section. From the positions of the brackets in the grave including the depth the objects were found and the grain direction of the wood, it is likely that these brackets fixed the east corner of the coffin with (f) forming a corner bracket and (e) a lid bracket.

Nails

Iron nails were found in several of the Buckland graves, usually in small numbers (Tables 3.1 and 3.5). For some of these graves at least, it can be suggested that the nails strengthened wooden coffins along their sides or at their ends. This appears to be the case with Graves 162, 163, 246, 247, 252, 256, 381 and 444. With a second series of graves (Graves 111, 260, 261, 265B, 281, 350B, 360, 391B and 392), the nails lay under the body and may have strengthened a coffin or bier on which the deceased was placed. In most of these graves the nails consist merely of one or two individual specimens, rather than any larger groups.

One exception to this situation lies with the two nails from Grave 260, which lay together, with two iron pins and a knife, under the right forearm of the deceased. It is difficult to understand what these nails were doing in that position, lying amidst a cluster of grave goods. Grave 246 produced seven nails, mostly in the area of the left shoulder. Four iron nails were recovered from Grave 444, arranged in a line down one side of the grave. They extended over a length of 1.20m and appear to correspond with the height of the deceased, who lay immediately to the side of them. They are not conventional nails with tapering shanks of square section, however. Their shanks are circular in section and do not taper, and they have discoidal heads. In effect, they resemble clench nails, for which the roves are absent. The two complete examples have shank lengths of 43 and 52mm below the heads.

The occurrence of small numbers of iron nails within the graves of Buckland 1994 recalls the situation with several of the burials in Buckland 1951–3 (Evison 1987, 99). Small numbers of nails have also been recovered from other graves within east Kent cemeteries (Table 3.6).

The general situation in Kent is similar to that at Buckland, with small quantities of nails arranged in a number of graves. The nails themselves are usually of small or medium size, although a larger category, which is mostly absent from Buckland, could be seen at both Gilton

Cemetery	Total length (mm)	Quantity of nails
Bekesbourne I	2	2–3
Bifrons	23	2–3
	26	2
	39	2
	45	1
Bourne Park		3 or 4 burials, each with 4 nails
Crundale	14	6
	20	4
	24	6
	25	4
Eastry		3
Holborough	18	1
Kingston	8	5
	9	5
	30	4
	33	4
	40	5
	41A	5
	45	4
	47	4–5
	231	2–3
Sarre	12	4
	200	unspecified
	259	unspecified
	287	2
Sibertswold	20	5–6
	33	3–4
Wickhambreux		2

Table 3.6. Iron nails from Anglo-Saxon graves in east Kent.

and Kingston (Faussett 1856). The nail (d) found by the right humerus of the male in Grave 381 represents the only example of this larger type to have come from the Buckland cemetery. It has a domed head and a tapering shank 95mm in length.

PART 4: THE GRAVE GOODS

Introduction

Ian Riddler

The grave goods from the 1994 excavations are described within functional categories, beginning with weapons and continuing with dress accessories, containers, textile manufacturing equipment, personal equipment, and amulets. The sequence of objects replicates that used in the Buckland 1951–3 monograph (Evison 1987), although the quantity and range of material is slightly different. There is no separate category for tools, for example, whilst the earlier report includes sharpening steels, awls, a possible mattock, firesteels and hones within that category. The 1994 excavations did not produce any sharpening steels, mattocks or hones. The awl-like objects fall into two types, both of which are dealt with as 'Personal Equipment', as are the firesteels or pursemounts. An additional category of prehistoric and Roman material has been added at the end of the chapter. Structural ironwork from graves has been considered above in Part 3 (pp 35–42).

A significant component of the analysis of objects from the cemetery has been their study in detail. This is emphasised throughout Part 4 and is particularly important in the absence of detailed, technological studies of objects from other Kent cemeteries. With the honourable exception of the Buckland 1951–3 excavations (Evison 1987) and some elements of the Mill Hill, Deal cemetery (Parfitt and Brugmann 1997; Parfitt 2003) detailed analyses of objects from Kent have been sparse and occasional, rather than customary. As noted below, the opportunity to examine technical aspects of object construction was available to this assemblage, and the results are included here. Technical

detail has usually been placed towards the end of each object category, with the majority of observations made by Fleur Shearman and Hayley Bullock.

Broader considerations of object technology, stemming from detailed analyses, follow in Part 6. Part 8 provides a detailed description and discussion of the various cemetery phasing systems into which the new evidence from Buckland has been added and readers may find it useful to refer to that section, particularly Table 8.4, in conjunction with Part 4 (see below). The suggested revised phasing for the Buckland cemetery is set out in the table below.

Phase	Evison date ranges	Phase	Revised date ranges
1	475–525	1a–1b	450–510/530
2	525–575	2a–2b	510/30–550/560
3	575–625	3a	550/60–580/600
4	625–650	3b	580/600–650
5	650–675		
6	675–700	5–7	650–750
7	700–750		

Table 4.0. Revised dating for Buckland cemetery phases.

Object conservation

Sarah Watkins-Kenney, Fleur Shearman and Hayley Bullock

The involvement of British Museum conservators with finds from the excavations began in 1994. Kent County Council's Heritage Conservation Group sent a draft specification for the excavation contract to the British Museum (BM), as holders of the 1950s Buckland archive. Leslie Webster of the then

Department of Medieval and Later Antiquities, in turn asked the Department of Conservation and Scientific Research for comments. This was a rare opportunity for archaeological conservators to have direct input to such a specification to try to ensure that there would be adequate conservation provision for the excavated artefacts. The final specification (Howard 1994) included a requirement that there be conservation involvement at all stages from planning to publication. When excavations began, the Canterbury Archaeological Trust team included an on-site conservator (*see* p 1).

In August 1994, the developers agreed that they would donate the artefacts from the excavations to the British Museum. Post-excavation conservation and much of any analyses that might be needed would be done by the museum as the finds would be part of its collection.

Of the 244 graves excavated 69 per cent contained artefacts. Altogether some 850 objects were found (of which 90 per cent were made of metal), plus approximately 2,300 beads (many of which were amber). Just over half the metal objects were iron (weapons, knives, buckles, coffin fittings) and a third were copper alloy (dress fittings, jewellery, coins) (Table 4.1). Objects made of glass (vessels and beads), ceramic (vessels), wood (a bucket with copper alloy bands), antler (a comb), and ivory (purse rings) were also found. All these finds would require some conservation.

On-site conservation

Archaeological artefacts are particularly vulnerable to damage and deterioration on and immediately following excavation due to the sudden change in their environment. Preventive conservation, to minimize deterioration, involved packing them on site in micro-environments appropriate to the type of material and its condition. Objects made of organic materials (ivory, amber, wood, bone) and of glass, were damp when excavated. Due to the way these materials degrade in the soil, it was essential that they were kept damp until they could be conserved. If allowed to dry out in an uncontrolled way they would suffer irreversible shrinkage, distortion or break up. In contrast, metal objects were packed dry as moisture promotes their corrosion.

On-site conservation was by the Trust's conservator but the museum's conservators were on standby in case additional assistance was needed. Very little interventive conservation was necessary on site, apart from some localised consolidation (for example the antler comb from Grave 420 with iron rivets) prior to lifting. Also, some fragile objects (eg the bucket from Grave 391) and some of the ceramic vessels were block lifted still surrounded by soil and wrapped with plaster bandage to hold the object and its contents together.

Post-excavation conservation assessment

Finds arrived at the Department of Conservation in October 1994. They were sorted by type of material and checked against finds lists. A brief inspection of their condition was made in case urgent remedial action might be needed. All wet and damp finds were transferred to a refrigerator. Metals were transferred to a dehumidified (45 per cent relative humidity) strong room. Most were also in dry micro-environments (approximately 18 per cent) created with silica gel in sealed polythene boxes (Watkinson 1987; Knight 1990). Indicator strips or data loggers were placed in the containers to record relative humidity and temperature.

By January 1995 most of the metal finds had been repacked, documented, x-rayed, photographed by grave groups, and assessed. All conservation treatments, as well as description and condition of all objects treated, are recorded on the museum's central computer database (Merlin). Mineral-preserved organic remains were recorded diagrammatically on 'technical information sheets' as well as by photography.

Most of the smaller objects were repacked, by grave group, in plastazote (polyethylene) foam cut-outs within polystyrene (crystal) boxes, which in turn were placed in polyethylene boxes with sufficient silica gel to create dry micro-climates. Some of the larger objects, such as the spearheads, swords and the weaving batten, had been packed on site into cut down lengths of plastic guttering, resting on foam. The foam was replaced with plastazote or covered with acid free tissue paper. Each length of gutter plus object was then sealed into polyethylene tubing with silica gel. These objects were repacked, after conservation, in correx boxes for long-term storage.

Early in 1995, following preliminary examination by x-ray and visually under magnification (x10–x20), it was estimated that conservation of the metal finds would take approximately 3,000 hours (3–4 hours on average per object). Conservation was completed in 2000, taking a total of 4,758 hours.

Post-excavation conservation strategy

Before launching into their conservation it was vital to decide on a strategy to take account not only of the preservation needs of the objects but also the objectives and different priorities of the various specialists involved in the post-excavation programme. Most critical was to establish at what stages of conservation, specialists, scientists and illustrators would want to examine, sample, study and record objects. For the archaeologists to understand the cemetery they would need the maximum amount of information possible for each and every grave; therefore all the objects would be conserved. Burial soil deposits were normally removed from the whole of each object.

A priority would be to reveal and record the full extent of mineral-preserved organic remains (MPOs) on metal objects. It was agreed that:

i) British Museum scientists with responsibility for identification of organic material would examine objects before conservation. Samples might be taken at this stage if visible. Further samples, if needed, would be collected by conservators during cleaning.

ii) Investigative cleaning to reveal, record, and preserve MPOs *in situ* would normally take precedence over revealing metal surfaces.

iii) Consolidation of MPOs would be avoided unless absolutely necessary to hold MPOs *in situ*. Samples would be taken before consolidation.

During conservation, finds listed as individual items in a grave by the excavators, may be found to be parts of one object, as for example, with a firesteel (Grave 300, p 148; Fig 10.31) which was reconstructed from miscellaneous unidentified fragments. For this reason the same conservator (if possible) would treat all the metal finds from a grave. Copies of grave plans with locations of individual finds marked, and photographs of the objects in the graves, also helped to make any connections between objects. The initial conservation strategy for the finds was described in Watkins *et al* (1998).

Condition

Metal finds were covered in thin calcareous deposits, derived from the burial soil. Gold objects were in excellent condition, as one would expect of the most stable metal. Some silver objects were covered in grey corrosion under the soil. Sheet silver was embrittled and fragile but cast silver objects were generally in a more sound condition. Base silver (ie silver mixed with some copper) objects had green and red copper corrosion obscuring the metal surface, gilding and other decoration such as niello. The condition of corrosion patinas on copper alloy objects varied from hard and sound to soft and friable. High-tin bronze buckles, were virtually uncorroded, appearing a dull silver-grey under soil deposits. None of the copper alloy finds showed signs of active corrosion.

Many of the iron objects were extensively corroded. The original surfaces of such objects would be found within the corrosion products; not at the surface of any surviving metal. Between 1994 and 1999 the iron generally showed no evidence of active corrosion. Most pieces appeared to be extensively mineralised, but without metallurgical examination of a cross-

section it can be difficult to accurately assess the degree of mineralisation. Many small objects appeared to be completely mineralised and many had also broken during burial. Most of the larger objects, such as the swords and spearheads, were unbroken. Mineral-preserved organics were most extensive on ironwork, and included horn knife handles; wood, leather and fleece scabbard remains on swords; textiles and leather on buckles and brooches (around iron pins); and, more unusually, remains of feathers on a number of objects.

Apart from the amber beads very few organic objects survived the burial conditions. Extensive traces did survive, however, where they had been in direct contact with iron or copper alloys. Copper corrosion products have a bacteriostatic effect, inhibiting the decay of organic materials, and original fibres or cell structures may be preserved. On iron, corrosion products may 'coat' or replace the organic material to varying degrees but morphological structures may still be identifiable. The presence of mineral-preserved organics restricted the extent of cleaning down to original surfaces that could be done on some objects.

Examination and treatments

Each metal object was x-rayed for identification, to assess its state of repair, and to give information on technical construction and any hidden decoration obscured by overlying soil and corrosion. Most of the objects were x-rayed, as grave groups, in a Torrex 150 machine. The film used was Kodak MX and exposures were in the region of 100–120 KV (5mA) for two to three minutes. X-radiography, particularly of iron finds, helped conservators assess shapes of objects within corrosion, ascertain the degree of mineralisation and physical condition, and identify the presence of technological information and of decoration or precious metal inlays obscured by overlying corrosion. For example, x-radiography revealed: sub-runic symbols, inlaid in base gold on each side of the blade of an iron spearhead from Grave 301 (p 66); the extent of silver and copper inlay on a buckle-plate from Grave 301 (p 128); and that the swords were pattern-welded (*see* pp 237–66).

After radiography, metal finds were cleaned using small hand tools and working under magnification. Original surfaces were revealed within or beneath corrosion, depending on the nature of the metal. Gold objects were rinsed with de-ionised water to remove soil deposits. On a couple of these, local application of dilute (15–30 per cent) formic acid was needed to soften hard calcareous deposits first.

Copper corrosion, overlying silver/gilt surfaces, was removed mainly with small hand tools, working under a binocular microscope (x10–20). In places corrosion was locally softened with dilute (15–30 per cent) formic acid, applied on cotton wool swabs. Chemical residues were removed by applying de-ionised water to the surface and touching with paper tissue, so drawing the residues into the tissue. Treated areas were dried with acetone on cotton wool swabs. When cleaning gilded objects care had to be taken to keep chemicals well away from non-gilded parts, particularly from backing pastes to garnet cloisonné.

Silver chloride was mainly removed manually with a scalpel. Where the corrosion was more powdery and over a good metal surface it could be removed with IMS on cotton wool swabs.

Burial soil and obscuring corrosion products on copper alloys and iron were removed with small hand tools, working under magnification, to reveal original surfaces within the corrosion. Air-abrasive cleaning was also done on most of the ironwork - removing concretions with a fine jet of compressed air (pressure varying from 40 to 80 psi), with or without abrasive powder (eg aluminium oxide or sodium carbonate) in the air stream, blown over the surface of the object. A compressed air pneumatic pencil was also used to remove hard corrosion concretions from iron. The composite iron, silver and garnet cloisonné jewellery proved to be very difficult to clean, with hard iron corrosion overlying softer copper alloy or silver sheet. MPOs were revealed by removing soil deposits with small hand tools or a low pressure air jet, without powder, in the air-abrasive machine.

Damp objects (such as bone, ivory, amber, glass) were cleaned, while still damp, using distilled water and soft brushes and working under a microscope. They were then either dried slowly in air, or via organic solvent baths to prevent drying stresses causing damage. Ivory purse rings (Graves 250 and 255) were dried through solvent baths but amber beads were air dried. Being a resin, amber will dissolve in many of the common organic solvents.

Block-lifted ceramic vessels were carefully excavated in the laboratory. Sherds were then cleaned to remove burial soil before reconstructing the vessels. Glass generally was in good, sound condition. Some of the glass objects were whole when excavated but others were found broken into many pieces. Once vessels were cleaned, it was possible to reconstruct them (both ceramic and glass) with reversible adhesives. Where it was necessary, missing areas were filled, to give physical stability, using materials that could be easily removed.

Fragile and friable surfaces, of all materials, were consolidated, if necessary, with 5 per cent Paraloid B72 in acetone/IMS (50/50 by volume), applied with a brush, or from a pipette. MPOs were only consolidated (locally) if absolutely necessary for their survival on the object and only after they had been sampled for identification.

Fragmentary objects were reconstructed using HMG (a cellulose nitrate adhesive). Some repairs, or particularly fragile objects, were supported with backings of nylon gossamer or fibreglass tissue secured with Paraloid B72 or HMG diluted in acetone for application. Some support fills on reconstructed objects were made with glass micro-balloons in Paraloid B72 or HMG.

As the copper alloy objects have shown no signs of active corrosion, no chemical stabilisation treatments have been done.

Over the years, many *interventive* stabilisation methods have been tried for archaeological iron. Such treatments can, however, compromise, if not destroy, archaeological and technological evidence within the objects and may not confer long term stability. The policy in the Museum generally is to establish environmental conditions within stores to minimize deterioration. Currently, there are a number of iron objects that are displaying signs of active corrosion. Research is being carried out by members of staff at the British Museum in relation to the corrosion of iron, and the most appropriate treatments for it. In the interim period all metal objects are stored in dry micro-environments, created with silica gel in sealed polythene boxes.

Research projects relating to the finds

Several projects have been undertaken by the Department of Conservation, Science and Documentation, including: extensive radiography of swords, spearheads and shield bosses to better understand their construction (see Part 6);

Metal	Percentage of total	Objects included
Iron (Fe)	52.0	weapons, knives, buckles, girdle-hangers, tools, coffin fittings
Copper alloy (CuA)	33.0	dress fittings & jewellery, coins, a scales & weights set, vessel fittings
Lead (Pb)	0.5	spindle-whorl
Silver (Ag)	2.5	crystal ball mounts, a spoon/skimmer, strap-ends, finger ring, pendants
Gold (Au)	2.0	pendants (including bracteates), braid
Ag/Au/CuA	10.0	brooches

Table 4.1. Summmary of metal finds buried in graves.

examination of metallographic structures of swords and knives; analysis of niello inlay on brooches; investigation of the technical construction and analysis of white inlay on cloisonné and garnet jewellery; identification of organic remains especially of woods in spearhead sockets and sword scabbards (Part 6). The MPOs and their conservation have formed part of two conservation student dissertations (Julien 1992; Didelot 1997).

Conclusions

Anglo-Saxon cemeteries tend to enjoy a brief period of celebrity and publicity when first excavated, but then all too often drift into an archaeological 'twilight zone', disappearing from public and academic view, as the enormity of the task of post-excavation study and recording sets in (Watkins *et al* 1998, 20). To counteract this 'drift', a study day on Buckland was held in April 1996, coinciding with a temporary exhibition of some of the finds at the British Museum. Several objects have been loaned to Dover Museum for local exhibition. Also, numerous visitors to the Department of Conservation were able to see the finds whilst conservation was in progress.

Objects excavated from burials are part of a total assemblage: the grave, the skeleton, and its associated artefacts. The challenge is not only to conserve the objects, but also to record and preserve information that they may retain, thus enabling archaeologists to interpret and understand the grave and its context.

Weapons

Weapons are considered to be male equipment and thirty-two of the adult and juvenile males in the 1994 excavations had been buried with them. Such items include swords, shields, spears, arrowheads, a seax and large knives, a fauchard and an axehead (Figs 4.1–4.15; Table 4.2). Weapon graves constitute 13 per cent of the total number of graves excavated in 1994. This figure may be compared with 20 per cent in the 1951–3 Buckland excavations and 25 per cent at Mill Hill, Deal[2] (Table 4.3). For a discussion of weapon combinations *see* pp 375–7.

In the 1994 excavations, the weapon graves were scattered throughout most of the plots, except the small Plots R and U. Seventeen of the graves contained just a spear; three more had a shield and a spear. Four contained a sword, a shield and a spear and two others, only a sword and spear. Grave 437 contained a sword but no spear or shield. Sword Grave

Grave	Phase	Sword	Spear	Shield	Large knife	Other
206	-				a	
218	-				e	
220	-		a		a	
230	2b-3a		b	d, e	s	
233	-		a			
240	-		a, b			
249C	2-3	a	c, e			
251	3		a			
256	-		c, e			
259	-		a			
262	2-3		a			
264	3	b	a	e-i		
265B	3a	b	a	c, d		
297	2		b, g	h, i	b	
299	-		a			
300	1b-2a		q			
301	-		a			
302	2-3a					b arrowhead
323	3		a	c-f		
337	-		c			
346	3	b	a			e axehead
363	-		a			
374	-		a			
375	3b	b	a	c		
381	1b-2a					a seax
393A	-		a		b	
400	-		b			
411	-		a			
414	2b-3a	b	a	g-k		
421	-					a arrowhead
423	2b-3a		a, b			
437	2	a				c fauchard

Table 4.2. Details of weapon combinations denoted by grave good letter.

	Buckland 1951–3	Buckland 1994	Mill Hill, Deal
Sword only		1	
Sword and fauchard		1	
Sword and shield			
Sword and spear	9	2	
Sword, shield and spear	9	4	4
Sword, axe and spear		1	
Spear only	13	15	8
Spear and shield	2	3	8
Spear and large knife	1	2	
Spear and seax	1		1
Seax	2		
Arrowhead only	1?	2	

Table 4.3. Comparison of weapon combinations at Buckland and Mill Hill, Deal.

---

2.   See Parfitt and Brugmann 1997, fig 1 for a map showing the distribution of the main Anglo-Saxon cemeteries in east Kent.

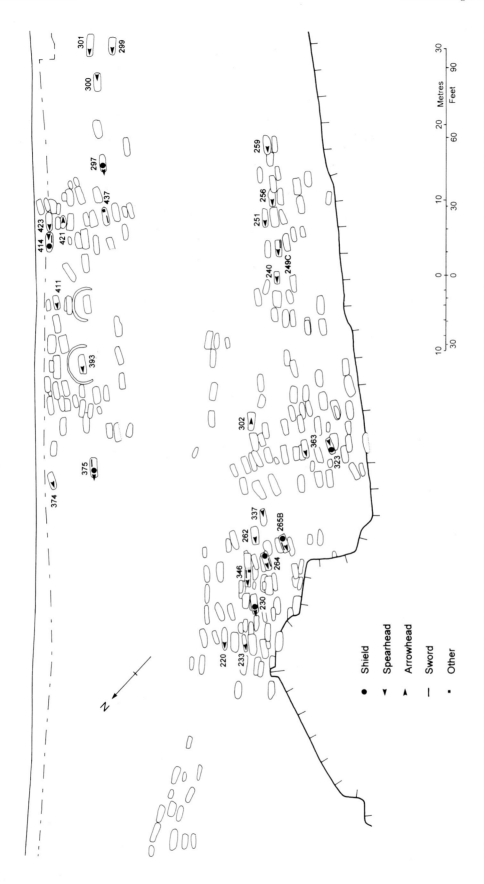

Fig 4.1. Plan of 1994 excavations showing distribution of weapon graves.

346 also contained an iron axehead and Grave 437 produced an uncommon type of socketed iron fauchard or bill-hook, in addition to the sword and a glass bowl. Graves 302 and 421 produced iron arrowheads. A seax was recovered from Grave 381. Large knives were found in Graves 206, 218, 297 and 393A (*see* pp 164–71). A further thirty-six weapon burials have been previously recorded by Evison, of which seventeen were males with swords (Evison 1987, 21).

Swords

Barry Ager

Seven swords were found, in Graves 249C, 264, 265B, 346, 375, 414 and 437. They are all of the long, double-edged type, with pointed tips and pattern-welded blades. None of them has any special embellishment, though three have small iron pommels of different forms: rectangular bar (Grave 264), truncated pyramid (Grave 375), and ovoid button (Grave 437); one has no pommel, but the end of the tang is burred over to secure the organic components of the hilt (Grave 249C). The pattern-welding of the swords and the mineral-preserved organic remains of the hilts and scabbards are discussed respectively by Janet Lang in Part 6 (pp 237–66) and by Fleur Shearman (pp 53–6) .

A detached, trapezoidal pommel (e) of copper alloy was found by the left pelvis in female Grave 360, where it had perhaps been contained in a pouch as a keepsake.

All the swords were found in the graves of adult males, their ages ranging between 25 and 50 years. Three of the sword graves are grouped close together in Plot S (Graves 264, 265B and 346) and it may be significant that the female Grave 360, with the detached pommel, is also located in their vicinity (Figs 2.2 and 4.1). The other sword graves do not show any particular concentration, but three lie towards the opposite end of the cemetery from the main group (Graves 249, 414, and 437), leaving Grave 375 on the edge of Plot X where no other swords were found, though it has a DNA link with Grave 437 (*see* p 322). There were no swords, either, in the areas at each end of the cemetery (Fig 4.1).

Position in grave

There is a fair degree of consistency in the placing of the sword in four cases, in agreement with general Anglo-Saxon practice, on the left of the body and upper leg, (ie on the owner's left, the side on which it would have been worn in life), overlying the arm in Grave 346 and underlying it in Grave 375, with the hilt in the region of the shoulder or upper arm (West 1988, 8; Härke 1992a, 127), and apparently

separate from any surviving belt (Graves 264, 346, 375 and 414). In one case, however, the hilt was on the level of the lower left body and the upper end of the scabbard may still have been attached to the waist belt worn by the deceased at burial (Grave 265B; Fig 10.83). In the other two cases (Graves 249C and 437) the swords were on the right of the body (although still next to the upper part of it, the hilt near the skull in Grave 437; Fig 10.116), comparable to the common practice in many Merovingian-period cemeteries on the Continent, eg at Dittenheim, Germany (Haas-Gebhard 1998, 19), although in France they were found on either the right or the left, more often the latter (Boulanger 1902–5, 118). Even at Dittenheim, grave 181, a sword was placed on the left, while at Straubing-Bajuwarenstraße I, Germany, two of thirty-five swords were on the left, the rest on the right (Geisler 1998). The placing on the right in Grave 437 perhaps reflects Frankish practice, especially in the light of the associated fauchard and glass bowl (Figs 10.67, 10.68 and 10.116). On the other hand, the position in Grave 249C need not have any special ethnic significance as the grave contains no specifically Frankish objects; the rule of position is not entirely hard and fast, and the spearhead is placed at the top of the grave, while in Frankish graves they are often placed pointing to the bottom (*see* p 63).

Six swords were combined with spears (Table 9.1), three on the same side of the body (Graves 264, 265B, and 414) and three on the opposite side (Graves 249C, 346, and 375). In four of these graves the weapon-set further included a shield (Graves 264, 265B, 375, and 414) and in two of these cases the shield would have overlapped one or other end of the sword (Graves 265B and 375). The placing of the boss of the shield directly over the hilt of the sword in Grave 375 may have been deliberate (Fig 10.103).

Blade dimensions

Overall sword lengths, including tang and pommel, range mainly from 870 to 920mm (approx), with one longer example at 944mm, minimum (Grave 265B). Blade widths, measured at the upper ends, range mainly between 43– 45mm (Graves 249C and 437) and 48–52mm (Graves 265B, 346, 375, 414); the widest is 55mm (Grave 264), at the upper limit for Behmer's narrow-bladed form (1939, 37). When the width is measured again at about 150mm from the tip, all of the blades show varying, slight degrees of taper, with a difference mainly between 5 and 8mm. This is most marked in the case of Grave 346, where the difference is 10mm, while Grave 437 is almost parallel-sided, with a difference of only 3mm. The maximum surviving thickness is around 3–4mm (but this compares with thicknesses of 4–5mm of early Anglo-Saxon swords housed in the British Museum with surviving original surfaces, eg from Waterbeach, Cambridgeshire, the Thames and London, and may possibly reflect some corrosion post-deposition).

Fullers are not always visible and may not have been present on all blades, although corrosion products of scabbards obscure the detail of the surfaces. Sectioning of the blades of Graves 264 and 265B shows fullers 2mm deep, but in the case of swords from Graves 346, 375 and 437 there is only a slight depression of 1–1.5mm. The other two blades were not sectioned: no fuller is visible on Grave 249C, but a central depression can be seen on Grave 414. Fullers were probably produced by hammering the blades between a shaped fuller tool, although grinding out was also used on the Continent (Engstrom *et al* 1989).

Pommels, grips and guards

Material and construction

The organic remains, surviving in most cases to some extent at least, show that the hilts comprised three main sections made of horn, where identification has been possible: a straight upper and lower guard and a grip section, held in place on the tang by either an iron or organic pommel, or by burring the end of the tang. However, not enough remains to reconstruct the precise form of the components.

Pommel forms

Three swords have iron pommels, all of different forms and no doubt secured by hammering out the end of the tang (Graves 264, 375 and 437); one with no trace of a pommel has only a slightly burred end to the tang to achieve the same result (Grave 249C); and one has the vestiges of an organic pommel above an upper guard of horn of a different colour (the contrast may or may not be deliberate; insufficient identifiable structure remains of the pommel though, to determine whether it is horn or ivory), although no evidence survives to show how it was fixed (Grave 414). In the case of Grave 346 no pommel survives, although there are organic traces of an upper guard, and both the end of the tang and any pommel are missing on Grave 265B.

The pommel of Grave 264 consists of a rectangular-section bar; surviving length, 37mm. The remains of bar-shaped, though more convex, pommels can be seen on fifth- to sixth-century swords from Lewes, Sussex, from Cursley Field, Bishopstone, Buckinghamshire and an example (with an unrecorded findspot) in Buckinghamshire County Museum (Baldwin Brown 1915a, pl 25, 2; Babb 1996, fig 1, 1 and 4).

A rectangular, bar-shaped pommel is used also on a weaving batten from Spong Hill, Norfolk, grave 24 (Gilmour 1984, fig 82, 3; Hines 1997a, fig 119e) and a late seventh-century seax from grave 85 at Polhill, Kent (Philp 1973a, fig 53, 482).

The pommel of Grave 375 is a low, truncated pyramidal cap with a slightly rounded top; length, 17mm. It is similar in form to the copper alloy pommel on a sword of Behmer's type VI from Barshalder, Gotland, Sweden (Behmer 1939, Taf 33, 1b), though this may be purely coincidental.

The pommel of Grave 437 appears from what survives to be a small, ovoid button, held by beating out the end of the tang; surviving length, 13mm. Swords from Shepperton, Middlesex; Chessell Down, Isle of Wight and Alfriston, Sussex, graves 1 and 86, have similar pommels (Baldwin Brown 1915a, pl 26, 2; Arnold 1982, fig 29, 99; Welch 1983, figs 3a and 35a). Similar pommels occur on the Continent, too, eg at Westheim, grave 31, of the sixth century, and Straubing-Bajuwarenstraße I, Germany, grave 486 (Reiß 1994, Taf 27, 1; Geisler 1998, Taf 177, 486: 1).

Sword 249C has merely a slightly expanded, burred end to the tang, probably to secure either an organic pommel or an upper guard/pommel alone. The form is common on early Anglo-Saxon swords, eg the fifth- to sixth-century swords from Croydon, Surrey, and Alton, Hampshire, grave 42, and the sword from Buckland Grave 96B (Evison Phase 4, *c* AD 625–650) (Baldwin Brown 1915a, 219, pl 25, 3; Evison 1987, fig 46, 10a, c; Evison 1988, fig 35: 42, 1a), and also on swords in the British Museum from Waterbeach, Cambridgeshire (registered no 69, 3–15, 1); Ashdown, near Lambourn, Berkshire (registered no 55,10–18,1), and Cumberland, with decorative mounts of the early seventh century (Baldwin Brown 1915a, pl 25, 9; Davidson 1998, 58–9, fig 63). The same form occurs on some continental swords, eg Straubing-Bajuwarenstraße I, grave 272 (Geisler 1998, Taf 79, 1).

Insufficient survives of the organic pommel of Grave 414 to suggest its original shape. Simple, rounded, elliptical, horn pommels doubling as upper guards are known from a few Anglo-Saxon and Germanic swords, most famously the one from Cumberland. A late fifth- to sixth-century sword with a horn pommel, grip and guard is recorded from Watchfield, Oxfordshire, grave 2 (Scull 1992, illus 26: 83, 10; 77; and 80), and a fine, early seventh-century example from Snape, Suffolk, with a largely intact, presumptively horn pommel, elliptical lower guard and tapering grip of oval section, shaped for the fingers, is also recorded (Cameron and Filmer-Sankey 1993, pl 1, fig 1). Seven swords from Dittenheim, Germany, originally had organic pommels (Haas-Gebhard 1998, 19).

The detached, copper alloy pommel (e) from Grave 360 is of a widespread and long-lived tang-held (unriveted) type.

A few examples are found in Anglo-Saxon and Scandinavian graves, but its main distribution is continental, particularly in the Rhineland, southern Germany and northern Italy (Menghin 1983, 76–7, 319–20, liste I. 3, karte 4). Menghin indicates the beginning of the type in his period B (AD 480–530), with most examples dating to around AD 600. It lasted into the early seventh century and at Dittenheim there is a late occurrence in grave 181 of *Schicht* 3a, around AD 620–630/40 (Haas-Gebhard 1998, Taf 98c, 1). But Evison (1988, 5) has queried Menghin's late start for the type and gains some support from an example of the simple form found with a late provincial-Roman buckle-loop in cremation grave K13/B1at Liebenau, Lower Saxony, Germany (Häßler 1985, Taf 63, K13/B1, 2), though Menghin (*op cit*, 77) dates this grave to the later fifth century. English occurrences include the sword from Collingbourne Ducis, Wiltshire, grave 2, with an unriveted pommel and late fifth- to early sixth-century associations (Gingell 1978, fig 14, 1); one from an early sword of Behmer's type VI from Bowcombe Down, Isle of Wight, graves 12–14 (Arnold 1982, fig 63, 12–14ib); and two others from Alfriston, Sussex, graves 26 (late fifth century; possibly a continental Germanic or Frankish 'import') and 89 (mid sixth century) (Evison 1965, 36, 80, fig 17a; Welch 1983, 119–20, figs 9c, and 37a).

Rivetless, copper alloy pommels of a more cocked-hat shape are also recorded, eg from grave 16 of the early seventh century at Alton, Hampshire (Evison 1988, fig 27/16.1b); and from the mid sixth-century horse and rider burial at Eriswell (RAF Lakenheath), Suffolk (Evans 2000, 28) on a sword with a whorl bead associated with the scabbard; the one on the sword from Chessell Down, grave 76, however, is regarded as a special, predominantly Scandinavian, pyramidal form of the late fifth century by Menghin (1983, 173, Karte 3; Arnold 1982, pl 9f, fig 17).

The hilt

The lengths of the tangs range from about 115 to 124mm and about half the swords have the transverse marks of the grain of upper and lower guards of organic material and, in a couple of cases, the vertical grain of the hand-grip. In all cases where traces of the guards remain, the lower one is between 1 and 3mm thicker than the upper one (thickness of lower guards: 11–14mm; of upper guards: 9–13mm). Where visible traces remain, the length of the grip between the upper and lower guards measures mainly between 92 and 96mm; the shortest is 90mm (approx); ie a single-handed grip.

There is no certain evidence for the use of ivory as on the sword from Buckland Grave 93/6, though there are perhaps ivory pommel remains on the hilt from Grave 414 (see

above and p 253). A late sixth-/seventh-century sword from Acklam Wold, North Yorkshire includes a hilt guard probably of ivory and possibly also a covering over the wooden grip (Ager and Gilmour 1988); and ivory was used for the front of the scabbard and probably also the grip of a Byzantine-Lombardic dagger of the late sixth or early seventh century from Castel Trosino, Italy (Paroli 2000, 142–6, fig 13.4–6). Ivory guards and grips are known on Roman swords, and on Germanic swords of the fifth and sixth centuries (Ager and Gilmour 1988, 15).

Pieces of wood varying in size from small to substantial have been observed on the hilts of swords beneath the horn of the upper and/or lower guards and the grip, which may have been inserted as packing pieces to secure the grip (Graves 265B, 375, 414 and 437; see below). These were also seen on the Acklam sword, where they were used to secure the grip (Ager and Gilmour 1988, 14).

Ribs on tangs (Graves 264 and 375)

On both sides of the tang of the sword from Grave 264 there is a slightly raised, but clear, midrib running the full length of the tang between, and perhaps under, the guards, although there is an offset discontinuity at one point (Fig 4.3). On both sides of the tang of the sword from Grave 375 there is a double, lengthwise rib (Fig 4.4 and 4.5) and a short, vertical rib is also present on one side of the upper guard of the sword from Grave 414; these ribs are mineral-preserved organic remains and not part of the metal of the tang (*see* pp 54–6). Although not previously remarked in discussions of early Anglo-Saxon swords, single midribs do occur on the tangs of swords, both from Buckland and at least two other sites, eg in the organic residue on both sides of the tang of the sword from Buckland Grave 91; more substantially on both sides of a sixth-century sword from Long Wittenham, Oxfordshire (British Museum registered no P&E 75, 3–10, 40); and a short section only on one side of the upper end of the tang of the sword from the seventh-century barrow at Bowerslow, Tissington, Derbyshire (British Museum registered no P&E 73, 6–2, 104). Although the ribs on these other swords have not been x-rayed, it seems that visually they are of a similar nature and the feature may be more widespread on Anglo-Saxon swords generally.

Sword fittings

Methods of suspension

The scabbard containing the sword from Grave 265B appears from its position to have been buried still attached to the buckled waist-belt (Fig 10.83). It shows no special mounts for attachment, so was probably suspended simply as illustrated by Menghin (1983, Abb 90). The remaining swords similarly show no clear evidence for the means of suspension. Assuming they had been worn in the same way as in Grave 265B, they appear from their high position within the grave to have been buried in their scabbards, but clearly detached from any waist belt (buckles were present in the region of the waist in Graves 249C, 375, 414 and 437).

Comparison with Buckland 1951–3

The position of the swords relative to the body is the same as with the earlier Buckland excavations where, out of the fourteen excavated examples, all but one was found on, or to, the left, with the hilt in the region of the shoulder; Grave 71 was on the right.

Early Anglo-Saxon swords in general show a correlation with male burials containing evidence for high status (Härke 1992a, table 25). But this is not always the case, as at Droxford, Hampshire, where six swords were found in a generally poor cemetery (Aldsworth 1978, 164). The earlier Buckland excavations had at least six examples of swords (Graves 27, 33, 71, 93, 96B and 131), out of a total of seventeen, with simple, shallow or convex iron pommels broadly comparable to Graves 249 and 437, although mostly longer. But the 1950s excavations also yielded four swords with more elaborate hilt-fittings, including a ring-sword, a sword with a silver lower guard, one with bronze-inlaid guards, and another with a silver band at each end of the grip, dating to the period AD 525–650 overall (Phases 2–4; Evison 1987, Graves C, 94B, 96A and 98), none of which are represented in the 1994 sample. Similarly, the scabbards of the swords from the 1994 excavations all lack metal fittings or braided openings, while with those from the earlier excavations two possibly have iron binding strips round the mouth (Graves 27 and 131), three have copper alloy or silver mouthpieces or binding strips (Graves C, 96A and 96B), and three have cords or braiding round the mouth (Graves C, 94B, and unstratified no 7). This would all appear to suggest that the sword-wearers in the 1994 part of the Buckland cemetery were of lower-ranking status than many, if not most, of those of the upper area, although age may also have been a factor. The 1951–3 excavations produced one sword that is definitely a Frankish import (Grave 96A), but it is uncertain if any from the 1994 excavations are from the Continent apart from the sword in Grave 414.

A further difference worth noting is that there is less evidence for sword belts with elaborate fittings from the 1994 excavations, compared with the previous assemblage.

With the 1950s assemblage, five of the sword graves had no belt fittings, while nine had belt-buckles surviving. Five of these were simple iron buckles, but one had a tinned bronze buckle with a punch-decorated triangular plate and a set of associated mounts (Grave 56), one was 'silvered' bronze (Grave 4), and two were accompanied by shoe-shaped rivets of Frankish derivation (Graves 91, of copper alloy, and 96A, of high-tin bronze ('silver-plated')); there was also a set of tinned bronze mounts, probably originally with a buckle-loop (Grave 98). With the 1994 excavations, one of the sword graves had no belt fittings while six did (Graves 249C, 264, 265B, 375, 414 and 437), but two are simple iron, two simple copper alloy, one iron with silver elements (Grave 264), and only in Grave 265B do they comprise a set, in copper alloy (*see* pp 405–6).

Lack of rich swords

In the sample of fifth- to seventh-century burials selected for analytical research by Härke (1992a, table 8), 10.8 per cent of all weapon graves, and 11.6 per cent of undisturbed weapon graves, contain a sword, although there is a slight fluctuation over the period (*ibid*, Abb 12). There are no fittings or ivory hilts (unlike Buckland Grave 93/6), though possibly ivory/horn pommel remains on the sword from Grave 414 would indicate higher status. However, swords themselves are a high-status marker and burials with axes, swords, or seaxes show the highest investment of labour and wealth of all male burials (Härke 1992a, table 25), although they may occur in otherwise poor graves, eg Droxford (Aldsworth 1978, 164 and fig 45), as noted above.

Dating implications

In view of the lack of diagnostic hilt or scabbard fittings it is not possible to date the Buckland 1994 swords, or their scabbards, closely and, although there are no certainly seventh-century features, this does not preclude such a date in some cases. The implication is that, although the likelihood is not high, some of the sword graves (Graves 265B, 346, 375 or 414) might possibly date to a later phase than the dating by other associations would seem to indicate.

Sword graves in Kentish cemeteries

Swords are comparatively rare in early Anglo-Saxon cemeteries, perhaps in part because of the 'heirloom factor' (Baldwin Brown 1915a, 207–9), though in east Kent they are nearly always present (Härke 1992a, 105). Because of the lack of completely excavated cemeteries, however, and often inadequate recording, it is possible to give only crude calculations of proportion. At Buckland itself perhaps as many as one hundred or more graves (possibly including another sword burial) were destroyed by the railway, although no clear records survive (*see* pp 4–6 and p 371). Based on the data given by Baldwin Brown (1915a, 207–8) and the evidence from the earlier excavations at Buckland, it has been suggested that the high proportion of weapon graves at Sarre and Buckland especially (both at 10 per cent, against the average for the region of 5.2 per cent) reflects the presence of military establishments of the king's port-reeves to protect trading centres (Chadwick Hawkes 1969, 191–2; Härke 1992a, 26). However, if the data now available for both parts of Buckland is combined, the proportion here is considerably reduced to 5.8 per cent, which is little above the average (compare the next highest at Mill Hill, with 5.3 per cent, or Alfriston, Sussex, with 5.2 per cent). The case for a royal military establishment at Dover becomes less persuasive accordingly (*see* p 369), while the status of Sarre is emphasised.

Sword scabbards and hilts　　*Fleur Shearman with Hayley Bullock, Eric Nordgren and Heidi Leseur*

In the following text each of the scabbards and hilts is reviewed in turn. Identification of wood and fleece samples taken by Caroline Cartwright has not been incorporated here but is noted in the grave catalogue (Part 10, pp 386–453).

Grave 249C

Scabbard (Fig 4.2)

There are extensive remains on the upper third of the blade of a wooden scabbard which was covered with leather. The wood is shaped and slopes down towards the edges of the blade from a central gully. The thickness of scabbard laths is no more than 1mm, measured at the exposed edge of the blade.

　　On one side of the blade, approximately one third of the way down from the shoulder, are the remains of at least three cords of plied fibre, probably of vegetable origin (Fig 4.2). These lie parallel to each other, along the length of the sword on the wood of the scabbard, in the form of three radiating lines. The outer two cords ray outwards, away from each other, with the widest part towards the middle of the blade. Residual traces and impressions of the third cord run down the centre of the scabbard. It is not possible to trace its full extent towards the lower end of the blade, where it may have continued, as the scabbard is not preserved in this area. Remains of the outer scabbard

0 _____ 5cm　　0 _____ 5cm

Fig 4.2. Radiating ribs on scabbard of sword from Grave 249C.

Fig 4.3. Upper part of sword from Grave 264.

leather, where this has survived, overlie the cords in this area and at the tip of the blade where it curves around the blade. The decorative cords would have been visible as raised ridges through the distortion of the thin scabbard leather. One small area at mid-blade retains the grain pattern which is suggestive of a bovine origin; from its thinness (at approximately 1mm) calfskin is indicated. There are two other areas where the upper scabbard leather retains shaped impressions, which may also be of decorative origin. Due to their ephemeral nature it is not possible to be more definite in their interpretation.

　　This unusual feature is similar in appearance to an unpublished example where three cords in a 'sun-burst' pattern have been recently revealed on a sword from the Sutton Hoo 2000 excavations. Scabbard decoration is discussed in detail by Cameron (2000, 35–6), where Anglo-Saxon and Scandinavian parallels either in the form of cords or carved detail, are given. At least two rayed cords are also preserved on the scabbard from Broomfield, Essex, in the collections of the British Museum (Cameron 2000, fig 11). What appears to be a triple ray in applied cords or carved in the wood of the scabbard is preserved on a sword from West Garth, Suffolk (Cameron 2000, fig 8i). This feature is drawn but not mentioned in the publication by West (1988, fig 75a).

A smooth layer of what may be interpreted as original adhesive or resin is present in some areas on the wood. An adhesive may have been used to stick the cords and perhaps the leather in place. There is no evidence for a fleece lining to the scabbard.

Hilt

There are only ephemeral traces of the organic parts of the grip, lower and upper guards. The grain direction runs parallel to the components of the hilt and would appear to be horn. The top of the tang has been burred over to form a rudimentary pommel (see above).

Grave 264

Scabbard

There are traces only of the wood from the scabbard, preserved on the edge of the blade. However, numerous detached fragments from the scabbard were retrieved with the sword. A number of these have been reconstructed to form the upper part of the scabbard lath on one side; the reconstructed fragment shows only minimal evidence for shaping. The thickness of scabbard laths, where they can be measured, are between 1.5 and 2mm. Traces of the fleece lining are present on the blade and the reverse of the reconstructed fragment. The cut edge of the fleece can be seen along the same edge of both sides of the blade. Halfway down the fleece on one side there are stitching threads running across the sword, indicating that the fleece has been repaired or added to in this area. There is a blackish layer between the wood and the fleece, which may be evidence for an adhesive layer. In several places there are remains of leather over the wood, probably from the upper scabbard leather. Traces of textile fibres over a fragment of leather on the upper third of the blade may be from an indirect association of body or possibly associated with a binding for the scabbard, although there is insufficient evidence to interpret this with confidence.

Hilt

Mineral-preserved organic remains surviving on the hilt of the sword indicate the lower and upper guards and the grip were made of horn. The grain direction runs parallel to the hilt components. The pommel is iron and only partially survives. The tang is broad and tapers toward the pommel. A central raised rib is present running down the centre front and back of the grip section of the tang (Fig 4.3). A feature similar in appearance has been noted by Barry Ager on the hilt of the sword from Long Wittenham in the collections of the British Museum (see above). A pair of ribs is present on the sword from Buckland Grave 375 and a short ridge is on the upper guard of the sword from Grave 414. Examination of the feature on the sword from Grave 264 suggests that it may have its origin in a channel cut with a U-shaped metal tool on the inside of the horn grip section. The channel has subsequently filled from behind with iron corrosion products which have preserved the horn in direct association with it, forming a positive cast of the groove. The line of the rib is broken and slightly offset, which would indicate that a gouge or bore has been introduced from either end of the grip section during its shaping for use. The function of this feature is not clear; it may be an accident of carving the grip section or, alternatively, a deliberate channel used to introduce an adhesive. The area of the grip where the horn has not been preserved was examined and no corresponding rib was found in the iron of the tang. Neither did x-radiography of this area (by Janet Ambers) from the side, show up any x-ray opaque areas indicating a ridge thicker than the tang itself.

Experimental replication of this feature using a U-shaped gouge on horn and casting the impression in dental putty produced a similar effect to that seen on the Buckland hilts. Examination of waste from horn working may throw more light on this feature.

Grave 265B

Scabbard

There are traces of mineral-replaced organics relating to the wooden scabbard, fleece lining and the upper leather of the scabbard. The staple on the fleece is about 10mm in length.

Hilt

The hilt is broken at the tip of the tang. Mineral-preserved horn is present on the lower and upper guards and grip. The grain direction runs parallel with the components of the hilt. There is a wooden packing piece under the tang; as elsewhere its purpose may be to pack out a hollow area under the horn hilt.

Grave 346

Scabbard

There are some remains of wood on the upper third of the blade; the evidence of the surviving fragment nearest the shoulder of the blade indicates the laths of wood may have been shaped, as the profile of the wood slopes down towards the edge of the blade from the edge of the remains of a central gully. The width of one of the laths, where it can be measured, is 1mm in thickness. There are extensive remains of a fleece lining. A defined edge on one side of the blade shows the fleece to have been cut back to about 100mm below the mouth of the blade. The opposing face of the blade does not show this feature but there is no evidence of surviving fleece either. The cut edge of the fleece is visible down opposite sides of the same edge of the blade. Remains of mineral-preserved leather over the wood in this area may suggest the wooden scabbard had a leather covering.

Hilt

Traces of mineral-preserved horn on the hilt suggest the lower and upper guards and the grip were made of horn. The grain runs parallel to the hilt components.

Grave 375

Scabbard

There are traces of mineral-preserved wood from the scabbard on both sides of the blade. Traces of mineral-preserved fibres from the fleece lining are also present on both sides of the blade. The upper layers of the scabbard do not survive.

Hilt

Mineral-preserved horn remains are present on the hilt forming the lower guard, grip and upper guard. The grain direction runs parallel to the hilt components. A double rib is present on both sides of the grip (Figs 4.4 and 4.5). This would appear to be the same feature as the single rib on the sword from Grave 264 and may relate to grooves introduced in the manufacture stage of the grip (see discussion on hilt

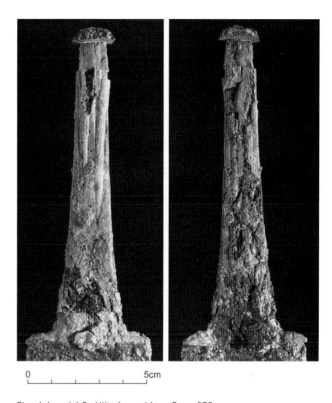

Figs 4.4 and 4.5. Hilt of sword from Grave 375.

from Grave 264 above). There is some evidence for 'chatter marks' from the tool used, which run at right angles to the ribbed impression. There are small pieces of wood present on the hilt of the sword beneath the horn, on the upper guard and the grip, and following their grain direction. These may have been inserted as on other swords from Buckland, as packing pieces to secure the grip. There is a cut notch at the top of the grip on one side.

Grave 414

Scabbard

There are remains of mineral-preserved wood along the edges and on one side of the lower half of the blade. The width of the lath can be measured near the shoulder of the blade and is 3mm in thickness. One side has a mineral-replaced fleece covering most of the blade. In areas, the flesh side of the skin is preserved. No fleece remains were found on the opposing side. A black layer between the wood and the fleece may be evidence for adhesive. Along one edge in three areas curving around the blade above the wood, there is evidence suggesting another scabbard leather.

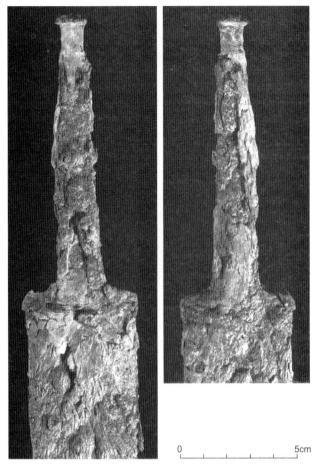

0   5cm

Figs 4.6 and 4.7. Hilt of sword from Grave 437.

Hilt

Traces of mineral-preserved horn on the hilt indicate the presence of the grip, upper and lower guards. Slight traces survive on the shoulder of the blade. The grain direction runs parallel with the orientation of the hilt components. The remains of a substantial wood packing piece lies against the tang below the horn on the grip, with the grain direction running parallel to it. There is a ribbed feature on the horn section of the upper guard which may replicate a tool groove made on the inside of this piece during manufacture (see hilts from Graves 264 and 375, above). There is some evidence that there was another shaped piece of horn, or possibly some other material of contrasting appearance such as ivory, above the upper guard, perhaps a shaped terminal or knop acting as a pommel.

Grave 437

Scabbard

There are traces of the wooden scabbard in one area. Extensive remains of fleece lining with a long staple are preserved on the blade. Two-thirds of the way down the blade there would appear to be a change in the fibre direction. This could indicate the mid-area of a fleece has been used. The cut edge of the fleece is clearly visible running along one edge of the blade. Ephemeral traces of leather above the wood and curving around the edge of the blade in isolated areas may indicate the scabbard had an upper leather. An area of surviving grain pattern suggests this is bovine and from the width of the skin and the pore distribution, calfskin is indicated. Associated with the sword is a fragment of stitched leather, although it is not clear whether this derives from the scabbard, the purse or knife sheath, all found in the vicinity of the sword.

Hilt

Traces of mineral-preserved horn on the hilt indicate the presence of the grip and upper and lower guards (Figs 4.6 and 4.7). The grain direction runs parallel to the components of the hilt. Three tabs of wood are present under the shoulder, grip and pommel sections of the hilt, under the horn. Where it is visible, the grain direction runs parallel to the grip. As above, these features would appear to relate to packing pieces or wedges to secure and wedge cavities in the horn sections of the hilt components.

Shields

Stephanie Spain[3]

(Graves 230, 264, 265B, 297, 323 and 414)

Shields were recovered from seven graves. These were distributed unevenly across the 1994 cemetery area, with some areas devoid of shields, while three occurred close together in Plot S (Graves 230, 264 and 265B; Figs 2.2 and 4.1). Two burials were well-spaced (Graves 375 and 297) and one, Grave 375, may have been covered by a barrow (*see* p 20), but the others occurred in densely-packed areas, sometimes cutting earlier interments (Figs 2.2 and 4.1). The clustering of shield burials is not uncommon and in part reflects the phases in which the various parts of the cemetery were used. At other east Kent sites, such as Finglesham, clusters occur in 'high status' plots which seem to have been reserved for élite

---

3. The information and analysis given here was made in 2003 and reflects the state of knowledge current at that time.

family or other groups within the burying community (Chadwick Hawkes 1982b; Chadwick Hawkes and Grainger 2006, 21–2).

The 1994 shields all fall within revised Buckland Phases 2 and 3 (AD 510/30–650). Evison assigned all the Buckland 1951–3 shield burials to her Phases 3 (AD 575–625) and 4 (AD 625–50) but recent work suggests that one shield, at least, dates to the mid sixth century and thus belongs in her Phase 2 (AD 525–575) (Evison 1987; Spain 2000). There is close agreement, then, between the two cemetery areas with regard to this rather limited period of shield burial.

In the graves excavated in 1994, two shields were positioned on the chest, two on the feet and one each on the pelvis, knees and face. It is significant that the predominant 'lower body habit' (pelvis, knees, feet) occurs in the densely packed areas, while the two chest positions occur in well-spaced burials, including possible barrow burial, Grave 375 (see above). This arrangement is also seen at Mill Hill, Deal, where chest positions occur in a string of well-spaced, probable barrow burials (Parfitt and Brugmann 1997, fig 8). Anglo-Saxon cemeteries tend to have one or two predominant shield positions, with the odd deviation from local custom (Dickinson and Härke 1992, 65). The single occurrence of a shield over the face in Buckland Grave 323 may reflect a deliberate attempt to emphasise difference in this grave, which is the only shield burial in Plot T (Figs 2.2 and 4.1).

The 'lower body habit' is also predominant in graves of the 1951–3 Buckland excavations, though superseded by vertical deposition for later shield burials; and there are single occurrences of the 'face' and 'chest' positions (Evison 1987, 35). The similarity between depositional patterns indicates local custom for the cemetery as a whole and the distributions reflect distinct burial plots for groups within this community (Dickinson and Härke 1992, 65).

Although shields are occasionally found with adolescents and young men, there is a general association of shield burial with adult and particularly mature males in Anglo-Saxon England (Dickinson and Härke 1992). Within the

graves of the 1994 excavations, shields were buried with adult males who died between the ages of 25 and 50. All had spears and four were also equipped with a sword (see above). Other associated grave goods mainly consist of knives and iron belt fittings, but two shield burials had copper alloy belt fittings and these graves included a set of scales and weights (Grave 265B) and a glass cone beaker (Grave 297).

The shield fittings

Six of the seven 1994 Buckland shields have bosses of the predominant type present in sixth-century east Kent burials, Dickinson's group 3 (Dickinson and Härke 1992). This is a Merovingian form and the earliest Anglo-Saxon examples found in east Kent burials, associated with long grips, are believed to have been imported (Spain 2000). Early examples are noticeably absent from both parts of the Buckland cemetery. As the Anglo-Saxons adopted group 3, it became smaller and lighter and was used with the more common strap grip (Spain 2000).

The shield in Grave 297 has a group 3 boss falling between the larger early examples and later standard ones, as its diameter is a little small for the former and its flange a little large for the latter (Table 4.2). An indication of early group 3 is its clear carination, however, and it was fitted with a long grip of a particular type found elsewhere with larger early group 3 bosses (see below). While the boss from Grave 414 is of a similar size, its carination is not pronounced and it was accompanied by the strap grip characteristic of shields with the smaller, more standard group 3 boss. The shield in Grave 264 bears a large group 3 boss which has been re-used: it was fitted to the shield board with small rivets noticeably out of keeping with its broad flange and was accompanied by a strap grip.

The remaining group 3 bosses belong to a sub-type 'b', characterised by a wide flange relative to diameter, with large flat or convex rivets. Examples have been found in several richly-furnished burials in east Kent, suggesting it had a certain prestige value and was used for display (Spain 2000). Further, its association with a resurgence of the long grip may indicate that the shields concerned were imported (Spain 2000). The Grave 265B shield boss can be identified as a particular variant with high wall and shallow convex cone, 3b(ii), which is identical to contemporary continental forms and has been found with strong Frankish associations at Saltwood and Broadstairs (Spain 2000). The shield was fitted with a long grip and the burial is notable for its copper alloy belt set, sword and scales and weights set (*see* pp 405–7).

Grave	Boss type	Grip type	Board mounts	Buckland phase	Kent phase
297	3	IIIb	Rivets	2	III
414	3	Ia1	Discs d 65mm	2b–3a	III/IV
264	3 (re-used)	Ia1	Discs d 40mm	3	IV/V
265B	3b (ii)	IIIb	Rivets	3a	IV/V
230	3b	IIIb		2b–3a	III/IV
323	3 (re-used)	Ia1	Rivets	3	IV/V
375	6	Ia2		3b	V

Table 4.4. Details of shield components.

Grave	Boss type	Diameter (mm)	Height (mm)	Flange width (mm)	Wall height (mm)	Rivet diameter (mm)	Apex diameter (mm)	Cone shape	Wall shape	Carination
297	3	150	75	25	20	20	23	Convex	Straight	Clear
414	3	155	77	23	22	20	20	Convex	Straight	Slight
264	3 (re-used)	160	80	22	25	8	20	Convex	Straight	Slight
265B	3b (ii)	170	85	25	25	22		Shallow convex	Straight	Slight
230	3b	160	80	27	20		22	Convex	Straight	Slight
323	3b (re-used)	165	80	25	25	10	20	Convex	Straight	Slight
375	6	120	70	10	10	6		Convex	Sloping	None

Table 4.5. Details of shield bosses.

The bosses from Graves 230 and 323 fit the sub-type 'b' dimensions but lack distinctive profiles. Such bosses may be the work of local smiths influenced by the particular continental-style bosses described above. However, it is also possible that they comprise further variants which are not yet recognised due to under-representation and difficulty distinguishing them from the mass of group 3 as a whole. The Grave 230 boss has a broad flange and the shield was fitted with a long grip. It may also be significant that this grave lay close to and aligned with Grave 265B in a cluster of burials (Plot S). The tall wall height and general dimensions of the boss from Grave 323 suggest type 3b, though the case is less clear-cut. It had, in any case, been re-used: fitted with small rivets and accompanied by a narrow strap grip.

The latest boss from the 1994 site was found in Grave 375 (Phase 3b) and can be identified as one of Dickinson's group 6. This is a small, convex type which evolved from the trend within group 3 for smaller, lighter cones. The lack of further group 6 bosses at both Buckland 1951–3 and 1994 is notable. Weapon burial in general and shield burial in particular declined from the seventh century, but other east Kent sites (eg St Peter's, Broadstairs) have produced a range of group 6 bosses (Härke 1992b, 159).

The long grips from the 1994 excavations are of two types, though both fall within Härke's IIIb category (Table 4.6). One type has clearly defined rivet plates either side of the central flanged handle section, from which they are separated by several millimetres of narrow grip. This type occurred with 3b bosses in Graves 230 and 265B and in Grave 91 from the earlier excavations (Evison 1987, 237). Elsewhere in east Kent, similar examples have been found in Finglesham grave G2 and Mill Hill, Deal grave 97 (Chadwick 1958; Parfitt and Brugmann 1997). The second type lacks separate rivet plates, its rivets situated at either end of a straight, rectangular flanged handle which continues as narrow grip extensions. This type occurred with the group 3 bosses in Buckland Graves 96A and 297. Similar examples have been found with large group 3 bosses at Mill Hill, grave 35 and Lyminge, grave 31, though the latter is not flanged (Evison 1987; Parfitt and Brugmann 1997; Warhurst 1955).

The Grave 375 shield was fitted with a straight, narrow strap grip of Härke's type Ia2, which is associated with group 6 bosses (Spain 2000). It is similar in size and shape to the Ia1 grip found with the re-used 3b boss in Grave 323 except that this expands at its terminals. The larger Ia1 strap grips from Graves 264 and 414 are characteristic of those found with standard group 3 bosses. It should be noted, however, that the pronounced curvature of the Grave 414 grip is unusual.

In the refined typology and chronology for east Kent, the development of shield boss form within Dickinson's groups 3 and 6 has been mapped onto the Kentish phases proposed by Brugmann in her discussion of the Mill Hill, Deal cemetery

Grave	Grip type	Description	Length (mm)	Width (central) (mm)	Width (terminals) (mm)
297	IIIb	Long, flanged - with defined rivet plates	275	30	10
414	Ia1	Strap - expanded terminals	160	20	60
264	Ia1	Strap - expanded terminals	140	20	40
265B	IIIb	Long, flanged	400	35	10
230	IIIb	Long, flanged	400	35	-
323	Ia1	Strap - expanded terminals	130	16	30
375	Ia2	Strap - narrow, straight	130	15	20

Table 4.6. Details of shield grips.

(Parfitt and Brugmann 1997). Large group 3 bosses with long grips are associated with Kentish Phases II (*c* AD 500–530/40) and III (AD 530/40–560/70), while standard group 3 bosses with strap grips occur in Phases III/IV and IV (*c* AD 560/70–580/90) (Spain 2000). Bosses with characteristics which are transitional between groups 3 and 6, and those belonging to group 6 itself, do not seem to occur before Kentish Phase IV and become common in Phase V, from *c* AD 580/90 into the first half of the seventh century (Spain 2000).

The group 3 boss with early features from Grave 297 therefore probably dates to Kentish Phase III (revised Buckland Phase 2; see Part 8, Tables 8.4–8.7, for a correlation of phasing systems), while the 'large' standard group 3 boss from Grave 414 belongs in Phase III/IV (= revised Buckland Phase 2b–3a). The re-used group 3 boss from Grave 264 was fitted with a strap grip, usually found with standard group 3 bosses, and with small rivets, as found with group 3/6 or 6 bosses. These date the shield to Kentish Phase IV or later (= revised Buckland Phase 3). The group 6 boss from Grave 375 is smaller than the Kentish Phase IV/V group 3/6 and 6 bosses at Buckland 1951–3 and Mill Hill, and it has a Ia2 strap grip which is associated with seventh-century contexts. It therefore probably dates later, rather than earlier, in Kentish Phase V (= revised Buckland Phase 3b).

Though the 3b subtype appears to date to Phases IV and V in east Kent, the 3b(ii) variant has yet to be firmly linked to the Kentish phase system. However, unpublished examples have been provisionally dated to the end of the sixth century and these include one from Broadstairs with dimensions similar to Buckland Grave 265B (Spain 2000). It therefore also probably belongs to Kentish Phase IV/V (= revised Buckland Phase 3a). The re-used 3b boss in Grave 323 was fitted with a narrow strap grip, similar in size to the Ia2 grip found with the group 6 boss in Grave 375, and small rivets, as usually found with small group 3 or transitional 3/6 bosses in Kentish Phases IV or IV/V. It too, then, belongs to Phase IV or V (= revised Buckland Phase 3b).

Around 50 per cent of Anglo-Saxon shields were provided with board mounts, but frequencies vary markedly between sites (Dickinson and Härke 1992). Only two of the eight shields from Mill Hill, Deal were supplied with board mounts, yet Buckland has a high proportion (combined figure 70 per cent). The 1994 Buckland mounts are all studs and discs of Härke's type 'a', however, and are in no way comparable with the gilt and silver figural appliqués from Buckland Grave 93 and Mill Hill grave 81 (Evison 1987, 32–5; Parfitt and Brugmann 1997, 87–8).

Large disc mounts, with diameters of 80 to 100mm, occur in sixth-century contexts in east Kent, at Buckland Grave 98, Lyminge grave 31, Mill Hill grave 89 and a newly discovered sword grave at Eastry, while a standard form with diameters of 40 to 45mm, seen at Buckland in Graves 27, 39 and 131, developed in the later sixth and seventh centuries (Spain 2000). With the 1994 Buckland excavations, sets of disc mounts were found with group 3 bosses and strap grips. In Grave 414, disc mounts with diameters of 60–65mm, falling between the outsize and standard types described above, were arranged in pairs on either side of the boss. In Grave 264 four standard discs were arranged on either side and below the boss.

Rivet-sized fittings, often domed or plated, are frequently found in association with group 3 and 3b bosses and are presumed to have been used to fasten a long grip to the board (Spain 2000). They were found with the earliest group 3 boss, the 3b(ii) boss and the re-used 3b boss in the 1994 excavations. A single silvered rivet secured each end of the long grip in Grave 297 and a set of four copper alloy rivets, identical to those on the boss flange, was arranged in pairs at either end of the long grip in Grave 265B. However, a set of four smaller copper alloy rivets in Grave 323 accompanied a strap grip. They are identical to the boss and grip rivets, all of which are 10mm in diameter and thus contemporary with the refitting of the 3b boss, so their function might have been purely decorative or served some practical purpose such as fixing leather patches to the board cover.

The shields show a high incidence of silvered or tinned fittings, including three sets of silvered or copper alloy rivets (Graves 297, 323 and 265B), plated flange rivets (Grave 414), apex disc and board mounts (Grave 264). This shows a certain amount of investment in the shields selected for burial. The rivets from the shield boss in Grave 264 have been scientifically investigated by Janet Lang, revealing that their surfaces were coated with a tinned layer which was heated to attach thin copper or bronze discs (*see* pp 267–9).

Materials and methods of construction

Shield bosses of the types found in the 1994 excavations were generally produced from a single iron block (Dickinson and Härke 1992, 31–5). A separate apex was sometimes 'inserted' into a boss, either during manufacture or as a repair, but some boss types were more prone to weakness at the apex than others (*ibid*). In both national and regional samples, no group 3 boss was observed with an inserted apex and bosses from Mill Hill, Deal have been x-rayed and shown to have integral apexes (Spain 2000; Parfitt and Brugmann 1997, 85). None of the Buckland 1994 bosses has the distinctive blob inside the cone indicating an inserted apex and the Grave 323 boss was sectioned through its apex, showing its integral construction.

The group 6 boss (Grave 375) has a repair at one of the rivet points on its flange. The flange rivet concerned has a disc, rather than knob, head and a very long shank which, having pierced the flange and board was hammered flush beneath the shield. A small copper alloy plate was fitted against the wall of the board aperture at this point, perpendicular to the flange, with tiny copper alloy rivets (see below).

With the exception of Grave 414, all the shield grips from the 1994 excavations have the remains of wooden handles (see below). Complex handle construction was used, in which board and handle are jointed as well as riveted together, as was found in the earlier Buckland excavations (Dickinson and Härke 1992, 35–41; Evison 1987, 35). Textile remains on the outer surface of three grips probably originated from clothing touching the grip in the burial (Graves 264, 297 and 414; see below and Part 5; Table 5.7). However, a narrow leather strip wound around the handle of the Grave 265B grip probably survives from the handle construction (see below).

The thickness of the shield boards, where this could be determined from rivet shanks, was consistently around eight millimetres (Graves 323, 375 and 264), in one case 8–10mm (Grave 414). This fits with Härke's average figure of 8.5mm for late sixth- and seventh-century boards (Dickinson and Härke 1992, 48). Evison recorded an average thickness of 10mm at Buckland 1951–3, though Graves 56 and 90 had boards only 6mm thick (Evison 1987, 34). Nearby, at Mill Hill, Deal board thickness ranged from 8 to 11mm (Parfitt and Brugmann 1997, 86). For details of the woods used in the Buckland 1994 shield boards see p 279 and Table 6.12.

Leather covers were used to strengthen and protect the wooden shield board (Dickinson and Härke 1992, 51). Evidence for board covering survives for at least five of the seven Buckland 1994 shields, in some cases both front and back (see below). Both the Mill Hill, Deal and Buckland 1951–3 shields showed evidence of leather board-covering and the Buckland Grave 39 shield had covering both front and back (Parfitt and Brugmann 1997, 86; Parfitt 2003, 78; Evison 1987, 35).

Some Anglo-Saxon shield boards curved towards the outer rim, though flat in the central area where the boss and grip were fitted. This can be detected in the shape of the long grip, which appears to have been preferred for convex boards, though not all boards with long grips were convex (Dickinson and Härke 1992, 44). Two shield grips are slightly curved, but neither necessarily suggests a convex shield board. A slight bow in the Grave 230 long grip may be due to earth pressure, as it is not well-defined and though the Grave 323 strap grip is very clearly curved, it was housed across the board aperture, directly beneath the boss, telling us nothing about the shape of the board itself.

Notes on mineral-preserved organic remains associated with shield bosses *edited by Hayley Bullock*

Investigative conservation and examination of the mineral-preserved organic remains using microscopy has enabled a range of technical observations to be made in relation to the shield fittings. Shields are made from a range of inorganic and organic material and whilst metal parts survive, organic material decays rapidly. However, in many cases organic remains may be preserved in a mineralised state where the shape, but not the composition of the organic material is retained (Cronyn 1990). It is the examination of this material that can reveal much about the structure, composition and nature of the Anglo-Saxon shield board.

Board shape and size

There is no direct evidence from the Buckland 1994 inhumations to suggest the shape of the shields, however, evidence from other sources including images, soil staining, edge binding and rare preservation of whole boards suggest that they would have been round (Dickinson and Harke 1992). However, an approximate estimate of the shield diameter can be made from the position of the appliqués (minimum diameter) and the proximity to the edge of the grave cut (maximum diameter). The board diameters from the seven graves range from 280 to 480mm (fitting into the small- to medium-sized board range of 450–660mm identified by Dickinson and Harke 1992).

Board covering

Examination of the underside of the shield fittings from five graves (264, 265B, 323, 375 and 414) confirms that the shield boards were made from wood, covered front and back with a thin layer of skin product. The remaining two (230 and 297) have possible skin product remains to the front and back. Preservation was poor (especially Graves 230 and 297) but there were areas of good preservation where fibre bundles were clearly visible. There was no evidence of seams, stitching or adhesion of skins as a means of attaching the board covers to the board as only very small areas were preserved.

Board hand hole

Evidence for the shape and size of the hand holes in the centre of the board is difficult to find due to a lack of material evidence, though Dickinson and Harke suggest that they were either D-shaped oval or figure of eight in shape. However, an area of hand hole interior edge did survive on one board from Grave 414. It measured 12mm and indicated that one side of the hand hole was straight and that the size of the hand hole was roughly the same as that of the inside of the boss. Graves 375 and 414 also displayed evidence for the exact location of their grips which were in an off centre position in the board hole, allowing a smaller space for the fingers and a larger space for the knuckles of the hand.

Grip and handle construction

All the shields have iron grips present. Graves 264, 323, 375 and 414 have short grips and 230, 265b and 297 have long grips. All the short grips (with the exception of Grave 414) have wooden handles with a lap joint construction and are type A1 according to Dickinson and Harke. These handles have grain direction running parallel to the length of the grip, which is inserted from the front into a recessed area in the board, the grain direction of which runs at a perpendicular angle to it. Evidence for this can be seen on the underside of the iron grips and on the shanks of the grip rivets where two different grain directions are present. Unusually, the edge of the wooden handle from Grave 323 is preserved showing that the handle was wider than the iron grip. The edge of the wooden handle from Grave 264 is also preserved in two areas and shows that the handle was straight-sided and was also roughly the same width as the iron grip.

The grip from Grave 414 shows no evidence of a wooden handle and although there are the remains of skin product and a loosely woven twill textile present on both sides of the grip there is not enough evidence to say with any confidence that this grip had either a leather or textile handle.

The remaining Graves 230, 265B and 297 all have wooden handles covered with skin product on the inside of the central flanged section of the long grips. In addition the grip in Grave 265B has the mineralised remains of a narrow leather strap wound round the grip either as a binding for the handle or from a carrying strap.

Two of the shield grips are attached to the boards in unusual ways. The boss in Grave 375 is attached to the shield board with just four rivets rather than the usual five, two of which attach the boss to the board and also hold the grip and handle in place. The grip in Grave 414 is attached to the back of the shield board using the two grip rivets, the ends of which were then riveted through the flange of the shield boss for extra strength. It is likely that the durability of such a shield would be poorer than the five rivet construction as the grip could become detached or weakened if the shield boss was damaged. The grips in the remaining graves are attached to the back of the shield board using two grip rivets in the usual way.

There is evidence of curvature to five of the grips (Graves 230, 264, 323, 375, 414), which could be indicative of a curve in the shield board but is probably more likely to be distortion due to soil pressure whilst buried.

Repairs

Boss 375 has a small, rectangular, copper alloy strip present on the underside of the shield boss at right angles to the wood of the board. There are two iron rivets through the strip that are covered with mineral-preserved wood. The purpose of this strip is unknown, but it may be a repair to one of the wooden shield board planks or may be a brace for strengthening.

Shield mounts

All the bosses have shield mounts within the graves (apart from Graves 230 and 375) and are copper alloy or iron. All are studs and discs. The iron shield mounts have mineral-preserved wood and skin products on the back that indicate they were riveted through the board and both the back and front shield covers. The function of the mounts is not known; they may have been decorative or have served a practical function strengthening plank joins or holding leather straps in position (Dickinson and Harke 1992).

Spearheads

Axel Kerep

(Graves 220, 230, 233, 240, 249C, 251, 256, 259, 262, 264, 265B, 297, 299, 300, 301, 323, 337, 346, 363, 374, 375, 393A, 400, 411, 414 and 423)

Twenty-six iron spearheads were recovered from the thirty weapon burials found at Buckland in 1994. Where possible, they have been assigned to one of seven types identified in Swanton's typology (Swanton 1973; 1974). In terms of date, all these types are contained within the revised Buckland Phases 1b–3b. Spears and other weapons are relatively common during Phases 2–3. Details of the number and chronology of the spear-types and other weapons within the 1994 sample are given in Tables 4.7 and 4.8. A detailed description of each spear is provided in the grave catalogue (Part 10).

Spears are, by far, the most numerous weapon type to be found in the Buckland cemetery and are one of the most common metal finds in male graves, alongside knives. The spears represent up to 57 per cent of all weapons in the 1994

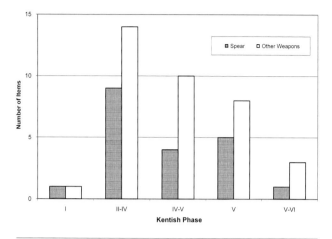

Fig 4.8. Quantity of spears and other weapons, by Kentish Phase (based on research by A Kerep).

part of the cemetery and occur amongst 87 per cent of the weapon burial/weapon combinations. This figure can rise to 100 per cent of the combinations in other Anglo-Saxon cemeteries, eg Alton, Hampshire; Burghfield, Berkshire; Norton, Cleveland; Saltwood and Mill Hill, Deal, both in Kent. This clearly makes spears important in studies of the male population of a cemetery.

The quantity of spears found in male graves is considerable but is not surprising in an Anglo-Saxon context. The graves in the Buckland cemetery are typical in following Anglo-Saxon burial practice. Studies by the writer indicate the important place granted to this type of weapon in Anglo-Saxon male object associations: around 52 per cent within Kentish cemeteries, 63 per cent for the rest of England (Fig 4.10). However, this does not seem to be the case on the Continent, with just 28 per cent for France and 26 per cent for southern Germany, where the seax appears as the most common weapon (Fig 4.11).

Due to its frequency in Anglo-Saxon cemeteries and to its nature, the spear also tends to be one of the most useful objects for the establishment of relative and absolute chronologies for male graves. Accordingly, some attention has been given in the discussion below to this aspect of spears, in relation to both Kentish and Merovingian examples.

Type series and phasing

In England the typology used to describe spearheads in Anglo-Saxon cemeteries is that produced by Michael Swanton in the 1970s (Swanton 1973; 1974). This typology was very important at the time, for spearheads had been constantly left to one side by previous researchers. However,

Swanton's typology has been criticised in more recent texts and it can be difficult to use. Høilund Nielsen's East Anglian spearhead typology may be of wider application, but has not been used here (Penn and Brugmann 2007, 17–23).

The references used to date most of the spears come from the dating originally given by Swanton. Most of that dating has been checked or reassessed by Evison (1987) and Härke (1992a) and they are not always in agreement. Here, recent continental references, taken particularly from the phases of Legoux and Périn for north-west France (Périn 1980; Legoux 1998), have also been added. Both the French systems and Swanton's chronology evolved essentially from Böhner's previous work (Böhner 1958). In addition, some of the types have been matched by reconsidering, via Swanton's typology, most of the spears from French and English published cemeteries nearest to Buckland. In addition, we have tried wherever possible to align the types with the new Rhineland phases proposed by Siegmund (1998, 97–105).

Knowing that Kent evolved with its own local traditions, it is perhaps unwise to use such a patchwork of chronological systems, but it remains the best way until the writer's own study of Kentish spearheads has been completed. In any case, much to Swanton's credit, our analyses indicate that his dating and technical evolution of types is essentially correct.

Location of spearheads within the grave

Figure 4.9 shows a schematically divided grave indicating the location numbers for spearheads that are listed in Table 4.7. Box 2 is at the head of the grave and Box 8 the foot. The grave is not oriented.

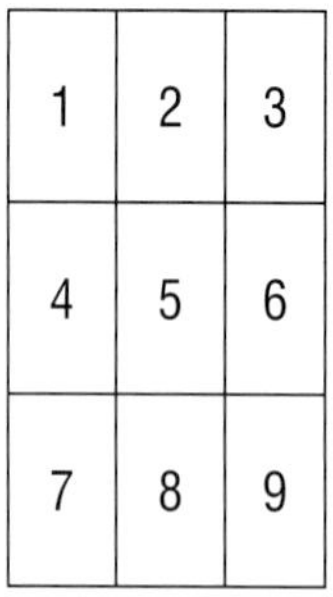

1	2	3
4	5	6
7	8	9

Fig 4.9. Location numbers for positions of spears in graves

For the 1994 Buckland excavations it does not seem that there is any clear pattern in the location of the spear within the grave. Almost all of them are placed either right or left of the body, usually beside the head or the shoulder, except for two burials (Graves 300 and 337) where the spearhead is located at the feet, reversed so as to point to the bottom

Grave	Type	Length (mm)	Ferrule	Buckland phase	Location	Finds gender	Sex	Category	Age	No of weapons in grave	No of objects in grave
220	H2	220		-	3	M	?	Grown	Adult	1	3
230	E3	390		2b–3a	3	M	?	Grown	Adult	2	4
233	G1/H3	295		-	3	M	No bone	?	?	1	2
240	D2/D3	270	#	-	2L	M	?	Juvenile	14–16	1	3
249C	H3	370	#	2–3	3	M	M	Adult	30–40	2	5
251	E3/G	390		3	3	M	M	Mature	40–50	1	4
256	C4	490		-	1	M	?M	Mature	40–45	1	2
259	G1	240		-	1	M	M	Adult	35–45	1	3
262	C2/H2	280		2–3	1	M	?	Adult	35–45	1	4
264	D2	448		3	3	M	M	Mature	40–45	3	5
265B	H2	335	#	3a	3	M	?M	Adult	25–30	3	14
297	H2	260	#	2	3	M	M	Adult	30–35	2	6
299	?	290		-	1	M	?F	Mature	40–50	1	2
300	E2/H3	250		1b–2a	7	M	M	Adult	30–40	1	3
301	G2	380		-	2	M	M	Adult	19–21	1	3
323	?	395		3	3	M	M	Mature	40–50	2	2
337	E3	380		-	9	M	?	Mature	40–45	1	4
346	E4	465		3	2	M	M	Mature	40+	3	5
363	H3	380		-	3	M	M	Mature	45–55	1	3
374	D2	250		-	2R	M	?	Juvenile	14–16	1	3
375	E3	350		3b	2R	M	M	Adult	25–30	3	4
393A	H2	400		-	3	M	M	Adult	25–30	1	2
400	H2	460		-	7	M	No bone	?	?	1	2
411	H2	290		-	3	M	?	Child	4–6	1	2
414	C2	410		2b–3a	3	M	M	Adult	35–40	3	8
423	H3	464	#	2–3a	3	M	M	Mature	40–50	1	5

Note: Location numbers are explained in Figure 4.9

Table 4.7. Details of spearheads.

Buckland phase	Spearhead type														
	C2/H2	C4	C2/H2	D2	D2/D3	E2/H3	E3	E3/G	E4	G1	G1/H3	G2	H2	H3	?
1b–2a						#									
2													#		
2b–3a	#						#								
2–3a														#	
2–3			#											#	
3a													#		
3b						#									
3				#			#	#							
unphased		#		#	#	#			#	#	#	#	#	#	#

Table 4.8. Spearhead types by phase.

of the grave. This last custom is said to be Frankish (Evison 1987, 28; Parfitt and Brugmann 1997, 84) and is rarely found in England, except in Kent, where it occurs more often, as at Mill Hill, Deal and Saltwood.

Spear types

The 'double' description, such as E2/H3, used for some spearheads in Table 4.7 reflects the difficulty of precisely

identifying finds according to Swanton's typology, and highlights the problem of fitting some spearheads into that system. Wherever possible the closest match has been given. But for many of them, uncertainty remains and where a single option cannot be assigned this has been noted.

Most of the spears have either a leaf-shaped or angular blade. Almost all of them are of lozenge-section, except two of lentoid section (Graves 300 and 374). Only two spearheads fall outside Swanton's typology (Graves 299 and 323); one is

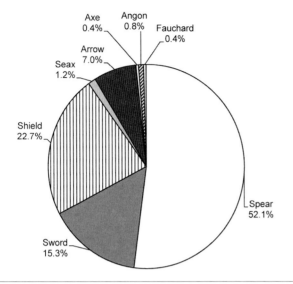

Fig 4.10a. Relative quantities of weapons from Anglo-Saxon cemeteries in Kent (based on research by A Kerep).

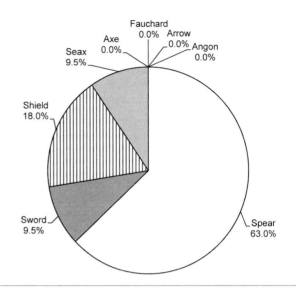

Fig 4.10b. Relative quantities of weapons from Anglo-Saxon cemeteries in England as a whole (based on research by A Kerep).

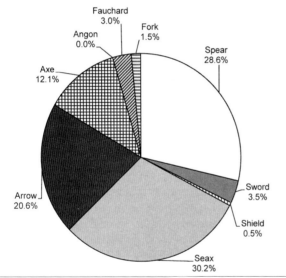

Fig 4.11a. Relative quantities of weapons from cemeteries in France (based on research by A Kerep).

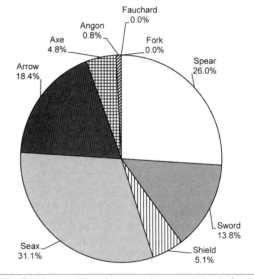

Fig 4.11b. Relative quantities of weapons from cemeteries in Southern Germany (based on research by A Kerep).

clearly of square-flat section (Grave 323). Traces of organic materials, such as textile or straw were found on a number of the blades (pp 53–6, Part 5 and pp 278–81). The textile remains, as well as showing the effects of oxidation, suggest that most of the spears were wrapped in cloth before being buried. It is logical to assume that this would have been the case during the spearhead's 'lifetime' as well, in order to avoid the effects of corrosion or prevent accidents.

All the spearheads have split sockets, with the possible exception of that from Grave 256 and most contain wood remains in their sockets (Table 6.12, p 281). On the Continent, split sockets usually indicate a post-Migration period date, although there are exceptions and local variations within the continental series. The shaft was pushed into the socket of the spearhead, sometimes without any fastening, but sometimes held with a rivet or nail (at least 36 per cent of the 1994

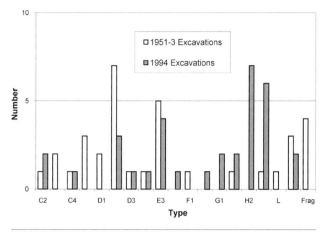

Fig 4.12. Spearhead types from Buckland cemetery.

sample) or with two nails (at least 30 per cent of the 1994 sample). Only three blades have their sockets bound with a ring (Graves 240, 249C and 301), usually made of copper alloy or, in the case of Grave 301, iron.

Six of Swanton's principal types of spearhead may be identified within the 1994 assemblage. The phasing of each type is given in Table 4.7. The most common spear types from the 1994 excavations are H2 and H3 (angular shape, side curving to the tip, nine examples), followed by E3 (straight-sided blade, three examples). By overall type, H, with 34 per cent of the total, is the most common, spanning all periods. Rare types, such as L, are not found in this sample. However, there are some typical insular spears such

as type G (G2). Type G seems to be associated with simple weapon combinations, unlike the situation with the previous Buckland excavations, where this type occurred with complex associations (Table 9.2). Figs 4.12 and 4.13 show the quantity of each type of spearhead from 1994, as well as a comparison with the previous excavations. Figure 4.14, combining the two cemetery areas, shows what can be found around Dover.

Following Swanton's typology, D2 (long leaf-shaped blade) is an early spearhead type, but this form continues for sometime and the dated example from Buckland 1994 is assigned to Phase 3 (Grave 264). It appears that type E3 (angular blade) is relatively late (Phases 2b–3b), whilst type E4 (sword-like), one of the longest of the types, lies in Phase 3. An (?)E2 (angular) type occurs during Phase 1b–2a, whilst one of the non-Swanton types falls within Phase 3 (Grave 323).

Types C2 (leaf) and H3 (angular curving) span most of the period, making it difficult to precisely date some of the graves; this is also the case with type H2 (angular curving). From the site dating, all these types occur during the sixth century (Phases 2–3a), which is reassuring because this is in accord with the chronological schemes drawn up by Swanton and Härke. Leaf-shaped blades gradually disappear, being replaced by the angular blade types. These evolve from angular to a straight-sided 'sword-like' blade.

Other spear types are relatively common in Kent. Within the sample from Buckland 1994 there is a lack of types E1, K1, J, H1 (found at Eccles) and L (present at Buckland 1951–3). In general, however, these are rare or else they are not found in Kent. Unlike Mill Hill at Deal, there are quite a few examples of type H2. What is striking when looking at

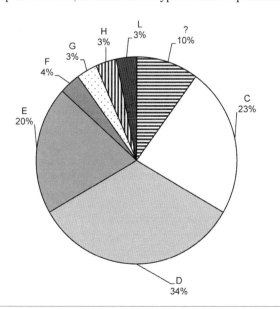

Fig 4.13a. Spearhead types from the 1951–3 excavations.

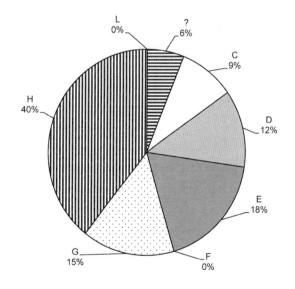

Fig 4.13b. Spearhead types from the 1994 excavations.

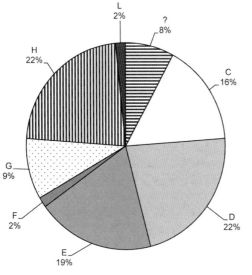

Fig 4.14. Main spearhead types from the entire cemetery.

the relative level of continental influence in Kent is that type G is not seen very much on the Continent, whilst occurring several times here.

The two excavated parts of the Buckland cemetery do not look the same when their spear types are compared (Figs 4.12 and 4.13). Apparently earlier leaf-shaped forms, like types C and D, tend to be the most numerous in Buckland 1951–3. The numbers of type H are limited in the 1950s excavations but it is the most numerous in the 1994 sample, where long angular to straight-sided blades of types G and E prevail. Types E and G appear in equal proportion within the two excavations, occurring in the most complex weapon combinations in both parts of the cemetery.

The blade from Grave 301 includes two inscriptions, one on each side, located at the bottom of the blade next to the shoulder (Figs 4.14a–b and 10.31). We have described these symbols here as ideograms (like Chinese or Japanese examples), meaning that in each case they bear a symbol with or without any magical nature. On one side the ideogram

Fig 4.14a. Spearhead from Grave 301, detail of ideogram – bow firing an arrow.

Fig 4.14b. Spearhead from Grave 301 detail of ideogram – clashing shield walls?

clearly represents a bow firing an arrow. This may be linked to hunting or to the concept of velocity. On the other side, the ideogram is rather more enigmatic. It looks like two convex lines facing each other. A possible interpretation is that these two lines schematically represent two shields facing each other, and it could be the symbol for two 'shield walls' clashing. Spears would be particularly relevant in any such opposition of shields.

Spearheads from Buckland and northern France

To enhance our discussion of the Buckland spear types, we can compare them with matching examples in Frankish cemeteries. The two published cemeteries used here are Nouvion-en-Ponthieux, Somme (Piton 1985) and Frénouville in Normandy (Pilet 1980). These two cemeteries have been phased following the system of Legoux and Périn (Périn 1980) for north-west France. This phasing has been recently reassessed (Delestre and Périn 1998).

At Frénouville the two C2 type spearheads (graves 9 and 42) are dated *c* AD 525–550, which equates with Phase 2 at Buckland. The example in Buckland Grave 262 (C2/H2) belongs to Phase 2–3, whilst that in Grave 414 falls within Phase 2b–3a. This dating is not incompatible as Swanton places the type in the last quarter of the sixth century through to the beginning of the seventh century. The C2 spears found in Nouvion also provide a broad range of dates, *c* AD 485–560; phase A/B/C–B/C/D.

The D2 spears of Frénouville also date to *c* AD 525–550. At least one of those from Buckland 1994 lies within Phase 3 (Grave 264) but one example from Grave 374 might be slightly earlier. The dating of Nouvion is too broad to help: A/B/C–C/D/E (*c* AD 485–580).

The two E3 spearheads at Frénouville are dated to around the middle of the seventh century (graves 436 and 458, unless a G1?). This dating corresponds to our type E3 in Phases 2b–3b. For Swanton, E3 spans all of the period from the beginning of the sixth to the end of the seventh century, which matches the dating proposed in Nouvion, *c* AD 485–560/70.

Unfortunately, it has not been possible to isolate closely dated H2–H3 types on the Continent (particularly in France), apart from the two supposed H3 spearheads at Nouvion (graves 333 and 429), which fall in phase A/B/C (*c* AD 475–525). This corresponds with Phase 1–2a for Buckland, whilst our H3 spears are more likely to lie in Phase 2 or 3.

A hint for the broad dating of the C4 (G2?) spear in Buckland Grave 256 is provided by the C3/C4 type in Nouvion (grave 244). There, it is more likely to fall within phase B/C/D–D/E (*c* AD 530–580), which would equate with Phase 2–3a at Buckland.

Some of the dates from these cemeteries match those given for Buckland 1994, whilst others differ or are too broad to be helpful, particularly those from Nouvion. At the same time, these are amongst the closest of the continental cemeteries to Buckland, where we can hope for some useful comparisons. However, it must be noted, firstly, that the Frankish spearheads are more standardised, with just four to six different types at a maximum, whereas Buckland has more than twelve different types. Secondly, Buckland does not have many types in common with the two Frankish cemeteries.

Type H2, and more specifically H3 and E3, are considered to be broad and long types of spearheads. Is this for any technical reason? There is no clear correlation with the type of spear and the nature of the association of weapons, but it does appear that a correlation exists between the length of the blade and its association with a shield. On average, the blades associated with the seven Buckland shield graves (see above) are 50mm longer than unaccompanied spearheads. The same is found if we look at the 1951–3 Buckland excavations where the blades found with at least a shield, or with a sword, are around 40mm longer than those found alone or associated with another type of weapon.

Thus, there is a clear positive correlation between the length of the spear and its association with a shield (and a sword). In the 1994 sample, it is in Phase 3 that we find the longer blade E3 with the latest type of bosses of the group 6 'low cones' (Grave 375) and this is true of the 1951–3 excavations as well (Grave 56). If we add the chronological dimension to this point, we find that the blades occurring after Phase 2 are 96mm longer than those occurring before it.

Can we draw any conclusions from this? At least we can say that blades are longer when found with a shield and generally became longer over time. Indeed, these spears become so long that it appears that they were made to be carried, sometimes two-handed, rather than thrown. It suggests, as Härke has emphasised, that there is a technological transformation of the spear/shield association, as well as their functionality, for obvious tactical reasons (Härke 1992a). Spears were adapted to the 'shield wall' tactic, with throwing-spears disappearing slowly in favour of carrying-spears. Weapons can thus inform us not only about sociology and social status, but also about battle tactics and functionality.

Spearhead types and technological analyses

With technical support provided by the British Museum, it has been possible to look closely through x-rays at the structure of the spearheads. It has been easier to find definitive matches for the blades in Swanton's typology, without having to deal with the problems of corrosion. Although type designations remain uncertain for six spearheads, this is not due to the x-rays but more to the criteria for the types. For example, one blade fits in a particular group for its proportions but not for its dimensions.

Study has also assisted in the suggestion that types like H3 or H2 with 'curving angular' blades might originally have been E2–E3 types, for their construction and proportions match very closely. Thus, it is likely that they were transformed from one type to the other through the processes of continual sharpening and use, and corrosion. The same situation can be seen with some examples of groups F1 and H1, or with the type where the socket is rather large in its proportions, where we can suggest that some of them are repaired and represent a reduction of a broader form (eg Grave 337).

Pushing the investigation further, sections of some of the spearheads have been provided. Those chosen have structures of particular interest. We move, then, from a two dimensional view to a three dimensional one, which is necessary for a further understanding of the crafting of blades. The initiative for this type of study came from the publication of the Edix Hill cemetery at Barrington, Cambridgeshire, where a large analysis of many of the spears was undertaken using radiographic 3D sections (Gilmour and Salter 1998). Our wish is to see that this kind of work is carried on and presented in other cemetery reports in order to provide a large collection of sections, transforming and improving the current two dimensional typology into a three dimensional one.

Details of the metallographic examination of four spearheads, from Graves 264, 299, 323 and 393A, are provided in Part 6. These spearheads were chosen because of apparent differences in construction, visible on radiographs. Two spearheads (Graves 264 and 299) appeared to have a layered structure, whilst the other pair did not. This was illusory, however, and the layered blades simply included large slag inclusions, which may have encouraged the spread of corrosion within the blade. The blade from Grave 323 is constructed from steel and is well-made 'with appropriate materials and technology' (p 272). It differs from the other spearheads of the Buckland cemetery both for its shape (which falls outside Swanton's system) and for the proficiency of its manufacture.

Analysis of the mineralised wood preserved in the sockets of the spearheads and their associated ferrules indicates that ash was the most commonly used wood for shafts, with a few examples of willow, field maple and beech (pp 279–80; Table 6.12). Ash is very frequently found to have been used for spear shafts (Evison 1987, 27). The ferrule from Grave 265B (ii) contained traces of yew wood in contrast to the

spearhead which contained ash. However, the ferrule was found under the skull, close to the spearhead (Fig 10.83) and it must now seem unlikely that these two items were part of the same weapon.

Ferrules

(Graves 240, 249C, 265B, 297 and 423)

Of the twenty-six spearheads, five were found in association with spear-butts or ferrules. There is also an unstratified example (Sf 1264), presumably from a destroyed grave. In each case, these were simple hollow cones, between 70 and 90mm in length. Ferrules, when still lying in position within the grave, allow us to estimate the length of a spear. Elsewhere in Kent, ferrules have been found in graves where spearheads are not present (Schuster 2011, 34).

At Buckland 1994 the three spears with undisturbed ferrules ranged in length from to 1.34 to 1.92m, which may be compared with 1.83 to 2.21m recorded in 1951–3 (Evison 1987, 28) and 1.63 to 2.29m at Mill Hill, Deal (Parfitt and Brugmann 1997, 84). The same calculation cannot be done for the spears without ferrules for it is known that some spears were broken before being buried, in order to fit into the grave.

The purpose of ferrules was largely technical. They helped to balance the weight of the spear, at the same time reducing the length of the shaft necessary. The ferrule was also useful as a means of pushing the spear in the ground, in a waiting position, without damaging the wood. It has also been suggested that the ferrule was used as a striking point in spear fights, with the spear used in a two-handed manner.

If there is a slight positive correlation between the wealth of the burial and the presence of a ferrule on a spear, there is a stronger correlation between the type of blade and the association of a ferrule. Four out of five ferrules are associated with an H type blade (H2/H3), the only exception is the ferrule in Grave 240, with a type D blade. The age of the owner does not seem to matter in terms of the distribution of the ferrules and the principal association lies with the type of blade.

The spearheads with other archaeological data

If we assume that age at death can be relied upon, then it is possible to correlate the presence of spears with the demography of the cemetery. For this purpose the males can be divided into four categories: child, juvenile, adult and mature. The results are striking for the 1994 sample. In the first instance, most of the spears concentrate in the adult-mature categories (79 per cent), as seen in Fig 4.15,

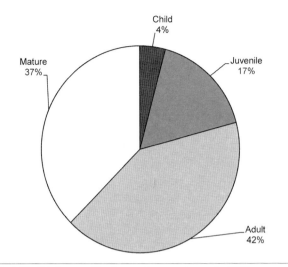

Fig 4.15. Relative quantity of spears by age category for 1994 excavations.

and only one spearhead was found in a definite young child grave (Grave 411).

What was important for Härke was to see if the length of the spears had any correlation with the age at death (Härke 1992a, 187–8 and Abb 37). There is a positive correlation of the length of the blade and the age of the bearer within the sample from the 1994 excavations. According to our calculations, the juvenile class has an average spearhead size of 282.5mm (the only spear in the child class is 290mm), adults reach 327mm, and the figure is greater for the mature category, at 370mm. Altogether, there is a 43mm difference between adult and mature, which is slight, but it is 80mm between juvenile and mature.

The sample is too small to extend these correlations. Comparing the size of the individual (also in relation to their age) could provide interesting results but the skeletal remains did not survive well enough to provide a good sample for study. Correlations of the type of spearhead and the wealth of the grave are given in the section on weapon combinations (*see* pp 375–7). There is no clear correlation between location within the cemetery and spear type.

In conclusion, the spear is the most important weapon type at Buckland, both for the number present and for technological reasons. Although the spear is not an accurate wealth marker, unlike the sword or the shield, it remains a very important indicator for social status, amongst the community. It is, as well, an indicator of the technical changes that might lead to a better understanding of contemporary battle tactics, and thus a more global vision of Anglo-Saxon sociology and warfare. The relationship between the weapon bearer and his weapons is further discussed in Part 9.

Evidence from the mineral-preserved organic remains on the spearheads and ferrules *Fleur Shearman*

The spearhead from Grave 264 has mineral-preserved feathers on the shaft, over a woven textile wrapping or binding. The position of the feathers above the textile would suggest an indirect association. This has been interpreted by as evidence for a pillow (p 203). At Mill Hill, Deal, mineralised traces of feathers found attached to the spear socket in grave 81 have been interpreted as relating to a down-filled pillow, with the pillow-case composed of a twill fabric (Parfitt 2003, 81). If feathers had been found in direct association with the spearhead as a decorative addition, with no associated textile, it might perhaps be interpreted by comparison with Roman military parallels where feathers tied to a spear were a sign of a courier or *pterophoros* (Plutarch, *Life of Otho* 4.2).

A number of other spearheads would appear to have been wrapped in textile, which in some cases is preserved on both sides of the blade, for example Graves 259 and 400 (*see* pp 195 and 197, Table 5.7). Leather was found in close association with the ferrule from Grave 265B and although unlikely in this position, may indicate a point of attachment to a carrying strap. A ferrule recovered from the spoilheap (Sf 1264) but presumably originally from a grave also had traces of leather, possibly from a strap.

Extensive remains of fibres were preserved on the surface of the spearhead from Grave 414. This spearhead was lying against the back of the skull so it is possible that the fibres are the remains of human hair.

A small patch of human hair, animal pelt or fleece was noted on the spearhead from Grave 220A. In this example there were no other adjacent grave goods and the spearhead was at the head end of a poorly-preserved skeleton. Possible remains of cordage are preserved on the socket of the spearhead from Grave 233.

Random plant matter was found on the ferrule and spearhead from Grave 240 and the spearheads from Graves 249, 259, 264 and 300. These remains may be evidence for a grave lining (*see* p 33).

Axehead

Axel Kerep

(Grave 346)

The axehead (e) found in Grave 346, was associated with an E4 type spearhead, as well as a sword, a knife, a looped iron rod and a buckle. According to studies made on the Continent by Böhner (1958), Périn (1980) and Böhme (2002), axes are quite numerous there, at least at the beginning of the Germanic migration. If this is the case on the Continent, it is not, however, true for England where axes have always been scarce in Anglo-Saxon cemeteries. The main chronological pattern is still followed, however, with the presence of the axe principally around the fifth and the sixth centuries, less so in the last quarter of the sixth century, then a slow diminution during the seventh century until they disappear completely.

This weapon type is so scarce that, like the arrows (see below), it is usually studied only through continental typologies. Axes are not well known in the Anglo-Saxon period and no historical English sources of the time discuss them (Härke 1992a, Tab 1). Recent studies show that archaeology supports the historical evidence. Within the corpus gathered by Härke of over 800 weapons, only fourteen axes were found. Of these fourteen axes, nine are *franciscas*, a very common type described in Böhner (1958), seven of which came from Kent. *Franciscas* were also found in the Burgh Castle and Morning Thorpe, Norfolk cemeteries (Penn and Brugmann 2007, 24). The axe from Buckland Grave 346 is, however, more sophisticated in construction.

Kent may not have produced many axes, but it is still the English region with the highest number of this type of weaponry. If England does not have a lot of axes, the opposite is true on the other side of the Channel, with almost 20 per cent of the total of weapons in a Frankish corpus (Siegmund 1998, 106–7; Kerep 2006, 90). The Buckland axe therefore links this cemetery to its Frankish counterparts, rather than to other cemeteries in England, outside of Kent.

The axe is made of iron, and is of T-shaped or axe-hammer type, with a symmetrically developed cutting-edge and a square to trapezoidal heel. It belongs to a type known as a 'Tüllenaxt' (literally 'heeled-axe') in the Böhner typology (Böhner 1958), and it has some common characteristics with the type Tüllenaxt B1, especially with the cutting-edge, as at Rittersdorf, Germany (grave 16). But if we look at the sophisticated heel with its trapezoidal shape, curving lines on top and bottom, it looks more like a B2 type, similar to that from Hohenfels, Germany (grave 1). This is a typical shape for the mid sixth to early seventh century (Böhner-Périn type 8; Stufe 3b *c* AD 560–600). In England it is mainly sixth century, following Härke, who dates it from the end of the fifth to the end of the sixth century (Härke 1992a, Abb 6).

The French chronology of Legoux (1998) places it usually in phase C/D/E of the mid sixth to early seventh century. However, if we look at more distant regions like the Rhineland, it is even later. We can find the same type in phase 6 (*c* AD 570–580/90) of Siegmund (1998), and even a very good parallel in his phase 7 (*c* AD 580–610).

Although Böhner notes that this type appears as early as the middle of the sixth century, a perfect match for our axe is present in grave 8 at Frénouville (Normandy), dated from *c* AD 525 to 600 (Pilet 1980). Another heel axe, but with an hypertrophied heel, Tüllenaxt B1, occurs in Nouvion-en-Ponthieux (grave 354), dated AD 530–570, Phase B/C/D of Legoux. In the original Böhner scheme (corrected however by Bakka in 1981 and Périn in 1998) type B2 comes after type B1, but between Nouvion and Frénouville the opposite is the case.

Tüllenaxt B1 occurs in the recently published cemetery of L'Isle Jourdan, near Toulouse, in the south France (Bach and Boudartchouk 1996). The site, apparently relating to a Frankish garrison of an expeditionary force contemporary with the battle of Vouillé (AD 507), includes a large number of these axes. There, the dating of the type is placed around the beginning of the sixth century. The heel of the Buckland example pushes it to a later date, as it is close to Tüllenaxt B2, even if the cutting-edge differs slightly. The Buckland axe, with its sophisticated cutting-edge, seems to lie between types B1 and B2.

Looking at the overall date range proposed, the Buckland axe can be placed around the middle of the sixth to the beginning of the seventh century. Axes of this type appear to represent the latest evolution of Merovingian axes, in graves at least. A very different type of axe, a 'war-axe' occurs in another Frankish 'expeditionary force' cemetery at Aldaieta, located in Spain (Böhme 2002). The Buckland axe is associated with an E4 spear type, proposed above as a late sixth-century type (*c* AD 530–580). This suggests that Phase 3 is an appropriate date range for Grave 346.

Arrowheads

Axel Kerep

(Graves 302 and 421)

The arrowhead in Grave 302 (b) has a small leaf-shaped blade with a lozenge-section and a split socket (Fig 10.31). It can be identified as a 'Pfeilspitzen A' in Böhner's typology (Böhner 1958). Böhner Type A arrowheads look almost like small C1 spearheads and are one of the most common types of arrowheads to be found in Merovingian cemeteries. Nonetheless, their dating is very broad, the type spanning almost all of the period from the fifth to the seventh century. The arrowhead from Grave 302 can be placed in Phase 2–3a on the basis of the buckle found in the grave, which is typical of the mid sixth century. There is mineralised ash wood in the socket (Table 6.12) and mineralised straw remains on the blade, which provides some indication of the furnishing of the grave.

The other arrowhead, from Grave 421 (a), could be called a 'mini spearhead' because of its length of 105mm. The diameter of the socket, at around 14mm, is also fairly large for the accommodation of an arrow shaft. Traces of mineralised wood in the socket indicate this shaft was of willow (Table 6.12). Moreover, the split socket includes a rivet, which is uncommon for an arrow construction. Nevertheless, arrowheads of a similar size, albeit, with a slightly narrower socket, can be found at Nouvion (Piton 1985). Even if the diameter of the socket is fairly large, it remains small for a spear, where the average socket size is around 24–30mm. This raises the question of whether this object served as a light javelin, or pique. The proportion of the blade in comparison with the socket, each taking up half of the object, makes this weapon very solid and very effective as a striking implement. For all of that, it is still best considered to be an arrowhead, but of a larger size than normal. Arrows from late medieval England show comparable diameters, as with those of types 18 and 21 in Riesch's classification (Riesch 1999, Abb 5).

As with the medieval weapons, it is possible to imagine for this period as well, that arrows had different or dual purposes, relating both to hunting and battle. Large arrows could have been employed to stop bigger prey in hunts, or to inflict maximum damage in battle. Not all arrows of this period are of the same shape: for example the torsaded-barbed example, type F (Böhner 1958), must have been very destructive and it can be imagined that it was used for a specific type of target.

Riesch's experimental study on Alamannic arrowheads shows the efficiency of each type of Merovingian arrowhead (Riesch 1999, Abb 1ff). Within that scheme, the Buckland arrowheads are respectively, type 3 for Grave 302 and close to type 9 for Grave 421. Riesch notes that the angular type 9 is almost one of the most efficient forms. The arrowhead from Grave 421 can also be placed in Böhner's type B (Böhner 1958). This type, like type A, is a reduction of a common spear type, in this case the angular form.

Type B arrows are usually dated to around the middle of the sixth century up to the end of the seventh, thereby following their respective spear counterpart's evolution. Similar, though smaller, arrows have been placed in phase A/B/C–C/D (*c* AD 485–560/70) at Nouvion, which would equate with Phases 1–2 at Buckland. The other objects in Grave 421 (an iron pin and a knife) do not help to establish a closer date. If the Nouvion dating is followed, then the grave should be placed slightly earlier. But the dating of the arrows at Nouvion is based only on the type of socket and it

can easily be criticised on that point. However, material in Nouvion buried with some B-type arrows is closer to phase ABC/CD, earlier than the dating proposed by Böhner. Our phasing therefore seems quite late compared to the French one. If we look at other chronologies (Siegmund 1998; Theune 1999; Burzler 2000), there is no closer dating for this type. It lies perhaps in phase 5 of the Rhineland chronology, if we consider the shape and proportion of one spear dated between AD 550 and 570. Within Scandinavian chronologies (Norgärd-Jorgensen 1999), the Götland system includes a similar shape dated between *c* AD 580–690 (Norgärd-Jorgensen 1999, Abb 111). This is quite a broad range but it does fit the 'sixth to seventh century' dating previously proposed by Böhner.

The arrowheads were found to the right of the skull in Grave 421 and to the left of the left femur in Grave 302. The latter is not an uncommon position and is the location of many of the arrowheads found in Nouvion and other Frankish cemeteries. The arrowhead in Grave 302 was found with an adult, whilst that in Grave 421 was buried with a child. Burying a weapon, particularly an arrow, with a child is a known custom (Crawford 1999). The fact that this arrowhead can be confused with a spear is probably not coincidental. Even if its size and proportion recall an arrowhead, it is still quite big to have been used by a child in archery. The child is believed to have died aged between 3 and 4 (*see* p 446). It is quite conceivable therefore, that this large arrowhead served as the tip to what we may view as a diminutive toy spear, accompanying a very young warrior. If it was a toy, with which the child was playing, he might have been one of the few children to possess such an object and to be buried with it. The arrow would have been the symbol for a spear, the symbol of the status of the child, and of his family. Another child (Grave 411) was buried with a weapon, a spear of small to average size, but the child was older than the occupant of Grave 421.

Fauchard

Axel Kerep

(Grave 437)

A single example of a fauchard was recovered from Grave 437 (c), the burial of an adult male assigned to Buckland Phase 2. The fauchard is an iron bill-hook-like implement, with a curving cutting-edge and straight back, and an 'axe-like' ergot. The section is triangular and knife-like. The present blade was attached to the shaft by a split socket. Wood remains are visible within the socket.

Within France this object would be described as a *'fauchard courbe'*, but its shape and size make it a less common type. Fauchards are not particularly common, but they are well-known on the Continent, though extremely rare in England. A second example is known from the Anglo-Saxon cemetery at Shrubland Hall Quarry, Coddenham, Suffolk (Penn 2011, 65–6). Its use in France starts as early as the fifth century but the Buckland example is more likely to date from the middle of the fifth to the middle of the sixth century, when compared to the continental examples.

Four examples (one fragmentary) have come from the cemetery of Nouvion-en-Ponthieux, (Somme). Here, two, in graves 177 and 388, were found without other grave goods, but the example in grave 429 was found with a spear and an arrow. All of them have a date range between the middle of the fifth to the middle of the sixth century. Although not exactly matching the shape of the Buckland fauchard, these are the closest examples. Other Merovingian fauchards have been listed by Piton (1985, 242–3) and Penn (2011, 66). On current understanding, the unusual presence of a fauchard in an Anglo-Saxon cemetery can make it nothing else but an import. The fauchard was not very fashionable outside the limits of the north-western region of France.

The fauchard is commonly considered to be a tool for cutting crops, or for other agricultural purposes. The presence of wood in the socket suggests an accompanying shaft. In this context, could it possibly be a substitute for a spear? Within burials it is mainly thought to be a pole weapon.

The presence of a fauchard at Buckland provides evidence for continental influence or contact, through trade, or migration. The location of Nouvion-en-Ponteux in the Somme, opposite southern England, with closely comparable objects to some of those found at Buckland, helps support this hypothesis.

Dress accessories

Brooches and a brooch model

Birte Brugmann

Thirty-eight graves produced a total of seventy-four brooches, one brooch model and one possible brooch. In the following, the various types and their provenance, distribution and dating is discussed. Reference to the use of the brooches is made only in relation to the types and their

combinations. For a more detailed discussion on costume, including textile evidence, see Part 5.

Cruciform and small-long brooches

(Graves 239, 254, 257 and 351B)

A single cruciform brooch and seven small-long brooches, three pairs and two single, all made of copper alloy, are among the earliest brooch types from the site. The majority of cruciform and small-long brooches discovered in Kent are recent metal-detector finds, suggesting that the small number known from graves is not representative (Chadwick Hawkes 1987; Richardson 2011). The generally early date of cruciform and small-long brooches within the Anglo-Saxon period[4] has been confirmed by a systematic study of the associated glass beads, which suggests that both small-long and cruciform brooches were common fifth-century types, further developed but less frequent in the sixth century (Brugmann 2004). In the correspondence analysis in Part 8 (Tables 8.2–8.3), cruciform brooches (type no 1) and small-long brooches (type no 5) form part of the definition of Phase 1.

The worn cruciform brooch Grave 351B (e) has knobs cast with the head-plate and two pin lugs. The half-round knobs, foot without lappets and animal head with half-round nostrils add it to the Kentish finds of Åberg's Group II (Åberg 1926). In Mortimer's typology the brooch falls into type B1 as part of an insular development of cruciform brooches, including an individualistic Kentish branch. Scientific analysis of the metal used for some Kentish and Frisian brooches suggests that they may come from the same source, possibly of late Roman origin (Mortimer 1990, 408). Two lugs for the spring are part of the insular development of cruciform brooches, and the Buckland brooch is the ninth example in Mortimer's corpus and the fourth Kentish find, after Faversham; Howletts grave 2 and Lyminge (*ibid*).

A correspondence analysis of the combination of thirty head-plate types, thirty-six bow types and fifty-four foot types used in 702 cruciform brooches from Scandinavia, England, Germany and the Netherlands has confirmed the existence of a specifically English typological development. Stylistically, this development as a whole was more closely related to the Continent than Scandinavia and is mainly dated to the last third of the fifth century and the first half of the sixth (Bode 1998, 23ff). Brooch Grave 351B (e) has a type 9 head-plate, a type 5 bow and a type 38 foot, a combination dated by Martina-Johanna Bode (pers comm) to the fifth century.

---

4.   For an overview on the state of research see Høilund Nielsen 1997a.

Some early cruciform brooches were produced in pairs to be worn at the shoulders; later ones were usually worn as single brooches on the chest, combined with a pair of small-long or annular brooches at the shoulders. Brooch Grave 351B (e) was found in a horizontal position in the pelvis area as part of a set of four brooches worn in a vertical row beginning at the chest (Fig 10.42). The use of a much abraded single brooch in combination with brooches in much better condition suggests it had been re-used for a Kentish costume marked more by its cut than the types of brooches used to keep it in place (*see* p 206).

Leeds' study (1945) shows small-long brooches from Kentish graves to be a heterogeneous group. They share few characteristics (mostly square-head plates and ring-and-dot decoration) which serve better to distinguish the majority of Kentish finds from the bulk of small-long brooches, especially from Anglian regions, rather than indicate a development of conventional designs produced in series. Some designs suggest that certain Kentish small-long brooches were not produced as a brooch type in their own right but as cheap versions of bow brooches, using ring-and-dot decoration instead of cast decoration and gilding (eg Webster 1995, 1036; and see below).

The pair of small-long brooches Grave 351B (a) and (d), associated with brooch (c) and the cruciform brooch (e) have square head-plates and foot-plates with lappets, common features of small-long brooches found in Kent (Leeds 1945, 38ff; fig 25; Evison 1987, 39; Evison 1994b, 5). The pair, however, was not worn as such but alternating with two other brooches to form a vertical row.

Small-long brooch Grave 257 (a) was found at the neck (Fig 10.18) but seems to have been barely functional. The pin-catch may have been already broken at the time of burial and lacks the hook that would hold the pin. The spring-holder is a replacement of the cast original, soldered on. The undecorated square head-plate, drop-shaped foot-plate and disc-shaped terminal of this brooch relate it to Leeds' series with a lozenge foot and square head-plate (Leeds 1945, 36ff) more than to any other of Leeds' series. A drop-shaped foot, however, seems to have been mostly used on Kentish finds, as is shown by a brooch from Grave 13 at Buckland, with a bi-lobed instead of a disc-shaped terminal, and the Kentish parallels discussed by Evison (1987, 39); also by a pair of small-long brooches from grave 77 at Bifrons with a spatula-shaped terminal (Chadwick Hawkes 2000, fig 34, 4).

The pair of brooches Grave 239 (b) and (c) are decorated with ring-and-dot punch-marks and were made to match by means of a repair. What seems to be a faulty casting of one head-plate was left plain and covered by copper alloy sheet with ring-and-dot decoration. Such decoration links the pair to other small-long brooches found in Kent, but the elongated square head-plate,[5] the oval platform on the bow and the tongue-shaped foot-plate recall the outline and roundels of some great square-headed brooches of Haseloff's 'Jutlandic Group'[6] and derivatives such as Buckland brooch Grave 281(e). Unlike the small-long brooches in Grave 351B (a) and (d) (see above), this pair was worn parallel, head-up on the chest, below a pair of annular brooches.

The particularly small pair of small-long brooches Grave 254 (d) and (e) also have ring-and-dot decoration and a roundel on the bow. They were apparently worn at the shoulders in the traditional way. The spatulate foot is a common feature among small-long brooches, but three flat knobs on the head-plate are found only among the 'abnormal' types defined by Leeds[7] and suggest they are another example of the lack of conformity in Kentish brooch fashion before the development of Kentish square-headed and disc brooches.

Annular and penannular brooches

(Graves 214, 237, 239, 250, 308, 326, 367 and 372)

Ten cast copper alloy annular brooches and one penannular ?brooch were found in eight graves at Buckland in 1994. Only two pairs of annulars, Grave 239 (d) and (e) and Grave 372 (b) and (c), were positioned at the shoulders and therefore worn in the 'Anglian' fashion. Single brooches Graves 308 (f) and 367 (g) were found at the neck. The matching pair of brooches Grave 237 (a) and (b) and the single brooch Grave 326 (b) were positioned at the left hip. The pair shows remains of iron pins and therefore was more likely kept in a bag, rather than being part of the bag itself. The single brooch Grave 326 (b) has no remains of a pin and may have been used for a bag instead of a copper alloy or iron ring, but equally might have been part of its contents. Wear on the ring opposite the pin housing, however, shows that the ring, at one time, was in use as an annular brooch.

The annular brooch Grave 250 (k), also positioned at the hip, had been repaired and was attached to an extremely worn clip. The diameter of the brooch itself is smaller than it was

---

5. Compare also Leeds 1945, fig 3c; 27c.
6. See, for example, a brooch from Pompey, Lorraine (Haseloff 1981, fig 26) and Evison (1987, 35ff).
7. See a brooch from Surrey, one from Norway and two from Kent (Leeds 1945, fig 26a–c; 27a). Three knobs are also found among the Elbe-Germanic bow brooches of Böhme's type 'Niederumstadt' dated in the last third of the fifth century (Böhme 1989). Though the type does not form a close parallel, the common element suggests a closer connection to the Continent than to Anglo-Saxon type developments. I am grateful to Johanna Brather for pointing out this parallel.

originally because the worn ring had apparently broken close to the pin housing and the two broken ends were then bent round to overlap and were secured by a copper alloy rivet.

The scrolled terminals of the copper alloy penannular ring (c) from the general fill of Grave 214 are overlapping, and as no remains of a pin were identified among the other objects recovered from the general fill, it seems most likely that the object was being used as a ring when buried. Scrolled terminals are known from Romano-British contexts (Leeds 1945, 44), and the object may have been old when buried.

A comprehensive analysis of annular brooch types and their distribution and dating is long overdue (MacGregor and Bolick 1993, 82; Stoodley 1999, 18)[8] and the Buckland finds are therefore dated mostly by their associated objects. Hirst's revision of Leeds' type description (Leeds 1945), however, is accompanied by a broad dating scheme for her groups I–VII (Hirst 1985, 55). None of the Buckland finds fall into her early groups I–III but into the later group IV, 'large brooches with narrow rings (Leeds type F)' (Graves 326 (b), 367 (g), 372 (b) and (c)), and into groups V, 'large brooches with rings decorated with groups of traverse furrows (Leeds' type G)', (Graves 239 (d) and (e), 250 (k)), and VI, 'large brooches with bead-and-reel moulded rings (Leeds' type G)' (Grave 237 (a) and (b)). Their date range is difficult to assess (*ibid*, 56). Groups IV–VI have a mostly Anglian distribution (*ibid*, 55) and owe some of their popularity in Kent to their re-use in the context of objects suspended from the belt (Evison 1987, 49; Parfitt and Brugmann 1997, 41). The large annular brooch Grave 308 (f) is the only one with a copper alloy, instead of an iron, pin and probably represents a variant of Group VI. At Buckland, annular brooches were used over a long period. Grave 239 is dated to Phase 1a, Grave 308 to Phase 1, Grave 372 to Phase 2a, and Grave 250 to Phase 3a.

Button brooches and a model

(Graves 219, 221, 254, 255, 290 and 384)[9]

The lead-alloy model Grave 384 (b) for a button brooch[10] unfortunately comes from the general grave fill and therefore need not be connected with the individual buried in the grave. It does, however, add to the rather meagre evidence for brooch production in early Anglo-Saxon England (see Dickinson 1993, 38; also Philp 2003, 13) and supports the idea generated by the distribution pattern of button brooches that they are a southern English and mainly Kentish type (Avent and Evison 1982).

It has been argued that lead models may have been cast from moulds, possibly in turn produced from primary models made of material easier to work, and that the lead models were only used to transfer and possibly refine the design of either the primary models or moulds to secondary moulds used for final casting (Coatswoth and Pinder 2002, 73ff). Model Grave 384 (b) does not seem to show any traces of the casting process itself and is in fact quite crude. If the idea was to improve the decoration of either the model itself or of the secondary mould before the final cast, this would presumably have required a correction to the uneven setting of the eyes.

The model was not, or at least not without correction of the secondary mould and/or the final product, used to produce any of the five copper-alloy gilt button brooches from the site or any of the brooches illustrated by Avent and Evison (1982). It has the pointed helmet and downward curving eyebrows of Avent and Evison's class Bii, combined with the round eyes mostly found with class Bi and the triangular face of class Dii.

Button brooch Grave 221 (a) falls within class Bi with nearly horizontal eyebrows, round eyes, eye-rings merged with the cheeks, a well defined mouth, a small diameter and high flange. Brooch Grave 255 (g) has its closest parallels in Class B, miscellaneous, including a brooch from Herpes (Dickinson 1993, pl XV, 21.1) with curved eyebrows beneath a straight helmet line and a ribbed nose. Class B is distributed mainly in Hampshire, Sussex and Kent.

Brooch Grave 290 (b) falls into Class Ai defined by a realistic representation of the human face, with a pointed helmet, curved eyebrows, small round eyes with curved eye-rings underneath them, flaring nostrils, a moustache indicated by the upper line of the mouth, rounded cheeks, punch-mark decoration around the inner part of the rim and on the helmet, an average diameter of 18.9mm and a relatively low flange. Brooch Grave 254 (b) is slightly smaller and matches Avent's and Evison's description of Class Aii with less rounded cheeks. The main distribution of classes Ai and Aii suggests that these brooches were made in Kent (Avent and Evison 1982, 80; fig 3).

Brooch Grave 219 (n) has its closest parallel in a pair of brooches from Vron in class A, miscellaneous (Avent and Evison 1982, pl XIV, 39.1, 2). The pair is remarkable for the

---

8. A severely criticised attempt at dating annular brooch types and other types of grave goods was made by Palm and Pind (1992).
9. This chapter was largely completed in 2004. For a more recent analysis of button brooches, including the Buckland examples, see Suzuki (2008).
10. The term 'button brooch' is used according to the definition: 'small saucer-shaped brooches whose main area of ornament consists of the representation of the human face and any other brooches which seem to be derived from this main type' (Avent and Evison 1982, 77).

absence of a helmet, the presence of thick and downward curving eyebrows, large eyes with curved eye-rings, full cheeks and a single bar moustache. Brooch Grave 219 (n), in contrast to the Vron pair, however, does not have a mouth beneath the moustache. Evison's assumption that the pair from Vron were made in France (*ibid*) is now challenged by the find of a very close parallel at Buckland. Brooch Grave 219 (n) is the only one of the button brooches from Buckland with a horizontal pin, a construction Avent and Evison (1982, 101) found to be commonly used for brooches of their earliest classes.

The button brooches from Buckland were found in the neck area (Graves 219 (n) and 254 (b)), in the area of the chest (Grave 290 (b)), or at the waist (Graves 221(a) and 255 (g)), positions known from other grave sites (see Avent and Evison 1982). For a detailed discussion on the individual positions of the pins in relation to the button brooch faces and implications this has on the costume, *see* p 184.

Avent and Evison (1982, 92ff; fig 13) dated button brooches to the fifth and first half of the sixth century on the basis of stylistic evidence and associated objects. According to Avent and Evison, Classes Aii and Bii fall mostly into the second half of the fifth century and the early sixth century, Classes Ai, Bi and B miscellaneous, in the late fifth and early/first half of the sixth century, and Class A miscellaneous in the early sixth century. Avent and Evison (1982, 99) points out the provisional character of these date spans stressing that 'The amount of positive evidence for dating brought forward above is sporadic, and will no doubt be extended by future finds'. The 1994 Buckland excavation adds substantially to the Kentish dating evidence, and in this new light the dates for the five button brooches and the model are reviewed (see Part 8). In the correspondence analysis (Table 8.1), button brooches of Class A form part of the definition of Phase 1a and brooches of other classes add to the definition of Phase 1b.

Saucer-shaped brooches with a central setting

(Graves 366, 428 and 440)

Graves 366, 428 and 440 produced two pairs and a single copper alloy gilt brooch with flange and slightly varying cast plaited decoration around a central garnet setting (brooches Graves 366 (a) and (b), 428 (a) and (b) and 440 (a)). These brooches are larger than the button brooches discussed above but smaller than most 'Saxon' saucer brooches. Arnold (1982, 52) noted that the same design was used for a disc

attached to the bow of a square-headed brooch from Tuxford, Nottinghamshire. Discs on bows, however, were produced without an upturned flange, and it seems more likely that the design of the Tuxford disc is related to the plait motif much used for square-headed brooches of Hines' Group XVI (Hines 1997a) rather than the garnet-set disc brooches found at Buckland.

Before the five new Buckland brooches of this type were discovered, the number found in Kent and on the Continent was almost even (Arnold 1982, fig 51), making it difficult to argue either for a Kentish or a continental provenance on the basis of their distribution. The flange of the Buckland brooches, however, indicates that they are more closely related to button and saucer brooches than to continental disc-shaped *Kleinfibeln* (see below). Close examination of both the insular and continental finds of brooches with a plait design and a central setting could show whether all such brooches were made with an upturned flange, or whether there might have been a continental type without.

Buckland Grave 366 is dated to Phases 1b–2 and Grave 428 to Phase 2. The only other pair of brooches from Kent with a known context come from grave 71 at Bifrons (Chadwick Hawkes 2000) and are associated with a buckle with club-shaped tongue, a type dated to Phases 1–2.

Brooch Grave 440 (a) is of exactly the same design as the pair in Grave 428 (a) and (b) but it is much worn and was found combined with a saucer-shaped brooch bearing Animal Style I decoration around a red enamel setting (b). Though the enamelled brooch is also worn, it seems likely that it represents a replacement for what was originally a pair of plait decorated brooches, or *vice versa*.

Brooch Grave 440 (b) combines the attributes of a 'Saxon' saucer brooch in size, shape and the use of Animal Style I design, but the cast ornament itself is not typical for this type of brooch. It shows a face-to-face design of two almost identical quadrupeds with their heads separated by a running spiral design, three spirals bordered by a V-shaped ornament, and their back feet separated by a simpler V-shaped design.[11] The combination of the heads, bodies and limbs of the quadrupeds would not stand out in the mirror design of a Kentish square-headed brooch but is not typical of saucer brooches ornamented with coherent creatures, which typically chase around the central field (see Dickinson 1993, 25). A disc brooch with mirror-image Style I is also known from Suffolk but the design is not part of the saucer brooch repertoire.

In a Kentish product, one would expect the use of a central inlay instead of enamel,[12] a method of decoration used for

---

11. This could be read as a simplified profiled head (Tania Dickinson, pers comm).
12. Such as for a round brooch with a flange and Animal Style I design found 'between Bridge and Bekesbourne' (Chadwick Hawkes 2000, fig 55, 1).

a small number of Anglo-Saxon objects found mostly in Cambridgeshire and Suffolk, and possibly a sign of Romano-British influence on brooch making (Scull 1985). The depiction of animals with angled upper and lower front and hind legs and articulated claws was used for Kentish bow brooches (eg brooch Grave 408 (c)) but not for Kentish disc brooches (see below), with more abstract animal designs (eg brooch Grave 222 (b)). A date for this brooch within Kentish Phases II or III, rather than IV, is on stylistic grounds, therefore, likely. Grave 440 is dated to Buckland Phase 1b–2a (Table 8.5).

Kentish disc brooches

(Graves 204, 222, 245, 353, 354 and 373)

Kentish disc brooches were exclusively made of silver and seem to match a development on the Continent that saw a change in fashion from the use of pairs of brooches to a single brooch at the neck, during the second half of the sixth century (Martin 1994). The 1994 Buckland excavations produced six Kentish disc brooches of Avent's Classes 1–3 (Avent 1975). At Mill Hill, Deal, Classes 1 and 2 were introduced during Kentish Phase III and were the main type in use during Phase IV. Class 3 at Buckland 1951–3 was dated by Evison to her Phase 3. In our revised Buckland chronology, Classes 1 and 2 (Table 8.3, type Kdbr1–2) are part of the definitions of Phases 2a–3a and Class 3 (Table 8.3, type Kdbr3) of Phases 3a and 3b.

Brooches Grave 222 (b), Grave 353 (b) and Grave 354 (b) were worn at the neck, brooches Grave 204 (b) and Grave 245 (e) in the chest area, combined with bracteates. Brooch Grave 245 (e) is the only one combined with another brooch.

Brooches Graves 204 (b), 353 (b) and 373 (j) fall in Avent's (1975) Class 1.1. Brooch Grave 204 (b) has a flat type 1.1 central garnet setting and three type 1 garnet keystone settings, one type 1.1 and two Animal Style ornaments showing heads of a type not classified by Avent (1975), and a type 4.1 nielloed rim. Brooches Graves 353 (b) and 373 (j) have a flat type 1.1 central shell setting, three type 1 garnet keystone settings, a plain type 1 inner ring, and three type 1.2 Animal Style I ornaments. Only the nielloed rims are different, type 4.3 in the case of brooch Grave 353 (b) and type 4.1 in the case of brooch Grave 373 (j). Around brooch Grave 353 (b) was a beaded silver-gilt rim (j), together with a fragmentary copper alloy possible pin-catch. The traces of possible solder on the inside of the ring and wear on the outside of the ring suggest that brooch Grave 353 (b) was re-used for the construction of a larger brooch possibly involving an additional rim partly made of organic material.

Brooch Grave 354 (b) falls into Class 1.2, with remains of a central setting and four type 2.1 keystone garnets, four Animal Style ornaments of types 2.5, 2.9, 3.1, and 3.3 with three, instead of two, parallel bars, and a type 4.1 nielloed rim. Brooch Grave 222 (b) is of Class 2.4 with a flat type 1.2 central garnet set in white magnesite and three type 2.1 garnet keystone settings, a double type 1 inner ring, three Animal Style ornaments roughly of type 6.13, and a type 4.1 niello rim surrounded by a type 1 outer rim cast as one with the brooch. The back of the brooch is decorated with a groove along the rim cut by a set of lines which has a vague resemblance to a beaded rim with the remains of gilding in the grooves. A Class 2.4 brooch from Faversham (Avent 1975, no 49) has similar decoration on the back.

Brooch Grave 245 (e) belongs to Class 3.5. It has a flat type 1.2 central glass inlay on gold foil set in bone and four garnet keystone settings, four Animal Style ornaments of type 9.3, two inner rings of types 2 and 1, and a type 4.3 nielloed rim. With a diameter of 32mm, it is the smallest brooch in this Class.

Continental types of *Kleinfibeln* (small brooches) with geometric design

(Graves 245, 247, 296, 372 and 391B)

The term *Kleinfibel*, 'small brooch', relates to the difference in size between the brooches used in fifth- and sixth-century Merovingian brooch fashion. The brooches worn at the neck, or on the upper chest fastened a tunic and are much smaller than the continental types of bow brooches (*Bügelknopffibeln*) worn at or below the waist. *Kleinfibeln* were first produced and worn in pairs and were replaced by larger single brooches during the course of the sixth century (Martin 1994). The most common Kentish brooch types apparently with the same function as *Kleinfibeln* are button brooches, saucer-shaped brooches with a central garnet and early Kentish disc brooches (see above).

There are not enough examples of the individual types of *Kleinfibeln* and *Bügelknopffibeln* in Kentish graves to be included as such in correspondence analyses in Part 8. Therefore, these brooches are summarised as 'Early Merovingian brooch types' (Table 8.3, *type impbro*) as an element of Kentish female dress forming part of the definition of Phases 1b and 2a.

The most common type of *Kleinfibeln* in the Merovingian West are 'cloisonné' brooches, a misleading term which refers to enamel decoration, instead of the cut settings made mostly of garnet, glass or bone in a usually copper alloy or silver setting. In the course of the sixth century, the design of 'cloisonné' brooches underwent a general development from small designs, with a simple central setting surrounded by a keystone setting, to larger brooches with more complex designs and more elaborate outlines such as rosettes and quatrefoil designs.[13] The earliest brooches were usually produced and worn as matching pairs, a fashion which in the second half of the sixth century changed to unmatched pairs (Martin 1994).

At Buckland, four single and one pair of 'cloisonné' brooches (Graves 245 (c); 247 (a); 296 (b); 372 (f) and 391B (d) and (e)) were found. The smallest brooch, Grave 372 (f), with eight keystone garnet settings, has an iron framework covered by silver sheeting. A brooch with six keystone garnet settings on an iron back from grave 105C at Mill Hill, Deal, and a brooch with eight keystone garnet settings on an iron back from Grave 92 at Buckland have been dated to Kentish Phase III (Brugmann 1999a, table 3.2).

The disc brooch Grave 247 (a) with a combination of red ?garnet and blue glass settings and an inlaid rim, has a close parallel in a disc ?brooch from Bifrons grave 42, with green instead of blue glass and a beaded rim, dated to Kentish Phase II (Brugmann 1999a, table 3.2). The quatrefoil brooch Grave 296 (b) has a more complex design than the quatrefoil brooches found in grave 158 at Sarre (Brent 1864–5, pl 6, 10) and grave 21 at Stowting (Brent 1867, pl 19, 6) and is of particularly high quality.

The pair of rosette brooches Grave 391B (d) and (e) and the single brooch Grave 245 (c) almost double the number of rosette brooches found in Kentish graves. The rosette brooch from grave 18 at Mill Hill, Deal, has been dated to Kentish Phases II/III (Parfitt and Brugmann 1997, fig 27, n) and the one from grave 203 at Finglesham to Kentish Phase III (Brugmann 1999a, table 3.2). The context of a rosette brooch from Ozengell (Roach Smith 1854, pl V, 9) is not recorded. On the Continent, small rosette brooches with a simple central setting can date from as early as the first quarter of the sixth century (U Koch 1990, 140). The Kentish rosette brooches, however, represent later designs. The brooch pair Grave 391B (d) and (e) may have been old when buried because they are worn and apparently also repaired. It seems that the fastening of brooch (e) is not cast with the back-plate but added on, while that of brooch (d) is broken and may have been repaired with the folded hook (s).

Disc brooch Grave 281 (a) does not have a central setting but two pairs of rounded ?green ?glass settings in a silver framework set on an iron back-plate. The workmanship of this brooch is poorer than that of brooch Grave 372 (f) but has an exact parallel

in the design of a glass-set brooch from Ozengell on Thanet (Powell Cotton Museum, Quex Park, unpublished).

The silver-gilt disc brooch Grave 419 (b) shows a cast geometric design around a garnet setting. Notched ridges frame four zones divided into sets of three raised triangles. The brooch does not have a flange, suggesting that its production is not closely related to the saucer-shaped brooches with a central setting discussed above. Disc brooches with a central setting and cast radiating geometric design framed by a flat, not a flanged rim, are a relatively rare continental type dated by U Koch (2001, 234) to phases SD 4–5 (see Part 8).

The silver-gilt whirl-shaped brooch Grave 347 (e) is comprised of six birds' heads radiating from a circular centre, set with discoloured and fragmented glass. According to U Koch (2001, 252), continental finds of such whirl-shaped brooches are set with garnets or yellow glass, suggesting that the inlays of brooch Grave 347 (e) may also have originally been yellow. Whirl-shaped brooches have been found mainly in France (*ibid*, 106) and are dated to Picardie phase C/D/E (Legoux 1998). U Koch (2001), however, assigned the most easterly find earlier, to phase SD 5 (see Table 8.4).

Rider-, animal- and S-shaped brooches

(Graves 223, 255, 419 and 433)

The rider-, animal- and S-shaped brooches are the only *Kleinfibeln* with figured shapes. The rider-brooch, Grave 223 (a), and the S-shaped brooch, Grave 255 (h) are continental types, whilst the bird brooch, Grave 419 (a) and possibly also the quadruped, Grave 433 (a) are Kentish types. The most striking difference between continental and Kentish animal brooches is the way the animals face. Continental animals are generally positioned so that they would move from left to right, according to Antique tradition (Martin 1991b, 645f), while bird brooch Grave 419 (a) and animal brooch Grave 433 (a) face to the left. A set of bird brooches identical in design to the silver-gilt bird brooch Grave 419 (a) but facing to the right was found in grave 30 at Bekesbourne. These bird brooches represent a Kentish production of *Kleinfibeln* dated to Kentish Phases II–III on stylistic grounds (Brugmann 1999a, 45).

The fine copper alloy gilt animal brooch Grave 433 (a) shows a crouching quadruped, possibly a horse from the elongated head but with toes instead of hooves, and is the only brooch of this shape known from Kent. Head, neck, body and the drop-shaped upper legs are more substantial

---

13. This development is well presented at Schretzheim (Phases 1–4; U Koch 1977).

and cohesive than the combined elements cast as ridges on the Kentish square-headed and disc brooches decorated with Animal Style I, and also on the unusual saucer brooch from Grave 440 (a) (see above). The closest parallels to the early Style I used for brooch Grave 433 (a) are found among the crouching quadrupeds framing the foot-plates of some great square-headed brooches of the 'Jutlandic Group' (Haseloff 1981). The depiction of the head of the animal with an eye framed by a semi-circle and an ?open mouth can also be seen on the upper foot-plate of a brooch from Skerne, Falster in Denmark (*ibid*, pl 5). The drop-shaped upper limbs, lines separating the hooves or claws from the lower legs and the substantial body with a raised centre can be seen on the lower foot-plate of the great-headed brooch from Gummersmark, Seeland (*ibid*, pl 23), and in a more compressed version, on the upper foot-plate of a brooch from Engers, Germany, which has its closest parallel in the great square-headed brooch from grave D3 at Finglesham (*ibid*, pl 12).

The close stylistic relationship of brooch Grave 433 (a) to the Danish finds of the 'Jutlandic Group' suggests a late fifth-century date for its manufacture (Karen Høilund Nielsen, pers comm). This is an unusually early date for the use of an animal-shaped ornament because Kent is better known for its sixth-century bird mounts showing a later and apparently specifically Kentish type of Animal Style (Parfitt and Brugmann 1997, 87ff; Brugmann 1999b). Brooch Grave 433 (a) may indicate that this development predates the standardised production of Kentish square-headed brooches and has its roots in the 'Jutish-Kentish' tradition expressed in some Kentish women's dress ornaments (see Parfitt and Brugmann 1997, 110ff). Grave 433 is dated to Phase 1 on the basis of these stylistic considerations.

The silver-gilt brooch Grave 223 (a) shows a rider on a horse, a motif of late Roman origin that found its way into Alamannic brooch production during the fifth century (U Koch 1993, 34 f) and in western Switzerland under Romanic influence was still used at the end of the sixth century (Marti 1990, 58). Among the two main types of silver rider-brooches, Grave 223 (a) belongs to the form where the rider has raised arms, which is dated to phase AM I (see A Koch 1998, 289, note 98). Buckland is the most north-westerly find of this kind made so far and is the first rider-brooch of any type known from Kent. The late context of the brooch (Part 8) suggests that this much worn and broken, but still functioning brooch was an heirloom, used as a surrogate for a silver Kentish disc brooch in Phases 2b–3.

S-brooches are defined by two animal heads with either an open or a closed beak attached to necks or bodies combined in an S-shape. They have a wide continental distribution (Kühn 1974–7, pl 63). According to Werner

(1962b) S-brooches as a type of *Kleinfibel* were to the Merovingian East what garnet disc brooches were to the Merovingian West. The design may have been copied in Anglo-Saxon England (Briscoe 1968).

S-brooches with open beaks and lines across the body, such as the copper alloy gilt brooch Grave 255 (h), according to Werner (1962b, 77) are among the earliest S-brooches. They are a rare type with a wide distribution and a design closely connected with Lombard S-brooches of the first half of the sixth century. Small brooches made of an elongated S-shape and without settings are generally dated to the late fifth and early sixth century, in particular Phase SD 3 (U Koch 2001, X20).

In southern England, a further two S-brooches with open beaks and lines along the 'body' have been found in grave 48 at Chessell Down, on the Isle of Wight (Arnold 1982, fig 16, 69ii) and in grave 33 at Lyminge (Warhurst 1955, pl 8, 5). The Chessell Down brooch was associated with a saucer-brooch with central garnet and cast plaited decoration (see above), whilst the Lyminge brooch occurred with eight blue out of nine glass beads - a combination which suggests that the grave belongs to the earliest phase of inhumations in Kent.

Kentish square-headed brooches

(Graves 255, 263B, 281, 347, 372, 391B and 417)

Kentish square-headed brooches seem to be the first type of brooch produced in Kent in numbers large enough to make the design immediately recognisable as 'Kentish'. Of the twelve Kentish square-headed brooches found at Buckland in 1994, ten belong to the Kentish-continental group (Graves 255 (c) and (i), 263B (b) and (c), 281(d), 347 (f), 391B (l), (m) and (n), 417 (c)) and two to the Jutish-Kentish group (Graves 281 (e), 372 (e); see Parfitt and Brugmann 1997, 35). Only two brooches, of the Kentish-continental group (Graves 255 (i) and 417 (c)), are more than 60mm long and therefore labelled as 'great' square-headed brooches, in contrast to the 'small' variant. Kentish square-headed brooches ceased to be used during Kentish Phase III (Brugmann 1999a, table 3.2).

For the correspondence analyses in Part 8, the Kentish square-headed brooches were sorted into three groups: brooches without garnets (Table 8.3, *type plainKsqh*), brooches with garnet settings (*type garnetKsqh*), and pairs with their foot-plate terminals shaped as roundels (*type Krundelpair*). The correspondence analysis suggests a chronological sequence: plain brooches were the earliest (Phases 1b–2a), followed by brooches with garnet settings (mostly Phase 2a), and pairs of brooches with roundels as a later development (Phase 2; Tables 8.2–8.3).

Kentish small square-headed brooches correspond in size to small-long brooches rather than continental bow brooches (*Bügelknopffibeln*, see below) but apparently were not worn at the shoulders to fasten a *peplos* garment. The great brooch Grave 255 (i) and the small brooch Grave 372 (e) were worn at the neck, presumably to hold a cloak in place, while the other brooches were used for vertical rows or pairs in the waist and pelvis area, usually combined with a brooch at the neck (*see* p 205).

Three of the copper alloy gilt brooches, the pair from Grave 263B and the single brooch Grave 255 (c), add to the relatively large group of small square-headed brooches of Åberg type 131 with a cruciform division on the foot-plate, half-circled side-terminals, and square foot-plate terminals (Parfitt and Brugmann 1997, 37; fig 14a)[14] dated to Kentish Phase II (Brugmann 1999a, 47). Brooch Grave 347 (f) is a silver-gilt variant with square garnets on the head-plate and a mushroom-shaped garnet on the foot-plate terminal, a rare shape among the drop-shaped, round, square, or leaf-shaped garnets more usually found on the foot-plate terminals of small Kentish square-headed brooches of this type.

The copper alloy gilt brooch Grave 281 (d) is a plain type without garnets, and has simple geometric decoration combined with Style I-elements on the upper foot-plate - features of Åberg type 131 - but it also has lozenge-shaped cast decoration on the foot-plate relating it to a brooch from grave 105C at Mill Hill, Deal (*ibid*, fig 13a), dated to Kentish Phase III (Brugmann 1999a, table 3.2), which has rounded side-terminals, and an unusual cross-shaped foot-plate terminal. Grave 281 is dated to Buckland Phase 1b (Table 8.5).

The pair of silver-gilt brooches Grave 391B (m) and (n) are of particularly high quality with carefully executed Style I-animals on the upper corners of the foot-plate and further elements on the head-plate, combined with well-cut garnets on hatched foil, niello and complex punched decoration. This hardly worn pair is combined with the much more abraded silver-gilt square-headed brooch (l) with the same decorative elements less well executed. The side terminals of the foot-plate are cast instead of garnet-set; the head-plate has only one central garnet, and cast, instead of garnet-set, leaf-shaped ornaments, and it has a rim punched with rings instead of garnet settings in the corners. The abrasion on brooch (l) suggests that it was longer, and more frequently used, or had a different function to the pair (m) and (n). It seems probable that brooch (l) was not produced to match

the pair, but that all three brooches were either made at the same time, or that the pair were a later addition.

The three brooches from Grave 391B combine decorative elements common in garnet-set Kentish small square-headed brooches and are part of a relatively large-scale production of similar, but not identical, designs. The same applies to the two Kentish great square-headed brooches Grave 255 (i) and Grave 417 (c). The copper alloy gilt brooch Grave 255 (i) and the silver-gilt brooch Grave 417 (c) show three carefully executed Style I-animals, one on the head-plate and one on each of the upper corners of the foot-plate. Head- and foot-plate are set with garnets, two of them in the upper corners of the head-plate framed by a lattice-work of triangles and semi-circles carried out as openwork on the silver brooch. The closest parallel to these brooches, with additional garnets on the side terminals of the foot-plate, is formed by a pair of brooches from grave E2 at Finglesham (Chadwick 1958, fig 11b).

On the head-plates of the two Jutish-Kentish brooches Grave 281 (e) and Grave 372 (e) Animal Style I was used for less obvious designs. The head-plate of the copper alloy gilt brooch Grave 281(e) is divided horizontally, with a mirror design of an animal on each side. The bow is decorated with a face, and the foot-plate with a lozenge-shaped geometric design, roundels on the terminals and the usual animal heads on the upper edges. The stylistic elements making up the brooch are a variation of designs used on brooches from Faversham, Stodmarsh, Bifrons and ?Kent (Åberg 1926, figs 138 f; Leigh 1980, pl 25–7; 56). Unfortunately, only the grave good associations of the pair of brooches from grave 64 at Bifrons are known. This pair was worn at the waist with a disc brooch at the neck (Chadwick Hawkes 2000). The closest parallel to brooch Grave 281(e) within the Buckland cemetery is the pair of brooches from Grave 20 with a mirror design on the head-plate, roundels on the foot-plate terminals and round settings on the bow, also worn in the waist area, with a disc brooch at the neck (Evison 1987, fig 12).

The silver-gilt brooch Grave 372 (e) has a similar design on the foot-plate with roundels on the foot-plate terminals and a lozenge design in the centre. The bow of the brooch, however, is plain and the head-plate is divided into three squares filled with Animal Style I-elements. The parallel partition of the head-plate is unique among the Kentish-Jutish brooches. However, it is basically a variation of the design used for Buckland brooch Grave 281 (e); and also pairs of brooches with animal style on the head-plate not divided into zones from Faversham, grave 30 at Bekesbourne (Leigh 1980, pl 31; 32) and grave 203 at Finglesham, or the brooch

---

14. A Koch (1998, map 23) shows the continental distribution of this type as 'Kentish little square-headed brooches Var A'.

with triangular zones on the head-plate from the same grave (Chadwick Hawkes and Pollard 1981, fig. 4; Chadwick Hawkes and Grainger 2006, 142–3, fig 2.142) dated to Kentish Phase III (Brugmann 1999a, table 3.2).

Bügelknopffibeln: radiate- and square-headed brooches with knobs

(Graves 263B, 266, 296, 347, 351B, 407, 408 and 417)

Brooches with three, (mostly) five, seven or nine knobs are common type of brooch on the Continent which developed in the fifth century. They have been the subject of extensive studies on Merovingian and related bow brooches.[15] In Table 8.3 these brooches are subsumed under 'Early Merovingian brooch types' (type 'impbro') as part of the definition of Phases 1b and 2a. The distribution of a few small types of *Bügelknopffibeln* suggests a Kentish origin.

The *Bügelknopffibeln* found at Buckland in 1994 were positioned the area of the lower chest, waist or pelvis with the exception of two graves. The miniature brooch Grave 417 (g) was positioned at neck, and the pair of bow brooches Grave 266 (i) and (j) were found on the upper and lower chest, with their head-plates pointing in opposite directions. These are positions also known from the Continent.

Brooch Grave 263B (a) is particularly small for a bow brooch. It has three knobs and is decorated with a cast zigzag line on the head-plate. The foot shows cast 'basketwork' decoration formed by sets of parallel lines set at a right angle. The foot-plate terminal is decorated with a row of V-shaped punches and separate ring-and-dot punches placed at each point of a 'V', a design suggesting a Kentish provenance for the brooch. V-shaped punch-marks, as much as the triangular punch-marks on brooch Grave 408 (d) discussed below, are found on cruciform brooches (see Mortimer 1990) and Kentish square-headed brooches (see Leigh 1980) among other Anglo-Saxon types of objects but they are not found on continental bow brooches.[16]

Close parallels to brooch Grave 263B (a) were found in mound 2 (a pair) and mound 6 at Chatham Lines (MacGregor and Bolick 1993, nos 16, 5.6) and grave 15 at Howletts (accession number BM 1936,5–11.51), with a variation in the decoration on the head-plates, showing radiating lines in the case of the single brooch from mound 6. The apparent lack of close parallels on the Continent also suggests that this is a brooch type produced in Kent. Presumably, its production is related to larger brooches with five knobs and similar cast designs, such as A Koch's type I.3.3.2.1.1 dated early in Phase AM I after Ament (1977; A Koch 1998, 78f; map 6).

If the records of grave 15 at Howletts are correct, the brooch from this burial was found with weapons including a Frankish axehead. The associations of the Chatham finds, however, are remarkably similar to Buckland brooch Grave 263B (a) because all of them involve Kentish square-headed brooches. Åberg's type 131 (see above) occurs in Grave 263 and Chatham Lines grave 2, whilst a similar type without garnets came from grave 6 at Chatham. Brooch Grave 263B (a) was worn as the top brooch in a vertical row across the waist. At Chatham Lines, all the brooches were also found at the waist.

The copper alloy gilt brooch Grave 408 (c) belongs to a small group of small bow brooches, with a triangular foot-plate and an animal in Style I on the radiate head-plate, distributed in Kent.[17] The only brooch with a known grave context, grave 102 at Mill Hill, Deal, is dated to Kentish Phase III (*ibid*, table 12). The Buckland brooch was worn in combination with a small continental-style bow brooch (d) at the waist.

The copper alloy gilt brooch Grave 408 (d) may also have been produced in Kent, not so much because there are no exact parallels on the Continent showing a comparable combination of cast and inlaid decorative elements, but because of the elaborate punch-marks on the trapezoid foot-plate. Rows of circles frame two triangular punch marks, each comprised of a dot framed by three smaller triangles. The punch-marks on brooch Grave 263B (a) are gilt and were therefore presumably produced when the brooch was made. It seems probable that the present brooch belongs to the same fifth-century experimental stage of brooch making in Kent as Grave 263B (a).

The copper alloy brooch Grave 351B (c) is a small radiate-headed brooch with five knobs and a trapezoid foot-plate, exclusively decorated with a multiple ring-and-dot (bull's-eye) motif. This type of decoration is of late Roman origin and is well known from late Roman belt sets.[18] In south-east England it was mostly used for 'Saxon' disc brooches distributed across Kent in small numbers (see Webster 1995). A brooch from Amiens, Somme (A Koch 1998, pl 8, 2) is a rare continental case of 'bull's eyes' used for a radiate-headed

---

15. For an overview on the history of research see Martin (1994) and A Koch (1998, 3ff).
16. According to A Koch (1998, 505ff) punched decoration was the main type of decoration on Germanic brooches of the first half of the fifth century in Gaul but became very rare towards the end of the fifth century (see also Evison 1965, 55). The punched decoration that was used for early types of Merovingian bow brooch is restricted to the simple designs of dots, circles and notches. This, of course, excludes the small and deeper triangular punch-marks used to produce niello decoration. For a discussion on 'basketwork' see Dickinson 1993, 22f.
17. See Parfitt and Brugmann 1997, 39, fig 12, and a further find from Mucking, Essex (Hamerow 1993, fig 151, 1).
18. See, for example, the plates in Bullinger (1969) clearly showing the grooves.

brooch. The ribbed bow of brooch Grave 351B (c) is of a design generally not used in Anglo-Saxon brooch making but it is found with some fifth-century bow brooches on the Continent, such as the radiate-headed Bulles/Krefeld-Gellep type (A Koch 1998). Both the grooved 'bull's eyes' and the ribbed bow suggest a fifth-century date for brooch Grave 351B (c). The brooch was worn in combination with a cruciform and a pair of small-long brooches (see above) and was presumably considered to be an adequate match to the latter both in size and decoration.

The silver-gilt brooch pair Grave 266 (i) and (j) belongs to the Bréban type, with a main distribution in the north of France dated by A Koch (1998, 217) to Phase AM II and by U Koch (2001) in phase SD 4. The only other Kentish find was given to the British Museum as part of the Howletts Collection (inventory number BM 1992,4-3.1).

The designs of the copper alloy gilt brooch Grave 417 (d) and of the silver-gilt brooches Grave 296 (e) and (f) and Grave 347 (k) are 'classic' examples of Merovingian bow brooch fashion, at its height during the first half and middle of the sixth century. Brooch Grave 417 (d) adds to the finds of the western variant of the Hahnheim type found in Kent, which according to A Koch (1998, 204f) is a type first produced towards the end of phase AM I and typical of phase AM II.[19] In Kent, the western variant, with a main distribution in France, is better represented than the eastern variant, with a main distribution pattern in the Rhineland (Parfitt and Brugmann 1997, 43). Brooch Grave 417 (d) is the fifth brooch find of this type to be made in Kent, after grave 18 at Chatham Lines (Douglas 1793, pl 15, 5), Faversham (inventory number BM 1067, 10), grave ?4 at Howletts (inventory number BM 1936, 16), and grave 16 at Lyminge (Warhurst 1955, pl 8, 5). At Mill Hill, Deal, the eastern variant Hahnheim type falls within Kentish Phase III (Parfitt and Brugmann 1997, 43).

Hahnheim type brooch Grave 417 (d) was combined with a silver variant (g) of the 'miniature' brooches of Weimar/Arcy-de-Sainte-Restitue and *Dreirundelfibeln* type, with triple sets of garnet inlays. Both have a main distribution in Thuringia and a remarkable number are found in northern France. These types were in use from the mid/second half of the fifth to the first half of the sixth century (early in phase AM II), mainly the late fifth century (A Koch 1998, 381ff). In northern France, the development of this type is put down to the influence of Thuringian immigrants (*ibid*).

Kentish finds of Weimar/Arcy-de-Sainte-Restitue type have been made at Howletts (unpublished, British Museum Howletts Collection), Ickham (Åberg 1926, fig 156) and Bifrons (Baldwin Brown 1915a, pl 35, 8). The Buckland find is the only variant known, so far, with three inlaid knobs to its semi-circular head-plate and a drop-shaped garnet combined with round garnets for a foot-plate. The Ickham find has been interpreted by A Koch (1998, 382) as a West Frankish import and the same might apply to the Buckland brooch, though it seems possible that it was part of the experimental phase of Kentish brooch making discussed above.

There is no pattern to the position of 'miniature' brooches of the Weimar/Arcy-de-Sainte-Restitue type in graves that would explain a specific function for such small bow brooches. Some, but not all, have been found in children's graves, so that it seems possible, but by no means certain, that they were originally produced for children and still worn in later life (see A Koch 1998, 380f). The much abraded brooch Grave 417 (g) was worn by an adult at the neck, presumably functioning as a *Kleinfibel* (see above).

The silver brooch pair Grave 296 (e) and (f) combine common cast geometric designs with round garnet inlays not only on the knobs but also on the bow and foot and therefore are of particularly high quality. A close parallel from Cormette, Pas-de-Calais, is not only decorated with the same combination of cast designs but also with inlays on the bow and foot. The brooch found at Cormette was associated with a radiate-headed brooch with cross-hatched decoration on the head-plate such as the one from Buckland Grave 347 (k), a combination dated by A Koch (1998, 80) to late in phase AM I or early in phase AM II after (Ament 1977).

The design on the bow and foot-plate of brooch Grave 347 (k), however, differs slightly from that of the Cormette brooch, and brooch Grave 347 (k) is, in fact, a further example of a large group of brooches that combines the cast decorative elements of a cross-hatched head-plate, a striped bow and zigzag borders on the foot-plate, dated by A Koch (1998, 111ff) to late in phase AM I and AM II after Ament (1977). Despite the wide distribution of brooches with hatched head-plates on the Continent, this seems to be the first find from Kent.

The matching pair of worn silver-gilt bow brooches Grave 407 (e) and (f) have their closest parallels in the Poysdorf type, named after an Austrian site that produced the grave of a smith, including models for brooches (see U Koch 1977, 49f). The overall design of the Buckland pair is the same as the Poysdorf type in regard to the square head-plate with short cast knobs and an animal-shaped foot-plate terminal. It seems that the Buckland brooches imitate the cast decoration of the Poysdorf type, which shows entwined zigzag bands on both the head- and the foot-plate. The design of the ornament

---

19. The evidence includes a coin-dated grave at Ciply (Hainaut) providing a *terminus post quem* of AD 524 (*ibid*).

on the head- and the foot-plate of the Buckland pair however, seems to have been only partially successful, because the zigzag bands are only partly entwined on the foot-plate and not entwined, but asymmetrical, on the head-plate.

In Anglo-Saxon contexts, unsuccessful or second-rate copies of original designs are best known from saucer brooches (see Dickinson 1993) and in this case do not necessarily suggest a Kentish product because they are also well known on the Continent. The east Meroviginan Poysdorf type may have been imitated in the Merovingian west (U Koch 1977, 49f), and, indeed, in Kent, if Kentish brooch production included straight (or near-straight) copies of non-Kentish brooch types. A slightly later variant of the Poysdorf type was associated with a rider-brooch (see above) at Rhenen, Utrecht and has been dated to late phase AM I–early AM II (after Ament 1977; A Koch 1998, 288f).

Pendants

Birte Brugmann

(Graves 245, 250, 391A, 391B and 413)

Graves of the Anglo-Saxon 'Early Phase' contain few types of pendants other than bracteates. Pendants with a loop attached for suspension became a regular part of Kentish female dress only after Kentish Phase IV.[20] This includes coins with a loop attached, such as Grave 232 (a) (p 394).[21] The correspondence analysis in Part 8 includes four types of pendants (Table 8.3): bracteates, scutiform pendants *(type scutiform)*, coin pendants with loops *(type 'coinpen')*, and inlaid pendants *(type 'inlaypen')*. Bracteates were mostly in use in Buckland Phases 2 and 3a, scutiform pendants mainly in Phase 3, coin pendants from Phase 3b, and inlaid pendants from Phase 5.

Regional Merovingian dress codes were less restrictive than Kentish, and pendants played a minor but relatively constant part in women's fashion from the fifth to the seventh century. At Buckland, nine pendants were found with five individuals (Graves 245 (d), 250 (cii and i), 391A (e), 391B (f/h/i), 413 (o)), all of them in the area of neck and chest with the exception of pendant Grave 250 (i) found at the waist and probably kept in a purse. The positioning of the large intaglio Grave 391B (f), in a sling at the lower chest, is the reason why this object is discussed here with the other pendants and not as a variant of a 'crystal ball', which would have been worn at or below the waist. Object Grave 350B

(b), a single copper alloy sling suspended from a loop and found at the waist, is discussed with the 'crystal balls' below also because of its position in the grave.

Two of the pendants listed above do not show evidence of a loop. The silver-gilt scutiform pendant Grave 245 (d) with bossed concentric decoration had a 'shield grip' soldered to its back instead. Scutiform pendants with 'grips' are a Scandinavian type introduced to Anglian England, and apparently also Schleswig-Holstein, during the fifth century (Bode 1998, 91). Pendant Grave 245 (d), however, is gilded, a feature found with a third of the scutiform pendants known from Kent but not from Anglian England (Hines 1984, 229). It is therefore not clear whether this pendant is a fifth-century type, re-used when scutiform pendants were introduced to Kent. The silver scutiform object Grave 339 (d) with punched ring-and-dot decoration shows no remains of a loop or 'grip' and has two perforations along the edge suggesting it was a mount rather than a pendant; this is discussed below (p 122).

Evison (1987, 55ff) interpreted the cross design on the scutiform pendants found in Graves 35 and 67 at Buckland as Christian symbols. The same symbols were found on the pair of silver scutiform pendants from Grave 250 (cii). The design on these two pendants is not only outlined with repoussé dots but also partially gilt. Only one of the pendants, however, has four gilt 'arms' of a cross, while the other has two gilded and two plain zones. The loops on the pendants from Graves 35, 67 and 250 show that the 'cross'-shape had to be worn as an 'X', and the additional standing cross scratched into the pendant from Grave 35 (Evison 1987, fig 21, 3) may as well indicate a Christian addition to a design of an unknown meaning.

The use of the copper alloy disc Grave 250 (i) with a central perforation and a double perforation at the edge, found in the same grave as the pair of pendants (cii) is not clear. Association with an ivory ring suggests the disc was carried in, or was part of, a purse. Pendants with a double perforation at the rim and a third perforation, or a raised boss in the centre and therefore scutiform pendants, have been found worn at the neck[22] but there are also examples of such pendants attached to buckets (Cook 2004).

Burials 391A and 391B produced four pendants, the copper alloy bulla pendant Grave 391A (e) and, in association, the silver pendant Grave 391B (i), the gold pendant Grave 391B (h) and the intaglio Grave 391B (f) set in a sling and attached to a slip-knot ring for suspension *(see pp 436–7)*. The silver pendant is made of two sheets folded

---

20. Brugmann 1999a, table 3.1; for a detailed discussion on chronology see Part 8.
21. This explains the general lack of sixth-century coins in sixth-century Anglo-Saxon graves.
22. See for example West Heslerton graves 50, 55, 86 and 111 (Haughton and Powlesland 1999).

and soldered and may have contained an amulet. The gold pendant is made of a coiled beaded wire with an open centre and a ribbed loop of the type used for bracteates.

Larger beaded-wire pendants with a cross set in the centre are known from grave 27 at Gilton and tumulus 5 on Chartham Downs (see Geake 1997, 37), both dated to post-Kentish Phase IV on the basis of their association with Kentish brooch types (Brugmann 1999a, table 3.1). On the Continent, however, the use of beaded gold wire for pendants and also beads (*see* p 119) is known from much earlier contexts, and the jewellery of the woman in Grave 391B may have been inspired by displays such as the extremely rich coin-dated[23] 'lady's' grave at Cologne Cathedral which included a pair of magnificent rosette brooches and a quartz ball in a sling. The terminal of a wound gold wire suspended from a silver slip-knot ring Grave 391B (j), apparently also worn on the chest as part of the arrangement of pendants and beads, may be a left-over from the production of pendant (h), suggesting a Kentish manufacture, commissioned by, or for the women.

The copper alloy bulla pendant Grave 391A (e) is the only pendant in the burial overlying Grave 391B and represents a Final Phase type mostly made of silver and distributed across Anglo-Saxon England (see Geake 1997, 36f, map 7). Though a scutiform pendant in design, most bullae are made from a single sheet of metal folded over to form a back-plate (*ibid*). The beaded wire pendant from grave 28 Harford Farm, Caister St Edmund, Norfolk was associated with bulla pendants, and in this context may have been an heirloom (Geake 1997, 37).

The silver cabochon pendant Grave 413 (o) is set with opaque turquoise glass. The colour is most unusual for glass from Anglo-Saxon graves and would have stood out in any context. Cabochon pendants oval, circular, triangular, rectangular, or trapezoidal in shape are a seventh-century type fairly evenly distributed across Anglo-Saxon England (see Geake 1997, 39f, map 9). With a glass setting in a silver mounting, pendant Grave 413 (o) is of lower quality than the majority of pendants, which have gold settings (see *ibid*).

Rock crystal pendant from Grave 391B   *Noël Adams*

Grave 391B included one of the most unusual finds in the cemetery - a recycled classical intaglio in rock crystal, mounted in a typical early Germanic suspension sling (f) (Fig 10.53; Fig 4.15a, 1, 6). The stone, flattened on one side

and convex on the other, is distinguished by its large size and ovoid shape. A representation of the mythical Lydian queen Omphale is engraved on the flat face. Its sling is composed of two ribbed silver-gilt bands, one wrapped around the circumference of the stone and the other looped vertically, running directly across the intaglio. These are soldered at the bottom and secured within a cylindrical sleeve at the top and were originally bordered with beaded wire, now heavily worn. The mounted intaglio was suspended from a copper alloy slip-knot ring threaded through a perforation in the capping sleeve. The stone has two conchoidal chips, one at the base on the flat side and the other on the convex face at the point where a section of the circumference sling is broken away.

The pendant was found slightly to the left of the stomach at the lower end of a large scatter of beads running the length of the torso, from the left shoulder to the waist (Fig 10.87). This position suggests that it formed part of a long necklace, which included two additional small pendants in gold (h) and silver (i) (Fig 10.52). The suspension of this sort of slung rock crystal as a pendant on a necklace (as opposed to a waist strap) is highly unusual and, together with the conspicuous wear on its sling mount, may be evidence for secondary use of an older object.

Sling-mounted crystals

The mount on the intaglio links it with the class of sling-mounted rock crystal balls whose archaeological distribution in the early medieval period is concentrated in high-status female graves in Kent, along the Rhine and Danube and across Merovingian Gaul (Hinz 1966; Richards 1980, 151–4, 431–43, table 18, figs 65–6; Meaney 1981, 84–5; Hugget 1988, 70, 72, fig 5). The woman in Grave 391B was buried with one of these as well (b). Its location on the outside of the lower right leg is consistent with the fashion for suspending crystal balls on a long strap from the waist. In Anglo-Saxon England sling-mounted rock crystals are predominantly a sixth-century phenomenon, although a small irregular rock crystal in a gold sling from grave 91, Edix Hill, Cambridgeshire may be from the first decades of the seventh (Malim and Hines 1998, 80–1, 128, 282, fig 3.60).

Amuletic stones set in crossed bands came into fashion in the late Roman period amongst the mixed Germanic and Sarmatian populations living in Central Europe (Martin 1997). Such mounts have early Hellenistic roots[24] and rock

---

23. With a *terminus post quem* of AD 526–534 (Siegmund 1998, 524).

24. Greifenhagen 1970, Taf 18.2, (Yalta, Antikensammlung, Staatliche Museen, Berlin, Massonneau collection, end of fourth century BC); Schiltz 2001, 127, no 101 (Kurgan 8, Stanica Elizavetovskaja, Don, second half of fourth century BC); OAK 1898, 155, fig 516 (Kurdžips Kurgan near Maikop, Kuban, fourth century BC).

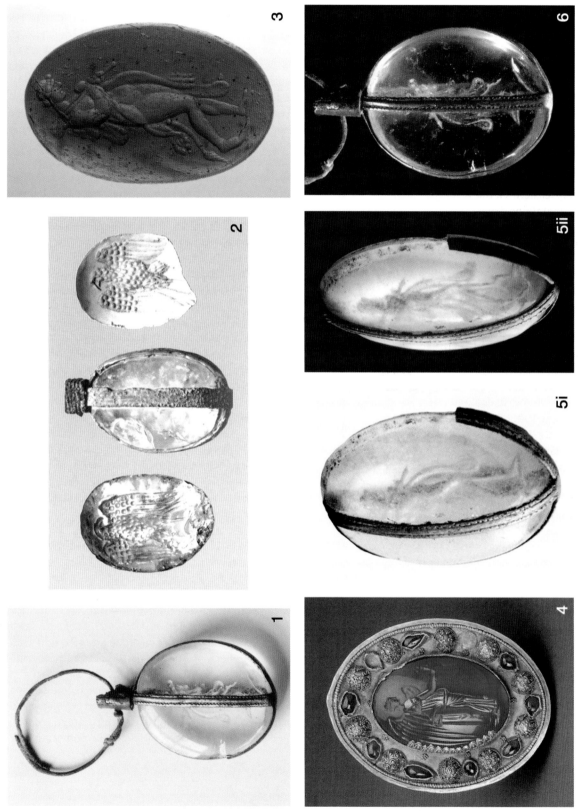

Fig. 4.15a. 1. Intaglio of Omphale, rock crystal, silver-gilt sling mount, Grave 391B, Dover Buckland, H (of crystal): 35mm. Photo: Noël Adams. 2. Intaglio of eagle with spread wings, rock crystal, copper alloy sling mount, Dettingen an der Erms (Kr Reutlingen), Germany, 5.1 x 3.5cm. After Veeck 1931, Bd II, Taf Ga–c. 3. Intaglio of Omphale, glass, H: 2.45cm. © Staatliche Museen zu Berlin, Antikensammlung FG 3088. Photo: Johannes Laurentius. 4. Brooch with intaglio of Nike, Peščanyi (Krasnodar krai, Russia), gold, carnelian, garnet, H: 6.1cm (Krasnodar Museum, inv F2 875). After Schlitz 2001, fig 179. 5i and 5ii. Buckland intaglio magnified. Photo: Noël Adams. 6. Buckland crystal in transmitted light. Photo: British Museum Laboratory.

crystal balls in gold slings were already used in the late first or early second century AD by the Maeotic Sarmatians living in the Kuban region of southern Russia (Mordvinceva and Treister 2007, II, 100, nr A312.2.1; Kurgan 42, burial no 1, Stanica Ust'-Labinskaja, Krasnodar krai). In the west slings were initially utilised for both organic and inorganic items, prized for their rarity or magical qualities, but from the later fourth century onwards were reserved primarily for highly-polished crystal spheres.[25] Martin (1997) has suggested that the western Germanic tradition of wearing crystal balls suspended from the waist may be traced back to fifth-century eastern Germanic ornaments such as the necklace or châtelaine from Szilágysomlyó (Şimleul-Silvaniei), Romania, with a rock crystal suspended at the centre of chains hung with golden amulets. Panthers holding the large crystal ball suggest that this piece had Dionysiac connotations.

The sling mount of the Grave 391B pendant is typical of early Anglo-Saxon and continental Germanic workmanship, but the use of an engraved rock crystal of this size and shape is highly unusual.[26] The best parallel is a continental piece – a slightly larger rock crystal intaglio in a copper alloy sling, with the rare subject of an eagle, from Dettingen an der Erms (Kr Reutlingen) in Bavaria (Fig 4.15a, 2; Veeck 1931, Bd I, 52, 309, Bd II, Taf G, 8; Christlein 1979, 114, Abb 91, 2; Ament 1991, 402, 417, Abb 2,13; Quast 2006, 202, Taf 12, 51-d). This was a stray find from the vicinity of a large Alamannic row-grave cemetery. Parallels for the engraving remain to be explored, but the rows of drilled pellets across the wings and breast of the Dettingen eagle can be paralleled on intaglios of the first century BC (cf Neverov 1976, 67–8, nos 81–3). It was set 'upside down' in its mount, intended to be seen in the correct orientation only by its owner looking downwards or when grasped by the sleeve at the top and held upright.

Subject matter and original setting

Omphale was a common glyptic subject from the late Republican era to the late Imperial period (Zwierlein-Diehl 1969, 175, no 473; Zazoff 1975, 82; Boardman 1994) (Fig 4.15a, 3). According to legend Omphale bought Herakles as a slave and assigned him various labours, one of which included exchanging clothes with her. They became lovers and she bore him a son. She is depicted on the Buckland crystal walking on a ground-line, her head lowered and hair drawn back in a knot; the pose is thought to copy a fifth-century sculptural type. Herakles' lion skin is slung over her shoulders, its tail and paws visible behind her; she carries his club over her right shoulder. Although considerably obscured by the sling, the visible areas of the engraving reveal wheel-cutting combined with rounded drills to define the body and the pelleted club. Some details of the classic representation have been rendered sketchily, for example the paws of the lion skin which normally swing at the front of Omphale's body are rendered here simply as drapery. The transformation from lion skin to looped drapery can already be detected on some glass pastes of the second half of the first century BC (Zwierlein-Diehl 1969, *loc cit*; Platz-Horster 1994, 189, no 299) (Fig 4.15a, 3). The domed ovoid shape of the gem is characteristic of the second and first century BC and the carving suggests a date in the first century BC or possibly the early first century AD.[27]

From a modern standpoint the Buckland rock crystal is an important addition to the early medieval corpus of re-used Roman intaglios and cameos.[28] But how was it regarded in the Anglo-Saxon period? In the period spanning the fifth to the seventh centuries, there is a considerable range in the degree of appreciation and understanding of these classical gems on the part of both clients and jewellers. Many, of course, were simply re-mounted in contemporary rings, worn in the Roman fashion (De Ricci 1912, pls XIV–XVI, nos 873, 903, 906, 978, 1012; Ament 1991, 413–24, Abb 2, nos 2, 5–7, 15–16, 19, 21, 26, 30, 33, 37; Henig 1978, 161, nos 205, 518; Filmer-Sankey and Pestell 2001, 195–8). A few were set on brooches or pendants (Henig 1978, *loc cit* and nos 97, 140, 231, 634, 734; Webster and Backhouse 1991, 54, no 35; Bierbrauer 1974, 269, tav XVII, 1a; Ament 1991, 414, 416) but whether these were valuable heirlooms or simply *objets trouvés* we cannot say. Others, however, were treated

---

25. Heege (1987, 32–8) discusses other materials (such as pyrites, haematite and meteorite) and reviews the evidence for the chronology of sling mounts on the Continent.

26. The rock crystal ball with a Gnostic inscription from a rich female grave (*c* AD 300) at Årslev, Fünen may or may not have had a sling mount (Storgaard 1990, 23–58, Abb 19). A rock crystal roughly engraved with a cross was found in the Bloodmoor Hill barrow, Gisleham, Suffolk (West 1998, 40, pl II.6). A first-century AD chalcedony intaglio of four erotes on a seashell in a sling mount, possibly from the area of a Frankish cemetery (Ober-Olm, Kr Mainz-Bingen) (Ament 1991, 422) may also be noted here.

27. Cf Mandrioli Bizzarri 1987, 46, no 15, dated first half of first century AD. I am grateful to Antje Krug for her opinion on the form and date of this gem, for which she prefers a BC date.

28. For examples in Anglo-Saxon England: Henig 1978, 159–61; on the Continent: Ament 1991, 413–24, Abb 2, nos 3–4, 8–9, 11–12, 14, 17–18, 20, 22–4, 27, 32, 34, 38–9, 41. Most recently: Sena Chiesa 2011 and Kornbluth 2011, the latter following the 2007 version of this paper. Early medieval re-use of gemstones was confined to individual examples on personal ornaments; relatively few of these have survived in comparison with the multiple gems assembled to decorate later liturgical objects (cf Krug 1993, 161–72).

as stones *qua* stones and set in a purely decorative fashion, orientated in unreadable positions and casually (or even brutally) trimmed to fit their new mounts. The latter treatment is particularly evident on gems incorporated onto buckle-plates (Henig 1978, no 264; Warhurst 1955, pl IX, 3; BM P&E 1900, 7–14.1). As there is no real way of determining how individual images from the classical past were viewed, the question of whether these had lost all significance, as has been argued,[29] must remain open. It is clear that there was a shift in values in the Early Medieval period, with the status imparted by the ownership of an ancient stone in many cases outweighing any potential meaning assigned to its iconography.

In the case of the Buckland rock crystal, the craftsman orientated the stone 'correctly' (ie upright as on a pendant), but at the same time partially concealed the engraving with the sling, apparently blind to both its subject matter and beauty. It is always possible that the orientation was arbitrary and that the stone simply served as an alternative to a rock crystal ball. Against this is the fact that the piece was not suspended on a girdle but worn as a pendant on a bead necklace, so the original perceptions of this large crystal and the question of how it may have found its way into an Anglo-Saxon context deserve exploration.

The large size (35mm) and elongated proportions of the Buckland crystal place it within the classical tradition of intaglios of full-length subjects, engraved vertically on varieties of quartz stones which naturally grow to large sizes. In general, coloured microcrystalline quartz (such as sardonyx and carnelian) was favoured over the translucent macrocrystalline stones (amethyst and rock crystal). The subject matter on these gems was often, but not exclusively, female, and not infrequently Heraklean or Dionysiac in content (Plantzos 1999, 66–7, 86, nos 165–71, 228–82). I know of no published examples of Omphale engraved on rock crystal, although the subject appears on several amethyst gems.[30] The Buckland gem, like the oversize rock crystal from Dettingen, is therefore also unusual within the

corpus of Greek and Roman engraved gems. Large rock crystal intaglios were relatively uncommon amongst classical gemstones,[31] in part because the cold and colourless stone is difficult to 'read' when engraved and, as Ogden (1982, 106) observed, can be unattractive in combination with gold metal. Craftsmen devised means of dealing with these problems which are explored further below. Although the engraving is not perhaps of the highest technical quality, the carving retains the fluid, pictorial character of the great Hellenistic intaglios. The Buckland crystal thus provides a rare example of a translucent gemstone whose glass imitations survive in far greater numbers (cf Zwierlein-Diehl 1969, 175, no 473; Zazoff 1975, 82, nos 313–5; Neverov 1976, 71–2, no 105; Plantzos 1999, 127, no 406) (Fig 4.15a, 3).

We cannot determine whether the crystal was originally set on a finger-ring or a piece of ornamental jewellery such as a pendant or brooch. The size of the Buckland and Dettingen crystal intaglios is a centimetre or more than the majority of those destined for ring settings (cf Chadour 1994, 31–2, nos 98–9, 102–3, the largest measuring 25 x 16mm), but oversized ringstone intaglios close to 4cm in size were produced, especially in the Hellenistic period (Platz-Horster 1995). Large oval gemstones engraved with female subject matter were also fashionable inlays on jewellery made from the late second century BC onwards. This Hellenistic tradition is well-represented on a sequence of excavated brooches from kurgan burials in the north-east Black Sea region, in the river valleys of the Kuban basin (Krasnodar krai) (Fig 4.15a, 4).[32] The populations living in this region are often referred to as the Maeotic Sarmatians after the ancient name for the Sea of Azov, Lake Maeotis. The brooches in these burials date primarily to the end of the second and first half of the first century BC and the engraved gemstones they display are for the most part contemporary with the mounts. The gold settings were richly embellished with gemstone and glass cabochons, granulation and filigree wire. Most of the Maeotian-Sarmatian brooches of this type are set with carnelians, sards or garnets, but at least one brooch and pendants mounted with un-

29. Cf Veeck 1931, 52, on the Dettingen crystal: 'Das Bild selbst hatte also für den Träger keine Bedeutung mehr'.

30. *Catalogue of the Story-Maskelyne Collection of Ancient Gems*, Sotheby's London 4 July 1921, lot no 111, pl III, ex-Marlborough collection; Sena Chiesa 1966, 215, no 487 (11 x 9mm); Vollenweider 1966, 42, 104, Taf 32, 3–5 (Duke of Devonshire, Chatsworth; 25 x 16mm).

31. A chronological range of examples in Zwierlein-Diehl 1969, 75–6, no 163 (scaraboid, ?Aphrodite with mirror, second half of fifth century BC); 73–4, no 156 (scaraboid with figure of Herakles, second quarter of fourth century BC); 169–70, no 456 (bust of Minerva en face, end of first century BC); and 180, no 493 (portrait of Nero, AD 64–8); also Boardman and Vollenweider 1978, 87, no 303 (Artemis, 21 x 20mm).

32. Excavated brooches set with large intaglios from Krasnodar krai: Stanica Brjuchoveckaja kurgan no 3, grave 13 (Artemis Phosphoros, agate, second quarter of first century BC; Mordvinceva and Treister 2007, II, 15, A25.1); Pesčanyj kurgan, grave 10 (Nike, sard, mid to second half of first century BC; *ibid* 2007 II, 72, A227.5); Stanica Achtanizovskaja, destroyed burial (Fortuna, sard or garnet; *ibid* 2007, II, 118, B1.7). Related brooches in museum collections: a Ptolemaic queen as Fortuna, carnelian, early first century BC (Cabinet des médailles, Bibliothèque nationale, Paris; Richter 1968, 142, no 545 (with the misidentification of the mount as 'Byzantine' by Chabouillet (1858, cat no 1724) uncorrected); Vollenweider 1995, no 136, 144, note 1, Mordvinceva and Treister 2007, II, 163, C/1.16.1); Artemis, first century BC (State Historical Museum in Moscow, Kerč, Crimea; *ibid* 2007, II, 159, C/1.11.1.15); a young woman with a parrot, carnelian (from Stanica Ščdritskaja; The Janashia Museum, Tbilisi, no 650; unpublished); seated Athena, garnet, first century BC (J Pierpont Morgan Library and Museum, New York; Adams 2012, cat no 1).

engraved, drilled rock crystal beads have also survived.[33] A gold pendant with a large intaglio of a nymph, possibly Amymone as she carries a hydria and trident, also belongs in this Kuban series.[34]

Brooches and pendants mounted with intaglios of female goddesses continued to be worn throughout the Roman period. Examples dated from the second to third century AD have been found across the Empire, from Italy to Pannonia and Syria, suggesting the fashion must have been more widespread and metropolitan than can be documented by archaeology.[35] As the production of ring-stone intaglios diminished in the course of the third century, antique stones became more precious and were treasured and re-set, as for example, the second half of the first-century BC amethyst intaglio mounted in a gold pendant from the late third century AD Beaurains Treasure, found near Arras, northern France (Walters 1926, no 1918; BM G&R 1924, 5-14.6). A brooch from the Massonneau collection of southern Russian material, now in Cologne, likewise displays a first-century BC intaglio of a young woman with a sacrificial tray and vase; the carnelian is set in a copper alloy mount covered with a silver-gilt sheet encircled with garnet and green glass inlays in simple square collets (Krug 1980, no 39). The latter has been dated to the first half of the fifth century (Damm 1988, 108–9, no 18, Abb 44–8), but the repoussé borders of the mount find earlier parallels in excavated material coin-dated to the second half of the third (grave 24, burial no 3) and first half of the fourth century (cf Archéologie de la mer Noire 1997, 62, Drouzhne (Crimea)). It is interesting to note that when originally found, the Massonneau intaglio was mounted upside down in its setting, that is, with the carved face down,[36] suggesting it was re-used simply as an attractive large stone.

Foil-backed intaglios

Two further intaglios in their original mounts throw light on the special requirements for successful presentation of translucent gemstones like the Buckland crystal. The first is a brooch with a topaz or citrine[37] with a deeply-cut frontal head of Helios; a stray find from the village of Usachelo near Kutaisi in the north-western Caucasus (Republic of Georgia), it has been dated to the first or second century AD (Neverov 1976, 78, no 136; Sulava 1996, 124–5, 138, Tab XXX, no 163). As on the Buckland and Dettingen rock crystal intaglios, the image was carved on the flatter side of the translucent stone. The stone was then mounted face down with the engraving on the underside. As it is viewed through the convex upper side of the stone, it appears magnified and in the same orientation as its impression. The intaglio is displayed in a gold brooch whose glass inlays, granulation and filigree wire represent a late variation of the Maeotic-Sarmatian-period settings found in the Kuban. Another rock crystal mounted in the same fashion decorated a necklace medallion included in a jewellery hoard found at Cihisdziri near Batumi, a port city on the east coast of the Black Sea in Adjara, Republic of Georgia. The superb intaglio, a portrait of the Emperor Lucius Verus (AD 161–9), is set in a late Roman-style palmette surround (Megow 1993, 237, no 124). A gold foil backing imparts depth and modeling to the image, enhancing the otherwise difficult to read engraving. The technique of pressing a metal foil against an engraving, used primarily with transparent stones like rock crystal, is first recorded in the classical period (Krug 1977) and numerous intact foiled crystals sandwiched with another un-engraved crystal or glass layer survive from the Late Antique and Early Byzantine periods (Spier 2007, 115–8, nos 666–701). These first and second century AD intaglios found in Georgia, although iconographically different to the Buckland crystal, suggest that it was originally set face down in a ring, pendant or brooch, with its shallow engraving backed with foil and slightly magnified through the domed convex 'lens' of the crystal (Fig 4.15a, 5i–ii).

Continental connections

It remains to be considered how the Omphale rock crystal found its way into Anglo-Saxon hands. As Antje Krug has observed (pers comm, April 2011), this is not an ordinary ringstone intaglio, plundered from a Roman cemetery, but

---

33. Cf a drilled ovoid rock crystal bead from the Stanica Achtanizovskaja find noted above (Mordvinceva and Treister 2007, II, 188, B1.6). Although identified in the modern catalogue as glass, on the basis of older publications and two further comparable drilled rock crystal beads in pendant settings in the same volume (*ibid*, 142, C4.3), this must be rock crystal. The beads have been dated to the second half of the second century BC.
34. *Bull Leapers to Picasso*, exhibition, 2 East 79th Street, New York, 6–16 December 2000, Robin Symes Ltd, London, np.
35. *Inter alia*: Becatti 1955, 216, no 527, tav CXLIX (sarcophagus of Crepereia Tryphena, second half of second century AD); Párducz 1935, 2, 108, Taf VI. 3 (Szcntes-Bökény); Fortin 1999, no 339 (Dura-Europos, third century AD). Some researchers have suggested the brooch from Pesčanyj (see note 32 above) was made in Alexandria but there would seem to be little convincing evidence for this; the origin of the intaglio is of course another matter.
36. It was 'restored' by the Römische-Germanischen Museum in 1955 with the intaglio face up (Damm 1988, *loc cit*); cf also Krug 1980, no 89 for another large carnelian with Apollo in the same collection, likewise set face down in a ?Scandinavian brooch.
37. The stone has been identified as a topaz, but as that mineral was only rarely used in antiquity, it is perhaps more likely to be a citrine, another crystalline variety of quartz (cf Ogden 1982, 106 and 111).

a long-distance import from the Mediterranean – perhaps Italy, Egypt or Asia Minor. Given the presence of another equally remarkable crystal in a sling mount from Dettingen in Alamannia, the possibility that these two gemstones emerged from the same workshop on the Rhine or Danube is worth considering. There is in fact additional evidence for contact with southern Germany in Buckland Grave 391B. The pair of garnet cloisonné rosette brooches in the grave (*see* p 77) relate to those from Schretzheim, Ulm, which Arrhenius (1985, 188–91) argued were manufactured in local south German workshops. Disc amulets with spiral filigree wire similar to that on the Buckland brooches were found in Schretzheim grave 300, one of the graves with related disc brooches (U Koch 1977, Bd 2, 73, Taf 195.8–10).

Whether the occasional evidence for connections between the Alamanni and Anglo-Saxons represents commercial transactions or immigration remains to be explored. Swanton (1967, 43–50) was among the first to document Alamannic influence in England, but was unsure as to whether the early Alamannic brooches he assembled were the result of late Roman trading contacts or continental settlement. Hills (1993, 16–17) has compared the brooches and combs found in two graves at Spong Hill with south German types and this author (Adams 2011, 28) has recently explored some parallels on high-status garnet cloisonné ornaments found in the two regions. Of course items of jewellery may simply represent a chain of trading relationships, but as the wholly exceptional rock crystal and disc brooches were found together in the same grave at Buckland it is tempting to suggest they document a continental ancestry.

Conclusions

With this background the Buckland crystal in its 'barbarian' metal sling begins to emerge in a new light. The first scholar to comment on the Dettingen intaglio felt that the 'disfiguring' mount had rendered it 'unsichtbar und unschädlich' (invisible and harmless) (Goeßler, cited in Veeck 1931, 52). While it can be argued that such mounts served to contain and conserve the 'power' of the stone (Kornbluth 2011), ultimately the use of a sling for suspension was a decorative treatment dictated by contemporary fashion.[38] As the Buckland crystal was worn as a pendant on a necklace it can hardly have been considered harmful and the engraving is not hidden as it can still be read simply by moving the crystal to catch the light (Fig 4.15a, 5i–ii, 6). It was perhaps obscure to the casual viewer, but not to its owner who could reveal her exclusive image whenever

she desired. Sling mounts were also thoroughly practical for precious or fragile stones. The Buckland crystal, like the Dettingen intaglio, may well have been chipped when it was removed from its first mount, particularly if it formed part of a sandwich. The crossed metal strips served to protect both these gems from further physical damage.

If rock crystal balls in sling mounts indeed had some ritual function associated with the serving of wine by women, as has been suggested (*see* p 163), it seems that in this role it was the supposed cooling properties of crystal that were appreciated. In the case of the large intaglios discussed here, the subject matter must also have enhanced the gemstones' natural qualities. The eagle as a symbol of Jupiter and imperial power is, of course, unambiguous. In a recent paper Véronique Dasen (2008) has explored the evolution of the iconography of Omphale and Herakles engraved on magical gems of the second and third centuries AD; these were intended to ensure the good health and vitality of the female womb. These often overtly sexual images are quite different to the type of chaste representation that appears on the Buckland gem and yet some representations of Omphale in the same classical pose do appear markedly pregnant.[39] It is possible therefore that the Omphale image was seen as specifically protective of female wellbeing.

We cannot imagine that such sophisticated associations between iconography and the medical/magical potency of stones, much less the nuances of the classical myth of the Lydian queen, survived intact into the sixth century in Anglo-Saxon England. The preservation of the Buckland crystal for so many centuries must be largely due to its remarkable size and material, but the possibility that its new owners found meaning in its elegant imagery should not be dismissed.

Coin pendant from Grave 232   *Gareth Williams*

The object (a) from Grave 232 is designed to appear like a Byzantine gold *tremissis* (Fig 10.8), but is in fact a plated imitation, which has been mounted for use as a pendant. It is not uncommon for genuine coins to be re-used in jewellery in the early Anglo-Saxon period, but this piece is clearly an imitation. The overall dimensions are similar to those of a genuine *tremissis*, but the gold plating has disappeared around the edge of the coin, revealing an interior apparently made of base metal. However, neither the dimensions nor the design are consistent with a bronze coin of the period, so it must have been created as an imitation *ab initio*, and cannot be a gold-plating of a genuine coin.

---

38. Cf Veeck 1931, 314–15, Taf D.1, Alamannic amethyst pendants from Altbierlingen wrapped with strips of gold.
39. Eg Zwierlein-Diehl 1973, 152, no 488; Boardman, February 2003, 'The Danicourt collection of gems in Péronne', no 54, first century BC–first century AD (http://www.beazley.ox.ac.uk/gems/danicourt).

The ultimate model for the coin is a *tremissis* of Justin I (AD 518–27) of the mint of Constantinople, of the VICTORIA AVGVSTORVM type. The obverse shows a diademed right-facing bust, with a crude but more or less accurate version of the legend DN IVSTINVS PP AVG. The reverse is more crudely imitative, with a very rough version of Victory advancing to the right holding a wreath and cross, with a star beneath the cross. The legend is completely blundered.

Byzantine gold coinage was widely imitated in western Europe in this period, and the Burgundians, Franks and Visigoths all issued imitations of this sort of coin for use in currency. Such currency imitations were in good gold, however, and it is unlikely that this piece could ever have passed inspection in regular currency usage. Imitative currency pieces tended to be issued in the name of the reigning emperor, and thus to be roughly contemporary with their official prototypes. However, since their circulation period could extend considerably beyond the date of issue, it is less certain that an imitation created only for re-use in jewellery need be imitating a contemporary model, and the object could therefore be somewhat later than the reign of Justin I.

Stylistically, the piece shows greater similarities with Visigothic coins of the period than with either the official issues or than with Burgundian or Frankish imitations. In itself, a Visigothic connection is not inherently unlikely in English soil. Stray finds of Visigothic coins are not unknown from England, and the Patching hoard of the late fifth century contained several gold coins of Visigothic origin. This could indicate that the piece is itself of Visigothic workmanship, but it could equally be a local imitation of a Visigothic imitation of an official Byzantine *tremissis*.

Traces remain of a copper alloy mount, which from its shape probably supported the piece as a pendant, although it is unclear whether it would have been a single pendant or part of a larger piece. The mount aligns poorly with the orientation of both obverse and reverse designs, but this is not especially unusual in Anglo-Saxon coin-jewellery.

To conclude, the piece was apparently made specifically for use in jewellery, and is likely to be either Visigothic, or a local imitation of a Visigothic model. The ultimate prototype provides a *terminus post quem* of AD 518–27, but the piece could plausibly have been made later in the sixth century.

Gold bracteates   *John Hines*

(Graves 204, 245 and 250)

The occurrence of gold bracteates in a small number of the more richly furnished women's graves is both a distinctive and an important feature of the archaeology of early Anglo-Saxon Kent. This type of pendant archaeologically represents the links eastwards across the North Sea between Kent and southern Scandinavia that were also reflected in traditions attributing the primary post-Roman Germanic settlement of this area to Jutes (Sørensen 1999, esp 97–113; Kruse 2007). The use of gold for these particular objects is a material embodiment of the symbolic value they had for the society in which they were produced and used.

The three specimens from the excavations at Buckland under consideration here are from female graves, as indeed are all but one of the examples from known contexts of deposition in England (cf Hines 1984, 204–20 and Behr 2010, 46–65, for finds outside of Kent). The conspicuous degree of abrasion on the loops and contiguous areas of the rim on the bracteates from Graves 204 (o) and 250 (a) in particular indicates that the pendants had been worn regularly as part of the women's costume. The deposition of bracteates in graves is otherwise paralleled as a regular practice only in Norway, where again the items are consistently found in women's burials (Bakka 1973). There are also examples of bracteates from graves on the Continent, even, in exceptional cases, associated with male graves, but these represent a more diffuse scatter, within which it is impossible to identify regular practices in any one locality (Axboe 1981, 79–87; Bakka 1981). In Denmark, northern Germany and southern Sweden, meanwhile, large quantities of bracteates have been recovered from hoards – many of them clearly of a ritual character (Hines 1989; Hedeager 1999; Behr 2010, 71–81).

From all of these sources in northern Europe together, several hundred bracteates are known, providing a large assemblage of comparable material. The principal collected and illustrated corpora are those of Mogens B Mackeprang (1952), updated by Morten Axboe (1981), and subsequently the highly detailed *Ikonographischer Katalog* supervised by the late Karl Hauck (Hauck *et al* 1985: bracteates may be referred to by numbers in this corpus, prefixed with IK; Axboe 2011). Mackeprang developed a thumbnail typology first used by Oscar Montelius (1869) that divided the pictorial designs of the pendants into Types A–F, identifying a considerable number of sub-types which he characterized by association with particular regions: eg the 'West Scandinavian' group of C-bracteates and two 'Jutlandic' groups of D-bracteates. Axboe further provided valuable observations of technical details of the production and construction of the bracteates, some of which also had their own distinctive distribution.

It is Montelius's Types A–D that have been the subject of extensive international research concerned with fifth- and sixth-century cultural history in Germanic Europe. Type E bracteates are a later form unique to the island of Gotland in the Baltic and Type F has proved to be a very minor variant. Excluded from Montelius's scheme and the other corpora, but of importance for the bracteate tradition in Kent in particular, are a number of gold bracteates with motifs in Salin's Style II (Speake 1980, 66–76). The earliest A-bracteates imitate imperial medallions of the late Roman period, and seem to be preceded as Scandinavian products by solid, two-sided, local copies of such medallions. The initial symbolic associations of these objects would therefore appear to have been with the prestige and power of the Roman Empire. Karl Hauck and his school's work has been concerned primarily with explorations of possible, peculiarly Germanic meanings of the 'iconographic' designs on the bracteates, suggested in light of the sources we have for pre-Christian, Germanic traditional religion. Much of this work (published largely in a series of articles *Zur Ikonographie der Goldbrakteaten* in the periodical *Frühmittelalterliche Studien*) has given rise to considerable controversy in ways that it is not appropriate to discuss further here. One perspective that should, however, be stated clearly is that the meaning and function of the bracteates may have changed substantially and even quite rapidly from the earliest examples in the fifth century to the Style-II bracteates of the seventh. In England especially, it still appears reasonable to interpret the sequence ending with those Style-II bracteates as one in which the secular, social-status marking character of the items gradually becomes predominant over whatever mythological and religious meanings they may originally have had (Hines 1984, 235–43). It is consequently relevant to consider how far along such a road our Kentish D-bracteates may lie.

The gold bracteates from Kent now consist of one B-bracteate and thirty D-bracteates, including the three under discussion here. There is also a gold filigree pendant from St Nicholas at Wade, Kent which is *stricto sensu* not itself a bracteate but which has the design of a D-bracteate (Behr 2010, 45–6). An impression of a C-bracteate die has been found on a silver vessel mount from Bradstow School, Broadstairs, grave 71, and a number of A- and C-bracteates are known from England north of the Thames. A major but curiously incomplete review of the bracteates in Kent was published by Sonia Chadwick Hawkes and Mark Pollard in 1981, and Axboe's supplement to Mackeprang's catalogue appeared the following year (though dated 1981), at the same time as further excavations in advance of the Thanet Gas Pipeline revealed more Anglo-Saxon burials at Monkton, including a man's grave (grave 26) with a gold D-bracteate, not worn as part of the costume but amongst a number of items apparently collected as valuables in a pouch worn by the waist (Perkins and Chadwick Hawkes 1984). The bracteates from the

Buckland excavations of 1994 were the first new finds from Kent after then, to which metal-detector finds of D-bracteates from Denton and Northbourne made in 2004 and 2005 respectively can now be added (Behr 2010, 43–5).

Chadwick Hawkes and Pollard's study was concerned largely with the dating of the bracteates and their burial contexts in Kent, as was a further study by Egil Bakka of Kentish and continental grave finds with bracteates published independently in the same year. An important if under-emphasized issue, though, is that at that time Chadwick Hawkes still continued to regard all of the Kentish finds of D-bracteates as imported items (Chadwick Hawkes and Pollard 1981, 351–2; cf Perkins and Chadwick Hawkes 1984, 105–7). Bakka was firmly of the opinion that some of them had been locally made, a suggestion previously made by Leslie Webster (Bakka 1981, 14 and ref). Comparison of the Anglian English silver D-bracteates with what appeared to be their Kentish models supported this view (Hines 1984, 215–16). This has subsequently received powerful corroboration from a thorough analysis of the entire D-bracteate series by Elisabeth Barfod Carlsen (1997; 2002), which concluded that some Kentish specimens are so little different from southern Scandinavian examples that they were probably imported while others are clearly of a distinctly local type. We may argue that the full sequence of bracteate history in Kent, from importation from southern Scandinavia to local imitation and further Kentish development of bracteate designs, is represented by these three specimens from the 1994 excavations at Buckland.

The D-bracteates from the Graves 204 and 250 at Buckland have no exact die-links with any other bracteates either in Kent or elsewhere. The primary, central zone of the bracteate from Grave 245 (b), conversely, is indistinguishable from that of the recent find from Denton, near Dover, and Behr reasonably judges these to have been pressed using the same die (2010, 43–4). These two bracteates are still different from one another in that the specimen in Buckland Grave 245 has a flan of wider diameter, producing a ring zone or 'outer border' that is decorated with punchmarks around the central zoomorphic motif. The loops of the two bracteates are similar but not identical. No links through punchmarks in the decorative outer border of the flans have been identified between any of the D-bracteates from Buckland that are the subject of this report and finds from any other sites.

The bracteates from Graves 204 and 250 represent Mackeprang's extensive Jutlandic group I (Mackeprang 1952, 56–7, pl 16, 1–31). That from Grave 204 (IK 580) finds a particularly similar counterpart in a D-bracteate from a large hoard found at Skonager, Næsbjerg parish, Skads district, Ribe *amt* in western Jutland in 1870 (Mackeprang 1952, no 101: pl 16,4). Within Kent, it has its closest parallels in a die-identical pair of D-bracteates from Finglesham grave 203 (Chadwick Hawkes and Pollard 1981, esp 333–9). Barfod Carlsen considers the Finglesham grave 203 bracteates to have been imported, not locally made. The loop of the Buckland Grave 204 bracteate, with its ribs of slightly varying thickness, is also most closely paralleled in Kent in Finglesham grave 203; this type of loop is familiar, though not especially common, on Scandinavian specimens (Axboe 1981, 31–3). Several Kentish and Jutlandic bracteates have one row of repoussé bosses around the edge of the flan alongside the rim (eg those from Finglesham grave D3, Bifrons 64, Lyminge 16, and Sarre 4), but the triple row on the bracteate from Buckland Grave 204 is extremely rare.

It can be relatively easily seen, too, that the design in the centre of the flan of the bracteate from Grave 250 (IK 582) is the result of a considerable loosening of the same original motif. This again is surrounded by a single ring of repoussé bosses, but the outer circuit of the broader flan of this bracteate is then decorated with two rows of neatly executed ring-and-triangle punchmarks. These are strongly characteristic of English rather than Scandinavian metalwork. The loop, with a broad central rib and two narrower ones on either side, is equivalent in form to those on bracteates from Buckland Grave 1, Bifrons grave 64 and Sarre 4, but not identical in execution. The face of the flan beneath the loop has been ornamented with applied wire volutes and spirals. A D-bracteate of unknown provenance but possibly from Kent (Axboe 1981, no 315a), and another bracteate from grave 4 at Sarre, with an equally unique central design, are Kentish parallels for applied wire decoration below the loop. In those two cases this takes the form of a single symmetrical double spiral unparalleled anywhere else, and thus suggesting English manufacture. Applied decoration on the face of a bracteate below the loop occurs sporadically on Scandinavian and continental bracteates, but there are no exact counterparts to the form found on the bracteate from Buckland Grave 250.

This bracteate is consequently a relatively individualistic piece, with no close parallels in matters of apparently significant detail. Perhaps its most unusual, and certainly its most problematic feature, however, is the beaded rim. Charlotte Behr and I have both discussed and re-examined this carefully, without coming to complete agreement about key details. It is clear that the beading of the rim in the segment opposite the loop (between 5 o'clock and 7 o'clock, if we treat the diameter as a clockface) is quite different from the remainder of the rim. It is extremely difficult if not impossible to see that the rim is in fact a separate piece of gold from the flan. Charlotte Behr identified a small arc only about 1mm long immediately to the right of the loop when viewed from the face where the beaded rim does appear to be separate from

the edge of the flan, but otherwise I suspect that this is rather a variant of the rare 'imitation beaded wire rim' noted by Axboe on a few C-bracteates, mostly from Skåne in southern Sweden, formed by rolling up the edges of the flan and then beading them (Axboe 1981, 38–40). Such a treatment of the rim might also explain the unusual series of nicks tangential to the circumference of the bracteate through both the rim and the flan at approximately 1, 5, 7 and 9 o'clock.

Behr's conclusion is rather that this is an example of the more frequent type of beaded wire applied 'on the front of the flan'; this type is found widely in Scandinavia, although in most regions as a minority variant (Axboe 1981, 41, fig 43). It would still be extremely unusual in England. I remain unconvinced that that is the case on Buckland Grave 250. It seems most appropriate here to outline the point of disagreement as an unresolved and important question. In whatever way it was formed, the rim partly overlies the attached wire volute and S-spirals by the loop. Again, the particular form of those appliqués on the Buckland Grave 250 bracteate appears to be unique.

The bracteate from Grave 245 (IK 581, 1; cf Denton: IK 581, 2) is the smallest and simplest of the three. The design has been reduced to five relatively simple elements; these appear, in fact, in a sharply and confidently executed form, although generally this bracteate displays the fewest signs of wear. No significant technical parallels can be identified on any other Kentish bracteates. This pair's nearest counterpart in terms of the simplification of the design is a D-bracteate from Ozengell in Kent (Axboe 1981, no 314f). Clearly visible on the Buckland Grave 245 specimen is the mark of the edge of the die used to impress the central design on the flan, as we also see on bracteates from Bifrons graves 29 and 64, Finglesham 203 and Sarre 90.

Altogether then, all three of these bracteates have some individual features. The example that would be most at home in southern Scandinavia, and which is therefore the most likely to have been imported from there, is that from Grave 204. Even this specimen, however, has one unusual feature in its triple row of repoussé bosses, and could have been manufactured in Kent. The technical peculiarities of the bracteate from Grave 250, and the unusual design of that from Grave 245 and its counterpart from Denton, point more conclusively towards Kentish production. There is no reason why the three together should not be taken, then, as representing the introduction and diversification of D-bracteate production within Kent. It is interesting to note that there is no correlation between the integrity or complexity of the central design and the technical quality of production or decoration: although the bracteates from Graves 245 and 250 have designs that could be characterized as degenerate or simplified, they also have punch-decorated borders, and a sharply executed design in one case and the applied wires and possibly skilfully rolled rim in the other. Purely on design grounds, one can suggest that the Grave 204 bracteate should be the earliest of the three; more tentatively, that from Grave 245 the latest. But it is not necessary for the sequence of production in each individual case to have followed the probable sequence in which the designs were derived.

Many aspects of the chronology of the bracteates of Types A–D are also the subject of intense debate. It is at least clear that these bracteates belong within the broad cultural horizon known as the Migration Period in Scandinavia and parts of Germany and England, running from the fifth to the sixth century. There is broad agreement that the earliest A-bracteates should start the whole series, perhaps not appearing much before the mid fifth century, with the addition of C- and probably B-bracteates constituting a second stage, and the emergence of D-bracteates a third. There must, however, have been a very high degree of overlap between A-, B-, C- and D-bracteates, and the successive stages at which new types were introduced could have followed one another very rapidly (Axboe 1999). Axboe's recent chronological analysis uses the technique of computerized correspondence analysis to search for a probable sequence within the A-, B- and C-bracteates. Barfod Carlsen likewise used that technique on the D-bracteates alone, and produced a sequence one end of which can be anchored to the characteristic C-bracteate horse-and-rider motif and which thus completely inverts Mackeprang's suggested sequence of development for the D-bracteates.

Other considerations to be brought to bear in attempting to establish a bracteate chronology are the finds with which bracteates are associated in closed deposits, and art-historical (stylistic) characteristics. At the time of her survey of the Kentish bracteates, Chadwick Hawkes was able to follow recent reassessments of the southern Scandinavian hoards combining bracteates with Byzantine gold coins to suggest that D-bracteate production began some way before the end of the fifth century. The one real problem that shrinking the period of introduction of all four main classes of bracteate in this way poses is that, in the Norwegian grave finds thoroughly discussed by Bakka (1973), we appear to have three quite distinct and substantial phases, including one that follows the early A-bracteates and is characterized by the presence of C-bracteates but virtually no D-bracteates. The availability and use of different types of bracteate in Norway need not have been the same as everywhere or anywhere else, but this evidence does warn us against too freely assigning the inception of the D-bracteates to a particularly early date.

In terms of style history, the introduction of the C-bracteates can be linked to the emergence of Salin's Style I,

and the development of the D-bracteates assigned at least a little time after that. The dating of the emergence of Style I has also had largely to be a matter of conjecture and debate up until very recently. Günther Haseloff (1974 and 1981) argued cogently for a date he estimated, by extrapolation, to be around AD 475; the most recent evidence and analyses have demonstrated, however, that a date close to *c* AD 450 should now be accepted (Rau 2010, 96–109 and 119–22; Kristoffersen and Magnus 2010, 75–81; cf Näsman 1984, 60–71). Barfod Carlsen has even identified possible links between the earliest D-bracteates and Nydam-style animals (1997; 2002). The relationships and possible overlaps between the relevant art-styles in the middle to later fifth century remain tantalizingly uncertain. Nonetheless it is practically impossible to assign any D-bracteate in a grave assemblage from England to a date any earlier than the sixth century, or even to the very early sixth century (Axboe 1999, fig 8.12).

Birte Brugmann's study of the chronology of Kentish grave groups (1999a) assigns the majority of such grave assemblages to her Phase III (*c* AD 530/540–560/570) although one from Buckland Grave 20 (Evison 1987, 220–1, figs 12–13) is of Phase II (*c* 500?–530/540). Also of Phase III is Finglesham grave 203 with the closest parallels to our bracteate of putatively earliest form, that from Grave 204. Chadwick Hawkes (Chadwick Hawkes and Pollard 1981, 339–40) would date Finglesham grave 203 to after AD 550. These three bracteates of themselves offer no finer dating evidence for the graves they were deposited in than can be obtained from other artefact-types there and the character of the whole assemblages. The radiocarbon dating and chronological modelling for this site (pp 360–6) includes datings of Graves 250 and 245 which are consistent with both the absolute and the relative datings implied here.

Beads

Birte Brugmann

(Graves 204, 207, 217, 218, 219, 221, 222, 223, 230, 232, 239, 245, 247, 250, 254, 257, 263B, 264, 281, 290, 293, 294, 296, 303A, 306, 308, 314A, 326, 327, 331, 334, 336, 339, 343, 347, 349, 350B, 353, 354, 360, 372, 373, 376, 377, 383, 389, 391A, 391B, 392, 404, 407, 408, 409, 412, 413, 415, 417, 419, 425, 427A, 428, 432, 440 and 441)

The 1994 excavations revealed sixty-four graves containing a total of 2,317 beads, together with the stray find of a quartz bead (Sf 970). The highest number was found in Grave 391B, with 178 individual beads. Fifty-nine per cent of the beads (a total of 1,366) are made of glass and 39 per cent (a total of

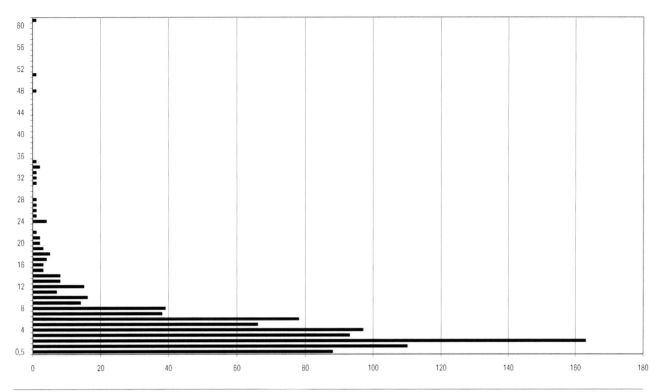

Fig 4.16. Buckland 1994. Amber beads sorted after their weight (0.05g–6.1g). The horizontal axis shows the number of beads, with the particular weight given in tenth of grams on the vertical axis.

923) are of amber. Only 2 per cent of the beads are made of other materials: fossils, jet, semi-precious stones (amethyst, carnelian and rock crystal), metal (copper alloy, silver and gold), or unidentified material.

Beads were generally worn by females. Two beads associated with the graves of males (Graves 230 and 264) were derived from their fills and need not have been associated with the deceased. The groups of eleven to sixty-six beads associated with individuals identified as being possibly male from the skeletal evidence (Graves 281, 350B and 373) were combined with other objects usually associated with females, such as brooches. The three beads in Grave 383 were also associated with a possible male skeleton and no other objects that would suggest a female are present. According to Stoodley (1999, 35), associations of more than one bead suggest female use. There is no evidence for beads at Buckland 1994 being used as sword beads.

Ninety-five per cent of all the beads were found above the (in some cases presumed) waist, in the area of the neck or chest, a position indicating they were part of necklaces or some other type of costume display. Groups of beads found in the central pelvis area such as in Graves 219 (d) and (l), 263B

(d–o), 373 (a) and 432 (e) and not associated with objects probably suspended from the belt, were presumably also part of the costume, while beads found with other objects between the waist and knees (including hollow vessel rim fragments) may have been part of the contents of pouches, or part of arrangements suspended from the belt (Graves 281 (m), 290 (e) and (f), 296 (h), 326 (k), 331 (e), 377 (k), 408 (i), 428 (e) and (f) and 432 (h)). In Graves 334 (b) and 383 (a) the beads were found in the area of the left waist/pelvis without any associated objects and they may have been associated with the costume or a pouch. Beads (e) in Grave 314A are associated with a knife (a) positioned above the waist and may, in fact, have been associated with either Skeleton A or B. Bead (b) in Grave 389 was probably given to a child of whom no bones remain. An unusual find was made in Grave 432: a group of beads (g) found with the remains of a glass vessel (f) positioned at the feet.

Among the beads that seem to have been used for châtelaines, or were possibly carried in a pouch, are some unusual types, suggesting that Anglo-Saxons did not only value amber beads of a particularly regular shape (see below) but also unusual glass bead types. In Grave 296 a translucent

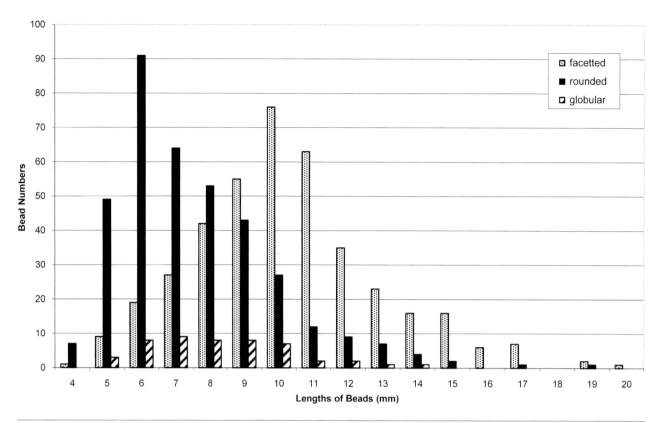

Fig 4.17. Buckland 1994. The total number of unfragmented facetted, rounded or globular amber beads sorted by their length of 4 to 20mm.

white bead (h) was present, an unusual colouring among almost always opaque white beads in Anglo-Saxon graves. In Grave 331 a translucent blue bead with a white trail (e) was singled out. This is an unusual colour combination for an Anglo-Saxon bead and is possibly of Iron Age or Roman origin. The hollow rims of glass vessels Graves 326 (k) and 428 (f1) may have been kept as scrap, though such objects in other contexts were worn with beads (see Brugmann 2004).

The 922 amber beads from the 1994 site have a total weight of 443g,[40] with an average weight of 0.5g per bead. The weight of the 867 complete beads ranges from less than 0.5 to 6g, and beads weighing 0.2g are actually the largest group, forming 19 per cent of the total. Figure 4.16 shows that beads made of more than 4g of amber are extremely rare (only Graves 417, 419 and 440 had one each) and there is no evidence for amber bead production that aimed at specific weight categories or bead sizes. The beads vary in size from

4mm in length and diameter to 12mm in length and 25mm in diameter.[41] The production of beads of more than 15mm in length and diameter may have been considered to require too much amber in proportion to beads not much smaller in size, and only twelve examples of such an 'extravagant' size were actually found among the unfragmented amber beads.

Most of the amber beads seem to have been made from natural lumps of amber with the intention of loosing as little raw material in the manufacturing process as was possible. This explains the irregular, facetted shape of 46 per cent of the Buckland beads, which were always perforated through their largest dimension. Another 42 per cent are rounded but not shaped regularly enough to be described as globular. It is impossible to draw clear distinctions between 'facetted' and 'rounded' and between 'rounded' and 'globular' amber beads. An attempt was made to differentiate between beads that have no rounded outline when viewed from any angle (facetted, Fig 4.17); beads that have a rounded 'display' side

---

40. All beads were weighed individually. As some amber beads from Anglo-Saxon graves weigh less than half a gramme, all beads were weighed in centigrammes and the numbers were added to the catalogue unedited. It is important to note, however, that the detail of the measurements should not be taken at face value. The amber was in different states of preservation, and in some cases the perforations were not cleaned out. While the following tables are based on the numbers in the catalogue, the text deals mostly with approximate numbers.
41. Measurements given in the catalogue record the maximum diameter of the beads.

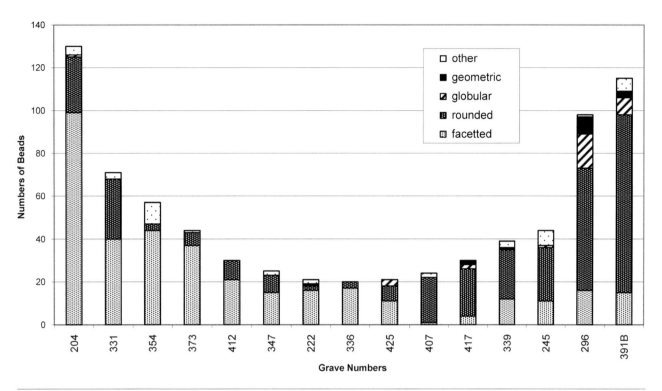

Fig 4.18. Buckland 1994. Graves with twenty to 130 amber beads. All types are represented. 'Other' includes amber bead fragments.

but an irregular outline when seen from a different angle (rounded, Fig 4.17); and beads which are almost globular, but have irregularities caused by the fact that the lump of amber was not large enough to allow for a fully globular bead of the intended size (Fig 4.17). Only 6 per cent of the Buckland amber beads are truly 'globular'. The remaining 6 per cent of unfragmented amber beads are barrel-shaped, cylindrical, spindle-shaped, wedge-shaped or irregular (Fig 4.17).

Figure 4.17 shows the facetted, rounded and globular amber beads sorted by length. On average, the rounded and globular beads are smaller than the facetted beads. This might not indicate that facetted beads were actually produced from larger lumps of amber than rounded and globular beads, but that, for the production of rounded and globular beads, more material was taken away to achieve a more regular shape. Only globular beads, however, are significantly more substantial than facetted beads. While it took an average of 0.41g of amber to produce one of the eight 8mm long globular beads found at Buckland, the fifty-three rounded beads of the same length required only 0.26g, which is actually slightly less than for the 119 facetted beads of this length, with an average of 0.28g. The difference between rounded and facetted beads of the same size may indicate different styles of bead making or possibly different sources of amber.

Graves with just one to three amber beads contained a proportionally high number of regularly-shaped, globular or other geometric types, namely barrel-shaped, cylindrical, spindle-shaped and wedge-shaped beads. In graves with up to six amber beads, the number of geometric and globular shapes is also relatively high. The high percentage of regular shapes among assemblages of one to three amber beads may indicate that single beads or small groups of amber beads did not necessarily represent 'poor' furnishing, but beads with a special, possibly amuletic function (Meaney 1981). Only three out of the total number of 923 amber beads from the 1994 site were found in the probable context of a pouch or châtelaine (Graves 281 (m) and 290 (f)) and it therefore seems that such 'special' amber beads were always part of a necklace, or directly attached to the dress.

Among the graves with between twenty and 130 amber beads, two different types can be defined (Fig 4.18). The associations from Graves 204, 331, 354, 373, 412, 347, 222, 336 and 425 are dominated by facetted beads, while Graves 407, 417, 339, 245, 296 and 391B are dominated by rounded types. The amber bead associations from Graves 204, 331 and 373, dominated by facetted types, have a total weight of between 50 and 60g. This is only to be expected considering that facetted beads tend to be larger than rounded ones (see

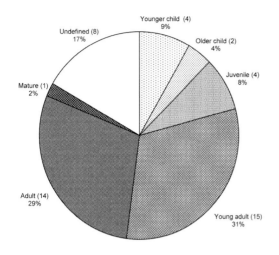

Fig 4.19. Buckland 1994. The total number and percentage of individuals of particular age groups buried with amber beads.

above). It is, however, noteworthy that the amber beads from Grave 331, comprising eighty-one mostly facetted types, weigh 59g and are therefore roughly three times heavier than the 115, generally rounded, amber beads from Grave 391B. This highlights the notion of weight and size being categories that should not be used in isolation to evaluate 'wealth' measured in amber beads.[42]

In their study of the Anglo-Saxon cemetery at Edix Hill, Barrington, in Cambridgeshire, Malim and Hines (1998, 211) compared the total weight of amber beads and noted the presence of possibly significant sets of 10–12g and 21–24g. Table 4.9 provides an overview of the total weight of amber bead assemblages found at Buckland in 1994. They may be divided into four groups: sets of up to 7g, sets of 11–19g, sets of 28–34g and sets of 50–60g. More data will be needed before any conclusions can be drawn on the possible implications of the total weight of amber used by individuals.

Table 4.9 presents the sorted matrix of a correspondence analysis of graves with well preserved beads and shows the association of beads of different weight groups in these graves. There is no pattern that would suggest amber beads were worn in clearly recognisable sets of sizes and numbers. The matrix does, however, reflect the differentiation between sets of beads dominated by rounded (mostly small) or facetted (mostly large) beads made in Fig 4.18. A grave not following this pattern is Grave 339, with a set of mostly rounded large beads.

Figure 4.19 and Table 4.9 demonstrate that amber beads were mostly buried with young adults and adults. This is not surprising considering that 82 per cent of the skeletons identified as female were also identified as young adult or adult. Table 4.9 indicates, however, that there is no significant difference in the distribution of facetted and rounded beads in the graves of young adult and adult women. In general, adult women wore no more amber than young adult women.

Larger amber beads usually have larger perforations than smaller ones but this may be a result of production rather than of wear. Most amber beads from Anglo-Saxon graves, however, show signs of wear on their perforated sides or around the perforation itself, an observation that suggests that amber beads generally had been used before they were buried. The type and grade of wear on an amber bead depends on its size, shape, weight and use. Evaluating this wear is difficult because it requires a quantification of the absence and not the presence of material. The most obvious sign of abrasion is the drop-shaped perforation of an asymmetrical bead. Rounded beads are mostly abraded on the perforated sides, resulting in a barrel-shaped profile (Figs 4.20–4.21). This type of abrasion is the rule and indicates rounded beads were usually strung and not individually attached to a garment. The irregular shape of a facetted bead often makes it difficult to say whether a plain part of the surface is an original facet or the result of wear.

For the purpose of this study, three types of wear have been defined and recorded for every amber bead, using a scale of '0', '1' or '2': abraded perforated sides and an oval or drop-shaped perforation at one or both ends. Additional features such as concave perforated sides and particularly worn edges around the perforation were recorded individually and added to the score. As there is no way of actually measuring the amount of wear, judgment on the presence or absence and the degree of abrasion had to be subjective. For the analysis, only amber beads were used that were well enough preserved to provide a full set of data (Figs 4.20–4.21). The data indicated, however, that larger beads tend to show more signs of abrasion than smaller ones, due to the greater pressure that a heavier bead puts on the string.

If women collected beads through their lifetime and were then buried with their sets, the amber beads in the graves of adult and mature women should generally be more abraded than beads in the graves of juvenile and young adult women. This was put to the test using two sets of data. A first test was run using rounded beads 0.1–0.2g in weight. The graph (Fig 4.20) does, in fact, show a higher proportion of wear on amber beads from the graves of adult women than in the graves of

---

42. See Malim and Hines (1998, 211) on this issue.

Grave	Osteological age	Total no of beads	Total weight in grams	weight categories in 10th of grams										2nd axis	Glass bead phase
				0.5–1	2–3	41–61	21–25	16–20	6–10	11–15	26–30	4–5	31–40		
293	infans II	7	0.5	7										-1.83	A2
327	adult	3	0.3	3										-1.83	
372	adult	1	0.1	1										-1.83	
441	infans II	1	0.1	1										-1.83	A2
245	adult	44	4.4	29	7									-1.61	(A2)
350B	young adult	14	2.0	10	3									-1.56	(A2)
223		8	0.9	4	2									-1.45	(A1)
239	adult	9	1.2	5	3									-1.40	(A1)
219	young adult	6	5.7	2	2									-1.26	(A1)
391B	young adult	115	18.3	54	51	3	1							-1.19	A2
407	young adult	24	3.7	9	13									-1.15	A2
281	young adult	11	5.5	3	5			1						-0.82	
247	young adult	2	0.3		1									-0.69	A2
417	mature	30	12.9	17	3	4	5	1					1	-0.62	(A)
314A	adult	9	2.4	2	4	1	1							-0.52	
296	adult	98	29.0	24	43	21	7	2				1		-0.45	A2
409	young adult	9	2.6	2	4	2	1							-0.39	A2
428	young adult	11	3.6	1	7	2	1							-0.34	A2
306		1	3.4									1		-0.18	A1
217		3	5.7				1					33		-0.15	(A1)
207	adult	4	1.4	2				2						-0.14	(A)
347	juvenile	25	15.0	3	8	11		1	1					0.05	A2
204	young adult	130	50.3	9	56	40	21			1	1			0.07	A2
392	infans III	3	1.4	1			2							0.43	A2
336	adult	20	11.6		8	5	3	4						0.52	A2b
412	juvenile	30	14.4		8	13	8	1						0.59	A2b
250	young adult	5	2.8		1	3		1						0.66	B1
254	infans II	1	0.4			1								0.68	(A2)
294		1	0.4			1								0.68	A
383	young adult	3	1.2			3								0.68	
263B	young adult	5	6.4		2			1			2			0.86	A1
339	adult	39	28.0	1	6	9	11	5	2					0.95	B1
425	young adult	21	16.9	1	4	2	10	2			2			0.95	A2
440	juvenile	2	5.2			1							1	1.04	A2
354	young adult	57	33.7		2	21	24							1.07	A2b
331		81	59.2		8	19	30	7	1		1		1	1.09	B1
222	adult	19	14.6			4	13	2						1.41	B2
290	young adult	2	1.6				2							1.56	
389		1	0.7				1							1.56	
353	adult	11	11.2				5	4	1					1.82	B2
373	adult	44	52.1			2	21	10	6	2	2			1.83	B1
419	adult	5	11.0				2		2				1	1.96	A2
391A	adult	1	1.8					1						2.64	C
1st axis				0.24	0.22	0.16	0.19	0.19	0.20	0.22	0.18	-4.86	0.22		

Table 4.9. The matrix of a correspondence analysis of bead associations using the total number of beads sorted into weight groups. Fragmented beads are given as part of the total number per grave but were excluded from the analysis. Bead associations dominated by rounded types are marked in blue, associations dominated by facetted types in yellow (after Fig 4.17). For the glass bead phases, see Table 4.14.

young adults. The number of beads from the graves of infants, juveniles and the mature individual is too small to produce any reliable results, but it is interesting to note that the beads buried with infants show wear, while there are relatively few signs of wear on the beads from the context of the mature woman. The wear on beads buried with children suggests these were handed down beads. This in turn implies that not everyone was buried with all the beads they had worn in their lifetime.

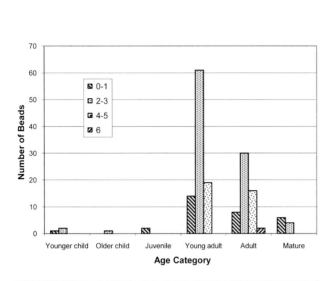

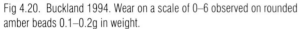

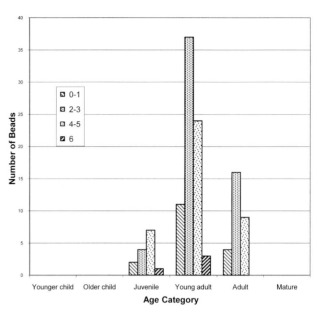

Fig 4.20. Buckland 1994. Wear on a scale of 0–6 observed on rounded amber beads 0.1–0.2g in weight.

Fig 4.21. Buckland 1994. Wear on a scale of 0–6 observed on facetted amber beads 0.4–0.6g in weight.

Facetted amber beads weighing 0.4–0.6g and with a full set of data available because of their good preservation, were only found in the graves of juveniles, young adult and adult women. Interestingly, the juvenile context produced the highest proportion of wear, followed by the young adults, while mature individuals are not represented. The pattern observed on the facetted beads therefore does not follow that of the rounded beads. The degree of wear on the bead sets buried with the females at Buckland therefore apparently does not clearly reflect the age of the owners. This may be connected with the way women acquired the bead sets they were buried with, or with the way the beads were worn, and in particular, how they were strung in combination with other beads. Heavy glass bead types presumably would have put particular stress on a necklace, especially if the beads were strung without a knot between individual beads. As rounded beads tend to be earlier than facetted amber beads (see below), it seems possible that there were changes over time that resulted in differences in the pattern of wear.[43]

Fifty-three graves dug in 1994 produced 1,366 glass beads, the numbers in a single grave ranging from one to 139. Roughly half these are covered by a typology developed for a chronological framework of glass beads from Anglo-Saxon graves (Table 4.10; Brugmann 2004). The purpose of the study of a national sample of glass beads, including Buckland 1951–3, was to develop a selective typology based on attributes marking related manufacture, and to use these types for a chronological analysis. If possible, the types were defined to match existing definitions of glass beads dated by contexts from continental graves, and so provide valuable links between Anglo-Saxon and continental chronological frameworks. It was therefore not possible to develop a systematic typology. This is reflected in the ranking of the criteria used to define types, forming a patchwork based on manufacturing techniques and further defined primarily by shape, colour or decorative pattern, and largely depending on existing typologies from various sources.

The selective choice of types covered in the main study accounts for roughly half the glass beads from the 1994 Buckland excavations. Additional types have been defined to cover the rest. About 100 beads can be defined as variants of types previously identified in the chronological study. The remainder are divided into three groups: monochrome drawn beads, monochrome wound beads and polychrome wound beads. These, were, if at all possible, divided into groups of beads apparently of related manufacture, leaving, however, a residue of about 300 beads which were grouped, for convenience only, according to their colour, shape

---

43. At Buckland 1994, the exact position of the beads could be recorded only in Graves 219, 222, 232, 250, 336 and 373. Similar data on the size, shape, weight and wear of the amber beads from the Eriswell, Lakenheath cemetery in Suffolk (site archive), with a larger number of detailed bead plans, may produce conclusive evidence on the wear and tear of amber beads.

or decorative pattern and are therefore not suitable for correspondence analysis, because they represent a fairly random selection of beads. The total number of beads of the types defined in Table 4.10 is listed by grave in Table 4.11.

The following variants of pre-defined types (Table 4.10; see Brugmann 2004) among the Buckland beads were defined (for a detailed type description see Table 4.10).

No 4, 'var Candy' (Table 4.10): a colour variation of 'Candy' beads with an opaque circumferential trail covering another opaque trail of a different colour on a translucent body, which is a pattern typical of fifth-century polychome beads from continental Saxon contexts.

Nos 7 and 8, 'light ConCyl' and 'discoloured ConCyl': light Constricted Cylinder beads are a variant of either light Constricted Segmented beads or of blue Constricted Cylinder beads. Discoloured Constricted Cylinder beads are poorly preserved and may originally have been light or blue.

No 9, 'CoilCyl': Coiled Cylindrical beads are blue wound beads very much like Constricted Cylinder beads in appearance and therefore mistakenly listed as (drawn) Constricted Cylinder beads in Brugmann 2004.

No 11, 'var CylPen': these two beads have the same attributes as the wound monochrome Cylinder Pentagonal beads with flattened perforated sides but are variations because they are decorated with applied and marvered in dots.

No 16, 'var Koch34': these wound beads with a type name referring to the type numbers used in the publication of the well-known Schretzheim cemetery (U Koch 1977) fall perfectly within the parameters of the Koch34 beads and therefore probably part of the same production,[44] but are variations because they are not decorated with applied narrow crossing trails and dots. The untidy spirals and wavy trails are probably careless variations of the common motif.

No 18, 'var Dot34': this bead is biconical instead of globular or barrel-shaped but the pattern and colour combination of the blue crossing trails and red dots on a white bead body suggests the bead is a variation made at a time when biconical beads were common.

No 22, 'var Melon': the size and colour of these translucent blue or yellow globular beads and the fact that they are often found with Melon beads suggest that they are part of the same series but they were not ribbed.

No 23, 'poly Melon-related': short dark beads with white or yellow zigzag are often found in combination with 'Melon' and 'var Melon' beads not only in Anglo-Saxon but also in continental graves, and it therefore seems probable that their production was related. Short dark beads with zigzag trails,

however, are also known from earlier contexts and the exact criteria that would differentiate between the various types have yet to be defined (Brugmann 2004). Table 4.10 gives the measurements for such beads associated with Melon beads as a first step towards such a definition.

No 26, 'Mosaic, ?Roman': some bead fragments appear not to be from early medieval Mosaic beads but from Roman types and are therefore listed separately.

No 32, 'var TL': beads with the colour combination of opaque yellow and translucent green, but without the opaque red that defines a 'Traffic Light' bead, are often found in association with the latter, and are therefore probably simpler versions.

No 38, 'RoSept?': this 'Roman Septagonal' bead is a translucent blue bead with a highly unusual septagonal cross section to a biconical shape; probably Roman.

No 40, 'single SegGlob': these 'Segmented Globular' beads have a sharp edge to the perforation on both perforated sides. This is a technical detail known from both fifth-, later sixth- and seventh-century contexts, so is therefore not suitable for dating purposes. Double segments, however, as they define the yellow Segmented Globular type, only occur in the later contexts. 'Single SegGlob' beads have exactly the same features in terms of shape, size and colour as the Segmented Globular beads, and as they exclusively occur in a grave that also has SegGlob beads, their manufacture is probably related. It would not, however, be possible to tell them apart from earlier types if occurring in a different context, as is the case with the larger beads of various colours summarized as No 62, 'sharp glob', under 'wound monochome' beads of 'other types'.

Kent seems to be the only Anglo-Saxon region in which drawn beads were reintroduced in the seventh century on a large scale. As with the wound 'No 40, single Segmented Globular' type discussed above, some technical aspects of late sixth- and seventh-century glass bead production seem to come full circle from the late Roman and fifth century, and it will take detailed studies of a larger sample of beads to evaluate the drawn monochrome types listed under 'other bead types' in Table 4.10.

Among the 'wound monochrome' beads which appear in Table 4.10, only Nos 54 and 55 are noteworthy. The 'blue almond' bead is rare in Anglo-Saxon graves but common on the Continent and is part of Ursula Koch's bead combination group F, partly contemporary with the Final Phase (U Koch 2001, 164; Brugmann 2004, table 3). The 'white/yellow cylinders' made of translucent whitish or light yellow glass and with a square cross section are probably quite common

---

44. In one case, the yellow bead body, which is rare among Koch34 beads.

Type no	Type name	No of beads	No of segs	Perf diam	Body diam	Body length	Proportion	Body tech	Shape	Translucency	Body colour	Dec technique	Motif
1	**Blue**	**24**	**1**	**3–6.5**	**7–13**	**3–9**		**wound**	**annular or coiled globular**	**translucent**	**blue**	**none**	**none**
2	**BlueGreen Spiral**	**1**	**1**	**2–2.5**	**7**	**6**	**medium**	**wound**	**globular**	**opaque**	**white**	**applied**	**translucent blue spiral**
3	**Brown**	**1**	**1**	**3**	**7**	**3**		**wound**	**globular**	**translucent**	**pink-brown**	**none**	**none**
4	var Candy	3	1	2–3	14	10–12	short or medium	wound	barrel-shaped		?white or dark	applied	opaque red circumferential trailed on translucent blue wavy trail (on ?white) or opaque red trail on bright green wavy trail (on dark)
5	**ConSeg**	**474**	**1–5**	**1.0–2.5**	**3–6**	**2–18**		**drawn layers, constricted perf sides**	**globular**		**light**	**none**	**none**
6	**ConCyl**	**50**	**1**	**1.0–2.0**	**2–5**	**11–21**	**very long**	**drawn, perf sides constricted, few cut**	**cylindrical**	**blue**	**blue**	**none**	**none**
7	light ConCyl	15	1	1.5–2.0	3–4	9–17	very long	drawn layers, constricted perf sides	cylindrical		light	none	none
8	discoloured ConCyl	8	1	1–2	2–3	11–14	very long	drawn layers, constricted perf sides	cylindrical	?	?	none	none
9	CoilCyl	6	1	1.0–2.0	3–4	8–15	very long	wound (coiled)	cylindrical	translucent	blue	none	none
10	**CylPen**	**64**	**1**	**2–5**	**6–10**	**8–15**		**wound, flat perforated sides**	**cylindrical, pentagonal cross-section**	**semi-trans-opaque**	**blue, red, white or yellow**	**none**	**none**
11	var CylPen	2	1	2–5	7–8	11		wound, flat perforated sides	cylindrical, pentagonal cross-section	opaque	red or white	applied	white, light blue or red splints marvered in
12	**CylRound**	**47**	**1**	**1.5–5**	**6–10**	**5–10**		**wound, flat perforated sides**	**cylindrical, round cross-section**	**semi-trans-opaque**	**blue, red, white or yellow**	**none**	**none**
13	**Hourglass**	**1**	**2**	**2–5.3**	**14**	**12**		**wound**	**barrel-shaped**	**translucent**	**green**	**applied**	**opaque yellow wavy trail**
14	**Koch20**	**16**	**1**	**1.5–4**	**6–11**	**6–10**	**medium**	**wound**	**barrel-shaped (or globular)**	**opaque**	**red (or dark)**	**applied**	**wide crossing trails & three dots (5 x white, 8 x yellow, 1 x lost); 1 x white var. without dots, 1 x white var. with lost trails& red dots)**
15	**Koch34**	**17**	**1–2**	**2.5–8**	**6–10**	**4–11**	**short to medium**	**wound**	**globular (or barrel-shaped)**	**opaque**	**white or red**	**applied**	**narrow crossing trails (7 x white, 8 x blue, 2 x lost)**
16	var Koch 34	15	1–2	2–4	6–8	4–11	short (or medium)	wound	globular (or barrel-shaped)	opaque	red (1 x yellow)	applied	white (1 x yellow) irregular or wavy trail or spiral
17	**Dot 34**	**1**	**1**	**4–6**	**15**	**12**	**medium**	**wound**	**barrel-shaped**	**opaque**	**white or red**	**applied**	**narrow translucent blue crossing trails and red dots**
18	var Dot 34	1	1	2–3	7	14	very long	wound	biconical	opaque	white	applied	wide translucent blue crossing trails and red dots
19	**Koch49/50**	**6**	**1**	**3–6**	**9–11**	**10–23**		**wound**	**cylindrical**	**opaque**	**red or white**	**applied**	**white or red combed spiral**
20	**Koch58**	**1**	**1**	**4–5**	**12**	**10**		**wound**	**barrel-shaped**	**opaque**	**red**	**applied**	**3 opaque yellow circumferential trails on white zigzag trail**

Type no	Type name	No of beads	No of segs	Perf diam	Body diam	Body length	Proportion	Body tech	Shape	Translucency	Body colour	Dec technique	Motif
21	Melon	18	1	2–6	10–15	6–11	short to medium	wound	globular to barrel-shaped, 5–12 ribbed cross-section	translucent	yellow or blue	none	none
22	var Melon	11	1	3–6	11–16	6–9	short	wound	globular	translucent	yellow or blue	none	none
23	poly Melon-related	7	1	3–4.5	11–15	7–13	short	wound	globular		dark	applied	white zigzag trail
24	MinDark	22	1	1–2	4–5	4–10	medium to long	wound	globular or coiled		dark	none	none
25	Mosaic	20	1	1.5–3.5	6–14	6–18	short to very long	mosaic	globular, cylindrical with hexagonal cross-section, biconical or spindle-shaped			mosaic	see catalogue figs
26	Mosaic, ? Roman	2	1				fragmented	mosaic	fragmented			mosaic	?translucent blue (now iridescent) & white radiating stripes ('eye') around lost core, or star pattern incl. translucent blue & white, possibly opaque yellow – if this is not discolouration
27	Mottled	1	1	5–5.5	13	8	short	wound	barrel-shaped	translucent	blue	applied	irregular dots, red applied on white
28	Reticella	10	1	3–6.5	13–20	10–19	short to long	wound	cylindrical, barrel-shaped or biconical	translucent	dark or green or not visible	applied	opaque red and yellow and translucent yellow twisted trails arranged in herringbone pattern
29	TLtw	7	1	1.5–3.5	7–15	7–15		wound	globular, barrel-shaped or cylindrical	opaque	red	applied	opaque yellow and translucent green twisted trails
30	TLlmi	3	1	2–4	10–17	11–13		wound	globular, barrel-shaped or cylindrical	opaque	red or yellow	applied	see catalogue figs
31	TLOth	3	1	1–3	5–13	6–12		wound	globular, barrel-shaped or cylindrical	opaque	red or green	applied	see catalogue figs
32	var TL	1	1	2.5–3	10	6		wound	barrel-shaped	opaque	yellow	applied	see catalogue figs
33	Orange	2	1	3.5–5.5	9–10	7–10	medium	wound	barrel-shaped/ biconical	opaque	orange	none	none
34	rim fragment	2	1	drop-shaped				hollow glass rim of vessel		translucent	blue-green	none	none
35	RoHexCyl	3	1	2–2.5	5–7	8–9	long	?	cylindrical, hexagonal cross-section	translucent	green	none	none
36	RoMelon	2	1	8–10	18–23	14–18	medium	?	globular, ribbed cross-section	opaque	turquoise	none	none
37	RoPoly	2	1	2.5	5	6	medium	?	polyhedral	translucent	blue	none	none
38	RoSept?	1	1	1–2	7	12	very long	?	biconical, heptagonal cross-section	translucent	blue	none	none
39	SegGlob	8	2	1–2	4	6–7	long	wound, edge of perf sharp	globular	opaque	yellow	none	none
40	single SegGlob	26	1	1–2	4	3–4	medium	wound, edge of perf sharp	globular	opaque	yellow	none	none

Other bead types

Drawn Monochrome

Type no	Type name	No of beads	No of segs	Perf diam	Body diam	Body length	Proportion	Body tech	Shape	Translucency	Body colour	Dec technique	Motif
41	blue ConSeg	2	1	2	5	4–5		drawn ?layers, constricted perf sides	globular	translucent	blue	none	none
42	blue Cylinder	1	1	3	10	9	medium	drawn?	cylindrical, rectangular cross-section	translucent	blue	none	none
43	red ConSeg	35	1–2	1.0–2.0	3–5	3–9		drawn ?layers, constricted perf sides	globular	opaque	inner and outer layer red	none	none
44	red Cyl	1	1	1.5	3	5		drawn ?layers, constricted perf sides	cylindrical	opaque	red	none	none
45	red barrel	1	1	4.0	8	4		drawn, perf sides cut	barrel-shaped	opaque	red	none	none
46	*other opaque red*	*2*	*1*	*3.5–5*	*7–8*	*5–6*	*short to medium*	*drawn?*	*?globular or cylindrical, perforated sides ?cut*	*opaque*	*red*	*none*	*none*
47	*green Seg*	*12*	*1–2*	*1–4*	*2–9*	*1–6*		*drawn*	*globular*	*transl. – opaque*	*green*	*none*	*none*
48	*green Cyl*	*10*	*1–2*	*1.0–2.0*	*3–5*	*2–12*		*drawn*	*cylindrical*	*semi-transl. – opaque*	*green*	*none*	*none*
49	*yellow Cyl*	*3*	*1*	*1.5–2*	*4*	*7–8*	*very long*	*drawn, constricted perf sides*	*cylindrical*	*opaque*	*yellow*	*none*	*none*
50	turquoise Cyl	65	1–3	1.0–2.0	2–3	2–8		drawn, perf sides cut or broken	cylindrical	opaque	turquoise	none	none
51	turquoise square Cyl	2	1	2–4	4–6	9–8	very long	drawn ?	cylindrical, square cross-section	opaque	turquoise	none	none
52	large ConSeg	12	1	1.5–2.0	5–9	7–10		drawn, one layer, constricted perf sides	globular	translucent	light or blue	none	none

Wound Monochrome

Type no	Type name	No of beads	No of segs	Perf diam	Body diam	Body length	Proportion	Body tech	Shape	Translucency	Body colour	Dec technique	Motif
53	*translucent green Cyl*	*3*	*1*	*2–3*	*3–9*	*4–6*	*short to very long*	*wound*	*cylindrical, round cross-section*	*translucent*	*green*	*none*	*none*
54	blue almond	1	1	2	8	10	long	wound	almond-shaped	translucent	blue	none	none
55	white/yellow Cyl	7	1	1.5–3	4–6	7–9	long to very long	wound	cylindrical, square cross-section	translucent	white or light yellow	none	none
56	*other Cyls*	*39*	*1–2*	*1–4.5*	*5–9*	*5–12*	*short to very long*	*wound, perf sides not flat, mostly not worked over*	*cylindrical, round cross-section*	*semi-transl. – opaque*	*blue, green, red, white, yellow*	*none*	*none*
57	*other barrel*	*22*	*1*	*2–5.5*	*7–13*	*4–8*	*short to medium*	*wound*	*barrel-shaped*	*transl. – opaque*	*blue, blue-green, dark, green red, white or yellow*	*none*	*none*

Table 4.10. Glass bead typology, covering all sufficiently preserved glass beads from the site. Bold script marks type definitions summarising beads with particular attributes but probably not of related manufacture. Types 1–40 types defined in Brugmann 2004. Italic script marks glass bead types defined in Brugmann 2004. Types 41–72 Other bead types: 41–52 - Drawn monochrome, 53–63 Wound monochrome, 64–71 - Wound polychrome, and 72 - Types neither drawn nor wound.

Type no	Type name	No of beads	No of segs	Perf diam	Body diam	Body length	Proportion	Body tech	Shape	Translucency	Body colour	Dec technique	Motif
58	*other annular*	3	1	4.5–9	9–14	3–5	very short	wound	annular	translucent or opaque	yellow	none	*none*
59	*other melon*	7	1	2–7	5–22	5–15	short to medium	wound	globular or barrel-shaped, ribbed cross-section	translucent or opaque	blue-green, dark green, red or yellow	none	*none*
60	*other coiled*	3	1	2–6	7–10	3–7	short	wound	coiled	semi-trans - opaque	blue, red or white	none	*none*
61	*biconical*	2	1	2–3	8–9	9–10	medium	wound	biconical	translucent or opaque	blue or yellow	none	*none*
62	*sharp glob.*	52	1	1–5	5–10	3–7	short to medium	wound, edge of perf sharp	globular	opaque	dark, green, red, white or yellow	none	*none*
63	*other glob.*	126	1–3	1–7	5–18	3–8	short to medium	wound	globular	opaque or translucent	dark, blue-green, blue, brown, green, red, white or yellow	none	*none*
Wound Polychrome													
64	blobby trail	2	1	5–5.7	6–7	15	short	wound	globular	dark	dark	applied	circumferential white blobby trail
65	wide crossing trail	5	1	2–4	9–11	5–8	short	wound	globular or barrel-shaped	opaque	white or light yellow	applied	red or blue wide crossing trails and blue or red dots
66	bicone	4	1	3–4.5	9–16	8–12	medium	wound	biconical	opaque	red	applied	yellow dots or wavy rails
67	*poly blue*	3	1	3–5.6	11–21	7–13	short to medium	wound	globular or barrel-shaped	translucent	blue	applied	white zigzag trail or lost circles, one open ring
68	*poly red*	5	1	1.5–5	9–14	9–13	short to long	wound	globular or barrel-shaped	opaque	red	applied	yellow or lost zigzag or spiral trail or 3 raised dots
69	*poly white*	1	1	1.5–2	8		short	wound	globular	opaque	white or light yellow	applied	red irregular trail
70	*poly dark*	3	1			5		wound	wedge-shaped globular		dark	applied	white zigzag trail or lost circles, one open ring
71	*poly mix*	1	1	3–4.5	11	10	medium	?	globular	opaque	red, black and white	applied	opaque yellow irregular zigzag
Other													
72	*folded?*	6	1	2–4	5–9	4–14	short to long	folded?	asym. biconical, barrel-shaped, cylindrical or globular	translucent to opaque	blue, green, orange or red	none	*none*

Abbreviations: var = variation; ConSeg = Constructed Segmented; Cyl = Cylindrical; ConCyl = Constructed Cylindrical; CoilCyl = Coiled Cylindrical; CylPen = Cylindrical Pentagonal; poly = polychrome; TLTw = Traffic Light Twisted; TLImi = Traffic Light Imitation; RoHexCyl = Roman Hexagonal Cylindrical; RoMelon = Roman Melon; RoPoly = Roman Polyhedral; RoSept = Roman Heptagonal (Septagonal); SegGlob = Segmented Globular; segs = segments; perf = perforations; diam = diameter; tech = technique; dec = decoration.

in continental graves (a survey would need to prove this), but they are rare in Anglo-Saxon graves. Both types 54 and 55 may be a result of the close contacts between Kent and the Continent.

Among the wound polychromes, only types 64 to 66 are remarkable. Short dark beads with a 'blobby' circumferential trail, often lost, are found mostly in fifth-century contexts. Beads with 'wide crossing trails' and dots are common in fifth- and early sixth-century Anglo-Saxon contexts but are rare on the Continent at that time. These beads are larger and mostly shorter than the probably imported later sixth- and seventh-century 'Koch20' beads with wide crossing trails and dots, and almost always have trails and dots in two different colours instead of the same colour used for 'Koch20' beads. The third type, biconical beads, both monochrome and globular, were produced in the later sixth and seventh centuries and are therefore useful for dating purposes.

The bead types used for an Anglo-Saxon chronological framework (Brugmann 2004) were sorted into Groups according to their associations in graves. Group A comprises Nos 1 (Blue), 2 (Blue-Green Spiral), 3 (Brown), 5 (Constricted Segmented), 6 (Constricted Cylindrical), 13 (Hourglass), 24 (Miniature Dark), and 29–31 (Traffic Light) and is subdivided into an earlier Group A1 dominated by Traffic Light and Hourglass beads, and a Group A2 dominated by 'Constricted Cylindrical' beads. 'Constricted Segmented' beads are also most numerous in Group A2, but as light drawn globular beads with constricted perforated sides in Kent come into fashion again later (see above), 'Constricted Segmented' beads are of limited use in a Kentish context. Beads of Group A2b, however, Nos 21 (Melon) and 28 (Reticella), are common in Kent. Group B comprises Nos 10 (Cylindrical Pentagonal), 12 (Cylindrical Round), 14 (Koch20), 15 (Koch34), 17 (Dot 34), 19 (Koch49/50), 20 (Koch58), 33 (Orange), and 39 (Segmented Globular) and is subdivided into Group B1 (Cylindrical Pentagonal and Cylindrical Round; Koch20 and 58 and Dot 34) and B2 (Koch34, SegGlob and Orange). Orange beads are also found in Group C, which is represented at Buckland 1994 only by amethyst beads (see below). Groups A–C represent a chronological development from the Early to the Final Phase, with Group A roughly covering the Early Phase, Group B the intermediate period and Group C the Final Phase (Brugmann 2004).

A correspondence analysis of the bead types used for the Anglo-Saxon framework in the graves at Buckland

1994 (nos 6 and 9, 10, 12, 14, 15, 19, 21, 24, 28, 29–31) was broken down into two completely separate groups of graves, representing Bead Groups A and B as defined in Brugmann 2004. Adding closely defined types (see above) among the rest of the Buckland glass beads to the matrix in Table 4.12 resulted in the same division. Graves 204, 223, 245, 254, 263B, 294, 306, 347, 372, 392, 407, 440 and 441 include only one of the types of Group A listed in Table 4.12 in their type associations and therefore cannot be used for a correspondence analysis. There are no graves with only one of the types listed in Group B of Table 4.12, but Graves 353, 360 and 376, with only No 33 (Orange) or 39 (Segmented Globular), cannot be included.

A correspondence analysis of the glass bead types in Table 4.12 and the two amber bead groups shown in Table 4.9 and Fig 4.18 (dominated by rounded or facetted types) shows that rounded amber beads are mostly associated with glass beads of Group A and facetted amber beads mostly with glass bead types of Groups A2b (Table 4.13). As in Table 4.9, Grave 339 forms an exception in the matrix in that it combines the rounded amber bead group with glass beads of groups A2b and B. Graves 204, 347 and 425 combine facetted amber beads with glass beads of Group A2. The amber bead group from Graves 204, 347 and 425 are in the middle range either in terms of type or weight combinations shown in Table 4.9 and Fig 4.18 and may represent a transition from the rounded to the facetted amber bead group. In this case, the change from rounded to facetted amber beads was made in the context of Group A.

It has generally been assumed that the amber buried in Anglo-Saxon graves increased during the middle of the sixth century and decreased towards the end of that century.[45] As glass bead Groups A–C represent an overlapping chronological sequence (Brugmann 2004), it is possible to test this idea in relation to Buckland 1994. The grave numbers that can be used, however, are quite small and represent only a proportion of the well-equipped individuals in any of the phases. Figure 4.22 shows the graves of juvenile to mature individuals whose graves that can be assigned to a particular bead group. Groups A1 and C are not well enough represented to be used in the table. Group A2 is represented by twelve graves,[46] Groups A2b, B1 and B2 by only three graves each.[47]

Figure 4.22 shows that the average number of beads in Groups A2 to B1 is roughly the same but it is considerably lower in Group B2. The average weight of amber, however,

---

45. For a discussion on the date of amber beads in Anglo-Saxon contexts see Hirst (1985, 68ff). The evidence, however, cannot contribute to the discussion on a general shift in Anglo-Saxon bead fashion from (blue) glass beads to amber beads (see Hirst 1985) because there is not enough substantial evidence from the site representing bead Group A1 (see Brugmann 2004).

46. Graves 204, 247, 296, 391B, 407, 409, 419, 425, 427A, 428, 432 and 440.

47. Group A2b: Graves 336, 354 and 412; Group B1: Graves 250, 339 and 373; Group B2: Graves 222, 353 and 360.

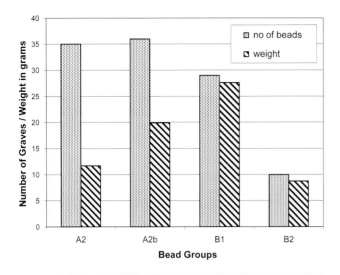

Fig 4.22. Buckland 1994. The average number of amber beads and their total weight in grams per grave in the graves of juvenile to adult individuals buried with beads of glass bead groups A2–B2 (after Brugmann 2004).

increases from Group A2 to B1 and then drops in Group B2. Group A2 can be roughly dated to AD 480–570; Group A2b, AD 530–580; B1, AD 550–600, and Group B2, AD 580–650 (Brugmann 2004). Figure 4.22 suggests that the number of amber beads at Buckland 1994 did not vary much throughout the sixth century, but that the actual amount of amber increased during the course of the sixth century and decreased only in the late sixth century. The data thus supports the general notion about amber from sixth-century contexts.

Analysis of glass bead colours from continental graves has shown that not only bead types but also colour combinations changed over time (see Siegmund 1998; Siegmann 2001), though continental fashion was not as much dictated by colour as some Scandinavian fashion (see Høilund Nielsen 1997b). A correspondence analysis of the glass bead colours from the Buckland graves (Table 4.14) roughly reflects those in the bead combination groups C–G of the lower Rhine region noted by Siegmund (1998, 57ff).[48]

Group A2 is dominated by light ('gold-in-glass'), blue and dark ('black') beads. Groups A1 and B have mostly red, yellow and white beads and also a small number of green beads. Group A1, however, is often dominated by blue and dark beads, as, for example, the associations from Graves 306, 308 and 349. Group B1 has a higher proportion of red and yellow beads (eg in Graves 339 and 250), and there is an overall increase of white beads in B2.

Turquoise beads are found at the extreme end of the negative part of both the first and the second axis due to the occurrence of a large number of small drawn cylinders (No 50) in Grave 360. The colour turquoise has an unfortunate affect on the analysis because it is found with very different bead types, among them Roman Melon beads (No 36) in Graves 222 and 263B (No 36 in Table 4.10). Two beads of a bright turquoise colour similar to the inlay in the pendant Grave 413 (o) and five green beads, one of them a Traffic Light bead, dictate the position of Grave 391B relatively close to Grave 360 despite the large number of light 'Constricted Segmented' beads in Grave 391B. The three orange beads represent two wound No 33 'Orange' beads and a ?folded bead (listed as No 72) probably related to the orange bead (h)12 from grave 71 at Mill Hill, Deal, in an Group A2 bead association (Parfitt and Brugmann 1997; Brugmann 2004) rather than No 33 'Orange' beads.

Though Table 4.14 shows that there are some colour combinations which are typical for certain bead groups, colours on their own are not safe guides to Kentish bead fashion. It is, however, noteworthy that Grave 372 contained eight green glass beads combined with a dark, a blue, a red and an amber bead. Such a large proportion of green beads is unusual for any group other than Group C dated in the Final Phase. The association, however, does not include any bead type known to date from the Final Phase. Three of the green beads are in fact Roman types, again an unusually high proportion of Roman beads in an Anglo-Saxon context.

Some bead type combinations from Buckland 1994 include none, or only a few, of the readily datable types in Table 4.12 but can be associated with one of the Groups discussed above and have their grave groups given in brackets in Table 4.14. This is the case especially in relation to Group A1, which is best defined in Anglian contexts because of the high number of readily recognisable 'Traffic Light' beads in these regions. Group A1 in Kent and the Saxon South and West is mostly comprised of monochrome beads. These include globular beads with sharp edges to the perforation, which also occur as part of Group B and are therefore not suitable for dating purposes (see above). On average, Group A1 was worn in smaller assemblages than Groups A2–B2, so that it is more difficult to define. The following graves, however, can be assigned to, or affiliated with, Group A1.

Grave 217 does not only have a 'Traffic Light' bead and an early bead with wide crossing trails (Table 4.12) but also a variation of a 'Traffic Light' bead (No 32) and globular beads with sharp edges to the perforation at both

---

48. For a more detailed discussion on the relevance of Siegmund's study on Kent see Brugmann 2004.

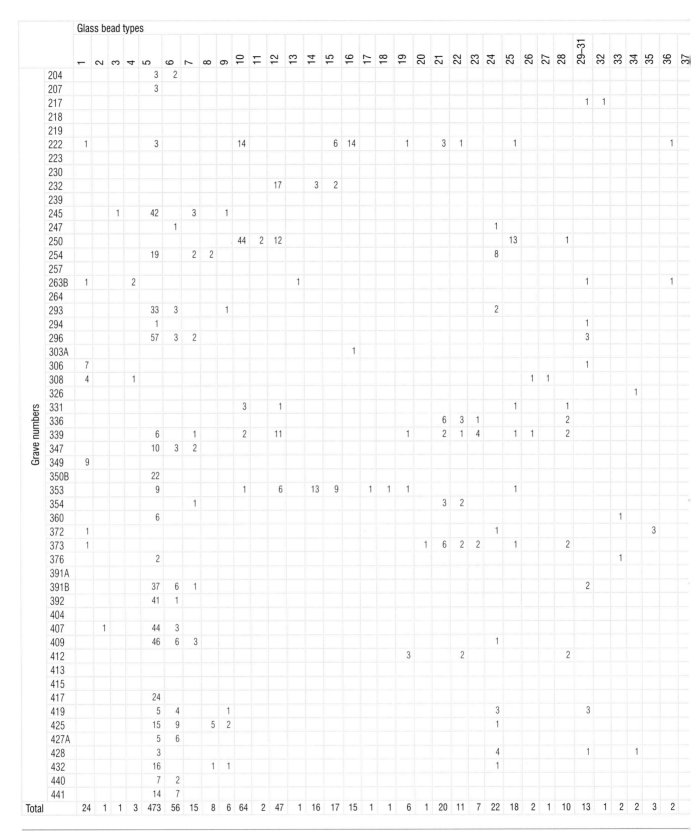

Grave	1	2	3	4	5	6	7	8	9	10	11	12	13	14	15	16	17	18	19	20	21	22	23	24	25	26	27	28	29–31	32	33	34	35	36	37
204					3	2																													
207					3																														
217																													1	1					
218																																			
219																																			
222	1				3					14					6	14			1		3	1		1										1	
223																																			
230																																			
232												17		3	2																				
239																																			
245			1		42		3		1																										
247						1																		1											
250										44	2	12													13		1								
254					19		2	2																8											
257																																			
263B	1			2									1																1						1
264																																			
293					33	3			1															2											
294					1																								1						
296					57	3	2																	3											
303A																1																			
306	7																												1						
308	4		1																		1	1													
326																																1			
331										3		1													1			1							
336																					6	3	1					2							
339					6		1			2		11							1		2	1	4	1	1			2							
347					10	3	2																												
349	9																																		
350B					22																														
353					9					1		6		13	9		1	1	1						1										
354							1														3	2													
360					6																										1				
372	1																							1									3		
373	1																			1	6	2	2	1				2							
376					2																										1				
391A																																			
391B					37	6	1																						2						
392					41	1																													
404																																			
407		1			44	3																													
409					46	6	3																	1											
412																			3			2						2							
413																																			
415																																			
417					24																														
419					5	4			1															3							3				
425					15	9		5	2															1											
427A					5	6																													
428					3																			4								1		1	
432					16		1	1																1											
440					7	2																													
441					14	7																													
Total	24	1	1	3	473	56	15	8	6	64	2	47	1	16	17	15	1	1	6	1	20	11	7	22	18	2	1	10	13	1	2	2	3	2	

Table 4.11. Graves and bead types. The total number of beads per grave of the types defined in Table 4.10a–d.

38	39	40	41	42	43	44	45	46	47	48	49	50	51	52	53	54	55	56	57	58	59	60	61	62	63	64	65	66	67	68	69	70	71	72	undef	Total
																				1					2											8
																																				3
																								4			2									8
																									4											4
																					1			4	2											7
									1						1				2	1				19	26			1							2	98
					1																				1		1									3
									1																											1
																			1						1											24
																						1														1
				1			1	1						12					2	1													1		1	67
																		2																		4
											1					1		13	2			2	1	19	27											129
			2						3																											36
1															1									1	1											4
																						1														7
																									1											1
																																				39
																																				2
																			1						1											67
																																				1
																						1									2					20
																			2									1			1				1	12
																																				1
																		2	8						11		1	1								29
																									1				1					2	16
																		8	1				1		35							1			78
										1											1														17
																									1	2								1	13
																																			22
	8	26																10	2				1	3	1				1				1		95
								1											2															3	13
					2							63	2																						74
															1				1		1			1	1										10
																			1						3				2					1	22
										6	3																								12
																		1							1										2
													2				2		1					4	2			1			1	2	62
																																			42
										4																									4
																		1				1			1				1						52
																																			56
					35																				1		2								45
									2																										2
																					1														1
																																			24
																	3																		19
																																			32
																																			11
									2																										11
																																			19
																																			9
																																			21
1	8	26	2	1	35	1	1	2	11	12	2	65	2	12	3	1	7	39	23	3	6	3	2	52	126	2	5	4	3	5	1	3	1	6	10	1360

Total numbers of glass beads per grave

Bead	ConCyl & CoilCyl	Min Dark	Traffic Light	White/ yellow cyl	Wide crossing trails	CylPen	CylRound	Koch20	Koch34	Koch49/50	Melon	var. Melon	Polychrome Melon-related	Mosaic	Reticella	Biconical	Bicone	
Type no	6 & 9	24	29–31	55	65	10	12	14	15	19	21	22	23	25	28	61	66	
Grave																		
217			X		X													
247	X	X		X														
293	X	X																
296	X		X															
391B	X		X	X	X													Group A
409	X	X																
419	X	X	X	X														
425	X	X																
428		X	X															
432	X	X																
222						X			X	X	X	X		X			X	
232							X	X	X									
250						X	X		X						X	X		
331						X	X		X						X		X	
336											X	X	X		X			Group B
339						X	X		X		X	X	X	X	X			
353						X	X	X	X	X				X		X		
354											X	X						
373											X	X	X	X	X			
412										X		X			X		X	

Table 4.12. Graves and bead types. The bead types defined in Brugmann 2004 and types defined for the rest of the glass beads are associated in the graves in two separate groups. The table shows the types in numerical order and not as they were shown in the matrix of the correspondence analysis.

sides (see above). The colour combination of two dark and two red globular beads in Grave 218 is a little unusual for an Anglo-Saxon grave, possibly because it is of an unusually early fifth-century date and related to 'barbarian' continental bead fashion of the fifth century making use mostly of short globular beads, a lot of them dark. Grave 219 combines red and green globular beads and an opaque yellow melon bead with four spindle-shaped amber beads considered to be a type of amber bead of an early date both in Anglo-Saxon England and on the Continent.[49] Grave 223 combines an early bead with wide crossing trails (No 65) with a blue-green and a red wound bead with eight mostly rounded amber beads, a combination also related to Group A1. In Grave 239, nine mostly rounded amber beads were

associated with a blue-green ribbed 'melon' bead, again an association that suggests an early date and affiliation with Group A1. Grave 257 combines two yellow globular beads with a green cylinder and an apparently Roman blue bead of a very unusual shape (No 38), a combination most likely related to Group A1.

Four graves, Graves 207, 254, 350B and 417, produced bead associations including 'Constricted Segmented' ('gold-in-glass') beads, but not the drawn or coiled blue Cylinders (Nos 6 and 9) that mark Group A2. The combination with four amber beads and a fossil with the 'Constricted Segmented' beads from Grave 207 however, suggests association with Group A2 rather than a later context. Grave 254 produced only light or discoloured drawn cylinders, some of which

---

49. See U Koch (2001, 162) bead combination group A.

Bead group		A1	Roman/A1	A2					A2b				A2b	B1	B1	B1	B1	B2	B1			
Bead type	wide crossing trails	Traffic Light	white/yellow cyl	MinDark	ConCyl & Coil Cyl	rounded	facetted	poly Melon-related	Melon	var Melon	Reticella	bicone	Koch49/50	Mosaic	CylPen	CylRound	Koch34	biconical	Koch20			
Type no	65	29-31	55	24	6&9	amber-r	amber-f	23	21	22	28	66	19	25	10	12	15	61	14			
Grave																						
217	1	1																		1.59	grown	
254		1		1																1.50	child	
428		1		1																1.50	young adult	
419		1	1	1	1															1.43	adult	
247			1	1	1															1.38	young adult	
391B	1	1	1		1	1														1.35	young adult	Group A1/2
293				1	1															1.31	child	
409				1	1															1.31	young adult	
432				1	1															1.31	adult	
296		1			1	1														1.20	adult	
245					1	1														1.02	adult	
407					1	1														1.02	young adult	
425				1	1		1													0.76	young adult	
204					1		1													0.42	young adult	
347					1		1													0.42	juvenile	
354							1		1	1										-0.63	young adult	
339						1		1	1	1	1		1	1	1	1				-0.66	adult	
336							1	1	1	1	1									-0.70	adult	
373							1	1	1	1	1				1					-0.73	adult	Group A2b/B
412							1			1	1	1	1							-0.74	juvenile	
331							1				1	1		1	1	1				-0.80	grown?	
222							1		1	1	1		1	1	1		1			-0.81	adult	
250												1		1	1	1		1		-0.93	young adult	
353													1	1	1	1	1	1	1	-0.97	adult	
232														1	1				1	-1.03	-	
	1.54	1.50	1.45	1.37	1.13	0.82	-0.33	-0.73	-0.74	-0.75	-0.80	-0.82	-0.83	-0.86	-0.87	-0.92	-0.98	-1.00	-1.05			

Table 4.13. The matrix of a correspondence analysis of the glass and amber bead groups from Table 4.9 and the bead types from Table 4.10.

may have been blue, and the beads therefore most likely represent Group A2. The 'Constricted Segmented' beads in Graves 350B and 417 were associated with amber beads but no other glass bead types and therefore can be considered to be part of Group A, rather than B.

Grave 245 presents a specific case because it combines beads of Group A2 ('Constricted Segmented' and 'Coiled Cylindrical') not only with amber beads, an early amethyst, a carnelian and a copper alloy bead (see below) but also with twelve large blue or light constricted segmented beads made of a single layer that do not seem to have parallels in other Anglo-Saxon graves. The amethyst bead suggests that the grave does not predate the last third of the sixth century (see below), and it therefore seems to be among the latest

Grave	blue-green	dark	light	blue	red	white	brown	green	yellow	orange	turquoise		Bead group
239	1											0.29	(A1)
326	1											0.29	
207			3									0.29	(A)
350B			22									0.29	(A2)
392			41	1								0.29	A2
417			24									0.29	(A)
427A			6									0.29	A2
407			44	6					1			0.28	A2
293		2	33	4								0.28	A2
296	1		59	3	3	1						0.28	A2
409		1	49	6								0.28	A2
432		1	16	1								0.28	A2
440			7	2								0.28	A2
245			52	7	7		1					0.28	(A2)
254		7	20	2				3				0.27	(A2)
347		1	12	3	1			1				0.27	A2
425		1	14	11								0.27	A2
441			14	7								0.27	A2
306		12		6								0.26	A1
218		2			2							0.26	(A1)
294			1	1								0.26	A
223	1	1			1	1						0.26	(A1)
428	1	4	3		1			2				0.25	A2
419		3	5	5	2				4			0.25	A2
308		1		6	2							0.25	A1
349		3		9		1						0.25	A1
336		1		7	2				3			0.24	A2b
303A					1							0.24	B2/C
204			2	2					3			0.24	A2
373		2		9	4				4			0.24	B1
339	1	12	7	7	19	9		1	17			0.24	B1
412				2	40	1						0.24	A2b
232				4	8	8		1	3			0.23	B2
331				1	10	9		1	6			0.23	B1
250				21	42	25		1	31			0.23	B1
247		1		1					2			0.23	A2
217					1	2			2			0.22	(A1)
353		1		7	18	15			42			0.22	B2
219					4			2	1			0.20	(A1)
415									1			0.20	
257				1				1	2			0.19	(A1)
391A					1			1				0.18	C
222		4	3	14	36	14		3	22		1	0.18	B2
372		1		1	1			8				0.16	
230								1				0.13	
404								4				0.13	
413								2				0.13	C
391B			38	7	1	5		5	2		2	0.11	A2
354			1	6	1	1		1	2	1		0.10	A2b
376			2					6	3	1		0.04	B2
263B				1	1			2			1	-0.72	A1
360									1	1	65	-4.24	B2
	0.28	0.26	0.28	0.24	0.23	0.22	0.29	0.12	0.19	-1.43	-4.17		

Table 4.14. The matrix of a correspondence analysis of glass bead colours. The colour of the bead bodies of both monochrome and polychrome beads are given. Composite and discoloured bead bodies are excluded. 'Dark' denotes apparently black beads. 'Light' describes the 'gold-in-glass' colour of Constricted Segmented beads. Jet is included as 'dark'. The right column gives glass bead groups after Brugmann 2004. For the bead groups listed see text.

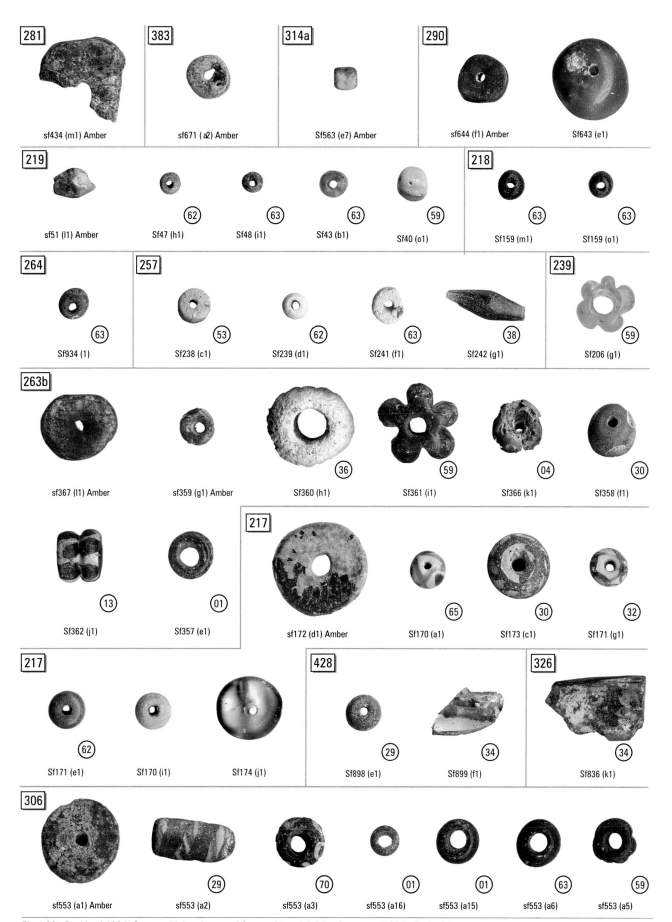

281 sf434 (m1) Amber

383 sf671 (a2) Amber

314a Sf563 (e7) Amber

290 sf644 (f1) Amber · Sf643 (e1)

219 sf51 (l1) Amber · Sf47 (h1) 62 · Sf48 (i1) 63 · Sf43 (b1) 63 · Sf40 (o1) 59

218 Sf159 (m1) 63 · Sf159 (o1) 63

264 Sf934 (1) 63

257 Sf238 (c1) 53 · Sf239 (d1) 62 · Sf241 (f1) 63 · Sf242 (g1) 38

239 Sf206 (g1) 59

263b sf367 (l1) Amber · sf359 (g1) Amber · Sf360 (h1) 36 · Sf361 (i1) 59 · Sf366 (k1) 04 · Sf358 (f1) 30

Sf362 (j1) 13 · Sf357 (e1) 01

217 sf172 (d1) Amber · Sf170 (a1) 65 · Sf173 (c1) 30 · Sf171 (g1) 32

217 Sf171 (e1) 62 · Sf170 (i1) · Sf174 (j1)

428 Sf898 (e1) 29 · Sf899 (f1) 34

326 Sf836 (k1) 34

306 sf553 (a1) Amber · sf553 (a2) 29 · sf553 (a3) 70 · sf553 (a16) 01 · sf553 (a15) 01 · sf553 (a6) 63 · sf553 (a5) 59

Fig 4.23. Buckland 1994. Graves with bead types of Groups A1 and A (after Brugmann 2004). Scale 1:1.

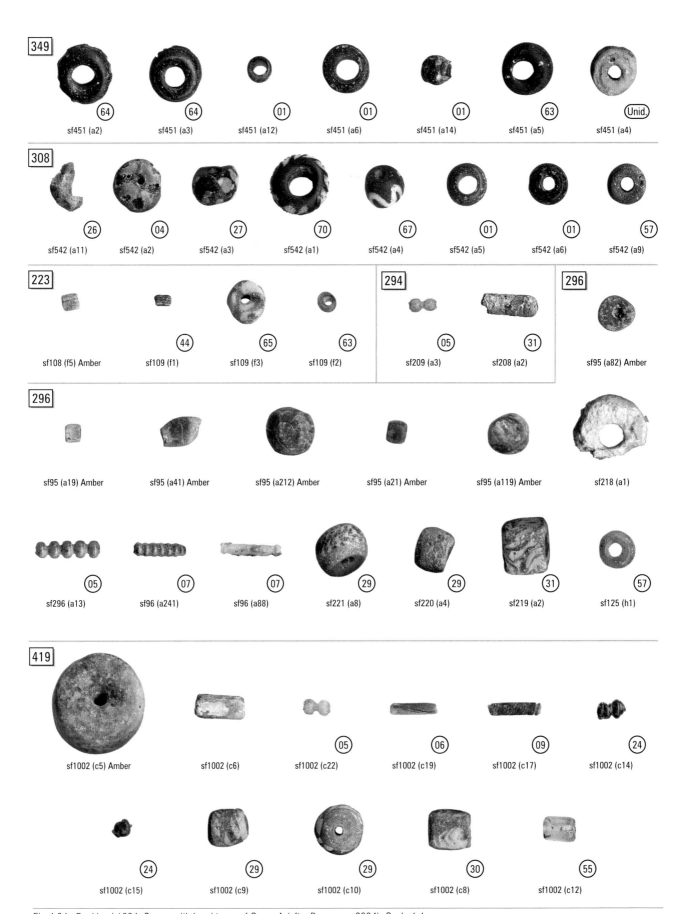

349

64 · sf451 (a2)   64 · sf451 (a3)   01 · sf451 (a12)   01 · sf451 (a6)   01 · sf451 (a14)   63 · sf451 (a5)   Unid. · sf451 (a4)

308

26 · sf542 (a11)   04 · sf542 (a2)   27 · sf542 (a3)   70 · sf542 (a1)   67 · sf542 (a4)   01 · sf542 (a5)   01 · sf542 (a6)   57 · sf542 (a9)

223

sf108 (f5) Amber   44 · sf109 (f1)   65 · sf109 (f3)   63 · sf109 (f2)

294

05 · sf209 (a3)   31 · sf208 (a2)

296

sf95 (a82) Amber

296

sf95 (a19) Amber   sf95 (a41) Amber   sf95 (a212) Amber   sf95 (a21) Amber   sf95 (a119) Amber   sf218 (a1)

05 · sf296 (a13)   07 · sf96 (a241)   07 · sf96 (a88)   29 · sf221 (a8)   29 · sf220 (a4)   31 · sf219 (a2)   57 · sf125 (h1)

419

sf1002 (c5) Amber   sf1002 (c6)   05 · sf1002 (c22)   06 · sf1002 (c19)   09 · sf1002 (c17)   24 · sf1002 (c14)

24 · sf1002 (c15)   29 · sf1002 (c9)   29 · sf1002 (c10)   30 · sf1002 (c8)   55 · sf1002 (c12)

Fig 4.24. Buckland 1994. Graves with bead types of Group A (after Brugmann 2004). Scale 1:1.

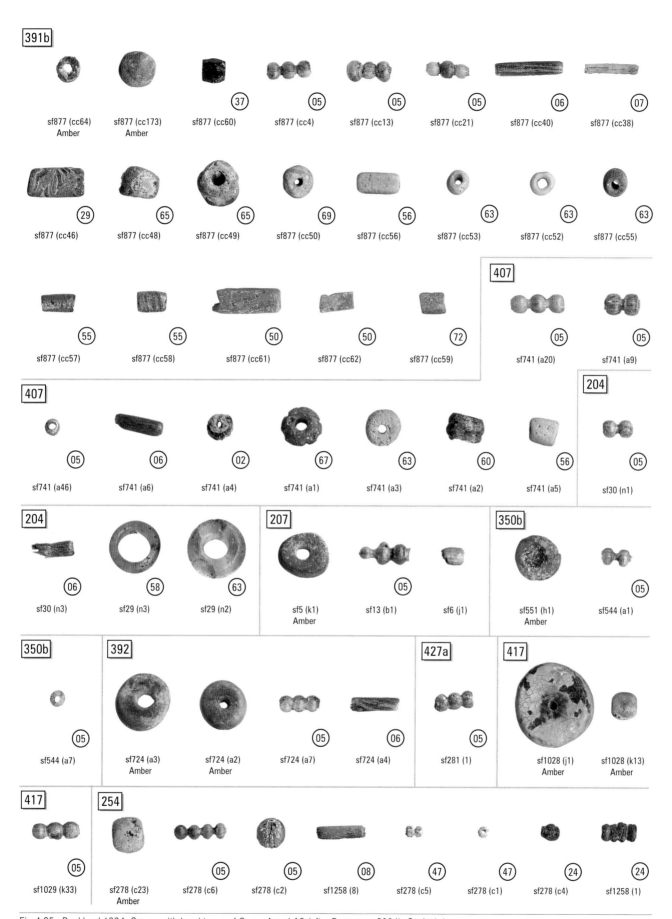

Fig 4.25. Buckland 1994. Graves with bead types of Group A and A2 (after Brugmann 2004). Scale 1:1.

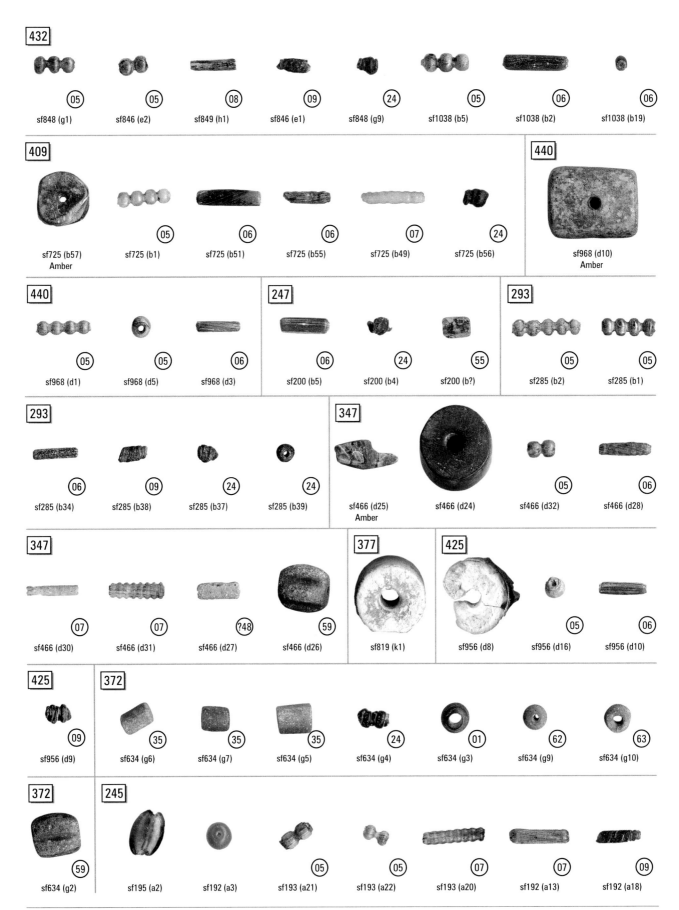

Fig 4.26. Buckland 1994. Graves with bead types of Group A2 (after Brugmann 2004). Scale 1:1.

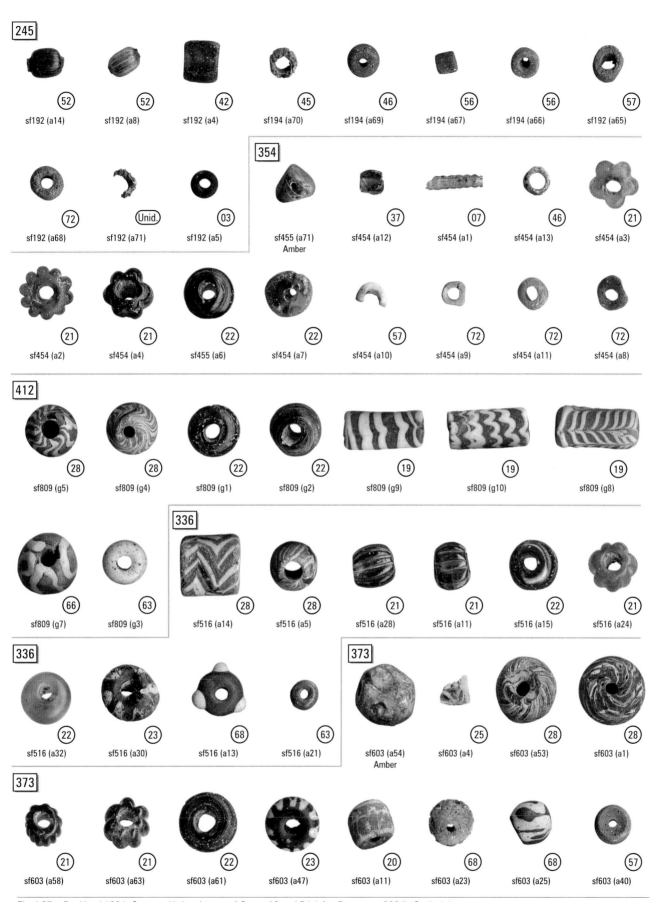

245

| sf192 (a14) ⓝ52 | sf192 (a8) ⓝ52 | sf192 (a4) ⓝ42 | sf194 (a70) ⓝ45 | sf194 (a69) ⓝ46 | sf194 (a67) ⓝ56 | sf194 (a66) ⓝ56 | sf192 (a65) ⓝ57 |

52 sf192 (a14)
52 sf192 (a8)
42 sf192 (a4)
45 sf194 (a70)
46 sf194 (a69)
56 sf194 (a67)
56 sf194 (a66)
57 sf192 (a65)

72 sf192 (a68)
Unid. sf192 (a71)
03 sf192 (a5)

354

37 sf455 (a71) Amber
37 sf454 (a12)
07 sf454 (a1)
46 sf454 (a13)
21 sf454 (a3)

21 sf454 (a2)
21 sf454 (a4)
22 sf455 (a6)
22 sf454 (a7)
57 sf454 (a10)
72 sf454 (a9)
72 sf454 (a11)
72 sf454 (a8)

412

28 sf809 (g5)
28 sf809 (g4)
22 sf809 (g1)
22 sf809 (g2)
19 sf809 (g9)
19 sf809 (g10)
19 sf809 (g8)

66 sf809 (g7)
63 sf809 (g3)

336

28 sf516 (a14)
28 sf516 (a5)
21 sf516 (a28)
21 sf516 (a11)
22 sf516 (a15)
21 sf516 (a24)

336

22 sf516 (a32)
23 sf516 (a30)
68 sf516 (a13)
63 sf516 (a21)

373

25 sf603 (a54) Amber
25 sf603 (a4)
28 sf603 (a53)
28 sf603 (a1)

373

21 sf603 (a58)
21 sf603 (a63)
22 sf603 (a61)
23 sf603 (a47)
20 sf603 (a11)
68 sf603 (a23)
68 sf603 (a25)
57 sf603 (a40)

Fig 4.27. Buckland 1994. Graves with bead types of Group A2 and B1 (after Brugmann 2004). Scale 1:1.

115

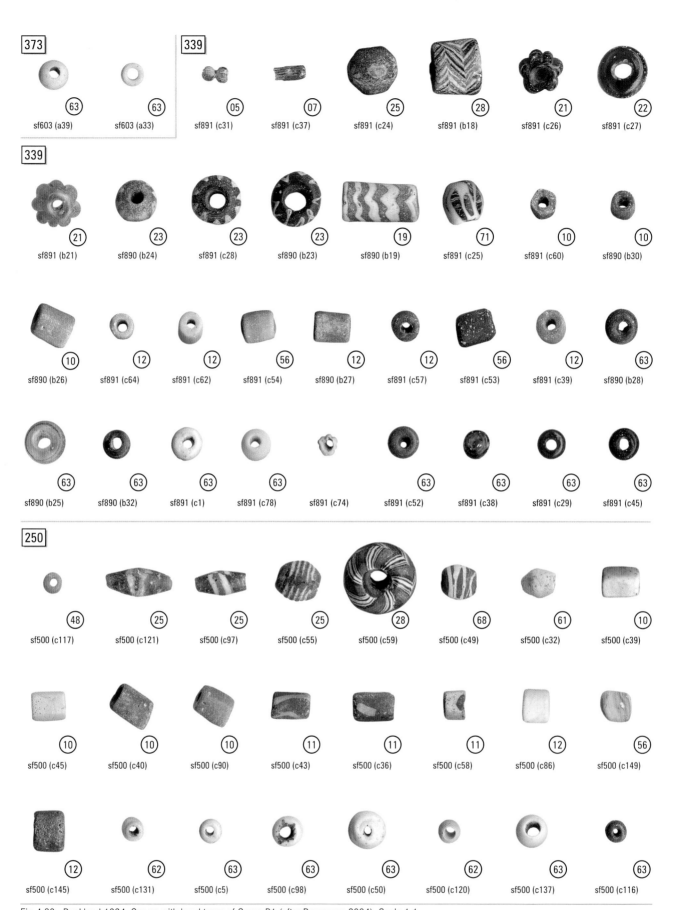

Fig 4.28. Buckland 1994. Graves with bead types of Group B1 (after Brugmann 2004). Scale 1:1.

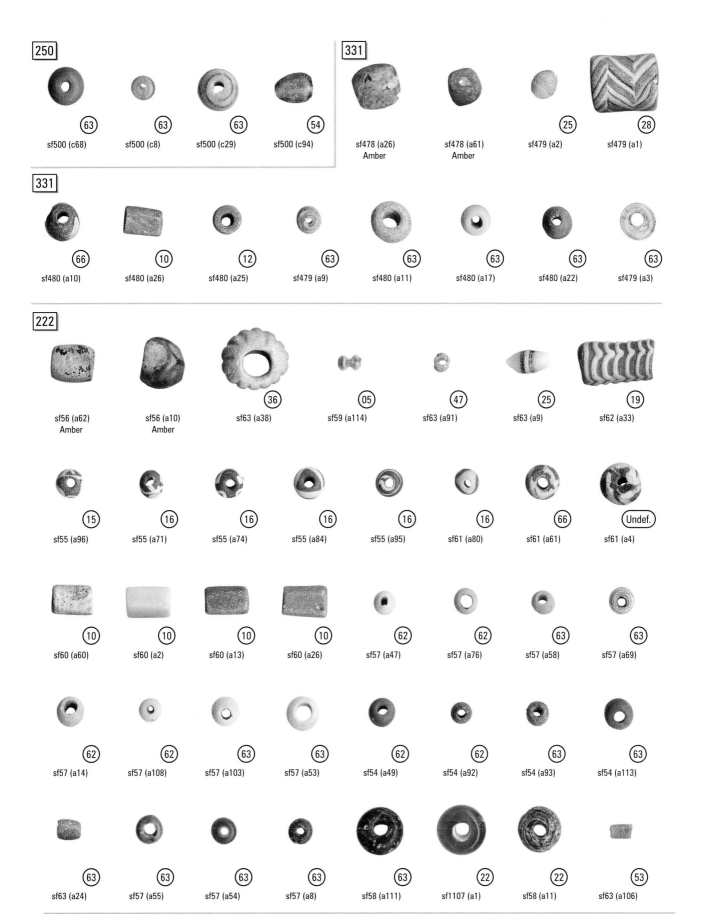

250

sf500 (c68) (63) sf500 (c8) (63) sf500 (c29) (63) sf500 (c94) (54)

331

sf478 (a26) Amber sf478 (a61) Amber sf479 (a2) (25) sf479 (a1) (28)

331

sf480 (a10) (66) sf480 (a26) (10) sf480 (a25) (12) sf479 (a9) (63) sf480 (a11) (63) sf480 (a17) (63) sf480 (a22) (63) sf479 (a3) (63)

222

sf56 (a62) Amber sf56 (a10) Amber sf63 (a38) (36) sf59 (a114) (05) sf63 (a91) (47) sf63 (a9) (25) sf62 (a33) (19)

sf55 (a96) (15) sf55 (a71) (16) sf55 (a74) (16) sf55 (a84) (16) sf55 (a95) (16) sf61 (a80) (16) sf61 (a61) (66) sf61 (a4) (Undef.)

sf60 (a60) (10) sf60 (a2) (10) sf60 (a13) (10) sf60 (a26) (10) sf57 (a47) (62) sf57 (a76) (62) sf57 (a58) (63) sf57 (a69) (63)

sf57 (a14) (62) sf57 (a108) (62) sf57 (a103) (63) sf57 (a53) (63) sf54 (a49) (62) sf54 (a92) (62) sf54 (a93) (63) sf54 (a113) (63)

sf63 (a24) (63) sf57 (a55) (63) sf57 (a54) (63) sf57 (a8) (63) sf58 (a111) (63) sf1107 (a1) (22) sf58 (a11) (22) sf63 (a106) (53)

Fig 4.29. Buckland 1994. Graves with bead types of Group B1 (after Brugmann 2004). Scale 1:1.

117

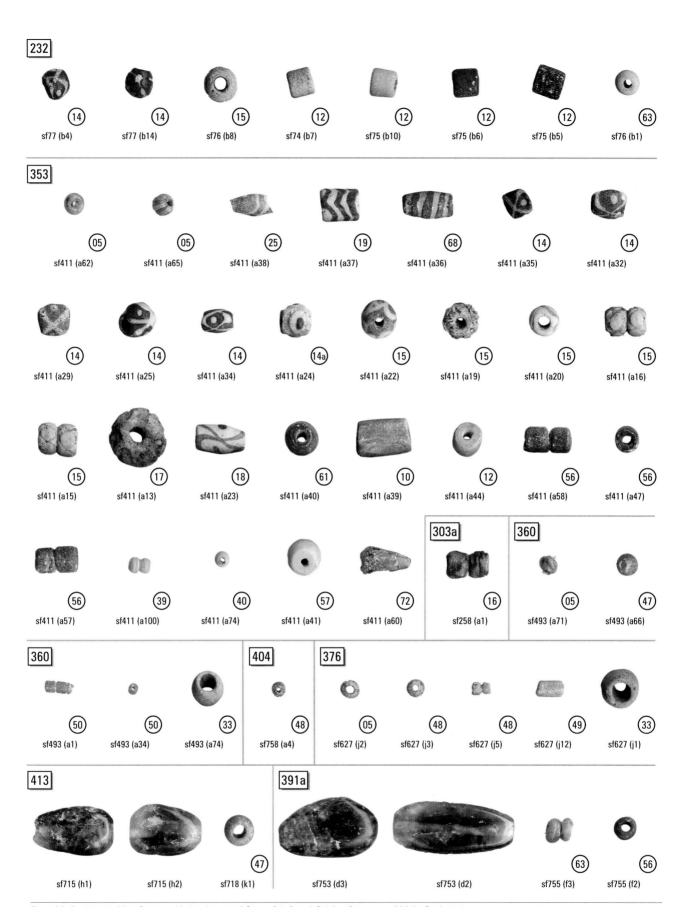

232

(14)	(14)	(15)	(12)	(12)	(12)	(12)	(63)
sf77 (b4)	sf77 (b14)	sf76 (b8)	sf74 (b7)	sf75 (b10)	sf75 (b6)	sf75 (b5)	sf76 (b1)

353

(05)	(05)	(25)	(19)	(68)	(14)	(14)
sf411 (a62)	sf411 (a65)	sf411 (a38)	sf411 (a37)	sf411 (a36)	sf411 (a35)	sf411 (a32)

(14)	(14)	(14)	(14a)	(15)	(15)	(15)	(15)
sf411 (a29)	sf411 (a25)	sf411 (a34)	sf411 (a24)	sf411 (a22)	sf411 (a19)	sf411 (a20)	sf411 (a16)

(15)	(17)	(18)	(61)	(10)	(12)	(56)	(56)
sf411 (a15)	sf411 (a13)	sf411 (a23)	sf411 (a40)	sf411 (a39)	sf411 (a44)	sf411 (a58)	sf411 (a47)

					303a	**360**
(56)	(39)	(40)	(57)	(72)	(16)	(05)	(47)
sf411 (a57)	sf411 (a100)	sf411 (a74)	sf411 (a41)	sf411 (a60)	sf258 (a1)	sf493 (a71)	sf493 (a66)

360 **404** **376**

(50)	(50)	(33)	(48)	(05)	(48)	(48)	(49)	(33)
sf493 (a1)	sf493 (a34)	sf493 (a74)	sf758 (a4)	sf627 (j2)	sf627 (j3)	sf627 (j5)	sf627 (j12)	sf627 (j1)

413 **391a**

		(47)			(63)	(56)
sf715 (h1)	sf715 (h2)	sf718 (k1)	sf753 (d3)	sf753 (d2)	sf755 (f3)	sf755 (f2)

Fig 4.30. Buckland 1994. Graves with bead types of Group B1, B and C (after Brugmann 2004). Scale 1:1.

118

graves with beads of Group A2.[50] The only grave that can be assigned to Group B, though it has none of the glass bead types that define it, is Grave 303 with a variant of type 'Koch34' (No 16) suggesting it is related to Group B2.

Just twenty-seven beads found at Buckland 1994 are made neither of amber nor glass. Bead Grave 223 (f4) is made of a black unidentified material. Bead Grave 347 (d24) is made of jet, a material used in Roman bead making. Whether the few jet beads from Anglo-Saxon contexts are Roman types or a sign of a small-scale early Anglo-Saxon output is not known. Two beads are made of the enigmatic white material often described as 'chalk'.[51] Cylindrical beads of this type are mostly associated with glass bead Group A2, as in Graves 296 and 425. Bead Grave 377 (k), however, was the only bead found in the grave. Bead 419 (c6) was possibly made of shell, though the grave is definitely too early to have contained a cowrie shell bead. Six beads were made from fossils.

Beads made of rock crystal (quartz) are usually short to medium and almost globular except for a ridge on their equator. If found with glass beads, they are usually associated with Group A1, or associations equally as early, as in Grave 217. Bead Grave 290 (e) appears to be a forerunner, or substitute for, a rock crystal ball in a sling (*see* pp 83–8) and bead Sf 970 is a stray find. Most almond-shaped amethyst beads found in Anglo-Saxon England are of the large, long, pale type imported into the Merovingian part of the Continent during the second half of the seventh century (see U Koch 1987, 346), and in the Final Phase to Anglo-Saxon England, where they were worn with glass bead Group C. Three each of this type of amethyst bead were found in Graves 391A and 413. The beads are 18–33mm long and weigh between 2 and 7g. A much smaller bead, only 13mm long and weighing less than 1 gramme, was found in Grave 245. These small beads were imported into the Frankish and Alamannic regions from the last third of the sixth century onwards (*ibid*) but are rare in Anglo-Saxon graves. The small globular carnelian bead from the same grave is probably Roman.

Buckland 1994 produced only four metal beads, two made of copper alloy, one of silver and one of gold. The copper alloy cylinder Grave 245 (a1) was found with 114 beads and was therefore presumably also used as one. The copper alloy wire wound into a coil Grave 425 (b) was also found with beads and was therefore probably used as a bead. Silver beads were introduced to Anglo-Saxon bead fashion towards the Final Phase. They are made of very thin sheets, hollow and usually double bell or almond-shaped (see Geake

1997, 42). Bead Grave 413 (n) is an almond-shaped one with a groove outlining its form. This type possibly imitated the shape of an amethyst bead, three of which were found in the same grave (see above).

The gold bead Grave 250 (c4) is made of beaded wire coiled around a tube made of gold sheet and is worn, particularly at its equator. The terminal of a beaded gold wire that may have been used for this bead was also found in the grave. Beaded wire beads made of copper alloy, silver or gold from Anglo-Saxon graves are generally dated to the Final Phase (see *ibid*). Bead Grave 250 (c4), however, is associated with glass beads of Group B1. The bead may actually be more closely related to the gold 'filigree' beads in use on the Continent during the sixth century (see U Koch 1990, 124), such as the four biconical beads in the 'Lady's Grave' under Cologne Cathedral (Doppelfeld 1960, pl 21, 13y) of earlier sixth-century date, which is also discussed above (p 83). The gold bead Grave 250 (c4) was not only associated with an enormous bracteate (above pp 89–92, Fig 10.13) but also with an impressive set of eleven spindle-shaped and two globular Mosaic beads (No 25) probably imported from the Continent as a set.[52]

In the chronological analysis in Part 8, 'Miniature Dark' beads form part of the definition of Phase 1 (type MinDark), 'Constricted Cylindrical' beads (*type ConCyl*) of Phases 1b–2, 'Reticella' and 'Melon' beads of Phases 2b–3a, 'Koch49/50' of Phase 3a, 'Cylindrical Pentagonal' and 'Cylindrical Round' beads (*types CylPen* and *CylRound*) and 'Koch20' and 'Koch34' beads of Phase 3, 'Segmented Globular' (*type SegGlob*) beads of Phase 3b, 'Orange' beads of Phases 3b–7, and cowrie shell, long amethyst (*type longam*) and Wound Spiral (*type WoundSp*) beads of Phases 5–7.

Pins and rods

Birte Brugmann

(Graves 204, 218, 222, 223, 232, 239, 240, 250, 254, 257, 260, 261, 266, 281, 290, 292, 308, 314, 326, 346, 353, 360, 376, 381, 391B, 407, 408, 409, 412, 413, 416, 419, 420, 423, 425, 431, 434, 437, 442 and 443)

In the context of early Anglo-Saxon grave goods, the term 'pin' is often used to describe anything from a needle to a substantial rod with a round–square section that may or may not have had a point. In the following, two categories of objects are discussed: copper alloy or iron pins or rods found on the upper

---

50. See Brugmann 2004 for an absolute date span for Group A2.
51. See Evison (1987, 60) on presumably the same material from the earlier excavations at Buckland.
52. For a colour reproduction of some of the beads and the bracteate *in situ* see Parfitt 1995a, 460.

part of the body, mostly close to beads or brooches, and other iron 'pins' and 'rods', mostly found at the waist with other objects such as knives. The likely use of many as fasteners for clothing is further discussed in Part 5 (p 181).

The graves of two adult males, a probable adult male and a child produced iron pins with scrolled heads (Graves 260 (a); 416 (b); 437 (d) and (h) and 442 (c)) 8–15mm long. Grave 442 is dated to Phase 1b–2 and Grave 437 to Phase 2. The distribution of this pin type, predominantly in Kent and East Anglia, suggests that scrolled pins were an Anglo-Saxon type mostly used by males.[53] Iron pins of this type from the 1951–3 Buckland excavations seem to have been used to fasten some cloth covering wrapped around spearheads (Evison 1987, 82). This, however, does not seem to have been the function of the pins found in 1994.

Pin Grave 260 (a) was found in a grave without weapons at the right waist together with other objects. Grave 437 has a sword but the two pins (d) and (h) were positioned below this. Pin (h) has a pair of tweezers and a piece of flint corroded onto it and mineral-preserved textile and cord attached to it. A tight fold of leather was wrapped around the shaft of pin (d). Pin Grave 442 (c) from a child's grave was aligned with a knife and a pursemount in what may have been a pouch or a sheath. Pin Grave 416 (b) was found above the skull together with a knife, suggesting that objects normally attached to a belt were in this case placed at the head.

Smaller pins with hooked heads were found in Grave 421 (b), on the right side of the decayed body and in Grave 434 (b) above the left pelvis. Fragments of rods with hooked ends that may have been pins were found in Grave 346 (d), above the left pelvis and in Grave 423 (c) under the right femur. Objects Graves 346 (d) and 421 (b) have mineral-preserved wood and textile attached, object Grave 434 (b) leather remains. The organics on Grave 423 (c) are not identified. Since Graves 346, 423 and 434 contained certain or probable adult males, it may be suggested that there was a specifically male use for hooked pins or rods.

Pin Grave 326 (l) has a slightly bent and possibly incomplete head and was buried with a female juvenile. The iron ?pin Grave 431 (b) found in the area of the decayed left body, with a knife has a globular head but the ?point is lost. Object Grave 443 (d) found above the left pelvis of an adult female is pointed at both ends and has attached mineral-preserved textile and leather remains. The use of these objects is not clear.

Plain iron pins (rods with points) *c* 90mm long were found left of the left femur in Graves 281 (l) and 412 (e), and between a buckle and a knife in Grave 314A (c). Possibly only the points of pins were preserved in the area of the decayed body in Grave 208 and over the left femur in Grave 409 (h). Rods, possibly originally pins, were found in Grave 281 (c) in the area of the decayed right chest and left of the left femur in Grave 266 (a). One end of rod Grave 218 (q) is woven through parallel slots cut into leather (see below) and rod Grave 266 (a) has wood remains attached to it. The copper alloy rod Grave 238B (c) is broken at both ends but narrows towards one, so that it seems likely it was originally a pin. It was found in the area of the decayed left pelvis and may have been kept in a pouch as scrap. The function of these objects from female contexts is not clear.

Iron pins found in fifteen graves in the area of the upper body and usually in combination with brooches or pendants and beads were probably used by females as dress pins.[54] The pin represented by fragments Grave 223 (d) and (e) has a hooked head, but most have globular heads[55] and some are too fragmented to tell.[56] Copper alloy pins found on the upper body presumably had the same function as the iron pins. The solid pin Grave 360 (b) has no head and is broken, but the shaft of hollow pin Grave 292 (a) rolled from a sheet of metal[57] is complete and may have had an organic head. The head of pin Grave 407 (j) is embedded in mineral-preserved textile and leather. A radiograph suggests a globular ribbed head. Pin Grave 239 (f) has a polyhedral head, a typical Roman decorative element still in use in the late fifth and possibly early sixth century, eg grave 5 at Bifrons (Chadwick Hawkes 2000, fig 4). This type is represented in Table 8.3 as 'pin with polyhedral head' (*type polypin*); Grave 239 is dated to Phase 1a.

Four pins 6–7mm in length, a pair from Grave 254 (f) and (g) and single pins from Graves 222 (c) and 257 (b), have perforated heads. Pins Grave 222 (c) and 254 (f) and (g) are flattened towards the perforation and therefore fall into Ross's type XVi.c, dated by him to the late fifth or early sixth century (Ross 1991). The pair from Grave 254 have rings attached to them, a feature also found with a pair of pins from grave 89 at Bifrons (Chadwick Hawkes 2000, fig 35) and known from earlier fifth-century inhumation burials at Sejflod in the north of Jutland.[58] Grave 254 is dated to Phase 1. Pin Grave 257 (b) was also associated with a small-long brooch and is the only perforated pin with spiral decoration,

---

53. See Ross (1991), *contra* R H White (1988). I am grateful to Seamus Ross for permission to use his unpublished PhD thesis.
54. Pins Graves 204 (l), 223 (d) and (e), 232 (c), 240 (d), 250 (c), 261 (a), 281 (c), 290 (a), 308 (d), 353 (c), 391B (g), 408 (b), 419 (g), 420 (b) and 425 (c). For details see Part 5.
55. Pins Graves 204 (l), 240 (d), 408 (b), 420 (b) and 425 (c).
56. Pins Graves 232 (c), 281 (c) and 419 (g).
57. Cf Grave 1 at Buckland 1951–3 (Evison 1987, 83).
58. See, eg, Graves D1, TO and TR (Nielsen 2000).

possibly a Roman type. Grave 257 is dated to Phase 1. The single pin in Grave 222 dated to Phase 3a may be an heirloom re-used when pins came into Kentish fashion again.

In an Anglo-Saxon context, pairs of pins are best known from graves of the late Final Phase. It seems, however, that pairs of pins were also used in the earliest Anglo-Saxon dress in Kent, as is suggested by Grave 254 at Buckland and grave 89 at Bifrons. The pair of pins and small brooches from Buckland Grave 254 were worn by a child 4–5 years old and may not represent a typical dress combination. Pairs of pins with attached rings are represented in Table 8.3 as *type 'pinpair'* forming part of the definition of Phase 1a.

It seems that the combination of a pair of pins and a pair of brooches has neither a Saxon nor a Frankish background. The best known continental parallel to the Kentish evidence is grave 421 at Altenerding in Bavaria (Sage 1984, pl 54), which produced a type of pin very close to the pair from Bifrons. Both pairs have perforated heads and rings attached to them, and a swelling below the perforation marking the beginning of the shaft. The pins from Altenerding, however, were associated with a brooch of the Ozengell type (see Parfitt and Brugmann 1997, 45f), a cross-bow brooch and a neck-ring, a combination Werner (1970, 78ff) labelled as Scandinavian, also on the basis of the pair of pins.[59] In the most recent study of the evidence from Altenerding, Magnus (forthcoming) points out that the use of pairs of pins in fifth- to sixth-century Scandinavian, Baltic and Anglo-Saxon contexts needs to be analysed in more detail before any conclusions can be drawn.

Graves 376 (i) and 413 (l) each produced short copper alloy pins decorated with mouldings. The pin from Grave 413 is only 24mm long and may originally have had an organic head. Pin Grave 376 (i) is 45mm long and has a flat disc-shaped head and a square cross section below the moulding. Evison dated pins shorter than 60mm in length 'usually in bronze, with a disc or spatulate head and moulding in the middle of the shaft to improve anchorage', mainly to her Phases 3–6 (Evison 1987, 84). Pins with mid-ribs are listed in Table 8.3 (*type ribpin*) as part of the definition of Phases 5–7. Pins with a plain discoid head, 30–60mm long and with lines incised into the shaft (type L, after Ross 1991) are known mainly from Kent, but also from southern East Anglia and the Upper Thames valley and do not seem to appear before the late sixth or early seventh century (Ross 1991).

Leather remains on pins and rods　　*Fleur Shearman*

Iron rod fragment Grave 218 (q) was associated with traces of textile and leather. This fragment retains evidence of

mineral-preserved leather including two cut loops in the leather through which the shaft passes. This rod fragment originally formed part of rod fragment (g). Other iron rods and pins have associated leather, including Grave 260 (a), with traces of leather thong around the head; Grave 414 (d) (*fiche à belière*), associated with leather around the head; Grave 434 (b), with remains of leather on shank; Grave 443 (d), with associated leather on one side; Grave 444 (f), with a leather suspension/attachment thong. Grave 437 (d) has associated leather which curves around the iron rod with the remains of stitching along one edge. Grave 391B (y) contains an iron strip with associated leather/skin product. Cordage is preserved on the head of an iron pin from Grave 260 (a).

Ear-rings

Birte Brugmann

(Graves 351 and 413)

Ear-rings were not a regular part of women's dress in Kent or elsewhere in Anglo-Saxon England, and the use of a copper alloy wire ring found by the skull of a girl buried in grave 18 at Mill Hill, Deal, is not clear (Parfitt and Brugmann 1997, 70; 116). The position of two silver wire rings (i) and (j) in Buckland Grave 413 (Phase 5–7), left and right of the skull of an adult female, however, revives the discussion on the use of silver wire rings in Final Phase graves (see Geake 1997, 48f). A third wire ring, Grave 413 (m), was found on the upper chest, apparently as an ornament in its own right. This is a common feature in Final Phase contexts (*ibid*). It seems possible that the wire rings Grave 413 (i) and (j) were part of the same decorative arrangement as ring (m), which had become dislocated, but it also seems possible that in this case the slip-knot rings were actually parts of ear-rings, a hair ornament or head-dress. U von Freeden (1979, 412f) points out that the term 'ear-ring' in a continental context relates to the position in which such objects are mostly found, that is close to the ears, but that the rings do not need to have been attached to the ear-lobes; they could equally have been elements of a hairstyle or head-dress.

The copper alloy polyhedral ear-ring in Grave 351A (c) was found at the waist of a grown male together with a knife, an iron fragment and a coin, suggesting it was contained within a purse. Cast penannular ear-rings with a pointed and a polyhedral-shaped terminal have a wide distribution in continental row-grave cemeteries but are not closely datable (*ibid*, 296f).

---

59. See also Jørgensen and Nørgård Jørgensen (1997, fig 46) on Sejlflod.

Bracelets

Birte Brugmann

(Graves 207, 219 and 388)

Bracelets were found with two adult females (Graves 207 (h) and 219 (m)) and possibly also with an infant less than one year old, Grave 388 (j). Slip-knot ring Grave 343 (b) was found in the left upper half of the grave. Bone preservation was poor, and though it seems possible that this ring was also used as a bracelet, its small diameter (only 37mm) and untidy manufacture, as well as its position at the upper, instead of the middle left of the grave, suggests that this was not the case. The copper alloy slip-knot ring Grave 433 (b) is large enough to have been used as a bracelet, but the remains of a leather ?thong attached to it and the position of the object, close to brooch (a) probably worn at the neck, renders this unlikely.

The bracelets worn by adults were positioned on the lower left arm, which confirms the use of Grave 207 (h) and Grave 219 (m). Bone preservation in Grave 388 was poor but the slip-knot ring (j) was positioned in the centre left of the grave and with a diameter of 42mm it is large enough to have been worn as an armlet by a child. Slip-knot rings with the same likely function were found in two children's graves at Mill Hill, Deal (Parfitt and Brugmann 1997, 69).

Bracelets were a common part of late Roman (Philpott 1991, 143) but not Anglo-Saxon female dress. In the upper Thames region, bracelets are found mostly with children and in fifth- and early sixth-century contexts (Dickinson 1976, 200). The same tendency is apparent in the Kentish material. Anglo-Saxon finds include late Roman glass bracelets[60] and are mostly found in graves of Kentish Phases I and II.[61] The use of bracelets may indicate Roman influence both in the earliest Anglo-Saxon graves and in the Final Phase.[62]

Bracelet Grave 219 (m) has a round cross-section and extremely worn stylised ?lion head-shaped terminals, flat on one side and decorated on the other. The same type found in grave 6 at Bifrons was interpreted by Kilbride-Jones (1980, fig 21, 13) as a re-used annular brooch with a missing pin. According to Baldwin Brown (1915b, 457), however, 'A close examination of the Bifrons piece has failed to disclose the slightest trace of the former presence of a hinged pin' and in view of comparative continental finds declared it 'under

reservation' to be a bracelet. Considering the existence of a late Roman bracelet type with round section and terminals of this form (see Konrad 1997, 59ff) it seems more likely the Bifrons and Buckland finds were actually produced as bracelets.[63] Table 8.3 lists them as type 'armlet' as part of the definition of Phase 1a.

Finger rings

Birte Brugmann

(Graves 204, 250, 253, 271, 288, 290, 298, 339, 408 and 409)

The 1994 excavations at Buckland produced nine finger rings (Graves 204 (i/j), 250 (c3), 253 (a), 271 (b), 288 (a), 290 (c), 298 (b), 408 (f) and unstratified find Sf 1235) and two possible finger rings (Graves 339 (e) and 409 (e)). All the rings from graves were found with adults, definitely or probably female. Six of the rings are made of silver (one with a garnet-set bezel), three are copper alloy and one is of iron. The iron ring Grave 288 (a) was found on the 'ring' finger of the skeleton, silver ring Grave 271 (b) around a finger and silver ring Grave 408 (f) with the 'ring' finger of the left hand. The silver ring with the garnet bezel Grave 204 (i/j) was positioned in the area of the left hand, as was the copper alloy ring Grave 290 (e). The silver wire rings Graves 298 (b) and 253 (a) were found in the presumed area of the decayed left hand. The copper alloy ring Grave 409 (e) with a white metal surface was positioned above the left hand, together with an iron lozenge and some fittings. As a finger ring, it would have been made for quite a large, presumably male, finger. The silver finger ring Grave 250 (c3) was found together with pendants on the upper chest and was presumably also suspended from the neck. The copper alloy ring Grave 339 (e) was also found at the neck, together with a scutiform mount (d), and may have been made, or at one time used, as a finger ring.

Finger rings worn on the left hand, usually by women, follow Roman tradition in the Gallo-Germanic provinces and are also found in Britain (Philpott 1991, 142ff). It seems that not only the habit, but also some of the types used, found their way into Anglo-Saxon fashion.[64] Most finger rings from Anglo-Saxon graves are made of metal strips or wires. The cast ring Grave 290 (c) with a bezel comes from one of the earliest graves on site, and is therefore particularly

---

60. Evison (1965, 21) and more recently, grave 2 at Orpington, Kent (Tester 1968).
61. Note that the bangle in grave 16 at Lyminge (Warhurst 1955, fig 10, 7) is too large for a bracelet and was found at the foot of the grave.
62. See Schulze-Dörlamm (1990, 184) and Geake (1997, 113).
63. A further find of a late Roman bracelet with a round section and ?lion head-shaped terminals was made at the Mucking settlement, Essex (Hamerow 1993, 61, fig 112.1).
64. See Schulze-Dörlamm (1990, 170), MacGregor and Bolick (1993, 169) and Konrad (1997, 85).

noteworthy. Finger rings made of wire coiled into a bezel such as Graves 250 (c3) and 298 (b) are not an invention of the early medieval period, but they are more common in Anglo-Saxon than in Roman graves and are therefore likely to have been produced during this period.

The most common type in Anglo-Saxon graves, however, are spiral rings made of decorated or undecorated strips of metal, mostly silver (Malim and Hines 1998, 217) Graves 253 (a), 271 (b), 408 (f) and Sf 1235. This type of ring is comparatively rare in Roman and continental row-grave cemetery contexts, despite being particularly practical because of its adjustable size and is therefore likely to be an insular product. The possible 'closed' finger ring Grave 409 (e) and the wire ring Grave 339 (e), with terminals that hardly overlap, however, are just as likely to be of Roman as Anglo-Saxon date.

Ring Grave 204 (i/j) is the only one from Buckland with an garnet-inlaid bezel in a silver framework soldered onto a strip of metal. This is a type well known from west Frankish row-grave cemeteries and is dated there to Böhner's phase II/early III (Schulze-Dörlamm 1990, 182f). However, ring Grave 204 (i/j) is the first ring of this type known from a Kentish context.[65] This is not surprising considering that finger rings on the Continent are not as commonly found as brooches, despite the fact that the production of a finger ring with an inlaid bezel requires considerably less material and skill than the production of a cast brooch. This suggests that finger rings had a more specific function than brooches in both Anglo-Saxon and Merovingian dress codes. At Buckland 1994, they were found in graves covering Phases 1b–3a.

Wrist-clasps

John Hines

(Grave 326)

Grave 326 contained unmatched hook- and catch-halves of wrist-clasps (Fig 10.34d and i), an artefact-type common in Anglian England, north of the Thames and the Chilterns, but alien to the material culture of Kent (Hines 1984, 35–109). In this case, the hook-piece could not fit in the catch-piece to form a functioning clasp.

The catch-piece (d) is a clasp-half of form B 7, altogether the commonest form known. This consists of no more than a single sheet of metal (copper alloy), with perforations through which it was sewn to the garment. The decoration

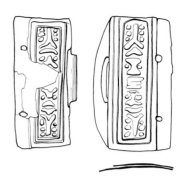

Fig 4.31. Pair of clasps from Cleatham, Lincolnshire. Scale 1:1.

comprises three rows of repoussé bosses, again the most familiar type (Hines 1993, 39–43 and 117–18). The hook-piece (i) is of a more complex but structurally closely related form, carrying an applied, thin copper alloy plate with repoussé ornament (form B 13 c; Hines 1993, 51–2). In this case the perforations for sewing pass through both the applied plate and the base-plate. Although the decoration in this case is severely rectilinear, the end panels contain stylized full-face masks (truncated at one end), and this specimen should therefore be counted amongst the examples with zoomorphic decoration rather than linear (which is in fact normally curvilinear). The closest known parallel is in two identical pairs of clasps from Cleatham, Lincolnshire (now South Humbside), grave 30 (Scunthorpe Museum), on which the nature of the masks is much clearer (Fig 4.31).

The occurrence of these two clasp-halves in a grave in Kent is unexpected, and points to a connection with the Anglian areas in the Midlands and further north in England. It is not entirely unparalleled, as two pairs of more elaborate Class C clasps are known from Bifrons: these pieces, however, had all been adapted and refitted for use as brooches on the costume (Hines 1993, 69–70). The two unmatched and non-fitting clasp-halves from Grave 326 were found with a group of metal items just below the waist of the skeleton in the grave, where they presumably formed part of a collection of scrap ready for recycling (cf Malim and Hines 1998, 216, for a particularly clear example of this practice in grave 3 at Edix Hill, Cambridgeshire). The collection also included a copper alloy annular brooch (b) of a form more familiar in Anglian England than in Kent (*see* p 74).

In any individual case, it seems idle to speculate on how objects such as these may have moved from one material-cultural province to another. Nonetheless, the presence of two different clasp-halves of relatively humble and common types

---

65. A gold ring with an inlaid quatrefoil bezel from a rubbish deposit at Dover (Philp 1973b, 10; 2003, 111) is of much better quality and a later date. For a comprehensive study see Filmer-Sankey (1989).

renders it reasonably likely that at some stage a woman who was dressed in Anglian style was resident in this part of eastern Kent (cf Hines 1996 for a similar case based on a clasp-half and other Anglian items found in a limited area of north Wiltshire). Such connections are also implied by the occurrence of an East Anglian form of great square-headed brooch at Faversham (Hines 1997a, 118–33, pl 61b). A full review of the evidence for Anglian material in, and influences on, Kent might now pay dividends. The chronological dimension could be significant here. All of the wrist-clasp-types concerned can be dated to the sixth century, more likely towards the middle of that century rather than earlier, a dating which also applies to the Faversham great square-headed brooch. There could conceivably be a context here for the curious phenomenon of the adoption of the scutiform pendant in Kent in the middle to later sixth century (as in Buckland Grave 245) while it is frequently found in earlier contexts in Anglian areas (Hines 1984, 225–32).

Buckles and belt fittings

Sonja Marzinzik

Ninety-one belt buckles were recovered from eighty-five different burial contexts, with six graves containing two examples. Some of the buckles were associated with additional fittings such as belt studs or other belt mounts (Figs 4.32 and 4.33) but another four contained fittings only. The graves belonged to men, women and children, and all age groups were present, although most buckles came from adult graves. In addition, there are six unstratified buckle finds (Sf 305, 409, 568, 923, 1236 and 1265). Amongst these Sf 568 is of medieval date and clearly post-dates the use of the cemetery. Out of the total of ninety-six Anglo-Saxon buckles recovered from the 1994 site, seventy-three consisted of a loop only and twenty-three were associated with a buckle-plate.

Buckles without plate

(Graves 204, 205, 207 (x 2), 209, 217, 223, 230, 248, 249C, 252, 255, 259, 262, 263A, 266, 296, 297, 302, 308, 311, 314A, 319, 327, 331, 333, 335, 336, 337, 339, 340, 344, 346, 350A, 350B, 354, 363, 367, 368, 372, 373, 374, 377, 381 (x 2), 391B, 392, 394, 395, 398 (x 2), 406, 407, 409, 412, 414, 417, 419 (x 2), 423, 426, 427A, 428, 432, 435, 436, 437, 442 and 443; Sf 409, 923, 1236 and 1265)

The majority of buckle-loops without plate are oval or D-shaped copper alloy loops with narrowed axis for the attachment of the tongue, and tongue shields of various shapes. Fourteen shield-tongue buckles represent the largest group among these. This originally Frankish buckle form is regularly found in Kentish cemeteries from the sixth century but is much less common in other regions of Anglo-Saxon England (Marzinzik 2003). The buckle from the Phase 2b Grave 204 has an unusual, recessed tongue shield with an inset Style I copper alloy sheet and three matching shoe-shaped studs. Another recessed shield-tongue comes from Grave 398 (c), although the ring-and-dot decoration is directly applied to the tongue shield in the same manner as in Frénouville, Calvados, grave 255 (Pilet 1980, pl 55). Recessed shield-tongues are unusual and two examples with inset ring-and-dot decorated sheets were found at Watchfield, Oxfordshire and Hérouvillette, Calvados with a *terminus post quem* of c AD 540/45 (Martin 1989, note to Abb 10). Recessed tongue shields with various insets seem to have been popular in Normandy, as there are many examples, eg from Saint-Martin-de-Fontenay (Pilet 1994, graves 108, 142 and 239) or Frénouville (Pilet 1980, graves 75, 197 and 255). The shield-tongue buckle (f) from Buckland Grave 222 was associated with a triangular copper alloy plate. At the nearby cemetery of Mill Hill, Deal, grave 63 produced a similar combination with a sub-triangular plate and buckle with trapezoid tongue shield (Parfitt and Brugmann 1997, 139). This grave is dated to Kentish Phase III/IV, which is earlier than the Kentish Phase V date of Buckland Grave 222 (belonging to Buckland Phase 3a; see Table 8.4). Silver, parcel-gilt sheet covers for a buckle of D-shaped outline, a shield-tongue and two shoe-shaped studs are all that remains of the buckle in the Phase 2–3a Grave 423 (f) (Fig 4.32). How they relate to the plain copper alloy tongue from this Kentish Phase III–V burial is unclear, as it is too narrow to fit well into the cover fragment for a shield-tongue. Although rare, silver sheet covers are not unknown. They occur, for instance, on a buckle with club-shaped tongue from Zürich Bäckerstraße with a *terminus post quem* of AD 536 (Moosbrugger-Leu 1971, Taf 22.9; Martin 1991a, 90, note 133). An interesting piece in the context of shield-tongue buckles is the Buckland stray find Sf 305. The kidney-shaped copper alloy loop features a flattened tongue base with lateral grooves. Such grooves are an indicator of a fifth-century date and are found on late and sub-Roman buckles with animal head decoration (eg Böhme 1974, Taf 92.7, 92.13) as well as early Germanic pieces (Hills and Hurst 1989, fig 1). They have been shown to later develop into the shield-tongues discussed above (Martin 1989, 132ff).

Twelve buckles feature a club-shaped tongue, ie one with a thickened base with cut-off end. Buckles with a club-shaped tongue are an originally eastern form that first appeared in the mid fifth century (Wieczorek 1987, 424) and became popular in Francia and north of the Alps. As opposed to shield-tongue

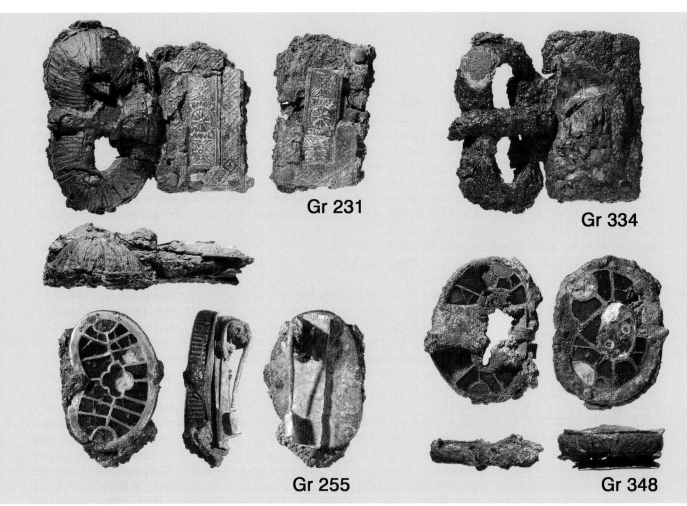

Fig 4.32. Buckland 1994. Buckles from Graves 231, 255, 334 and 348. Scale 1:1.

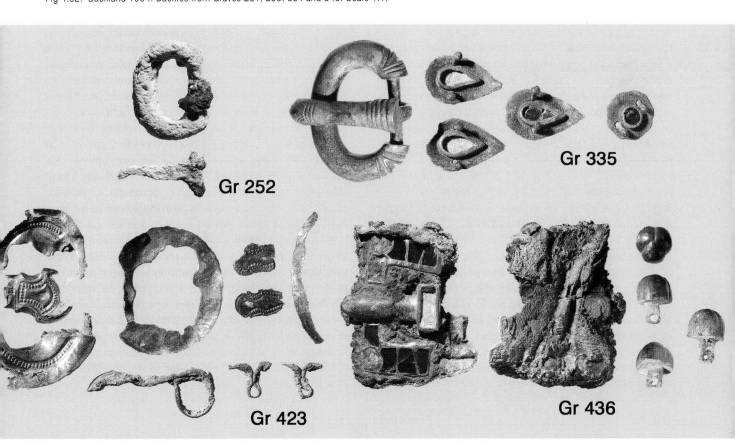

Gr 252

Gr 335

Gr 423

Gr 436

Fig 4.33. Buckland 1994. Buckles from Graves 252, 335, 423 and 436. Scale 1:1.

buckles they are also found throughout the Mediterranean (Martin 1989, 133). In Anglo-Saxon England they are most frequent in Kentish contexts, just like shield-tongue buckles (Marzinzik 2003). Club-shaped tongues can be strongly waisted, such as in Buckland Grave 409 (d), which is an indication of a sixth-century date (Moosbrugger-Leu 1971, 121). If the back of the tongue forms a ridge and the loop cross-section is round or hollow, as with the buckle with plate from Grave 417 (e), an early date, in the later fifth or early sixth century is likely (Wieczorek 1987, 424; Siegmund 1998, 21). Grave 252 (b) contained one of the exceptional bone buckles known from Anglo-Saxon England (Fig 4.33). Two similar bone pieces came from the mid or late fifth- to sixth-century graves at Petersfinger grave 26 (Leeds and Shortt 1953) and Pewsey grave 94 (Marzinzik 2003; 2010), in Hampshire and Wiltshire, respectively. Traces of a white metal finish, possibly tinning, marks out the buckle from Grave 381 (e). The unstratified buckle Sf 1236 shows extensive traces of gilding. Although standard on brooches, this is a rare feature of Anglo-Saxon buckles.

In the male Grave 297 a buckle with a club-shaped tongue and three dome-headed studs (c) was apparently associated with a translucent light-blue glass cabochon in a copper alloy setting with beaded wire rim (d). The stud (d) was secured by means of a metal wire bent into a loop, the ends of which were fed through a slot in the base-plate of the mount and hammered flat. Six set cabochon garnets were found in female graves from the earlier Buckland excavations. They differ from the mount here not only in their use as pendants, but apart from one were all set in precious metal (cf Evison 1987, 56). Cabochon pendants are typical of female costume of the 'Conversion Period' (Geake 1997, 39f). There are, however, no parallels for belt studs from this period.

On the other hand, the attachment of stud Grave 297 (d) by a copper alloy wire loop at the back is rather more characteristic of early finds. Périn illustrates a heart-shaped, garnet-inlaid belt stud from Bourcq, Ardennes with such an attachment (Périn 1980, fig 51). It is dated to his Phase A/B/ D1 for north-eastern France, which finishes around AD 475. It appears that some of the garnet studs from Childeric's grave had such or very similar loops on the back as well (Evison 1965, fig 8). Other studs set with garnet or glass cabochons of various shapes are known from the Crimea, Tunisia, Hungary, Bohemia, Switzerland and the Netherlands. They may have either rivets or loops for attachment and their use is unclear as they seem to have been associated with belts and pouches as well as seax sheaths (Quast 1993, 55). Their dating is centred on the Flonheim-Gültlingen Phase (Ament

1970, 65; Quast 1993, 54),[66] ie between about AD 480 and 510 (U Koch 2001, 83). Many of these finds share not only a similar attachment, but also the beaded wire rim around the setting. These finds are very different from the massive U-shaped wire sunk into a circular disc attached to the back of the sword-scabbard buttons from Sutton Hoo mound 1 (Bruce-Mitford 1978, fig 222, a–f).

Another seven buckles have tongue shields varying from rectangular or square over stepped to trapezoid. Dates range from the later fifth or early sixth century in Grave 437 (Phase 2) to the late sixth century in Grave 354 (Phase 2b). The rectangular tongue shield from Grave 209 (a) is particularly interesting. It is ornamented with grooves that imitate the appearance of tongue bases set with rectangular garnets. On the Continent, unconstricted tongues with such bases have been dated from the later fifth into the early sixth centuries (Wieczorek 1987, 422f). There are also a number of buckles, normally with garnet-inlaid plates of the later fifth to early sixth centuries, with a rectangular tongue base set with two garnets. Northern French-Belgian examples are a buckle from Eprave (Böhme 1994, Abb 20.20), or Bourcq, Ardennes (Périn 1998, fig 8). Buckles with a number of different tongue shield forms also occur on other Kentish sites. Examples are a trapezoid tongue shield from Buckland 1951–3 Grave D (Evison 1987, 215) and other forms from Mill Hill, Deal, grave 63 (Parfitt and Brugmann 1997, 139), Lyminge grave 42 (Warhurst 1955) and a late find from Polhill, grave 28 (Philp 1973a). Grave 30A at Westgarth Gardens, Suffolk, contained a buckle with rectangular, now empty tongue base, which was probably already old when buried (West 1988; Marzinzik 2003). There are thirteen loops which resemble in their shape and narrowed axis the buckles discussed above. They have, however, either lost their tongue or they have a simple, indistinct tongue, most likely a replacement.

Two of the buckle-loops from the earlier Buckland excavations were rectangular and there is a rectangular copper alloy frame from Grave 207 (c), possibly a buckle that has lost its tongue. The adult of indeterminate sex in Grave 436 was buried with an extraordinary garnet and glass cloisonné buckle with a gilt tongue (b) (Fig 4.33). No close parallels are at present known from Anglo-Saxon England.

A number of similar buckles with a narrowed axis and an inlaid tongue base are known, albeit normally associated with a rectangular or kidney-shaped cloisonné plate. The find from Grave 436 should therefore be seen in the context of the buckle from Grave 348 (c) and the brooch made from a buckle-plate from Grave 255 discussed below. A close parallel to Grave 436 is the late fifth-century rectangular

---

66. I would like to thank Patrick Périn, for drawing these finds to my attention.

loop with kidney-shaped plate from grave 68 at Charleville-Mezières, Ardennes (Périn 1975). The garnet-inlaid loop shares the semi-circular insets in two of its corners and the gilt tongue. While these two cells contain now deteriorated glass at Buckland, the French buckle has ivory inlays.

The heavy, high-tin buckle from Grave 331 (b) belongs to a small group of very similar buckles from southern England. All have a narrowed axis for the attachment of the tongue, which is often shield-shaped and usually has a strongly curved tip. A decorated example came from Buckland Grave 31 while other nearby examples are Mill Hill, Deal graves 65 and 81 (Parfitt and Brugmann 1997). On the Continent, similar buckles have been found from Switzerland, over the Rhineland into northern France. Many of those buckles are narrower, however, and were connected with pouches or knife sheaths (Marti 1990, 80). This buckle type mainly dates to the sixth century, but occasionally continues into the seventh (Moosbrugger-Leu 1971, 128; Siegmund 1998, 40).

The remaining loops are oval, D-shaped or round, mostly iron pieces. Only the iron loops from Graves 426 (a) and 311 (a) stand out. The former has an applied copper alloy sheet on the upper face of both loop and tongue while radiographs of the latter show transverse wire inlay. The round copper alloy buckle from Grave 308 (b) is extremely unusual, as it has a central transverse bar through which the iron tongue is fixed. With the flat loop cross-section and the decoration of punched crescents this buckle closely resembles an annular brooch. As it was found by the left waist of the old woman, associated with the knife, there is no doubt of the use as a buckle. There are no good parallels and the closest comparison can be drawn with a small number of buckle-loops from the later Roman Iron Age, which have been found in southern and eastern Germany and in Poland (Garbsch 1966, 69, Taf 26.14; Madyda-Legutko 1987, 81, map 10). They are, however, figure-of-eight-shaped and not round with a central bar and the tongue is in all cases looped around the central axis rather than fixed through it.

Buckles with plate

(Graves 222, 228A, 231, 245, 251, 261, 264, 265B, 281, 287, 289, 301, 324, 325, 334, 340, 345, 347, 348, 375, 408 and 417; Sf 305)

Only twenty-three buckles had a plate attached to, or at least closely associated with, the loop. In contrast to the buckles without plates, a much larger variation occurs. Many forms are only present in one or two examples, even though they belong to well-defined types found elsewhere.

Among the earliest pieces with plate are three buckles with a decorative sheet applied to the iron plate. In Grave 408 a

copper alloy loop (e) was covered with silver sheet and the separate plate, (j) and (k), had an applied copper alloy sheet with a tendril border. The decoration of the central field is now illegible. The plate with copper alloy sheet from Grave 334 (a) was associated with a kidney-shaped loop (Fig 4.32). The decorative sheet with traces of white metal plating is strongly deteriorated but the composition appears similar to Grave 408 with a border and central panel. Grave 231 produced a complex suite of similar type (a). In addition to the wire-inlaid kidney-shaped loop with plate, there is a matching belt fitting (Fig 4.32). Both the iron plate and fitting carry an applied copper alloy repoussé frame surrounding a central repoussé silver sheet. Although kidney-shaped buckles with and without plate, in iron or copper alloy and with or without inlay, are common finds on the Continent, buckle-plates with applied decorative sheet as at Buckland are an Anglo-Saxon characteristic. A small number of similar buckle-plates are known from Anglo-Saxon England. The closest parallels are a find from grave 41 at Kingsworthy/Worthy Park, Hampshire, with an applied sheet with tendril ornament around a central field and a buckle-plate with similar composition in exquisite repoussé from Alfriston grave 24 (Evison 1965, fig 16d, pl 5c; Hawkes with Grainger 2003, fig 2.28.1.1; Welch 1983, fig 8c). The Sussex cemeteries of Alfriston and Highdown and the cemetery at Droxford, Hampshire, moreover produced several iron buckles with wire-inlaid plates including tendril ornament (Welch 1983, figs 4, 120; Aldsworth 1978, fig 48).

A stunning and unusual piece is the oval garnet inlaid loop with garnet inlaid tongue base and a now separate rectangular plate with extensive remains of gilding and set with five garnet roundels from Grave 245 (g). The buckle-loop can be compared to the oval loop from Grave 348 (c) and to the rectangular loop from Grave 436 (b) and has numerous counterparts on the Continent, from northern France, into Hungary and the Mediterranean (Werner 1966, Abb 2 and 7; Böhme 1994, Abb 22). As opposed to that, there are no exact matches for the buckle-plate. It has to be seen in the tradition of high-rectangular buckle-plates inlaid with garnets of various forms, often drop-shaped, set flush and sometimes without backing foils. These individual high-quality pieces of the late fifth century can be made from exotic materials, such as the amber plate from Straubing Bajuwarenstraße, Bavaria (Geisler 1998, Taf 99, Gr 16.1). Other similar plates are known from Picardie, via Italy, the Rhineland and Hungary (Böhme 1994, Abb 20.22–20.24, 21.15) to Asia Minor and the Caucasus (Quast 1993, liste 6, Abb 50, map Abb 51). This technique of setting stones, which differs from the common Mediterranean and northern European cloisonné, has been traced back to Sassanian or Afghan origins (Ament 1970, 55ff).

Apart from Grave 245 (g) and the rectangular buckle-loop discussed above, there are another two garnet-inlaid pieces from the 1994 Buckland excavations. One is the cloisonné buckle with kidney-shaped plate from Grave 348 (c) (Fig 4.32), whereas the other, from Grave 255, is a kidney-shaped buckle-plate that was transformed into a brooch (b). The inlay on the buckle (c) from Grave 348 is a composition of glass, garnet and a central shell slip (Scientific BM report 6710.52697R). The plate from Grave 255 was at some point equipped with a copper alloy pin and iron spring mechanism on a copper alloy plate (Fig 4.32). Again, for these cloisonné pieces numerous parallels from northern France, over the Rhineland to the Mediterranean, can be quoted (eg Werner 1957, 327ff and map fig 27; Kazanski 1994, List I.1; Böhme 1994, Abb 21.1, 22.7–8). Closer to home, two buckles with inlaid kidney-shaped plates were excavated at Lyminge (Warhurst 1955, pls IX, X); one was found at the King's Field, Faversham (Åberg 1926, fig 178; de Baye 1893, pl 12.2) and another one comes from Finglesham grave 204 (Chadwick Hawkes 1982b, fig 2; Chadwick Hawkes and Grainger 2006, 152, fig 2.148).

The buckle with semi-circular iron plate and wire-inlaid oval loop from Grave 261(b) is another early piece, dated to Phase 1. The narrow transverse brass inlay on the loop indicates a fifth-century date (Evison 1958, 243; Martin 1976, 87) and good parallels from Essex and Sussex, as well as from continental cemeteries, exist. Often, such buckles have a semi-circular to kidney-shaped decorative sheet applied to the iron plate, as on the buckles from Petersfinger grave 29 (Leeds and Shortt 1953, pl VI) and Highdown, Sussex, grave 9 (Welch 1983, fig 92) but there are no traces of such a feature here.

The two buckles from Graves 265B (e/f) and 281 (g) both have moulded decoration on the plate. The male burial Grave 265B contained a copper alloy, white metal-plated belt suite. It consisted of a buckle with stepped tongue shield (f), a cast rectangular box with hollow back applied to the plate and three dome-headed rivets arranged along the rear plate edge, plus two matching fittings. This suite is typical for a group of belt sets known as Type *Ennery* after a find from the French Moselle area. An almost identical set, but with only two rivets along the plate and fitting edges, was excavated in Bifrons grave 43 during the nineteenth century, while another set with three rivets but slightly differing grooving of the plate came from grave 74 there (Chadwick Hawkes 2000). Other suites of Type *Ennery*, which so far are only known from male graves, come from north-eastern France and southern Germany and were often used in connection with the sword belt (Windler 1989, 195f, Fundliste 3). There is indeed a sword in this grave, although it seems to have been deposited by the left side of the body rather than being linked to the belt (*see* p 49, Fig 10.83). Bifrons graves 43 and 73 appear to have contained seaxes, judging by the descriptions of a 'dagger' and 'hunting knife' both found with smaller knives in one sheath (Chadwick Hawkes 2000, 35, 52).

The exact reconstruction of the suite is not possible now, as it cannot be confirmed that all fittings were found face-up. Continental belt suites often have a fitting that is worn at waist height behind the back and consequently found face down in the grave. Buckland sword Grave 98 contained a similar tinned suite of three fittings and a bayleaf-shaped strap-end. However, no buckle was found, the fittings have only two rivets at each end and their decoration of crossed bands is rather different from Type *Ennery* (Evison 1987, fig 47). In this grave, all fittings were found at waist height, but as one of them was indeed face-down, it had probably been fixed to the back part of the belt (cf reconstruction in Evison 1987, 88).

The buckle from Grave 281 (g) was decorated with a half-cylinder on both tongue shield and plate. Two very similar buckles, however with ribbed decoration covering a larger proportion of the half-cylinders, were found in Mill Hill, Deal, graves 71 and 86 and were dated by Brugmann to Kentish Phase II, which corresponds to Buckland Grave 281 (assigned to Buckland Phase 1b). Like the Buckland burial, the Mill Hill graves were female. In Buckland Grave 38 a more complex buckle with a Style I decorated half-cylinder was found, which belongs to the late sixth century (Evison 1987, 89).

Grave 264 at Buckland contained an unusual iron buckle with applied silver decoration (d). The plate is rectangular near the loop, then narrows to a strip and has an enlarged terminal. The large disc-headed silver rivets relate this piece to a group of buckles almost exclusively distributed north of the Thames (Marzinzik 2003). They have a rectangular plate and usually two large rivets made from a material different to the plate to produce a visual contrast. At Buckland, such a buckle was found in Grave 301 (b). The best parallel to the buckle from Grave 264 (d) is, however, a buckle from Lechlade, Gloucestershire, grave 112 (Boyle *et al* 1998, fig 5.79). Radiograph evidence suggests that grave 20 at Snape in Suffolk contained a belt buckle with matching counter-plate similar to Grave 264 (d) and the Lechlade find (Filmer-Sankey and Pestell 2001, 61, fig 98).

Later types from the 1994 Buckland excavations include five buckles with triangular plates. Two are iron, the other three copper alloy. The largest and most elaborate piece comes from Grave 251 (c). The iron plate carries the remains of three rivets, two of which still have their lead-filled copper alloy domes and notched collars. For the Trier and Moselle areas, hollow copper alloy rivets with notched collars from seax sheaths have been dated to the seventh century, occasionally even later (Schulze-Dörrlamm 1990, 300). Ursula Koch (2001, 284), however, suggested that such rivets already are widespread in her South German Phase 5, ie from about AD 530 to 555. The mushroom-shaped tongue shield of buckle Grave 251 (c) contains remains of an inset identified as glass by scientific examination (BM Laboratory Report 6710-100). Examples of such tongue shields occurred in copper alloy in the male Grave 4 at Buckland and garnet-inlaid at Harford Farm, Norfolk, grave 12 (Penn 2000) and Alton, Hampshire, grave 16 (Evison 1988). Other buckles with such tongues have been found mainly in Kent, but also in Essex, Cambridgeshire and Buckinghamshire (Speake 1980, pl 6–8). Mushroom-shaped tongue shields, rare in Anglo-Saxon England but common on the Continent, indicate a date around AD 600, or in the early seventh century (Schulze-Dörrlamm 1990, 240f).

Graves 289 and 345 produced two similar miniature copper alloy buckles with fixed triangular plate. Dating is complicated. There were no other grave goods to assist with the chronological evaluation of the damaged burial Grave 345 and additionally the buckle (a) was found in the south corner of the grave pit. Grave 289 contained a number of châtelaine items and a knife. These would be in keeping with the dates of four similar buckles from St Peter's, Broadstairs, grave 76; Finglesham grave 95 (Evison 1979, fig 36k; Hawkes and Grainger 2006, fig 2.102.8.1–8.5) and Holborough grave 7 (Evison 1956, fig 6). Buckles with fixed triangular plate occur in southern Germany already in the second half of the sixth century (U Koch 2001, Abb 16), but all three English parallels are dated to the seventh century. On site, Grave 289 was thought to be cut by Grave 290 but analysis of the grave goods has suggested that the order should be reversed because Grave 290 is datable to *c* AD 450–510/530, Phase 1 (*see* p 30). This then allows for a later dating of buckle Grave 289 (h).

The remaining buckles have plain rectangular copper alloy or iron plates. The most recent buckle from the site is the gilt copper alloy stray find Sf 568. Its axis is partly concealed by the buckle-plate, but the loop is identical to a find from Exeter (Goodall 1984, fig 190.70). Its narrow, D-shaped, copper alloy loop is slightly thickened either end of the axis. These minute protrusions are often found on medieval buckles and the Exeter loop came from a late thirteenth- or early fourteenth-century context (Goodall 1984, 347). I Fingerlin (1971, 49, no 27) illustrates a similar loop with ribbed decoration on the tongue rest from Strasbourg, which she dates to the third quarter of the thirteenth century. This ties in with the notion that D-shaped buckle-loops were more common in the thirteenth and fourteenth centuries, while later, rectangular, trapezoidal and loops with a transverse

internal bar became popular (Whitehead 1996, 16). The use of the Buckland stray find is difficult to determine, as similar buckles were used as dress-fittings, for sword belts, armour and horse harnesses in the medieval and post-medieval era (Margeson 1993, 24), although copper alloy was probably more common with dress accessories than horse equipment (Egan and Pritchard 1991, 50). Whatever its precise function, it seems certain that this buckle is not derived from any Anglo-Saxon grave and it must be connected with subsequent medieval activity (*see* pp 12–14).

The belt studs

(Graves 204, 271, 245, 255, 271, 296, 297, 319, 327, 331, 335, 339, 350, 373, 381, 391B, 407, 412, 419, 423, 428 and 436)

Decorative studs of various forms, mainly shoe-shaped and dome-headed, were found in twenty-two graves. They were normally associated with buckles without plate and served to fasten the end of the leather strap which had been looped over the axis of the buckle. There are exceptions, as no buckle was found in Grave 271 and Grave 245 contained a buckle with a plate as well as one shoe-shaped and two disc-headed studs. Judging by their positions in the grave, however (Fig 10.78), none of these three studs was associated with the belt fastened by the buckle. Between one and three studs could occur in association with the belt and the four small disc-headed studs from Grave 419 (e) were part of a bag or châtelaine complex by the left thigh of the deceased. Four studs were also found in Grave 335 (a). Three of them are drop-shaped, while one is round (Fig 4.33). They all share a central setting, which still contains a garnet with one of the drop-shaped studs and a red glass cabochon in the case of the round stud. Their individual character links them to the gilt mount with a semi-circular garnet set without backing foil from Buckland Grave 21.

Shoe-shaped studs are rarely found before the mid sixth century (Martin 1989, 135) and large examples, such as those from Grave 331(b) are more characteristic of the second half of the century. On the Continent, they often occur in threes but are also found in pairs or even singly, which does not necessarily imply a loss in antiquity (*contra* Evison 1987, 87). Dome- and cone-headed studs are more recent types of belt stud from Buckland 1994. Both varieties are rare in Anglo-Saxon England and, depending on the type, on the Continent date to the second half of the sixth and on into the seventh century (cf above). The flanged studs with ribbed cone from Grave 327 (d) have few insular parallels, for instance from Bifrons, in grave 11 and in the Conyngham Collection nos 184–5 (Chadwick Hawkes 2000). No good comparative pieces are known for the two heart-shaped studs with applied silver sheets from Grave 381 (c).

The use of belt studs, as well as their shoe-shaped and dome-headed forms, follow continental fashions. Indeed, all studs were found in graves which contained originally continental buckle types, ie with copper alloy loops with shield- or club-shaped tongue or other tongue shield forms and with the rectangular buckle from Grave 331. Interestingly, of the twenty-two graves with studs, seventeen belonged to women, judging by their finds' gender. Only two burials were male, the remainder indeterminate, although three of the archaeologically female graves were osteologically sexed as possibly male. The high proportion of women reflects the situation at Buckland 1951–3 and Anglo-Saxon England in general. This is a major difference to the Continent, where belt studs are more typical of male costume (Marzinzik 2003).

Iron lozenges are another type of fitting or mount, which are occasionally found in association with the belt (*see* p 162).

Strap-ends

(Graves 204, 222, 255, 265B, 290, 373, 412 and 417)

Of the eight graves which produced strap-ends, three (the female Graves 204 and 417 and the male burial Grave 265B) each contained two strap-ends. The two in Grave 204 (h) form a proper pair and were found between the deceased's calves, and the almost identical pieces from Grave 417 (b) were found fused together next to a silver-mounted crystal ball between the knees. The strap-ends in Grave 265B (g) and (h) are similar but not a pair and were located at the left side, at approximately waist height. One of them was above the belt set while the other one was below it and perhaps associated with the belt end (Fig 10.83).

Six of the strap-ends have the shape of bay leaves. They hardly occur outside Kent (Marzinzik 2003) but are more widespread on the Continent and also in Scandinavia and often made from silver (Parfitt and Brugmann 1997, 75). Early forms of such strap-ends are already present in the third-century 'Princess Grave' from Haßleben in Thuringia (Schulz 1933, Taf 7). It is here and in Bohemia that leaf-shaped strap-ends were most popular during the Migration period (Schulze-Dörrlamm 1990, 234). In Kent, they are most typical of the sixth century (Evison 1987, 90) and several bay-leaf-shaped strap-ends were excavated at Bifrons. One of them, from grave 73, has cast ridges on the back (Chadwick Hawkes 2000), similar to those from Buckland Grave 373. Bay-leaf-shaped strap-ends were

found in the 1951–3 Buckland excavations, for instance in Grave 98.

U-shaped strap-ends made from two sheet metal plates riveted together, such as in Grave 204, were particularly common north of the Thames in the sixth century (Marzinzik 2003). They appear to represent a development independent of the continental-type strap-ends with split end and two rivets (Parfitt and Brugmann 1997, 76). The two strap-ends from Grave 417 follow this construction principle, but have only one rivet. Finally, there is a rectangular strap-end from Grave 290 (g), made from one sheet of metal bent over and riveted together, which was associated with a group of objects that was presumably suspended from the belt and found outside the woman's left thigh.

As to the function of strap-ends, pairs are often part of shoe or garter fittings, while single pieces can belong to belts, pouches or even horse harnesses (Schulze-Dörrlamm 1990, 279).

Gender

Buckles from male graves were less common than those from female graves, whether the osteological sex or the gender displayed through grave goods, is examined (Table 4.15).

The proportion of the genders is interesting in view of the buckles without loop, which belong to originally continental types. Judging by finds' gender, ten out of the fourteen shield-tongue buckles and half, or just over half, of all buckles with a different tongue shield or club-shaped tongue were found in female graves. This reflects the general situation on Anglo-Saxon sites, where shield-tongue and buckles with club-shaped tongue, similar copper alloy loops and rectangular buckles are more common in female than male (or indeterminate) burials (Marzinzik 2003). On the Continent, the situation is exactly the opposite and, particularly, shield-tongue buckles are more typical of male graves (Parfitt and Brugmann 1997, 74). Burials with indeterminate grave goods at Buckland 1994 are represented among most buckle types, but constitute only a minority of the continental buckle types.

	Finds gender	Osteological sex
Female	33	22
?Female	4	13
Male	18	22
?Male	1	14
Indeterminate	29	14
Total	85	85

Table 4.15. Sex and gender for the graves with buckles.

Grave	Object letter	Details
209	a	leather around tongue
228A	b	leather noted, no details
230	a	leather near tongue
231	a	leather between plates
245	g	amorphous organic remains
252	b	leather on hinged tongue
259	c	leather on edge of buckle
261	b	leather on rivet side of back-plate
262	d	leather on the inside of the back-plate
263A	b	leather strap
264	d	shield buckle; leather on tongue, between plates, strap stiffener and rivets
265B	e	leather on counter-plate of buckle
281	g	leather between plates
296	c	possible leather on tongue
301	b	leather between plates
302	a	leather on bar, loop and tongue
311	a	leather on bar, loop and tongue
314A	b	leather strap
319	a	leather on bar, loop and tongue
319	b	shoe-shaped rivet with associated leather
319	c	tinned domed-headed stud with associated leather
324	a	leather between plates
325	a	leather between plates
327	d	associated leather
331	b	pair of shoe-shaped belt-rivets associated with buckle, possible remains of leather
333	a	leather inside loop and on tongue
334	a	possible leather between plates
339	a	leather on bar and tongue, in association with; three shoe-shaped belt-rivets with remains of leather
340	b, c	leather between plates and over tongue
344	a	leather on buckle bar and loop
344	b	belt-rivet with remains of leather
345	a	possible leather around tongue; possible leather, evidence for sewing thread through back-plate perforations
347	i	leather between plates
350A	b	associated leather
350B	c	associated leather
363	c	possible leather on bar
367	d	amorphous organic remains
373	h	leather around hinge bar, back of tongue and shoe-shaped rivets
375	d	associated leather
377	g	leather around bar
391B	o	leather on back of loop; separate fragment of a double thickness of leather in close association with textile
394	a	leather remains on loop and across tongue
395	b	leather on both sides of the loop
398	b	leather around bar
406	b	leather on inside of loop
409	d	leather on inner loop, bar and tongue
412	b	leather on bar and tongue, leather also found with the associated pair of shoe-shaped rivets
414	f	leather on the inner face of the surviving half of the back-plate and on the tongue
417	e	leather between the plates, strap-ends associated leather retrieved from the knee area
419	e	leather on back of loop and reverse of associated rivets of buckle
419	f	buckle with three associated rivets, associated leather
427A	g	leather on inside of loop and across tongue
428	c	buckle and rivets with associated leather
432	d	leather on bar and underside of loop
435	a	leather on back of tongue plate
443	b	leather on back of tongue plate
Sf 1265		(unstratified find) associated leather

Table 4.16. Occurrence and position of leather on buckles.

Age groups

Seventy-eight graves with buckles belonged to adults and there are another two possibly adult graves. This includes all graves with more than one buckle and the four burials which only contained belt fittings other than buckles. The youngest of the five children buried with a buckle was only 3 to 4 years old. The 8- to 10-year old girl in Grave 392 was the only child with a grave assemblage indicative of gender that included a shield-tongue buckle. It is one of the rare children's graves with a continental buckle (Marzinzik 2003, 72). In general, children tend to be buried without grave goods (Crawford 1993, 85) and buckles were no exception. The iron buckle with a kidney-shaped loop from Grave 334 (a), which was found with the disturbed burial of a 6- to 8-year old is therefore all the more remarkable. It has been pointed out, however, that if the burials of sub-adults were furnished at all, they could be furnished quite lavishly (Crawford 1993, 85). Another example might be the girl's burial, Grave 20, from Buckland, which contained a shield-tongue buckle and two disc-headed rivets, but doubts have been raised as to whether this was a child, or that of a juvenile (Crawford 1993, 85).

Leather found in association with iron and copper alloy buckles   *Fleur Shearman*

Of the ninety-seven buckles from the 1994 excavations over half were recorded as retaining surviving evidence of the material used for a strap or belt. The organic material was noted either around the rivets, between the plates where the belt was fastened, in those buckles which had a back-plate, or in the tongue area of the buckles where the opposing end of the belt or strap was passed through. In simple forms of buckle there is evidence for leather both on the tongue and on the hinged axis where the belt was attached. The occurrence of leather around the tongue area on buckles is an indicator that the buckles were fastened onto the dressed body at the time of burial. Buckles found at waist level may be interpreted as belt buckles.

To ascertain whether any of the buckles were fixed to a textile rather than a leather belt, all associated organic remains were carefully examined under magnification to discriminate between and identify the multiple layers. Organic material in direct association with the buckles proved to be exclusively from leather belts and straps, while that in indirect association was more commonly related to layers of garment textiles worn under or over the buckles

and adhering to upper, lower or both surfaces. Where there were separate belt-rivets, the occurrence of organic remains around the shanks and the inside faces of the rivet-heads were examined for evidence in the same way.

The miniature buckle and plate from Grave 345 (a) has traces of fibres instead of rivets passing through two of the three rivet-holes. Amorphous remains of possible leather under the plate would indicate that the buckle was secured to its strap by a sewing thread.

Of a total of fifty-four buckles which retained evidence for the associated strap or belt, forty-six could be identified as leather on the basis of the identification of one or more diagnostic features. An additional five were identified as probably leather where this was strongly indicated using the criteria of Archaeological Leather Group guidelines, as formulated by Esther Cameron. No evidence for belts made wholly of textile was noted. There is a very close textile association with a detached fragment of two layers of leather, possibly from a folded strap from a leather belt, associated with a high-tin buckle and three shoe-shaped studs, from Grave 391B (o). The textile appears to partly encircle the leather fragment rather than merely to adhere to its surface and what appear to be large stitching threads are also present on an area of the woven textile. This initially raised the possibility of an unusual leather textile composite but Penelope Walton Rogers (*see* p 182) interprets the evidence as garment textile lying in close association. Although there is no positive evidence, the possibility that some belts may have been made up of a textile band with reinforced leather ends cannot be entirely discounted by the localised evidence preserved on the buckles themselves. Garment textile remains found in indirect association with the buckles have been identified and interpreted by Walton Rogers in Part 5.

Vessels and containers

Ceramic vessels

Ailsa Mainman[67]

(Graves 219, 234, 238B, 251, 295, 307, 308, 338, 371, 376, 377, 384, 387, 388, 389, 392, 418, 422 and 441; context 390)

Nineteen pots have survived from the 244 graves in the Buckland 1994 excavations, representing only 8 per cent of

---

67. Report submitted in 2003.

Category based on osteology	Grave nos	No of vessels
Children	307, 376, 388, 392, 422, 441	6
Juveniles	234, 418	2
Adult females	238B, 308	2
Adult ?females	219, 387	2
Adult males	338	1
Adult ?males	251, 295, 371	3
Indeterminate (?child)	377, 384, 389	3

Table 4.17. Sex and age category for graves with ceramic vessels.

the burials; single pots were found in each of these nineteen graves. Substantial parts of a twentieth vessel came from a hillwash layer above the Upper Terrace, and was possibly also originally associated with a grave. Further sherds found in the soils over the cemetery might relate to other vessels which have been shattered and destroyed. It seems clear, however, that here, placing pots in graves was not common practice. Similarly, from the Buckland 1951–3 excavations, 171 graves produced only eight vessels, all but one being imported wheel-thrown pots (Evison 1987), the majority of which are likely to be later in date than the vessels considered here.

Of the nineteen graves with pots, fourteen had other grave goods and five (Graves 234, 307, 338, 371 and 418) had no other furnishings. Only three of the graves which included pots amongst their grave goods could be described as well-furnished (Graves 219, 376 and 377). Two of the graves had some evidence for internal structural features (Graves 388 and 392; Table 3.1). In the 1951–3 excavations all the graves with pots had some other grave goods, though none was richly furnished.

Most of the vessels recovered in 1994 were associated with children, juveniles and females. This is summarised in Table 4.17.
Although few, if any, bones survive from Graves 377, 384 and 389 the size of the grave cut suggests that they are of children (*see* pp 21–2). Thus, only four graves with pots are males or possible males, four are of females or possible females and the rest are children or juveniles, suggesting that this was a rite most commonly associated with the young. In Grave 87 (1951–3) the hand-made vessel was from an adult male, the remainder included male, female and juvenile burials and Evison concludes that most were associated with young people (Evison 1987, 94).

Position of pots in graves

Pots were found placed either beside the skull (eleven examples) or near the feet (eight examples). There is no correlation of age or gender and position of the vessel in the grave, which might suggest that the positioning of the pot was insignificant. The two imported bottles, however, are both placed near the legs, a position favoured by all but two of the vessels from Buckland 1951–3. The two exceptions are Grave 139, where the pot appears to be near the head but very few bones survived, and Grave 87 where the single hand-made vessel was placed to the left of the skull, a common position for the 1994 vessels.

Decoration on pottery

Five vessels are undecorated (Graves 307, 371, 384, 388 and 389) and the rest have some form of decoration. Four of the undecorated vessels are associated with children or possible children (Graves 307, 384, 388 and 389) and one with a possible male (Grave 371). Two of the graves with undecorated vessels had no other grave goods (Graves 307 and 371). There may, therefore, be some correlation between undecorated pottery and age, but only slight evidence of an association between plain forms and lack of wealth or status.

Pottery forms

The pottery forms allow some groups to be identified.

Group 1: small plain cups (Graves 307, 384 and 389)

This group includes small, undecorated cups of similar size, one of which has the remains of a handle, Grave 307, Plot T. Insufficient of the other two (from Graves 384 and 389, both in Plot X) survives to know whether these originally had handles or not. All three are from children's or supposed children's graves.

Group 2: small biconical vessels (Graves 441, 422, 238 and context 390)

This group of small biconical forms includes pottery from two children's graves (Graves 441 and 422, both Plot Y), one adult female (Grave 238, Plot V) and from the hillwash layer, context 390. The vessels from Grave 238 and 422 have very similar decoration, paired stabs on the neck, with bunches of grooved decoration arranged below on the carination and lower body, but the fabrics are distinct (see below). The vessels from Grave 441 and 422, however, have similar fabrics but somewhat different schemes of decoration. The fragmentary vessel from context 390 is decorated with a series of bosses and linear grooves.

Fig 4.34. Grave 388, child's feeding vessel *in situ*. Scale 10cm.

Group 3: biconical vessels (Graves 308, 418, 338, 377, 392 and 219)

This group of biconical and sub-biconical vessels is clearly related in terms of form to Group 2, but the size of the vessels is greater. It includes vessels from Graves 308 (an adult female) and 338 (an adult male), 418 (a juvenile ?female), 377 (a female, on the basis of grave goods) and 392 (a child). Apart from a similarity of form, those from Graves 308, 418 and 338 share similar decorative schemes of neck rings or grooves below which are various arrangements of vertical bunches of line and groove decoration. The vessel from Grave 377 is unusual as it has a 'fret' or 'wurm' pattern on the neck ring, and the wide-mouthed vessel from Grave 392 is something of an outlier to the group; the decoration in this case is a continuous pattern of line and groove below a neck ring. The handful of surviving sherds from Grave 219, an adult ?female, may be from a vessel of this type.

Group 4: rounded forms (Graves 388, 371, 295 and 387)

These vessels with rounded forms were all found within graves in Plot X. Two vessels of this group have plain rounded forms and everted rims (Graves 388 and 371). The vessel from Grave 388 is remarkable for the infant's feeding spout which has been attached to the rounded body of the vessel (Fig 4.34). This had apparently been used in an unsuccessful attempt to nourish an infant of 6–12 months buried in a simple box or coffin (*see* p 34 and Fig 10.107).

On the grounds of form, the vessel from Grave 387 can also be included with this group; it is somewhat larger and is simply decorated with a neck groove, and grooves or slashes around the body. Grave 387 is that of a ?female; Grave 371 is the unfurnished grave of an adult ?male. The sherds with another adult male grave, Grave 295, suggest a rounded form, again simply decorated with shallow incised neck rings and chevron decoration. Apart from the pot only an iron knife was recovered from this grave.

Group 5: imported bottles (Graves 251 and 376)

Only two imported bottles were recovered from the 1994 excavations as opposed to seven in 1951–3. One came from Grave 251 in Plot W and the other, from Grave 376 in Plot X. These two wheel-thrown bottles are similar in shape, but that from Grave 251 is substantially larger than that from

Grave 376. Both are quite simply decorated with incised line decoration; wavy lines in the case of the harder fired vessel from Grave 376, and concentric rings in the case of the softer fired vessel from Grave 251. Grave 251 is that of a ?male buried with an iron spearhead, knife, buckle and plate, whilst Grave 376 is that of a child (aged 7–8) whose grave is the most richly furnished of all those which contain pottery. The character of the grave goods suggests a girl. In this case, therefore, there is an apparent association between an imported vessel and inherited wealth or status in the community.

Group 6: shouldered vessel (Grave 234)

The vessel from the juvenile Grave 234 in Plot S has a distinctive shouldered form not seen amongst the other vessels. It is decorated very simply with shallow neck grooves and bunched scratched lines, and the surface has not been lavishly burnished. The grave had no other grave goods.

Pottery fabrics

Examination of the fabrics has been restricted to some extent by the completeness of the vessels; they were either found intact or have been reconstructed, masking breaks. Of the latter, however, there are often non-joining sherds which could be examined. The surface burnishing of some of the complete vessels has also made examination of the fabrics difficult, although abraded patches have allowed some features to be remarked.

Hand-made wares

The vessels from Graves 377 (Plot X), 418 (Plot Y), 308 and 338 (Plot T), 441 (Plot Y) and context 390 (area of Plot X) group together on the basis of the appearance of the fabric, but also on the grounds of surface treatment and technology. They have in common a reddish sandy matrix with some large rounded and sub-rounded quartz sand grains. All have pin-prick voids on the surface resulting from calcareous inclusions leaching out. Several have organic impressions on the surfaces.

Grave 238B (a) is a harder sandier fabric unlike any of the others, although it still has small surface voids and organic impressions. Graves 371 (a) and 384 (a) have a very dense scatter of quartz sand in a fabric which is reduced throughout, and has fewer less obvious calcareous inclusions. Grave 219 (g) and Grave 295 (a) have greater amount of calcareous inclusions; in the case of Grave 219 (g) these are visible in the surviving sherds, in Grave 295 (a) they have largely

leached away. The feeding bottle from Grave 388 (i) has many leach holes but is virtually free of organic impressions on the surfaces.

The other vessels are all of similar fabrics though there are variations in the amount of quartz sand and calcareous inclusions, probably chalk. Some have occasional fresh or patinated flint inclusions and either unworked clay, mudstones or grog.

With the exception of the imported bottles the vessels are likely to be Kentish products, a conclusion reached by analysis of the single hand-made vessel from Buckland 1951–3, where the inclusions were 'consistent with a derivation from Kentish sediments' (Evison 1987, 93).

Imported wares

The two bottles from Graves 251 and 376 occur in what Evison has defined as Fabric I (Evison 1979, 24) and are both red in colour, a common feature of Kentish examples (*ibid*, 46). Fabric I is described as 'normal' and occurs in a variety of colours, red, grey, buff with rounded sand grains of fairly equal in size, some grog and smoothed or burnished surfaces. Analytical work on this broad fabric type showed that it clustered with an example from Wierre Effroy in northern France and with sherds from a kiln site at Huy in Belgium (Evison 1987, 93).

Position of graves with pots in the cemetery

Of the nine burial plots identified in the 1994 cemetery area (Plots R to Z), six produced graves with pots. No pots were found within graves in Plots R, U or Z, and only one each in Plots V and W (Graves 238 and 251, respectively). Two graves with pots were found in Plot S (Graves 219 and 234) and three in Plot T (Grave 307, 308 and 338). These seven graves with vessels include two males, three females, a juvenile and a child. They are spread across Plots S, T, V and W, which are situated on the lower part of the excavated area, with burials similarly aligned, and include a number of well-furnished graves.

The majority of the pots came from graves in Plot X (Graves 295, 371, 376, 377, 384, 387, 388, 389 and 392) and Plot Y (Graves 418, 422 and 441) on the upper part of the site. These twelve graves include seven women and children, one ?male, on the western fringes of the grave cluster (Grave 371), and another male to the south of this cluster (Grave 295); the other three, all children, (Graves 418, 422 and 441) are in the two rows of graves at the eastern edge of Plot Y.

From Buckland 1951–3, the earliest grave with a pot (Grave 87) is in Plot A, which is described as 'a tight-packed early section' (Evison 1987, 94). Grave 43 is in Plot B and Grave 109 from Plot H while the other five graves with pots (Graves 156, 157, 137, 139 and 129) are in Plot G. Evison concludes that the tradition of placing pottery in inhumations was rare and belongs mostly to her Phase 5 (AD 650–675), and maybe limited to one family (Evison 1987, 94). Clearly the new evidence from 1994 shows that, while the custom is still not common, it extends back for perhaps a century and is quite widespread across the burial plots. Perhaps the concentration seen, for example, in Plot X, supports the idea of family or kin-group traditions.

In the 1994 excavations there is little spatial patterning to the distribution of the pottery form groups described above. Two of the small plain cups (Graves 384 and 389) are near each other in Plot X while the third, the handled cup (Grave 307) is on the edge of Plot T. Similarly, two of the small biconical vessels in Group 2 (Graves 441 and 422) are from Plot Y, while the third (Grave 238) is in Plot V. The other biconical vessels (Group 3) occur in Plot S (Grave 219), Plot T (Graves 308 and 338), Plot X (Graves 377 and 392) and Plot Y (Grave 418). The three rounded forms (Group 4) are all from Plot X.

One of the imported bottles (Grave 376) was also recovered from Plot X, while the other (Grave 251) was from Plot W. The single shouldered vessel (Grave 234) was from Plot S. In the same way, any grouping seen in the fabrics of the vessels is not reflected in the spatial patterning of the graves from which the pots were recovered.

Discussion

The pottery as a group can be dated broadly to the sixth century. There is nothing distinctive to suggest any of the vessels are definitely fifth century and, with the possible exception of the imported bottles, nothing which would confirm a date later than the sixth century. At Buckland 1951–3, with the exception of the hand-made vessel from Grave 87, most of the pots have been dated to the mid to late seventh century.

The group of small vessels (Groups 1 and 2) are, in five out of the six cases, associated with children and small pots may have been selected for burial on that basis. Small cups, with and without handles, or handled vessels generally, are not common but other Kentish examples are known. Small, more rounded, forms were recovered from early levels (above Hut 1) east of Marlowe Theatre, Canterbury by Sheppard Frere (Stow 1995, fig 345) and subsequently by Canterbury Archaeological Trust at the same site (Macpherson-Grant 1995a). This group included a rounded form with rectilinear decoration over much of the body and under the base (fig 368.199), as well as a plain undecorated handled vessel

(fig 368.202). Myres examined this group and ascribed it a fifth-century date (Stow 1995, 825); however, a very similar handled vessel later in the sequence (Macpherson-Grant 1995b, fig 357.62) belongs to Period 6IV which is dated to the seventh century, although residuality cannot be ruled out as a contributing factor. Neither of these vessels is identical with the Buckland example, however, as the handles are attached to the rim not just below as in the example from Grave 307.

Myres also illustrates a handled form from Bekesbourne (Myres 1977, corpus no 1079, fig 74), which he connects with 'Jutish' traditions, but it is clear from his own illustrations, as well as more recent research, that handled vessels are neither exclusively 'Kentish' nor 'Jutish'.

Common to many of the vessels from Buckland are simple arrangements of linear decoration around the neck and on the upper body. At its most typical this comprises concentric neck grooves and bunches of linear incised lines or shallow grooves arranged vertically around the centre of the body. Variations of this simple decoration scheme occur on many of the different sizes and forms of vessels from Buckland. Two of the smaller biconical vessels (Grave 238 and 422) have pairs of stabbed decoration on the neck whilst another vessel (Grave 338) has a neckline of 'wurm' or 'fret' pattern. Grave 295 has a chevron arrangement of incised lines and grooves, whereas Grave 392 alternates vertical grooves with small bosses.

This scheme of decoration falls with Myres' Group II.6 which includes pots with 'Grouped vertical lines' on a variety of forms (Myres 1977, figs 212–15) and, in one or two cases, simple examples of his 'Bossed linear panel decoration' (*ibid*, fig 218–25). These simple arrangements, on a variety of forms, can be paralleled in a number of cemeteries in eastern England as far north as Sancton in East Yorkshire, typically in cemeteries of Anglian traditions. The excavations at the Marlowe sites in Canterbury have produced examples of these, both with the diagonal arrangement of line and grooves (Stow 1995, fig 345 FI; Macpherson-Grant 1995b, fig 353.4), and the vertical bunched arrangement (fig 356.52). These are variously from contexts dated to the fifth, sixth and seventh centuries illustrating the difficulties in trying to establish a tight chronology for these types.

Bossed linear panel decoration, such as occurs as shallow bosses on the pot from Grave 392 and as a more pronounced features on the vessel from the hillwash, context 390, can also be seen on sherds recovered by the Kent Archaeological Rescue Unit from occupation sites in Dover (Keller 2003; no 47, fig 44 and no 55, fig 45), together with sherds of a Frankish import. It is believed that the structure from which they were recovered was abandoned in the sixth century, although Keller follows Myres's chronology and places the sherds with linear decoration vessels in the fifth century. The single example of a hand-made vessel from Buckland 1951–3 (Grave 87) is a large biconical form with this type of decoration arranged underneath a neck ring decorated with diagonal lines chevron fashion in groups of three. Evison notes the very marked similarity between the fabrics of the vessel from Grave 87 and those referred to above from Dover. She suggests a date at the very end of the fifth century for the pot from Grave 87 and places it in her Phase 1 (AD 475–525). The vessel from Grave 87 is very similar in terms of decoration to that from context 390 having the same number of bosses and grooves between the bosses, albeit on a larger form. It may be that the vessel from context 390 is of a comparable date; its lack of association with any particular grave hampers further analysis. The slashes around the collar on the Buckland 1951–3 vessel are reminiscent of the slashes on the small biconical vessels from Graves 238 and 422 where they are more crudely executed.

In two cases from Buckland 1994 (Graves 234 and 387), the decorative scheme used is so simple and so carelessly applied as to be almost symbolic, representing schematically the better executed patterns seen on some of the other vessels. Whether this is indicative of a chronologically later degenerating stylistic tradition can only be guessed at.

The infant's feeding bottle (Grave 388) is clearly a unique form shaped for a particular use (Fig 4.34). A parallel in terms of purpose, but not form, was recovered from an Anglo-Saxon cemetery at Castledyke South, Barton-on-Humber, Lincolnshire (Drinkall and Foreman 1998, 309–11). There, grave 133, a presumed infant grave, produced a pottery vessel described as mammiform (fig 141, no 26) with a teat positioned at one side of the base. The fact that the teat was heavily worn has lead to speculation that this vessel may have been initially, or also, used for feeding animals, such as hand-reared lambs. The teat on the Buckland example does not exhibit the same evidence of heavy or prolonged use, and the more traditional jar form would have been less easy to handle if feeding animals. As far as the author is aware, however, these are the only two Anglo-Saxon examples known in this country.

Imported Frankish pottery in Kent is best known from graves, with fewer examples from domestic contexts. The two bottles from Graves 251 and 376 are tall-necked examples with simple line and wavy line decoration; Grave 251 conforms to Evison's group 1b, concentric line decoration, while Grave 376 is a Group 1c with wavy line decoration (Evison 1979, 9). Both have parallels in Kent; Grave 251 can be matched with bottles from graves in Sarre, Folkestone and Finglesham (*ibid,* fig 1); Grave 376 has parallels from

Howletts and Strood (*ibid*, fig 2). The spalled-off footring seen on Grave 251 is an unusual feature although a bottle from Sarre grave 70 (*ibid*, fig 1d) has a slightly swollen base, though not a true footring as seen on an example from Armentières, in the Somme region (*ibid*, fig 28b). Evison's dating for the bottles suggests they belong to the second half of the sixth century (*ibid*, 45); a fragmentary early quoit brooch found with the vessel from Howletts mentioned above she dismisses as a possible heirloom.

The bottles from Buckland 1994 are quite distinct from the bottles and imported bowl recovered from Buckland 1951–3 (Evison 1987, 92–4) which invariably have rouletted decoration (with the possible exception of Grave 129 where only the bottom half survived). The earliest of the bottles (from Grave 43) she dates to her phase 4 (AD 625–650), the rest (Graves 129, 137,139,156 and 157) to phase 5 (AD 650–675) and one (Grave 109) possibly as late as phase 6 (AD 675–700). These vessels are grey, buff or black with no examples of the more typical red vessels like those recovered from Buckland 1994.

Work by the Kent Archaeological Rescue Unit in Saxon Dover has recovered fragments of at least nine Frankish vessels including bottles and biconical jars, all with rouletted decoration. One of the bottles (Keller 2003, no 100, fig 53) can be paralleled closely with two bottles found in Graves 109 and 157 at Buckland 1951–3. This is useful new information as it demonstrates that these vessels were in quite common usage and not simply prestigious items associated with funerary rites. Frere's excavations at Canterbury Marlowe (Hut 2) produced a copy of a Frankish rouletted biconical vessel (Wilson 1995, fig 348, F45) while later in the sequence there is what appears to be a simple copy of a bottle form (Macpherson-Grant 1995b, fig 359, 97). Analysis of other, more clumsily produced, bottles from Dover, Margate and from Buckland 1951–3 (Grave 156) showed that they too were Kentish copies, dated to the later seventh century (Evison 1987, 93).

Summary

The group of pottery vessels from Buckland 1994 makes a useful contribution to the corpus of Anglo-Saxon vessels from east Kent. Their association with other artefact types, some more closely datable than the pottery vessels, helps to refine the dating of the pottery. This, in turn, contributes to understanding the chronological framework for the recent discoveries from occupation sites in Canterbury and Dover, and to move the subject forward.

Most of the vessels from the graves at Buckland 1994 appear to be local products, as are most of those from the occupation sites referred to above. The new evidence from Canterbury and Dover indicates that the same vessels were being used in domestic as well as funerary contexts, dispelling the idea that vessels, especially decorated vessels, were being made especially for funerary use. How far the similarity noted in the decorative schemes and their arrangement reflects fashion, kinship or even ethnic origin, remains unclear, although the similarity of style seen on vessels in Anglian cemeteries in eastern England is worth noting.

Similarly, some progress has been made in understanding the role of the imported Frankish bottles. Although only two were found in Buckland 1994, these were not associated with the richest graves; while they might be indicators of wealth or status they might also indicate the taste, or kinship connections of the dead or owner (who may or may not be the same person). Their recovery from occupation sites in Dover emphasises that these vessels too have a domestic role.

Fewer than 10 per cent of the burials at Buckland 1994 contained pottery vessels and their role in the funerary rituals and beliefs of the community buried there is unclear. As demonstrated above, there is some evidence for the correlation between the presence of pottery in the grave and the burial of children, juveniles or women suggesting, perhaps, the offering of nourishment in the afterlife for the weaker members of the community; but there are more burials of these age and gender groups without pottery than with pottery, and perhaps this custom too might be better seen as having its origin in kin group or family traditions.

Glass vessels

Vera Evison[68]

(Graves 250, 254, 297, 347, 353, 355, 372, 420, 422, 432 and 437)

Five glass vessels were found in the Buckland 1951–3 excavations, but there were as many as thirteen from the 1994 excavations. The date of production of the vessels from the 1994 excavations ranges from the beginning to the end of the pagan period, but most were made before the middle of the sixth century (Phases 1–3a). The earliest is the thin-walled bowl with unsmoothed rim (a) found in Grave 355 (Fig 10.43), where it was the only object in the burial. This type of bowl was broken off from the blowing iron and the rim was not smoothed by reheating but was left unfinished or ground. This technique did not continue long after the fourth century as all forms of vessel were then

finished by transfer to a punty rod so that the rim could be smoothed by reheating.

This form corresponds to Isings Type 96 which began in the third century and survived into the fifth century (Isings 1957, 113; U Koch 1987, 53–5; Cabart and Feyeux 1995, 31, nos 45, 48). A later date of mostly AD 450–490 with later occurrences is allocated to it in France (Feyeux 1995, 118, pl 3, T 80; Périn 1995, fig 5). Four occurred in early Saxon graves, at Bifrons and Sittingbourne in Kent, Great Chesterford in Essex and High Down in Sussex, and a number of bowl or cup fragments were found in the Anglo-Saxon settlement site at West Stow, Suffolk (Evison 2000b, 58, 73, group 1, fig 2, 1, 3–13; Price 2000, 12).

Grave 422 contained a bell beaker (b) with vertical wall, everted rim and knobbed base, decorated with two zones of horizontal trails (Fig 10.63). The shape is not well formed and the decoration is untidy. The type occurs in northern France, with some in Germany and a few in Belgium, dated mid fifth to mid sixth century (Périn 1995, fig 5, T 56; Alénus-Lecerf 1995, 64–5, fig 13, 1). The shapes of this type vary in width and height (Feyeux 1995, pl 12, T 56) and the decoration, usually by white trails, is in horizontal zones and sometimes with a zone of trails drawn into arcades. The Buckland vessel was decorated with white horizontal trails, but they have almost completely decomposed and only the channels remain. There are only five of the general type from Anglo-Saxon graves, of which three are decorated with horizontal trails (Evison 2000b, group 28, fig 2, I, 25) and two have in addition a zone of arcading (Evison 2000b, group 29, fig 2, I, 26).

Another type of bell beaker (c) which occurred in Grave 420 (Fig 10.63), also retains a knob at the tip but the walls are incurved and widen slightly into a carination at the base. This is decorated with white glass on the knob and as parallel trails near the rim.

The type is most common in northern France and Belgium, with very few outside this area (U Koch 1996, distribution map Abb 470, 3 and 4). They belong mostly to the period AD 520–600 (Alénus-Lecerf 1995, 66 (a) fig 14, T 45 and T 91, fig15, 1 and 2, fig 16; Périn 1995, fig 4, T 52; Feyeux 1995, 116, T 52.1a, T 52.1ae, pl 10). Although they occur very frequently in continental Merovingian graves, in England there are only a few of this general type of bell beaker, and only the beaker from Monkton, grave 5 is similar in proportions and decoration (Evison 2000b, group 30, 2, fig 2, I, 27).

Fragments of a cone beaker (a) decorated with a narrow zone of white horizontal trails found in Grave 254 (Fig 10.16), belong to a type known mostly from Belgium and northern France with some in Germany, which is dated from

---

68. Report submitted in 2003.

the late fifth to early sixth century (U Koch 1987, 73–7, Abb 26; Feyeux 1995, 116, pl 10, T 51.1a; Périn 1995, fig 4, T 51; Alénus-Lecerf 1995, 63a).

The cone (b) in Grave 347 (Fig 10.39) is fragmentary and the colour of the trails has been affected by decomposition so that, although there is a possibility that it also might have had white trails, it was probably decorated with self-colour trails and the width of the trail zone is unknown. This type had a similar distribution to the cone in Grave 254 and belongs to the same period (U Koch 1987, 73, 76, Abb 26, 28; Feyeux 1995, T 51.2f, pl 10).

The cone beaker (f) in Grave 432 (Fig 10.66) has a zone of white trail decoration, but in addition, a zone of trails applied in the middle of the vessel has been drawn into arcade shapes. This has been called Type *Haillot*, and was mostly confined to Belgium and northern France at the end of the fifth century into the sixth century (U Koch 1987, 149–51, Abb 64; Feyeux 1995, pl 10, T 51.1ac; Alénus-Lecerf 1995, 64c, fig 10, 5). Three others occur in England, at Bifrons, Kent; High Down, Sussex and Loveden, Lincolnshire (Evison 2000b, group 21, 1–3).

The same type of decoration by white trails in horizontal zones and as arcades is to be seen on the bowl (b) from Grave 437 (Fig 10.67). Bowls like this occur mostly in northern France and the upper Rhine in the late fifth to early sixth century (U Koch 1987, 226k, distribution map Abb 96; Feyeux 1995, 118, pl 14, T 81.1acp; Périn 1995, fig 5, T 81; Alénus-Lecerf 1995, 60c, fig 5, 11, map fig 6). In England one occurred in grave 200 at Mitcham, Surrey, and one in grave 22 at High Down, Sussex.

Cone beakers with a zone of self-colour horizontal trails below the rim and thicker trails in vertical loops below are named the Kempston type after one find spot. There is one example from Grave 297 (a) (Fig 10.29) and this is comparable in size to the single example from Buckland Grave 22, which is the tallest of this cone beaker type (Evison 1972, 62; Evison 1987, 94, fig 14, Grave 22, 1; Evison 2000b, 62, group 26, 35 and 15). They are not common in France (Feyeux 1995, 116, pl 10.51, 2fh). Both Buckland vessels are light green and of similar proportions: in Grave 22 the workmanship is not of the highest standard possible as shown by the comparative superiority of the Kempston and Howletts beakers (Evison 2008, nos 36 and 37) for the horizontal trails are irregular and overrun by the ten vertical loops. In Grave 297 the trails at the top are slanting out of the horizontal and only four vertical loops were attempted, as opposed to twelve on the Kempston beaker, and these are very irregular. It hardly seems likely that both Buckland cones were made by the same glass blower as the vessel in Grave 297 is a very inferior product. Distribution maps of the type show main

concentrations and possible production centres in Kent and the Rhineland, with other finds in northern France, Belgium, Holland, Germany and Czechoslovakia (Evison 1972, fig 23; Evison 1987, 94–6, fig 114; U Koch 1987, 116–49, Abb 47; Evison 2008, map 3).

As many as forty-nine have been found in England and they occurred in both male and female graves (Evison 1972, 62; Evison 2000b, 62, groups 24–6). Larger concentrations of fragments on one spot are noted at the settlement site of the Runde Berg bei Urach in Germany where twenty-six were found (U Koch 1987, 120) and in England at the cremation cemetery at Spong Hill, Norfolk, with six definite and six probable fragments (Evison 1994b, 30, figs 6 and 7; Evison 2008, map 3). These cone beakers occurred mostly in the late fifth to early sixth century. On the Continent they occur mostly in graves of high-ranking armed men in the second half of the fifth century (U Koch 1987, 120) and the man in Buckland Grave 297 possessed a spear and shield, while Grave 22 contained a spear and sword.

Grave 372 contained a brown claw beaker (h) (Fig 10.45) which belongs to Type 3a (Evison 1982, 47–8), a type moderately tall and of slender proportions with a flared rim, a zone of horizontal trails below the rim and another near the foot with two rows of claws applied in the lower part of the space between. It is very similar indeed to the claw beaker in Buckland Grave 20 (Evison 1987, 96–7, 221, fig 13, 16; Evison 2000b, group 35, 3; Evison 2008, nos 61–2), both are blown very thin, the trails are unevenly applied and the foot carelessly formed. There are further minor points of similarity which might indicate the same glass blower: the foot is carelessly pushed in with a pointed tool, off-centre on one and pushed in twice on the other, and in the top row of claws two opposite claws are applied higher than the intervening two. There are four beakers of this particular type and all were found in Kent, one from Lyminge and one from Sarre (Evison 1982, map fig 2; Evison 2008, map 4). Both at Buckland were in well-furnished female graves, Grave 20 being allocated to the period AD 475–525. This type appears to have been produced in England and a possible export was found at Hermes, Oise, France (Evison 1982, 71, pl VI, c).

All of these nine beakers of various types from the 1994 excavations were in use before the middle of the sixth century. The remaining four are from the late sixth to seventh century, and Grave 250, a well-furnished female grave, contained three of them, a bowl (e) and two bell beakers (f) and (g) (Fig 10.14). This bowl type occurred in the Rhineland from the late fifth century to the seventh century (U Koch 1987, 198–207, Abb 84–7), there are some in Belgium but in France an undecorated bowl was a rarity (Feyeux 1995, 118, pl 14, T 81. 0; Alénus-Lecerf 1993, 101, no 7; Alénus-Lecerf

1995, 59a, fig 4, 5). One other bowl of this type was found in England in grave 190 at Ozengell, Kent (Evison 2000b, group 43/1, misprinted as from 'Kent' only).

Tall bell beakers with vertical ribbing and a knob on the base like the pair in Grave 250 at Buckland occurred most frequently in the Meuse valley with some elsewhere in northern France and the Rhineland, but these are the only two which reached England (Feyeux 1995, pl 11, T 52.3ke; Périn 1995, fig 4, T 52; U Koch 1996, 614–7, Abb 470). Two others included in group 48 (Evison 2000b, group 48, 1–2) differ in having rounded bases without a point, and they probably originated in the Rhineland.

The blue claw beaker in Grave 353 (f) (Fig 10.42), which consists of the foot part of the grave only (*see* p 30 for a discussion of the interpretation of this grave) is one of the latest type to appear in Anglo-Saxon graves. It is tall, with a straight, unflared rim and two rows of four claws each. It belongs to Type 4c (Evison 1982, 51) and the best preserved example was found in a well-furnished grave at Wickhambreaux in east Kent (Evison 1982, 51, 70, pl XIII, b). This also has a straight rim, but with two rows of three claws and a row of blown knobs above, characteristics which ally it to the four olive green beakers from Taplow. Fragments of another blue claw beaker were found at Faversham, as well as part of a single claw, which seems to represent a separate beaker (Evison 1982, 70, nos 52 and 53, fig 12f). Fragments of one other blue claw beaker were found amongst the cremated remains at Spong Hill, Norfolk, but these appear to belong to Type 3c, of the early sixth century, which had a flared rim. It is unique as the blue claws were decorated with a vertical indented trail in light green glass (Evison 1994b, 29–30, fig 4, 2948/2, SF 1521, SF 1612, 2921/1, Archive Catalogue 1). Other blue beakers of the later Type 4c however have been found, one in Gotland (Nerman 1969, II, Taf 84, 737) and one at Nettersheim, Germany (Wieczorek *et al* 1996, Teil I, 19, Abb 14, Teil II, 977, no 17). A small fragment of a blue claw from a beaker of unknown type was also found in 1988 at the presumed site of Quentovic in France (Evison forthcoming, NI 475/630).

The Buckland claw beaker has much in common with other vessel shapes in blue glass which were blown in England in the late sixth to early seventh century such as bag beakers (Evison 2000a, map fig 55; Evison 2000b, group 13; Evison 2008, map 9), with zigzag trail decoration as from Broomfield (Evison 2000b, group 66, fig 3, II/17; Evison 2008, map 7) and other globular beakers, both plain and decorated with vertical notched trails (Evison 1989, 341–5; Evison 2000b, 69, group 67, fig l, II, 18). A few of these blue vessels have continental find spots and these beakers were no doubt exported to these destinations from England.

The change of types of glass vessel in England which occurred in the middle of the sixth century detected in the forms and colours (Evison 2000b, figs 2 and 3) has also been noticed in the chemical composition. Amongst a small group of vessels which have been analysed, a blue globular beaker with neck trails from Faversham corresponds to the analyses of other Period II vessels (AD 550–700) which differ from those in Period I (AD 400–550) (Evison 2000b, group 62, 6; Evison 2008, no 134). Analyses of the Broomfield blue globular beakers, however, (Evison 2000b, group 66, 1–2; Evison 2008, nos 150–1) and of three other vessels were found to be unusual and different from those from both Period I and Period II (Freestone *et al* 2008, 32–42).

Clear ring-shaped punty marks are to be seen on all the vessels discussed here with the exception of the cone (b) in Grave 347 which had suffered from decomposition, and the bowl (a) from Grave 355 where transfer to a punty rod was unnecessary as the rim was not smoothed. Use of the blowing pipe for empontilling is therefore clear in all cases and was particularly efficient in the case of the knobbed bases where it encircled the knob and enabled the punty to be attached without disturbing the contour of the vessel.

The glass vessels from Buckland were mostly in female graves, the only exceptions being three weapon graves, Graves 22, 297 and 437. A similar pattern is to be seen at Mill Hill, Deal, where there were five glass vessels. There the sex of two of the accompanying skeletons is not known, and of the remaining three, two were female. However, the other glass vessel, a bell beaker, was in the grave of a man with a sword (grave 93) (Parfitt and Brugmann 1997, 153–4, fig 50c).

The graves from the 1994 Buckland excavations containing glass vessels were not dispersed in a haphazard manner, but there is a certain amount of clustering which suggests connections between these individuals. Graves 250, 254, 372 and 432 all occur in Plots V and W; Graves 295, 420, 422 and 437 in Plots X and Y; Grave 355 has the only glass in Plot T, but Graves 347 and 353 are near together in Plot S.

Most of the glass vessels from the 1994 excavations belong to the period before the middle of the sixth century and are imports from northern France, particularly the Meuse valley. Two vessels, however, the Kempston cone and the claw beaker in Grave 372, were probably produced in England. In the period after the mid sixth century, the blue claw beaker was also produced in England, but the three vessels in Grave 250 were imported from the Meuse or Rhine valleys. Similar origins are noted for the vessels from the 1951–3 excavations where before AD 550 a cone beaker was imported from northern France and a cone and claw beaker made in England. In the later period a bell beaker came from the Rhine valley and a palm cup may have been an Anglo-Saxon or imported product. The high total of eighteen glass vessels in Buckland is in keeping with the quantity and high quality of the other grave goods in this cemetery.

Caskets and boxes

Ian Riddler and Hayley Bullock

(Graves 246, 255 and 353)

Fittings indicating the presence of a casket with bone mounts and a wooden box were recovered from Graves 255 and 353. A series of small nails from Grave 246 may possibly indicate the presence there of a wooden box as well, although no other box fittings were recovered from that grave. Within Grave 255, the burial of an adult female, a series of over forty small copper alloy and bone pins lay above the head of the deceased (m). In a few cases, decayed strips of bone or antler present in this assemblage include the vestiges of rivet-holes. A fragmentary copper alloy staple lay in the general area of the pins. In addition, three plain copper alloy mounts were located on the right side of the skull (k), (l) and (n). Each of these mounts includes at least two copper alloy rivets. One of the mounts is triangular in shape (k), whilst the others are rectangular, with rounded corners. Each mount is lightly curved in profile. Thirty-one of the pins are made of copper alloy, in each case from a small piece of folded, tapering sheet. Complete examples vary from 11–15mm in length. The eleven bone pins are similar in shape, although they are a little shorter, with lengths of 8–11mm. A rectangular strip includes a slot that contains a spring mechanism for the box. It consists of a segment of bone or antler, which is secured in its slot by two copper alloy pins, and ends below in an abraded, hooked terminal. Too little survives of the box for its shape and arrangement of mounts to be accurately determined, and the assemblage was not recorded in detail during excavation.

The copper alloy mounts appear to have accompanied a casket of bone or antler, formed largely of thin, narrow rectangular strips, secured by pins to a wooden former. No trace of the wooden former survived. The small copper alloy and bone pins and the plain sections of copper alloy sheet are paralleled by examples discovered in association with the casket from the burial at Swallowcliffe Down, Wiltshire. The sheet mounts there are thought to have been added as later reinforcements for the casket (Speake 1989, 29 and fig 26).

Bone or antler caskets occur throughout the Anglo-Saxon period (MacGregor 1985, 197). In most cases, decorated strips of bone or antler were fastened to a wooden backing,

and that was probably the situation here. Scarcely any decoration is visible on the remaining bone elements of the casket from Grave 255, but they survive in poor condition and their original form is difficult to distinguish. A largely undecorated casket with bone or antler mounts would be very unusual for this period; virtually all examples carry extensive areas of decoration.

Substantial elements of early Anglo-Saxon bone or antler caskets are known from Abingdon, Berkshire; Caister-by-Norwich and Illington, Norfolk (Myres and Green 1973, 85–7; Davison *et al* 1993, fig 44). Fragments almost certainly from a casket of seventh-century date came from the Asthall Barrow, Oxfordshire (Leeds 1924; Dickinson and Speake 1992, 105 and pl 5). One example is known also from the Old Park, Whitfield cemetery (Kendrick 1937, 448 and pl XCVII), a little to the north-west of Buckland (*see* p 4; Fig 1.1), and Evison noted that several graves from the 1951–3 Buckland excavations may have contained caskets with bone mounts, to judge from the presence of small, flat fragments of bone or antler within them (Evison 1987, 106). Caskets are common on the Continent within graves of Merovingian and later date and, as with the Anglo-Saxon sample, most are decorated with ring-and-dot and linear designs (Goessler 1932; Schoppa 1953; Roes 1963, 79–80 and pl LXIII,1–11; Werner 1962a, 153; Elbern 1972; Vanhaeke 1997).

The iron fittings for a wooden box were recovered from Grave 353 (g), which was the burial of an adult, probably female. The set consists of a handle (g1), four complete corner fittings, four incomplete corner fittings, three fragmentary pieces (possibly belonging to corner fittings) and a spring mechanism (g10). The objects were found around the left foot of a female skeleton along with a glass claw beaker (f) and silver rim-bindings (h) belonging to a wooden vessel. During the excavation, it was not possible to determine the exact association of these objects but it seems likely that the claw beaker and the wooden vessel had been placed within the wooden box.

The corner brackets are L-shaped and are pierced by two iron rivets, one at each end. There are mineral-preserved wood remains on the inside of the brackets. The wood remains were examined at x40 magnification. The wood of the box was identified (p 279; Table 6.12) as beech (*Fagus sylvatica*). The corner brackets showed an alternating wood grain at the corners, which suggests comb jointing (Evison 1987, 102). From the evidence it seems that a pair of the corner fittings were attached to the comb jointed corners for further support. Some of the corner fittings showed small traces of mineral-preserved tabby woven textile. This textile probably relates to a garment or covering which it was in contact with during burial (*see* p 195; Table 5.7).

There is no evidence present on the fittings to indicate the construction of the base of the box. It is possible the base was fitted by a system of dowelling or by means of a rebate into the sides of the box. The thickness of the side walls of the box was approximately 11–12mm as indicated by the wood remains on the bracket rivets.

There is little evidence for the construction of the lid. The handle was found inside the perimeter of the outer fittings and is thought to have been secured to the lid of the box. The depth of the lid, 12mm, was indicated by the mineral-preserved wood remains found on the handle. No hinges were recovered; the lid may have slid into recesses in the side walls (Evison 1987, 101). The iron handle showed evidence of twisted construction/decoration.

The only evidence for a latch or locking mechanism is a small iron object that was secured into wood at one end with a nail. A similar object appeared in Buckland Grave 32 (Evison 1987, 101). This is thought to be a spring. It is possible that the spring was secured into either the lid or side wall of the box. Wood remains are present on the opposite side of the spring. It is thought that the wood remains are from a wooden bolt/catch plate as no iron bolt plate was found. The spring would have held the bolt in a locked position thus preventing removal of the lid (Evison 1987, 101).

The assemblage was not lifted in a block so the dimensions of the box cannot be exactly defined. It was impossible to identify the fittings (except for the handle) from black and white photos of the grave and assemblage. Only five of the fittings were recorded individually and associated finds numbers were subsequently mixed up off site. Therefore, it is not possible to attempt an exact reconstruction for the box. From the scatter of the objects recorded on the grave plan (Fig 10.98) it appears that the dimensions of the box were approximately 230mm wide and up to 390mm long.

The shape of this box and the type of iron fittings present recall those described by Evison for several other graves within the earlier Buckland excavations (Evison 1987, 100–3 and table XVI). Although a handle and corner brackets were retrieved, there were no metal hinges, and this situation occurs with several of the boxes from Buckland (Evison 1987, 101). The presence of a handle, alongside the absence of any iron bolt fittings, allows this box to be compared with those from Buckland Graves 43 and 143, in particular (Evison 1987, table XVI). The spring mechanism, however, is best paralleled by the example from Grave 32.

Wooden boxes first occur in graves of the later sixth century, and are reasonably common in east Kent, although most discoveries were made in the nineteenth century and details of their construction and fittings are sparse (Meaney and Chadwick Hawkes 1970, 46; Geake 1997, 81–2; Lucy 2000, 57–8). The majority have been found in the graves of women and they were usually placed, as here, at the foot of the grave, although occasionally they were located by the head. Amongst those recovered from east Kent cemeteries are the fittings for wooden boxes from Gilton, Kingston and Sarre (Douglas 1793, pl 10, fig 8; Faussett 1856; Brent 1868, 314; Evison 1987, 103).

A fragmentary nail (i) was found towards the foot of Grave 246. At the other end of the grave, to the side of the head, lay eight small iron nails, mostly 13–15mm in length, although two examples, (f) and (h) extend to 26–28mm. Traces of wood are visible on several of them (one specimen (c) has been identified as oak; Table 6.12). They were arranged in a line to the left of the skull, with three examples placed a little further to the right. Their original function remains unclear. They might be coffin nails, although they are relatively insubstantial; they had clearly been driven into wood along most, if not all, of their length. They are similar in size to a series of nails retrieved from a grave at Harford Farm, Norfolk in association with a wooden box (Penn 2000, 64–5 and fig 83). No other fittings for a wooden box were recovered from this grave, however, and the nails may possibly have secured another item, like a gaming board, for example.

Bucket

Birte Brugmann and Jean M Cook[†]

(Grave 391B)

The bucket (a) from Grave 391B was examined by Jean Cook[69] in 1996 for a publication on Anglo-Saxon buckets, posthumously published in 2004, which includes the finds from Buckland Graves 28, 53 and 391B (Cook 2004, nos 98–100). She planned to examine the most recent find again before writing it up but sadly died before a second visit to the British Museum could be arranged. The following notes made on the first visit are printed with kind permission of the literary executors of the Jean M Cook Archive at the Oxford Institute of Archaeology.

Bucket description   *Jean M Cook[†]*

Copper alloy bound bucket with iron handle.
Height: 135mm. Top diameter: 139–142mm. Straight-sided, so bottom diameter is the same. Three hoops. Four uprights, two were extended to take the handle.

---

69. As a student Jean had taken part in the first Buckland excavations (Evison 1987, 11).

Top hoop, width: 35mm, up to the top which overlapped the top of the staves to make the rim. Most of this overlap is now broken away. No separate rim. One strip, with one overlapping join behind one of the extended uprights (the one broken off at the rim). Complete. Decorated along lower edge with repoussé arches and a row of repoussé dots. Arches are separate, stamped individually judging by varying spaces between them.

Middle hoop, width: 20mm. Single strip, one overlapping join behind same upright as top hoop. Undecorated. Small piece missing.

Bottom hoop, width: 21mm. Single strip, with a break (cannot quite see how it joined). I think the overlapping join is behind the same upright as the other two, but this is difficult to see. Undecorated.

Four uprights, two terminating below top hoop and two extending above rim for handle.

Short uprights. Height: 95mm, width: 18mm. No taper. Decorated with four central repoussé bosses in pairs, 7mm in diameter and a row of repoussé dots parallel to long edges but with gaps where the repoussé bosses are and not along the bottom edge. These dots look smaller and less well lined up than those in the top hoop. Attached to middle hoop by single tack-type rivet and to bottom hoop by two such rivets.

Long uprights. Height: 135mm (minimum) but actual top broken off the one which retains part of handle and the other is broken off at the rim. Width: 18mm. Decorated with four repoussé bosses in pairs, in central line and a row of repoussé dots parallel to long edges with breaks where the repoussé bosses are.

Attached to top hoop by a single tack-type rivet which seems to have passed through hoop (including the overlapping join on the one side) stave and base of internal fish-plate; to middle hoop by one tack-type rivet (this is missing on the upright with broken-off top); and by two tack-type rivets to the bottom hoop.

Handle, only a fragment remains. Iron, suspended by tack-type rivet of which inside end seems to have been burred over. This rivet goes through top of extended upright, end of handle and top of internal fish-plate. Only one fish-plate remains: 27 x 11mm. Handle width at attachment: 9mm.

Staves, a lot remaining. Looks as if there were eight, approximate width: 50mm. Remains of basal groove, width: 3mm; 9mm from base. Staves chamfered at top, but edges look clean-cut. Staves project up to 7mm below bottom of bottom hoop. Wood subsequently identified as oak (Table 6.12).

All uprights, base is aligned with bottom edge of bottom hoop. This probably means that the basal groove

was supported by bottom hoop, that is, it exerted pressure on it.

Discussion of the bucket　　*Birte Brugmann*

The bucket is of a simple design characterised by extended uprights instead of handle mounts such as the one from Buckland Grave 28, repoussé decoration and an absence of decorative triangular appliqués. Extended uprights and repoussé decoration are more commonly found with buckets from 'Saxon' contexts than in buckets from 'Anglian' graves, which tend to have punched decoration and bifurcated handle mounts, such as found on the bucket from Grave 28 (see Cook 2004).

The use of the arcade motif for the present bucket and some further buckets from early Anglo-Saxon contexts[70] suggests the influence of late Roman workshops on Anglo-Saxon bucket production and a fifth-century date for the bucket in Grave 391B. The short bows with the line of dots underneath are probably based on more elaborate late Roman designs such as illustrated by Arnold (1982, fig 54, m, n). If buckets were produced in Kent, regional workshop characteristics have not yet been recognised (see Parfitt and Brugmann 1997, 79ff).

The bucket in Grave 391B was positioned at the head of a female buried during Phase 2, as was probably the copper alloy bound bucket from Grave 28, dated to Phases 2–3a. The iron bound bucket from Grave 53, dated to Phases 5–7, was positioned at the feet of the female in that grave. The position of the three buckets and the dates of the associated grave goods support the notion that copper alloy buckets in Anglo-Saxon graves tend to be earlier than iron buckets and that earlier ones tend to be buried by the heads of males or females, while a larger proportion of the late buckets were positioned at the feet (see Cook 2004).

Rims and mounts from organic vessels

Keith Parfitt

(Graves 228A, 228B, 249C, 326, 348, 353, 381, 413, 424, 427B and 436)

Metal rim-bindings and other fittings from otherwise decayed organic vessels were recognised in eleven graves. These occurred in burials dating from throughout the period of use of the 1994 cemetery area and were found with both males and females.

---

70. See Arnold (1982, 58) on arcades and similar motifs on Anglo-Saxon and continental finds and Cook (2004) on further examples. The term 'arcade' applies to a row of joint standing arcs, often combined with dots. C- and U-shaped or 'horseshoe' motifs are far more common.

The somewhat miscellaneous group of metal items discussed here may be grouped into three main types: rims, bases and repairs. Silver rim-bindings and associated attachment clips (h) came from a small wooden vessel originally contained in Grave 353. This had been placed adjacent to the glass claw beaker (f) and both vessels seem to have been housed in a small wooden box (g) (*see* p 141). Another small silver rimmed wooden vessel had been contained within Grave 413 (b). Copper alloy rim-bindings found with these silver fittings may be derived from a second wooden vessel. Small copper alloy rim clips came from Graves 381 (h) and 436 (c). ?Wall repair clips, all of copper alloy, were recovered from Graves 228A (c), 249C (g), 326 (c), 424 (a), 436 (c) and 427B (a). Only the two in Grave 436 were associated with a rim fitting.

Two other items were of more particular interest. From Grave 348 came a complete copper alloy base and side mount from a circular wooden container (b), whilst Grave 228B produced a copper alloy triangular sheet (b1), originally a 'vandyke' from a drinking vessel, but re-used as a rim repair.

Textile manufacturing equipment

Penelope Walton Rogers

Three spindle-whorls and a sword-beater (weaving batten), representing the crafts of spinning and weaving respectively, were recovered from four graves. As is usual (Walton Rogers 2007, 45–6) all four were female burials. It is obvious from historical sources that textile production was considered the responsibility of women, although it was not regarded as menial. Charlemagne himself made sure that his daughters were taught to 'spin and weave wool, use the distaff and spindle and acquire every womanly accomplishment' (Einhard: *Life of Charlemagne*, Thorpe translation 1970, 59).

Spindle-whorls

(Graves 204, 207 and 347)

A single spindle-whorl was recovered from each of three graves, Graves 204 (Phase 2b), 207 (unphased) and 347 (Phase 2a). The women ranged in age from teenage to early thirties and the two younger ones were well-provided with grave goods, while the eldest, in Grave 207, had only a small necklace, a bracelet, buckles and a knife. The whorls were positioned by the skull in Grave 347, by the left hip in Grave 207 and by the left thigh in Grave 204.

Two of the whorls have been cast from lead or lead alloy, with a former for the spindle hole. Both are rather shallow; Grave 207 (e) has a flattened hemispherical shape and Grave 347 (m) is flattened biconical. Both have the typical spindle hole diameter of this period, 7–8mm (Walton Rogers 1997, 1731; and 2007, 23–4) and may be compared with a third lead whorl of rounded conical shape, Sf 588, from an unstratified deposit. Its 7–8mm spindle hole suggests that it originated in the same period. The weights of the whorls are 36g for Grave 207 (e), 42g for Sf 588 and Grave 347 (m) may be reconstructed as 20g. The whorl from Grave 204 is fragmentary and made from shale.

Lead whorls made in these shapes were used in the Iron Age and Roman period, although these early whorls tend to have narrower spindle holes, to fit the thinner spindles of the time (Walton Rogers 1997, 1731). Lead whorls have also been noted in Grave 48 of the 1951–3 excavations (Evison 1987, 112–13) and at the Anglo-Saxon village of Mucking, Essex (Hamerow 1993, 65, 70), in similar shapes to those recorded here. Shale is a less common material for whorls, but there are two examples, thought to be oil shale, from Buckland Grave 21 (Phase 1) and Grave 60 (Phase 3) (Evison 1987, 112–13), two from Canterbury, one dated to the fifth century and the other middle Saxon (Blockley *et al* 1995, 1170–1, 1177) and five from Mucking (Hamerow 1993, 65), while Evison notes shale whorls from late Roman Portchester, Hampshire and Shakenoak, Oxfordshire and another from a seventh-century context at Chamberlain's Barn, Leighton Buzzard, Bedfordshire. These are not necessarily from the same source, however, since there are different shales in different parts of the south of England; and some may be reworked from Roman objects (Walton Rogers 2007, 25).

When spinning yarn, whorls are fitted on the end of a wooden spindle, to weight it and to keep up the spin momentum. The weights of the three complete whorls (20g, 36g and 42g) fall within the standard range for Anglo-Saxon spindle-whorls. Those at Mucking were 14–60g, but mostly 25–45g (Hamerow 1993, 65), which compares with those from Anglo-Scandinavian Coppergate, York, which were mostly 10–55g (Walton Rogers 1997, 1743–75). Only the whorls from middle Anglo-Saxon Flixborough, Lincolnshire, a high status site with a number of features suggesting specialised textile production, were lighter, at 10–20g (Walton Rogers 2009, 25).

To spin good quality yarn takes skill and dexterity, but such skills were probably quite commonplace among Anglo-Saxon women. Spinning would keep a large number of them busy for much of the year, if they were to prepare enough wool and linen yarn for weaving. Anyone who spins on a regular basis will have at least two spindles and three or four whorls, from which a spindle and whorl can be selected for the job in hand. A single whorl in a grave will not, therefore, represent the only spindle-whorl that the woman used in life. Three whorls in a box at the feet of a woman in grave 121 at Burwell, Cambridgeshire (Lethbridge 1931, 67–9) are more likely to represent a typical spinner's kit.

Sword-beater (weaving batten)

(Grave 250)

A long iron sword-beater or weaving batten (d) had been placed at the side of the woman in Grave 250. It was positioned by the left lower leg, with its tip pointing towards the head and it was probably wrapped for burial. The coarse plain twill preserved on one face of the blade is very like the textiles used to wrap spearheads in men's graves (*see* p 197). The burial is particularly well furnished and dated to Phase 3a. The woman was aged 25–30 years and wore an elaborate beaded collar in the Byzantine style (*Dress Style V*; *see* pp 187–8).

The sword-beater is 615mm long, of which 135mm is the tang for the handle and 15mm the tongue-like projection at the opposite end. The tang ends in a suspension ring, now broken, on which the conservator noted the remains of a leather strap. The surviving areas of wood on the tang suggest that the handle was oval or elliptical in section, narrow under the hand, but flaring to meet the blade. The blade is 46–49mm wide, and pattern-welded (*see* pp 273–5).

There is an almost identical sword-beater from Buckland Grave 46 (1), 623mm long x 43mm wide, with a suspension ring at the end of the tang (Evison 1987, 111–12). This was in a grave allocated by Evison to Phase 1 (AD 475–525), although the extensive beading around the woman's neck and the bead types of Group B2 seem at odds with this date. As will be shown, sword-beaters lengthen with time and this example would be better fitted to a date in the late sixth or early seventh century, as would the beaded collar. The grave might therefore be re-dated to Phase 3b. The two other sword-beaters from Buckland 1951–3 are shorter: Grave 20 (1), dated by Evison to Phase 1 and redated to Phase 2a (AD 510/30–*c* 540) is 376 x 46mm and Grave 38 (11) dated by Evison to Phase 3 and redated to Phase 2b/3a (AD *c* 540–580/90) is 411 x 42mm.

Iron sword-beaters with a tang for the handle and a tongue-like projection at the tip have been found in eleven graves in east Kent, two from Finglesham (graves D3 and 203), two from Bifrons, two from Sarre (1860 and grave 4), one from Ozengell, one from outside Ramsgate, possibly also Ozengell, and three from Buckland 1951–3 (surveyed

in Chadwick 1958; updated in Chadwick Hawkes 1969; reviewed in Evison 1987). A recent find from grave C3762 at Saltwood can be added to the list (Walton Rogers and Riddler 2006). Outside this region there are six examples from cemeteries, from Chessell Down, Isle of Wight; Holywell Row, Suffolk; Luton, Bedfordshire; Mitcham, Surrey (*op cit*); Spong Hill, Norfolk (Gilmour 1984), and Edix Hill, Barrington, Cambridgeshire (Malim and Hines 1998, 52, 219, 234, 282–7). There is also an incomplete example from the Anglo-Saxon village at West Stow, Suffolk (West 1985, vol I, 138–40). In the north Anglian region there is a spear-shaped form with a cleft socket instead of a tang, which presages the long spear-shaped beaters of Viking Age Norway (Walton Rogers 1998, 292–4). This type has been identified only recently, due to confusion with spears with parallel-sided blades of Swanton's series G, and its exact distribution has yet to be explored.

Sword-beaters were used to beat the weft upwards on the warp-weighted loom and should be seen as companions to the loomweights and double-ended (cigar-shaped) pin-beaters which are found in the Anglo-Saxon settlements. On the Continent they are found especially amongst the Alamanni, the Lombards and the peoples of Thuringia and Bohemia (Werner 1962b; Chadwick Hawkes 1969, 20; Banck-Burgess 1997, 373–5). The rarity of these artefacts in the core Frankish areas (except for the Kent-influenced cemetery at Herpes in western France) is due to the survival there of the Gallo-Roman two-beam vertical loom, which requires a toothed weft-beater and single-ended pin-beater (*see* p 198; Walton Rogers 2001). The warp-weighted loom was also in use in Scandinavia, but the beaters from the three zones (England, the Continent and Scandinavia) seem to follow independent lines of development. In Scandinavia the earliest are dated to the fourth, fifth and sixth centuries, are 200–500mm long and have tangs and tongue-like tips (Hoffmann 1974, 279–82). They lose the tongue-like tip in the later sixth century, gradually lengthen and at some stage acquire a socketed handle like the northern English finds, so that they emerge in the Viking Age in the fully fledged spear-shaped form, 600–800mm long. The continental examples come from graves with jewellery suggesting dates in the second half of the sixth and early seventh centuries, and they are mostly less than 500mm long, with a bar or retaining knob at the end of the tang (Behrens 1947; Werner 1962b), although Marta Hoffmann refers to an example from Weimar that is 660mm long (Hoffmann 1974, 380).

In Britain most sword-beaters are later than *c* AD 550 and the earliest at Buckland 1951–3 is also one of the shortest (Grave 20, Phase 2a, 376mm long). Several of the beaters were excavated some time ago and have become separated from any datable evidence, but the Chessell Down example comes from a mid sixth-century grave and is 510mm long, the Saltwood example is 530–40mm long and dated to the mid to late sixth century, the Holywell Row beater is 535mm and dated to the second half of the sixth century, while the Edix Hill example is 765mm and comes from a Final Phase bed burial. The sword-beater from West Stow, Suffolk, is over 630mm long (tip missing) and was found outside a late sixth-/seventh-century hall (Hall 7, West 1985, vol I, 138–40). Among the spear-shaped forms in the north, a sixth-century example from Searby, Lincolnshire, is 262mm long (Swanton 1974, 79), a seventh-century beater from Castledyke is 350mm (Walton Rogers 1998, 292–4), and then a ninth-century example from York is 535mm long (Walton Rogers 1992, 887–8; 1997, 1753–5). The evidence suggests a lengthening of the beater in both the tang-and-tongue and the socketed forms, although a graph plotting length against date would not give a smooth curve. A good sword-beater only improves with age and the fact that some were probably kept in use for a generation or so may explain the staggered nature of the data.

The iron beaters are unlikely to represent the full range of beaters used by Anglo-Saxons, since at sites where organic materials are preserved, such as the Frisian terps or Irish bogs, wooden weaving battens are found in a variety of sizes and shapes (Morris 1985). Sonia Chadwick Hawkes has pointed out how frequently those sword-beaters made from iron occur in well-furnished graves and has suggested that they are indicative of social status appropriate to the mistress of an aristocratic house (Chadwick Hawkes 1969, 21). In the author's experience, weaving with the warp-weighted loom proceeds best with two or three people working together, especially when making the fine diamond-patterned twills described below (*see* pp 195–7). It is possible that the woman with the sword-beater had a supervisory role, deciding the weave, maintaining the quality and ensuring that plenty of appropriately spun yarn was ready for the work.

Personal equipment

Fiche à bélière

Ian Riddler and Axel Kerep

(Grave 414)

A single example of a *fiche à bélière*, or *fiche patte*, was recovered from Grave 414 (d). It consists of an iron object with a tapering shaft of square section, surmounted by a broad, closed loop. Three similar examples came from Buckland

Grave 65, and two further *fiches* are recorded from Grave 9 (Evison 1987, 110 and figs 8 and 36). Evison rightly noted that objects of this type are common on the Continent, but are rare in Anglo-Saxon England. Several types can be noted within the Buckland assemblage. The *fiches* from Graves 65 and 414 are plain, with broad loops and shafts of square section, and they correspond well with the definition of the type provided by Joffroy and Pilet (Joffroy 1974, 32; Pilet 1980, 55). One of the *fiches* from Grave 9, however, has a shaft of circular section, which is twisted just below the loop. Twisted shafts are seen on continental examples where, however, the shaft is normally of square section (Joffroy 1974, fig 13.49 and 289).

Fiches à bélière are widespread in graves from the fifth century onwards, and they cannot be closely dated (Pilet 1980, 56; U Koch 2001, 273). On the Continent *fiches* occur both in cemeteries and settlements (Cuisenier 1988, no 312; Catteddu 1992, 81 and fig 27.7). They are confined to male graves, where they are normally found in the belt area, often close to a knife. Within Grave 9, the two *fiches* lay at the waist, with the tips pointing towards the head. In Grave 65, two of the *fiches* were positioned with the knife at the left waist, whilst the third example lay with the buckle at the right waist. In Grave 414 the *fiche* lay beside the knife, with the tip towards the feet. The deceased in Grave 9 was an adult male, as was the elderly skeleton in Grave 65. Grave 414 was also the burial of an adult male.

A few examples of *fiches à bélière* have been found in Anglo-Saxon graves. A *fiche* with a spiral twisted shaft came from grave 5 at the Mount Pleasant cemetery on the Isle of Thanet (Riddler 2008, 285, 297). This was a male burial of seventh-century date. *Fiches* were found also within the Mill Hill, Deal cemetery, in graves 63, 97 and 105 (Parfitt and Brugmann 1997, figs 35, 53 and 56). A further example is known from the middle Saxon site at Dorney Reach, near Maidenhead, Berkshire (Foreman *et al* 2002, iron object no 25).

Fiches à bélière have been regarded as awls, or as objects fulfilling a variety of utilitarian functions (Joffroy 1974, 32; Ament 1976, 115; Evison 1987, 110; U Koch 2001, 273). Their close association with knives has led recently, however, to a return to an earlier interpretation, as culinary implements. The principal objection to this interpretation has been their absence from women's graves (Joffroy 1974, 32) but it remains, nonetheless, a plausible explanation of their function.

It is noted above (p 120) that some of the iron pins from the cemetery were found at the waist of the deceased, particularly in male graves. Where they have been found in this position they are often in close proximity to knives, allowing for the possibility that they served a similar purpose to the *fiches à bélière*.

Awl-like firesteels

Ian Riddler

(Graves 265B, 414 and 423)

Iron awl-like objects were retrieved from three graves, each of which was the burial of an adult male. The object from Grave 265B (hh) was found under the skull of the deceased. The two objects from Grave 414 (e) and the single example from Grave 423 (d2) were beside the iron knives from those graves, lying above the waist.

Evison referred to iron awls in relation to three objects from Grave 65 at Buckland (Evison 1987, 110). The objects from that grave are, in fact, *fiches à bélière*, and further examples from Buckland and other cemeteries in east Kent have been noted above. The objects from Grave 57 include an iron object (Evison 1987, fig 32) of a similar shape and size to the example from Grave 414, as well as a second example, which is fragmentary. Grave 57 was the burial of a male, possibly a juvenile, assigned to Evison's Phase 3 and contemporary therefore with the other awls from the cemetery. The awls lay, once again, around the area of the skull. The small 'spike' from Grave 149 is also likely to be a similar type of object, as Evison suggested (1987, 30). It came from another male grave, assigned in this instance to Phase 6, and it was located under the lower left arm, close to the waist.

The six objects from the cemetery as a whole are small items which include the vestiges of wooden or horn handles, with shafts of square or round section which taper to a point. Four of the handles are wood and two are horn. This contrasts noticeably with the whittle tang handles of the iron knives, almost all of which are made of horn.

On the basis of continental parallels, these objects can be identified as awl-like firesteels (Ilkjaer 1993, 242–6; Schuster 2006, 99–101).

Few examples have been identified from cemeteries in east Kent and this is undoubtedly a consequence of their small size, together with a relative lack of understanding of the nature of the object type. Without the use of radiography and the specialist identification of wood and horn remains, small iron firesteels are difficult items to find and identify. Two possible iron tools from Monkton grave 26 have shafts of square section and could be fragmentary firesteels (Perkins and Chadwick Hawkes 1984, 91 and fig 7). They came from a sixth-century male grave, 'the most important male burial' excavated in that particular cemetery (Perkins and Chadwick Hawkes 1984, 102).

Awl-like firesteels from early Anglo-Saxon burials are generally (though not invariably) associated with the graves of male adults. A firesteel from Snape, for example, came from grave 47, one of the more auspicious boat burials within that cemetery, of late sixth- or early seventh-century date (Filmer-Sankey and Pestell 2001, 107, 111 and fig 110, Ovi). A similar firesteel came from grave 5 at Westgarth Gardens, Bury St Edmunds, Suffolk (West 1988, fig 58.5F). Awl-like firesteels were discovered also within two late seventh-century graves at Harford Farm, Caister St Edmund, Norfolk (Penn 2000, 18, 25 and figs 86 and 92). Whilst grave 25 was that of a male, grave 18 contained grave goods appropriate for a female. Two firesteels came from Harford Farm grave 25, reflecting the presence of two in Grave 414 at Buckland, and two iron tools in Monkton grave 26. Two iron firesteels came also from Spong Hill grave 1244 (Hills 1977, 48). An object from a seventh-century grave at Burghfield, Berkshire, has also been regarded as an awl (Butterworth and Lobb 1992, 23, 57 and fig 12). Their occurrence as single items in four graves at Basel-Bernerring was noted by Martin (1976, 69). They were restricted there to male graves and were found at the waist, usually close to a knife, as at Buckland.

Each of the iron firesteels from Buckland is relatively small, with a slender, tapering shaft. Several 'awl-like' objects from West Heslerton, North Yorkshire, were found in association with tweezers, suggesting that they may have functioned as toilet implements (Haughton and Powlesland 1999, 120). Small firesteels were recovered also from several cremation graves at Spong Hill where, once again, they may have been used as toilet items, and that is the likely function of the Buckland sample (Hills 1977, fig 124.1244; Hills *et al* 1994, fig 114.3059/2b).

Pursemounts and firesteels

Birte Brugmann

(Graves 228A, 300, 381, 437 and 442)

Five graves produced iron objects which according to Brown (1977) were used as firesteels and also as pouch mounts if they have a buckle attached. Four of the Buckland finds have attached buckles (Graves 228A (d); 300 (o); 381 (g2); 437 (k)) and one, Grave 442 (d), is plain. As it seems likely that the iron of which the backs of Anglo-Saxon knives were made was suitable for the production of sparks,[71] a knife would probably have fulfilled the same function as

---

71. For a scientific analysis of firesteels see Seeberger (1985).

an additional firesteel among personal possessions. Thus, firesteels were perhaps 'luxury' items, possibly signalling social status, which may explain the garnet-set firesteel buried with a small girl at Lyminge (see Parfitt and Brugmann 1997, 76). The firesteels at Buckland were found with a ?boy (Grave 442), a ?female juvenile (Grave 228A) and three adults, all certainly or probably male (Graves 300, 381 and 437). Unlike continental row grave cemeteries, firesteels in Anglo-Saxon graves are not mainly found with males, but with both sexes (Stoodley 1999, 22), although males clearly predominate in the present sample.

The firesteels with buckles from Graves 228A and 300 were found at the waist and not associated with other objects that might have formed the possible contents of a pouch. In Grave 437, the firesteel with buckle was covered by a sword, together with a knife and a Roman coin, the latter most likely kept in a container. In Grave 442, the plain firesteel lay side by side with a knife and an iron pin. The firesteel with attached buckle from Grave 381 was found with a knife, an iron rod, a pin and a nail, and the copper alloy mounts of a purse, flat strips of copper alloy with rivet-holes and short rivets, presumably attached to the organic material of a purse.

Few early medieval pursemounts are known, apart from the famous example from Sutton Hoo (Brown 1977). The sixth-century find of a purse from München-Aubing (Dannheimer 1998, pl 82, 19), however, 'suggests that the large size and precise form of the Sutton Hoo purse were already well established by the date of its burial' (Bruce-Mitford 1978, 517). This is supported by the date of Grave 381 to Phase 1b–2a. Though a number of curved iron, copper alloy or silver purse-'frames' have been published in the last two decades,[72] none of them were reconstructed in combination with a firesteel-pursemount. Most of them are of later sixth- and seventh-century date when purses were attached to the belt set with mounts, presumably designed specifically for this purpose (see Vogt 1960) and when firesteels with buckles were no longer in use. The seventh-century firesteel from Buckland Grave 53, however, has three rivet-holes, which 'means that it could be attached to the tinder container by rivets or thongs, although it would seem to be unnecessary in this case for it was found with an iron diamond inside an ivory ring (bag-holder)' (Evison 1987, 111).

More recent Anglo-Saxon finds comparable to the purse frame from Buckland come from Droxford, Hampshire; Apple Down, Sussex and Edix Hill, Cambridgeshire (Malim and Hines 1998, fig 3.67 no 45). Mounts from Chessel Down,

Isle of Wight excavated in the nineteenth century were found with a firesteel with buckle judged by the excavator to be part of the purse (Arnold 1982, fig 20). The firesteel with a buckle and the pursemount at Droxford were recorded *in situ* but unfortunately the grave had been disturbed.[73] The pursemount from Apple Down was found together with the fragment of a firesteel that may or may not have had a buckle (Down and Welch 1990, 103). It would probably take an excavation *en bloc* to prove beyond doubt that a firesteel was attached to, or placed within a purse.

Brown (1977) divided firesteels with animal head terminal into two types, attached to a pouch in different ways – those with bird heads and those with horse heads. The firesteels Grave 381 (g2) and Grave 228A (d) have horse head-shaped terminals suggesting they were attached to the purse with the buckle suspended (see Brown 1977, fig 4). The iron firesteel with buckle Grave 381 (g2) was associated with part of a mineral-preserved leather strap attached to the buckle-loop (see below). Mineralised textile and ?straw remains are attached to one side, wood on leather to the other. Mineralised leather remains are also preserved on the plain side of the copper alloy mounts, but there is no clear evidence that the mounts and the firesteel are part of the same object. If the wood attached to the back of the firesteel were placed between the leather and the iron, it would seem to indicate a wooden back-plate covered by leather, to which the mounts were fixed with short copper alloy rivets. The remains of leather between the iron and the wood, however, could either indicate the leather lining of a wooden back-plate to the purse, or a leather purse lying on, or covered by a wooden object. A purse from grave 10 at Köln-Müngersdorf (Fremersdorf 1955, pl 92, 1) is of particular interest in this context, because in this case a copper alloy back-plate and frame was preserved with a decorated leather cover and an opening through the leather, presumably for a leather strap.

The firesteels Grave 300 (o) and Grave 442 (d) have bird head terminals, Grave 300 (o) with longer curved beaks than those of Grave 442 (d), and, according to Brown (1977) attached to a pouch so that the birds' heads would be positioned upright. Long narrow firesteels with the birds' heads folded over were in use during Phases SD 3–4, AD 480–530, and at Mill Hill, Deal, are dated to Kentish Phase II (Parfitt and Brugmann 1997, table 12). Graves 300 and 442 are dated to Phases 1b–2.

Firesteels with horse heads are a fifth-century development with the best dated example, in Childerich's grave, also one

---

72. Some of them U-shaped with rim-clips. For more recent publications of purse frames see Martin (1991a, 128), Sasse (2001), Pescheck (1996) and Haas-Gebhard (1998, 43) and Fleury and France-Lanord (1998, 11f).
73. 'This object [pursemount] appears to have been damaged [...] and it is difficult to reconstruct its original form, but an associated dark stain suggests that it is the remains of a purse or tinder pouch with associated firesteel and knife' (Aldsworth 1978, 118, fig 19, 2).

of the earliest (Brown 1977, 470). A sixth-century typological development seems to reduce the horse head terminals to simple pointed ends such as those of firesteel Grave 437 (k) with a slightly curved back, a type dated at Mill Hill, Deal to Kentish Phase III.[74] The horse head terminals of firesteel Grave 228A (d) are less contoured than those of firesteel Grave 381(g2) and may represent such a typological development. Grave 437 is dated to Phase 2 and Grave 228 to Phases 3a–7.

Mineral-preserved organic remains associated with pursemounts and firesteels   *Hayley Bullock and Fleur Shearman*

Grave 228A (d)

Investigative cleaning revealed extensive mineral-preserved organic remains on the object including leather, wood and textile. The remains indicate that the purse bar was probably attached to a leather purse that may have had a textile lining and a wood frame. There are mineral-preserved remains of leather passing through the buckle indicating the presence of a strap. This probably relates to the way in which the pursemount was attached or fastened. Hair follicle pattern is visible on the leather and was tentatively identified as bovine (with the assistance of C Calnan). There are no rivet-holes or evidence of stitching to indicate how the purse bar was held in position. Remains of woven textile are also present but under the leather. This would indicate that the fragments were a lining for, or stored inside the purse. The wood present on the purse bar would appear to be part of the structure of the purse.

In the soil lifted with the firesteel/pursemount was a copper alloy buckle, seven loose garnets, a beak-shaped garnet, a piece of millefiori glass and a flint-like stone. The copper alloy buckle (b) had traces of mineral-preserved leather remains between the plates but no clear evidence from around the tongue of the object. It is presumed these objects were enclosed within the purse when deposited in the grave.

Grave 300 (o)

There is extensive mineral-preserved leather present on the object. This probably relates to the purse to which it was attached. A follicle pattern is visible in one area of the leather that suggests an identification of sheep-skin. There are mineral-preserved remains of leather passing through

the central buckle indicating the presence of a strap. This probably relates to the way in which the pursemount was attached or fastened. There is mineral-preserved coarse twill weave textile present on the back of the object on top of the leather. This textile probably relates to garments in which it was in contact with during burial. Traces of mineralised wood were identified as oak (Table 6.12). This wood does not appear to be associated with the pursemount and may be incidental to it.

Grave 381 (g2)

Investigative cleaning revealed extensive mineral-preserved organic remains on the object including leather, wood and textile. There is a band of mineralised leather in the centre of the object. This indicates that the purse or pouch may have been closed by a leather strap which would have fastened to the buckle. The iron pursemount has no rivet holes present for attachment to the purse and there is no evidence of stitching. The front of the firesteel/pursemount is covered with at least three layers of woven textile (see Table 5.7, p 228). This may be associated with the purse/pouch or may be incidental to it; probably from garments with which it was in contact during burial. The back of the pursemount has a single layer of mineralised leather covering the surface. This probably relates to the leather from the purse/pouch. There is also a small area of mineralised wood. The function of this is not known but it may either relate to a wooden reinforcing frame for the pursemount or to an object within the purse or in close association to it. Note that a coffin nail from the same grave (*see* p 434) was also identified as associated with wood remains of ash.

Associated with the firesteel/pursemount are a set of copper alloy bindings or frame for the pursemount. There are six fragments that join to form three fittings. They are flat in section, one fitting is straight and two are curved. They have incised line and dot and circle punched decoration on the front. There are small copper alloy rivets present that may have been used to fasten the frame in position on the purse or pouch. The rivets are 6mm long and may indicate the thickness of the leather to which it was attached. There are mineralised remains of leather in various places on the back of the fittings which indicates that they were fastened to the leather of the purse/pouch. On the right hand terminal there are mineralised remains of vegetable fibres, perhaps straw. These are on top of the woven textile and may relate to a grave covering or lining.

---

74. Parfitt and Brugmann (1997, 76). For the continental chronological background of this date see Schulze-Dörrlamm (1990, 288) and U Koch (2001).

Fig 4.35. Grave 265B, scales and weights *in situ*. Scale 10cm.

Grave 437 (k)

There are mineral-preserved remains of leather passing through the central buckle indicating the presence of a leather strap. This indicates that the purse or pouch may have been closed by a strap which would have fastened to the buckle in the centre of the object. The iron pursemount has no rivet-holes present for attachment to the purse but there is a piece of leather with a line of stitching along the loop of the central buckle. This may indicate the method in which the firesteel was attached to the pursemount, ie by stitching.

On the radiograph there is a denser structure along the bottom of the purse bar which may be the striking edge of the firesteel. In addition a worked flint adhering to a fragment of rod found under the sword is probably associated with the firesteel/pursemount.

Grave 442 (d)

Investigative cleaning revealed mineral-preserved woven textile (Table 5.7) and amorphous skin product remains upon its surface. There is insufficient material evidence to suggest exactly how this firesteel/pursemount was attached to the purse.

Scales and weights

Christopher Scull

(Grave 265B)

Complete balances are rare finds from early Anglo-Saxon graves. The find from Grave 265B brings the number of known examples to ten, nine of which were found with assemblages of weights, ingots and pre-Saxon coins. These earlier finds have been catalogued and discussed in detail, with a metrical analysis of the weight assemblages, in Scull 1990. All but two of the known examples are from Kentish cemeteries, the exceptions being those from burials at Watchfield, Oxfordshire, and Castledyke South, Barton-on-Humber (Scull 1986; 1990; 1992; Drinkall and Foreman 1998). This is the second example known from Buckland, the other being from Grave C (Evison 1987). Balances and weights are also known from two separate burials at Gilton, Kent (Scull 1990; Boys 1792, 868–9; Douglas 1793, 48–52, pl 12; Faussett 1856, 22–3, pl 17).

The disposition in the ground of the balance and weights from Grave 265 (Fig 4.35), and the associated organic remains, suggest that they were buried wrapped in wool or fleece in a rectangular organic container. Although

Sf no	Object letter	Weight (g)	Value in units of 1.56g (ideal weight in parentheses)	Value in units of 1.32g (ideal weight in parentheses)	Deviation from ideal weight (g)	Percentage error	Mineral-preserved organic?	Markings
398	r	24.99	16 (24.96)		+ 0.03	0.12	present	
				19 (25.08)	− 0.11	0.55		
400	s	19.70		15 (19.80)	− 0.10	0.51	present	single dot
402	v	18.32		?14 (18.48)	− 0.16	0.87	present	
408	bb	15.57	10 (15.60)		− 0.03	0.19	present	
393	k2	12.54	8 (12.48)		+ 0.06	0.48	present	
392	k1	9.34	6 (9.32)		+ 0.02	0.21		6 dots
397	q	9.22	6 (9.32)		− 0.10	1.07		double arcade punches
				7 (9.24)	− 0.02	0.22		
403	w	9.11		7 (9.24)	− 0.13	1.41	present	23 line cross
399	t	6.24	4 (6.24)		0.00	0.00	present	
394	m	3.19	2 (3.12)		+ 0.07	2.24		
396	o	2.69		2 (2.64)	− 0.05	1.89		
405	p	1.73	?1 (1.56)		+ 0.17	10.90		
407	aa	1.72	?1 (1.56)		+ 0.16	10.26		
404	y	1.65	1 (1.56)		+ 0.09	5.77	present	10 dot border
401	u	0.79	1/2 (0.78)		+ 0.01	1.28		
406	z	0.46	1/3 (0.52)		− 0.06	11.53	present	

Table 4.18. Regression analysis of weights from Grave 265B.

positive identification has not been possible (see below) it seems likely that the container was a pouch or case of leather or hide like that known from grave 67 at Watchfield, Oxfordshire (Scull 1986; 1992). The Watchfield case, which was sufficiently well-preserved to allow a reconstruction, had angled copper alloy fittings at either end, and it is tempting to suppose that the copper alloy strip, Grave 265B (x), is a similar fitting, albeit broken and incomplete at the time of burial. The balance and weights from Buckland Grave C were found associated with 'dark peaty stuff', probably the remains of an organic pouch or case (Evison 1987, 120).

The assemblage buried with the balance from Grave 265 is very similar in its composition to the other known examples. They typically consist of two or three copper alloy or lead ingots and a number of pre-Saxon coins which have often been filed or abraded, and marked, presumably to adapt them for use as weights. These are mostly Roman but Iron Age coins are known from Watchfield and Gilton grave 66, and a Greek civic coin from Watchfield. Weights of Byzantine form are also known from Watchfield and Gilton grave 66.

These assemblages have been interpreted as collections or sets of weights on three grounds: their occurrence with balances; the occurrence of clearly-recognisable weights as at Watchfield and Gilton; and the re-use of pre-Saxon coins, which retained no monetary value, often with marks which may indicate a specific weight. This interpretation is supported by metrical analysis indicating coherent structures based on weight standards equivalent to those of contemporary continental and Byzantine gold coins, which in turn suggests that these balances and weights were used to weigh coins and bullion to these standards (Scull 1990). The occurrence of touchstones with both balance assemblages from Gilton supports the suggestion that these were used to weigh gold.

The result of metrical analysis of the assemblage from Grave 265 (see below) conforms to the pattern observed in the other assemblages, with weight standards equivalent to 1.56g and 1.32g. It does not follow that this was a complete set when buried – it is possible that the assemblage selected for burial may include tokens, counters or discards – but there is strong evidence that the assemblage includes a high proportion of genuine weights and that the balance set from Grave 265B served the same function as the other known examples.

The balance assemblage from Barton-on-Humber is from a seventh-century female grave. Otherwise, all balances and weights from early Anglo-Saxon graves, where associations are known, are from male weapon burials which may be dated to the second and third quarters of the sixth century (Scull 1990, 186; Brugmann, p 376). Grave 265B reinforces this pattern and the overwhelmingly Kentish distribution of finds.

None of the other known examples can be convincingly interpreted as a smith's or jeweller's balance (Scull 1990, 196–7) and the small assemblage of ?tool(s) and scrap items buried next to the balance set in Grave 265B resembles a bag or purse collection rather than a tool kit and is at best equivocal evidence for any direct link with craft working. It therefore seems likely that the social identity of the individuals buried with these balances and weights was linked to their handling of bullion, coined or uncoined, for use as currency (Scull 1990, 196–208). Balances have been interpreted as direct evidence of commercial activity and those buried with them as merchants or traders. There is, though, no reason to assume that currency use need have been restricted to commercial transactions rather than social, judicial or jurisdictional payments (Scull 1990, 196–208 and refs) and it has been suggested that the man buried in Buckland Grave C may be a good candidate for royal port-reeve or similar official (Evison 1967, 63; 1987, 120–1). However, while the link with bullion and the likely contexts of currency use would support the identification of balances and weights as an attribute of higher-status burial, the precise social identity of any single individual buried with them must remain conjectural.

Metrology of the weights

Successful metrical analysis depends upon the extent to which valid inferences about the original weight may be drawn from current weight and the precision which may originally have been expected.

For the purposes of this exercise, as with the previous analysis of earlier finds, the weight after investigative cleaning is used and it is assumed that copper alloy items with good surface condition are still close to their original weight when buried; 0.20g is adopted as the maximum limit of tolerance (for details of the reasoning behind this, including a discussion of the precision which might be expected from early medieval balances, and the constraints and method used see Scull 1990, 187–90). One item Grave 265B (n) is incomplete and so has been excluded from the analysis. In nine other cases the weight includes that of mineral-preserved organic material adhering to the item but in only one case (s) is this likely to have a significant affect.

The results of a simple regression analysis are presented in Table 4.18. Twelve of the items correspond to simple fractions or multiples of a unit equivalent to 1.56g within an acceptable limit of tolerance and nine of these correspond to within 0.10g. Six correspond to simple multiples of a unit equivalent to 1.32g. Two items (q) and (r) may have had dual values. There is therefore a strong prior case that the assemblage includes a high proportion of genuine weights. At the very least it can be said that the assemblage contains nine items which could be used today to weigh against a standard of 1.56g to within 0.09g or better.

The identification of a weight standard of 1.56g within the assemblage is supported by the marking of six dots on

(k1) for which a value of six units is proposed. There is, however, no apparent relationship between the markings on (q), (s), (w) and (y) and their proposed weight values and these may be interpreted as private markings rather than numerical indicators.

Mineral-preserved organic remains associated with the scales and weights　*Hayley Bullock*

Investigative cleaning revealed mineral-preserved organic remains on the objects. These indicate that the scales set may have been contained in a leather pouch or container, secured in place with an organic packing material and that

Sf no	Object letter	Description	Organic material A	B	C
389	ee	Balance beam	#	#	#
391	dd	Scale pan	#	#	#
390	cc	Scale pan			#
408	bb	Coin/Weight			#
407	aa	Coin/Weight			#
406	z	Coin/Weight			#
405	p	Coin/Weight			
404	y	Coin/Weight			#
403	w	Coin/Weight			#
402	v	Coin/Weight			#
401	u	Coin/Weight			
400	s	Coin/Weight			#
399	t	Coin/Weight			#
398	r	Coin/Weight			#
397	q	Coin/Weight			
396	o	Coin/Weight			
395	n	Weight			
394	m	Coin/Weight			#
393	k1	Coin/Weight			
392	k2	Coin/Weight			
386	jj	Weight			
387	kk	Weight			
388	ll	Shaft			Leather
385	ii	Ferrule			Wood shaft
384	hh	Awl			Wood handle
383	gg	Shaft (chisel)			Wood handle
382	x	Strip			#

A = A dark brown crumbly organic material. This material has yet to be identified but based on similar scales sets from Buckland 1951–3 Grave C and Watchfield this material may be leather from a purse/pouch in which the scales set was held

B = Mineral-preserved spun threads around the suspension rings of the scale pans and loops of the balance beam. These threads suspended the scale pans from the balance beam

C = Thin, fine, short, unwoven, random fibres. The fibres have not been identified but may relate to an organic packing material used to hold the objects in the scale set together

Table 4.19. Mineral-preserved organic remains on objects from Grave 265B.

the scale pans were suspended from the balance beam with thread (Table 4.19).

During investigative cleaning three types of mineral-preserved organic remains were revealed: a dark, crumbly material (A); spun fibres (B); and a fine unwoven, unspun material (C). There are mineral-preserved spun threads (B) wound around the suspension rings of the scale pans; through one of the oval loops of the balance beam and on the detached suspension loop of the balance beam. In addition, there is a distinct spun thread present on the surface of the scale pan (dd) and on one side of the balance beam. From their location it would appear that these mineral-preserved fragments are the remains of threads which suspended the scale pans from the balance beam and suspended the whole weighing system from the detached suspension loop.

A dark brown crumbly material (A) is present in areas on the surface of the scale pan (dd) and the balance beam. Similar scales sets from the Anglo-Saxon burials of Watchfield and Buckland, Grave C were held in leather cases (Scull 1986), the remains of which appear to be similar to the remains in this grave. This material has yet to be conclusively identified, but may be leather remains relating to a purse/pouch or box in which the scales set was held.

There are also thin, fine, short, unwoven, random fibres (C) present on many of the objects within the set, including the scale pans, balance and eleven of the other objects. The identity and function of this material is not clear but it may relate to an organic packing material used to hold the objects in place.

Keys and châtelaines

Angela Care Evans

(Graves 204, 222, 245, 250, 289, 314A, 318, 347, 348, 360, 376, 381, 387, 391A, 407 and 444)

Sixteen graves, mainly female, with two probable male exceptions (Graves 348 and 381), contained keys and other elements associated with the wearing of a châtelaine. Many are in poor condition with their functional end damaged but, where this survives, the majority of the 'keys' have finger-crooked wards and variations may reflect temporal difference. Although they span Phases 1 to 5–7 of the cemetery's use, the keys are generally similar in style, made with looped heads and rounded, squared or rectangular shafts, occasionally with a twist in their length. Two graves (Graves 376 and 387) contained keys or latch-lifters with T-shaped terminals, in both cases associated with keys with finger-crooked wards. Two graves contained the fittings

of complex châtelaines, one (Grave 407) with a variety of copper alloy tubes and lozenges, the other (Grave 376) with short iron rods, all perhaps fittings from pendent straps.

The function of keys and their role as an indicator of status have been examined in previous excavation reports (eg Meaney 1998, 268ff; for keys at Buckland 1951–3 see Evison 1987, 116–17). It seems probable that keys with both finger-crooked wards and T-shaped terminals can be thought of as functional, capable of unfastening both doors and the closing devices of cupboards and chests. Whether they are keys in the strictest sense, or latch-lifters, is uncertain as domestic architecture and furniture is generally missing in the context of early Anglo-Saxon graves. The question of keys in relation to the status of the women with which they are buried is also one that is difficult to interpret, although it is generally assumed that the presence of keys in a grave is a pointer to the status of the dead woman. However, given the very different material attributes in graves containing keys (eg Graves 376 and 407), it would seem that the possession of a key or several keys may reflect social rather than material standing.

Only two graves (Graves 376 and 407), contained fittings that can be associated with the wearing of a châtelaine with metal fittings, perhaps originally the links on pendent straps. The fittings of the two are stylistically different and this may be a reflection of the temporal difference between them. Grave 407 is assigned to Phase 2 and the surviving châtelaine fittings are made up of copper alloy tubes separated by iron lozenges. In contrast the fittings in Grave 376, assigned to Phase 5–7, are made of twisted iron rod which is associated with a mineralised leather thong and a bone/ivory bag ring. These fittings can be compared with fittings from an equivalent châtelaine found in the robbed out grave of a high status woman beneath mound 14 in the high status cemetery at Sutton Hoo (Evans 2005). Whether they belong to a waist belt or pendent straps is unclear as in both cases they were found clustered in the region of the left pelvis and the upper left femur. They may, however, belong to pendent straps in the style of some continental châtelaines, for example those from Gimbsheim, Kreiz Alzey-Worms, (graves 7 and 1; Die Franken, cat ix.2.19, 40, 1026).

Phase 1–2 keys, found in Graves 348 and 444, are singletons. The key found in Grave 444 (f) has a rolled head and a shaft with a flattened, rectangular cross section. This expands as it moves away from the loop head and appears to flare just before it ends at a break. Although identified as a potential key, it is possible that it represents the terminal and shaft of some other object although its associated finds give no clue to its identity. The single key in Grave 348 (a) was associated with an inlaid kidney-shaped buckle (c), a cylindrical organic container with metal fittings (b) and an iron knife (d). It has a round-sectioned shaft that develops from three flattened 'wards' (one missing), tapering to a narrow neck where it breaks. Also of Phase 1–2 is possible male Grave 381, which contained the remains of two, perhaps three, keys found in two complexes of iron. The first (g5) consists of a probable key with a looped head ending in a curlicue. Its shaft is rounded and broken. To it is corroded a section of shaft also with a rounded cross-section, which ends in a serpentine hooked ward ending in a curlicue. This fragment is probably the terminal belonging the loop head although no clear join survives. Also in the grave is a fragment of iron rod with a rounded cross section and a tightly coiled head (g7), possibly the remains of a second key. The three graves with keys that belong to Phases 1–2 vary in status but are linked by the absence of beads, the presence of which are a distinguishing feature of graves containing keys or châtelaines in later phases.

Rich Grave 347, of Phase 2a, contained forty-one beads and three keys (j). The keys have simple loop heads and flattened rectangular shafts. Two end in semi-circular 'wards' which face in the opposite direction to the loops, while the third ends in a small hook which faces forwards from the front of the shaft. One key has a fragment of its suspension ring still in the loop and one has a small patch of mineral-replaced textile on one surface at the junction of shaft and 'ward'. Another high status grave of Phase 2 (Grave 407) has the remains of copper alloy and iron elements, which can be interpreted as fittings from the pendent strands of a châtelaine (i; below). These were found on the left side of the pelvis. The grave also contained 115 beads.

Definite keys are a rare attribute in Phase 2b graves, with only one burial (Grave 204) containing the remains of two keys with loop heads and damaged wards (k). These were found associated with copper alloy suspension rings and are covered with mineral-replaced textile. The associated finds in the grave include a keystone garnet disc brooch (b), a garnet inlaid ring bezel (i and j) and 135 beads, (a) and (n).

It is in Phase 3a that the only cluster of temporally associated graves occurs with three high status burials (Graves 222, 245 and 250) containing a total of seventeen keys between them. These graves also contained over 100 beads each. Grave 222 produced the remains of four fragmentary keys placed on the left femur (h). Each has a shaft with a flattened rectangular cross section. Three end in a simple rolled loop and two of these are associated with suspension rings, one partial ring of iron, the other a complete ring of copper alloy, suggesting perhaps that the keys belong to two different groups. Only one of the four keys survives in more or less complete form with the beginnings of a

narrow finger crook ward placed at right-angles to the shaft. Mineral-replaced textile remains on one side of three of the shafts and also on a large iron ring associated with the keys, possibly for suspending the two groups. In contrast to the two groups of keys in Grave 222, Grave 245 contained a bunch of six keys corroded to each other (k). These have thin rectangular shafts with simple loop heads with fragments of an iron slip-knot ring still *in situ*. The keys are damaged but all have angular finger-crook wards. Small patches of mineral-replaced textile is present on both shafts and wards, suggesting that the keys, which were found near the left arm, were loose and not contained in a bag. Two distinct clusters of keys on rings (o) of different weights were found in Grave 250. One consists of four keys with an associated lightweight iron ring, all heavily covered with mineral-replaced textile on one surface. The keys have loop heads and rectangular shanks, two with barley-twist, and rounded finger-crook wards. The second cluster is made up of three keys with flattened rectangular shafts attached to a heavy iron ring. Two of the wards are missing, but the third may have been rounded and similar to those of the first cluster. Amongst the associated finds is an angular ward, which may also belong to this cluster.

These three graves, all high status, contain not only clusters of similar style keys, but large numbers of beads. In contrast, Grave 360, a grave assigned to Phase 3b, contains two keys (f) that were found on the left pelvis. Both have tightly looped heads with the remains of the suspension ring still *in situ* and short square shafts that terminate in one case with an angular finger-crook ward and in the other with a semi-circular ward similar to those in Grave 347. The grave also contained seventy-four beads (a) and a copper alloy sword pommel, perhaps a keepsake (e).

In Phase 5–7, child Grave 376 contained one of the most remarkable assemblages of keys and châtelaine fittings in the cemetery. Found in a complex on the left femur were a cluster of five, perhaps six keys and connecting rods (b)–(g) from a châtelaine belt or cord associated with fragments of bone/ivory, from a bag ring (h). The keys were probably suspended as two, perhaps three, units as three are associated with the remains of copper alloy rings of two thicknesses and two with an iron ring. The latter, although having different terminals, appear to be a pair (g1 and g2). One has a barley-twist shaft and ends in a typical angular finger-crook ward (g1) but the other has a tightly curled loop and a flattened rectangular shaft, which ends in a double finger crook ward (g2). The three keys associated with copper alloy suspension rings consist of a pair corroded to each other, with looped ends, square sectioned shafts and angular finger-crook wards (b). The third has a looped head, barley-twist shaft with a distinctive S/Z twist. This key ends in rising wards to either side of the shaft forming a T-shaped terminal (c).

All five keys are covered with patches of mineral-replaced textile and are associated in the complex with iron châtelaine fittings of barley-twist rods with looped terminals alternating with lengths of flattened rod also with looped ends (d and e). The complex contained a sixth fitting, which although small, may also be a key (f). This has a looped head above a double collar, a flattened rectangular shaft and a curved terminal with a slight backward kick, perhaps originally a semi-circular ward in the style of those found in Graves 347 and 360. The two keys in the latter grave are similar in size to this example.

Four graves with keys fall outside the phasing sequence of the cemetery (Graves 289, 314A, 318 and 387). Stratigraphically early Grave 289 contains a figure-of-eight iron ring, a second iron ring and the remains of four fragmentary keys, (b)–(d). Two are still attached to an iron ring and a third with a swan neck loop is associated with a length of iron wire. All four keys have looped heads, squared shafts with traces of twisting in the corrosion and semi-circular finger-crook wards. Four, perhaps five, keys were found in Grave 318 (b) and two of these have looped heads and squared shafts with traces of twisting on one, one has a semi-circular finger-crook ward while the other is more angular. These two keys share the same iron suspension ring and are associated with three smaller keys. Two with rectangular shafts and the remains of distorted finger-crook wards are attached to a second iron ring. The third fitting in this group has a ring head, a rounded shaft and a hooked terminal that is bent back against the shaft – its identification as a key is uncertain. All have traces of mineral-replaced textile on the loops and wards. In contrast to the keys with squared shafts, Grave 314A contained two, perhaps three, keys with flattened rectangular shafts and small rounded loops (d). One has an angular finger-crook ward, while the second terminates in two small hooks reminiscent of the single hooked key also with a tapering flattened rectangular shaft in Grave 347 (j). Grave 387 also contains a key with two forward facing hooks (b), which is associated with a second key with missing wards. Both were found together with a third key, corroded to an iron knife, with a flattened rectangular shaft which develops into upward facing wards so that, although probably functional, it resembles a T-shaped 'girdle-hanger' in the same way as the key with S/Z twisted shaft in Grave 376.

Leather and associated mineral-preserved organics found with keys/girdle-hangers   *Fleur Shearman*

In Grave 314A there are three iron keys/girdle-hangers. Mineral-preserved leather thongs are preserved on each of the three suspension loops. They were possibly strung together and hung at the waist. The feature is also found on the key/girdle-hangers from Grave 318. Remains of a leather thong suspension/attachment loop were present on two items from the group of keys. In Grave 413 a mass of iron key/girdle-hangers and associated iron rings were found. The associated leather relates to remains of thongs for suspension/attachment. In the example from Grave 381 leather on keys is extensive and not localised on the suspension terminals. It has therefore been interpreted as leather associated with the adjacent purse (*see* p 148). Feathers preserved on the latch lifters from Grave 376 are interpreted as evidence for an eiderdown or feather mattress by Walton Rogers (p 203).

Tweezers, toilet sets and nail cleaners

Angela Care Evans

(Graves 215, 218, 237, 262, 281, 306, 331, 336, 349, 351B, 367, 423 and 437)

Thirteen graves contained objects that can be associated with personal care, the majority are copper alloy tweezers (11), but one nail cleaner and one toilet set were also found. These toilet accessories are found in graves of Phases 1–3 of the cemetery and are found in both male and female graves, with eight occurrences in the graves of women and three in male graves. All the examples are functional and were presumably used to remove unwanted hair (but see MacGregor and Bolick 1993, 220 for a discussion on non-functional tweezers) and for personal cleansing.

In Phases 1 and 2 seven toilet accessories were recorded, six tweezers (Graves 237 (c), 281 (o), 336 (b), 349 (c), 351B (b), 437 (f)) and one toilet set (Grave 306). Apart from the male with a sword (Grave 437) all are from female graves. The copper alloy tweezers from the undated but stratigraphically early Grave 237 (c) were associated with two annular brooches (a) and (b); they were found on the left pelvis and have parallel-sided arms decorated with mouldings below the spring head and above the incurved terminals. They are 65mm long and are the largest of the copper alloy tweezers.

Grave 281, a well-furnished female grave, which included a disc brooch (a), contained a small tweezers placed near the left femur, (o), 38mm. This has broad arms and gently incurving terminals. Immediately below the spring head on one arm is a band of mineral-replaced textile. Traces of this survive in the corrosion on the other arm and it is probably the remains of a textile loop.

The well-furnished woman's grave, Grave 336, contained plain copper alloy tweezers with delicate arms springing from a ring head and expanding to sharply incurved terminals (b). The tweezers in Grave 349 (c) were found on the chest together with a copper alloy ring and a small group of fourteen glass beads (a). They are 47mm long and plain with narrow, slightly expanding arms and incurved terminals. Grave 351B, a grave containing two small-long brooches, (a) and (d), a miniature digitated brooch (c) and a cruciform brooch (e), also contained a small copper alloy tweezers (b), 31mm long, found by the right humerus. Its arms are plain, broad in relation to their length and expand slightly from the head to the incurved terminals. Male grave, Grave 437, belonging to Phase 2, contained copper alloy tweezers (c) alongside the right femur.

The toilet set in Grave 306 produced a single two-implement toilet set (b) (MacGregor and Bolick 1993, 216–18, esp 37.6). This was found on the right collar bone and consists of a tinned pick (b1) and a second implement (b2) whose terminal is missing. The pick has a ring above shoulders cut from the flat-sectioned strip that forms the top of the shaft. This is twisted below the shoulders for a length of 48mm before flattening out to a point. The second instrument, also tinned, has an oval loop with a curlicue. The shaft, like the pick, is made from a flat strip of copper alloy, which is broken at the beginning of the twisted section. Both implements are associated with a copper alloy slip-know ring (b3), which is not tinned. Apart from the toilet set the grave contained only twenty-one beads (a), twenty glass and one amber.

In Phase 2–3 of the cemetery a male grave (Grave 262) had large iron tweezers (c), 78mm, at the waist. These have a broad angular head and splaying arms with sharply incurved terminals. Another male of Phase 2–3a is represented by Grave 423, provided with a pair of copper alloy tweezers (e), 60mm long. Tweezers were also found in two more probable male burials, Graves 215 (c) and 367 (b). These graves are both unphased. Phase 3a produced only one set of tweezers in Grave 331. The grave, which is that of a woman, also contains a swag of amber and glass beads, (a) and (e). The tweezers (d) are made from a thick strip of copper alloy that is bent to form an oval ring head, before developing into arms that expand to the incurved terminals. They were found on the left femur.

A toilet instrument, in this case a nail cleaner, was found in an unclassified grave of a juvenile female. The grave, Grave 218, is amply furnished and the nail cleaner is distinctively made of copper alloy with a ring head and a flat rectangular shaft that expands to a scalloped waist. The terminal is slotted in much the same way as a modern cuticle trimmer (for other examples of these, see MacGregor and Bolick 1993, 225–6, esp 39.2 and 39.5).

Antler comb and case

Ian Riddler

(Grave 420)

A near-complete antler single-sided composite comb and an accompanying case (d) came from Grave 420 (Fig 4.36). The comb lay by the left ankle of the deceased, close to a glass bell-beaker (c). The grave was the burial of a probable adult female, aged 20–25.

The comb is single-sided, with a small projecting handle at the centre of its back. It is decorated on one side by double ring-and-dot patterns, confined by quadruple diagonal lines. The other connecting-plate is more restrained and merely includes double framing lines and two further incised lines across its centre. The decoration of one of the connecting-plates of the comb case reflects that of the display side of the comb, and suggests that they were designed to be used together. Elsewhere in early Anglo-Saxon England, combs were not necessarily deposited with their original cases (Hills 1981).

Combs were also recovered from Buckland Graves 30 and 110, and possibly from a further nine graves, where vestiges of bone or antler, or small iron rivets, indicate their former presence (Evison 1987, 119). Little can be said, however, of the combs from those graves. The three remaining combs from the cemetery include a double-sided composite (Grave 110), a single-sided composite (Grave 420) and a comb (Grave 30), which may have begun as a double-sided composite, but was deposited as a single-sided object (Evison 1987, 119). Although several double-sided composite combs of middle Saxon date have been re-used as single-sided combs, it is more likely, however, that this comb was always intended to be a single-sided composite. Two of the three combs were accompanied by cases. The comb from Grave 30 was found in the grave of an adult female assigned to Evison's Phase 3, and the example from Grave 110 came from the burial of an adult woman with an unborn child. Two *sceattas* found in the grave allow it to be dated to the late seventh century (Evison 1987, 181).

All three objects include features that are unusual for combs produced in early Anglo-Saxon England and they are briefly reviewed here as a group. The single-sided composite from Grave 420 (d) has a small handle above the line of the comb back. To avoid confusion with other comb forms (and handled combs in particular), this type can be described as centre-handled. A similar device can be seen on a comb from Castledyke South (Lincolnshire), which is thought to be of seventh-century date (Drinkall and Foreman

Fig 4.36. Grave 420, antler comb *in situ*. Scale 10cm.

1998, 329 and fig 93). The device is not seen on any other combs of early Anglo-Saxon date and it is more common on contemporary examples from the Continent. Brynja has published a series of centre-handled combs, which come from the Mälaren region of Sweden and belong largely to the first part of the sixth century (Brynja 1997). Some were intended to fit into comb cases (Brynja 1997, fig 2). Combs of this type are known also from Broa, in Gotland, Sweden (MacGregor 1985, 85).

Closer parallels are provided by single-sided composite combs with small projecting handles which come from Merovingian contexts. They include combs from Oberflacht and Schretzheim (Petitjean 1995, pls III.2 and V.2; U Koch 1977, 92 and Taf 50.17). The same feature can also be seen on a comb from Frisia (Roes 1963, 17 and pl XVIII.1). The Schretzheim comb was also accompanied by a case. As a group, these combs share common characteristics, including broad connecting-plates that taper only a little towards each end, an absence of projecting wings and small projecting handles at the centre of the comb back. The handles are decorative, rather than functional (Petitjean 1995, 150).

The sample of combs is relatively small and they cannot be closely dated. It is likely that they were produced around the middle or the second half of the sixth century, although the comparable Scandinavian evidence might indicate a slightly earlier date.

The double-sided composite comb from Grave 110 was enclosed within a case and the general type is well-known from Merovingian contexts (eg Behrens 1947, Abb 12, 15, 19, 22 and 27; Bertram 1996, 86), although the addition of a copper alloy band to retain the comb is a little unusual. The type is rarely seen in Anglo-Saxon cemeteries or settlement contexts, however, although one example is attested from Driffield, Yorkshire, grave 21 (Mortimer 1905, 281 and fig 799). Both should perhaps be considered as Merovingian combs deposited in Anglo-Saxon England.

The comb from Grave 30 is altogether more enigmatic, particularly for the manner in which it utilises doubled connecting-plates (Evison 1987, fig 18). Only the central part of the comb survives and it lacks both the comb teeth and the end segments. Both sides include thin plates of copper alloy positioned between the connecting-plates. The rectangular shape of the comb is paralleled by an example from Frisia, as Evison noted (Evison 1987, 120; Roes 1963, pl XX.2), and also by an undecorated single-sided composite from *Hamwic* (Southampton) which, however, lacks a second set of connecting-plates (Holdsworth 1980, fig 15.1.1).

During the period from the fifth to the seventh century few combs were buried with accompanying cases in graves. Less than 20 per cent of the sample of Merovingian combs considered by Petitjean included cases, whether for single- or double-sided combs (Petitjean 1995, 158). On the Continent the deposition of combs reached a peak around the middle of the sixth century and declined rapidly by the seventh century (Petitjean 1995, 170; Sasse 2001, 101).

Ivory rings

Ian Riddler

(Graves 250, 255, 376, 419 and 432)

Fragments of ivory rings were found in five of the graves from the 1994 excavations. In two cases only small pieces of ivory remain, some of which nonetheless retain an indication of their original curvature (Table 4.20). In contrast, the ivory ring from Grave 250 (b) is virtually complete, as also is the example from Grave 432 (b). In each case the ring has been cut to a circular or oval form, with a rounded square section.

The discovery of five ivory rings from the 1994 excavations complements earlier finds from the Buckland cemetery, where Evison noted their presence in a further five graves. They were located either by the left femur or between the knees of the deceased, all of which were females (Evison 1987, 118 and figs 5.8, 29.6, 38.4 and 62.4). The ivory rings from the 1994 excavations also come entirely from the burials of women, usually adults, and they had

been placed in similar positions in the grave, either beyond the left leg, or a little above the pelvis, but with no examples placed as low as the knees.

The graves cover all phases within the cemetery as a whole, which reflects the situation across the other cemeteries of early Anglo-Saxon England (Geake 1997, 81; Hills 2001, 138–9). In general, rings of this form and material seem to occur throughout most of the early Anglo-Saxon period (Myres and Green 1973, 101).

Other Kentish finds of ivory rings include examples from Bifrons, Kingston, Ozengell and Sarre (Chadwick Hawkes 2000, 60; Faussett 1856, 66–7; Millard *et al* 1969, 22–4 and fig 3.1; Perkins 1992, 91; Huggett 1988, fig 3). A perforated fragment from Sarre illustrated by Brent is likely to have formed part of an antler burr ring, of the type described below, rather than an ivory ring (Brent 1864–5, 182). The fragments from Kingston come from a grave of the second half of the seventh century, whilst those from Ozengell and Sarre are likely to be earlier in date (Millard *et al* 1969, 23).

Ivory rings are commonly found both in inhumation and cremation cemeteries, and occasionally in settlement contexts. Green provided a comprehensive list of cemeteries in which ivory rings had been encountered (Myres and Green 1973, 101 note 1) and they have been found in a large number of other cemeteries published in recent years (Hills 2001), including Apple Down, Sussex (Down and Welch 1990, 103); Barrington, Cambridgeshire (Malim and Hines 1998, 218); Beckford, Worcestershire (Evison and Hill 1996, 22); Berinsfield, Oxfordshire (Boyle *et al* 1995, 90); Castledyke, Lincolnshire (Drinkall and Foreman 1998, 285–6); Illington, Norfolk (Davison *et al* 1993, fig 46); Lechlade, Gloucestershire (Boyle *et al* 1998); Newark-on-Trent, Nottinghamshire (Kinsley 1989, 18); Portway, Hampshire (Cook and Dacre 1985, 92); Sancton, East Yorkshire (Timby 1993, 279); Spong Hill, Norfolk (Hills 1977, 30; Hills and Penn 1981, fig 180; Hills, Penn and Rickett 1987, fig 118);

Grave	Grave	Object number/ letter	Sf no	Preservation	Internal diam (mm)	Gender	Phase	Location
1951–3	1	8		Near-complete	124	Female	3	Outside left femur
	38	10		Fragmentary		Female	3	Under knives, between femurs
	53	6		Incomplete	86	Female	5	Inside Left femur
	75	4		Incomplete	98	Female	7	Between knees
	160	7		Incomplete	89	Female	6	By left knee
1994	250	b	340	Near-complete	94	Female	3a	Outside left femur
	255	p	334–5	Incomplete	115	Female	1b	Above left pelvis
	376	h	625	Fragmentary		Female	5–7	Outside left femur
	419	d	1003	Fragmentary		Female	2a	Above left pelvis
	432	b	843	Incomplete	105	Female	1b–2	Under left elbow, above pelvis

Table 4.20. Details of ivory rings.

Grave	Glass bead	Copper alloy brooch	Copper alloy ring	Copper alloy disc	Copper alloy mount	Antler burr disc	Iron knife	Iron keys	Iron lozenge	Iron ring	Iron rods/ girdle-hanger	Iron pursemount	Bone pin-beater	Garnets
1			x				x	x		x				
38														
53							x	x				x		
75													x	
160											x			
250				x					x					x
255		x	x											
376								x			x			
419					x	x			x					
432	x						x							

Table 4.21. Objects found in the vicinity of ivory rings.

Thurmaston, Leicestershire (Williams 1983, 170) and West Heslerton, North Yorkshire (Haughton and Powlesland 1999, 117). They occur in continental burials from the second half of the fourth century onwards, through to the seventh century (Heege 1987, 142; Bode 1998, 96). Ivory rings from cremation burials are associated strongly but not invariably with females, as is the case with the finds from the inhumation burials at Buckland (Richards 1987, 128; Hills 2001, 141). On rare occasions, fragments of ivory rings have also been found in settlement contexts, at Waterbeach, Cambridgeshire and Sutton Courtenay, Berkshire (Lethbridge 1927, fig 4.8; Leeds 1923, pl XXVIII.1.h; Myres and Green 1973, 101).

Huggett provided provisional figures for their occurrence in early Anglo-Saxon graves, but these are inaccurate and they underestimate the totals known from cremation cemeteries, in particular (Huggett 1988, 68 and fig 3; cf also Arnold 1988, 52–3; Hills 2001). Fragments of forty-two ivory rings came from the cremation cemetery at Loveden Hill, Lincolnshire and well over 100 pieces are now known from Spong Hill, Norfolk alone (Bond 1994; Hills 2001; Catherine Hills, pers comm).

Some of the latest examples from Anglo-Saxon England appear in the Buckland cemetery. Thereafter, ivory rings disappear from the archaeological record in England. They are not seen amidst the collections of material from the pre-Viking trading and production centres, and they have not come from settlement contexts of middle Saxon date. A comparable item from the Anglo-Saxon monastery at Jarrow is a ring which has a diameter of approximately 125mm (Riddler 2006). It is made from whale bone however, and not from ivory.

Merovingian examples of ivory rings have been described by a number of authors (Vogt 1960, 85–90; Myres and Green 1973, 101; Renner 1970, 52–3; Meaney 1981, 250–3; MacGregor 1985, 111–12; Heege 1987, 141–2). They occur both in Frankish and in Alamannic graves, and they are found on occasion in Italian graves. They are generally accompanied by openwork copper alloy discs, as at Bülach, Cividale or Marktoktoberdorf, for example (Meaney 1981, fig VII.j; Menghin 1983, Abb 159; Menis 1992, pl X.49h; MacGregor 1985, fig 62c). In some cases the discs are joined to the rings by copper alloy bands and the two elements may have worked together to secure and close the pouch opening (MacGregor 1985, 102).

It appears that the ivory rings themselves were used in a similar manner in Anglo-Saxon England, but the absence of accompanying copper alloy openwork discs in insular contexts suggests that they did not follow continental fashions precisely (Meaney 1981, 252). Several openwork discs have been found in early Anglo-Saxon graves, but not with ivory pouch rings. None of the ivory rings from Buckland includes any surviving attachments, either of metal or other materials. In one case, however, in Grave 376, the looped end of a pair of girdle-hangers (e) encloses part of the ivory purse (h) from the grave.

Ivory rings have been discussed in some detail by Green, who has also provided a reconstruction of the method of their use (Myres and Green 1973, 100–3 and text fig 3; Meaney 1981, 252–3; MacGregor 1985, 40, 110–12 and fig 62). Hills has reviewed the Anglo-Saxon series recently (Hills 2001). They formed the frames for pouches and at Buckland, as elsewhere, a number of objects were found in their vicinity, which may have been contained within the pouch. They include rings and discs of antler, copper alloy and iron, iron lozenges and keys (Table 4.21). There is a general absence, however, of items that could be described as amuletic.

Ivory rings have been considered to reflect trade with East Anglia and Lincolnshire, rather than Kent, and the possibility has been raised that they were made from fossil (mammoth) ivory or from walrus (Huggett 1988, 68). There is no doubt, however, that the examples from the Buckland cemetery are made from elephant ivory. The same can be said for those from other cemeteries in Kent, as well as the samples from Spong Hill and Schmalstede (Bond 1994; Bode 1998, 96; Hills 2001, 134–5). They can be readily distinguished from the ivory of walrus but it is more difficult to differentiate them from mammoth ivory. At least one contemporary continental object is considered to be made from mammoth ivory (Hampel and Bannerjee 1995, 150–3).

Hills has drawn attention both to the considerable numbers of ivory rings from early Anglo-Saxon cemeteries, and to the fact that, as bag rings, they may have been obscured when worn on the body (Hills 2001, 142–3). At Castledyke South, north Lincolnshire, it was suggested that whole bags may have been imported, including the textiles (Drinkall and Foreman 1998, 285–6), and this might explain why the ivory ring was not necessarily a prominent part of the bag (Hills 2001, 143).

Antler burr discs and rings

Ian Riddler

(Graves 250, 336, 350B and 419)

Discs or rings produced from naturally-shed antler burrs were found in four graves, all certainly or probably those of women, aged between 20 and 40 years old. There are no examples from the earlier excavation of the cemetery. Two distinct types of object can be identified. The first consists of antler rings, for which the central part of the burr has been removed, which were recovered from Graves 336 (h) and 350B (e). The second comprises antler discs (Graves 250 (m) and 419 (j)), which have been cut from the central part of the burr, with the coronet still present, but usually trimmed.

Antler rings were found in Graves 336 and 350B. These utilise naturally-shed burrs but the central area has been hollowed in each case, leaving a ring which consists largely of the coronet. One of the rings (from Grave 350B) is near complete, whilst the other survives only as a small fragment. Both examples are undecorated and are little modified from the natural shape of the antler.

Grave	Find	Phase	Object	Gender	Category	Age
250	b	3a	Antler burr disc	Female	Adult	25–30
419	j	2a	Antler burr disc	Female	Adult	30–35
336	h	2b	Antler burr ring	Female	Adult	30–40
350B	e	1b–3a	Antler burr ring	Female	Adult	20–25

Table 4.22. Details of antler burr discs and rings.

Similar rings have been found in both cremation and inhumation burials, principally of sixth-century date. They include examples from Barrington (Malim and Hines 1998, 218 and fig 3.58.5); Empingham, Rutland (Timby 1996, 62 and fig 149); Little Wilbraham, Cambridgeshire; Long Wittenham, Berkshire (Meaney 1981, 139 and fig IV.cc); Loveden Hill, Lincolnshire; Newark-on-Trent, Nottinghamshire (Kinsley 1989, 21); Sancton, East Yorkshire (Timby 1993, 277); Snape, Suffolk (West and Owles 1973, fig 19d); Spong Hill, Norfolk (Hills 1977, fig 136; Hills and Penn 1981, fig 178; Hills *et al* 1987, fig 117; 1994, figs 127 and 133) and Thurmaston, Leicestershire (Williams 1983, 17). A fragmentary example is known from Sarre and a near-complete ring came from Bifrons, but the object type appears to be rare in east Kent (Brent 1864–5, 182; Chadwick Hawkes 2000, 23 and fig 15.32.2). The survival of bone and antler is generally fortuitous, however, and there may be no significance in their scarcity in Kentish graves.

It has been suggested that antler rings served as bracelets, but some would have been too small for that purpose and their precise function remains uncertain (Roes 1963, 73; Williams 1983, 17; Timby 1996, 62; but cf Hills 1977, 28; Bode 1998, 95). The example from Grave 336 (h) lay at the left waist, beside an iron ring. The antler ring from Grave 350B (e) was in a similar position and was also close to an iron ring, with a bead, stud, glass vessel fragment and nail between the femurs, possibly enclosed within a bag. Accordingly, at Buckland both antler rings may have been used as suspension devices.

The two examples of antler discs differ in terms of their decoration. One (Grave 250) is decorated by double ring-and-dot patterns, which originally adorned most or all of the space available. The object survives in poor condition and the full extent of the decoration is no longer clear. The second disc (Grave 419) is undecorated, and is little modified from the original shape of the slice across the burr, with some of the accompanying coronet still present. The decorated disc has been perforated at its centre. A series of natural holes of the coronet fringe its circumference, but a fractured aperture may have served as a suspension hole.

At Buckland, the phasing of the two graves with antler discs is basically confined to the sixth century (Phases 2a–3a). In conformity with this, antler burr discs from Schretzheim and other continental sites are thought to belong essentially to the second half of the sixth century (Martin 1976, 98 and note 166; U Koch 1977, 81–2; 2001, 198; MacGregor 1985, 107; Sasse 2001, 103). Within England, similar types of antler disc are largely found, however, in seventh-century contexts. Examples are known from Eccles, Finglesham (graves 8 and 203) and Polhill within Kent (Chadwick Hawkes 1973, 196 and fig 51.490; Detsicas and Chadwick Hawkes 1973, 280–1 and fig 4). By implication at least, they are thought to be discs from graves of seventh-century date, although one example (from Finglesham grave 203; 12.2) has been assigned to the sixth century (Detsicas and Chadwick Hawkes 1973, 281; Chadwick Hawkes 1976, 35; Meaney 1981, 140; Chadwick Hawkes and Grainger 2006, 145). Comparable examples from Burwell, Cambridgeshire; Standlake and Yelford, Oxfordshire emphasise the predominantly seventh-century dating of the object type within Anglo-Saxon cemeteries (Lethbridge 1931, 61–5 and figs 31–3; Meaney 1981, 140; Speake 1989, 72). An undecorated disc with a large central aperture from Droxford, Hampshire may, however, be of sixth-century date (Aldsworth 1978, 125, 171 and fig 25.4). Some examples are therefore contemporary with those seen on the Continent, whilst others are later.

The choice of material for these discs has led to a general belief that they have an amuletic character, a suggestion that has been made also for antler rings (Ament 1992, 19–20; U Koch 1977, 82; 2001, 199; Meaney 1981, 140–2; MacGregor 1985, 106–8). Antlers were renewed by male deer each year, providing symbols of immortality and power. Within the context of their graves, however, decorated antler discs performed practical tasks. Each example includes at least one suspension hole and several, including those from Burwell, were attached by clasps or loops to other objects (Lethbridge 1931, 62 and 64–5). Those from Burwell and Yelford acted in effect as suspension devices for a châtelaine, and the same purpose can be suggested for the Buckland example from Grave 250 (Speake 1989, 73). It lay just inside the left elbow of the deceased and it was very close to a cast copper alloy ring and mount, with an iron châtelaine below, within the lower arm. It may have been attached, originally, to the copper alloy ring and possibly to the iron châtelaine, although the antler disc from Burwell grave 83 was linked merely to small, thin loops of copper alloy wire (Lethbridge 1931, fig 33). In contrast, the discs from Standlake and Eccles have been plausibly interpreted as parts of the fastening mechanisms for satchels (Speake 1989, 72; but cf Cameron 2000, 4). The discs from Standlake, Oxfordshire and Eccles, Kent both have broad central apertures, unlike the examples from Buckland, Burwell grave 83 and Yelford.

The antler disc from Grave 419 (j) is undecorated and it has no central perforation. A fragmentary segment at the circumference may represent a fractured suspension hole. It was found within the ivory ring in the grave and its location suggests that it may either have lain within a pouch, or formed a part of its suspension mechanism. A similar association, albeit of an ivory ring and an antler ring, occurred at Empingham (Timby 1996, 63). Undecorated

antler discs are rare in early Anglo-Saxon and continental graves. Comparable discs, which have not been perforated at the centre, have come from Barrington and Castledyke (MacGregor 1985, fig 61g; Drinkall and Foreman 1998, fig 113). However, both of these are decorated with ring-and-dot motifs and they lack any trace of the coronet. Closer parallels are provided by continental examples, as with the antler burr disc from Lavoye grave 354, which is not decorated and lacks a central perforation. It came from a grave of the second half of the sixth century (Joffroy 1974, 65, 94 and pl 35). An undecorated disc of similar date came from Basel-Bernerring grave 42 (Martin 1976, 98) and another is known from Pleidelsheim grave 126 (U Koch 2001, 239–40 and Taf 50.9). They are usually found in female graves (U Koch 2001, 240) as are the decorated examples, which occur both with juveniles and adults (U Koch 2001, 198–202 and Tab 3).

Iron lozenges

Ian Riddler with Fleur Shearman

(Graves 218, 245, 250, 289, 293, 294, 326, 347, 353, 373, 377, 407, 409, 419 and 428)

Iron lozenges, the exact purpose of which remains unclear, were encountered in fifteen graves excavated in 1994. In most cases a single lozenge was present, although in four graves (Graves 218, 377, 407 and 428) pairs of lozenges were discovered, usually in close proximity. In each case they consist of small diamond-shaped plates of iron, pierced by single central perforations. Their shape is similar to that of the roves associated with iron clench nails, although they generally lack any central iron fittings (Evison 1987, 118).

Fifteen iron lozenges were recovered from eleven graves within Buckland 1951–3 (Evison 1987, 118). Again, most of the graves contained a single iron lozenge, although Graves 20 and 38 produced two and Grave 28 included three. Details of both assemblages are provided in Table 4.23. Within the cemetery as a whole, iron lozenges occur in graves of Phase 1 through to Phase 7 and they are spread evenly across those phases (Table 4.23). Where two or three lozenges occurred in a grave, they were invariably found close to each other.

With the 1994 excavations, iron lozenges were largely found in the graves of females, including children and juveniles. Grave 373 was thought to be possibly a male on osteological grounds, but includes grave goods appropriate for a female. The same can be said for Graves 218, 293, 294 and 377. Grave 139 from the earlier excavations, however,

Grave	Object number/letter	Phase	No	Location in grave	Gender	Category	Age
1	11	3	1	By ivory ring, outside left femur	Female	Adult	45+
12	2	1	1	Left hip	Female	-	-
14	10	2	1	Under left pelvis	Female	Adult	20–30
20	14, 15	1	2	Left hip	Female	Child	0–6
28	5, 6a, 6b	2	3	At waist	Female	Adult	20–30
38	9f, 9g	3	2	Between femurs	Female	Adult	20–30
48	9	1	1	Left hip	Female	Juvenile	12–18
53	4	5	1	Inside left femur	Female	Adult	20–30
60	8	3	1	Within wooden box to right of feet	Female	-	-
74	1	7	1	Near teeth	Female	Child	0–6
139	2	5	1	Area of waist	Male	Juvenile	-
218	c	-	2	Area of left pelvis	Female	Juve/Grown	12+
245	l	3a	1	Area of left pelvis	Female	Adult	35–45
250	j	3a	1	By left femur, just below pelvis	Female	Adult	25–30
289	g	-	1	By left femur, just below pelvis	Female	Adult	17–20
293	a	1b-2	1	Chest area	Female	Child	2–3
294	b	1 ?	1	Towards right side of grave	-	-	-
326	f	2-7	1	Centre of pelvis	Female	Juvenile	14–16
347	j	2a	1	Area of left pelvis	?Female	Juvenile	14–16
353	e	3a	1	Lower part of left femur	?Female	Adult	30–35
373	c	2b-3a	1	To side of left pelvis	Female	Adult	35–40
377	i, j	1-2	2	Central area of grave	-	-	-
409	f	1b	1	Area of left pelvis	Female	Adult	22–27
419	h	2a	1	Area of left pelvis	Female	Adult	30–35
428	i, k	2	2	Over left lower arm, just above left pelvis	Female	Adult	20–25

Table 4.23. Buckland 1951–3 and 1994. Distribution of iron lozenges.

includes a lozenge accreted to a pursemount, together with a knife, an arrowhead, a ceramic vessel and part of an iron horseshoe, the latter possibly of Roman date. The grave is thought to be that of a male juvenile; there were no surviving human remains (Evison 1987, 248).

Iron lozenges have been discovered in graves at Bifrons and Mill Hill, Deal within east Kent (Godfrey-Faussett 1876, 309 and 311; 1880, 553; Evison 1987, 118; Parfitt and Brugmann 1997, 68–9; Chadwick Hawkes 2000, 23, 35, 43 and figs 14.17, 21.13 and 27.3). They are largely absent from 'Final Phase' cemeteries, both in Kent and elsewhere, although one example came from Buckland Grave 74, one of the latest graves from the cemetery. They occur also in continental cemeteries, as at Frénouville and Giberville (Pilet 1980, pls 38, 60 and 150; Pilet *et al* 1990, pl 15.11).

Grave 407 contained a pair of iron lozenges and copper alloy tubes (i) strung together on a leather thong, remains of which survive. The strung items were found with other items on the left hip. A loose copper alloy fragment may possibly be a lace end. Near the group were pin fragments with associated textile and leather including a fragment of a needle with thread wrapped round. In Grave 409 cordage was noted passing through the central perforation of an iron lozenge (f). Grave 326 contained a fragment of an iron

lozenge (f); remains of a leather thong pass through the central perforation. Leather suspension thongs were found on iron rings from this grave near the lozenge. Grave 353 and Grave 373 both contained iron lozenges, which also retain remains of leather thongs passing through their central perforations. A lozenge from Mill Hill, Deal also included a leather strip at its centre (Parfitt and Brugmann 1997, 68). A further lozenge retained an iron rivet within its perforation (Evison 1987, fig 13).

As seen in Table 4.23, the iron lozenges were mostly discovered about the waist or by the femurs of the deceased. In a number of cases they were found close to ivory pouch rings (Graves 1, 53, 250 and 419; and probably also Grave 38), to rings of copper alloy and/or iron (Graves 1, 12, 28, 245 and 377) or to iron keys, usually by their wards (Graves 1, 20, 53, 218, 245 and 289). In several cases (Graves 139, 218 and 289) they were discovered in close proximity to pursemounts. Equally, there are graves where the iron lozenge is positioned as if it was fixed to a belt around the waist (Graves 14, 245, 326, 347 and 409; possibly also Grave 419) and others where the lozenge appears to have lain within a bag (Graves 48, 250, 419 and 428). Lozenges may have been attached to belts in other Anglo-Saxon cemeteries as well (Filmer-Sankey and Pestell 2001, 74 and fig 100). In one case at Buckland

(Grave 60) the lozenge had been placed in a wooden box at the feet of the deceased (Evison 1987, 118).

The deposition of lozenges differs noticeably within the child graves. In Graves 74 and 139 they lay below the teeth, in the region of the neck and in Grave 293 the lozenge lay over the presumed area of the chest. The lozenge in Grave 294 lay towards the eastern side of the burial.

Skimmers and quartz balls

Birte Brugmann

(Graves 290, 350B, 391B and 417)

Women's graves with either a skimmer or a quartz ball are widely distributed in continental row-grave cemeteries. The combination of a skimmer ('spoon') and a quartz ball in a sling ('crystal ball') presumably suspended from a belt, is typical for Anglo-Saxon graves of Kentish Phases II and III (Brugmann 1999a). The skimmers were probably used for wine, but the use of the crystal balls in this context is not clear (see Parfitt and Brugmann 1997, 67f). The free-swinging copper alloy single sling Grave 350B (b) suspended from a very worn loop shows a construction entirely different to that of the double silver slings used for quartz balls and, in fact, could not have been used for a quartz ball without additional means of fixing the ball. The object was found at the left waist of an adult probable female. A similar construction was found at Bifrons (Chadwick Hawkes 2000, 64, fig 39, 26) but has no known context.

The silver skimmer (d) found at the upper left leg of the woman buried in Grave 290 was not associated with a quartz ball in a sling but with a rock crystal bead (e) and a strap-end (g). The skimmer (Fig 4.37) was probably attached to the copper alloy slip-knot ?ring (incomplete, as the skimmer) and suspended from a belt. The quartz ball (b) was found as the only object to the right of the lower legs of the women buried in Grave 391B, with the attached slip-knot ring in a position suggesting that the ball was suspended probably from a belt.

Ball Grave 417 (a) weighs a little less and was found between the knees of the woman in the grave, together with the pair of strap-ends (b). The association of strap-ends and skimmers and balls in Graves 290 and 417 and also in grave 25B at Mill Hill, Deal, with a skimmer and a ball (Parfitt and Brugmann 1997, 74) suggests the strap-ends were used for straps suspending these objects from the belt.

Skimmer Grave 290 (d) belongs to Martin's English type B2 with a flat broad handle (Martin 1984, 104ff). Of the three

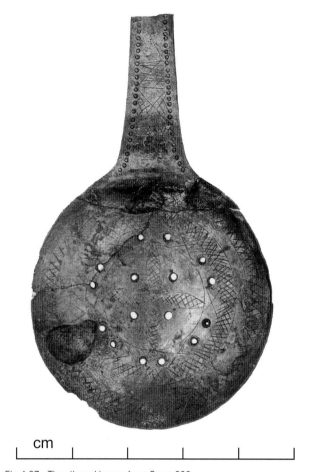

cm

Fig 4.37. The silver skimmer from Grave 290.

skimmers of this type from Bifrons, the one from grave 6 is made of tinned bronze (Chadwick Hawkes 2000, fig 5, 8), the two unassociated ones of white metal (*ibid*, fig 39, 24.25). The only skimmer in this group with garnet settings and gilding was found in grave 2 at Chatham Lines (Douglas 1793, 6ff). The decoration of the Bifrons skimmers of type B2 is punched while the Buckland skimmer has punched and incised decoration, some of it produced with dividers. Dividers were also used for the decoration of the bowl of a skimmer from grave 51 at Bifrons, set with a raised central garnet on the flat part of the handle (Chadwick Hawkes 2000, fig 24,6), probably a proto-type of skimmer type B1, dated to Kentish Phases II–IV (Parfitt and Brugmann 1997, 67; Brugmann 1999a, table 3.2).

All Kentish finds of type B2 skimmers with known grave contexts were associated with quartz beads[75] and not with balls. Though quartz beads may be no more than 'cheap' variants of

---

75. In grave 2 at Chatham Lines six quartz beads were found near an arm. The skimmer is worn and repaired (Douglas 1793, 6ff).

crystal balls, the fact that these were found in earlier graves than balls associated with skimmers suggests the association of skimmer and ball was not just a more elaborate version but also a later development: Grave 290 is dated to Phase 1, Grave 417 to Phase 2a and Grave 391B to Phase 2.

Knives

Ian Riddler

(Graves 205, 206, 207, 209, 214, 215, 217, 218 (x 2), 220, 222, 223, 224A, 228A, 228B, 230, 233, 239, 240, 245 (x 2), 248, 249C, 250, 251, 255, 259, 260, 262, 263A, 264, 265B, 266, 269, 271, 272, 281, 282A, 285, 286, 289, 295, 296, 297, 298, 299, 300, 301, 303A, 308, 314A, 318, 321, 326, 327, 330, 331, 336, 337 (x 2), 340, 346, 348, 350A, 351A, 353, 358, 360, 363, 366, 367, 372, 373, 374, 376, 379, 381 (x 2), 386B, 391A, 391B (x 2), 392, 393A, 395, 397, 398, 399, 400, 405, 406, 407, 408, 409, 411, 412, 413 (x 2), 414, 416, 417, 421, 422, 423, 427A, 428, 431, 432, 433, 434, 436, 437, 438, 439, 440, 442, 443 and 444)

One hundred and eighteen iron knives were recovered from 112 of the graves in the 1994 excavations, making them one of the most common artefact types to have come from the cemetery, with the exception of buckles and beads. In most cases a single knife was found in each grave, but there were two knives in Graves 218, 245, 337, 381, 391B and 413.

The knives have been catalogued in accordance with the type series of Evison, Härke and Drinkall (Evison 1987, 113–15; Härke 1992a, 90–1; Drinkall and Foreman 1998, 279–84). Evison's system for Buckland was based on the shape of the knife blade. It has been used subsequently for knives from early Anglo-Saxon cemeteries and settlements (Evison 1987, 113–15). Härke's scheme, in contrast, subdivides knives into four groups by size alone and allows for correlations to be made between knife sizes, broad dating, gender and age at death (Härke 1989a; 1992a, 89–91). The

Buckland 1951–3

| Evison phase | No | Type | | | | | | |
		A	B	C	D	E	F	Indet
1	9	3	1				1	4
1/2	2	1						1
2	5	4		1				
3	21	10	1	2		1	1	6
3?	3	2						1
4	19	6	2	3	1	3		4
4?	5	3		1				1
5	16	5		3		5		3
5?	2	1			1			
6	21	4	1	3	1	3	2	7
6?	11	1		1	1	2		6
7	14	4		1	4	2		3
Unphased	8			1	1	1		5
Total	136	44	5	15	9	17	5	41

Buckland 1994

| Phase | No | Type | | | | | | |
		A	B	C	D	E	F	Indet.
1	8	6						2
1-2	18	13	3	1				1
2	11	9	1					1
2-3	9	5	2			1		1
3	12	8	1		1			2
3-7	2	1	1					
5-7	4				2			2
Unphased	54	37	7	1	1		3	5
Total	118	79	15	2	2	2	4	14

Table 4.25. Knives by phase and types.

examination of the knives from the 1994 excavations has, however, led to a revision of Härke's size categories for knives, as noted below. Drinkall's system is based on that devised by Vera Evison for the Buckland cemetery, where the diagnostic attribute is the shape of the blade, rather than the size of the knife. Drinkall has also incorporated the Härke scheme of knife sizes, however, thereby providing an integrated typological scheme. Definitions of larger knives and seaxes are those outlined by Härke, Geake and Cameron, which follow earlier texts (Härke 1992a, 90–1; Geake 1997, 14–15 and 72–4; Cameron 2000, 50; Evison 1961, 226; Chadwick Hawkes 1973, 188–90; Gale 1989). There is one seax from the 1994 excavations and two examples came from the 1951–3 excavations (Graves 65, 93 and 381).

Evison identified six types of knife amidst the assemblage from the earlier Buckland excavations and all of these types are also present within the sample from 1994, although Table 4.24 indicates that the relative percentages of each are different across the two sections of the cemetery (cf Evison 1987, text fig 22).

| | Buckland 1951–3 | | Buckland 1994 | | 1951–3 & 1994 |
Type	No	% of total	No	% of total	Overall total
A	44	32.3	79	67.0	123
B	5	3.7	15	12.7	20
C	15	11.0	2	1.7	17
D	9	6.6	2	1.7	11
E	17	12.5	2	1.7	19
F	5	3.7	4	3.4	9
indet	41	30.2	14	11.8	55

Table 4.24. Relative totals of knives identifiable by type for Buckland cemetery.

Grave	1951–3 Phase	1994 Phase	Types	Blade Lengths (mm)		Category	Gender	Age
38	3	2b-3a	A A	130	125	Adult	Female	20-30
65	6	3a	A B	302	125	Adult	Male	-
83	7	-	A D	125	75	-	Female	-
87	1	1-2	A A	-	90	-	Male	-
91	3	2-3a	A A	115	90	Adult	Male	20-30
93	3	2b-3a	A F	275	155	Adult	Male	30-45
135	4?	3-7	A A	185	90	Adult	Male	25-35
137	5	5-7	A A	80	55	Juvenile	Male	-
162	6	-	-	-	-	Juvenile	Male	-
218		-	A A	172	99	Juve/Grown	?Female	12+
245		3a	A -	96	96	Adult	Female	35-45
337		-	A A	132	91	Adult	Male	40-45
381		1b-2a	A B	205	106	Adult	Female	30-40
391B		2	A A	120	105	Adult	Female	20-25
413		5-7	E E	88	80	Adult	Female	22-27

4.26 Pairs of knives.

Iron knives were found in graves of all phases. A summary of knives by phase (Table 4.25) indicates that the majority belong to the same type; it also serves to show when particular forms may have come into use. The table incorporates the work of Evison on the knives from the earlier Buckland excavations (Evison 1987, table XVII).

Knives of Type A dominate the assemblage from the 1994 excavations, forming 67 per cent of the sample of 104 examples that can be identified to type. They are present across all phases and if they appear to be scarce in Phases 5–7, it should be remembered that very few graves have been assigned to these phases. Knives of Type A were prominent in the earlier excavations, although they formed less than 44 per cent of that sample (Table 4.25).

The fifteen knives of Type B occur within graves of Phases 1b to 3a, suggesting that it is essentially a sixth-century form. The five examples from the earlier excavations were found in Evison's Phases 1, 3, 4 and 6, however, indicating that the type was found in at least a small number of seventh-century graves. Evison has noted that Type B corresponds with Böhner's type B, which was largely a sixth-century form (Evison 1987, 115; Böhner 1958, 214–15 and Taf 60.3–4).

Type C knives were relatively common in the earlier excavations but are scarce within the 1994 assemblage. Knives of this type are similar in form to those of Types A and E and the distinction between them is often a small and subtle one. The type is related to Böhner's type C, a seventh-century form, and the principal characteristic of the angled back is shared by Buckland Type E, also of seventh-century date. Evison noted, however, that in the 1951–3 sample the type occurred in both sixth- and seventh-century contexts, suggesting that it is earlier than type E (Evison 1987, 115).

The two examples from the 1994 excavations came from Graves 224A and 300 (Phase 1b–2a).

The two knives of Type D came from Graves 264 (Phase 3) and 314A and the phasing generally corresponds with the larger sample from the earlier excavations, where the type was thought to be of seventh- and eighth-century date (Evison 1987, 115). However, the presence of a Type D knife in Grave 314A, alongside amber beads, perhaps indicates that the type goes back a little into the sixth century.

Type E is rare within the 1994 sample but was common in the earlier excavations, where it was found largely in seventh-century graves. The type became the most common form for knives of middle and late Saxon date within east Kent (Riddler 2001, 232–4). The two examples from the 1994 excavations came from the same grave (Grave 413), which belongs to Phase 5–7 of the cemetery, well into the seventh century.

Four examples of knives of Type F came from the 1994 excavations, against five examples of the same type from the earlier excavations. Evison argued that this type belonged to the seventh and eighth centuries and that an outlier in an early phase represented a variant of the type (Evison 1987, 115). Knives of Type F from the 1994 excavations included one from a grave (Grave 271) dated to Phase 2–3a, however, indicating once again that the object type may have its origins in the sixth century.

As noted above, two knives came from Graves 218, 245, 337, 381, 391B and 413. Pairs of knives were also found in Buckland Graves 38, 65, 83, 87, 91, 93, 135, 137 and 162. Details of the knives from these graves are presented in Table 4.26. They occur across most of the phases within each section of the cemetery. Within the 1994 sample, pairs of knives were largely found in female graves; with the earlier excavations

Grave	Length (mm)	Phase	Sex	Gender	Category	Age
299	164	-	?Female	Male	Adult	40–50
393A	170	-	Male	Male	Adult	25–30
218	172	-	?	Female	Juve/Grown	12+
206	180	3–7 ?	?	?	Juvenile	13–15
381	205	1b–2a	?Male	Male	Adult	30–40

Table 4.27. Buckland 1994. Details of occurrence of the larger knives.

the reverse is the case. No child was buried with two knives, although this was the case with several juveniles. It has been noted previously that child burials are invariably restricted to a single knife (Härke 1989a, 147). At Buckland the customary situation was for a knife with a blade length of over 100mm to be accompanied by a smaller knife, and the pair placed together or in close proximity. In Grave 93 the smaller knife (itself with a blade length of 155mm) lay on top of a seax, imitating the situation seen in some graves, where a knife has been placed on top of a sword. In some cases, however (Graves 38, 91, 391B and 413), there was little appreciable difference in the size of the knives that had been placed together. Pairs of knives have been found in a number of graves within other east Kent cemeteries, including Monkton and Sarre (Perkins 1985, 53; 1991, 147; 1992, 109, 111, 114 and 117).

Grooves are visible along the backs of knives from Graves 263A, 271, 295 and 372. No inlays are now present in any of the grooves. Similar grooves were seen on a number of the knives from the earlier excavations, across Phases 2–5 (Evison 1987, 114). They are commonly seen on knives of middle and late Saxon date (Riddler 2001, 232–3). It has been suggested that they first occur in the seventh to eighth century (Cameron 2000, 53) but they are clearly present in small numbers with some knives of sixth-century date.

The lengths of the blades of the knives from the 1994 excavations vary between 58 and 205mm (Fig 4.38). The tangs extend from 32 to 108mm. Härke identified three broad groups of knife on the basis of the length of the blade, with a fourth group designated as a *Kurz-/Schmalsaxe* (Härke 1992a, Tab 5). Under his system, knives of Group 1 have blades of 60–99mm, whilst those of Group 2 extend in blade length from 100–129mm and Group 3 from 130–170mm (Härke 1992a, Tab 5). Cameron has subsequently extended the range of large knives from 170–5 to 179mm, thereby closing an awkward gap (Cameron 2000, 49). Figure 4.38 shows that the majority of the knives from the 1994 excavations fall into the smallest two groups, with only eight examples exceeding 129mm in blade length. Figures 4.38 and 4.39 also indicate that the division between knives

of Groups 1 and 2, with blades of 99mm or less belonging to the first group, is entirely arbitrary for this cemetery. In reality, for the 1994 excavations there is a continuum in blade lengths between 58 and 136mm. The same can be said also for the remaining knives of the cemetery, whose blades vary between 55 and 302mm in length (Fig 4.39). The concept of the large knife remains valid, but the division by size into two smaller groups does not, for this cemetery at least. The distinction to be made in terms of the size of knives lies between the majority, which have blades up to 136mm in length, and the small number with longer blades.

In general terms, within the sample from the 1994 excavations, the length of the tang reflects the length of the blade (Fig 4.38), although there are several occasions where the tangs are disproportionately short. Similarly, the length of the blade is generally proportional to its width, with the longer knives once again providing more variability than those with blade lengths of up to 140mm (Fig 4.40).

Five knives can be placed into the long category (Table 4.27). Three of these belong to Härke's Group 3 of large knives and one can be defined as a short seax.[76] The knife from Grave 206 has a blade length of 180mm, but a width of just 16mm, and it is regarded as a large knife, rather than a seax. On blade length alone, it would be a seax. There is a suspicion that knives of type A with blades over 130mm in length from the 1994 excavations became increasingly common over time, in accordance with Härke's assertion (Härke 1989a, 145 and table 2). The phasing is generally imprecise, however and the suggestion can only be tentative. No changes are visible in the relative sizes of knives with smaller blades. It has also been suggested that the deposition of knives of Group 3 (with blades of 130–179mm) was restricted to the graves of males of later sixth- or seventh-century date (Härke 1989a, 146; 1992a, 90 and 188–9; Drinkall and Foreman 1998, 282). Most of those from the 1994 excavations - but not all - appear to have come from the graves of males. In several graves (Graves 299 and 393A) the knife was accompanied merely by a spearhead and in one further example (Grave 337) the grave goods included a spearhead, a second knife and a buckle. These burials appear to reflect one stage in the male burial rite at Buckland, where large knives were still associated with weapons (Härke 1989a, 147). A later stage, where weapons are absent and appear to be replaced by large knives, may be represented by Grave 340 and possibly also by Grave 206.

The seax in Grave 381 (a) includes a blade of over 200mm and has an overall length of 280mm. It comes from the grave possibly of a male, on osteological grounds, buried with a simple knife and buckle combination, but with a group

---

76. Härke 1989a, table 1, defines large knives as a blade length of 130–175mm, but his revised table (Härke 1992a, table 5) shortens this length to 130–170mm. With both tables, short seaxes begin with blade lengths of 180mm.

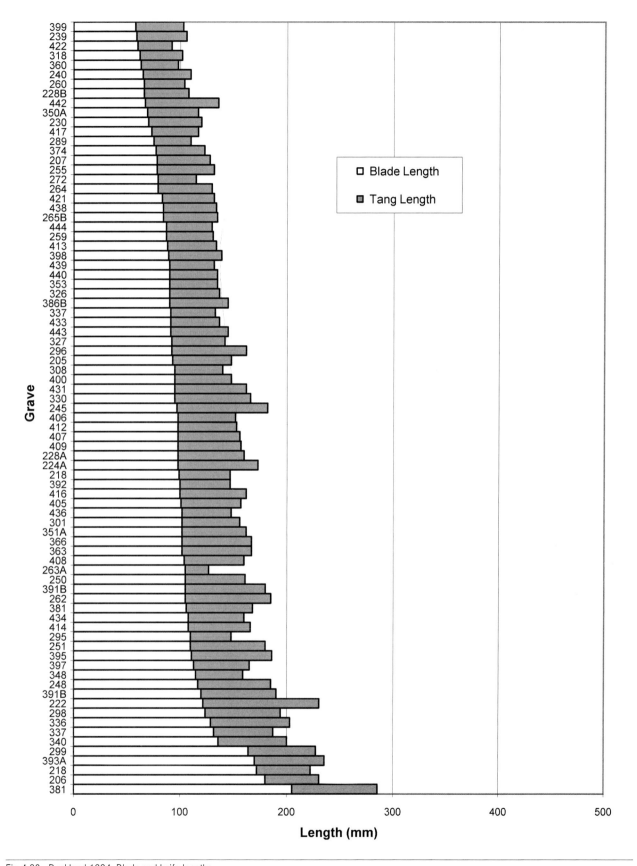

Fig 4.38. Buckland 1994. Blade and knife lengths.

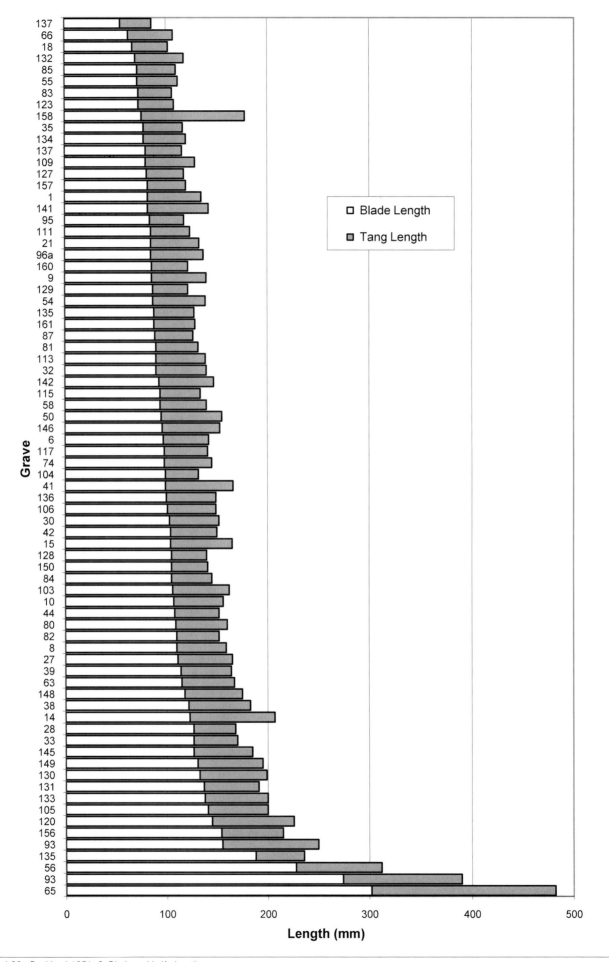

Fig 4.39. Buckland 1951–3. Blade and knife lengths.

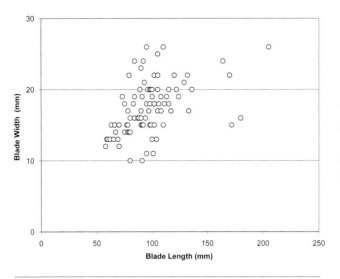

Fig 4.40. Buckland 1994. Knives: blade length against width.

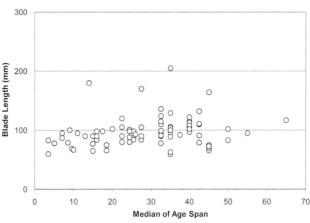

Fig 4.41. Buckland 1994. Length of knife blade against median of age span.

of objects lying under the seax, which include a second (smaller) knife, a pursemount/firesteel with further mounts of a definite purse, and an iron rod. Anglo-Saxon seaxes are themselves divided into three groups, reflecting narrow, broad and long forms, and this example belongs to the narrow group (Böhner 1958, 135–45; Chadwick Hawkes 1973, 188–90; Gale 1989, 72–4; Härke 1992a, 89; Geake 1997, 72–4 and table 4.14). Geake has rightly noted, however, that the current classification of seaxes is inadequate for Anglo-Saxon England (Geake 1997, 72–3).

The lozenges found in Grave 218 may suggest that the occupant was a female and the size of the grave indicates the presence of an adult. Two knives were found in this grave. The smaller example belongs to type A and includes the unusual feature of a rivet passing through the tang, towards its end. The handle is made of horn and the rivet may conceivably have held two sections of that material together. It is also possible, if less likely, that the rivet acted as a means of suspension for the knife. A second knife from the cemetery, recovered from Grave 391B, also has a rivet placed through its tang, although in this case it lies close to the blade.

The knife from Grave 206 was enclosed within a wooden sheath. The wood was covered in leather, with a cord running down the centre of the scabbard on one side only, although it may simply be missing on the other side, which is slightly more degraded in the area where the cord might have been. Sheaths with the cord underlying the wood and beneath a layer of leather have been noted on sword scabbards of this date (Cameron 2000, 39–40). The sword from Grave 437 exhibits this feature (*see* p 204), a simpler form of which may be noted in the construction of this knife sheath.

Metal chapes secured the ends of knives from Graves 206, 245 and 391B. The copper alloy chape from Grave 206 was accompanied by a mount of the same material, positioned at the top of the sheath. In contrast, the chape from Grave 391B is silver, with stamped decoration across the centre band and no mount for the top of the sheath. The fragmentary chape for the knife from Grave 245 is also silver, with incised lines in a band across part of the edging strip. The knife was the only object to be found in Grave 206 and its size suggests that this may have been a grave reflecting the late stages of weapon burial, as noted above.

A copper alloy sheath with a central band was found on a knife from Sarre grave 138 and a similar example, lacking the band but with a mount at the top of the sheath, was recovered from a grave at Chessell Down on the Isle of Wight (Brent 1864–5, 178; Arnold 1982, 33, 69 and fig 18). A fragmentary copper alloy chape came from a late grave at Polhill (Chadwick Hawkes 1973, 190 and fig 54.515). A seax from Shudy Camps, Cambridgeshire, grave 36 included a chape that is similarly devoid of any centre plates (Lethbridge 1931, 14 and fig 36). Chapes are also known from seaxes within graves at Ford (Wiltshire) and Dunstable (Bedfordshire) and the Ford example, in particular, is an ornate silver example (Musty 1969, 106, 114–6 and figs 5h and 6; Matthews 1962, fig 2.2). An elaborate chape with edging mounts also secured the sheath on a knife from Brighthampton, Oxfordshire. (MacGregor and Bolick 1993, 235). More locally, an example accompanies a fragmentary knife from Faversham (Cameron 2000, 55 and fig 36.iv). Chapes are more commonly seen on seaxes and swords, but the evidence from Buckland shows that they also adorned larger knives. It is worth noting also that the seax from Grave 381 has a transverse bar at the end of the tang, echoing the design of sword hilts and pommels, and the same feature can be seen on the knife from Grave 245, which otherwise belongs to the group of small knives.

Härke has also suggested that the length of a knife blade might be related to the age at death of the deceased (Härke 1989a, 146–7). In particular, children and juveniles

Age band (years)	0–5	6–10	11-14	15–29	30–44	45+
No	3	6	6	24	32	5
Av length (mm)	73.7	82.8	83.4	91.1	100.5	93.4

Table 4.28. Buckland 1994. Average length of knives by age band.

Adult	Overall knife length (mm)	No	Overall knife length (mm)	No
Male	167.18	11	102.92	13
?Male	166.82	11	107.50	14
Female	151.00	15	92.00	22
?Female	163.80	10	103.00	11

Table 4.29. Average length of knives for adult males and females.

Sex	No	Gender	No
Female	26	Female	45
?Female	16	?Female	2
Male	21	Male	25
?Male	17	?Male	0
Indet	32	Indet.	40

Table 4.30. Sex and gender attributions for graves with knives.

Grave	1951–3 phase	1994 phase	Category	Gender	Age
34	4	3a	Child	Indet	0–6
52	5	5–7	Adult	Male	45+
85	7	-	Juvenile	-	-
108	6	-	Juvenile	-	-
146	7	5–7	Adult	Male	20–30
209		1b–2	Adult	Male	40–50
215			Adult	?Male	25–30
228B		-	Adult	?Male	17–20
248		-	Adult	Male	60+
263A		1b–2a	Grown	?Male	20+
340		-	Adult	Male	30–35
350A		1b–3	Child	Indet.	9–10
395		-	Adult	?Male	40–45
406		1b–7	Grown	?Male	20+

Table 4.31. Graves with knives and buckles.

appear to have been buried with smaller knives than adults. This correlation has been disputed subsequently, however, particularly on the basis of the precise definition of the terms 'child' and 'juvenile' in relation to early Anglo-Saxon burial (Crawford 1999, 21–7 and 71–2). A distribution diagram of blade length against the median of the age span for the knives from the 1994 excavations (Fig 4.41) highlights the presence of small knives with the youngest of the deceased, but knives of a similar size occur with adults as well, and no significant distinction can be inferred from this figure. The average size of knives (Table 4.28) does seem to increase across age bands, for the 1994 excavations as much as for other cemeteries (Crawford 1999, 72).[77]

Sasse has noted that knives from women's graves in southern Germany were shorter than those recovered from male graves (Sasse 2001, 98). The same situation prevails also within the sample considered here, at least for skeletons identified as definitely male or female (Table 4.29).

All the knives from the Buckland cemetery have whittle tangs. The two tangs that include rivets, described above, were probably intended to fasten sections of bone, antler or horn together. Several of the knives were deposited in the grave in the general area of iron or copper alloy rings and the same situation occurred with a number of those from the earlier excavations (Evison 1987, 114). With the graves of the 1994 sample, however, the rings are not located by the tangs of the knives and they do not appear to have been placed in the grave in a position that would allow them to have functioned as suspension rings specifically intended for the knives, rather than for other implements. As noted below (pp 276–8), a number of the knives were encased in sheaths, and these may have been suspended from a belt.

The majority of the knives from the 1994 excavations were found close to the waist, and usually on the left side of the body. In some cases they were at the level of the pelvis and in others they were a little higher, beside the lower left arm. Exceptions include the two knives from Grave 413, one of which was placed at the foot of the grave, and the knife from Grave 416, located above the skull. In some cases the tip of the blade was pointing towards the head of the deceased or across the body and in others it faced towards the foot of the grave, either directly, or on a diagonal alignment. The general impression from their location in the grave is that the knives were placed there and were not necessarily worn by the deceased. They may, however, have been placed in the position that they were worn during life. Within the earlier Buckland excavations almost all of the knives were placed at the left waist. The knife from Grave 57, however, lay

---

77. The largest knives or short seaxes, with blade lenghts of 170mm or more, are excluded from Table 4.29. If they were included, the would create a considerable bias in the material..

beside the upper right arm, in a similar position to a knife from Holborough grave 7 (Evison 1956, fig 21).

Knives were found in both male and female graves within the 1994 excavations, apparently in reasonably equal numbers, to judge from attributions of sex, but with more females identified from a consideration of the grave goods (Table 4.30). In both cases there are significant quantities of indeterminate graves.

Penn has noted that where knives and buckles occur as the only goods in a burial this is often a characteristic of male graves (Penn 2000, 55) and this is confirmed from the Buckland cemetery as a whole (Table 4.31).

Where knives were the only grave goods, the evidence is more equivocal, and the sex of most of the deceased of these graves from the 1994 excavations could not be securely identified. Three were male and three others may have been male, whilst one may have been female and eight were indeterminate.

Copper alloy and iron rings

Birte Brugmann

(Graves 207, 214, 218, 222, 245, 250, 255, 266, 281, 289, 293, 297, 303A, 326, 336, 339, 347, 349, 350B, 354, 367, 373, 377, 381, 391B, 409, 412, 417, 419, 427A, 428 and 444)

Metal rings with no obvious function were mostly found as a part of female equipment, usually worn at the left hip or waist, together with objects such as knives or lozenges (see above), or in the area of the chest in combination with dress accessories, mostly beads. The only ring (e) in the grave of a definite male, a weapon grave (Grave 297), is cast of copper alloy, 28mm in diameter and was found right of the right femur of the adult buried with a shield and a spear. The buckle in this grave was positioned at the right waist and it seems possible that the copper alloy ring was attached to a leather strap which caused wear on the inner edge of the ring and was part of some construction to do with the belt. A cast copper alloy ring, 32mm in diameter, in the weapon grave Grave 93 was found in a similar position and was interpreted by Evison (1987, 238) as possibly part of the spear in this grave. Such a function would be unlikely in the case of Grave 297 because the spear and ferrule in this grave were found on the other side of the skeleton.

The cast copper alloy ring, 38mm in diameter (g) found below the buckle in Grave 222, between the femurs and also worn on the inner edge, may have been used by the adult female in this grave in a way similar to that of the male in

Grave 297 and possibly also in Grave 93. The rings in weapon graves 81 and 91 at Mill Hill, Deal are smaller than the finds from Buckland and were found at the feet of the skeletons in association with a possible lyre and possibly with a mounted wooden bowl (Parfitt and Brugmann 1997, 147–8, 150–1).

The rings positioned in the area of the chest in Graves 293 (b2), 303A (b), 349 (b) and 412 (f) are made of copper alloy, and of a strip of silver sheet (h) in Grave 347. Iron fragments of a possible ring (a) were found in the area of the decayed chest of a young adult female in Grave 354. None of the copper alloy rings are slip-knot wire rings but are either cast (Graves 349 (b) and ?412 (f), or made of wires with open terminals (Grave 293 (b2), coiled). The rings found in the chest area are smaller (7–21mm diameter) than the ones found at the waist or hip of other females and are likely to have been part of some arrangement connected with beads, brooches or tweezers that was used by, or for, children (Graves 293 and 303A), juveniles (Graves 347 and 412) and possibly also adults (Graves 349 and 354).

Cast copper alloy rings as part of arrangements worn at the left hip or waist were found with adults only (Graves 245 (l), 266 (g), 373 (e), 377 [undetermined] (l), (n) and (p), 417 (i) [mature], and 428 (o) [young adult]). The diameters of these rings vary from 21 to 55mm. Some of the rings show wear on the inner edge and therefore were probably suspended from the belt rather than being the contents of a bag. Most of the cast copper alloy rings are remarkably solid, probably more solid than was required by their function and therefore were possibly re-used or status objects. Ring Grave 245 (l) was associated with two penannular rings fused to an iron lozenge; ring Grave 373 (e) with a larger iron ring (g); and the three rings Grave 377 (l), (n) and (p) were associated with copper alloy spiral wire rings (o) and (q) and an iron ring (h). The adult female in Grave 427A had an association of a copper alloy wire ring (i) and two iron rings (d) and (e). A set of copper alloy rings (z) and (aa), with a fluted and gilt show-side, 42 and 50mm in diameter, was found in Grave 391B, that of a young adult female, and may be of Roman rather than early medieval manufacture because of their unusual decoration. The child in Grave 444 had a single undecorated copper alloy wire ring (g).

Iron rings found at the waist or hip of females tend to be larger (24–70mm) than copper alloy rings found in the same position (21–55mm) and therefore probably had a different function. Some, at least, may represent a type of variant bag fastening. The juvenile in Grave 326 was buried with four iron rings varying in diameter from 24mm (coiled) to 60mm, (a), (e) and (h). The young adult in Grave 281 had three rings 33–45mm in diameter (j), and the adult in Grave 207 two rings 29 and 35mm in diameter (e) and (f). The variation in sizes suggests that these individual used sets of rings rather than being buried with 'spare' rings or amulets (cf Evison 1987, 119 and Parfitt and Brugmann 1997, 69). Iron rings were also found in Graves 218 (b), in Graves 336 (e) and 367 (f) of adults, and in Grave 350B (d) of a young adult. The ring in Grave 336 was combined with a tube made of a copper alloy sheet and ?bound with iron (g).

Evison's excavations at Buckland produced relatively few rings with no obvious function, positioned at the waist or hip (Evison 1987, 119), while Mill Hill, Deal, included fourteen women's graves with such rings (Parfitt and Brugmann 1997, 69). This seems to be a matter of date-spans, rather than local differences. It seems likely that combinations of rings, probably suspended from the belt, were replaced in the seventh century by châtelaines made of linked rods (*see* p 329).

Evidence from mineral-preserved leather found in association with the iron or copper alloy rings
Fleur Shearman

Strips of mineral-preserved leather were noted on nineteen iron or copper alloy rings; the position in all cases was in close association and encircling or wound round the rings (Graves 214, 250, 281, 326, 347, 367, 373, 377, 419 and 427A). In the case of the iron ring from Grave 427A (d) the leather was wound round twice. Leather and additional cordage was present on the rings from Graves 326 (e), 367 (a) and 377 (n). The function of suspension or attachment, perhaps to a belt worn around the waist, would seem probable. Groups of rings in one grave all with associated leather (Graves 326, 377 and 427A) may have been additionally linked together to each other by the thongs or strips.

Copper alloy and iron chains

Birte Brugmann

(Graves 214, 296, 336, 347, 354, 409 and 419)

Remains of iron or copper alloy chains were found in seven graves, four of them in the area of chest or neck of juvenile or (young) adult females, together with beads and brooches (Graves 347 (g), 354 (c), 419 (g)) and a pair of tweezers (Grave 336 (c)). Iron chain fragments were also found between the femurs of an adult female together with a bead (Grave 296 (g)) and close to the skull of a young adult female (Grave 409 (a)). The iron chains Graves 336 (c), 347 (g) and 409 (a) are

made of rings with overlapping terminals fitted with iron or copper alloy rivets, a technique known from chain mail of the period.[78] A ring of this type was also found in the fill of Grave 214 (d). The copper alloy chain Grave 354 (c) is made of folded double loops of wire, a type of chain found attached to a brooch from grave 44 at Lyminge.[79]

A chain from grave 71 at Bifrons (Chadwick Hawkes 2000, 51) and possibly also a chain from grave 44 at Lyminge linked the pairs of brooches from these graves. There is no specific evidence for such an arrangement in any of the Buckland graves, none of which produced a matching pair of brooches, but the copper alloy chain from Grave 354 may have been suspended from a brooch at the neck, together with beads. The chain is extremely abraded where the loops touch, as if it had been worn for a long time, or a considerable weight had been suspended from it. The chain Grave 419 (g) may have been attached to the bird brooch (a) found close to it at the neck. Grave 366 produced no brooch but copper alloy tweezers were attached to the chain, as was an ear pick from the chain in grave 71 at Bifrons.

Iron chains found around the lower body, such as Grave 296 (g) between the femurs of the woman in this grave and an iron chain below brooches at the right hip of a woman in grave 73 at Mill Hill, Deal (Parfitt and Brugmann 1997, 69), may have had the same function as chains found on the chest. The Mill Hill chain was discovered with a bead but at some distance from the iron rings and knife found at the left waist. A copper alloy chain found at the left hip of a female, apparently attached to a knife, in grave 64 at Bifrons (Chadwick Hawkes 2000, 50f), however, may have had the function of a châtelaine.

With the exception of Grave 214, which is undated, and Grave 409 dated to Phase 1b, all graves with chains at Buckland are dated to Phase 2. As grave 44 at Lyminge, grave 71 at Bifrons and possibly grave 73 at Mill Hill can be dated to the same period, it seems that the use of chains as dress accessories by women was a fashion of Buckland Phase 2, although it may have started in Phase 1.

Copper alloy sheet mounts

Birte Brugmann

(Graves 250 and 278)

The copper alloy mount Grave 250 (l) is roughly shaped like a pursemount/firesteel and has a rivet with a washer. It was found associated with objects typically found at the

---

78. See, for example, the chain mail attached to a helmet from the 'boy's grave' from under Cologne Cathedral, in this case without rivets (Doppelfeld 1964, 24).
79. Warhurst (1955, 29), with further examples.

left waist or hip of women, such as a châtelaine and an antler burr pendant (see above). The mount may have been a substitute for a functional pursemount/firesteel or may have been amuletic.

The function of the copper alloy sheet Grave 278 (a) with a curved cross section and perforations in the corners is not obvious. The punched decoration suggests a decorative function and the associated wire that it was only a part of an object, probably mainly organic. It was found at the north-west end of the probable grave of a child.

Copper alloy sheet

Ian Riddler

Small portions of copper alloy sheet were recovered from several graves. In each case they are small and fragmentary, undecorated sections of sheet, and it is not possible to establish their original function.

Prehistoric and Roman grave objects

As with most early Anglo-Saxon cemeteries, a small number of objects of earlier date were recovered from the graves. As well as the items described below and the rock crystal pendant (*see* pp 83–8), a small piece of porphyry veneer and fragments of Roman pottery and tile were discovered in the general filling of several graves and the infilling of certain terraces. Reports on this material by Nigel Macpherson-Grant and Louise Harrison remain in the site archive.

Iron Age toggle

Keith Parfitt

(Grave 407)

A copper alloy toggle of Iron Age date was recovered from Grave 407 (Fig 10.56). Found by the knife at the left waist, the object (c) is barrel-shaped in overall form with plain, disc-shaped terminals and a projecting rectangular loop for attachment on one side.

Such objects have been rarely found in Kent, although a broadly similar example has recently been published from Wrotham (Lewis *et al* 2002). It seems fairly certain that the present object had been acquired as a curio or amulet by the deceased. Another late Iron Age object, in the form of a potin

coin, came from Grave 331 (see below). We are grateful for confirmation of the identification of the toggle by J D Hill.

Iron Age coin

Ian Riddler

(Grave 331)

An Iron Age potin coin (f) (weight: 1.43g. Sf 482) was recovered from Grave 331. It was discovered in the area of the left femur, with other objects that were probably contained in a purse or pouch. The coin may be identified as a British Iron Age potin of Class I (Hobbs 1996, 674, etc), datable to the first century BC. Such finds are well known in Kent and were probably made here (Holman 2000).

Crossbow brooch

Don Mackreth

(Grave 264)

This brooch come from the general filling of Grave 264 (Sf 679; Fig 10.21) and is a member of Böhme's Group 582–613, more specifically 592–599 (Böhme 1972, 23, Taf 14), and dated by her to the later second, into the third century (*ibid*, 24). The general type was used largely by the army and this shows to a great measure in its distribution in Britain, bearing in mind that the native habit of wearing bow brooches had largely died out by AD 200, if not almost completely by AD 175. Looking at the general type, the distribution runs from the south coast to the military north, with by far the greatest concentration in the Hadrian's Wall zone. Thereafter, military sites such as Dover, including the present example, Beauport Park, Sussex; Richborough, Caister on Sea, Norfolk; Caerleon, south Wales and Brancaster, Norfolk, predominate. Others may be counted as military, Charterhouse, or government managed, Stonea, or *civitates* and *colonia* where government officers entitled to wear military uniform could be expected, Lincoln, Colchester, Cirencester and Silchester. There is so little representation on proven rural sites, including villas, that one might almost describe their occurrence as marking the presence of someone wearing the brooch as part of his insignia of office. There is a fairly high proportion made of silver and parcel gilt, and real bullion or its imitations is surely another pointer in this direction. In which case, the terminal date should be strongly related to the introduction of the earliest hinged Crossbows, which take up the same position in the hierarchy, which appear more or less in the second quarter of the third century.

Horse harness pendant

Ian Riddler

(Grave 377)

The cast copper alloy pendant Grave 377 (m) includes a suspension loop at the top, a tear-shaped cut-out area within the oval-shaped, decorated disc with a small circular perforation below and a knop at the base of the disc. It is almost certainly of early Roman date and probably served as a horse harness pendant. Its near-circular form is not common for this type of object, and early forms tend, in contrast, to be crescentic, heart-shaped, lunate or leaf-shaped (Bishop and Coulston 1993, 105 and fig 65; Oldenstein 1976, Taf 29–31; Deschler-Erb 1999, Taf 21–31). Circular or 'teardrop' forms are known, however (Oldenstein 1976, 234–9 and Taf 88–90) and in this case the shape may be derived from a 'Trophen' form, one of the simplest types of pendant (Deschler-Erb 1999, 57). Pendants formed a part of military costume and were suspended from horse harness, although some hung from soldiers' belts, and it can be difficult to distinguish between the two types (Deschler-Erb 1999, 48). They served no practical purpose and were merely decorative, albeit imbued in some case with amuletic significance (Deschler-Erb 1999, 49).

Roman coinage

Ian Riddler

(Graves 204, 205, 218, 265B, 351A, 391B, 392, 407, 408, 427A, 428, 437 and 440)

Roman coins were found in thirteen of the graves from the 1994 excavations. The group of fourteen coins and possible coins from Grave 265B are noted above (p 151). The remaining graves produced smaller quantities of Roman coins, with single examples from Graves 205, 351A, 392, 407, 437 and 440, two coins from Graves 204, 391B, 408 and 427A, three coins from Grave 428 and five from Grave 218. The coins are principally of late Roman date. A first-century coin came from Grave 204 and a second-century coin was recovered from Grave 408. Third-century radiates came from Graves 204, 391B, 427A, 428 and 437, and fourth-century coinage from Graves 205, 218, 351A, 392, 407, 427A, 428 and 440.

Graves 204 and 205 were adjacent in Plot R. Graves 265B and 351A were close together in Plot S, with Grave 218 some distance away to the north. Graves 391B and 392 were close

to each other in Plot X, with Graves 407 and 408 nearby, and Grave 427 as well as Grave 428 a little further to the east. Graves 437 and 440 lay in the southern part of Plot Y.

Roman coins were also found in Buckland Graves 14, 15, 129, 138 and 141, the majority of types differing from those encountered in the 1994 excavations (Evison 1987, 122 and 181). In each case, a single coin had been deposited in the grave; those from Graves 14, 129 and 141 had been perforated for suspension.

The coins from Graves 15 and 138 were found amidst objects deposited in a bag or purse. This appears to have been the case also for coin (c) from Grave 204, as well as the coins from Graves 205 (c) and 428 (g) and (n), and possibly those from Graves 408 (h) and 440 (c). The two coins in Grave 391B (p) and (q) lay with a lead object (r1) and several nails (r2– r5) to the side of the left knee, possibly in a wooden container. The coin from Grave 407 (g) lay under the Roman intaglio (h) in that grave, below a deposit of textile and leather at the waist that also included the Iron Age toggle (see above). Several other locations for coins can be identified. The five coins (h–l) from Grave 218 were deposited at the foot of the grave. The coin from Grave 351A (b) lay on the right side of the chest, with the other objects from that grave. The two coins from Grave 427A (a) and (b) also lay over the arm but in this case they were situated above several iron rings (d) and (e) and it is possible that these coins were also enclosed within a purse.

Most of the Roman coins were found with adult females. The exceptions are the juvenile in Grave 440 and the child in Grave 392. Coins were found in male graves Graves 351A (b) and 437 (j). In the case of Grave 437 the coin was underneath the sword (a), alongside a knife (i) and a pursemount/firesteel (k).

Glass

Ian Riddler

(Graves 208, 238B, 266, 326, 350B, 367, 377 and 428)

Thirteen fragments of Roman vessel and window glass were recovered from eight graves. A fragment from Grave 208 was retrieved from the fill of the grave (Sf 924). The remaining glass was located in each grave beside the body of the deceased, either by the lower arm or the pelvis, or lying between the femurs.

The glass consists largely of small fragments of vessels, including several body sherds and a handle fragment from a bottle, as well as body sherds and a base from thin-walled, naturally coloured vessels. There are also several pieces of window glass, trimmed in each case to a rectangular shape. The glass from Grave 377 (b)–(d) and (f) also includes the upper part of a naturally coloured stirring rod (e). The hollow rim fragments from Graves 326 (k) and 428 (f) may have been used as beads (*see* p 94).

Small fragments of glass of Roman origin were also found in Buckland Graves 15, 48, 49 and 59 (Evison 1987, 98–9). It was noted at the time that the fragments from Graves 15, 48 and 49 were 'in the earliest part of the cemetery' (Evison 1987, 99). The fragments described here come mostly from Phases 1 and 2, suggesting that they too, are moderately early in date.

The two fragments of glass in Grave 266, (b) and (c), lay with a number of other objects to the side of the waist of the deceased. These objects include an iron staple (e) and a rod (a), all of which have traces of wood remains on them, suggesting the possible presence of a small wooden container of some description in this area of the grave. Aside from the staple, there is no structural ironwork that would suggest the presence of a box, which would in any case be unusual for a burial of this period. The glass sherd from Grave 326 (k) lay within a cluster of objects, including several iron rings and rod fragments, as well as jewellery, and all of these objects may have been deposited originally in a bag. A similar cluster of objects, including several nails and a bead, lay in the vicinity of the glass sherd (i) from Grave 350B, between the femurs of the deceased.

The glass fragment from Grave 367(c) was arranged with a knife (a), a pair of copper alloy tweezers (b) and an indistinct fragment of iron (e), all of which lay beside the left arm of the deceased. The largest collection of Roman glass, amounting to five separate pieces, lay at the centre of the Grave 377 (b–f), the burial of a child or juvenile. A copper alloy harness pendant (m) of Roman date was also present in this grave, and is described above. It lay with a bundle of copper alloy rings, as well as two iron lozenges. The single sherd of glass in Grave 428 (f) was situated by the lower left arm of the body alongside a knife (h), several Roman coins (d), (g) and (n), two iron lozenges (i) and (k) and another copper alloy ring (o). Some of the objects lay over the arm and others were below it. Once again, they may have been contained within a bag or pouch.

Both the arrangement of objects in the grave and the associations with the glass are repeated in the other Buckland graves. Within Grave 15 a small assemblage including a sherd of Roman glass, a Roman coin, a fragment of copper alloy sheet metal and several beads lay in a group beside the left pelvis of the body. The objects from Grave 48 were placed in a similar position and include beads, copper alloy fragments and a lozenge, with a knife nearby (Evison 1987, 230). The fragment of glass from Grave 49, however, lay at the neck, close to a bead, and the fragment from Grave 59 was also close to a string of beads.

Meaney has noted that fragments of Roman glass were regularly deposited in the amulet bags of early Anglo-Saxon women and White echoed the same sentiments (Meaney 1981, 227; White 1988, 160–1). Within east Kent, examples are known from graves at Barfreston; Chatham Lines; Mill Hill, Deal; Sarre; Sibertswold and Stowting (Meaney 1981, 227–8; Parfitt and Brugmann 1997, 78). Graves 86 and 95 from Mill Hill, Deal, which included fragments of Roman

Grave	Object letter	1994 Phase	Sex	Gender	Age	Object	Element
15	4	2	Female	Female	30–45	Vessel	Body sherd
48	11	1b	Female	Female	12–18	Vessel	Rim or body sherd
49	b	1	Female	Female	Adult	Vessel	Body sherd
59	3q	3a	Female	Female	20–30	Vessel	Body sherd
208	c	-	?Female	?	20–30	Vessel	Body sherd
238B	b	1-2	Female	?	30–40	Window	
266	b	1b-2a	?Female	Female	30–35	Window	
266	c	1b-2a	?Female	Female	30–35	Bottle	Body sherd
326	k	2-7	?Female	Female	14–16	Vessel	Rim sherd
350B	i	1b-3a	?Male	Female	20–25	Bottle	Body sherd
367	c	-	?Male	Female	30–40	Bottle	Handle
377	b	1-2	-	Female	-	Window	
377	c	1-2	-	Female	-	Vessel	Body sherd
377	d	1-2	-	Female	-	Vessel	Base
377	f	1-2	-	Female	-	Vessel	Body sherd
377	e	1-2	-	Female	-	Rod	Upper part
428	f	2	Female	Female	20–25	Vessel	Body sherd

Table 4.32. Details of Roman glass.

glass, were assigned to Kentish Phases II and IV, which echoes the situation with Buckland and suggests that Roman glass was largely deposited in east Kent graves during the sixth century. The practice was restricted to the graves of females, most of whom were adult.

A similar situation prevailed nearby on the Continent, although the practice was not common there. The cemetery at Lavoye, for example, produced just one grave with a fragment of the rim of a vessel (Joffroy 1974, 78, 122 and pl 23.205). Further fragments, again occurring only in small numbers, are known from Frénouville, Krefeld-Gellep and Eichstetten, amongst other sites (Pilet 1980, pls 24 and 150; Pirling 1979, 143; Sasse 2001, 105).

Miscellaneous

Amulets

Ian Riddler

(Grave 204, 205 and 246)

Possible amulets from individual graves include the antler discs and rings described above (pp 160–1), for which the amuletic value lay in the symbolism attached to deer and their antlers (as Joffroy 1974, 65; MacGregor 1985, 107–8). Roman glass may have been kept by adult women of the sixth century simply for its colour and translucence or for other reasons described by Meaney (1981, 228). The mythology of the rock crystal pendant in Grave 391B may not have interested its Anglo-Saxon owner (*see* pp 85–6), but rock crystal itself possessed properties conceivably of amuletic value (Meaney 1981, 82–8).

A stone pebble (e) from Grave 204 was found together with a shale spindle-whorl (d), a fragment of marine shell (f) and a Roman coin (m) beside the left femur of the female skeleton. The pebble is grey in colour with yellow banding. Pebbles were also found in Graves C, 11 and 147 of the earlier Buckland excavations (Evison 1987, 122). The example from Grave 147 probably lay in a bag at the waist of the deceased, together with the other objects. As with the Roman glass, it may have been retained from a fascination with its colour and shape, but could also have had a broader significance for its owner.

A fossil shark's tooth (d) lay by the waist of the deceased in Grave 205. Meaney has previously noted that fossil shark's teeth were absent from early Anglo-Saxon graves, and this may be the first recorded example (Meaney 1981, 12–13). It was retrieved from the pelvis area of the deceased

(an adult, probably a female), close to a Roman coin (c) which, alongside several fragments of copper alloy, may have been kept in a bag or pouch. As such, it cannot be easily reconciled with the 'tongue of a serpent' hung from the neck of a man in an eighth-century source, although it may have been retained for its amuletic significance (Meaney 1981, 12). The fish vertebra from Grave 246 (j) probably represents food debris (*see* p 31), although they were occasionally strung together as parts of necklaces, a tradition that continued throughout the Anglo-Saxon period, and can be seen with several graves at Dunstable, Bedfordshire (Meaney 1981, 147). *Elasmobranch* or shark-type vertebrae are amongst the species suspended and worn as amulets.

Faunal remains

Robin Bendrey

(Grave 372)

Grave 372 produced a small collection of animal bones from over the right femur of the skeleton (a). The bones were generally well-preserved, though there was variable presence of root-etching recorded. In a few cases the root-etching had caused significant destruction to the surfaces of bones, which had become quite brittle. The material appears to represent two distinct groups of bones.

Firstly, there is a collection of nineteen foot bones that are consistent with coming from the four feet of a single sheep (*Ovis* sp domestic). This includes left and right metacarpals and metatarsals, a left carpal (magnum), seven proximal phalanges, three medial phalanges and four distal phalanges (Table 4.33).

Secondly, there are seven right ribs that have been identified as probably sheep (cf *Ovis* sp domestic) and are also consistent with deriving from a single animal (not necessarily the same one as the feet bones). One rib has a small healed fracture.

Grave 372 was that of a female and it has been dated to Phase 2a. The animal bones from this grave appear to represent two distinct deposits: a set of seven sheep ribs, and the four feet of a single sheep. The absence of any other sheep bones, in particular the more robust limb bones, and the presence of the rib mid-blades which have a relatively low structural density, indicates that the recovered bone is a true representation of the bones deposited and not a product of differential preservation.

The ribs are all from the right side of the animal, and may represent a joint of meat. The deposition of joints of meat in

Taxon	Element	Side	Fusion	>50%	<50%	GL	Bp	SD	BatF	Bd	a	1	2	3	b	4	5	6	DLS	Ld	MBS	Comment
Ovis	magnum	l																				GB = 14.7mm
Ovis	metacarpal	r	f	1, 2, 3, 4, 5, 6, 7, 8		115.9	20.7	11.7	22.4	23.0	10.8	9.8	14.5	12.5	10.7	9.1		12.4				
Ovis	metacarpal	l	f	1, 2, 3, 4, 5, 6, 7, 8		116.7	20.7		22.3	22.9	10.8	9.8	14.5		10.6	9.1						
Ovis	metatarsal	r	f	1, 2, 3, 4, 5, 6, 7, 8		127.0	18.9	9.8	21.4	21.9	10.1	8.7	14.3	11.8	9.4	8.4	13.8	12.1				
Ovis	metatarsal	l	f	1, 2, 3, 5, 6, 7, 8							10.0	8.7										
Ovis	1st phalanx		f	1, 2, 3		30.8	11.8	9.0														
Ovis	1st phalanx		f	1, 2, 3		30.2	10.9	8.2		10.4												
Ovis	1st phalanx		f	1, 2, 3		30.0	11.2	8.1		10.3												
Ovis	1st phalanx		f	1, 2, 3		31.4	10.7	7.7		10.2												
Ovis	1st phalanx		f	1, 2, 3		30.9	11.5	8.9		11.8												
Ovis	1st phalanx		f	1, 2, 3		31.0	11.6	9.0		11.5												
Ovis	1st phalanx		f	1, 2, 3		30.8				9.7												
Ovis	2nd phalanx		f	1, 2, 3		19.5	10.4	7.1		8.0												
Ovis	2nd phalanx		f	1, 2, 3		19.7	10.0	7.2		7.9												
Ovis	2nd phalanx		f	1		18.0	11.1	9.0		9.4												
Ovis	3rd phalanx		f	1, 2															26.0	21.5	5.6	
Ovis	3rd phalanx		f	1, 2															25.2	20.8	5.2	
Ovis	3rd phalanx		f	1, 2															27.8	22.3	5.3	
Ovis	3rd phalanx		f	1, 2															26.8	21.5		
cf Ovis	rib	r		2, 3																		
cf Ovis	rib	r		2, 3																		healed break
cf Ovis	rib	r		2, 3																		
cf Ovis	rib	r		2, 3																		
cf Ovis	rib	r		2, 3																		
cf Ovis	rib	r		2, 3																		
cf Ovis	rib	r			2, 3																	

Notes:
1 – bones recorded using the diagnostic zones of Dobney and Reilly (1988)
2 – measurements follow Davis (1992, fig 2) for metapodials and von den Driesch (1976) for other elements
3 – in the case of the 1st and 2nd phalanges GL refers to GLpe as defined by von den Driesch (1976, figs 45 and 46)
NB. All elements were positively identified to sheep (Ovis sp domestic) (Boessneck 1969) except for the mid-shaft rib fragments which were identified to probably sheep (cf Ovis sp domestic)

Table 4.33. Full catalogue of animal bones from Grave 372.

177

Anglo-Saxon graves may be as food offerings (Nicholson 1998, 240; Lucy 2000, 94).

The metapodials, carpal and phalanges represent the four feet of a single animal. This deposit does not represent a food offering, as the feet are not a meat-bearing area of the body. They may, however, indicate the presence of a sheep-skin as a grave offering, on which the feet had been left. Prummel (2000, 77) records cremated parts of metapodials or carpus or tarsus bones of cattle, roe deer and sheep/goat in some early medieval graves in the Netherlands as the only bones of these species, and suggests that skins of the animals were burnt on the cremation pyre. A similar collection of sheep foot bones was also recovered from cremation 5 at the cemetery at Illington, Norfolk (Green and Milligan 1993, 22).

The Buckland sheep had a height at the withers of 57cm, calculated following Teichert (1975), which is at the lower end of the size range of Anglo-Saxon sheep. Eighteen metacarpals from sixth-century West Stow, for example, produced a range of 117.1–142.1mm and a mean of 128.7mm (Crabtree 1989, table 29), compared to measurements of 116.7mm from the left metacarpal and 115.9mm from the right metacarpal of the Buckland animal.

PART 5: COSTUME AND TEXTILES

Penelope Walton Rogers

Introduction

It is evident from the remains of textile adhering to brooches and buckles that many of the people buried at Buckland were placed in the grave fully clothed. This chapter examines how that clothing may have looked. In working towards a reconstruction of costume styles, the following elements have been considered: the arrangement of garment-fasteners such as brooches, buckles and pins on the body; the position of decorative accessories such as necklaces, bracelets and rings; the range of fabrics used to make the clothing; and the borders and fastening loops which mark the edges of garments.

Not all graves have yielded evidence. Of the 260 bodies excavated in 1994, seventy-nine were buried without grave goods and thirty-one with objects, such as pots and glass vessels, which have no bearing on the clothing. The best evidence comes from the 120 bodies (in 244 graves) buried with garment-fasteners, of which a large proportion are female (Fig 5.1). A further sixteen bodies, again mainly

female, had decorative accessories (beads, rings, and so on), but no garment fasteners. In fifteen graves with neither garment fasteners nor dress accessories, there were still textile remains adhering to metal objects, such as knives, spears, keys and girdle-hangers. In other words, 151 bodies (58 per cent of the cemetery) have yielded costume evidence of some sort.

The pie-graphs in Fig 5.1 show this evidence divided by sex and age, according to osteological study. The group labelled 'adults, sex unknown' includes a certain number where the gender can be interpreted from the grave goods, and in the following pages, burials with swords, spears and shields have been classed as male, and those with brooch-suites, beads, keys, girdle-hangers and textile tools as female. In Graves 281, 350B, 367, 373 and perhaps also Grave 381, there may be biological males in women's clothing, but in those cases the artefact evidence has been given precedence. It is the gender role encapsulated in the clothing that is the main concern here.

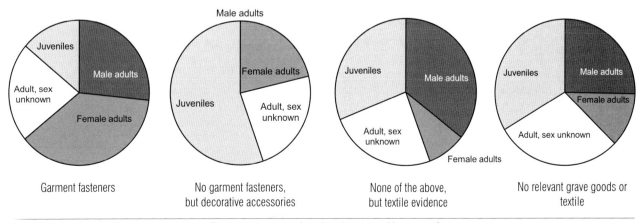

Fig 5.1. Buckland 1994. The costume evidence. The best data comes from female graves with garment fasteners.

Layout of graves

Men's burials

Men prove to have been buried with a limited range of garment fasteners and no decorative accessories. There were forty-eight skeletons confidently identified as biologically male, eighteen more tentatively so, and six where the sex was unknown but male-gender weapons were present. In thirty-two of these seventy-two burials there was a single buckle present at the waist, in a position that suggests a waist-belt. One further burial, Grave 381, had two buckles at the waist, one perhaps a pouch-fastener, although here the sex identification was uncertain.

There seems to have been little chronological change in how the buckles were used, although three examples set low on the hips, in Graves 302, 333 and 337, are all from early phases (Phases 1–3). The buckle was usually placed centrally or a little to the left and where the direction of the buckle pin was recorded it pointed to the body's right. Among the buckles worn at the waist there are seventeen iron, twelve copper alloy, one silver, one bone and one composite metal (*see* pp 124–9). Several had ornamental rivets behind the buckle, but strap-ends were absent, except in one double burial, Grave 265, where the strap-end attributed to the male, Sk 265B, may in fact represent the end of a girdle worn by his partner (sex not established), Sk 265A. Where

the material of the strap has been preserved, it is always leather. The nature of the garments that these belts are likely to have clasped is discussed in relation to the textile evidence, below (pp 203–4).

Two further buckles, both very small, were found in men's graves, close to the feet. One is iron, from Grave 340 (c), and the other copper alloy, from Grave 345 (a). Small buckles, and the aglets (lace-tags) with which they are often associated, do not appear at the feet until the seventh century (Geake 1997, 64–5, 137–8), when they seem to represent an introduction from the Continent (Owen-Crocker 2004, 190). The buckles mainly occur as matched pairs which suggests that a second buckle has been lost by the two Buckland men. They are found in both male and female burials, and most are thought to be shoe-fasteners, although some may relate to leg-bands.

In seven of the male burials, Graves 240 (a teenager), 260, 351A, 381, 416, 434 and 437, there was a single iron pin, of which five are coil/scroll-headed (*see* p 120). The position of these pins in the grave could be anywhere from the head to the knee, but in six of the burials the pin lay alongside the knife (Fig 5.2a) (for pins in the burials of women and children, see below). Where dated, they are from Phases 1–2 and can be compared with iron pins with knives in other sixth-century male burials in Kent, such as grave 97 at Mill Hill, Deal, Kentish Phase III (AD 530/40–560/70), and Graves 50 and 33 at Buckland, Phases

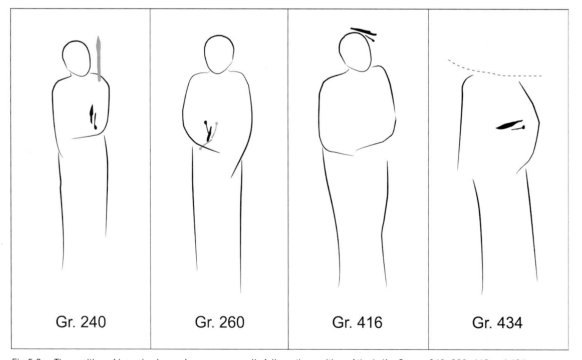

Fig 5.2a. The position of iron pins in men's graves generally follows the position of the knife. Graves 240, 260, 416 and 434.

2 and 3, respectively. Evison (1987, 82–3) also noted three pins in positions that suggested they were fastening textile wrappers for spearheads in seventh-century burials, but this seems to be a later development. In the sixth century they were more probably connected with the carrying or use of the knife. At any rate, they can be discounted as part of the clothing ensemble for men.

No brooches, apart from a Roman crossbow brooch (j) from the fill of Grave 264, were found in male graves. The large rectangular wool cloaks worn by Germanic men from the Roman Iron Age to the eighth or ninth centuries were often fastened by a brooch or buckle on the shoulder (Hald 1980, 322, 331; Bender Jørgensen and Wild 1988, 72, 82–6; Owen-Crocker 2004, 78), but, for some reason, these cloak-fasteners rarely appear in Anglo-Saxon burials (Walton Rogers 2007, 207–9).

Women's burials

The costume of women is better represented than men's, in terms of garment fasteners and the textiles adhering to them. Forty-three skeletons were confidently identified as biologically female and many of the thirty-nine tentative identifications have been confirmed by the grave goods. A further four bodies had no sex attribution but female-gender garment fasteners and, as already described, three or four skeletons tentatively described as male had female

accessories. A small number of children buried with female accessories also have some relevance, although brooches and pins were not necessarily used in the same way by youngsters (*see* pp 212–13). The graves with garment fasteners and dress accessories fall into natural groups, here called '*Dress Styles*'. Before considering these groups some general remarks may be made concerning individual artefact groups (for further details of objects, *see* pp 119–32).

Pins

Thirty pins were recovered from twenty-seven women's graves, but three, all of iron, were closely associated with a knife, in Graves 223, 281, 412 (Phases 1b–3a), just as they were in men's graves (Fig 5.2b). Two pin fragments with a cluster of objects at the hip in Grave 413 may have been in a pouch. There were, therefore, only ten copper alloy and fifteen iron pins, one in each of twenty-five graves, which could be regarded as garment pins. The pins were spread evenly through all phases. They most frequently appeared crossways at the neck, often on top of any beads lying there, but also occurred vertically or diagonally on the chest, and in three instances in Phases 1b–2 (Graves 427A, 407 and 408) they were worn in the region of the waist and upper thigh. These last formed part of the shift of focus to the waist and hip, which coincided with the arrival of *Dress Style IV*. With the appearance of *Dress Style V*, they returned to the upper chest and, although many

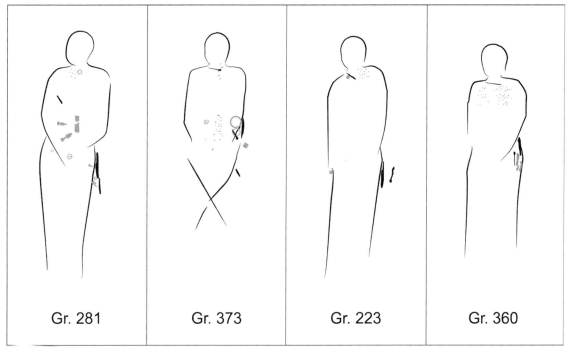

| Gr. 281 | Gr. 373 | Gr. 223 | Gr. 360 |

Fig 5.2b. In women's graves, the pin is usually in a position that suggests a garment fastener, except where there is a second pin by the knife. Graves 281, 373, 223 and 360.

of these later pins are incomplete, they have the appearance of being shorter than the earlier ones, 90mm or less in length, as compared with 100–150mm in Phases 1–2.

Buckles and strap-ends

All except one of the buckles in women's graves lay in the vicinity of the waist or hip, in a position that suggested a belt. Most were worn singly (twenty-five graves) but in two Phase 2a burial (Graves 417 and 419) there were two buckles at the waist, one larger than the other. A particularly small iron buckle in Grave 372 lay under the right hip, where it may have been displaced by, or had some connection with the small sheep placed in the woman's lap on the right-hand side (*see* pp 176–8). One further buckle loop, without a pin, was recovered from the foot of Grave 336, but it is assumed to be intrusive, as it was well away from the feet and its large size would be unusual for a shoe buckle.

Where the direction of the pin in the belt buckles had been recorded, it pointed to the body's right, except for Grave 324 where it pointed to the left. Where the belt strap had survived it was always leather and shield-on-tongue buckle Grave 391B (o) has a well-preserved strap, 21mm wide, which tapers inwards to meet the buckle loop. The buckles were iron or copper alloy in the early phases, but, with the exception of the silver-inlaid iron buckle from Grave 245, all the later buckles were copper alloy, including some silver-coloured high-tin bronze. This distinguishes the women's burials from the men's, where iron buckles were still common in later graves.

Most of the buckles were in the normal waist position, but several examples seem to be set on the hips in Phases 2b-3a (eg Graves 204, 223, 350B, 373 and 412). This coincides with the use of strap-ends, which are likely to represent the long pendent end(s) of the belt. Strap-ends occur as a pair between the knees in Grave 417 and between the calves of Grave 204; and singly by the ankle in Grave 373, between the upper thighs in Grave 412 and on the upper right thigh in Grave 222. The person in Grave 373 was particularly small (and tentatively identified as a male), which may explain why the strap-end hangs so low. Pairs of strap-ends below the knee have sometimes been interpreted as the ends of garters or hose-binding straps, but the paired ends in Grave 417 and Grave 204 both lie so close together that it seems more likely that they represent either the split ends of the same strap, or the two ends of a knotted girdle. At any rate, the single female burial with strap-ends from Buckland Grave 14 (Phase 2; Evison 1987, 90) and the seven from Mill Hill, Deal, (graves 25B, 33, 38, 69, 71, 94, 105; Kentish Phases II–IV; Parfitt and Brugmann 1997, 74–5) confirm that these

are a feature of sixth-century women's dress and that the early examples all hang below the knee, while the late ones tend to be on a level with the thigh.

Bracelets, rings and ear-earings

Bracelets are rare in Anglo-Saxon cemeteries and mostly occur in children's graves, but a thin copper alloy bracelet was found on the left forearm of two adult women in Graves 207 and 219 (*see* p 122). Grave 207 (h) is a simple sliding-knot form and Grave 219 (m) is a heavily worn late Roman type. Finger rings were recovered from seven adult women's graves, always in the vicinity of the left hand and in Graves 271 and 288 still *in situ* on the bone. Four are silver; Graves 250 (h), 253 (a), 271 (b), 298 (b); one copper alloy, Grave 408 (f); one iron, Grave 288 (a) and one silver with a garnet-set bezel, Grave 204 (i) and (j). In four graves they were the only costume item present and the burials were therefore difficult to date, but in Grave 408 the woman was wearing *Dress Style IV* in Phase 1b, in Grave 204 *Dress Style V* in Phase 2b, and in Grave 250 *Dress Style V* in Phase 3a.

There is no clear evidence that ear-rings were worn by women at Buckland. One certain continental-style ear-ring was found with other items likely to be the contents of a purse in a man's grave, Grave 351A (*see* p 121), but the wire rings by the head of the woman in Grave 413, of Phase 5–7, match a third on her chest alongside some beads, and are perhaps more likely to be part of an encircling beaded collar, pulled upwards when the body was placed in the grave, or the fixing for a veil (*see* p 210). Beads, worn as collars, necklaces and festoons between brooches will be considered in relation to the different *Dress Styles*, along with the brooches.

Dress Style I

Dress Style I is defined by annular brooches at the shoulders. The brooches appear as a pair, one on either shoulder, in Graves 239 and 372, and as a singleton on the right shoulder in Graves 308 and 367 (Fig 5.3). Where the pin direction has been recorded, it is always vertical. These brooches would have clasped the tubular gown, or 'peplos', which was worn by Germanic women in the Roman and Migration Periods (Walton Rogers 2007, 144–54). In Britain, paired annular brooches were typically combined with a crossways pin at the throat (Graves 239 and 308) and a modest number of beads strung between the brooches (Graves 239 and 372). A pair of brooches is the norm, but single brooches on the right shoulder also occur, with beads strung in a short loop from the shoulder brooch (Grave 308); and a second pair of brooches lower on the chest (Grave 239), is not unusual (discussed further below,

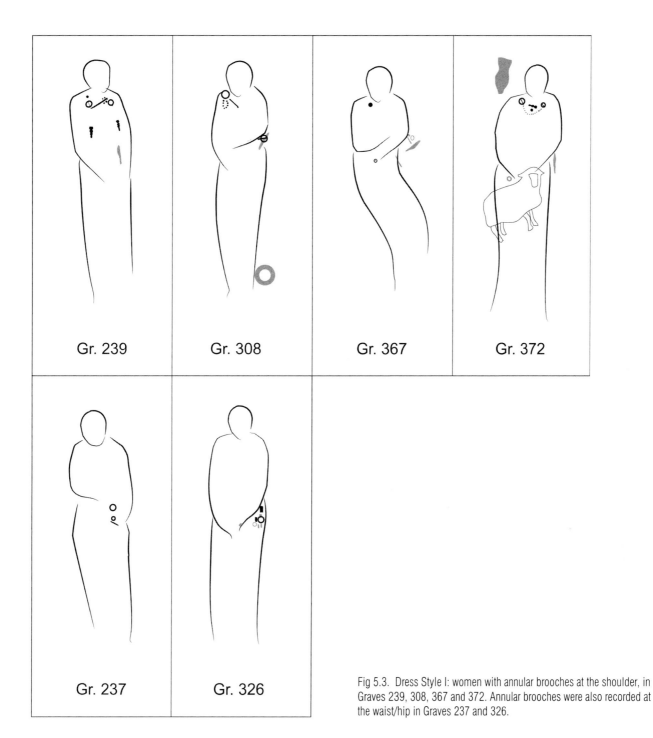

Fig 5.3. Dress Style I: women with annular brooches at the shoulder, in Graves 239, 308, 367 and 372. Annular brooches were also recorded at the waist/hip in Graves 237 and 326.

p 205). At least two of these burials, Graves 239 and 308, belong to Phase 1. The tubular gown probably went out of fashion in east Kent in the early decades of the sixth century and the woman-with-sheep (Grave 372; Phase 2a) seems to be wearing a late fusion of styles, with non-matching annular brooches at the shoulders, combined with a Frankish disc

brooch (f) and small Kentish square-headed brooch (e) under the chin, where a pin would normally be.

In two graves, annular brooches were found at the left hip; two in Grave 237 and one in Grave 326. It is possible that these represent brooches that had gone out of fashion and were being held as keepsakes in a pouch at the hip, but

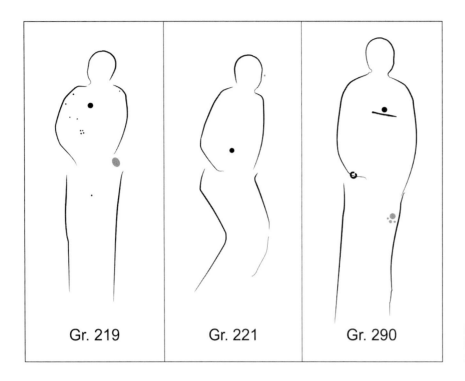

Fig 5.4. Dress Style II: women with a single button brooch placed centrally, Graves 219, 221 and 290.

in Scandinavia objects comparable with annular brooches, *ringspenner*, were also used on the belt, as a buckle or as a means of attaching objects to the belt (Fig 5.19b) (Hines 1984, 266–8). The tentatively identified remains of a linen tablet weave on the back of brooch Grave 237 (a) might represent such a belt. The sleeve clasps from Grave 326 represent the fasteners, which would have been attached to the cuffs of the garment worn underneath the tubular gown. Due to the poor preservation of the bones, it was not possible to tell whether they were still on the wrists, which lay across the waist or in a bag with the annular brooches.

Dress Style II

Dress Style II is represented by three burials (Graves 219, 221 and 290) in which there is a single button brooch placed centrally somewhere between the throat and the lower chest, with no other brooch present (Fig 5.4). These are early graves, possibly all from Phase 1. They are broadly contemporary with *Dress Style I* and there is a link between the two styles in a child's grave from Phase 1, Grave 254, where a single button brooch appears at the neck, combined with what is often a feature of the tubular gown ensemble, a pair of vertical small-long brooches on the upper chest (cf Grave 239). Beads lie on the upper chest (Grave 219 and 254), where they may have been strung around the neck, but three by the left leg in Grave 290 seem to be associated

with the silver spoon placed there. There is a pin in only one grave, at the neck of the woman in Grave 290.

The orientation of the brooch pins in relation to the body was generally not recorded during excavation, but on brooch Grave 219 (n) it is vertical to the human face depicted on the front, with the pin pointing up, while in all other examples, including a fifth button brooch which appears later, in *Dress Style IV*, Grave 255, the pin is roughly horizontal (pin orientation kindly recorded by Kate Morton). Assuming that the face was meant to be upright, a horizontal brooch pin would point across the body and is likely to have fastened a garment with a vertical front opening. This contrasts with the larger button brooches found elsewhere in southern England (Avent and Evison 1982, 100–1; Evison 1987, 48; Suzuki 2008, 336–43). They have vertical pins, and were sometimes worn as an alternative to saucer brooches on the shoulders, as fasteners on another version of the tubular peplos-style gown (eg Alton, Hampshire, grave 35, Evison 1988, 10, 114).

Dress Style III

Dress Style III is defined by showing two brooches, worn as a matching or non-matching pair at neck and centre chest. In three burials, Graves 366, 428 and 440 in Phases 1b–2, the brooches are small saucer brooches (Fig 5.5); in Grave 266 they are two matching radiate-headed bow brooches

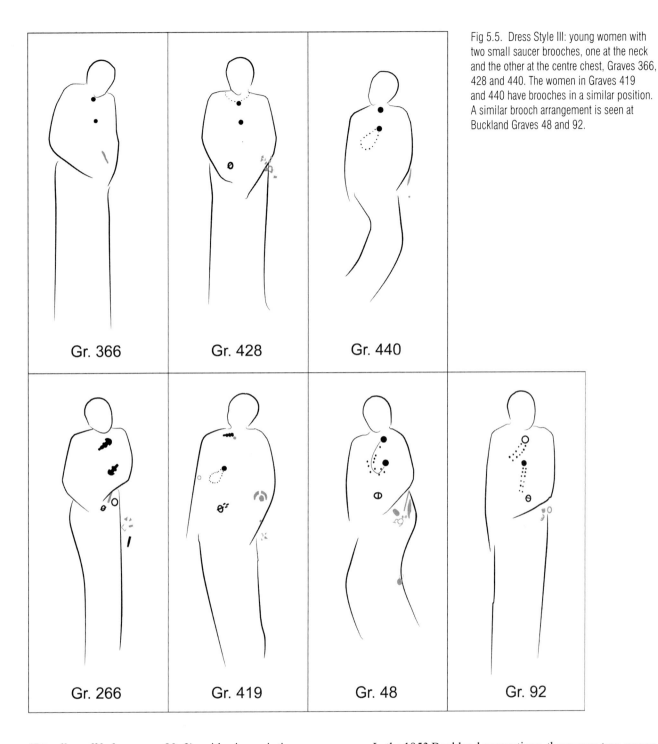

Fig 5.5. Dress Style III: young women with two small saucer brooches, one at the neck and the other at the centre chest, Graves 366, 428 and 440. The women in Graves 419 and 440 have brooches in a similar position. A similar brooch arrangement is seen at Buckland Graves 48 and 92.

Gr. 366

Gr. 428

Gr. 440

Gr. 266

Gr. 419

Gr. 48

Gr. 92

(*Bügelknopffibeln, see* pp 80–2), with pins pointing across the body in opposite directions; and in Grave 419 there is a bird brooch at the neck and a silver-gilt disc brooch (*Kleinfibel, see* pp 76–7) on the chest. The radiate-headed brooches and the disc brooch mark the introduction of continental garment-fasteners.

In the 1953 Buckland excavations, there were two graves which may represent early and late examples of this style (Fig 5.5). Grave 48 (Phase 1b) has a button brooch at the neck, which harks back to the button brooches of *Style II*, combined with a saucer brooch on the chest, the two brooches being connected by a metal chain and a string of beads.

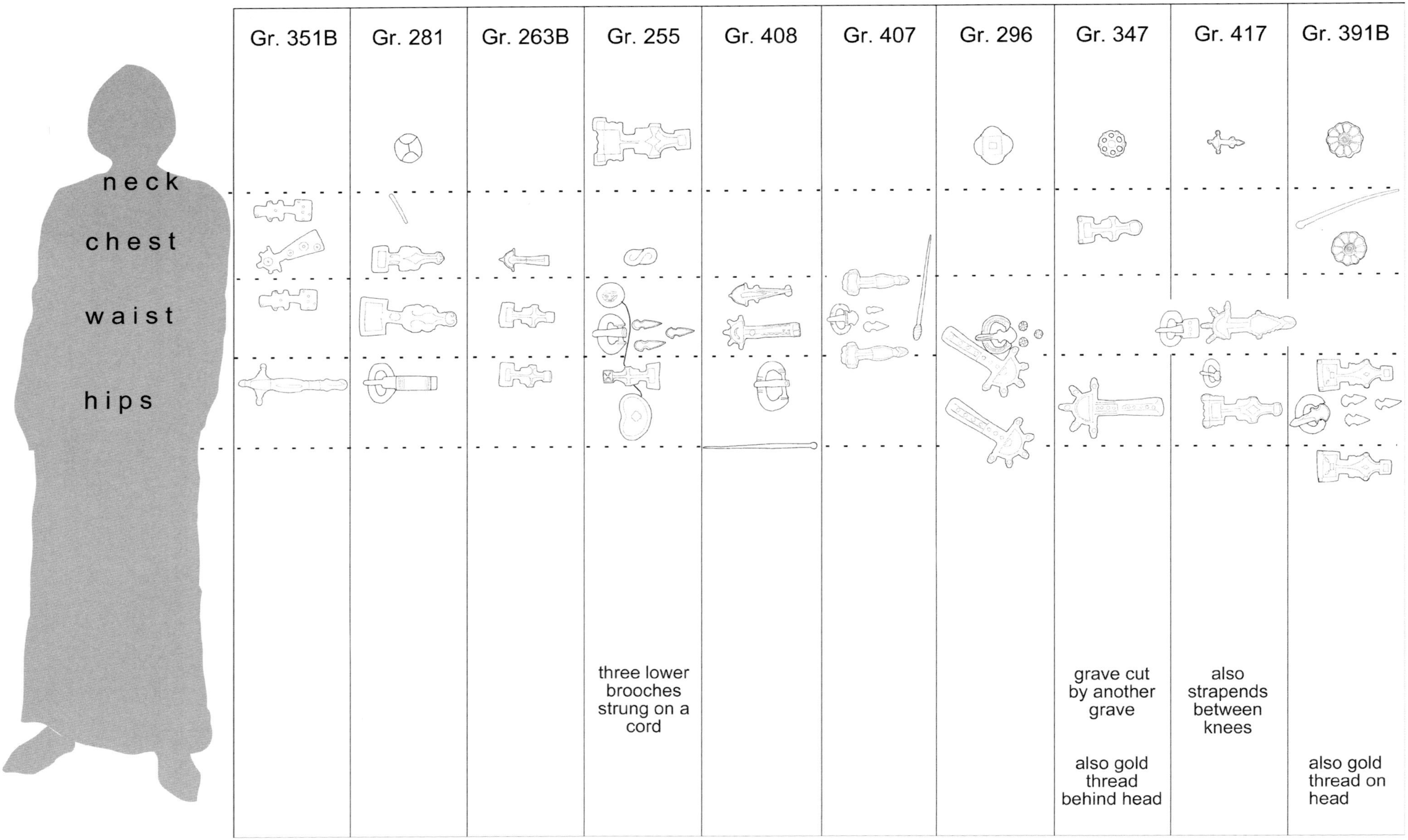

Fig 5.6. Dress Style IV. There is a column of brooches worn vertically on the body in ten women's graves. The pins of the brooches are almost all horizontal to the body and larger brooches are generally set low on the body. Grave 255 is aberrant, with a large brooch at the neck and the three lower brooches tied together with cords (see p 207).

Grave 92 (Phase 2) has at the neck a Kentish disc brooch of *Dress Style V* (see below) combined with a small Frankish disc brooch on the chest.

Beads start to play a more prominent role with *Dress Style III*, and in Graves 419 and 440 twenty or so have been suspended in a loop from the lower of the two brooches. This is part of the shift in emphasis away from the neck and shoulders in *Style I* and *II*, to the lower chest, waist and hips in *Dress Styles III* and *IV*. *Dress Styles III* and *IV* are contemporary with each other in Phases 1b–2 and it will be argued that *Style IV* is simply a second garment worn on top of a *Style III* gown.

Dress Style IV

Dress Style IV is represented by ten graves of Phases 1b–2a, in which there is a vertical column of brooches with the emphasis set low, in the region of the waist, and brooch-pins pointing across the body (Fig 5.6). The brooches at waist and hip are mostly radiate-headed or square-headed bow brooches, often worn in pairs pointing in the same direction, but among the earliest examples, from Phase 1, there are substitutions in the form of a very worn cruciform brooch at the bottom of the column in Grave 351B, an iron pin at the bottom of Grave 408, and a re-used buckle-plate at the bottom of Grave 255. Smaller fasteners appear at the neck and centre chest in five graves, a Frankish disc brooch and an iron pin in Grave 281, a single quatrefoil brooch in Grave 296, an openwork rosette brooch in Grave 347, a pair of garnet rosette brooches at throat and chest in Grave 391B, and a small radiate-headed brooch in Grave 417.

The position of the upper brooches often matches that already seen in *Dress Style III* and the theory that they represent the same gown, worn inside the garment fastened by the larger brooches at waist and hip, will be explored below in the light of the textile evidence. It may be noted at this stage, however, that the three women wearing pairs of small saucer brooches (*Style III*) were under the age of 25, while from the 1951–3 excavations the occupant of Grave 48 was a teenager and the woman in Grave 92 was 20–30 years old. In contrast, seven of the ten women wearing *Style IV* were over 25, and two were over 40, so that age and/or status may have played a part in who acquired the extra brooches and the garment which went with them.

Beads in *Dress Style IV* could be suspended from one of the brooches at the waist, either in a small cluster (Grave 263B) or as a singleton (Grave 296), while others were at the neck (Grave 281). Five of the later *Style IV* graves (Phase 2) had more numerous beads stretching between neck and waist, 164 beads in Grave 296, 41 in Grave 347, 115 in Grave 407, 53 in Grave 417 and 174 in Grave 391B (for the stringing of the beads on cords, *see* p 202). These long bead strings continue to be a feature of *Dress Style V*, but in *Style IV* the bead groups are dominated by light 'gold-in-glass' and rounded amber beads, whereas the *Style V* necklaces have more coloured glass and faceted amber beads (*see* p 105).

Dress Style V

Dress Style V belongs to Phases 2b and 3a and is represented by six burials, Graves 204, 222, 245, 353, 354 and 373, with a single Kentish disc brooch at the throat or upper chest, and necklaces which incorporate particularly numerous beads, combined with new elements such as bracteates, pendants and large faceted amber beads (Fig 5.7). In four of these graves there was also a small iron or copper alloy pin on the upper chest, below the brooch, pointing across the body, and in five graves a buckle at the waist, often combined with a strap-end. Four further graves from the same phases, Graves 250, 331, 339 and 412, lack any brooch or pin, but have been placed with the *Style V* group because of obvious similarities in the necklaces. The *Style V* graves are listed in Table 5.1. Birte Brugmann has suggested that Grave 223 represents an example of *Style V*, where a silver rider brooch has been substituted for a Kentish disc brooch.

The beads have been arranged in different ways and fashions can be seen evolving from the late *Style IV* graves through *Style V* (Fig 5.8). Among the necklaces in late *Style IV* graves, one, from Grave 391B (Phase 2) had 174 beads in a column between the neck and waist. The bead cords have not survived, but it is possible that they were similar to those in Grave 347, where several different cords run vertically down the body and are anchored to, or twisted round, the pins of the vertical column of brooches. In Grave 296 (Phase 2a) there was another vertical column of beads, but in this instance they probably represent a very long single loop, suspended from a single row of beads which encircle the neck, with a cluster of larger beads weighting the loop at the bottom. This fashion is repeated in a *Style V* Grave 373, where there is another necklet with a long vertical loop reaching to the waist. In Grave 222 the beads are more broadly arranged across the chest, but there is again a small necklet at the top and larger beads clustering lower down. In Grave 339 the small necklet has developed into a wide collar of beads, circling the neck and shoulders, with a wide vertical band reaching a short way down the front, to mid chest. In Grave 250, the vertically arranged beads have disappeared and the collar has developed so that it covers the whole of the upper shoulders and chest on front and back of the body.

Style V graves with Kentish disc brooches and multiple beads, often arranged vertically on the body, occur in the

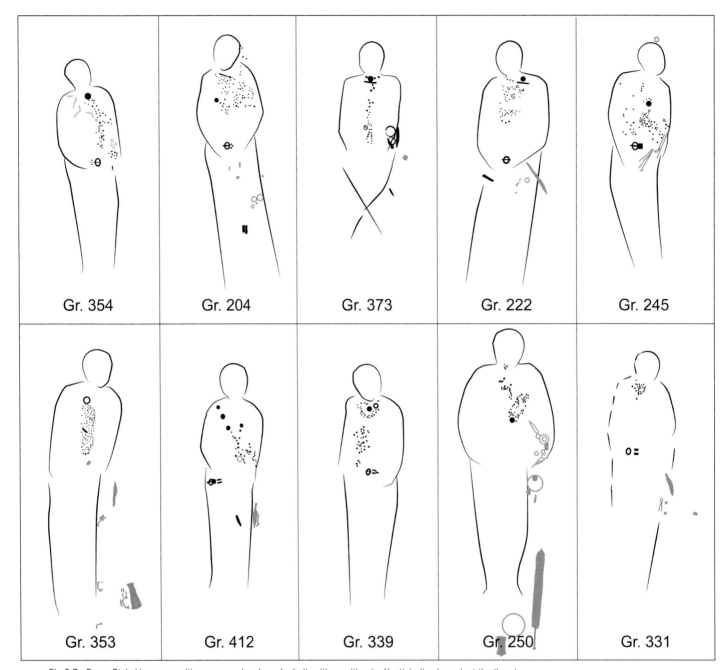

Fig 5.7. Dress Style V: women with numerous beads and a belt, with or without a Kentish disc brooch at the throat.

earlier Buckland excavations during Phase 3, although two burials, Graves 14 and 92, may be a little earlier. At Mill Hill, Deal the overlap between *Style IV* and *Style V* is represented in Kentish Phase III (AD 530/40–560/70), by a number of intermediate graves, most notably grave 105C, where the vertical column of brooches, *Dress Style IV*, incorporates a pair of Kentish disc brooches at neck and left waist and 132 beads. *Style V* seems to begin somewhere around the middle

of the sixth century and continues with changes in bead arrangement into the early decades of the seventh.

Dress Style VI

Phases 3b and 5–7 see a return to smaller necklaces, combined with a small pin on the upper chest, but no buckle or belt fittings (Fig 5.9). One early burial, Grave 360 (Phase

Grave no	Phase	Age	Beads	Dominant type	Additions	Other garment accessories
With Kentish disc brooch at throat						
354	2b	25–30	75	blue + faceted amber (A2b)		Buckle, gold thread
204	2b	22–27	133	faceted amber (A2)	Gold bracteate	Buckle, strap-end, pin
373	2b-3a	35–40	65	blue + red + faceted amber (B1)		Buckle, strap-end, pin
222	3a	35–45	118	red + faceted amber (B2)		Buckle, strap-end, pin
245	3a	35–45	150	pale + rounded amber (A2)	Gold bracteate, silver-gilt scutiform pendants, small amethyst, carnelian (?Roman), copper alloy cylinder	Large buckle
353	3a	30–35	104	yellow + red + white (A2)		Pin
Without Kentish disc brooch						
412	2b-3a	15–20	76	red + faceted amber (A2b)		Buckle, strap-end
250	3a	25–30	150	red + yellow + white (B1)	Gold bracteate, gold bead, 2 silver scutiform pendants, ?bucket pendant	Buckle
339	3a	27–32	118	red + yellow (B1)		Buckle
331	3a	?adult	111	red + yellow (B1)		Buckle

Table 5.1. Beads and pendants in *Dress Style V*.

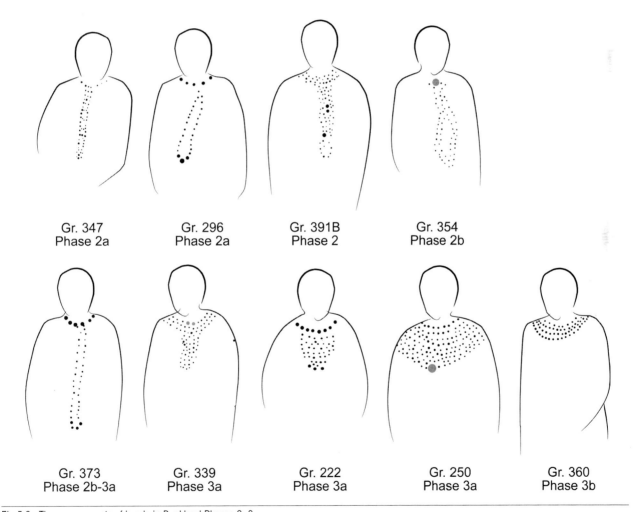

Fig 5.8. The arrangements of beads in Buckland Phases 2–3.

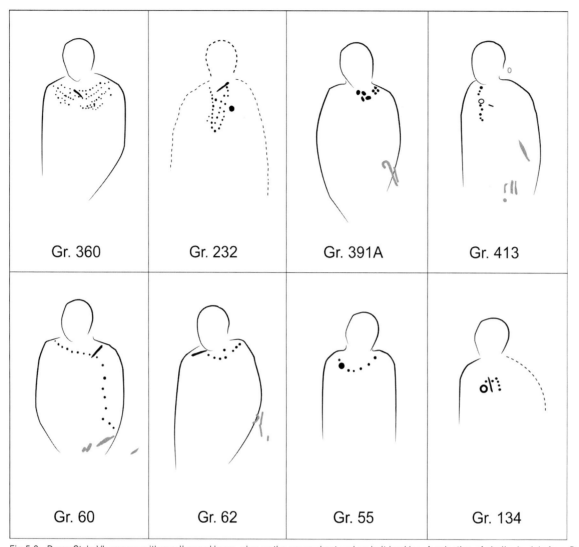

Fig 5.9. Dress Style VI: women with smaller necklaces, pins on the upper chest and no belt buckles. A selection of similar burials from Buckland 1951–3 are illustrated on the bottom row.

3b) has the most beads, seventy-four in all, arranged over the upper chest and shoulders in a reduced version of the beaded collar already seen in Grave 250 (Phase 3a). In Grave 232 (Phase 3b) there were twenty-four beads in a cluster with a gold coin pendant, although here the position on the body could not be recorded because the skeleton had decayed. The woman in Grave 391A (Phase 5–7) had three amethysts, a silver bulla and two glass beads around the neck, while the woman in Grave 413 (Phase 5–7) had three amethysts, a glass-inlay pendant, two silver sliding-knot rings and some fragments of sheet silver, seemingly arranged vertically below the right shoulder.

These four are the only representatives of *Dress Style VI* from the 1994 excavations, but in the earlier excavations,

where late graves were more numerous, burials with no brooches and few buckles but moderate numbers of beads, combined with a small pin at the neck, occur throughout later phases (Fig 5.9). Here, too, were amethysts, pendants of different sorts and silver-wire rings incorporated into the necklaces. Vera Evison has suggested that the amethysts were mounted in such a way as to point outwards from the line of the necklace, in imitation of the jewelled collars worn at the Byzantine court (Evison 1987, 69).

Burials of other women

Roughly half of the identifiable women's burials have been incorporated into this scheme of *Dress Styles*, which

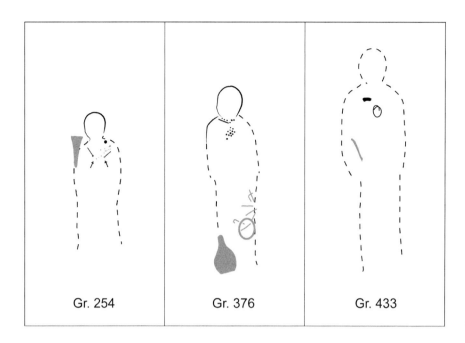

Gr. 254   Gr. 376   Gr. 433

Fig 5.10. A small number of juvenile graves have garment fasteners.

includes all the graves with brooches and significant quantities of beads. There remains outside this group, women who wear, perhaps a single buckle, or a pin, or no garment fasteners at all. Although textile remains adhering to knives and other metal goods may indicate the kinds of fabrics these women wore, there is little that can be said of their garment styles.

Burials of juveniles

There were fifty-six burials of under 16 year olds, identified by the osteology or the small size of the grave. With a few exceptions, these were poorly equipped in terms of costume accessories. Buckles of iron or copper alloy were found at the waist in seven graves, in which were buried children ranging in age from 3–4 (Grave 287) to 14–16 years old (Grave 374). Pins were recorded in five graves, but the four iron examples, from Graves 240, 421, 431 and 442, were all associated with knives and only the copper alloy pins from Graves 254 and 376 may be regarded as garment pins. Beads occurred in thirteen graves, sometimes as a single item in the middle of the grave (eg Graves 294 and 334) or sometimes as a necklace (Graves 254 and 404). Copper alloy bracelets, which are generally more common in children's graves than in adults', were found in three graves, Graves 343, 388 and 433, one of them (Grave 388) the burial of an infant less than one year old. Some of these items may have been toys or trinkets, as in Grave 377, where there were five copper alloy rings (l), (n) – (q), a buckle loop (g), a pendant (m) and a bead (k).

A few child burials were better equipped (Fig 5.10). The 4–5 year old in Grave 254 had a pair of ring-headed pins at the throat, a button brooch at the left neck and a pair of vertical small-long brooches on her chest. The 7–8 year old in Grave 376 had a small copper alloy pin at the neck, beads on her chest and a set of adult female accessories incorporating keys and a purse ring at her left hip. In Grave 433 a juvenile had a lying-horse brooch near the throat and a bracelet below. While these share some characteristics with adult graves, only the late burial, Grave 376, from Phase 5–7, can be regarded as duplicating the style of adult women of the period.

The textiles

Introduction

Where the clothing of the dead had touched metal objects, such as brooches and pins, small areas of the textile were often preserved within the corrosion crust. Textiles have been shown to survive in this situation partly by the process of copper salts acting as a biocide on the micro-organisms that attack organic fibres, and partly by the replacement of the decaying textile by minerals (Jakes and Sibley 1983; Jakes and Howard 1986; Sibley and Jakes 1984; Walton Rogers 2007, 50–60). In the Buckland (1994) cemetery, textiles were preserved in this way in 112 of the 244 graves (or 114 of the 260 bodies). In some instances only a few threads

Textile type	Wool	Linen	No fibre identified	Total
ZZ tabby	1	25	18	44
ZZ tabby repp	0	12	5	17
ZS tabby repp	1	0	0	1
ZZ 2/2 twill	9	6	23	38
ZZ 2/2 diamond or chevron twill	0	1	2	3
ZS 2/2 twill	7	0	13	20
ZS 2/2 diamond or chevron twill	5	0	13	18
Spin-patterned 2/2 twill	1	0	0	1
ZZ 2/1 twill	0	1	0	1
Spin-patterned 2/1 twill	0	0	1	1
Tablet-woven and warp-faced bands	0	5	11	16
Total	24	50	86	160

Table 5.2a. Summary of Buckland 1994 textiles, from 114 graves.

Textile type	Total
ZZ tabby	33
ZZ tabby repp	5
ZS tabby repp	1
spin-patterned tabby	1
tabby with soumak	1
ZZ 2/2 twill	0
ZZ 2/2 diamond or chevron twill	2
ZS 2/2 twill	1
ZS 2/2 diamond or chevron twill	10
ZZ 2/1 twill	0
spin-patterned 2/1 twill	0
tablet bands	4
Total	58

Table 5.2b. Summary of textiles from Buckland 1951–3, from fifty-six graves (data extracted from Crowfoot 1987).

have survived, but in 160 textiles, full details of weave, spin and thread-count (number of threads per centimetre) could be recorded (Table 5.2a and Fig 5.11). To these may be added a number of cords used to string beads and tie objects together, some needle-worked button loops and four examples of gold thread.

This sizeable collection is the largest so far from Kent and can be added to the fifty-eight textiles identified by the late Elisabeth Crowfoot for Buckland 1951–3 (Crowfoot 1987 and summarised here in Table 5.2b). Other collections from Kent, mostly recorded by Crowfoot, are available in an on-line database (Walton Rogers 2007). Thanks are due to the Department of Conservation and Scientific Research at the British Museum for facilitating the research.

Fibre identification

The application of modern microscopy techniques, including polarised light microscopy and Scanning Electron Microscopy (SEM), has allowed a distinction between wool and linen in seventy-five textiles (Scanning Electron Micrographs of fifteen samples were kindly prepared for the author by Margaret Brooks, English Heritage Centre for Archaeology). Twenty-six samples could be identified as wool by this means, but if it is accepted that the combination of Z and S spin (ZS twills) is an indicator of a wool textile, as has been shown for other Anglo-Saxon cemeteries (Walton Rogers 1999, 145; 2007, 72), then the totals in Table 5.2a can be revised to fifty wool, fifty linen and sixty not identified.

The term 'linen' is used here in its loosest sense, for a textile made from plant fibre. In mineral-preserved textiles it is difficult to distinguish between the different plant fibres, although in five cases, Graves 228, 245, 255, 294 and 351A, flax from *Linum usitatissimum* L could be confidently identified by the fine lumen, well-spaced cross-markings, prominent dislocations and clockwise drying twist. In one case, Grave 281, hemp, from *Cannabis sativa* L, was thought likely from the thick cuticle and close cross-markings. More significantly, in a textile on a knife at the waist of the man in Grave 340, nettle fibre, from *Urtica dioica* L, was identified by its flattened cross-section and close, regular cross-banding (knife (a)). Apart from some probable threads in grave 81 at Mill Hill, Deal (Parfitt 2003, 81), this is the first time that nettle has been positively identified in an early Anglo-Saxon burial, despite extensive microscopy of textiles from other Anglo-Saxon cemeteries (Walton Rogers 2007, 15, 62). Nettle-fibre textiles are more frequently found in Scandinavia, where flax was a late arrival, although a single example was tentatively identified among some charred textiles from Anglo-Scandinavian York (Walton 1989, 312). More recently, a nettle-fibre textile, technically almost identical with the Buckland example, has been identified on the back of a copper alloy belt-plate found at the waist of a child buried with seventh-century female accessories at Flurlingen (Kanton Zürich), Switzerland (Windler *et al* 1995).

No attempt was made to identify dyes, the textiles being in every case too small and too firmly fixed to the artefact to allow successful sampling.

The main textile types

Although there are many variables involved in the preservation of textiles, within the larger cemeteries they seem to be evened out, and the ratios between fabric-types

tabby

2/1 twill

tabby repp

2/2 twill

2/2 diamond twill

Fig 5.11. The main weaves of the Buckland 1994 textiles.

are remarkably consistent. From the data acquired for the Anglian region it is possible to demonstrate a rise in the use of tabby-weave textiles made with Z-spun yarn (ZZ tabby) and a corresponding decline in ZZ 2/2 twill over the fifth to seventh centuries (Walton Rogers 2007, 104–7). At West Heslerton, North Yorkshire, for example, where most textiles came from fifth- and sixth-century graves, ZZ tabby represented 28 per cent of the collection and ZZ twill 38 per cent (Walton Rogers 1999, 144–7). At Castledyke, north Lincolnshire, a mainly sixth- and seventh-century cemetery, ZZ tabby represented 54 per cent and ZZ twill 32 per cent, and in the graves that could be closely dated ZZ tabby rose from 44 per cent in the sixth century to 63 per cent in the seventh (Walton Rogers 1998, 274–5). These changes are mirrored at Buckland (Table 5.3).

Other Kent cemeteries with textiles, such as Updown at Eastry (Crowfoot 2008), also have a high ratio of ZZ tabby and this has been interpreted elsewhere as a regional characteristic (Bender Jørgensen 1989, 26–38; 1992, 37). In

	ZZ tabby (including repp)	ZZ twill	ZS twill	Other
Buckland 1994 Phases 1–3 (up to mid 6th century)	34%	27%	25%	14%
Buckland 1994 Phases 4–7 (mid 6th–mid 8th century)	56%	11%	18%	15%
Buckland 1951–3 all phases (mostly late 6th and 7th century	65%	4%	20%	11%

Table 5.3. Changes in the use of textiles at Buckland over the sixth and seventh centuries.

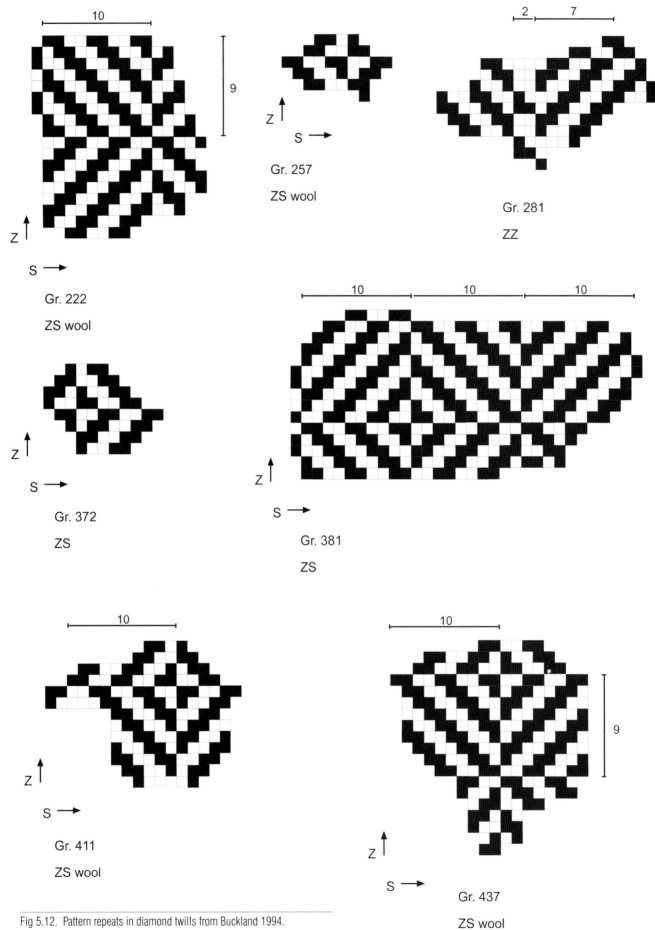

10

9

Z

S

Gr. 222

ZS wool

Z

S

Gr. 257

ZS wool

2   7

Gr. 281

ZZ

Z

S

Gr. 372

ZS

10   10   10

9

Z

S

Gr. 381

ZS

10

Z

S

Gr. 411

ZS wool

10

9

Z

S

Gr. 437

ZS wool

Fig 5.12. Pattern repeats in diamond twills from Buckland 1994.

fact, it can now be shown to be a reflection of the late date of much of the previously recorded Kent evidence. The shifts in textile use seen at Buckland are exactly the same as occur in other parts of the country. What lies behind this rise in the use of ZZ tabby seems to be partly a moderate increase in the use of linen for burial textiles, a feature which can be matched elsewhere in north-west Europe (Walton Rogers 2007, 107) and partly a greater degree of standardisation, as linens came to be made most commonly in ZZ tabby and wool cloth in ZS twill.

If Buckland resembles the cemeteries of other regions in its range of textile-types, it out-ranks them in terms of the fine quality of the fabrics. Broadly speaking, thread-counts are higher in finer textiles and in the Buckland 1994 graves approximately forty out of the 144 textiles (excluding narrow bands) had counts of 16 x 16 threads per centimetre or higher, while in the earlier excavations the number was twenty-five out of fifty-four. This compares with 29 out of 95 at Finglesham II, but contrasts with only fourteen out of 129 textiles at West Heslerton, five out of forty-eight at Castledyke and three out of twenty-three at Market Lavington, Wiltshire (Walton Rogers 2006). This supports the evidence of the metalwork, that the dead at Buckland, and elsewhere in east Kent, were provided with particularly valuable material goods.

Plain ZZ tabby

Most of the simple tabby-weave textiles are linens. They occur through all phases and were used equally by men, women and children. Thread-counts mostly fall within the range 12 x 10 (Grave 264) to 22 x 20 per centimetre (Graves 347 and 353) and there is no change in quality with time. They appear in positions that allow them to be interpreted as inner and outer garments and veils or scarves. One linen tabby, on the back of a buckle in *Dress Style IV*, proves to be made from part-processed fibre. This would have given the fabric a harder feel than usual and in this it resembles the tabby repps described below. Two particularly coarse examples of tabby-weave textiles made from plant fibre have paired threads in one system, Graves 376 and Grave 413 (Phases 5–7). Both were in association with feathers and, from their position in the grave, are assumed to represent bedding.

One tabby-weave textile, arranged in folds under and around the iron objects by the left knee of the woman in Grave 353, Phase 3a, has a fine, open, net-like appearance and proves to be made from wool. This distinctive textile-type has been noted in two graves in Anglian north Yorkshire, at West Heslerton (grave 143, Walton Rogers 1999, 147), and Scorton (Walton Rogers unpublished), in both cases over the top of

brooches and other textiles on the upper chest, in a position that suggests a veil or scarf. Similar net-like wool tabby-weaves have been recorded at seventh-century Hessens, north Germany (Walton Rogers 1995), Viking Age Dublin (Heckett 1990) and York (unpublished data). The finds from the British Isles are the most complete and are often narrow loom pieces, 150–240mm wide. If the Buckland example is also from a narrow piece, then the position would suggest the ends of a sash hanging down on the left-hand side of the body.

Tabby repp

Tabby repp is a tabby weave in which one system of threads dominates over the other, to give a slightly ribbed fabric. There are seventeen examples from the 1994 excavations, with an eighteenth on an unstratified spear ferrule, Sf 1264. They range in thread-count from 6–8 x 10 to 16 x 24 and at least eleven are linen, while three of the coarser examples are wool. They occur in both male and female graves, through most phases of the site, but there seems to be a consistent use for them at the waist in Phases 2–3, when they appear on the backs of buckles or in contact with other objects at the waist, in six female burials, Graves 204, 228, 336, 347, 350B and 436, and three male burials, Graves 259, 346 and 414. The rib always runs across the body, parallel to the belt, and they are rare elsewhere on the body. In Grave 347 a relatively fine tabby repp forms part of *Dress Style IV* and in Grave 204 part of *Style V*, but in other graves the dead seem to be simply dressed, with few accessories.

Tabby repp makes a strong, hard-wearing material and is used nowadays for textile belts and linings. In Anglo-Saxon reports, tabby repp has not always been distinguished from plain tabby, but at Sutton Hoo its use has been described for tapes and straps, and the inner cover of a pillow (Crowfoot 1983, SH11, SH13, SH16). At Buckland, tabby repps on spears in Graves 400, 421 and unstratified Sf 1264, and on the bucket in Grave 391B may be explained as straps, but the nine examples on the backs of buckles are more puzzling. It is possible that they represent a sash comparable with the *fascia ventralis* worn by Roman soldiers under the military belt (Ubl 1989), although in Graves 347 and 407 the repp re-appears higher up the body (*see* p 207). In these two cases it seems to represent a solidly made inner gown.

2/2 ZZ twill

2/2 ZZ twill was the major fabric-type of north-west Europe in the Roman Iron Age ('Haraldskjaer twills' in Bender Jørgensen 1992, 126ff). It survived in a variety of forms in Scandinavia into later periods, but in England it declined through the sixth

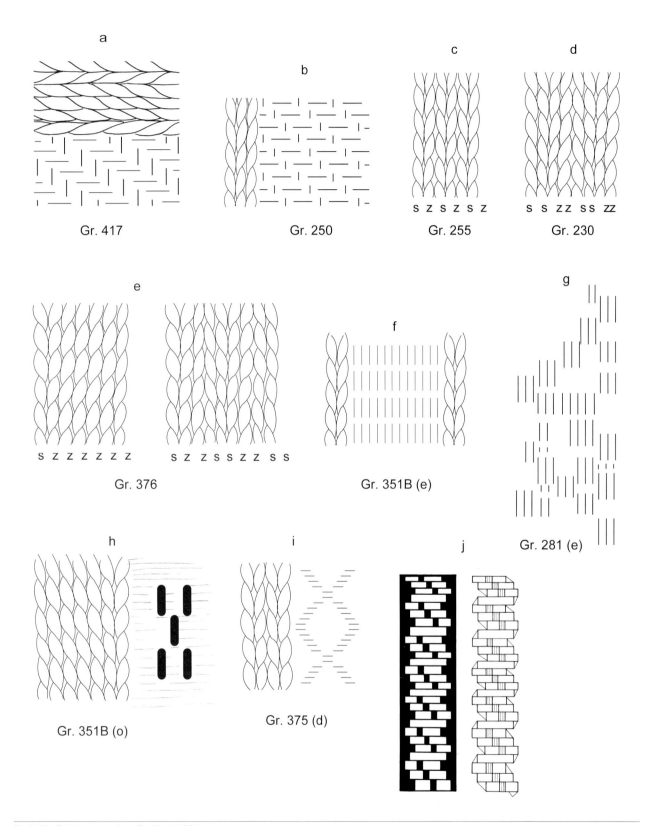

Fig 5.13. Tablet weaves from Buckland 1994.

century, and played only a minor role in late Anglo-Saxon clothing. The examples made in wool at Buckland 1994 are coarse and medium-weight fabrics, with thread-counts of 6 x 6 to 14 x 14 per centimetre. The medium-weight wool twills were used for women's gowns in the early phases, Graves 239, 308 and 367, a cloak or cover in Grave 381, for the outer belted garment of a child, Grave 287, and for what is probably a cloak, clasped at the neck by the large square-headed brooch in Grave 255. The coarsest ones may have been used as wrappers, as they appear either on spearheads (Graves 240, 256, 363 and 421), or on the weaving batten (Grave 250), with none in positions where clothing is likely.

The linen ZZ twills are mostly medium and fine fabrics, ranging from 9 x 10 to 20 x 20 threads per centimetre, and include a number of diamond patterned weaves. Fine linen twill and diamond twill seem especially associated with the garments of *Dress Styles III* and *IV*, in Graves 266, 281, 296, 326 and 391B, but are rare in men's graves.

2/2 ZS twill

2/2 ZS twill is largely the successor to ZZ twill for wool clothing fabrics. It was worn by men, women and children, in a range of qualities, from 9 x 9 (Grave 259) to 28 x 16 (Grave 257) per centimetre, and was often diamond-patterned. The finer types of diamond twills were especially espoused by the women wearing Kentish disc brooches, *Dress Style V*, Graves 222, 245, 353 and 373. In these graves it was not possible to reconstruct the orientation of the textile on the body, but in an earlier example used for a *Style IV* garment from Grave 417, the Z-spun warp runs across the body, with the starting band (Fig 5.13a) running vertically down the body, so that the loom width must run from shoulder to hem.

In men's graves ZS twill was often at the waist and upper body in a position that suggested a tunic, but the coarse example on both faces of the spearhead from Grave 259 is probably another wrapper. The medium-weight diamond twill on the man's legs in Grave 414 may represent his trousers, or perhaps a cloak laid over the body. The ZS spin combination particularly lends itself to felting and there is a matted example from Grave 231, on the back of a buckle. A matted effect can be the result of over-zealous washing, but some wool twills with a deliberate nap were recorded at West Heslerton, their position being suggestive of cloaks (Walton Rogers 1999, 146).

Patterning

Anglo-Saxons generally confined obvious patterning to the tablet-woven bands that edged their garments. More subtle pattern effects were achieved in the full-size cloths by reversing

the twill diagonal when weaving, to give chevron and diamond patterns, or by using alternating yarns of different spin, to give a textured effect called spin-patterning. The pattern units of the diamond weaves could be worked out in four examples (Fig 5.12), and in each case the reverse in the diagonal is after 10Z and 9S threads (= 20Z x 18S per diamond), a pattern which can also be seen at Fordcroft, Orpington (Crowfoot 1969, 51). There are many different pattern repeats recorded in Anglo-Saxon diamond twills, but this is the most common type, especially in the finer range of fabrics. Bender Jørgensen, in her survey of north European textiles, pointed out that it appears in the Roman Iron Age (as the 'Virring type') and is distributed at sites around the North Sea in the Germanic Iron Age (as 'Hessens/Elisenhof type C') (Bender Jørgensen 1992, 134–43). She suggests it was produced in specialist centres and puts it forward as a candidate for the 'Frisian cloth' recorded in Carolingian documents.

Spin-patterning was noted in a wool 2/2 twill from a man's burial, Grave 262, Phase 2–3, a twill of unknown fibre, possibly a 2/1 twill, from a woman's grave, Grave 204, Phase 2b and the wool tabby repp on the unstratified ferrule. The earliest Anglo-Saxon examples of spin-patterning were all wool twills, and probably native products, but in the late sixth and seventh centuries, a group of fine, spin-patterned tabby-weaves, thought to represent the import of fine linens from the Continent, appeared (Walton Rogers 2007, 74–5). The example from Grave 262 belongs in the first group, but it is less easy to categorise the example from Grave 204.

2/1 twill

2/1 twill is difficult to identify in mineral-preserved finds, where only one face is presented to the viewer. For this reason, only one example of 2/1 twill could be confidently identified, from Grave 250, Phase 3a, but a further five may exist in Graves 204, 247, 255, 263B and 420, from Phases 1b–3a. All of these are from women's graves and made with Z-spun yarn. The example from Grave 250 is a relatively fine linen, which falls in close vertical folds or gathers over the objects to the left of the body (j), (m) and (o). It reaches from the inner left elbow to the outer left hip, with a tablet-woven selvedge running over iron ring (o) (Fig 5.13b) (*see* p 210). The position of this loosely pleated textile with a corded border suggests the edge of a long head-veil, open at the front and reaching at least to the hip.

In Grave 255, Phase 1b, a twill of similar quality had been edged with a separately worked tablet-woven band (p 210) in a similar position on the body to that in Grave 250 (Phase 3a). It runs over the button brooch at the left waist as well as the châtelaine equipment, and perhaps also the belt buckle. In Grave 263B, Phase 1b, the linen twill was clearly the material of the *Style IV* gown fastened by the crossways brooches at waist and hip (a) and (c). The spin-patterned example in Grave 204, Phase 2b, is part of a complex layering of textiles beside the body and may represent another long veil, or some sort of coverlet or bedding beneath the body. In Grave 420, Phases 2–3a, the textile is on the chest, in contact with the iron pin pointing across the body. One last example comes from the back of the brooch worn at the throat of the woman in Grave 247, Phase 2a. This is so fine, at 54–72 x 36–48 threads per centimetre, and smoothly made, that the possibility that it is silk may be considered (Fig 5.27b).

2/1 twills were comparatively rare in the early Anglo-Saxon period, but some early examples from more northerly sites, are thought to represent the survival of Romano-British technology (Walton Rogers 2007, 110). The weave structure is commonly associated with the two-beam vertical loom, which is known to have existed in Roman Gaul and to have survived in northern France into the Merovingian period (Walton Rogers 1997, 1760–1; *et al* 2001, 163–6), whence it may have spread into the linen-producing areas of the Rhineland. Some of the 2/1 twills from Kent, therefore, which include fine examples from Riseley and Ozengell, may be imported textiles, or textiles produced with imported technology.

Tablet weaves

Tablet weaves were recovered from seventeen graves, representing adults, teenagers and children of both sexes (Tables 5.4 and 5.5). Some had been woven as an integral border on a full-size cloth, but most had been made as separate bands and then stitched to the fabric. In either case, the tablet weave is likely to mark the edge of the garment, whether at neck, cuff, front-opening or veil-edge, and its route over the body has significance for interpretation of the clothing.

Tablet weaving is worked with a set of thin square plates or 'tablets', which have a circular hole at each corner. Every hole is threaded with a separate warp thread, four threads per tablet (four-hole tablet-weaving), so that as the tablets are rotated, each tablet forms a four-strand cord. By introducing a weft yarn, the cords are held together in a flat band. Depending on whether the warp threads pass through the tablet from the left or from the right, the cords will twist clockwise or anti-clockwise, defined as Z or S twist. The technique may be worked with only two holes threaded per tablet (two-hole tablet weaving), to give a thinner band. In the Buckland (1994) cemetery, there were ten or eleven of these plain corded bands (Table 5.4; Figs 5.13c and 5.13d), and one example, Grave 376, where four-hole cording had

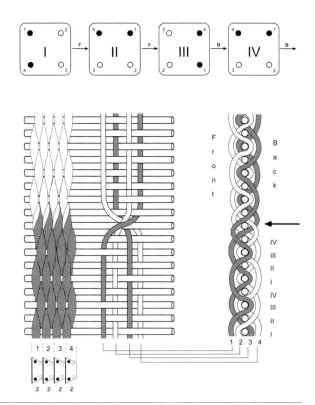

Fig 5.14. Weaving double-faced 3/1 repp on four-hole tablets (after Collingwood 1982, fig 147, 228).

been combined with two-hole cording to give a textured effect (Fig 5.13e). They were all of similar quality, with 10–14 warp cords per centimetre and were mostly made from S-ply yarn.

Patterning can be introduced in a variety of ways. One of the most common in the Buckland (1994) cemetery was a weave in which the tablets are rotated forwards and back, so that the corded appearance disappears and in its place are cross-ways ribs. Hansen calls this 'double-faced 3/1 repp' (Hansen 1990, 23–4, 47–9, 65). It appears in five graves, all *Dress Style IV*, and in Grave 351B the complete width of *c* 16mm wide is present, including a pair of corded borders flanking the central ribbed panel (Fig 5.13f). This is a popular weave amongst modern tablet weavers, who thread the four yarns that enter each tablet with two different colours, one pair on the top and the other pair below (Collingwood 1982, 227ff). By turning the tablets forward two turns then back two turns, the weave becomes one colour on the front and another on the back (Fig 5.14). By manipulating the tablets so that the opposite colour comes to the front, blocks of contrast can be made, a technique especially used for producing text. Although no colour has survived in any of the Buckland

Grave	Phase	Sex	Age	Function	Fibre	Width	Threading	Twists	Position
(i) woven borders									
250	3a	Female	25–30	selvedge on linen 2/1 twill	F/H	2.5mm	3 x 2-hole	SZZ	Diagonally over chatelaine at left hip
417	2a	Female	40–50	starting border on wool 2/2 ZS diamond twill	W	5.0mm	6 x 4-hole	SSZZZS	Vertical on back of brooch 1022d at centre waist
(ii) separately made									
230	2b–3a	(Male)	grown	-	F/H	38mm	2-hole	alternating SSZZ	Vertical on back of buckle 139a at waist
237	unphased	Female	30–40	-	F/H	-	-	-	On back of annular brooch at waist
255	1b	Female	30–35	attached to fine ??2/1 twill	?	-	-	alternating ZS	On objects at left waist
297	2	Male	30–35?	-	?	39mm	-	SSS	Tablet band or fringe on chest under shield
347	2a	Female	14–16	-	?	35mm	-	?	Vertical on back of brooch 468f on chest
373	2b–3a	Female	35–40	-	?	33mm	-	SSS	Pair of tablet bands at opposite ends of disc brooch 612j at neck
391B	2	Female	20–25	-	?	314mm	-	?	Vertical on back of brooch 862n between upper legs
408	1b	Female	30–40	In association with button loop	?	37mm	2-hole	?	Vertical on back of brooch 791c at waist
409	1b	Female	22–27	-	?	312mm	2-hole	SSS	Cords, possibly tablet weave across rods on left thigh
443	1b–2	Female	30–35	In association with ZS diamond twill	?	311mm	4-hole	alternating ZS	On iron rods at left hip

Notes: (Male) = male, implied by grave goods; F = flax; H = hemp

Table 5.4. Plain corded tablet weaves.

Grave	Phase	Sex	Age	Function	Fibre	Width	Weave	Position/Notes
281	1b	Female	25–30	in association with button loop	H prob.	39mm	double-faced repp	Vertical on back of (d) Sf 461 and (e) Sf 462
296	2a	Female	35–45	bordering fine ZZ linen twill	F/H	35mm	double-faced repp	Vertical on back of brooch (f) Sf123 at waist and pierced by pin
351B	1	Female	40–45	(i) ?	F/H	16mm	double-faced repp with corded ZS border	Vertical on back of brooch (e) Sf 578 at hips, pierced (c) Sf 576 on lower chest. See Fig 5.13f and Fig 5.6.
351B	1			(ii)	F/H	16-20mm	double-faced repp	Vertical on back of brooch (c) Sf 576c on lower chest. See Fig 5.13f.
351B	1			(iii)	F/H	311mm	corded SSSSSZ with warp-patterned zone	Vertical at centre chest, clasped by brooch (a) Sf 574 (different from (i) and (ii))
375	3b	(Male)	14–16	?	H prob.	313mm	diamond pattern with corded ZSZS border	Vertical on back of buckle (d) Sf 763 at left waist
376	5-7	Child	7–8	poss. bordering fine linen tabby	F/H	320mm	2-hole panel with 4-hole corded border	Vertical over objects at left waist, parallel to leg
407	2	Female	23–28	stitched to fine ZZ twill	F/H	38mm	part 4-hole SSSSSS, part double-faced repp	Two bands, parallel, vertical, clasped by 746f at waist and another on (e) Sf 745 where stitched to twill
417	3	Female	40–50	bordering fine ZZ weave	F/H	36mm	double-faced repp	Vertical, on back of brooch (c) Sf 1021, with second area crossways along pin

Notes: (Male) = male, implied by grave goods; F = flax; H = hemp

Table 5.5. Patterned tablet weaves.

examples, the way in which front and back yarns exchange places is typical of this form of two-colour patterning. The best-preserved area of patterning is illustrated in Fig 5.13g. This weave does not seem to have been recorded previously in Anglo-Saxon tablet-weaving, but there is an early variation in a girdle dated to the second or third century AD from Dätgen in north Germany (Collingwood 1982, 267; Hansen 1990, 47, 60). In the Dätgen weave the tablets are given a half turn, where the Buckland ones are given a quarter turn, but otherwise they are the same double-faced weave. The technique may, then, have arrived in Kent with early immigrants from northern Germany.

Another form of patterning was recorded on brooch (a) from Grave 351B. It has a broad corded border and then a patterned zone which incorporates a repeating pattern worked on three warp cords (Fig 5.13h). The ground weave of the patterned zone is too abraded to distinguish the technique, but there is a clear four-spot motif repeating down the centre, worked in darker yarn. If the motif is the centre of the band, it may be reconstructed as 16mm wide. Another poorly-preserved patterned tablet weave occurs on the back of a buckle (di) in male Grave 375. Here, a fine diamond pattern of uncertain construction has been worked on a paired S-ply warp, with a border of ordinary tablet cords (Fig 5.13i). This band ran vertically down the back of the buckle.

The role of tablet-woven bands within clothing suites will be discussed further below in relation to other costume evidence.

Gold thread

Gold threads were found in the graves of three young adult women, Graves 354 (e), 391B (c) and 420 (a), and one teenage girl, Grave 347 (a), from Phases 2–3a (Table 5.6).

The threads were always close to the head, on the skull itself in Graves 347 and 420, reaching down the side of the jaw and neck in Grave 391B, and in patches on the head and chest in Grave 354. No organic fibres were found on any of these threads, but the way that they zigzag back and forth, with regular indentations, is typical of thread that has been used for surface brocading in a tablet-woven band. The indentations represent the tie-down points, where the gold thread engaged with the ground weave. The pattern the tie-down points make could be reconstructed in the bands from Graves 391B and 420 and both proved to be the same weave (Fig 5.13j), although the gold strips from Grave 420 are wider and more yellow than the strips from Grave 391B. All the threads are flat strips cut from gold foil, 25–55 microns thick, evenly cut in Graves 391B and 420, but irregularly cut in Graves 347 and 354. The width of the zigzag represents the width of the patterned zone within the woven band. In all four examples the patterning is 5–6mm wide, which, allowing for corded edges, probably represents a band of about 10mm width. The greatest amount of thread came from Grave 420, where the different pieces added up to a total band length of over 300mm.

Roman gold thread was mainly 'spun gold', that is, a strip twisted around a core yarn, and that type began to re-appear at the end of the sixth century, in the grave of Queen Arnegunde at Saint-Denis. The simpler flat strips seen at Buckland were used on the Continent in the fifth, sixth and seventh centuries, in men's and women's graves within the areas of Frankish influence (Crowfoot and Chadwick Hawkes 1967). In Britain, most examples come from twenty or so sixth-century women's graves in Kent. There are four further specimens from outside Kent, two from sixth-century female burials with Kentish connections at Chessell Down, Isle of Wight, and Holywell Row, Suffolk and two in male

Grave	Phase	Sex	Age	Dress style	Location	Pattern width	Length	Details
347	2a	Female	14–16	IV	(a) Sf 467 at back of head	6.0mm	36mm long and loose pieces = c 50mm	Strip 330–440 microns wide, 30–40 microns thick, variable
391B	5–7	Female	20–25	IV	(c) Sf 851 side of jaw and left neck	5.5mm	individual pieces 10–18mm, total c 80–90mm long	Strip 320–350 microns wide, 40 microns thick, evenly made
354	2b	Female	20–25	V	(e) Sf 459 on head and chest	5.0–6.0mm	individual pieces 6–11mm, total c 30–40mm long	Strip 450–700 microns wide, 30–55 microns thick, extremely irregular
420	2–3a	Female	20–25	none (pin on chest only)	(a) Sf 1035 & Sf 1279 at right of head and on skull	5.5mm	mostly 20–25mm, total over 300mm long	Strip 400–520 microns wide, mostly 450 microns, varying thickness. Pattern as 391B, but gold is more yellow and strip wider

Table 5.6. Buckland 1994. Gold thread from four graves.

burials, at Taplow Barrow, Buckinghamshire, and Prittlewell, Essex, which belong to the seventh century (Walton Rogers 2007, 96–7).

The patterns formed by the tie-down points vary, but the two Buckland examples are worked in a simple design which matches an example from Sarre, in a grave there dated to the second quarter of the sixth century (Crowfoot and Chadwick Hawkes 1967, grave 90, fig 14,12).

The Sarre example comes from around the woman's head and most of the other pieces from Kent have been found on or near the skull, which has led to their identification with the *vittae*, narrow hair bands worn by girls and married women in the Roman period (Sebesta 1994). Less frequently, gold brocading appears at other positions on the body, such as around the wrist, and on the Continent, there are examples where the brocading may represent borders on tunics, cloaks, or veils. Since the first twenty Kent graves were published, another from Mill Hill, Deal has appeared, grave 105C, in which much more extensive gold thread is present, reaching over the head and shoulders and down to the hips (Parfitt and Brugmann 1997, 31–2; and see below Fig 5.25). This almost certainly represents a long head veil. The less extensive gold thread from Buckland Graves 391B and 354 would fit the front edging on such a veil (*see* p 210).

Button loops

Linen button loops were recorded on the pins of ten brooches from nine burials, Graves 222, 223, 281, 347, 408, 417, 419, 433 and 440. The button loops have been made by taking a bundle of fine yarns and binding them with another thread, in a tightly worked row of what a modern needle-woman would call button-hole stitch (Figs 5.15a and 5.28b). The work is curved round into a loop and the ends anchored to the edge of a textile. The work is all finely done, with about twenty stitches per centimetre. The loops are mostly 2–3mm thick and made with S-ply yarn binding bundles of 20–30 fine Z-spun yarns, except for the example from Grave 347 which is the reverse, Z-spun yarn binding a bundle of S-ply threads.

The button loops come from the graves of women aged from 14–15 to 40–50 years old. Some early loops from Grave 408 appear on brooches at the waist, but the remaining seven are all on small brooches from the neck. These brooches are from Phases 1–3 and they mostly form part of *Dress Styles III* and *IV*, with one example of *V* (Grave 222). Most examples are preserved at the hinge end of the pin, but there is often a hint of a second loop at the opposite end, and in Grave 440 there are two loops associated with the brooch, one now detached. On the brooch from Grave 281, a bundle of fine

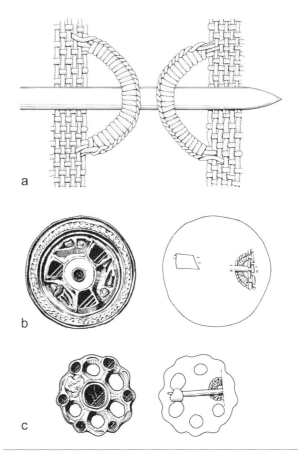

Fig 5.15. Button loops.
(a) The construction of a button loop.
(b) On the back of small disc brooch Grave 222 (b).
(c) On the back of small openwork brooch Grave 347 (e).

Z-spun yarns, probably the core of a threadbare button loop, is attached to a fine ZZ twill and the opposite end of the pin pierces the twill itself. In Grave 222 the button loop is attached to fine textile, its structure uncertain (Fig 5.15b); in Grave 347 the textile seems to be a tabby or tabby repp (Fig 5.15c); and in Grave 408 the loop was in association with a tablet band, although not necessarily attached to it. In Grave 366, plain cords, and in Grave 373 a three-cord-wide tablet band, looping round the pins of brooches at the throat may be regarded as an alternative form of button loop.

Button loops do not seem to have been recorded previously in Britain, nor are there any from the German cemeteries meticulously recorded by H J Hundt. Recently, however, examples from three sites have emerged on the Continent. A pair of button loops has been noted on an S-shaped brooch from Waging am See, in south Bavaria, in the sixth-century burial of a woman who had a similar arrangement of brooches to that of our *Dress Style IV* (grave 115, Bartel and Knöchlein 1993). There are further examples on two bird brooches from a single Migration Period burial of the Thuringian region, at Grossengottern, near Erfurt, Kr Muhlhausen, where they are attached to the stitched edge of a linen tabby garment (Färke 1991). There are also later examples from seven seventh- and eighth-century graves at Nørre Sandegård Vest, on the island of Bornholm, in the western Baltic (Mannering 1997, 130–1). Each of these was on a single central brooch at the neck, associated with linen tabby and interpreted as a fastener on the front neck slit of a chemise. This chemise was worn inside the typically Scandinavian dress-with-shoulder-straps. It is not possible to draw conclusions from this scattered distribution of finds, especially as so few textiles have been recorded from cemeteries of northern France, but the spread of linen chemises with button-loop fasteners through the widening influence of the Franks would be credible.

Cords

Plied cords serving a variety of purposes were recorded in four male and fifteen female graves. Thick cords running diagonally over the sockets of spearheads in Graves 233 and 297 are clearly there to bind in place the textile wrapper, of which there are remains on both faces of the blade in Grave 233 and on the socket in Grave 297. Finer cords wound around the fold of a pair of tweezers in Grave 281 are probably to suspend the tweezers from the belt or châtelaine and another cord was found close to tweezers on a chain in Grave 336, while in Grave 351B the tweezers on the upper right arm were probably suspended from the cords on the brooch (a) on the upper chest. The cord running across the iron rod at the man's thigh in Grave 437 may have been used for binding or tying also, while the cords criss-crossing the square-headed brooch Grave 372 (e) (Fig 10.45) are plainly holding in place the detached pin-catch. Fine plied threads wrapped around a link of metal chain (g) on the chest of the woman in Grave 347 may have been to attach the chain to the garment below. Knotted cords on the spring at the back of two bow brooches from Grave 391B and further cords tied to the pin of bow brooch Grave 408 (d) may be connected with the fastening of the garment (*see* p 207). Further cords lying parallel to each other at the waist in a man's burial, Grave 351, and on the legs of a woman in Grave 413 seem to represent finely worked fringes, perhaps the ends of a sash or scarf in the case of Grave 413.

Most of the other cords are tied around the pins of brooches and many of these are likely to represent the ends

of bead strings. This is especially clear in Grave 372, where the two ends of an S-ply cord are caught in the pin-catches of both the annular brooches on the shoulders (Fig 10.103) and a row of eleven glass and amber beads runs between. A thicker Z-ply cord tied to the pin of the small-long on the breast of the woman in Grave 239, however, runs down the pin and points directly towards the knife lying below (Fig 10.10). In this grave the beads are, as before, in a row between the annular brooches on the shoulders and the function of the cord on the small-long brooch must be to suspend the knife. At a later date, Scandinavian women would hang accessories from one of the two tortoise brooches on their chest in the same way.

In Grave 419, the disc brooch worn on the centre chest had a loop of twenty-two beads below and to the side, and the two ends of the linen bead string are clearly both tied to the pin of the brooch. This forms part of the migration of garment fasteners and decorative accessories downwards on the body in Phases 2 and 3, in *Dress Styles III* and *IV*. In Grave 263B (*Style IV*) there are eleven beads still lower, between the upper legs, and these were probably suspended from the S-ply cord tied to the pin of the radiate-headed brooch at the waist. In four further graves, Graves 428 (*Style III*) and 281, 296 and 408 (*Style IV*), there are single beads in the region of the waist, and in Grave 296 the bead may have been suspended from the S-ply cord tied to a radiate-headed brooch at the waist, although the others may have been held in a pouch.

In Grave 347 there is a spread of forty-one glass and amber beads down the body from mid-chest to waist and a number of different cords tangled up with each of the brooches, three on brooch (e) at the throat, two on brooch (f) at centre chest and one on brooch (k) at the waist (Fig 10.82). This grave was cut by another, so that it is not possible to see the relationship of beads to brooches in its entirety, but the evidence suggests a very complex stringing of the beads. Similarly, in Grave 391B, although only one cord has been found, knotted around the rosette brooch (e) at centre chest, there must have been further cords to help suspend the weight of the 174 beads and two pendants distributed down the body. Further plied cords were found knotted round the pin hinge of Kentish disc brooches on the upper chest in Graves 204 (b) and 353 (b) and on a rosette brooch at centre chest in Grave 245 (c), all with beads in the vicinity.

Where the fibre could be identified, these cords were all linen, except for a wool or hair cord used to bind the spear wrapper in Grave 297. In several instances, under the microscope, the plant fibre could be seen to lie in bundles, which indicates that it had not been processed to its full extent, as it would be for a linen textile. The purpose of leaving the fibre half-processed would be to give a strong, slightly stiff thread, easier to thread through beads and better able to withstand rubbing.

Feathers

Fine feathers, identified by their fine arching fibres with barbs visible at high magnification, were identified on objects from three relatively late graves. In Grave 264, Phase 3, they were on a linen tabby on a spearhead next to the man's head, in a position that suggested the head had been on a pillow. In a child's grave, Grave 376, Phase 5–7, they were in several dense patches, in contact with a flat layer of coarse plant-fibre tabby, under the left thigh and against the left waist, where they probably represent an eiderdown or feather mattress under the body. In a woman's burial, Grave 413, Phase 5–7, they are on a similarly coarse plant-fibre textile, on iron rods between the thighs, which again suggests some form of bedding.

Fleece

Tufts of animal fibre, arranged in a way that suggests a fleece or other animal pelt, were noted in three men's graves, Graves 264 and 346 (Phase 3), Grave 340 (unphased). In Grave 346 they were on the blade of the sword and will represent the fleece lining for the scabbard, which is a common feature of swords from Anglo-Saxon burials. The other two were both on knives at the waist. Remains of animal pelts have been detected in a similar position, on objects at the waist, in a small number of male and female burials elsewhere (Walton Rogers 2007 103–4). The fibre side usually faces outwards and they have been interpreted as the remains of an animal skin placed over the body. Animal pelts are surprisingly rare in Anglo-Saxon burials, considering that they are likely to have been used quite widely for cloaks, capes and furnishings (Owen-Crocker 2004, 181–2).

Reconstructing the clothing

By combining the evidence of the textiles with that of the garment accessories, it is possible to reconstruct at least some of the clothing worn by the men and women buried at Buckland. That these were costumes worn in life seems highly likely, judging from the wear visible on both textiles and brooches, although it must remain an open question as to

whether they represent everyday clothes, or dress for formal occasions. It is inevitable that the best evidence comes from those graves with the greatest number of metal artefacts, and therefore the burials of those people, especially women, with enough wealth and/or status to merit grave goods of this sort. There remains a whole class of people whose clothing styles are as yet unknown.

Men's clothing

It has been demonstrated that the iron pins in men's graves are unlikely to be connected with their clothing (pp 180–1). This leaves only the buckles at the waist as the main source of costume evidence, together with remains of textile adhering to spears, knives and other grave goods. Before examining these, some general remarks may be made about men's clothing in the fifth to seventh centuries.

Roman sculptures show Germanic men wearing thigh-length belted tunics, trousers and a cloak fastened on the right shoulder (Fig 5.16). Complete examples of these garments have been found in Roman Iron Age sites in Schleswig-Holstein and other parts of Free Germany, most notably in the votive deposit at Thorsbjerg in Angeln, where there is a long-sleeved close-fitting tunic with slits up the sides, trousers which are essentially leggings-with-feet and a large rectangular cloak (Hald 1980, 328–35, 338–40; Nockert 1991, 120–3). The trousers have a band at the top

Fig 5.16. German warriors on the second-century column of Marcus Aurelius. The man on the right has trousers and arm-coverings; the man on the left has the full suite of trousers, belted tunic and a cloak fastened on the right shoulder. Courtesy of the National Museum of Denmark.

and loops for the passage of a belt. In English manuscript illustrations of the ninth and tenth centuries, this suite of clothing, incorporating a long-sleeved tunic (now with a fuller, knee-length skirt), close-fitting trousers or leggings and rectangular cloak, re-appears (Owen-Crocker 2004, 232–3; Walton Rogers 2007, 199–207), so that it seems reasonable to suppose that something similar was worn in the intervening centuries. Where buckles occur at the waist in the burials of Anglo-Saxon men, therefore, they may represent belts used on tunics *or* trousers, and, although no cloak fasteners have been found, a large rectangular cloak could have been laid out as a cover over or under the body.

The coarse twills on spearheads from Buckland (1994) are almost certainly wrappers for the spear and can be discounted as clothing fabrics. Setting these aside, the most common textile-type in men's graves is wool ZS 2/2 twill, generally in plain, medium-quality fabrics, but sometimes finer and diamond-patterned (eg Grave 264). These twills appear on the upper body in positions suggesting an over-tunic or cloak in Graves 262, 363 and 379, on the backs of buckles in Graves 264 (d) and probably 337 (d), and on a pin at the waist in Graves 260 (a). They also occur on the legs in Graves 249C and 414. Plain linen tabby was used for inner garments, being worn inside a coarse ZZ twill in Grave 395 and inside a matted wool textile in Grave 231. It was also on the back of a belt buckle in Grave 301 (b) and a knife at the waist in Grave 321 (a). Tabby repp was on the backs of buckles in Graves 259 (c), 346 (f) and 414 (f), just as it was in women's graves of the period (*see* p 195).

In Grave 437 (Phase 2) there was an elaborate combination of textiles which was difficult to interpret. The man had been buried with an iron fauchard and a sequence of textiles was preserved along the side of the weapon where it lay against his left leg. The textiles were a coarse ZS diamond twill at the thigh, a plain ZZ tabby above the knee and a coarse ZZ twill inside the curve of the fauchard blade, at the knee. A much finer ZS diamond twill was found on the firesteel (k) at centre chest and a linen tabby repp lay in folds sandwiched between the bone and tweezers complex (f), (g) and (h) by the right thigh, where it was associated with cords and a leather thong.

Finally, in Graves 230 (Phase 2b–3a) and 375 (Phase 3b), there was a tablet-woven band running across the back of the buckle, and therefore vertically down the body (Fig 5.17). The example from Grave 230 was a plain corded band with plied threads crossing its surface, thought to be sewing stitches rather than a weft pattern. The band from Grave 375 had a corded border with a diamond-patterned area beside it on the belt-plate (p 200). Similar, but more extensive,

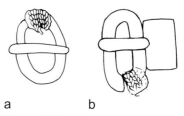

Fig 5.17. Vertical tablet bands on the backs of buckles from male graves: a) Grave 230 (a) b) Grave 375 (d).

Fig 5.18. Warriors in belted wrap-over jackets depicted on the helmet plaques from Sutton Hoo. After Ahrens 1978, fig15.

remains were found in a man's grave at Castledyke, north Lincolnshire, grave 126, where a tablet-woven band formed the edging on a linen twill which recurred in patches over the upper body, and a second flap of the same linen twill passed in front of the tablet weave at the waist (Walton Rogers 1998, 278–9). This was interpreted as a warrior's jacket of the sort depicted in the Sutton Hoo helmet plaques (Fig 5.18), Vendel period helmets from Sweden (Almgren 1982), and in the *guldgubbar*, impressed plates from Bornholm (Munksgaard 1990, 89–99). These were knee-length wrap-over garments, rather like a modern martial arts jacket, with ornamental bands along the front edges and hems, and a belt at the waist. The Castledyke grave and Buckland Grave 375 are dated to the seventh century, as Grave 230 may also be, and they are therefore contemporary with the metalwork images. This garment derives ultimately from the Asiatic riding coat, which reached the west via the Sasanian Empire and which may have been brought into north-west Europe by Germanic soldiers who had served in the Byzantine army (Walton Rogers 2007, 213–14).

Women's clothing

Early fashions

The costume of the women in east Kent seems to evolve from the mixed styles of the early Migration Period, through suites of clothing influenced by the Franks, to a more unified fashion in the seventh century. One of the early styles is represented by Grave 13 at Buckland, where there are two different square-headed brooches, one at least made in Scandinavia, worn crossways on the upper chest (Fig 5.19a) (Evison 1987, 68–9) and an annular brooch/buckle at the waist. A similar arrangement can be seen in women's graves in Jutland in the fourth and fifth centuries (Jørgensen and Nørgård Jørgensen 1997, 59) and an example from Sejlflod is illustrated in Fig 5.19b. There are no examples of this style from the 1994 Buckland excavations, but it may have echoes in the pair of ring-headed pins on the upper chest of the child in Grave 254 from Phase 1 (Fig 5.10). Pins were not worn in this way by Anglo-Saxon women until the seventh century, but in Jutland, pairs of ring-headed pins or small brooches were worn on either side of the neck, where they supported a metal chain or a string of beads (Fig 5.19b).

A more common early style in Kent was the tubular gown, fastened on the shoulders with a pair of matching brooches. This gown was a large tube of material which the woman stepped into, pulled up to her armpits and then clasped at front and back top edge on the shoulders. Roman sculptures depicting women of the northern tribes represent it as a loose, full-length gown, girdled at the waist and clasped on the shoulders with a variety of paired brooches (Walton Rogers 2007, figs 5.9 and 5.12; Wild 1968, 199–208; Hald 1980, 357–67). It was often worn over a long-sleeved under-gown, or sometimes with separate detachable sleeves, and the sleeves generally had cuff-bands. These garments arrived in Britain in the fifth century and became standard dress in the 'Anglian' and 'Saxon' regions (Walton Rogers 2007, 144–52).

In the Buckland (1994) cemetery, the tubular gown is represented by annular brooches on the shoulder, worn singly or as a pair (*Dress Style I*; Fig 5.3). The fabrics of these early garments are the medium-weight wool ZZ twills, which were so common in earlier centuries, so that both the garment and its material can be seen as survivors from the north continental Roman Iron Age. The later example of the gown, Grave 372, Phase 2a, which combines the shoulder annulars with Frankish and Kentish brooches at the neck, uses the 'newer' ZS wool twill for its material. In the Anglian region, where the tubular gown was in use long after it had disappeared from east Kent,

the paired shoulder brooches are sometimes combined with a second pair of brooches lower on the breast, and at Buckland, there is a pair of vertical small-long brooches in this position in Grave 239 (b) and (c). The Anglian second pair of brooches seems to have been used in different ways, but generally fastened back an outer garment to an inner. In the Buckland grave the small-long brooches fasten loose folds of linen tabby, perhaps a shawl or head-veil back to the wool twill gown. Annular brooches at the hip in the later graves, along with sleeve clasps (previously wrist clasps) in Grave 326 (d) and (i) (*see* pp 123–4), may have been heirlooms, or re-used as belt accessories, after the fashion had disappeared in east Kent in the early decades of the sixth century (Chadwick 1958, 39–40).

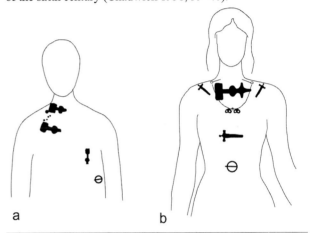

Fig 5.19. (a) An old woman buried at Buckland 1951–3, Grave 13, in Phase 1b; (b) woman buried at Sejiflod in the Early Germanic Iron Age, *c* AD 425–450 (after Jørgensen and Nørgård Jørgensen 1997, fig 46).

A third form of costume from the early period is represented by *Dress Style II*, a single button brooch worn centrally (Fig 5.4). These brooches may appear anywhere between the neck and the lower chest. If each of these burials represents the same garment, it must have been a loose one, which allowed the brooch to float around on the body. It is difficult to suggest what that garment might be and the textile evidence is regrettably silent. A costume which would fit the evidence can be seen in Roman sculptures depicting women of the Ubii, a tribe of the Lower Rhineland. Essentially, it is a voluminous, lightweight, half-moon mantle worn over a tunic and under-tunic and clasped at the front above the waist (Wild 1968, 210–6; Vierck 1978, 250–1). The same costume was worn by the Germanic goddess Nehelennia, who had a temple at the end of one of the Roman trade routes into Britain (Wild *ibid*). The question of the *Dress Style II* costume cannot be settled, however, until more textile evidence is recovered from comparable graves.

The arrival of Frankish fashions

In Phases 1b and 2 there are firstly graves with two small brooches, one above the other at neck and centre chest (*Dress Style III*; Fig 5.5), and secondly graves with two bow brooches worn crossways at or below the waist, often combined with small brooches at neck and chest (*Dress Style IV*; Fig 5.6). It will be argued that these represent two garments, one fastened with the upper small brooches, the other with the lower bow brooches, and that these were often worn together, the small-brooch dress inside the bow-brooch garment. The belt represented by the buckle at the waist clasps the inner garment. This theory is based on the position of the textiles on the metal garment fasteners, which may now be reviewed (Figs 5.20–5.23).

In Grave 351B there is an early variation of the standard arrangement, with a cruciform brooch (e) acting as a substitute for one of the bow brooches and the paired small brooches (a) and (d) set lower on the body than usual (Fig 5.20). A pair of matching rib-weave tablet-woven bands, *c* 16mm wide, is clasped edge-to-edge by the bow brooch (c) and the cruciform (e) below. A different tablet-woven band, with corded border and a repeating pattern, is pinned by the upper small, square-headed, brooch (a) and the orientation of this band lines up with the matching square-headed brooch below (d). This allows interpretation as two garments, both with vertical front openings, but edged with different borders, one clasped by the small square-headed brooches, the other clasped by the larger brooches.

In Grave 281 the lower brooches are again non-matching (d) and (e) and again clasp a pair of tablet bands edge-to-edge (Fig 5.21). The Frankish disc brooch at the neck (a) fastens a worn button loop attached to a linen 2/2 twill at one end of the pin, with a fold of the same textile at the other end. The twill is almost certainly the same as the linen diamond twill which appears on the back of the buckle (g). This may be reconstructed as a garment of linen diamond twill, fastened by the belt at the waist and clasped at the neck by the Frankish disc brooch. A second garment with a vertical front opening edged with tablet-woven borders is clasped by brooches (d) and (e) at the waist. A medium-weight wool twill which appears on one face of the iron rings at the left hip may represent the main fabric of this front-opening gown.

In Grave 296 a pair of matching bow brooches at waist and pelvis (e) and (f) both clasp a fine linen 2/2 twill, which, on one brooch (f), has remains of a band or border (Fig 5.22). The border passes over the pin at an unusual angle, which is explained by the diagonal orientation of the brooches in the grave (Fig 5.22). The buckle (c) lies directly behind the brooch (f) with its textile complex, and the belt therefore must have fastened an inner garment. The quatrefoil brooch

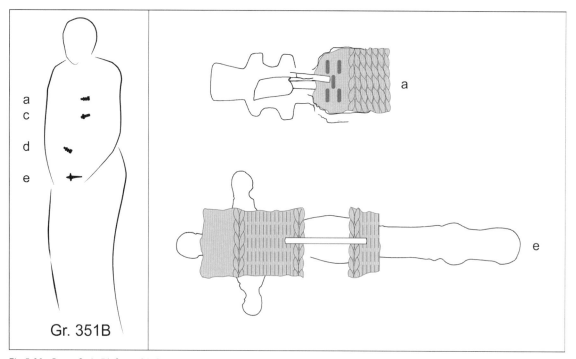

Fig 5.20. Dress Style IV: Grave 351B and the textiles on the back of brooches (a) and (e).

at the neck (b) has a button loop fastener, but no evidence for the garment that it fastened.

In Grave 347 (Fig 5.22) a metal chain (g) on the chest is sandwiched between a tabby repp on one face and a plain tabby on the other (and seemingly stitched to one of the two, *see* p 202). The tabby repp re-appears on the back of the buckle at the waist. The plain tabby re-appears on the front of brooch (e) at the neck and is clasped by bow brooch (k) at the lower waist (a second bow brooch may have been lost when Grave 347 was cut into by Grave 264). It may be surmised from comparison with Grave 281 that the button loop on the back of the brooch at the neck belongs with the tabby repp garment fastened by the belt. The plain tabby garment was worn outside this and was fastened by the bow brooches at the waist. Traces of a tablet-weave pierced by the pin of small square-headed brooch (f) may represent a narrow border on either of these gowns. The chain lay between the inner and outer garments.

In Grave 407 the matching bow brooches at the waist (e) and (f) clasp a pair of tablet-woven bands attached to a fine ZZ twill and these both recur on one face of the complex of objects with the pin on the chest (Fig 5.23). On the back of the buckle, however there is a linen tabby repp, which also appears on the pin complex, suggesting that the pin complex, like the chain in Grave 347, was sandwiched between the two garments. There is no brooch at the neck in this grave.

In Grave 391B the two small bow brooches below the waist (m) and (n), clasp a tablet-woven band edging a fine ZZ diamond twill. On the back of the buckle there is a linen tabby which also appears on the pin across the centre chest. No significant remains could be found on either of the two rosette brooches (d) and (e), but a small square-headed brooch placed upright above the bow brooches at the waist (l) clasped a third textile, a ZS twill, back to the fine ZZ twill clasped by the bow brooches. The role of this ZS twill is not known, but the other textiles indicate an inner gown of linen tabby fastened by the belt, worn inside a gown of fine diamond twill clasped by the bow brooches.

Two anomalous graves can be added to this group. In Grave 255 the lower three brooches (g), (c) and (b) are laid out over a fine twill, which they do not clasp, and are tied together by lengths of plied cord, so that they sit in the position they would have been in if they were fastening the garment (Fig 5.28a). The functioning garment fasteners in this grave are a large square-headed brooch at the neck (i), which clasps a heavy wool twill, and an S-brooch (h) which is covered by the same wool twill. The S-brooch in turn clasps the finer twill on which the tied brooches have been placed. In Grave 417 (Fig 5.22) the two lower bow brooches (c) and (d) clasp the edges of two different garments, one made from a ZS diamond twill with a tablet-woven border doing service

as front edge of the gown (brooch d), the other a fine ZZ twill with a separately worked tablet-woven border (brooch c). This grave also has two buckles at the waist, making interpretation difficult, but there is an interesting technical detail on brooch (c), where a small tab cut from a piece of tablet-weaving was attached at right angles to the main band on the back of the ZZ twill, presumably to strengthen the garment at the point where the brooch would cause wear.

The evidence has been used to show that there was an inner linen gown, which might be twill, tabby or tabby repp, with a long vertical front slit clasped by small brooches at neck and/or chest, often by means of button loops. This gown was belted. Over the top there was a garment that opened down the front and this was often made from fine diamond-patterned twill, bordered with tablet bands of the double-faced repp technique, and clasped by the lower two bow brooches.

There are cross-references between this clothing suite and the *Style III* arrangement with two brooches at neck and chest, in that they both share fine linen twills and button loops on the brooch at the neck. The *Style III* dress fastened by the small upper brooches, was not worn alone, however. There is evidence for a second garment inside the gown with button loops in Grave 428 and the textile pinned by the brooch on the chest in Grave 419 was different from the textiles found elsewhere in the grave. Thus, the *Style III* garment is not an undergarment, but a gown in its own right. This gown must have had a front slit opening, but it seems not to have required fastening below the belt, and the slit may have reached to just below the waist, in the manner of a slightly later long-sleeved woman's tunic from Moščevaja Balka in the Caucasus (Ierusalimskaja and Borkopp 1996, 28–9). The outer garment fastened by the larger bow brooches is more likely to have been open all the way down the front.

The coat-like garment with a vertical front opening (*Style IV*) is obviously not part of the Anglo-Saxon repertoire and its origin must be sought elsewhere. Since front-opening garments are common among the horse-riding people of the Steppes, it is possible that ultimately it derives from the westerly movement of Asian tribes such as the Huns into Europe. Be that as it may, by the sixth century, the *Style IV* arrangement of brooches had spread throughout the middle zone of Europe, appearing in graves from the Channel to the Carpathian Basin (Böhme 1988; Bóna 1976, 39–43). At the western end of its distribution, the 'four-brooch costume' (*Vierfibeltracht*), with a pair of small brooches above and a pair of matching bow brooches below, was established in Frankish, Thuringian, Alamannic, Baiuwarian and Langobard territories (Martin 1991b). In graves in these regions, the two lower brooches often lie vertically, pin pointing up, a puzzling arrangement which spawned a number of different

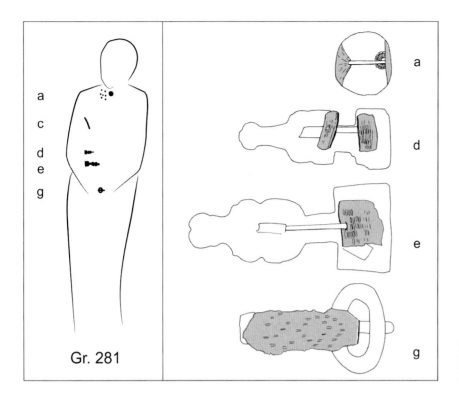

Fig 5.21. Dress Style IV: Grave 281 and the textiles on the backs of brooches (a), (d), (e) and buckle (g).

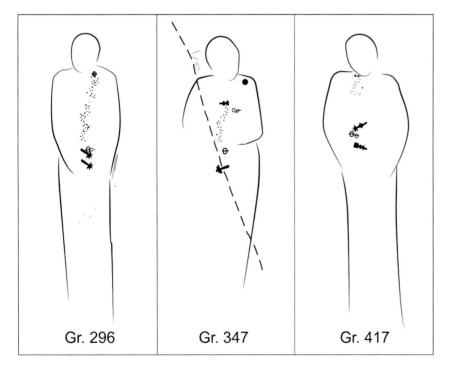

Fig 5.22. Three more women wearing Dress Style IV, Graves 296, 347 and 417.

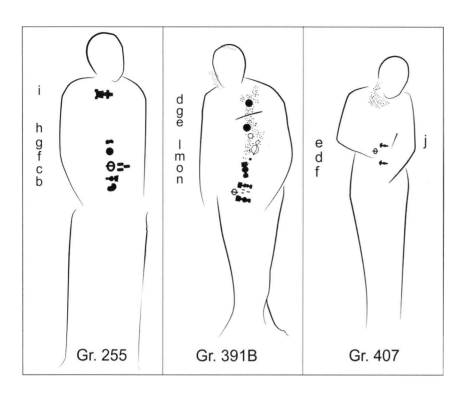

Fig 5.23. Dress Style IV: Grave 255, 391B and 407.

reconstructions (Martin 1998; Marti 1994; Zeller 1996), until finds from Waging am See provided the answer (Bartel and Knöchlein 1993). Here, in grave 105, well-preserved textile evidence revealed that the vertical opening of the garment had two pairs of crossways tabs jutting out from the edge. Each brooch pinned the loose ends of two tabs to the opposite garment edge. Thus, even vertically arranged brooches fastened a front-opening gown.

The Waging am See garments had supplementary fasteners in the form of leather thong ties, in association with the brooches (Bartel and Knöchlein 1993, 436–7). These provide an explanation for the fragment of leather thong which is visible behind the tablet band on Grave 281 (e). The pairs of knotted cords on the pin springs of Grave 391B (m) and (n) and tied to the pin on Grave 408 (d) may represent similar secondary fasteners.

Max Martin has plotted the position of the bow brooches on the body in relation to the brooch length (Martin 1991b, 655–8). His work has shown that while most brooches are arranged vertically, pin pointing up, and often quite low on the body, the shorter bow brooches tend to be worn higher, at or immediately below the waist. More importantly, within the Frankish region west of the Rhine, these smaller bow brooches are clasped horizontally. The bow brooches at Buckland seem to have been worn in this Frankish style.

The four-brooch costume appears exclusively in graves of Phases 1b and 2a, which corresponds to the first half of its period of use on the Continent. As described above, there are a number of hybridised examples, incorporating substituted brooches and variations on the standard arrangement (Fig 5.6; see also Parfitt and Brugmann 1997, 114–16). If the two lower brooches represent a second, outer garment, this would explain anomalies such as Mill Hill, Deal grave 86, where a mature woman was buried with three very worn annular brooches, two at the shoulders and one at the neck, combined with a much newer set of bow brooches (unusually, a matching set of three), crossways lower down. Presumably, this woman was wearing the tubular gown of her youth, underneath a more modern Frankish coat. The same process can be seen elsewhere in Anglo-Saxon England, at Castledyke grave 160, for example, where an elderly woman, who must have been buried in the seventh century to judge from her jewellery, wore a pair of annular brooches at her shoulders at least twenty years after they had disappeared from other graves (Drinkall and Foreman 1998, 274). This combining of old and new styles by the elderly may explain why the costume of Arnegunde at Saint-Denis has proved so difficult to categorise (Périn 1991) for she was probably in her 80s when she died at the end of the sixth century.

There is one last piece of evidence for the coat-like garment hypothesised here, in another of the *guldgubbar*, this time from seventh-century Helgö, near Stockholm (Fig 5.24). It is

Fig 5.24. Seventh-century impressed gold foil from Helgö, Ekerö, Uppland, Sweden, in the Statens Historiska Museum, Stockholm, depicting an embrace between the god Frey and giantess Gerðr. Gerðr is wearing a short front-opening jacket, possibly sleeveless. After Magnus 1997, fig 94c, catalogue no 6.

believed to depict the meeting between the god Frey and the giantess Gerðr (Magnus 1997, 205–7) and shows Gerðr in a short, probably sleeveless, jacket. A cursory examination of Scandinavian burials has not revealed any examples of the 'four-brooch costume', but the linen chemises with button loop fasteners at Nørre Sandegård Vest show that the inner garment of the clothing suite could have reached South Scandinavia by the seventh century. Furthermore, Bender Jørgensen, commenting on the appearance of new textile types in Scandinavian graves in the later sixth and seventh centuries, attributed them to the Scandinavian nobility adopting Frankish fashions (Bender Jørgensen 1992, 136). Thus, it is conceivable that Gerðr is wearing a Frankish coat. The fact that the coat is relatively short may be significant. It was noted above that in Grave 417 the warp of the fabric used for the coat ran across the body and the loom width must have been from shoulder to hem. The wide warp-weighted looms of the Anglo-Saxon settlements would have had no difficulty in producing a width equal to a woman's dress length, but the two-beam vertical loom of northern France was often used for narrower pieces (Walton 1989, 1824; 2001). The length of the coat may have been based originally on a Frankish loom width.

Veils

A long head veil seems to appear at about the same time as *Dress Styles III* and *IV* and continues into later periods. The extensive area covered by gold thread in Mill Hill, Deal grave 105C, Kentish Phase III (AD 530/40–560/570), probably marks the outline of such a veil, reaching from head to hip (Fig 5.25) (Parfitt and Brugmann 1997, 31–2). The gold thread at Buckland covers a smaller area, but in Grave 391B it runs down the side of the head and in Grave 354 it reaches down to the upper chest (Fig 5.25), so that a gold border on a veil seems likely. The length of the gold does not necessarily represent the full length of the tablet-weaving, for patches of gold could have been alternated with coloured silks within the band. The top edge of a veil of this type was recorded at West Heslerton, in a sixth-century burial, grave 123 (Walton Rogers 1999, 154–5). The folded edge of a lightweight tabby fabric, dyed red, ran back across the temple and over the ear and was bordered with a fine wool tablet-woven band, which, at 9mm, was a similar width to the Buckland gold-brocaded bands. Moving down the body, in four burials, Graves, 250, 255, 409 and 443, there are further narrow tablet bands running diagonally over objects at the left hip, in a position well away from the front opening of the garment. In two instances, Graves 250 and 255, the band is identifiable as the border on a lightweight fabric and other fine fabrics often appear in the same position, even when no border has been preserved. The fabric of these veils is in several instances 2/1 twill, a weave thought to have been introduced from the Continent, either as an imported textile, or as new technology.

Such veils are referred to by Merovingian and Carolingian commentators and in *De Virginitate*, Aldhelm described veils *quae vittarum nexibus assutae talotenus prolixius dependunt*, 'which, stitched to clips on the head-bands, fall sumptuously to their ankles' (author's translation). Long veils would need to be anchored by some means and ribbon ties, perhaps an extension of the headband, seem likely, since hair pins are absent from these graves. The pair of closed wire rings found by the ears in Grave 413, (i) and (j), are wide enough to allow a 10mm band to be threaded through and may mark the point at which the ties were attached. In the Mill Hill, Deal grave, some of the gold thread lay behind the brooch at the throat, which led Birte Brugmann to suggest that the veil had been clasped by the brooch. That is unlikely to be the case where there are button loops on the brooches at the throat, because button loops would be an encumbrance on the fluttering edges of a veil, and at sites with more extensive textile evidence (*see* p 202), button loops have always been shown to be the fastener on a chemise.

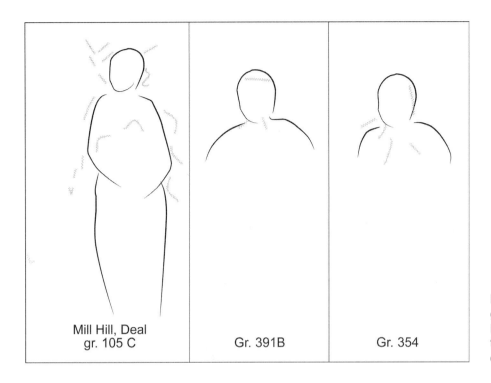

Mill Hill, Deal
gr. 105 C

Gr. 391B

Gr. 354

Fig 5.25. Gold thread in three women's graves; Mill Hill, Deal grave 105C, Buckland Graves 391B and 354. The thread may have formed the ornament on a head veil.

Later styles

The evidence for the Frankish coat at Buckland disappears with the ending of Phase 2a, when the vertical column of brooches is replaced with a single Kentish brooch at the neck (*Dress Style V*; Fig 5.7). It is possible that the linen chemise continued to be worn, as there is a button loop on the brooch in Grave 222 - although tablet bands edged the front slit in Grave 373 and the brooch was pinned straight through a plain linen tabby in Grave 353. Buckles were still present at the waist. The numerous beads of Phase 2 continued to be worn as vertical strings in Phase 3, but they were now also worn as large encircling collars.

The textiles from *Style V* graves (Phases 2b–3a) include fine wool ZS diamond twill in four graves, in positions that suggest an outer garment. They are on the group of châtelaine objects at the left hip in Graves 222 and 245, in the latter sandwiching the objects between the diamond twill and the fine linen thought to represent the veil; ZS diamond twill also appears on the pin on the chest in Grave 353 and outside the buckle in Grave 373. Inner garments are suggested by the linen tabbies on the backs of buckles in Graves 222 and 373. Long veils have been identified in Graves 204, 245, 250 and 354, as described above, and the gathers of fine linen clasped by the rosette brooch (c) at the centre chest in Grave 245 may represent a lightweight shawl. An open gauzy weave on and around objects by the left hip was thought to represent the ends of a sash in Grave 353 (*see* p 195).

In time, the brooch at the throat disappeared, buckles became scarce and necklaces reduced down to small strings of large beads and pendants, which were mostly worn around the neck and combined with a single short pin on the upper chest (*Style VI*). Because of the scarcity of metalwork in these graves, there is little textile present, but surviving remains are mostly very fine, including plain linen tabby and ZS wool twill. In Grave 413 there is also a fine row of cords on the iron rods between the thighs, which suggests the fringe on another sash. The presence of textile sashes in late graves would help explain the rarity of belt buckles.

The wide encircling collars of beads and the necklaces with pendants are reminiscent of the necklaces worn at the court in Byzantium, as depicted in an ivory relief of about AD 500 at Bargello, Italy, and in sixth-century mosaics at S Vitale, Ravenna. In these images the women wear long, belted tunic-like garments with lightweight mantles falling from the shoulder to the ankles. The ends of sashes peep out from beneath layers of fabric. The jewellery is also depicted in embroidery on a garment attributed to Queen Bathild (d AD 680/681) at Chelles, which is a round-necked tabard-like garment made from spin-patterned tabby, with embroidery representing a wide bead collar and a pectoral cross together with a lower necklace of pendants (Laporte 1982; Berthelier-Ajot *et al* 1985).

Helen Geake has proposed that the late sixth and seventh century saw a revival of Roman culture in Britain, beginning in Kent and spreading out to the other regions (Geake 1997). She argues that the objects appearing at this time are not just borrowed from contemporary Byzantine culture, but are referring back to an earlier classical model. If this is the case, then Roman women's clothing, essentially a full, loose long-sleeved tunic with a horizontal neckline, girdled with a narrow sash, may also have appeared in Britain. With the addition of the long cloak, this would be close to the Byzantine court dress

and it would not be possible on the evidence of textiles from graves to draw a distinction between the two.

Juveniles

In the graves of under 16 year olds, clothing styles are poorly represented by both garment fasteners and textiles, although decorative items such as beads and bracelets are more common. Only one child has any number of brooches and they are in an unusual arrangement, in combination with

Fig 5.26. Reconstruction of clothing styles at Buckland: (a) Dress Style I; (b) Dress Styles III and IV; (c) Dress Style V; (d) Dress Style VI.

Fig 5.27a. Grave 255, mineral-preserved textile on brooch (h).

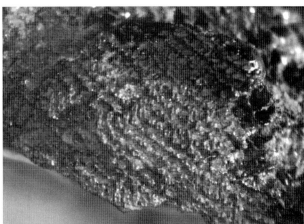

Fig 5.27b. Grave 247, textile (?silk) on back of brooch (a).

Fig 5.28a. Grave 255, knotted cord on back of brooch (g).

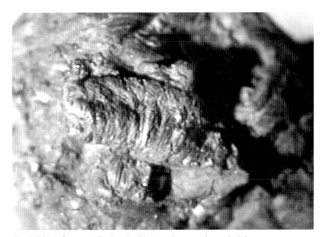

Fig 5.28b. Grave 417, detail of button loop on brooch (g).

an anachronistic pair of ring-headed pins (p 191). Among the few children buried with brooches elsewhere in Kent, there is a 5 year old at Lyminge with a pair of equal-armed brooches of a type and in a position (on the shoulders) not often seen on adults in this country (grave 24, Warhurst 1955). This suggests that children were sometimes dressed differently from adults, perhaps in a variation of the old tubular gown.

The textiles in the graves of juveniles are of the same types and qualities as are found in adult graves and share some characteristics, such as tabby repp on the back of the buckle (a) in Grave 334 and at the waist in Grave 377. Linen twill, tentatively identified as 2/1 twill, appears in the better furnished graves, Graves 254 and 377, as it does in older women. A wide, apparently free-hanging tablet-woven band parallel to the left leg of a 7 or 8 year old in Grave 376, Phase

5–7, may represent the end of a girdle, comparable with the sashes in late adult graves, Graves 353 and 413. This child wears the same pin and necklace as older women of the same period and it is possible that in this particular instance the girl has been dressed as an adult.

Conclusion

The aim of this chapter has been to focus on the function of the garment fasteners and to put them in alliance with the textiles, with a view to reconstructing the clothing styles of the people buried at Buckland. This has proved moderately successful for women's costume. The number of well-dated and well-equipped women's graves has allowed a sequence of '*dress styles*', from the later fifth to the seventh century to be established (Fig 5.26). When this sequence is compared with dated women's graves from previously published cemeteries of east Kent, it becomes clear that the sequence applies there, but previous attempts to make a logical order from the evidence have been foiled by a number of graves which fall at the turning point between fashions and which include both earlier and later features. In addition, it has been shown that more mature women had a tendency to retain styles of their youth at the same time as acquiring more recent accessories, and this has easily confused the picture. It is useful to note, for the purposes of future research, that fashion changes seem to be represented in their purest form in the graves of young adults.

The picture for men and children is more shadowy. There is tentative evidence for a warrior jacket in two seventh-century graves and there is data which suggests that children may have been dressed differently from adults. Even among women, however, only the better-equipped burials allow reconstruction. It is inevitable that any study of this kind raises as many questions as it answers and the research has been taken further with the more recently excavated site at Saltwood. The purpose of this assiduous collection and sorting of data is not just to produce an accurate reconstruction for museum displays and re-enactment societies. How we dress reflects who we are, how we see ourselves, our gender role and our status within the community. Once costume styles have been fully characterised, the study of clothing - who wears it and how - has the capacity to contribute to a much broader knowledge of the social and economic relationships within Anglo-Saxon society.

	Dress fittings, etc	Fibre	Weave	Count/Spin	Position of textile	Interpretation
Grave 204 female age 22–27 extended supine, hands on groin Phase 2b *Dress Style V*	With textile: (b) Kentish disc brooch Sf 23 (g) tinned cu alloy buckle Sf 26 (l) iron pin Sf 25 (k) châtelaine complex Sf 38 (m) coin Sf 39 Without textile: glass beads and Au bracteate on chest, garnet-inlaid mount on left thigh and strap-end between lower legs	flax/hemp	tabby	18–20/Z x 18–20/Z	In thick folds on back of buckle (g) at lower waist; and on châtelaine complex (k)/(m), to left of left hip	A gown of linen tabby fastened by a belt at lower waist, with strap reaching to mid calf. The textiles to the left of the left hip, sandwiching the ironwork, may include bedding/covers as well as clothing. They lie in four layers: - spin-patterned 2/1 twill - linen tabby repp - iron châtelaine etc - linen plain tabby - coarse wool twill
		flax/hemp	tabby repp	15/Z x 20–24/Z	On châtelaine complex (k)/(m), consistently on opposite face to plain tabby	
		not ident	twill, ?2/1	16/Z x 16/Z+S	Next to tabby repp on châtelaine	
		?wool	?	coarse Z x Z	Next to plain tabby on châtelaine	
		flax/hemp	?	medium Z x Z	On iron pin (l) at lower jaw	
		flax/hemp	cord	S-plied, 2.5mm diameter	Cord knotted around pin hinge on back of disc brooch (b), on right breast	
Grave 205 ?female age 23–28 extended supine	With textile: (a) cu alloy buckle Sf 18 Without textile: knife, coin, object	?	?2/2 twill	16–20/Z x 16–18/S	In association with buckle (a) at right waist, but detached	
Grave 206 sex unknown age 13–15 extended supine	With textile: (a) iron knife Sf 17	?	?tabby	12/? x 12/?	In association with knife and leather scabbard at pelvis	
Grave 218 (female) juv/gr? incomplete skeleton	With textile: (b) two iron rings Sf 148 (d) iron chain link Sf 150 (g) iron rod or pin Sf 152 (r) iron ring fragment Sf 929 Without textile: knife, lozenge, beads in neck region	?	tabby	12/Z x 12/Z	On iron link at left hip, iron rod at left lower leg and ring fragment (r)	
		?	?twill	?/Z x ?/S	On iron ring (d) at left hip	
Grave 220 (male) grown incomplete skeleton	With textile: (a) iron spearhead Sf 144	wool	?	5–7/Z x 5–7/Z	On blade of spearhead at left of head	Probably wrapper for spearhead
Grave 222 female age 35–45 extended supine Phase 3a *Dress Style V*	With textile: (b) Kentish disc brooch Sf 71 (h) iron key/girdlehanger & ring Sf 64–65 Without textile: beads on chest cu alloy pin below jaw cu alloy buckle centre-left pelvis cu alloy strap-end on thigh	wool	2/2 diam twill	20/Z x 14/S	On one face of iron complex (h), on left thigh	A garment fastened at throat with disc brooch and linen button loop. This, or another gown, of fine wool diamond twill. Belt set low with strap reaching to upper thigh.
		flax/hemp	button loop	yarn S-plied	On back of brooch (b) at throat, in loop around hinge of pin	

	Dress fittings, etc	Fibre	Weave	Count/Spin	Position of textile	Interpretation
Grave 223 female adult extended supine Phase 2b–3? *Dress Style* possibly variant of V	With textile: (a) Ag horse-and-rider brooch Sf 101 Without textile: beads at neck iron pin fragment at neck second fragment at left hip	not ident	?button loop	S-plied yarn binding Z's	On back of horse-and-rider brooch (a) at throat	
Grave 228A ?female age 15–17 flexed, on left side Phases 3a–7	With textile: (b) iron buckle and plate Sf 111 (d) iron firesteel/pursemount Sf 113	flax	tabby repp	16/Z x 24/Z	On back of belt-plate of buckle (b) at left centre waist, and perhaps also on firesteel/ pursemount (d) at left waist	
Grave 230 (male) adult extended supine Phase 2b–3a	With textile: (a) iron buckle Sf 139 Without textile: spearhead, shield and knife	flax/hemp coarse	tablet band, 2-hole	14/S-plied x ?/Zs	Vertically behind buckle at centre left waist; belt is leather. Band is either stitched or weft-patterned	Front-fastening jacket, belted at waist, with tablet band edging front opening
Grave 231 male age 40–55 extended supine Phase 3b	With textile: (a) composite iron buckle Sf 593	flax/hemp ?wool	tabby ?twill	18/Z x 16/Z ?/Z x ?/S	On back of buckle (a) at left waist Matted textile between back of buckle and fine linen tabby	Inner garment of fine linen, outer of matted wool textile. Both fastened by belt
Grave 232 (female) age unknown body decayed Phase 3b *Dress Style VI*	With textile: (c) iron pin tip Sf 73 Without textile: beads and coin pendant	not ident	?	30/Z x 20/Z	On one face of pin (c), north end of grave	
Grave 233 (male) age unknown body decayed	With textile: (a) iron spearhead Sf 116	not ident not ident	? cord	medium–fine, Z x ? Z, 1.0–1.2mm	On both faces of spearhead (a), probably to left of head Diagonally across socket of spearhead	Wrapper for spear, bound in place with cord
Grave 237 female age 30–40 extended supine	With textile: (a) small cu alloy annular brooch Sf 525 (b) small cu alloy annular brooch Sf 525 (c) cu alloy tweezers Sf 526	flax/hemp not ident flax/hemp	?tablet weave ? ?	14–16/S-ply x 12/S-ply fine Z x Z fine	Over hinge on back of brooch (a) at left waist On iron pin of brooch (b), lower left Inside fold of tweezers (c), left waist	Unusually positioned brooches, perhaps fixed to a tablet-woven belt, with tweezers suspended

	Dress fittings, etc	Fibre	Weave	Count/Spin	Position of textile	Interpretation
Grave 239 female age 30–40 extended supine Phase 1a *Dress Style I*	With textile: (b) cu alloy small-long brooch Sf 201 (c) cu alloy small-long brooch Sf 201 (d) cu alloy annular brooch Sf 202 (e) cu alloy annular brooch Sf 202 Without textile: cu alloy pin with ornamented head at throat vertical knife at left waist	wool	2/2 plain twill	12–14/Z x 10–12/Z	Pierced by pin of brooch (b) on lower right breast, inside linen tabby A (which is also pierced by pin). On back of brooch (c) on lower left breast, in association with tabby A. On pin of brooch (d) at right shoulder, outside linen tabby B. Probably also on back of annular brooch (e) on left shoulder.	A tubular gown of wool twill clasped by annular brooches on shoulders. An inner gown of linen tabby B. An outer garment, possibly a head-veil, in full folds, linen tabby A, reaches down to lower breast, where it is fastened back to the wool tubular gown with the pair of vertical small-long brooches. The thick cord running vertically down the body from the left small-long brooch may have suspended the knife at the left waist. The purpose of the crossways pin at the throat is not known. It may have held the front of the veil together.
		flax/hemp	tabby A	20/Z x 16–18/Z	Pierced by pin of brooch (b), outside wool twill. Also, in folds, pierced by pin of small-long brooch (c)	
		flax/hemp	tabby B	Z x Z	On front and back of pin of brooch (d) at right shoulder, inside wool twill	
		not ident	cord	Z-ply 2.0–2.5	Looped around pin of brooch (c) and then running towards tip of brooch	
Grave 240 (male) age 14–16 extended supine	With textile: (a) iron spearhead Sf 287	not ident	2/2 twill	7–8/Z x 7/Z	On socket of spearhead (a), left of head	Wrapper for spear
Grave 245 female age 35–45 extended supine Phase 3a *Dress Style V*	With textile: (c) Frankish rosette brooch Sf 187 (e) Kentish disc brooch Sf 185 (g) garnet inlay buckle Sf 100 (k) iron keys/girdle-hanger and suspension ring Sf 190 (l) three cu alloy rings and iron lozenge Sf 184 Without textile: Beads, bracteate and pendant on chest; Ag studs left arm and thigh	flax	tabby	25/Z x 18/Z	On back of disc brooch (e), at centre lower chest	Tentatively An outer gown of wool diamond-patterned twill. Underneath this a medium-weight linen gown fastened by a belt at lower waist. The fine linen tabby fastened by the Kentish disc brooch at centre chest may represent a veil or shawl. The fine plain twill covering the objects at the left hip may be a veil or shawl.
		flax/hemp	tabby	12/Z x 10/Z	On back of buckle (g) at centre waist	
		wool	2/2 diamond twill	14–16/Z x 12–14/S	On one face of iron lozenge and rings (l), at left hip and on keys, etc (k) at left hip	
		not ident	2/2 plain twill	16–20/Z x 16/Z	On hooked ends of keys (k), on opposite face to ZS diamond twill	
		flax/hemp	cord	?	Around pin hinge of rosette brooch (c) at centre upper waist	
Grave 247 female age 23–28 extended supine Phase 2a	With textile: (a) Frankish cloisonné brooch Sf 198 Without textile: beads in head/neck area	not ident	2/1 or 2/2 twill	54–72/? x 36–48/?	Around edges and on back of disc brooch (a) at throat	Very fine (silk?) twill garment possibly fastened at throat by Frankish brooch.
		not ident	cords	S-ply, 1.2mm diam	On back of disc brooch, running across pin catch	
		not ident	cord	S-ply, 0.8mm diam	On back of disc brooch, knotted, at hinge end of pin	
Grave 249C male age 40–50 extended supine Phase 2–3	With textile: (e) iron spear ferrule Sf 292 Without textile: sword, spearhead, knife, buckle at waist, clips by head	not ident	?	Z x S	Poor remains on tip of spear ferrule by left calf	

	Dress fittings, etc	Fibre	Weave	Count/Spin	Position of textile	Interpretation
Grave 250 female age 25–30 extended supine Phase 3a *Dress Style V*	With textile: (d) iron weaving batten Sf 509 (j) iron objects Sf 505 (n) knife Sf 506 (m)–(o) châtelaine complex Sf 504 Without textile: bracteate at centre chest, pin fragment at neck, buckle etc at left waist	not ident	2/2 twill	7–8/Z x 7–8/Z	On one face of blade of weaving batten (d), flat to surface, by left leg	The fine linen twill with tablet border may represent a long head-veil, open at the front, reaching to waist. The coarser textile on the knife perhaps the outer gown. The coarse twill on the weaving batten probably a wrapper.
		flax/hemp	2/1 twill with tablet border	16–18/Z x 16–18/Z	On one face of iron objects (j) In diagonal folds across châtelaine complex (m)–(o) at left waist	
		not ident	?	10/Z x 9/Z	On blade of knife (n) by left lower arm	
Grave 254 sex unknown age 4–5 skeleton decayed Phase 1	With textile: (b) gilded button brooch Sf 277 (e) small-long brooch Sf 281 Without textile: second small-long brooch (d) on chest two cu alloy pins on chest beads at neck	not ident	2/1 or 2/2 twill	20/Z x 12/Z	On back of button brooch (b) at neck over pin hinge	
		not ident	threads	coarse	Coarse textile on back of small-long brooch (e) at centre chest	
Grave 255 female age 30–35 extended supine Phase 1b *Dress Style IV*	With textile: (c) small square-headed brooch Sf 318 (b) cloisonné buckle-plate/brooch Sf 317 (e) iron knife Sf 320 (f) & (p) iron objects Sf 321 & 334/5 (g) gilded button brooch Sf 322 (h) gilded cu alloy S-brooch Sf 323 (i) gilded square-headed brooch Sf 324 (o) cu alloy ring Sf 330 (q) iron objects Sf 331 Without textile: cu alloy strap-end between knees cu alloy objects at right of head ivory purse ring at left waist	not ident	?2/1 twill	18–20/Z x 16–18/Z	On front of button brooch (g) at left waist; on one face of other objects at left pelvis, knife (e), (q), (f) and (o)	A fine wool inner gown is fastened by the S-brooch and the buckle-plate brooch. An outer garment, perhaps a cloak, is fastened by the square-headed brooch at the throat and passes over the S-brooch at the waist. The fine ?2/1 twill passing over the objects at the left waist, and bordered by the tablet band, may represent a long veil, open at the front. The brooches at the left hip seem to be connected by cords.
		wool [SEM]	2/2	fine Z x Z	On back and edge of buckle brooch (b) and on back of S-brooch (h) at lower left chest.	
		not ident	tablet-woven: ZSZS	16 cords/? x ?	On top of fine ZZ twill on (f) at left waist	
		wool [SEM]	2/2 twill	12–14/Z x 12/Z	On back of square-headed (i) at throat; on front of S-brooch (h) at lower left chest.	
		flax	cord	S-ply 1.0–1.5mm diameter	On back of button brooch (g) around hinge; and on back of small square-headed brooch (c), both on left hip; and knotted around pin hinge of (b).	
		not ident	cord	Z-cabled, Z2S2Z	On back of S-brooch (h), wrapped around spring of hinge and knotted; emerges on both sides of brooch	
Grave 256 male age 35–45 extended supine	With textile: (c) spearhead Sf 300	imprint	2/2 twill	7/Z x 8/Z	Around most of socket of spearhead (c) to right of right shoulder	Wrapper for spear
Grave 257 (female) adult twisted supine Phase 1	With textile: (a) small-long brooch Sf 236 Without textile cu alloy pin and beads	wool [SEM]	2/2 diamond twill	28/Z x 16/S	On back of small-long brooch (a) on right ribs, on pin hinge and pin catch	

	Dress fittings, etc	Fibre	Weave	Count/Spin	Position of textile	Interpretation
Grave 259 male age 23–28 extended supine	With textile: (a) spearhead Sf 272 (b) knife Sf 271 (c) small iron buckle Sf 270	flax/hemp	tabby repp	16–18/Z x 12/Z	In two layers on back and around edges of buckle (c) in pelvic region and on knife (b) at left waist	Linen garment fastened by belt; knife worn outside this. Spear probably wrapped in coarse wool twill.
		?wool	2/2 twill	9/Z x 9/S	On both faces of spearhead (a) to right of right arm	
Grave 260 ?male age 40–50 extended supine	With textile: (a) large iron pin Sf 346 Without textile: nail and knife at right waist	imprint	?twill	12/Z x 14/S	On one face of head of pin (a) at right waist	
Grave 261 ?female age 15–17 extended supine Phase 1	With textile: (b) iron buckle with brass inlay Sf 213 Without textile: Pin on right chest, two nails	not ident	?	fine, Z x ?	On back of buckle (b) at centre-right waist	
Grave 262 (male) age 35–45 extended supine Phase 2–3	With textile: (a) iron spearhead Sf 336 (b) iron knife Sf 337 (c) iron tweezers Sf 338 Without textile cu alloy buckle at left waist	wool	2/2 twill	10/Z x 10/S	On socket of spearhead (a) to right of head, where socket touched shoulder	Tunic or cloak of plain wool twill and second garment of spin-patterned wool twill, either tunic or trousers. This second garment probably fastened by belt.
		wool	spin-patterned 2/2 twill	12/Z+S x 12–14/S	On knife (b) and centre waist and on tweezers (c) at left waist	
Grave 263B female age 25–30 extended supine Phase 1b Possibly *Dress Style IV*	With textile: (a) gilded bow brooch Sf 353 (c) gilded square-head brooch Sf 355 Without textile: (b) small square-headed Sf 354, crossways at left waist string of beads between legs	flax/hemp	?2/1 twill	16–18/Z x 12/Z	On back of brooch (a), crossways at left waist and pierced by pin of small square-headed brooch (c), crossways on left hip	The vertical row of three crossways brooches running down the left centre waist suggest a front-opening garment. This garment is made of fine linen ?twill.
		not ident	cord	S-ply 2.0mm	On back of brooch (a) outside ?2/1 twill	
Grave 264 male age 40–45 extended supine Phase 3	With textile: (a) iron spearhead Sf 252 (c) iron knife Sf 260 (d) iron buckle Sf 259 (e) iron shield fitting Sf 253 Without textile: boss and other shield fittings	wool	?twill	12–16/Z x 8/S	On back of shield fitting (e) at ankles and possibly on front of buckle (d)	Head on feather pillow with coarse linen cover. Tunic or trousers of fine patterned wool twill, fastened by belt. A cover or long cloak of coarser plain wool twill, with shield on top. Fleece may represent sheath lining.
		flax/hemp	tabby	12/Z x 10/Z	On spearhead (a) in flat layer above layer of feathers	
		?wool	chev/diam 2/2 twill	16/Z x 16/S	With knife (c) at waist and on back of buckle (d) at left waist	
		fibre tufts	?fleece	–	On blade of knife (c)	
Grave 266 ?female age 30–35 extended supine Phase 1b–2a *Dress Style III*	With textile: (i) & (j) pair of silver-gilt radiate-headed brooches, Sf 243 and 244 Without textile: iron pin etc outside left thigh iron buckle mid pelvis	flax/hemp	2/2 twill	16–18/Z x 16–18/Z	In two folds, both pierced by pin of ?brooch (i) on upper chest; and on back of brooch (j) on left lower chest	The position of the two radiate headed brooches suggests that they fasten a front-opening gown of fine linen twill, which has pulled to the left.

	Dress fittings, etc	Fibre	Weave	Count/Spin	Position of textile	Interpretation
Grave 269 sex unknown age 20–25 extended supine	With textile: (a) iron knife Sf 266	not ident	?	fine Z x S	On one face of knife blade (a) at right hip	
Grave 272 child age 8–9 extended ?supine	With textile (a) iron knife Sf 275	not ident	tabby	18/Z x 16/Z	On one face of knife (a) at left waist	
		not ident	?	medium-coarse	Between knife (a) and tabby	
Grave 281 (female) age 25–30 extended supine female from finds but ?male from osteology Phase 1b *Dress Style IV*	With textile: (a) small disc brooch Sf 460 (d) small square-headed brooch Sf 461 (e) larger square-headed brooch Sf 462 (g) cu alloy buckle Sf 463 (j) three iron rings Sf 431 (o) cu alloy tweezers Sf 465 Without textile: beads at neck iron pin fragment on right breast and 2nd fragment by knife by left leg cu alloy mount right waist misc objects at left hip	not ident	2/2 diamond twill	16–18/Z x 10/Z	On back of buckle (g) at centre pelvis; with a possible selvedge vertically behind buckle hoop.	A garment of medium-fine diamond twill, possibly with vertical opening, has been fastened at the lower waist with a belt. Loops have been used to fasten a garment at the throat, probably the belted garment. The patterned band(s) which run vertically down the body and are fastened by the two crossways square-headed brooches on the lower torso, may be edging a different front-opening gown. The objects at the left hip may be in a bag or purse of coarse plain twill. The tweezers seem to have been hung from a suspension cord.
		hemp	warp-faced patterned band	28–36/Z2S x 10–12/?	Across back of, and pierced by, ?brooch (d), which is horizontal at right upper waist, and (e), which is horizontal and directly below (d)	
		flax/hemp	button loop	bundle of *c* 30 Z-spun	Probably as on buckle (g). On and around pin of disc brooch (a).	
		coarse flax/hemp	2/2 twill	Z x Z	In two loops around pin of disc brooch (a), at catch and at hinge end	
		not ident [SEM]	2/2 twill	8/Z x 9/Z	On one face of each of three rings (j) at left hip, in association with leather thong	
		flax/hemp, part-processed	cord	6 S-plied	wrapped around folded end of tweezers (o) outside left hip.	
Grave 286 female age 45+ extended supine	With textile: (a) iron knife Sf 449	not ident	tabby	12/Z x 14/Z	On one face of knife (a), outside leather sheath	
Grave 287 child age 3–4 body decayed	With textile: (a) iron buckle Sf 436	not ident	?twill	14/Z x 14/Z	On back of buckle (a) in centre of grave	
Grave 288 female age 30–40 extended supine	With textile: (a) iron finger-ring Sf 474	not ident	tabby	14/Z x 12/Z	On outer face of ring (a) on finger	
		not ident	?	18/Z x ?	Finer textile on opposite side of ring (and finger)	

	Dress fittings, etc	Fibre	Weave	Count/Spin	Position of textile	Interpretation
Grave 289 female age 17–20 extended supine *Dress Style VI*	With textile (c) iron key or latch-lifter Sf 533	imprint	?	fine, Z x ?	On one face of iron key (c) at left hip	
Grave 290 female age 19–22 extended supine Phase 1 *Dress Style II*	With textile: (a) iron pin Sf 639 (d) perforated spoon or skimmer Sf 642 Without textile: button brooch on left breast finger ring crystal and beads by spoon	flax/hemp flax/hemp	tabby ?	16/Z x 12/Z fine Z x Z	On back of bowl of spoon (d) to left of left thigh On pin (a) horizontal on left breast	
Grave 293 child age 2–3 extended Phase 1b–2	With textile: (a) iron lozenge Sf 286 (b2) iron fragment with cu alloy ring Sf 1084–5 Without textile: beads at neck	wool [SEM]	2/2 twill	18/Z x 12/S	On one face of lozenge (a) at neck and on iron with cu alloy ring Sf 1084–5 (b2) at neck	
Grave 294 (female) age unknown skeleton absent Phase 1?	With textile: (b) iron lozenge Sf 210 Without textile: four beads at head end of grave	flax	2/2 twill	15/Z x 14/Z	On one face of iron lozenge (b) at left of body	
Grave 295 ?male age 30–35 extended supine	With textile (b) iron knife Sf 225	flax/hemp Wool [SEM]	tabby 2/2 twill	16/Z x 14/Z 12/Z x 12/Z	In folds on one face of knife (b) vertically on chest On opposite face of knife from tabby	Not clear which side of knife was against body
Grave 296 female age 35–45 extended supine Phase 2a *Dress Style IV*	With textile: (b) quatrefoil brooch Sf 119 (e) & (f) radiate-headed brooches Sf 123 (g) iron chain Sf 124 (i) iron stud Sf 122 Without textile: beads on neck and chest buckle at waist	flax/hemp part-processed flax/hemp flax/hemp not ident not ident	2/2 twill warp-faced tabby band cord tabby threads	20/Z x 20/Z 20/S x 10/? S-ply (Z6–8S), 1.5mm diam 15/Z x 15/Z Around pin-hinge of quatrefoil brooch (b) at throat	On back of radiate-headed brooch (f), which is horizontal at centre waist, and on back and pierced by radiate-headed brooch (e), which is horizontal at centre pelvis. On back of brooch (f), running vertically down body and bordering linen twill Twisted around and knotted to hinge of pin of brooch (f) On both faces of iron stud (i) at left hip and on both faces of chain (g) at inside left thigh	A front-opening gown of fine linen twill, with vertical borders of warp-faced weave: fastened with two crossways radiate-headed brooches, one above other at lower waist. Threads around hinge of quatrefoil brooch at throat may represent a button-loop. The medium-weight tabby enveloping the objects at the lower left side may represent a bag, wrapper, or the folds of an inner gown. The function of the cord on brooch (f) is not known.

	Dress fittings, etc	Fibre	Weave	Count/Spin	Position of textile	Interpretation
Grave 297 male age 30–35 extended supine in coffin Phase 2	With textile: (b) iron spearhead Sf 314 (i) shield on chest Sf 313 Without textile: iron buckle at waist cu alloy fittings to right of right arm	not ident	?tablet weave	Z2S x ?	Parallel cords near shield boss (i) on centre-left chest, possibly tablet band	Spear wrapped, and wrapper bound with cords
		not ident	?	?	Lengthways folds of unidentifiable textile on socket of (b) left of skull	
		wool/hair	cords	S, 1.0–2.0mm	Cords binding textile on socket (b)	
Grave 298 ?female age 30–35 extended supine	With textile: (a) iron knife Sf 114 Without textile: finger ring on left hand	?flax/ hemp	tabby	20/Z x 14/Z	In two layers on one face of knife (a) which is vertical at left waist	
Grave 299 (male) age 40–50 extended supine ?female from osteology	With textile: (a) iron spearhead Sf 773 Without textile: knife at left waist	?flax/ hemp	?	coarse Z x Z	On tip of spearhead (a) to right of head	
Grave 300 male age 30–40 extended supine body possibly on slab of ship's timbers Phase 1b–2a	With textile: (o) iron firesteel/pursemount Sf 93 (q) iron spearhead Sf 92	wool/hair	plain 2/2 twill	7/Z x 7/Z	On one face of firesteel/ pursemount (o) at left waist	
		?wool	?2/2 twill	9/Z x 6/Z	On socket of downward pointing spearhead (q) at right ankle	
Grave 301 male age 19–21 extended supine	With textile: (b) iron buckle Sf 137 Without textile: knife at waist, spearhead on left side	flax/hemp	?tabby	20/Z x 16/Z	On back of belt-plate (b)	
Grave 308 female age 50+ extended supine Phase 1 *Dress Style I*	With textile: (b) cu alloy buckle Sf 541 (d) iron pin Sf 543 Without textile: annular brooch at right shoulder, beads at neck	wool [SEM]	2/2 twill	14/Z x 12/Z	Caught on to pin of buckle from back (b), at left waist. Also along shank of pin (d) at neck	
Grave 311 male age 40–50 extended supine	With textile (a) iron buckle Sf 564	imprint	?	?/Z x ?/Z	On back of buckle (a) at left waist	

	Dress fittings, etc	Fibre	Weave	Count/Spin	Position of textile	Interpretation
Grave 314A female age c 40 extended supine	With textile: (b) iron buckle Sf 560 (d) iron keys Sf 562 Without textile: iron knife, rod, beads at waist	flax/hemp	tabby	16–18/Z x 14–16/Z	On front and sides of buckle (b) and on both faces of keys (d), both at waist	
		flax/hemp	2/2 twill	8–9/Z x 10/Z	On one face of keys (d) at waist	
Grave 318 (female) age unknown skeleton decayed	With textile: (b)/(d) iron latch-lifters Sf 706/708 Without textile: knife near to latch-lifters	not ident	2/2 twill: diam/chev	14/Z x 12/S	Along one face of latch-lifters (b)/(d) at centre of grave	Objects at waist are sandwiched between two different textiles, but not known which is uppermost.
		not ident	tabby	14/Z x 12/Z	On opposite face of latch-lifters (b)/(d)	
Grave 319 ?male age 25–30 extended supine Phase 1b–3a	With textile: (a) cu alloy buckle 764	?flax/hemp	?	?	Back of buckle (a) at right waist	
Grave 321 ?male age 25–30 extended, most decayed	With textile: (a) iron knife Sf 435	not ident	tabby	16/Z x 15/Z	On blade of knife (a) at left of body	
Grave 324 female age 40–45 extended supine Phase 1–3	With textile: (a) cu alloy buckle Sf 653	flax/hemp	tabby	15/Z x 15/Z	On back of buckle (a) at right waist	
Grave 326 female age 14–16 extended supine Phase 2–7	With textile: (a) iron ring Sf 826 (b) cu alloy annular brooch Sf 827 (c) cu alloy folded, riveted mount Sf 826 (e) & (h) iron rings Sf 830 & 833 (i) cu alloy wrist clasp Sf 834 Without textile: second wrist clasp on right wrist cu alloy belt fittings at waist second iron buckle lower waist	wool [SEM]	2/2 twill	20/Z x 18/Z	On one face of ring/buckle (a) at left hip	Tentatively, an inner gown of fine ZZ twill; an outer gown of fine tabby; and a third item, perhaps a cloak or a textile bag made from ZS twill. Wrist clasps usually belong with the undergown.
		not ident	tabby	20–22/Z x 14–16/Z	On upper face of large ring (e) at left hip and on ring (h), sandwiched between ZS twill and metal	
		not ident	2/2 twill	12/Z x 12/S	On one face of ring (h) at left hip	
		not ident	?	?	Further fibrous remains on annular (b) on left hip and wrist clasp (i) on left wrist, and cu alloy mount (c) on left	
Grave 334 child age 6–8 extended supine Phase 1a	With textile: (a) large iron and cu alloy buckle Sf 422 Without textile: amber bead at left hip	?flax/hemp	tabby repp	18/Z x 12/Z	On back of buckle (a) on pelvis	
		?wool	?2/2 twill	12/Z x 10/Z	On back of buckle (a) between tabby repp and belt-plate	

	Dress fittings, etc	Fibre	Weave	Count/Spin	Position of textile	Interpretation
Grave 336 ?female age 30–40 extended supine Phase 2b	With textile: (c) iron chain Sf 515 (f) iron object with suspension ring Sf 511 (g) cu alloy tube with iron binding Sf 517 Without textile: misc. objects at chest and left hip; beads	flax/hemp	tabby	12/Z x 10/Z	On chain (c) at centre chest	
		not ident	?twill	12/Z x ?/S	On end opposite to suspension ring of object (f) at left hip	
		wool	tabby repp	10/Z x 6–8/S	On one side of cu alloy tube (g), left hip	
		not ident	cords	Z2S 1.0mm	Two cords running across chain (c)	
Grave 337 (male) age 40–45 extended supine	With textile: (d) iron buckle Sf 770 Without textile: iron knives at waist and spearhead at left ankle	not ident	?	14/Z x 12/S	On one face of buckle (d) on left hip	
Grave 340 male age 30–35 extended supine	With textile: (a) iron knife Sf 879 Without textile: large iron buckle at waist and small iron buckle on left foot	nettle fibre	tabby	14/Z x 14/Z	In several folds across knife (a) at waist	
		?wool ident	?fleece	?	On tip of knife (a)	
Grave 344 female age 30–35 extended supine Phase 1b	With textile (a) small cu alloy buckle Sf 437	not ident	2/2 twill	12/Z x 11/Z	On back of buckle (a) at centre waist	
Grave 346 male age 40+ extended supine Phase 3 with grave 353, Phase 3a	With textile: (b) sword Sf 499 (f) iron buckle Sf 1265	?wool	?fleece	–	On blade of sword (b)	
		flax/hemp	tabby repp	16/Z x 10/Z	On back of buckle Sf 1265 (f)	

	Dress fittings, etc	Fibre	Weave	Count/Spin	Position of textile	Interpretation
Grave 347 female age 14–16 extended supine but upper body turned to left Phase 2a *Dress Style IV*	With textile: (a) gold threads Sf 467 (e) gilded openwork brooch Sf 440 (f) small square-headed brooch Sf 468 (g) iron chain Sf 441 (i) iron buckle Sf 443 (j) iron keys, lozenge, ring Sf 444 (k) radiate-headed brooch Sf 469 Without textile: miscellaneous iron objects of uncertain function at waist and hip bronze wire at left skull small silver object centre lower chest 41 beads at left of neck and skull	gold	brocading	strip	Brocading from ?tablet band (a), from back of head (body's right)	Because the body is twisted, the brooches down the left are probably from the front of the clothing. An outer gown of fine tabby, edged with vertical tablet band(s) and fastened by crossways brooches (small square-headed on chest and radiate-headed at lower waist). An inner gown of linen tabby repp, belted. It is perhaps this gown which has the button loop fastened by the wheel-shaped brooch at the throat. The function of the twill on the iron objects at the left hip is not known, but, from comparison with other burials, it may represent a long veil. The beads in regions of neck seem to be worn as several strings, some of which may be anchored to brooches. Function of other cords lower on body not known Hair or headdress bound with textile band brocaded with gold
		flax/hemp	tabby repp	18–26/Z x 12–14/Z	In contact with chain (g) on left chest and on back of buckle (i) at left centre waist	
		flax/hemp	tabby	22/Z x 20/Z	On front of wheel brooch (e) at left shoulder; in association with chain (g) on left chest; probably pierced by pin of radiate-headed brooch (k), crossways at centre pelvis; and on hook of key (j) at left waist	
		not ident	tablet band	?	Running vertically down body, pierced by pin of small square-headed brooch (f) crossways at centre left chest	
		not ident	2/1 or 2/2 twill	?/Z x ?/Z	On second latch-lifter (j) at left waist	
		flax/hemp	button loop	2.0mm thick	Looped around pin of wheel-shaped brooch (e) at left shoulder	
		flax/hemp	cords	Z2S 0.6mm	Three cords around pin hinge on wheel-shaped brooch (e)	
		not ident	cord	Z2S 0.6mm	Cord wrapped around one link of chain (g) on left chest	
		not ident	cords	2 S-ply, 1 Z-ply	Caught between tablet band and square-headed brooch (f)	
		not ident	cord	S-ply 0.8–1.2mm	Wound around pin and hinge of radiate-headed brooch (k) and passing across front of brooch	
Grave 348 male age 30–35 extended supine in coffin Phase 1b–2a	With textile: (a) iron key/girdle-hanger Sf 487 (d) iron knife Sf 490 Without textile: garnet buckle at right waist cu alloy object at right elbow	wool	chev/diam 2/2 twill	12/Z x 12/S	Around shank of iron key/girdle-hanger (a) on left shoulder and in folds across one face of knife (d) vertical at left waist	An inner garment of fine ?tabby. An outer of coarser wool twill, reaching from shoulder to waist. The key/girdle-hanger on left shoulder is closely caught up in its folds.
		not ident	?tabby	20/Z x 18/Z	On opposite face of knife (d)	
Grave 350A child age *c* 8 skeleton decayed	With textile: (a) iron knife Sf 491 Without textile: iron buckle above knife	wool	chev/diam 2/2 twill	10/Z x 8/S	On both faces of knife (a) at centre of grave below buckle	Knife at waist caught in folds of wool twill garment
Grave 350B (female) age 20–25 female from finds but ?male from osteology extended supine cuts female grave 351B (Phase 1–2)	With textile: (d) iron ring and Sf 547 Without textile beads at neck and between legs belt fittings at waist	not ident	tabby repp	20/Z x 12/Z	Around edges of iron ring (d) at left hip	

	Dress fittings, etc	Fibre	Weave	Count/Spin	Position of textile	Interpretation
Grave 351A male grown extended supine Phase 1–2	With textile: (a) iron knife Sf 555 Without textile: cu alloy ring, iron pin, coin	flax	threads	?	Three threads running diagonally across knife (a) which is diagonally across waist	Possibly remains of fringe in area of waist
Grave 351B female age 40–45 extended supine; lower spine twisted to right Phase 1 *Dress Style IV*	With textile: (a) cu alloy small-long brooch Sf 574 (c) small radiate-headed brooch Sf 576 (e) cruciform brooch Sf 578 Without textile: second cu alloy small-long brooch at right hip above cruciform brooch; tweezers on right upper arm	flax	patterned tablet bands with two-cord (ZS) border	warp 32–40 (= 8–10 warp cords) per cm x weft ?/Z2S	Two parallel tablet-woven bands run vertically down body, on back of radiate-headed brooch (c), on lower chest, and pierced by pin of cruciform brooch (e) crossways at lower right pelvis.	There appear to be two sets of tablet-woven bands, representing the borders on two different front-opening garments, both fastened by crossways brooches.
		flax/hemp	tablet band, cords SSSSSSZ, with adjacent patterning	Z2S x Z2S	Vertically on body and pierced by small-long brooch (a) crossways on chest	
		flax/hemp	2 cords	Z2S 1–1.5mm	On back of brooch (a), one parallel to band and other between band and brooch	
Grave 353 female age 30–35 extended supine; head and arms decayed and possibly disturbed (this grave is an extension at foot end of Grave 346) Phase 3a *Dress Style V*	With textile: (b) disc brooch Sf 413 (d) iron rod Sf 415 (e) iron lozenge Sf 416 (g) iron box fittings Sf 419 (i) iron pin Sf 418 (j) silver penannular ring Sf 613, around disc brooch (b) Without textile: iron knife at left thigh and beads close to pin on chest	flax/hemp	tabby	20/Z x 20/Z	Two folds of textile, at opposite ends of pin, and both pierced by pin, of disc brooch (b) and on penannular (j), both on upper chest; also in three layers (folds) on one side of pin (i) on centre chest	A gown of fine linen tabby. Outside this a cloak or other outer garment of patterned wool twill. The beads may have been attached to the disc brooch. The net-like tabby on the objects at the left knee may represent the ends of a sash, but the function of the coarse linen tabby on the box by the foot is not known.
		wool	chev/diam 2/2 twill	18/Z x 12/S	On pin (i), on opposite side from fine linen tabby	
		wool [SEM]	net-like tabby	14/Z x 8–9/Z	On both faces of iron rod (d) at left knee and on one face of iron lozenge (e) above left knee	
		flax/hemp	tabby	12/Z x 12/Z	On one face of corner fitting of box (g) at left of left foot	
		flax/hemp	cord	Z2S 0.8mm	Knotted cord around hinge of disc brooch (b) on upper chest	
Grave 354 ?female age 25–30 skeleton mostly decayed Phase 2b *Dress Style V*	With textile: (e) gold thread Sf 459 Without textile: Kentish disc brooch at throat, cu alloy chain and a vertical string of beads on chest; cu alloy buckle at pelvis	gold	brocading	strip	Brocading from ?tablet band (e) in head and chest area	

	Dress fittings, etc	Fibre	Weave	Count/Spin	Position of textile	Interpretation
Grave 360 ?female age 30–40 extended supine Phase 3b *Dress Style VI*	With textile: (f) iron latch-lifters/keys Sf 498 Without textile: Cu alloy pin crossways at neck, beads on chest, knife at left waist, sword pommel on hip	wool	twill	14/Z x 12/Z	On one face of latch-lifters/ keys (f) at left hip	
Grave 363 male age 45–55 extended supine	With textile: (a) spearhead Sf 522 (b) iron knife Sf 523 Without textile: iron buckle at centre left waist	wool	2/2 plain twill	7/Z x 5/Z	Around socket of spearhead (a) at left shoulder	Spear probably wrapped
		wool	chev/diam 2/2 twill	10/Z x 10/S	On lower end of knife (b), vertical at right waist	
Grave 366 ?female age 20–25 extended supine Phase 1b–2 *Dress Style III*	With textile: (a) saucer brooch Sf 636 Without textile: saucer brooch matching (a) on centre chest; knife at left hip	not ident	cord	S-twist, 1.0–1.2mm	Thick cord looped around hinge of pin of saucer brooch (a) at throat	
Grave 367 (female) ?male age 30–40 female from finds but ?male from osteology supine, slightly flexed, arms folded across chest *Dress Style I*	With textile: (f) iron ring Sf 651 (g) cu alloy annular brooch Sf 652 Without textile: iron buckle at waist and knife and tweezers at left hip	? wool	2/2 twill	10/Z x 9/Z	On one face and sides of ring (f) at left hip; and at hinge on back of annular brooch (g) on right shoulder	Gown of coarse wool twill, fastened on right shoulder by annular brooch. The finer linen textile may be undergown or head-veil
		flax/hemp	?	finer ?/Z x ?/Z	Close to pin tip of annular (g)	
Grave 372 female age 30–35 extended supine Phase 2a *Dress Style I*	With textile: (b) cu alloy annular brooch Sf 629 (c) cu alloy annular brooch Sf 630 (non-matching pair) (e) square-headed brooch Sf 632 (f) Frankish disc brooch Sf 633 (i) iron buckle Sf 635 Without textile: beads at neck	wool	diamond 2/2 twill	16/Z x 12/S	Folds pierced by pin of annular brooch (c) on left shoulder; also on back of annular (b) on right shoulder and on back of buckle (i) under right hip	Anglian style tubular gown made from patterned wool twill and fastened on shoulders with non-matching annular brooches. A fine linen undergown is fastened at throat with the Frankish disc brooch and touches other brooches at neck and shoulder. Beads worn as festoon(s) between shoulder brooches. The square-headed brooch has been repaired.
		flax/hemp	?	fine Z x Z	Folds pierced by pin of Frankish disc brooch (f) at throat and probably also on back of square-headed brooch (e) immediately above disc brooch; also in association with annular (b) on shoulder	
		not ident	cord or plait	S-ply, 2.5mm	Emerging from pin catch of annular brooch (b) on right shoulder	
		not ident	cord	S-ply, 1.5mm	Emerging from pin catch of annular brooch (c) at left shoulder	
		flax/hemp	cord	Z-ply, 0.8mm	Criss-crossing square-headed brooch (e), binding pin catch-plate to brooch	

	Dress fittings, etc	Fibre	Weave	Count/Spin	Position of textile	Interpretation
Grave 373 ?male (female) age 35–40 female from finds but ?male from osteology extended supine, legs crossed Phase 2b–3a *Dress Style V*	With textile: (c) iron lozenge Sf 605 (g) large iron ring Sf 609 (h) cu alloy buckle Sf 610 (j) disc brooch Sf 612 Without textile: beads at waist, cu alloy pin at throat, strap-end outside left leg below knee	wool	diamond 2/2 twill	16/Z x 14/S	On sides and both faces of large ring (g) at left waist, on front of buckle (h) at right- centre waist and perhaps also on lozenge (c) at left thigh	An outer gown or cloak of fine patterned wool twill. Inside this, a gown fastened by belt. Garment fastened by tablet bands on disc brooch at throat. It is perhaps this garment which is belted at waist.
		not ident	tablet band, SSS	fine, S-ply	In two loops around pin of disc brooch (j) at throat	
Grave 375 (male) age 25–30 extended supine Phase 3b	With textile: (d1) iron buckle Sf 763 Without textile: spearhead, sword and shield	warp =?, weft = flax/hemp	tablet band, patterned (see text)	Z-plied x S-spun	On back of belt-plate of buckle (d1) at left waist, running across line of belt.	A belted, front-fastening jacket with a vertical tablet-woven border
Grave 376 (female) age 7–8 extended supine, but skeleton mostly missing Phase 5–7 *Dress Style VI*	With textile: (a) iron knife Sf 618 (b)–(e) iron châtelaine complex Sf 619–622 (g) iron key Sf624 Without textile: purse ring at knee, below châtelaine cu alloy pin and beads at throat	flax/hemp	tablet band (see text)	12/Z2S x ?	Band over 22mm wide running parallel to left femur, on upper face of châtelaine item (c)	Linen garment with wide vertical tablet-woven border. Body laid on mattress or bedding which has a coarse cover and is stuffed with feathers
		flax/hemp	tabby	16/Z x 14/Z	In folds at ends of châtelaine objects (b), (c) and (e) under left thigh and on knife (a) at left waist. Also in folds on top of key (g)	
		coarse plant fibre	tabby (some paired threads)	10/Z x 7/Z	In smooth layer beneath all châtelaine objects and linen tabby at left thigh. Feathers underneath	
Grave 377 (female) age unknown skeleton decayed Phase 1–2	With textile: (h) iron ring Sf 816 (i) iron lozenge Sf 817 (q) cu alloy spiral Sf 825 Without textile: bead, Roman pendant, cu alloy buckle	not ident	tabby repp	14–15/Z x 10–12/Z	On one face of lozenge (i) and ring (h) at centre grave	
		not ident	2/1 or 2/2 twill	11/Z x 10/Z	On opposite face of ring (h) from tabby repp, and on outer face of spiral (q)	
Grave 379 male age 30–35 extended supine	With textile: (a) iron knife Sf 757	not ident	chev/ diam2/2 twill	12/Z x 10/S	On knife (a) on lower chest	
Grave 381 ?male 30–40 Phase 1b–2a	With textile: (g2) pursemount/firesteel Sf 882 Without textile: Knife and pin at left waist two cu alloy buckles at waist cu alloy fitting left of head	not ident	2/2 plain twill	8/Z x 7/Z	Outside diamond twill on pursemount/firesteel (g2) at left waist	Garment of patterned twill worn underneath cloak or cover of coarse plain twill
		not ident	diamond 2/2 twill	12/Z x 9/S	On pursemount (g2) inside plain ZZ twill	

	Dress fittings, etc	Fibre	Weave	Count/Spin	Position of textile	Interpretation
Grave 387 ?female age 20–25 Phase 2–7	With textile: (b) iron keys and a girdle-hanger Sf 733	flax/hemp	chev/diam 2/2 twill	18/Z x 18/Z	On both faces of one of group of iron objects (b) at left waist/hip	
Grave 391A female age 35–45 Phase 5–7 *Dress Style VI*	With textile: (c) iron hooks and key Sf 752 Without textile: knife, beads and bulla pendant	not ident	2/2 twill	16/Z x 14/S	On hook (c) by left elbow	
Grave 391B female age 20–25 extended supine, head facing front Phase 2 *Dress Style IV*	With textile: (a) bucket iron handle and cu alloy fittings Sf 788 (c) gold strip Sf 851 (e) rosette brooch Sf 853 (g) iron pin Sf 855 (l) square-headed brooch Sf 860 (m) square-headed brooch Sf 861 (n) square-headed brooch Sf 862 (o) high-tin cu alloy buckle Sf 863 (t) iron strip Sf 868 loose organics Sf 878 Without textile: second rosette brooch (d) at throat 174 beads, pendants etc arranged vertically on chest	gold	brocading	strip	Brocading from ?tablet-woven band, top of skull, side of jaw and left neck	Inner gown of linen tabby fastened by belt on hips. The iron pin on the chest passes over this but does not necessarily pierce it. The rosette brooches may have fastened it. Over this a close-fitting gown of fine diamond-patterned twill with a vertical front opening, the opening edged with tablet-woven bands. The front opening is clasped by the crossways square-headed brooches (m) and (n). On the head, a veil with a gold-brocaded border. The cording or braiding on the pin on the chest may be connected with this or with the elaborate necklace and pendants. The function of the ZS wool twill and the upright brooch (l) that fastens it is unknown. The tabby repp and the coarse wool twill seem to be separate from the clothing and perhaps part of a grave lining or cover
		flax/hemp	tabby	14–16/Z x 14/Z	On iron pin (g) crossways at centre chest, in folds on iron strip (t) on left hip, in two layers on back of buckle (o) at lower hips, and inside wool ZS twill on brooch (l) at waist.	
		not ident	tablet band or braided border	S-ply x ?	Running along iron pin (g), on opposite face from linen tabby	
		not ident	tablet band	S-ply x ?	Behind square-headed brooch (n), between legs, running vertically down body and pierced by brooch pin.	
		wool	2/2 twill	12–14/Z x 16–18/S	On back of square-headed (l), upright at lower waist	
		not ident	2/2 chev/diam	24/Z x 16/Z	On back of square-headed (m), bordered by tablet band as on (n)	
		kempy wool	2/2 plain twill	6/Z x 5/Z	On handle of bucket (a) at left shoulder	
		flax/hemp	tabby repp	14–16/Z x 10–12/Z	On bucket fitting (a) at left shoulder and at left of left thigh (Sf 788)	
		not ident	cord	Z-cabled, 2.5mm	On one face of cu alloy bucket mount (a) at left shoulder	
		flax/hemp	cord	?	Knotted around hinge on back of rosette brooch (e), lower centre chest, and on back of brooch (l) inside ZS twill.	
Grave 394 male age 40–50 extended supine	With textile: (a) iron buckle Sf 756	not ident	?	relatively coarse	On back of buckle (a) at right waist	
Grave 395 ?male age 40–45 extended supine	With textile: (a) iron knife Sf 699 (b) iron buckle Sf 700	flax/hemp	tabby	15/Z x 12/Z	On one face of knife (a), outside leather sheath, at left waist	
		imprint	twill	8/Z x 8/Z	On opposite face of knife from linen tabby	
		imprint	?	?/Z x ?/Z	On back of buckle (b)	

	Dress fittings, etc	Fibre	Weave	Count/Spin	Position of textile	Interpretation
Grave 398 female age 30–40 extended supine Phase 2b–3a	With textile: (a) iron knife Sf 736 (b) high-tin cu alloy buckle Sf 737 (d) iron rod with loop Sf 739 Without textile: second buckle close to first	not ident	tabby	12/Z x 12/Z	On knife (a) between upper legs, on front of buckle (b) underneath knife, and on iron rod (d) between knees	The medium-weight tabby-weave textile seems to be the outer of two belted garments
Grave 400 (male) age unknown skeleton decayed	With textile: (b) iron spearhead Sf 735 (c) iron knife Sf 702 Without textile: belt fitting probably at waist	flax/hemp	tabby repp	15/Z x 22–26/Z	On one face of spearhead (b), probably at left shoulder	A tunic of fine linen tabby and perhaps a cloak of coarse wool twill. Function of tabby repp not clear
		flax/hemp	tabby	20/Z x 20/Z	In loose fold across knife (c), probably above waist	
		coarse wool	chev/diam 2/2 twill	10/Z x 10/S	On socket of spearhead (b), where touched shoulder	
Grave 405 ?male age 22–27 extended supine	With textile: (a) iron knife Sf 838	imprint	?	relatively coarse Z x Z	On one face of knife (a) at left hip, under left wrist	
Grave 407 female age 23–28 extended supine, right arm on waist, left on pelvis Phase 2	With textile: (d) buckle with shoe rivets Sf 744 (e) silver-gilt bow brooch Sf 745 (f) silver-gilt bow brooch Sf 746 (j) rod and cu alloy pin Sf 750 and associated complex Without textile beads at neck coin, intaglio and knife at left hip	flax/hemp	tablet band (see text)	12 cords/Z2S x 14/S (=24/Z2S x 14S)	Tablet bands on back of bow brooches, (e) crossways at centre-left waist and (f) directly below. Lies between back of brooches and fine twill: probably stitched to twill on (e). Also on cu alloy object (j) at upper left waist	The main gown is made of fine twill and is front-opening, with linen tablet-woven bands running down the front edges. The edges have been clasped by two crossways bow brooches, one above the other at the waist. A second garment made of a medium-weight linen tabby is belted at the waist: this is likely to be inside the other garment. The coarse ZZ twill at the left waist may be a bag for the group of objects there.
		not ident	twill	20/Z x ?	On back of bow brooches (e) and (f), inside tablet band; also in association with cu alloy pin (j) at upper left waist	
		part-processed flax/hemp	tabby	14–15/Z x 10–12/Z	On back of buckle (d) at centre waist and on one face of iron lozenge (j) at left waist	
		not ident	twill	10/Z x 10/Z	In association with cu alloy pin (j) at left waist	
Grave 408 ?female age 30–40 extended supine Phase 1b *Dress Style IV*	With textile: (c) miniature brooch Sf 791 (d) radiate-headed brooch Sf 792 Without textile: cu alloy buckle on left hip long iron pin crossways between upper legs ring on left hand	not ident	tablet band (see text)	12 /? x 10/?	On back of miniature brooch (c) which is crossways at centre- left waist. Band runs across line of pin and is pierced by it. ?Stitching.	Main gown is front-opening and bordered with vertical tablet bands which are clasped by crossways brooch(es) at waist. This, or another garment, has button loops on the front opening.
		flax/hemp	button loop	S-ply binding a bundle of Zs	Detached from miniature brooch (c). Another is in position around hinge of radiate-headed brooch (d) at centre-left waist	
		flax/hemp	threads	fine Z	Loosely twisted together and knotted around pin hinge of radiate-headed brooch (d)	
Grave 409 female 22–27 extended supine Phase 1b	With textile: (f) iron lozenge Sf 729 (h) iron pin Sf 731 Without textile: miscellaneous objects at left waist and hip; iron links left of head; 50 beads at neck	?wool	?2/2 twill	12/Z x 12/Z	On one face of iron lozenge (f) at left hip	
		flax/hemp	2 threads	fine Z	Emerging from perforation of iron lozenge (f)	
		not ident	?tablet band	Z2S x ?	Parallel cords across pin (h) on left thigh, probably the remains of a vertical tablet band	

	Dress fittings, etc	Fibre	Weave	Count/Spin	Position of textile	Interpretation
Grave 411 (male) age 4–6 child, extended supine	With textile: (b) knife Sf 802 Without textile: spearhead at left of head	wool flax/hemp	diamond 2/2 twill tabby repp	10/Z x 9/S 16/Z x 24/Z	On one face of knife (b) at centre waist On opposite face of knife (b)	Inner garment of fine linen and an outer, perhaps cloak, of patterned wool twill.
Grave 412 ?female age 15–20 extended supine Phase 2b–3a *Dress Style V*	With textile: (e) iron pin Sf 807 Without textile: buckle at right waist, cu alloy strap-end, 78 beads etc at neck and chest	not ident	tabby	15/Z x 12/Z	Around one end and down shank of iron pin (e), vertical at left hip	
Grave 413 female age 22–27 extended supine Phase 5–7 *Dress Style VI*	With textile: (c) & (d) iron girdle-hanger Sf 711 & 723 (e) & (f) iron pin fragments, Sf 712 & Sf 713 Without textile: beads, pendant etc around head and neck	not ident not ident ?wool not ident	cords tabby tabby repp tabby	8/Z2S 14/Z x 12–14/Z 4–8/? x 16–18/S (or S-ply) 6/? x 6 pairs/?	Fringe or tablet band underneath iron girdle-hanger (c) between thighs In several layers arranged in tight folds or gathers on iron pin (e)/(f), both on left thigh; and probably also underneath cords on girdle-hanger (c) between thighs Deep underneath girdle- hanger (c) & (d) at left hip Underneath tabby repp on (c); a layer of feathers and plant material lies below this	The clothing seems to be made up of a medium-weight tabby- weave textile, arranged in close folds, and a ribbed wool textile. Both of these seem to be on front and back of the body and the wool repp is probably the outermost. The coarse tabby with paired threads is probably the cover for a mattress. The fringe or tablet band outside the other textiles on the thigh may represent the end of a sash.
Grave 414 male 35–45 extended supine, in coffin Phase 2b–3a	With textile: (f) iron buckle Sf 990 (g), (h), (i),(j) & (k) iron shield fittings Sf 991–994 & 983 Without textile: spearhead, sword, knife and iron objects	wool [SEM] flax/hemp	chev/diam 2/2 twill tabby repp	12/Z x 12/S 20/Z x 13/Z	On shield grip and detached in association with other shield fittings on lower legs On back of buckle (f) at left upper waist	Tunic of linen tabby repp and second garment, trousers, cloak or cover, of patterned ?wool twill
Grave 416 male age 30–40 extended supine, head turned to left	With textile: (b) Iron pin Sf 938	not ident	2/2 twill	15/Z x 15/Z	On one face of pin (b) above forehead, next to knife	

	Dress fittings, etc	Fibre	Weave	Count/Spin	Position of textile	Interpretation
Grave 417 female age 40–50 extended supine Phase 2a *Dress Style IV*	With textile: (c) small square-headed brooch Sf 1021 (d) radiate-headed brooch Sf 1022 (g) small bow brooch Sf 1025 (i) large cu alloy ring Sf 1027 Without textile: one large buckle and one small close to each other at waist, 58 beads on chest, strap-ends (with leather) and crystal ball between knees	flax/hemp	button loop	spin not clear, 1.8mm wide	Looping over pin hinge on back of bow brooch (g) at lower neck	A front-opening gown made from fine patterned wool twill, with tablet-woven border running vertically down front edge; fastened by radiate-headed brooch at waist. It is possible that the fine ZZ twill represents a second gown, bordered by the warp-faced band and fastened by the small square-headed brooch. Both gowns may have been belted. It is not clear which of these garments was fastened at the throat with the button loop(s) and the small bow brooch.
		flax/hemp	c.4 threads	Z-spun	Knotted bundle of threads parallel to button loop on (g)	
		wool [SEM]	2/2 diamond twill with starting border	20–24/Z x 18–22/S	In and around large cu alloy ring (i) at left waist; and pierced twice by pin of crossways radiate-headed brooch (d) at centre waist. It has a tablet-woven starting border running across the pin of (d)	
		flax/hemp	warp-faced band	fine, spin not clear	Two areas, one running across pin, other running along pin, at hinge, on back of crossways small square-headed brooch (c) at lower waist	
		not ident [SEM]	twill	fine, Z x Z	Inside warp-faced band and also touching back of brooch, on back of small square-headed brooch (c). Remains of stitching.	
Grave 419 female age 30–35 extended supine Phase 2a *Dress Style III*	With textile: (a) bird brooch Sf 1000 (b) disc brooch Sf 1001 (f) buckle with shoe-shaped studs Sf 1005 (g) iron pin, chain and ring with bead Sf 1006 (h) iron lozenge Sf 1007 Without textile: antler burr pendant and ivory purse ring on left hip beads on chest	not ident	button loop	S-plied, 4mm wide	On back at pin hinge of bird brooch (a) at throat	Three garments, one of medium twill, one of fine linen tabby and one of fine wool twill. It is not clear which is fastened by the button loop at the throat, or which is belted.
		not ident	2/2 twill	16/Z x 12/Z	On back of disc brooch (b) at middle of chest, pierced by pin	
		part-processed flax/hemp	two cords	S-ply, 1.5mm	Two cords, one with three knots, on back of disc brooch (b), between twill and brooch	
		?flax/hemp	tabby	18/Z x 14–16/Z	In association with buckle (f) at right waist and on ring (g) at throat	
		not ident	?2/2 twill	20/Z x 16/S	Around pin and on link of chain (g) at throat	
		leather	thong	7mm wide	Threaded through perforation of iron lozenge (h)	
Grave 420 (female) age 20–25 extended supine, head facing forward Phase 2–3a	With textile: (a) gold Sf 1035 & 1279 (b) iron pin Sf 1037	gold	brocading	strip	Gold brocading from tablet-woven band at right of head	
		not ident	tabby or 2/1 twill	14/Z x 14/Z	Along one side of shank of iron pin (b), crossways on right chest	
Grave 421 (male) age 3–4 skeleton mostly decayed	With textile: (a) iron arrowhead Sf 939 (b) iron pin Sf 940 Without textile: knife	?flax/hemp [SEM]	2/2 twill	9/Z x 9/Z	On one face of socket of arrowhead (a) above head and possibly also along pin (b) on right of body	
		not ident	tabby repp	20/Z x 12–15/Z	On socket of arrowhead (a) and along pin (b), in both cases on opposite face from the twill	

	Dress fittings, etc	Fibre	Weave	Count/Spin	Position of textile	Interpretation
Grave 423 male age 40–50 skeleton decayed Phase 2–3a	With textile: (b) large iron ferrule Sf 959 Without textile: spearhead, iron rod, buckle, knife, etc	?wool	2/2 plain twill	8/Z x 8/Z	Next to open end of iron ferrule (b) to left of left foot	
Grave 425 female age 20–25 extended supine Phase 1b–2	With textile: (c) iron pin Sf 955 Without textile: beads on shoulder and left of body	not ident	?	?/Z x ?/Z	On pin (c) on left chest	
Grave 426 ?female age 40–50 extended supine Phase 2	With textile: (a) buckle Sf 985	not ident	tabby repp	10/Z x 16/Z	On back of buckle (a) on chest	
Grave 427A female age 30–35 extended supine Phase 1b–2	With textile: (d) large iron ring Sf 1012 (e) small iron ring Sf 1013 Without textile: cu alloy pin centre pelvis, buckle and knife at right waist	not ident not ident	tabby 2/2 twill	12/Z x 10/Z 14/Z x 14/S	On one face of large iron ring (d) by left elbow On (d) on opposite face to tabby and on small iron ring (e) nearby	
Grave 428 female age 20–25 extended supine Phase 2 *Dress Style III*	With textile: (a) & (b) saucer brooches Sf 894 & 895 (h) long-handled knife Sf 901 (i) & (k) iron lozenges Sf 902 & 904 Without textile: beads further objects on left hip	flax/hemp flax/hemp leather flax/hemp	?twill ? thong tabby	12/Z x 12/Z ?/S x ?/S folded lengthways 16/Z x 13/Z	On back of saucer brooches (a) at neck and (b) mid chest, both pierced by pins; and on handle of knife (h) under lower left arm On back of saucer brooch (b) inside linen twill A strip of leather under wire of pin spring of brooch (a) On iron lozenges (i) and (k) between left hip and lower left arm	A front-opening gown of linen ?twill, fastened by two saucer brooches, one above the other. An inner gown, again of linen. The function of the linen tabby at the left hip is not known – perhaps a bag. The folded leather thong may be a repair to the brooch, or an alternative to a linen button loop.
Grave 432 female age 20–25 extended supine Phase 1b–2	With textile: (d) cu alloy buckle Sf 845 Without textile: cu alloy pin at skull, ivory purse ring; beads and knife at waist	not ident	2/2 twill	14/Z x 13/Z	On back of buckle (d) at left-centre waist	

	Dress fittings, etc	Fibre	Weave	Count/Spin	Position of textile	Interpretation
Grave 433 sex unknown juv/gr skeleton decayed Phase 1	With textile: (a) small gilded 'horse' brooch Sf 910 Without textile: cu alloy bracelet and iron knife	flax/hemp	button loops	bundle of Zs	Remains of two button loops at either end of pin of 'horse' brooch (a)	
Grave 436 sex unknown age 35–45 extended supine Phase 1b–2	With textile: (b) buckle with glass and garnet inlay Sf 951	flax/hemp	tabby repp	22/Z x 14/Z	Arranged in vertical folds across back of buckle (b) at centre waist	
Grave 437 male 35–40 extended supine Phase 2	With textile: (c) iron fauchard Sf 973 (d) (f), (g) (h) (i), (j) tweezers complex, including iron pin, knife, ring & coin Sf 974, 976–8, 1042, 1043 (k) iron pursemount/firesteel Sf 979 Without textile: sword, buckle at left waist, iron pin at right knee	wool	diamond 2/2 twill	10/Z x 8–10/S	Along one face of socket of fauchard (c) where against mid left thigh	Five different textiles, but relationship not clear. The coarse wool diamond twill is perhaps the tunic and the medium-weight tabby the trousers
		not ident	tabby	16/Z x 14/Z	On blade of fauchard (c) where against upper knee	
		flax/[SEM]	2/2 twill	8/Z x 7/Z	Inside curve of blade of fauchard (c)	
		flax/hemp	tabby repp	9/Z x 20/Z	In folds on iron pin (d) at right thigh	
		flax/hemp	cord	S-ply, 1.5mm	Diagonally across pin at right thigh	
		leather	thong		On pin at right thigh	
		not ident	thread	Z, 0.8mm	Wrapped around tweezers (f)	
		?wool	diamond 2/2 twill	20–24/Z x 18–20/S	In two layers on pursemount/firesteel (k) under sword at right side	
Grave 438 male age 15–17 extended supine	With textile: (a) iron knife Sf 886	imprint	?	fine, Z x ?	On knife (a), outside leather sheath on lower chest	
Grave 440 (female) age 15–17 supine, turned to left, slightly flexed Phase 1b–2a *Dress Style III*	With textile: (a) & (b) saucer brooches Sf 965 & 966 Without textile: beads at right upper arm	flax/hemp	button loops	2.0mm thick, fine Z-spuns bound together	On back of saucer brooch (a) at throat, in two loops, one around pin, the other now detached	The knotted bundle of threads on the lower of the two saucer brooches is probably a repaired button loop.
		flax/hemp	threads	Z, 0.3–0.4mm	A bundle of Z-spun threads, knotted together and looped over hinge of pin on saucer brooch (b), on centre chest. More threads in pin catch	
Grave 442 child age 9–11 skeleton mostly decayed Phase 1b–2	With textile: (d) iron firesteel Sf 1034 Without textile: cu alloy buckle, iron pin and knife	imprint	twill	16/Z x 20/S	On iron firesteel (d) on left side	

	Dress fittings, etc	Fibre	Weave	Count/Spin	Position of textile	Interpretation
Grave 443 ?female age 30–35 extended supine Phase 1b–2	With textile: (c) iron nail Sf 998 (d) iron pin Sf 999 Without textile: cu alloy buckle centre-right waist, iron knife inside left arm	not ident not ident	diamond 2/2 twill tablet band	20/Z x 16/S 12–14/S-ply x ?	On one face of iron pin (d) and iron nail (c) on left hip Running diagonally across iron pin (d) on left hip, on opposite face from diamond twill	
Grave 444 sex unknown age 6–8 skeleton mostly decayed Phase 1–2	With textile (f) iron ?key Sf 947	not ident	?tabby	12–16/Z x 12–16/Z	On curved end of iron ?key (f) at left hip	
Unstratified sex unknown age unknown	With textile iron spear ferrule Sf 1264	wool	tabby repp	12/Z x 8/Z＋S	Spin-patterned textile along one side of iron spear ferrule Sf 1264	

Notes:
TEXTILES
Fibres were identified at The Anglo-Saxon Laboratory with a transmitted-light microscope fitted with a polarising analyser.
[SEM] indicates that a sample has been identified with the aid of scanning-electron micrographs prepared at English Heritage Centre for Archaeology.
'Counts' are the numbers of threads per cm
Z and S indicate the lie of the fibres in a yarn, when the yarn is held vertically: Z = / and S = \
Z2S indicates a two-ply yarn or cord, twisted in the S direction from two Z-spun yarns
For weaves see Figs 5.11–5.12

COSTUME
The clothing has been described as if the person were alive and standing upright.
'Left' and 'right' indicate the body's left and right.
'Above' and 'below', mean worn higher or lower on the body.
'Inside' and 'outside' mean as worn, 'inside' being closer to the body.
The terms for living body parts – head, neck, breast, arm, waist, hip – replace strict osteological terms, except where they cause ambiguity.

Table 5.7. Buckland 1994. Textile and costume evidence.

PART 6: OBJECT TECHNOLOGY

Introduction

Ian Riddler

The 800 objects and 2,300 beads recovered from the 1994 excavations at Buckland have been described in Part 4 in terms of their function, typology, dating and possible provenance, as well as for the indications they provide of gender and social affiliation. In Part 5 these studies are further developed by an analysis of the garment fasteners and mineralised textile remains to reconstruct clothing styles. In this chapter a selection of objects is investigated scientifically to examine their technology. In essence, these are detailed analyses carried out by staff of the British Museum in response to specific questions raised by object specialists. These are presented in broadly the same sequence as in Part 4 begining with weapons and the examination by Janet Lang of five iron swords, the shield boss from Grave 323, the shield boss rivets from Grave 264 and spearheads from Graves 264, 299, 323 and 393 with the weaving batten from Grave 250.

A note on the examination of the gilt silver quatrefoil brooch from Grave 296 by Susan La Niece (pp 275–6) is followed by a summary of the technology of the knives from the cemetery by Ian Riddler and Fleur Shearman (pp 276–8), particularly in terms of the organic remains that survived on their tangs and blades.

The chapter concludes with a contribution by Caroline Cartwright on the mineral-preserved wood remains discovered on a wide range of objects from the cemetery, including knives, sword scabbards, shield boards, spearheads and ferrules, but also awl-like firesteels, caskets, brooches and clench nails.

Metallographic study: five swords

Janet Lang

(Graves 264, 265B, 346, 375 and 437)

Seven swords were found during the 1994 excavations, all of which appear to be pattern welded. This form of decoration is achieved by forge-welding the blade from composite bars or strips, some or all of which have been twisted prior to welding. The finished blade, when polished and etched, exhibits a pattern on the surface which may take the form of a herringbone, straight and twisted elements or curving patterns. Thålin Bergman and Arrhenius (2005) have suggested that it was developed for practical reasons, to utilise the perhaps small pieces of metal available, and then became an art, conferring status on the smith and his client. Mechanical tests indicate that composite structures, if the metal and welds are sound, are more resistant to impact and bending stresses than low carbon iron and wrought iron, although not as effective as steel (Lang in press). There is evidence for the technique being introduced during the Iron Age (Pleiner 1993). Pattern welding has been extensively studied, initially by Neumann (1927–8), followed twenty years later by Maryon (1948). Subsequent studies have been carried out by a number of workers, probably the most well-known being by Ypey (1982–3). Numerous examples were also examined metallographically and illustrated by Tylecote and Gilmour (1986) while Thomsen (1989, 1994) and Buchwald (2005) have studied some of the extensive finds from Illerup and Nydam. A study of Swedish Vendel and Viking weapons, including metallography and radiography, was published by Thålin Bergman and Arrhenius (2005). A radiographic survey of Anglo-Saxon swords (including those from the 1951–3 Buckland excavations) was carried out by Lang and Ager (1989). Gilmour (2007) has made a number of studies and has reviewed pattern welding for edged weapons in England from the late Roman to the Anglo-Saxon period. He also (2010) considered the wider implications of pattern welding in sixth-century swords from Kent.

Five of the Buckland swords have been studied metallographically and analysed in the British Museum. This provided an opportunity to examine a small group of swords from the same site, with similar dates. Comparison of the micro-sections would show similarities or differences in composition and construction and might indicate if the blades had a common origin, or perhaps came from the same tradition of fabrication. The metallographic sample from each sword is here referred to by an individual Specimen number (eg SN 1019). The swords are from: Grave 264 (SN 1019); Grave 265B (SN 1020); Grave 346 (SN 1021); Grave 375 (SN 1022) and Grave 437 (SN 1023). A pattern-welded weaving batten from Grave 250 (SN 1024) was also examined and has been reported separately (*see* pp 273–5).

The study has underlined the importance of phosphoric iron in making blades, especially those which have been pattern welded. Its use has been observed by Schürmann (1959), Bühler and Straßburger (1966), Tylecote and Gilmour (1986), McDonnell (1989), Ottaway (1992), Gilmour (1996, 2010), Thomsen (1989, 1994), Weimer (1996), Thålin Bergman and Arrhenius (2005) and others. Phosphoric iron was used in the construction of all five Buckland blades. It is clear that its use was deliberate and intended to produce a visual contrast with the darker-etching carbon iron or steel. The hardness values of both these iron alloys were similar and the use of phosphoric iron would not necessarily have a deleterious effect upon the mechanical properties (Goodway and Fisher 1988; Balasubramaniam 2003; Gilmour 2007).

Experimental

Radiography revealed the swords' structure (albeit imperfectly) and condition. On the basis of the radiographs, suitable areas were selected for sampling from five of the swords, determined in consultation with a metals conservator specialising in the preservation of organic surface remains on metal objects, as some of the blades had traces of wood and fabric which were not to be disturbed. At the agreed point, a wedge was cut in sound metal from the cutting-edge inwards to the centre of each sword blade (sometimes referred to as the *central rib*, although the blades do not have a marked rib; *see* p 51), no more than 2mm at its widest at the cutting-edge. The length of each section was approximately 20mm. The saw blade was cooled in order to avoid unintentional heat treatment. Each

sample was mounted in a cold setting epoxy resin. The surface was ground using carborundum paper (250- to 1000-grade) with water lubrication and then polished with 6 and 1 micron diamond pastes with a proprietary lubricant. The polished samples were examined before etching with nital (2 per cent concentrate nitric acid in ethanol) to reveal the structure. They were re-examined after etching and photographed. They were then coated with carbon to ensure conductivity and examined in a scanning electron microscope (SEM) with an energy dispersive X-ray spectrometer (EDXA), allowing analysis of the slag inclusions and the body metal. The precision is taken to be 2 sigma, which is 1.5 per cent or less for iron and less than 0.5 per cent for other elements. The accuracy is ± 1–2 per cent. Detection limits are less than 0.07 per cent for all elements analysed (except iron). Results were calculated as oxides. A total of 600 analyses were carried out. To reduce the length of the tables, the analysis figures for each strip or area examined have been averaged and appear in Tables 6.7a–e. Elemental mapping, amplified by line scan analyses (ie making a series of point analyses across the specimen along a predetermined line), was also carried out. When microscopy was complete, hardness tests were carried out using a Vickers diamond pyramid micro-hardness tester with a 100g load ($HV_{0.1}$).

The non-metallic inclusions visible in the micro-sections may be waste products from the smelting or smithing processes, iron oxides, fragments of fuel ash or furnace lining (usually containing clay). As each inclusion may be derived from more than one source (eg interaction between the waste ore minerals or gangue and the furnace lining) the source of individual inclusions cannot readily be determined in most instances. The majority of the inclusion analyses revealed small quantities of compounds of magnesium (Mg), aluminium (Al), potassium (K), calcium (Ca) and titanium (Ti), as well as iron (Fe), and were measured as oxides. All these should be taken as present unless an inclusion is referred to as a specific oxide (silica, SiO_2 for example) and the elements are normally only mentioned when the quantity seems unusual. Generally, the presence and quantity of phosphorus (P) and/or manganese (Mn) seem to be the most significant in distinguishing different batches of metal. Trace amounts of nickel (Ni), cobalt (Co), chromium (Cr), vanadium (V) (not always tested), arsenic (As), sulphur (S) and barium (Ba) were also found.

The diagram (Fig 6.1) indicates the terminology employed in this report to describe the various components of the blade. As far as possible the parts of the blade which were distinguished microscopically are referred to by the terms shown in the diagram. The term *band* is usually employed to describe a feature which is a result of segregation during metallurgical processes, such as extraction or cyclical heating

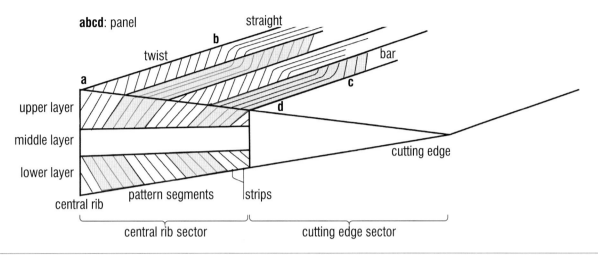

Fig 6.1. Terminology used in sword technology discussion.

and working, rather than the result of the deliberate joining of pieces of metal. The piles of strips welded together are termed *bars*.

Sword: Grave 264

(SN 1019) (Figs 6.2, 6.3 and 6.4)

The blade has a central pattern-welded panel 26.1mm wide. On the radiograph the pattern appears to be unusual: it consists of four rods with twists and straights; the segments are arranged so that two lengths of twists are next to each other, while the other two segments are straight (type C2a, Lang and Ager 1989). It is very difficult to distinguish, but it is possible that the surface of this blade has been ground, as there is a suggestion of curving elements in the pattern of the twists. The cutting-edge is plain.

The section was removed 330mm from the shoulder of the blade. The dimensions were: length of section 25.5mm; thickness at rib 2mm; maximum thickness 4mm. The depression in the centre of the blade was more marked than in SN 1021, SN 1022 and SN 1023. This would be consistent with grinding down a fuller to remove the top layers of the twists to reveal a curving pattern. Pitting corrosion is present at the cutting-edge and at the join between the central rib and edge sectors and at several points on the surface of the central sector. The surfaces were corroded but not deeply. Sound metal extends to the cutting-edge. A crack, bordered by corrosion extends inwards for about 0.25mm in the central sector.

It was noted that the blade was very hard and had to be cut with a diamond wheel.

Unetched, microscopy and semi-quantitative analysis

The sample showed a variety of inclusions, mainly in bands or groups. In comparison with the other sword cross-sections, the inclusions were relatively few and small. The grouping of the inclusions suggested that the blade had been constructed from a number of bars of metal, some of which were themselves fabricated from more than one component. Many of the inclusions were aligned parallel to the blade surfaces as a result of working, but other groups were transversely oriented, showing that some of the metal had been worked in a different direction before being fire-welded together to make the blade. The slags were mainly featureless, some were slightly translucent, while a few contained a second phase, wüstite (low valence form of iron oxide, with a variable composition approximating to FeO).

Spot analysis in the SEM showed that the composition of a number of the inclusions in the central sector includes phosphorus, whereas those found in the cutting-edge area do not (Table 6.7a). There are no marked differences between the average inclusion composition in the rib and edge sectors (Table 6.5). The inclusions found in the joins are iron oxides, often combined with silicon and occasionally with phosphorus. A weld might be expected to contain iron oxide and the presence of silicon suggests that silica was used as a flux during welding to assist in removing the oxides and making welding easier.

The results show that the metal of the components in the middle layer (M), the edge sector, strips U1(4), L1(2), L3(5), L5(4) and L5(5) contained traces of nickel mainly in the metal (as might be expected). The amounts are small, but suggest that these components were made from metal

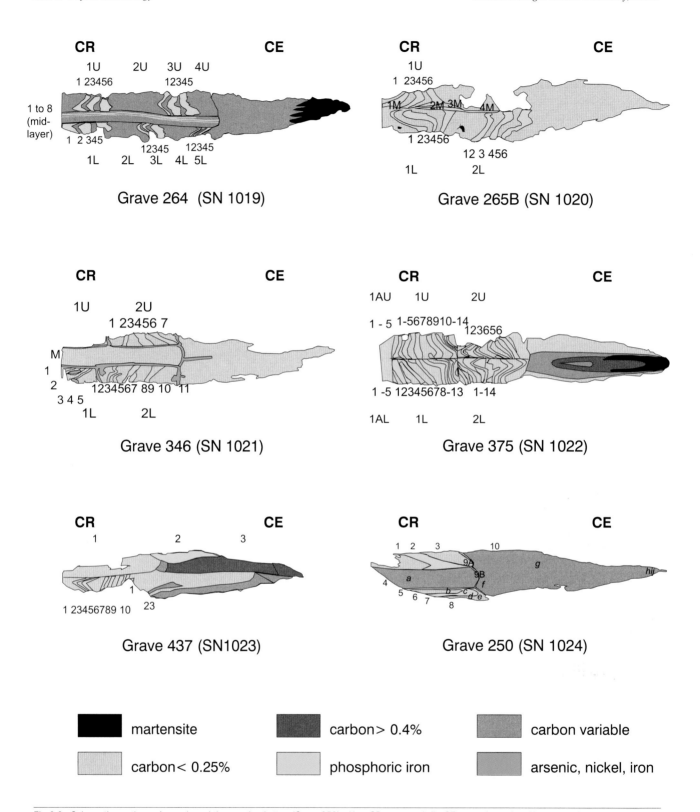

Fig 6.2. Schematic sections of swords and the weaving batten (Grave 250). Key: CR = central rib; CE = cutting-edge; U = upper layer; L = lower layer; M = middle layer; A = part of other half of blade not sectioned; a, b, c, etc, location of hardness test readings (see Table 6.11).

at least partly from the same source. About half the metal containing phosphorus also contains nickel, while 11 per cent shows traces of nickel but no phosphorus; this might imply that ores were being mixed before smelting.

Etched, microscopy and semi-quantitative analysis

The etched specimen shows a very inhomogeneous structure with bands of different composition (Figs 6.2–6.4). The cutting-edge comprises just under half the section. There is a marked transition between the edge sector and the central part of the blade. At least eleven regions with different characteristics can be distinguished, half of which consist of strips of different composition. This was seen not only in the orientation and the elongation of the inclusions but also in the changes of composition and morphology of the ferrous metal.

Cutting-edge section

The cutting-edge itself has a martensitic structure (Figs 6.3.4 and 6.4.1). This hard metastable phase is normally produced by rapidly quenching iron with carbon contents even as low as 0.3 per cent C. The structure is coarser nearer to the edge where the section is thin which is perhaps surprising, but may be a result of heavy prior work, making transformation quicker. The edge was only lightly tempered, indicated by the slow response to etching, but the temper increased further from the edge, where etching was more rapid. Characteristically, untempered martensite is extremely slow to respond to etching. It is probable that the blade was quenched and then withdrawn from the quenching medium so that the residual heat left in the centre of the blade was sufficient to temper the blade (about 250°C), except in the immediate vicinity of the cutting-edge which is hard and

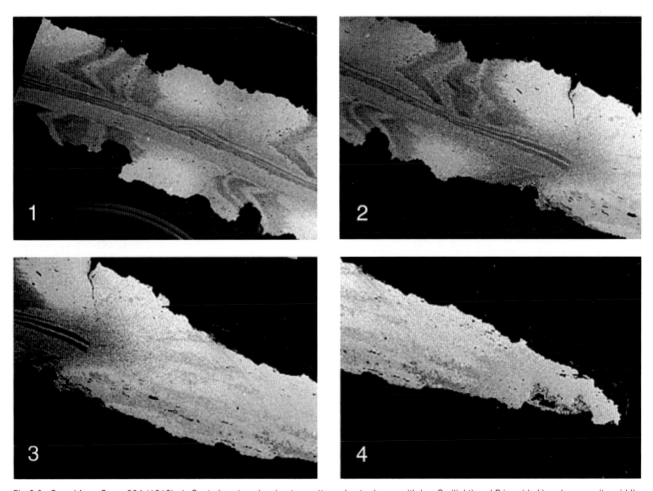

Fig 6.3. Sword from Grave 264 (1019). 1: Central sector, showing two patterned outer layers with low C- (light) and P-iron (dark) and composite middle layer. 2: Central sector join with the edge sector. 3: Edge sector. 4: Cutting-edge, dark martensite and light pearlite (width of view 16mm).

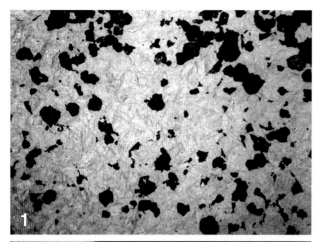

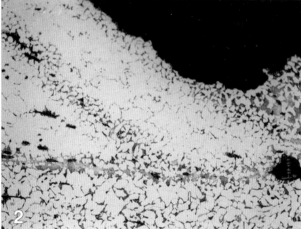

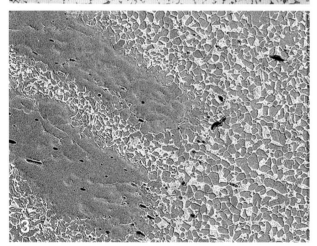

Fig 6.4. Micrographs of sample 1019 from Grave 264. 1: Nodules of pearlite in a martensitic matrix, near the cutting-edge (width of view 280 microns). 2: Two strips of P-iron (light) and low C-iron (dark) in the upper layer close to the join with the edge sector (width of field 720 microns). 3: Termination of the middle layers at the join between the central and edge sectors (width of view 740 microns).

barely tempered (see below). The process is sometimes termed slack quenching. Martensite spreads inwards unevenly from the cutting-edge to extend over about a third of the edge section, nearer one surface than the other. There also appear to be small areas of carbides precipitated at the prior austenite grain boundaries where the carbon content may be more than the eutectoid composition of 0.8 per cent C. Moving away from the cutting-edge itself, nodules of dark etching pearlite have precipitated in four to five finger-shaped bands (Figs 6.2 and 6.3.4). The nodules increase in frequency until they merge to become a continuous area of pearlite (Fig 6.4.1). The size of the pearlite grains also varies in bands aligned parallel to the surface of the blade, probably due to micro differences in composition (ie below detection limits). There are also some narrow light etching bands; these may result from dissolved elements (eg oxygen, silicon) which are present in amounts which are also often below detection limits in the SEM. Arsenic, phosphorus and nickel and possibly other elements can also cause this effect, but were not detected either in the bands or in the body metal of the edge sector.

Central section

The transition to the central sector of the blade is marked by a series of oxide inclusions (Fig 6.4.3) and a light-etching band running transversely and somewhat irregularly across the section, from surface to surface. The central sector is more complex and has been constructed from three main components; a composite core layer running parallel to the surfaces of the blade, with a patterned surface layer on either side (Fig 6.3).

The core layer is composed of strips of different thickness, consisting of two outer layers, one considerably wider than the other, and five narrow inner strips, three of which are virtually carbon free. These three strips show 'ghosting', indicating the presence of phosphorus (Fig 6.4.3). The terms 'ghosting' or 'ghost' structure are used to describe the uneven response to etching around the grain boundaries, mainly in ferrite, which is the result of dissolved phosphorus present in the body metal. Areas with phosphorus are less readily attacked by the etchant and tend to be in the middle of the grains rather than the grain boundaries (Stewart *et al* 2000). This appearance is often termed a 'ghost' structure. The outer edges of this composite layer are defined by slag stringers and an almost continuous line of small pearlite grains, a feature which often indicates a join (Fig 6.4.2). The composite layer ends abruptly at the edge sector (Fig 6.4.3).

Each outer layer consists of five pattern segments. Frequent slag inclusions (oxides) mark the joins between the outer layers and the mid section. The segments are either twists or straights (mainly low carbon steel) and are often delineated by slag inclusions (Fig 6.4.2). There are variations between the composition and the grain size of the segments which also make them clearly distinguishable after etching. The carbon content varies between negligible and about 0.5 per cent. In some of the low-pearlitic areas, the grain boundaries are somewhat flattened in the transverse direction, an effect probably produced by working. Pearlite has precipitated around the grain boundaries, consistent with the blade being heated to above 723°C and allowed to cool slowly.[80] In a number of the segments the presence of phosphorus is indicated by 'ghost' structures.

Semi-quantitative energy dispersive analysis, elemental mapping and line scans of the metal (EDXA-SEM) show that phosphorus is present in the central sector (Fig 6.3). Although the analyses did not include all segments, the results obtained, together with those from the microscopic examination, are sufficient to confirm that the central sector was constructed using alternating strips or rods of phosphorus-rich and phosphorus-free metal. Generally carbon was present, but to a lesser extent in the phosphorus-rich areas (which is not surprising as carbon uptake and cementation are inhibited by the presence of phosphorus).

Hardness

The cutting-edge is extremely hard (+900 $HV_{0.1}$) which indicates that the carbon content is in the region of 0.8 per cent. The hardness in the pearlitic areas of the edge section varies between 260 and 500 $HV_{0.1}$. The hardness of the central section is lower, varying between 170 and 310 $HV_{0.1}$, measured mainly near the surfaces. When average values are calculated for the hardness of the phosphorus-rich and low-phosphorus twisted bands, they are similar, being 264 $HV_{0.1}$ and 244 $HV_{0.1}$ respectively.

Summary

The blade was made with a complex centre sector and an edge sector. The central sector is a sandwich, consisting of two outer layers of alternating twisted and plain segments on either side of seven strips of different thickness, lying parallel to the surfaces of the blade. The composition of the strips and segments generally seems to alternate phosphorus-rich (up to 4 per cent P) and low phosphorus (down to the undetected

level) ferrous metal. The carbon content varied between negligible and 0.4 per cent. Joins were often characterised by iron oxide inclusions and silicon, probably indicating that sand was used as a flux. Phosphoric iron may have been used to facilitate welding and (or) to provide a contrast on etching when it would appear white. There was little difference in the hardness between the layers (average overall 250 $HV_{0.1}$). The edge sector was made from phosphorus-free high carbon iron, quenched to martensite and partially tempered. The cutting-edge itself was extremely hard.

It is probably the earliest in the group and the pattern appears to have curving elements: this suggests that it could have been imported. Wherever it was made, it is the work of a skilled craftsman.

Sword: Grave 265B

(SN 1020) (Figs 6.2, 6.5 and 6.6)

The blade has a pattern-welded centre panel 22.9mm wide. The pattern is not easily distinguished on the radiograph. It consists of two layers of three bars with alternating coincident twists and straights (type B2a or C2a). It is not easy to see if the twists and straights are coincident within both layers. The cutting-edge is plain.

The specimen was cut from the blade 280mm from the shoulder of the blade. The dimensions were: length of section 21mm; thickness at rib 2mm; maximum thickness 4mm. The central depression was more marked than in SN 1021, SN 1022 and SN 1023. It is very difficult to distinguish, but it is possible that the surface of this blade has been ground, as there is a suggestion of curving elements in the twists. The overall length of the section, including corrosion, is 24mm.

The section is corroded at the cutting-edge and near to the centre a large corrosion pit penetrates from the surface to the middle of the blade.

The specimen does not etch as readily as SN 1019. It also shows evidence of a complex construction but the carbon content is not high. The section is again divided into slightly uneven halves, consisting of a relatively simply constructed edge sector and a more complex central sector.

Unetched, microscopy and semi-quantitative analysis

The unetched section shows a number of inclusions throughout, varying in average diameter from 0.2mm to

---

80. 723°C is the *transformation* temperature, at which iron or iron-carbon alloys change from the low temperature phases *ferrite* and *pearlite* (alternating lamellae of ferrite and iron carbide, Fe_3C) to the high temperature phase *austenite*. On cooling, the change is reversed, unless the metal is quenched and cools too fast for the reaction to take place, when a hard metastable phase, *martensite,* forms, instead.

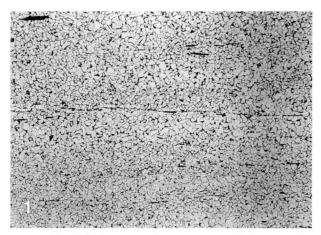

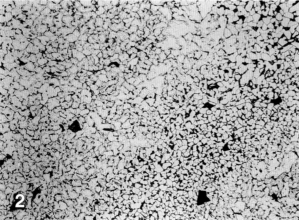

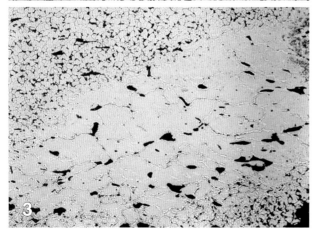

Fig 6.5. Micrographs of sample 1020, Grave 265B. 1: Line of inclusions and faint 'ghost' band near cutting-edge, variable, small grains (width of view 720 microns). 2: Strips in central sector, variations in carbon and phosphorus content (width of view 720 microns). 3: P-iron band with 'ghost' grain boundaries, inclusions; some grains elongated by working (width of view 720 microns).

0.04mm. Some of them appear to be associated with joins and boundaries. Many are elongated parallel to the surfaces. A curving transverse line of inclusions, terminating at one of the most deeply corroded parts of the section, midway between the rib and the cutting-edge, indicates the join between the two sectors.

Analysis showed that the larger inclusions are either fayalitic slag with wüstite dendrites or iron oxides. Although apparently not connected to the surface, some of the iron oxides may be corrosion which has penetrated from it. Some of the small, less rounded, inclusions appear to be largely alumina (57 per cent) with a trace of titanium, indicative of clay minerals, probably from the furnace or hearth linings. The large pale inclusions associated with changes in composition or morphology are iron oxides. There are few, if any, silica inclusions in these areas.

The majority of the inclusions in the edge sector are aligned parallel to the surfaces and are thin and elongated. Unusually they also contain traces of sulphur, presumably remaining after the extraction process, possibly derived from ore or fuel ash, together with the normal slag elements and manganese.

Trace amounts of chromium, vanadium, cobalt, nickel and arsenic were detected. Chromium, vanadium and arsenic occur together and seem to be associated with raised levels of alumina, but as arsenic is part of this grouping, it seems more likely to come from an ore source rather than the furnace lining. Nickel traces are also present in some components, but not ones containing chromium, vanadium and arsenic (with one exception, in the middle strip 1). These observations seem to suggest that more than ore source was in use and some ore mixing took place. There may have been variations in the processes as well. It is clear that, apart from using phosphoric and non-phosphoric iron, different batches of metal were being utilised.

Etched, microscopy and semi-quantitative analysis

The response to the etching was not very rapid. It revealed an inhomogeneous structure. Areas with different compositions were not so clearly marked as they were in SN 1019 (Fig 6.2).

Cutting-edge

Etching confirms that the edge sector is divided from the central sector by a very narrow band, consisting of pearlite with small globular inclusions, a feature often seen at welds. The join is not very distinct. The edge sector also has a single line of small pearlite grains (Fig 6.5.1), possibly indicating

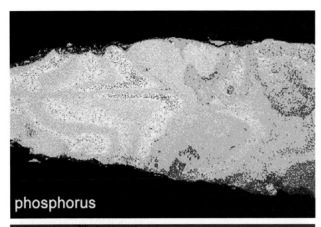

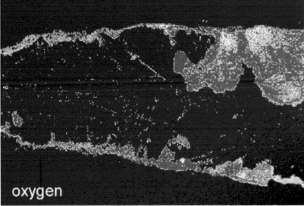

Fig 6.6. Element maps, sword from Grave 265B (1020) (width of view 10mm). White indicates maximum concentration of element.

a join, running parallel to the surfaces, close to the middle. 'Ghost' bands, indicating the presence of phosphorus, also run parallel to the surfaces. The grain size is variable and the carbon content is between 0.01 per cent and 0.25 per cent, increasing towards the surfaces and the cutting-edge. This suggests that the blade may have been carburised but unfortunately the outermost surface layers have been removed by corrosion.

More detailed examination near the surface, not far from the join, showed elongated inclusions, containing both phosphorus and manganese and signs of working, as the grain size decreased towards the surface. In the middle of the sector, a little closer to the cutting-edge, narrow bands of ferrite with somewhat spheroidised pearlite at the grain boundaries alternate with ferritic bands containing trace amounts of phosphorus. In the area which appears to be a remnant of a lost surface layer, the grains are small (0.02mm average diameter) and equiaxed and the carbon content is slightly higher than elsewhere. Nearer to the remaining surface and the cutting-edge, the ferrite grains are equiaxed, and very small

(0.004mm) with little variation. The carbon content is not high (0.25 per cent C or less) and the carbides are spheroidised or located in the grain boundaries, probably as a result of heating for a short while above about 750°C and cooling fairly slowly within the hearth. The body metal does not contain phosphorus, although it is present in a few of the inclusions, together with manganese. The cutting-edge itself has a small grain size (0.01mm), slightly increased carbon content (c 0.3 per cent C) and the morphology of the grains (acicular ferrite) suggests air cooling, probably from just above 730°C.

Central rib sector

The central sector of the blade is much more complex, and is partly corroded. It appears to have consisted of two layers with four twist segments in each layer (only two are visible in each layer in the mounted specimen as it is a half blade section). One of the twists is almost completely missing. There is also a small, thin layer in the middle (1mm maximum thickness, 4.8mm in length). This is outlined by a line of pearlite grains with some small inclusions. It might be either a small core layer or even part of the next twist on the upper side. Each twist alternates strips of phosphoric iron (with or without a small amount of carbon) with low carbon iron (0.2–0.3 per cent C) which can be distinguished by different responses to etching (Fig 6.5). Oxide inclusions from the welding process are found in the transitional area between adjacent segments. The grain size in the phosphorus-rich strips is generally larger than the non-phosphoric ones and they show 'ghosting' (Fig 6.5.3). In several areas, phosphoric inclusions were found in the pearlitic strips (ie non-phosphorus strips), whereas in the phosphoric iron (ferritic with phosphorus) bands, the inclusions contained manganese but not phosphorus.

A comparison between the compositions of the inclusions in the upper and lower twist layers with the middle layer does not show any obvious similarities. It is possible that it was part of the missing, corroded twist, but is more likely to have been a separate core layer.

The SEM map of the phosphorus distribution (Fig 6.6) shows some phosphorus concentration within the corroded areas which appear to relate to the original, uncorroded phosphorus-rich strips.

Hardness

The hardness of the section varied between a maximum of 226 $HV_{0.1}$ (one of the twists) and 130 $HV_{0.1}$ (close to the cutting-edge). A sequence of hardness measurements was made across the twist segments (157: 204: 135: 187: 145: 226: 130 $HV_{0.1}$). The first, third and fifth were low carbon strips (less than 0.2 per cent), the seventh contained slightly more carbon (0.25 per cent) while the second and fourth were ferritic with phosphorus. The hardness values clearly reflect the composition. With these compositions it would have been difficult to achieve greater hardness, although it is possible that corrosion has removed work hardening or even carburisation on the surfaces.

Summary

The blade section is constructed with a complex pattern-welded centre panel and an edge sector. The central sector consists of four twists (one of which is almost completely missing, as a result of corrosion) with a very thin core layer. The twists are made from alternating strips of phosphoric iron (up to 1.7 per cent P_2O_5) and low carbon iron (0.25 per cent C with low phosphorus). The edge sector has a light etching band and may have originally consisted of more than one strip. The blade is hardest in some of the twist segments but the cutting-edge is has a carbon content of 0.25 per cent C or less, and has not been hardened. Although this sword appears to have curving elements in the pattern, and could have been imported, it would not have been as effective a weapon, as the previous sword (SN 1019).

Sword: Grave 346
(SN 1021) (Figs 6.2, 6.7, 6.8 and 6.9)

The pattern-welded central panel is 20.01mm wide. The radiograph shows that the pattern consists of three continuously twisting elements. It is possible that there are some straight elements at the edge of the pattern but this is not confirmed by the micro-section (type B1). It is possible that there is some twisting in the cutting-edge.

　　The specimen was cut 270mm from the shoulder of the blade. The dimensions are: length of section 23mm; thickness at rib 3mm; maximum thickness 4mm. The depression in the centre of the blade is not very marked. The specimen surfaces are corroded in places. The upper part of the cutting-edge is missing and there are also some cavities close to the surface resulting from corrosion penetration. Corrosion attack has completely removed part of the surface layer on the upper side and also penetrated transversely in the central sector along the twists.

Unetched, microscopy and semi-quantitative analysis

Unetched, a considerable number of inclusions are visible, especially in the central sector (Figs 6.7 and 6.8). The distribution, orientation and size of the inclusions are heterogeneous. Throughout the section the majority of the inclusions are two-phased with a dendritic or globular wüstite phase in a fayalitic matrix (Fig 6.7). A transverse division into an edge sector and a central sector is suggested by a series of small rounded oxide inclusions running somewhat irregularly from surface to surface, midway between the central rib and the cutting-edge. The small rounded inclusions associated with the boundaries (Fig 6.8.2) are iron oxides, silicates and may contain some phosphorus. The majority of the inclusions in the edge sector are thin, dark and glassy slags with a higher proportion of silica, alumina and more manganese than phosphorus (see Table 6.1). Other inclusions resemble those in the middle layer of the central sector and there may be some relationship between the ore sources for these two areas, because both contain inclusions

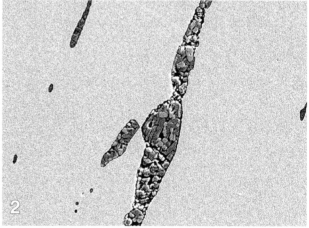

Fig 6.7. Micrographs (SEM), sword Grave 346 (sample 1021). 1: Pale grey iron oxide and mid-grey iron silicate phases in an inclusion in the middle layer (width of view 610 microns). 2: Inclusions in the middle layer, pale grey iron oxide globules and dendrites, matrix analyses: <30% silica, 2–7% phosphorus (oxide) and 1–2% manganese (oxide) (width of view 610 microns).

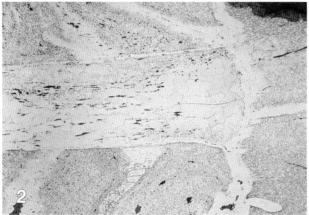

	Al$_2$O$_3$	SiO$_2$	P$_2$O$_5$	K$_2$0	CaO	MnO	BaO
central, edges	6.2	23	3.5	1.1	1.8	1.6	0.12
central, mid (a)	5.6	27	5.3	1.2	2.0	2.2	0.56
central, mid (b)	4.4	28	3.4	1.3	0.8	1.0	0.00
edge sector	14.5	40	3.1	3.3	6.2	5.4	1.20

Table 6.1. Sword from Grave 346: average inclusion composition.

with barium (0.25–1.8 per cent BaO). It is unlikely that they come from the same batch or smelt, however, because the alumina, silica, lime (CaO) and manganese oxide contents are significantly different.

The central sector is divided into three layers parallel to the surfaces (Fig 6.8). The middle layer contains a large number of mid-grey, somewhat fragmented inclusions, elongated parallel to the surfaces. Some are iron oxides, but the others can be divided into two groups, one with barium, the other without. The analyses are given in the table above (Table 6.1). The inclusions in the outer layers are of similar composition, except that there is little or no barium present.

The main analytical table also shows the presence of small but significant quantities of arsenic and nickel, both in inclusions and the body metal. The distribution of these elements is shown in Table 6.2. Occasional traces of vanadium, chromium and cobalt were also noted.

Etched, microscopy and semi-quantitative analysis

The response to etching with nital was weak, but showed quite clearly that the blade had been constructed from several component pieces. Narrow light etching bands indicated joins between an edge sector and a central sector and between some of the strips in the outer, surface layers (Fig 6.2).

Cutting-edge

The edge sector is ferritic and contains a small amount of phosphorus (less than 1 per cent). The interface between the two sectors is a light etching, well-defined transverse band (Fig 6.8). From this, another band extends at right angles, towards the cutting-edge for a short distance before gradually disappearing: small inclusions outline the bands on both sides.

The ferritic grain size is smaller at the interface and towards the surfaces of the sector. The grains appear to be flattened near one of the surfaces, indicating low temperature (ie cold) working took place. This sector appears to have been constructed with a narrow strip at the centre and thicker

Fig 6.8. Micrographs of sample 1021 from Grave 346. 1: Central ferritic layer with inclusions, lower layer with twisted strips and light-etching bands at the joins (width of view 5.76mm). 2: Join between the pattern-welded sector (left) and the cutting-edge sector (right), large inclusions, variable grain size and C content; alignments of small inclusions in the light-etching bands and 'ghosts' in some grain boundaries (width of view 5.76mm). 3: In the cutting-edge sector the grain size is large except at the lower surface and nearer to the central sector (left); the light-etching band at the left extends from the transverse join between the central and edge sectors (width of view 5.76mm).

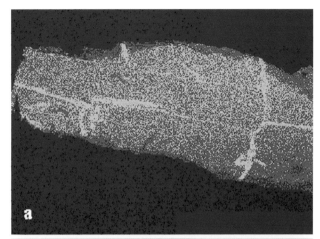

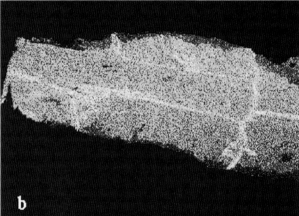

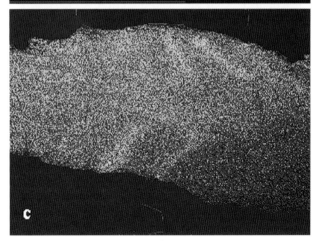

Fig 6.9. Element maps, sword from Grave 346 (1021).
a: Nickel; b: Arsenic; c: Phosphorus (width of view 10mm).

layers on either side. At the cutting-edge itself, the average ferrite grain diameter is large (between 0.3 and 0.45mm). The carbon content at the cutting-edge is negligible except for some coarse carbides precipitated at the grain boundaries.

Central sector

The central sector consists of a broad, ferritic core layer (2.6mm wide), parallel to the surfaces, bounded on either side by a layer of twists and straights, confirming the structure suggested by the inclusion distribution (Fig 6.8). The twists also appear to be joined by light etching bands similar to the join between the sectors. Line scan analyses for silicon, aluminium, oxygen, manganese, potassium, phosphorus, arsenic and nickel were carried out to try to understand the element distribution. The analysis results for some elements are incorporated in the diagram (Fig 6.2) and the element maps (Fig 6.9), from which it can be seen that the light etching bands contain arsenic and nickel. Part of the surface was so corroded that one of the twists was missing at the central rib. The twists consist of alternating strips of phosphoric iron and low-carbon (less than 0.25 per cent C) iron. The average grain size of the central layer tends to be large (0.2mm average diameter), whereas the grain size of the twists is smaller (eg 0.09mm). Small amounts of grain boundary carbides can be seen. The grains in the twists are elongated with respect to the surfaces. The broad central layer is somewhat featureless ferrite, although some sub-grain boundaries are visible.

Hardness

The hardness throughout the section is low, ranging between 134 $HV_{0.1}$ and a maximum of 266 $HV_{0.1}$ near the surface in the pattern-welded panel. Two sets of adjacent strips were tested in this sector, giving the results 195:195:215 $HV_{0.1}$ and 153:217:158 $HV_{0.1}$. The hardness probably depends on the phosphorus content as well as the carbon content. The average hardness (three values) at the cutting-edge is 160 $HV_{0.1}$.

Summary

The sword was made with a central panel consisting of pattern-welded twisted layers, using alternating phosphoric iron and low carbon/low phosphoric iron with an iron core layer. The edge sector contains little phosphorus or carbon. Arsenic and nickel enrichment has occurred at the joins and is discussed further below. The hardness of the blade throughout is low. The composition makes this blade slightly unusual, its properties were not outstanding.

	centre u layer (i)	centre u layer (b)	centre l layer (i)	centre l layer (b)	mid (i)	mid (b)	edge sector (i)	edge sector (b)
NiO	yes	yes	yes	yes	yes	yes	no	yes
As_2O_3	yes	yes	no	yes	no	yes	no	yes

Note: i = inclusion; b = body metal; u = upper; l = lower.

Table 6.2. Sword from Grave 346: summary of arsenic and nickel distribution.

Sword: Grave 375

(SN 1022) (Figs 6.2, 6.10 and 6.11)

The pattern-welded central panel is 21.7mm wide and is difficult to distinguish on the radiograph. The pattern is unusually fine (ie small) and may consist of three or four elements which have coincident twisted and straight sections (type B2a or C2a). The cutting-edge is plain.

The specimen was cut 330mm from the shoulder of the blade. The dimensions are: length of section 22mm; thickness at rib 2mm; maximum thickness 3.5mm. The depression in the centre of the blade is not very marked. The width of the blade, including corrosion, is 25mm.

Unetched, microscopy and semi-quantitative analysis

The unetched section shows a number of inclusions. These are generally quite small although some are long and extended, tending to break up. Both single and two phased inclusions are present. The majority of the inclusions are slags (20 per cent< SiO_2 <70 per cent). The section is clearly divided transversely by an extensive inclusion (almost certainly part of a weld) into edge and central sectors (Fig 6.10). The large inclusions in the edge sector are elongated and are either pale grey slag (30 per cent silica with 1 per cent P_2O_5) or darker silica-rich inclusions with manganese contents of between 3–14 per cent (MnO) and no phosphorus (Fig 6.10, 2 and 3). The siliceous inclusions have broken into smaller pieces all of which have similar compositions.

The central sector is divided into two more or less equal halves by fairly continuous iron oxide inclusions running down the middle parallel to the surfaces (Fig 6.10). The orientation of the inclusions in the central sector appears more random, some being at an angle to the surfaces while others are at right angles, presumably as a result of twisting. All the inclusions analysed in the central sector contain phosphorus (between 1 and 16 per cent P) but very few contain manganese, in contrast to the cutting-edge, indicating that different batches of metal must have been used. Also, a few traces of nickel were found in the body metal of two strips in the second twist (7, 14) as well as in the

body metal and some inclusions in the cutting-edge sector. Trace quantities of cobalt were found in the body metal and inclusions of several components, but arsenic and barium were not identified. Generally the slag has a ratio of 1:2 silica to iron oxide and the proportion of the other elements is low relative to the other sections.

Etched, microscopy and semi-quantitative analysis

Cutting-edge

The edge sector consists of a core with a high carbon content (*c* 0.8 per cent C) with lower carbon surface layers, one of which is thicker than the other (Fig 6.10). The surface layers near the cutting-edge have alternating carbon-rich bands with some areas which are rich in phosphorus (Fig 6.11) as indicated by 'ghost' structures and confirmed by analysis. Oxide inclusions follow the weld lines

The cutting-edge itself is martensitic (Figs 6.10 and 6.11), produced by quenching. Lath martensite and retained austenite can be seen (eg Samuels 1980, 90.4), suggesting that the carbon content is not more than 0.6 per cent. Martensite extends inwards towards the rib in two spurs. Extremely fine pearlite has precipitated at the martensite interface and also along the axis (F.ig 6.11). It is probable that the blade was withdrawn from the quenching medium well before quenching was complete to allow it to be slack quenched., reducing the hardness slightly but increasing the toughness. The uneven banded response to etching suggests that there may be some small variations in composition or structure, which could indicate that centre of the sector had been constructed from several layers (Fig 6.10.3). Some elongated inclusions follow the changes in morphology between the layers.

The presence of phosphorus in the outer layers has inhibited carbon uptake and also suggests that the edge sector was made from several pieces of metal.

Central sector

The etched microstructure and the element distribution maps show clearly that the central sector is constructed with two

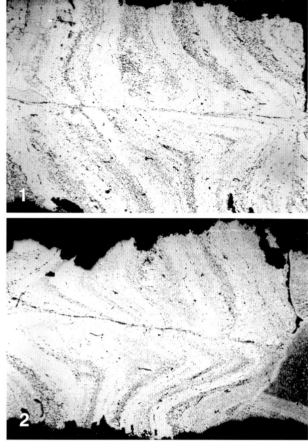

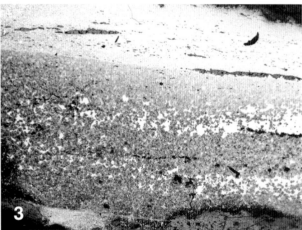

Fig 6.10. Micrographs of sample 1022 from Grave 375. 1: Central sector, two patterned layers with alternating strips of P-iron (light) and low C-iron (dark) (width of view 5.76mm). 2: Join between central edge sectors, showing change in composition and grain size (width of view 5.76mm). 3: Edge sector, C-rich middle layer, with some martensite (light) and elongated slag inclusions (width of view 5.76mm).

layers, each having two segments of twists (Fig 6.10) with alternating strips of carbon-free phosphoric iron and low carbon iron. The carbon is present as small areas of coarse pearlite which tended to nucleate at the inclusions and the grain boundaries. The ferritic strips have 'ghost' structures (Fig 6.11.2) and the grains tend to be larger and elongated parallel to the surfaces, consistent with the presence of phosphorus. The section has been cut so that the transverse join down the centre of the blade is visible and includes a small amount of the other half of the blade, which appears to be similar in construction. Corrosion has penetrated down the join between two of the twist segments to within about 200 microns of the join at the centre. One of the adjacent twisted segments has been partly corroded away.

Hardness

The edge section was considerably harder than the central section. In the martensitic areas hardness values reached more than 900 $HV_{0.1}$, while the pearlite nodules were 270 $HV_{0.1}$. Some of the high carbon areas (c 0.8 per cent C), had very fine or irresolveable pearlite, possibly with some bainite, the hardness being 500 $HV_{0.1}$. The hardness values of the bands in the central section varied between 190 and 250 $HV_{0.1}$. Where the response to etching was uneven, indicating the presence of dissolved phosphorus, the hardness was higher, whereas in other areas, even those with some pearlite (up to 0.2 per cent C), the hardness was lower.

Summary

The section shows a distinct join between the cutting-edge and the central sectors. As a whole, the section does not exhibit extensive slag. The edge sector may have been constructed from a carbon-rich core (c 0.8 per cent C) with a layer of lower carbon-iron containing some phosphorus on either side. Quenching has resulted in a hard martensitic structure near the edge and irresolvable pearlite in the carbon-rich areas away from the cutting-edge. The central section is divided into two layers, with alternating phosphoric and low-carbon iron bands making the pattern. The join, in the middle of the blade, is distinct and consists of a very narrow band of almost continuous small pearlite grains. Pale grey slag is associated and is present extensively in some of the joins. The carbon content varies, but does not rise above 0.3 per cent.

Apart from the inherent weakness in having coincident transverse joins in the pattern-welded layers, without a central layer to absorb impact shock, the edge of this blade is hard, and if the welds were sound, would have been an effective weapon.

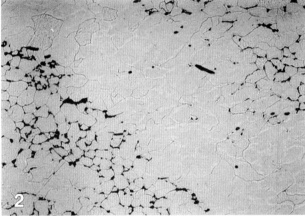

Fig 6.11. Micrographs of sample 1022 from Grave 375. 1: Transition between martensite (light grain on right), very fine pearlite and eutectoid ferrite (width of view 144 microns). 2: Detail of strips in the central sector, with dark grain boundary pearlite in the low-C bands and a 'ghost' structure in the ferrite bands, indicative of phosphorus (width of view 720 microns).

Sword: Grave 437

(SN 1023) (Figs 6.2, 6.12 and 6.13)

The pattern-welded central panel is 20.05mm wide and is rather indistinct on the radiograph, but appears to consist of twists and straights. The cutting-edge is plain.

The sample was removed 560mm from the shoulder of the blade. The dimensions were: length of section 16mm; thickness at rib 2mm; maximum thickness 3mm. The depression in the middle of the blade was not marked.

A considerable part of the surface of the section has been lost to corrosion, reducing the thickness to almost half at one point (Figs 6.12,1 and 6.12.2). Both surfaces of the central sector exhibit pitting attack and it appears that about one third

of the centre part of the blade on one side is missing. There are a number of inclusions visible in the unetched section, mainly orientated parallel to the surface.

Unetched, microscopy and semi-quantitative analysis

Nearer the cutting-edge surface the inclusions are thin, small and elongated, some consisting of iron oxide with phosphorus-rich 'tails' at each end. A group of larger, less elongated, dark, glassy inclusions lies about three-quarters along the section towards the cutting-edge and these contain more silica (50–75 per cent).

The inclusions in the central rib areas were much more numerous and varied in composition, morphology, size and orientation. The majority are extended parallel to the surface, especially in the upper half.

Analysis of both inclusions and body metal showed that phosphorus is present both in some inclusions and in parts of the body metal. Some inclusions contain manganese (1.5 per cent or less). Variations in the phosphorus content occur within small groups of inclusions which are clearly associated, both morphologically and spatially). A few traces of nickel were found mainly in the rib sector, while cobalt was present in the metal and inclusions of both sectors.

Etched, microscopy and semi-quantitative analysis

The section does not divide readily into two sections like the others in this study (Fig 6.12). This may be fortuitous, because of the position of the sample in the pattern or because of the pattern itself, which is not easily distinguished on the radiograph.

Central sector

The central sector is divided into two layers by a very thin light etching band, parallel to the surfaces and accompanied by a line of single pearlite grains. The grain sizes are generally small and the phosphorus content is variable in the lower part and contains rather indistinct twisted pearlitic and ferritic strips. Line scans suggest that the twist segments probably consist of alternating strips of phosphoric iron and low carbon iron, but the difference in composition is very small (heavy etching showed phosphorus ghosts in the ferrite), which accounts for the difficulty in distinguishing them microscopically and the lack of clarity on the radiograph. There are few inclusions in the patterned area and even with analysis and mapping, it was difficult recognize the outlines of the strips with any precision. The elemental map shows an increase in the phosphorus content in the area of the twists,

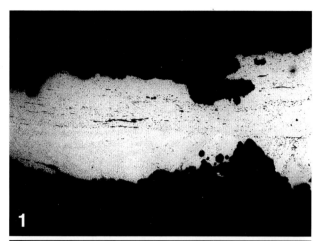

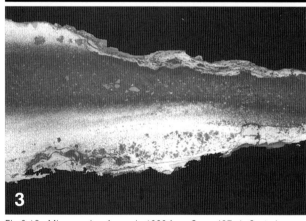

Fig 6.12. Micrographs of sample 1023 from Grave 437. 1: Central sector, showing inhomogeneous inclusion distribution indicating two layered structure (width of view 5.76mm). 2: Transition between central and central sectors, inhomogeneous inclusion distribution and C-rich layer in edge sector (width of view 5.76mm). 3: Cutting-edge showing a dark etching C-rich band between lower carbon bands (width of view 5.76mm).

but it is not as marked as in the other sections (Fig 6.13). In what appears originally to have been the central layer, all the inclusions are orientated parallel to the surfaces and the structure consists of variably sized equiaxed ferrite grains which have been slightly elongated parallel to the surface. A third, upper layer was probably lost to corrosion. At the transition to the edge sector, the middle layer seems to be joined to a carbon-rich layer which extends to the cutting-edge (Fig 6.12).

Cutting-edge

The cutting-edge sector appears to have consisted of a carbon-rich layer sandwiched between two phosphorus-rich layers (Fig 6.12), one of which is partially missing. Oxide inclusions can also be seen at the join between the carbon-rich layer and the outer layers. The middle, dark etching layer has the eutectoid composition (0.8 per cent carbon) and consists of very fine or irresolvable nodular pearlite. Some of these areas are very hard, suggesting that they may have been quenched quickly enough to transform into martensite. Next to the carbon-rich layer, the grain size is very small, increasing towards the surface as the carbon content decreases. The outer layers contain less carbon and are of unequal size (Fig 6.12). The upper surface is corroded so that little remains, but the lower surface shows a banded structure with light etching 'ghost' bands and carbon-rich bands where pearlite has accumulated in irregular bands of nodules. Some extremely acicular ferrite is associated with the large pearlite nodules which have formed (this would occur if the temperature dropped from perhaps 850°C, above the transition temperature, and remained, briefly at about 650°C, plausibly, during slack quenching). Very fine carbides have precipitated within the grains and pearlite forming in the grain boundaries.

Hardness

The hardness of the central area is low, varying between 110 $HV_{0.1}$ and 215 $HV_{0.1}$. In the high carbon areas of the edge sector, however, values of between 440 $HV_{0.1}$ and 520 $HV_{0.1}$ are found. The lower carbon areas have hardness values of between 212 $HV_{0.1}$ and 280 $HV_{0.1}$.

Summary

The surface of the blade is corroded and it is possible that one of the pattern-welded layers has been lost from one of the surfaces, or it might have been made with pattern welding on only one surface. Because of the corrosion, it is difficult

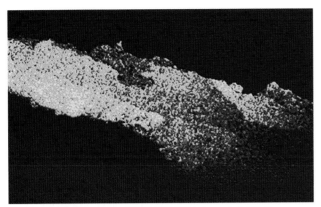

Fig 6.13. Sword from Grave 437 (1023) SEM element distribution map: phosphorus.

to be certain which construction is the more likely to have been used. The pattern-welded twists are probably alternating bands of phosphoric and low carbon iron. The cutting-edge consists of a carbon-rich (0.8 per cent C) core, with phosphorus banding and lower carbon bands towards the surfaces. The cutting-edge is hard (520 $HV_{0.1}$ maximum).

It is difficult to assess this blade as the section appears to be incomplete: it was probably soundly constructed and would have been a good weapon.

Discussion

The Buckland swords have patterned panels running down the blades from the hilt to the tip. These can be seen on the radiographs, although not all the details are easily distinguishable. All appear to consist of various combinations of twists and straight sections, but the pattern on the swords from Grave 437 and 414 (not sectioned) could not be distinguished. It was difficult to tell if the swords from Graves 265B and 375 were types B2a or C2a (Lang and Ager 1989). The sword from Grave 249 (not sectioned) was interesting because it had a two layered B2a pattern in which the straight part of the patterned layer near the hilt was 20mm longer on one side than the other. The smith reduced the length of the straights, until at about 270mm from the hilt, the twists on both sides coincided. Another feature of interest was the faint possibility of curved elements in the patterns on the swords from Graves 264 and 265B, since these are more commonly found in swords from the Continent. It is sometimes difficult to see the number of bars present, especially when there are two patterned layers. Plain core layers are not normally visible on radiographs and can best be recognised in micro-sections, or, if the blade is badly corroded, the number of layers is revealed when splits occur

between them along the old weld lines. The choice of the area to be sectioned is largely determined by conservation considerations, so an atypical cross-section may result; for example, in an extreme case, if the sample is taken from a blade with alternating twists and straights, so that all the straights are lined up across the blade and all the twists likewise, the cross-section may show only twists or straights. As Pleiner (1993, 146) has pointed out, the use of small metallographic sections has its limitations, particularly the half-blade sections used here, because only a slice through the structure at that small region is represented accurately. The structure and especially the surface treatment may differ over the whole length of a sword blade. For curatorial reasons, however, it would be unreasonable to use more or larger samples and radiography provides some indication of macro-scale differences in structure and composition. The micro-sections identify plain central layers in SN1021 and SN1023, and a composite central layer in SN1019, a possible one in SN1020 and none in SN1022.

Sources

The iron ores which were extracted in antiquity included the various iron oxides (limonite, haematite, goethite, magnetite), carbonates (siderite) and possibly some weathered marcasite nodules found in chalk (Tylecote and Clough 1983). Bog iron ores (sedimentary deposits of iron hydroxides and limonite, frequently containing phosphorus and manganese) and nodules were widely available in small quantities and readily exploitable. Bog ores have the advantage that they regenerate and can be 'harvested' again after 20 to 30 years (www.mcvsd.org). Tylecote (1986, 124–5) lists the composition of examples of excavated iron ores from British sources. An interesting account, by Evenstad (1968), of extracting iron from bog sources in eighteenth-century Norway describes the characteristics of the bog ores to be found and their transformation into iron using charcoal (with coal) and a simple furnace, sited close to the ore source. Evenstad also recounts using mixtures of different bog ores to make ductile iron. The analyses given in Table 6.7 in this report suggest that bog ore, usually rich in phosphorus and manganese (Buchwald 2005, 135) provided at least some of the metal for the Buckland swords, although it is not available locally.

Producing the iron

Iron was produced in hand-blown (or possibly natural draft) furnaces by heating and reducing the iron ores with charcoal so that the gangue or waste materials were removed

	Total no inclusions	No MnO inclusions	No inclusions MnO>0.5%
Grave 264 (1019) edge sector	9	5	5
Grave 264 (1019) central sector	59	41	35
Grave 265B (1020) edge sector	23	16	16
Grave 265B (1020) central sector	80	44	29
Grave 346 (1021) edge sector	12	11	11
Grave 346 (1021) central sector	39	28	25
Grave 375 (1022) edge sector	28	18	17
Grave 375 (1022) central sector	28	6	3
Grave 437A (1023) edge sector	25	8	7
Grave 437A (1023) central sector	35	26	19

Table 6.3. Buckland 1994 swords: proportion of inclusions with manganese oxide contents of more than 5 per cent.

as a liquid slag at about 1200°C (Paynter 2007), leaving a somewhat porous and heterogeneous lump of iron, known as a bloom. The processes have been described by (amongst others) Tylecote (1986) Pleiner (2000) and summarised by Dungworth (2011). The different methods of furnace design and operating the extraction processes have been widely discussed by archaeometallurgists (eg Tylecote 1962; 1976; 1986; Craddock 1995, Pleiner 2000 and Dillmann *et al* 2003, 2007). Smelting and smithing experiments have been carried out by Crew and others (Crew 1991; 1998; Crew and Crew 1990; 1997; Crew and Salter 1991; 1993; Serneels and Crew 1997; Crew and Charlton 2007).

The metal might also contain up to 0.8 per cent carbon or more (Tylecote 1986, 169; Gassman 1998; Pleiner 2000; Salter and Crew 2003). Buchwald (2005,166) demonstrated the heterogeneity of a bloom by cutting a series of sections through it, showing phosphorus-rich ferritic iron at one end and pearlitic steel (0.3 per cent to 0.7 per cent C) with phosphorus-rich inclusions at the other.

Materials other than iron are acquired from the ore, fuel, furnace lining and flux, if used. Some elements, such as copper, nickel and cobalt are reduced into the metal, while potassium, sodium, calcium and magnesium always pass into the slag as oxides. Another group of elements may be found in both the metal and the slag (arsenic, phosphorus, manganese, sulphur and silicon), depending on the smelting conditions. Of these, manganese only enters the metal at higher temperatures, so the presence of manganese in the metal provides a useful identifier for high temperature extraction (eg blast furnace) (Starley 1999). Some compounds, such as magnesia, alumina, silica or lime (MgO, Al_2O_3 SiO_2, CaO) are not reduced in the furnace and are termed 'non reduced compounds' (NRCs), although they are essential for the extraction processes.

Blooms contain cavities, entrapped slag, oxides, charcoal and fragmentary material acquired during extraction, so the metal is consolidated and impurities removed by heating to bright yellow heat *c* 1100°C in a blacksmith's hearth and then forging it. The slag melts and is expelled, porosities and cavities are welded up and some homogenisation takes place. The blooms might be smithed more or less complete or they might be heated, broken up and harder or more ductile pieces separated. Using smaller pieces can make the smithing process quicker and more effective (Sim1998). The metal could be used directly to make artefacts, or be consolidated into ingots or currency bars for trade or storage. During smithing, impurities can also be introduced from the fuel, flux and hearth linings (Crew 1998, Blakelock *et al* 2009). Crew (1991) has considered the resources required to make bars (similar to currency bars) from ore and has also shown that the processes result in considerable metal loss as oxide.

Analysis: inclusions

In a finished artefact, such as a sword, inclusions are almost invariably present. Apart from small differences caused by human operational decisions (Rehren *et al* 2007, Blakelock *et al* 2009), the inclusion compositions within a single piece of metal can be very varied, because small differences occur in gas composition and temperature in the furnace, resulting in very local differences in equilibria affecting the inclusion composition (Buchwald 2005,162).

It is therefore problematical to try to use slag inclusions to provenance the ore source unless the chemical signature is unusual. In any case, ores may have been mixed in making a single bloom. Blakelock *et al* (2009) comment that iron blooms from the same smelter, worked by smiths using different fuels, would produce different inclusion compositions. Studies devoted to slag and inclusion analysis are very numerous: Morton and Wingrove (1969); Hedges and Salter (1979); Todd and Charles (1977); McDonnell (1991; 2000); Gordon (1997); Buchwald and Wivel (1998); Starley (1999); Whiteman and Okafor (2003); Kronz (2003); Paynter (2006; 2007) and Blakelock *et al* (2009), are some of many. Desaulty *et al* (2009) showed that it was possible to find a chemical signature for an archaeological iron making site using selected ratios of rare earth elements (REE).

Slags with similar compositions are produced using similar materials and conditions. The ratios of non-reduced compounds (eg MgO, Al_2O_3 SiO_2, CaO) can be used to characterise these 'smelting systems' (Paynter 2006; Dillman and L'Héritier 2007; Blakelock *et al* 2009). These ratios are best used when ores, slag and metal remains are available, which is not possible here. Facilities for in-depth trace analysis

Specimen no	Location	MgO	Al$_2$O$_3$	SiO$_2$	P$_2$O$_5$	SO$_3$	K$_2$O	CaO	TiO$_2$	MnO	FeO	V$_2$O$_5$	Cr$_2$O$_3$	CoO	NiO	As$_2$O$_3$	BaO
1019	Rib inclusions	0.68	12.01	46.86	1.43	0.05	1.46	3.19	0.54	0.79	32.22			0.02	0.02		
1020	Rib inclusions	1.22	24.66	30.45	0.62	0.01	1.34	2.19	0.33	0.33	36.04	0.09	0.19	0.01	0.03	0.26	
1021	Rib inclusions	0.54	4.74	20.84	3.37	0.11	0.93	1.33	0.23	1.38	65.17	0.01	0.13	0.01	0.02	0.03	0.05
1022	Rib inclusions	0.54	2.89	21.59	6.67	0.18	1.16	2.77	0.20	0.07	63.05			0.01			
1023	Rib inclusions	0.37	5.65	33.46	1.35	0.12	0.85	2.41	0.33	0.46	53.31			0.10	0.01		
1019	Rib body metal	0.19	0.24	0.64	0.55		0.03	0.06	0.01	0.01	96.88			0.01	0.16	0.02	
1020	Rib body metal	0.04		0.02	0.37						98.86			0.03	0.04		0.01
1021	Rib body metal	0.34		0.02	0.18						97.77			0.01	0.13	0.37	
1022	Rib body metal	0.08	0.01		0.27			0.01			98.26	0.01		0.07			
1023	Rib body metal	0.05	0.02	0.06	0.04						98.38						
1019	Edge inclusions	0.68	10.68	55.72	1.23	0.05	1.44	4.45	0.65	0.94	23.33			0.07			
1020	Edge inclusions	0.33	10.16	33.58	1.34	0.26	0.99	3.39	0.48	1.38	47.16			0.02	0.01		
1021	Edge inclusions	0.84	10.05	33.05	2.57		2.34	4.04	0.41	4.31	39.29	0.13	0.04			0.11	0.49
1022	Edge inclusions	0.81	2.20	47.21	0.95		1.18	2.37	0.15	3.67	44.07		0.01	0.06			
1023	Edge inclusions	0.35	3.20	40.96	2.62	0.04	1.35	3.07	0.16	0.22	46.74			0.08			
1019	Edge body metal	0.28		0.04							98.35				0.08		
1020	Edge body metal	0.03	0.01	0.06	0.02						98.56			0.02	0.05		0.02
1021	Edge body metal	0.21									96.49				0.44	1.01	
1022	Edge body metal	0.07	0.03	0.04	0.28						98.22						
1023	Edge body metal	0.11	0.04		0.21	0.01					98.24		0.01	0.08	0.03		

Table 6.4. Buckland 1994 swords: averages of analyses.

Specimen no	Location	MgO	Al$_2$O$_3$	SiO$_2$	P$_2$O$_5$	SO$_3$	K$_2$O	CaO	TiO$_2$	MnO	FeO	V$_2$O$_5$	Cr$_2$O$_3$	CoO	NiO	As$_2$O$_3$	BaO
1019	Rib inclusions	0.68	12.01	46.86	1.43	0.05	1.46	3.19	0.54	0.79	32.22			0.02	0.02		
1019	Rib body metal	0.19	0.24	0.64	0.55		0.03	0.06	0.01	0.01	96.88			0.01	0.16	0.02	
1019	Edge inclusions	0.68	10.68	55.72	1.23	0.05	1.44	4.45	0.65	0.94	23.33			0.07			
1019	Edge body metal	0.28		0.04							98.35				0.08		
1020	Rib inclusions	1.22	24.66	30.45	0.62	0.01	1.34	2.19	0.33	0.33	36.04	0.09	0.19	0.01	0.03	0.26	
1020	Rib body metal	0.04		0.02	0.37						98.86			0.03	0.04		0.01
1020	Edge inclusions	0.33	10.16	33.58	1.34	0.26	0.99	3.39	0.48	1.38	47.16			0.02	0.01		
1020	Edge body metal	0.03	0.01	0.06	0.02						98.56			0.02	0.05		0.02
1021	Rib inclusions	0.54	4.74	20.84	3.37	0.11	0.93	1.33	0.23	1.38	65.17	0.01	0.13	0.01	0.02	0.03	0.05
1021	Rib body metal	0.34		0.02	0.18						97.77			0.01	0.13	0.37	
1021	Edge inclusions	0.84	10.05	33.05	2.57		2.34	4.04	0.41	4.31	39.29	0.13	0.04			0.11	0.49
1021	Edge body metal	0.21									96.49				0.44	1.01	
1022	Rib inclusion	0.54	2.89	21.59	6.67	0.18	1.16	2.77	0.20	0.07	63.05			0.01			
1022	Rib body metal	0.08	0.01		0.27			0.01			98.26	0.01		0.07			
1022	Edge inclusions	0.81	2.20	47.21	0.95		1.18	2.37	0.15	3.67	44.07		0.01	0.06			
1022	Edge body metal	0.07	0.03	0.04	0.28						98.22						
1023	Rib inclusions	0.37	5.65	33.46	1.35	0.12	0.85	2.41	0.33	0..46	53.31			0.10	0.01	0.01	0.01
1023	Rib body metal	0.05	0.02	0.06	0.04	0.01					98.38				0.02		
1023	Edge inclusions	0.35	3.20	40.96	2.62	0.04	1.36	3.07	0.16	0.22	46.74			0.08			
1023	Edge body metal	0.11	0.04		0.21	0.01					98.24		0.01	0.02	0.03		

Table 6.5. Buckland 1994 swords: comparison of analysis of inclusions and body metal in sectors.

(eg REE analysis) were not available for the present study either, but it seemed reasonable to compare the analyses of the body metal and inclusions of the different components to see if there were clear similarities or variations between them. This proved to be rather problematic, especially with the inclusions, because, apart the possibility of micro differences within the furnace, as mentioned above, the inclusions are sometimes small, few in number, or clearly derived from the break-up of a single larger inclusion or associated with a weld.

Some of the blades contained low but detectable amounts of one or more of the elements arsenic, nickel, barium, chromium, cobalt and vanadium. Where this occurred, the fact that several components contained trace amounts, suggested that their metal came from the same ore source and possibly even the same smelt. There did not seem to be sufficient trace element similarities between the swords, however, to suggest a shared primary source. A summary of the analyses of the inclusions and body metal are given in Table 6.7 and the average values in Tables 6.4–6.6.

Manganese was only present in the inclusions, as the reaction temperatures were not high enough for it to be reduced into the iron. The presence of manganese oxide (MnO) (and iron oxide) in the slags indicates relatively low melting points (Crew and Charlton 2007). Manganese passes into the slag, substituting for some of the iron and combining with silica, thus making the reduction of iron and its carburisation easier according to Pleiner (2000, 136), although Dillmann *et al* (2003) have expressed some doubts on a link between manganese and carburisation. McDonnell (1988) has suggested that the main distinction to be made between extraction and smithing slag is the presence of more than 0.5 per cent MnO in the extraction slags, because manganese minerals are not found in refractories, fuel or flux in greater quantities, although there is some evidence for manganese mineral being used as flux in the Migration Period (Joosten *et al* 1996). Up to 0.5 per cent MnO may come from fuel ash, beech being especially rich in the element (Evans and Tylecote 1967).

The number of inclusions with manganese oxide contents of more than 0.5 per cent MnO are shown in Table 6.3. The number of inclusions in both sectors of SN 1021 with more than 0.5 per cent MnO is high, suggesting a manganese-rich source. Different ore sources may be indicated for the central and edge sectors of 1022 (the latter is manganese-rich, the former low in manganese), although it could simply be a result of the central section being more extensively smithed (see below). Both sectors of SN 1019 have virtually identical proportions of manganese-rich inclusions, indicating perhaps that the same types of ore were used. SN 1020 shows the same trend. The negative correlation between manganese and phosphorus in the

Anglo-Saxon knives from Cannington found by McDonnell (2000) was not present in the Buckland swords: presumably different types of ore were used.

Table 6.4 gives the average contents and shows that the potassium content of the inclusions for all the swords is fairly similar (average K_2O is less than 2 per cent, except for SN 1021). Lime (CaO) contents lie between 4.5 per cent and 0.2 per cent, while the alumina varies between 3 per cent and 25 per cent. Generally, the results do not differ greatly from those of Hedges and Salter (1979) for inclusions in currency bars.

Table 6.5 compares the differences for the average values of the inclusion and body metal analyses in the sectors for all the swords, showing that there are no major differences except that the alumina contents of SN 1019 and SN 1020 are noticeably higher than in the other swords, especially in the central sectors. This suggests different smelting systems.

Table 6.6 contrasts the analysis of the central and edge sectors for each sword. The higher average values for the inclusions are summarised below:

Al_2O_3 CR (central sector except SN 1021)
SiO_2 CE (edge sector)
P_2O_5 CR (SN 1019, SN 1021, SN 1022), CE (SN 1020, SN 1023)
K_2O CR (SN 1020), E (SN 1021, SN 1023), little difference (SN 1019, SN 1022)
CaO CE (except SN 1022)
MnO CE (except SN 1023)

This also shows that there is little difference throughout in the potassium content, while the lime, manganese and silica slag contents are generally higher in the cutting-edges. Apart from SN 1020 and SN 1023, the phosphorus content is generally higher in the body metal and the inclusions of the central sectors. The distribution maps show that phosphorus is distributed widely but more diffusely in the central sectors, which is reflected in the radiographs as both have less easily distinguished patterns. The tendency for phosphorus-rich inclusions to be found in phosphoric iron (McDonnell 2000) was not observed to be strictly the case in the Buckland swords. For most of the sections, there is a wide variation in the alumina content and its distribution, more being found in the central sectors.

The differences (generally higher per cent weights of the minor elements in the edge sector) between the central and edge sector inclusions (noted in Table 6.6) might result from the use of different batches of metal, but as it seems to be a consistent feature, it might be attributable to the fact

Specimen no	Location	MgO	Al$_2$O$_3$	SiO$_2$	P$_2$O$_5$	SO$_3$	K$_2$O	CaO	TiO$_2$	MnO	FeO	V$_2$O$_5$	Cr$_2$O$_3$	CoO	NiO	As$_2$O$_3$	BaO
1019	Rib	0.68	12.01	48.86	1.43	0.05	1.46	3.19	0.54	0.79	32.22			0.02	0.02		
1019	Edge	0.68	10.68	55.72	1.23	0.05	1.44	4.45	0.65	0.94	23.33			0.07			
1020	Rib	1.22	24.66	30.45	0.62	0.01	1.34	2.19	0.33	0.33	36.04	0.09	0.19	0.01	0.03	0.26	
1020	Edge	0.33	10.16	33.58	1.34	0.26	0.99	3.39	0.48	1.38	47.16			0.02	0.01		
1021	Rib	0.54	4.74	20.84	3.37	0.11	0.93	1.33	0.23	1.38	66.17	0.01	0.13	0.01	0.02	0.03	0.05
1021	Edge	0.84	10.05	33.05	2.57		2.34	4.04	0.41	4.31	39.29	0.13	0.04			0.11	0.49
1022	Rib	0.54	2.89	21.59	6.67	0.18	1.16	2.77	0.20	0.07	63.05			0.01			
1022	Edge	0.81	2.20	47.21	0.95		1.18	2.37	0.15	3.67	44.07		0.01	0.06			
1023	Rib	0.37	5.65	33.46	1.35	0.12	0.85	2.41	0.33	0.46	77.31			0.10	0.01	0.01	0.01
1023	Edge	0.35	3.2	40.96	2.62	0.04	1.36	3.07	0.16	0.22	46.74			0.08			

Table 6.6. Buckland 1994 swords: comparisons of inclusion analyses in rib and edge sectors.

that the metal in the central sector had been subjected to more extensive working, first to form strips, then welded to make the composites, forged and then welded to make the blade: perhaps a higher proportion of the gangue minerals from the initial processes was eliminated as slag. This would mean that the majority of the remaining inclusions are relicts of the initial extraction process rather than subsequent smithing processes. Hedges and Salter (1979) suggested that because the most heavily worked currency bars in their study contained fewer, smaller inclusions than those which were less worked, material had been lost during the smithing process rather than being added, which accords well with the results in the present study, except for the alumina content. This is higher in all the central section inclusions (except SN 1021 which is anomalous, in any case). According to Blakelock *et al* (2009), smithing introduces material from the hearth and flux. As the metal usually contains siliceous inclusions flux is not always used and as the metal is in a solid, consolidated form, additions could only be acquired at the surfaces, by dissolution in the iron or by absorption. The sword with the least inclusions (Grave 264) is the most likely to have been fluxed, perhaps the others were self-fluxing during welding. The alumina may come from the lining of the smithing hearth. It is difficult to envisage any other process to account for its presence, unless, of course, it was associated with the phosphorus-rich ore (potassium and calcium may be found in clays but there is no significant relationship between CaO or K$_2$O and Al$_2$O$_3$ here; the clay mineral might be the alumino-silicate kaolinite, however). It is probable, of course, that phosphoric and carbon-iron bars were being made by different workers, using different extraction regimes.

Silica, aluminium, potassium, manganese, calcium and phosphorus may come from fuel ash or ores. Fuel ashes vary considerably in composition, because of the diversity of materials which may be used (from plants and wood to animal dung), and each of these is by no means constant in composition, as this depends partly on where and from what the nutrients were obtained. The compositions of a number of fuels which demonstrate these variations have been listed by Sanderson and Hunter (1981) and Tylecote (1986). The latter showed that most of the peat, wood and leaf ash contents included 10–20 per cent calcium (lime, CaO) and the fuel used in Blakelock's experiments contained 22.1 per cent K$_2$O and 58.9 per cent CaO (2009). The calcium (lime) content of the inclusions in the Buckland swords sections is less than 5 per cent, which suggests that the ash contribution may not have been very large.

Analysis: metal: iron, carbon, phosphorus

Three types of ferrous metal were selected to make the swords: low carbon iron, phosphoric iron and steel (up to 0.8 per cent C). The first two were present in all the Buckland sword sections. Steel was absent in the sections SN 1020 and SN 1021. We have no evidence to suggest how the metal was chosen, but it is clear from the structures that some, if not all, smiths were capable of discriminating between these alloys. Thålin Bergman noted the capacity of contemporary Swedish smiths to select effectively (Thålin Bergman and Arrhenius 2005, 79) and Gilmour, likewise Anglo-Saxon smiths (2007; 2010). Evenstad's much later description of choosing the appropriate bog ore on the basis of colour, structure, association and even taste is instructive (Evenstad

Position	Material	Layer	Twist	Strip	No an	MgO	Al2O3	SiO2	P2O5	SO3	K2O	CaO	TiO2	MnO	FeO	V2O5	CoO	NiO	As2O3
e	m				6	0.3									98.3			0.1	
e	inc				9	0.7	10.7	55.7	1.2		1.4	4.5	0.6	0.9	23.3		0.1		
r	m	L	1	1	1				1.6						97.7				
r	m	L	1	2	5	0.2									98.3			0.2	
r	inc	L	1	2	3	0.9	17.1	50.9	0.5		2.8	5.2	0.6	0.9	20.3				
r	m	L	1	3	2				1.2						97.7				
r	inc	L	1	3	1	1.5	9.9	56.8	3.9		2.0	4.8	0.9	2.3	16.4	0.3			
r	m	L	1	4	1										97.7				
r	inc	L	1	4	3	0.8	25.4	46.2		0.2	1.4	3.6	0.6	0.7	19.9				
r	m	L	1	5	1				0.5						96.9				
r	m	L	2		3	0.6									98.1				
r	inc	L	2		9	0.8	19.8	62.7			2.3	6.0	1.0	1.0	5.8				
r	m	L	3	1	1				0.6						97.0				
r	m	L	3	3	1				0.5						98.9				
r	inc	L	3	3	1	1.0	19.8	59.5			2.3	6.3	1.0	2.7	7.4				
r	m	L	3	4	1				1.5						97.9				
r	inc	L	3	4	1		3.2	89.9			0.4	1.3	0.6	0.4	3.4				
r	m	L	3	5	1				0.6						97.6			0.5	0.3
r	m	L	5	3	2	0.2			0.2						98.5				
r	m	L	5	4	2	0.5			0.8						97.5		0.1	0.1	
r	inc	L	5	4	2	0.6	4.5	51.5	2.0		2.5	1.3	0.2	0.2	36.2		0.2		
r	m	L	5	5	5	0.5	0.1		0.6						97.4				
r	inc	L	5	5	2	0.2	6.3	44.0	8.8		2.0	2.5	0.2	0.1	35.1				
r	m	L	1	2	1										96.8		0.7		
r	inc	L	1	2	1	0.6	6.0	25.2	1.7		0.4		0.5		64.4				
r	m	M		1	4	0.2		0.1	0.1						98.5			0.2	
r	inc	M		1	6	0.5	5.0	28.8	1.3	0.1	0.9	2.2	0.2	0.3	59.5			0.1	
r	m	M		2	3	0.1		0.1	0.7						97.7			0.1	
r	inc	M		2	2	0.6	5.8	22.0	6.2	0.3	0.8	0.9	0.2	0.4	61.1			0.1	
r	m	M		3	2	0.2			0.5						98.3				
r	m	M		4	2	0.5			2.2					0.1	96.9			0.1	
r	inc	M		4	1	1.3	12.2	59.6	2.0		1.8	4.2	0.6	2.0	16.9				
r	m	M		5	3				0.5						98.0			0.1	
r	m	M		6	3			0.1	1.2						97.7			0.1	
r	inc	M		6	1	1.0	7.4	35.5	14.8	0.5	1.2	3.6	0.6	3.6	31.6				
r	m	M		7	8	0.1			0.2						97.6			0.6	0.1
r	inc	M		7	10	0.7	9.4	44.4	1.3	0.1	1.1	3.1	0.4	0.6	38.2				
r	m	U	1	4	3				0.8						97.4			0.1	
r	inc	U	1	4	1	0.7	10.8	61.9			2.0	2.8	0.7	0.8	19.9				
r	m	U	1	5	1										99.4				
r	m	U	2		1										98.7				
r	inc	U	2		10	0.8	14.7	55.4	0.3		1.1	3.0	0.7	1.2	22.2				
r	m	U	3	1	1	0.4			1.3						97.0			0.3	
r	m	U	3	3	1				1.6						97.6				
r	m	U	3	4	1				1.7						97.0				
r	inc	U	3	4	2	0.6	10.9	74.2	0.5		1.3	3.3	0.5	1.0	7.5				
r	inc	U	4		1	0.8	31.5	58.2			1.7	4.4	1.4	0.3	1.3				

Table 6.7a. Sword from Grave 264: summary SEM-EDXA results (average values) (SN 1019) sword section (Cr2O3, BaO not quantifiable). Key: (see Fig 6.1) r = central rib sector; e = cutting-edge sector; m = metal; inc = inclusion; L = lower layer; M = middle layer; U = upper layer; No an = number of analyses.

1968). Breaking up the bloom, as he describes, would also make it possible to select the appropriate lumps from what is often a very inhomogeneous whole, by appearance, scratching, resistance to hammering or cutting, treating with the etching acid or other simple tests. Similar processes may have been used from the Iron Age onwards. Certainly, modern blacksmiths also distinguish effectively between different iron bars by observation and simple tests (sound and rebound when dropped on a stone floor, filing etc). As carbon-rich areas are well attested in blooms (Tylecote 1986, 169; Gassman 1998; Pleiner 2000; Salter and Crew 2003; Buchwald 2005), it is very likely that this source of steel was utilised from the Iron Age onwards. Cast iron has been found at a number of sites, also from the Iron Age (see Tylecote 1986, 167) and later, for example the late Roman and early medieval sites at Ponte di Val Gabbia near Bienno, northern Italy where there is evidence that cast iron was being made and decarburised to make steel (Fluzin 1999; Mack *et al* (2000) suggested that steel was produced from cast iron in Saxon Southampton, but Salter and Crew (2003) consider that Iron Age, Roman and post-Roman steel generally came from bloomery iron rather than cast iron. Both may have been used contemporaneously, in different places. In the eighteenth century Evenstad (1968) describes making steel blooms from rich bog ores in a small air-blown furnace.

The carbon content varies between approximately 0.1 per cent and 0.8 per cent carbon (or possibly slightly more) while phosphorus varies between negligible and approximately 2 per cent.

The body metal analyses and the elemental distribution maps show that the central sectors consist of alternating strips of phosphoric iron and low-carbon iron, confirming that the construction of the patterned panels follows the methods which have been identified in a number of studies (eg Tylecote and Gilmour 1986; Thomsen 1994; Gilmour 1996). The body metal of the strips contains traces of other elements which do not appear to be in any way out of the ordinary. The construction of the sword from Grave 346 (SN 1021), however, shows some unusual features and is discussed below.

Phosphorus-rich iron seems to have been used from the Iron Age like carbon-rich iron, ie as a hardened iron, both in tool-making (Ehrenreich 1986; Pleiner 1982), and also on the Continent to make swords (Pleiner 1993). There are many examples of late Romano-Barbarian pattern-welded blades with phosphorus-rich layers alternating with steel (eg Tylecote and Gilmour 1986; Ottaway 1992). Thomsen (1966) concluded that a piece of phosphoric iron was deliberately chosen to make the cutting-edge of a Danish Migration Period axe. The reasons for using phosphoric iron and low

carbon iron for the patterned panels probably have to do with their availability, the appearance of the blade when it was finished and the properties of the two materials. Using strips of different composition would ensure that the pattern is easily visible after polishing and etching. On etching, the low carbon strips darken and the phosphoric iron remains white and shiny, thus revealing the pattern. Phosphorus may remain as iron phosphide, even when the metal has corroded completely (see Fig 6.5.3): this may contribute to the visibility of patterns in completely corroded swords which can be seen on radiographs.

It has been suggested that iron containing phosphorus cannot be carburised or welded (Rolsch and Kuhm 1976), but this is clearly not the case. Crew and Salter (1993) have stated that an experimental bar with a high phosphorus content and up to 0.7 per cent carbon could be smithed and welded without difficulty. Apart from being relatively hard, phosphorus-rich iron may be more easily weldable because the melting point is lowered by phosphorus. This may explain the use of alternating phosphoric and wrought iron sheet or strips (0.7 per cent P and 0.06 per cent P, respectively) to weld Roman iron glass-blowing tubes (Lang and Price 1975). Rollason (1973) mentions that one of the advantages of phosphorus being present is that it assists fire welding.

Hardness tests on the pattern-welded panels suggest that there is little difference in the hardness values between the phosphoric iron and the low carbon strips which would ensure that the surfaces resisted scratching and wear equally. Without carrying out mechanical tests it is difficult to judge how the response to deformation would be affected. From the extensive use of the combination in antiquity, it is unlikely that noticeably deleterious effects were experienced. The effects of the use of phosphorus have been discussed in a number of studies, eg Ehrenreich (1986), Piaskowski (1989) and Vizcaino *et al* (1998). 'Ghosting' has been investigated by Stewart *et al* (2000). Nowadays phosphorus is always avoided, as it causes *temper brittleness* by segregating at the grain boundaries during heating in the range 375–575° C, or if the metal is slowly cooled through this range (Samuels 1980, 379–80). Presumably, in antiquity blades were normally cooled quite quickly (in air) at these temperatures, and so phosphorus was not a problem. Also work by Hopkins and Tipler (1958) has shown that carbon (frequently present in the phosphorus-rich areas of the swords) has an ameliorating effect on embrittlement. According to Gordon (1984), up to 0.2 per cent phosphorus can be tolerated in wrought iron before the metal becomes *cold short* with a loss of strength. This means that the metal cannot be cold worked (ie below

100°C), which is probably not a problem for a sword which would normally be forged above this temperature. However, Godfrey *et al* (2005) state that ancient smiths could cold work phosphoric iron and that it is easier to forge than P-free iron above 900° C. Goodway and Fisher (1988) have pointed out that phosphorus does not make low carbon iron (less than 0.1 per cent C) cold short, but can have a

strengthening effect. Segregation of carbon to form graphite can occur, according to Kronz (2003).

Iron, nickel, arsenic

Traces of nickel, arsenic, vanadium, chromium, cobalt and barium were also found. All these elements were below 1

Position	Material	Layer	Twist	Strip	No an	MgO	Al2O3	SiO2	P2O5	SO3	K2O	CaO	TiO2	MnO	FeO	Cr2O3	V2O5	CoO	NiO	As2O5	BaO
e	m				21			0.1							98.6						
e	inc				23	0.3	10.2	33.6	1.3	0.3	1.0	3.4	0.5	1.4	47.2						
r	m	L	1	1	1				0.4						99.5						
r	m	L	1	2	1										99.9						
r	m	L	1	4	1										99.5						
r	m	L	1	5	3		0.1		0.4						98.7						
r	m	L	1	6	1	0.4			0.8						97.9						
r	m	L	2	2	3				0.1						98.3				0.3		
r	m	L	2	3	1										99.5						
r	m	L	2	4	1				0.5						99.5						
r	m	L	2	5	2				0.0						99.5						
r	m	L	2	6	7			0.1	0.4						99.2						0.1
r	m	L	2	7	4				0.3						99.5						
r	m	L	2	8	8	0.1		0.1	0.7						98.8						
r	inc	L	1	1	3	0.3	21.2	19.8	0.7		0.8	1.5	0.3	0.1	53.2	0.2	0.4	0.2		0.5	
r	inc	L	1	2	2	0.2	2.9	29.5	2.5		1.5	2.1		0.2	60.0				0.1		
r	inc	L	1	3	2	0.8	11.8	65.9	0.9	0.1	2.3	2.8	0.6	0.2	13.8	0.1					
r	inc	L	1	4	3	3.1	37.0	32.6	0.6		1.2	2.8	0.3	0.8	19.7	0.5	0.7				
r	inc	L	1	5	1	1.3	55.3								38.7	0.8	0.9			1.6	
r	inc	L	1	6	1	1.0	12.8	69.7			4.7	6.3	0.7	0.5	3.4						
r	inc	L	2	1	2	1.0	12.3	69.3			4.9	6.2	0.8	0.4	4.3						
r	inc	L	2	2	8	0.3	4.2	25.5	0.5		1.0	1.4	0.2	0.1	60.5				0.1		
r	inc	L	2	3	2	1.0	9.7	69.2			6.0	6.2	0.7	0.6	5.7						
r	inc	L	2	4	6	2.1	43.7	33.5	0.3	0.1	1.0	2.1	0.2	0.5	15.5					0.3	
r	inc	L	2	5	2	1.1	8.5	73.3			3.4	8.3	0.6	0.5	3.5						
r	inc	L	2	6	11	1.3	47.0	23.1	0.6		0.7	1.7	0.4	0.3	23.0	0.3	0.4			0.7	
r	inc	L	2	7	5	1.1	26.1	27.9	1.1		1.3	2.5	0.5	0.1	37.1		0.5			0.3	
r	inc	L	2	8	5	1.5	13.6	56.6	0.4		1.9	4.1	0.4	0.6	19.9						
r	m	M		1	2				0.3						98.6				0.2		
r	inc	M		1	6	0.6	29.7	17.1	1.0		0.8	0.9	0.1	0.2	47.4		0.5		0.1	0.5	
r	m	M		2	7	0.1			0.4						98.7			0.1			
r	inc	M		2	4	0.6	19.2	1.5	0.2	0.1	0.1	0.3	0.2		76.0	0.1				0.4	
r	m	M		3	1										98.3						
r	inc	M		3	1		1.6	4.3	1.1			1.0	0.6		90.5						
r	m	U	1	1	1				0.4						99.2						
r	m	U	1	2	5	0.1			0.6						98.3				0.1	0.1	
r	m	U	1	3	3				0.2						98.9						
r	m	U	1	5	2										98.8				0.2		
r	m	U	1	6	3	0.1			0.3						98.1			0.2	0.1		
r	inc	U	1	2	4	0.7	7.4	47.6	1.1		1.7	2.1	0.2	0.3	32.2				0.2		
r	inc	U	1	3	4	0.8	34.4	27.5	1.0		2.0	2.3	0.2	0.3	23.7						
r	inc	U	1	4	5	2.2	24.3	14.5	0.4		0.4	0.7	0.3	0.4	54.9	0.1	0.4			0.6	
r	inc	U	1	5	2	6.4	51.1	26.8			0.8	2.0	0.2	1.1	10.6	0.4					
r	inc	U	1	6	1	1.6	26.9	52.9			2.0	3.3	0.5	0.5	11.3						

Table 6.7b. Sword from Grave 265B: summary SEM-EDXA results (average values) (SN 1020) sword section.

Position	Material	Layer	Twist	Strip	No an	MgO	Al2O3	SiO2	P2O5	SO3	K2O	CaO	TiO2	MnO	FeO	Cr2O3	V2O5	CoO	NiO	As2O5	BaO
e	m		4		4	0.2									96.5				0.4	1.0	
e	inc		12		12	0.8	10.0	33.0	2.6		2.3	4.0	0.4	4.3	39.3	0.1			0.1		0.1
r	inc	L	1	4	3	0.5	3.9	13.8	0.3	0.7	0.5	0.8	0.2	1.1	75.9				0.2		
r	m	U	2	4	4	0.3			0.1						98.2				0.2	0.3	
r	m	L	2	2	1										95.4				0.7	2.3	
r	m	L	2	11	3			0.1							95.9			0.2	1.1	2.6	
r	inc	L	1	2	1	0.7	6.2	25.7	10.5		0.3	5.2	0.3	3.1	45.9		0.3				
r	m	L	1	3	1	0.4									98.0						
r	m	L	2	1	1	0.6									98.8						
r	inc	L	2	5	1	0.5		0.5	0.5	1.8					95.7						
r	m	L	2	6	3										98.3						
r	m	L	2	9	3	0.7		0.1	1.0						96.3						
r	inc	L	2	10	1	0.7	9.8	31.8	13.4		1.6	5.5	0.4	3.7	30.7						
r	m	L	2	10	7	0.4			0.1						98.0						
r	inc	L	2	11	3	0.5	6.6	17.7	0.1		1.4	2.2		1.0	68.6						
r	inc	M			23	0.5	4.1	20.7	3.5		0.9	1.1	0.2	1.3	66.8				0.1	0.2	
r	m	M			17	0.4			0.2						97.9				0.2	0.1	
r	m	U	2	2	3	0.7			0.2						97.4						
r	inc	U	2	3	1	0.4	1.6	4.7	0.4			0.3		0.7	90.7						16.6
r	inc	U	2	4	2	0.8	9.3	24.1	3.8		0.6	1.2	0.8	2.3	53.3						
r	m	U	2	5		0.7			3.6		2.1	1.6	0.4	2.3	39.3						
r	m	U	2	5	2				0.4						99.5						
r	inc	U	2	7	1		4.2	26.7	7.1		1.3	0.5			57.9						
r	m	U	2	7	2										99.5						

Table 6.7c. Sword from Grave 346: summary SEM-EDXA results (average values) (SN 1021) sword section.

per cent except in SN 1021. The sword found in Grave 346 (SN 1021) shows unusual features; it contains significant quantities of nickel (1–2 per cent) and arsenic (1–4 per cent), as well as phosphorus (Fig 6.9) in the welds. An Anglo-Saxon sword from Lowbury Hill, Berkshire with phosphorus with arsenic and nickel in the welds is another example (Salter 2004) and Gilmour (2010) noted weld boundaries enriched in arsenic, nickel and cobalt in one of the Saltwood swords. The presence of arsenic in blades from elsewhere has been noted and discussed by Rosenqvist (1968), Tylecote and Thomsen (1973) and Tylecote (1976; 1990). Nickel has been studied by Piaskowski (1960; 1961) and Hermelin *et al* (1979). Segebade (1996) has reported both elements on two tenth-century AD swords found in the Rhine. Navasaitis *et al* (2010) have studied trace elements (including arsenic, nickel, cobalt and phosphorus) in the bloomery products of Lithuanian bog ores. They found that because the oxides of these elements are more readily reduced by carbon than iron, they became concentrated in the iron in the bloom. Arsenic, cobalt and nickel also concentrated in welds. Suzuki and Yangihera (2002) have also shown that when iron containing nickel is oxidised, the surface layer below the oxide becomes enriched in nickel, which is evidently what happened at the welds in SN 1021.

Sources of nickel are also magmatic sulphide ores containing pentlandite (Ni,Fe)S (almost always with copper pyrites); weathering products from the hydrous Ni-Mg-silicate, garnerite or the iron rich deposit laterite; hydrothermal veins with nickel as sulphides and arsenides.

Arsenic may also come from ferruginous gossans. Both elements can occur together, in marcasite nodules or as the hydrothermal minerals niccolite (NiAs), found in Saxony and rammelsbergite $(NiAs_2)$ found in small deposits in Germany, France, Austria and Switzerland. Both elements can also be found in Lithuanian bog ores (Navasaitis 2010).

Arsenic and nickel produce light etching bands (as does phosphorus), usually as a result of segregation during cyclical treatments, forging and welding. During heating in air, iron is lost from the surface as iron oxide and iron can become enriched in elements such as arsenic or nickel. Arsenic in iron segregates to the surface at temperatures of 800ºC and above (Busch *et al* 1999). An arsenic enriched layer can even be used to braze iron and steel, although the bond has little strength (Kosec *et al* 1969; Tylecote and Thomsen 1973). It was also observed that arsenical iron has a remarkable facility for removing iron scale, acting somewhat like a flux.

Piaskowski (1960) examined a socketed axe from the Carpathians which had nickel-rich bands and concluded that it had been made by welding together an irregularly carburised soft steel and an iron containing 8–10 per cent nickel. This suggestion does not seem to explain the structures in the sword from Grave 346 (SN 1021), however, as they do not have the same appearance.

Rosenqvist (1968) examined several swords, including a Roman pattern-welded blade with inlaid copper alloy Victory and Mars figures and a pattern-welded sword from a fourth-century grave at Dynna, Gran in Opland. She suggested that the cutting-edge components of the inlaid sword were joined together using a welding paste or solder, containing arsenic,

cobalt and nickel and the cutting-edge of the Dynna sword was also partly welded together with a substance of a similar arsenic content. The pattern-welded centre panels appeared to have been welded with a phosphorus paste, according to Rosenqvist. The arsenic and nickel enriched joins on the mid sixth- to mid seventh-century Lowbury Hill, Berkshire sword has already been mentioned, and Gilmour (2010) found that the sword from grave 3885 at the Saltwood Tunnel presents the same unusual appearance, suggesting that the joins had been brazed. However, since spot and line analyses

Position	Material	Layer	Twist	Strip	No an	MgO	Al2O3	SiO2	P2O5	SO3	K2O	CaO	TiO2	MnO	FeO	NiO
e	m				21	0.1			0.3						98.2	
e	inc				28	0.8	2.3	48.9	1.0		1.2	2.5	0.2	3.8	42.1	0.1
r	inc	AL	1		2	0.6	4.7	25.7	10.9		2.6	7.5	0.2		46.3	
r	m	AU	1	5	1	0.2			0.9						97.7	
r	inc	AU	1	4	1	1.6	5.1	57.5	2.2	0.2	5.1	6.1	0.3		20.7	
r	m	L	1	4	2				0.2						97.7	
r	inc	L	1	4	1	0.6		27.4	3.4			0.3		0.5	66.8	
r	m	L	1	5	3	0.1			0.7						97.9	
r	inc	L	1	5	1		6.3	25.9	13.1		2.3	2.2			49.5	
r	m	L	1	6	2	0.2			0.5						98.5	
r	inc	L	1	6	1		6.1	21.5	20.2	0.8	0.9	2.5	0.5	0.4	46.4	
r	inc	L	1	9	2	0.8	7.9	26.5	8.5	1.1	2.4	5.1	1.2		44.9	
r	inc	L	1	10	1	0.5	5.8	19.6	10.3	0.5	1.2	2.4	0.4	0.4	57.7	
r	inc	L	2	8	1	0.4	0.7								98.0	
r	m	L	2	9	1	0.4			0.5						98.2	
r	inc	L	2	9	1		0.5								97.4	
r	m	L	2	10	1										98.8	
r	inc	L	2	10	3	0.6	2.5	28.7	7.8		1.4	5.2	0.1		52.4	
r	inc	L	2	11	1	0.4	6.7	20.2	9.5	2.5	1.2	1.7	0.9	0.5	96.1	
r	m	L	2	12	1				1.2						96.5	
r	inc	L	2	12	3	0.3	3.9	27.7	11.5		0.8	1.5	0.2		52.5	
r	m	L	2	13	1										98.8	
r	inc	L	2	13	3	0.4	4.1	28.0	5.3	0.2	1.0	1.0	0.1	0.1	58.1	
r	m	L	2	14	1										97.8	0.5
r	inc	U	1	12	2	0.4	4.7	24.2	9.8		3.9	7.3	0.1		48.1	
r	m	U	2	1	1				0.4						97.9	
r	inc	U	2	1	1	0.3	0.5	7.9	0.5		0.1	0.2	0.4		88.9	
r	inc	U	2	2	2	1.1	0.8	28.4	2.7		0.6	1.6	0.3		63.4	
r	m	U	2	3	2		0.2		0.3						98.1	
r	m	U	2	4	1										98.7	
j	m	U	2	5	1				0.8						97.7	
r	m	U	2	6	1				0.5						98.9	
r	inc	U	2	6	1	1.1		30.6	1.3		0.2	0.5			64.6	
r	m	U	2	11	1										98.8	
r	inc	U	2	11	1	1.6		31.6							64.8	
r	m	U	2	12	1										98.8	
r	inc	U	2	12	3	0.9	3.2	28.0	16.9		1.6	7.6			40.8	
r	m	U	2	14	1				0.5						97.9	
r	inc	U	2	14	3	0.2	0.1		0.3			0.1			91.7	

Table 6.7d. Sword from Grave 375: summary SEM-EDXA results (average values) (SN 1022) sword section (Cr_2O_3, CoO, As_2O_3, BaO not quantifiable). Key: AL = lower layer beyond middle of blade; AU = upper layer beyond middle of blade.

Position	Material	Layer	Twist	Strip	No an	MgO	Al2O3	SiO2	P2O5	SO3	K2O	CaO	TiO2	MnO	FeO	CoO	NiO	BaO
e	m	L	2	1	7	0.1			0.3						98.2	0.1	0.1	
e	inc	L	2	1	4	0.2	1.1	22.9	1.5		0.6	0.9			71.7			
e	inc	L	2	2	4	0.4	0.8	69.6	0.3		0.2	1.1		0.1	27.0			
e	m	L	2	3	8	0.2	0.1		0.2						98.2	0.1		
e	inc	L	2	3	8	0.4	2.7	29.0	7.2		1.5	3.5		0.2	53.2	0.1		
e	m	U	2		5	0.1			0.4						98.1	0.1		
e	m	U	3		13	0.1	0.1		0.1						98.4	0.1		
e	inc	U	2		1	0.0	1.9	2.6	0.8	0.7	0.5	0.2			89.8	0.5		
e	inc	U	3		9	0.5	5.8	51.1	0.3		2.2	4.8	0.5	0.4	33.9			
r	inc	L	1	1	4	0.1	2.9	18.3	1.5		0.9	0.7	0.3	0.1	73.4	0.2		
r	m	L	1	2	2	0.1			0.2						98.3			
r	inc	L	1	4	1		3.5	35.6	4.6		0.8	2.1	0.4	0.5	51.5			
r	inc	L	1	5	1		1.5	24.2	6.8		0.4	0.9			63.8			
r	inc	L	1	6	1	0.4	2.2	29.9	4.9		0.6	0.9	0.4		59.5			
r	m	L	1	8	1										98.5			
r	inc	L	1		4	0.8	5.4	57.5	1.2		1.7	2.6	0.5	0.6	27.8			0.07
r	inc	L	1		4	0.3	2.3	27.9	3.2		0.7	1.1	0.2	0.2	62.4			
r	m	U	1		11										98.4			
r	inc	U	1		20	0.4	7.0	32.7	0.8	0.2	0.8	3.0	0.3	0.5	52.6	0.1		

Table 6.7e. Sword from Grave 473A: summary SEM-EDXA results (average values) (SN 1023) sword section (Cr_2O_3, As_2O_3 not quantifiable).

of SN 1021 (Grave 346) confirm that nickel and arsenic are present in the body metal, not just the joins, it is likely that it is an enrichment effect rather than a brazing addition. As the joins become enriched in arsenic, there is a change in the temperature (A_1) at which the transition from one crystallographic form of iron (the ferrite phase) to another (the austenite phase) takes place (this is normally 723°C,) but if up to 4 per cent arsenic is present, the equilibrium diagram for arsenic and iron shows that the change occurs at 910°C. This means that when the temperature drops below 910°C, arsenic-rich ferrite forms as a visibly distinct phase. Low concentrations of nickel have little effect on this reaction.

A source of arsenic and nickel might be marcasite nodules which are found in chalk in the Dover area. Iron ores, in the form of siderite (iron carbonate) nodules, were exploited in the Weald. If the blades were made in the Dover area (for which there is no strong evidence), it is possible some of the ores might have been obtained locally.

Construction

The construction of the swords has already been mentioned and may be summarised: the blades were made with pattern-welded panels bounded by plain cutting-edges although sometimes these could be twisted as well (Gilmour 2010). Core layers, sometimes composite, were often incorporated; the advantages were that the patterned layers could be relatively thin, some strengthening and toughness could be

added, especially if the pattern welding was not completely sound. It is likely that the construction of all the swords followed three main stages. Firstly, phosphoric iron and carbon iron and steel (not always) strips were selected for both sectors and the surfaces prepared. The smiths may have made their own metals from local resources or they may have obtained their metals by trade. There is plenty of archaeological evidence for the metal trade in currency bars from the Iron Age onwards which has been reviewed by Pleiner (2000) and their compositions analysed by Hedges and Salter (1979) and Buchwald (2005), amongst others. In antiquity, the metal would have been selected by experience, both of appearance and source. Some of the possible tests have been discussed already. Then the second stage, a sequence of welding operations was carried out, cleaning and flattening the surfaces to be joined to ensure a good contact, between each operation. Modern smiths secure the bars or strips together with twisted wire or clips and it is likely that the Anglo-Saxon smiths had some similar arrangement. Radiographs show that the bars making the pattern were drawn down, with the bars making the edges (also possibly composite), and extended to make the tang. A small cavity can be seen between the top of the pattern-welded section of the weaving batten and the edge strips around it, as both were drawn up to make the hilt or handle. The point of the blade was usually made in a similar fashion, although it is possible that sometimes a continuous edge bar might have been used, going all the way round: it would have been inconveniently long, however.

263

The final main stage was finishing the blade, including heat-treatment, filing, polishing and etching and also, of course, adding the fittings. Fullers were either forged or ground. If the surface of the twists was ground, curving patterns were produced. An experienced modern smith, Vince Evans (pers comm), has suggested that a layer of twisted bars could be split, and the curved patterned surface mounted facing outwards. The initial selection of the materials,

Position	Material	Layer	Twist	Strip	No an	MgO	Al2O3	SiO2	P2O5	SO3	K2O	CaO	TiO2	MnO	FeO	V2O5	CoO	NiO
e	m				6	0.3									98.3			0.1
e	inc				9	0.7	10.7	55.7	1.2		1.4	4.5	0.6	0.9	23.3		0.1	
r	m	L	1	1	1				1.6						97.7			
r	m	L	1	2	5	0.2									98.3			0.2
r	inc	L	1	2	3	0.9	17.1	50.9	0.5		2.8	5.2	0.6	0.9	20.3			
r	m	L	1	3	2				1.2						97.7			
r	inc	L	1	3	1	1.5	9.9	56.8	3.9		2.0	4.8	0.9	2.3	16.4	0.3		
r	m	I	1	4	1										97.7			
r	inc	L	1	4	3	0.8	25.4	46.2		0.2	1.4	3.6	0.6	0.7	19.9			
r	m	L	1	5	1				0.5						96.9			
r	m	L	2		3	0.6									98.1			
r	inc	L	2		9	0.8	19.8	62.7			2.3	6.0	1.0	1.0	5.8			
r	m	L	3	1	1				0.6						97.0			
r	m	L	3	3	1				0.5						98.9			
r	inc	L	3	3	1	1.0	19.8	59.5			2.3	6.3	1.0	2.7	7.4			
r	m	L	3	4	1				1.5						97.9			
r	inc	L	3	4	1		3.2	89.9			0.4	1.3	0.6	0.4	3.4			
r	m	L	3	5	1				0.6						97.6		0.5	0.3
r	m	L	5	3	2	0.2			0.2						98.5			
r	m	L	5	4	2	0.5			0.8						97.5		0.1	0.1
r	inc	L	5	4	2	0.6	4.5	51.5	2.0		2.5	1.3	0.2	0.2	36.2	0.2		
r	m	L	5	5	5	0.5	0.1		0.6						97.4			
r	inc	L	5	5	2	0.2	6.3	44.0	8.8		2.0	2.5	0.2	0.1	35.1			
r	m	L	1	2	1										96.8			0.7
r	inc	L	1	2	1	0.6	6.0	25.2	1.7		0.4		0.5		64.4			
r	m	M		1	4	0.2		0.1	0.1						98.5			0.2
r	inc	M		1	6	0.5	5.0	28.8	1.3	0.1	0.9	2.2	0.2	0.3	59.5			0.1
r	m	M		2	3		0.1	0.1	0.7						97.7			0.1
r	inc	M		2	2	0.6	5.8	22.0	6.2	0.3	0.8	0.9	0.2	0.4	61.1			0.1
r	m	M		3	2	0.2			0.5						98.3			
r	m	M		4	2	0.5			2.2				0.1		96.9			0.1
r	inc	M		4	1	1.3	12.2	59.6	2.0		1.8	4.2	0.6	2.0	16.9			
r	m	M		5	3				0.5						98.0			0.1
r	m	M		6	3		0.1		1.2						97.7			0.1
r	inc	M		6	1	1.0	7.4	35.5	14.8	0.5	1.2	3.6	0.6	3.6	31.6			
r	m	M		7	8	0.1			0.2						97.6		0.6	0.1
r	inc	M		7	10	0.7	9.4	44.4	1.3	0.1	1.1	3.1	0.4	0.6	38.2			
r	m	U	1	4	3				0.8						97.4			0.1
r	inc	U	1	4	1	0.7	10.8	61.9			2.0	2.8	0.7	0.8	19.9			
r	m	U	1	5	1										99.4			
r	m	U	2		1										98.7			
r	inc	U	2		10	0.8	14.7	55.4	0.3		1.1	3.0	0.7	1.2	22.2			
r	m	U	3	1	1	0.4			1.3						97.0			0.3
r	m	U	3	3	1				1.6						97.6			
r	m	U	3	4	1				1.7						97.0			
r	inc	U	3	4	2	0.6	10.9	74.2	0.5		1.3	3.3	0.5	1.0	7.5			
r	inc	U	4		1	0.8	31.5	58.2			1.7	4.4	1.4	0.3	1.3			

Table 6.7f. Weaving batten from Grave 250: summary SEM-EDXA results (average values) (SN 1024) batten section (Cr_2O_3, CoO, NiO not quantifiable).

	Grave 264 (1019)	Grave 265B (1020)	Grave 346 (1021)	Grave 375 (1022)	Grave 437A (1023)
central sector min.	170	130	143	181	127
central sector max.	310	226	207 (266)#	490	215
edge sector min.	260	130	133	119	171
edge sector max.	500 (900)*	177	195 (239)#	490 (900+)*	490

Notes: * martensite; # in area containing As and Ni

Table 6.8. Buckland 1994 swords: hardness values (diamond pyramid micorhardness 100g weight).

welding to make the blade, and the final heating treatments are important metallurgically and require the skills of an experienced smith.

From the presence of silica in welds, it can be inferred that sand flux was sometimes used to clean the surfaces to be welded (eg SN1019, Grave 264). The welding temperature depends on the composition, ferritic (wrought) iron requiring the highest temperature (*c* 1200°C, white sparking heat) while steel and phosphoric iron can be welded at lower temperatures depending on their compositions (720–1200°C). The necessary tools, such as tongs, hammers and files, were available from the Iron Age onwards, and have been excavated in hoards, such as the Tattershall Thorpe hoard, Lincolnshire (Hinton and White 1993) and smiths' graves (400 Viking Age smiths' graves have been found in Norway alone: Munksgaard 1984). Illustrations on Roman funeral monuments (eg Sim 1998) and the Frank's Casket depiction of Wayland the Smith (Webster 1982, pl 22) show tools and forges.

The role of carburisation has already been discussed; it is often difficult to recognise its deliberate use, partly because surface layers are frequently corroded. The cutting-edge of SN1020 (Grave 265B) has an increased carbon content, indicating carburisation. Decarburisation (probably unintentional) is often observed: for example, on the surfaces of SN 1022 (Grave 375) (Fig 6.10.3) and SN 1023 (Grave 437) (Fig 6.12.3). Tylecote (1987, 259) suggested that because the solid-state diffusion of carbon is slow (eg 1.5mm depth after heating for eight hours in charcoal), steel was made by carburising sheets of iron which were piled and folded to make the banded or multi-layered structures familiar from Iron Age iron artefacts. However, it is more likely that carbon-rich fragments from iron blooms were used. Carburisation was employed more erratically for surface hardening in the Iron Age (Fell and Salter 1998).

Heat treatment can improve the properties of carbon iron and steel if carried out with care. If a carburised ferrous metal blade is heated to well above 727°C (the eutectoid temperature) and then quenched by plunging it into water, brine, urine, or oil, the normal crystallographic transformations are suppressed; instead a hard metastable

phase (*martensite*) forms, hardening the blade. Final quenching treatments were carried out on two of the five swords (Fig 6.4, 1; Fig 6.10, 3) with high-carbon contents in the edge sectors, with the result that the edges are very hard. A third (1023) had also been quenched, not rapidly enough to form martensite but the structure is extremely fine and sufficiently hard to make a good edge. Table 6.8 shows the results of the hardness tests.

Bealer (1995, 150) describes how a rural blacksmith would work out the correct quenching temperature by heating a strip of the steel to be used at one end to white heat, noting the different colours along the length and then quenching it. Fragments were broken off with a hammer and the appearance at the break observed. The correct temperature is indicated by the colour at the point where the broken surface is very close textured (unlike the coarse textured break at the hottest part). Early smiths could have made use of similar tests and observations to supplement their experience.

Martensite is very hard, but is also apt to be brittle: some of the strains can be relieved by reheating to a moderate temperature, (eg *c* 300°C), to temper the metal. If a blade is quenched in water and withdrawn before the quench is completed, heat is retained in the middle of the blade where the cross-section is greater, and this then reheats the thin cutting-edge, tempering it (auto-tempering). It will be appreciated that the thickness of the metal section affects the rate of cooling, as thicker parts retain heat longer. The swords from Graves 264 and 375 were probably auto-tempered, although this could have been fortuitous. The other blades appear to have been air cooled: although the carbon contents at the cutting-edges were not high (ie less than 0.4 per cent C), it would still have been possible to harden the edge by a water quench (Samuels 1980, 348). None of a group of ten British Iron Age swords (Stead 2006) have unequivocally quenched martensitic structures, unlike contemporary tools such as files (Fell 1997) and Roman swords and daggers (Lang 1988; 1995). Heat treatment is sometimes regarded as a measure of technical advancement (McDonnell 2000); its presence confirms mastery but its absence does not necessarily indicate a lack of technical skills. It seems that some smiths did not quench blades even in the Anglo-Saxon period, whether from a lack of knowledge or from a lack of belief in the value of the technique for swords (where brittleness could be catastrophic) it is hard to say.

One of the last operations would be to add a fuller, if desired. Fullers were either forged (before the final heat treatment) or ground. If the surface of a twist was ground, curving patterns were produced as the surface layers were removed. Vince Evans (pers comm) has suggested that the layer of twisted bars could be split, and the resulting curved-patterned surface mounted face up. Lang and Ager (1989) found that the fullers on the Anglo-Saxon swords in the British Museum collections had been forged not ground, as the curving elements displayed in the fullers of continental swords were absent. To produce a good curving pattern, the coincidence of the adjacent twists must be accurate and a considerable amount of energy expended in removing the surface to a depth sufficient to reveal a pleasing partly curved pattern. Some of the sections (SN1021 and SN1022) showed slight depressions in the middle of the blades which may be the remains of forged fullers, but the surface is corroded, removing any evidence. Radiographs of the swords from Graves 264 (SN 1019) and 265B (SN 1020) hint at the possibility that their surface may have been ground as there appear to be curving elements in the twisted areas.

After filing, grinding, polishing and etching the blade to bring out the patterns, the final stage of making the sword would be to add the fittings, which might have been carried out by another artisan, but equally the smith himself may have furnished the hilt as suggested by some of the items in the smith's hoard from Tattershall Thorpe (Hinton and White 1993; Hinton 2000).

Chronology

The swords cannot be dated by technology, analysis or pattern and are discussed in this context by Ager (*see* p 52) who has kindly provided the information which follows. Normally the fittings, blade shape and associations would give some guidance, but the swords are sparsely endowed and it appears that all the blades can be dated to the sixth century AD, on the basis of their typology or the phasing of the graves.

Grave 264. Typology: mid fifth to sixth century. Grave phasing: Phase 3
Grave 265B. Typology: mid fifth to seventh century. Grave phasing: Phase 3a
Grave 346. Typology: mid fifth to seventh century. Grave phasing: Phase 3

Grave 375. Grave phasing: Phase 3b
Grave 437. Typology: sixth century. Grave phasing: Phase 2

The swords themselves do not provide any stylistic indication of their origins either. Four of the swords could have similar sources of metal (Graves 264, 265B, 375 and 437), while the remaining sword (Grave 346), containing nickel and arsenic, may have a continental origin, although it might have been locally made: the grave includes a Frankish axe (e) which suggests continental connections although the layout of the grave is typically Anglo-Saxon.

The dates of the swords do not relate to what might be considered as technical development (eg from soft unquenched cutting edges to heat treated, hardened cutting edges). The sword which is probably the earliest (Grave 264), and the later two swords (Graves 375 and 437) have hardened edges, while the others do not. The sample is too small to be significant in any case.

It is difficult to know if the swords were continental or insular in origin. It has been thought that Anglo-Saxon blades were generally imported (Davidson 1998, 34), but Gilmour (2010; forthcoming) considers that the Saltwood Tunnel swords provide evidence for insular production, suggesting a different, indigenous smithing tradition, producing swords with straight and twisted elements to make the patterns, whereas on the Continent, patterns with curved elements predominated. The study of the pattern-welded swords in the British Museum collection noted the same division (Lang and Ager 1989). It does not seem unreasonable to suppose that swords were made in Anglo-Saxon England, even though archaeology has not yet provided direct evidence of this. Some of the Dover swords could have been made locally, using some traded phosphoric iron bars and perhaps some locally produced iron or steel, while others may have been imported.

Scientific examination of the apex of a shield boss

Janet Lang

(Grave 323)

A radiograph of the shield boss from Buckland Grave 323 (Fig 10.33) showed a cavity in the apex which appeared to penetrate from the interior of the boss, through the neck, to the flat top surface. A cross-section of the neck and apex was studied metallographically, using optical and scanning electron microscopy, in order to investigate the method of construction.

Experimental

The cross-section through the head and neck of the apex or knob of the shield boss shows a number of elongated, large inclusions or cavities, mainly filled with iron oxides. The cavities are parallel to the sides in the neck and more or less parallel to the top surface in the head. The inclusions are iron oxide and phosphorus, present in both the inclusions and the body metal (up to 1.4 wt per cent P_2O_5).

Etching revealed a heavily banded structure, with varying grain sizes; some bands contained carbon (not more than 0.3 per cent C) in the form of pearlite with ferrite. Nearer the top of the apex there are some very fine, needle-like carbide precipitates and cementite in the grain boundaries. There are also light etching bands and 'ghost' grain boundaries, which indicate the presence of phosphorus in the metal. An elemental distribution map shows that phosphorus is fairly well distributed throughout the whole section with very minor differences between the bands. The grains also show considerable distortion and compression parallel to the surfaces, indicating heavy working. Some heating, resulting in partial annealing, has taken place, as the ferrite shows a small amount of re-crystallisation.

The cavity within the neck of the apex does not appear to have been sealed by forge welding and it penetrates through to the flat top surface of the apex. To judge by the distorted grains, a considerable amount of work has been completed without a full, final annealing process, leaving it in a somewhat hardened state. The top of the apex has been hammered down, but a lap has formed and it has not fused completely, leaving a flap with oxides and corrosion underneath it.

Discussion

The microstructure of the apex section suggests that the boss was produced from inhomogeneous bloomery iron containing phosphorus. The structure and composition, although inhomogeneous, do not suggest a piled structure, but rather the use of a sheet made from an inhomogeneous bloom product. The number of inclusions in the metal is small, which indicates that it was probably heavily worked, although it has been suggested that the overall number of inclusions does not greatly change because additions from fuel ash, flux and the hearth occur during smithing operations (Blakelock *et al* 2009).

Härke and Salter (1984) and Härke (1992a) have discussed the fabrication of shield bosses, suggesting two main methods of fabricating a boss, either in one piece, starting from a single billet, or by making the cone and wall separately and welding the two pieces together. Radiographs and low-magnification microscopy do not give indications of any joins in the cone or walls. The apex was not added as a separate piece of metal, another method described by Härke and Salter (1984) but appears to have been made by pinching or crimping the metal together at the neck. There is no evidence that the metal was ever joined completely at the apex, which seems to rule out the methods suggested by Härke and Salter (1984) and Härke (1992a). Radiographs of the shield bosses from Graves 264, 265B and 414, show similar tiny cavities in the middle of the apices, which indicates that they were all probably made in a similar way. A possible method might have been to start with a flat rectangular sheet, make it into a cylinder and then forge one edge outwards to make the flange and the other edge inwards to make the conical shape and the apex.

Another method which appears to have been used to make the apex of at least one of the Tranmer House (Sutton Hoo) bosses (Lang and Wang forthcoming) was to start with a circle of flat sheet, make a cone shape, and then decrease the internal angle at the centre until the metal could be crimped to make the apex. The Tranmer House bosses showed striations on radiographs due to working and cavities were found within the top and neck of a section from the boss from Tranmer House grave 614, but there was no indication that the cavities penetrated to the upper surface of the apex. If, as Härker and Salter (1984) suggested, the tip of a cone (made from a disc) was extended considerably to make the apex, it is possible the inner surface remained partially unfused, leaving the cavities. It seems clear that a number of different methods of shield boss construction were used. Directional working in the neck producing a fibred structure and increased hardness would increase strength and resistance to transverse blows.

Scientific examination of plated rivets from a shield boss

Janet Lang

(Grave 264)

The three disc-headed rivets from the shield boss in Grave 264 which were examined (Fig 10.20) are badly corroded; two (h) and (i) are incomplete while (f) is complete and has the remains of a shaft or pin on the back. Fragments of wood adhere to the back surfaces. Copper corrosion products were noted during conservation, as well as the outline of a disc applied to the top surface of rivets (h) and (i). Both green and white corrosion as well as the normal iron corrosion products could be seen and a scientific examination was undertaken to discover how the rivets had been decorated.

Examination and results

As the rivets are extremely corroded and fragile, it was not possible to make a taper section at the edge to reveal the layers, so they were examined using binocular microscopy and scanning electron microscopy (SEM) with energy dispersive X-ray analysis facilities (EDXA). The results are qualitative rather than quantitative because of the geometry and the condition of the rivets. Rivet (f) was not examined in the SEM because it was larger and more awkwardly shaped than the fragments.

An irregular arrangement of layers can be seen at the edges of the rivet-heads, which are thin and flat. Some layers have split away from each other, leaving gaps (h). Reddish, rust-coloured iron corrosion is seen throughout the layers and on all the surfaces. The layers appear to be whitish, greenish or dark brown and shiny. Examination in the SEM also allowed the complex layered structure to be analysed as small areas (see Table 6.9) or by using a line scan (for details of analytical procedures *see* pp 238–9), or elemental distribution maps.

The major metallic element present was iron, which permeated the whole of two rivets examined. Copper and tin was within detectable limits while line scans showed that trace amounts of lead were associated with tin. Analyses of the edges (achieved by placing the rivet so that the edge of the head was presented to the detector) did not produce a very clear-cut picture of the elemental distribution. A lump on the upper surface of rivet (h) did show an increased tin content in comparison with the rest of the section, however, which suggests that the surface of the rivet was tinned.

Another set of analyses was carried out on the flat top surface of the rivet (h); in this position it can be seen that a flat disc covers the centre which has a slightly different texture compared with the periphery. There are some cavities in the surface of both the discs. Analysis of the central disc indicates an increase in the copper content. The central areas of the rivet-heads contain a small proportion of tin (eg 1–2 per cent) with larger quantities of copper (3–11 per cent), the remainder being iron and non-metallic elements (eg oxygen), while the peripheral area contains proportionally more tin and the tin content in the cavities was also higher.

Line scans carried out on the edge of the rivets indicated clearly the presence of low levels of lead associated with

No	Rivet	Fe	Cu	Sn	Pb	Location
2	i	5	88	0.4	tr	top, near edge (1)
3	i	80	11	4	tr	top, edge (2)
4	i	92	<2	3	tr	top, under surface layer
5	i	92	7	1	tr	top edge
6	i	73	8	14	tr	top, surface
7	i	78	15	2	tr	top, inner area
8	i	57	12	31	tr	top, hole in surface
9	i	86	11	2	tr	top, surface
10	i	91	7	1	tr	top, surface
11	h	88	2	3	tr	top, surface (1)
12	h	92	7	1	tr	top, edge (2)
13	h	98	1	1	tr	edge, under surface (1)
14	h	96	3	1	tr	edge, middle layer (2)
15	h	93	6	1	tr	edge, top surface (3)
16	h	94	5	1	tr	edge, under surface (1)
17	h	3	86	9	3	edge, middle layer (2)
18	h	2	96	1	tr	edge, intermediate layer (3)
19	h	91	6	2	tr	edge, top surface (4)
20	h	95	3	3	tr	edge, under surface layer (1)
21	h	92	5	2	tr	edge, laminated layer (2)
22	h	93	4	3	tr	edge, thicker powdery layer (3)
23	h	93	5	2	tr	edge, more consolidated dark layer (4)
24	h	92	5	3	tr	edge, light layer (5)
25	h	96	4	2	tr	edge, mixed layer (6)
26	h	93	4	3	tr	edge, sub-top surface layer (7)
27	h	91	2	8	tr	edge, raised lump on top surface (8)
28	h	96	1	3	tr	top, outer area (1)
29	h	96	4	tr	tr	top, close to join outer and inner layers (2)
30	h	96	3	1	tr	top, inner area (3)
31	h	95	2	3	tr	top, hole in surface, inner area (4)

Note: Numbers in brackest indicate that the analyses were made in the same area, eg analyses nos 28–31 are from the same area of the top surface of rivet (h). tr = trace.

Table 6.9. Semi-quantitative analyses of rivets (h) and (i), Grave 264.

the tin near the upper surface of the rivet (h). The rivet (i) showed a similar distribution. Copper was found not only at the surface on both rivets but also throughout the cross-section of rivet (h).

Discussion

The analysis results at the edges of the rivet-heads are not very clear, partly due to their fragmentary state and partly due to the geometry. One set of analyses shows a tin-rich surface layer, a second showed a maximum tin content at the middle of the section while a third shows equal amounts of tin across the section.

The area analysis did not reveal quantifiable amounts of lead although the line scans of the edges show that it is present in trace proportions, probably combined with tin. The spread of the corrosion products throughout the section made it difficult to understand what the original configuration was. The flat surfaces of rivet (i) and rivet (h), shows a clear boundary between the central disc where there is more copper and the periphery where the proportion of tin is higher.

Despite these inconsistencies, the results suggest that the top surface of the rivets was coated with a low melting point alloy, consisting mainly of tin with a little lead. In the case of rivet (i) a thin copper or bronze disc was attached to the surface by heating the tinned layer to act as a solder. Rivet (h) was almost certainly treated in the same way; the edge of the disc is clearly visible on the top surface but the copper content is low, no doubt, as a result of corrosion.

According to Dickinson and Härke (1992, 27–9), studs or disc-headed rivets are the most commonly found shield board fittings. Although usually made of iron, they are less frequently made of copper or tinned copper. This suggests that the rivets (h) and (i) from Grave 264 are unusual in being made from iron with tinned heads decorated with copper discs. Rivet (h) seems to have had a copper disc which was surrounded by a narrow band of tinning: it is not obvious if this was an intentional arrangement or simply a mistake in making the copper disc too small to cover the top of the tinned rivet-head completely. As the top of other rivet examined (i) appears to have been more or less completely covered by its copper disc, it seems more likely that the tinned periphery on (h) was accidental, but disc-headed rivets with bronze washers are known (Evison and Hill 1996, grave 64).

Metallographic study: four spearheads

Janet Lang

(Graves 264, 299, 323 and 393A)

All the spearheads from the excavation were radiographed and have been examined in detail elsewhere in this report (pp 61–9). In order to minimise intrusive examination, the radiographs were examined in order to select four spearheads which appeared to be in a sufficiently sound condition to sample for metallography and which also indicated that they might provide representative structures from a technical point of view. The structures visible on the radiographs suggested that some of the blades had layered or piled structures while others appeared to be more homogeneous. Two blades were

selected from each type: the spearheads from Graves 264 and 299 appeared to be layered, while those from Graves 323 and 393 did not.

Experimental

The areas selected for sampling were determined in consultation with a metals conservator who specialised in the preservation of organic surface remains on metal objects. A wedge was cut in sound metal from the cutting-edge inwards to the centre of each blade at the agreed point, no more than 2mm at its widest at the cutting-edge. The length of each section was approximately 15mm. Hardness test results are shown in (Table 6.10). The experimental procedures are described above (pp 238–9).

Test position	Grave 264	Grave 299	Grave 323	Grave 393
centre	211	147	290	148
edge	260	203	382	165

Table 6.10. Hardness tests on selected spearheads (all results are an average of three; diamond pyramid microhardness 100g weight).

Spearhead: Grave 264 (a)

The micro-section (Fig 6.14) showed a number of relatively large inclusions, elongated in the direction of working. Etching shows that the metal is ferritic iron and contains some phosphorus 'ghosts' (Fig 6.15). A small quantity of carbide is present in the grain boundaries, mainly near the cutting-edge of the blade. The ferrite grains and 'ghosts' are elongated, showing that the blade was not annealed after the final forging process. The few remaining areas of surface metal showed marked distortion from cold working.

Fig 6.14. Spearhead from Grave 264 (montage – section long axis 14.7mm).

Fig 6.15. Spearhead from Grave 264 (micro-section, width of view 1120 microns), large ferrite grains with inclusions and an uneven response to etching, indicating phosphorus.

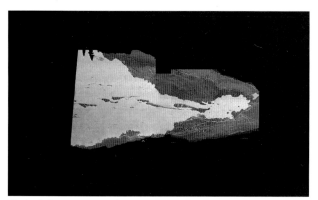

Fig 6.16. Spearhead from Grave 299 (montage – section long axis 12.6mm).

Fig 6.17. Spearhead from Grave 299 (micro-section, width of view 280 microns), large ferrite grains with uneven texture indicating the presence of phosphorus, cavity left by inclusion.

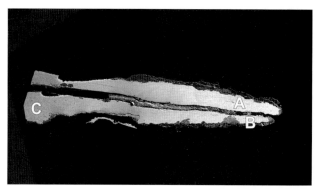

Fig 6.18. Spearhead from Grave 323 (montage – section long axis 14.3mm).

It was not possible to confirm that the blade was made by piling, although the distribution of the inclusions does not rule this out.

Spearhead: Grave 299 (a)

The micro-section (Fig 6.16) shows an irregular series of very large inclusions which run from the middle of the blade towards the cutting-edge. They are two-phased, elongated parallel to the surfaces and are somewhat angular and fragmented. The metal consists of large-grained ferrite (eg 1mm diameter maximum) with some phosphorus (Fig 6.17). A very small quantity of carbide is present in the grain boundaries.

Spearhead: Grave 323 (a)

The sample appears to split in two parts, from middle to edge, with a gap containing corrosion between the two (Fig 6.18). There are several large inclusions associated with the split, which may be the result of the penetration of corrosion during burial. Elsewhere the elongated inclusions are much smaller, glassy and single-phased. The carbon composition of the metal is close to the eutectoid proportion (0.8 per cent C) with a little spheroidisation. The grain size is larger near the middle of the blade and very fine nearer the edge (Fig 6.19).

Spearhead: Grave 393A (a)

There are few inclusions of any size in this section, except for a group near the surface (Fig 6.20). A band of much smaller, mainly two-phased inclusions appears to run from the middle to the edge and may represent a join or interface. The composition is not homogeneous and the carbon content is variable (Fig 6.21). The structure is mainly ferrite with

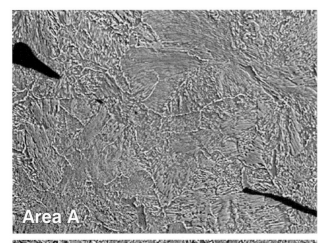

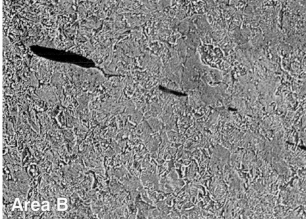

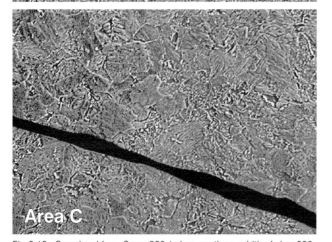

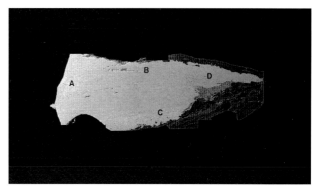

Fig 6.20. Spearhead from Grave 393A (montage – section long axis 12.6mm).

Fig 6.19. Spearhead from Grave 323 (micro-sections, width of view 280 microns). Area A: near edge, upper segment (see montage), pearlite with elongated single phased glassy inclusion. Area B: near edge, lower segment (see montage), slightly smaller pearlite grains, some spheroidisation, elongated single phased glassy inclusions. Area C: near middle of blade, pearlite, slightly slower cooling has resulted in coarser and larger grains than near the edge.

some carbides at the grain boundaries with coarser pearlite. The carbon content increases towards the surface and the edge of the blade. There are also bands of ferritic iron. This blade appears to have a layered structure.

Hardness test

A 100 gram weight was used with the Vickers micro-hardness tester. In all cases, hardness increased at the edge of the spearhead blades. The layered blade from Grave 393A was the least hard while, not unexpectedly, the carburised blade from Grave 323 was the hardest. As the blade from Grave 264 is almost carbon-free, it might have been expected to be very soft, but cold working and the presence of phosphorus accounts for the higher than expected hardness values. The presence of phosphorus has also increased the hardness of the blade from Grave 299.

Discussion

The blades were examined in order to see if there were differences in construction which mirrored the apparent differences visible on the radiographs and to see if the metallographic structures were related in any way to the shape of the spearheads. The micro-sections of the two blades from Graves 264 and 299 (which appeared layered in the radiographs) are similar in construction: both contain relatively large inclusions strung out irregularly from the middle of the blade to the cutting-edge, and it is this feature which evidently gives rise to the appearance of a piled structure on the radiographs. Generally the blades are simply made, only one is constructed from steel (Grave 323). This is a wide, thin blade, tapering to the point, with a larger surface area than the others. Using a harder material would have meant that it retained its shape well, despite being

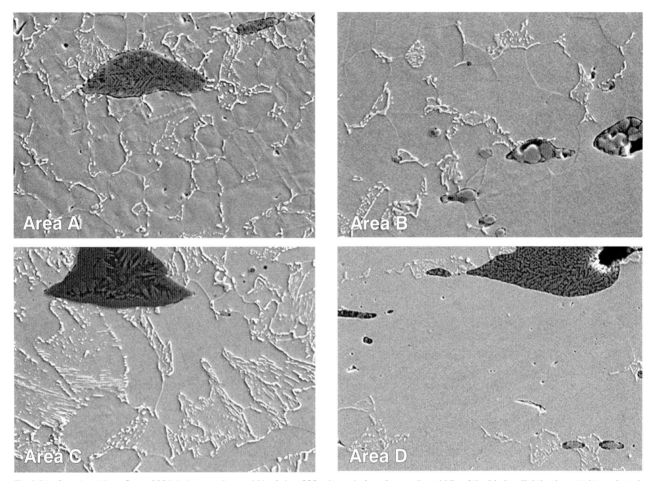

Fig 6.21. Spearhead from Grave 393A (micro-sections, width of view 280 microns). Area A: near the middle of the blade, slightly elongated two phased inclusion, low carbon content, with carbides precipitated at the grain boundaries and an uneven response to etching in the ferrite, due to phosphorus. Area B: near one surface, about midway between the edge and the middle of the blade, inclusions with a globular second phase are part of a long series of inclusions stretching back towards the middle of the blade, larger grain size than A with grain boundary carbide and a small amount of coarse spheroidised pearlite. Area C: near the opposite surface, two phased inclusion with a cavity in the middle and a slightly higher carbon content than at A or B. Area D: near the cutting-edge, two phased inclusion, low carbon content, with carbides at the grain boundaries.

relatively thinner in section. It could be used to penetrate or slice. In fact, the hardness could have been further increased by quenching, but such a heat treatment might have resulted in brittleness and fracture or shattering. It can be concluded that this spearhead (Grave 323) was made with appropriate materials and technology, from a technical point of view.

The other blades do not show such clear relationships between shape, construction and composition. They would all have been effective as stabbing weapons although the blade from Grave 393 would have been less sharp than the one from Grave 264. The shape of the latter might be considered consistent with a spear which could be thrown as it would be sharp enough to penetrate flesh and to stick

in a shield, perhaps. It also appears to have a narrow shaft, which might be consistent with a weapon intended at least in part for throwing.

The blade from Grave 393 contains fewer, much smaller inclusions and the microstructure is layered, but the differences in radiographic density are not sufficiently marked to show on the radiographs. It is impossible to draw any conclusions with regard to the chronology of the blades from the technology: similarly, the sword blades from the Buckland graves which have been examined, as described in Part 4, do not give any indication of technological development. With regard to the radiographs, it seems (on this rather slender evidence) that apparently layered structures may indicate of the presence of large slag inclusions which can encourage the spread of corrosion within the structure.

Comparison with results from the examinations of a group of twenty spearheads from Edix Hill (Barrington A) carried out by Gilmour and Salter (summarised in Malim and Hines 1998), with others from Flixton (in press), Boss Hall (Fell and Starley 1999) and Tranmer House, Sutton Hoo (Lang and Wang forthcoming) leads to the conclusion that the quality of material and construction used for the spearheads was not particularly good in comparison with other iron weaponry, such as knives or swords. An examination of the schematised diagrams of the Edix Hill spearheads, for example, suggests that between a half and a quarter of the spear blades were constructed so that the cutting-edge was harder than the rest of the spearhead, whereas about two-thirds of the knives increased in hardness at the edge and more than half of the knives contained steel, unlike the spearheads. On the information available at present, there seems to be little correspondence between Swanton's typology and technology. For example, the spearhead from Grave 264 (D2 type, Swanton 1974) consists of ferritic iron with some phosphorus, as does one of the two D2 types from Sutton Hoo (grave 967) although the other Sutton Hoo spearhead (grave 857) has a central band of iron containing 0.3–0.4 per cent carbon, with wrought iron and phosphoric bands on either side (in press), using optical and scanning electron microscopy.

Metallographic study: weaving batten

Janet Lang

(Grave 250)

The weaving batten, found in Grave 250 (d), is 480mm in length. Radiographs show a pattern which is not very distinct but appears to consist of two layers, one made from two twisted bars (type A) and the other layer with three bars with straight and twisted sections (B2a). The bars constituting the blade are drawn out at both ends, the more substantial forming the tang. A single curved element or motif can be seen on the radiograph, 220mm below the shoulders of the blade, but it is difficult to confirm that this is part of an inlaid pattern-welded circle or merely part of the main pattern. It is almost as if the batten is a test piece of the smith's art.

The sample was removed 200mm from the shoulder, mounted, polished and etched in exactly the same way as the sword cross-sections (see above). The length is 15.8mm.

Unetched microscopy

The unetched section shows a number of inclusions distributed throughout without any obvious indication of an underlying structure. The inclusions vary in size and shape but most are single phased, dark and glassy and elongated to a greater or lesser extent parallel to the surfaces of the blade.

Etched microscopy and semi-quantitative analysis

Etching with nital (2 per cent nitric acid in ethanol) revealed a macrostructure which was not very distinct. Light-etching bands accompanied by small inclusions indicate the junction between the cutting-edge sector and the central sector. The latter consists of three layers; the central layer is plain, but the outer layers are twisted. The cross-section comprises slightly less than half the blade width, which may contribute to the difficulty of understanding the pattern. The micro-section indicates that it consists of a twist in each surface layer. An elemental distribution map suggests that each twist is made up from a phosphoric iron strip sandwiched between two strips of steel. The carbon content varies between 0.3 per cent C and 0.1 per cent C, with much less in the phosphoric iron. Inclusions are found throughout, but a number accompany the light etching joins. The various areas which can be distinguished are indicated on Fig 6.2, together with the hardness values.

Area 1 consists of pearlite and ferrite (0.4 per cent–0.6 per cent C) and single phased somewhat elongated inclusions with very similar compositions with high manganese (c 11 per cent MnO) and silica contents (c 66 per cent SiO_2). There are traces of barium in some of the inclusions. No phosphorus was detected in the body metal.

Area 2 is phosphoric iron with a higher proportion of ferrite than in Area 1 but some fine, mainly spheroidised pearlite grains. It also contains a number of single-phased inclusions, all of which contain phosphorus (P_2O_5) and have relatively high silica contents (50–70 per cent SiO_2) and lower manganese contents (MnO<5 per cent). The average alumina content is 11 per cent (Al_2O_3) but in each of the other oxides (calcium, potassium and titanium) it is less than 2 per cent. Two of the inclusions in this area are attached to iron oxide inclusions.

Area 3 is the third strip in the twist in the upper layer, adjacent to the join with the cutting-edge sector (Areas 9, 10). It contains ferrite and pearlite, the carbon content is about 0.5 per cent. A large inclusion within Area 3 has a manganese content of 8 per cent MnO and a trace of barium, apart from the usual oxides of potassium, calcium, titanium and silicon. Phosphorus was not detected in the inclusions or the body metal.

The central layer, Area 4, was not analysed in detail but the elemental maps (Fig 6.2) showed that it does not have a detectable phosphorus content and the inclusions contain appreciable amounts of silicon. The carbon content is about 0.6 per cent or more, and the structure consists of pearlite and ferrite.

The join between two of the strips in the lower layer shows that one strip (Area 6) is steel with a structure of ferrite and pearlite (0.4 per cent C content) and phosphorus is not detected in the inclusions or the body metal, while the other strip (Area 7), as shown in the elemental maps, contains phosphorus in the body metal (but not the inclusions). The 'ghost' grain boundaries, often found in ferritic phosphoric iron, are absent but some fine, spheroidised pearlite is present. Two of the three inclusions tested in Area 7 contain traces of barium, one also had a trace of arsenic. The manganese content in both areas is less than 5 per cent (MnO).

Area 8 consists of fine pearlite with some distortion a result of working.

Area 9 (A, B) is the narrow, light etching band which appears to mark the boundary between the central and cutting-edge sectors. It contains a number of inclusions which elemental distribution maps show to have high silica and alumina contents: the two analysed inclusions in the join have low manganese contents. The body metal contains phosphorus. The ferrite and pearlite grains in the adjoining areas extend across the band, becoming faint and diffuse as they do so.

The edge sector, Area 10, has a near-eutectoid composition (0.6 per cent–1 per cent C) consisting of mainly fine or unresolvable pearlite. The pearlite lamellae are distorted near the surface as a result of working. Below the distorted surface, the structure consists of pearlitic grains, many outlined with proeutectoid cementite, sometimes accompanied with a little proeutectoid ferrite, replacing the prior austenite grain boundaries. This is likely to occur when austenitisation has only been partial and the grain size not small. According to the phosphorus distribution map, the sector appears to be divided into at least three layers, consisting of two phosphorus rich layers with low phosphorus layers between, but the etched structure, viewed with an optical microscope, shows no evidence of layering. This suggests that either the cutting-edge sector was made from a single piece of steel containing both carbon and inhomogeneously distributed phosphorus which tended to segregate as a result of repeated working and annealing cycles, or that it was skilfully forge-welded from several pieces of steel, some with phosphorus and some without, so that the joins were not visible. According to Salter (1999, 25) this is perfectly possible. Almost all the inclusions

are single phased and featureless, with high silica and alumina contents (Al_2O_3> 11 per cent; SiO_2> 60 per cent). Many of the inclusions contain tiny globules of iron metal suggesting that they are extraction slags. The iron oxide content is low in most of the inclusions in the cutting-edge sector; the only exceptions are found near the join on the upper side.

About 90 per cent of the inclusions contain more than 0.5 per cent manganese oxide which probably comes from the ore. This supposition is supported by the MnO results for Area 9 (the light-etching join between the central and cutting-edge sectors), all of which are below 0.5 per cent.

Summary

The weaving batten has a pattern-welded structure which was constructed in a similar manner to the swords from the same site. The pattern is made by using strips of different composition (steel and phosphoric iron), welded together and then partially twisted. The blade is constructed with steel cutting-edges and a steel central layer between two patterned layers, which consist of composite bars with twisted and straight sections. Both ends are drawn out, one of which makes the tang. It is clear that the blade was not intended to be a full-length sword blade at the time when the bars were welded together. It may have been an experiment, an apprentice piece or made in answer to a request for a prestigious item for domestic use. It was not a cut-down sword, and thus resembles the Saltwood batten and others (Walton Rogers and Riddler 2006). It is physically dissimilar to the spear-shaped sword-beater from Coppergate (Walton Rogers 1992). The carbon content of some of the steel is high (up to 1 per cent carbon, or perhaps slightly more) but no attempt has been made to harden the blade by quenching. This is appropriate for its function if it was to be used in weaving. However, not all the sword blades examined from this site were fully hardened so this may not be significant. The pattern itself is less complex than the other Buckland patterns, and is slightly unusual because the two layers appear to be different. The metal is generally of good quality, and the presence of traces of barium in some areas but not others suggests that different batches of metal were used, with more than one ore source. Although detectable trace amounts of barium might link the source to that of the anomalous sword from Grave 346, the absence of nickel in the batten shows that there is no real similarity between them. The presence of moderate quantities of manganese (the effect of which generally has been discussed above) in many of the inclusions and metallic globules in some indicates that the majority are probably derived from the ores in the initial extraction process rather than subsequent smithing operations.

The metallurgy of the ironwork: conclusions

The uses of ferrous metals, methods of fabrication and treatment from the second excavation at Buckland, Dover are technologically consistent with other reported groups of Anglo-Saxon ironwork. The origins of the metal and the artefacts themselves are more difficult to determine in the absence of archaeological evidence of metal extraction and working in the area. It is clear that metals from different ore sources were being used, and if some of the swords were made locally, metal had been obtained from elsewhere, probably as billets or trade bars. If the practice of grinding rather than forging fullers (making curving patterns) is a criterion, then two of the swords may have been imported (Graves 264, 265B). The metal in the sword from Grave 346 has a distinctive composition which might mean that it, too, was imported, but it is also possible that it is related in some way (by the ore source perhaps) to swords from the Lowbury Hill and Saltwood Tunnel burials.

Fabrication and smithing techniques seem to have been generally understood, although not always applied successfully. A mistake in the relative length of the twists in the sword from Grave 249 was corrected, however. Firewelding was generally achieved with skill (the composite cutting-edges and twisted bars) although completing the assemblage of the layers and the cutting-edge was more difficult. It is possible that sand flux was used, but it is not necessary. Heat treatment appears to have been carried out with caution, perhaps in order to avoid expensive mistakes leading to weapon failure. When the welds are sound, the complex construction is more resistant to bending and impact than low carbon iron. The quality of the swords is variable, but they would make useful weapons, and generally fine looking, high status objects. Three have hardened edges which would be sharper and more effective against harder materials than flesh and bone than the others. There is no reason to suppose that they were not intended for use.

The construction of shield boss apices seems to vary between sites: the Buckland bosses were not constructed in the same way as those from Flixton or the bosses discussed by Härke and Salter (1984). This suggests localised traditions with smiths working out their own practical solutions. The quality of the materials and work in the spearheads (apart from the Grave 323 spear which may have had a specialised use) is poor in comparison with the swords or the batten,

which are also consistent with other hoards (eg Gilmour and Salter 1998).

In summary, it seems that the smiths who made these objects, whether they were local or not, had access to a variety of materials. Most had the knowledge and skills to make use of them effectively when required and probably did not use more time and resources on simpler, lower status items than was necessary.

Quatrefoil brooch: Grave 296

Susan La Niece

The gilt silver quatrefoil brooch, Grave 296 (b), which is one of several from the richly furnished grave of a female, has a broken edge. One garnet and its foil were dislodged on excavation so the opportunity was taken to examine the setting before the garnet was replaced.

The backing paste

The cell for the garnet is partly filled with a firm reddish-brown paste, which still retains the impressions of the foil which rested on it, suggesting that it had not suffered any significant loss during burial. The backing paste has a coarse, sandy structure with a waxy texture. Small flakes of charcoal are embedded in it. X-ray diffraction (XRD) analysis of the paste identified quartz (SiO_2) as the main component, with some calcite ($CaCO_3$). FTIR analysis confirmed the presence of an organic material, possibly a binder, but the sample was inadequate for full identification.

The foil

The foil has a simple grid pattern and is made of mercury gilded silver sheet. It was cut slightly larger than the cell and bent up around the lower edge of the garnet.

Central white inlay

The inlay is in a very decayed state but sufficient structure was visible under magnification to identify it as ivory (identification by Caroline Cartwright).

Material in the small circular cells

There is a pale, fine-grained fill in the bottom of these cells which was examined for evidence of their original settings. XRD analysis of a small sample from the bottom of one of these cells identified calcite with quartz and some cassiterite (SnO_2) and silver chloride (AgCl). It is possible that all of these components are contaminants from the burial soil and metal corrosion, rather than evidence for the original setting.

Discussion

The garnet was set in a cloisonné cell, over a mercury gilded, patterned silver foil. The bottom of the cell was packed with fine sand mixed with calcite and probably an organic binder. Analysis and examination of backing pastes from both continental and English garnet jewellery at the British Museum over the last few years has not identified any which are comparable with this one from Buckland Grave 296. This type of backing paste was classified by Birgit Arrhenius (1985) as sand paste. She too believed it was held together with an organic binder, suggesting egg white rather than wax. She proposed that sand paste was introduced from Rhenish workshops which were operating between AD 520 and 580. She mentions a few examples of this type of backing paste from south-east England: from Taplow, Bifrons, Milton, Buckland and Sutton Hoo. However, the garnet work from the Sutton Hoo ship burial has been very thoroughly examined by Mavis Bimson at the British Museum (Arrhenius 1985, appendix) and no backing pastes at all were found in any of the accessible cells in the gold and garnet regalia from the ship burial assemblage. Nevertheless, the backing pastes behind the garnets from the more recently excavated grave (Sutton Hoo mound 17) are of the calcite paste type.

In conclusion, the sand putty backing paste found in this brooch is unusual, though whether this is because it is fragile and more likely to be damaged, lost during burial, or mistaken for contamination than the finer grained, more consolidated backing pastes, is not clear.

The technology of the knives

Ian Riddler and Fleur Shearman

The knives from the 1994 excavations are described in Part 4 and are summarised by type. Their relationship to broader social studies is also noted. In this contribution, emphasis has been placed on the technology of the knives, and in particular, on their handles and sheaths. No scientific examination of the knife blades has been carried out, and although these techniques have been used on a variety of knives of Anglo-Saxon date, studies have seldom been

centred on early Anglo-Saxon knives from east Kent, with the notable exception of several knives from Canterbury (Wall 1990).

The majority of the knives, where organic remains have survived, have remains of leather sheaths and simple whittle tangs made of horn. There are a few exceptions, however, including the knives from Graves 249C, 285 and 391A, which have wooden handles (*see* pp 279–81). Two knives have riveted handles Graves 391B (w) and 218 (a). The knife from 391B (w), has a handle of riveted horn and that from Grave 218 B (a), where both wood and horn may be present, is also held in place by the single rivet. A similar riveted tang came from a grave at Berinsfield, Oxfordshire (Boyle *et al* 1995, 75 and fig 64). The detached knife tang fragment from Grave 209 (b) has horn over wood but it is not clear whether this is a handle replacement or a slip of wood introduced to secure a loose horn handle. Wooden packing pieces or wedges have been found under the horn handles from three swords from the cemetery (*see* pp 55–6) where their function would appear to be to secure or pack out the hilts. In other cases, summarised below, wood remains are associated with knives, but not specifically with their handles. It is unclear why three knives should have wooden handles, whilst over 100 have handles of horn. With one exception (Grave 249C) they were the graves of adult females. By the late Saxon period most knives had wooden handles, with comparatively few including horn handles, and an increased number utilising bone or antler. The graves listed above, however, include those of both sixth- and seventh-century date. Small numbers of early Anglo-Saxon knives with wooden handles have been noted at other cemeteries, including Beckford (one of six knives), Castledyke (one of seventy-three) and Sewerby (three of twenty-two) (Evison and Hill 1996, 70; Drinkall and Foreman 1998, 283).

The knife from Grave 391B (x) appears to be unique in having a barbed terminal to the end of the iron tang; this is now exposed where the horn is only partially surviving. It is presumed that this internal structure was designed to ensure the handle was firmly fixed in place.

Sheath construction

Fleur Shearman.

A number of the sheaths have traces of textile remains adhering to them, which are often found above the remains of the leather, indicating they may be from garments or possibly cloth bags in the vicinity of the knives. A few knives have no evidence for leather sheaths and human bone and textiles are preserved on their surfaces. It is possible that a

Grave	Details
206	horn handle, wood lined leather scabbard with a single line of string lining decoration under the leather, copper alloy chape and scabbard mouth band
209	horn handle, leather sheath
218	two-part horn handle (a)
218	wooden scabbard (e)
220	horn handle, amorphous organics on blade
223	horn handle
224A	horn handle
228B	horn handle
230	horn handle, leather sheath
233	horn handle, leather sheath
239	horn handle
248	horn handle, leather sheath
249C	wood handle
250	horn handle, leather sheath
259	horn handle, leather sheath
260	horn handle, leather sheath
262	horn handle, leather sheath
263A	horn handle, amorphous deposit on blade probably leather
264	horn handle
265B	horn handle, leather sheath
266	horn handle, leather sheath
269	horn handle, leather sheath
271	horn handle, leather sheath
272	leather sheath
281	horn handle, leather sheath
282A	horn handle, possible traces of leather
285	wood handle, leather sheath
286	horn handle, leather sheath
289	horn handle, leather sheath
295	horn handle, no evidence for sheath
296	organic handle, hide and hair/animal pelt sheath
297	horn handle, organic traces on blade
298	horn handle, no evidence for leather sheath (but see textiles)
299	horn handle, leather sheath
300	horn handle fragment
301	horn handle, leather sheath
308	horn handle
314A	horn handle, leather sheath
303A	horn handle, leather sheath
318	leather sheath
321	horn handle
326	horn handle, leather sheath
327	horn handle, leather sheath
330	horn handle, leather sheath
331	horn handle, leather sheath
336	horn handle, leather sheath with wood ?reinforcement
337	horn handle, leather sheath (a)
337	horn handle, leather sheath (b)
340	horn handle, leather sheath
348	horn handle, leather sheath
350A	horn handle
351A	horn handle, leather sheath
353	horn handle, leather sheath
363	horn handle, leather sheath

Grave	Details
366	horn handle, leather sheath
367	horn handle, leather sheath
372	horn handle, leather sheath
373	horn handle, leather sheath with possible wood/plant stem stiffener on one edge
374	horn handle
376	blade fragment with associated leather
379	leather sheath
381	horn handle, leather sheath (knife, g3)
381	horn handle, leather sheath, traces of associated wood from scabbard or edge stiffener (seax, a)
386B	horn handle, leather sheath
391A	wood handle, no evidence for a sheath
391B	riveted wood handle, no evidence for leather sheath (w)
391B	horn handle, leather sheath, silver and niello chape with a pair of rivets which fasten the leather (x)
392	horn handle
393A	horn handle, wood lined leather sheath
395	horn handle, hide and hair/animal pelt sheath
397	horn handle
398	horn handle, leather sheath
399	organic handle, leather sheath
400	horn handle, no remains of sheath
405	horn handle, leather sheath
406	horn handle, leather sheath
408	horn handle, amorphous organics possibly leather on blade
409	horn handle, leather sheath
411	horn handle, leather sheath with puckering along stitch edge
412	horn handle, leather sheath
413	horn handle, leather sheath
414	horn handle, leather sheath
416	horn handle, leather sheath
417	horn handle
421	horn handle, leather sheath
422	horn handle, leather sheath
423	horn handle, leather sheath with possible internal wood/plant stem stiffener on blade edge
427A	horn handle, leather sheath
428	horn handle, leather sheath
431	horn handle, leather sheath
433	horn handle, leather sheath with possible internal wood/plant stem stiffener on blade edge
434	horn handle, leather sheath
436	horn handle, amorphous organics on blade
437	horn handle, amorphous organics on blade
438	horn handle, decorated leather sheath impressed with geometric designs
439	horn handle, leather sheath
440	horn handle, leather sheath
442	horn handle, leather sheath
443	horn handle, leather sheath
444	leather sheath
Sf. 760	horn handle, leather sheath
Sf. 1285	horn handle, leather sheath

Table 6.11. Knife sheath and handle construction.

proportion of these knives were enclosed without sheaths in cloth wrappings, placed in a cloth bag or placed with the clothed body. However, as the survival of the leather is only partial in many cases, the lack of evidence for sheaths on some knives should not discount the explanation that they were originally present and have subsequently decayed. The knife from Grave 432 has associated leather on the surface. It appears from its grave position, adjacent to an ivory purse ring, to have been enclosed in a purse. Although a cloth bag might be expected, the possibility that leather adhering to the surface may relate to a pouch enclosure, rather than that of a sheath, cannot be eliminated.

The sheaths, where well preserved, have a visible fold edge and an opposing stitched edge. Although the stitching itself is rarely preserved, there is evidence in the form of puckering to confirm the sheaths were stitched rather than stuck, for example the knife from Grave 411 where this evidence survives in good condition. Remains of a possible hide and hair sheath were noted on knives from Graves 296 and 395.

The most elaborate sheath from the long knife in Grave 206 is a scaled down version of a sword scabbard construction with shaped wooden laths covered in leather. As with the decorative string-lining on the scabbard from Grave 249C (*see* pp 53–4), and other examples of string-lining reported by Cameron (2000), the single line of cord is applied to the wood but is covered by a layer of leather. The skin is so thin that the ridged line of the cord would have been intentionally visible on the object. Wood samples were taken from this scabbard and have been identified as willow (*Salix* sp), see below. Wood was also found on both sides of the knives from Graves 393A and 218 in association with leather which would indicate a wood-lined leather sheath. The scabbards from Grave 206 and 391B both have chapes; copper-sheet in the case of Grave 206 and niello-inlaid silver in the example from the rich female Grave 391B.

Knives from Graves 336, 373, 381 and possibly Graves 407 and 433 had fragments of wood or plant stem parallel to one edge. If this is in direct rather than incidental relationship with the sheaths, it is possible that the narrow strip has been incorporated as a form of stiffener or protection from damage from proximity with the blade-edge. This feature has been noted elsewhere on knives from the St Peter's, Broadstairs cemetery (Shearman, unpublished notes). In the case of Grave 381 there are other possible sources for wood in the vicinity, which would need to be taken into account.

Two detached fragments of leather with circular stamped decoration and a line of two stitch-holes were found under a knife from Grave 428. Although these small leather pieces may have originally been part of a sheath, which has become

Fig 6.22. Grave 428, decorated leather fragments found under knife (h).

detached, it is tentatively suggested that they may be from a decorated openwork bag or pouch (Fig 6.22). A coin found in the same area as the leather fragments, under the left arm, would appear to support evidence for the latter.

More compelling evidence for a decorated sheath is present on the fragment of leather preserved on the knife from Grave 438, where impressed designs of zigzags, lines and circles are evident. Longitudinal grooves running along the blade edges were recorded by conservators on knives from Graves 263A and 372 and additionally by Riddler on the knives from Graves 271 and 295. This feature is not necessarily disclosed by x-radiography and as most of the knives have partial remains of a leather sheath, other examples may be at present obscured by the mineralised organic remains.

Mineral-preserved wood: selection and choice of timber

Caroline R Cartwright

Introduction and methodology

Sampling of mineral-replaced wood was carried out on a significant proportion of artefacts from Buckland 1994 (see catalogue, Part 10 and summary below). Artefacts were submitted to the author prior to any conservation treatment and at various stages thereafter; close collaboration with the conservation team is therefore gratefully acknowledged. This report focuses on the properties of the woods identified and why they might have been selected for a particular purpose. The technological significance and chronology of the artefacts with which the wood is associated is described in specific artefact reports (see above and Part 4).

Standard techniques of wood identification and terminology, as set out by the International Association of Wood Anatomists (IAWA), are usually adopted for the identification of modern wood as exemplified by Wheeler *et al* (1986) and Wheeler *et al* (1989). For each sample, the key features are compared with reference collection specimens and textual descriptions (eg Schweingruber 1990). This methodology can often be applied to archaeological wood, providing it is modified to accommodate the effects of the conditions of burial, eg mineral-preservation, waterlogging, desiccation or charring. In all cases, each sample needs to be prepared to expose transverse, radial longitudinal and tangential longitudinal sections or surfaces for identification. For modern and certain types of archaeological wood (such as waterlogged) thin sections of approximately 12–14°m are cut on a base-sledge microtome, mounted on glass slides and examined by transmitted light optical microscopy. In the case of mineral-preserved wood, the cutting of thin-sections is usually prevented by the condition of the wood and the degree of mineral-replacement. For the Buckland cemetery wood, therefore, the method adopted for most of the material was the technique usually used for charcoal identification. This method uses reflected light optical microscopy with darkfield and polarising capabilities and a range of objectives comprising magnifications from x20 to x1000. Fresh transverse, radial longitudinal and tangential longitudinal surfaces were exposed and the characterisation of the anatomical features examined microscopically followed the above-mentioned standardised definitions published by IAWA (Wheeler *et al* 1989). It is worth emphasising that the number of features available for characterisation was restricted because of the high shrinkage, distortion and alteration of the cellular structure during the burial history.

Results and discussion

Despite the very specific problems associated with the identification of mineral-preserved wood, over eighty identifications were possible (see Table 6.12 and Part 10), with nine taxa represented (eight hardwood and one softwood). The predominantly-used wood for most categories of artefacts was *Fraxinus excelsior*, ash, particularly in association with iron artefacts such as swords, spearheads, ferrules, arrowheads, awl-like firesteels, shafts, rods, the weaving batten and shields. Ash had already been recorded from artefacts recovered during earlier excavations at Buckland, eg for spearheads and a ferrule (Watson 1987).

It is not surprising that ash should be a prime choice for handles, scabbards, shafts, hafts and such artefacts; the timber is well-known for its pliability and toughness. Ash wood has sufficient elasticity to absorb shock or strain without fracturing. Ash trees are generally hardy enough to survive in most habitats, although they prefer valley bottoms and river edges – an environment existing in the immediate area of the Buckland cemetery. As a common component of mixed oak forest in Britain, they are readily available. If ash trees are cut before reaching maturity they coppice freely; these quickly-grown coppice poles are highly suitable for weapon and tool handles, spear shafts and the like. Coppiced poles with their long straight grain may well have been the source for much of the ash wood present in the Buckland assemblage. Like oak, ash has the potential for being deliberately split along the radial plane when required for shaft lengths and handles. Ash is suitable for all types of general carpentry; during this period it may be regarded as the next most important timber after oak and beech. It is interesting to find ash wood and *Salix* sp, willow wood associated with copper alloy rivets for an iron shield board (Grave 265B); could the shield have been composed of both ash and willow sections? Watson (1994) has noted that shield boards of this period were usually made of lime, alder, ash, birch, field maple and willow/poplar, with a few in beech or oak. Despite the traditional popularity of lime wood, willow or poplar wood has been identified for many shield boards. At Buckland, here is another example of willow wood used (alongside ash) for this purpose.

Salix sp, willow was selected as a source of wood in the Buckland assemblage for iron artefacts such as knives, spearheads, a spear ferrule, an arrowhead and on the above-mentioned shield board. Whilst nowhere near as important a choice as ash wood, willow was selected when a lightweight but very resilient raw material was required. Ash wood consistently out-performed willow wood for spear shafts and sword scabbards and hilts, but willow wood was often quite adequate for knife handles, as can be seen in the Buckland assemblage. Willow (or poplar) was identified in the previous Buckland excavations, too, in association with the ring-sword, a seax and a knife with composite handle (Watson 1987). Willow was particularly sought after as withies for strips, small branches and materials for basketry and hurdling. Wilson (1987) notes its use for a belt.

Fagus sylvatica, beech wood was present in the Buckland assemblage in very specific instances: as a wooden box (Grave 353), as part of a composite casket (Grave 255), and in association with a couple of iron spearheads, knives and a fragment of iron binding. It is interesting to note the use of beech wood for two boxes from the earlier Buckland excavations (Cutler 1987). Beech wood was widely available in England during this period and could often be split like oak, when required. Beech timber was particularly useful for the manufacture of furniture and small tools, where a strong, even grain was essential. Seasoning of the wood was needed for best results.

Other components of mixed oak forests and riversides were present in the wood assemblage eg *Corylus avellana*, hazel, which was used for iron rod and awl-like firesteel handles. Cutler (1987) noted hazel in association with an iron fragment. In the present Buckland assemblage, hazel wood was also found in association with two copper alloy brooches (Grave 239) and a loop (Grave 350B), but it is not clear what the relationship of the hazel wood might be with respect to these artefacts. It is possible that these hazel wood fragments relate to wooden artefacts which only survived in fragmentary form where they rested on, and were preserved by, metal artefacts. Like willow and ash, hazel coppices easily and is often used in this form for basketry, casks, hoops, hurdles, wicker-lined pits and fencing. There is a long history of use of hazel wood in the British Isles (from Neolithic and Bronze Age times particularly) when it provided the material of choice where toughness and flexibility were concerned for spears, arrow shafts and bows. Such usage in the Buckland assemblage, however, was obviously replaced by ash wood.

Acer campestre, field maple wood was used in connection with three iron spearheads from the present Buckland assemblage. Cutler (1987) records earlier examples of field maple wood from a scabbard and spear. Field maple wood is compact, fine-grained and takes a high polish; for this reason, it is sought after at the present-day for cabinet-making, inlay and fine items such as violin cases. Coppiced field maple branches would have yielded the best timber for Buckland weaponry purposes.

Also in the decorative wood and inlay category was *Prunus* sp (plum/cherry) wood. At Buckland it was found in the present assemblage associated with two copper alloy buckles. As in the case of hazel, it is most likely that these fragments represent wooden artefacts which only survived in fragmentary form where they rested on, and were preserved by, the copper alloy buckles. Cutler (1987) noted the presence of Rosaceae-type wood (which includes the genus *Prunus*) at the foot of a grave in the earlier Buckland assemblage, presumably with a similar contextual interpretation. *Prunus* wood is of medium density, firm, strong, with a fine, uniform texture and generally straight grain. It is easy to work, is dimensionally stable, and can be polished to a smooth finish. Useful for handles, boxes, small artefacts and fine furniture, there may have been specific (and decorative) uses for *Prunus* wood in the Buckland assemblage.

Quercus sp (oak) wood, although widespread and an excellent all-purpose timber in many periods throughout the British Isles and Europe was only represented at Buckland in the form of the wooden bucket from Grave 391B and associated with iron firesteels/pursemounts, iron nails and cleats. Its apparent scarcity may be misleading, however. For example, if the graves had contained oak coffins, conditions of preservation in the burials might mean that the only surviving traces of such usage would be where the wood had been preserved by the iron corrosion products on nails. Is this perhaps what we are seeing? The presence of oak wood under bronze bowls and near a skull in burial contexts from the earlier excavations (Cutler 1987) might be seen as reinforcing this possibility. There is no doubting the usefulness of oak wood for its stiffness, medium density and resistance. Its straight growth and ability to be split cleanly along the radial plane make it very suitable for laths, staves, beams and planks. Its choice for the Buckland bucket is clearly an informed and specific one, designed to make best use of oak wood properties. Oak would also have made ideal coffin timber for the Buckland graves (*see* p 34).

The only remaining hardwood in the Buckland assemblage is *Tilia* sp, lime, present in association with an iron shield boss (Grave 264). It has already been noted above that lime wood was traditionally chosen for shield boards and its presence in this particular context seems to indicate this usage here. The presence of lime wood in the earlier Buckland excavations is less clear; it was found on the back of a copper alloy buckle (Watson 1987) and near the pelvis of a skeleton (Cutler 1987). *Tilia*, often known as the 'carver's tree', has a straight grain and fine, even texture. It can be worked easily and is very stable in all forms of carpentry despite being relatively lightweight.

The only softwood present in the Buckland assemblage is *Taxus baccata*, yew, found in association with iron artefacts such as a buckle and spear ferrules. Yew wood is perhaps best known prehistorically as the choice raw material for making bows and spear points. It is moderately heavy and hard with medium strength and has relatively low stiffness and shock resistance. Yew wood reacts well to steam bending, and has good stability and decay-resistance over time. Its even, medium texture also makes it suitable for turnery and carving, whether in its typically straight grained form, or curly, knotty and irregular.

Conclusions

The wood represented in the Buckland cemetery is largely associated with metal weaponry, tools and some functional or decorative artefacts. Consequently, timbers have been very carefully and specifically chosen for their particular properties to suit the function of the object. *Fraxinus excelsior*, ash wood, was by far the most popular choice for the range of weapons and tools present. Its ready availability locally, pliability, toughness and reliability made it an obvious favourite for the Buckland carpenters. Other components of mixed oak forest, such as willow, hazel, field maple, beech, lime, plum/cherry

and yew were also used, but even with all their numbers of identifications combined, they do not amount to a higher percentage of use than is displayed by ash wood. Little in the way of direct evidence for coffin wood has survived. There is a possibility that *Quercus* sp, oak wood may have furnished the raw material for Buckland coffins, but (to date) no intact wooden oak coffin has survived (*see* pp 34–5).

Grave	Find	Object	Wood	Wood
205	a	Buckle	*Prunus*	Plum/Cherry
206	a	Knife sheath	*Salix*	Willow
209	b	Knife	*Fraxinus excelsior*	Ash
220	a	Spearhead	*Acer campestre*	Field maple
224A	a	Knife	*Fraxinus excelsior*	Ash
230	b	Spearhead	*Fraxinus excelsior*	Ash
231	a	Buckle	*Taxus baccata*	Yew
239	b, c	Brooches	*Corylus avellana*	Hazel
239	d, e	Brooches	*Fraxinus excelsior*	Ash
240	a	Spearhead	*Fraxinus excelsior*	Ash
240	b	Ferrule	*Fraxinus excelsior*	Ash
246	c	Nail	*Quercus*	Oak
249C	a	Sword scabbard	*Fraxinus excelsior*	Ash
249C	c	Spearhead	*Fraxinus excelsior*	Ash
249C	d	Knife	*Fraxinus excelsior*	Ash
249C	f	Ferrule	*Fraxinus excelsior*	Ash
250	d	Weaving batten	*Fraxinus excelsior*	Ash
250	k	Ring	*Fraxinus excelsior*	Ash
250	n	Knife	*Fraxinus excelsior*	Ash
251	a	Spearhead	*Acer campestre*	Field maple
255	m	Casket	*Fagus sylvatica*	Beech
256	c	Spearhead	*Fraxinus excelsior*	Ash
262	a	Spearhead	*Fraxinus excelsior*	Ash
264	a	Spearhead	*Salix*	Willow
264	b	Sword scabbard	*Fraxinus excelsior*	Ash
264	e	Shield boss	*Tilia*	Lime
265B	a	Spearhead	*Fraxinus excelsior*	Ash
265B	b	Sword scabbard	*Fraxinus excelsior*	Ash
265B	d	Shield board rivets	*Fraxinus excelsior and Salix*	Ash and willow
265B	f	Buckle and plate	*Prunus*	Plum/Cherry
265B	i	Knife	*Fraxinus excelsior*	Ash
265B	gg	Iron shaft	*Fraxinus excelsior*	Ash
265B	hh	Awl-like firesteel	*Fraxinus excelsior*	Ash
265B	ii	Ferrule	*Taxus baccata*	Yew
266	a, e	Rod and staple	*Fraxinus excelsior*	Ash
281	i	Knife	*Fraxinus excelsior*	Ash
297	g	Ferrule	*Salix*	Willow
299	a	Spearhead	*Fraxinus excelsior*	Ash
300	a-n	Clench nails	*Quercus*	Oak

Grave	Find	Object	Wood	Wood
300	o	Firesteel/pursemount	*Quercus*	Oak
300	p	Knife	*Fagus sylvatica*	Beech
300	q	Spearhead	*Fraxinus excelsior*	Ash
301	a	Spearhead	*Fraxinus excelsior*	Ash
302	b	Arrowhead	*Fraxinus excelsior*	Ash
323	a	Spearhead	*Fraxinus excelsior*	Ash
336	d	Knife	*Salix*	Willow
336	g	Iron binding	*Fagus sylvatica*	Beech
337	c	Spearhead	*Acer campestre*	Field maple
346	a	Spearhead	*Fagus sylvatica*	Beech
346	b	Sword scabbard	*Fraxinus excelsior*	Ash
346	d	Rod	*Corylus avellana*	Hazel
350B	b	Copper alloy loop	*Corylus avellana*	Hazel
353	g	Casket	*Fagus sylvatica*	Beech
363	a	Spearhead	*Salix*	Willow
374	a	Spearhead	*Fraxinus excelsior*	Ash
375	a	Spearhead	*Fagus sylvatica*	Beech
375	b	Sword scabbard	*Fraxinus excelsior*	Ash
375	d2	Cleat	*Quercus*	Oak
381	g2	Firesteel/pursemount	*Quercus*	Oak
388	a-h	Angle-irons	*Quercus*	Oak
391B	a	Bucket	*Quercus*	Oak
391B	w	Knife	*Fagus sylvatica*	Beech
391B	x	Knife	*Fraxinus excelsior*	Ash
393A	a	Spearhead	*Fraxinus excelsior*	Ash
400	b	Spearhead	*Fraxinus excelsior*	Ash
411	a	Spearhead	*Fraxinus excelsior*	Ash
414	a	Spearhead	*Fraxinus excelsior*	Ash
414	b	Sword scabbard	*Fraxinus excelsior*	Ash
414	c	Knife	*Salix*	Willow
414	e1	Awl-like firesteel	*Corylus avellana*	Hazel
414	e2	Awl-like firesteel	*Corylus avellana*	Hazel
417	h	Knife	*Salix*	Willow
421	a	Arrowhead	*Salix*	Willow
423	a	Spearhead	*Fraxinus excelsior*	Ash
437	a	Sword scabbard	*Fraxinus excelsior*	Ash
444	b	Nail	*Quercus*	Oak

Table 6.12. Summary of mineralised wood remains.

PART 7: THE HUMAN SKELETONS

Trevor Anderson[†] with John Andrews and Ian Hodgins[81]

Two hundred and forty-four graves were excavated in 1994. In twenty-seven of these no bone was recovered. Fourteen graves contained two skeletons and one (Grave 249) contained three individuals. As such, 233 skeletons were available for study. Bone preservation was very poor due to the high alkalinity of the chalk subsoil. The majority of the skeletons were represented by eroded long bone shafts and fragmented crania. Just over 11 per cent of all the skeletons (n = 26) were reasonably complete (Table 7.1a). All the immature skeletons were incomplete, with over half the sub-adults represented by less than 20 per cent of the skeleton. All sub-adult and almost 90 per cent of the total sample were classed as fragmented or highly fragmented (n = 207). There was evidence that the younger adult skeletons were less fragmented than the older adults (Table 7.2a).

Poor bone preservation appears to be a frequent finding in Anglo-Saxon cemeteries (Anderson 1990; Anderson and Andrews 1997; Anderson and Birkett 1989; Cox 1990; Haughton and Powesland 1999; Chadwick Hawkes and Hogarth 1974, 85; Hirst 1985; Marlow 1992; Mays 1990; McKinley 1987; Philp 1973a; Waldron 1994). At Empingham (Mays 1990) and West Heslerton (Haughton and Powesland 1999) skeletal condition was so poor that sexing had to be attempted using dental metrices.

Demography

One hundred and eighty three skeletons were assessed as adult. Males and females were equally represented in the sample as a whole (Figs 7.1 and 7.3). However, twenty-seven poorly preserved adults could not be sexed on osteological evidence. There is no clear evidence for sexual segregation, males and females appear to be randomly distributed throughout the cemetery (Fig 7.1). Almost two-thirds of all adults died before they were 45 years old and approximately one sixth were definitely classed as mature (Figs 7.1 and 7.2). There is some evidence that males were living longer than females. Almost 40 per cent of females were dead before the age of 30 years and just over 12 per cent (n = 7) were classed as elderly. Over a quarter of males (n = 21) reached old age (Tables 7.1b and 7.2b). As far as adults are concerned, age at death does not appear to have influenced burial location. The osteological data coupled with the lack of chronological grouping supports a polycentric growth pattern. Similar independent plots have been recognised at Alfriston; Andover; Holywell Row; Polhill; Sewerby and the burials at Spong Hill (Härke 1997).

Over 20 per cent of the Buckland 1994 population failed to reach adulthood (Tables 7.1b and 7.2b). Only one child (Sk 388) under 1 year old was recovered (Fig 7.1). The other three sub-adult age groups are almost equally represented (Tables 7.1b and 7.2b; Fig 7.2). Out of twenty-seven graves with no bones, twenty-three, by size, probably contained children, giving a sub-adult mortality of over 28 per cent (73/260) (Table 7.3; Fig 7.2). The greatest concentration of sub-adult skeletons occurs in the higher, north-eastern portion of the 1994 cemetery area (Plots X and Y). When seven short graves without bones are included, the sub-adult mortality for this area reaches almost 36 per cent. It also contains three child graves in close proximity (Graves 422; 442 and 444), which are all dated to the earlier phases of the cemetery (Phases 1–2).

---

81. This study was completed by the late Trevor Anderson in 2002 and is presented with very little alteration to his manuscript.

Code	Sub-adult	Adult			
	All	All	Male	Female	? Sex
1	0.0 (0)	4.4 (8)	5.1 (4)	5.2 (4)	0.0 (0)
2	0.0 (0)	9.8 (18)	15.4 (12)	7.8 (6)	0.0 (0)
3	14.0 (7)	31.7 (58)	38.5 (30)	36.3 (28)	0.0 (0)
4	18.0 (9)	26.8 (49)	24.4 (19)	29.9 (23)	25.0 (7)
5	12.0 (6)	13.1 (24)	11.5 (9)	13.0 (10)	17.8 (5)
6	14.0 (7)	7.7 (14)	3.8 (3)	3.9 (3)	28.6 (8)
7	42.0 (21)	6.6 (12)	1.3 (1)	3.9 (3)	28.6 (8)

1: >95%; 2: 80–95%; 3: 60–80%; 4: 40–60%; 5: 20–40%; 5: 20–40%; 6: 5–20%; 7: <5%

Table 7.1a. Buckland: bone completeness.

	Sub-adult	Adult			
Code	All	All	Male	Female	? Sex
a	0.0 (0)	0.5 (1)	1.3 (1)	0.0 (0)	0.0 (0)
b	0.0 (0)	2.7 (5)	2.6 (2)	3.9 (3)	0.0 (0)
c	0.0 (0)	10.9 (20)	17.9 (14)	7.8 (6)	0.0 (0)
d	12.0 (6)	40.4 (74)	43.6 (34)	48.0 (37)	10.7 (3)
e	88.0 (44)	45.5 (83)	34.6 (27)	40.3 (31)	89.3 (25)

a: excellent, all solid; b: very good, mainly solid; c: good, some fragmented, repairable; d: largely fragmented; e: very badly fragmented; f: powdery stain, some bone; g: stain only.

Table 7.2a. Buckland: bone condition.

Sub-adult

Age	Total	Completeness						
		1	2	3	4	5	6	7
Sub-adult	50	-	-	7	9	6	7	21
0–1 years	1	-	-	-	-	-	-	1
1–6 years	13	-	-	-	-	1	2	10
6–12 years	16	-	-	-	5	2	2	7
12–20 years	20	-	-	7	4	3	3	3

Adult

Male

Age	Total	Completeness						
		1	2	3	4	5	6	7
All	78	4	12	30	19	9	3	1
Young adult	23	3	6	8	5	1	-	-
Adult	24	-	4	11	6	1	2	-
Mature	21	1	2	11	6	1	-	-
Grown	10	-	-	-	2	6	1	1

Female

Age	Total	Completeness						
		1	2	3	4	5	6	7
All	77	4	6	28	23	10	3	3
Young adult	30	4	3	12	6	3	1	1
Adult	31	-	3	11	12	2	1	2
Mature	10	-	-	5	3	2	-	-
Grown	6	-	-	-	2	3	1	-

? Sex

Age	Total	Completeness						
		1	2	3	4	5	6	7
All	28	-	-	-	7	5	8	8
Young adult	3	-	-	-	1	-	1	1
Adult	5	-	-	-	2	2	-	1
Mature	2	-	-	-	2	-	-	-
Grown*	18	-	-	-	2	3	7	6

Total adults: 183; Graves with no bones: 27
* includes 4 poorly preserved skeletons, either juvenile or grown

1: >95%; 2: 80–95%; 3: 60–80%; 4: 40–60%; 5: 20–40%; 5: 20–40%; 6: 5–20%; 7: <5%

Table 7.1b. Buckland: bone completeness by age and sex.

Sub-adult

Age	Total	Condition				
		a	b	c	d	e
Sub-adult	50	-	-	-	6	44
0–1 years	1	-	-	-	-	1
1–6 years	13	-	-	-	-	13
6–12 years	16	-	-	-	1	15
12–20 years	20	-	-	-	5	15

Adult

Male

Age	Total	Condition				
		a	b	c	d	e
All	78	1	2	14	34	27
Young adult	23	1	2	5	8	7
Adult	24	-	-	4	12	8
Mature	21	-	-	4	11	6
Grown	10	-	-	1	3	6

Female

Age	Total	Condition				
		a	b	c	d	e
All	77	-	3	6	37	31
Young adult	30	-	3	4	13	10
Adult	31	-	-	-	18	13
Mature	10	-	-	2	4	4
Grown	6	-	-	-	2	4

? Sex

Age	Total	Condition				
		a	b	c	d	e
All	28	-	-	-	3	25
Young adult	3	-	-	-	-	3
Adult	5	-	-	-	-	5
Mature	2	-	-	-	-	2
Grown*	18	-	-	-	3	15

Total adults: 183; Graves with no bones: 27
* includes 4 poorly preserved skeletons, either juvenile or grown

a: excellent, all solid; b: very good, mainly solid; c: good, some fragmented, repairable; d: largely fragmented; e: very badly fragmented; f: powdery stain, some bone; g: stain only.

Table 7.2b. Buckland: bone condition by age and sex.

The lack of perinatal and early infant burials has been noted in other Anglo-Saxon cemeteries. Only a single perinatal burial was discovered at West Heslerton (Cox 1990). At Empingham, Leicestershire, only two children under 2 years were buried (Mays 1990) and at both Mill Hill, Deal and Burgh Castle, Norfolk the youngest burials were over 2 years old (Anderson and Andrews 1997; Anderson and Birkett 1989). In the Buckland 1951–3 excavations five children (Sk 20, Sk 34, Sk 55, Sk 74 and Sk 119) under 6 years of age were recorded along with a mother buried with her unborn foetus (Sk 110). Eleven graves with no bones, by size, also probably contained children (Evison 1987, 18), suggesting a sub-adult mortality of around 9 per cent (16/171) for this part of the cemetery.

At Abingdon, only 8 per cent (4/48) of sub-adults were under 1 year old (Leeds and Harden 1936). The only early Anglo-Saxon cemetery with a high perinatal mortality is Great Chesterford in Essex, where almost a third of the total sample, some fifty-five infants, died before their first birthday (Waldron 1994). A small sixth-century cemetery at Oakington, Cambridgeshire displays an extremely high sub-adult mortality (60 per cent) with two infants under 1 year old (Taylor *et al* 1997). Also, a cemetery at Butler's Field in Gloucestershire, with a wide date range, has revealed a high sub-adult mortality, with forty-two children dying before the age of 5 years, including five new born babies (Boyle *et al* 1998).

There is some evidence that burial of young infants in cemeteries became more common in the middle and later Anglo-Saxon period. Although the eighth-century Christian cemetery at Nazeingbury did not contain any children under eighteen months (Huggins 1978), middle Saxon Raunds (Powell unpublished), had sixty-seven infants under 1 year (18.1 per cent of the population); Castledyke South (seventh to eighth centuries) had nine children under 2 years and a mother buried with her unborn foetus, about three weeks before full term (Drinkall and Foreman 1998, 225). Late Anglo-Saxon Red Castle (Wells 1967) had fourteen infants under 2 years old (16.5 per cent of the sample).

Allowing for problems of ageing and sexing poorly preserved skeletal remains, the overall demographic pattern revealed in our sample appears to be fairly normal.

Burial practice: multiple and prone burials

From the 217 graves in which bones were recovered, the majority (n = 202) contained a single supine individual. Fourteen graves contained two skeletons and one (Grave 249) contained three individuals (*see* pp 26–8; Table 7.4). As such, almost 7 per cent of graves (n = 15) with preserved skeletal material were classed as multiple. A lower figure, 1.3 per cent (2/156) was recorded in the earlier Buckland excavations (Evison 1987, Graves 96 and 110). The combined figure for both areas is just over 4.5 per cent (17/373). In three of the multiple graves (Graves 224, 228 and 314) the skeletons were buried side by side. Grave 224 contained two unsexed adults; Grave 228 held a 15–17 year old possible female (Sk A) and a possible male 17–20 years old (Sk B), facing each other (p 25; Fig 7.1; Fig 7.4). Grave 314 contained a female about 40 years old (Sk A) and an unsexed child, aged 7–9 (Sk B).

The other twelve multiple graves contained skeletons buried directly above each other, the stacked graves (*see* pp 26–9; Table 7.4). The majority contained only adults. In four cases these appeared to be of the same sex: two with certain or possible females (Graves 238 and 391) and two with certain or possible males (Graves 282 and 393). In two cases, a male was buried above a female (Graves 263 and 351) and the triple grave contained a possible female buried above two males. In two other cases, the lower skeleton was male but the upper burial was unsexed (Graves 265 and 386). In the two graves with sub-adults, the children were buried above an adult (Graves 303 and 350). As noted elsewhere (Stoodley 1999, 54–5), the demography of the multiple graves at Buckland appears to reflect that of the overall sample, although sub-adults seem to be slightly under-represented (Table 7.6). At several sites, the opposite finding is demonstrable (Tables 7.7a, 7.7b). There is evidence that sub-adult material is more frequent in contemporary side by side burials (Table 7.7a) than in double-stacked graves (Table 7.7b). A review of other Anglo-Saxon cemetery sites indicates that deliberate deposition of more than one body in a grave is not uncommon (Table 7.5a and b).

Only one prone burial (Grave 263A) has been noted at Buckland, an un-aged grown male buried directly above a 'rich' young adult ?female (Sk B). The prone skeleton had been partially cut away by a later grave (Grave 264) and was only represented by leg bone diaphyses. Such burials are a well-recognised finding in many Anglo-Saxon cemeteries (Tables 7.9 and 7.10). Although never frequent, their prevalence is normally higher than recorded at Buckland.

Metric analysis

Stature

The fragmented nature of the 1994 Buckland sample meant that living stature, based on long bone lengths of sexed individuals (Trotter and Gleser 1958), could only be calculated for twenty-four males and eighteen females. The mean male

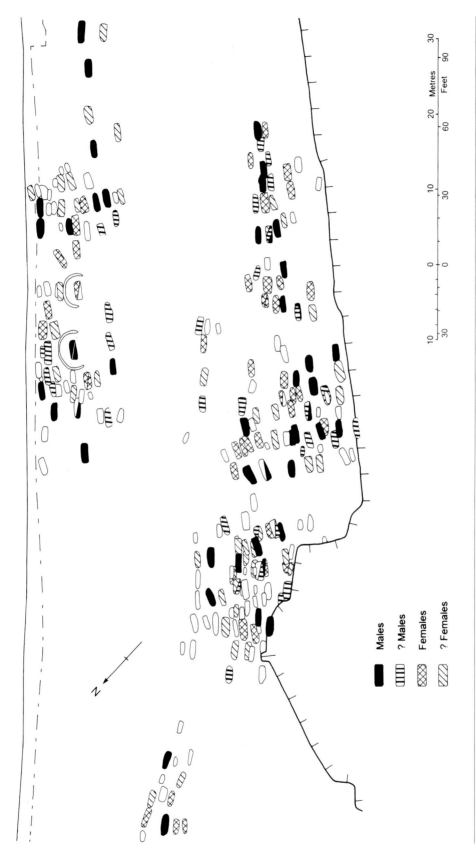

Fig 7.1. Plan of 1994 excavations showing distribution of male and female skeletons based on osteological evidence.

Males
? Males
Females
? Females

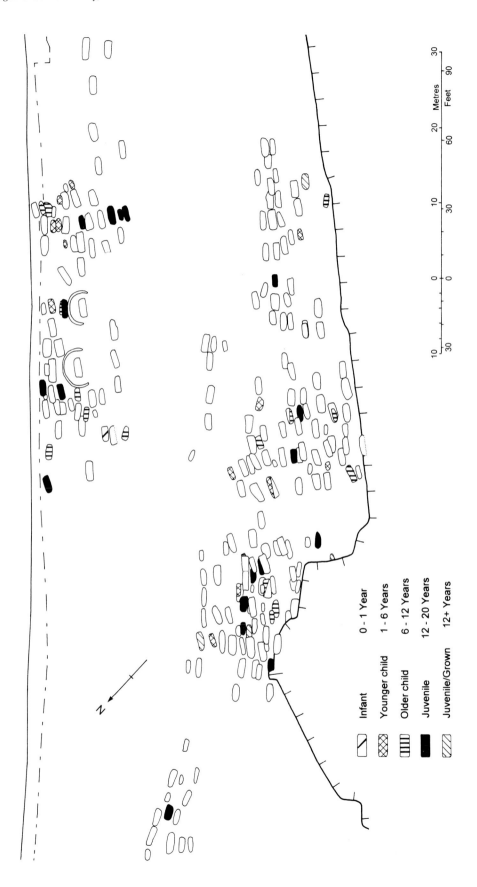

Fig 7.2. Plan of 1994 excavations showing distribution of sub-adult skeletons.
Infant (0–1 year), Younger child (1–6 years), Older child (6–12 years), Juvenile (12–18 years) and Juvenile/Grown (12+ years).

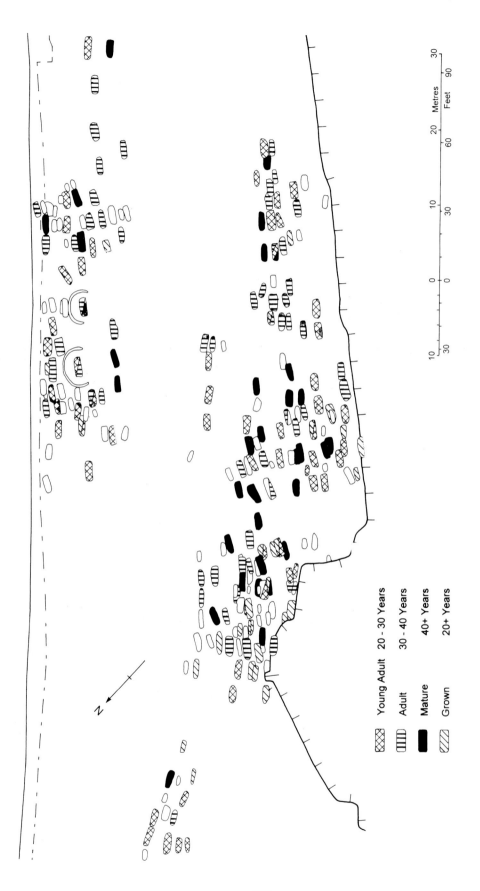

Fig 7.3. Plan of 1994 excavations showing distribution of adult skeletons.
Mature (40+ years), Adult (30–40 years), Young adult (18–30 years) and Grown (18+ years).

Young Adult 20 - 30 Years

Adult 30 - 40 Years

Mature 40+ Years

Grown 20+ Years

stature was 1.758m (5ft 9¼in), with a range from 1.674m (5ft 6in) [Sk 351A] to 1.876m (6ft 1¾in) [Sk 301]. The mean female stature was 1.642m (5ft 4¾in), with a range from 1.543m (5ft ¾in) [Sk 372] to 1.763m (5ft 9½in) [Sk 426].

Detailed examination of British height, from the mid eighteenth century to the present, suggests that stature attainment is related to childhood nutritional status (Floud *et al* 1990); with stunting occurring before 5 years of age

(*ibid*, 232). As such, it appears valid to consider that short stature in archaeological material may be related to lower social status and poorer levels of nutrition, especially during the first years of life.

The tallest male (Sk 301) and female (Sk 426) were both buried in the north-eastern part of the 1994 cemetery area (Plots Z and Y). However, there is no definite relationship between height and burial location. The shortest female (Sk 372) may

Sub-adult mortality (%)	Site	Source
5.2 (3/58)	Finglesham, Kent	Chadwick (1958)
5.3 (1/19)	Monkton, Thanet, Kent	Denston (1974)
11.1 (17/153)	Nazeingbury, Essex	Huggins (1978)
12.5 (1/8)	Crane Down, Jevington, Sussex	Holden (1969)
13.6 (8/59)	Sewerby, Yorkshire	Hirst (1985)
15.5 (30/194)	Burgh Castle, Norfolk	S Anderson & Birkett (1989)
17.6 (34/193)	West Heslerton, Yorkshire	Cox (1999)
18.2 (32/176)	Eccles, Kent	Manchester (unpublished)
18.6 (8/43)	Holborough, Kent	Evison (1956)
18.9 (39/206)	North Elmham, Norfolk	Wells (1980)
19.0 (4/21)	Ports Down, Hampshire	Corney *et al* (1967)
19.5 (8/41)	Droxford, Hampshire	Aldsworth (1978)
20.0 (9/45)	Winnall, Hampshire	Meaney & Chadwick Hawkes (1970)
20.7 (6/29)	Orpington, Kent	Tester (1968)
20.7 (68/328)	St Peter's, Broadstairs, Kent	Duhig (1996)
21.4 (6/28)	Little Eriswell, Suffolk	Wells (1966)
21.5 (50/233)*	Buckland 1994, Dover, Kent	present report
22.2 (8/36)	Lyminge, Kent	Warhurst (1955)
22.2 (35/158)	Staunch Meadow, Brandon, Suffolk	S Anderson (1990)
23.0 (32/139)	Caister-on-Sea, Norfolk	S Anderson (1991)
23.1 (46/199)	Castledyke South, Humberside	Drinkall & Foreman (1998)
24.0 (30/125)	Polhill, Kent	Philp (1973a)
24.1 (35/145)	Buckland 1951–3, Dover, Kent	Evison (1987)
25.0 (7/28)	Melbourn, Cambridgeshire	Wilson (1956)
28.2 (24/85)	Red Castle, Norfolk	Wells (1967)
28.4 (19/67)	Petersfinger, Wiltshire	Leeds & Shortt (1953)
29.6 (24/81)	Broughton Lodge, Nottinghamshire	Harman (1993)
29.8 (14/47)	Alton, Hampshire	Evison (1988, table 12)
30.4 (38/125)	Norton, Cleveland	Marlow (1992)
30.6 (37/121)	Apple Down & the Mardens, Chichester, Sussex	Harman (1990)
31.1 (46/148)	Edix Hill, Barrington, Cambridgeshire	Duhig (1998)
35.7 (10/28)	Ocklynge Hill, Sussex	Stevens (1980)
35.9 (55/153)	Empingham II, Rutland	Timby (1996)
38.6 (44/114)	Abingdon, Oxfordshire	Harman (1995)
38.9 (42/108)	Berinsfield, Oxfordshire	Harman (1995)
39.3 (48/122)	Abingdon, Berkshire	Leeds & Harden (1936)
40.3 (31/77)**	Mill Hill, Deal, Kent	Anderson & Andrews (1997)
41.9 (93/222)	Butler's Field, Gloucestershire	Harman (1998)
46.2 (171/370)	Raunds, Northants	Powell (unpublished)
46.7 (78/167)	Great Chesterford, Essex	Waldron (1994)
27.5 (1291/4699) Mean		

* 23 of 27 graves without bones appear, by size, to contain children. Including these gives a sub-adult mortality of 28.1% (73/260)

** in Burials Nos 8, 13, 58 & 62, no bones were recovered. Based on the length of these graves, they originally contained children. Inclusion of these individuals would result in a sub-adult mortality of 43.2%

Table 7.3. Sub-adult mortality in Anglo-Saxon England.

be regarded as 'rich' from the grave goods. Similarly, at Mill Hill, Deal two of the richest females (Sk 25A and Sk 105C), were of short stature: 1.532m (5ft ¼in) and 1.509m (4ft 11½in), respectively (Anderson and Andrews 1997). Compared to other Anglo-Saxon cemeteries, the mean stature of both sexes at Buckland is relatively tall (Tables 7.11 and 7.12). Both sexes are as tall as their modern day counterparts in Kent.

Cranial metrics

Metric analysis could be undertaken on forty-seven largely fragmented and incomplete, adult crania. The metrics and calculated indices fall within the accepted range for the

Anglo-Saxon period. The sample of intact crania is too small to establish any definite spatial variation in the cranial indices.

The mean adult cranial index (74.0) based on only seventeen skulls, falls within the dolichocranic (long-headed) range. Male crania (mean 72.6) were predominantly long-headed (mean 74.0), while female crania (mean 75.3) were medium-headed. The most dolichocranic skull (66.5) was from a male (Sk 328) buried in Plot T. The most brachiocranic (round-headed) (80.7) skull was that of a young adult male (Sk 385; Plot X). Brachycephalisation has been related to both cold climate (Beals 1972) and improved nutrition (Lasker 1946; Miki 1990).

Side-by-side graves			1.38% (3/217)	
Grave	Sex	Age	Phase	Notes
224A	?	grown	-	side-by-side
224B	?	grown	-	truncated, left femur and tibiae only
228A	?Female	15–17	3a–7	side-by-side facing right
228B	?Male	17–20	3a–7	side-by-side facing left
314A	Female	c 40	-	side-by-side
314B	?	7–9	-	side-by-side

Double-stacked graves			5.07% (11/217)	
Grave	Sex	Age	Phase	Notes
238A	?Female	grown	1–2	above 238B
238B	Female	30–40	1–2	below 238A
263A	Male	grown	1b–2a	upper half cut away, prone, above 263B
263B	?Female	25–30	1b	below 263A
265A	?	grown	3–7	cut by machine, left tibia only, above 265B
265B	?Male	25–30	3a	below 265A, sword
282A	?Male	grown	-	above 282B
282B	Male	25–30	-	below 282A
303A	?	c 3	3b	slightly higher at side of left knee Sk 303B
303B	Male	30–35	1–3	partially healed cranial weapon wound
350A	?	c 8	-	above 350B
350B	?Male	20–25	-	below 350A, grave goods imply female
351A	Male	grown	1–2	above 351B
351B	Female	40–45	1	below 351A
386A	?	grown	-	cut by machine, left arm only, above 386B
386B	Male	20–25	-	below 386A
391A	Female	35–45	5–7	very rich, above 391B
391B	Female	20–25	2	very rich, below 391A
393A	Male	25–30	-	above 393B
393B	Male	35–45	-	below 393A
427A	Female	30–35	1b–2	above 427B
427B	?	20–25	1–2	below 427A

Triple grave			0.46% (1/217)	
Grave	Sex	Age	Phase	Notes
249A	?Female	35–45?	-	only frags of mandible, cervical vertebrae and left shoulder surviving; upper burial
249B	Male	grown	-	middle burial
249C	Male	40–50	2–3	primary burial with weapons

Table 7.4. Buckland: multiple burials.

Fig 7.4. Grave 228: two juvenile skeletons, buried side by side, facing each other.

The unaccompanied skeleton in Grave 385 had been buried, in an atypical manner (*see* pp 24–5) close to the north-west boundary of the plot. He was interred very deeply and was one of the few individuals found buried on his right side, with his left arm lying in front of the body. The skeleton displayed a well-healed fracture just above the left wrist, probably the result of a fall rather than direct trauma. The same individual also displayed the narrowest nose (42.4) and narrowest male internal palate (78.7). Nasal morphology, appears to be influenced by climate, with narrower noses related to cold and dry conditions (Davies 1932; Thomson and Buxton 1923). As such, the nasal and cranial morphology all might suggest the possibility that this individual had grown up in a country with a cold and dry climate.

Post-cranial metrics

Metric analysis could be undertaken on less than 60 per cent of adult skeletons and the available metrics and indices fall within the bounds of normality. There was no obvious spatial distribution of the various indices. Only the meric and cnemic indices are available for comparison from other excavated Anglo-Saxon cemeteries (Tables 7.13a and 7.14a).

The meric index records the degree of antero-posterior (front-to-back) flattening of the upper femoral shaft. An index of under 85 is platymeric (marked flattening). Both

sexes were affected equally with just over three quarters (141/187) of the adult femora classed as platymeric (Table 7.13b). In both sexes, flattening was more marked (85/101) on the left side. A similar laterality has been noted from Mill Hill, Deal (Anderson and Andrews 1997). Other Anglo-Saxon sites all display a greater degree of flattening. Indeed, there is definite evidence that femora from Kentish sites (75.4 per cent to 82.8 per cent) are less platymeric than those from other Anglo-Saxon kingdoms, all over 90 per cent (Table 7.13a).

The cnemic index records the degree of transverse flattening of the upper tibial shaft. An index of under 63 is platycnemic, marked flattening. Only 5 per cent of tibiae are platycnemic, with no sexual variation. However, examples were confined to the lower cemetery plots. Two cases were noted in poorly equipped males buried in Plots T and S (Sk 327 and Sk 402). Kentish sites display relatively low levels of platycnemia (Table 7.14a). Whereas over a quarter of bones at Caister-on-Sea, Norfolk (S Anderson 1991) and almost two thirds of bones at Staunch Meadow, Suffolk (Anderson 1990) were platycnemic.

Both platymeria and platycnemia occur more frequently in pre-industrial and modern primitive societies. There is no significant reduction in the amount of bone present and the flattening develops due to repeated antero-posterior bending strain (Lovejoy *et al* 1976). Such strain could possibly occur

	Site	Source
0.4 (1/238)	Mitcham, Surrey	Bidder & Morris (1959)
0.6 (1/161)*	Great Chesterford, Essex	Evison (1994a)
1.0 (1/104)	Linton Heath, Cambridgeshire	Neville (1854)
1.2 (1/86)	High Down, Sussex	Read (1895)
1.3 (2/156)	Buckland 1951–3, Dover, Kent	Evison (1987)
1.5 (2/130)	Beckford, Hereford & Worcester	Evison & Hill (1996)
1.6 (1/63)	Bergh Apton, Norfolk	Green & Rogerson (1978)
1.6 (3/187)	Bidford-on-Avon, Warwickshire	Humphries *et al* (1923)
1.7 (2/115)	Camerton, Somerset	Meaney (1964, 218)
1.7 (1/58)	Sewerby, Yorkshire	Hirst (1985)
2.0 (2/102)	Valetta House, Broadstairs, Kent	Hurd & Smith (1911); Meaney (1964, 111)
2.0 (5/248)	Finglesham, Kent	Chadwick Hawkes & Grainger (2006)
2.1 (4/188)	Long Wittenham, Berkshire	Akerman (1862; 1863)
2.5 (5/199)	Castledyke South, Humberside	Drinkall & Foreman (1998)
2.6 (1/39)	King Harry Lane, St. Albans	Ager (1989)
2.7 (1/37)	Holborough, Kent	Evison (1956)
3.1 (1/32)	Barrow Furlong, Northamptonshire	Dryden (1849)
3.1 (2/65)	Westgarth Gardens, Suffolk	West (1988)
3.2 (1/31)	Gunthorpe, Norfolk	Osborne (1987, unpublished)
3.3 (3/91)	Bifrons, Kent	Godfrey-Faussett (1876; 1880)
3.4 (1/29)	Holdenby, Northamptonshire	Harman *et al* (1981)
3.4 (8/236)	Sleaford, Lincolnshire	Thomas (1887)
4.2 (5/119)	Apple Down & the Mardens, Chichester, Sussex	Down & Welch (1990)
4.2 (1/24)	Oakington, Cambridgeshire	Taylor *et al* (1997)
4.3 (2/46)	Beckery Chapel, Somerset	Rahtz & Hirst (1974)
4.4 (2/45)	Winnall, Hampshire	Meaney & Chadwick Hawkes (1970)
4.6 (5/108)	Alfriston, Sussex	Griffith & Salzmann (1914)
5.1 (6/117)	Norton, Cleveland	Sherlock & Welch (1992)
5.3 (5/94)	Burwell, Cambridgeshire	Lethbridge (1924-1928)
5.3 (4/76)	Mill Hill, Deal, Kent	Parfitt & Brugmann (1997)
5.7 (7/122)	Abingdon, Oxfordshire	Leeds & Harden (1936)
5.8 (16/274)	Sarr, Kent	Brent (1862-3)
5.9 (2/34)	Luton, Bedfordshire	Austin (1928)
6.5 (15/217)	Buckland 1994, Dover, Kent	present report
7.1 (2/28)	Melbourn, Cambridgeshire	Wilson (1956)
9.1 (5/55)	Brighthampton, Oxfordshire	Akerman (1857; 1860)
9.2 (10/109)	Broughton Lodge, Nottinghamshire	Dean & Kinsley (1993)
9.2 (27/295)	St Peter's, Broadstairs, Kent	Duhig (1996)
9.4 (6/64)	Harnham Hill, Wiltshire	Akerman (1853); Meaney (1964, 298)
9.5 (19/199)	Butler's Field, Gloucestershire	Harman (1998)
10.0 (3/30)	Finglesham, Kent	Chadwick (1958); Whiting (1929)
10.0 (2/20)	Swaffham, Norfolk	Hills & Wade-Martins (1976)
10.4 (14/135)	Empingham II, Rutland	Timby (1996)
10.5 (6/57)	Nassington, Northamptonshire	Leeds & Atkinson (1944)
11.1 (1/9)	Cassington, Oxfordshire	Meaney (1964, 205–6)
12.0 (3/25)	Stowting, Kent	Brent (1867)
15.9 (17/107)	Polhill, Kent	Philp (1973a)
18.2 (2/11)	Darenth Park, Kent	Batchelor (1990); Walsh (1981)
23.1 (3/13)	Ozengell, Ramsgate, Kent	Meaney (1964, 131)
23.1 (3/13)	Roche Court Down III, Wiltshire	Meaney (1964, 272)
25.0 (2/8)	Little Wilbraham, Cambridgeshire	Lethbridge & Carter (1926/27)
27.1 (10/37)	Caistor-by-Norwich, Norfolk	Myers & Green (1973)
50.0 (1/2)	Buckland Denham, Somerset	Meaney (1964, 218)
5.0 (255/5106) Mean		

* The Great Chesterford case is an adult female with an *in situ* foetus

Table 7.5a. Multiple burials in Anglo-Saxon cemeteries.

Multiple graves (%)	Site	Source
Anglo-Saxon triple graves		
0.5 (1/217)	Buckland 1994, Dover, Kent	present report
0.9 (1/117)	Norton, Cleveland	Sherlock & Welch (1992)
0.9 (1/107)	Polhill, Kent	Philp (1973a)
1.0 (1/102)	Valetta House, Broadstairs, Kent	Meaney (1964, 111)
1.1 (2/187)	Bidford-on-Avon, Warwickshire	Humphreys *et al* (1925)
1.3 (1/76)	Mill Hill, Deal, Kent	Parfitt & Brugmann (1997)
1.4 (4/295)	St Peter's, Broadstairs, Kent	Duhig (1996)
1.6 (1/63)	Bergh Apton, Norfolk	Green & Rogerson (1978)
2.2 (3/135)	Empingham II, Rutland	Timby (1996)
2.6 (1/39)	King Harry Lane, St Albans, Hertfordshire	Ager (1989)
3.1 (1/32)	Barrow Furlong, Northamptonshire	Dryden (1849)
3.1 (2/64)	Harnham Hill, Wiltshire	Akerman (1853); Meaney (1964, 298)
3.7 (4/109)	Broughton Lodge, Nottinghamshire	Dean & Kinsley (1993)
7.7 (1/13)	Roche Court Down III, Wiltshire	Meaney (1964, 272)
12.5 (1/8)	Little Wilbraham, Cambridgeshire	Lethbridge & Carter (1926/27)
15.4 (2/13)	Ozengell, Ramsgate, Kent	Meaney (1964, 131)
1.7 (27/1576) Mean		
Anglo-Saxon quadruple graves		
0.3 (1/295)	St Peter's, Broadstairs, Kent	Duhig (1996)
0.7 (1/135)	Empingham II, Rutland	Timby (1996)
1.0 (1/102)	Valetta House, Broadstairs, Kent	Meaney (1964, 111)
2.7 (1/37)	Caistor-by-Norwich, Norfolk	Myers & Green (1973)
Anglo-Saxon quintuple graves		
1.1 (1/91)	Bifrons, Kent	Godfrey-Faussett (1876; 1880)
4.0 (1/25)	Stowting, Kent	Brent (1867)
12.5 (1/8)	Little Wilbraham, Cambridgeshire	Lethbridge & Carter (1926/27)
Anglo-Saxon sextuple graves		
2.9 (1/34)	Luton, Bedfordshire	Austin (1928)

Table 7.5b. Anglo-Saxon multiple burials.

when walking over rough terrain or as a result of habitual squatting. However, as at North Elmham, the vast majority of tibiae from the 1994 Buckland excavations (81.8 per cent) display lateral squatting facets (see below), which shows that a direct relationship between platycnemia and habitual squatting may be too simplistic.

Cranial non-metrics

Based on the definitions in Berry and Berry (1967) and the detailed text of Hauser and de Stefano (1989), thirty-seven different cranial non-metrics were recorded as present, absent, or unscoreable (bone area unavailable for study). The prevalence of each trait, subdivided by sex, is presented as Table 7.15. The following traits display evidence of possible familial grouping.

Metopism (Trait 1)

The two halves of the frontal bone begin to unite during the second year and between the third and the eighth year, at the latest, the suture is obliterated (Williams and Warwick 1980, 334). Occasionally the suture persists throughout life; this condition is known as metopism. The overall frequency of 10 per cent, is similar to the prevalence found in large samples of English medieval and post-medieval crania (Parsons 1908; Hooke 1926; Molleson *et al* 1993, table 2.15).

The trait is thought to be largely genetic (Schultz 1929; Torgersen 1951) and a higher than normal frequency may suggest a familial group. However, environmental factors, including malnutrition (Reimann *et al* quoted in Cross and Bruce 1989); bone resorption (Manzanares *et al* 1988) and frontal breadth (Bolk 1917) may influence the persistence of

	Total sample	Single burials	All multiple burials
All sub-adult	21.5% (50)	22.8% (46)	12.9% (4)
Children	12.9% (30)	13.4% (27)	9.7% (3)
Juvenile	8.6% (20)	9.4% (19)	3.2% (1)
All adult	78.5% (183)	77.2% (156)	87.1% (27)
Male	33.5% (78)	32.2% (65)	42.0% (13)
Female	33.0% (77)	33.6% (68)	29.0% (9)
? Sex	12.0% (28)	11.4% (23)	16.1% (5)
Total	100.0% (233)	86.7% (202)	13.3% (31)

Table 7.6. Buckland: demography of the multiple burials.

Sub-adult %	Site	Source
0.0 (0/2)	Gunthorpe, Norfolk	Osborne (unpublished)
0.0 (0/2)	High Down, Sussex	Read (1897)
0.0 (0/2)	Melbourn, Cambridgeshire	Wilson (1956)
0.0 (0/2)	Westgarth Gardens, Suffolk	West (1988)
0.0 (0/14)	Sleaford, Lincolnshire	Thomas (1887)
14.3 (1/7)	Stowting, Kent	Brent (1867)
25.0 (1/4)	Beckery Chapel, Somerset	Rahtz & Hirst (1974)
25.0 (1/4)	Buckland 1951–3, Dover, Kent	Evison (1987)
25.0 (1/4)	Darenth Park, Kent	Batchelor (1990); Walsh (1981)
25.0 (2/8)	Castledyke South, Humberside	Drinkall & Foreman (1998)
27.6 (8/29)	Polhill, Kent	Philp (1973a)
28.3 (17/60)	St Peter's, Broadstairs, Kent	Duhig (1996)
28.6 (2/7)	Brighthampton, Oxfordshire	Akerman (1857; 1860)
28.6 (4/14)	Broughton Lodge, Nottinghamshire	Dean & Kinsley (1993)
30.0 (3/10)	Apple Down & the Mardens, Chichester, Sussex	Down & Welch (1990)
33.3 (1/3)	Farthing Down, Surrey	cited in Hirst (1985)
33.3 (1/3)	Little Wilbraham, Cambridgeshire	Lethbridge & Carter (1926/27)
33.3 (1/3)	Swaffham, Norfolk	Hills & Wade-Martins (1976)
33.3 (2/6)	Buckland 1994, Dover, Kent	present report
37.5 (3/8)	Luton, Bedfordshire	Austin (1928)
42.9 (3/7)	Valetta House, Broadstairs, Kent	Meaney (1964, 111)
42.9 (3/7)	Mill Hill, Deal, Kent	Parfitt & Brugmann (1997)
46.2 (6/13)	Norton, Cleveland	Sherlock & Welch (1992)
50.0 (1/2)	Great Chesterford, Essex	Evison (1994a)
50.0 (5/10)	Burwell, Cambridgeshire	Harman et al (1981); Lethbridge (1924–8)
51.9 (14/27)	Empingham II, Rutland	Timby (1996)
52.2 (12/23)	Butler's Field, Gloucestershire	Harman (1998)
64.3 (9/14)	Harnham Hill, Wiltshire	Akerman (1853); Meaney (1964, 298)
66.7 (2/3)	Barrow Furlong, Northamptonshire	Dryden (1849)
66.7 (2/3)	King Harry Lane, St. Albans	Ager (1989)
75.0 (3/4)	Winnall, Hampshire	Meaney & Chadwick Hawkes (1970)
100.0 (2/2)	Bassett Down, Wiltshire	Meaney (1964, 265)
100.0 (2/2)	Camerton, Somerset	Meaney (1964, 218)
100.0 (2/2)	Cassington, Oxfordshire	Meaney (1964, 205-6)
100.0 (2/2)	Oakington, Cambridgeshire	Taylor et al (1997)
100.0 (4/4)	Beckford, Hereford & Worcester	Evison & Hill (1996)
37.9 (118/311) Mean		

Table 7.7a. Anglo-Saxon sub-adult multiple burials: side-by-side.

the suture. In general, there is very little evidence for a sex bias in metopism (Hauser and de Stefano 1989, 44).

Metopic crania are spread throughout the 1994 site: in the upper area (Sk 297, Plot Z; Sk 419 and Sk 423, Plot Y) and in the lower area (Sk 255 and Sk 260, Plot W; Sk 312, Sk 327 and Sk 329, Plot T; Sk 223, Sk 263B and Sk 265B, Plot S). Two of these graves were in close proximity (Sk

327 and Sk 329, Fig 2.2). Metopism is absent from Plots R, U, V and X.

Foramen at inion

This is an additional foramen located in the squamous portion of the occipital bone inferior to the highest nuchal

Sub-adult %	Site	Source
0.0 (0/2)	Mill Hill, Deal, Kent	Parfitt & Brugmann (1997)
0.0 (0/2)	Ferrybridge, Yorkshire	Meaney (1964, 288)
0.0 (0/2)	Holdenby, Northamptonshire	Harman *et al* (1981)
0.0 (0/2)	Little Wilbraham, Cambridgeshire	Lethbridge & Carter (1926/7)
0.0 (0/2)	Melbourn, Cambridgeshire	Wilson (1956)
0.0 (0/2)	Mitcham, Surrey	Bidder & Morris (1959)
0.0 (0/2)	Sewerby, Yorkshire	Hirst (1985)
0.0 (0/2)	Sleaford, Lincolnshire	Thomas (1887)
0.0 (0/2)	Westgarth Gardens, Suffolk	West (1988)
8.0 (2/25)	Buckland 1994, Dover, Kent	present report
10.0 (1/10)	Broughton Lodge, Nottinghamshire	Dean & Kinsley (1993)
16.7 (1/6)	Empingham II, Rutland	Timby (1996)
25.0 (1/4)	Alfriston, Sussex	Griffith & Salzmann (1914)
25.0 (1/4)	Castledyke South, Humberside	Drinkall & Foreman (1998)
33.3 (2/6)	Polhill, Kent	Philp (1973a)
50.0 (1/2)	Brighthampton, Oxfordshire	Akerman (1857; 1860)
50.0 (1/2)	Holborough, Kent	Evison (1956)
52.4 (11/21)	Butler's Field, Gloucestershire	Harman (1998)
21.6 (21/97) Mean		
9 cases foetal/newborn	2 Apple Down & the Mardens, Chichester, Sussex	Down & Welch (1990)
	1 Buckland 1951–3, Dover, Kent	Evison (1987)
	3 Butler's Field, Gloucestershire	Harman (1998)
	1 Great Chesterford, Essex	Evison (1994)
	1 Harnham Hill, Wiltshire	Akerman (1853); Meaney (1964, 298)
	1 St Peter's, Broadstairs, Kent	Duhig (1996), side by side
7.6 (9/118) Mean		
33 cases juvenile	1 Barrow Furlong, Northamptonshire	Dryden (1849)
	1 Beckford, Hereford & Worcester	Evison & Hill (1996)
	2 Broughton Lodge, Nottinghamshire	Dean & Kinsley (1993)
	2 Butler's Field, Gloucestershire	Harman (1998)
	2 Buckland 1994, Dover, Kent	present report
	1 Darenth Park, Dartford, Kent	Batchelor (1990); Walsh (1981)
	2 Mill Hill, Deal, Kent	Parfitt & Brugmann (1997)
	5 Empingham II, Rutland	Timby (1996)
	1 Harnham Hill, Wiltshire	Akerman (1853); Meaney (1964, 298)
	2 Luton, Bedfordshire	Austin (1928)
	3 Norton, Cleveland	Sherlock & Welch (1992)
	1 Oakington, Cambridgeshire	Taylor *et al* (1997)
	2 Polhill, Kent	Philp (1973a)
	2 King Hary Lane, St Albans, Hertfordshire	Ager (1989)
	6 St Peter's, Broadstairs, Kent	Duhig (1996)
28.0 (33/118) Mean		

Table 7.7b. Anglo-Saxon sub-adult multiple burials: double-stacked.

Site	Source	Grave	Sex	Age	Details
Alfriston, Sussex	Griffith & Salzmann (1914)	16a			Bones disturbed
Brighthampton, Oxon	Akerman (1857; 1860)	32a–b			Two skeletons; much deranged side-by-side?
		44a		child	Above 44b, male with sword
		44b	M		Child below 44a, disturbed (evidence of re-opening?); spear
		49a	F	"elderly"	Crystal spindle-whorl; ivory ring
		49b			Disturbed to make room for 49a
Broughton Lodge, Nottinghamshire	Dean & Kinsley (1993)	103	M	25–30	Buried W, facing left, legs slightly flexed; lying over head and torso of Sk 104. Spearhead, grave partially full when inserted. Nine packing stones over legs of Sk 103
		104	M	25–30	Buried W, facing left, legs flexed. Spearhead; shield boss
Butler's Field, Lechlade, Gloucestershire	Boyle *et al* (1998)	33/1		9-10	Later insertion over 33/2 & 33/3
		33/2	F	30–35	33/2 & 33/3 side by side; brooches 2; pin; knife
		33/3		4-5	Respecting 33/2; beads; pin; keys
		38/1	M	30–35	Primary burial disturbed by 38/2. 38/1 disarticulated on top of 38/2
		38/2		5½–6½	No finds
		80/1			Primary burial disturbed by 80/2. 80/1 disarticulated bones on top of 80/2. Brooch
		80/2	M	20–25	No definite finds
		81/1	F	18–21	Primary burial, below 81/2, 81/4, 81/5. Skull cut away by 81/2. Beads; brooches; toilet set; spindle-whorls; bag; key
		81/2		2½–3	No definite finds
		81/3		6–7	2 brooches beads; 2 pierced coins
		81/4	F	25–30	2 brooches; 2 beads; pierced coins; buckle; comb
		81/5		15–18 months	No definite finds
		172/1	M	30–35	2 spears; seax; knife; bucket
		172/2		2½–3½	At side of 172/1 but disturbed not contemporary? Beads; glass; silver sheet
Darenth Park, Dartford, Kent	Batchelor (1990); Walsh (1981)	5a	M	juvenile	Skull damaged in antiquity
		5b	M	grown	Disturbed, 5a later insertion?
		6a	F	35–45	6a-6b mixed together
		6b	M	?	Un-aged; lower L. tibia, raised lesion
Mill Hill, Deal, Kent	Parfitt & Brugmann (1997)	85a	M	20–30	Above 85b; bones muddled; spear; knife
		85b	?M	30–35	Bones muddled; spear. Later insertion, disturbs 85a
Melbourn, Cambridgeshire	Wilson (1956)	11a	M	grown	Skull lying on a sheep's jaw; buckle; 2 knives
		11b	F	grown	Moved to one side to make room for 11a, still articulated so only short interval; beads; rings
Norton, Cleveland	Sherlock & Welch (1992)	36	M	15–21	Buried NW/SE, primary burial, extended. Iron knife; potsherd. Associated with disarticulated bones of a 13-17 year old
		37	F	mid age	Buried NW/SE, overlying 36, right arm under body; left over chest. No grave goods. Associated with disarticulated bones of a 7-11 year old
		38	F	20–30	Buried NW/SE, crouched at south end, a later insertion disturbing 36 & 37. Iron knife; buckle; belt-plate. Osteological evidence suggest a MNI of 5
Polhill, Kent	Philp (1973a)	63a	?	*c* 34	Lying over Sk 63b. No grave goods
		63b	?	*c* 15	Primary burial. Right arm flexed. No grave goods. Not contemporary, has cut into Sk 63a. Skull of Sk 63a placed between legs of upper skeleton
Roche Court Down III, Wiltshire	Meaney (1964, 272)				2 double and one triple; in each case primary burial disturbed
Sleaford, Lincolnshire	Thomas (1887)	16a	?F	grown	Much intermixed with 16b; later insertion?
		16b	?M	grown	Much intermixed with 16a; shield & spear; brooch intermixed
		124	?	grown	Much intermixed
		125	?	grown	Much intermixed
Westgarth Gardens, Bury St Edmunds, Suffolk	West (1988)	63	?M	grown	Immediately above 64; spear
		64	?	grown	Left side missing, cut by 63?; knife
Winkelbury II, Wiltshire	Meaney (1964, 278)				One grave, bones of earlier burial replaced in a heap at the head of a later insertion

Table 7.8. Anglo Saxon multiple burials: evidence for re-opening.

line. The trait was confined to two individuals (Sk 316 and Sk 328) both classed as 'poor' by grave goods, buried in close proximity in Plot T (Fig 2.2). This foramen has rarely been recorded and very little data is available on either its inheritance pattern or intra-population variation (Boyd 1930; Hauser and de Stefano 1989, 112–4).

Zygomatico facial foramen absent

The foramen is variable in position, located on the facial aspect of the zygomatic bone, inferior or lateral to the orbit. It may be multiple or, as scored here, absent. In our material it was absent in just over 16 per cent of the sample, with a slight male bias. In a sample of modern London crania, the foramen was rarely absent (Berry 1975). There is no definite evidence for sexual predilection in this trait (Hauser and de Stefano 1989, 225). This foramen transmits the zygomatico facial nerve and artery (Williams and Warwick 1980, 299) and is reported to develop during the third month of foetal life (Hauser and de Stefano 1989, 224). In the upper part of the 1994 site, four individuals with this trait, two of which

were also metopic (Sk 419 and Sk 428), were found in close proximity (Sk 416, Sk 419, Sk 420 and Sk 428, Plots X and Y). However, low heritability estimates have been postulated for this trait (*ibid;* Rösing 1984).

Hypoglossal canal bipartite

When viewed from the posterior aspect of the foramen magnum, these canals, right and left, can be visualised, under the occipital condyles. They transmit the twelfth (hypoglossal) cranial nerve and occasionally present as a double canal. In our sample, the trait was only scored if bipartition was complete. The overall prevalence was 18.9 per cent with a high sub-adult prevalence (36.4 per cent). In modern London crania a prevalence of 22.2 per cent was recorded for the trait (Berry 1975). Earlier work by Lille (1917) found a frequency of 11.4 per cent with a slight preference for bipartition to occur on the left side in European material. A high degree of heritability has been estimated for this trait in man and animals (Hauser and de Stefano 1989, 122). The lack of environmental influence for this trait and its

%	Site	Source
0.5 (1/217)	Buckland 1994, Dover, Kent	present report
0.8 (1/119)	Frilford, Berkshire	Harman *et al* (1981); Rolleston (1870)
0.8 (1/121)	Broughton Lodge, Nottinghamshire	Dean & Kinsley (1993)
0.9 (1/113)	Burwell, Cambridgeshire	Harman *et al* (1981)
0.9 (1/117)	Camerton, Somerset	Harman *et al* (1981); Meaney (1964, 218)
1.2 (2/161)	Great Chesterford, Essex	Evison (1994)
1.5 (3/198)	Butler's Field, Gloucestershire	Harman (1998)
1.7 (1/58)	Sewerby, Yorkshire	Hirst (1985)
1.7 (4/138)	Mitcham, Surrey	Bidder & Morris (1959)
2.1 (2/94)	Worthy Park, Hampshire	Harman *et al* (1981); Chadwick Hawkes & Wells (1975)
2.2 (1/46)	Wheatley, Oxfordshire	Harman *et al* (1981); Leeds (1916–17)
2.2 (1/46)	Bekesbourne, Kent	Harman *et al* (1981); Meaney (1964, 109)
2.3 (3/132)	Beckford, Hereford & Worcester	Evison & Hill (1996)
2.6 (1/38)	Totternhoe, Bedfordshire	Harman *et al* (1981); Meaney (1964, 41)
3.2 (3/94)	Dunstable, Bedfordshire	Dunning & Wheeler (1931); Harman *et al* (1981)
3.4 (1/29)	Holdenby, Northamptonshire	Harman *et al* (1981); Meaney (1964, 190)
4.0 (2/50)	Caistor-by-Norwich, Norfolk	Myers & Green (1973)
4.0 (8/199)	Castledyke South, Humberside	Drinkall & Foreman (1998)
5.2 (8/153)	Empingham II, Rutland	Timby (1996)
5.6 (7/126)	Norton, Cleveland	Sherlock & Welch (1992)
6.9 (2/29)	Farthing Down, Surrey	Harman *et al* (1981); Meaney (1964)
7.7 (1/13)	Toddington, Bedfordshire	Harman *et al* (1981); Meaney (1964, 40)
8.0 (2/25)	Oakington, Cambridgeshire	Taylor *et al* (1997)
11.8 (2/17)	Roche Court Down I, Wiltshire	Harman *et al* (1981)
12.0 (3/25)	Ruskington, Lincolnshire	Harman *et al* (1981)
13.0 (6/46)	Beckery Chapel, Glastonbury, Somerset	Rahtz & Hirst (1974)
20.0 (2/10)	Meon Hill, Hampshire	Harman *et al* (1981); Liddell (1934)
2.8 (70/2488) Mean		

Table 7.9. Anglo-Saxon prone burials.

possible relationship to manifestation of an occipital vertebra suggest that it could be a useful genetic marker (Anderson 1996a). Both skeletons in double Grave 228 (Plot S) and two other skeletons buried next to each other (Sk 250 and Sk 256, Plot W), displayed division of the canal.

The data from the fragmented crania provide only very limited evidence for any genetic groupings. Also, most traits are inherited on a multifactorial basis, with incomplete penetrance (Hauser and de Stefano 1989). It may be possible to recognise genetic groupings, such as siblings; brothers and sisters. However, it must be remembered that non-metric variation will not establish non-genetically related individuals, such as husbands and wives.

Post-cranial non-metrics

Based on the definitions in Finnegan (1978) and in Anderson (1987), twenty-nine different post-cranial non-metrics were recorded as present, absent, or unscoreable (bone area unavailable for study). The prevalence of each trait, subdivided by sex, is presented as Table 7.16. The following traits display evidence of unusual clustering.

Hypotrochanteric fossa

This is a distinct fossa, located on the lateral aspect of the superior gluteal ridge. It has only been scored when an

Site	Source	Grave	Sex	Age	Details
Empingham II, Rutland	Timby (1996)	113a	M	17–25	Prone, hands tied in front of face? Iron frags (2)
		113b	?	3–4	Prone, below legs of Sk 113a
Farthing Down, Surrey	quoted in Hirst (1974)	?	M	young adult	With weapons
		?	M	boy	Buckle
		?	F	mid age	Prone, lying between two males
Holdenby, Northants	Harman *et al* (1981, 187)	?	F	?	Prone, buried above an older female
		?	F	"older"	Buried below a prone burial of a younger female
Mitcham, Surrey	Bidder & Morris (1959)	44	F	?	Prone. Beads; buckle; knife. Above Sk 45
		45	F	?	Supine, belt fittings; brooch; comb. Below Sk 44
Norton, Cleveland	Sherlock & Welch (1992)	98	M/F	20–30	Crouched, lying on left side, legs flexed; R. arm extended; left flexed. Buried N/S. Annular brooch; copper strip; copper fragment. Buried on shelf to East side of grave, above Sk 99
		99	F	15–21	Prone, buried N/S, primary burial, lower legs bent double. Bone comb internal to the upper right arm
		47	?F	?mid age	Prone, buried E–W, fragmented, only lower half survived. No grave goods
		116	?	infant	Prone?, buried E–W, v fragmented. No grave goods. Situated to N of thigh and pelvis of Sk 47
Oakington, Cambridgeshire	Taylor *et al* (1997)	12a	?	8	Prone, side-by-side; no grave goods
		12b	F	15	Prone. Brooch; bone pin; beads
Sewerby, Yorkshire	Hirst (1985)	41	F	35–45	Prone, arms and lower legs flexed (live burial trying to rise up from the grave); Buried E/W; limestone block between shoulders; quern fragment just below pelvis. Flint flake; iron buckle; iron knife; jet bead/spindle-whorl; annular brooches (2); pierced iron frag; pierced bronze plates (2); bronze frag; glass and amber beads (16)
		49	F	17–25	Extended, buried E/W; Below Sk 41 in wood coffin. Bronze cauldron; box of wood and shale; animal bones (ribs); sleeve clasps (2); girdle hangers (2); purse ring; knife; small-long brooches (2); square headed brooch; glass, amber & crystal beads (206); bronze pendants (2); flint flake. No evidence of re-cutting: suggests contemporary burials

Note: Norton, Cleveland, Grave 98; Male by osteological evidence; Female by grave goods

Table 7.10. Anglo-Saxon prone burials from multiple graves.

obvious fossa was present. The aetiology of the variant is not fully understood. It is uncommon in animals, except for non-human primates (Hrdlička 1934). Its occurrence in the latter is related to the insertion of the accessory adductor, a muscle not normally developed in man (Appelton 1922). The fact that it has been reported in foetal material (Hrdlička 1934), however, suggests that its manifestation may not be completely due to bone robusticity or musculature.

The variant was not uncommon, involving 38 per cent of all adult femora, with evidence for a male preference (Table 7.16). A lower frequency (26 per cent) was recorded at Great Chesterford (Waldron 1994, table 21). Unfortunately, the variant has not been included by other workers who have examined Anglo-Saxon skeletal material. In a large sample (n = 810) of post-medieval British material, 33.9 per cent displayed the fossa (Pearson and Bell 1919); a slightly higher prevalence (44 per cent) was noted in a Neolithic sample (Hrdlička 1934).

It occurs throughout the cemetery but is clearly more frequent on the lower part of the 1994 site. A very high concentration occurs in Plot W, where a group of eleven skeletons (Sk 248, Sk 249C, Sk 250, Sk 252, Sk 253, Sk 256, Sk 259, Sk 260, Sk 319, Sk 340 and Sk 432) display the trait. This group includes a sword burial (Sk 249C). Indeed, four of the seven 1994 sword burials (Sk 249C, Sk 264, Sk 265A and Sk 375) present with the variant. Although, it might be tempting to suggest a relationship between strenuous muscular activity or occupation and trait manifestation, the sample of males with swords is too small to uphold a definite correlation.

Calcaneal facet form

The three talar articular surfaces of the calcaneus display morphological variations (Bunning 1964). The different forms are classified as below. Type A is generally the most frequent presentation (Bunning 1964; El-Eishi 1974; Forriol Campos and Gomez Pellico 1989; Laidlaw 1905; Padmanabhan 1986; Trinkaus 1975). Types C and D are both rare presentations.

Type A: single antero-medial facet. The middle and anterior facets form a continuous, possibly waisted, surface (Bunning Type B).

Mean stature			Range	Site	Source
1.660	5' 5¼"	(n28)	1.510–1.830	Great Chesterford, Essex	Waldron (1994)
1.697	5' 6¾"	(n16)	1.613–1.754	Red Castle, Norfolk	Wells (1967)
1.700	5' 7"	(n42)	1.590–1.850	Butler's Field, Gloucestershire	Harman (1998)
1.708	5' 7¼"	(n33)	1.570–1.858	Caister-on-Sea, Norfolk	S Anderson (1991)
1.713	5' 7½"	(n84)	1.578–1.830	Raunds, Northants	Powell (unpublished)
1.714	5' 7½"	(n?)	?	Bidford-on-Avon, Warwicks	White (1988)
1.716	5' 7½"	(n24)	1.608–1.865	Staunch Meadow, Brandon, Suffolk	S Anderson (1990)
1.716	5' 7½"	(n29)	1.654–1.786	St Peter's, Broadstairs, Kent	Duhig (1996)
1.720	5' 7¾"	(n?)	1.630–1.860	Jarrow, Tyne & Wear	Wells *et al* (forthcoming)
1.720	5' 7¾"	(n24)	?	Castledyke South, Humberside	Drinkall & Foreman (1998)
1.721	5' 7¾"	(n45)	1.623–1.807	North Elmham, Norfolk	Wells (1980)
1.729	5' 8"	(n64)	?	Eccles, Kent	Manchester (unpublished)
1.730	5' 8"	(n24)	?	Berinsfield, Oxfordshire	Harman (1995)
1.730	5' 8"	(n?)	1.610–1.920	Monkwearmouth, Tyne & Wear	Wells *et al* (forthcoming)
1.732	5' 8¼"	(n6)	1.667–1.796	Mill Hill, Deal, Kent	Anderson & Andrews (1997)
1.733	5' 8¼"	(n35)	1.600–1.840	Edix Hill, Barrington, Cambridgeshire	Duhig (1998)
1.735	5' 8¼"	(n?)	1.641–1.828	Norton, Cleveland	Marlow (1992)
1.737	5' 8½"	(n11)	1.640–1.800	Droxford, Hampshire	Aldsworth (1978)
1.740	5' 8½"	(n?)	1.610–1.850	Empingham II, Rutland	Mays (1990)
1.740	5' 8½"	(n38)	1.640–1.860	Apple Down & the Mardens, Chichester, Sussex	Harman (1990)
1.744	5' 8¾"	(n6)	1.690–1.820	Buckland 1951–3, Dover, Kent	Powers & Cullen (1987)
1.744	5' 8¾"	(n15)	?	Broughton Lodge, Nottinghamshire	Harman (1993)
1.753	5' 9"	(n?)	1.700–1.810	Nazeingbury, Essex	Huggins (1978)
1.758	5' 9¼"	(n24)	1.674–1.876	Buckland 1994, Dover, Kent	present report
1.759	5' 9¼"	(n?)	?	Porchester Castle, Hampshire	White (1988)
1.759	5' 9¼"	(n53)	1.657–1.861	Burgh Castle, Norfolk	Anderson & Birkett (1989)
1.880	6' 2"	(n3)	1.830–1.910	Oakington, Cambridgeshire	Taylor *et al* (1997)

Table 7.11. Adult male stature in Anglo-Saxon England.

Mean stature			Range	Site	Source
1.562	5' 1½"	(n?)	?	Bidford-on-Avon, Warwicks	White (1988)
1.574	5' 2"	(n39)	1.424–1.697	North Elmham, Norfolk	Wells (1980)
1.581	5' 2¼"	(n17)	1.519–1.670	Red Castle, Norfolk	Wells (1967)
1.583	5' 2¼"	(n6)	1.519–1.649	Mill Hill, Deal, Kent	Anderson & Andrews (1997)
1.590	5' 2½"	(n?)	1.490–1.660	Jarrow, Tyne & Wear	Wells *et al* (forthcoming)
1.599	5' 3"	(n64)	1.478–1.744	Raunds, Northamptonshire	Powell (unpublished)
1.600	5' 3"	(n26)	?	Castledyke South, Humberside	Drinkall & Foreman (1998)
1.600	5' 3"	(n?)	1.540–1.690	Monkwearmouth, Tyne & Wear	Wells *et al* (forthcoming)
1.610	5' 3½"	(n79)	1.500–1.740	Butler's Field, Gloucestershire	Harman (1998)
1.610	5' 3½"	(n38)	1.460–1.710	Great Chesterford, Essex	Waldron (1994)
1.610	5' 3½"	(n15)	1.478–1.777	Staunch Meadow, Suffolk	S Anderson (1990)
1.611	5' 3½"	(n39)	1.486–1.723	Caister-on-Sea, Norfolk	S Anderson (1991)
1.612	5' 3½"	(n17)	1.520–1.700	Droxford, Hampshire	Aldsworth (1978)
1.617	5' 3¾"	(n12)	1.556–1.716	St Peter's, Broadstairs, Kent	Duhig (1996)
1.620	5' 3¾"	(n37)	1.520–1.700	Apple Down & the Mardens, Chichester, Sussex	Harman (1990)
1.620	5' 3¾"	(n17)	?	Berinsfield, Oxfordshire	Harman (1995)
1.631	5' 4¼"	(n37)	1.515–1.762	Burgh Castle, Norfolk	Anderson & Birkett (1989)
1.631	5' 4¼"	(n30)	1.510–1.710	Edix Hill, Barrington, Cambridgeshire	Duhig (1998)
1.639	5' 4½"	(n44)	?	Eccles, Kent	Manchester (unpublished)
1.640	5' 4½"	(n30)	1.520–1.790	Empingham II, Rutland	Mays (1990)
1.641	5' 4½"	(n?)	1.483–1.761	Norton, Cleveland	Marlow (1992)
1.642	5' 4¾"	(n18)	1.543–1.763	Buckland 1994, Dover, Kent	present report
1.645	5' 4¾"	(n9)	?	Broughton Lodge, Nottinghamshire	Harman (1993)
1.651	5' 5"	(n?)	?	Porchester Castle, Hampshire	White (1988)
1.656	5' 5¼"	(n5)	1.610–1.730	Oakington, Cambridgeshire	Taylor *et al* (1997)
1.666	5' 5½"	(n8)	1.610–1.710	Buckland 1951–3, Dover, Kent	Powers & Cullen (1987)
1.682	5' 6¼"	(n?)	1.585–1.740	Nazeingbury, Essex	Huggins (1978)

Table 7.12. Adult female stature in Anglo-Saxon England.

Adult femora				
All* %	Male %	Female %	Site	Source
75.4 (141/187)	75.0 (72/96)	75.8 (69/91)	Buckland 1994, Dover, Kent	present report
77.8 (77/99)	82.3 (51/62)	70.3 (26/37)	Eccles, Kent	Manchester (unpublished)
80.7 (-)	-	-	St Peter's, Broadstairs, Kent	Duhig (1996)
82.8 (24/29)	81.2 (13/16)	77.8 (7/9)	Mill Hill, Deal, Kent	Anderson & Andrews (1997)
90.6 (116/128)	86.5 (64/74)	96.3 (52/54)	Staunch Meadow, Suffolk	S Anderson (1990)
91.4 (53/58)	88.9 (24/27)	93.5 (29/31)	Great Chesterford, Essex	Waldron (1994)
94.7 (124/131)	93.3 (56/60)	95.8 (68/71)	Caister-on-Sea, Norfolk	S Anderson (1991)
98.1 (155/158)	96.5 (83/86)	100.0 (72/72)	North Elmham, Norfolk	Wells (1980)

* including adults of uncertain sex

Table 7.13a. Anglo-Saxon England: meric indices.

	All %	Right %	Left %
All	75.4 (141/187)	65.1 (56/86)	84.2 (85/101)
Male	75.0 (72/96)	67.4 (31/46)	82.0 (41/50)
Female	75.8 (69/91)	62.5 (25/40)	86.2 (44/51)

Table 7.13b. Buckland: meric indices: detail.

Type B: bipartite antero-medial facet. The middle and anterior facets are discontinuous and present as two distinct facets (Bunning Type A).

Type C: absent anterior facet. The anterior facet is missing (rare).

Type D: facets all fused. All three facets are fused and present as a single continuous surface (Bunning Type C) (rare).

Both of the common types of facet occur throughout the cemetery. Based on individual adult calcanei, in both sexes, the discontinuous facet (Type B) was more frequent than the continuous (Type A) form (Table 7.16). Based on a small sample, the discontinuous facet appears to be more frequent on the upper part of the 1994 site, with some evidence of a cluster in the western half of the upper area.

Other anatomical variants

Mandible

A young adult female (Sk 247) in Plot V presented with bilateral absence of the mandibular mental foramen. Based on a sample of eighty-three intact mandibles, this represents a prevalence of 1.2 per cent.

The foramen transmits the inferior alveolar nerve (Williams and Warwick 1980, 1067). Complete absence is a very rare finding (Hauser and de Stefano 1989, 230). In a large series de Freitas *et al* (1979) reported a prevalence of 0.2 per cent (3/1435). Interestingly, a unilateral (left side) absence has been reported in an Iron Age male (grave 31) from Mill Hill, Deal (Anderson 1995, 117).

Atlas bifid arch

One individual, a young adult female (Sk 409) presented with a bifid posterior arch of the first cervical vertebra. Based on the number of atlases, the prevalence is 3.9 per cent (1/39). The variant is not uncommon. Nine examples (5.8 per cent) are known from a late Roman to early Saxon cemetery at Cannington (Brothwell *et al* 2000, 197, fig 142).

Additional vertebra

One individual, a mature male (Sk 291), presented with six lumbar vertebra. Based on the number of lumbar spines, including fragmented remains, the prevalence of additional vertebra is 1.7 per cent (1/60). This is not an uncommon variant. At medieval York, based on complete spines, 7.1 per cent and 3.9 per cent presented with an additional, or a congenitally absent, vertebra (Stroud and Kemp 1993, 196).

Transitional vertebra

Two young adults, a male (Sk 375) and a female (Sk 409) displayed attempted fusion of the lowest lumbar vertebra to the

Adult tibiae				
All* %	Male %	Female %	Site	Source
0.0 (0/38)	0.0 (0/21)	0.0 (0/14)	Mill Hill, Deal, Kent	Anderson (1997)
5.0 (9/181)	5.0 (5/100)	4.9 (4/81)	Buckland 1994, Dover, Kent	present report
7.1 (9/127)	6.8 (5/73)	7.4 (4/54)	North Elmham, Norfolk	Wells (1980)
7.8 (5/64)	13.8 (4/29)	2.9 (1/35)	Great Chesterford, Essex	Waldron (1994)
10.6 (11/104)	10.8 (7/65)	10.2 (4/39)	Eccles, Kent	Manchester (unpublished)
14.9 (-/-)	-	-	St Peter's, Broadstairs, Kent	Duhig (1996)
28.2 (35/124)	32.7 (17/52)	25.0 (18/72)	Caister-on-Sea, Norfolk	S Anderson (1991)
65.7 (44/67)	74.3 (26/35)	56.2 (18/32)	Staunch Meadow, Suffolk	S Anderson (1990)
* including adults of uncertain sex				

Table 7.14a. Anglo-Saxon England: cnemic indices.

	All %	Right %	Left %
All	5.0 (9/180)	4.6 (4/87)	5.4 (5/93)
Male	5.0 (5/100)	4.1 (2/49)	5.9 (3/51)
Female	5.0 (4/80)	5.6 (2/38)	4.8 (2/42)

Table 7.14b. Buckland: cnemic indices: detail.

sacrum and attempted separation of the upper sacral element, respectively. Such variants, examples of cranial/caudal shifting are not uncommon findings (Barnes 1994, 79–116), with the lumbo-sacral junction being the site of preference (Barnes 1994, 108).

Palaeopathology

The very poor preservation and fragmented nature of the material severely limits the value of the sample for diagnosing the true prevalence of skeletal disease. An accurate level of arthritic degeneration cannot be assessed since very few hands or feet, or even large articular surfaces were available. Similarly the eroded nature of the diaphyses

(long bone shafts) mean that osteitic reaction, evidence of infection, cannot be accurately diagnosed. The following is a basic summary of the pathological conditions that could be recognised.

Arthritic conditions

Osteoarthritis

Three skeletons displayed evidence of extra spinal degeneration. An adult male (Sk 381) presents with unilateral degeneration of the hip (right). A 'rich' mature female (Sk 417) displays degeneration of the right hand (first metacarpal-phalangeal joint) and the left knee. The most advanced degeneration occurs in a mature male (Sk 291).

Trait no	All adult*	Male	Female	Sub-adult
1	11.3% (11/97)	8.2% (4/49)	14.9% (7/47)	0.0% (0/13)
4	1.2% (1/80)	0.0% (0/37)	2.3% (1/43)	0.0% (0/4)
5	2.4% (1/42)	0.0% (0/21)	4.8% (1/21)	0.0% (0/2)
6	25.0% (17/68)	25.0% (9/36)	25.0% (8/32)	0.0% (0/0)
7	0.0% (0/65)	0.0% (0/35)	0.0% (0/30)	20.0% (1/5)
8	4.8% (3/62)	6.2% (2/32)	3.3% (1/30)	0.0% (0/0)
9	17.9% (10/56)	17.2% (5/29)	18.5% (5/27)	0.0% (0/0)
11	5.3% (1/19)	0.0% (0/10)	11.1% (1/9)	0.0% (0/0)
13	17.3% (23/133)	17.9% (12/67)	16.9% (11/65)	0.0% (0/10)
14	34.6% (46/133)	33.3% (22/66)	36.4% (24/66)	40.0% (4/10)
15	10.3% (11/107)	13.8% (8/58)	6.1% (3/49)	0.0% (0/1)
16	32.0% (16/50)	28.6% (8/28)	36.4% (8/22)	0.0% (0/0)
17	57.1% (20/35)	47.6% (10/21)	71.4% (10/14)	0.0% (0/0)
18	3.6% (2/55)	3.7% (1/27)	3.7% (1/27)	0.0% (0/1)
19	16.2% (13/80)	20.0% (7/35)	13.6% (6/44)	33.3% (1/3)
20	6.2% (1/16)	12.5% (1/8)	0.0% (0/8)	0.0% (0/0)
23	1.9% (1/52)	0.0% (0/31)	5.0% (1/20)	0.0% (0/2)
24	3.1% (3/98)	3.6% (2/55)	2.3% (1/43)	0.0% (0/5)
25	4.8% (1/21)	0.0% (0/10)	9.1% (1/11)	0.0% (0/4)
27	16.7% (14/84)	16.7% (9/45)	13.5% (5/37)	36.4% (4/11)
28	50.0% (11/22)	60.0% (6/10)	41.7% (5/12)	50.0% (1/2)
29	1.8% (1/55)	3.1% (1/32)	0.0% (0/23)	0.0% (0/4)
30	1.4% (1/69)	2.8% (1/36)	0.0% (0/32)	0.0% (0/7)
31	2.3% (1/44)	3.8% (1/26)	0.0% (0/17)	0.0% (0/4)
37	3.4% (3/89)	2.2% (1/46)	4.7% (2/43)	0.0% (0/9)

* includes unsexed individuals; sides have been pooled

Key: Trait no: (1) Metopism; (2) Metopic ossicle; (3) Bregmatic bone; (4) Coronal ossicle; (5) Sagittal ossicle; (6) Lambdoid ossicles; (7) Os inca; (8) Asterionic ossicles; (9) Parietal notch bone; (10) Squamo-parietal ossicles; (11) Epipteric bone; (12) Os japonicum; (13) Supra orbital foramen; (14) Frontal notch present; (15) Parietal foramen present; (16) Mastoid foramen absent; (17) Mastoid foramen exsutural; (18) Foramen at Inion; (19) Zygomatico-facial foramen absent; (20) Accessory infra orbital foramina; (21) Anterior ethmoid foramen exsutural; (22) Posterior ethmoid foramen absent; (23) Foramen ovale complete; (24) Foramen of Hushke; (25) Accessory Palatine foramina; (26) Jugular foramen bipartite; (27) Hypoglossal canal bipartite; (28) Posterior condylar canal patent; (29) Condylar canal facet double; (30) Pre-condylar tubercle; (31) Third condyle; (32) Para condyloid process; (33) Maxillary tori; (34) Palatal tori; (35) Mandibular tori; (36) Mental foramen multiple; (37) Mylo-hyoid bridge

The following cranial traits were not seen in the Buckland 1994 material: 2; 3; 10; 12; 21; 22; 26; 32; 33; 34; 35; 36

Table 7.15. Buckland: cranial non-metrics.

The left shoulder, both wrists and the right hip were involved. The gross deformities of the femoral head and the associated juxta-articular new bone buttressing would suggest that his movement was painful and severely limited.

Vertebral degeneration

From a total of sixty-one incomplete spines, eight displayed osteoarthritic degeneration; sixteen displayed osteophytes and eight displayed typical Schmorls' nodes or narrower linear defects. However, the highly fragmented and incomplete nature of the few available spines means that the true prevalence of vertebral degeneration cannot be accurately assessed.

Osteoarthritis

Male: mature Sk 248; Sk 291; Sk 346; Sk 394; Sk 401; female: adult: Sk 304; Sk 313; mature: Sk 324

Based on a detailed study of individual facets, only 1.3 per cent of all articular surfaces displayed osteoarthritic changes,

with males involved seven times more frequently than females (Table 7.17). In both sexes, the site of predilection was the cervical spine (Table 7.17). The only individual with sacral degeneration was a male with an additional lumbar vertebra (Sk 291). Practically all the diseased facets, 91.4 per cent (n = 32) occurred in mature individuals. The marked sexual dimorphism (only three female joint surfaces were involved; Table 7.17), is probably related to the lack of elderly females in the sample.

Osteophytes

Male: young adult: Sk 338; Sk 350B; Sk 375; Sk 381; adult: Sk 416; Sk 435; mature: Sk 291; Sk 292; Sk 311; Sk 363; female: young adult: Sk 250; adult: Sk 288; Sk 313 mature: Sk 316; Sk 351B; Sk 417

Based on available vertebral body surfaces, subdivided into right and left; superior and inferior, some 18.5 per cent displayed osteophytic outgrowths (Table 7.17). Just over three-quarters (87/115) occurred in mature individuals. In both sexes, the site of predilection was the lumbar and sacral

Trait no	All adult*	Male	Female	Sub-adult
1	6.9% (5/72)	7.9% (3/38)	5.9% (2/34)	0.0% (0/4)
2	4.9% (3/61)	9.4% (3/32)	0.0% (0/29)	0.0% (0/3)
4	5.0% (2/40)	9.1% (2/22)	0.0% (0/18)	0.0% (0/3)
8	28.6% (2/7)	28.6% (2/4)	0.0% (0/3)	0.0% (0/0)
10	4.8% (1/21)	0.0% (0/10)	9.1% (1/11)	0.0% (0/4)
12	14.3% (1/7)	0.0% (0/5)	50.0% (1/2)	0.0% (0/0)
14	2.1% (1/48)	0.0% (0/30)	5.6% (1/18)	0.0% (0/1)
16	25.4% (15/59)	27.8% (10/36)	21.7% (5/23)	0.0% (0/1)
17	11.1% (2/18)	14.3% (2/14)	0.0% (0/4)	0.0% (0/1)
18	3.6% (1/28)	4.5% (1/22)	0.0% (0/6)	0.0% (0/1)
19	6.9% (2/29)	8.7% (2/23)	0.0% (0/6)	0.0% (0/0)
20	1.3% (1/80)	2.0% (1/50)	0.0% (0/28)	0.0% (0/5)
21	38.0% (68/179)	42.4% (39/92)	30.8% (24/78)	11.1% (2/18)
22	8.3% (4/48)	13.8% (4/29)	0.0% (0/19)	0.0% (0/1)
23	2.1% (1/48)	3.4% (1/29)	0.0% (0/19)	0.0% (0/1)
25	81.8% (18/22)	71.4% (5/7)	86.7% (13/15)	100.0% (1/1)
26A	44.4% (28/63)	42.3% (11/26)	45.9% (17/37)	100.0% (1/1)
26B	54.0% (34/63)	53.8% (14/26)	54.1% (20/37)	0.0% (0/1)
26C	1.6% (1/63)	3.8% (1/26)	0.0% (0/37)	0.0% (0/1)
28	6.0% (3/50)	0.0% (0/23)	11.1% (3/27)	0.0% (0/1)

* includes unsexed individuals; sides have been pooled

Key: Trait no: (1) Atlas facet double; (2) Atlas posterior bridge; (3) Atlas lateral bridge; (4) Atlas retro-articular bridge; (5) BFT CV3; (6) BFT CV4; (7) BFT CV5; (8) BFT CV6; (9) BFT CV7; (10) Accessory Sacral Facets; (11) Sternal foramen; (12) Os acromiale; (13) Supra scapular formen; (14) Septal aperture; (15) Supracondylar spur; (16) Acetabular crease; (17) Poirier's facet; (18) Plaque; (19) Allen's Fossa; (20) Third trochanter; (21) Hypotrochanter fossa; (22) Vastus notch; (23) Emarginate patella; (24) Squatting facets medial; (25) Squatting facets lateral; (26) Calcaneus facet form (A-D); (27) Calcaneus secundarius; (28) Os trigonum; (29) Cuneiform I Facet Doublee

The following cranial traits were not seen in the Buckland 1994 material: 3; 5; 6; 7; 9; 11; 13; 15; 24; 26D; 27; 29

Table 7.16. Buckland: post-cranial non-metrics.

(Table 7.17). Overall, males were more prone to osteophyte development, with all regions of the spine affected (Table 7.17). In females, osteophytic outgrowths were largely confined to the lower spine (Table 7.17).

Schmorls' nodes

Male: young adult: Sk 375; adult: Sk 416; mature: Sk 291; female: young adult: Sk 420

Linear defects

Male: young adult: Sk 342; Sk 385; female: young adult: Sk 420; adult: Sk 313; mature: Sk 351B

Based on available vertebral body surfaces, subdivided into superior and inferior, some 6.3 per cent displayed Schmorls' nodes or linear defects (Table 7.17). Almost 60 per cent (22/38) occurred in young adults and the favoured sites are the thoracic and lumbar spine (Table 7.17). Females present with a higher prevalence of nodes (10 per cent) than males (4.2 per cent). This is due to the widespread presence of nodes in one female (Sk 420). It is generally accepted that node formation is directly related to severe strain, especially compressional forces, which cause the intervertebral disc to rupture (Knowles 1983). It is possible that the cavitations will more readily develop during adolescence, while the vertebral bodies are still plastic (*ibid*). Based on large medieval samples, node formation displays a male bias (Mays 1991; Stroud and Kemp 1993, 214). A similar bias has been noticed at Anglo-Saxon sites, including Castledyke South (Boylston *et al* 1998, 231); Barrington (Duhig 1998, 168). No sexual dimorphism was noted in a small sample from Norton, Cleveland (Birkett 1992).

Intervertebral osteochondrosis [IVO]

Male: adult: Sk 381; mature: Sk 29; female: mature: Sk 417

Based on available vertebral body surfaces, subdivided into superior and inferior, only 1 per cent displayed intervertebral osteochondritis (IVO), with no sexual dimorphism (Table 7.17). The site of predilection, in both sexes, was the cervical spine (Table 7.17). Based on an extremely small sample, IVO was strongly aged related, with 85.7 per cent (6/7) of lesions occurring in mature individuals. IVO has received less attention than other spinal degenerative changes. However, as in our sample, a distinct preference for cervical involvement and clear age-related distribution has been demonstrated in

	All	Male	Female
Osteoarthritis			
All	1.3% (35/2689)	2.1% (32/1524)	0.3% (3/1165)
Cervical	3.5% (21/607)	5.9% (19/321)	0.7% (2/286)
Thoracic	0.3% (4/1328)	0.4% (3/768)	0.2% (1/560)
Lumbar	1.2% (8/661)	2.1% (8/386)	0.0% (0/275)
Sacral	2.2% (2/93)	4.1% (2/49)	0.0% (0/44)
Osteophytes			
All	18.5% (115/623)	20.4% (85/416)	14.5% (30/207)
Cervical	10.3% (24/233)	13.0% (19/146)	5.7% (5/87)
Thoracic	19.3% (53/274)	22.8% (43/189)	11.8% (10/85)
Lumbar	29.6% (32/108)	26.3% (20/76)	37.5% (12/32)
Sacral	75.0% (6/8)	60.0% (3/5)	100.0% (3/3)
Schmorls' nodes			
All	6.3% (38/602)	4.2% (16/381)	10.0% (22/221)
Cervical	0.0% (0/166)	0.0% (0/101)	0.0% (0/65)
Thoracic	9.5% (25/263)	4.9% (8/163)	17.0% (17/100)
Lumbar	8.8% (13/148)	7.8% (8/102)	10.9% (5/46)
Sacral	0.0% (0/25)	0.0% (0/15)	0.0% (0/10)
Intervetebral osteochondosis			
All	1.0% (6/602)	1.0% (4/381)	0.9% (2/221)
Cervical	2.4% (4/166)	3.0% (3/101)	1.5% (1/65)
Thoracic	0.0% (0/263)	0.0% (0/163)	0.0% (0/100)
Lumbar	0.7% (1/148)	0.0% (0/102)	2.2% (1/46)
Sacral	4.0% (1/25)	6.7% (1/15)	0.0% (0/10)

Table 7.17. Buckland: vertebral degeneration.

both large medieval assemblages (Stroud and Kemp 1993, 207) and post-medieval material (Waldron 1991).

Spondylolysis (neural arch separation)

This condition was noted in only one individual (Sk 328, Plot T), a mature male buried without grave goods. The defect was bilateral occurring at the normal site, the fifth lumbar vertebra (Frederickson *et al* 1984; Hensinger 1989). Based on the number of intact lumbar vertebrae, this represents a prevalence of 4.5 per cent. Most other Anglo-Saxon sites present with a higher prevalence: Eccles (6.6 per cent; Manchester, unpublished); Apple Down (6.9 per cent; Harman 1990); Mill Hill, Deal (7.7 per cent; Anderson and Andrews 1997, 228).

The condition is reported to affect 3–7 per cent of modern day populations (Resnick and Niwayama 1981, 2253). As long as no displacement occurs (spondylolisthesis) the condition is frequently asymptomatic. Cases with displacement have been reported from Burgh Castle, Eccles and Buckland 1951–3 (S Anderson and Birkett 1989; Manchester 1982; Powers and Cullen 1987).

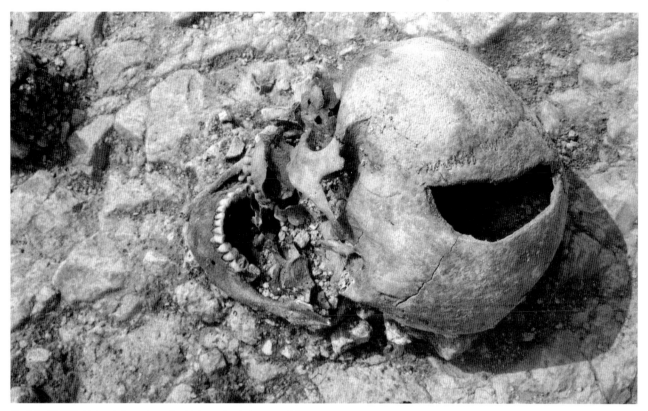

Fig 7.5. Sk 348: Male adult cranium, displaying unhealed weapon injury.

The favoured interpretation of spondylolysis is a stress or fatigue fracture that fails to heal (Resnick and Niwayama 1981, 2253). As such it appears that the prevalence of the condition may give a clue to levels of vertebral stress in earlier populations. The possibility that a genetic weakness in the spine may predispose to neural arch separation cannot be ignored (Hensinger 1989).

Trauma

Weapon injuries

Two adult males (Sk 348 and Sk 303B) display cranial weapon injuries. Both are typical extended burials and neither were buried with weapons. In the former, dated to Phase 1b–2a, the only pathology was the absence of a large portion of the left parietal (Fig 7.5). The sharp-edged defect is 98mm long (arc measurement) with a maximum width of 36mm. The most anterior point is 10mm posterior to the middle of the coronal suture and posteriorly it reaches the sagittal suture 40mm from the bregma. The posterior edge presents as a

sharp, cleanly cut edge, with no evidence of remodelling. The anterior edge, although still sharp, is slightly irregular and not so well-defined. *Post mortem* erosion has lead to a slight rounding of the outer edges of the defect. The internal edges are sharp with no evidence of healing. The absent portion of the vault was not present in the grave.

The sharp edges, as well as the lack of micro-fracture, suggest that a sharp-edged weapon, most probably a sword, inflicted this injury. The position of the defect, sharpness and angle (*c* 40 degrees) of the posterior edge suggest that the blow was inflicted by a right-handed assailant swinging the sword from above (Anderson 1996b). The sword sliced through the bone; penetrating to 10mm; the angle of the blow flattened; the blade was twisted; the bone was traumatically excised, breaking with slight irregularity anteriorly. There is no evidence of remodelling or secondary infection. The individual had not survived long enough for the healing process to begin. Remodelling would probably be visible within five days (Wenham 1989). As such, the injury was probably fatal or, technically, perimortal.

In Grave 303, the primary, adult, skeleton (Sk 303B) displayed a sinuous cleft involving the vertex of the

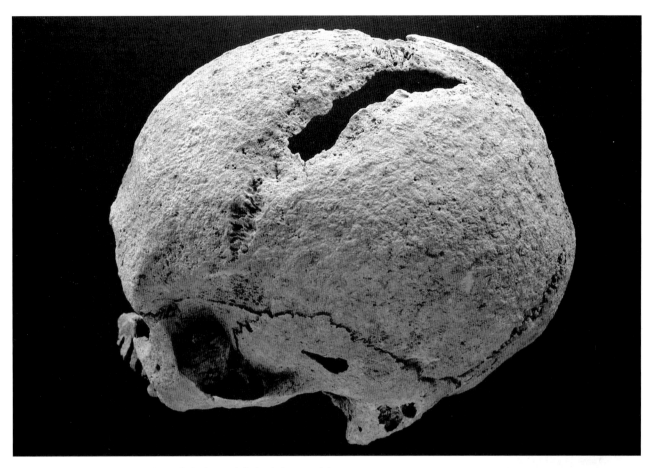

Fig 7.6. Sk 303B: Male adult cranium, displaying partially-healed weapon injury.

cranial vault (Fig 7.6). The linear defect is 78mm long (arc measurement) with a width of 6–10mm. The most anterior point is on the coronal suture, 15mm from the bregma. Posteriorly, it extends to the sagittal suture 65mm from the bregma. Externally, the bone surrounding the defect is depressed, despite the extensive *post mortem* erosion of the vault, this is clearly visible both anteriorly and posteriorly. Both internal and external edges of the cleft are smooth and rounded – evidence of *ante mortem* remodelling. Internally, several small foramina are visible marginal to the defect.

The smooth edges of the defect and the highly vascularised internal surface argue for direct trauma which was not immediately fatal (Anderson 1996b). The area surrounding the linear defect is depressed and micro-fracture is visible anteriorly and posteriorly. A blunt instrument, such as a wooden club would probably present with a circular depressed fracture rather than a sinuous cleft. It is probable that the blow was inflicted with a heavy blade weapon, possibly a small axe.

Several Anglo-Saxon sites have revealed definite evidence of weapon injury (Boylston 2000, table 3; Brothwell 1967; Smith 1884). Crania at Brandon and Caister-on-Sea display unhealed cut marks (S Anderson 1990; 1991); a weapon injury was noted at Norton (Marlow 1992) and an unhealed sword cut was reported from the Burgh Castle site (Anderson and Birkett 1989). At Great Chesterton, Essex two cases of cranial weapon injury, a sword and a blunt instrument, were noted (Waldron 1994). Three examples of cranial trauma at Butler's Field, Gloucestershire, have been attributed to weapon injuries (Harman 1998, 45–6). Direct violence, a broken nose, was reported from Caister-on-Sea (S Anderson 1991).

In Kent, a fatal sword blow, removing a portion of cranial vault similar to Sk 348, is known from Finglesham (Chadwick 1958; Chadwick Hawkes and Grainger 2006, 333, 339, grave 94). At Eccles, 7.8 per cent of the adult males (6/77) display unhealed sword injuries to the skull (Wenham 1989) and in one, an arrowhead was found embedded in

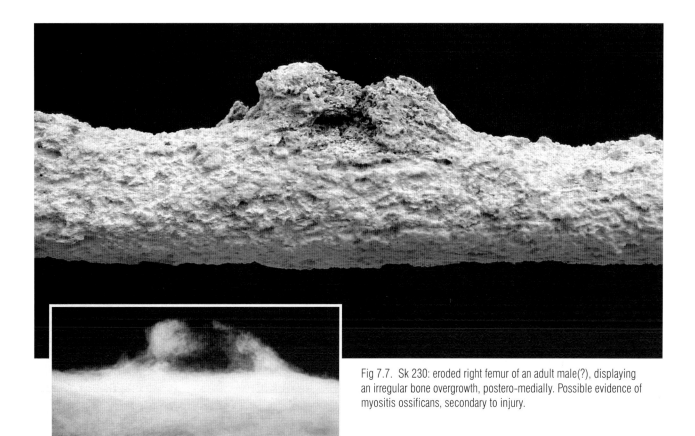

Fig 7.7. Sk 230: eroded right femur of an adult male(?), displaying an irregular bone overgrowth, postero-medially. Possible evidence of myositis ossificans, secondary to injury.

Fig 7.8. Sk 230: Radiograph of the femur, showing a dense overgrowth which has not invaded the medullary cavity.

the lower spine (Manchester and Elmhirst 1980; Wenham 1989).

The majority of weapon injuries occur on male crania (Boylston 2000, table 3). An exception is a tall (1.762m), possible female, from Burgh Castle (Anderson and Birkett 1989). Prior to our example (Sk 303B), the two cases from Great Chesterton (Waldron 1994), two males from Barrington (Duhig 1998) and a male from Alton, Hampshire (Powers and Brothwell 1988, fig 14) display evidence of healing.

Three males, all from the upper part of the 1994 cemetery area, presented with fractures. All had solidly re-united without any evidence of complications. The young adult male (Sk 385, Plot X) buried without grave goods, in an atypical posture (*see* pp 24–5), presents with a well-healed fracture of the distal left radius, associated with avulsion of the ulnar styloid process. This is a very common fracture site, first described by Abraham Colles in 1814 (Adams 1965, 155). It is nearly always caused by a fall on an outstretched hand. The only unusual feature is the young age of the individual,

since Colles' fractures are rare presentations under the age of 40 years (Adams 1965, 155).

An older ?male (Sk 395, Plot X) presents with a healed oblique fracture of the left distal tibia. The bone is solidly re-united with slight medial angulation. The distal fibula was not available for examination. The fact that the bone has successfully re-united would suggest that adequate immobilisation was carried out (Watson-Jones 1943, 764). An adult male (Sk 414, Plot Y), buried with a sword, appears to have suffered a mid-shaft left clavicular fracture during life.

Other trauma

A mature male (Sk 423, Plot Y) presents with a cystic cavitation of the superior aspect of the acetabular rim. The defect, some 10mm (a–p) by 6mm (sup-inf) and *c* 3mm deep (damaged), appears to represent a condition known as an acetabular flange lesion (Knowles 1983). Most workers have overlooked this defect, which normally affects the acetabulum but spares the femoral head. The favoured interpretation is one of acute trauma (Knowles 1983).

An unaged individual from Plot S (Sk 230), probably male on the evidence of the grave goods, presents with an irregular bone overgrowth on the postero-medial aspect of the proximal shaft of the right femur. The surface of the femur and the exostosis have been eroded in the ground (Figs 7.7 and 7.8). It is estimated that the exostosis was *c* 50mm in length; 25mm in width and its greatest height was 14mm. The radiographic evidence shows a dense overgrowth which has not invaded the medullary cavity (Fig 7.8). The most plausible diagnosis is one of myositis ossificans, which may occur as a complication of trauma in which the periosteum is ruptured (Watson-Jones 1943, 66–71). The irregular surface of the exostosis means that one would need to consider a low grade malignant neoplasia. However, the intact medullary cavity does not support this diagnosis. On balance, the lack of a smooth external surface that would be expected in myostis ossificans is considered to be the result of *post mortem* damage and erosion.

Infection

Apart from dental abscesses and sinus formation, there was no definite evidence of infection at Buckland 1994. Although many of the bone surfaces were eroded and would not permit identification of osteitic reaction, other contemporary sites with poor bone preservation have produced evidence for infective lesions. At Norton and Raunds the frequency of tibial osteitis was 7.7 per cent (Birkett 1992; Powell 1982). At Brandon the figure was 13 per cent and a case of femoral osteomyelitis was reported (Anderson 1990). At Eccles, a much higher figure, 23.6 per cent, was reported with

both sexes involved equally (Manchester, unpublished). However, a similar lack of bone infection was noted in poorly preserved material from Mill Hill, Deal (Anderson and Andrews 1997).

Metabolic (nutritional)

There was no evidence for rickets, scurvy or malnutrition in our sample. Five individuals, three males (Sk 319, Sk 394 and Sk 414); a female (Sk 255) and a juvenile (Sk 440) displayed porosity of the eye sockets, so-called cribra orbitalia. Three were buried in the upper area, one (Sk 394) in Plot X and two in Plot Y (Sk 414 and Sk 440). The other two (Sk 255 and Sk 319) were buried near to each other in Plot W. From grave-good evidence, three (Sk 255, Sk 414 and Sk 440) may be classed as 'rich'. Based on a small sample of orbits, the adult prevalence is 9.5 per cent (Table 7.18). A similar figure has been reported from other Anglo-Saxon cemeteries in Kent (Table 7.18). Much higher frequencies, with a sub-adult bias, have been observed in larger Anglo-Saxon samples from Suffolk, Norfolk and Yorkshire (Table 7.18).

Earlier work has suggested that cribra orbitalia may be evidence for iron deficiency (Carlson *et al* 1974; Cybulski 1977; Fornaciari *et al* 1982; Hengen 1971). Marked cranial porosis presenting with a radiological 'hair on end' appearance is pathognomonic for anaemia (Moseley 1965; 1966). However, both avitaminosis C (Holck 1987) and folic acid shortage, as a result of drinking goat's milk (Janssens 1981), have been considered influential in diploic expansion. It must be stressed that other non-dietary factors can lead to iron shortage (Von Endt and Ortner 1982; Walker 1986); perhaps the most frequent is parasitic infestation (Hengen 1971; Kent 1987).

| All % | Adult | | Sub-adult | | |
	male %	Female %	All	Site	Source
4.3% (?/??)	-	-	16.6% (-/-)	Castledyke South, Humberside	Drinkall & Foreman (1998)
7.1% (3/42)	13.6% (3/22)	0.7% (0/20)	33.3% (1/3)	Buckland 1994, Dover, Kent	present report
7.4% (5/68)	10.8% (4/37)	0.2% (1/31)	??? (??/??*)	Eccles, Kent	Manchester (unpublished)
7.7% (1/13)	33.3% (1/3)	0.0% (0/10)	0.0% (0/5)	Mill Hill, Deal, Kent	Anderson & Andrews (1997)
8.7% (2/23)	-	-	-	Norton, Cleveland	Birkett (1992)
18.3% (15/82)	-	-	-	Edix Hill, Barrington, Cambridgeshire	Duhig (1998)
23.2% (19/82)	25.0% (11/44)	21.1% (8/38)	41.7% (5/12)	Brandon, Suffolk	S Anderson (1990)
24.8% (35/141)	25.0% (17/68)	24.7% (18/73)	32.4% (12/37)	Caister-on-Sea, Norfolk	S Anderson (1991)
27.8% (??/??)	-	-	66.6% (??/??)	West Heslerton, Yorkshire	Cox (1990)

* one case in a 6-8 year old child, but sub-adult sample size not stated

Table 7.18. Ango-Saxon cribia orbitalia.

Vascular

Only one individual, a young adult ?female (Sk 420, Plot Y) displayed definite evidence of osteochondritis dissecans (OD), involving both knee joints. In modern Europeans OD may give rise to painful swelling, typically presenting at the knee in adolescent and young adult males (Barrie 1987). A frequency of about 8 per cent was noted in femora from Norton (Birkett 1992). At both Brandon and Caister-on-Sea, six osteochondrotic defects were recorded (S Anderson 1990; 1991). According to Wells (1974) the lesion is more frequent in the Roman and Anglo-Saxon periods and is rarer in Bronze Age and more recent material.

At Mill Hill Deal, the only definite OD defect was noted at an atypical ankle location (Anderson and Andrews 1997, 228–31). At Eccles almost a quarter of osteochondrotic defects (8/33) were located at the ankle (Manchester, unpublished). Lesions at atypical sites may indicate greater stress and strain of the involved joints (Anderson 2000a; 2001a; 2001b; During *et al* 1984).

An adult ?female (Sk 336) presents with an irregular central defect on talar surface of the left navicular (an ankle bone). A young adult female (Sk 290) presents with a circular cavitation on the proximal articulation of the first proximal pedal phalanx. Detailed osteological study indicates that such minor defects are not an infrequent finding and may involve a wide range of articular surfaces (Cardy 1998, 534–7).

Neoplasm

A possible case of benign neoplastic disease was noted in a 30–40 year old male from Plot Y (Sk 416). The sacral body displays a well-demarcated, slightly-lobulated, bone overgrowth involving the central anterior surface of the first and second elements and also, to a lesser extent, the left ala (Fig 7.9). The maximum dimensions are 79mm (mediolateral) and 53mm (cranial-caudal). The central surface of the expanded lesion presents as coarse trabecular, highly vasularised, bone (Fig 7.10).

The sacral arch was unavailable for study and the posterior body was severely eroded *post mortem*. However, there is evidence that the lower central border of the posterior body displays evidence of new bone formation and was originally enlarged. Directly inferior to this, the lesion is damaged and is represented by coarse trabecular bone.

The radiograph picture is complicated by the *post mortem* damage. However, the centrally-placed lesion presents as irregular coarse bone, with a triangular lytic area (*post*

mortem?) and a well-defined sclerotic margin, bounding the superior and right-superior margins (Fig 7.10).

The available data, indicates a slow-growing indolent lesion producing an overall bone increase with some evidence of reduced mineralisation and coarsening of trabeculae. This suggests the possibility of a benign largely bone-forming neoplasm. Benign neoplasia known to favour the spine include osteoblastoma and haemangioma (Anderson 2000b, table 7a; Bullough and Boachie-Adjei 1988, 176–8; Schajowicz 1981, 36–52, 303; Sutton 1975, 146).

Benign osteoblastoma favours the cervical and lumbar regions, involving the vertebral arches, spinous and transverse processes, rather than the vertebral bodies (Bullough and Boachie-Adjei 1988, 176; Marsh *et al* 1975). Typically, it presents with a central lytic focus (nidus) of over 20mm with little sclerosis (Schajowicz 1981, 48). It may occasionally be found in the sacrum, as a well-defined lesion including evidence of both bone formation and bone loss (Bullough and Boachie-Adjei 1988; fig 13.10; Marsh *et al* 1975). In some cases, areas of mineralisation may appear similar to that seen in Paget's disease (Schajowicz 1981, 49). Clinically, the vast majority of cases present by the age of 30 years, with a male (3:1) bias (Anderson 2000b, table 7a).

Haemangioma, is one of the most common spinal tumours, most frequently affecting the bodies of the lower thoracic region; occasionally it occurs in the sacrum (Bullough and Boachie-Adjei 1988, 178). It typically presents with loss of horizontal trabeculae and overall decrease in bone quantity, honeycomb appearance (Schajowicz 1981, 303), with possible bulging of the end-plates (Bullough and Boachie-Adjei 1988, 178). However, the vertebral body itself does not normally increase in size (Sutton 1975, 146). Clinically, both sexes are equally involved with all ages of adults involved (Anderson 2000b, table 7a).

Other benign neoplasia which may rarely affect the spine include osteoid osteoma (Bullough and Boachie-Adjei 1988, 182; Sutton 1975, 117), which is also known as circumscribed osteoblastoma (Schajowicz 1981, 36–47). However, the majority occur in the lower limb; hands; feet and ankle; only 5.6 per cent (11/214) are located in the spine (Schajowicz 1981, 36–47). Typically, it presents as a small lesion (less than 10mm) with a well-defined sclerotic nidus and favours the vertebral arches (Sutton 1975, 117; fig 5.6). Less than 0.5 per cent of cases occur in the sacrum (Schajowicz 1981, 36–47).

Neurofibroma and Schwannoma, arising within spinal nerve tissue, can be excluded since the only bone changes would be pressure erosion of the dorsal vertebral body (Bullough and Boachie-Adjei 1988, fig 14.42; Sutton 1975,

Fig 7.9. Sk 416: the sacrum of an adult male displaying bone overgrowth of the anterior surface of the first and second elements. Possible evidence of a benign neoplasm.

Fig 7.10. Sk 416: A-P radiograph of the sacrum, displaying coarse irregular trabeculae with evidence of a peripheral sclerosis. Suggestive of a slow-growing bone overgrowth.

150). A well-defined external bone overgrowth (hyperostosis) is known to occur in about 20–25 per cent of intracranial meningiomata (T Anderson 1991; 1992; 1993; 2000b). However, the much rarer vertebral meningioma, which strongly favours the thoracic spine (Russell and Rubenstein 1989, 452–6; Sutton 1975, 1314), can be excluded since a tumour of the spinal cord would not result in hyperostosis of the anterior aspect of the sacral body.

Differential diagnosis would need to include Paget's disease, a condition of obscure aetiology which leads to bone resorption and excessive, structurally deficient, disorganised new bone formation (Hamdy 1991, 31–5). The sacrum is the most frequent site for Paget's disease (Hamdy 1991, table 2-6). Clinically, the disease is rarely seen in patients under the age of 55 years, though cases have been detected, by

radiology, as early as 35 years of age (Hamdy 1991, table 2-2). A lobulated bone overgrowth, however, appears to be a very unusual presentation.

One other Anglo-Saxon case is known, occurring in an elderly male from Jarrow (Wells and Woodhouse 1975). One case is known from the Roman period (Molleson 1993). Other examples are known from the medieval (Mays and Turner-Walker 1999; Stirland 1991) and the post-medieval periods (Waldron 1993).

A definite diagnosis, based on examination of fragmented dry bone material, is not possible. A strong contender would be a benign, bone-forming tumour, possibly an osteoblastoma, located at a somewhat atypical location. However, an early manifestation of Paget's disease should be considered as a differential diagnosis.

Adult oral health

The dental remains were examined and recorded by John Andrews. The standard of adult oral health is based on the examination of 147 dentitions, with a total of 2,845 teeth. Over a third of the teeth were recovered as loose elements (986/2,845) with no jaw bone surviving; with maxillary teeth (571/1,307) more likely to be loose than mandibular (415/1,538).

Ante mortem tooth loss

In the 1994 Buckland material 15 per cent of adults with dental remains displayed *ante mortem* tooth loss (Table 7.19). The most advanced tooth loss was seen in a mature male (Sk 328) (17/24), classed as 'poor' by grave good evidence. Based on erupted tooth positions, it was possible to ascertain, for all adults, an overall *ante mortem* tooth loss of 2.3 per cent, with no sexual dimorphism (Table 7.20). Almost three-quarters of teeth lost, occurred in mature individuals. A higher frequency of mandibular teeth was lost during life; this was most marked in females (Table 7.20). An identical pattern was noted at Mill Hill, Deal (Anderson and Andrews 1997, table 24). Compared to most other Anglo-Saxon sites, Buckland presents with a very low *ante mortem* tooth loss (Table 7.20). Only West Heslerton displays a similarly low level of *ante mortem* tooth loss, which appears to be related to the high percentage of young adults in the sample (Cox 1999, table 75).

Caries

Over 30 per cent of adults presented with carious cavities, with evidence of a female bias (Table 7.19). However, the most widespread involvement, occurred in a young adult male (Sk 386B, Plot X), with all mandibular molars involved.

	No	Ante-mortem Loss	Caries	Calculus	Abscess	Hypoplasia	Congenital absence
Sub-adult							
Total	43	2.3%	4.7%	0.0%	0.0%	16.3%	4.7%
1–6	13	0.0%	0.0%	0.0%	0.0%	0.0%	0.0%
6–12	11	0.0%	9.1%	0.0%	0.0%	9.1%	0.0%
Juvenile	19	5.3%	5.3%	0.0%	0.0%	31.6%	10.5%
Adult - all							
Total	147	17.0%	29.3%	32.0%	17.7%	15.6%	16.3%
Young adult	55	3.6%	23.6%	29.1%	7.3%	16.4%	16.4%
Adult	61	19.7%	32.8%	36.1%	16.4%	16.4%	16.4%
Mature	30	36.7%	33.3%	30.0%	40.0%	13.3%	16.7%
Grown	1	0.0%	0.0%	0.0%	0.0%	0.0%	0.0%
Adult - male							
Total	68	16.2%	23.5%	27.9%	20.6%	16.2%	17.6%
Young Adult	23	8.7%	26.1%	34.8%	13.0%	13.0%	17.4%
Adult	24	12.5%	29.2%	29.2%	16.7%	20.8%	16.7%
Mature	21	28.6%	14.3%	19.0%	33.3%	14.3%	19.0%
Adult - female							
Total	70	18.6%	35.7%	38.6%	15.7%	14.3%	17.1%
Young adult	29	0.0%	20.7%	27.6%	3.4%	17.2%	17.2%
Adult	32	25.0%	37.5%	46.9%	15.6%	12.5%	18.7%
Mature	8	62.5%	87.5%	50.0%	62.5%	12.5%	12.5%
Grown	1	0.0%	0.0%	0.0%	0.0%	0.0%	0.0%
?Sex							
Total	9	1.1%	22.2%	11.1%	11.1%	22.2%	0.0%
Young adult	3	0.0%	33.3%	0.0%	0.0%	33.3%	0.0%
Adult	5	20.0%	20.0%	0.0%	20.0%	20.0%	0.0%
Mature	1	0.0%	0.0%	100.0%	0.0%	0.0%	0.0%

Table 7.19. Buckland: dental health based on individuals.

Based on individual teeth it was possible to ascertain, for all adults, an overall caries frequency of 3.5 per cent, with no marked sexual variation (Table 7.21). In the female dentition, maxillary caries was slightly more frequent than mandibular (Table 7.21). In both sexes, interstitial caries (mesial and distal) were by far the most frequent presentation (Table 7.22a). Almost half the cavities could be classed as large or extensive, with no sexual variation in cavity size (Table 7.22b). However, it was very noticeable that large cavities were more likely to be encountered in the lower jaw (Table 7.22b).

A similar overall caries frequency has been reported from other Anglo-Saxon sites (Table 7.21). However, the true level of carious experience will be under-represented in samples, such as Raunds, with a high *ante mortem* tooth loss. Consequently, a combination of carious teeth and *ante*

mortem tooth loss may give a more accurate picture of oral health. This derived figure suggests that Buckland dentitions were very healthy (Table 7.23).

Calculus

A third of adults presented with calculus deposits (Table 7.19). Based on individual teeth, the overall adult frequency was 10.1 per cent, with females twice as likely to be involved as males (Table 7.24). In both sexes, the lingual/palatal surfaces were the site of predilection (Table 7.25a). The majority of deposits were small and minimal (Table 7.25b). When compared to other Anglo-Saxon material the level of calculus appears very low (Table 7.24). However, the badly eroded nature of the dental remains means that many friable deposits of calculus

All

All %	Maxilla %	Mandible %	Site	Source
1.2 (21/1744)	-	-	West Heslerton, Yorkshire	Cox (1999)
2.3 (73/3195)	1.4 (20/1450)	3.0 (53/1745)	Buckland 1994, Dover, Kent	present report
2.6 (31/1204)	-	-	Berinsfield, Oxfordshire	Harman (1995)
4.1 (-/-)	-	-	Norton, Cleveland	Marlow (1992)
4.8 (146/2264)	5.5 (59/1080)	6.8 (87/1284)	Brandon, Suffolk	S Anderson (1990)
5.5 (45/822)	2.3 (9/399)	8.5 (36/423)	Mill Hill, Deal, Kent*	Anderson & Andrews (1997)
5.8 (44/758)	-	-	Broughton Lodge, Northants	Harman (1993)
6.5 (159/2441)	-	-	Caister-on-Sea, Norfolk	S Anderson (1991)
7.7 (209/2731)	-	-	Castledyke South, Humberside	Drinkall & Foreman (1998)
11.1 (272/2457)	9.9 (104/1047)	11.9 (168/1410)	North Elmham, Norfolk	Wells (1980)
11.7 (448/3840)	12.5 (225/1797)	10.9 (223/2043)	Raunds, Northants	Powell (unpublished)

*includes unsexed individuals

Male

All %	Maxilla %	Mandible %	Site	Source
0.9 (3/333)	0.0 (0/155)	1.7 (3/178)	Mill Hill, Deal, Kent	Anderson & Andrews (1997)
2.1 (31/1511)	1.8 (12/679)	2.3 (19/832)	Buckland 1994, Dover, Kent	present report
2.7 (-/-)	-	-	Norton, Cleveland	Marlow (1992)
6.2 (76/1216)	9.2 (55/601)	3.4 (21/615)	Caister-on-Sea, Norfolk	S Anderson (1991)
7.7 (99/1280)	7.4 (46/621)	8.0 (53/659)	Brandon, Suffolk	S Anderson (1990)
9.5 (72/755)	-	-	Castledyke South, Humberside	Drinkall & Foreman (1998)
9.8 (114/1155)	8.0 (38/474)	11.2 (76/681)	North Elmham, Norfolk	Wells (1980)
13.1 (296/2256)	15.9 (173/1086)	10.5 (123/1170)	Raunds, Northants	Powell (unpublished)

Female

All %	Maxilla %	Mandible %	Site	Source
2.5 (39/1585)	0.7 (5/723)	3.9 (34/862)	Buckland 1994, Dover, Kent	present report
4.3 (47/1084)	2.8 (13/459)	5.4 (34/625)	Brandon, Suffolk	S Anderson (1990)
4.6 (-/-)	-	-	Norton, Cleveland	Marlow (1992)
6.8 (83/1225)	7.7 (47/609)	5.7 (35/616)	Caister-on-Sea, Norfolk	S Anderson (1991)
9.6 (152/1584)	7.3 (52/711)	11.5 (100/873)	Raunds, Northamptonshire	Powell (unpublished)
12.1 (158/1302)	11.5 (66/573)	12.6 (92/729)	North Elmham, Norfolk	Wells (1980)
12.4 (105/849)	-	-	Castledyke South, Humberside	Drinkall & Foreman (1998)
13.6 (42/309)	7.3 (9/124)	17.8 (33/185)	Mill Hill, Deal, Kent	Anderson & Andrews (1997)

Table 7.20. Anglo-Saxon dental disease: *ante mortem* tooth loss.

have been lost *post mortem*. Consequently, the true prevalence of *in vivo* calculus is grossly under-represented.

Abscesses

Less than a fifth of adults presented with abscesses, with a female bias (Table 7.19). However, based on individual teeth the overall adult frequency was 1.7 per cent, with both sexes and upper and lower jaws equally involved (Table 7.26). The majority of abscesses are small radicular (Tables 7.27a and 7.27b). In the lower jaw several cases have led to the formation of buccally draining sinuses (Table 7.27a). Other Anglo-Saxon cemeteries display a higher frequency of abscess formation (Table 7.26).

Hypoplasia

Hypoplastic lines represent defects in the enamel formation during the growth of the tooth. They occur in response to childhood stress, such as malnutrition or fever (Dobney and

All adults

All %	Maxilla %	Mandible %	Site	Source
1.0 (17/1623)	1.3 (9/716)	0.9 (8/907)	Brandon, Suffolk	S Anderson (1990)
1.8 (31/1759)	1.4 (11/774)	2.0 (20/985)	Caister-on-Sea, Norfolk	S Anderson (1991)
2.4 (41/1723)	-	-	West Heslerton, Yorkshire	Cox (1999)
3.2 (32/986)	-	-	Berinsfield, Oxfordshire	Harman (1995)
3.4 (-/-)	-	-	Norton, Cleveland	Marlow (1992)
3.5 (98/2836)	4.3 (55/1288)	2.8 (43/1548)	Buckland 1994, Dover, Kent	present report
3.8 (26/676)	6.7 (21/315)	1.4 (5/361)	Mill Hill, Deal, Kent*	Anderson & Andrews (1997)
4.3 (139/3257)	4.6 (68/1481)	4.0 (71/1776)	Raunds, Northamptonshire	Powell (unpublished)
4.5 (64/1431)	-	-	Empingham II, Leicestershire	Mays (1990)
5.1 (-/-)	-	-	Porchester Castle	White (1988)
5.7 (32/562)	-	-	Broughton Lodge, Northamptonshire	Harman (1993)
6.5 (102/1577)	4.4 (28/630)	7.8 (74/947)	North Elmham, Norfolk	Wells (1980)
6.6 (-/-)	-	-	Castledyke South, Humberside	Drinkall & Foreman (1998)

*includes unsexed individuals

Male

All %	Maxilla %	Mandible %	Site	Source
0.7 (6/906)	0.5 (2/412)	0.8 (4/494)	Brandon, Suffolk	S Anderson (1990)
1.7 (16/923)	1.2 (5/415)	2.2 (11/508)	Caister-on-Sea, Norfolk	S Anderson (1991)
2.7 (-/-)	-	-	Norton, Cleveland	Marlow (1992)
2.8 (37/1323)	3.1 (18/583)	2.6 (19/740)	Buckland 1994, Dover, Kent	present report
3.9 (30/767)	-	-	Empingham II, Leicestershire	Mays (1990)
4.2 (79/1873)	4.2 (35/826)	4.2 (44/1047)	Raunds, Northamptonshire	Powell (unpublished)
4.5 (-/-)	6.0 (-/-)	4.2 (-/-)	Eccles, Kent	Manchester (unpublished)
6.4 (21/326)	11.4 (17/149)	2.3 (4/177)	Mill Hill, Deal, Kent	Anderson & Andrews (1997)
6.8 (53/778)	5.0 (15/302)	8.0 (38/476)	North Elmham, Norfolk	Wells (1980)
7.1 (-/-)	-	-	Castledyke South, Humberside	Drinkall & Foreman (1998)

Female

All %	Maxilla %	Mandible %	Site	Source
1.5 (11/717)	2.3 (5/723)	1.0 (4/413)	Brandon, Suffolk	S Anderson (1990)
1.8 (15/836)	1.7 (6/359)	1.9 (9/477)	Caister-on-Sea, Norfolk	S Anderson (1991)
2.1 (5/235)	3.7 (4/109)	0.8 (1/126)	Mill Hill, Deal, Kent	Anderson & Andrews (1997)
4.2 (60/1420)	5.4 (36/663)	3.2 (24/757)	Buckland 1994, Dover, Kent	present report
4.3 (-/-)	-	-	Norton, Cleveland	Marlow (1992)
4.3 (60/1384)	5.0 (33/655)	3.7 (27/729)	Raunds, Northamptonshire	Powell (unpublished)
5.1 (34/664)	-	-	Empingham II, Leicestershire	Mays (1990)
6.2 (49/799)	4.0 (13/328)	7.6 (36/471)	North Elmham, Norfolk	Wells (1980)
6.3 (-/-)	-	-	Castledyke South, Humberside	Drinkall & Foreman (1998)
6.3 (-/-)	5.6 (-/-)	6.9 (-/-)	Eccles, Kent	Manchester (unpublished)

Table 7.21. Anglo-Saxon dental disease: caries.

All adults

Location	All	Maxilla	Mandible
1	8.1% (8)	0.0% (0)	18.6% (8)
2	4.0% (4)	1.8% (1)	7.0% (3)
3	2.0% (2)	3.6% (2)	0.0% (0)
4	31.3% (31)	30.4% (17)	18.6% (14)
5	43.4% (43)	51.8% (29)	32.6% (14)
6	11.1% (11)	12.5% (7)	9.3% (4)

Male

Location	All	Maxilla	Mandible
1	5.4% (2)	0.0% (0)	10.5% (2)
2	10.8% (4)	5.6% (1)	15.8% (3)
3	0.0% (0)	0.0% (0)	0.0% (0)
4	32.4% (12)	38.9% (7)	26.3% (5)
5	43.2% (16)	50.0% (9)	36.8% (7)
6	8.1% (3)	5.6% (1)	10.5% (2)

Female

Location	All	Maxilla	Mandible
1	9.8% (6)	0.0% (0)	25.0% (6)
2	0.0% (0)	0.0% (0)	0.0% (0)
3	3.3% (2)	5.4% (2)	0.0% (0)
4	31.1% (19)	27.1% (10)	37.5% (9)
5	42.6% (26)	51.4% (19)	29.2% (7)
6	13.1% (8)	16.2% (6)	8.3% (2)

Caries location: 1: buccal/labial; 2: occlusal; 3: lingual/palatal; 4: mesial; 5: distal; 6: widespread.

Table 7.22a. Buckland: caries location.

Goodman 1991). Once formed, they remain visible in the enamel throughout life. In the adult Buckland skeletons, less than 10 per cent of available dentitions displayed enamel hypoplasia (Table 7.19). Involvement of a single tooth may be evidence of localised trauma. Widespread defects would argue for a systemic health problem.

There was evidence that individuals with hypoplastic defects were more likely to die earlier (Table 7.19). The most advanced case, with twenty-eight teeth involved, occurs in the young adult male (Sk 385, Plot X). This man, as previously noted, was the most broad-headed and narrow-nosed individual, who had been buried in an atypical position (*see* pp 290 and 24–5). Possibly a foreigner, and with serious childhood health problems, he ended his short life at Buckland.

A concentration of individuals with hypoplastic defects was noted in Plot Y: four adults (Sk 413 (Plot X), Sk 416, Sk 419 and Sk 425) and two juveniles (Sk 438 and Sk 439, see below). This, coupled with the high childhood mortality in this portion of the cemetery, as well as two cases of possible iron deficiency (cribra orbitalia), suggests that this group was

markedly less healthy than those interred in other areas. The available dating evidence indicates that these burials are not all contemporary, which argues against a single episode of famine, starvation or malnutrition. Burials in close proximity of rich males (Sk 414 and Sk 437); females (Sk 420 and Sk 428) and a juvenile (Sk 440), all without hypoplasia, is possible evidence for social stratification within this plot.

When compared to other Anglo-Saxon sites the level of hypoplasia at Buckland 1994 is extremely low (Table 7.28). At Norton, over half the dentitions were reported to display hypoplastic defects (Marlow 1992). At Brandon, in Suffolk, almost half the children displayed defects (Anderson 1990) and at Nazeingbury hypoplasia was recorded on all sub-adult dentitions (Huggins 1978). At Caister-on-Sea, almost three quarters of sub-adult dentitions presented with enamel hypoplasia (S Anderson 1991).

Detailed examination of individual teeth shows that males displayed a higher level of hypoplasia (3.5 per cent) than females (1.4 per cent) (Table 7.29). This is probably biased by the fact that one male (Sk 385) displayed widespread hypoplasia. In both sexes, the canines, followed by the incisors, are most frequently involved (Table 7.29).

Malocclusion

The high percentage of loose teeth in the whole sample, coupled with the poor quality of the available bone, means

All adults

Severity	All	Maxilla	Mandible
a	18.2% (18)	21.4% (12)	14.0% (6)
b	36.4% (36)	46.4% (26)	23.3% (10)
c	45.4% (45)	32.1% (18)	62.8% (27)

Male

Severity	All	Maxilla	Mandible
a	21.6% (8)	27.8% (5)	15.8% (3)
b	35.1% (13)	50.0% (9)	21.1% (4)
c	43.2% (16)	22.2% (4)	63.2% (12)

Female

Severity	All	Maxilla	Mandible
a	16.4% (10)	18.9% (7)	12.5% (3)
b	37.7% (23)	45.9% (17)	25.0% (6)
c	45.9% (28)	35.1% (13)	62.5% (15)

NB: Sk 237, female adult R max 7 has two carious cavities, therefore total number of cavities is 99 although only 98 teeth involved

Caries severity: a: minimal; b: moderate; c: extensive.

Table 7.22b. Buckland: caries severity.

All adult

All %	Maxilla %	Mandible %	Site	Source
2.8 (171/6031)	2.7 (75/2738)	2.9 (96/3293)	Buckland 1994, Dover, Kent	present report
4.1 (163/3987)	3.8 (68/1796)	4.3 (95/2191)	Brandon, Suffolk	S Anderson (1990)
4.7 (71/1498)	4.2 (30/714)	5.2 (41/784)	Mill Hill, Deal, Kent*	Anderson & Andrews (1997)
8.3 (587/7097)	8.9 (293/3278)	7.7 (294/3819)	Raunds, Northamptonshire	Powell (unpublished)
9.3 (374/4034)	7.9 (132/1677)	10.3 (242/2357)	North Elmham, Norfolk	Wells (1980)

*includes unsexed individuals

Male

All %	Maxilla %	Mandible %	Site	Source
2.4 (68/2834)	2.4 (30/1262)	2.4 (38/1572)	Buckland 1994, Dover, Kent	present report
3.6 (24/659)	5.6 (17/304)	2.0 (7/355)	Mill Hill, Deal, Kent	Anderson & Andrews (1997)
4.8 (105/2186)	4.6 (48/1033)	4.9 (57/1153)	Brandon, Suffolk	S Anderson (1990)
8.6 (167/1933)	6.8 (53/776)	9.9 (114/1157)	North Elmham, Norfolk	Wells (1980)
9.1 (375/4129)	10.9 (208/1912)	7.5 (167/2217)	Raunds, Northamptonshire	Powell (unpublished)

Female

All %	Maxilla %	Mandible %	Site	Source
3.2 (58/1801)	2.6 (20/763)	3.7 (38/1038)	Brandon, Suffolk	S Anderson (1990)
3.3 (99/3005)	3.0 (41/1386)	3.6 (58/1619)	Buckland 1994, Dover, Kent	present report
7.1 (212/2968)	6.2 (85/1366)	7.9 (127/1602)	Raunds, Northamptonshire	Powell (unpublished)
8.6 (47/544)	5.6 (13/233)	10.9 (34/311)	Mill Hill, Deal, Kent	Anderson & Andrews (1997)
9.9 (207/2101)	8.8 (79/901)	10.7 (128/1200)	North Elmham, Norfolk	Wells (1980)

Note: excludes teeth that are broken down by caries

Table 7.23. Anglo-Saxon dental disease: combined *ante mortem* tooth loss and caries.

that the true level of malocclusion in this sample cannot be assessed.

Abnormalities

There were very few abnormalities in the available fragmented dentitions. It would appear that a deciduous canine had been retained for several years (between the left upper canine and first premolar) in a young adult ?male (Sk 281) in Plot T.

Impactions

Maxillary canine impaction occurred in a male (Sk 416) and an unsexed mature adult (Sk 337). Excluding the loose canines, this represents a prevalence of 2 per cent. A single case of a third molar impaction could be identified in the fragmented lower jaw of a 'rich' adult female (Sk 255), even though the tooth in question had been lost *post mortem*. The remains of the socket shows that this was a horizontal impaction, much rarer than the normal mesio-angular impaction (Stones 1957, 123–5). Based on the number of lower third molars in adult jaws, this represents a prevalence of 0.85 per cent (1/118). These figures largely mirror modern clinical data, in which mandibular molars (n = 231), followed by maxillary canines (n = 99) and maxillary third molars (n = 62) are the most frequent impactions (Stones 1957, table 2).

Congenital absence

Some 16.3 per cent of adult dentitions displayed congenital absence of one or more teeth (Table 7.19). Twenty-two individuals, nine males (Sk 281, Sk 291, Sk 292, Sk 295, Sk 300, Sk 348, Sk 363, Sk 416 and Sk 423) and thirteen females (Sk 239, Sk 250, Sk 253, Sk 288, Sk 296, Sk 327, Sk 344, Sk 347, Sk 349, Sk 351B, Sk 355, Sk 366 and Sk 428) are involved. A high percentage (54.5 per cent) of adult dentitions dated to Phases 1 or 1–2 display congenital absence of third molars (Sk 239, Sk 281, Sk 348, Sk 349, Sk 351B and Sk 355). This may suggest a founding group of closely related family members. However, no definite familial groupings could be detected. The skeletons in question are dispersed throughout the cemetery, in Plots S, T, V and Y.

Some 8.2 per cent of available third molars were congenitally absent, with mandibular molars more frequently absent (11.7 per cent) than maxillary (3.7 per cent) (Table

All adult

All %	Maxilla %	Mandible %	Site	Source
10.1 (279/2776)	7.5 (96/1228)	16.9 (183/1548)	Buckland 1994, Dover, Kent	present report
22.4 (146/653)	19.7 (60/304)	24.6 (86/349)	Mill Hill, Deal, Kent*	Anderson & Andrews (1997)
41.6 (-/-)	-	-	West Heslerton, Yorkshire	Cox (1999)

*includes unsexed individuals

Male

All %	Maxilla %	Mandible %	Site	Source
6.4 (85/1323)	5.1 (30/583)	7.4 (55/740)	Buckland 1994, Dover, Kent	present report
19.0 (61/321)	9.6 (14/146)	26.9 (47/175)	Mill Hill, Deal, Kent	Anderson & Andrews (1997)
78.6 (-/-)	-	-	Caister-on-Sea, Norfolk	S Anderson (1991)

Female

All %	Maxilla %	Mandible %	Site	Source
13.5 (191/1420)	9.5 (63/663)	16.9 (128/757)	Buckland 1994, Dover, Kent	present report
38.7 (84/217)	45.5 (46/101)	32.8 (38/116)	Mill Hill, Deal, Kent	Anderson & Andrews (1997)
82.3 (-/-)	-	-	Caister-on-Sea, Norfolk	S Anderson (1991)

Note: excludes teeth that are broken down by caries

Table 7.24. Anglo-Saxon dental disease: calculus.

All adults

Location	All	Maxilla	Mandible
1	27.4% (119)	39.4% (54)	21.8% (65)
2	0.2% (1)	0.0% (0)	0.3% (11)
3	51.3% (223)	34.3% (47)	59.1% (176)
4	9.0% (39)	11.7% (16)	7.7% (23)
5	12.2% (53)	14.6% (20)	11.1% (33)

Male

Location	All	Maxilla	Mandible
1	22.2% (32)	40.0% (14)	16.5% (18)
2	0.0% (0)	0.0% (0)	0.0% (0)
3	70.1% (101)	60.0% (21)	73.4% (80)
4	1.4% (2)	0.0% (0)	1.8% (2)
5	6.3% (9)	0.0% (0)	8.3% (9)

Female

Location	All	Maxilla	Mandible
1	29.2% (84)	37.4% (37)	24.9% (47)
2	0.3% (1)	0.0% (0)	0.5% (1)
3	42.4% (122)	26.3% (26)	50.8% (96)
4	12.8% (37)	16.2% (16)	11.1% (21)
5	15.3% (44)	20.2% (20)	12.7% (24)

Abscess location: 1: buccal/labial; 2: occlusal; 3: lingual/palatal: 4: mesial; 5: distal.

Table 7.25a. Buckland: calculus location.

All adults

Severity	All	Maxilla	Mandible
a	70.3% (308)	81.3% (109)	65.5% (199)
b	27.2% (119)	17.9% (24)	31.6% (95)
c	2.5% (11)	0.7% (1)	3.3% (10)

Male

Severity	All	Maxilla	Mandible
a	73.6% (106)	88.6% (31)	68.8% (75)
b	26.4% (38)	11.4% (4)	31.2% (34)
c	0.0% (0)	0.0% (0)	0.0% (0)

Female

Severity	All	Maxilla	Mandible
a	69.1% (199)	78.8% (78)	64.0% (121)
b	27.8% (80)	20.2% (20)	31.7% (60)
c	3.1% (9)	1.0% (1)	8.1% (8)

Abscess severity: a: minimal; b: moderate; c: extensive.

Table 7.25b. Buckland: calculus severity.

All Adult

All	Maxilla	Mandible	Site	Source
0.7 (-/-)	-	-	Norton, Cleveland	Marlow (1992)
0.8 (-/-)	-	-	Castledyke South, Humberside	Drinkall & Foreman (1998)
1.7 (33/1930)	1.9 (14/748)	1.6 (19/1182)	Buckland 1994, Dover, Kent*	present report
2.3 (53/2344)	-	-	Brandon, Suffolk	S Anderson (1990)
2.9 (33/1129)	-	-	Berinsfield, Oxfordshire	Harman (1995)
4.5 (22/488)	4.8 (10/209)	4.3 (12/279)	Mill Hill, Deal, Kent*	Anderson & Andrews (1997)
4.8 (31/646)	-	-	Broughton Lodge, Nottinghamshire	Harman (1993)
5.0 (133/2655)	5.9 (76/1294)	4.2 (57/1361)	Raunds, Northamptonshire	Powell (unpublished)
5.4 (131/2441)	-	-	Caister-on-Sea, Norfolk	S Anderson (1991)

Male

All	Maxilla	Mandible	Site	Source
2.0 (20/980)	2.6 (10/390)	1.7 (10/590)	Buckland 1994, Dover, Kent*	present report
2.3 (29/1270)	-	-	Brandon, Suffolk	S Anderson (1990)
5.0 (91/1832)	7.1 (56/785)	3.3 (35/1047)	Raunds, Northamptonshire	Powell (unpublished)
8.0 (17/213)	6.6 (7/106)	9.3 (10/107)	Mill Hill, Deal, Kent*	Anderson & Andrews (1997)

Female

All	Maxilla	Mandible	Site	Source
1.3 (12/934)	0.9 (3/342)	1.5 (9/592)	Buckland 1994, Dover, Kent*	present report
2.0 (5/249)	2.9 (3/103)	1.4 (2/146)	Mill Hill, Deal, Kent*	Anderson & Andrews (1997)
2.2 (24/1074)	-	-	Brandon, Suffolk	S Anderson (1990)
5.1 (42/823)	3.9 (20/509)	7.0 (22/314)	Raunds, Northamptonshire	Powell (unpublished)

* includes unsexed individuals

Table 7.26. Anglo-Saxon dental disease: abscesses.

All adults

Location	All	Maxilla	Mandible
1	28.1% (9)	30.8% (4)	26.3% (5)
2	62.5% (20)	61.5% (8)	63.2% (12)
3	3.1% (1)	7.7% (1)	0.0% (0)
4	0.0% (0)	0.0% (0)	0.0% (0)
5	6.3% (2)	0.0% (0)	10.5% (2)

Male

Location	All	Maxilla	Mandible
1	30.0% (6)	20.0% (2)	40.0% (4)
2	65.0% (13)	70.0% (7)	60.0% (6)
3	5.0% (1)	10.0% (1)	0.0% (0)
4	0.0% (0)	0.0% (0)	0.0% (0)
5	0.0% (0)	0.0% (0)	0.0% (0)

Female

Location	All	Maxilla	Mandible
1	25.0% (3)	66.7% (2)	11.1% (1)
2	58.3% (7)	33.3% (1)	66.7% (6)
3	0.0% (0)	0.0% (0)	0.0% (0)
4	0.0% (0)	0.0% (0)	0.0% (0)
5	16.7% (2)	0.0% (0)	22.2% (2)

Abscess location: 1: buccal/labial; 2: apical; 3: lingual/palatal; 4: mesial; 5: distal.

Table 7.27a. Buckland: abscess location.

All adults

Severity	All	Maxilla	Mandible
a	78.1% (25)	69.2% (9)	84.2% (16)
b	12.5% (4)	15.4% (2)	10.5% (2)
c	9.4% (3)	15.4% (2)	5.3% (1)

Male

Severity	All	Maxilla	Mandible
a	75.0% (15)	60.0% (6)	90.0% (9)
b	15.0% (3)	20.0% (2)	10.0% (1)
c	10.0% (2)	20.0% (2)	0.0% (0)

Female

Severity	All	Maxilla	Mandible
a	83.3% (10)	100.0% (3)	77.8% (7)
b	8.3% (1)	0.0% (0)	11.1% (1)
c	8.3% (1)	0.0% (0)	11.1% (1)

Abscess severity: a: minimal; b: moderate; c: extensive.

Table 7.27b. Buckland: abscess severity.

7.30b). A similar prevalence and mandibular bias was noted at Mill Hill, Deal (Anderson and Andrews 1997). At other Anglo-Saxon sites, a higher frequency of congenital absence has been recorded (Table 7.30a). Based on 2,500 dentitions the frequency of third molar absence in southern England today is 12.7 per cent (Shinn 1976).

Five individuals displayed congenital absence of a mandibular second premolar (Sk 282B, Sk 289, Sk 327, Sk 338 and Sk 350B). In all but Sk 338, the left premolar was absent. Based on available erupted tooth positions, this represents a prevalence of 2.1 per cent, a figure which is in accord with established clinical data for congenital absence (Sylvester 1984, 225). A more unusual absence, that of a maxillary second premolar (left) was noted in the juvenile female (Sk 347) who

was also missing both mandibular third molars. This represents a prevalence of 0.4 per cent of available maxillary second premolar positions. Three individuals in Plot T (Sk 282B, Sk 327 and Sk 338) were buried in close proximity. Also, Sk 347 and Sk 350B were buried next to each other in Plot S.

Sub-adult oral health

Sub-adult oral health, based on forty-three dentitions, subdivided into permanent and deciduous teeth. Two individuals, an 8–11 year old child (Sk 305) and a 15–20 year old juvenile (Sk 412) presented with caries cavities. In the former, one medium sized cavity was noted on the distal

Adult			Sub-adult	Site	Source
All	Male	Female			
6.1% (2/33)	6.2% (1/16)	10.0% (1/10)	4.2% (1/24)	Mill Hill, Deal, Kent	Anderson & Andrews (1997)
15.6% (23/147)*	16.2% (11/68)	14.3% (10/70)	16.3% (7/43)	Buckland 1994, Dover, Kent	present report
61.1% (44/72)	70.0% (28/40)	50.0% (16/32)	46.7% (7/15)	Brandon, Suffolk	S Anderson (1990)
64.0% (55/86)	65.9% (27/41)	62.2% (28/45)	37.5% (3/8)	Caister-on-Sea, Norfolk	S Anderson (1991)
* includes unsexed individuals					

Table 7.28. Anglo-Saxon dental disease: hypoplasia.

All Teeth	Sub-adult	Adult			
	All	All	Male	Female	?Sex
All	3.7% (18/486)	2.7% (77/2847)	3.5% (47/1361)	1.4% (20/1385)	0.0% (0/101)
Maxilla	3.3% (8/239)	1.8% (24/1299)	2.8% (17/606)	1.1% (7/648)	0.0% (0/45)
Mandible	44.0% (10/247)	3.4% (53/1548)	4.0% (30/755)	1.8% (13/737)	0.0% (0/56)
Incisors					
All	2.8% (4/145)	2.7% (16/603)	3.8% (14/294)	1.3% (2/296)	0.0% (0/13)
Maxilla	5.3% (4/76)	2.6% (7/269)	4.7% (2/128)	0.7% (1/137)	0.0% (0/4)
Mandible	0.0% (0/69)	2.7% (9/334)	3.8% (8/166)	1.3% (2/159)	0.0% (0/9)
Canines					
All	6.8% (5/73)	4.1% (16/393)	7.0% (6/368)	1.6% (3/191)	0.0% (0/15)
Maxilla	5.7% (2/35)	2.7% (4/183)	4.7% (2/178)	1.1% (1/92)	0.0% (0/6)
Mandible	9.5% (3/38)	5.2% (11/210)	8.8% (4/202)	2.0% (2/99)	0.0% (0/9)
Premolars					
All	4.4% (5/114)	2.1% (16/779)	2.7% (10/368)	1.6% (6/380)	0.0% (0/31)
Maxilla	3.6% (2/56)	1.1% (4/362)	1.2% (2/169)	1.1% (2/178)	0.0% (0/15)
Mandible	5.2% (3/58)	2.9% (12/417)	4.0% (8/199)	2.0% (4/202)	0.0% (0/16)
Molars					
All	2.6% (4/154)	1.8% (19/1072)	2.0% (10/512)	1.7% (9/518)	0.0% (0/42)
Maxilla	0.0% (0/72)	1.6% (8/485)	2.2% (5/224)	1.2% (3/241)	0.0% (0/20)
Mandible	4.9% (4/82)	1.9% (11/587)	1.7% (5/288)	2.2% (6/277)	0.0% (0/22)

Table 7.29. Buckland: hypoplasia sub-divided by individual tooth.

All	Male	Female	Site	Source
7.6% (11/145)	4.2% (2/48)	17.3% (9/52)	Mill Hill, Deal, Kent*	Anderson & Andrews (1997)
8.2% (30/368)	6.6% (12/182)	9.7% (18/186)	Buckland 1994, Dover, Kent	present report
-	9.1% (-/-)	14.4% (-/-)	Brandon, Suffolk	S Anderson (1990)
16.4% (47/286)	9.5% (13/137)	22.8% (34/149)	North Elmham, Norfolk	Wells (1980)
17.6% (51/290)	11.0% (-/-)	24.3% (-/-)	Caister-on-Sea, Norfolk	S Anderson (1991)
24.1% (13/54)	-	-	West Heslerton, Yorkshire	Cox (1999)

* includes unsexed individuals

Table 7.30a. Anglo-Saxon dental disease: third molar congenital absence.

	All %	Male	Female
All	8.2 (30/368)	6.6 (12/182)	9.7 (18/186)
Maxilla	3.7 (6/163)	3.8 (3/79)	3.6 (3/84)
Mandible	11.7 (24/205)	8.7 (9/103)	14.7 (15/102)

Table 7.30b. Buckland: third molar congenital absence.

surface of the right maxillary first molar. In the latter, large interstitial cavities affected the right maxillary second and third molars.

Hypoplastic defects were noted in seven sub-adults: a child (Sk 272) and six juveniles (male: Sk 438; female: Sk 289, Sk 382, Sk 440; ?Sex: Sk 310 and Sk 439). Over 30 per cent of juveniles displayed hypoplastic defects, which strongly suggest that there is a direct link between childhood stress and early death. Indeed, two of the juveniles (Sk 439 and Sk 440) each presented with ten hypoplastic teeth, apparently evidence of systemic disease.

Very few reports have been published on Anglo-Saxon sub-adult oral health. At Caister-on-Sea (S Anderson 1991) and West Heslerton (Cox 1990) the deciduous dentition was also free from caries. The level of oral health appears to be much higher than is found in more recent material. The children at medieval Cuddington presented with carious lesions in 12.2 per cent of deciduous and 5.7 per cent of permanent teeth (James and Miller 1970) and a similar frequency (9.2 per cent) has been reported from medieval Coldstream (Williams and Curzon 1985). In modern day children, approximately a third of deciduous teeth are carious (James and Miller 1970).

Conclusions

A total of 233 skeletons, mainly dating to the late fifth and sixth centuries, was recovered. Bone preservation is very poor, the majority of the skeletons are represented by eroded long bone shafts and fragmented crania. Over three-quarters (n = 183) were assessed as adult, with both sexes equally represented and no sexual segregation. Male life expectancy was greater than female. Over 20 per cent of the sample failed to reach adulthood. Only one child under 1 year old was recovered. In the north-eastern portion of the cemetery (Plot Y), sub-adult mortality reaches almost 36 per cent.

Some 7.5 per cent of graves contained more than one skeleton; one (Grave 249) contained three individuals. Compared to other Kentish cemeteries, multiple burials are infrequent. With one probable exception (Grave 391), there was no definite archaeological evidence that any of the multiple graves had been re-opened. Only one prone burial (Sk 263A) was noted, an un-aged grown male buried directly above a 'rich' young adult ?female (Sk 263B).

The mean stature of both sexes is relatively tall, similar to modern day stature. One young adult male (Sk 385), buried in an unusual posture, has an atypical cranial morphology and widespread enamel hypoplasia - possible evidence for a sickly childhood in a foreign country. A young adult female (Sk 247) displayed a rare variant, absence of both mandibular foramina.

The very poor preservation and fragmented nature of the material severely limits the value of the sample for diagnosing the true prevalence of skeletal disease. Vertebral degeneration was the most frequently encountered pathology. Two adult males display marked cranial weapon injury. Three males, including Sk 385 and all from the upper part of the 1994 cemetery area, presented with well-healed fractures, which were probably due to accidents. A ?male from the lower part of the cemetery presents with an irregular femoral overgrowth, a possible sequelae of trauma. Five individuals, three buried in the upper area, displayed cribra orbitalia, a condition which has been related to iron deficiency. A possible case of benign neoplasia was noted in a male from the early phase of the upper part of the cemetery.

Oral health was good, only West Heslerton, with many young adults, displays a similar low level of *ante mortem* tooth loss. Interstitial caries were by far the most frequent presentation, larger cavities were more likely to be encountered in the lower jaw. The combined figure of carious teeth and *ante mortem* tooth loss supports a good standard of oral health. Also, the level of abscess formation and enamel hypoplasia is lower than that seen at other Anglo-Saxon cemeteries.

Individuals with enamel hypoplasia had a shorter life expectancy. A concentration of hypoplastic defects was noted in Plot Y. These burials are not contemporary, which argues against a single episode of famine, starvation or malnutrition. A high percentage (58.3 per cent) of adult dentitions, dated to the earlier phases of the site, display congenital absence of third molars. This may suggest a founding group of closely related family members. However, the skeletons in question are dispersed throughout the cemetery in different plots.

In Plot Y, burials with enamel hypoplasia and 'rich' burials without dental defects provide possible evidence for social stratification in this group. However, grave good evidence suggests that no 'poor' individuals were buried in this area of the cemetery (see Part 9). The tallest male and female were both located in this plot. Several of the 'poor' males are buried on the periphery of the plots, including two who displayed marked flattening of the lower legs – a condition which may be related to walking over rough terrain or habitual squatting.

Apart from enamel hypoplasia, there was no definite evidence that health problems displayed marked variation between different plots. However, high status was no barrier to health problems: of the five cases of possible iron deficiency, three occurred in 'rich' graves. Also, the only example of widespread Schmorls nodes, in a 'rich' young adult female, suggests that she had to carry out repetitive activities which put her back under severe strain.

DNA analysis

Ana Töpf

No formal resources were available for extensive research, but a limited study of DNA preserved within the skeletal material recovered from the 1994 excavations was undertaken in 2003 at the School of Biological Sciences, University of Durham. Samples from thirty-one individual skeletons with reasonably well preserved teeth were chosen

for analysis. These included a range of men, women and children, perceived to be of both 'high' and 'low' status, selected from different plots across the site. It was hoped that examination of these might be able to identify familial relationships and perhaps distinguish between groups of Anglo-Saxon incomers and people descended from Romano-British stock.

Introduction and scientific background

During decades of molecular research, long-term DNA-preservation was not expected in archaeological remains, as it was believed that total degradation occurred soon after death. When an organism dies, deprived of the *in vivo* repair systems, hydrolytic and oxidative processes damage its genetic material, leading to the degradation of the DNA molecule into small fragments (Lindahl 1993). However, the use of very sensitive protocols has proved that these short DNA strands can still be recovered and made available for analysis. In particular, the field of molecular archaeology was boosted by the development of the PCR (Polymerase Chain Reaction) technique (Mullis and Faloona 1987). This molecular technique allows the quantitative amplification of specific DNA regions, starting from just a few DNA molecules. Since its invention, it has been possible to detect and characterize (ie sequence) minimal traces of DNA present in archaeological material or museum samples. Thus, DNA sequences of non-living and/or extinct samples can be compared to those of living ones.

In a mammalian cell, most of the genetic material is located in the nucleus. In addition, a separate compartment, the mitochondria, also contains DNA. This DNA encodes for proteins involved in metabolic processes which occur inside the mitochondria, such as the energy production system. Whereas there are two copies of DNA in the nucleus (each one inherited from each parent), there are >500 copies in the mitochondria (Robin and Wong 1988). This makes mitochondrial DNA (mtDNA) more likely to be isolated from archaeological material. In addition, mitochondrial DNA analysis is a useful tool in genetic population studies due to its high mutation rate (Brown *et al* 1979). This means that mitochondrial DNA evolves rapidly, giving rise to much variation between the mtDNA sequences from different individuals. In addition, as opposed to nuclear DNA which is inherited from both parents, mitochondrial DNA is inherited maternally (Giles *et al* 1980) and therefore does not undergo recombination. As a result, individuals maternally related present identical mtDNA types. Moreover, relationships between mtDNA

Grave	Sex	Gender	Age	Phase	Variable sites	Type
264	Male	Male	40–45	3	16126, 16294, 16296, 16304	1
265B	?Male	Male	25–30	3a	16126, 16294, 16296, 16304	1
281	?Male	Female	25–30	1b	16192, 16223 16274, 16301	2
313	Female	-	*c* 40	2–7	16189	3
316	Female	-	65+	-	16311	4
375	Male	Male	25–30	3b	16162, 16292	5
437	Male	Male	35–40	2	16162, 16292	5

Table 7.31. Buckland 1994. Authenticated mitochondrial DNA sequences for seven skeletons.

haplotypes can be traced phylogenetically to reconstruct maternal genealogies.

Study methods

Samples

Teeth were chosen as a tissue for the DNA extraction due to their unique histological and anatomical organization. Dental hard tissue physically encloses the pulp, offering a structure of great durability and preventing the degradation due to microbial attack (Smith *et al* 1993). The coronal pulp chamber is the main target for DNA sampling, as cell remnants of the pulp may remain attached to the chamber walls, allowing recovery by grinding (Drancourt *et al* 1998). A total of sixty-two dental samples, derived from thirty-one Buckland skeletons, were used for the DNA analyses.

Preparation of the samples

To eliminate possible external contamination, teeth were cleaned by soaking in 3 per cent hydrogen peroxide for thirty minutes (Ginther *et al* 1992) and exposed to Ultra Violet light for twenty minutes (Sarkar and Sommer 1993). Dental samples were broken lengthways using a manual vice and pulp cell remnants were collected by grinding the walls of the pulp chamber with an electric drill. Several fractions were collected from each tooth. A total of 103 fine-powdered dental samples were subjected to the DNA extraction protocol.

DNA extraction

The method used was based on a protocol previously described by Schmerer *et al* (1999), consisting of a 48-hour enzymatic digestion followed by two organic (phenol/chloroform) extractions and a silica-based concentration. Extensive precautions to avoid contamination with modern material were taken (see below).

Polymerase and sequencing reaction

As DNA strands from archaeological material are likely to be degraded, only a small fragment of the most variable region of the mtDNA, namely the hypervariable segment I (HVS-I), was amplified by PCR. A specific set of primers designed for this study (L16098/H16329) and optimised PCR conditions were used for the amplification reaction. The resulting PCR product was a mtDNA fragment of 207 units (base pairs). These PCR products were subjected to a subsequent reaction to determine their DNA sequence. All DNA sequences were compared to a reference sequence (the Cambridge Reference Sequence, CRS; S Anderson *et al* 1981) to determine the number and position of distinctive sites (variable nucleotides).

Precautions against contamination

DNA analysis of human archaeological material is highly susceptible to contamination, as traces of modern cells are likely to present larger amounts of DNA than the ancient tissue. To avoid contamination with PCR products, pre- and post- PCR analyses were carried out in spatially separated rooms and where human DNA analysis was not previously undertaken. In addition, protective clothing (ie lab coat, gloves, face mask and hair net) was worn throughout all procedures. Disposable material and reagents were sterilised and tools and benches thoroughly cleaned with bleach and irradiated under UV light. Several controls to detect possible remaining contamination were carried out. Lastly, to identify the most likely source of contamination with modern DNA (ie through dead skin cells dispersed in the air) nucleotide sequences of lab workers were determined for comparisons.

Authentication of ancient DNA

To authenticate the DNA sequences from the archaeological material, each sample was analysed at least twice, including double DNA extraction, PCR amplification and DNA sequencing. Only replicate samples yielding identical sequences were included in the data analysis.

Results

DNA extraction, amplification and authentication

Of the total thirty-one samples from Buckland, seven yielded authenticated DNA sequences (DNA from another five samples was obtained but could not be authenticated, see below). This success rate (17 per cent) was within the range expected for ancient DNA analyses. In addition, several DNA extracts showed DNA artefacts, a typical ancient DNA behaviour (Hofreiter *et al* 2001). A fragment of 207 base pairs of the hypervariable segment I (HVS-I) of the mtDNA was obtained for all the samples. None of the DNA extracts yielded amplification for larger fragments, suggesting a high level of degradation, as is expected for genetic material from archaeological samples. DNA sequences were considered to be authentic when different extracts from different dental samples from the same skeleton yielded identical DNA sequences.

Mitochondrial DNA sequence data

The obtained DNA sequences extended from nucleotide position 16123 to 16330. Variable sites were identified by comparisons with the reference sequence (CRS). Three

sequences (from Sk 264, Sk 265B and Sk 281) presented three variable sites; two sequences (from Sk 375 and Sk 437) presented two variable sites and two sequences (from Sk 313 and Sk 316) presented one variable site. None of the sequences was identical to the CRS (see Table 7.31).

Among the seven mtDNA sequences obtained, five different mtDNA variants or haplotypes were observed. Sk 264 and Sk 265B, males aged respectively 40–45 and 25–30, share the same mtDNA haplotype (mtDNA sequences presenting the same variable sites), type 1. Likewise, Sk 375 and Sk 437 (two males, aged respectively 25–30 and 35–40) share mtDNA type 5. As mtDNA is maternally inherited, sharing mtDNA haplotypes may indicate maternal relationship between these pairs of individuals, either pairs of siblings or cousins (through the maternal line). As haplotype 1 (belonging to Sk 264 and Sk 265B) is very frequent among modern European populations, it is possible that these individuals shared such a mtDNA variant by chance rather than actual biological bond. Despite this, the close location of these two burials and their similar (Phase 3) dating would support the idea that they were related.

In contrast, haplotype 5 is extremely rare. Among >6,500 DNA sequences from a large number of modern populations this haplotype was observed exclusively only in these two individuals from Buckland (Töpf 2003). Thus, despite having been buried some 35 metres apart, in different plots (Plots X and Y), the DNA data strongly indicates that the individuals represented by Sk 375 and Sk 437 were maternally related.

PART 8: BUCKLAND CEMETERY CHRONOLOGY

Birte Brugmann

In 1987 Buckland (1951–3) was the first substantial Kentish cemetery with a long date range to be published in detail since the nineteenth century. As a Kentish site rich in regional material culture and in continental imports, the cemetery was particularly promising for chronological studies. For ease of reference back to the first Buckland report, the detailed phasing set out by Vera Evison (1987, Phases 1–7) has been retained here, with only minor amendments (Table 8.0 and 8.6). The first three Phases (c AD 475–625) are particularly well represented in the 1994 area, and it has been possible to subdivide a number of these graves into earlier ('a') and later ('b') groups. No burials have been assigned to Phase 4 (c AD 625–650), whilst graves of Phases 5–7 (c AD 650–750) are treated collectively as only three burials of this date were found in 1994 (Table 8.5).

Phase	Evison date ranges	Phase	Revised date ranges
1	475–525	1a–1b	450–510/530
2	525–575	2a–2b	510/30–550/560
3	575–625	3a	550/60–580/600
4	625–650	3b	580/600–650
5	650–675		
6	675–700	5–7	650–750
7	700–750		

Table 8.0. Revised dating for Buckland cemetery phases.

Amendments to the chronological phases in the first Buckland report are based on the small finds analyses in this volume and on correspondence analysis of a corpus of grave goods from Kentish graves. Shifts in the absolute chronological dates given to the phases draw on the state of research on Anglo-Saxon and Merovingian chronology in 2003; the calibrated and modelled radiocarbon dates discussed below were not available at the time. While they indicate that some absolute date ranges suggested for the phases below are too late, both the unmodelled and the modelled calibrated radiocarbon dates correspond well with the relative chronological sequence: Grave 391B assigned to Phase 2 has an earlier calibrated date range than Grave 414 assigned to Phases 2b–3a and Graves 222, 250 and 339 assigned to Phase 3a. Grave 264 assigned to Phase 3 has a slightly later calibrated date range than the graves assigned to Phase 3a, and Graves 323 and 375 assigned to Phase 3b have again slightly later calibrated ones. Grave 391A assigned to Phase 5–7 has the latest calibrated date range.

Methodology

Evison used the layout of Buckland 1951–3 for the dating of graves which could not be dated on the basis of grave goods. The method made use of the overall shift from west to east in the utilisation of space across the hillside. Horizontal stratigraphy was also employed to date individual graves at Mill Hill, Deal (Parfitt and Brugmann 1997). The layout of Buckland 1994, however, is more complex, and a review of the phasing of Buckland 1951–3 has shown that the stratigraphy in that part of the cemetery is not quite as obvious as it once seemed (see below). In the following discussion graves have been dated purely on the basis of the grave goods they contained, not on their position and orientation within the plots, unless useful stratigraphic relationships occurred (Fig 8.4).

Though eighty-nine graves at Buckland 1994 are either double graves, cutting, or cut by other graves, the stratification contributes little towards a chronological framework

Table 8.1. Sorted matrix of the correspondence analysis for Buckland graves. For abbreviations of type names see Table 8.3.

Grave	club	smbr	buttonBff	Ksqhgarnet	impbro	MinDark	ConCyl	shieldbu	shoerivet	Melon	Reticella	Kdbr1-2	bracteate	Koch49/50	CylPen	scutiform	CylRound	Koch20	Kdbr3	keybunch	Koch34	SegGlob	box	coinpen	Orange	inlaypen	cowrie	longam	ribpin	bottle	châtelaine	WoundSp		Evison Phase	Kentish Phase	Buckland Phase
DBC417	1			1	1																												1.81			2a
DBC254		1				1																											1.70			1
DBC255	1		1	1	1				1																								1.66			1b
DBC013		1					1																										1.63	1		1b
DBC347			1		1		1																										1.61			2a
DBC048			1				1																										1.61	1		1b
DBC409	1					1	1																										1.59			1b
DBC372					1	1																											1.57			2a
DBC247					1	1	1																										1.50			2a
DBC391B			1			1	1	1	1																								1.39			2
DBC296						1	1	1																									1.36			2a
DBC407						1	1	1	1																								1.27			2
DBC419					1	1		1	1																								1.24			2a
DBC020						1	1	1				1																					1.14	1		2a
DBC092						1	1				1	1																					1.03	2		2
DBC204							1	1	1			1	1																				0.90			2b
DBC373								1	1	1	1	1																					0.77			2b/3a
DBC354								1	1			1																					0.72			2b
DBC412								1	1		1		1																				0.70			2b/3a
DBC038								1			1					1																	0.63	3	IV	2b/3a
DBC339								1	1	1	1	1		1	1	1	1																0.53			3a
DBC331									1		1				1	1																	0.39			3a
DBC060					1	1											1	1		1		1											0.27	3		3
DBC245									1			1				1			1	1													0.23			3a
DBC222											1	1			1		1			1													0.16			3a
DBC250										1		1	1		1		1																0.14			3a
DBC042										1		1	1				1	1		1	1												0.11	4		3
DBC353												1	1		1	1				1													0.03			3a
DBC059												1	1			1						1											-0.03	3	IV	3a
DBC030												1				1			1	1													-0.05	3	IV	3a
DBC062										1						1			1														-0.11	4		3a
DBC001									1	1						1	1	1	1	1					1								-0.18	3	V	3b
DBC035															1	1		1	1		1	1											-0.27	3	V	3b
DBC032															1	1		1	1	1	1	1											-0.27	3		3b
DBC232																1	1	1					1										-0.35			3b
DBC029										1						1	1		1		1			1									-0.42	3	V	3b
DBC133													1			1									1		1						-0.62	5		3b-5
DBC360																1									1								-0.67			3b
DBC055																	1				1		1		1						1		-0.74	4		3b-5
DBC018																	1	1							1		1						-0.78	4		3b-5
DBC067															1	1									1	1	1	1					-0.84	5	V	3b-5
DBC124																							1					1					-1.01	6		3b-5
DBC006																								1		1	1				1		-1.12	5		5-7
DBC134																					1				1	1		1			1		-1.12	5		5-7
DBC053																									1			1					-1.22	5		5-7
DBC00F																							1				1				1		-1.22	3		5-7
DBC043																							1						1		1		-1.24	4		5-7
DBC157																									1		1			1	1		-1.35	5		5-7
DBC132																									1			1	1		1		-1.37	5		5-7
DBC110																								1							1	1	-1.38	6		5-7
DBC413																										1	1	1			1		-1.41			5-7
DBC376																									1			1	1		1		-1.41			5-7
DBC160																										1						1	-1.50	6		5-7
DBC138																												1			1		-1.51	6		5-7
DBC044																												1			1		-1.51	4		5-7
DBC075																													1			1	1	-1.57	7		5-7
DBC127																													1			1	1	-1.58	7		5-7
DBC155																																1	1	-1.67	5		5-7
DBC107																																1	1	-1.67	6		5-7
	1.81	1.78	1.75	1.73	1.53	1.40	1.26	1.01	0.95	0.58	0.56	0.49	0.48	0.11	0.08	0.02	-0.12	-0.13	-0.13	-0.25	-0.28	-0.42	-0.60	-0.77	-1.00	-1.14	-1.18	-1.29	-1.38	-1.42	-1.45	-1.67				

because few of these graves produced datable grave goods. Significantly, however, Grave 232, cutting Grave 223 and cut by Grave 231, contained an imitation *tremissis* of Justin I with a *terminus post quem* of AD 518–527 (*see* pp 88–9). This adds to the small number of previously recorded Anglo-Saxon graves containing sixth-century coins (see Hines 1999). The few apparent contradictions between the stratigraphic evidence and the conventional dating of grave goods are discussed below (*see also* p 30).

The relative chronological framework presented for the grave goods of females is largely based on the small finds analyses of the authors in this volume and on a correspondence analysis of objects from the 1951–3 and 1994 parts of the cemetery, together with details provided by modern excavations of fifth- and sixth-century graves at Finglesham (Chadwick 1958; Chadwick Hawkes and Grainger 2006), Lyminge (Warhurst 1955), Bekesbourne (Jenkins 1957), Mill Hill, Deal (Parfitt and Brugmann 1997), and (with kind permission of the late Dave Perkins) a fifth-century grave at Ozengell, Thanet. The search for further fifth-century material has led to the addition of Bifrons to the sample, excavated in the nineteenth century and republished by Chadwick Hawkes (2000). For correspondence analysis, the programme KVARK1.0 developed by T Madsen (University of Aarhus) was used (Høilund Nielsen 1995). The phasing of grave goods from male burials is based on small finds analysis only because there are too few grave-good associations at Buckland which are suitable for correspondence analysis.

Some of the absolute dates assigned to Evison's phases have been revised (Table 8.0) on the basis of the small finds analyses of the authors in this volume, on the basis of previous research on Kentish absolute chronology (Parfitt and Brugmann 1997; Brugmann 1999a), on the basis of a national framework for the dating of glass beads from Anglo-Saxon graves (Brugmann 2004), and on the basis of a correlation with continental frameworks, in particular René Legoux's and Patrick Périn's framework for Picardie and the north-east of France (Legoux 1998; Périn 1998), Frank Siegmund's framework for the Lower Rhine region (Siegmund 1998) and Ursula Koch's recent framework for the south of Germany (Koch 2001).

Matches in the relative sequence of objects in these frameworks give reason to assume that Kent was not a region with a particularly high proportion of 'heirlooms' in use. Therefore, it seems unlikely that, as far as imports and possible imitations were concerned, Kent systematically lagged behind to the extent that it would have a noticeable effect on any absolute Kentish chronology correlated with continental frameworks.

The layout of the cemetery

Nine plots have been defined on the lower part of Buckland cemetery, designated plots 'R–Z', following 'A–N' used on the upper part of the site (pp 15–16; Fig 2.4). In general, the plots on Buckland 1994 are more obvious than Plots C–N at Buckland 1951–3. The only grave on Buckland 1994 that causes any real problem in terms of its position is Grave 428, which lies between Plots X and Y. It is further away from the ring gully F571 than Grave 413 in Plot X and falls in line with neighbouring graves in Plot Y. For convenience, it has been listed under Plot X throughout this volume.

Most plots include some graves which cut into others (*see* p 29), which raises questions about the former presence of grave markers and lack of space. This is relevant to the dating of individual graves because the accidental cutting of an earlier grave implies that the later grave was dug only when the first was no longer visible on the ground and all memory of it was lost. This could imply a time period of at least one generation had elapsed between the two episodes of burial. There are some indications that on Buckland 1994, earlier graves were deliberately cut as part of the burial practice. Figure 8.1 shows the position of three types of graves here: graves 1.90m or more in length not cutting other graves (Group 1, unshaded), graves 1.90m or more in length cutting other graves (Group 2, solid), and graves up to a length of 1.90m (Group 3, shaded). The plan of the cemetery (Fig 2.2) shows that the graves of Group 1 by themselves have an orderly and mostly spacious layout. The graves of Group 3 are comprised almost exclusively of children and juveniles. Most of these graves are either around the edge of the space used by graves of Group 1, for example Graves 216 and 241 in Plot R, or fill gaps in the orderly layout of Group 1 burials, as for example in Plot Y. The graves of Group 2 either cut graves along their length, or touch their end, in most cases a corner.

From this, it would seem that space, rather than the lack of space, played an important role in the burial practice at Buckland 1994. An individual was either given his or her own space (as a 'primary' grave) or a space affiliated to an existing grave (in a 'secondary' position). Intercutting graves do not seem to indicate a 'return', when the space allotted to a plot ran out and the re-use of old ground was required, but that primary and secondary graves were part of an ongoing burial practice. Intercutting graves dated to the same or immediately following phase on the basis of their grave goods (see below) support this interpretation.

This is all relevant to the chronological framework in so far as it implies that intercutting graves can be of the same phase and that there is very little hope for the kind

	Bifr15	Bek16	DBC351B	DBC239	Oz174	Bifr06	Bifr89	DBC219	Bif05	DBC254	Bifr77	DBC013	Lym60	MH061	DBC409	DBC417	DBC255	DBC372	MH073	MH071	DBC247	DBC048	DBC347	DBC419	Lym16	Bifr42	DBC296	MH105	MH025B	DBC391B	Bifr41	DBC407	DBC020	Lym44	Fing203	DBC092	FingE2	Bifr29	Bek22	DBC204	Bifr74	Bifr64	Bek24	DBC038	DBC373	MH064	DBC354	MH102	DBC412	DBC339	DBC060	
Buckland Phase			1	1				1a		1		1b			1b	2a	1b	2a			2a	1b	2a	2a			2a			2		2	2a			2				2b				2b/3a	2b/3a		2b		2b/3a	3a	3	
Kentish Phase														II					II	II						II		III	III		II			III	III			III	IV		IV			IV		III-IV		III				
Evison Phase												1										1											1			2								3							3	
	3.94	3.94	3.62	3.40	3.40	3.21	2.97	2.94	2.50	2.29	2.15	1.70	1.68	0.80	0.75	0.64	0.55	0.53	0.52	0.51	0.46	0.39	0.34	0.28	0.27	0.25	0.24	0.23	0.22	0.22	0.20	0.20	0.16	0.14	0.14	0.12	0.10	0.09	0.09	0.06	0.04	0.03	-0.02	-0.06	-0.07	-0.07	-0.08	-0.11	-0.12	-0.18	-0.19	
WoundSp																																																				-1.14
châtelaine																																																				-1.05
bottle																																																				-1.04
ribpin																																																				-1.02
longam																																																				-0.98
cowrie																																																				-0.95
inlaypen																																																				-0.93
Orange																																																				-0.86
coinpen																																																				-0.76
box																																																			1	-0.68
SegGlob																																																				-0.62
Koch34																																																			1	-0.53
keybunch																																																				-0.51
Kdbr3																																																				-0.49
CylRound																																																		1	1	-0.44
Koch20																																																			1	-0.44
scutiform																																												1						1		-0.41
Koch49/50																																																	1	1		-0.38
CylPen																																																		1		-0.37
Melon																																													1	1	1			1		-0.23
Reticella																																				1					1		1		1	1		1	1	1		-0.16
Kdbr1-2																												1	1					1		1	1	1	1	1	1	1		1	1	1	1	1				-0.05
bracteate																									1								1		1			1		1												-0.05
shieldbu																								1		1	1	1		1	1	1	1				1		1	1	1		1		1	1			1	1		0.04
shoerivet																	1		1					1				1		1	1	1					1		1	1	1		1		1	1	1		1	1		0.06
Ksqhrundepair																																	1		1							1										0.11
ConCyl												1			1				1	1	1	1	1	1	1		1	1		1		1	1			1			1	1	1			1						1	1	0.30
Ksqhgarnet																1	1			1			1			1			1	1	1			1			1															0.33
impbro														1		1	1	1	1	1	1		1		1	1	1		1	1	1	1	1		1	1		1														0.35
buttonBff																	1		1			1			1																											0.45
MinDark										1					1			1	1	1	1			1																											1	0.67
Ksqhplain													1	1			1			1								1																								0.79
club									1		1			1	1	1	1		1																																	1.18
buttonA								1	1	1			1																																							2.45
pinpair							1			1																																										2.74
smbr			1	1	1	1	1			1	1	1																																								2.96
armlet						1		1																																												3.20
polypin	1	1		1	1				1																																											3.58
cruciform	1	1	1																																																	3.99

Table 8.2. Sorted matrix of the correspondence analysis for Buckland and east Kent graves. The columns are graves (grave numbers at foot), rows are bead/artefact types (row scores at right).

Type	DBC331	MH094	DBC245	MH010	MH068	DBC250	DBC222	MH106	DBC042	DBC353	DBC030	DBC059	MH095	DBC062	DBC001	DBC032	DBC035	DBC232	DBC029	DBC133	DBC360	DBC055	DBC018	DBC067	DBC124	DBC134	DBC006	DBC00F	DBC053	DBC043	DBC157	DBC132	DBC110	DBC376	DBC413	DBC160	DBC044	DBC138	DBC075	DBC127	DBC155	DBC107	Score
Buckland Phase	3a		3a		3a	3a		3	3a	3a	3a	3a		3a	3b	3b	3b	3b	3b	3b-5		3b-5	3b	3b-5	3b-5		5-7	5-7	5-7	5-7	5-7	5-7	5-7	5-7	5-7	5-7	5-7	5-7	5-7	5-7	5-7	5-7	
Kentish Phase		III-IV	IV	III-IV				III-IV		IV	IV	IV			V		V		V					V																			
Evison Phase								4		3	3			4	3	3	3		3	5		4	4	5	6	5	5	3	5	4	5	5	6			6	4	6	7	7	5	6	
Column score	-0.24	-0.24	-0.29	-0.29	-0.34	-0.34	-0.34	-0.37	-0.38	-0.38	-0.40	-0.40	-0.43	-0.46	-0.48	-0.55	-0.55	-0.56	-0.61	-0.69	-0.71	-0.74	-0.76	-0.79	-0.86	-0.91	-0.92	-0.95	-0.96	-0.96	-1.01	-1.02	-1.02	-1.03	-1.04	-1.07	-1.08	-1.08	-1.10	-1.10	-1.14	-1.14	
WoundSp																															1						1		1	1	1	1	-1.14
châtelaine																1						1	1	1				1	1	1	1	1	1				1	1			1	1	-1.05
bottle																								1	1						1												-1.04
ribpin																						1				1		1			1		1	1					1	1			-1.02
longam																			1					1	1			1				1				1			1	1			-0.98
cowrie																								1			1				1												-0.95
inlaypen																		1								1	1									1	1						-0.93
Orange															1						1	1	1	1	1					1													-0.86
coinpen																		1	1														1										-0.76
box												1				1	1					1		1																			-0.68
SegGlob														1		1	1					1					1																-0.62
Koch34									1		1	1		1		1		1				1	1		1																		-0.53
keybunch		1	1		1					1					1	1	1		1		1		1																				-0.51
Kdbr3			1																																								-0.49
CylRound	1	1		1	1	1			1	1	1			1	1	1	1	1	1					1																			-0.44
Koch20		1		1					1								1					1																					-0.44
scutiform			1													1	1							1																			-0.41
Koch49/50								1	1		1			1		1			1																								-0.38
CylPen	1			1	1				1				1						1																								-0.37
Melon		1			1	1							1																														-0.23
Reticella	1	1			1	1			1																																		-0.16
Kdbr1-2		1			1					1	1	1																															-0.05
bracteate			1		1										1																												-0.05
shieldbu				1					1																																		0.04
shoerivet	1	1	1																																								0.06
Ksqhrundepair																																											0.11
ConCyl																																											0.30
Ksqhgarnet																																											0.33
impbro																																											0.35
buttonBff																																											0.45
MinDark																																											0.67
Ksqhplain																																											0.79
club																																											1.18
buttonA																																											2.45
pinpair																																											2.74
smbr																																											2.96
armlet																																											3.20
polypin																																											3.58
cruciform																																											3.99

Table 8.2. Sorted matrix of the correspondence analysis for Buckland and east Kent graves. For abbreviations of type names, see Table 8.3. Abbreviations of sites combined with grave numbers: Bek = Bekesbourne; Bifr = Bifrons; DBC = Buckland; Fing = Finglesham; Lym = Lyminge; BM = Mill Hill; Oz = Ozengell.

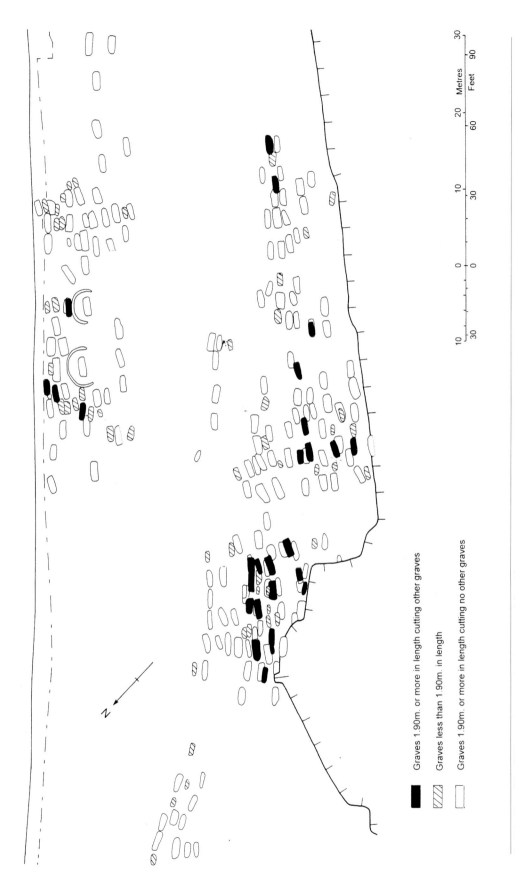

Graves 1.90m. or more in length cutting other graves

Graves less than 1.90m. in length

Graves 1.90m. or more in length cutting no other graves

Fig 8.1. Plan of the 1994 cemetery area showing grave relationships.

of horizontal stratigraphy evident in the later phases at Buckland or at Mill Hill, Deal.

A chronological framework for the graves of females and males without weapons

Correspondence analysis

Females were buried with a wide range of grave goods and grave good combinations. Graves of males with objects from the same range, for example buckles, can be correlated with a framework for female graves and are therefore integrated into the framework for female graves. Weapon graves are discussed separately below.

Table 8.3 gives a list of types of grave goods from female graves which test runs proved to be useful for correspondence analysis and which can be argued to have a limited date range. The types chosen or newly defined for the purpose of the analysis include, if possible, types of objects used in Evison's framework for Buckland 1951–3 as a basis for later correlation.

As regional products, Kentish types of brooches can be used for correspondence analysis in some detail, while Early Merovingian types have to be used collectively because individual types are represented in too small numbers (Table 8.3). The date range of the individual types on the Continent, however, can be used to correlate the Kentish framework with continental frameworks.

Buckles with club-shaped tongues and shield-on-tongue buckles, with or without shoe-shaped studs, are useful types of objects for chronological analysis, not only because they are included in continental frameworks but also because in Kent they were a regular part of women's dress accessories and can therefore be used to correlate frameworks for Kentish male and female chronology to an extent that is not possible on the Continent. The type range of shield-on-tongue buckles worn in Kent is, however, smaller than on the Continent and does not include types of the very early sixth century. A division of shield-on-tongue buckles into sub-types for the purpose of the correspondence analysis therefore did not prove to be useful. The Kentish material does, however, include early types of buckles with club-shaped tongue (see below).

The bead types in the analysis (Table 8.3) represent types used for a national framework for glass beads from Anglo-Saxon graves (Brugmann 2004). The national sample includes the beads from Buckland 1951–3 and the results

are confirmed by the beads from the 1994 part of the site (*see* p 98 and below).

The correspondence analysis includes four types of pendants: bracteates, scutiform, looped coins, and objects set in a frame (Table 8.3). The coins are all post-Roman and thus connect aspects of relative and absolute chronology. The only pin types at Buckland that proved to be useful for analysis were those with a polyhedral head, pairs of pins with attached rings, and pins with a mid-rib on the shaft (*see* pp 120–1). Solid cast armlets are another type of dress accessory used in the correspondence analyses.

Apart from dress accessories, personal equipment is listed in the form of bunches of three or more iron keys and iron châtelaines including linked rods. The only containers used in the analysis are wooden boxes with iron fittings and imported pottery bottles.

Most functional types of objects in the analysis are represented by more than one design. If for the definition of these type's attributes primarily related to quality had been used, such as differences in material like gold or copper alloy, quality groups would have been the most likely result of a correspondence analysis. Most of the types, however, define designs considered to have a limited date range. It is, therefore, possible to relate the sequence produced by the correspondence analysis in Table 8.1 with Evison's framework for Buckland 1951–3 and with continental systems.

Figure 8.2 shows that the correspondence analysis has not produced the perfect parabola that would be the result of ideal data but it does come reasonably close. Figure 8.2b shows Buckland Grave 60 to be somewhat out of place, and Table 8.1 with the sorted matrix, indicates the reason for this. This grave combines an iron bound wooden box with a range of bead types that were apparently heirlooms.

Next to the sorted matrix of the correspondence analysis, Table 8.1 lists the phases into which Evison dated the graves at Buckland 1951–3, and the Kentish Phases to which some of the same graves have been assigned (see Brugmann 1999a). The positive part of the matrix includes only a few graves from Buckland 1951–3, including three graves dated to Evison's Phase 1 and one grave dated to her Phase 2. The negative part lists almost exclusively Buckland 1951–3 graves, dated to Phases 3–7 and Kentish Phases IV and V.

In the matrix, the Buckland 1951–3 graves are only partly sorted in the order suggested by Evison's phasing. In Evison's scheme, iron fittings of wooden boxes are dated to Phases 3 and 4, inlaid pendants to Phases 3–6, Frankish bottles to Phases 4 and 5, pins with a mid-rib to Phases 4–6, and amethyst beads to Phases 5–7. Grave 81 in Plot I contains the lock of a box but is dated to Phase 7.

Category	Abbreviation	Details	1a	1b	2a	2b	3a	3b	5-7
Brooches									
	cruciform	cruciform brooch	x						
	smbr	small brooch	x						
	buttonA	button brooch Cl. A	x						
	buttonBff	button brooches Cl. B ff.		x					
	Ksqhplain	Kentish square-headed brooch without garnets		x					
	Ksqhgarnet	garnet-set Kentish square-headed brooch		x	x	x			
	Ksghrundelpair	pair of Kentish square-headed brooches, foot-plate terminals shaped as roundels			x	x			
	Kdbr1-2	Kentish disc brooch Cl. 1-2			x	x	x		
	Kdbr3	Kentish disc brooch Cl. 3					x	x	
	impbro	Early Merovingian brooch types		x	x				
Buckles									
	club	buckle with straight club-shaped tongue	x						
	club	buckle with raised club-shaped tongue		x	(x)	(x)			
	shieldbu	shield-on-tongue buckle		(x)	x	x	x		
	shoerivet	shoe-shaped rivet		(x)	x	x	x		
Beads									
	MinDark	bead type MinDark	(x)	x					
	ConCyl	bead type ConCyl		x	x	x			
	Reticella	bead type Reticella				x	x		
	Melon	bead type Melon				x	x		
	Koch49/50	bead type Koch49/50					x		
	CylPen	bead type CylPen					x		
	CylRound	bead type CylRound					x	x	
	Koch20	bead type Koch20					x	x	
	Koch34	bead type Koch34					x	x	
	SegGlob	bead type SegGlob					x		
	Orange	bead type Orange						x	x
	cowrie	cowrie shell rim bead							x
	longam	long amethyst bead							x
	WoundSp	bead type Wound Spiral							x
Pendants									
	bracteate	bracteate		(x)	x	x			
	scutiform	scutiform pendant				(x)	x	x	
	coinpen	coin pendant with loop						x	x
	inlaypen	pendant made of framed setting							x
Pins									
	polypin	pin with polyhedral head	x	x					
	pinpair	pins with attached ring	x						
	ribpin	pin with midrib							x
Armlet									
	armlet	armlet with animal heads	x						
Objects suspended from the waist									
	keybunch	bunch of iron keys (3 or more)					x	x	
	châtelaine	châtelaine made of iron links							x
Containers									
	box	wooden box with iron fittings						x	x
	bottle	Frankish bottle							x

Table 8.3. Types of grave goods from female burials useful for correspondence analysis.

Evison 1987 Buckland 1951–3	Buckland 1994	Brugmann 2000 Kent	Koch 2001 S Germany	Siegmund 1998 Lower Rhine	Legoux 1998 Picardie	Périn 1998 NE France
	AD 450		AD 460	AD 440	AD 450	AD 540
	1a	I	2	2	ABC 1	
AD 475			AD 480	AD 485		ABD 1
1		~ AD 500	3		AD 470/80	AD 475
	1b	II	AD 510	3	ABC 2	
AD 525	AD 510/30		4			ABD 2
	2a	AD 530/40	AD 530	4	AD 420/30	AD 525
		III	5	AD 530		
2	2b	AD 560/70	AD 555	AD 555	BCD	BCD/DE
AD 575	AD 550/560	IV	6	5	AD 550/60	AD 550
	3a		AD 580	6	CDE	DEF
		AD 580/90	7	7		
3			AD 600	AD 610	AD 600/610	AD 600
	3b	V	8	8		
AD 650	AD ?650			9		
5-7	5-7			10		
				AD 705		

Table 8.4. Buckland and continental phasing schemes.

Most graves of females are assigned to Phase 4 on the basis of the position of their graves in the cemetery. Grave 42 combines a shield-on-tongue buckle with a knife, a pin and bead types assigned to Group B2 (Brugmann 2004, table 11). Knife and pin are not closely datable but shield-buckles without plates were generally out of use by the end of the sixth century. An absolute date of the grave somewhere in the second quarter of the seventh century would make the buckle not only an heirloom but also an heirloom worn at a time when decorative buckles were not required for the dress worn (pp 188–90). A re-dating of this grave to Phase 3 would therefore seem more appropriate.

In the sorted matrix, Grave 62 appears among the graves of Phase 3 as another grave of Evison's Phase 4. The grave is sorted in the matrix on the basis of two bead types and a bunch of keys. The complete bead association from this grave represents Group B1, generally earlier than Group B2 (Brugmann 2004, table 11). Evison dated the wearing of keys in numbers of more than two to Phases 3–7 (Evison 1987, 117). The keys would therefore be within the assigned date range if the grave was shifted back from Phase 4 into Phase 3.

Grave 18, as the latest grave in Plot A, combines beads of Group B2 with a pin with a mid-rib, a functional type otherwise regularly associated with beads of Group C, dated to the second half of the seventh century and later (see Brugmann 2004). The other pin with a mid-rib of this phase is from Grave 44 in Plot B, assigned to Phase 4 because of the positioning of the grave in the cemetery but containing the knife of a type otherwise assigned to Phases 6 and 7 (Evison 1987, table XVII) and an iron buckle with a narrow loop and square plate which is more common in the second half of the seventh century.

In her overview of the Buckland 1951–3 framework (*ibid* 138f) the only dress accessory exclusively dated to Phase 4 is the strap-end from Grave 34. This makes it difficult to relate this phase to the evidence from Buckland 1994. Scutiform and inlaid pendants fall into Phases 3 and 5 but not in Phase 4. The correspondence analysis shows that only Grave 67 combines scutiform pendants, cowrie shells and amethyst beads and an inlaid pendant. The other scutiform pendants are associated with beads of Group B and brooches of Phase 3. This suggests that scutiform pendants fall within Phase 3 and that the pendants in Grave 67 are late exceptions. The buckle from Grave 8 with an oval plate and three rivets, dated to Phase 5, may be placed in Périn's Phase DEF, Siegmund's Phase 7 and Koch's SD Phases 7–8 and is thus re-dated as a late sixth-/early seventh-century type. The associated spearhead is not closely datable, and it would therefore seem that Grave 8 falls into Evison's Phase 3 rather than Phase 5. In all of this, Phase 4 does not feature and does not now seem to exist as an identifiable phase.

For Phase 5 more types of objects are listed, in particular beads and pottery. Silver bell beads in Anglo-Saxon graves are associated with glass beads of both Groups B2 and C, and large amethyst beads and cowrie shell rim beads with

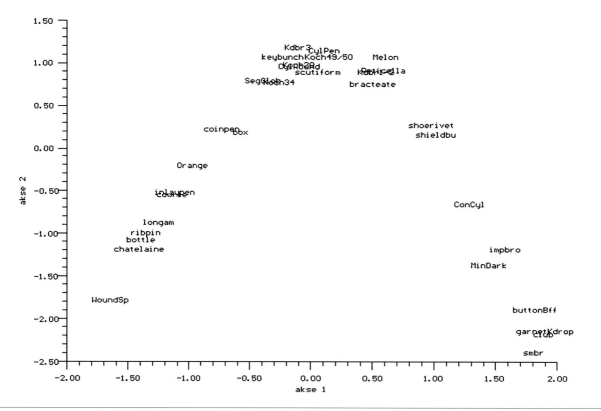

Fig 8.2a. Buckland 1951–2 and 1994. Correspondence analysis of grave goods. For abbreviations of type names see Table 8.3.

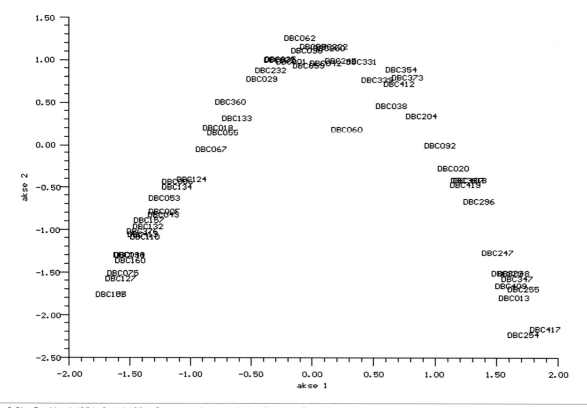

Fig 8.2b. Buckland 1951–3 and 1994. Correspondence analysis of graves. For abbreviations of type names see Table 8.3.

332

glass beads of Group C (Brugmann 2004). Group C is dated to the second half of the sixth century and later, mainly on the basis of continental dates for amethyst beads, but the date was also considered to be supported by Evison's chronology (*ibid*), so that a circular argument needs to be avoided.

Most of the wheel-thrown pottery from Buckland 1951–3 is dated to Phase 5, to some extent on the basis of the small finds analysis suggesting a seventh-century date for certain types (Evison 1987, 92ff). One pot falls within Phase 4 (Grave 43), five in Phase 5 (Graves 129, 137, 139, 156 and 157) and one in Phase 6 (Grave 109) on the basis of associated grave goods and the positioning of the graves in question (*ibid*). The bottle in Grave 43 was associated with a wooden box and a châtelaine almost exclusively found in graves dated by Evison to Phases 5–7. The pot in Grave 109 is of the same type as the pot from Grave 157 dated to Phase 5 (Evison 1979; 1987, 92) but tentatively dated in Phase 6 on the basis of the position of the grave (Evison 1987, 176). A date in the second half of the seventh century for Graves 139 and 157 is supported by the associated firesteels with curled terminals. It would seem that if the layout of the graves is ignored, all the pots would fall into Phase 5.

An analysis of the mostly unpublished cemeteries at Finglesham; St Peters, Broadstairs and Lord of the Manor, Ozengell, would probably allow the Buckland Phases 4/5–7 to be related to a regional framework for late sixth- and seventh-century graves. Buckland 1994 has only three graves of females with grave goods that can be related to Phases 5 and 6: Grave 376 with beads of the late Group B2, pins with a mid-rib, a châtelaine and a wheel-thrown pot; Grave 391A with beads of Group C including amethyst beads and a bulla pendant; and Grave 413 with beads of Group C including amethyst beads, a pin with a mid-rib, an inlaid pendant and a châtelaine. The horizontal stratigraphy at Buckland 1994 can add nothing definite to a closer dating of these graves.

Evison's Phases 1 and 2 are much better represented on the 1994 part of the site than in the 1951–3 area. The correspondence analysis includes Graves 13, 20 and 48 dated to Phase 1 and Grave 92 dated in Phase 2. Grave 13 includes two worn square-headed brooches, a small-long brooch, an annular brooch and beads of Group A2 (Brugmann 2004, table 11), Grave 20 has two square-headed brooches with a garnet disc brooch, a bracteate and a shield-on-tongue buckle associated with a claw beaker and a copper alloy bowl with beaded rim. Grave 48 has beads of Group A2 with a button brooch, a saucer brooch and a dolphin buckle with a replacement tongue. The buckle with club-shaped tongue shown in Evison's overview (1987, 138f) is from Grave 21. Grave 92, dated to Phase 2, combines a garnet disc brooch

with a Kentish disc brooch of Class 2 and beads of Groups A2 with a reticella bead (Group A2b).

The sorted matrix in Table 8.1 shows that beads of Group A2 (*MinDark*, *ConCyl*) and A2b (Reticella and Melon), Early Merovingian brooches, Kentish disc brooches and shield-on-tongue buckles were found in a number of graves on Buckland 1994. Cone and claw beakers are not included in the matrix but were also found on the 1994 site. The matrix does include buckles with club-shaped tongue, button brooches, small-long brooches, bracteates and additionally garnet-set Kentish square-headed brooches and shoe-shaped studs. The matrix indicates that Buckland 1994 also includes a number of graves with objects not dated before Phase 3 on the upper part of the site: scutiform pendants, another Kentish disc brooch of Class 3 and some bead types, in particular Koch Type 20.

Analysis of the Mill Hill, Deal, cemetery and well-equipped female graves from other sites has allowed a subdivision of the sixth century into three phases, Kentish Phases I–III covering all of Evison's Phase 2 and part of her Phases 1 and 3 (Parfitt and Brugmann 1997, table 11; Brugmann 1999a). Despite the substantial number of sixth-century graves, Buckland 1994 produced only two burials with the set of four brooches (including at least one Kentish square-headed brooch) that defines Kentish Phase II (Graves 255 and 391B), none that combine Kentish disc brooches with other types of brooches (Kentish Phase III) and four graves with single Kentish disc brooches (Kentish Phase IV: Graves 204, 222, 354 and 373). A correspondence analysis of the Buckland graves to include finds from modern excavations at Mill Hill, Deal; Finglesham; Lyminge; Bekesbourne and Ozengell (Table 8.2) as well as graves from Bifrons (see above) suggests that the sequence of grave good associations suggested by the Kentish Phasing system is largely correct (*ibid*, column 'Kentish Phase'). The broader basis now available, in the shape of the 1994 Buckland site suggests, however, a revision of the (always artificial) lines between the phases. For convenience in the present report, this has been done in the form of a redefinition of Evison's original phases, including sub-phases.

The small finds analysis of the grave goods from Buckland 1994 suggests that this part of the cemetery includes graves predating Kentish Phase II as it was defined for Mill Hill, Deal. This may also be the case with Grave 21 at Buckland 1951–3, which has a particularly early type of club-shaped buckle and inlaid plate but it is probably not the case with Graves 13 and 48, and certainly is not so with Grave 20. The square-headed brooches from Grave 13 are much abraded and associated with beads of Group A2. Grave 20 includes a shield-on-tongue buckle and a garnet rosette

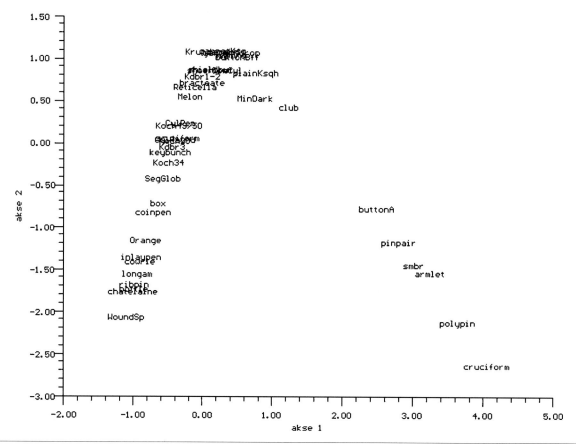

Fig 8.3a. Correspondence analysis of east Kent grave goods. For abbreviations of type names see Table 8.3.

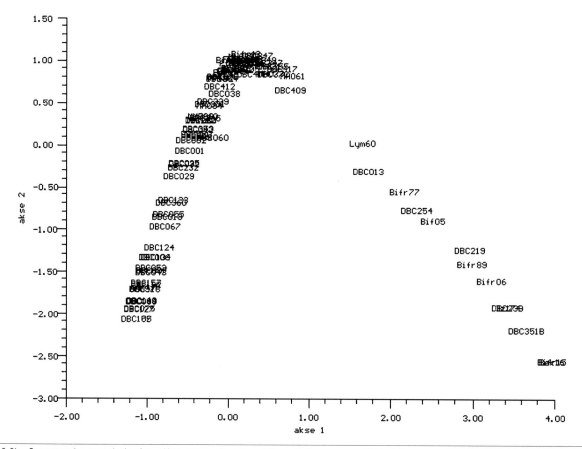

Fig 8.3b. Correspondence analysis of east Kent graves. For abbreviations of site names see Table 8.2.

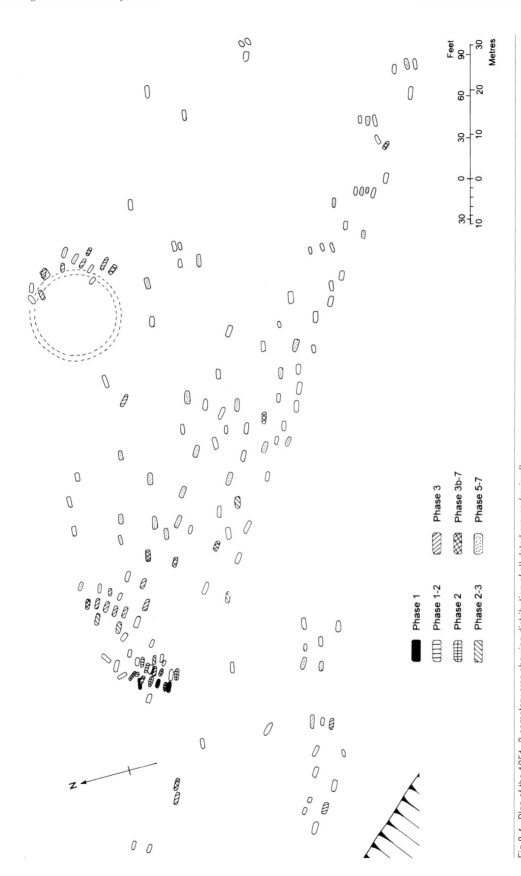

	Phase 1		Phase 3
	Phase 1-2		Phase 3b-7
	Phase 2		Phase 5-7
	Phase 2-3		

Fig 8.4. Plan of the 1951–3 cemetery area showing distribution of all dated graves (revised).

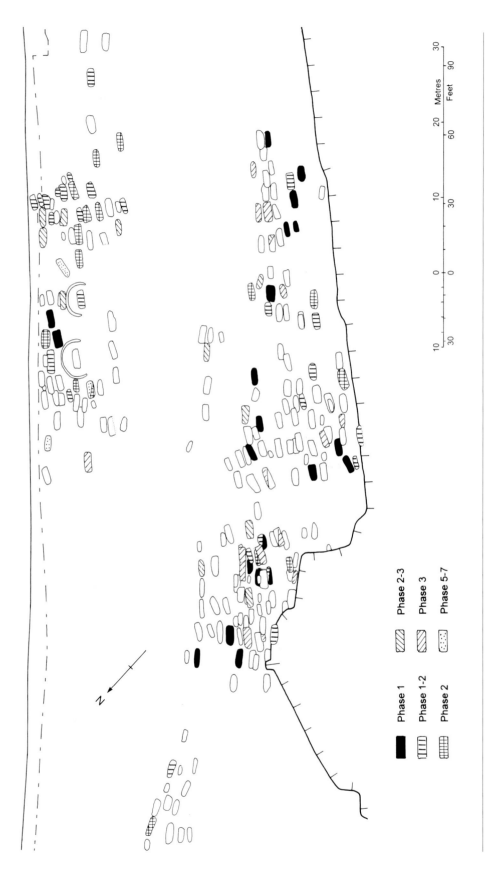

Fig 8.5. Plan of the 1994 cemetery area showing distribution of all dated graves.

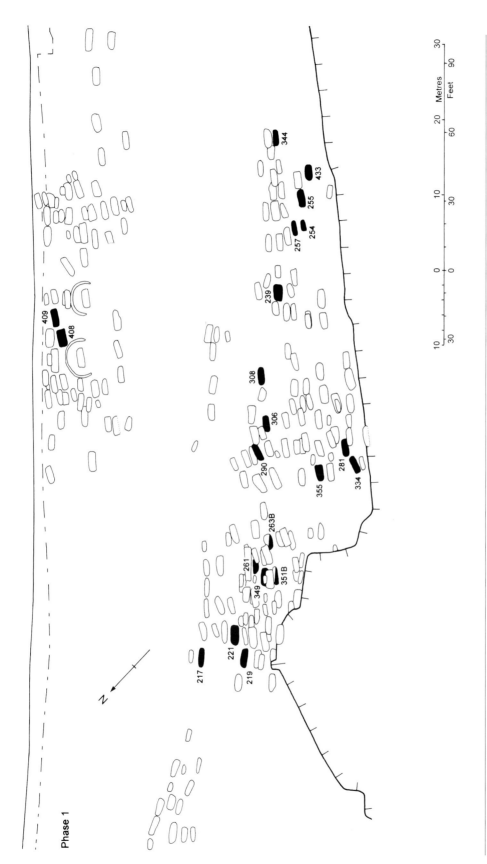

Phase 1

Fig 8.6. Plan of the 1994 cemetery area showing distribution of all graves dated to Phase 1.

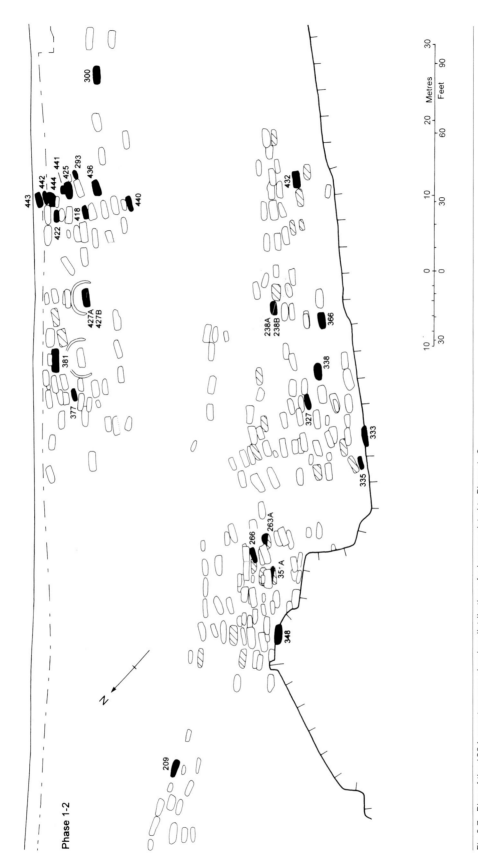

Fig 8.7. Plan of the 1994 cemetery area showing distribution of a I graves dated to Phase 1–2.

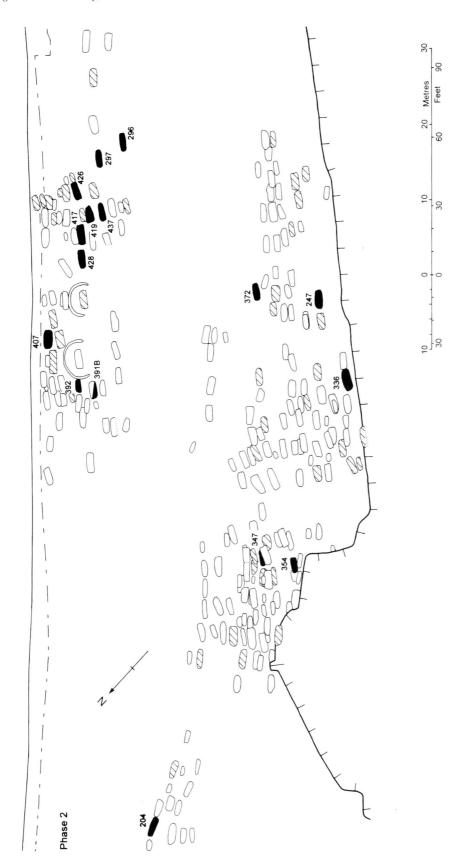

Fig 8.8. Plan of the 1994 cemetery area showing distribution of all graves dated to Phase 2.

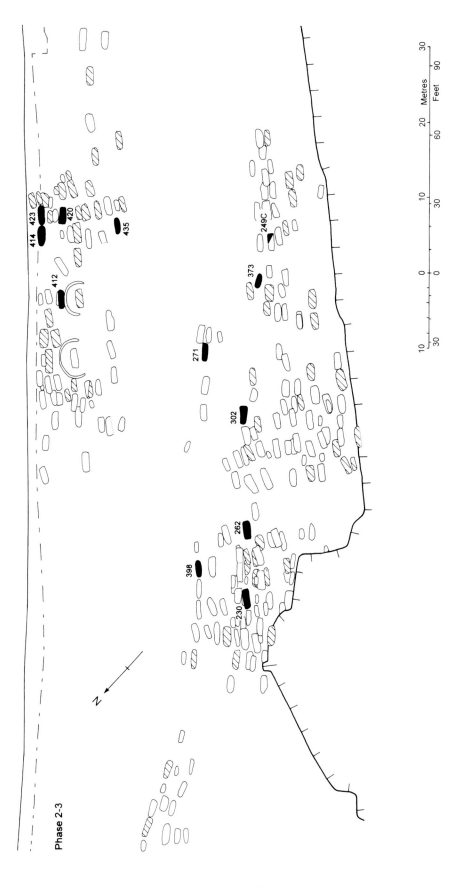

Fig 8.9. Plan of the 1994 cemetery area showing distribution of all graves dated Phase 2–3.

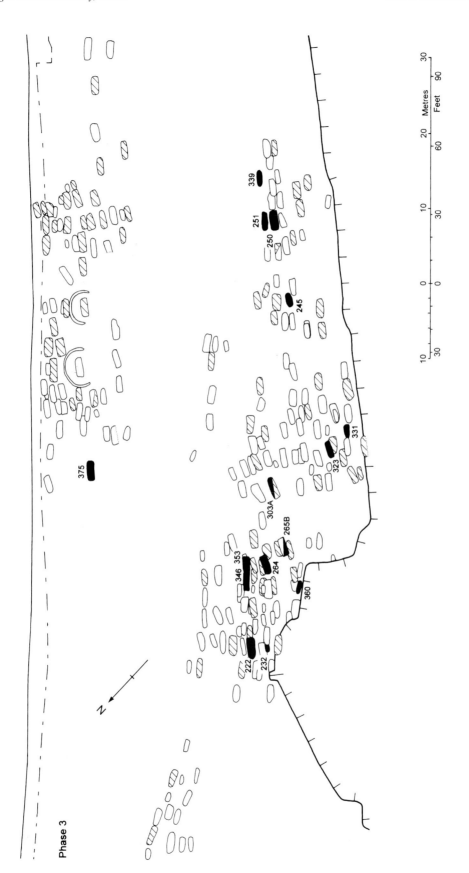

Fig 8.10. Plan of the 1994 cemetery area showing distribution of all graves dated to Phase 3.

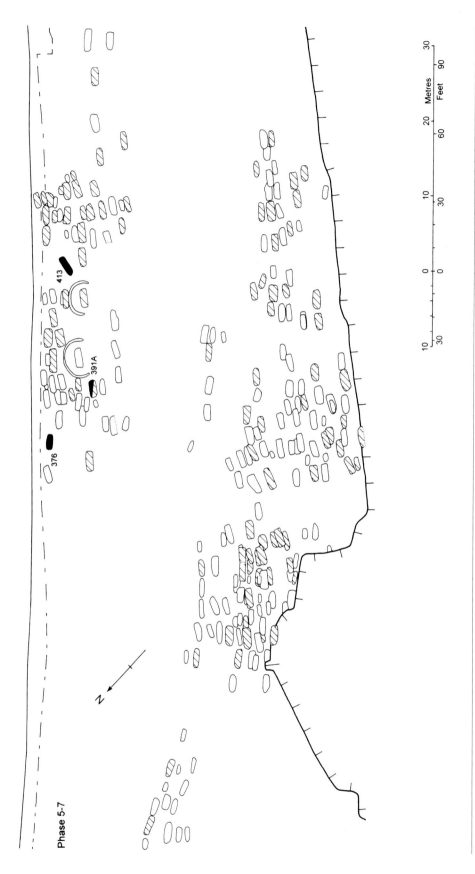

Fig 8.11. Plan of the 1994 cemetery area showing distribution of all graves dated to Phases 5–7.

Phase 1a

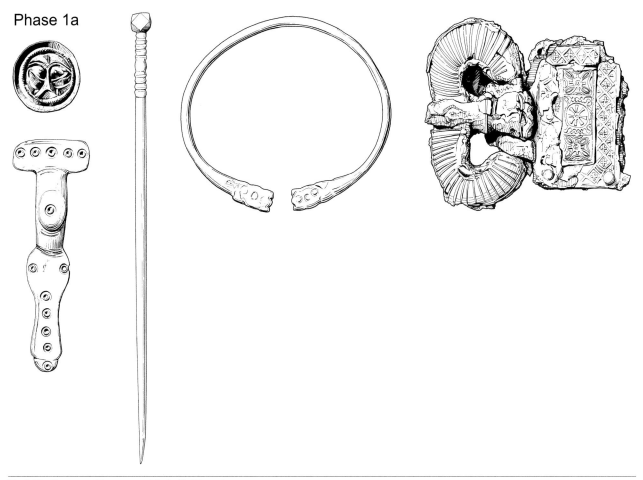

Fig 8.12. Grave good types associated with Phase 1a.

brooch, neither considered to predate the sixth century. Grave 48 includes a dolphin buckle with a replaced tongue and a saucer brooch with five scrolls, but also a button brooch of Class B and beads of Group A2.

The graves with cruciform, small-long and button brooches of Class A, pins with polyhedral heads or perforated heads with small wire rings attached to them (not slip-knot as in the Final Phase), cast armlets and beads of Group A1 are best paralleled at Bifrons, Bekesbourne and Lyminge and also at Ozengell. It will be argued below that these graves actually represent the elusive Kentish Phase I.

The sorted matrix of the correspondence analysis in Table 8.2 adds thirty-four graves to the Buckland graves analysed in Table 8.1. Most of these are from Mill Hill and Bifrons but they also include some Buckland graves whose grave good combinations can now be added. Figures 8.3a–b show not a perfect parabola but a decent curve. The sorted matrix

in Table 8.2 shows variations in grave good combinations interpreted as a gradual change over time.

The matrix is, however, not suitable as the sole basis for the dating of a grave. The attributes cannot necessarily include every single datable object in each grave, and a grave may be insufficiently represented by the selection that has been the basis for matrix. Another aspect that needs to be taken into consideration is that this is a presence/absence matrix and that the number of objects representing an attribute is not taken into account. A single 'heirloom' on a bead string has as much of an effect on the sorting of the matrix as, for example, a Kentish disc brooch.

The sorted matrix demonstrates that any phasing of grave goods from the grouping of grave good associations on the basis of similarity and dissimilarity can be nothing but artificial. Some changes in the material culture, however, are a little more pronounced than others, and this is best

Phase 1

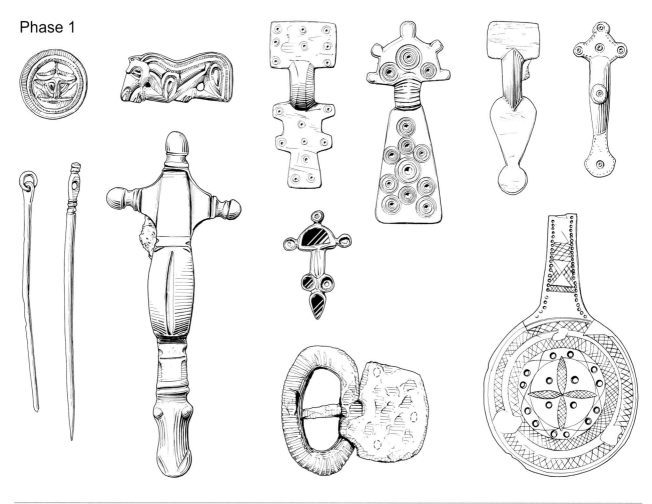

Fig 8.13. Grave good types associated with Phase 1 (AD 450–510/30).

demonstrated by the curve in Fig 8.2a. The gap between button brooches of Class A (button A) and buckles with club-shaped tongue (club) is considerable and dominates the curve. Another line, though nowhere near as obvious, can be drawn between graves only with beads of Group A2b (Reticella and Melon) and graves with additional or only beads of Group B1 (*CylPen*, Koch49/50, Koch 20, *CylRound*).

Table 8.4 correlates the attributes of the correspondence analyses with Evison's and the Kentish Phases, dividing Evison's Phases 1 to 3 into the sub-phases 1a and 1b, 2a and 2b and 3a and 3b. Phases 5 to 7 are treated as one. Phase 4 is omitted in relative terms because it is too difficult to define outside its Buckland 1951–3 context (see above). Table 8.5 assigns the graves at Buckland to a phase or phases if possible, taking both the sorted matrix and additional dating

evidence into account, such as objects not presented in the matrix or the intercutting of graves. The position of the graves on the burial site is shown in Figs 8.6–11.

Most types of objects listed in Table 8.3 are assigned to more than one phase, and only some graves with a combination of grave goods are assigned to a particular sub-phase. Shield-on-tongue buckles, for example, are assigned to Phases 2a, 2b and 3a. A grave with only a shield-buckle therefore is assigned to Phases 2–3a.

A subdivision of buckles with club-shaped tongues was not possible in the correspondence analysis because there are too few buckles in the matrix. It is, however, interesting to note that the buckle associated with objects in Phase 1a is a particularly early type, while the buckles associated with objects assigned to Phase 1b are later typological developments. There are only a few buckles

Phase 1b

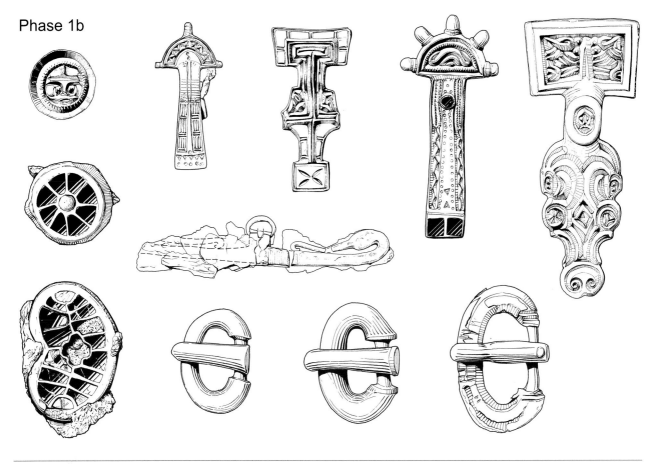

Fig 8.14. Grave good types associated with Phase 1b.

with club-shaped tongues in the matrix, and all of them appear to be 'early'. On the Continent, however, buckles with club-shaped tongues are represented in a large number of sub-types covering the same overall date span as shield-on-tongue buckles (see below), which in Table 8.3 is denoted by ticks in brackets.

The bead type *MinDark* is mainly associated with objects assigned to Phase 1b, but is also known to have been in use in Roman times. Therefore, it would seem unwise to assume that a grave with this type of bead could not date earlier than in Phase 1b. Thus, the tick for Phase 1a is also given in brackets.

Bracteates are mainly associated with grave goods assigned to Phase 3. A bracteate associated with a button brooch and an imported brooch of the Hahnheim type in grave 16 at Lyminge (Table 8.2), is an exception (denoted by the tick in brackets for Phase 1b in Table 8.3). Considering the typological and cultural background of bracteates (see pp 89–92) it seems likely that the framework

relates to a fashion rather than the bracteates themselves. Pendants are not a regular component of Kentish women's dress accessories in Phases 1 and 2 but are common from Phase 3 onwards.

The six dress styles defined by Penelope Walton Rogers (pp 182–90) as such, have not been used to date graves, in order to avoid a circular argument but Walton Rogers's interpretation of their development over time does seem to be confirmed. *Dress Style II* falls in Phase 1, *Dress Styles III* and *IV* in Phases 1b–2, with the possible exception of Grave 351B that represents the earliest appearance of Style IV and may date to Phase 1a. *Dress Style V* develops during Phase 2b and lasts until Phase 3a; Style VI has one grave in Phase 3a (Grave 250) and two in Phases 5–7 (Graves 413 and 391A). Walton Rogers's study of Kentish dress has added a new dimension to Kentish chronological studies that is particularly important because it shows that changing brooch designs were an aspect of female dress fashion that went along with changes in the types of garments worn.

Phase 1b-2

Fig 8.15. Grave good types associated with Phase 1b–2.

Phase 2

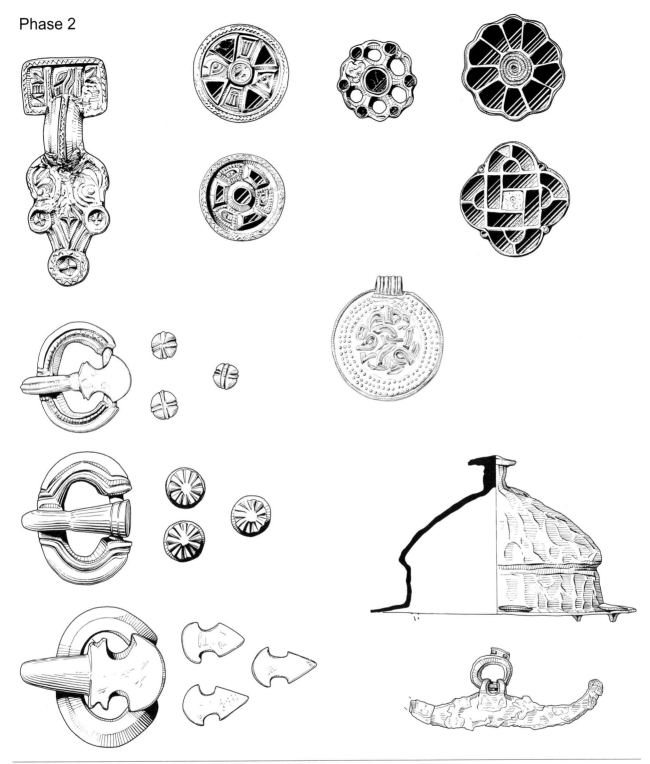

Fig 8.16. Grave good types associated with Phase 2 (AD 510/30–550/560).

Phase 2b-3a

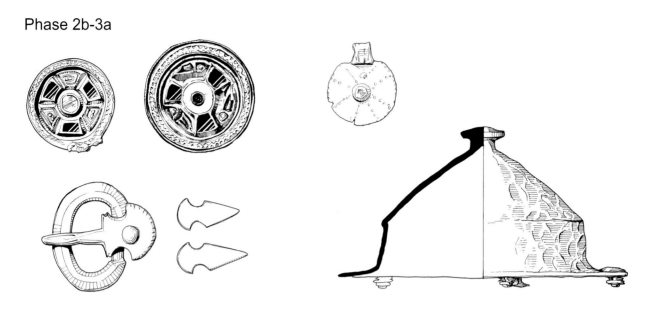

Fig 8.17. Grave good types associated with Phase 2b–3a.

Two graves with brooches seem to represent variations of the dress styles defined by Walton Rogers. Grave 433 had a single brooch with a design probably contemporary with button brooches of Type A and may have been used as a variation of *Dress Style II*. The rider brooch in Grave 233 is much worn and may have substituted a Kentish disc brooch as part of Style V. The beads in this grave, unfortunately, are not closely datable but it would seem that they correspond with the date of the brooch, rather than that of Style V. A closer date for the associated buckle type unfortunately is not available.

Grave goods and vertical stratigraphy

In most cases the stratigraphy of double graves and intercutting graves supports the chronological framework derived from grave-good combinations:

Grave 18 (Phase 3b–5) *cuts* Grave 22 (Phase 1)
Grave 58 (Phase 3) *cuts* Grave 59 (Phase 3a)
Grave 266 (Phase 1b–2a) *cuts* Grave 261 (Phase 1)
Grave 350B (Phase 1b–3a) *cuts* Grave 349 (Phase 1) and 351A *above* 351B (Phase 1)
Grave 391A (Phase 5–7) *above* Grave 391B (Phase 2)
Grave 412 (Phase 2b–3a) *cuts ring-gully of* Grave 427A (Phase 1b-2)
Grave 441 (Phase 1b–2) *cuts* Grave 425 (Phase 1b–2)

There are two cases which are more problematic, with apparent conflicts between the recorded field evidence and the dating of the grave goods:-

Grave 231, with a buckle of Phase 1a, *cuts* the coin-dated Grave 232 (Phase 3b). Thus, the buckle may have been an heirloom, or the field evidence was misinterpreted.

Grave 290 (Phase 1) *cuts* Grave 289 (Phase 2b–7). Grave 290 is firmly dated to Phase 1 by the combination of a button brooch of Class A with an early type of strainer associated with amber and a rock-crystal bead and a Roman finger-ring. Grave 289 contained a bunch of keys and a buckle type considered not to predate Phase 2b. Contrary to the recorded field evidence, the positioning of Graves 289 and 290 in relation to the neighbouring graves suggests that Grave 290 was the earlier one because it was dug at a regular interval in a row (Fig 2.2). Grave 289 fills the space between two graves of the same row in the manner of a 'secondary' grave (see above). The possibility of a misinterpretation of the evidence in the field thus needs to be noted (*see* p 30).

Absolute chronology

Absolute dates for Phases 1 to 7 were given by Evison in schematic steps of fifty and twenty-five years. A correlation of Phases 1 to 3 with the Kentish Phases and continental frameworks (Parfitt and Brugmann 1997, table 11; Brugmann 1999a, table 3.3) show that the dates given are still to be

Phase 3a

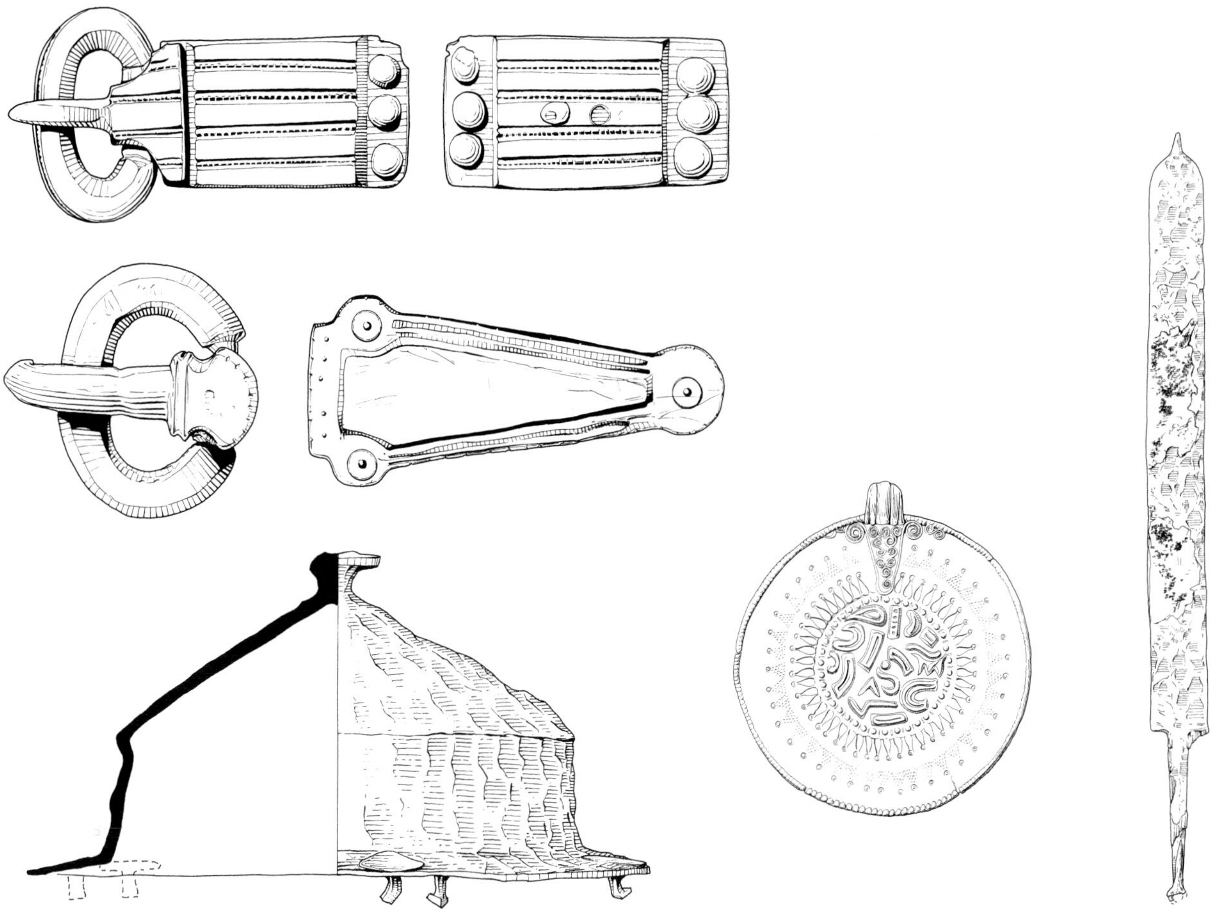

Fig 8.18. Grave good types associated with Phase 3a.

considered quite accurate. The revised definition of Phases 1–3, however, also requires a review of the absolute dates assigned to them (Figs 8.6–8.20).

Buckland 1994 adds only one coin-dated grave to those of Buckland 1951–3. The post-Roman coins at Buckland have been integrated in the correspondence analysis in the form of 'looped coins'. Overall, it seems likely that sixth-century coins are rare in Anglo-Saxon graves for the same reason that bracteates are rare before Phase 3; that is, the minor role pendants play in sixth-century Anglo-Saxon fashion. The *termini post quos* of the three associated Buckland coins are discussed below.

Cruciform, small-long and button brooches are notoriously difficult to date in absolute terms. Pins with a polyhedral head and bracelets with animal-head terminals

are late Roman types suggesting an element of continuity in the earliest Kentish fashion. Among the earliest datable types of objects found at Buckland are the dolphin buckle in Grave 48, with a replacement tongue, and the inlaid iron buckle from Grave 231 which cut a coin-dated grave with a sixth-century *terminus post quem* (see above). The buckles with club-shaped tongues from Grave 21 (not in the correspondence analysis) and from Bifrons grave 5 in the correspondence analysis can date as early as the mid fifth century according to the continental frameworks of Legoux (1998), Périn (1998), Siegmund (1998) and Koch (2001). In the present state of research, the beginning of Phase 1a is thus best put at *c* AD 450.

The Early Merovingian brooch types in the matrix cover Phases A/B/C 2 to C/D/E in Picardie (Legoux 1998), Phases

Phase 3

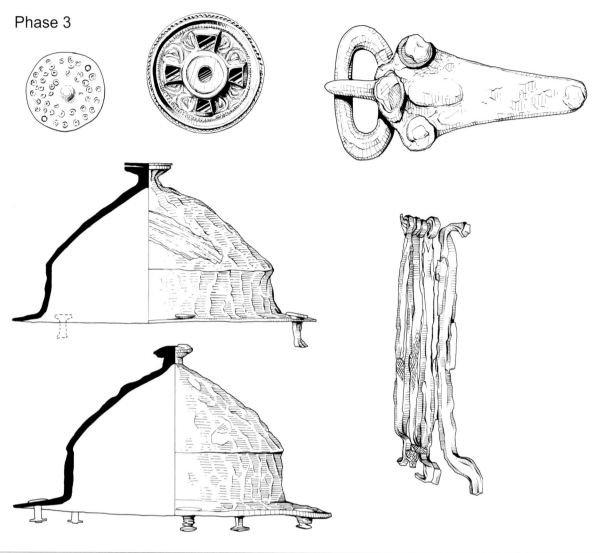

Fig 8.19.　Grave good types associated with Phase 3 (AD 550/560–?650).

A/B/D 1 and B/C/D-D/E in north-east France (Périn 1998), Phase 3 in the Lower Rhine (Siegmund 1998) and Phases 3/4–5/6 in south Germany (Koch 2001). In Buckland Phase 1b the bead type *ConCyl* and buckles with raised club-shaped tongues (see above), also suggests a correlation with Koch's Phases 3/4 and Siegmund's Phase 3. A beginning for Phase 1b in the 480s therefore seems likely.

Fully developed shield-on-tongue buckles and shoe-shaped studs fall within Phase BCD in Picardie, in Phase A/B/D 2 in the north-east of France, Phase 4 at the Niederrhein and Phases 4/5 in south Germany. Though there is some evidence for shoe-shaped studs associated with grave good combinations dated to Phase 1b (see above), shield-on-

tongue buckles become a regular dress accessory only in Phase 2a. Previous research on this buckle and stud type and associated continental types of brooches in Kentish graves (Brugmann 1999a) has suggested that the bulk of shield-on-tongue buckles date to the second and third quarters of the sixth century. A precise date for the beginning of Phase 2a is difficult to determine from the present evidence but it appears to lie early in the sixth century.

Buckland Phase 2, characterised by shield-on-tongue buckles, shoe-shaped studs, Kentish disc brooches and various types of Kentish square-headed brooches, can only be tentatively divided into two sub-phases. The correspondence analysis, however, suggests an overall

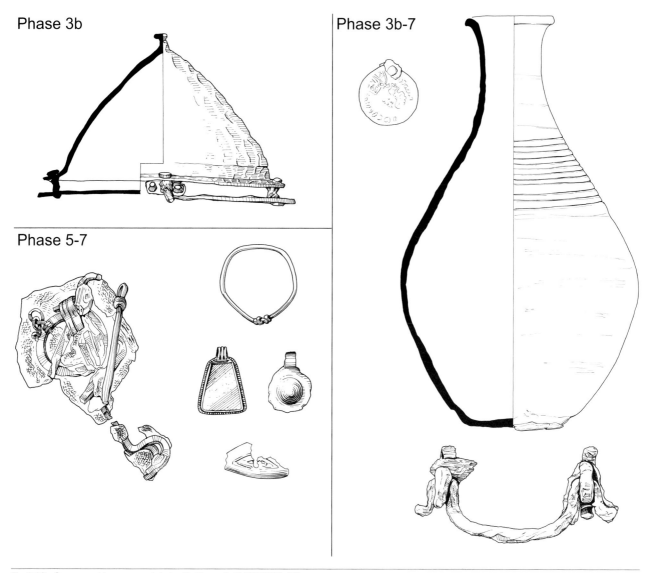

Phase 3b

Phase 5-7

Phase 3b-7

Fig 8.20. Grave good types associated with Phase 5–7 (AD ?650–??).

development that sees continental brooch types coming to end and Reticella and Melon beads being introduced. Precise dating of a grave to Phase 2a or 2b, rather than Phase 2 in general, is only possible if it is well equipped and includes brooch or buckle types with a well-defined date range or well-dated bead types.

The beginning of Phase 3a at Buckland can be correlated with continental frameworks with the aid of probably imported bead Group B, which includes bead types introduced in Koch's Phase 6 and Legoux's Phase C/D/E. This suggests that the beginning of Buckland Phase 3 is datable to the mid sixth century, or soon after. The correspondence analysis in

Table 8.2 shows the changes in bead fashion during Phase 3 that led to a subdivision of Bead Group B (Brugmann 2004) to have been too gradual to be used for subdividing Buckland Phase 3. Only the introduction of Orange beads coincides with marked changes in the combination of grave goods, which include shield-on-tongue buckles and various types of beads running out (see Brugmann 2004). The beginning of Phase 3b can thus be correlated with Koch's and Siegmund's Phases 8 and put around AD 600, or early in the seventh century.

The difficulties of adapting Buckland Phase 4 to the revised framework have been discussed above. The phase

Grave	Phasing basis	Stratigraphy	Overlap phases
A			
B			-
C	spear; sword		
D			-
E			
F	CA		5–7
1	CA		3b
2			-
3			-
4	buckle		3a
5			-
6	CA		5–7
7			-
8	buckle		3
9			-
10	pin		5–7
11			-
12			-
13	CA		1b
14	brooch; beads		2
15	belt set; beads		2
16			-
17			-
18	CA	cuts 22	3b–5
19			-
20	CA, glass vessel, cu-alloy vessel		2a
21	buckle		1a
22	glass vessel	cut by 18	1
23	brooch		2a
24			-
25			-
26			-
27	spear; shield		-
28	belt set; bucket		2a–3a
29	tpq c. 560–70; CA		3b
30	CA		3a
31			-
32	CA		3b
33	buckle; pin; (spear)		3–7
34	strap-end		3a
35	CA		3b
36			-
37			-
38	CA		2b–3a
39	spear; shield; buckle		
40			-
41	firesteel; (spear)		1b–2a
42	CA		3
43	CA		5–7
44	CA		5–7
45			-
46	beads; weaving batten	cuts 49	3b
47			-
48	CA	cuts 49, cut by 90	1b
49		cut by 46 and 48	1
50	buckle set; (spear)		2–3a
51			-
52	buckle		5–7

Grave	Phasing basis	Stratigraphy	Overlap phases
53	CA; firesteel; bucket		5–7
54	key bunch		3
55	CA		3b–5
56	belt set		3a
57	spear		-
58	key bunch	cuts 59	3
59	CA	cut by 58	3a
60	CA		3
61	buckle; ((spear))		((??))
62	CA		3a
63	spear		-
64			-
65	seax, belt set; (spear)		3a
66	beads		1–3
67	CA		3b–5
68			-
69			-
70		cut by 92	1–2
71	spear, shield		-
72			-
73			-
74			-
75	CA		5–7
76	bead group C		5–7
77			-
78			-
79			-
80	knife		5–7
81	box		3b–5
82			-
83			-
84	châtelaine		5–7
85			-
86			-
87	pot; (spear)		1–2
88			-
89			-
90		cuts 48	-
91	belt set; (spear, shield)		2–3a
92	CA	cuts 70	2
93	seax, bead; (spear, shield)		2b–3a
94A		over 94B	
94B	sword	under 94A	2–3
95			-
96A	buckle set; (spear, shield)	next to 96B	2–3a
96B	(sword; spear)	next to 96A	2–3a
97			-
98	shield; belt set		3
99			-
100			-
101			-
102			-
103	knife; belt mount		3–7
104			-
105			-
106			-
107	CA		5–7
108			-

Grave	Phasing basis	Stratigraphy	Overlap phases
109	bottle		5–7
110	tpq *c* 660–70; CA		5–7
111			-
112			-
113	buckle; châtelaine; belt mount; shoelace tag		5–7
114	spear		-
115			-
116			-
117			-
118			-
119			-
120	shoelace tag		5–7
121			-
122			-
123			-
124	CA		3b–5
125			-
126	brooch		3b
127	CA		5–7
128	buckle; (spear)		3–7
129	beads		5–7
130			-
131	spear		-
132	CA		5–7
133	CA		3b–5
134	CA		5–7
135	buckle; (spear)		3–7
136			-
137	buckle; bottle; (spear)		5–7
138	CA		5–7
139	firesteel, pot		5–7
140			-
141	bead group C		5–7
142			-
143			-
144	shoelace tag?		5–7?
145			-
146	buckle		5–7
147			-
148			-
149	buckle		3–7
150			-
151			-
152			-
153			-
154			-
155	CA		5–7
156	bottle; strap-end; (spear)		5–7
157	CA; firesteel		5–7
158	buckle		5–7
159			-
160	CA		5–7
161	pin		5–7
162			-
163			-
164			-
165			-

Grave	Phasing basis	Stratigraphy	Overlap phases
201			-
202			-
203			-
204	CA; *dress style V*		2b
205	buckle		(2–3?)
206	knife		(3–7?)
207	beads		(1–2?)
208			-
209	buckle		1b–2
210			-
211			-
212		cut by 213	-
213		cuts 212	-
214			-
215			-
216			-
217	beads; buckle loop		1
218			-
219	CA; pot 3; *dress style II*		1a
220	spear		-
221	brooch; *dress style II*		1b
222	CA; *dress style V*	cuts 235	3a
223	beads; brooch; buckle; *dress style V?*	cut by 232	2b–3?
224A		over 224B	-
224B		under 224A	-
225		cuts 234	-
226			-
227			-
228A	buckle; firesteel	over 228B, cuts 237	3a–7
228B		under 228A, cuts 237	-
229		cut by 230	-
230	shield; (spear)	cuts 229	2b–3a
231	buckle	cuts 232	3b
232	CA; coin-pendant, prov. tpq 518	cuts 223, cut by 231	3b
233	spear		-
234		cut by 225	-
235		cut by 222	1–3a
236			-
237		cut by 228, 346 and 358	-
238A		under 238B	1–2
238B	pot 2	over 238A	1–2
239	CA; *dress style I*		1a
240	spear		-
241			-
242			-
243			-
244			-
245	CA; *dress style V*		3a
246			-
247	beads, brooch		2a
248			-
249A			-
249B			-
249C	buckle; (spear)		2–3

Grave	Phasing basis	Stratigraphy	Overlap phases
250	CA; *dress style VI*; bell beakers; antler burr disc		3a
251	buckle; (spear)		3
252			-
253			-
254	CA; *dress style II*; cone beaker		1
255	CA; *dress style IV*		1b
256	spear	cut by 340	
257	brooch; beads; pin		1
258			-
259	spear	cuts 260	-
260		cut by 259	-
261	buckle	cut by 266	1
262	buckle; (spear)		2–3
263A		over 263B	1b–2a
263B	beads; brooches; *dress style IV*	under 263A	1b
264	shield (spear)	cuts 263 & 347	3
265A		over 265B; cuts 359	(3–7)
265B	buckle set; shield; scales; (spear)	under 265A; cuts 359	3a
266	brooches; *dress style III*	cuts 261	1b–2a
267			-
268			-
269	knife		(3–7?)
270			-
271	shoe-shaped rivets		2–3a
272		cuts 320	
273			-
274			-
275			-
276		cuts 349 & 350	(2–7)
277			-
278			-
279			-
280			-
281	brooches; buckle; *dress style IV*	cut by 325	1b
282A		over 282B	-
282B		under 282A	-
283			-
284			-
285			-
286			-
287			-
288			-
289		cut by 290	-
290	brooch; spoon; *dress style II*	cuts 289	1
291			-
292			-
293	beads		1b–2
294	beads		(1?)
295			-
296	CA; *dress style IV*		2a
297	shield; glass vessel; buckle set; (spear)		2
298			-
299	spear		
300	firesteel; knife; (spear)		1b–2a

Grave	Phasing basis	Stratigraphy	Overlap phases
301	spear		-
302	buckle		2–3a
303A	beads	over 303B	3b
303B		under 303A	1–3
304			-
305			-
306	beads		1
307			-
308	beads; pot 3; *dress style I*		1
309			-
310		cuts 311	-
311		cut by 310 and 363	-
312			-
313		cuts 326	-
314A	knife	adjacent 314B	(3–7?)
314B		adjacent 314A	(3–7?)
315			-
316			-
317		cuts 318	-
318		cut by 317	-
319	buckle; shoe-shaped stud		(1b–3a)
320		cut by 272	-
321			-
322			-
323	shield; (spear)	cuts 324	3
324		cut by 323	(1–3)
325	buckle	cuts 281	(2b–3?)
326	knife?; brooch; wrist clasps	cut by 313	(2–7)
327	buckle & studs		1b–2a
328			-
329			-
330		cuts 365	-
331	CA; buckle & rivets; beads		3a
332			-
333	buckle		1b–2
334	buckle		1a
335	buckle & studs		1b–2
336	beads; antler burr ring		2b
337	spear		-
338	pot 3		1–2
339	CA		3a
340		cuts 256	-
341			-
342			-
343			-
344	buckle		1b
345	buckle in fill	cuts 357	(2b–7)
346	axe; (spear)	cuts 237	3
347	CA; brooches; cone beaker; *dress style IV*	cut by 264	2a
348	buckle		1b–2a
349	beads	cut by 276 & 350	1
350A	knife & iron buckle	cut by 276; over 350B, cuts 349 & 351	(1b–3)
350B	beads; buckle; studs; antler burr ring	cut by 276, under 350A, cuts 349 & 351	(1b–3a)

Grave	Phasing basis	Stratigraphy	Overlap phases
351A	*earring does not help*	cut by 350 & 276; over 351B	1–2
351B	CA; *dress style IV*	cut by 350 & 276; under 351A	1
352		cut by 353	(1–3a)
353	CA; claw beaker late 6th–7th; *dress style V*	cuts 352	3a
354	CA; *dress style V*	cuts 361	2b
355	glass bowl		1
356			–
357		cut by 345	–
358		cuts 237	–
359		cut by 265	(1–3)
360	CA	cuts 361	3b
361		cut by 354 & 360	(1–3b)
362			–
363	spear	cuts 311	–
364			–
365		cut by 330	–
366	brooch; *dress style III*		1b–2
367	*dress style I*	cuts 378	–
368			–
369			–
370			–
371			–
372	CA; claw beaker; *dress style I*		2a
373	*dress style V*; beads B1		2b–3a
374	spear		–
375	shield; (spear)		3b
376	CA		5–7
377	pot 3		1–2
378		cut by 367	–
379			–
380		cut by 404	–
381	firesteel/pursemount; buckle	cuts 406	1b–2a
382			–
383		cut by 405	–
384	brooch model in fill	cuts 384; cut by 405 check	(1b–7)
385			–
386A		over 386B; cut by 387 & 431	–
386B		under 386A; cut by 387 & 431	–
387	shoe-shaped stud	cuts 386	(2–7)
388			–
389			–
390			–
391A	beads; pendant; *dress style VI*	over 391B	5–7
391B	CA; pendants; *dress style IV*	under 391A	2
392	shield-on-tongue buckle; pot 3		2
393A	spear	over 393B	–
393B		under 393A	–
394			–
395			–
396			–

Grave	Phasing basis	Stratigraphy	Overlap phases
397			–
398	buckle		2b–3a
399			–
400	spear		–
401			–
402			–
403			–
404		cuts 380	–
405		cuts 383	(1b–7)
406		cuts 381	(1b–7)
407	CA: *dress style IV*		2
408	brooches; buckle; *dress style IV*		1b
409	CA		1b
410			–
411	spear		–
412	CA	cuts 430 and ring gully of 427	2b–3a
413	CA; knife; *dress style VI*		5–7
414	shield; (spear)		2b–3a
415			–
416			–
417	CA; brooch type Hahnheim; *dress style IV*		2a
418	pot 3		1–2
419	CA; antler burr pendant		2a
420	comb; bell beaker		2–3a
421			–
422	bell beaker; pot 2		1–2
423	buckle; (spear)		2–3a
424		cuts 444	–
425	beads	cut by 441	1b–2
426	buckle		2
427A	beads	over 427B; ring gully cut by 412	1b–2
427B		under 427A; ring gully cut by 412	1–2
428	brooches, beads; buckle & studs; *dress style III*		2
429			–
430		cut by 412	(1–3a)
431		cuts 386	–
432	beads, cone beaker		1b–2
433	brooch; *dress style IV?*		1
434			–
435	buckle		2–3a
436	buckle		1b–2
437	buckle; firesteel; fauchard; glass vessel		2
438	knife		(3–7?)
439			–
440	brooches, beads; *dress style III*		1b–2a
441	beads; pot 2	cuts 425 & 444	1b–2
442	firesteel, buckle	cuts 444	1b–2
443	shield-on-tongue buckle		1b–2
444		cut by 424 & 442	1–2

Table 8.5. Buckland 1951–3 and 1994. Revised phasing of all graves.

Grave	Plot	Sex	Evison	Brugmann	Notes
A					
B	D	F	?3		
C	D	M	3		
D	D	?M	3		
E	D	-	?3		
F	D	F	3		
1	D	F	3		
2	D	-	?3		
3	D	M	3		
4	D	M	3		
5	D	M	?3		
6	C	F	5		
7	C	-	?5		
8	C	M	5		
9	C	M	?5		
10	C	M	5		
11	C	F	-		
12	A	F	1		
13	A	F	1	1b	
14	A	F	2	2	
15	A	F	2	2	
16	A	-	?1–2		
17	A	-	?1–2		
18	A	F	4	3b–5	cuts Gr 22
19	A	-	?1–2		
20	A	F	1	2a	
21	A	F	1	1a	
22	A	M	1	1	cut by Gr 18
23	A		2	2a	
24	C	F	?5		
25	B	F	?4		
26	D	-	?3		
27	B	M	4		
28	A	F	2	2–3a	
29	B	F	3	3b	
30	B	F	3	3a	
31	B	-	-		destroyed
32	B	F	3	3b	
33	B	M	3	3–7	
34	B	-	4	3a	
35	B	F	3	3b	
36	J	M	?5		
37	J	F	?5		
38	F	F			
39	F	M	4		
40	H	-	?6		
41	D	M	3		
42	B	F	4	3	
43	B	F	4	5–7	
44	B	F	4	5–7	
45	A	-	?1–2		
46	A	F	1	3b	
47	B	-	-		destroyed
48	A	F	1	1b	
49	A	F	2		cuts Grs 46, 48
50	A	M	2	2–3a	
51	-	-	-		destroyed

Grave	Plot	Sex	Evison	Brugmann	Notes
52	E	M	5		
53	E	F	5		
54	E	F	?4		
55	E	F	4		
56	K	M	3		
57	K	M	3		
58	E	F	4		cuts Gr 59
59	E	F	3		cut by Gr 58
60	E	F	3		
61	E	M	3		
62	E	F	4		
63	E	M	3		
64	E	M	4		
65	E	M	4		
66	E	F	4		
67	E	F	5		
68	N	F	7		
69	J	M	?5		
70	A	-	1	1–2	
71	F	M	4		
72	I	-	7		
73	I	?M	7		
74	I	F	7		
75	I	F	7		
76	I	F	7		
77	I	-	7		
78	I	-	7		
79	I	-	7		
80	I	?M	7		
81	I	F	7		
82	I	F	7		
83	I	F	7		
84	I	F	7		
85	I	-	7		
86	I	-	7		
87	A	M	1	1–2	
88	A	-	?1-2		
89	A	-	?1-2		
90	A	M	4		
91	B	M	3		
92	A	F	2	2	
93	B	M	3	2B–3A	
94A	A	F	3		
94B	A	M	2	2–3	
95	A	F	6		
96A	F	?M	4		
96B	F	F	4		
97	F	-	?4		
98	D	M	3		
99	I	F	7		
100	I	F	7		
101	H	F	6		
102	H	-	?6		
103	H	M	6		
104	H	M	?6		
105	H	-	?6		
106	H	M	?6		

Grave	Plot	Sex	Evison	Brugmann	Notes
107	H	F	6		
108	H	-	6		
109	H	-	?6		
110	H	F	6		
111	H	M	?6		
112	H	F	?6		
113	H	F	6		
114	H	M	6		
115	D	F	?3		
116	D	-	?3		
117	I	-	7		
118	H	-	?6		
119	H	-	?6		
120	I	M	7		
121	H	F	?6		
122	D	F	?3		
123	D	-	?3		
124	H	F	6		
125	H	M	?6		
126	B	F	3	3b	
127	I	F	7		
128	G	M	5		
129	G	F	5		
130	G	-	?5		
131	F	M	4		
132	G	F	5		
133	G	F	5		
134	G	F	5		
135	F	M	?4		
136	F	M	?4		
137	G	M	5		

Grave	Plot	Sex	Evison	Brugmann	Notes
138	H	F	6		
139	G	M	5		
140	H		?6		
141	H	F	6		
142	H	F	?6		
143	H		?6		
144	H	?M	6		
145	N	M	7		
146	N	M	7		
147	H	F	?6		
148	H	M	6		
149	H	M	6		
150	H	M	6		
151	N	-	7		
152	M	M	7		
153	M	-	7		
154	M	-	7		
155	G	F	5		
156	G	M	5		
157	G	F	5		
158	H	?M	6		
159	H	-	6		
160	H	F	6		
161	L	F	6		
162	L	M	6		
163	L	-	6		
164	L	F	6		
165	N	M	7		

Table 8.6. Revised phasing for Buckland 1951–3.

is therefore omitted in Table 8.4, and Phases 5–7 are collectively correlated with the disputed 'Final Phase' (see Geake 1997), dated to the mid seventh century by Evison's small finds analysis and bead Group C (see above). To fill the gap, Phase 3b is extended to *c* AD 650.

Phase 3b has the first two coin-dated graves at Buckland, Grave 29 (*c* AD 560–570) and Grave 323 (*c* AD 518–527, or later). Though the latter could date Grave 323 as early as Phase 2b, the item itself is actually a plated imitation of a Byzantine gold *tremissis*, seemingly designed as a piece of jewellery. A later date for the production of the piece thus seems entirely possible (*see* pp 88–9). The other grave goods suggest that this burial is about half a century later than the date of the coin. The coin-dated Grave 110 was assigned by Evison to Phase 6 and is placed here in the 'collective' Phase 5–7.

The absolute dates for Evison's Phases 1 to 3 have shifted only slightly (Table 8.0): Phase 1 has been pushed back to the mid fifth century in order to accommodate the early material found in 1994. The schematic date of the beginning of Phase

2 is within the date range set for the beginning of Phase 2a. The redefinition of Phase 3 requires a slightly earlier date than AD 575, whilst the omission of the relative Phase 4 extends Phase 3 to the mid seventh century.

Weapon graves

The twenty-six spears, seven shields, the axe and fauchard from Buckland 1994 and their grave associations do not comprise a dataset substantial enough to merit correspondence analysis. The dating of weapon graves, therefore, has to rely largely on small finds analysis. The only stratigraphic evidence for a weapon grave is provided by Grave 264 which cuts Graves 263 and 347. Grave 263 is dated to Phases 1b–2a and Grave 347 to Phase 2a. This suggests that weapon Grave 264 is no earlier than Phase 2a.

In her small finds analysis, Stephanie Spain gives relative and absolute date ranges for shield fittings based on an analysis of a Kentish sample of shields (Spain 2000), updated with the 1994 Buckland evidence (*see* pp 56–7).[82] The dates for the twenty-six spearheads from Buckland 1994 given by Axel Kerep in Table 4.7 are not only based on his small finds analysis of the spearhead types but incorporate his dating of associated objects. This leads to widely varying date ranges of some spearhead types, for example for Types D2 and E3, while Type H2, dated by Swanton in the very late fifth and sixth centuries, remains undated if not associated with other datable objects. This suggests that spearheads are more difficult to date than hitherto appreciated and that we must wait for Kerep's forthcoming analysis of Kentish spearheads for further illumination on the subject. To what extend this will lead to a revision of Evison's dates for spearheads from the Buckland 1951–3 site remains to be seen.

Kerep's small finds discussion on the axe from Grave 346 allows the weapon to be assigned to Buckland Phase 3. The absolute date range given for the fauchard suggests a date within Buckland Phases 1–2 (see also Legoux's Phase A/B/C 2). Swords and arrowheads cannot add to the dating of the graves (p 52, p 70).

The correlation of male graves with the phases developed for the grave goods of females in Table 8.5 relies mostly on buckles (see above).

Horizontal stratigraphy

Of the 260 burials recorded at Buckland in 1994, ninety-six have been dated to within one or two of the Buckland Phases. These include sixty-one graves of females, seventeen graves of males and eighteen indeterminate graves. Figure 8.3–8.4

shows the distribution of these dated graves across Buckland 1951–3 and 1994. Table 8.7 gives the numbers of graves per plot. In this table, Plots Y and Z are combined as one plot because the similar layout of Plot B at Mill Hill, Deal, suggests that the Buckland Plot Z is actually a spin-off of Plot Y. Table 8.7 additionally lists Plots A and B at Buckland 1951–3 as the only two plots with graves of the same date as the bulk of graves at Buckland 1994. Plot A mostly has graves of Phases 1 to 3 while Plot B is also laid out in rows but has a later date range mostly covering Phase 3 (Tables 8.8 and 8.9).

On the 1994 Buckland site, just Plot X clearly spans Phases 1 to 5–7 (Table 8.14). The datable graves of Plots S, T, V, and W cover only Phases 1 to 3. In Plots S, T and W Phase 2 would appear to be under represented (Tables 8.10, 8.11 and 8.13). Measured in years, this phase is, however, considerably shorter than Phases 1 and 3 and therefore can be expected to be represented by fewer graves. In Plot Y–Z only Phase 2 is strongly represented or particularly well identifiable (Table 8.15), suggesting that this plot developed in a way different from Plots S, T and W but similar to the contemporary plot A at Mill Hill, Deal. Plot U with seven graves has only one dated burial (Phases 2–3); Plot R, with fourteen graves, has one dated to Phase 1–2 (Grave 204) and one to Phase 2 (Grave 207).

In the larger plots, the sub phases are sufficiently evenly distributed to suggest that there are no substantial gaps in the development of these plots over time (Table 8.7). The only exception is found in Plot X where there is a clear under-representation of Phase 3. This is the only plot with graves dated to the 'Final' Phase 5–7. The plot is almost certainly truncated by the site boundary and may have included graves of Phase 3 in its north-eastern part. Alternatively, the late graves in this part of the cemetery may indeed mark a

	Phase 1	Phase 1–2	Phase 2	Phase 2–3	Phase 3	Phase 3–7	Phase 5–7	Total of phased graves	Total no of graves in plot
Plot A	4	2	5	3	1	1		16	27
Plot B				1	7	1	2	11	15
Plot R	1	1						2	14
Plot S	7	4	2	3	7			23	74
Plot T	6	4	1	1	3			15	54
Plot U				1				1	7
Plot V	1	3	2	1	1			8	14
Plot W	4	2		1	3			10	22
Plot X	1	5	4	1	1		3	15	42
Plot Y-Z		11	6	4				21	33
Total	24	32	20	16	23	2	5	122	302

Table 8.7. Phasing of Buckland 1995 (with 1950s Plots A and B).

---

82. I am most grateful to Stephanie Spain for the teamwork involved in correlating the Buckland framework with her previous work on a Kentish sample.

Grave no	Sex	Phase
21		1a
22		1
87	M	1–2
70		1–2
48	F	1b
13	F	1b
20		2a
23		2a
92	F	2
15		2
14		2
50	M	2–3a
28	F	2–3a
94B	M	2–3
46	F	3b
18	F	3b–5

Table 8.8. Sub phases in Plot A.

Grave no	Sex	Phase
93		2b–3a
34		3a
30		3a
42	F	3
33		3–7
126		3b5
35	F	3b–5
32		3b–5
29	F	3b–5
44	F	5–7
43		5–7

Table 8.9. Sub phases in Plot B.

Grave no	Sex	Phase
219	F	1a
217	F	1
351B	F	1
349	F	1
261		1
351A	M	1–2
263B	F	1b
221	F	1b
263A		1b–2a
266	F	1b–2a
348	F	1b–2a
347	F	2a
262	M	2–3
354	F	2b
230	M	2b–3a
398		2b–3a
222	F	3a
265B	M	3a
353	F	3a
264	M	3
346	M	3
360	F	3b
232	F	3b

Table 8.10. Sub phases in Plot S.

Grave no	Sex	Phase
334	F	1a
355		1
308	F	1
306	F	1
290	F	1
338	M	1–2
281	F	1b
327	F	1b–2a
335		1b–2
333		1b–2
302	M	2–3a
336	F	2b
331	F	3a
323	M	3
303A		3b

Table 8.11. Sub phases in Plot T.

Grave no	Sex	Phase
239	F	1a
238B	F	1–2
238A	F	1–2
366	F	1b–2
372	F	2a
247	F	2a
373	F	2b–3a
245	F	3a

Table 8.12. Sub phases in Plot V.

Grave no	Sex	Phase
433	F	1
257	F	1
254	F	1
255	F	1b
344	F	1b
432	F	1b–2
249C	M	2–3
339	F	3a
250	F	3a
251	M	3

Table 8.13. Sub phases in Plot W.

Grave no	Sex	Phase
427B		1–2
377	F	1–2
409	F	1b
408	F	1b
381	F	1b–2a
427A	F	1b–2
428	F	2
407	F	2
392	F	2
391B	F	2
412	F	2b–3a
375	M	3b
413	F	5–7
391A	F	5–7
376	F	5–7

Table 8.14. Sub phases in Plot X.

Grave no	Sex	Phase
418		1–2
422		1–2
444		1–2
300	M	1b–2a
293	F	1b–2
425	F	1b–2
436		1b–2
440	F	1b–2
441	F	1b–2
442		1b–2
443		1b–2
296	F	2a
419	F	2a
417	F	2a
297	M	2
426		2
437	M	2
435		2–3a
420	F	2–3a
423	M	2–3a
414	M	2b–3a

Table 8.15. Sub phases in Plot Y–Z.

started in the fifth century, but only three (Plots S, T and X) seem to have been still in use in the seventh century.

The layout of the individual plots does not show much evidence that could be interpreted as a 'micro'-horizontal stratigraphy. Most of the intercutting graves are of the same or immediately following phases (see above and pp 29–30). The only clear evidence of a time gap between two stratigraphically related graves is the double stacked Grave 391 (*see* p 28). Figure 8.5 shows what, on first sight, appears to be a random scatter of graves dated to Phases 1–3 across the plots. On further study, some individual patterns may be discerned: a shift from south-west to north-east in Plot W and what seems to be a fringe of late graves around a cluster of earlier ones in Plot S. The practice of 'stacking', however, was already taking place during Phase 1 (Grave

'return', focussed on the barrows in this area. This later phase of use also seems to have included the re-opening of Grave 391 to allow the insertion of a second burial (Sk 391A).

The chronological framework set out above gives relatively close dates for about one third of the graves on the 1994 Buckland site. These dates suggest that most, if not all the plots (Plot U has only one dated grave out of seven) were

351; *see* p 28) and the cutting of earlier graves by later ones was occurring by Phase 2a (Grave 266). The latter may account for the internal structure of the individual plots, which appears random but may reflect a complex burial practice with grave goods as one dimension and the use of space as another, just as meaningful, dimension. The layout of the upper part of the Buckland cemetery (Fig 8.4) shows the change from compact plots to more widely spaced graves during Phase 3.

Radiocarbon dating and chronological modelling

Alex Bayliss, Nancy Beavan, John Hines, Karen Høilund Nielsen and Gerry McCormac

Radiocarbon dating

Nine samples of human bone from articulated skeletons (Sk 222, Sk 250, Sk 264, Sk 323, Sk 339, Sk 375, Sk 391A, Sk 391B, Sk 414) have been radiocarbon dated from the cemetery at Buckland. All were dated at the Queen's University, Belfast Radiocarbon Laboratory, and were pre-treated using a method based on that of Longin (1971), combusted to carbon dioxide and converted to benzene (Pearson 1983; McCormac *et al* 2011), and dated by high-precision liquid scintillation spectrometry (McCormac 1992; McCormac *et al* 2001; Wilson *et al* 1995). Errors have been calculated as described by McCormac *et al* (2011).

The results are conventional radiocarbon ages (Stuiver and Polach 1997) and are listed in Table 8.16. The calibrated date ranges for the samples have been calculated using the probability method (Stuiver and Reimer 1993) and are quoted in the form recommended by Mook (1986) with end points rounded outwards to five years. The probability distributions of the calibrated dates are shown in Fig 8.21. They have been calculated using OxCal v4.1.7 (Bronk Ramsey 2009) and the current internationally-agreed atmospheric calibration dataset for the northern hemisphere, IntCal09 (Reimer *et al* 2009).

Stable isotope measurements

Carbon and nitrogen stable isotope measurements were carried out at Rafter Radiocarbon as described by Beavan-Athfield *et al* (2001). The results are shown in Table 8.17. Both pairs of replicate $\delta^{13}C$ values are statistically consistent (T'=0.3; T'(5%)=3.8; v=1 for both; Ward and Wilson 1978), as are both pairs of replicate $\delta^{15}N$ values (T'=0.2; T'(5%)=3.8; v=1 for both).

All the samples fall in the optimum C:N ratio range for well-preserved bone protein of 2.9 to 3.6 established by DeNiro (1985). The %N values for these samples do not indicate protein degradation, and the %C values do not indicate contamination with exogenous carbon. The protein in these samples is therefore suitable for accurate radiocarbon dating.

Fig 8.22 shows the isotopic ratios of the dated human skeletons from Buckland in relation to regional dietary

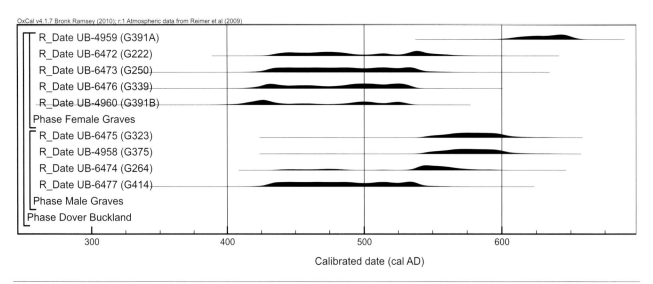

Fig 8.21. Probability distributions of calibrated radiocarbon dates from Buckland.

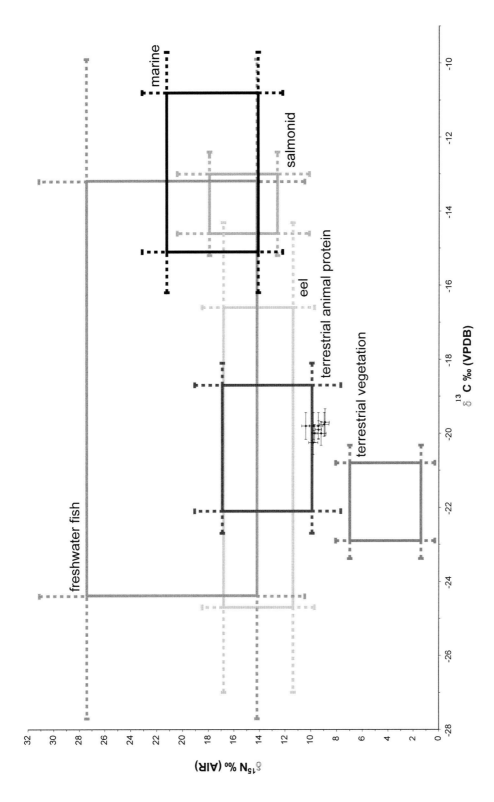

Fig 8.22. Stable isotope values for individuals from Buckland fit well within parameters for a mainly terrestrial animal protein diet. Diet-to-collagen value boxes are those reported by Beavan and Mays (forthcoming), using a trophic enrichment factor of 1‰ based on ¹³C upon enrichments in herbivores (Jay and Richards 2006) and 4‰ for ¹⁵N, based on evidence for trophic enrichments in breastfeeding children and nursing women (Richards *et al* 2002).

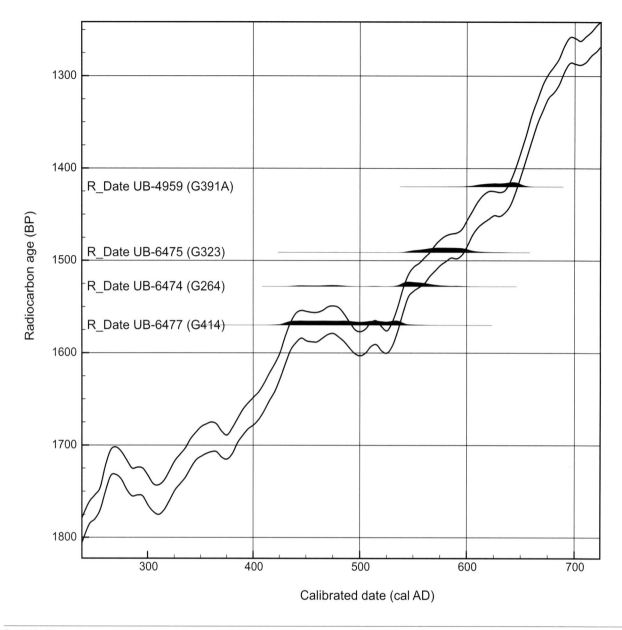

Fig 8.23. The calibration curve of Reimer *et al* (2009) for the early Anglo-Saxon period, showing the effect of the plateau in radiocarbon ages covering much of the fifth and early sixth centuries AD on the precision calibrated radiocarbon dates in this period.

sources. The diet-to-collagen value boxes are those reported by Beavan and Mays (forthcoming), using a trophic enrichment factor of 1‰ based on ^{13}C on enrichments in herbivores (Jay and Richards 2006) and 4‰ for ^{15}N, based on evidence for trophic enrichments in breastfeeding children and nursing women (Richards *et al* 2002). No trophic enrichment factor has been applied to the 'terrestrial vegetation' box as the cattle values used to construct this act as a proxy for where

human collagen values would be with a vegan diet. The plot indicates that all skeletons are enriched in δ^{13}C and δ^{15}N to points well above pure 'terrestrial vegetation' ranges, and the human values sit well within the range of 'terrestrial animal protein' sources, yet they do not necessarily exclude small components of freshwater or marine fish in the human diets. If there was a freshwater or marine component in the diet at Buckland (*see* p 31), it was probably small enough not to

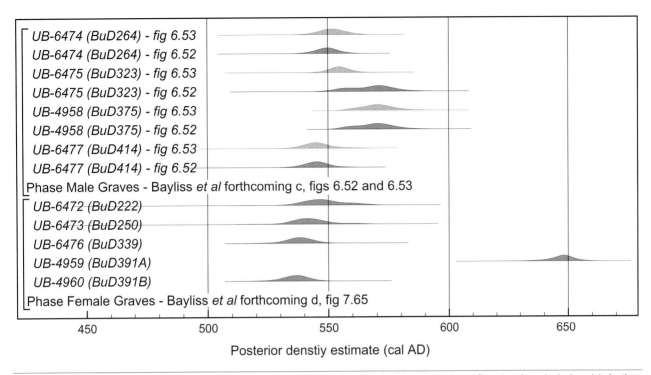

Fig 8.24. Probability distributions of dates for burials from the cemetery at Buckland, derived from the preferred Bayesian chronological models for the two alternative partitions of the male sequence (Bayliss *et al* forthcoming c, figs 6.52–3) and from the preferred Bayesian chronological model for the female sequence (Bayliss *et al* forthcoming d, fig 7.65).

affect radiocarbon ages significantly. This justifies our use of the fully atmospheric calibration curve in calibrating the radiocarbon measurements from the site.

Further discussion of the stable isotope results from Buckland is provided in Beavan and Mays (forthcoming), Beavan *et al* (2011), and Mays and Beavan (2011).

Chronological modelling

The simple calibrated date ranges of the radiocarbon measurements (Table 8.16) are accurate estimates of the dates of the samples, but they derive from the scientific information alone, taking no account of other information which we may have about the date of the burials, and so are imprecise. We do, however, have a range of other information relevant to the date of these burials. Most simply, this includes the fact that all the radiocarbon dates are related, as the dated skeletons all came from the same cemetery. We also know, from stratigraphy, that Grave 391A was later than Grave 391B, and can additionally consider dating information derived from the typologies of artefacts contained within some of the graves, and from the pattern of co-occurrence of artefact-types in burials.

In order to utilise this additional information to refine the date estimates provided by the simple calibrated radiocarbon dates, we have adopted a Bayesian approach for the interpretation of the chronology of the dated burials (Buck *et al* 1996). Unfortunately, a site-based approach to modelling the chronology of the cemetery, which has recently proven effective for seventh-century groups of burials at Boss Hall/Buttermarket (Bayliss *et al* 2009) and Bloodmoor Hill, Carlton Colville (Marshall *et al* 2009), is unlikely to produce dating that is sufficiently precise to be of practical use in the archaeological interpretation of this site. This is because of the small number of radiocarbon dates available from Buckland, the scarcity of stratigraphic relationships between burials, and a plateau in the available calibration data covering much of the fifth and earlier sixth centuries AD. The effect of calibration on the precision of calibrated radiocarbon dates in this period is illustrated in Fig 8.23, where the date from Grave 414 covers a much wider range than the dates from the other, later, graves shown on this graph.

For this reason, we report here the results from a wider study of the chronology of Anglo-Saxon grave assemblages, which has combined seriation of the grave assemblages and artefact-types by correspondence analysis with a larger

Laboratory number	Context	Radiocarbon age (BP)	δ13C (‰) [14C]	Calibrated date (95% probability)	Calibrated date (68% probability)
UB-6472	Grave 222, human bone from female skeleton	1550±19	−20.1±0.5	cal AD 430–565	cal AD 435–490 (48%) or cal AD 510–515 (1%) or cal AD 530–550 (19%)
UB-6473	Grave 250, human bone from female skeleton	1572±22	−20.1±0.5	cal AD 425–545	cal AD 435–495 (50%) or cal AD 505–520 (11%) or cal AD 525–540 (7%)
UB-6474	Grave 264, human bone from male skeleton	1528±17	−20.0±0.5	cal AD 435–490 (22%) or cal AD 530–600 (73%)	cal AD 470–490 (22%) or cal AD 535–575 (64%)
UB-6475	Grave 323, human bone from male skeleton	1491±18	−20.1±0.5	cal AD 540–620	cal AD 560–600
UB-6476	Grave 339, human bone from female skeleton	1592±17	−20.0±0.5	cal AD 420–540	cal AD 425–445 (14%) or cal AD 455–465 (4%) or cal AD 480–535 (50%)
UB-4958	Grave 375, human bone from male skeleton	1493±18	−20.0±0.5	cal AD 540–615	cal AD 560–600
UB-4959	Grave 391A, human bone from female skeleton (stratigraphically later than Grave 391B)	1420±20	−20.5±0.5	cal AD 600–660	cal AD 615–650
UB-4960	Grave 391B, human bone from female skeleton (stratigraphically earlier than Grave 391A)	1611±18	−20.3±0.5	cal AD 405–535	cal AD 410–440 (32%) or cal AD 485–535 (36%)
UB-6477	Grave 414, human bone from male skeleton	1570±20	−20.1±0.5	cal AD 425–545	cal AD 435–495 (50%) or cal AD 505–520 (10%) or cal AD 525–540 (8%)

Table 8.16. Radiocarbon dates and δ13C values used for age calculation.

Laboratory number	Grave	%C	δ13C (‰)	error (±)[1]	total error (±)[2]	%N	δ15N (‰)	error (±)[1]	total error (±)[2]	Atomic C:N[3]
UB-6472	Grave 222	43.5	−19.8	0.2	0.36	16.1	+9.8	0.2	0.32	3.2
UB-6472	Grave 222 (replicate)	38.4	−20.1	0.1	0.32	14.1	+9.6	0.2	0.32	3.2
	Grave 222 (weighted means)		−20.0		0.24		+9.7		0.23	
UB-6473	Grave 250	39.5	−19.8	0.2	0.36	14.4	+10.4	0.2	0.32	3.2
UB-6474	Grave 264	39.2	−19.7	0.2	0.36	14.4	+9.3	0.2	0.32	3.2
UB-6474	Grave 264 (replicate)	42.6	−20.0	0.1	0.32	15.9	+9.5	0.2	0.32	3.1
	Grave 264 (weighted means)		−19.9		0.24		+9.4		0.23	
UB-6475	Grave 323	37.4	−19.8	0.2	0.36	13.8	+9.8	0.2	0.32	3.2
UB-6476	Grave 339	41.9	−19.7	0.2	0.36	15.6	+8.9	0.2	0.32	3.1
UB-4958	Grave 375	43.0	−19.8	0.12	0.32	15.9	+9.0	0.26	0.36	3.2
UB-4959	Grave 391A	28.5	−20.3	0.12	0.32	10.3	+9.8	0.26	0.36	3.2
UB-4960	Grave 391B	48.3	−20.0	0.1	0.32	17.3	+9.2	0.3	0.39	3.3
UB-6477	Grave 414	40.0	−19.8	0.2	0.36	14.8	+9.4	0.2	0.32	3.2

Table 8.17. Stable isotope results (including two replicate samples). 1) Error on stable isotope analysis is determined from mean std dev at 1σ on EDTA standards within the stable isotope analysis run; 2) Total error reported for 15N and 13C includes analytical error and variation in stable isotope results associated with chemistry preparation of the bone protein; 3) Atomic CN ratio = (%C/%N)*(14/12).

sample of radiocarbon dates from England (Bayliss *et al* forthcoming a). In that study, it has been necessary to conduct the seriation and chronological modelling of the male and female sequences separately because of the very small degree of overlap in chronologically significant artefact-types between the two sets of grave assemblages. Bayliss *et al* (forthcoming b) provide an introduction to how we have used these diverse methodologies to construct the reported chronologies.

The final analysis of the male burials from England includes 272 grave assemblages and seventy-eight artefact-types, and contains twenty-eight graves which have radiocarbon dates. Two alternative chronologies are proposed, based respectively on the partition of the correspondence analysis according to leading artefact-types (Bayliss *et al* forthcoming c, fig 6.52) and on the partition of the correspondence analysis according to the two-dimensional map of grave assemblages (Bayliss *et al* forthcoming c, fig

6.53). The results from the two approaches are very similar: both divide the grave assemblages into five, non-overlapping, sequential phases. The date estimates for the boundaries between equivalent phases in the two models vary by no more than 5 years (Bayliss *et al* forthcoming c, table 6.9). There are greater differences between the date estimates for certain burials, however, where grave assemblages lie in the liminal areas of the sorted data-matrix (Bayliss *et al* forthcoming c, e-fig 6.6): ie where non-equivalent phases of the two alternative partitions overlap.

The posterior density estimates for the four dated male graves from Buckland are shown in Fig 8.24, with the highest posterior density intervals given in Table 8.18. The date estimates for Graves 264, 275, 414 produced by the two approaches are almost identical, although those provided for Grave 323 are more different. This is because this grave can be allocated to a single phase in the partition based on the two-dimensional map of grave assemblages (Bayliss *et al* forthcoming c, fig 6.49; AS-Mp), but can only be allocated to within a pair of sequential phases in the partition based on leading artefact-types (AS-MB or AS-MC). This means that the model based on the two-dimensional map of grave assemblages contains more information about this grave, and so the resultant date estimate is both more precise and lies towards the earlier end of the date estimate provided by the model based on the leading-types partition.

The final analysis of the female burials from England includes 300 grave assemblages and eighty-one artefact-types, and contains fifty-two graves which have radiocarbon dates. The two alternative approaches to the partition of the correspondence analysis produce exactly the same division into four, non-overlapping, sequential phases (Bayliss *et al* forthcoming d, fig 7.62a). The resultant preferred chronological model for the female sequence is shown in Bayliss *et al* (forthcoming d, fig 7.65). The posterior density estimates for the five dated female graves from Buckland are shown in Fig 8.24, with the highest posterior density intervals given in Table 8.18.

Discussion

The nine samples from this site discussed here were selected for dating in two separate batches and with different purposes in view. This inevitably limits the collective significance of the results. The samples from Graves 375, 391A and 391B were submitted in 2003 by the Canterbury Archaeological Trust. Grave 375 was selected because it appeared to be 'one of the latest' graves that had been excavated, and the superimposition of female Grave 391A over another female grave, 391B, was considered remarkable in light of the wide difference in their dates that the beads with which the women were buried seemed to imply.

Both the seriation of Anglo-Saxon male graves by correspondence analysis referred to above (Bayliss *et al* forthcoming c) and the radiocarbon date of the skeleton confirm that Grave 375 is probably the latest of the male burials sampled for radiocarbon dating from this site (see Fig 8.24 and Table 8.18) although the correspondence analysis assigns Grave 251 from the more recently excavated burial area at Buckland to the same phase (AS-MC/AS-Mq). The

		Bayliss *et al* forthcoming c, fig 6.52 (leading artefact-types) MALE		Bayliss *et al* forthcoming c, fig 6.53 (2D map of grave assemblages) MALE		Bayliss *et al* forthcoming d, fig 7.65 (leading artefact-types =2D map of grave assemblages) FEMALE	
Laboratory number	Grave	Highest posterior density interval (95% probability)	Highest posterior density interval (68% probability)	Highest posterior density interval (95% probability)	Highest posterior density interval (68% probability)	Highest posterior density interval (95% probability)	Highest posterior density Interval (68% probability)
UB-6472	Grave 222					*cal AD 530–570*	*cal AD 535–555*
UB-6473	Grave 250					*cal AD 525–565*	*cal AD 530–550*
UB-6474	Grave 264	*cal AD 540–560*	*cal AD 540–555*	*cal AD 540–565*	*cal AD 545–560*		
UB-6475	Grave 323	*cal AD 545–585*	*cal AD 555–580*	*cal AD 545–565*	*cal AD 550–560*		
UB-6476	Grave 339					*cal AD 525–550*	*cal AD 530–545*
UB-4958	Grave 375	*cal AD 550–585*	*cal AD 560–580*	*cal AD 555–585*	*cal AD 560–580*		
UB-4959	Grave 391A					*cal AD 635–660*	*cal AD 640–655*
UB-4960	Grave 391B					*cal AD 520–550*	*cal AD 530–545*
UB-6477	Grave 414	*cal AD 530–560*	*cal AD 540–555*	*cal AD 530–560*	*cal AD 540–555*		

Table 8.18. Highest posterior density intervals for the radiocarbon-dated graves, derived from the preferred models for the seriation of the male grave assemblages partitioned according to the leading artefact-types (Bayliss *et al* forthcoming c, fig 6.52) and the two-dimensional map of the grave assemblages produced by correspondence analysis (Bayliss *et al* forthcoming d, fig 7.65).

radiocarbon dates of Graves 391A and 391B, combined with phasing on the basis of seriation by correspondence analysis and Bayesian modelling of the radiocarbon dates, confirm that these two interments were very probably made around a century apart, if not even more (Fig 8.24 and Table 8.18). Whether the relationship between them was deliberate, accidental, or simply opportunistic, is therefore a matter for further consideration. Both burials are relatively well furnished for their periods: Grave 391A has amethyst beads and bulla pendants, characteristic of phase AS-FE of the middle or later seventh century, while Grave 391B contained, *inter alia*, a belt-set of the early to mid sixth century and amber beads that were most common at that time too.

The six samples from Graves 222, 250, 264, 323, 339 and 414, three males and three females, were selected in May 2005 by the chronology project team for their relevance in the national perspective rather than to contribute directly to a chronological model of the cemetery at Buckland. It was initially thought that it might be possible to define sequential chronological phases within the female series in the earlier to mid sixth century on the basis of assemblages such as those in Graves 222, 250 and 339, with Grave 339 in an earlier sub-phase than the other two. This idea has proved unsustainable on the basis of the evidence we have at present. It is clear that the Highest Posterior Density intervals of the dates of burial of these graves overlap considerably, even if the medians of the distributions hint at an order in which Grave 339 precedes Grave 250 and then Grave 222 in turn. Grave 250 is important in a wider perspective as it contains a glass bowl of Evison's (2008) Group 43 and two bell beakers of her Group 48, together with a gold D-bracteate. In all of these cases, the posterior density estimate for this burial in the second quarter or around the middle of the sixth century (Fig 8.24; Table 8.18) is valuable corroborative and supplementary evidence for dates of currency of these types assigned by Vera Evison (2008, 13) and in bracteate studies (see p 92).

The majority of the radiocarbon dates reported here represent burial within the sixth century: only Grave 391A belongs in the seventh century, and indeed the probability that any of the dated burials was made in the first or final decades of the sixth century is extremely small. This cannot, however, support any inference that burial in this area of Buckland might have been discontinuous, so that the superimposition of Grave 391A over Grave 391B represents either oblivion of the presence of the earlier burial or an extraordinary return to the area, to re-open and re-use a much earlier grave. Although we have no identified male graves later than Graves 251 and 375, four female graves from this area of the cemetery are assigned in the national correspondence analysis scheme to phases between Grave 222 and Grave 391A: Grave 232 in phase AS-FC and Graves 245, 376 and 413 in AS-FD. Particularly noteworthy in this regard is the presence of a further gold D-bracteate in Grave 245 (*see* pp 89–92). In fact, though, Grave 245 can only be incorporated in the correspondence analysis by treating the presence of the gold bracteate in it, and the single shoe-shaped rivet, as anachronistic survivals. The latest dated artefact-type in Grave 245 according to this national scheme is the amethyst beads. Within the national scheme, Grave 245 might be dated to the very late sixth century, but is more probably a burial of the first half of the seventh century (Bayliss *et al* forthcoming d).

PART 9: DISCUSSION

Buckland cemetery in its local setting

Keith Parfitt

Late Roman and early Anglo-Saxon settlement in the Dour Valley: the transition

The available historical and archaeological evidence indicates that Anglo-Saxon colonisation in east Kent first began during the mid fifth century AD. Certainly by the late sixth century, if not sometime before, a fully independent and powerful kingdom had developed, which had expanded from its original base, across the Medway as far as the south bank of the Thames (Chadwick Hawkes 1982a; Brooks 1989; Welch 2007, 189, figs 6.5 and 6.6; Brookes and Harrington 2010, 49, fig 10). Sonia Chadwick Hawkes (1989a, 88) suggested that the growth of this prosperous kingdom owed much to a surviving Roman substructure and Alan Everitt, in his extensive landscape studies, reached much the same conclusion (Everitt 1986, 95). Stuart Brookes and Sue Harrington in their more recent review, however, are less certain on the point (Brookes and Harrington 2010, 25–30). Either way, the nature of the latest Roman occupation in and around Dover must be significant in any consideration of early Anglo-Saxon settlement of the region (Fig 1.1).

In the Dover area, the main focus of fourth-century Roman activity seems to have been within the strongly walled Shore fort, first erected around AD 275 at the mouth of the River Dour on the Channel coast (Philp 1989, 283; *see* p 2). There was apparently no associated extra-mural *vicus* here then (Pearson 2002, 155) and there are presently no known late Roman rural occupation sites within 4km

of the fort. About 1.75km up the valley inland from the Shore fort, the first Anglo-Saxon burials at Buckland may be dated to the second half of the fifth century (*see* p 323; Evison 1987, 142f), implying that the settlement which the cemetery served had been established in that area perhaps as early as *c* AD 450.

Presumably, the very first Anglo-Saxon settlers arrived by boat, taking advantage of the narrow gap that the valley of the River Dour offered as a means of access into the hinterland of east Kent. If this is correct, it immediately raises the question as to whether the Roman Shore fort was still garrisoned and its adjacent harbour still functioning when these Anglo-Saxon colonists landed. This becomes of key significance if there is any truth in the long held view that the primary function of Roman Shore forts was to defend against Anglo-Saxon raiders and pirates who were attempting to gain a foothold on British soil (eg Johnson 1976; Mann 1989, 9–10; Pearson 2002, 131–5). More questions follow. Did the early Anglo-Saxon colonists specifically by-pass the fort and settle further up the Dour valley? Was a settlement of incoming Anglo-Saxons this close to the fort acceptable to any remaining Roman garrison? Was that garrison in any position to oppose incoming Anglo-Saxons?

Exactly how and when the Dover garrison's military duties were discontinued remains unknown. Esmonde Cleary (1989, 140) has rightly observed that if a government ceases paying its soldiers those soldiers will, in due course, cease to serve. As the Imperial administration of Roman Britain started to disintegrate during the early fifth century, this is quite possibly what happened at Dover, the garrison here never being issued with orders either to redeploy or stand down. What would be the plight of such redundant soldiers who were by this time most probably married into, and largely integrated with, the local population?

Fig 9.1. Imaginative reconstruction of the Anglo-Saxon settlement at Buckland overlooked by its hillside cemetery. From an original drawing by the late Michael Copus, reproduced here by courtesy of Dover Museum.

The currently available archaeological evidence indicates that Roman occupation within the Shore fort continued until the earlier part of the fifth century (Wilkinson 1994, 75), although full publication of all the excavated evidence is still awaited. At present, there are no clear answers to any of the questions posed above. In the absence of evidence to the contrary, however, it seems most logical to assume that when the first Anglo-Saxon settlers arrived, the Shore fort defending the Dover gap was no longer manned by any functioning Imperial military unit. The incomers found room enough to settle in the Dour valley, presumably having in some way agreed terms with any existing local population, which might have included descendants of the former Shore fort garrison troops. Anglo-Saxon re-occupation of the old Roman fort itself eventually occurred, but not much before the start of the sixth century (Philp 2003; *see* pp 2–4).

Anglo-Saxon Buckland

As is so often the case in east Kent, Anglo-Saxon cemetery sites must deputise as evidence for settlements (cf Chadwick Hawkes 2000, 2). The cemetery at Buckland, with its discrete burial plots, provides evidence of use over three centuries (*c* AD 450–750) by a well-established local community most probably made up by several separate family/household groups. The presence of some skilled craftsmen in the area is suggested by quality metalwork placed in a number of the burials (see Part 6).

The precise location of the settlement associated with the cemetery at Buckland remains uncertain. Most probably, it was situated somewhere in the valley below Long Hill (Figs 1.2 and 9.1; Evison 1987, 173) and it perhaps lay in the general area of the Norman and later medieval parish church

368

of St Andrew. The church is recorded in the Domesday Book, where it is listed under the possessions of the Canons of St Martin, an important monastic establishment founded at Dover during the seventh century AD (Philp 2003; see below). Church dedications to St Andrew often tend to be relatively early, although they are generally quite rare in Kent (Everitt 1986, 242). The place-name 'Buckland' is of a well-known origin, being derived from 'book land', ie land held by a deed or charter. Similar names occur quite commonly across southern England but there is no documentary record of the present place before 1086.

Somewhere near Buckland church, the old Roman road leading from Dover to Canterbury (later Watling Street; Margary 1967, Route 1a) must have originally crossed the River Dour (Fig 1.2). Such a crossing could have provided a natural focus for settlement (Fig 9.1). A large sherd from an Anglo-Saxon wheel-thrown pottery bottle discovered during the nineteenth century close to the junction of St Radigund's Road with London Road (Watling Street) south-east of the church, might be derived from such a settlement (Evison 1979, 84–5; 1987, 171; Fig 1.2) but there is currently no other evidence for Anglo-Saxon occupation anywhere in the area.

The presence of other valley-side burial grounds on Durham Hill, Priory Hill, Old Park Hill, at Lousyberry Wood, Waters End and Wolverton, clearly implies the existence of further Anglo-Saxon groups occupying portions of the Dour valley adjacent to the Buckland folk, and continuing on into the adjoining Alkham valley (*see* p 4; Fig 1.1; Evison 1987, text fig 36). The cemetery at Buckland, however, presently provides the clearest evidence for the presence of Anglo-Saxon settlers as early as the fifth century. At least twenty-five Buckland graves, including burials of men, women and children, fall within the period *c* AD 450–530 (Phase 1, *see* p 323; Fig 9.2; Table 8.8–8.14) and these are scattered throughout six burial plots, mostly on the lower (1994) part of the excavated site. Datable material found at the other burial places noted above largely belongs to the sixth and seventh centuries but given the much more limited nature of the evidence recovered, this cannot preclude a fifth-century origin for at least some of these other sites. Previous suggestions that the Buckland cemetery reflects the location of an unusually well-armed community strategically positioned close to an Anglo-Saxon port at Dover (Chadwick Hawkes 1969, 191–2) may now be dismissed (Evison 1987, 173), not least on the grounds of distance and the likely existence of other contemporary settlements closer to the sea (*see* p 4; *see also* p 53).

A general model for Anglo-Saxon settlement of the hinterland of Dover, similar to that previously envisaged by Everitt (1986, 75–6), may now be put forward with some reasonable confidence. The evidence implies that by the start of the seventh century a series of occupation sites, presumably in the form of hamlets and farmsteads, were spaced at intervals up the Dour valley, each probably placed close by the old Roman road to Canterbury and the river (Figs 1.1 and 9.1; Parfitt and Dickinson 2007). Cemeteries for these sites were established on the adjacent valley-side, overlooking the settlements, at intervals of between 0.75 and 2km (Parfitt and Dickinson 2007, fig 2). The valley settlements and their associated lands must have soon become firmly established and eventually developed into the medieval parishes of Dover, Charlton, Buckland, River, Ewell and Lydden, several of which are recorded in Domesday. Expansion out of the valley, onto the surrounding high chalkland, also seems to have occurred during this period, with a hamlet founded at Church Whitfield, close by the Roman road from Dover to Richborough, sometime during the sixth century (*see* p 4; Fig 1.1; Parfitt *et al* 1997; Parfitt forthcoming).

A broadly similar settlement pattern has been suggested for the valley of the Little Stour, a short distance to the northwest of the Dour valley. Here, long established villages and hamlets in the valley bottom, such as Barham, Kingston, Patrixbourne and Bekesbourne, are also overlooked by a number of early Anglo-Saxon hillside cemeteries, set between 1 and 3km apart, again implying that these present-day settlements were first established between the fifth and seventh century (Chadwick Hawkes 1982a, 74; Everitt 1986, 79–82; Chadwick Hawkes 2000, 4–6).

The field lynchets on Long Hill

The number and richness of its Anglo-Saxon burials now makes the Buckland site one of the most important post-Roman cemeteries to be excavated anywhere in southern Britain (see below). Nevertheless, the Anglo-Saxon cemetery represents just one phase within a much longer sequence of human activity on this hillside. The available evidence indicates that the slopes of Long Hill had been quite intensively cultivated at times both before and after the cemetery period (*see* pp 9–15 and Figs 2.1 and 2.3). It is clear that the Bronze Age barrow mound above the Anglo-Saxon cemetery (apparently still visible when the cemetery was in use) must have subsequently been completely removed by ploughing, along with a number of smaller Anglo-Saxon mounds (see below). Evison believed that the 1951–3 site had been significantly reduced by post-Saxon ploughing (1987, 11) and the evidence from the 1994 excavations indicates the same for this area.

The use of Long Hill for an Anglo-Saxon burial ground would thus seem to constitute a relatively short interlude within a much longer sequence of agricultural activity here that extended across many centuries. The first ploughing of these slopes apparently occurred in the prehistoric period, during the early Iron Age, if not before, leading to the formation of a series of field lynchets. Further remains of lynchets and cultivation terraces have been noted at several other locations on the sides of the Dour valley. Still preserved on Long Hill itself, in a field to the south-east of Hobart Crescent, are two slight terraces set one above the other and following the contour of the hillside. Large scale nineteenth-century Ordnance Survey maps record the former existence of more lengths of lynchet on this hillside. Other terrace earthworks have been recorded on nearby Old Park Hill (Cross and Parfitt 1999), in Lousyberry Wood above Temple Ewell (Phillips 1964) and at Lydden. Collectively, these surviving lynchets and terraces provide positive evidence for the former cultivation of substantial areas on the south-facing slopes of the Dour valley. Today, none of these slopes are under the plough and most are occupied by rough grassland, scrub and trees. Although the dating is generally uncertain, many of the terraces recorded are likely to be medieval but others are quite possibly of prehistoric origin (see below).

At the foot of Long Hill, colluvium containing prehistoric pottery and struck flints, together with some Roman finds, was exposed during building work in the late nineteenth century (Osborne White 1928, 68). More recently, down-washed sediments that must also have been eroded from the valley slopes, very probably as a result of agricultural activity, have been identified at several more localities in the bottom of the Dour valley (Barham and Bates 1990; Bates *et al* 2008, 325). A site at Dryden Road, about 500 metres to the north-west of Long Hill, on the lower slopes of Old Park Hill, revealed prehistoric colluvial soils containing finds which suggested that cultivation of the valley slopes there began during the late Bronze Age–early Iron Age period (Corke and Parfitt 1997).

The prehistoric lynchets excavated on Long Hill may be interpreted as representing part of a more extensive ancient field system (Fig 2.1). Frequently remaining as earthworks on the chalklands of central southern England, surviving prehistoric field systems are virtually unknown across the intensively farmed county of Kent (Fowler 1983, 96), where most have probably been destroyed by later agricultural activity. It now seems likely that the Anglo-Saxon cemetery at Buckland was specifically established on this part of Long Hill in order to take advantage of the slightly more level areas of ground that an old field-system had left on this steep slope.

The later cultivation terraces identified on Long Hill, together with some of the surviving earthwork remains on other local slopes may be more readily identified as being medieval strip lynchets. There are many examples across the country of hillsides where prehistoric fields have subsequently been cut across by such later field systems (Bowen 1969, 19; Taylor 1975, 155); Long Hill appears to be another example of this. The steep, chalky slopes of the Dour valley can never have been prime agricultural land and their cultivation in both pre- and post-Anglo-Saxon times must be indicative of periods when there was considerable pressure for farmland. This, in turn, implies the presence of very substantial populations in the immediate area during these periods.

The cemetery

Keith Parfitt

Size and extent

There can be no doubt that the Anglo-Saxon burials recorded at Buckland in 1994 relate to the same cemetery site as those which were excavated in the 1950s (Fig 1.3). It is now equally apparent, however, that this cemetery had distinct burial areas or plots contained within it, which reflect social groups and/or chronological developments. Evison has discussed such arrangements for the upper part of the cemetery in some detail but her findings must now be reconsidered in the light of the more extensive recent discoveries.

The excavations of 1994 dramatically demonstrated that the cemetery at Buckland was very much larger than had been envisaged during the 1950s work. Present day Hobart Crescent, following a prominent shoulder on the middle slopes of the Long Hill spur, seems to mark the northern, uphill edge of the burial area and much of this part of the site was fully examined before its destruction in the 1950s. From here graves extended south-westwards, down the hillside, at least as far as Mayfield Avenue which formed the south-western limit of the 1994 Castle View site. An unknown number of graves were destroyed in this area during an earlier phase of building work. Members of the Kent Archaeological Rescue Unit had visited the site on several occasions during the early stages of the work here during the 1980s, without result (Peter Keller, pers comm). Clearly, the cemetery area had been reached sometime after the site visits ceased, and graves went unrecorded. Workers employed at the site have since confirmed their discovery of 'old bones' and 'iron daggers'.

It is also now apparent that a significant number of graves must also have been destroyed during the construction of the Dover–Deal railway line cut through Long Hill during 1879–1880 (*see* pp 4–5). The width of the railway cutting ranges between 25 and 45 metres and although no certain record of any burials being found during its creation survives (but *see* p 5), it seems possible from the grave density on some other parts of the site that 100 burials or more could have been then destroyed. In overall terms, the complete cemetery on Long Hill must have once covered an area measuring at least 230m (north-east to south-west) by 190m (north-west to south-east), over 4 hectares in extent, and contained well in excess of 500 graves.

Thus, even though extensive excavations have now been undertaken at Buckland, a complete plan of the cemetery has not been recovered. Damage caused by medieval ploughing, the nineteenth-century railway cutting and building work during the 1950s and the 1980s means that an unknown number of graves have been destroyed without record. Moreover, it seems very likely that another significant group of burials remain to be located under the half hectare of uncultivated scrubland that lies between the railway line and the back gardens of houses fronting onto Napier Road (Fig 1.3). Nor can it be certain given the difficult circumstances that the 1950s excavations succeeded in locating all the burials within the areas examined. Overall, then, it seems probable that not much more than half the total number of graves originally present on the site might have actually been recorded (Fig 1.3). Whilst more burials may yet be excavated, a substantial number of others have already gone. When given up around AD 750, the complete burial ground may perhaps have held close to 1,000 men, woman and children taken from a local Anglo-Saxon community over a period of about 300 years. An average interment rate for the entire cemetery might thus perhaps have been as high as three or four bodies per year.

Even though they do not represent the complete population of the cemetery, a total of 415 individual graves has now been fully excavated and recorded at Buckland (Fig 1.3). The large assemblage of skeletal and artefactual material recovered constitutes a major resource for future research into early Anglo-Saxon cemeteries. It is to be hoped that evolving scientific analyses, such as DNA testing of human bone (*see* pp 320–2) and Oxygen Isotope analysis of tooth enamel, and continually developing artefact studies will, in the future, provide further insights into the social structure and evolution of this important Anglo-Saxon burial ground.

Layout and evolution

The excavations in 1951–3 revealed the remains of a Bronze Age round barrow on the northern edge of the cemetery and this seems to have acted as a local focus for some of the late sixth- to seventh-century Anglo-Saxon graves (principally those of Plot E; Fig 1.3; Evison 1987, fig 98). Nevertheless, it would seem that this prehistoric monument did not specifically exert any direct influence on many other (earlier) parts of the cemetery. Elsewhere in England, the association of Anglo-Saxon burial areas with prehistoric barrows is now firmly established (Williams 1997; 1998; Lucy 2000, 126) and is particularly well illustrated locally by the Mill Hill cemetery at Deal (Parfitt and Brugmann 1997, 12). Less frequently, other ancient structures such as enclosures, linear earthworks and route ways, also had some influence on cemetery positioning and layout (Williams 1997; 1998; Lucy 2000, 128). In this context the presence of an ancient field system (see above), which had existed on the side of Long Hill centuries before the Anglo-Saxon cemetery was established, may also have been considered to be significant.

The reason for the association of Anglo-Saxon cemeteries with earlier monuments and earthworks has now been studied in some detail. It would seem that such places were widely viewed by the Anglo-Saxons as being sacred sites, often endowed with supernatural forces and providing links to ancient ancestors, as well as demonstrating long held rights to the local land (Williams 1997, 25; Lucy 2000, 130). The early barrow at Buckland may have been seen in exactly this way, with the ancient field system adjacent perhaps imparting a further spiritual significance to the general area, as well as conveniently providing some relatively level areas for graves needing to be placed on a steep chalk hillside.

Comparison of the respective cemetery plans for the 1951–3 and 1994 excavations indicates some significant differences in grave spacing and layout, although orientations were all broadly the same (Fig 1.3). It is immediately apparent that the density of graves was generally very much higher on the 1994 part of the site (Fig 2.2). Taken with the evidence from other east Kent cemetery sites, it would now appear that the spacing of graves has some broad chronological significance (*see* pp 325–9; Parfitt and Brugmann 1997, 121). Late fifth- and sixth-century graves are frequently arranged more closely than later burials (*see* pp 29–30 and below).

The wider spacing of late graves may have been to allow the erection of a covering mound over individual burials. Cemeteries of such small Anglo-Saxon barrows once survived in some numbers across east Kent, including the local burial sites at Old Park (*see* p 4 and Fig 1.1; Hasted 1800, 438) and Bay Hill, St Margaret's (Douglas 1793, 119). Today, virtually all these barrow fields, with the exception of that on Breach Down near Barham, have been destroyed by ploughing. The majority of the examples excavated by early antiquaries contained graves datable to the later sixth and seventh centuries (Douglas 1793; Faussett 1856; Parfitt and Brugmann 1997, 121; Richardson 2005, i, 68–9; 112–16). It now seems quite possible that another Anglo-Saxon barrow field once existed on part of Long Hill, mostly covering the later graves on the upper part of the cemetery but with a few in the lower (1994) area. In this context, it is of interest to recall a comment made by William Stukeley who noted 'many barrows on the hills around Dover' (Stukeley 1776, 128).

Areas with either close or widely spaced graves identified at Buckland indicate discrete zones, used for burials during either the fifth to sixth or seventh to eighth centuries (Figs 1.3, 8.3 and Evison 1987, figs 101–7). Thus, the majority of the earlier graves occur on that part of the site excavated in 1994 (Fig 9.2), with the bulk of the later burials lying further uphill in the 1950s area. On the upper part of the site, a general easterly drift along the hillside is also apparent, so that the eighth-century graves tend to lie at a considerable distance from the earliest graves. Evison has previously suggested that this eastward drift was following the edge of a trackway (1987, 145). This certainly remains possible but in the light of the 1994 excavations it may be alternatively suggested that it reflects the influence of another early cultivation terrace.

Within the very broad chronologically defined zones indicated by the grave spacings the Buckland cemetery may be further subdivided into twenty-three separate burial plots of varying size and density of burial, based on grave distribution (pp 15–19; Fig 2.4; Evison 1987, fig 98). Most of these plots are probably best interpreted as family/household burial areas, which remained in use for differing lengths of time (see below for further discussion). A mixture of variously aged men, women and children had been buried within these areas, such as might reflect the range of mortalities amongst a family or household group over the years. The most important men are identifiable by the provision of a sword, an expensive and prestigious weapon throughout the Anglo-Saxon world. Seven males armed with swords were recorded in 1994, with no less than three contained within Plot S (see pp 17 and 49). The 1950s work had recovered a further seventeen sword burials, including one (Grave C) comprising an ornately decorated ring-sword, which must have been the possession of a particularly important man, perhaps a head-man or elder (Evison 1967).

Some of the smaller plots identified seem to contain too few graves to represent standard family/household plots

and these may have been special burial areas, specifically set apart from the main area used by a particular group (see p 16, and below).

Six plots, mostly situated in the 1994 excavated area, contain graves assignable to Phase 1 (c AD 450–510/30; Table 8.7). Plot A, located on the north-western edge of the known cemetery, seemingly stood apart from the rest (Fig 3.1; Fig 9.2). Its full extent could not be established and a number of related graves may well have been destroyed by the initial building work in 1951 (Evison 1987, 172). In view of the unknown extent of the graves lost to building and the railway, it must remain uncertain whether this plot originally stood in isolation from the other early grave groups. Despite the presence of an early sword grave here (Grave 22), there is no clear evidence from the grave finds to suggest that the occupants of this plot were generally of any higher social status than others buried further downhill. Either way, the graves assigned to Phase 1 must represent the burials of the earliest Anglo-Saxon inhabitants of the Buckland area. It may be tentatively suggested that a minimum of half a dozen separate family/household groups founded the cemetery here sometime during the second half of the fifth century (see above).

The results of DNA tests (see pp 320–2) have provided two examples of familial relationships, which help shed some light on the nature and use of the burial plots. The well-equipped men with swords buried in adjacent Phase 3 Graves 264 and 265B (Plot S) were perhaps brothers from a family of some status. A family connection between Plots X and Y is provided by another pair of well-equipped males provided with swords. The individual in Phase 2 Grave 437 of Plot Y seems to have been a relative of the Phase 3b warrior in possible barrow Grave 375 on the western edge of Plot X. Detailed analysis of the skeletal remains has also occasionally hinted at other possible family connections (see pp 315 and 320).

It thus seems possible that something of the original social structure of the associated settlement is reflected within the layout of the Buckland cemetery. However, this settlement need not have been a nucleated one; perhaps families were more dispersed, with the cemetery on Long Hill providing a focus for the burial of a number of scattered family/household groups occupying different parts of the valley below.

With time, fresh burial plots were founded in the cemetery as it moved further up the hillside, although whether these were set up by newcomers in an expanding community, or were fresh plots belonging to long-established families who had used up the available space in their traditional areas, is less clear (see below).

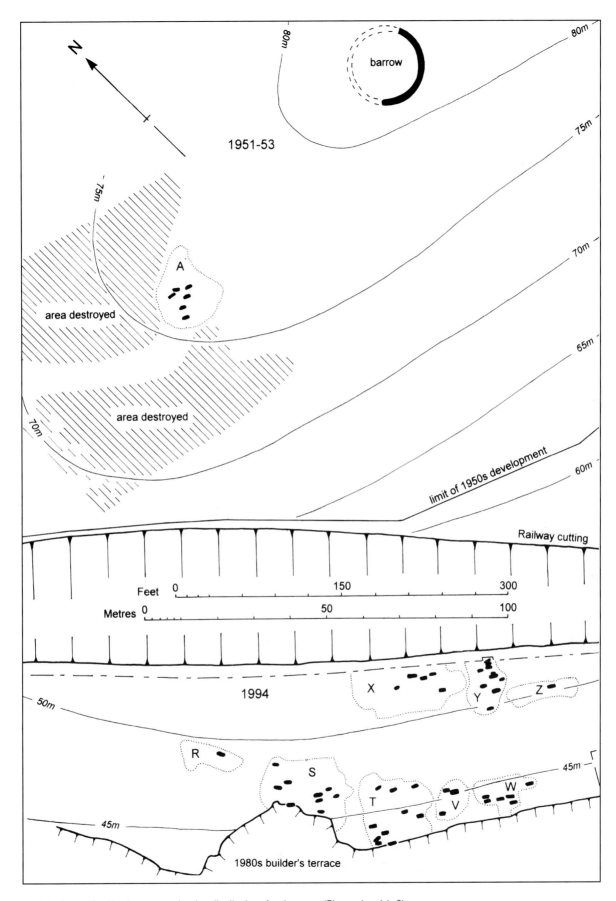

Fig 9.2. Plan of Buckland cemetery showing distribution of early graves (Phases 1 and 1–2).

Population size

As part of the cemetery analysis some attempt was made to estimate the size of the living population that the substantial burial ground at Buckland might represent. The number of unknown variables in relation to the quantitative data available, however, combined to make any conclusions reached little more than speculation. Figures arrived at suggested that the cemetery might have drawn from a living population of around 50–100 individuals, but whether this in anyway reflects the true situation must remain unknown.

Male graves and weapon combinations

Ian Riddler and Axel Kerep with Stephanie Spain

The ownership of weapons during the Anglo-Saxon period was a matter of legal right; consequently, their burial with an individual male may be a reflection of his status within the community. The spear seems to have been carried by all freemen (Swanton 1973, 3); men of higher status would also possess a double-edged broad sword. Nevertheless, the deposition of such weapons within graves also seems to be partially dictated by fashion, so that weapon burials tend to be rare in the fifth century but become much more common in the sixth, before declining again in the seventh century.

Forty-eight of the skeletons within the graves from the 1994 excavations have been identified as males on the basis of the osteological study by the late Trevor Anderson (see Part 7). A further thirty-two individuals were initially classed as possibly male. Analysis of the grave goods suggests that five of the questionable males could, in fact, have been female, and nineteen are indeterminate. Three have male gender from the grave goods, and five others are probably male on that basis. Equally, eight of the graves where bone survival was poor or non-existent appear to be male, judging from the grave goods alone and three others may also be male.

Male graves without weapons

If the sex of the individual is taken to be the most reliable attribute, with grave goods a secondary criterion, a corpus of around eighty burials can be assembled, which may have been the interments of males, virtually all of whom were adults. This is slightly larger than the sample noted in Part 5, but it does include several graves that are not certainly male. Twenty-one of these burials have no grave goods at all. Of those males with grave goods, the first group consists of those buried with a single item, for which a total of sixteen

graves can be identified from the 1994 excavations. Within this sample that object is a knife (six graves), a buckle (nine graves) or a pin (one grave). For the purposes of this analysis structural ironwork is considered to be part of the burial arrangement, rather than the grave goods. Five of the six graves with knives on their own include simple examples with whittle tangs and horn handles (Graves 321, 379, 386B, 405 and 438). Grave 206 is distinguished from the remainder by the presence of a large knife, and it is considered below as a weapon burial. Three graves from the earlier excavations (Graves 111, 120 and 125) also fall into this category. Most of these graves contained adult males, the only exception being Grave 438 (young adult, aged 15–17).

Nine graves merely contained buckles, either of copper alloy or iron, with one example of bone. As noted above (p 130) these buckles do not include shield-tongue or club-shaped tongue forms, which only occur at Buckland in the graves of females. This type of grave was not common in the earlier excavations, and only one example was recorded (Grave 36). They are all graves of adults, aged at least 25–30, with most of them over 30. One male grave (Grave 292) merely contained a copper alloy pin (a), of an unusual, hollow type (Fig 10.28).

Eleven graves include two items, usually both of iron, one of which is a knife. It has been noted above (p 171) that the combination of a knife and a buckle is characteristic of a male grave. In the same way, where the grave goods are limited to a pin and a knife, that also signifies a male grave. Four examples of 'knife and pin' graves are known from the 1994 excavations, and there are two from the earlier excavations. Grave 434 is the burial of a male adult and Graves 136, 260 (which included two pins) and 416 are mature adult males. A knife and pin combination also accompanied the child burial in Grave 431. The pins are invariably made of iron (p 120). In each case the pin and the knife were found in close proximity and usually at, or near to the waist, although in Grave 416 both the pin and the knife had been positioned above the skull. Grave 351A is similar, although a miscellaneous collection of an ear-ring and a Roman coin were also in the grave, alongside the pin and the knife. The two graves from the earlier excavations (Graves 136 and150) were both placed into the seventh century by Evison (1987, 175–6).

Graves with a combination of a knife and a buckle are a little more common with seven examples (Table 4.32); ten graves of this type came from the earlier Buckland excavations. The deceased within this group range from children (Graves 34 and 350A) to adult and mature adults, the latter including two graves (Graves 149 and 248) with skeletons aged at least 60 years at death.

Several male graves included knives in addition to other miscellaneous grave goods, but with an absence of buckles. Grave 228B included a knife and a copper alloy mount, possibly from a box, which lay near the left shoulder of the deceased. Beyond the head of Grave 246 lay an arrangement of small nails, possibly from a box or a gaming board, again by the left shoulder. A ceramic vessel lay in the same position in Grave 295, with a knife situated at the waist.

Male graves can therefore be identified from the combinations of knife and buckle or knife and pin, but not with the combination of buckle and pin without a knife, which does not occur at Buckland. Three further male graves provide combinations of a knife, a buckle and a pin, and other items were also present in one of those graves. In Grave 442 a firesteel lay with a knife and a pin, with a buckle nearby. Tweezers are present in two graves (Graves 215 and 367). Where tweezers are present, pins are absent.

In functional terms, the male graves without weapons include several categories of object. The principal items are the knife and the buckle. The knife is sometimes accompanied by a pin and some of these pins are placed at the waist and are likely to echo a Frankish fashion for the use of the *fiche* or *fiche patte*, an object which accompanies the knife. The buckle often represents the sole item of dress within these graves, unless the pin is at the neck or skull. Personal grooming is reflected in the presence of tweezers.

Weapon combinations

Thirty-two graves from the 1994 excavations included a weapon of some form. Six groups of weapon combinations have been outlined by Härke (1989b, table 4.3; 1992a, 109 and table 9) and these are all represented within the Buckland cemetery (Table 9.1). In addition, Härke has suggested that large knives may represent a late form of the weapon rite (Härke 1989a, 147; 1992a, 89–90). Accordingly, a category of Knife Combinations has been added to Tables 4.2 and 9.1. The quantity of weapons for the 1994 excavations is shown in Table 9.2.

Graves containing a spear alone are the most common, both within the sample from the 1994 excavations and the cemetery as a whole. In relative terms, there are fewer examples from the 1950s excavations, although that is a reflection of the increased number of sword combinations (Fig 9.1). They form around 40 per cent of the overall sample of weapon combinations, a similar figure to the 46.4 per cent provided by Härke (1989b, fig 4.4) for Kent as a whole. They represented the most common combination at Mill Hill also (Parfitt and Brugmann 1997, 90). Spear graves are generally limited to adult males but there are exceptions, including

Group	1951–3 excavations	1994 excavations
Spear combinations		
Spear only	12	15
Shield combinations		
Shield and spear	3	3
Sword combinations		
Sword and spear	5	1
Sword and fauchard		1
Sword, shield and spear	7	4
Sword, shield, spear and large knife	1	
Sword, seax, shield and spear	1	
Sword, Axe and Spear		1
Seax combinations		
Seax only		1
Seax and spear	1	
Arrow combinations		
Arrow only	1	2
Knife combinations		
Large knife only		2
Large knife and spear	1	2

Table 9.1. Buckland: weapon combinations.

Weapon	No of burials with this weapon	% of all weapon burials
Spear	26	89.7
Shield	7	24.1
Sword	7	24.1
Seax	1	3.4
Axe	1	3.4
Arrow	2	6.9
Fauchard	1	1.6
Large knife	2	6.9

Table 9.2. Buckland 1994. Frequency of weapon types. (Total number of weapon burials = 29.)

the possible adolescent in Grave 57 and the juveniles in Graves 137, 240 and 400, as well as the child aged 4–6 in Grave 411.

Seax combinations are confined to a burial where it is the only weapon (Grave 381) and a grave where it occurs with a spear (Grave 65). A seax was found with a sword, shield and spear in Grave 93. These combinations reflect those recorded by Geake (1997, 75). The two seax combination graves contained adult males, aged at least 30 at death, and the same is true also for Grave 93. The large knife combinations follow the same pattern as those for the seax, with a large knife on its own in Grave 206, and large knives with spears in Graves 135, 299 and 393A. Several *fiches* and a set of tweezers also came from Grave 65 and two clench nails were present in Grave 135. Three of these graves contained adult males aged at least 25–30, but Grave 206 was that of a juvenile, aged 13–15. Thus, whilst seax combination graves are confined to adult males, male graves with large knife combinations can encompass younger individuals. This contrasts with the situation envisaged by Härke (1992b, 162), under which the large knife is regarded as a symbol of male adult status. For the purposes of this study (and in slight contrast to Härke 1992b, 162) large knives are defined as having blades of 140–180mm, not 130–170mm (*see* p 166).

Single arrowheads came from Graves 139, 302 and 421. Two of the three graves were the internments of children or juveniles, whilst the other (Grave 302) contained an adult. The association of children with arrowheads, or 'miniature' spears, has been noted by Härke (1992a, 86 and 190–5; 1992b, table 4). The presence of a single arrowhead in an adult male grave, with the head pointing towards the foot of the grave, is unusual. Evison's hand list suggests that in adult graves they usually occurred with other weapons (Evison 1987, 30).

Shield and spear combinations were found in six graves altogether (Graves 5, 39, 90, 230, 297 and 323). One of the graves (Grave 5) was disturbed but the others were not and they contain few other grave goods beyond a knife and buckle (Graves 39 and 230), a knife and wooden bowl (Grave 90), and a knife, buckle and cone beaker (Grave 297). Where the age of the deceased could be determined (in three of the six graves), it was an adult of at least 30 years. Shield combinations are less common in Kent and Sussex than the rest of England but Kent has the highest proportion of swords and seaxes, effectively providing an alternative burial rite (Härke 1992a, Tab 9 and Abb 16; Dickinson and Härke 1992, 70). The figures suggest that 'the sword and the shield may have been used as alternatives in the burial ritual'. Kent's preference for swords over shields may be due to its wealth or its close links with the Continent, as 'Kentish frequencies of weapon types in burials are closer to the continental figures than are the frequencies in any of the other English regions' (*ibid*).

Sword combinations are prominent, particularly within the 1951–3 sample, but also from the 1994 excavations. There are six forms of sword combination in Table 9.1 but four of these are represented by single graves. Evison has noted that some of the graves from her excavations were disturbed, so that the quantity of sword and spear graves could be a little high and some of those graves may originally

have included shields as well (Evison 1987, 15, 16). The overall total of sword combinations within the weapon graves from Buckland may seem reasonably high but Ager has rightly noted that the percentage of swords from the cemetery as a whole is roughly average and no more than would be expected (*see* pp 52–3) and Härke has established that sword combinations are more common in Kent than elsewhere (Härke 1992a, 111 and Abb 16).

In six graves (Graves 22, 33, 41, 94B, 96B and 249C) a sword is accompanied by a spear and in one further grave the associated weapon is a fauchard (Grave 437). As with the knife, seax and shield combination graves, there were few other grave goods in these burials. They are limited to a cone beaker (Grave 22), iron pins at the waist (Grave 33) or neck (Grave 96B), tweezers (Grave 41), a wooden vessel (Grave 249C) and a copper alloy strip (Grave 94B). The grave with the fauchard differs markedly from this sample, however. It contained a glass bowl, two iron pins, tweezers, a Roman coin and a pursemount or firesteel. This is possibly a Frankish grave, although it is more appropriate to highlight its continental elements and to note the differences between it and the other sword combination graves.

Grave 346 included an axe, in addition to a sword and spear, as well as a knife, buckle and iron rod. The rod may well represent another iron pin, situated at the waist. The grave contained a male aged at least 40 at death. Axes are much more common in Frankish graves than in Anglo-Saxon burials, as Kerep has noted above (pp 69–70). They are limited both geographically and in terms of their distribution, occurring only in southern England, during the fifth and sixth centuries (Härke 1992a, 105, 106 and Abb 14).

Sword, shield and spear graves outnumber those of other combinations at Buckland, as they do in early Anglo-Saxon England as a whole (Härke 1989b, table 4.3). The combinations from Buckland include sword, shield and spear alone (Graves C, 27, 71, 91, 96A, 98, 131, 264, 265B, 375 and 414), or in association with a seax (Grave 93) or large knife (Grave 56). Most of these graves contain little else, beyond the typical addition of a knife and buckle. An iron pin lay by the spearhead in Grave 96A and may have secured textile around the blade. A small iron cleat in Grave 375 was probably used in the construction of the coffin for that grave. A *fiche à bélière* and two awl-like firesteels were recovered from Grave 414 (*see* pp 146–7). The deceased in male graves with sword combinations from Buckland were invariably adults, aged at least 20–30 years at death. The body in Grave 131 was described, however, as a 'young adult' (Evison 1987, 125 and 245).

Two graves (C and 265B) are distinguished from the remainder by the presence of scales and weights (*see* pp 150–3) and these represent the most auspicious of the male graves from the cemetery. Grave 265B also included an awl-like firesteel and a fragment of a Roman lead object. In general, weapon burials possess more grave goods than male graves without weapons, in conformity with the general trend in early Anglo-Saxon England (Härke 1992b, 150–1). A whole level of male grave is missing from the Buckland cemetery, however, notwithstanding the excavation of over 400 burials. There are no examples of the larger male graves of late sixth- or early seventh-century date, which could have included horse equipment, angons, Byzantine bowls, gaming pieces or, very occasionally a second shield, as well as iron-bound wooden buckets (Härke 1992a, 91–4). Some of these burials were enclosed within barrows and lay within chambers; they are entirely absent here.

A further aspect of the male graves lies with burials containing obvious injuries; these have been summarised by Anderson (1996b, and pp 305–8 above). Two graves (Graves 303B and 348) showed evidence of cranial weapon injuries, probably caused by a sword (Grave 348) and an axe (Grave 303B). Neither grave is a weapon burial. There were no objects in Grave 303B, and Grave 348 included a knife, buckle and pin.

Age thresholds

The graves with weapon combinations conform to some extent with the age thresholds established by Härke (1992b, table 4; 1997, 127–9). The first archaeological threshold is represented by the child of 4–6 years from Grave 411 (buried with a spear) and the child of 3–4 years from Grave 421 (buried with an arrowhead). These follow the pattern established by Härke (1992b, table 4). The second threshold, in archaeological terms, is provided by males aged *c* 12 years (Härke 1997, 128), at which point they can be buried with swords and shields. However, 'the shield was deposited primarily in adult burials, and only very occasionally with juveniles' under the age of 18 years (Dickinson and Härke 1992, 69). It is believed to have been 'deposited … mostly as a token of male adult status within those families or social groups which practised weapon burial' (*ibid*).

At Buckland, males between 4 and 18 years are provided only with a spear (Graves 240 and 374) or a large knife (Grave 206), with the exception perhaps of the young adult from Grave 131. Similarly, the graves with weapon combinations from Mill Hill, Deal were entirely confined to male adults, the youngest estimated at 18–20 years (Parfitt and Brugmann 1997, table 8).

Only adults aged 18–20 onwards appear to be buried with axes, seaxes or scales and weights (Härke 1992b, table 4; 1997, 128) and this is the case at Buckland. Indeed, with the

exception of Grave 265B, the deceased are aged at least 30, and fall into the 'senior adult' category, as noted also by Härke (1997, 128). The deceased buried with a seax at Mill Hill died aged 25–35 (Parfitt and Brugmann 1997, table 8).

Senior adults (aged 30 onwards) were granted access to the full range of weapon combinations. Buckland also included the graves of several male individuals who died at the age of at least 50 (Graves 227, 248, 291, 328 and 401). Only one of these graves included any grave goods at all (Grave 248) and comprising a knife and a buckle. This age group was not included in Härke's calculations (Härke 1992b, table 4; 1997, 129).

Plots and founder graves

Evison associated the sword graves from Buckland with their plots, which she interpreted as family groups (Evison 1987, 145–6). The sword graves could be regarded as the founder burials in most of the plots. Subsequently, it has rightly been noted that the plots are better regarded as households, rather than families (Härke 1997, 139; Stoodley 1999, 129; see above). As noted above (p 322), there is a DNA link between Graves 375 and 437, both of which provided swords but belonged to different, if adjoining plots. This may reflect Härke's work on epigenetic traits, under which weapon burials are linked together (Härke 1992b, 155). Härke observed patterns at Finglesham and Berinsfield, Oxfordshire, in certain genetically transmitted skeletal traits used to identify family relationships. For example, 'individuals buried with weapons have some traits which do not appear among individuals without weapons' (Härke 1990, 41). At three further cemeteries for which data was gathered the evidence was inconclusive.

At Buckland, Grave 206 is prominent at the centre of Plot R but, as a relatively late male burial equipped only with a large knife, it is unlikely to have been the founder burial for this plot. A number of burials with weapon combinations are gathered together in Plot S, including Graves 220, 230, 233, 262, 264, 265B, 337, 346 and 400. This plot includes three of the seven burials with swords. According to the chronological system, however, none of these graves can be as early as the accompanying females, some of which go back to Phase 1 (*see* p 379). The layout of this burial plot is difficult to interpret, given the loss of burials to the south. It does resemble oval-shaped burial plans which (accepting the vagaries and uncertainties of phasing) may devolve from a central focus. The Anglo-Saxon cemetery at Mount Pleasant on the Isle of Thanet is a good example of this type; the dispersed burials to the north of the barrow at Holborough are also similar, as well as the lower part of Plot D at Buckland 1951–3 (Riddler

2008; Evison 1956, fig 3; Härke 1992, Abb 59; Evison 1987, fig 98). Grave 230 lies towards the centre of Plot S and it would be a perfect candidate for a founder burial; but as with Grave 206, it appears to be relatively late (Phase 2b–3a). Both plots may therefore have begun with inauspicious male and female burials, suggesting that weapon burial is not a feature of the earliest phases of the cemetery, and does not become prominent until the sixth century.

Plot T has very few weapon burials and includes only Graves 302, 323 and 363. Grave 302 lies on the periphery of the plot, whilst Graves 323 and 363 sit within one of its rows. Here, as with almost all of the plots, the female graves go back to Phase 1, whilst the weapon burials are scarcely seen before Phase 3. This may reflect the changing circumstances of weapon burial, highlighted once again by Härke, with marked changes in its later phases (Härke 1992b, 159–64). Buckland forms a good illustration both of sixth-century weapon burial and of its decline across the middle and second half of the seventh century. The late sixth- to early seventh-century transition is not well represented, however. As well as the missing rich burials there is also a noticeable lack of the smaller group 3 and transitional group 3/6 shield bosses, which typify the more average burials around this time.

By the late sixth century male burial wealth had become concentrated in a small number of adult graves (Härke 1992b, 162); but those graves themselves had become more significant and some of them (as at Saltwood, Kent, for example) formed foci for later burials, either within a burial plot, or within a complete cemetery. As noted above, this situation is not reflected at Buckland.

There are no weapon burials from the small Plot U and there is merely a grave with a spear (Grave 240) from Plot V. Plot W includes one grave with a sword (Grave 249C), as well as two graves with spears (Graves 251 and 256). Grave 375, perhaps a barrow burial (*see* p 372), lies on the edge of Plot X, with Graves 393 and 427 enclosed within penannular ditches. They may have formed a focus of burial. The two graves with spears (Graves 374 and 411) are equally peripheral to this plot.

Plot Z consists of just six graves but amidst these are, one grave with a shield and spear (Grave 297), two with spears (Graves 300 and 301) and one with a large knife and spear (Grave 299). Four of the six graves are thus weapon burials. The other two graves are those of females. With this plot (unlike any other from the 1994 excavations) the earliest grave could be a weapon burial, with Grave 300 provided with the earliest phasing (Phase 1b–2a). But if Plot Z is considered to be nothing more than an extension to Plot Y (*see* p 16), then none of the earliest, founding graves within the 1994 part of the cemetery are weapon burials.

Buckland in its continental context

Birte Brugmann

In her analysis of Buckland 1951–3, Vera Evison (1987, 142f) saw Plot A as the one which 'contains the earliest settlers whose possessions suggest a mixture of Franks and Danes or Jutes, with perhaps an Angle and a Saxon'. This puts in a nutshell what much of the research on early medieval Kent in a continental context has been concerned with: aspects of migration and ethnicity. Research carried out since the publication of Buckland 1951–3 has emphasised the difficulties associated with identifying the provenance or ethnic identity of an individual on the basis of grave goods (Brugmann 2011).

Ethnic identification becomes difficult once it is not assumed that only Saxons would have worn saucer brooches, only Anglians annular brooches and only women of Kent, Kentish disc brooches. It has been argued that, though Kentish material culture includes a range of object types mainly distributed on the Continent and Scandinavia, the grave context of these objects would make most well-equipped fifth- and sixth-century Kentish women's graves conspicuously odd in a contemporary continental or Scandinavian context, and that the use of imported brooch types therefore was a feature of regional female dress styles (Parfitt and Brugmann 1997, 110ff). A plot-by-plot survey of those Buckland graves well enough equipped to be closely dated to a phase, or sub-phase, no later than Phase 3a on the basis of their grave goods, confirms this pattern.

Plot A

Nine graves in this plot contained objects for which analysis has provided information about dating and provenance. During Phase 1, some individuals were buried with objects that have a main distribution in Kent, 'Saxon' England or the Continent; in Phase 2 'Kentish' and 'Frankish' types dominate. None of the graves provides a particularly compelling case for an immigrant, on the basis of the grave goods. Their combinations, rather, suggest a heterogeneous material culture, particularly during Phase 1:

Grave 21   (Phase 1a): The buckle with a gilt and garnet-set plate is probably a continental product and a type of object one would expect to find with a well-equipped male. As such, it is an unusual accessory in the grave of a child also buried with a spindle-whorl and therefore probably female.

Grave 22   (Phase 1): The cone beaker found with this armed male may have been produced in the Rhineland, Northern France, or in Kent (Evison 1987, 94ff).

Grave 13   (Phase 1b): the two 'Jutish-Kentish' square-headed brooches in this grave were made in Kent (Evison 1987, 35ff).

Grave 48   (Phase 1b): the juvenile in this grave would be conspicuous in a Saxon context because the button brooch and the saucer brooch were not worn at the shoulders but in the manner of *Dress Style III* (*see* pp 184–7).

Grave 20   (Phase 2a): this child was buried with Frankish types of brooch and buckle, and with Frankish types of vessels, but also with a bracteate and Kentish types of brooches.

Grave 23   (Phase 2a): the young adult in this grave with a rosette brooch would probably not stand out in a continental row-grave cemetery.

Grave 92   (Phase 2): this young adult combined a Frankish disc brooch with a Kentish disc brooch.

Grave 15   (Phase 2): a ?male adult combined a shield-on-tongue buckle with an armlet, an inconclusive combination.

Grave 14   (Phase 2): a young adult with a Kentish disc brooch.

Plot S

Phase 1 includes mainly Kentish brooches; Phase 2 is dominated by Kentish and continental brooch types and shield-on-tongue buckles:

Grave 219   (Phase 1a): the young adult was buried with a button brooch.

Grave 261   (Phase 1): a juvenile with an inlaid buckle would not seem conspicuous in a continental context.

Grave 351B (Phase 1): the small-long brooches include a variation of a bow-brooch with five knobs and were combined with a cruciform brooch. None of the brooches were worn at the shoulders but in *Dress Style IV* (*see* p 187). This grave, of a mature adult, would be considered unusual in any context.

Grave 221   (Phase 1b): the adult was buried with a button brooch.

Grave 263B (Phase 1b): the dress of this young adult includes small Kentish square-headed brooches.

Grave 266   (Phase 1b–2a): the grave of this adult would probably not be conspicuous in a continental row-grave context, though it is well equipped. The pair of Frankish bow brooches is not combined with other brooch types.

Grave 348   (Phase 1b–2a): this adult was buried with a high-quality belt set, as it would usually be found in a well-equipped male grave on the Continent. The organic and copper alloy container in the grave (b) would be unusual in any context (quiver?).

Grave 347   (Phase 2a): continental types of brooches are combined with a Kentish small square-headed brooch.

Grave 354   (Phase 2b): a shield-on-tongue buckle is combined with a Kentish disc brooch.

Grave 398   (Phase 2b–3a): the shield-on-tongue buckle was not used for a belt but associated with a knife and other objects above the knees, probably suspended from a belt.

Plot T

Phase 1 is represented by Kentish brooches, an annular brooch and an assortment of continental types of buckle.

Grave 334   (Phase 1a): a child buried with a large and ornamental buckle would be noteworthy in a continental context, but not identifiable as Kentish.

Grave 290   (Phase 1): this young adult buried with a button brooch and a strainer would be recognised as Kentish in a continental or Scandinavian context.

Grave 308   (Phase 1): in an Anglian context, the buckle associated with the annular brooch would be recognised as unusual, but not as Kentish.

Grave 355   (Phase 1): this young adult buried with a glass bowl would not stand out in a continental context.

Grave 281   (Phase 1b): this young adult was buried with two Kentish types of brooch among other objects.

Grave 327   (Phase 1b–2a): this adult female, buried with a buckle possessing a club-shaped tongue and matching studs but no other dress accessories except beads, probably would not look out of place in a continental row-grave context.

Grave 336   (Phase 2b): the adult with the bead set and buckle loop associated in this grave would probably not stand out in a row-grave cemetery context.

Plot V

Grave 239　(Phase 1a): this adult buried with a pair of annular brooches at the shoulders and a pair of small-long brooches would stand out in a Scandinavian context.

Grave 372　(Phase 2a): a Frankish type of disc brooch and a pair of annular brooches are associated with a Kentish type of square-headed brooch.

Grave 247　(Phase 2a): this young adult, buried with a Frankish type of disc brooch and beads of Group A2, would probably not appear conspicuous in a row-grave cemetery.

Grave 373　(Phase 2b–3a): a shield-on-tongue buckle and shoe-shaped studs are associated with a Kentish disc brooch.

It is noteworthy that both a grave dated to Phase 1 (Grave 239) and a burial from Phase 2 (Grave 372) have annular brooches worn at the shoulders, though neither individual would make a convincing Angle.

Plot W

Grave 433　(Phase 1): the animal brooch is probably a Kentish product.

Grave 257　(Phase 1): this grave would need to be evaluated on the basis of a survey of Anglo-Saxon and continental small-long brooches.

Grave 254　(Phase 1): sets of pins and small-long brooches were combined with a button brooch.

Grave 255　(Phase 1b): a shield-on-tongue buckle, shoe-shaped studs and an S-brooch are associated with a button brooch and two different types of Kentish square-headed brooches. The set includes an inlaid belt-plate worked into a brooch.

The secondary use of the buckle-plate in Grave 255 may underline what seems to be a Kentish penchant for elaborate belt settings during Phase 1.

Plot X

Grave 408　(Phase 1b): a continental type of buckle set and a radiate-headed brooch are associated with a Kentish bow brooch.

Grave 381　(Phase 1b–2a): the buckle with club-shaped tongue in this grave is associated with a continental type of pursemount/firesteel and a rare purse frame, but also with an iron pin with scrolled head, apparently an Anglo-Saxon type.

Grave 428　(Phase 2): the buckle with club-shaped tongue from this grave is associated with a pair of probably Kentish brooches.

Grave 407　(Phase 2): the young adult in this grave combined a pair of continental type brooches with a shield-on-tongue buckle and shoe-shaped studs. Though this combination is not common in row-grave cemeteries, it would probably not be enough to argue for a Kentish connection. It would seem, however, that the iron lozenges from this grave, which were combined with copper alloy tubes, give away the Kentish background of the deceased.

Grave 392　(Phase 2): the child in this grave was buried with a shield-on-tongue buckle, beads and a hand-made pot. Though the combination of buckle and beads would be unusual but not conspicuous in a row-grave context, the pot would probably give away a Kentish background.

Grave 391B (Phase 2): a shield-on-tongue buckle with shoe-shaped studs and a pair of rosette brooches are combined with Kentish square-headed brooches.

Grave 412　(Phase 2b–3a): the combination of a shield-on-tongue buckle and shoe-shaped studs with beads (Group A2b) is typically Kentish but a single grave such as this would probably not be conspicuous in a continental context.

Plot Y–Z

Grave 296　(Phase 2a): this grave combines a Frankish disc brooch with a shield-on-tongue buckle.

Grave 419　(Phase 2a): a shield-on-tongue buckle was combined with a Frankish disc brooch and a Kentish bird brooch.

Grave 417　(Phase 2a): a buckle with club-shaped tongue was worn in combination with a Thuringian miniature brooch, a Frankish brooch type and a Kentish bow brooch.

Grave 297　(Phase 2): this male was buried with a buckle with club-shaped tongue but the shield and spearhead types seem to be more Kentish, than continental.

Grave 426　(Phase 2): the ?shield-on-tongue buckle was associated only with potsherds.

Grave 437   (Phase 2): the buckle, fauchard and glass vessel may have been imported but the iron pin with scrolled head seems to be an Anglo-Saxon type.

Grave 414   (Phase 2b–3a): the four iron discs forming part of the shield fittings in this grave suggest an Anglo-Saxon background.

This survey of the Buckland plots suggests that by the sixth century, continental material culture was integrated into the life-style of the wealthier part of the Kentish population, a larger part than is suggested by furnished Anglo-Saxon graves outside Kent. However, this does not provide overwhelming evidence for immigrants transplanting every aspect of their previous life-style into Kent (see Evison 1987, 172f). At Buckland, Phase 1 is represented mostly by Kentish brooch types such as button and square-headed brooches, and by Anglo-Saxon types such as annular brooches, a saucer brooch, and small-long brooches, the latter requiring an updated survey before they can contribute to the discussion. These objects suggest links with Anglo-Saxon neighbours, Scandinavia and the near-Continent, and it appears that this phase sees the development of Kentish brooch types from a Scandinavian, rather than Frankish, background. Button brooches of Class A, dated to Phase 1a, represent the earliest brooch type in Kent that does not have its main distribution pattern outside the region. This is followed by the small square-headed brooches of Phase 1b. Scandinavian inspiration not only for the development of both 'Jutish-Kentish' great square-headed brooches but ultimately also the

smaller 'Kentish-continental' types (Parfitt and Brugmann 1997, 35), possibly via the Anglo-Saxon tradition of wearing small-long brooches in pairs, is suggested by the square head-plate of these brooches.

The elaborate buckles buried with children and a juvenile and the glass vessels in Phase 1 probably are Frankish products but appear to be luxury items invested in burials, rather than the kind of personal possessions brooches are assumed to have been. Brooch types with a main distribution in Merovingian row-grave cemeteries are a typical feature of Phase 2, combined with Kentish types of brooches and shield-on-tongue buckles or buckles with a club-shaped tongue. In terms of workmanship, the imported brooch types are not superior to contemporary Kentish products. It cannot, therefore, be argued that imports provided quality otherwise unattainable locally. Gold bracteates in Kentish graves of Phases 2 and 3 suggest that Scandinavian links were maintained throughout the sixth century, and the Kentish evidence is consistent with an interpretation which sees an essentially Anglo-Saxon population integrate continental objects, manufacturing techniques and art styles into their own material culture. More gold and silver was invested in Phase 2 than previously, mostly in the form of gilding, gold braid and silver brooches (Table 9.3).

During Phase 3, Kentish women's dress changed in a way that required only a single Kentish disc brooch at neck (*see* p 187). What looks like the consolidation of a genuinely Kentish fashion that abandoned the wide variety of brooch types previously used, is in fact a development that probably follows continental fashion, which was also

Plot	Silver decorated	finger rings	brooches	pendant	other	Gilt object	Gold braid	pendant	No of graves in plot
R		204	204			204		204	1
S	231, 264, 353, 400		222, 223, 266, 347, 353, 354		347, 353	219, 221, 222, 223, 232, 263B, 266, 347, 348, 353, 354	347, 354		14
T	281				290	281, 290			2
U		271							1
V	245, 372		245, 372, 373	245	245	245, 366, 372, 373		245	4
W		250, 253		205, 339	255	250, 251, 254, 255		250	6
X	381, 391B, 408, 413	408	391B, 407	391B, 413	391B, 413	391B, 407, 408, 413, 428	391B	391B	6
Y–Z	298, 301, 419, 423, 436		296, 417, 419		297, 417	296, 301, 417, 419, 423, 436, 440	420		10
								Total	44

Table 9.3. Buckland 1994. Distribution of silver and gold.

changing to a single brooch at neck, usually a continental type of disc brooch. The use of Kentish disc brooches for this fashion in Kent, however, was probably a deliberate choice because the bead fashion of the time, among other types of objects in the graves, suggests that trade links with the Continent were still in place. The use of shield-on-tongue buckles for this fashion during Phase 3a is a continuation of a Kentish peculiarity that made use of a type of object in women's dress which on the Continent was mostly used by men (see Parfitt and Brugmann 1997, 113). Towards the end of Phase 3, well-furnished burial had become the exception, and this is probably the main reason why the 'continental connection' in the burial evidence is less pronounced. The Frankish bottles in some graves of the following phases, however, suggest that cross-Channel trade was maintained during the seventh century. Kentish women's fashion does not seem to lose touch with the Continent because amethyst beads and châtelaines made of linked rods were worn on both sides of the Channel.

The 'cosmopolitan' character of Kentish female dress, in particular during Phases 1b and 2, is not matched by the evidence from the male graves to the same extent. There are no objects in the graves suggesting Scandinavian influence, and there is relatively little of obvious continental character. The relatively low number of fifth-century weapon graves in comparison to the sixth century is, however, in accordance not only with Anglo-Saxon burial practice (*see* p 378) but also with Merovingian burial practice. Buckles, a regular dress accessory in continental graves of males, are relatively rare in the graves of males at Buckland, though the common occurrence of the relevant buckle types in sixth-century female graves demonstrates that they were available. Almost all the spears have split sockets (*see* p 64), a technical feature suggesting a common standard in the production of the spears which is not found with sixth-century continental spears, though split sockets do predominate in the Rhineland and further west (Siegmund 2000, 183ff). According to Kerep (*see* p 67) the range of spearhead shapes, however, is wider than in neighbouring Frankish cemeteries. The high percentage of spears among the weapons from Buckland is typical of Anglo-Saxon burial practice, which seems to have been different from both continental and what is known of Scandinavian burial practice (Siegmund 2000, 175ff, 299f).[83] Seaxes are more common in Kent than in other Anglo-Saxon regions but they are not as common as on the Continent (*ibid*). This provides another example of Kent superficially

appearing as being more continental than other Anglo-Saxon regions but in detail, not really so.

There seems to be some evidence for the Kentish production of shield bosses (Spain 2000) and of sword-ring-pommels (Evison 1987, 21ff), together with some types of spearhead. Amongst the Buckland 1994 weapons, this leaves only the axe from Grave 346, the fauchard from Grave 437, the seax from Grave 381 and the large knife from Grave 206, as likely candidates showing continental influence. Additionally, the metal composition of the sword from Grave 346 could suggest that it also is of continental origin (*see* p 266). None of the weapon graves from Buckland, however, can yet be dated to Phase 1 with certainty and, therefore, there is little room for any discussion concerning male 'founder graves' in Plots R–Z, either of immigrant or local stock (*see* pp 377–8). The 1994 excavations at Buckland have provided no new evidence to challenge the argument, previously put forward, that status-goods in the graves of Kentish males have relatively little in common with the status-goods found with continental males (Parfitt and Brugmann 1997, 117).

The only bucket from Plots R–Z was found with a female (Grave 391B) in Plot X and is of an Anglo-Saxon type. There are no copper alloy bowls in any of the male graves, nor any Kentish ring-sword-pommels among the plain swords from Plots R–Z. Of the two cone beakers from weapon graves, the Kempston type from Grave 297 is of remarkably poor workmanship (*see* p 139). Gold or silver decoration is a rare feature among the weapon graves, in contrast to the use of gold and silver for female dress accessories. In comparison with Merovingian row-grave cemeteries (see Siegmund 2000, 129ff), pottery is a rare feature in Kentish graves, despite the relatively high number of pots found in the graves of children (Stoodley 1999, 108). Buckland is no exception in this respect (*see* p 138), despite the importation of wheel-thrown pottery during the seventh century, which post-dates the probably Kentish hand-made ceramic vessels from graves of the fifth and sixth centuries.

The polycentric layout of Buckland 1994 (Fig 2.2) is a common feature of cemeteries on both sides of the Channel but a clear definition of fifth- and sixth-century plots may turn out to be a Kentish feature if more cemeteries like Mill Hill, Deal, with its two obvious plots (Parfitt and Brugmann 1997) and Buckland 1994 are located. There is no clear indication of differences in the material culture from the various plots at Mill Hill and Buckland that could indicate settlers from particular, or even different, regions of the Continent, such as

---

83. The discussion of weapon combinations earlier in this chapter was not available at the time of writing. For differences between Kent and other Anglo-Saxon regions *see* p 376.

the Rhineland, Alamannia or Thuringia. A mixed settlement on a very small scale, with few, if not individual, Jutes, Angles, Saxons and Franks using the same burial ground, as suggested for Buckland 1951–3 (see above), seems unlikely, however, as migration was probably a process that required some strength derived from numbers (cf Scull 1993, 71). It seems more likely that burial grounds such as Bifrons, Buckland, Lyminge, and Mill Hill, Deal, producing a mix of Frankish, Scandinavian, Anglian and Saxon objects, are the result of inter-regional exchange occurring on a scale not found in other Anglo-Saxon regions, although no formally organised network need necessarily be implied. Buckland 1994 confirms the interpretation of the Mill Hill cemetery in this respect (see Parfitt and Brugmann 1997, 110ff). The

wealth displayed at the sites may be the result of a fortunate alliance between a native population holding on to the last strands of the economic and political structure of the late Roman province (*see* p 367) and the political and economic network of enterprising immigrants. The Kentish economy would not have needed to greatly excel the Merovingian in order to produce the surplus taken out of circulation during the sixth century, but it may have taken, for example, Kentish workshops producing glass vessels for export to stand out from the rest of Anglo-Saxon England. There is, as yet, no evidence of a Kentish social élite comparable to the so-called 'princely' graves of the Continent (see, for example, Doppelfeld and Pirling 1966). Nevertheless, their discovery is likely to be just a matter of time.

PART 10: GRAVE CATALOGUE

Ian Riddler, Keith Parfitt, Barry Corke and Cathy Haith

with Barry Ager, Birte Brugmann, Hayley Bullock, Angela Care Evans, Caroline Cartwright, Vera Evison, Duncan Hook, Axel Kerep, Susan La Niece, Don Mackreth, Sonja Marzinzik, Christopher Scull, Fleur Shearman, Stephanie Spain and Penelope Walton Rogers

The graves in the 1994 excavation were numbered in sequence from 201 to 444 in order not to duplicate numbers allocated to graves excavated during 1951–3. Following the grave number, the sex (M, F) and age of the individual based on the osteological evidence is given (uninfluenced by the associated grave goods), then the grave orientation, primary burial deposit context number and phase if known. Plot location and measurements of the grave length, width and depth occur next: the depth figures are for the distance into the natural chalk rather than from ground surface, since the cuts generally could not be traced through the overlying soils. A description of the grave fill is also given. Grave axes given are foot to head alignments, calculated in degrees from true north. Unless otherwise stated, all the bodies were laid in an extended, supine position. Left and right refer to the body's left and right.

The radiocarbon dates have been calibrated using the probability method (Stuiver and Reimer 1993) and IntCal09 (Reimer *et al* 2009). Further interpretation of these data, including refined date estimates for each of the burials sampled for radiocarbon dating, is provided in Part 8 (pp 360–6).

Various categories of finds are discussed in the preceeding chapters, with detailed descriptions of the swords in Part 4 and technological analysis of them in Part 6. An extensive catalogue of the textile remains appears as Table 5.7 in Part 5. The beads are discussed in Part 4 (pp 92–119); their catalogue entries are as follows:

Descriptions are based on visual examination under fluorescent light.

Measurements. Diameters are given in 5mm ranges: 2–5mm; 6–10mm; 11–15mm; 16–20mm; 21–25mm. Bead proportions indicate their length: very short, 1:4; short, 1:2;

medium, 1:1; long, 1.5:1; very long, 2:1. For size ranges of individual glass bead types see Table 4.10.

Segments. The beads are made of a single segment if not described otherwise.

Shapes. The outline of the longitudinal section of most of the glass beads is rounded or square. A rounded section is described as globular or annular depending on the proportion of the bead and the size of the perforation. Short or very short beads with a perforation that measures circa half the diameter of the cross-section of the bead or more are described as annular; all other beads with a rounded longitudinal section are described as globular or barrel-shaped. Beads with a square longitudinal section are described as cylinders. The cross-section is described only if it is not round but ribbed or square. Some beads are described as polyhedral in reference to both their longitudinal and cross-sections. The shape of the amber beads is described in the text (pp 94–5).

Perforations. With one exception (in Grave 391B) perforations of glass beads have a round cross-section. Abrasions on amber beads that have changed cross-sections are not described. For the diameter of perforations of glass beads in relation to bead sizes see *Shapes.* For a discussion on the abrasion of amber beads see p 96.

Colours. The colour descriptions are based on visual examination in artificial light and differentiate between white, yellow, green, blue, red (brown/ 'terracotta'/brick-red) for opaque beads and brown (including 'pink') for translucent beads, 'light' used for the colour variations in so-called 'gold-in-glass' beads, and 'dark' for any beads that appear black in daylight. For the difficulties that would be attached to a more detailed description see Brugmann 2004.

Bead types. The glass bead types referred to in the catalogue in italics are described in detail in Table 4.10 and for brevity, the catalogue omits attributes of glass beads if these are defined as part of the type description given the table.

For glass *bead making techniques* see the type descriptions in Table 4.10.

For *opacity and translucency* see the type descriptions in Table 4.10.

THE CATALOGUE

Grave 201 (Fig 10.71) M 25–30. 327°. Context 50. Plot R. 2.76m x 0.97–1.17m x 0.32m.
Cream-grey loam with very frequent small and medium chalk. Poorly-preserved skeleton; skull half left. No grave goods.

Grave 202 (Fig 10.71) F 20–25. 324°. Context 56. Plot R. 2.05m x 0.88m x 0.21m.
Cream-grey loam with frequent small and medium chalk. Moderately well-preserved skeleton; skull right; legs bent to right; left arm bent across body. No grave goods.

Grave 203 (Fig 10.71) F 25–30. 315°. Context 54. Plot R. 1.93m x 0.75m x 0.20m.
Cream-grey loam with frequent small and medium chalk containing one sherd of Roman pottery. Poorly-preserved skeleton; skull largely decayed; left arm slightly bent. No grave goods.

Grave 204 (Figs 10.1, 10.2, 10.71) F 22–27. 343°. Context 48. Phase 2b. Plot R. 2.58m x 0.92m x 0.43m.
Pick and mattock marks on base and north-east side. Cream-grey loam with very frequent small, medium and large chalk containing several iron fragments. Moderately well-preserved skeleton; skull half left; arms bent across pelvis.

a   Scatter of around 130 **beads**. Chest area, neck and skull (see below).
b   Silver-gilt cast Kentish **disc brooch**. Garnet settings not on hatched foil; some cast ridges nicked; rim decorated with niello triangles. Cast spring-holder and pin-catch. Iron remains of spring with mineral-preserved textile remains. Diameter: 23mm. Weight: 6g. By right humerus. Sf 23.
c   Copper alloy Roman **coin**. Copper *as* of Vespasian (AD 69–79), PROVIDENT SC type (RIC 494), AD 71. Weight: 10.88g. By left femur. Sf 32.
d   Fragmentary shale **spindle-whorl**. Extremely fragile, in poor condition. Biconical form. Diameter: 33mm. By left femur. Sf 31.

e   Small grey, oval stone **pebble** with yellow banding. Length: 25mm. Width: 18mm. By left femur. Sf 34.
f   Fragment of **marine shell**. By left femur. Sf 33.
g   Cast high-tin copper alloy **buckle**. Faceted loop with narrowed axis for attachment of shield-tongue. The tongue shield which is deeply recessed for an inset appliqué with repoussé ornament. Plus three high-tin **shoe-shaped studs**, similarly recessed with remains of sheet copper alloy inset appliqués with repoussé ornament and with one attachment lug each. Mineral-preserved organic remains on loop and tongue. Width of loop: 35mm. Length of stud: 22mm. Centre waist. Sf 26.
h   Pair of copper alloy **strap-ends**, tongue-shaped. Upper plate cast, lower plate of sheet metal. Serrated edge on upper plate at split end, central disc-headed rivet in centre of incised diagonal cross with two incised transverse lines below. Length: 32mm. Between lower legs. Sf 28.
i, j   **Finger-ring** with hoop made of silver sheet decorated with grooves; terminals show remains of tin-based solder. Silver bezel, 12mm square, set with four garnets on hatched foil; beaded rim around setting made of silver wire. Width: 5mm. Weight: 1.6g. Area of left hand. Sf 24 and Sf 27.
k   Iron and copper-alloy **châtelaine** covered in mineral-replaced textile. The complex contains the remains of two **keys** with loop heads, largely obscured by mineral-preserved textile, and squared shanks associated with ?copper-alloy suspension **rings**. It is associated with the fragment of a hooked 'ward'. Associated with coin (m). Left of left femur. Sf 38.
l   Iron **pin** with globular head. Mineral-preserved textile on surface. Length: *c* 90mm. Under lower jaw. Sf 25.
m   Copper alloy Roman **coin**. Debased (silvered bronze) radiate, late third century. Details illegible. Pierced, broken around top of piercing. Covered with mineral-preserved organics, especially textile. Weight: 1.77g. Left of left femur with châtelaine (k) and including also small iron object. Sf 39.
n   6 glass **beads** (see below).
o   Gold **bracteate** with ribbed suspension loop. Triple concentric rings of repoussé bosses surround central motif. Diameter: 32mm; weight 3.3g. Under lower jaw (right side). Sf 1082.
p   Nine small and indistinct iron **fragments**. Mineral-preserved textile on surface. In general filling of grave. Sf 37.

Grave 204 beads (Sf nos 29, 30, 35, 36, 1081)
a
amber: 125–130 beads
1	short, wedge-shaped, diam 11–15mm
1	medium, globular, diam 6–10mm
2	medium, rounded, diam 11–15mm
18	medium, rounded, diam 6–10mm
2	medium, rounded, diam 2–5mm
15	medium, facetted, diam 11–15mm
85	medium, facetted, diam 6–10mm
1	fragments

probably also from this group:
1	medium, rounded, diam 6–10mm
1	medium, facetted, diam 11–15mm
3	medium, facetted, diam 6–10mm

glass: 2 beads
Constricted Segmented (no 5)
2	two segments, long, diam 2–5mm

n
glass: 6 beads
Constricted Segmented (no 5)
  1   two segments, very long, diam 2–5mm. Fig 4.25, Grave 204, Sf 30 (n1)
Constricted Cylindrical (no 6)
  2   very long, diam 2–5mm. Fig 4.25, Grave 204, Sf 30 (n3)
other annular (no 58)
  1   very short, diam 11–15mm, translucent, green (yellow). Fig 4.25, Grave 204, Sf 29 (n3)
other globular (no 63)
  2   short, diam 11–20mm, translucent, yellow. Fig 4.25, Grave 204, Sf 29 (n2)

Grave 205 (Figs10.2, 10.72) ?F 23–28. 335°. Context 60. Plot R. 2.32m x 0.75m (min) x 0.14m.

Cream-grey silty loam with frequent small and medium chalk. Poorly-preserved skeleton; skull damaged; left arm slightly bent.

a   Cast copper alloy **buckle** with mineral-preserved traces of *Prunus* sp plum/cherry wood. D-shaped loop with hollow back, narrowed axis for attachment of iron tongue or anchorage, only fragments of which remain. Width of loop: 24mm. Inside right forearm. Sf 18.
b   Iron **knife**, lacking tip of blade. Tang set at an angle in relation to blade. Straight back, slightly sinuous cutting-edge. Length: 148mm. By lower left arm. Sf 22.
c   Copper alloy Roman **coin**. Silvered bronze *nummus* of AD 330–335. Possibly Constantine II. cf RIC VII, Lyon 244. Chipped edge. Weight: 2.00g. Top of left femur. Sf 21.
d   Fossil shark's **tooth**. Triangular, including part of root channel, tapering to point. Length: 22mm; width: 14mm. Top of left femur. Sf 19.
e   Fragments of a copper alloy **object**. Three pieces of cast strip, with flange on one side, and T-shaped fragment. Length: 32mm. Width: 6mm. Top of left femur, beside coin (c). Sf 20.

Grave 206 (Figs 10.2, 10.72) ? 13–15. 330°. Context 52. Plot R. 1.91m x 1.10m x 0.48m.

Mattock marks on north-east side. Cream-grey loam with frequent small and medium chalk. Large chalk lumps under surviving bones. Skull and leg bones only.

a   Iron **knife** (large). Short tang, long slender blade, back straight with cutting-edge curving up to tip. Leather covered, wooden scabbard with a string lining decoration running down centre under the leather. Also, traces of mineral-preserved textile. At top of scabbard is a copper alloy strip (mouth band), 7mm wide, folded over willow wood (*Salix* sp) and secured with small copper alloy rivet. Copper alloy **chape** survives at end of scabbard, formed from undecorated sheet. Length: 232mm; blade length: 180mm. Area of pelvis. Sf 17.

Grave 207 (Figs 10.3, 10.72) F 30–35. 333°. Context 62. Plot R. 2.20m x 0.75m x 0.20m.

Light-brown loam with frequent small and medium chalk. Moderately well-preserved skeleton; left arm slightly bent; legs crossed at ankle (left over right).

a   Two amber **beads**. Right side of skull. Sf 14 (see below).
b   Three glass **beads**. Above right shoulder. Sf 13 (see below).
c   Cast copper alloy ?**buckle** loop, rectangular, of square section. No wear marks or any other traces of a tongue. Width of loop: 22mm. Right shoulder. Sf 12.
d   Remains of iron **buckle**. Oval loop and plain tongue. Width of loop: 20mm. Right waist. Sf 3.
e   Lead or lead-alloy **spindle-whorl**, cast, shallow hemispherical shape. Diameter: 29mm. Height: 9mm; spindle hole 7–8mm diameter, widest at flat face. Weight: 36.1g. Small iron **ring**, accreted to (e). Under left lower arm, below (f). Sf 11.
f   Iron **ring**. D-shaped section, split at one point. Diameter: 35mm. Under left lower arm, above iron ring (e). Sf 10.
g   Iron **buckle** loop, circular. Width of loop: 30mm. Under left forearm, adjacent to iron ring and lead spindle-whorl (e). Sf 9.
h   Copper alloy slip-knot wire **bracelet**. Diameter: 61–68mm. Weight: 8.2g. Around lower left arm. Sf 8.
i   Iron **knife**. Back straight and curving to tip, cutting-edge sinuous and worn. Length: 127mm. Under lower left arm. Sf 7.
j   Fossil **bead**. Unidentified. Right chest. Sf 6 (see below).
k   Amber **bead**. Right shoulder. Sf 5 (see below).
l   Amber **bead**. Right shoulder. Sf 4 (see below).

Grave 207 beads
amber: 4 beads
a   2   medium, facetted, diam 6–10mm
k   1   short, cylindrical, diam 11–15mm. Fig 4.25, Grave 207 (k1)
l   1   medium, facetted, diam 11–15mm
glass: 3 beads
b
Constricted Segmented (no 5)
       1   three segments, very long, diam 2–5mm. Fig 4.25, Grave 207, Sf 13 (b1)
       2   short, diam 2–5mm
fossil: 1 bead
j   1   (unidentified). Fig 4.25, Grave 207, Sf 6 (j1)

Grave 208 (Figs 10.3, 10.72) ?F 20–30. 345°. Context 66. Plot R. 2.04m x 0.72–0.76m x 0.20m.

Cream-brown clay with very frequent small chalk containing a small glass fragment. Poorly-preserved skeleton; left arm slightly bent.

a, b   Six fragments of iron, including four identifiable objects: 1, part of a **rod** of circular section. Length: 23mm; diameter: 5mm; 2, the point of a **pin**. Length: 14mm; 3, part of an **implement tang**, probably for a knife. Length: 28mm; 4, a folded piece of iron **sheet**. Length: 32mm. Sf 162 and Sf 163.
       Small fragment of **vessel glass**. Roman. From general filling of grave. Sf 924.

Grave 209 (Figs 10.3, 10.72) M 40–50. 333°. Context 64. Phase 1b–2. Plot R; 2.49m x 0.75–0.88m x 0.35m. Mattock marks on north-east side.
Cream-brown loam with frequent small and medium chalk. Poorly-preserved skeleton; right arm completely decayed. Left femur over large chalk lump.

a   Cast copper alloy **buckle**. Oval loop of D-shaped section with narrowed axis for attachment of tongue, which has rectangular shield at base, which is ornamented with transverse grooves, apparently imitating similar tongue shields with two inset rectangular garnets. Iron anchorage for attachment to loop. Remains of mineral-preserved leather around tongue. Width of loop: 39mm. Centre waist. Sf 16.
b   Iron **knife** with mineral-preserved traces of ash wood (*Fraxinus excelsior*) under remains of horn on the handle. Fragmentary, lacking part of blade and tang. Straight back, curving to tip, straight cutting-edge. Length: 131mm. Across body, above waist. Sf 15.

Grave 210 (Fig 10.73) ? grown? 332°. Context 58. Plot R. 2.02m (min) x 0.55m (min) x 0.10m (min).
Cream-grey clay with very frequent small chalk. Fragmentary arm bones only. No grave goods.

Grave 211 (Fig 10.73) ? grown. 321°. Context 68. Plot S. 2.43m x 0.92m (min) x 0.25m.
Cream-brown loam with frequent small chalk. Very poorly-preserved skeleton. No grave goods.

Grave 212 (Fig 10.73) ?F grown. 328°. Context 70. Plot S. 2.28m x 0.97m x 0.22m.
Cut by Grave 213. Light-brown loam very frequent small and medium chalk. Poorly-preserved skeleton; skull right. No grave goods.

Grave 213 (Fig 10.73) ? grown? 323°. Context 72. Plot S. 1.95m (min) x 0.70m (min) x 0.10m (min).
Cuts Grave 212. Light-brown loam with frequent small chalk. Fragmentary long bones of left side only. No grave goods.

Grave 214 (Fig 10.3, 10.73) ? 12–18? 319°. Context 74. Plot S. 1.60m (min) x 0.80m (min) x 0.22m.
Partially destroyed by modern terrace. Cream-brown loam with frequent small and medium chalk containing two copper alloy objects (c and d) and two intrusive medieval pot-sherds. Leg bones only; left leg slightly bent to right.

a   Iron **knife**. Fragmentary, lacking most of tang and end part of blade. Back straight and curving to tip, cutting-edge curved. Length: 110mm. Area of pelvis. Sf 160.
b   Part of an iron **staple**. Length: 75mm. By left lower leg. Sf 161.

c   Copper alloy penannular **brooch** with scrolled overlapping terminals. No remains of pin. Diameter: *c* 30mm. Weight: 4.0g. Skin product remains surviving on one side of the ring. From general fill of grave. Sf 926.
d   Fragment of a copper alloy **ring** made of two overlapping terminals fastened by a copper alloy stud. Estimated diameter: 15mm. Weight: 0.2g. From general fill of grave. Sf 925.

Grave 215 (Fig 10.4, 10.74) ?M 25–30. 311°. Context 76. Plot S. 2.40m x 0.90–1.07m x 0.22m.
Cream-grey clay loam with very frequent small and medium chalk containing two iron fragments (d) and (e). Poorly-preserved skeleton; fragmentary skull; arms bent across pelvis area.

a   Iron ?**belt fitting**, rectangular, in form of recessed tray, now empty, with an inset copper alloy frame, and iron back-plate with remains of four rivets. Length: 44mm. Weight: 3.4mm. Left of skull. Sf 164.
b   Small iron **nail**, square section, rectangular head. Length: 35mm. Chest area. Sf 165.
c   Iron **tweezers**, fragmentary with spring head and straight arms with slight flare. Both terminals are missing. Length: 45mm. Area of left shoulder. Sf 166.
d   Large, fragmentary iron **nail** with discoidal head and shank of rectangular section. Length: 36mm. General filling of grave. Sf 927.
e   Iron **knife**, consisting merely of fragmentary section of blade. Length: 40mm. General filling of grave. Sf 928.

Grave 216 (Fig 10.74) ? grown. 346°. Context 78. Plot R. 1.70m x 0.70–0.80m x 0.23m.
Mattock marks on base and north-east side. Cream-brown loam with very frequent small and medium chalk. Single femur fragment only. No grave goods.

Grave 217 (Fig 10.4, 10.74) ? grown. 327°. Context 80. Phase 1. Plot S. 2.35m (min) x 0.50m (min) x 0.20m.
Pick and mattock marks on base. Cream loam with frequent small and medium chalk. Poorly-preserved skeleton.

a   Blue and white **bead**. Area of neck and right shoulder. Sf 170 (see below).
b   Blue and white **bead**. Area of neck and right shoulder. Sf 170 (see below).
c   Decorated **bead**. Area of neck and right shoulder. Sf 173 (see below).
d   Amber **bead**. Area of neck and right shoulder. Sf 172 (see below).
e   **Bead**. Area of neck and right shoulder. Sf 171 (see below).
f   **Bead**. Area of neck and right shoulder. Sf 170 (see below).
g   **Bead**. Area of neck and right shoulder. Sf 171 (see below).
h   **Bead**. Area of neck and right shoulder. Sf 170 (see below).
i   **Bead**. Area of neck and right shoulder. Sf 170 (see below).
j   Rock crystal **bead**. Area of neck and right shoulder. Sf 174 (see below).

k   Cast high-tin copper alloy **buckle** loop, circular, with narrowed section for attachment of tongue, which is now missing. Width of loop: 26mm. Centre waist. Sf 167.

l   Iron **knife**. Fragmentary, only tang and small part of blade survives. Length: 82mm. Area of left pelvis, below buckle loop (k). Sf 168.

m   Fragmentary iron **rod**. Thin rod of square section, bent back at one end. Length: 54mm. South-west side of grave. Sf 169.

n   not allocated.

o   Amber **bead**. Area of neck. Sf 172 (see below).

p   Amber **bead** fragments. Area of neck and right shoulder. Sf 172 (see below).

Grave 217 beads
amber: 3 beads

d   1   very short, barrel-shaped, diam 21–25mm. Fig 4.23, Grave 217, Sf 172 (d1)

o   1   short, globular, diam 11–15mm

p   1   fragments

glass: 8 beads
a-b
wide crossing trails (no 65)
     2   short, globular, diam 6–10mm, translucent blue wide crossing trails and red dots on white. Fig 4.23, Grave 217, Sf 170 (a1)

c
Traffic Light Imitation (no 30)
     1   medium, globular, diam 16–20mm, opaque red circumferential trail on equator, perforated sides probably originally completely covered with opaque red (remains of peripheral ?stripes), on combed translucent green zigzag. Fig 4.23, Grave 217, Sf 173 (c1)

e
sharp globular (no 62)
     1   short, diam 6–10mm, opaque, red. Fig 4.23, Grave 217, Sf 171 (e1)

f
sharp globular (no 62)
     1   short, diam 6–10mm, discoloured

g
variation Traffic Light (no 32)
     1   short, barrel-shaped, diam 6–10mm, translucent green irregular trail on opaque green. Fig 4.23, Grave 217, Sf 171 (g1)

h
sharp globular (no 62)
     1   short, diam 6–10mm, discoloured

i
sharp globular (no 62)
     1   short, diam 6–10mm, white. Fig 4.23, Grave 217, Sf 170 (i1)

rock crystal: 1 bead

j   1   short, globular with ridge on equator, diam 16– 20mm. Fig 4.23, Grave 217, Sf 174 (j1)

Grave 218 (Fig 10.4, 10.74) ? juvenile/grown? 310°. Context 82. Plot S. 2.40m x 0.70–0.95m (min) x 0.35m. Mattock marks in north corner.
Cut by plough-score of Middle Terrace. Cream-brown

loam with frequent small and medium chalk containing a few iron fragments (q) and (r). Fragmentary leg bones only.

a   Iron **knife**. Back straight and curving to tip, cutting-edge straight and curving in same way. Abundant organic remains on tang, suggesting a two-part horn handle, secured by an iron rivet, 11mm in length. Overall length: 147mm; blade length: 99mm, Area of left pelvis. Sf 147.

b   Two iron **rings**. One complete, other lacking small part of circumference. Diameters: 40mm and 56mm. Area of left pelvis. Sf 148.

c   Two iron pierced **lozenges**, fused together. Length: 44mm. Pelvic region, left side. Sf 149.

d   Iron **chain link** of figure-of-eight form. Mineral-preserved textile and ?leaves. Length: 83mm. Area of left pelvis. Sf 150.

e   Iron **knife** (large). Fragmentary, lacking tip of blade, some of cutting-edge and end part of tang. Long, lightly curved blade, sinuous and fragmentary cutting-edge. Length: 205mm; blade length: 172mm. Over left femur. Sf 151.

f   Copper alloy ?**nail cleaner**. Flat rectangular section, expanded scalloped mid-point, flat ring head with recessed band beneath. The foot is in the form of a slotted terminal providing a good implement for cuticle removal (equivalent to modern toilet equipment). Length: 60mm. Thickness: 2mm. Above right femur. Sf 153.

g   Iron **rod** or **pin** with traces of mineralised leather thong (see also q). Length: 76mm. Area of left lower leg. Sf 152.

h   Copper alloy Roman **coin**. Silvered bronze *nummus* of AD 330–335. CONSTANTINOPOLIS type. cf RIC VII, Trier 554. Near south-east end of grave. Weight: 1.48g. Sf 154.

i   Copper alloy Roman **coin**. Silvered bronze *nummus* of AD 323–324. DN CONSTANTINI MAX AVG (Constantine I), mint illegible. Near south-east end of grave. Weight: 1.59g. Sf 155.

j   Copper alloy Roman **coin**. Silvered bronze *nummus* of AD 323. BEATA TRANQVILLITAS (Constantine I), RIC VII, Trier 390. Near south-east end of grave. Weight: 2.27g. Sf 156.

k   Copper alloy Roman **coin**. Silvered bronze *nummus* of AD 323–324. CAESARVM NOSTRORVM (Crispus), RIC VII, Trier 440. Near south-east end of grave. Weight: 2.80g. Sf 157.

l   Copper alloy Roman **coin**. Silvered bronze *nummus* of AD 323. BEATA TRANQVILLITAS (Constantine I), mint illegible. Near south-east end of grave. Weight: 2.82g. Sf 158.

m–p   Group of four **beads**. Chest area. Sf 159 (see below).

q   Iron **rod** woven through minimum of four slots cut into leather. Part of rod or pin (g). Length: 26mm. General filling of grave. Sf 929.

r   Iron **ring** fragment. Small fragment of circular cross-section with traces of mineral-preserved textile. Diameter: 32mm. General filling of grave. Sf 929.

Grave 218 beads
glass: 4 beads
m, n
other globular (no 63)
     2   short, diam 6–10mm, dark or red. Fig 4.23, Grave 218, Sf 159 (m1)

o, p
other globular (no 63)

    2   medium, diam 6–10mm, opaque, red. Fig 4.23, Grave 218, Sf 159 (o1)

Grave 219 (Fig 10.5, 10.74) ?F 20–25. 327°. Context 84. Phase 1a. Plot S. 2.45m x 0.83m (min) x 0.29m. Grey-brown loam with frequent small chalk containing two amber beads. Very poorly-preserved skeleton.

a   Amber **bead**. Area of right shoulder. Sf 46 (see below).
b   Glass **bead**. Chest area. Sf 43 (see below).
c   Small, indistinct fragment of curved copper alloy **sheet**. Length: 13mm. Weight: 11mm. Chest area. Sf 45 (see below).
d   Glass **bead**. By left femur. Sf 44 (see below).
e   Amber **bead**. Right of skull. Sf 42 (see below).
f   Amber **bead**. Left of skull. Sf 41 (see below).
g   **Ceramic vessel**. Thirty-eight small sherds, mostly from the centre of the body, suggesting a carinated or biconical form. Impossible to reconstruct size or shape of the vessel. Decoration includes well-executed vertical line and deep groove decoration on the carination. It is unclear whether the scheme is continuous or arranged in bunches. Right of skull. Sf 177 and Sf 180.
h–k   Group of four glass **beads**. Chest area. Sf nos 47, 48, 49 and 50 (see below).
l   Amber **bead**. By left femur. Sf 51 (see below).
m   Copper alloy cast **bracelet** with expanded ?lion head-shaped terminals and decorated on one side with punched ?rings; worn. Diameter: 57mm. Weight: 9.7g. Around lower left arm. Sf 53.
n   Copper alloy gilt cast **button brooch**. Ridge around face nicked. Gilding worn only on central ridges and flange. Cast spring-holder and pin-catch with remains of iron spring. Axis vertical in relation to face decoration. Diameter: 18mm. Height of flange: 4mm. Weight: 6.8g. Area of upper chest. Sf 52.
o   Melon **bead**. Area of right chest. Sf 40 (see below).

Grave 219 beads
amber: 6 beads
a   1   very long, spindle-shaped, diam 6–10mm
e, l   2   long, spindle-shaped, diam 6–10mm. Fig 4.23, Grave 219, Sf 51 (l1)
p   1   long, spindle-shaped, diam 6–10mm
     1   fragments
f   1   fragments
glass: 7 beads
d, h, j, k
sharp globular (no 62)
     4   medium, diam 2–5mm, opaque, red. Fig 4.23, Grave 219, Sf 47 (h1)
i
other globular (no 63)
     1   medium, diam 2–5mm, semi-translucent, green. Fig 4.23, Grave 219, Sf 48 (i1)
b
other globular (no 63)
     1   short, diam 6–10mm, translucent, green. Fig 4.23, Grave 219, Sf 43 (b1)

o
other melon (no 59)

     1   medium, globular, 6-ribbed cross-section, diam 6–10mm, opaque, yellow. Fig 4.23, Grave 219, Sf 40 (o1)

Grave 220 (Fig 10.5, 10.75) ? grown. 319°. Context 86. Plot S. 2.96m x 0.70–1.02m x 0.26m. Cut by plough-scores of Middle Terrace. Cream-brown loam with moderate small and medium chalk. Leg bones only.

a   Iron **spearhead**. Small angular/leaf-shaped blade, concave side, with a lozenge-section and a small split socket. Remains of field maple wood (*Acer campestre*) in socket; mineral-preserved textile on blade; traces of human hair, animal pelt or fleece from sheath. Fragment of iron shaft? Left of skull. Length: 220mm. Sf 144.
b   Two small iron fragments, possibly from a **pin**. Length: 44mm. Area of left pelvis. Sf 145.
c   Iron **knife**. Fragmentary, missing front section of blade. Straight back, curved cutting-edge with no sign of wear. Well-defined junction of handle and blade. Mineral-preserved horn handle. Length: 120mm. Area of left pelvis. Sf 146.

Grave 221 (Fig 10.5, 10.75) ?F 30–40? 319°. Context 92. Phase 1b. Plot S. 2.65m x 1.08–1.20m x 0.36m. Mattock marks on north-east side. Cut by plough-score of Middle Terrace. Cream-brown loam with frequent small and medium chalk containing a few prehistoric struck flints. Very poorly-preserved skeleton; fragmentary skull and long bones; leg bent to right.

a   Copper alloy gilt cast **button brooch**. Ridge around face nicked. Gilding worn only on ridges and flange. Cast spring-holder and pin-catch with iron spring. Axis of pin diagonal to face decoration with pin pointing down. Diameter: 18mm. Height of flange: 4mm. Weight: 6.2g. Area of body. Sf 129.
b   Fossil **bead**. Left of skull. Unidentified. Diameter: 6–10mm. Sf 130.

Grave 222 (Fig 10.5–6, 10.76) F 35–45. 318°. Context 94. Phase 3a. Plot S. 2.75m x 1.12–1.20m x 0.45m. Cuts Grave 235. Brown loam with frequent small and medium chalk containing iron fragments (i) and an Anglo-Saxon pot-sherd dated *c* AD 575/600–700, together with an intrusive medieval sherd. Poorly-preserved skeleton; right arm decayed. Radiocarbon date: 1550 ± 19 BP (UB 6472), cal AD 430–565 (95%).

a   Scatter of 119 amber and glass **beads**. Area of neck and right chest. Sf nos 54–63 and 132 (see below).
b   Silver-gilt cast Kentish **disc brooch**. Central garnet in ?copper alloy frame surrounded by white magnesite set in cast frame; keystone garnets ?partly on hatched foil; zigzag pattern on rim produced by double row of opposing silver-copper triangular niello triangles; gilding worn on ridges. Back decorated with groove along the rim, cut with a set of lines creating vague

resemblance to beaded wire rim; remains of gilding in grooves. Iron pin on back, with remains of cordage knot, probably a button loop, tied around the spring. Diameter: 30mm. Weight: 10.1g. Neck. Sf 71.

c   Copper alloy **pin**. Tapering shaft of circular section. Head flattened and lightly rounded; pierced by a circular perforation. Point missing. Length: 70mm. Weight: 2.0g. Neck. Sf 67.

d   Iron **knife**. Long tang, straight back curving to tip, sinuous cutting-edge. Well-defined junction of handle and blade. Length: 230mm. Area of left pelvis. Sf 66.

e   Cast high-tin copper alloy bay leaf-shaped **strap-end**, with a central rib, and a slightly up-curved pointed tip. The split end which is stained with iron, has two disc-headed rivets for attachment to the strap and on the back a third, larger rivet-hole is visible. The surface is worn, there is a diagonal cut from one of the rivets and the back is covered with transverse scratches. Length: 67mm. Lying over top of right thigh. Sf 68.

f   Cast high-tin copper alloy **buckle** and separate **triangular plate**. Heavy, oval, faceted loop with a narrowed axis for the attachment of the strongly curved tongue, which was secured by an iron anchorage. Shield-shaped tongue has notches along the basal edge, and is decorated with swallow-tailed lateral finials and two incised transverse lines. Plate has a frame in relief with two crude ridges around a plain central sunken field, too shallow for inlay, and a line of five punched dots along the edge nearest the loop. The three lobes are each decorated with a ring-and-dot. On back along central axis are two pierced lugs for attachment, one with the remains of ?leather. Width of loop: 32mm. Plate length: 57mm. Centre waist. Sf 69 and Sf 128.

g   Copper alloy cast **ring**. Wear on inner edge. Diameter: 38mm. Weight: 22.9g. Between femurs. Sf 70.

h   Remains of 3 or 4 iron flat shafted **keys**, one with patches of mineral-replaced textile and a partial iron ring, a second with an expanding shaft and mineral-replaced textile on one side associated with a copper alloy suspension **ring**; the third is missing its upper end but has the remains of a hooked 'ward', the fourth has a flattened oval terminal loop and a damaged shaft, with mineral-replaced textile on the ring terminal and along one side of the shank. Possibly the third and the fourth originally joined. Also found associated with the keys is a large and featureless iron **ring**. Length overall of most complete: 119mm. External diameter of copper alloy ring: 25mm. External diameter of iron ring; 60mm. By left femur. Sf 64 and Sf 65.

i   Iron **object**. Two fragments join ring (h). From general filling of grave. Sf 931.

Grave 222 beads
a: 119 beads
amber
a62
    1   medium, cylindrical, diam 6–10mm. Fig 4.29, Grave 222, Sf 57 (a62)
a22, 79
    2   medium, rounded, diam 11–15mm
a3, 5, 7, 10, 11, 17, 21, 25, 28, 36, 37, 63, 105
    13   medium, facetted, diam 11–15mm. Fig 4.29, Grave 222, Sf 56 (a10)
a12
    1   long, facetted, diam 11–15mm

a39, 99
    2   medium, facetted, diam 6–10mm
a34, 94
    2   fragments
glass
a38
Roman Melon (no 36)
    1   medium, globular, multi-ribbed cross-section, diam 16–20mm, opaque, turquoise. Fig 4.29, Grave 222, Sf 63 (a38)
a89, 114, 116
Constricted Segmented (no 5)
    3   segment, long, diam 2–5mm. Fig 4.29, Grave 222, Sf 54 (114)
a91
green segmented (no 47)
    1   short, globular, diam 2–5mm. Fig 4.29, Grave 222, Sf 63 (a91)
a9
Mosaic (no 25)
    1   very long, spindle-shaped, diam 6–10mm, yellow, blue and white stripes. Fig 4.29, Grave 222, Sf 63 (a9)
a33
Koch49/50 (no 19)
    1   very long, cylindrical, diam 6–10mm, opaque yellow spiral combed in one direction applied on red body and not marvered flush. Fig 4.29, Grave 222, Sf 62 (a33)
a31, 42, 43, 57, 72, 96
Koch34 (no 15)
    6   short, globular, diam 6–10mm, white on red. Fig 4.29, Grave 222, Sf 55 (a96)
a15?, 32, 51, 65, 67, 68, 71, 74, 82, 84, 90, 95, 97
variation Koch34 (no 16)
    13   short, globular, diam 6–10mm, opaque, applied white wavy or zigzaggy (irregular or narrow) trail or wide crossing trails or white streaked spiral on red body. Fig 4.29, Grave 222, Sf 55 (a71), (a74), (a84); Fig 4.29, Grave 222, Sf 54 (a95)
a80
variation Koch34 (no 16)
    1   medium, globular, diam 6–10mm, red irregular wide crossing trail on yellow body. Fig 4.29, Grave 222, Sf 61 (a80)
a61
polychrome biconical (no 66)
    1   medium, diam 6–10mm, yellow irregular zigzag trail on opaque red body. Fig 4.29, Grave 222, Sf 61 (a61)
a4
undefined
    1   medium, biconical, diam 11–15mm, dark irregular application?, partly lost? or: bead body made of yellow and dark? glass, or dark and lost decoration on yellow body? Fig 4.29, Grave 222, Sf 61 (a4)
a6, 27, 50, 60
Cylindrical Pentagonal (no 10)
    4   medium or long, diam 6–10mm, opaque, white. Fig 4.29, Grave 222, Sf 60 (a60)
a1, 2, 18, 100
Cylindrical Pentagonal (no 10)
    4   medium, long or very long, diam 6–10mm, opaque, yellow. Fig 4.29, Grave 222, Sf 60 (a2)

a13, 16, 23, 35, 81
Cylindrical Pentagonal (no 10)
> 5   one long or very long, diam 6–10mm, opaque, red.
> Fig 4.29, Grave 222, Sf 60 (a13)

a26
Cylindrical Pentagonal (no 10)
> 1   long, diam 6–10mm, opaque, blue. Fig 4.29, Grave
> 222, Sf 60 (a26)

a29, 47, 59, 76
sharp globular (no 62)
> 4   short or medium, diam 6–10mm, opaque, white (one
> greenish). Fig 4.29, Grave 222, Sf 57 (a47); 222
> Sf 57 (a76)

a14, 45, 48, 52, 70, 75, 108, 118
sharp globular (no 62)
> 8   short or medium, diam 6–10mm, opaque, yellow.
> Fig 4.29, Grave 222, Sf 57 (a14); Fig 4.29, Grave
> 222, Sf 57 (a108)

a41, 49, 86, 92, 104, 117
sharp globular (no 62)
> 6   short or medium, diam 2–10mm, opaque, red.
> Fig 4.29, Grave 222, Sf 54 (a49); Fig 4.29, Grave
> 222, Sf 54 (a92)

a19, 58, 98, 102
other globular (no 63)
> 4   short or medium, (asymmetrically) globular, diam
> 6–10mm, opaque, white. Fig 4.29, Grave 222, Sf 57 (a102)

a44
other globular (no 63)
> 1   long, diam 2–5mm, opaque, white with dark streaks

a69
other globular (no 63)
> 1   short, diam 6–10mm, opaque, white with dark
> streaks. Fig 4.29, Grave 222, Sf 57 (a69)

a64, 83, 85, 87, 103, 107
other globular (no 63)
> 6   short, diam 6–10mm, opaque, yellow. Fig 4.29, Grave
> 222, Sf 57 (a103)

a46
other globular (no 63)
> 1   short, diam 6–10mm, translucent, yellow

a30, 78, 93, 113
other globular (no 63)
> 4   short, diam 6–10mm, opaque, red. Fig 4.29, Grave
> 222, Sf 54 (a93); Fig 4.29, Grave 222, Sf 54 (a113)

a24
other globular (no 63)
> 1   short or medium, diam 2–5mm, semi-translucent,
> blue. Fig 4.29, Grave 222, Sf 63 (a24)

a55, 66
other globular (no 63)
> 2   short, diam 6–10mm, semi-translucent, blue.
> Fig 4.29, Grave 222, Sf 57 (a55)

a54, 56, 112
other globular (no 63)
> 3   short, diam 6–15mm, translucent, blue. Fig 4.29,
> Grave 222, Sf 57 (a54)

a88
other globular (no 63)
> 1   short, diam 6–10mm, opaque, blue (greenish 'petrol'
> with red streaks)

a8, 73, 77
other globular (no 63)
> 3   short or medium, diam 6–10mm, opaque, dark. Fig
> 4.29, Grave 222, Sf 57 (a8); Fig 4.29, Grave 222,
> Sf 54 (a73)

a53
other annular (no 58)
> 1   very short, diam 6–10mm, opaque, yellow. Fig 4.29,
> Grave 222, Sf 57 (a53)

a110
other barrel (no 57)
> 1   short, diam 11–15mm, dark

a111
other barrel (no 57)
> 1   short, diam 11–15mm, translucent, green (dark), Fig
> 4.29, Grave 222, Sf 58 (a111)

a20
Blue (no 1)
> 1   short, annular, diam 6–10mm, translucent, blue

a1, 2, 11, 101/109?
variation Melon (no 22)
> 4   short, globular, diam 11–15mm, translucent, blue. Fig
> 4.29, Grave 222, Sf 1107 (a1), Fig 4.29, Grave 222,
> Sf 58 (a11)

a106
translucent green cylindrical (no 53)
> 1   very long, diam 2–5mm, bluish green. Fig 4.29,
> Grave 222, Sf 63 (a106)

a115
unidentified
> 1   fragments, translucent, blue

Grave 223 (Figs 10.6, 10.76, 10.120) F grown. 315°. Context 96. Plot S. 2.58m x 1.05m x 0.22m.
Cut by Graves 231 and 232 (Phase 3b). Cream-brown loam with frequent small and medium chalk containing an intrusive medieval pot-sherd. Fragmentary skull and leg bones only.

a   Silver-gilt openwork 'rider' **brooch**. Base decorated with punched triangles, presumably nielloed originally; ring-and-dot punch mark used for eye of horse. Rim of brooch worn, gilding preserved in crevices only; parts of base, hind leg and tail of horse broken off. Cast spring-holder and pin-catch. Remains of iron pin and mineral-preserved textile. Remaining width. 24mm. Weight: 3.7g. Neck. Sf 101.

b   Cast high-tin copper alloy **buckle**. Oval, faceted loop with narrowed axis for attachment of tongue. Stepped, trapezoidal tongue shield, ornamented with transverse ridges, remains of iron anchorage on the back. Tip of tongue missing. Mineral-preserved textile on back. Width of loop: 31mm. Right hip. Sf 102.

c   Iron **knife**. Fragmentary, lacking end of tang. Long, broad tang, back straight and curving to tip, cutting-edge sinuous. Well-defined junction of handle and blade. Mineral-preserved horn handle. Length: 185mm. Area of left pelvis. Sf 103.

d, e   Fragments of iron ?**pin** with hooked head (e) and the point (d). Length of (d): 52mm.; length of (e): 65mm. Neck (d) and left pelvis (e). Sf 104 and Sf 105.

f   Scatter of 12 amber and glass **beads**. Neck area. Sf nos
        106–9.

Grave 223 beads
f
amber: 8 beads
    1   medium, cylindrical, diam 2–5mm. Fig 4.24, Grave
            223, Sf 108 (f5)
    1   medium, globular, diam 2–5mm
    1   medium, rounded, diam 6–10mm
    1   medium, rounded, diam 2–5mm
    2   medium, facetted, diam 6–10mm
    2   fragments
glass: 3 beads
red cylindrical (no 44)
    1   long, diam 2–5mm. Fig 4.24, Grave 223, Sf 109 (f1)
wide crossing trails (no 65)
    1   short, barrel-shaped, diam 6–10mm, translucent
            turquoise trails and 3 opaque red dots on white. Fig
            4.24, Grave 223, Sf 109 (f3)
other globular (no 63)
    1   short, irregularly globular, diam 2–5mm, translucent,
            blue-green.Fig 4.24, Grave 223, Sf 109 (f2)
(unidentified material): 1 bead
    1   short, semi-globular, diam 6–10mm, dark

Grave 224 (Figs10.7, 10.75) 318°. Context: Sk A, 98; Sk
B,166. Plot S. 2.15m (min) x 0.74m (min) x 0.20m.
Grey-brown loam with moderate small and medium chalk.
Severely truncated double grave (Sk A adjacent Sk B).

Sk 224A ? grown. Poorly-preserved skeleton.

a   Iron **knife** with mineral-preserved traces of horn handle and
        traces of ash wood (*Fraxinus excelsior*). Tang slightly bent
        upwards. Straight back with distinct change of angle towards
        tip. Cutting-edge sinuous and curving to tip. Length: 173mm.
        By left pelvis. Sf 118.

Sk 224B ? grown. Lower leg bones only, other bones
previously removed. No grave goods - ?previously
removed.

Grave 225 (Fig 10.76) ?F grown. 317°. Context 100.
Plot S; 1.10m (min) x 0.30m (min) x 0.03m.
Cuts Grave 234. Light-brown loam with frequent small and
medium chalk. Poorly-preserved skeleton. No grave goods.

Grave 226 (Fig 10.75) ?F 30–40. 310°. Context 102. Plot
S. 1.97m x 0.85m x 0.16m.
Cut by plough-score of Middle Terrace. Light-brown
loam with frequent small and medium chalk. Very poorly-
preserved skeleton. No grave goods.

Grave 227 (Fig 10.75) M 50+. 302°. Context 104. Plot S.
2.51m x 0.91–1.04m x 0.36m.

Cut by plough-scores of Middle Terrace. Light-brown loam
with frequent small and medium chalk. Moderately well-
preserved skeleton; skull right. No grave goods.

Grave 228 (Figs 10.7, 10.77) 327°. Context: Sk A, 106; Sk
B, 140. Phase 3a–7. Plot S. 2.20m x 0.99–1.10m x 0.28m.
Cuts Grave 237. Cream-brown loam with frequent small and
medium chalk. Double grave (Sk A adjacent Sk B).

Sk 228A ?F 15–17. Moderately well-preserved skeleton.

a   Iron **knife** with mineral-preserved traces of ash wood (*Fraxinus
        excelsior*). Lacking tip of blade. Straight back, sinuous cutting-
        edge curving to tip. Well-defined junction of handle and blade.
        Length: 155mm. Over left pelvis. Sf 110.
b   Remains of iron **buckle** and **plate**. Oval loop with a long,
        narrow, triangular plate with a disc-headed rivet at the basal
        end. A dome headed rivet seems to be visible towards the loop
        end of the plate. Mineral-preserved textile and leather. Width
        of loop: 25mm. Width of plate 19mm. Overall length: 70mm.
        By left elbow. Sf 111.
c   Three copper alloy vessel **repair-clips**. Largely complete,
        rectangular, with tapered terminals. Lengths: 22, 17 and 20mm.
        Width: 6mm. Over left lower leg. Sf 112.
d   Iron **firesteel/pursemount** with a hinged buckle held by folded
        iron sheet. Extensive mineral-preserved remains indicate a
        wood-framed leather purse with a possible lining. Remains
        of leather strap on buckle. Length: 130mm. By left elbow.
        Sf 113.

Sk 228B ?M 17–20. Moderately well-preserved skeleton.

a   Iron **knife** with traces of mineral-preserved horn handle. Back
        curves towards tip with slight uplift at end. Sinuous cutting-
        edge. Well-defined junction of handle and blade. Length:
        108mm. By right elbow. Sf 126.
b   1, Copper alloy, triangular sheet, originally a 'vandyke' from
        a drinking vessel, re-used as a **rim-repair**. One corner of the
        vandyke is broken at the rivet-hole and the fragment is now
        loosely folded and secured with a replaced rivet. Light traces
        of rounded punch marks are visible along the margins of the
        mount and across its corners. Width: 30mm. Length unfolded:
        40mm. Over left shoulder. Sf 127a.
        2, Copper alloy sheet, fragmentary, loosely folded and secured
        by a small copper alloy rivet. The fragment now forms part of
        a right-angled '**frame**' - the ?containing frame for a flat-edged
        buckle loop. Width: 16mm. Length of rivet: 3mm. Over left
        shoulder. Sf 127b.

Grave 229 (Fig 10.77) ? grown. 315°. Context 108. Plot S.
1.40m (min) x 0.38m (min) x 0.22m (min).
Cut by Grave 230 (Phase 2b–3a). Cream-brown loam with
frequent small and medium chalk. Bones of left arm only.
No grave goods.

Grave 230 (Figs 10.7–8, 10.77) ? grown. 324°. Context 110.
Phase 2b–3a. Plot S. 2.65m x 0.93–1.04m x 0.40m.

Cuts Grave 229. Cream-brown loam with frequent small and medium chalk containing a bead (Sf 932) and two iron nails or rivets (Sf 933). Poorly-preserved skeleton; fragmentary skull and long bones only.

a   Iron **buckle**, oval to D-shaped loop and plain tongue. Mineral-preserved textile on loop. Leather on either side of hinged tongue, from strap. Width of loop: 30mm. Centre lower chest. Sf 139.

b   Iron **spearhead**. Long angular straight-sided blade with a lozenge-section and a long split socket. No shank. Rivet and rivet-hole. Ash wood (*Fraxinus excelsior*) in socket. Length: 390mm. Left of skull. Sf 140.

c   Iron **knife**. Straight back curving to tip, sinuous cutting-edge. Well-defined junction of handle and blade. Mineral-preserved horn handle and leather sheath. Length: 120mm. Under shield boss (e). Sf 141.

d   Iron **shield grip**. Incomplete, terminals of narrow extensions missing. Long grip with flanged central section (length: 70mm, width: 35mm) flanked by pair of lozenge-shaped plates (width: 50mm, length: 30mm), one of which accommodates plated disc-headed rivet (diameter: 20mm), continuing as narrower tapering extensions (length: 130mm). Overall legth: 400mm. Slight convex bow. Wooden handle with leather on inside of central flanged section. Under boss (e) over left elbow. Sf 142.

e   Iron **shield boss**. Incomplete, flange rivets missing. Slightly carinated convex cone with straight wall (height: 20mm), disc-headed apex (diameter: 22mm) and large flange (width: 27mm) with five equally-spaced rivet-holes. Possible leather remains on underside of flange. Diameter: 160mm. Height: 80mm. Over left elbow. Sf 143.

    Glass **bead**. Green glass segmented (no 47) short, globular, diam 2–5mm, translucent, bluish-green. From general filling of grave (probably derived from Grave 229). Sf 932.

    Two iron **nail heads** or **rivets**, with a disc-shaped head. Remains of mineral-preserved wood and leather on the underside of the object. The leather is closest to the iron which may suggest that the objects were fixed to a leather covered wooden object. From general filling of grave. Sf 933.

Grave 231 (Figs 10.9, 10.76) M 40–55. 323°. Context 112. Phase 3b. Plot S. 2.45m x 0.75–0.83m x 0.40m.
Cuts Grave 223 and 232 (Phase 3b). Cream-grey silty loam with frequent small and medium chalk. Flint packing stones at ends of grave indicate a coffin. Poorly-preserved skeleton; skull half right; left arm over pelvis.

a   Iron **buckle**, **plate** and **counter-plate**. Convex, kidney-shaped loop and club-shaped tongue inlaid with transverse copper alloy wires, plate and counter-plate decorated with applied repoussé sheets in Quoit Brooch style. High rectangular plate with copper alloy repoussé frame, soldered onto surface and decorated with geometric pattern comprising row of lozenges, each containing four dots, within double line border. Set into this frame is a repoussé silver strip divided into three square panels. Two show a four-petalled floral motif, the middle one resembles a sun with a notched border. Remains of knob-headed

corner rivets visible on both plates. On back of counter-plate large copper alloy washers for holding back-plate are visible. Traces of mineral-preserved yew wood (*Taxus baccata*), found associated with back of buckle in close proximity to flax fibres (*Linum usitatissimum*) and mineral-preserved textile. Width of loop: 50mm. Width of plate 41mm. Overall length: 57mm. Counter-plate: 41 x 27mm. Under left elbow. Sf 593.

Grave 232 (Figs 10.8, 10.76, 10.120) No bone. 315°. Context 114. Phase 3b. Plot S. 1.15m (min) x 0.67m x 0.27m.
Cuts Grave 223; cut by Grave 231. Cream-brown loam with frequent small and medium chalk. No bones survived.

a   Plated gold **coin pendant**, copying a *tremissis* of Justin I (AD 518–527). Weight: 1.20g. Central part of grave. Sf 72.

b   Scatter of 24 glass **beads**. Central part of grave. Sf nos 74–77 (see below).

c   Iron **pin**, with shaft of circular section. Traces of mineral-preserved textile on tip. Length: 39mm. Central part of grave. Sf 73.

Grave 232 beads
glass: 24 beads
Koch20 (no 14)
    1   medium, globular, diam 6–10mm, white on red. Fig 4.30, Grave 232, Sf 77 (b4)
    1   medium, globular, diam 6–10mm, yellow on red. Fig 4.30, Grave 232, Sf 77 (b14)
    1   short, globular, diam 6–10mm, lost trails on red
Koch34 (no 15)
    2   short, globular, diam 6–10mm, lost trails on white. Fig 4.30, Grave 232, Sf 76 (b8)
Cylindrical Round (no 12)
    5   medium, diam 6–10mm, opaque, white. Fig 4.30, Grave 232, Sf 74 (b7)
    3   medium, diam 6–10mm, opaque, yellow. Fig 4.30, Grave 232, Sf 75 (b10)
    4   medium, diam 6–10mm, opaque, red. Fig 4.30, Grave 232, Sf 75 (b6)
    1   medium, diam 6–10mm, opaque, green (yellowish)
    4   medium, diam 6–10mm, translucent, blue. Fig 4.30, Grave 232, Sf 75 (b5)
other cylindrical (no 56)
    1   medium, diam 6–10mm, opaque, red
other globular (no 63)
    1   diam 6–10mm, opaque, white. Fig 4.30, Grave 232, Sf 76 (b1)

Grave 233 (Figs 10.8, 10.77) No bone. 315°. Context 116. Plot S. 2.15m (min) x 0.40m x 0.26m.
Cream-brown loam with frequent small and medium chalk. No bones survived; grave length suggests a grown individual.

a   Iron **spearhead**. Medium, slightly angular blade with lozenge-section, long split socket and short solid shank. Two small rivets on the socket. Wood in socket and remains of cordage on socket; mineral-preserved textile remains on blade. Length: 295mm. North-west end of grave. Sf 116.

b   Iron **knife**. Fragment, lacking end of tang and tip of blade. Long blade, straight back curving to tip, cutting-edge shows little wear. Mineral-preserved horn handle and traces of leather on blade, from a sheath. Length: 172mm. Central part of grave. Sf 117.

Grave 234 (Figs 10.9, 10.77) ? 13–15. 138°. Context 118. Plot S. 1.67m x 0.58–0.62m x 0.20m.
Cut by Grave 225. Cream-grey loam with frequent small and medium chalk. Fragmentary skull and leg bones only; head at south-eastern end.

a   **Ceramic vessel**. High shouldered, with hollow neck and wide mouth. Traces of very faint shallow neck grooves above the shoulder, below which are simple vertical thin incised scratched lines starting from edge of shoulder, extending onto central body. Arranged in nine bunches of three, seven or ten simple scratches. Fabric appears to have sandy matrix with some large grits (both quartz sand and flint, in one or two cases up to 10mm. in size) on surface as well as voids where grits have fallen out and/or organic material has burned out during firing. Surface pin-prick holes where calcareous inclusions have leached out and voids where short pieces of organic material have burned out of the surface. Coil built and both interior and exterior surfaces smoothed, rather than burnished. Rim diameter: 93mm. Height: 130mm. Right of skull. Sf 581.

Grave 235 (Fig 10.76) ? juvenile/grown? 320°. Context 120. Phase 1–3a. Plot S. 1.88m (min) x 0.70–0.80m x 0.20m.
Cut by Grave 222 (Phase 3a). Cream-brown loam with frequent small and medium chalk. Long bones only. No grave goods.

Grave 236 (Fig 10.78) ? 4–5. 301°. Context 122. Plot S. 1.93m x 0.67m x 0.33m.
Cream silty loam with frequent small and medium chalk. Poorly-preserved skeleton. No grave goods.

Grave 237 (Fig 10.9, 10.77) F 30–40. 325°. Context 124. Plot S. 2.26m x 0.98m x 0.38m.
Cut by Graves 228, 346 and 358. Light-brown loam with frequent small and medium chalk. Poorly-preserved skeleton; legs crossed at ankle (right over left).

a, b   Matching pair of cast copper alloy **annular brooches** with remains of iron pins; decorated with traverse grooves partly worn away on top and outer rim. Mineral-preserved woven textile remains on both. Diameter: *c* 33mm in each case. Weights: (a) 3.9g.; (b) 4.7g. Left pelvis. Sf 525.

c   Copper alloy **tweezers**. Arms with parallel sides, decorated with a pair of transverse mouldings below the head and four towards the incurved terminals and series of incised lines. Traces of mineral-preserved textile inside fold. Length: 65mm. Width: 4mm. Left pelvis. Sf 526.

Grave 238 (Figs 10.9, 10.78) 134°. Context: Sk A, 126; Sk B, 410. Phase 1–2. Plot V. 1.87m x 0.89–0.99m x 0.22m.
Cream-brown loam with frequent small and medium chalk. Double-stacked grave (Sk A 0.05m above Sk B).

Sk 238A ?F grown. Right leg bones only; bent to right; head at south-eastern end. No grave goods.

Sk 238B F 30–40. Poorly-preserved skeleton; skull right; head at south-eastern end.

a   **Ceramic vessel**. Small biconical vessel, Forty per cent complete, rim and most of upper body missing. Decoration on surviving part comprises horizontal broad shallow groove on shoulder above carination. Pair of oval stab marks above groove presumably continued around vessel as traces of two further stabs survive. On angle of carination itself vertical broad shallow grooves arranged in bunches (of at least two grooves, possibly three) around carination. Produced in hard fine sandy fabric. An abraded break shows matrix densely packed with sub-angular and sub-rounded quartz sand. Calcareous inclusions visible on surface and pin-prick holes where these have leached out. Coil built, thin-walled, clear finger-nail impressions where the shoulder and rim were added to lower coil. Surfaces smoothed rather than burnished. Height: 50mm. Base diameter: *c* 40mm. Left of skull. Sf 694.

b   Two fragments of Roman **window glass**, one drawn. Thickness: 2mm. Area of left pelvis. Sf 673.

c   Copper alloy ?**rod/pin** broken at both ends, narrowing towards one. Length: 44mm. Weight: 1.4g. Area of left pelvis. Sf 674.

Grave 239 (Figs 10.10, 10.78) F 30–40. 315°. Context 128. Phase 1a. Plot V. 2.26m x 1.25m x 0.32m.
Cream loam with frequent small and medium chalk. Poorly-preserved skeleton; skull left; right arm bent.

a   Iron **knife**. Tang leads directly to blade, which curves to tip with slight uplift at end. Cutting-edge curves to tip, no obvious wear. Well-defined junction of organic handle and blade. Mineral-preserved horn handle. Length: 106mm. Area of left pelvis. Sf 203.

b, c   Matching pair of copper alloy cast **small-long brooches**. Punched ring-and-dot decoration framed by incised lines. Elongated square head-plate of (b) appears particularly worn at upper left corner; signs of wear also on right side of line decoration on lower bow. Head-plate of (c) has hole, seemingly the result of faulty casting and originally covered by copper alloy sheet with matching punched ring-and-dot decoration. Remains of solder on faulty head-plate. No evident signs of wear on head or bow of (c). Both brooches showed traces of mineral-preserved *Corylus avellana*, hazel wood and textile. Length of (b): 62mm; weight: 7.8g. Length of (c): 62mm; weight: 9.1g. Width of decorative sheet: 2mm; weight: 0.2g. Right and left chest. Sf 201.

d, e   Pair of cast copper alloy **annular brooches** with iron pins; not matching. Ring (d) decorated on show side with bosses flanked by lines, inner rim worn around pin point, outer rim to both sides. Both rings showed traces of mineral-preserved *Fraxinus excelsior*, ash wood. Ring (e) decorated on show side with groups of lines; small groove to hold pin point in place, decoration worn on top to both sides. Both pins show traces of mineral-preserved textile. Diameter of (d) : *c* 40mm; weight: 7.2g. Diameter of (e): *c* 39mm; weight: 7.5g. Right and left shoulder. Sf 202.

f   Copper alloy **pin** with polyhedral head and decorated shaft. Length: 117mm. Weight: 5.9g. Chest, between (d) and (e), over (h). Sf 204.

g   Glass **bead**. Right shoulder. Sf 206 (see below).

h   Group of nine amber **beads**. Chest, under pin (f). Sf 205.

Grave 239 beads

g

glass: 1 bead

other melon (no 59)

    1   short, globular, 5-ribbed cross-section, diam 11–15mm, translucent, blue-green. Fig 4.23, Grave 239, Sf 206 (g1)

h

amber: 9 beads

    1   medium, globular, diam 6–10mm
    3   medium, rounded, diam 6–10mm
    2   medium, rounded, diam 2–5mm
    2   medium, facetted, diam 6–10mm
    1   fragments

Grave 240 (Figs 10.10, 10.78) ? 14–16. 319°. Context 130. Plot V. 1.88m x 0.88m x 0.17m.

Cream-brown loam with frequent small and medium chalk. Poorly-preserved skeleton; left arm bent.

a   Iron **spearhead**. Leaf-shaped blade of lozenge-shaped section, with long shank and split socket. Copper alloy binding ring on socket. Remains of ash wood (*Fraxinus excelsior*). Traces of mineral-preserved plant/vegetal material including flax fibres (*Linum usitatissimum*). Length: 278mm. Left of skull. Sf 287.

b   Iron **ferrule**. Simple conical short ferrule associated with spear (a). Closed socket containing traces of ash wood (*Fraxinus excelsior*). Also, traces of mineral-preserved plant/vegetal material. Length: 90mm. Below knee. Sf 288.

c   Iron **knife**. Definite shoulder, back straight and curving to tip. Sinuous cutting-edge. Slight traces of junction between organic handle and blade. Length: 110mm. Area of left chest. Sf 289.

d   Iron **pin** with scrolled head. Length: 106mm. Area of left chest. Sf 290.

Grave 241 (Fig 2.2) No bone. 328°. Context 161. Plot R. 1.39m x 0.73m x 0.26m.

Cream-brown silty loam with frequent small and medium chalk. No bones survived; grave length suggests a child. No grave goods.

Grave 242 (Fig 2.2) No bone. 335°. Context 162. Plot R. 1.26m x 0.68m x 0.19m.

Brown loam with frequent small and medium chalk. No bones survived; grave length suggests a child. No grave goods.

Grave 243 (Fig 2.2) No bone. 333°. Context 163. Plot R. 1.17m x 0.54m x 0.28m.

Brown loam with frequent small and medium chalk. No bones survived; grave length suggests a child. No grave goods.

Grave 244 (Fig 2.2) No bone. 323°. Context 164. Plot S. 1.52m x 0.53m x 0.17m.

Pick marks on base. Brown loam with frequent small and medium chalk. No bones survived; grave length suggests a child. No grave goods.

Grave 245 (Figs 10.11, 10.78) F 35–45. 316°. Context 148. Phase 3a. Plot V. 1.94m x 0.79m x 0.16m.

Brown loam with frequent small and medium chalk. Poorly-preserved skeleton; arms slightly bent.

a   Scatter of 114 amber, amethyst, carnelian, copper alloy and glass **beads**. Over neck and chest. Sf nos 191–6 (see below).

b   Gold **bracteate**. Ribbed suspension loop, beaded wire rim, outer border of double crescents surrounding a central zoomorphic motif. Diameter: 28mm; weight: 3.8g. Chest area. Sf 276.

c   Silver-gilt **rosette brooch** with garnet inlays on hatched foil. Outer beaded rim part of back-plate, nicked to imitate beaded wire. Beaded rim worn, one of central garnets cracked. Iron spring with mineral-preserved textile. Diameter: *c* 28mm. Weight: 8.0g. Area of body. Sf 187.

d   Silver-gilt scutiform **pendant** with shield grip originally soldered on. Decoration embossed from back side, gilding only on display side. Gilding on bosses worn. No evidence of loop. Diameter: *c* 17mm. Weight (including handle): 0.5g. Chest area. Sf 188.

e   Silver-gilt cast Kentish **disc brooch**. Central translucent colourless glass inlay on hatched foil; set in gold case within bone inlay, all within a cast frame. Surrounding garnets on hatched foil. Ridge around animal style decoration nicked. Niello in outward pointing triangles on rim lost. Gilding on garnet framework presumably worn off. Cast spring-holder and pin-catch. Remains of iron spring with mineral-preserved textile. Diameter: *c* 32mm. Width: 12.7g. Below (b). Sf 185.

f   Circular object with calcified textile remains. Diameter: 0.33–35mm. Above skull. Sf 181.

g   Iron, silver, and copper alloy garnet-inlaid **buckle** and **plate**. Oval iron loop, with iron frame inlaid with vertical ?copper wires. Upper face of loop carries silver cloisons inlaid with garnets set on cross-hatched foil, probably gilded silver. Cast copper alloy waisted tongue with rectangular base set with garnet on two foil panels. One panel has very different stamp pattern with larger cross-hatching with one raised circle inside. Two small copper alloy attachment straps, still folded over axis, originally held loop and plate together. High-rectangular, cast, copper alloy, box-shaped plate with traces of gilding on upper and outer faces. Decorated with punched circlets which still retain gilding. Five circular flat-cut garnets set flush with the surface without backing foil. Plate attached to sheet metal back-plate by four white metal alloy rivets, possibly silver. Mineral-preserved textile on back. Width of loop: 41mm. Width of plate: 25 x 21mm. Centre waist. Sf 100.

h Cast copper alloy **shoe-shaped stud**, tinning on surface. Pierced attachment lug on back. Length: 15mm. Adjacent to (k), iron keys. Sf 186.

i Three fragments of silver **chape**, including part of edging, with a silver rivet *in situ*, decorated by band of five incised lines, and section of undecorated central plate. Edging length: 15mm, central plate 14 x 13mm. Left elbow. Sf 183.

j Two iron **knives**.

   1, lacking tip of blade. Unusual tang, long with expanded cross-member to secure handle, similar to sword construction. Lightly curved back, sinuous cutting-edge. Slight traces of junction of organic handle and blade. Length: 174mm; blade length: 96mm.

   2, lacking end of blade. Broad tang leading to slender blade. Back straight and curving to tip, cutting-edge similar. Length: 174mm; blade length: 98mm.

   Area of left lower arm. Sf 189.

k Iron **keys**, cluster of 6 corroded together with thin, flattened rectangular shafts and damaged hooked 'wards', some with re-curved hooks. Length of longest key: 150mm. One iron ring, flattened oval in shape, diameter 30mm, and fragment of slip-knot iron ring; length 30mm. Mineral-preserved textile on keys. Area of left pelvis. Sf 190.

l Three copper-alloy **rings**, two fused to pierced iron **lozenge**. One ring is penannular with slightly expanded terminals. Associated mineral-replaced textile. Diameter of penannular ring: 25mm. Diameter of second ring: 22mm. Third ring incomplete. Lozenge length: 40mm. Area of left pelvis. Sf 184.

m Silver **stud** with small, plain discoidal head. Length: 4mm; diameter: 6mm. Area of left pelvis. Sf 182.

n Silver **stud** with small, plain discoidal head. Length: 4mm; diameter: 6mm. Above left elbow. Sf 182.

Grave 245 beads

a

amber: 44 beads

1	medium, globular, diam 6–10mm
17	medium, rounded, diam 6–10mm
8	medium, rounded, diam 2–5mm
5	medium, facetted, diam 6–10mm
6	medium, facetted, diam 2–5mm
1	fragment, diam 6–10mm
1	fragments, diam 2–5mm
5	fragments

amethyst: 1 bead

1 almond-shaped, diam 6–10mm, pale. Fig 4.26, Grave 245, Sf 195 (a2)

carnelian: 1 bead

1 medium, globular, diam 6–10mm. Fig 4.26, Grave 245, Sf 192 (a3)

glass: 67 beads

Constricted Segmented (no 5)

2 two segments, very long to long, diam 2–5mm, light. Fig 4.26, Grave 245, Sf 193 (a21, a22)

18 medium, diam 2–5mm
23 short, diam 2–5mm

light Constricted Cylindrical (no 7)

2 very long, one beaded, diam 2–5mm. Fig 4.26, Grave 245, Sf 192 (a13)2; Fig 4.26, Grave 245, Sf 193 (a20)

Coiled Cylindrical (no 9)

1 very long, diam 2–5mm. Fig 4.26, Grave 245, Sf 192 (a18)

large Constricted Segmented (no 52)

4 long, diam 6–10mm, light. Fig 4.27, Grave 245, Sf 192 (a8)A

3 long to very long, diam 2–5mm, light

5 medium to long, diam 6–10mm, translucent, blue. Fig 4.27, Grave 245, Sf 192 (a14)

blue cylinder (no 42)

1 medium, square cross-section, diam 6–10mm. Fig 4.27, Grave 245, Sf 192 (a4)

red barrel (no 45)

1 short, diam 6–10mm. Fig 4.27, Grave 245, Sf 194 (a70)

other opaque red (no 46)

1 short, cylindrical, asymmetrical cross-section, diam 6–10mm. Fig 4.27, Grave 245, Sf 194 (a69)

other cylindrical (no 56)

1 medium, diam 2–5mm, opaque, red. Fig 4.27, Grave 245, Sf 194 (a67)

1 short, diam 6–10mm, opaque, red. Fig 4.27, Grave 245, Sf 194 (a66)

other barrel (no 57)

1 short, diam 6–10mm, opaque, red. Fig 4.27, Grave 245, Sf 194 (a65)

folded? (no 72)

1 short, barrel-shaped, diam 6–10mm, opaque, red. Fig 4.27, Grave 245, Sf 194 (a68)

unidentified

1 fragments, diam 6–10mm, opaque, red. Fig 4.27, Grave 245, Sf 194 (a71)

Brown (no 3)

1 short, globular, diam 6–10mm. Fig 4.27, Grave 245, Sf 192 (a5)

copper alloy: 1 bead

1 very long, cylindrical, diam 6mm; 14mm long. Fig 10.11 (a)

Grave 246 (Figs10.12, 10.78) M 30–40. 319°. Context 150. Plot V. 2.22m x 0.81m x 0.09m.

Cream-brown loam with frequent small and medium chalk. Poorly-preserved skeleton; right arm decayed.

a Fragment of the shank of an iron **nail**. Unidentified mineral-preserved wood remains on shank. Length: 15mm. Left of skull. Sf 226.

b Small iron **nail** with a flat, oval head. Unidentified mineral-preserved wood remains on shank. Length: 14mm. Left of skull. Sf 227.

c Small iron **nail** with oval head, shank covered in oak wood (*Quercus* sp) remains. Length: 14mm. Left of left shoulder. Sf 228.

d Small rectangular iron **strip**. Unidentified mineral-preserved wood remains on shaft. Length: 15mm. Chest area. Sf 229.

e Small iron **nail** with a square head and a shank of rectangular section. Unidentified mineral-preserved wood remains on shank. Length: 13mm. Left of skull. Sf 230.

f   Lightly curved **strip** of iron, of square section. Unidentified mineral-preserved wood remains on shaft. Length: 28mm. Left of skull. Sf 231.

g   Iron **nail** fragment, for which only the shank survives. Unidentified mineral-preserved wood remains on shank. Length: 13mm. Left of skull. Sf 232.

h   Iron **nail** with rectangular head and shank of square section. Unidentified mineral-preserved wood remains on shank. Length: 26mm. Left of skull. Sf 233.

i   Discoidal head of an iron **nail**. Unidentified mineral-preserved wood remains on shank. Diameter: 13mm. By right ankle. Sf 234.

j   Small **vertebra** from a fish (unidentified). Area of body. Sf 235.

Grave 247 (Figs 10.12, 10.79) F 23–28. 316°. Context 152. Phase 2a. Plot V. 2.40m x 1.00m x 0.24m.
Brown loam with frequent small and medium chalk. Poorly-preserved skeleton; skull left.

a   Garnet-inlaid **disc brooch**. Central white inlay. Semi-circular inlays made of ill-fitting blue glass on hatched foil; remaining inlays, garnet on hatched foil in crudely made framework. Iron brooch core inlaid with copper alloy strips along the edge. X-ray suggests a strip with spring-holder and pin-catch was soldered to the back. Mineral-preserved fine woven textile on back of brooch. Twisted cord and knot on lug and catch-plate. Original diameter: *c* 25mm. Weight: 10.0g. Neck area. Sf 198.

b   Group of two amber and four glass **beads**. Neck area. Sf 199 and Sf 200 (see below).

c   Iron **nail** fragment. Rectangular head, bent shank. Mineral-preserved wood on shank. General filling of grave, north corner. Sf 197.

Grave 247 beads
b: 6 beads
amber
        1   medium, globular, diam 6–10mm
        1   fragment, diam 6–10mm
glass
Constricted Cylindrical (no 6)
        1   very long, diam 2–5mm. Fig 4.26, Grave 247, Sf 200 (b5)
Miniature Dark (no 24)
        1   long, coiled, diam 2–5mm. Fig 4.26, Grave 247, Sf 200 (b4)
white/yellow cylindrical (no 55)
        2   long to very long, diam 2–5mm, yellow. Fig 4.26, Grave 247, Sf 200 (b?)

Grave 248 (Figs 10.12, 10.79) M 60+. 319°. Context 154. Plot W. 2.08m x 0.87m x 0.26m.
Brown loam with frequent small and medium chalk. Flint packing stones along north-east side of grave indicate a coffin. Moderately well-preserved skeleton.

a   Iron **knife**. Relatively short tang. Straight back tapering to tip, very sinuous and worn cutting-edge. Well-defined junction between mineralised horn handle and blade, traces of mineralised leather from sheath. Length: 185mm. Right pelvis. Sf 298.

b   Iron **buckle**. Oval loop, plain tongue. Width: 38mm. Above pelvis. Sf 299.

Grave 249 (Figs 10.12–13, 10.79, 10.118) 315°. Context: Sk A, 156; Sk B, 57; Sk C, 158. Sk C, Phase 2–3. Plot W; 2.21m x 0.71–0.87m x 0.34m.
Cream-brown loam with frequent small and medium chalk. Triple stacked grave (Sk A 0.07m above Sk B; Sk B 0.03m above Sk C).

Sk 249A ?F 35–45? Fragmentary vertebrae and ribs only. No grave goods.

Sk 249B M adult. Right side of body only; skull missing; arm bent double, leg bent to right, appears to be lying on right side. No grave goods.

Sk 249C M 40–50. Poorly-preserved skeleton; legs crossed at ankle (right over left).

a   Iron **sword**. End of tang burred over in place of pommel; tip of blade missing. Extensive remains on the upper third of the blade of wooden scabbard covered with leather. The wood is shaped and slopes down towards the edges of the blade from a central gully. Wooden scabbard made from ash (*Fraxinus excelsior*) with traces of calfskin leather. The thickness of scabbard laths is no more than 1mm, measured at the exposed edge of the blade. Scabbard remains preserve the lines of three vertically radiating cords on one side. Organic remains of grip, lower and upper guards; possibly horn. Length: 900 x 43mm (37); grip length: 96mm (min). Thickness of upper and lower guards: 9 and 11mm respectively. Over right arm, 'pommel' by shoulder. Sf 332.

b   Copper alloy **buckle**. D-shaped loop decorated with incised transverse lines, acute wear on inner edge in one corner. XRF analysis identifies it as an alloy of copper with zinc, tin and lead with no evidence for tinning. Width: 30mm. By right lower arm. Sf 294.

c   Iron **spearhead**. Angled blade, curving side up to the tip, lozenge-section, with split socket and short solid shank. X-ray shows presence of binding ring (copper alloy or iron). Ash wood (*Fraxinus excelsior*) remains in socket. Length: 370mm. Left of skull. Sf 291.

d   Iron **knife**. Fragmentary, lacking part of tang. Straight back with slight curve to tip, curved cutting-edge with little wear. Well-defined junction between organic handle and blade. Mineral-preserved ash wood (*Fraxinus excelsior*) of handle. Length: 75mm. Under left elbow. Sf 293.

e   Iron **spear ferrule**. Conical ferrule associated with spear. Closed socket containing traces of yew wood (*Taxus baccata*). Mineral-preserved textile on tip and plant/vegetal material on surface. Length: 86mm. Below left knee, upside down. Sf 292.

f   Copper alloy rectangular sheet **repair clip**, folded over and fastened by two rivets showing traces of mineral-preserved ash wood (*Fraxinus excelsior*). Length: 20mm; width: 11mm. Right of skull. Sf 295.

g   Four copper alloy **repair-clips** for wooden vessel. Rectangular with slightly tapered ends. Length: 14–17mm. Right of skull. Sf 297.

Grave 250 (Figs 10.13–15, 10.80) F 25–30. 315°. Context 160. Phase 3a. Plot W. 2.84m x 1.13m x 0.69m.

Cream-brown loam with frequent small and medium chalk. Well-preserved skeleton; skull dislocated left; arms bent outwards slightly. Radiocarbon date: 1572 ± 22 BP (UB-6473), cal AD 425–545 (95%).

a   Gold **bracteate**. Ribbed suspension loop. Applied beaded wire border, broken in three places. Beneath loop is tongue-shaped panel outlined in plain wire containing filigree spirals, flanked by one large and two small spirals at top. Outer border of stamped, hatched triangles surmounted by circles, apices pointing outwards. Inner border of plain stamped triangles surmounted by circles. Concentric ring of repoussé dots surrounds central motif. Diameter: 41mm; weight 9.9g. Left lower chest. Sf 370.

b   Ivory **purse ring**. Rounded square section, undecorated, no fittings attached. Diameter: (external) 110mm; (internal) 90mm. Width: 10mm. By left femur. Sf 340.

c   1, Iron ?**pin/rod** with looped head; ?point missing. Remaining length: 70mm. Area of neck and chest. Sf 500.
2, Pair of silver scutiform **pendants**. Bosses punched from back, producing a cruciform pattern and a border. The pendant with a preserved ribbed loop soldered on has four segments gilded, forming an X in relation to the loop; the other pendant has two oppose opposed gilt segments. Fragments of the ?loop are preserved but not shown. Diameter of pendant with preserved loop: 19mm. Weight: 0.8g. Area of neck and chest. Sf 500.
3, Silver wire **finger ring** with coiled bezel. Diameter: *c* 25mm. Weight: 2.2g. Area of neck and chest. Sf 500.
4, Scatter of five amber, one gold and 139 glass **beads**. Area of neck and chest. Sf 500 (see below).

d   Iron sword-shaped **weaving batten** with small projecting tip and tang for handle; tang ends in remains of a broken iron suspension ring. Pattern welded. Ash wood (*Fraxinus excelsior*) on tang and remains of leather strap on suspension ring. Extensive mineral-preserved textile on one face of blade. Length of whole object: 615mm. Blade: 480mm, tang: 135mm (+ ring), projecting tip 15mm with sloping shoulders 32mm. Width of blade (at tang end): 49mm, tapering to 46mm towards tip. Thickness of blade: *c* 7.5mm. throughout. Thickness of tang: 5mm (+ wood = 9mm). By left foot. Sf 509 (SN 1024; pp 273–5).

e   Glass **bowl**. Broken and restored, with one large gap at the rim and another smaller in the wall. Light olive green, rim thickened and cupped, convex wall with base indented by a pointed tool. The bowl is higher on one side than the other. Mostly small bubbles, but some large, some adhesions and iridescence. Oval remains of punty metal on the base. Diameter: 15 x 22mm. Height: 45–55mm. Diameter: 131–5mm. South-east (foot) end of grave. Sf 471.

f   Glass **bell beaker**. Broken and restored with a few gaps. Light olive green, tall, nearly cylindrical body, slightly thickened rim, corded carination, convex base with centre knob, vertical ribbing from carination to within 40mm of rim. Clear scar of ring punty, diameter: 19mm each side of the knob. Small bubbles, some iridescence and discolouration. A pair to (g). Height: 125mm; diameter: 62mm. Thickness: 0.5mm; 2mm at rim. South-east (foot) end of grave. Sf 472.

g   Glass **bell beaker**. Broken and restored with small gaps. Light olive green, rim rolled in, tall, cylindrical body, corded carination, convex base and knob, close vertical ribbing from carination to near rim. Oval punty traces round knob 11 x 15mm, and scar on knob caused by removal of punty. Few small bubbles, but some inclusions. A pair to (f). Height: 132mm; diameter: 62mm. Thickness: 0.5mm; 2.5mm at rim. South-east (foot) end of grave. Sf 473.

h   Group of seven loose, flat-cut **garnets**. Roughly shaped, seemingly chipped. Length: 16mm (largest example). By left femur. Sf 508.

i   Copper alloy ?bucket **pendant** with a central and two peripheral holes. Brown material attached to rim appears to be wax. Diameter: *c* 23mm. Weight: 2.9g. By left femur. Sf 501.

j   Iron pierced **lozenge** with iron **ring-binding**. Centrally-pierced lozenge, incomplete. Mineral-preserved textile on one side. Length: 31mm. Inside ivory ring (b). Sf 505.

k   Copper alloy **ring** with clip. Ring made from cast annular brooch presumably broken close to the narrowed part originally holding the pin; two ends now overlapping and secured by copper alloy rivet. Incised decorative lines on display side of brooch worn. Clip worn and partly broken where it bends around ring; clip held by one remaining rivet, presumably there was originally another one in the hole with edges ?broken on one side. Traces of mineral-preserved ash wood (*Fraxinus excelsior*). Ring diameter: 30mm. Width of clip 13mm. Weight: 6.6g. By left lower arm. Sf 507.

l   Copper alloy **mount** roughly in the shape of a pursemount/firesteel. Decorative sheet and washer clipped into shape. Mineral-preserved organic remains on surface. Length: 42mm. Weight: 1.6g. By left lower arm. Sf 502.

m   Antler burr **pendant**. Poor condition. Thin disc of naturally-shed burr with part of coronet. Square hole at centre and suspension hole towards edge. Decorated by double ring-and-dot patterns, originally over most of available surface. Length: 50mm. Width: 54mm. Thickness: 3mm. By left lower arm. Sf 503.

n   Iron **knife**. Straight back curving to tip, cutting-edge similar with little wear. Well-defined junction between organic handle and blade. Mineral-preserved horn handle and leather sheath. Mineral-preserved woven textile and traces of ash wood (*Fraxinus excelsior*). Length: 161mm. By left lower arm. Sf 506.

o   Iron **châtelaine**: two clusters of keys on rings of different weights. By left lower arm. Sf 504.
1, cluster of 4 **keys** on light weight **ring**, with associated shank corroded to it, perhaps from second cluster. All are heavily covered with mineral-replaced textile on one surface. The shafts are broadly rectangular, two of the four are barley-twist. The wards are rounded. Length overall: 180mm. Diameter of ring: 3mm.
2, cluster of three **keys** on heavier weight **ring**, shafts flattened rectangular, the wards missing on two, the third may be

associated with a curved ward, but this could also belong to the associated shaft from Cluster 1. Length overall: 80mm. Diameter of ring: 5mm.

Associated fragments as follows:

　　i, fragment of iron slip-knot **ring**: Length: 29mm;

　　ii, **key ward** with flat section and angular hook: Length: 42mm;

　　iii, fragment of iron **rod** with mineral-replaced textile on one face: Length: 54mm;

　　iv, fragmentary iron flattened **oval ring** and part of round sectioned **rod** attached to it with tight ring head:　Diameter of ring: 24mm. Length of rod: 32mm; thickness of rod: 4mm;

　　v, fine copper alloy slip-knot **ring**, broken and distorted, corroded to length of thin iron rod with one rounded end (joins iron rod iv). Diameter of ring: 21mm. Length of rod: 35mm; thickness of rod: 4mm. Sf 504.

Grave 250 beads
c4
amber: 5 beads
　1　medium, rounded, diam 6–10mm
　1　medium, facetted, diam 11–15mm
　3　medium, facetted, diam 6–10mm
glass: 139 beads
green Cylindrical (no 48)
　1　short, diam 2–5mm. Fig 4.28, Grave 250, Sf 500 (c117)
Mosaic (no 25)
　4　very long, spindle-shaped, diam 6–10mm, mirror stripes: translucent blue white, opaque red. Fig 4.28, Grave 250, Sf 500 (c121, 97)
　3　very long, spindle-shaped, diam 6–10mm, mirror stripes: translucent green (bluish), white, opaque red
　4　very long, spindle-shaped, diam 6–10mm, mirror stripes: translucent greenish blue (petrol), semi-translucent white
　2　medium, globular, diam 6–15mm, opaque white (5) and translucent blue (5) striped glass, opaque red ('sealing wax red') 'slip' on both perforated sides, applied before folding. Fig 4.28, Grave 250, Sf 500 (c55)
Reticella (no 28)
　1　medium, diam 16–20mm, translucent green (dark) trails twisted with alternating bundles of opaque yellow and bundles of opaque red stripes on translucent green body. Fig 4.28, Grave 250, Sf 500 (c59)
polychrome red (no 68)
　1　medium, globular, diam 6–10mm, opaque yellow spiral trail on opaque red. Fig 4.28, Grave 250, Sf 500 (c49)
monochrome biconical (no 61)
　1　medium, diam 6–10mm, opaque, yellow. Fig 4.28, Grave 250, Sf 500 (c32)
Cylindrical Pentagonal (no 10)
　8　medium to very long, diam 6–10mm, opaque, white. Fig 4.28, Grave 250, Sf 500 (c39)
　10　medium to very long, diam 6–10mm, opaque, yellow. Fig 4.28, Grave 250, Sf 500 (c45)
　1　very long, diam 6–10mm, opaque, red
　12　medium to long, diam 6–10mm, opaque, red. Fig 4.28, Grave 250, Sf 500 (c40)

　10　medium to very long, diam 6–10mm, opaque or semi-translucent, greyish or light blue. Fig 4.28, Grave 250, Sf 500 (c90)
variation Cylindrical Pentagonal (no 11)
　1　long, diam 6–10mm, opaque, light blue with red trails. Fig 4.28, Grave 250, Sf 500 (c43)
　1　long, diam 6–10mm, discoloured
　1　diam 6–10mm, opaque, white, with two opaque red scraps marvered in. Fig 4.28, Grave 250, Sf 500 (c58)
　1　long, diam 6–10mm, opaque, red, with two opaque white and one opaque light blue scrap of glass marvered in. Fig 4.28, Grave 250, Sf 500 (c36)
Cylindrical Round (no 12)
　3　short to long, diam 6–10mm, opaque, white. Fig 4.28, Grave 250, Sf 500 (c88), (c46)
　2　medium to long, diam 6–10mm, opaque, yellow. Fig 4.28, Grave 250, Sf 500 (c86)
　6　medium, diam 6–10mm, opaque, red. Fig 4.28, Grave 250, Sf 500 (c145)
　1　medium, diam 6–10mm, opaque, greenish blue
other cylindrical (no 56)
　2　short or medium, diam 6–10mm, opaque, white with dark streaks
　7　short or medium, diam 6–10mm, opaque, yellow. Fig 4.28, Grave 250, Sf 500 (c149)
　4　medium, diam 6–10mm, opaque, red
sharp globular (no 62)
　6　short, globular, diam 6–10mm, opaque, white (one bluish). Fig 4.28, Grave 250, Sf 500 (c131)
　6　short, globular, diam 6–10mm, opaque, yellow. Fig 4.28, Grave 250, Sf 500 (c120)
　7　short to medium, globular, diam 6–10mm, opaque, red
other globular (no 63)
　5　short, globular, diam 6–10mm, opaque, white (one bluish). Fig 4.28, Grave 250, Sf 500 (c5), (c50), (c98), (c15)
　5　short, globular, diam 6–10mm, opaque, yellow. Fig 4.28, Grave 250, Sf 500 (c137)
　10　short, diam 6–10mm, opaque, red (two irregularly globular, one with dark streaks). Fig 4.29, Grave 250, Sf 500 (c116), (c68)
　6　short, globular, diam 6–10mm, translucent, blue. Fig 4.29, Grave 250, Sf 500 (c8)
　1　short, diam 11–15mm, opaque, (light) blue with dark streaks. Fig 4.29, Grave 250, Sf 500 (c29)
other barrel (no 57)
　2　medium, barrel-shaped, diam 6–10mm, semi-translucent, (light) blue
other coiled (no 60)
　1　short, coiled, diam 6–10mm, opaque, red
　1　short, asymmetrically coiled, diam 6–10mm, opaque, white with translucent green streak
blue almond (no 54)
　1　diam 6–10mm, translucent, blue. Fig 4.29, Grave 250, Sf 500 (c94)
gold: 1 bead
　1　medium, barrel-shaped, diam 2–5mm

Grave 251 (Figs 10.15, 10.79) ?M 40–45. 317°. Context 172. Phase 3. Plot W. 2.46m x 0.75–0.88m x 0.27m.

Cream-brown silty loam with frequent small and medium chalk. Poorly-preserved skeleton; arms bent across pelvis.

a　　Iron **spearhead**. Straight-sided angular, sword-like blade. Lozenge-section. Short split socket, no shank. Field maple wood (*Acer campestre*) remains in socket. Length: 390mm. Left of skull. Sf 341.

b　　Iron **knife**. Lacking tip of blade. Straight back, curving to tip, sinuous and worn cutting-edge. Length: 168mm. Area of left pelvis. Sf 342.

c　　Iron **buckle** and **plate**. Oval loop, remains of tongue with mushroom-shaped shield now fused to plate. Remains of cross-hatched gold foil visible inside tongue shield, implying that it was originally recessed and contained an inset garnet. Triangular plate with broken end and remains of two copper alloy rivets, dome-headed rivets with tin-lead cores and notched collars. Remains of a small copper alloy back-plate are visible on the back of the plate. Width of loop: 36mm. Width of plate (including rivets): 30mm. Overall length: 70mm. Centre waist. Sf 343.

d　　Tall necked **ceramic bottle**. Twelve concentric neck rings on the lower neck and upper shoulder. Parts of applied footring survive, rest spalled off. Fine sandy oxidized fabric with occasional inclusions of grog or un-worked clay (1–2mm in size). Wheel-thrown, quite soft-fired and now very crumbly. Surface smoothed, not burnished. Rim diameter: 70mm; base diameter: 85mm. Height: 330mm. South corner of grave. Sf 616 and Sf 1045.

Grave 252 (Figs 10.16, 10.80) M 30–40. 310°. Context 176. Plot W. 2.38m x 0.97m x 0.27m.

Cream-brown loam with frequent small and medium chalk. Well-preserved skeleton; skull right; left arm bent across pelvis.

a　　Iron **nail**. Discoidal head, shank of rectangular section. Mineral-preserved wood on shank. By right femur. Length: 50mm. Sf 344.

b　　Bone **buckle** with bone tongue (now separate). D-shaped loop, very similar to copper alloy loops with shield-tongue. Narrowed axis with fragment of iron anchorage. Waisted club-shaped tongue is carved from bone and has remains of iron anchorage through its base. Mineral-preserved leather remains on iron hinge. Centre waist. Width: 26mm. Sf 345.

Grave 253 (Figs 10.16, 10.80) ?F 25–30. 314°. Context 178. Plot W. 2.01m x 0.60–0.92m x 0.14m.

Cream-brown silty loam with frequent small and medium chalk. Poorly-preserved skeleton; left arm bent across pelvis.

a　　Silver spiral **finger ring** decorated with punched dots and triangles; worn. Coil now crumpled, one end broken off. Width of silver strip: 3.5mm. Weight: 2.8g. Below left pelvis. Sf 265.

Grave 254 (Figs 10.16, 10.80) ? 4–5. 131°. Context 174. Phase 1. Plot W. 1.39m x 0.63m (min) x 0.15m.

Cream-brown loam with frequent small and medium chalk. Skull and chest fragments only; at south-eastern end.

a　　Glass **cone beaker**. Broken and restored with a few small gaps. Light green, slightly thickened and out-bent rim, straight wall and flat tip. A fine white trail, now decomposing, dropped on and turned nine times towards the rim. Bubbles, some striations and adhesions. Height: 174mm. Diameter: 70mm. Punty ring diameter: 14mm. Area of right shoulder. Sf 284.

b　　Gilt copper alloy cast **button brooch**. Ridge around face notched. Gilding worn on ridges and flange. Cast spring-holder and pin-catch. Axis of pin horizontal in relation to face decoration. Remains of iron spring with mineral-preserved textile. Diameter: 18mm. Area of left shoulder. Sf 277.

c　　Group of one amber and 22 glass **beads**. Area of upper left chest. Sf 278 and Sf 279.
　　NB: Fourteen additional glass **beads** were recovered from the skull and chest bones during off-site cleaning. Sf 1258.

d, e　Matching pair of cast copper alloy **small-long brooches**. Punched dotted lines and ring-and-dot decoration on head-plate, roundel on bow, spatulate foot with single central ring-and-dot decoration. Bows are worn. Cast spring-holder and pin-catch. Remains of iron spring. Mineral-preserved textile on pin of (e). Length of (d): 40mm; weight: 4.6g. Length of (e): 41mm; weight: 3.9g. Left and centre of chest. Sf 280 and Sf 281.

f, g　Matching pair of copper alloy **pins** with wire ring attached to head. Points missing. Remaining length (without ring) of (f): 61mm; weight: 1.1g. Length of (g): 60mm; weight: 1.1g. Left shoulder and diagonally below jaw. Sf 282 and Sf 283.

Grave 254 beads
c
amber: 1 bead
　　1　　medium, barrel-shaped, diam 6–10mm. Fig 4.25, Grave 254, Sf 278 (c23)
glass: 22 beads
Constricted Segmented (no 5)
　　1　　four segments, very long, diam 2–5mm. Fig 4.25, Grave 254, Sf 278 (c6)
　　1　　three segments, very long, diam 2–5mm
　　6　　two segments, long, diam 2–5mm
　　4　　medium, diam 2–5mm. Fig 4.25, Grave 254, Sf 278 (c2)
discoloured Constricted Cylindrical (no 8)
　　1　　very long, cylindrical, diam 2–5mm, originally blue? (now apparently light).
green segmented (no 47)
　　1　　two segments, long, diam 2–5mm, opaque? Fig 4.25, Grave 254, Sf 278 (c5)
　　2　　short, diam 2–5mm, opaque? Fig 4.25, Grave 254, Sf 278 (c1)
blue Constricted Segmented (no 41)
　　2　　medium, diam 2–5mm
Miniature Dark (no 24)
　　4　　medium, coiled, diam 2–5mm. Fig 4.25, Grave 254, Sf 278 (c4)
glass: 14 beads
Constricted Segmented (no 5)
　　1　　four segments, very long, diam 2–5mm
　　2　　two segments, long, diam 2–5mm
　　4　　short to medium, diam 2–5mm

light Constricted Cylindrical (no 7)
    2   very long, cylindrical, diam 2–5mm. Fig 4.25,
        Grave 254, Sf 1258 (8)
discoloured Constricted Cylindrical (no 8)
    1   very long, diam 2–5mm
Miniature Dark (no 24)
    3   medium to very long, coiled, diam 2–5mm. Fig 4.25,
        Grave 254, Sf 1258 (c1, 4)

Grave 255 (Figs 10.16–18, 10.80) F 30–35. 309°. Context 180. Phase 1b. Plot W. 2.34m x 0.98m x 0.19m.
Brown loam with frequent small and medium chalk. Poorly-preserved skeleton.

a   Cast copper alloy, silver-gilt **strap-end** with discoloured niello inlay. Tongue-shaped, with central ridge. Two knob-headed rivets at split end with associated mineral-preserved organic remains. The back is concave and has a fastening mechanism in the form of small rectangular plate pierced by the two rivets at the split end, from which descends a pin of rectangular section with a spatulate end, thus forming a flexible clip on the back. Length: 59mm. Between knees. Sf 316.

b   Silver, kidney-shaped cloisonné **buckle-plate with brooch mechanism** on the back. Turned at some point into a brooch by addition of copper alloy pin and iron spring mechanism on rectangular copper alloy plate. Kidney-shaped, iron box overlain by kidney-shaped silver frame containing silver-gilt cloisons. Filled with garnets, some on cross-hatched gold foil. Two semi-circular green glass inlays, one of which is subdivided into two halves. Central quatrefoil cell now empty. Outer, iron face of frame inlaid with vertical copper gilt strips, which are cross-cut by remains of one vertical strip. Semi-circular copper alloy back-plate has three rivets. Mineral-preserved textile and traces of knotted cordage on the detached pin fragment. Width: 37mm. Width of spring mechanism: 9mm. Over left waist. Sf 317.

c   Gilt copper alloy cast small **square-headed brooch**. Gilding worn on bow. Cast spring-holder and pin-catch. Remains of iron spring. Mineral-preserved textile on back. Length: 44mm. Weight: 8.6g. Over left pelvis. Sf 318.

d   Cast copper alloy **ring**. Semi-circular section, with projection on one side. Diameter: 29mm. By left pelvis. Sf 319.

e   Iron **knife**. Long and slender. Straight back, sinuous cutting-edge, heavily worn. Length: 141mm. By left pelvis. Sf 320.

f   Small curved section of **iron strip**, of rectangular section. Associated mineral-preserved textile. Length: 60mm. Width: 18mm. Next to left pelvis. Sf 321.

g   Gilt copper alloy cast **button brooch**. Gilding on face not worn. Cast spring-holder and pin-catch, axis of pin diagonal to face decoration. Remains of iron spring. Mineral-preserved woven textile on back, near hinge including flax cordage. Diameter: *c* 21mm. Height of flange: 3mm. Weight: 4.6g. Above left pelvis. Sf 322.

h   Copper alloy gilt cast openwork **S-brooch**. Gilding hardly worn. Cast spring-holder and pin-catch. Remains of iron spring. Extensive mineral-preserved textile on front and back. Length: 25mm. Weight: 3.5g. Above left pelvis. Sf 323.

i   Gilt copper alloy cast openwork Kentish **square-headed brooch**. Garnet inlays not on hatched foil. Hole in foot-plate apparently from faulty cast repaired before gilding. Gilding worn on bow and presumably on garnet frames. Foot-plate cast without central ridge. Cast pair of spring-holders and pin-catch. Remains of iron spring with mineral-preserved textile. Length: 75mm. Weight: 17.3g. Neck. Sf 324.

j   Cast copper alloy **buckle**. Oval loop of D-shaped section, with extensive traces of gilding and narrowed axis for attachment of club-shaped tongue. Three cast copper alloy **shoe-shaped studs**, with gilt upper faces and simple incised line borders, deep pierced lugs on backs. Width of loop: 30mm. Length of studs: 22mm. Right waist. Sf 325.

k   Copper alloy **mount**. Triangular, plain sheet mount, curved in profile, with two rivet-holes and two rivets *in situ*. Right of skull, over (n). Sf 326.

l   Copper alloy **mount**. Rectangular, plain sheet mount, curved in profile, retaining three rivets. Under right side of skull. Sf 327.

m   Bone, wood and copper alloy **casket** fragments. 19 casket mount fragments, probably of bone (rather than antler), all stained green and several with one or more rivets holes. One copper alloy rivet *in situ*, 7mm long, protruding 5mm into beech wood (*Fagus sylvatica*). Part of spring mechanism, including strip of bone or antler with rectangular slot, in which section of bone or antler has been placed and secured with two small copper alloy rivets. Also thirty-one copper alloy rivets, all made from folded sheet metal, lengths between 11 and 15mm, and eleven bone pegs, 7.5–10mm in length. Above skull. Sf 328 and Sf 333.

n   Copper alloy **mount**. Rectangular strip with rounded ends. Two rivet-holes, rivet remaining in one. Under (k). Sf 329.

o   Iron **key/girdle-hanger**. Rectangular section of iron with loop, as well as cast copper alloy **ring** of flat section, accreted to second iron **strip** with loop. Extensive mineral-preserved textile. Lengths: 110mm. and 40mm. Above left pelvis. Sf 330.

p   Ivory **purse ring** and **iron object**. Ivory ring incomplete. Rounded square section. Heavily laminated. Undecorated with no attached fittings. Also an iron strip, with mineral-preserved textile on surface. Width: 13mm. Above left pelvis. Sf 334 and Sf 335.

q   Two pieces of iron **strip**, flat, rectangular section. Possibly part of girdle-hanger (o). Mineral-preserved textile on surface. Lengths: 58 and 88mm. Above left pelvis. Sf 331.

Grave 256 (Figs 10.18, 10.81) M 35–45. 314°. Context 182. Plot W. 2.38m x 0.93–1.07m x 0.25m.
Cut by Grave 340. Cream-brown silty loam with frequent small and medium chalk. Well-preserved skeleton; skull half left; right arm bent across pelvis.

a   Iron **nail**. Fragmentary, part of the head and shank only. Unidentified mineral-preserved wood on shank. Length: 18mm. By left foot. Sf 301.

b   Iron **pin**. Shaft of rectangular section, ring-form head, now fractured. Unidentified mineral-preserved wood on shaft. Length: 38mm. By right femur. Sf 302.

c   Iron **spearhead**. Long, thin, angular-shaped blade, lozenge-section, and fragmentary closed (?) socket. No shank. Ash wood (*Fraxinus excelsior*) remains in socket. Mineral-preserved textile on socket. Length: 490mm. Right of skull. Sf 300.

d　　Iron **nail**. Fragmentary, curved shank only. Unidentified mineral-preserved wood on shank. Length: 30mm. By left foot. Sf 303.

Grave 257 (Figs 10.18, 10.80) ?F grown. 135°. Context 184. Phase 1. Plot W. 1.94m x 0.64–0.70m x 0.20m.
Brown loam with frequent small and medium chalk. Poorly-preserved skeleton; decayed skull at south-eastern end; right arm bent. Surviving ribs suggest body was slightly twisted lying on its left side.

a　　Copper alloy cast **small-long brooch**. Undecorated head- and drop-shaped foot-plate with disc-shaped terminal. Pin-catch cast with brooch; incomplete and not functional; ?secondary spring-holder made of folded copper alloy sheet soldered on to head-plate. Remains of iron spring. Mineral-preserved textile on spring and pin-catch. Length: 46mm. Weight: 6.6g. Chest area. Sf 236.
b　　Copper alloy **pin**. Perforated head with spiral decoration. Length: 73mm. Weight: 2.4g. Left chest. Sf 237.
c, d　Two glass **beads**. Left chest. Sf 238 and Sf 239 (see below).
e　　Small, unperforated **metallic sphere**. Not a metal bead, probably natural, ?iron pyrites nodule. Left chest. Sf 240.
f, g　Two glass **beads**. Above left chest. Sf 241 and Sf 242.

Sf 1262 Iron **nail** fragment with associated mineral-preserved wood. Length: 29mm. Retrieved from skeletal material. *Not illus.*

Grave 257 beads
glass: 4 beads
c
translucent green cylindrical (53)
　　1　　short, cylindrical, diam 6–10mm. Fig 4.23, Grave 257, Sf 237 (c1)
d
sharp globular (no 62)
　　1　　short, diam 6–10mm, opaque, yellow. Fig 4.23, Grave 257, Sf 239 (d1)
f
other globular (no 63)
　　1　　short, diam 6–10mm, opaque, yellow. Fig 4.23, Grave 257, Sf 241 (f1)
g
Roman Septagonal? (no 38)
　　1　　very long, biconical, heptagonal cross-section, diam 6–10mm, translucent, blue. Fig 4.23, Grave 257, Sf 242 (g1)

Grave 258 (Fig 10.81) ?M 30–35. 329°. Context 186. Plot U. 2.10m (min) x 0.93m x 0.18m.
Brown loam with frequent small and medium chalk. Poorly-preserved skeleton; left arm bent across pelvis area. No grave goods.

Grave 259 (Figs 10.18, 10.81) M 23–28. 313°. Context 188. Plot W. 2.68m x 0.93–1.07m x 0.30m.
Cuts Grave 260. Light-brown loam with frequent small and medium chalk. Moderately well-preserved skeleton; skull half left; right arm slightly bent across pelvis.

a　　Iron **spearhead**. Small angular to straight-sided blade, lozenge-section, with broad, solid split socket. Mineral-preserved wood remains in socket. Traces of mineral-preserved plant/vegetal material. Coarse woven textile on blade and socket possibly from wrapping or clothing. Length: 240mm. By right shoulder. Sf 272.
b　　Iron **knife**. Back straight and curving to tip, cutting-edge similar. No signs of wear. Mineral-preserved horn handle. Leather and textile on blade from clothing or sheath. Length: 138mm. Above left pelvis. Sf 271.
c　　Iron **buckle**. Simple D-shaped loop with iron tongue. Mineral-preserved textile on back and edges. Mineral-preserved leather near hinge from a leather strap. Width: 27mm. Waist area. Sf 270.

Grave 260 (Figs 10.119, 10.810) ?M 40–50. 321°. Context 190. Plot W. 1.86m x 1.05m x 0.20m.
Cut by Grave 259. Cream silty loam with frequent small and medium chalk. Poorly-preserved skeleton; right arm bent across pelvis area.

a　　Iron **pin** with scrolled head. Mineral-preserved textile and possible traces of leather thong around head of pin. Length: 132mm. Inside right forearm. Sf 346.
b　　Iron **nail**. Incomplete. Square-sectioned shank, discoidal head. Length: 100mm. Inside right forearm. Sf 347.
c　　Iron **pin**. Incomplete. Ring-form head leading to shaft of circular section, point missing. Traces of mineral-preserved wood and cordage. Length: 105mm. Inside right forearm. Sf 348.
d　　Iron **nail**. Discoidal head, short tapering shank of square section. Length: 38mm. Under right forearm. Sf 349.
e　　Iron **knife**. Short and thin tang. Back curving to tip, cutting-edge sinuous. Well-defined junction of organic handle and blade, set diagonally. Mineral-preserved horn handle and leather on blade from sheath. Length: 114mm. Area of body. Sf 350.

Grave 261 (Figs 10.19, 10.82) ?F 15–17. 321°. Context 192. Phase 1. Plot S. 1.89m x 0.83m x 0.19m.
Cut by Grave 266 (Phase1b–2a). Cream-brown loam with frequent small and medium chalk. Moderately well-preserved skeleton; skull right; left arm bent across body; right arm bent across pelvis.

a　　Iron **pin**. Bent. Amorphous mineral-preserved organic remains on surface. Length: *c* 125mm. Right chest. Sf 212.
b　　Iron **buckle** and **plate**. Oval loop with transverse brass wire inlay and plain tongue. The semi-circular plate has three rivets, which are visible on the back. The back-plate is now lost. Mineral-preserved leather remains present on back-plate from a leather strap. Textile remains on back. Width of loop: 33mm. Width of plate 29mm. Overall length: 41mm. Above right waist. Sf 213.

c   Iron **nail**. Discoidal, oval head and shank of square section. Mineral-preserved, amorphous, organic remains on surface. Length: 49mm. Above left pelvis. Sf 214.

d   Lightly curved shank of an iron **nail**. Fragmentary. Mineral-preserved, amorphous, organic remains on surface. Length: 43mm. Under left waist. Sf 215.

Grave 262 (Figs 10.19, 10.88) ? 35–45. 316°. Context 194. Phase 2–3. Plot S. 2.43m x 1.07–1.13m x 0.30m.
Cream-brown loam with frequent small and medium chalk. Flint packing stones along north-east side of grave indicate a coffin. Poorly-preserved skeleton; left arm slightly bent across pelvis area.

a   Iron **spearhead**. Medium, angular blade, lozenge-section, with a split socket. Two rivets on the socket. Mineral-preserved ash wood (*Fraxinus excelsior*) in socket. Mineral-preserved leather on blade and woven textile on socket. Length: 280mm. Over skull. Sf 336.

b   Iron **knife**. Incomplete, lacking tip of blade. Large, broad tang. Back curves to tip, cutting-edge sinuous. Well-defined junction of organic handle and blade, slightly angled. Mineral-preserved horn handle. Traces of leather and textile on blade from sheath and/or clothing. Length: 188mm. Area of body. Sf 337.

c   Iron **tweezers**. Incomplete. Arms with even splay from broad and angular head to incurved terminals. Undecorated. Mineral-preserved textile and leather thong. Length: 78mm. Inside left elbow. Sf 338.

d   Cast copper alloy **buckle**. D-shaped, faceted loop of D-shaped section, narrowed axis for attachment of tongue, which is missing. Upper and outer faces of loop decorated with six groups of three incised lines. Width of loop: 30mm. Right waist. Sf 339.

Grave 263 (Figs 10.20, 10.82, 10.118) 309°. Context: Sk A, 196; Sk B, 211. Sk A, Phase 1b–2a. Sk B, Phase 1b. Plot S. 2.27m x 1.21m x 0.41m.
Cut by Grave 264 (Phase 3). Light-brown loam with frequent small and medium chalk. Double-stacked grave (Sk A 0.18m above Sk B).

Sk 263A M grown. Prone, leg bones only.

a   Iron **knife**. Fragmentary, lacking part of tang. Back straight and curving to tip. Shallow incised groove on both sides of blade, parallel with back. Mineral-preserved horn handle. Amorphous organic remains on blade, probably leather. Length: 143mm. Area of pelvis. Sf 216.

b   Cast copper alloy **buckle**, D-shaped loop, tongue missing. It was possibly iron due to iron staining found on the loop. Remnants of mineral-preserved leather strap. Width of loop: 24mm. Above spine of Sk B. Sf 217.

Sk 263B ?F 25–30. Poorly-preserved skeleton; skull half right; arms bent across pelvis area.

a   Gilt copper alloy cast small **bow brooch**. Punched ring-and-dot decoration on foot-plate, row of V-shaped punches on foot-plate, cast basketwork decoration on bow. Cast zigzag line/open triangles on the head-plate. Gilding worn on bow and knobs and on ridges of cast decoration. Cast spring-holder and pin-catch. Remains of iron spring with mineral-preserved textile. Length: 39mm. Weight: 4.8g. Left of spine. Sf 353.

b   Gilt copper alloy cast Kentish small **square-headed brooch**. Border of head- and foot-plate punched with ring-and-dot motif. Gilding worn on bow and ridges of cast decoration. Edge of foot-plate partly broken away. Cast spring-holder and pin-catch; copper alloy pin piercing mineral-preserved textile. Length: 43mm. Weight: 6.9g. In area of left pelvis. Sf 354.

c   Gilt copper alloy cast Kentish small **square-headed brooch**. Ridges on border of head- and foot-plate nicked. Gilding worn on ridges. Cast spring-holder and pin-catch. Iron spring with mineral-preserved textile. Length: 42mm. Weight: 8.2g. In area of left pelvis. Sf 355.

d–o   Five amber and seven glass **beads**. Between femurs. Sf nos 356–367.

Grave 263 beads
amber: 5 beads

d	1	short, facetted, diam 16–20mm
g	1	medium, barrel-shaped, diam 6–10mm. Fig 4.23, Grave 263B, Sf 359 (g1)
l	1	short, wedge-shaped, diam 21–25mm. Fig 4.23, Grave 263B, Sf 367 (l1)
n	1	short, facetted, diam 16–20mm
o	1	short, globular, diam 6–10mm

glass: 7 beads
e
Blue (no 1)

      1   very short, annular, diam 11–15mm. Fig 4.23, Grave 263B, Sf 357 (e1)

f
Traffic Light Imitation (no 30)

      1   medium, globular, diam 11–15mm, three opaque yellow and translucent green streaked dots on opaque red body. Fig 4.23, Grave 263B, Sf 358 (f1)

h
Roman Melon (no 36)

      1   medium, diam 21–25mm, discoloured. Fig 4.23, Grave 263B, Sf 360 (h1)

i
other melon (no 59)

      1   short, barrel-shaped, 5-lobed cross-section, diam 21–25mm, translucent, green (light). Fig 4.23, Grave 263B, Sf 361 (i1)

Hour-glass (no 13)

      1   two segments, medium, barrel-shaped, diam 11–15mm, translucent, green, opaque yellow wavy trail Fig 4.23, Grave 263B, Sf 362 (j1)

k, m
variation Candy (no 4)

      2   medium, barrel-shaped/globular, diam 11–15mm, opaque red trail on the equator on translucent blue wavy trail on discoloured body (one fragmented). Fig 4.23, Grave 263B, Sf 366 (k1)

Grave 264 (Figs 10.20–21, 10.82, 10.121) M 40–45. 302°. Context 198. Phase 3. Plot S. 2.57m x 0.93–1.12m x 0.51m.

Cuts Graves 263 (Phase 1b–2a) and 347 (Phase 2a). Brown loam with frequent small and medium chalk containing two residual pot-sherds, one Iron Age and one Roman, one bead (k) and a crossbow brooch (j); see below. Poorly-preserved skeleton; right arm bent across pelvis. Traces of textile and feathers may denote head was laid on a feather pillow. Radiocarbon date: 1528 ± 17 BP (UB-6474) cal AD 435–490 (22%) or cal AD 530–600 (73%).

a   Iron **spearhead**. Leaf-shaped, lozenge-section, with a medium shank and a split socket, rivet (nail). *Salix* sp, willow wood in socket. Traces of mineral-preserved feathers on the socket overlying remains of mineralised textile and plant/vegetal material from a possible pillow. Length: 444mm. Left of skull. Sf 252.

b   Iron **sword**. Pommel of short, rectangular iron bar (37mm surviving); remains of organic grip and guards, with a slight midrib to the broad tang on both sides between the guards; fuller; organic scabbard remains including leather. Wood from the scabbard preserved on edge of the blade with traces of mineral-preserved *Fraxinus excelsior*, in association with sheep's wool and *Linum usitatissimum*, flax fibres. Traces of a horn hilt. Length: 890 x 55mm (47); grip length: 9mm; thickness of upper and lower guards, 13 and 14mm respectively. On the left, pommel by shoulder. Sf 369 (SN 1019; pp 239–43).

c   Iron **knife**. Broad, short tang. Back curves to tip, cutting-edge straight, blade relatively wide. Mineral-preserved horn handle. Fibre tufts on blade possibly represents a fleece-lined sheath. Length: 130mm. Above left pelvis. Sf 260.

d   Iron **buckle** and **plate**, now strongly distorted. Round or d-shaped iron loop with the tongue piercing a fragment of mineral-preserved leather from belt or suspension strap. The plate is rectangular near the loop, then narrows to a strip and has an enlarged terminal. The narrow part of the plate is decorated with a silver strip. The terminal and rectangular section each carry a large disc-headed silver rivet each. On the underside of the terminal there is a copper alloy rivet and a diamond-shaped washer. Mineral-preserved textile back of buckle. Width of loop: 24mm. Width of plate 16mm. Length of plate: *c* 49mm. Lying next to knife (c). Sf 259.

e   1, Iron **shield boss**. Incomplete. Slightly carinated convex cone with high, sloping wall (height: 25mm), silver-plated disc-headed apex (diameter: 20mm) and five small disc-headed flange rivets (diameter: 8mm), one with a silvered disc and another with a washer *in situ* on its shank. On opposite face to mineralised *Tilia* sp, lime wood, diagonally across iron band, loosely woven textile. Mineralised wood and leather remains indicate a covering of leather to the front as well as the back of the wooden shield board. Diameter: 160mm. Height: 80mm. Between feet. Sf 253.

e   2, Iron **shield grip**. Incomplete, end of one terminal broken. Strap grip (width: 20mm) expanding towards terminals (width: 40mm). Fastened to shield board by a rivet at each end. Mineralised wood remains indicate a wooden handle with a lap joint construction. Length: 140mm. Under shield boss between feet. Sf 254.

f–i   Four iron **shield board mounts**. Set of four identical tin-plated disc mounts positioned over feet, around shield boss (e). Only mount (f) complete. Mineral-preserved wood and leather from shield board. Diameter: 40mm. Sf nos 255–258. (See pp 267–9).

j   Copper alloy Roman **crossbow brooch**. Spring is mounted on an iron axis bar in plain open-backed spring case which is rounded front and back but has a slightly flattened top. Bow has flat back whose section has sides tapering in toward the front which has a flat front down which runs a cabled line. Bow is stopped top and bottom by cross-moulding. Top one has a groove above and below a concave surface, lower cross-moulding has only a concave surface running back to the top of the foot which has a slot for the pin. The front has a flat central face and a chamfer on each side. The whole is tinned. From the general filling of grave. Length: 109mm. Sf 679.

k   Glass **bead**. *Other globular (no 63)*, short, diam 6–10mm, opaque, red. Fig 4.23, Grave 264, Sf 934 (1). From the general filling of grave. Sf 934.

Grave 265 (Figs 10.21–24, 10.83) 300°. Context: Sk A, 200; Sk B, 212. Sk B, Phase 3a. Plot S. 2.55m x 0.87–0.92m x 0.31m.

Cuts Grave 359. Brown loam with frequent small and medium chalk. Double-stacked grave (Sk A 0.20m above Sk B).

Sk 265A ? grown. Lower leg bones only. No grave goods.

Sk 265B ?M 25–30. Poorly-preserved skeleton.

a   Iron **spearhead**. Broad angular blade, lozenge-section, with a short thin shank and a split socket with rivet. Traces of *Fraxinus excelsior*, ash wood remains in socket. Length: 335mm. Left of skull. Sf 371.

b   Iron **sword** with traces of mineral-preserved wood scabbard made of *Fraxinus excelsior*, ash with a sheep's wool fibre lining. Traces of horn and ash wood survive on the hilt. End of tang missing; no pommel; wood packing pieces on tang; fuller. Length: 944mm (surviving) x 52mm (45); grip and guards not measurable. On left, hilt by lower end of upper arm. Sf 368 (SN 1020; pp 243–6).

c   Iron **shield boss**. Incomplete, broken apex. Large, slightly carinated shallow convex cone with high straight wall (diameter: 25mm), disc-headed apex (diameter: 20mm) and five large copper alloy disc-headed flange rivets (diameter: 22mm). Mineralised wood and leather remains indicate a wooden board with a leather covering front and back. Diameter: 170mm. Height: 85mm. Between knees. Sf 372.

d   1, Iron **shield grip**. Incomplete. Long grip with flanged central handle section (length: 70mm, width: 35mm) flanked by two circular plates (diameter: 35mm, diameter: 32mm) each accommodating a rivet. Narrower tapering extensions (length: 100mm and 120mm; width: 10mm) detached from central section. Mineralised wood and leather remains indicate a wooden handle covered with leather. Remains of a narrow leather strap wound round the grip either as a binding for the handle or from a carrying strap. Under boss, between knees. Sf 373.

2, Iron **shield board rivets** with traces of mineral-preserved *Fraxinus excelsior*, ash and *Salix* sp, willow wood on backs. Set of four copper alloy disc-headed rivets. Identical to flange rivets on shield boss. Associated with long shield grip. Positioned in two pairs on shield board at either end of long grip extensions to either side of shield boss. Diameter: 22mm. Between legs. Sf 375.

e   Pair of copper alloy **buckle counter-plate**. Rectangular. Central raised field has four groups of double incised lines running across plate, each flanged end has line of three dome-headed rivets for attachment. Mineral-preserved leather. Length: 38mm. Width: 21mm. Above right pelvis. Sf 376.

f   Copper alloy **buckle** and **plate**. Oval facetted loop, pentagonal shield-on-tongue. Rectangular plate with same decoration as (e). Sheet metal back-plate with central slot and two tongue-shaped projections folded over loop, between two plates. Traces of mineral-preserved plum/cherry wood (*Prunus* sp) and wool fibres. Length: 52mm. Width: 28mm. Above right pelvis. Sf 377.

g   Copper alloy **strap-end**. Leaf-shaped with central ridge. Split end with two disc-headed rivets. Double line incised border at top, diagonal cross beneath, repeated below. Length: 60mm. Above pelvis. Sf 378.

h   Copper alloy **strap-end**. Leaf-shaped with central ridge, adorned with two lines of punched dots. Split end with two disc-headed rivets. Not a pair for (g). Length: 55mm. Above pelvis. Sf 379.

i   Iron **knife**. Short tang leading to straight back, curved to tip. Sinuous cutting-edge. Well-defined junction of organic handle and blade. Mineralised remains of horn handle and leather sheath; also, traces of ash (*Fraxinus excelsior*) (intrusive?). Length: 135mm. Above pelvis. Sf 374.

j   Three copper alloy **fragments**. Possibly part of buckle (e). Above pelvis. Sf 380.

k, m   Copper alloy **balance** and **pans**, with seventeen discs, ingots
–ee   and Roman coins which probably functioned as weights (k, m–w, y–bb), and probable case fitting (x), found below and to the left of the skull. Disposition of these items and associated organic remains suggests that balance and assemblage of coins, discs and ingots were placed together in a leather case, and that they were wrapped or packed in fleece within it.

     A small group of tools and scrap items (gg–ll) tightly clustered adjacent to but below the balance and weights and appears to represent a separate assemblage.

k   1, **coin**, *Aes dupondius* or *as* (first, second or third century). Detail uncertain as coin has been filed to make it flatter and rounder, probably to adapt the coin for use as a weight, but traces of the bust and a standing figure on the reverse are discernible; line of six triangular punch marks on reverse. Weight: 9.34g. Diameter: 25mm. Accreted to (k2) by corrosion. Sf 392.

     2, copper alloy **disc**, probably a weight, possibly cut down and shaped from a Roman *sestertius*. Both faces and edge have been filed flat. Weight: 12.54g. Diameter: 24mm. Accreted to (k1) by corrosion. Sf 393.

     Both located at the left of skull.

l   Copper alloy belt **mount**, similar to (e) with remains of sheet copper alloy back-plate. Length: 39mm. Above pelvis. Sf 381.

m   Domed copper alloy **ingot**, probably a weight. Mineralised remains of fine, unspun, unwoven fibres which may be a

packing material. Weight: 3.19g. Diameter: 12mm. Sf 394.

n   Lead and copper alloy **object**, probably a weight. Incomplete. Cast copper alloy band around lead core which is mineralised and incomplete, original form is uncertain. Weight: 14.90g. Diameter: 19mm. Sf 395.

o   Copper alloy **coin**. Silvered bronze *nummus* of AD 367–375. GLORIA NOVI SAECVLI (Gratian). RIC IX, Arles 15. Under skull. Weight: 2.70g. Sf 396.

p   Copper alloy **coin**, debased *radiate*, possibly barbarous, AD 260s–270s (probably a Gallic usurper). Both faces and edge have been filed, probably to adapt the coin for use as a weight, but details survive on both obverse and reverse. Weight: 1.73g. Diameter: 14mm. Sf 405.

q   Copper alloy **disc**, probably a weight, possibly cut down and shaped from a Roman *sestertius*. Both faces and edges have been filed flat; one face has a border of sixteen or possibly seventeen double-arcade punch marks. Weight: 9.22g. Diameter: 17mm. Sf 397.

r   **Coin**, brass *sestertius* of Trajan (AD 98–117). Both faces and edge have been filed, probably to adapt the coin for use as a weight, removing detail. Mineralised remains of fine, unspun, unwoven fibres which may be a packing material. Weight: 24.99g. Diameter: 31mm. Sf 398.

s   **Coin**, brass *sestertius* of Trajan (AD 98–117). Both faces and edge filed have been filed, probably to adapt the coin for use as a weight, removing detail; single punched or drilled dot on reverse. Mineralised remains of fine, unspun, unwoven fibres which may be a packing material. Weight: 19.70g. Diameter: 30mm. Sf 400.

t   Copper alloy **disc**, probably a weight, possibly cut down and shaped from a Roman *sestertius*. Mineralised remains of fine, unspun, unwoven fibres which may be a packing material. Weight: 6.24g. Diameter: 14mm. Sf 399.

u   Copper alloy **washer** or **rivet-head**. Remains of rivet shank in centre. Weight: 0.79g. Diameter: 19mm. Sf 401.

v   **Coin**, brass *sestertius* of Septimius Severus (AD 193–211). Reverse: standing female figure holding cornucopia. Both faces and edge have been filed, probably to adapt the coin for use as a weight, removing detail and reducing the original diameter of the coin. Mineralised remains of fine, unspun, unwoven fibres which may be a packing material. Weight: 18.32g. Diameter: 28mm. Sf 402.

w   Copper alloy **disc**, probably a weight, probably adapted from a Roman *dupondius*. Both faces and edge have been filed flat; one face has a cross of twenty-three punched lines. Mineralised remains of fine, unspun, unwoven fibres which may be a packing material. Weight: 9.11g. Diameter: 26mm. Sf 403.

x   Sub-rectangular copper alloy **strip**, possibly a fitting from a case or bag. Mineralised remains of fine, unspun, unwoven fibres which may be a packing material and possible mineralised leather remains relating to case. Length: 57mm. Sf 382.

y   Copper alloy **disc**, probably a weight, possibly adapted from a Roman coin. One side has a border of ten punched dots. Mineralised remains of fine, unspun, unwoven fibres which may be a packing material. Weight: 1.65g. Diameter: 10mm. Sf 404.

z   Copper alloy **disc**, probably a weight, possibly adapted from a Roman coin. Mineralised remains of fine, unspun, unwoven fibres which may be a packing material. Weight: 0.46g. Diameter: 6mm. Sf 406.

aa   Copper alloy **coin**. Silvered bronze *nummus* of AD 330–335. CONSTANTINOPOLIS type. Mint illegible. Weight: 1.72g. Diameter: 17mm. Sf 407.

bb   **Coin**, brass *sestertius* of the second century (Hadrianic or Antonine). Both faces and edge have been filed flat, probably to adapt the coin for use as a weight. Mineralised remains of fine, unspun, unwoven fibres which may be a packing material. Weight: 15.57g. Diameter: 28mm. Sf 408.

cc   Copper alloy **balance pan**. Raised metal sheet; three suspension rings of copper alloy wire. Scratches on the interior surface appear to have been caused by use. Mineralised remains of fine, unspun, unwoven fibres which may be a packing material. Diameter: 42mm. Sf 390.

dd   Copper alloy **balance pan**. Raised metal sheet; three suspension rings of copper alloy wire. Mineral-preserved spun fibres on suspension ring. Possible mineralised leather remains relating to case. Mineralised remains of fine, unspun, unwoven fibres which may be a packing material. Diameter: 42mm. Sf 391.

ee   Copper alloy **balance beam**. Incomplete, top suspension ring detached. The suspension shears are pivoted through the indicator with a copper alloy rivet; above this a hole (diameter: 2.5mm) has been drilled through the indicator. The beam ends are flattened and pierced to take suspension rings of copper alloy wire. Mineral-preserved spun fibres on suspension ring. Possible mineralised leather remains relating to case. Mineralised remains of fine, unspun, unwoven fibres which may be a packing material. Length: 132mm. Sf 389.

ff   not allocated.

gg   Iron **shaft** of oval section with traces of mineral-preserved ash wood (*Fraxinus excelsior*). Length: 63mm. Under skull. Sf 383.

hh   Iron **awl-like firesteel**. Incomplete, lacking end part of ash wood (*Fraxinus excelsior)* handle. Slender, tapering shaft of iron, circular section, point possibly broken. Length: 43mm. Under skull. Sf 384.

ii   Iron **spear ferrule**. Yew wood (*Taxus baccata*) remains in socket. Mineral-preserved traces of leather may denote a carrying strap. Length: 76mm. Under skull. Sf 385

jj   Lead or silver **lump**. Copper alloy clip in centre. Under skull. Sf 386.

kk   Roman lead **fragment** in form of bird of prey, seen in profile. Iron staining on one side. Length: 32mm. Under skull. Sf 387.

ll   Iron **nail**. Square section, shank only. Mineral-preserved leather remains. Length: 18mm. Under skull. Sf 388.

Grave 266 (Figs 10.24–25, 10.82, 10.121) ?F 30–35. 303°. Context 202. Phase 1b–2a. Plot S. 2.28m x 0.74m x 0.45m.

Cuts Grave 261 (Phase 1). Grey-brown loam with frequent small and medium chalk. Moderately well-preserved skeleton; arms bent across upper pelvis.

a, e   Iron **rod** (a), broken at one end, fused to incomplete, U-shaped iron **staple** (e). Ash wood (*Fraxinus excelsior*) remains attached to both sections (a) and (e). Length of rod: 63mm. Width of staple: 38mm. Left of left femur. Sf 247 and Sf 248.

b   Fragment of **window glass**. Naturally coloured blue-green and rectangular in shape. Sandy texture on one side. Length: 33mm. Width: 16mm. Left of left pelvis. Sf 250.

c   Fragment of **vessel glass**. Body sherd from Roman bottle. Length: 24mm. Width: 16mm. Left of left pelvis. Sf 352.

d   Fragment of dark green **porphyry** marble veneer, bevelled on one edge. Length: 29mm. Width: 31mm. Left of left pelvis. Sf 351.

f   Iron **buckle** fragments, D-shaped loop, plain tongue. Width: 38mm. Centre waist. Sf 246.

g   Cast copper alloy **ring**. Extreme wear on inner ridge. Diameter: 39mm. Weight: 15.5g. Above left pelvis. Sf 245.

h   Iron **knife**. Fragmentary and lacking most of tang. Straight back curving to tip, sinuous and worn cutting-edge. Well-defined junction between organic handle and blade. Mineral-preserved horn handle with leather from sheath. Length: 115mm. Above left pelvis. Sf 249.

i, j   Matching pair of silver-gilt cast openwork **radiate-headed brooches** set with garnets not on hatched foil. Punched triangles on head- and foot-plate and ring-and-dot decoration on bow copper-nielloed. Rims on edges of bow worn, possibly also edge of head-plate. Cast pair of spring-holders and pin-catch with hatched decoration. Remains of iron pins with mineral-preserved folds of textile. Length of (i): 83mm; weight: 21.3g. Length of (j): 83mm; weight: 19.2g. Area of decayed chest. Sf 243 and Sf 244.

Grave 267 (Fig 10.82) ? 15–18. 320°. Context 204. Plot S. 2.07m x 0.72m (min) x 0.12m.

Grey-brown clay loam with frequent small and medium chalk. Very fragmentary skull and long bone fragments only. No grave goods.

Grave 268 (Fig 10.83) ? juvenile/grown 313°. Context 206. Plot S. 0.91m (min) x 0.55m x 0.06m.

Partially destroyed by modern terrace. Grey-brown clay loam with frequent small and medium chalk. Fragmentary femurs only. No grave goods.

Grave 269 (Figs 10.25, 10.83 ? 20–25. 327°. Context 208. Plot S. 1.90m (min) x 0.52m (min) x 0.06m.

Cream-brown loam with frequent small chalk. Fragmentary pelvis and long bones only.

a   Iron **knife**. Fragmentary, lacking end of tang which is noticeably broad. Back curves and rises slightly to tip, cutting-edge sinuous. Mineral-preserved horn handle with mineralised leather remains from sheath. Textile remains on one side. Length: 125mm. Diagonally across right waist. Sf 266.

Grave 270 (Fig 10.83) F grown. 304°. Context 210. Plot S. 2.05m x 0.71–0.85m x 0.23m.

Cream-brown loam with frequent small and medium chalk. Poorly-preserved skeleton; skull decayed; left arm bent across pelvis; right arm decayed. No grave goods.

Grave 271 (Figs 10.25, 10.84) F 23–28. 327°. Context 222. Phase 2–3a. Plot U. 2.20m x 0.80m x 0.42m.
Cream silty loam with very frequent small and medium chalk. Moderately well-preserved skeleton; skull half left; right arm bent across body; left arm slightly bent across pelvis.

a　　Iron **knife**. Fragmentary, lacking part of tang. Straight back, curving and rising slightly to tip. Slight groove running parallel with back on one side. Well-defined junction between handle and blade. Mineral-preserved horn handle with leather from sheath. Length: 113mm. Over left lower arm. Sf 269.
b　　Silver spiral **finger ring**. Decorative grooves not showing on rear side of silver strip; worn on side opposite to terminals. Diameter: *c* 2mm. Weight: 2.8g. Around finger of left hand. Sf 267.
c　　Two cast copper alloy **shoe-shaped studs**, with remains of white metal plating. The pierced attachment lugs at the back have the same length although the studs are of different sizes. Lengths: 17 and 20mm. Centre waist. Sf 268.

Grave 272 (Figs 10.25, 10.84) ? 8–9. 319°. Context 224. Plot S. 1.78m x 0.52–0.70m x 0.15m.
Cuts Grave 320. Cream loam with very frequent small and medium chalk. Fragmentary skull and long bones only.

a　　Iron **knife**. Back curves to tip, sinuous cutting-edge, trace of junction between organic handle and blade. Mineral-preserved leather from sheath and remains of textile on one face of blade. Length: 115mm. Left side of decayed body. Sf 275.

Grave 273 (Fig 2.2) No bone. 319°. Context 213. Plot S. 2.51m x 0.62m (min) x 0.15m.
Pick marks on base. Cream-brown loam with frequent small and medium chalk. No bone survived, grave length suggests a grown individual. No grave goods.

Grave 274 (Fig 2.2) No bone. 308°. Context 214. Plot S. 1.70m (min) x 0.57m (min) x 0.11m.
Brown loam with frequent small and medium chalk. No bones survived; grave length suggests a grown individual. No grave goods.

Grave 275 (Fig 2.2) No bone. 319°. Context 215. Plot S. 1.25m (min) x 0.44m (min) x 0.19m.
Cream-brown loam with frequent small and medium chalk. No bones survived. No grave goods.

Grave 276 (Fig 10.121) No bone. 322°. Context 216. Plot S. 1.10m x 0.52m (min) x 0.14m.
Cuts Graves 349 (Phase 1) and 350 (Phase 1b–3). Brown loam with frequent small and medium chalk. No bones survived; grave length suggests a child. No grave goods.

Grave 277 (Fig 2.2) No bone. 330°. Context 217. Plot S. 1.06m (min) x 0.49m (min) x 0.16m.

Brown loam with frequent small and medium chalk. No bones survived. No grave goods.

Grave 278 (Figs 10.25, 10.84) No bone. 319°. Context 220. Plot S. 1.39m x 0.81m x 0.27m.
Brown loam with frequent small and medium chalk. No bones survived; grave length suggests a child.

a　　Copper alloy **sheet** with punched ring-and-dot decoration; some of the dots created holes in the sheet. Perforations in two corners, third corner bent, perforation torn, forth corner broken off. Copper alloy wire ring in one hole, broken. Associated wire does not match. Width of sheet 38mm; weight: 4.1g. Length of wire: 38mm; weight: 0.4g. North-west end of grave. Sf 273.
b　　Seven iron fragments of flat section with flattened triangular apex. Length of fragments: 88mm; max width: 17mm. North-west end of grave. Sf 274.

Grave 279 (Fig 10.84) M 40–50? 321°. Context 226. Plot T. 2.27m x 0.98m x 0.35m.
Cream-brown loam with very frequent small and medium chalk. Poorly-preserved skeleton; left arm bent across pelvis area. No grave goods.

Grave 280 (Fig 10.84) ?F 20–25. 316°. Context 228. Plot T. 2.35m x 0.90m x 0.30m.
Light-brown loam with frequent small and medium chalk. Moderately well-preserved skeleton; right arm bent across pelvis; left arm bent across body; legs crossed at ankle (right over left). No grave goods.

Grave 281 (Figs 10.25–26, 10.85) ?M 25–30. 311°. Context 230. Phase 1b. Plot T. 2.30m x 0.96m x 0.32m.
Cut by Grave 325. Cream-brown loam with frequent small and medium chalk. Moderately well-preserved skeleton; skull half right; arms bent across pelvis area.

a　　Iron **disc brooch** with translucent (greenish?) inlays separated by silver strips. X-ray suggests spring-holder and pin-catch made of folded iron strips. Mineral-preserved textile on and around pin, hinge and catch. Diameter: *c* 20mm. Neck. Sf 460.
b　　Group of 10 amber **beads**. Neck area. Sf 426 (see below).
c　　Fragments of an iron **pin/rod**. Length: 40mm. Right chest. Sf 427.
d　　Gilt copper alloy cast Kentish small **square-headed brooch**. Punched dots on border of head- and foot-plate, ridges nicked. Gilding worn. Head-plate border partly broken off. Cast spring-holder. Remains of iron spring with mineral-preserved textile. Length: 55mm; weight: 11.6g. Right side of body. Sf 461.
e　　Gilt copper alloy cast Kentish great **square-headed brooch**. Gilding worn mostly on ridge framing face on bow, right and upper frame of animal decoration on head-plate, and edges of foot-plate. Iron spring. Mineral-preserved leather (thong or strap) and textile on back. Length: 74mm; weight: 20.5g. Right side of body. Sf 462.

f   Two cast copper alloy **mounts**, rectangular, with a rivet in each corner. Width: 22 x 14–16mm. Outside right wrist. Sf 428.

g   Cast copper alloy **buckle** and **plate**. Oval loop of convex section, tongue with semi-cylindrical base. Rectangular plate with matching raised moulding of semi-cylindrical section with three grooves either end. The three small dome-headed rivets on the flanged rear end of the plate reach into the iron back-plate. Towards the loop end, one rivet shank is visible between plate and back-plate. Mineral-preserved textile on back. Width of loop: 30mm; width of plate 10mm. Overall length: 48mm. Centre waist. Sf 463.

h   Iron **nail**. Small discoidal head. Length: 26mm. Left of left pelvis. Sf 429.

i   Iron **knife** with traces of mineral-preserved ash wood (*Fraxinus excelsior*) on blade. Fragmentary, lacking end of blade; noticeably long and slender. Well-defined junction between organic handle and blade. Back straight, cutting-edge sinuous and fragmentary. Mineral-preserved horn handle with traces of leather on blade. Length: 134mm. Area of left waist, over brush handle (k). Sf 430.

j   Three iron **rings**. Mineral-preserved leather and textile on one side of each ring. Leather indicates possible suspension thong. Diameters: 45mm, 40mm and 33mm. Left of left femur. Sf 431.

k   Copper alloy sheet **brush handle**, curved to form hollow cone. Length: 60mm. Left of pelvis, under knife (i). Sf 432.

l   Iron **pin**. Strip wound round shaft. Length: 95mm. Left of left femur. Sf 433.

m   Large amber **bead**. Left of left femur. Sf 434 (see below).

n   Copper alloy **armlet**. Length: 51mm. Left of left femur. Sf 464.

o   Copper alloy **tweezers** with plain, slightly expanding arms below a constricted head and lightly incurved terminals. A band of degraded cord is visible on the arm immediately below the loop, with evidence in the corrosion of its continuation on the other - perhaps from a suspension cord? Length: 38mm. Left of left femur. Sf 465.

Grave 281 beads
b
amber: 10 beads
- 2   medium, globular, diam 6–10mm
- 1   medium, rounded, diam 6–10mm
- 1   medium, facetted, diam 11–15mm
- 2   medium, facetted, diam 6–10mm
- 2   medium, facetted, diam 2–5mm
- 1   medium, fragment, re-used, diam 6–10mm
- 1   fragments

m
amber: 1 bead
- 1   short, fragment. **Fig 4.23**, Grave 281, Sf 434 (m1)

Grave 282 (Figs 10.27, 10.84) 312°. Context: Sk A, 232; Sk B, 354. Plot T. 2.42m x 0.89m x 0.40m.
Cream-brown loam with frequent small and medium chalk. Double-stacked grave (Sk A 0.25m above Sk B).

Sk 282A ?M grown. Leg bones only; legs bent to right.

a   Iron **knife**. Two small fragments of blade and tang. Mineral-preserved remains of horn handle and possible leather from sheath on blade. Length of fragments: 55mm (broken). Area of pelvis. Sf 263.

Sk 282B M 20–25. Moderately well-preserved skeleton; skull right; right arm bent across upper pelvis; left arm bent across body. No grave goods.

Grave 283 (Fig 2.2) No bone. 339°. Context 233. Plot U. 1.40m x 0.60m x 0.15m.
Grey-brown loam with frequent small and medium chalk. No bones survived; grave length suggests a child. No grave goods.

Grave 284 (Fig 2.2) ?M 25–30. 317°. Context 236. Plot U. 2.22m x 1.10m x 0.44m.
Cream-brown loam with frequent small and medium chalk. Poorly-preserved skeleton; skull half right. No grave goods.

Grave 285 (Figs 10.27, 10.85) ?F 20–25. 327°. Context 238. Plot U. 2.38m x 1.00m x 0.20m.
Brown loam with frequent small and medium chalk. Poorly-preserved skeleton; left arm bent across body.

a   Iron **knife**. Fragmentary, lacking most of blade. Long tang, traces of junction between organic handle and blade. Mineral-preserved wood handle and traces of leather on blade from sheath. Length: 100mm. Left chest. Sf 447.

Grave 286 (Figs 10.27, 10.86) F 45+. 306°. Context 240. Plot T. 2.10m x 1.03m x 0.47m.
Brown loam with frequent small and medium chalk containing an Iron Age pot-sherd. Poorly-preserved skeleton; left arm bent across pelvis area.

a   Iron **knife**. Fragmentary, lacking part of tang. Back straight and curving to tip; cutting-edge similar, no obvious wear. Well-defined junction of organic handle and blade. Mineral-preserved horn handle and remains of leather from sheath which is overlain by mineral-preserved textile remains on one face. Length: 118mm. By left elbow. Sf 449.

b   Two copper alloy **repair-clips**. One is U-shaped, with tapering terminals, the other is fragmentary with incurved terminals. Length: 11mm; terminals 7mm. By left foot. Sf 450.

Grave 287 (Figs 10.27, 10.86) ? 3–4. 295°. Context 242. Plot T. 1.65m x 0.72m x 0.63m.
Cream-brown loam with frequent small and medium chalk. Lower jaw fragment only.

a   Iron **buckle** and **plate**. Oval loop, tongue missing. Tapering fragmentary plate, now separate. Mineral-preserved textile on back. Width of loop: 23mm; width of plate: 16mm. Centre waist. Sf 436.

Grave 288 (Figs 10.27, 10.86) F 30–40. 298°. Context 244. Plot T. 2.42m x 0.80m x 0.65m.
Light-brown loam with frequent small and medium chalk. Moderately well-preserved skeleton.

a   Iron **finger ring**. Remains of mineral-preserved textile and possible human skin product. Diameter 25mm. Around fourth metacarpel of left hand. Sf 474.

Grave 289 (Figs 10.27, 10.86, 10.120) F 17–20. 310°. Context 246. Plot T. 2.52m x 0.88m x 0.44m.
?Cut by Grave 290 (Phase1). Brown loam with frequent small and medium chalk. Moderately well-preserved skeleton.

a   Iron **knife**. Broad tang, slightly bent. Back curves to tip, cutting-edge similar. Trace of junction between organic handle and blade. Mineral-preserved horn handle and remains of leather from sheath on blade. Length: 111mm. Left of left pelvis. Sf 531.
b–d Iron **châtelaine**: remains of figure-of-eight iron **ring** (d) in poor condition and 4 **keys** (b, c), two are fragmentary and made from thin rod. Two remain attached to an iron **ring**, a third, with a swan's neck curve, is attached to a length of iron **wire**, of which 17mm survives. Four hooked 'wards' remain. Associated mineral-preserved textile on one face of (c). Length of most complete key: 124mm. Diameter of ring: 25mm. Left of left pelvis. Sf nos 532–534.
e   **Limpet shell**. Left of left femur. Sf 535.
f   Iron **ring**. Incomplete, D-shaped section. Found with three fragments of copper alloy sheet. Diameter: 37mm. Left of left femur. Sf 536.
g   Iron pierced **lozenge** with fragmentary iron ring. Length: 46mm. Left of left femur. Sf 537.
h   Cast copper alloy miniature **buckle** and **plate**. Oval loop with fixed triangular plate. There is one rivet-hole at the pointed end of the plate. Two pierced lugs on the back of the buckle provided further means of attachment. Traces of white metal plating and iron staining on the back of the buckle. Width of loop:13mm; width of plate: 14mm. Overall length: 30mm. By left pelvis. Sf 538.

Grave 290 (Figs 10.27, 10.86, 10.120) F 19–22. 304°. Context 248. Phase 1. Plot T. 2.57m x 1.00m x 0.75m.
?Cuts Grave 289; relationship to Grave 292 unclear. Cream-brown loam with frequent small and medium chalk. Moderately well-preserved skeleton.

a   Iron **pin**. Associated mineral-preserved textile. Length: 150mm. Left chest. Sf 639.
b   Gilt copper alloy cast **button brooch**. Ridges around face and of upper part of face nicked. Gilding worn only on flange, nose and brow of face. Punch-mark decoration around the inner rim and on helmet. Cast spring-holder and pin-catch. Remains of iron spring. Axis of pin almost horizontal in relation to face

decoration. Mineral-preserved textile on lug. Diameter: 19mm. Height of flange: 3mm. Weight: 4.0g. Left chest. Sf 640.
c   Gilt copper alloy **finger ring**. Plain with oval bezel and hoop of semi-circular section. Diameter: 22mm. Area of left hand. Sf 641.
d   Silver perforated **spoon** or **skimmer** and fragment of copper alloy ?suspension wire ?ring. Break on spoon handle fresh. Holes ?drilled/punched on display side of bowl. Punched ring decoration; circles incised with dividers. Length: 69mm. Weight: 7.9g. Copper alloy ?**ring** made of three wires, two held together by loops, one of them intertwined with a third wire in slip-knot fashion. It seems a slip-knot ring made of a single wire broke and was repaired. Missing part of ring marked by fresh breaks. Mineral-preserved textile on back. Mineral-preserved leather, textile and vegetable fibres under spoon. Width: 18mm. Weight: 0.5g. Outside left thigh. Sf 642.
e   **Rock crystal bead**. Left of left femur. Sf 643 (see below).
f   Two amber **beads**. Left of left femur. Sf 644 (see below).
g   Copper alloy **strap-end** made from a single folded strip. Leather originally fixed by copper alloy rivet. Length: 25mm. Weight: 1.6g. Under spoon (d). Sf 645.

Grave 290 beads
e
rock crystal: 1 bead
1   medium, asymmetrically globular, ridge on equator, diam 21–25mm. Fig 4.23, Grave 290, Sf 643 (e1)
f
amber: 2 beads
1   short, wedge-shaped, diam 11–15mm. Fig 4.23, Grave 290, Sf 644 (f1)
1   short, facetted, diam 11–15mm

Grave 291 (Fig 10.87) M 50+. 291°. Context 250. Plot T. 2.77m x 1.25m x 0.65m.
Cream loam with very frequent small and medium chalk. Moderately well-preserved skeleton; skull right; legs bent to right. No grave goods.

Grave 292 (Figs 10.28, 10.86) M 40–50. 302°. Context 252. Plot T. 2.53m x 1.07–1.13m x 0.58m.
Relationship to Grave 290 (Phase 1) unclear. Cream-brown loam with frequent small and medium chalk. Moderately well-preserved skeleton; right arm slightly bent across pelvis.

a   Copper alloy **pin** made from sheet coiled into a hollow tube. Incised spiral or series of incised fine lines at wide end. Length: 72mm. Weight: 1.6g. Right shoulder. Sf 448.

Grave 293 (Figs 10.28, 10.87) ? 2–3. 310°. Context 144. Phase 1b–2. Plot Y. 1.60m x 0.60m x 0.45m.
Cream-brown loam with frequent small and medium chalk containing a Roman pot-sherd. Fragmentary skull only.

a   Iron pierced **lozenge** with central piercing. Associated mineral-preserved textile on one face. Length: 39mm. Chest area. Sf 286.

b   1, group of seven amber and 39 glass **beads**. Chest area. Sf 285 (see below).

2, copper alloy wire coiled into a **ring** and iron hook-shaped **fragment**. Mineral-preserved textile. Diameter of ring: *c* 7mm. Length of fragment: 13mm. Weight: <0.1g. Chest area. Sf 1084 and Sf 1085.

Grave 293 beads

b

amber: 7 beads

3   medium, rounded, diam 6–10mm

4   medium, rounded, diam 2–5mm

glass: 39 beads

Constricted Segmented (no 5)

1   five segments, very long, diam 2–5mm. Fig 4.26, Grave 293, Sf 285 (b2)

1   four segments, very long, diam 2–5mm. Fig 4.26, Grave 293, Sf 285 (b1)

4   three segments, very long, diam 2–5mm

7   two segments, long to very long, diam 2–5mm

20   short to medium, diam 2–5mm

Constricted Cylindrical (no 6)

3   very long, diam 2–5mm. Fig 4.26, Grave 293, Sf 285 (b34)

Coiled Cylindrical (no 9)

1   very long, diam 2–5mm, blue. Fig 4.26, Grave 293, Sf 285 (b38)

Miniature Dark (no 24)

2   medium, coiled, diam 2–5mm. Fig 4.26, Grave 293, Sf 285 (b37), (b39)

Grave 294 (Figs 10.28, 10.87) No bone. 313°. Context 146. Plot Y. 1.00m x 0.55m x 0.22m.

Cream-brown loam with frequent small and medium chalk. No bones survived; grave length suggests a child.

a   Group of one amber and two glass **beads**. North-west end of grave. Sf nos 207–209 (see below).

b   Iron **lozenge**. Diamond-shaped with central piercing. Mineral-preserved textile on one face. Length: 42mm. North-east side of grave. Sf 210.

Grave 294 beads

a

amber: 1 bead

1   medium, globular, diam 6–10mm.

glass: 2 beads

Constricted Segmented (no 5)

1   two segments, very long, diam 2–5mm. Fig 4.23, Grave 294, Sf 208 (a3)

Traffic Light Other (no 31)

1   very long, cylindrical, diam 2–5mm, translucent green and opaque yellow twisted or streaked spiral trail on opaque red body. Fig 4.23, Grave 294, Sf 208 (a2)

Grave 295 (Figs 10.28, 10.88) ?M 30–35. 310°. Context 136. Plot X. 2.17m x 0.86–1.10m x 0.35m.

Cream-brown loam with frequent small and medium chalk. Poorly-preserved skeleton; skull half right.

a   **Ceramic vessel**. Rounded form, over sixty per cent complete. Parts of rim and lower body are missing. Decoration includes two or three very shallow narrow incised neck rings. Below these on rounded body, scheme of chevron patterns formed by groups of three incised narrow, shallow lines. Fine, dense sandy fabric with lots of calcareous inclusions on the surface and in section. Occasional larger (1–2mm) quartz sand grains as well as holes (1–2.5mm in size) where calcareous inclusions have leached out, on both exterior and interior surfaces. Hand-made, probably coil built. Exterior surface smoothed but not burnished, interior surface wiped. Surviving height: 130mm. By left shoulder. Sf 1044.

b   Iron **knife**. Incomplete, lacking tip of blade. Straight back with groove running parallel on one side, cutting-edge sinuous and curving to tip. Well-defined junction of mineral-preserved horn handle with blade. Traces of textile on blade in association with human skin and bone. No evidence for sheath. Length: 37mm. Area of left chest. Sf 225.

Grave 296 (Figs 10.28, 10.87) ?F 35–45. 315°. Context 142. Phase 2a. Plot Z. 2.30m x 0.80m x 0.20m.

Cream-brown loam with frequent small and medium chalk. Poorly-preserved skeleton.

a   Scatter of one chalk, one fossil, 98 amber and 66 glass **beads**. Area of neck and chest. Sf nos 95–99 and 218–224 (see below).

b   Silver-gilt garnet **quatrefoil brooch**. 'Beaded' rim part of back-plate nicked on show side; worn. Cast spring-holder and pin-catch. Remains of iron pin with associated mineral-preserved textile. Diameter: *c* 30mm. Weight: 7g. Neck area. Sf 119.

c   Cast copper alloy **buckle**. Rounded loop with a hachured bands on upper face and flanking the tongue-rest. Narrowed axis for attachment of the waisted shield-tongue. The tongue shield has swallow-tailed lateral finials and the pin is decorated with a hachured band similar to the loop. Mineral-preserved organic remains on back, possibly leather. Plus three cast copper alloy **dome-headed studs** bearing cast bands similar to the buckle loop. Pierced lugs for attachment, two of which are broken. Width of loop: 29mm. Height of complete stud: 14mm. Centre waist, above (f), copper alloy radiate-headed brooch. Sf 120.

d   Iron **knife**. Long slender tang, back straight and curving to tip, cutting-edge similar, little wear. Distinct junction between organic handle and blade. Mineral-preserved organic remains on hilt. Hide and hair possibly from an animal skin sheath on blade. Length: 162mm. Left of left pelvis. Sf 121.

e, f   Matching pair of silver-gilt cast **radiate-headed brooches**. Some garnets on hatched foil, some lost. Central ridges on head-plate and bow nicked. Gilding much worn on ridges, foot-plate worn especially at base, bow on top, knobs on head-plate at terminal and on top. Cast pair of spring-holders and pin-catch. Remains of iron spring. Mineral-preserved textile on back of both and cordage on pin of (f). Length (e): 74mm; length (f): 75mm. Weight (e): 18.1g.; weight (f): 17.6g. Area of pelvis. Sf 123.

g   Iron **chain** fragments. Rings ?solid. Mineral-preserved textile. Diameter of individual rings: *c* 15mm. Between femurs. Sf 124.

h   Glass **bead**. Between femurs. Sf 125 (see (a) above).

i   Iron **stud**. Mineral-preserved textile on both faces. Diameter: 7mm. Length: 15mm. Left of left pelvis. Sf 122.

Grave 296 beads

a

amber: 98 beads

    1   short, cylindrical, diam 6–10mm. Fig 4.24, Grave 296, Sf 82 (a82)

    1   medium, cylindrical, diam 2–5mm. Fig 4.24, Grave 296, Sf 95 (a19)

    4   long to very long, spindle-shaped, diam 6–10mm. Fig 4.24, Grave 296, Sf 95 (a41)

    5   short to medium, globular, diam 11–15mm. Fig 4.24, Grave 296, Sf 95 (a212)

    11   medium, globular, diam 6–10mm

    52   medium, rounded, diam 6–10mm

    1   medium, rounded, diam 2–5mm

    2   short to medium, barrel-shaped, diam 6–10mm. Fig 4.24, Grave 296, Sf 95 (a21)

    1   medium, facetted, diam 2–5mm

    17   medium, facetted, diam 6–10mm

    1   medium, facetted, diam 6–10mm. Fig 4.24, Grave 296, Sf 95 (a119)

    1   medium, facetted, diam 11–15mm

    1   fragment, diam 6–10mm

'chalk': 1 bead

    1   cylindrical, diam 16–20mm. Fig 4.24, Grave 296, Sf 218 (a1)

fossil: 1 bead

    1   unidentified

glass: 66 beads

Constricted Segmented (no 5)

    1   five segments, very long, globular, diam 2–5mm. Fig 4.24, Grave 296, Sf 96 (a13)

    1   four segments, very long, globular, diam 2–5mm

    22   three segments, very long, globular, diam 2–5mm

    18   two segments, long to very long, diam 2–5mm

    15   short to medium, diam 2–5mm

Constricted Cylindrical (no 6)

    3   very long, diam 2–5mm

light Constricted Cylindrical (no 7)

    2   very long, beaded, diam 2–5mm. Fig 4.24, Grave 296, Sf 96 (a241), (a88)

Traffic Light Twisted Trail (no 29)

    2   short, barrel-shaped, diam 11–15mm, translucent green and opaque yellow twisted trail on opaque red body. Fig 4.24, Grave 296, Sf 220 (a4), Sf 221 (a8)

Traffic Light Other (no 31)

    1   medium, cylindrical, square cross-section, diam 11–15mm, opaque red frame on translucent green and opaque yellow twisted or streaked coat on opaque red body. Fig 4.24, Grave 296, Sf 219 (a2)

other barrel (no 57)

    1   medium, diam 6–10mm, translucent, blue-green. Fig 4.24, Grave 296, Sf 97 (a7)

h

glass: 1 bead

other globular (no 63)

    1   short, diam 6–10mm, translucent (clear). Fig 4.24, Grave 296, Sf 125 (h1)

Grave 297 (Figs 10.29–30, 10.88, 10.118) M 30–35. 313°. Context 138. Phase 2. Plot Z. 2.34m x 0.78–0.86m x 0.44m. Cream-brown loam with frequent small and medium chalk containing four residual Iron Age pot-sherds. Flint and chalk packing around sides of grave indicate a coffin 2.10 x 0.45–0.65m. Moderately well-preserved skeleton; skull right; left arm slightly bent across pelvis.

a   Glass **cone beaker**. Kempston type, tall, narrow shape, with everted, thickened rim. Trail dropped on and wound horizontally but slightly slanting, upward to rim fifteen turns. Four vertical loops, irregular, slanting and melting in near tip. Flat tip with residual metal and chipped traces of ring punty; diameter: 18mm. Striated, some iridescence, small bubbles, discoloured patches. Height: 290mm. Diameter: 30mm. By left shoulder. Sf 304.

b   Iron **spearhead**. Angular, concave-sided blade, lozenge-section, with a split socket with rivet. Mineralised wood remains in socket; textile and associated cordage on the outside. Length: 272mm. By left shoulder. Sf 314.

c   Cast high-tin copper alloy **buckle** with D-shaped loop. Narrowed axis with iron concretion from the anchorage of the now separate club-shaped tongue. Plus three cast high-tin copper alloy **dome-headed studs**, with ribbed flange, and only traces of the iron attachment shanks or lugs left. Width of loop: 36mm. Height of highest stud 11mm. Inside right elbow. Sf 306.

d   Copper alloy **mount**. Oval translucent blue glass cabochon in a cast copper alloy frame with narrow flange. Sheet copper alloy back-plate now separate with wire loop for attachment, the ends of which are slotted through the plate and hammered out flat. Length: 20mm; width: 15mm. Centre waist. Sf 307.

e   Copper alloy **ring**, wear on inner edge. Diameter: 2.8mm. Weight: 8.7g. Right of right femur. Sf 308.

f   Iron **knife**. Fragmentary, lacking part of tang and end of blade. Back curving to tip, cutting-edge similar, little wear. Mineralised horn handle and degraded organic material on blade. Length: 114mm. Under left lower arm. Sf 311.

g   Iron **spear ferrule**. Hollow conical. willow wood (*Salix* sp) remains in socket. Mineral-preserved textile on tip. Length: 72mm. Left of left lower leg. Sf 315.

h   Iron **shield grip**. Fragmentary, lacking terminal of grip extension. Rectangular, flanged central handle section (length: 85mm; width: 30mm) with one narrow long-grip extension (length: 80mm; width: 10mm) *in situ*, the other having become detached (see (i)). Wooden handle with leather on inside of central flanged section. Mineralised fibres on outside grip. Over chest. Sf 312.

i   Iron **shield boss**. Incomplete. Carinated convex cone with straight wall (height: 20mm), disc-headed apex (diameter: 23mm) and five disc-headed flange rivets (diameter: 20mm). Wood and possible leather remains on underside of flange. Diameter: 150mm. Height: 75mm. Over chest. Sf 313.

Iron **shield grip** fragment. Narrow long-grip extension belonging to shield grip (h), lacking terminal. Length: 90mm. Width: 10mm. Over chest. Sf 313.

Iron **shield grip rivet**. Disc-headed rivet with silvered face and thin rectangular washer. One of pair used to secure central handle section of long grip (h) to shield board. Diameter: 17mm. Over chest. Sf 313.

Iron **shield grip rivet** fragments. Fragments of second disc-headed rivet with silvered face and thin rectangular washer. One of pair used to secure central handle section of long grip (h) to shield board. Diameter: 17mm. Over chest. Sf 313.

j   Copper alloy sheet **mount**. Two rectangular plates, secured by iron rivets in each corner. Organic material in between the plates. Length: 20mm. Width: 15mm. Overall height: 21mm. By right shoulder. Sf 310.

k   Set of five ?copper alloy **rivets** with fragments of copper alloy sheet. Height: 7mm. Right of right humerus. Sf 309.

Grave 298 (Figs 10.30, 10.88) ?F 30–35. 308°. Context 132. Plot Z. 2.41m x 1.15m x 0.21m.
Cream clay with very frequent small and medium chalk. Poorly-preserved skeleton; left arm bent across pelvis area.

a   Iron **knife**. Straight back curving to tip, cutting-edge similar but damaged close to handle. Well-defined diagonal junction between organic handle and blade. Mineral-preserved horn handle. Extensive mineral-preserved textile on one face of blade together with skin-product and bone. Length: 193mm. Under left lower arm. Sf 114.

b   Silver wire **finger ring** with coiled wire bezel. Bezel worn on inside and on show side. Diameter: 22mm. Weight: 2.4g. Area of left hand. Sf 115.

Grave 299 (Figs 10.30, 10.88) ?F 40–50. 323°. Context 254. Plot Z. 2.30m x 0.89m x 0.11m.
Brown loam with frequent small and medium chalk. Poorly-preserved skeleton; skull half right; arms bent across pelvis.

a   Iron **spearhead**. Broad angular-shaped blade and split socket. Rivet/iron nail. Remains of ash wood (*Fraxinus excelsior*) in socket. Mineral-preserved textile on tip of blade. Length: 290mm. Right of skull. Sf 773.

b   Iron **knife** (large). Incomplete, lacking part of tang. Straight back curving to tip, sinuous cutting-edge. Slight traces of junction of handle and blade. Mineral-preserved horn handle and remains of leather on blade from sheath. Length: 234mm; blade length: 164mm. By left lower arm. Sf 774.

Grave 300 (Figs 10.30–31, 10.89) M 30–40. 317°. Context 88. Phase 1b–2a. Plot Z. 2.35m x 0.98–1.07m x 0.11m.
Brown loam with moderate small chalk. Poorly-preserved skeleton; skull half right; left arm slightly bent across pelvis. Two rows of seven clench nails under body.

a–n   Two rows of iron **clench nails**. Traces of mineral-preserved oak wood (*Quercus* sp). Between legs. Sf 94

o   Iron **firesteel/pursemount**. Traces of mineral-preserved oak wood (*Quercus* sp). Fragmented and incomplete. Mineral-preserved leather from purse and strap through buckle. Associated textile remains on one side. Remaining lengths: 54 and 81mm. Reconstructed length: 140mm. By left elbow. Sf 93.

p   Iron **knife** fragments with traces of mineral-preserved horn from the handle on the tang fragment. Beech wood (*Fagus sylvatica*) found in association with the knife fragments but probably not from a direct association. Fragmentary. Part of broad tang survives, as well as end section of blade with straight back and distinct angle towards tip. Cutting-edge straight and curving to tip. Length: 100mm. Area of decayed left shoulder. Sf 91.

q   Iron **spearhead**. Straight angular ?repaired blade, lentoid section. Split socket with rivet showing traces of ash wood (*Fraxinus excelsior*). Random vegetable fibres on blade. Mineral-preserved textile on socket. Length: 250mm. Area of right foot. Sf 92.

Grave 301 (Figs 10.31, 10.89) M 19–21. 320°. Context 90. Plot Z. 2.57m x 0.81–0.93m x 0.27m.
Brown loam with frequent small and medium chalk. Poorly-preserved skeleton; right arm bent across pelvis.

a   Iron **spearhead**. Long straight-sided angular blade of lozenge-section, with a solid cylinder split socket closed by a binding ring of iron. Decorated with a different rune-like ideogram/symbol on each side. One represents a bow and an arrow being thrown. On the other side the interpretation is much more difficult. Ash wood (*Fraxinus excelsior*) remains. Length: 383mm. Left of skull. Sf 136.

b   Iron **buckle** and **plate**. Rectangular plate with two large iron disc-headed rivets which have silver sheet covers. Mineral-preserved textile on back and leather between plates. Width of loop: 36mm. Width of plate: 24mm. Overall length: 49mm. Lower body left of spine. Sf 137.

c   Iron **knife**, lacking tip of blade. Straight back curving to tip, fractured, irregular cutting-edge. Traces of junction between organic handle and blade. Mineral-preserved horn handle and remains of leather sheath. Length: 153mm. Above left pelvis. Sf 138.

Grave 302 (Figs 10.31, 10.89) ?M 20–25. 322°. Context 256. Phase 2–3a. Plot T. 2.35m x 1.00m x 0.65m.
Light-brown loam with frequent small and medium chalk. Poorly-preserved skeleton; right arm bent across pelvis area.

a   Cast copper alloy **buckle**. D-shaped loop of roughly D-shaped section with narrowed axis for attachment of the iron tongue. Mineralised leather remains on narrowed bar, iron tongue and back of loop. Width of loop: 24mm. Excavated from under the left pelvis. Sf 601.

b   Iron **arrowhead**. Leaf-shaped blade, lozenge-section, split socket containing ash wood (*Fraxinus excelsior*) fragments. Random remains of mineral-preserved vegetal material preserved on one side of the arrowhead. Length: 88mm. Left of left femur. Sf 602.

c   Fragmentary iron **staple**, now lacking its terminals. Length: 21mm. Width: 8mm. Area of body. Sf 663. *Not illus.*

Grave 303 (Figs 10.32, 10.90, 10.118) 296°. Context: Sk A, 258, Sk B, 378. Sk A, Phase 3b. Sk B, Phase 1–3. Plot T. 2.80m x 0.90–1.00m x 0.63m.

Brown loam with frequent small and medium chalk. Double-stacked grave (Sk A 0.10m above Sk B).

Sk 303A ? *c* 3. Fragmentary bones of a small child by left knee of Sk B.

a   Glass **bead**. Chest area. Sf 528 (see below).

b   Copper alloy wire **ring**. Sections touch. Diameter: *c* 10mm. Weight: 1.0g. Chest area. Sf 529.

c   Iron **knife**, lacking end of blade. Broad tang, straight back curving to tip, sinuous cutting-edge. Well-defined junction between organic handle and blade. Mineral-preserved horn handle and remains of leather from sheath. Length: 107mm. Chest area. Sf 530.

Grave 303 beads
a
glass: 1 bead
variation Koch34 (no 16)
   1   2 segments, long, globular, diam 6–10mm, yellow trail ?irreg. applied and partly lost, on opaque red body. Fig 4.30, Grave 303A, Sf 528 (a1)

Sk 303B M 30–35. Poorly-preserved skeleton; skull half right; arms bent across pelvis. No grave goods.

Grave 304 (Fig 10.90) F 35–40. 297°. Context 260. Plot T. 2.19m x 1.03m x 0.69m.
Cream silty loam with very frequent small and medium chalk. Poorly-preserved skeleton; skull half right; left arm slightly bent across pelvis. No grave goods.

Grave 305 (Fig 10.89) ? 8–11. 305°. Context 262. Plot T. 1.81m x 0.73–0.87m x 0.74m.
Cream loam with very frequent small and medium chalk. Poorly-preserved skeleton; skull half left. No grave goods.

Grave 306 (Fig 10.32, 10.90) ?F 50+. 310°. Context 264. Phase 1. Plot T. 2.15m x 0.96m x 0.88m.
Cream-grey loam with frequent small and medium chalk. Poorly-preserved skeleton; skull half right.

a   Group of one amber and twenty glass **beads**. Neck area. Sf 553 (see below).

b   Tinned copper alloy **toilet set** and slip-knot ring.
1, **pick**, oval ring head (broken) and shoulders formed from cutaway section of strip, with flat section immediately below ring turning into barley-sugar twist for 38mm before flattening out to point. Length overall: 78mm; width: 3mm.
2, **implement** with head as above, looped to form oval, with tail of strip curving back on itself into a curlicue. Shaft is broken at beginning of barley-twist. Length: 33mm.
3, **slip-knot ring** made of copper alloy wire, not tinned, 1mm thick. Diameter: 20mm. Area of right shoulder. Sf 554.

Grave 306 beads
a
amber: 1 bead
   1   short, globular, diam 21–25mm. Fig 4.23, Grave 306, Sf 553 (a1)
glass: 20 beads
Traffic Light Twisted Trail (no 29)
   1   very long, cylindrical, diam 6–10mm, translucent green and opaque yellow twisted trail on opaque red body. Fig 4.23, Grave 306, Sf 553 (a2)
polychrome dark (no 70)
   2   short, asymmetrically globular, diam 11–20mm, white wavy trail on dark body. Fig 4.23, Grave 306, Sf 553 (a3)
Blue (no 1)
   6   short, annular, diam 6–10mm. Fig 4.23, Grave 306, Sf 553(a16)
   1   short, globular, diam 11–15mm. Fig 4.23, Grave 306, Sf 553(a15)
other globular (no 63)
   6   short to medium, annular, diam 11–15mm. Fig 4.23, Grave 306, Sf 553 (a6)
   3   short, globular, diam 6–20mm
other melon (no 59)
   1   short, barrel-shaped, 6-ribbed cross-section, diam 11–15mm, dark. Fig 4.23, Grave 306, Sf 553 (a5)

Grave 307 (Figs 10.32, 10.90) ? 3–5. 339°. Context 266. Plot T. 1.68m x 1.00m x 0.68m.
Cream-brown loam with frequent small and medium chalk. Teeth only.

a   **Ceramic vessel**. Small, wide-mouthed undecorated handled cup with slightly everted rim. Ninety per cent complete with only part of rim and much of handle missing. Only lower stump of the handle survives but scar on body shows that it re-joined the body again just below the rim. Dense fine sandy fabric reduced throughout. Abraded break on handle shows fine dense quartz sand inclusions with occasional quartz sand grains to 0.75mm. Hand-made, probably coil built and external surface shows vertical smoothing or shallow knife trimming, especially under rim. Base has also been knife-trimmed. Sooting on surface and soot marks on body and near rim. Rim diameter: 99mm; base diameter approx. 65mm. Height: 75mm. South-east end of grave. Sf 614.

Grave 308 (Figs 10.32, 10.90) F 50+. 315°. Context 268. Phase 1. Plot T. 2.12m x 0.94m x 0.65m.
Cream-brown loam with frequent small and medium chalk. Poorly-preserved skeleton; skull half right; arms bent across pelvis.

a   Iron **knife**, lacking tip of blade. Straight back curving to tip, sinuous cutting-edge. Well-defined junction of organic handle and blade. Mineral-preserved horn handle. Length: 137mm. Above left pelvis, over buckle (b). Sf 540.

b   Cast copper alloy **buckle**. Unusual oval loop of flat section, very worn in places with a central bar on which the iron tongue is hinged. Decoration in form of punched crescents. Mineral-preserved textile. Width of loop: 51mm. Under iron knife (a). Sf 541.

c   Twelve glass **beads**. Right shoulder. Sf 542 (see below).

d   Iron **pin**. Neck area. Mineral-preserved textile. Length: *c* 120mm. Sf 543.

e   **Ceramic vessel**. Biconical. 90 per cent complete with only parts of rim and upper shoulder missing. Much of upper shoulder is worn and abraded. Decoration carefully executed, comprises broad neck groove bordered by two incised lines below which vertical incised line and broad shallow groove decoration is arranged regularly in eleven groups around the carination and extending onto lower body. Fresh break shows fine reddish sandy matrix with scatter of rounded and sub-rounded quartz sand grains. Under exterior burnishing, on surface, there are a few voids left by calcareous inclusions leaching out and other inclusions abrading out. Coil built. Exterior surface was once finely burnished but is now abraded and flaking off. Interior wiped. Rim diameter: 94mm; base diameter: 55mm. Height: 90mm. By left lower leg. Sf 615.

f   Copper alloy cast **annular brooch** with copper alloy pin. No obvious signs of wear. Diameter: *c* 44mm. Weight: 13.8g. Under lower jaw. Sf 600.

Grave 308 beads

c

glass: 12 beads

Mosaic, ?Roman (no 26)
1   fragments, light ?translucent blue (now iridescent) and white radiating stripes around lost core on light? blue? body. Fig 4.24, Grave 308, Sf 542 (a11)

variation Candy (no 4)
1   short, barrel-shaped, diam 11–15mm, opaque red trail on bright green wavy trail on discoloured body. Fig 4.24, Grave 308, Sf 542 (a2)

Mottled (no 27)
1   short, barrel-shaped, diam 11–15mm, opaque red mottles on white mottles on translucent blue body. Fig 4.24, Grave 308, Sf 542 (a3)

polychrome dark (no 70)
1   short, globular, diam 16–20mm, white circumferential zigzag trail on dark body. Fig 4.24, Grave 308, Sf 542 (a1)

polychrome blue (no 67)
1   medium, asymmetrically barrel-shaped, diam 11–15mm, white zigzag on translucent blue body. Fig 4.24, Grave 308, Sf 542 (a4)

Blue (no 1)
2   short, annular, diam 6–10mm
2   short, annular, diam 11–15mm. Fig 4.24, Grave 308, Sf 542 (a5), (a6)

other barrel (no 57)
2   short, diam 11–15mm, opaque, red. Fig 4.24, Grave 308, Sf 542 (a9)

unidentified
1   annular, translucent? blue?

Grave 309 (Fig 10.91) ?F 20–25. 307°. Context 270. Plot T. 2.44m x 0.88m x 0.80m.
Cream loam with very frequent small and medium chalk. Well-preserved skeleton; skull half left. No grave goods.

Grave 310 (Fig 10.91) ? 14–16. 314°. Context 272. Plot T. 1.96m x 0.93m x 0.48m.
Cuts Grave 311. Cream-brown loam with frequent small and medium chalk. Poorly-preserved skeleton. No grave goods.

Grave 311 (Figs 10.32, 10.91) M 40–50. 306°. Context 274. Plot T. 2.00m x 0.73m (min) x 0.34m.
Cut by Graves 310 and 363. Cream loam with very frequent small and medium chalk. Well preserved but damaged skeleton; skull right; right arm bent across pelvis.

a   Iron **buckle**. D-shaped to oval loop and plain tongue. Three small impressions on front of the buckle are remains of a deteriorated, decorative, metal inlay, only visible under the microscope when the object is held at an oblique angle. Further remains of transverse wires are present on both tongue and loop. X-ray fluorescence revealed the presence of a small amount of tin. Mineral-preserved leather on tongue, loop and bar from strap and traces of textile adhering to the outside of the loop and tongue. Width of loop: 32mm. Above left pelvis. Sf 564.

Grave 312 (Fig 10.92) ?F 25–30. 307°. Context 276. Plot T. 2.17m x 0.68–0.90m x 0.50m.
Cream loam with very frequent small and medium chalk. Poorly-preserved skeleton; right arm slightly bent across pelvis. No grave goods.

Grave 313 (Fig 10.92) F *c* 40. 308°. Context 278. Plot T. 2.19m x 0.87m x 0.47m.
Cuts Grave 326. Cream loam with very frequent small and medium chalk. Poorly-preserved skeleton. No grave goods.

Grave 314 (Figs 10.32, 10.91) 302°. Context: Sk A, 280; Sk B, 384. Plot T. 2.05m x 0.89m x 0.23m.
Cuts pit F 386. Cream-brown loam with frequent small and medium chalk. Double grave (Sk A adjacent Sk B).

Sk 314A F *c* 40. Poorly-preserved skeleton; skull left; partially decayed arms bent across pelvis.

a   Iron **knife**, lacking tip of blade and most of tang. Straight back curving to tip, slight wear on cutting-edge. Well-defined junction between organic handle and blade. Mineral-preserved horn from the handle and remains of leather on blade from sheath. Length: 136mm. Area of body. Sf 559.

b   Iron **buckle**. Oval loop and plain tongue. Mineral-preserved leather and leather thong. Mineralised textile. Width of loop: 39mm. Centre of body. Sf 560.

c   Iron **pin**. In three pieces, head missing. Length: *c* 90mm. Area of body. Sf 561.

d   Iron **keys**. Suspension loop, shaft of rectangular section, hooked terminal. Two similar shafts with suspension loops fused together. Length: 107mm. Area of right pelvis. Sf 562.
1, iron **key** with expanding flattened rectangular shaft and

angular hooked 'ward'. Terminal tapers to small loop which springs from edge. Length: 175mm. Area of right pelvis. Sf 562.

2, iron ?**key** and **terminal loop** with expanding flattened rectangular shaft ending in two forward pointing hook-like 'wards'. Length: 109mm. Area of right pelvis. Sf 562.

3, iron **shank** and **terminal loop**, similar to 2, broken at end. Length: 104mm. Area of right pelvis. Sf 562. Mineral-preserved leather thong on the suspension loops. Associated textile adhering to both surfaces.

e   Nine amber **beads**. Under and around (a). Sf 563.

Grave 314 beads

e

amber: 9 beads

    1   medium, cylindrical, diam 6–10mm. Fig 4.23, Grave 314A, Sf 563 (e7)
    3   medium, rounded, diam 6–10mm
    4   medium, facetted, diam 6–10mm
    1   facetted?, diam 6–10mm

Sk 314B ? 7–9. Fragmentary skull and leg bones only. No grave goods.

Grave 315 (Fig 10.91) ? 6–12. 327°. Context 282. Plot W. 1.72m (min) x 0.72m (min) x 0.09m.
Cream loam with very frequent small and medium chalk. Fragmentary leg bones only. No grave goods.

Grave 316 (Fig 10.92) F 65+. 319°. Context 284. Plot T. 2.25m x 1.06m x 0.45m.
Cream loam with very frequent small and medium chalk. Moderately well-preserved skeleton. No grave goods.

Grave 317 (Fig 10.93) ? 50+. 309°. Context 286. Plot T. 2.15m x 0.87m x 0.18m.
Cuts Grave 318. Cream-brown loam with frequent small and medium chalk. Poorly-preserved skeleton; skull half left; right arm bent across body. No grave goods.

Grave 318 (Figs 10.33, 10.93) No bone. 315°. Context 288. Plot T. 2.05m x 0.77m x 0.09m.
Cut by Grave 317. Cream-brown loam with frequent small and medium chalk. No bones survived; grave length suggests a grown individual.

a   Iron **knife**. Straight back curving to tip, sinuous cutting-edge. Trace of junction of handle and blade. Mineral-preserved leather on blade from sheath. Length: 104mm. Centre of grave. Sf 705.

b–d   Iron **keys** (5) from **châtelaine**. Two, large, heads looped onto iron ring, with square shafts, one barley-twist, with angular hooked 'wards'. Mineral-replaced textile on ends of shafts. Two, small, looped over ring, rectangular shafts and the remains of hooked 'wards' bent back against shaft. Traces of mineral-replaced textile. One with a ring head, round shaft and hooked 'ward' bent back against shaft. Mineral-replaced textile

above 'ward'. Mineral-preserved leather thong for suspension in loops; associated textiles. Lengths overall: 70mm and 35mm. Centre of grave. Sf nos 706–708.

Grave 319 (Figs 10.33, 10.92) ?M 25–30. 315°. Context 290. Plot W. 2.21m x 0.85m x 0.25m.
Light-brown loam with frequent small and medium chalk. Moderately well-preserved skeleton; skull half right.

a   Cast copper alloy **buckle**. Oval loop of approximately semi-circular section with narrowed axis for attachment of the tongue. Faceted tongue has a rectangular shield and iron anchorage is still intact. Traces of mineral-preserved textile on back. Width of loop: 30mm. Above right pelvis. Sf 764.

b   Cast copper alloy **shoe-shaped stud**, white metal-plated and of unusual size and proportions. Equally unusual is the method of attachment, which consists of two rivet shanks on the back with an oblong washer plate. Mineral-preserved leather on back. Length: 12mm. Above pelvis. Sf 765.

c   Small copper alloy **knob-headed stud** with circular shank, piercing a sheet metal strip, possibly forming a similar arrangement to (b) above. The shank has a white shiny surface that may be the remains of white metal plating. Mineral-preserved leather on back. Height: 9mm. Above right pelvis. Sf 766.

Grave 320 (Fig 10.93) ? 9–11. 315°. Context 292. Plot S. 2.30m x 0.98m x 0.28m
Cut by Grave 272. Cream-brown loam with frequent small and medium chalk. Poorly-preserved skeleton; partially decayed arms bent across pelvis. No grave goods.

Grave 321 (Figs 10.33, 10.93) ?M 25–30. 320°. Context 294. Plot T. 1.52m x 0.49m x 0.07m.
Brown loam with frequent small and medium chalk. Fragmentary ribs and long bones only.

a   Iron **knife**. Fragmentary, lacking end of blade and part of tang. Broad tang, back straight and curving to tip, cutting-edge sinuous. Mineral-preserved horn handle. Associated textile remains on blade. Length: 117mm. Above area of left waist. Sf 435.

Grave 322 (Fig 10.93) ? 2–3. 317°. Context 296. Plot T. 1.21m x 0.75m x 0.22m.
Light-brown loam with frequent small and medium chalk. Teeth and fragmentary leg bones only. No grave goods.

Grave 323 (Figs 10.33, 10.94) M 40–50. 299°. Context 300. Phase 3. Plot T. 2.41m x 0.90m x 0.26m.
Cuts Grave 324; cut by modern trench. Cream-brown loam with frequent small and medium chalk. Damaged skeleton. Radiocarbon date: 1491 ± 18 BP (UB-6475) cal AD 540–620 (95%). Sf 936 and Sf 1280 found in modern trench probably derive from this grave (*see* p 452).

a   Iron **spearhead**. Angular to triangular blade, flat to lozenge-section. Long split socket containing ash wood (*Fraxinus excelsior*) remains. Unique type of blade. The shoulder of the blade offers a very distinctive angle of aperture. Length: 400mm. By left shoulder. Sf 680.

b   Copper alloy disc-headed **shield board rivet**. Face plated with white metal. One of a set of four rivets (with d–f) identical to boss and grip rivets associated with shield board. Diameter: 10mm. Sf 681.

c   Iron **shield boss**. Carinated convex cone with straight wall (height: 25mm), disc-headed apex (diameter: 20mm) and four of original set of five tinned-copper alloy disc-headed rivets (diameter: 10mm), all with circular washers, in a broad flange (width: 25mm). Mineralised wood and leather remains indicate a covering of leather to the front and back of the wooden shield board. Diameter: 165mm. Height: 80mm. Over jaw and left shoulder. Sf 682.
     Iron **shield grip**. Incomplete, broken edges at terminals. Straight, narrow (width: 16m) strap grip expanding at each end (width: 30mm) to accommodate a single tinned-copper alloy disc-headed rivet (diameter: 10mm). Grip exhibits a slight curve. Rivet-heads angled to reflect slight curve. Mineralised wood remains indicate a wooden handle with a lap joint construction. Length: 130mm. Over jaw and left shoulder. Sf 682.

d–f Three copper alloy disc-headed **shield board rivets** with circular washers. Faces plated with white metal. With b, form a set of four, identical to boss and grip rivets associated with shield board. Diameters: 10mm. Sf 683–685.

Grave 324 (Figs 10.33, 10.94) F 40–45. 317°. Context 302. Plot T. 2.34m x 1.13m x 0.34m.
Cut by Grave 323 (Phase 3). Cream-brown loam with frequent small and medium chalk. Legs and pelvis fragments only.

a   Copper alloy **buckle** and **plate**. Cast, oval loop of rounded section with iron tongue with curved tip. Sheet copper alloy rectangular plate folded over the axis and secured by two knob-headed rivets. It is broken on the back. Mineral-preserved leather between plate from strap; textile remains on the back. Width of loop: 34mm. Width of plate: 18mm. Overall length: 41mm. Above right waist. Sf 653.

Grave 325 (Figs10.34, 10.85) M 25–30. 315°. Context 298. Plot T. 2.36m x 0.78m (min) x 0.15m.
Cuts Grave 281 (Phase 1b). Brown loam with frequent small and medium chalk. Poorly-preserved skeleton; skull right; partially decayed right arm bent across upper pelvis.

a   Cast copper alloy miniature **buckle** and **plate**. Convex oval loop with narrowed axis. The tongue has a rectangular to trapezoid tongue shield. The damaged sheet metal plate has the shape of a soft triangle and is folded over the loop, secured by three knob-headed rivets. Mineral-preserved leather strap between plates. Width of loop: 19mm; width of plate: 13mm. Overall length: 26mm. Adjacent to lower left arm. Sf 264.

Grave 326 (Figs 10.34, 10.92) F 14–16. 318°. Context 304. Plot T. 2.36m x 0.79m x 0.34m
Cut by Grave 313. Cream-brown loam with frequent small and medium chalk. Poorly-preserved skeleton; arms bent across pelvis.

a   Fragment of iron **ring**. Mineral-preserved textile on one side of the object and remains of a leather suspension thong around the ring. Diameter: *c* 33mm. Area of left pelvis. Sf 826.

b   Copper alloy **annular brooch**. Decorated with punched half-circles and lines on show side. No remains of pin. Brooch especially worn in area of original pin point. Mineral-preserved textile. Diameter: *c* 37mm. Weight: 5.7g. Area of left pelvis. Sf 827.

c   Copper alloy **mount** or patch, flat, rectangular sheet, folded over and pierced for two rivets, now missing. No curve to suggest from the rim of a vessel. Two thin copper alloy rivets with 1mm diameter shanks in secondary repair holes. Traces of organic remains. Width: 29mm; height: 16mm, length of rivets: 6mm. Area of left pelvis. Sf 828.

d   Copper alloy **wrist clasp**. Rectangular with two rivet-holes, narrow slot, decorated with three rows of repoussé dots. Possible mineral-preserved leather. Length: 35mm. Area of left pelvis. Sf 829.

e   Two iron **rings**. Larger ring incomplete. Smaller ring coiled with tapering ends. Both rings have mineral-preserved leather suspension thongs around the object. Additional remains of cordage wound round twice around one of the rings. Diameters: 32mm and 24mm. Area of left pelvis. Sf 830.

f   Fragmentary iron pierced **lozenge** with trace of leather thong through perforation. Length: 25mm. Central pelvis area. Sf 831.

g   Iron **knife**, lacking tip of blade. Back curves to tip, cutting-edge sinuous. Trace of junction of handle and blade. Mineral-preserved horn handle and leather on blade from sheath. Length: 125mm. Area of left pelvis. Sf 832.

h   Oval open iron **ring** with wedge-shaped section. Traces of mineral-preserved textile on one side. Maximum diameter: 44mm. Area of left pelvis. Sf 833.

i   Copper alloy **wrist clasp** fragments with traces of fibrous remains. One hooked section with two rivet-holes and fragment of top repoussé sheet. Stylised full-face masks on end panels. Lengths: 41mm and 35mm. Central pelvis area. Sf 834.

j   Iron ?**pin**, ?point only. Length: 46mm. Area of left pelvis. Sf 835.

k   Glass **bead** made from rim fragment of a Roman vessel, translucent blue-green colour. Area of left pelvis. Sf 836 (see below).

l   Iron **pin** with slightly bent, possibly incomplete head. Length: 52mm. Area of left pelvis. Sf 837.

Grave 326 beads
k
glass: 1 bead
rim fragment (no 34)
     1   fragment of blue-green vessel glass with hollow rim.
          Fig 4.23, Grave 326, Sf 836 (k1)
Also, amber 1 bead
     1   fragments found during conservation. Sf 1277

Grave 327 (Figs 10.35, 10.93) F 35–45. 309°. Context 306. Phase 1b–2a. Plot T. 2.03m x 0.79m x 0.29m.
Cream-brown loam with frequent small and medium chalk. Moderately well-preserved skeleton; right arm bent across pelvis. Iron rod fragment recovered from general filling of Grave (Sf 935).

a–c Three amber **beads**. Right of skull. Sf 597 (see below).
d   Cast copper alloy **buckle**. Oval with narrowed axis and club-shaped, waisted tongue with remains of the iron anchorage. Two cast ridges decorate the upper face of the loop and flank the tongue-rest. The thickened end of the now separate tongue has two incised transverse lines. Mineral-preserved leather on back. Plus three cast copper alloy, **cone-headed studs** with ribbed top and plain flange and a pierced lug for attachment on the back. Width of loop: 36mm. Height of highest stud 16mm. Area of waist. Sf 598.
e   Iron **knife**, lacking tip of blade. Back straight and curving to tip, cutting-edge similar. Well-defined junction of organic handle and blade. Mineral-preserved horn handle and leather on blade from sheath. Length: 135mm. Over left lower arm. Sf 599.
Iron **rod** fragment, square section. Length: 53mm. From general filling of Grave. Sf 935

Grave 327 beads
amber: 3 beads
    2   medium, rounded, diam 6–10mm
    1   long, facetted, diam 6–10mm

Grave 328 (Fig 10.94) M 50+. 319°. Context 308. Plot T. 2.15m x 0.74–1.02m x 0.37m.
Cream-brown loam with frequent small and medium chalk. Well-preserved skeleton; skull left. No grave goods.

Grave 329 (Figs 10.94, 10.118) M 25–30. 312°. Context 310. Plot T. 2.23m x 1.06m x 0.40m.
Light cream-brown loam with frequent small and medium chalk. Flint packing stones mainly along north-east side of grave indicate a coffin. Poorly-preserved skeleton; skull left; right arm bent across body. No grave goods.

Grave 330 (Figs 10.35, 10.99, 10.101) ? 10–12. 309°. Context 312. Plot T. 1.58m x 0.52m x 0.15m.
Cuts Grave 365. Cream-brown loam with frequent small and medium chalk. Fragmentary long bones only.

a   Iron **knife**, lacking tip of blade. Elongated, narrow shape, back straight and curving to tip, cutting-edge sinuous. Well-defined junction of handle and blade. Mineral-preserved horn handle and leather on blade from sheath. Length: 151mm. Under left lower arm. Sf 539.

Grave 331 (Figs 10.35, 10.94) ? grown? 315°. Context 314. Phase 3a. Plot T. 1.85m x 0.79m x 0.10m.

Brown loam with frequent small and medium chalk. Fragmentary leg bone only.

a   Group of 81 amber and 28 glass **beads**. North-west (head) end of grave. Sf nos 478–481 (see below).
b   Cast high-tin copper alloy **buckle**. Rectangular loop of rectangular section with narrowed round axis for attachment of the tongue, which is missing. Loop is damaged on one side and has marked groove to accommodate presumably curved tip of tongue. Amorphous organic remains. Plus two cast high-tin copper alloy **shoe-shaped studs**, pierced lugs on back, both broken. Width of loop: 31mm. Length of studs: 22 and 26mm. Area of right waist. Sf 483.
c   Iron **knife**, lacking part of tang. Back curves to tip, cutting-edge similar. Well-defined junction of organic handle and blade. Mineral-preserved horn handle and leather on blade from sheath. Length of fragments: 129mm. Area of left pelvis. Sf 484.
d   Copper alloy **tweezers** formed from thick strip bent over to form oval ring head. Arms gently expand to incurved terminals. Length: 55mm; width: 6mm; thickness: 1.5mm. Over left femur. Sf 485.
e   Glass **bead**. By left femur. Sf 481 (see below).
f   Iron Age **coin**. Potin, class I (Hobbs 1996, 674 etc.). First century BC. Weight: 1.43g. By left femur. Sf 482.

Grave 331 beads
a
amber: 81 beads
    1   medium, rounded, diam 16–20mm
    14   medium, rounded, diam 11–15mm. Fig 4.29, Grave 331, Sf 478 (a26)
    13   medium (one long), rounded, diam 6–10mm
    1   rounded
    2   medium, facetted, diam 16–20mm
    18   medium (one long), facetted, diam 11–15mm
    20   medium (one long), facetted, diam 6–10mm. Fig 4.29, Grave 331, Sf 478 (a61)
    3   facetted
    9   fragments
glass: 28 beads
Mosaic (no 25)
    1   medium, globular, diam 6–10mm, bright green and opaque yellow. Fig 4.29, Grave 331, Sf 479 (a2)
Reticella (no 28)
    1   long, cylindrical, diam 11–15mm, 3 translucent, opaque yellow and opaque red twisted trails. Fig 4.29, Grave 331, Sf 479 (a1)
polychrome biconical (no 66)
    1   medium, diam 6–10mm, 3 dots on equator on red body. Fig 4.29, Grave 331, Sf 480 (a10)
Cylindrical Pentagonal (no 10)
    3   long to very long, diam 6–10mm, opaque, red. Fig 4.29, Grave 331, Sf 480 (a26)
Cylindrical Round (no 12)
    1   medium, diam 6–10mm, opaque, red. Fig 4.29, Grave 331, Sf 480 (a25)
other cylindrical (no 56)
    1   short, cylindrical, diam 6–10mm, opaque, white.
    1   short, cylindrical, asymmetrical cross-section, diam 6–10mm, opaque, red.

other globular (no 63)

4   short, globular, diam 6–15mm, white, one asymmetrically. Fig 4.29, Grave 331, Sf 479 (a9); Fig 4.29, Grave 331, Sf 480 (a11)

2   short, globular, diam 6–10mm, opaque, yellow. Fig 4.29, Grave 331, Sf 480 (a17)

4   short, globular, diam 6–10mm, opaque, red. Fig 4.29, Grave 331, Sf 480 (a22)

1   short, globular, diam 6–10mm, translucent, green, very pale. Fig 4.29, Grave 331, Sf 479 (a3)

other barrel (no 57)

4   short, diam 6–10mm (one 11–15mm), white

4   short, diam 6–10mm, opaque, yellow

e

glass: 1 bead

polychrome blue (no 67)

1   short, globular, diam 21–25mm, white circumferential zigzag on translucent blue body

Grave 332 (Fig 10.95) ?F 20–25. 318°. Context 316. Plot T. 2.55m x 1.13m x 0.48m.
Cream loam with frequent small and medium chalk. Poorly-preserved skeleton. No grave goods.

Grave 333 (Figs 10.35, 10.95) ?M grown. 315°. Context 318. Phase 1b–2. Plot T. 2.72m x 0.83m (min) x 0.48m
Partially destroyed by modern terrace. Cream-brown silty loam with frequent small and medium chalk.
Damaged skeleton.

a   Cast copper alloy miniature **buckle**. D-shaped loop of D-shaped section, narrowed axis for attachment of the club-shaped tongue. Mineral-preserved leather over tongue from strap. Width of loop: 19mm. To left of waist. Sf 475.

Grave 334 (Figs 10.36, 10.95) ? 6–8. 292°. Context 320. Phase 1a. Plot T. 2.46m x 0.72–0.90m x 0.14m.
Grey-brown loam with frequent small and medium chalk. Leg bones only.

a   Iron **buckle** and **plate**. Kidney-shaped loop of convex section. Base of tongue is decorated with two ridges. High-rectangular plate has an applied copper alloy sheet but only traces of a stamped or incised decoration remain. In one place the corner of a central panel is visible and there are minute traces of white metal plating. Mineral-preserved textiles on back. Four iron rivets, three of them still with their copper alloy heads are visible on the corners of plate. Width of loop: 51mm. Width of plate: 49mm. Overall length: 57mm. Area of pelvis. SF 422.

b   Amber **bead** (fragments). Above left femur. Sf 423.

Grave 335 (Figs 10.36, 10.95) ? grown. 307°. Context 322. Phase 1b–2. Plot T. 1.81m x 0.57m x 0.07m.
Light grey-brown loam with frequent small and medium chalk. Poorly-preserved skeleton; skull and right arm decayed.

a   Cast copper alloy **buckle**. D-shaped loop of D-shaped section, with cast and notched bands either side of the axis. Club-shaped tongue with ridged back has similar decoration on its tip and base and a large copper alloy anchorage.
Also four copper alloy **belt mounts**.
i, Sheet metal drop-shaped plate and raised cloison cell containing a ?garnet. Base-plate is notched around the cell in a similar way to the buckle loop. Two attachment rivets with knob heads, shanks of circular section and sheet metal washers at the base.
ii, Similar, cell empty, slightly damaged in one corner.
iii, Similar, cell empty.
iv, Octagonal sheet metal stud with raised round cloison cell surrounded by notching and set with a red glass cabochon. Width of loop: 35mm. Length of stud with (i): 22mm. Diameter of stud (iv): 13mm. Above left waist. Sf 527.

Grave 336 (Figs 10.36–37, 10.96) ?F 30–40. 313°. Context 324. Phase 2b. Plot T. 2.76m x 1.30m x 0.58m.
Brown loam with frequent small and medium chalk. Moderately well-preserved skeleton. Right arm bent across pelvis.

a   Twenty amber and sixteen glass **beads**. Neck and chest. Sf 516 (see below).

b   Copper alloy **tweezers**. Narrow arms lightly expanded to incurved terminals. Length: 46mm. Chest area. Sf 518.

c   Iron **chain** complex; rings fastened by copper alloy rivets. Extensive mineral-preserved organic remains including textile, cordage, leather/skin product and fragment of bone. Diameter of individual rings: *c* 14mm. Chest area. Sf 515.

d   Iron **knife**. Poor condition. Straight back curving to tip, sinuous cutting-edge. Well-defined junction of horn handle. Traces of willow wood (*Salix* sp) on edge of blade under the leather possibly indicating reinforcement for the sheath. Length: 210mm. Left pelvis. Sf 513.

e   Iron **ring**. Diameter: 70mm. Left pelvis. Sf 512.

f   Iron, possible **key/girdle-hanger** with expanding shaft and missing terminal. Head folded over large iron wire **ring**. Mineral-preserved textile. Length: 135mm. Ring diameter: 52mm. Left pelvis. Sf 511.

g   Iron **binding** around copper alloy **tube** made of copper alloy folded sheet. Binding split open as a result of corrosion. Traces of mineral-preserved beech wood (*Fagus sylvatica*). Mineral-preserved textile on one side. Length of tube: 37mm. Left pelvis. Sf 517.

h   Antler burr **ring**. Fragment of an antler burr coronet, with burr removed from centre. Width: 10mm. Left pelvis. Sf 514.

i   Cast high-tin copper alloy **buckle**. D-shaped loop of convex section, narrowed axis for attachment of tongue, which is missing. The tongue rest is worn and traces of iron on the axis may suggest that it was an iron tongue or had an iron anchorage. Width of loop: 40mm. Right of right foot. Sf 510.

Grave 336 beads

a

amber: 20 beads

3   medium, rounded, diam 6–10mm

1	medium, facetted, diam 16–20mm
6	medium, facetted, diam 11–15mm
10	medium, facetted, diam 6–10mm

glass: 16 beads

Reticella (no 28)

1   medium, cylindrical, diam 16–20mm, 3 translucent, opaque yellow and opaque red twisted trails. Fig 4.27, Grave 336, Sf 516 (a14)

1   medium, biconical, diam 11–15mm, two translucent, opaque yellow and opaque red twisted trails. Fig 4.27, Grave 336, Sf 516 (a5)

Melon (no 21)

4   short to medium, globular, 8–13 ribbed cross-section, diam 11–15mm, translucent, blue. Fig 4.27, Grave 336, Sf 516 (a28), (a11)

1   medium, globular, 13-ribbed cross-section, diam 6–10mm, translucent (originally), blue (badly preserved, iridescent)

1   medium, globular, 7-ribbed cross-section, diam 11–15mm, translucent, yellow. Fig 4.27, Grave 336, Sf 516 (a24)

variation Melon (no 22)

1   short, globular, diam 11–15mm, translucent, blue with white streak. Fig 4.27, Grave 336, Sf 516 (a15)

2   short, globular, diam 11–15mm, translucent, yellow (one greenish). Fig 4.27, Grave 336, Sf 516 (a32)

polychrome Melon-related (no 23)

1   short, irregularly globular, diam 11–15mm, white circumferential zigzag trail on dark body. Fig 4.27, Grave 336, Sf 516 (a30)

polychrome red (no 68)

1   short, globular, diam 11–15mm, 3 yellow raised dots on equator on red body. Fig 4.27, Grave 336, Sf 516 (a13)

other globular (no 63)

1   short, irregularly globular, diam 6–10mm, opaque, red. Fig 4.27, Grave 336, Sf 516 (a21)

unidentified

1   fragments, opaque, blue

1   short, globular, diam 11–15mm, discoloured

Grave 337 (Figs 10.37, 10.96) ? 40–45. 315°. Context 326. Plot S. 2.21m x 0.80–0.94m x 0.29m.
Cream-brown loam with frequent small and medium chalk. Poorly-preserved skeleton.

a   Iron **knife**, lacking tip of blade. Tang tapers sharply and is bent out of alignment. Back rises before curving to tip, cutting-edge slightly sinuous. Mineral-preserved horn handle and leather on blade from sheath. Length: 181mm; blade length: 132mm. Area of left pelvis. Sf 767.

b   Iron **knife**, lacking tip of blade. Back straight and curving to tip, cutting-edge similar. Trace of junction of handle and blade. Mineral-preserved horn handle and leather on blade from sheath. Length: 129mm; blade length: 91mm. Area of left pelvis. Sf 768.

c   Iron **spearhead**. Long angular to straight-sided blade of lozenge-section with a medium shank and split socket. The shoulder of the blade has an hypertrophy, possibly a repair, making the blade knife-like. Field maple wood (*Acer campestre*) remains in socket. Mineral-preserved leather on blade. Length: 388mm. Left of left lower leg. Sf 769.

d   Iron **buckle** fragment. Fragment of loop with part of the tongue fused to it. Mineral-preserved textile. Length: 34mm. Above left femur. Sf 770.

Grave 338 (Figs 10.37, 10.96) M 19–21. 313°. Context 328. Phase 1–2. Plot T. 2.21m x 1.00m x 0.20m.
Cream-brown clay loam with frequent small and medium chalk. Well-preserved skeleton; skull half left.

a   **Ceramic vessel**. Wide-mouthed, rounded vessel with hollow neck and a slightly everted rim. Decorated with simple horizontal 'fret' or 'wurms' pattern in zone between two narrow incised horizontal neck grooves. Originally nine or ten 'frets' or 'wurms'. Below this zone on the upper shoulder and body are bunches of shallow grooves and incised lines, originally eight or nine, extending onto the lower body. Fresh break on non-joining sherd shows a reddish sandy matrix quite densely packed with rounded, sub-rounded and sub-angular quartz sand grains (up to 1mm in size). Some calcareous inclusions and occasional holes where they have leached out of the surface. Probably coil built. Burnished on exterior and interior rim, now worn. Rest of interior wiped smooth. Rim diameter: 102mm; base diameter: 55mm. Height: 119mm. Right of skull. Sf 689.

Grave 339 (Figs 10.37, 10.95) F 27–32. 132°. Context 33. Phase 3a. Plot W. 2.10m x 0.67–0.84m x 0.58m.
Cream-brown loam with frequent small and medium chalk. Poorly-preserved skeleton; skull half right; head at south-east end. Radiocarbon date: 1592 ± 17 BP (UB-6476) cal AD 420–450 (95%).

a   Cast copper alloy **buckle**. D-shaped loop of convex section with a narrowed axis for attachment of the now separate shield-tongue. Three groups of three incised lines decorate the loop. Mineral-preserved leather on bar and tongue. Plus three **shoe-shaped studs**, each with a pierced attachment lug. One stud with an unusual round finial. Mineral-preserved leather on the underside of all studs. Width of loop: 29mm. Length of studs: 19mm, 21mm, 23mm. Waist area. Sf 889.

b   Scatter of sixteen amber and sixteen glass **beads**. Right chest. Sf 890 (see below).

c   Cluster of 61 glass and 23 amber **beads**. Neck area. Sf 891 (see below).

d   Silver scutiform ?**pendant**. No remains of grip or loop; two perforations. Central boss punched from back; ring-and-dot decoration punched on front. Max diameter: *c* 21.5mm. Weight: 1.0g. Neck. Sf 892.

e   Copper alloy wire **ring**, broken; ends bent to overlap. Diameter: 20mm. Weight: 1.2g. Neck. Sf 893.

Sf 1276 Glass cylinder bead. Found in skull.

Grave 339 beads
b
amber: 16 beads

4   medium, rounded, diam 11–15mm
5   medium, rounded, diam 6–10mm
6   medium, facetted, diam 11–15mm
1   medium, facetted, diam 6–10mm

glass: 16 beads
Reticella (no 28)
2   medium, cylindrical, diam 11–15mm, 3 translucent, opaque yellow and opaque red twisted trails. Fig 4.28, Grave 339, Sf 890 (b18)
Melon (no 21)
1   medium, globular, 8-ribbed cross-section, diam 11–15mm, translucent, yellow. Fig 4.28, Grave 339, Sf 890 (b21)
polychrome Melon-related (no 23)
3   short to medium, globular, diam 11–15mm, white circumferential zigzag trail on dark body. Fig 4.28, Grave 339, Sf 890 (b23), (b24)
Koch49/50 (no 19)
1   very long, cylindrical, diam 11–15mm, opaque yellow spiral combed in one direction on opaque red body. Fig 4.28, Grave 339, Sf 890 (b19)
Cylindrical Pentagonal (no 10)
3   medium, diam 6–10mm, opaque, greyish blue. Fig 4.28, Grave 339, Sf 890 (b26), (b30)
Cylindrical Round (no 12)
2   medium, diam 6–10mm, opaque, red. Fig 4.28, Grave 339, Sf 890 (b27)
other globular (no 63)
1   short, diam 6–10mm, opaque, red. Fig 4.28, Grave 339, Sf 890 (b28)
1   short, diam 11–15mm, translucent, green-blue with black streak. Fig 4.28, Grave 339, Sf 890 (b25)
2   short, (one asymmetrical), diam 6–10mm, dark. Fig 4.28, Grave 339, Sf 890 (b32)

Bead
b or c
glass: 1 bead
Mosaic, ?Roman (no 26?)
1   fragments, star pattern including translucent blue and white and ?opaque ?yellow

c
amber: 23 beads
1   medium, rounded, diam 16–20mm
11   medium, rounded, diam 6–10mm
1   medium, facetted, diam 16–20mm
2   medium, facetted, diam 11–15mm
4   medium, facetted, diam 6–10mm
3   fragments
1   very short, wedge-shaped, diam 16–20mm

glass: 61 beads
Constricted Segmented (no 5)
4   two segments, long to very long, globular, diam 2–5mm. Fig 4.28, Grave 339, Sf 891 (c31)
2   medium, globular, diam 2–5mm
light Constricted Cylindrical (no 7)
1   diam 2–5mm. Fig 4.28, Grave 339, Sf 891 (c37)
Mosaic (no 25)
1   medium, globular, diam 11–15mm, 2 yellow 8-leafed stars in translucent ?green square alternating with 2 ring-and-dot motifs: white centre, opaque red ring,

white ring, red slip around perforation in translucent ?blue square. Fig 4.28, Grave 339, Sf 891 (c24)
polychrome mix (no 71)
1   medium, globular, diam 11–15mm, opaque, red/black/white melange, opaque yellow irreg. circumferential zigzag. Fig 4.28, Grave 339, Sf 891 (c25)
Melon (no 21)
1   medium, globular, 6-ribbed cross-section, diam 11–15mm, translucent, blue. Fig 4.28, Grave 339, Sf 891 (c26)
variation Melon (no 22)
1   short, globular, diam 11–15mm, translucent, blue. Fig 4.28, Grave 339, Sf 891 (c27)
other melon (no 59)
1   medium, asymmetrically globular, 8-ribbed cross-section, diam 2–5mm, opaque, yellow. Fig 4.28, Grave 339, Sf 891 (c74)
polychrome Melon-related (no 23)
1   short, globular, diam 11–15mm, white circumferential zigzag trail on dark body. Fig 4.28, Grave 339, Sf 891 (c28)
Cylindrical Pentagonal (no 10)
2   diam 6–10mm, opaque, red. Fig 4.28, Grave 339, Sf 891 (c60)
Cylindrical Round (no 12)
1   short, diam 6–10mm, opaque, white. Fig 4.28, Grave 339, Sf 891 (c64)
2   short to medium, diam 6–10mm, opaque, yellow. Fig 4.28, Grave 339, Sf 891 (c62)
3   short to medium, diam 6–10mm, opaque, red. Fig 4.28, Grave 339, Sf 891 (c57)
1   short, diam 6–10mm, opaque, greyish blue. Fig 4.28, Grave 339, Sf 891 (c39)
other cylindrical (no 56)
2   medium, diam 6–10mm, opaque, white (one bluish). Fig 4.28, Grave 339, Sf 891 (c54)
1   medium, diam 6–10mm, opaque, yellow
3   medium to long, diam 6–10mm, opaque, red. Fig 4.28, Grave 339, Sf 891 (c53)
sharp globular (no 62)
1   short, diam 6–10mm, opaque, dark
other globular (no 63)
6   short, one asymmetrically globular, diam 6–10mm, opaque, white. Fig 4.28, Grave 339, Sf 891 (c1)
11   short, diam 6–10mm, opaque, yellow (one greenish). Fig 4.28, Grave 339, Sf 891 (c78)
7   short to medium, diam 6–10mm, opaque, red. Fig 4.28, Grave 339, Sf 891 (c52)
1   short, diam 6–10mm, translucent, green (yellowish). Fig 4.28, Grave 339, Sf 891 (c38)
1   short, diam 6–10mm, translucent, blue. Fig 4.28, Grave 339, Sf 891 (c29)
5   short, diam 6–10mm, dark. Fig 4.28, Grave 339, Sf 891 (c45)
other cylindrical (no 56)
1   medium, cylindrical, diam 6–10mm, opaque, yellow (greenish)

Grave 340 (Figs 10.38, 10.81) M 30–35. 318°. Context 332. Plot W. 2.25m x 0.85m x 0.40m.

Cuts Grave 256. Cream-brown loam with frequent small and medium chalk. Moderately well-preserved skeleton; skull rolled forward.

a Iron **knife**. Back straight and curving to tip, cutting-edge similar. Well-defined junction of organic handle and blade. Mineral-preserved horn handle and leather on blade from sheath. Several folds of nettle fibre textile are preserved on the blade, possible traces of fleece on tip. Length: 200mm. Left pelvis. Sf 879.

b Iron **buckle**. Oval loop and plain tongue. Mineral-preserved leather on loop and over tongue. Width of loop: 33mm. Over left foot. Sf 880.

c Iron **buckle** and **plate**. Miniature oval loop with a rectangular plate folded over the loop. Remains of two iron knob-headed rivets along the rear edge of the plate. Mineral-preserved leather between plates and over tongue. Width of loop: 11mm; width of plate: 10mm. Overall length: 19mm. By left foot. Sf 881.

Grave 341 (Fig 10.96) ?M 35–40. 315°. Context 334. Plot W. 1.98m x 0.72m x 0.15m.
Light-brown loam with frequent small and medium chalk. Fragmentary skull and upper body only. No grave goods.

Grave 342 (Fig 10.97) ?M 20–25. 303°. Context 336. Plot T. 2.38m x 0.94m x 0.23m.
Cut by modern trench. Brown loam with frequent small and medium chalk. Moderately well preserved; skull right. No grave goods.

Grave 343 (Figs 10.37, 10.96) No bone. 323°. Context 338. Plot T. 1.34m x 0.49m x 0.16m.
Brown loam with frequent small and medium chalk. No bones survived; grave length suggests a child.

a Amber **bead** fragments. North-west end of grave. Sf 579.
b Copper alloy slip-knot ?**bracelet**. Maximum diameter: 37mm. Weight: 2.8g. North-east side of grave. Sf 580.

Grave 344 (Figs 10.38, 10.97) F 30–35. 316°. Context 340. Phase 1b. Plot W. 2.10m x 0.70–0.81m x 0.13m.
Cream-brown loam with frequent small and medium chalk. Moderately well-preserved skeleton; skull left; arms bent across body.

a Cast copper alloy **buckle**. Oval loop of D-shaped section with a narrowed axis for attachment of a club-shaped tongue with iron anchorage. Mineral-preserved leather on bar and loop from strap. Textile remains on back. Width of loop: 28mm. Under lower left arm. Sf 437.

b Sheet copper alloy **belt-mount**. An elongated oval plate with a disc-headed rivet at each end. The shanks are of circular section, and one has a sheet metal washer at the base. Mineral-preserved leather. Width: 15mm. South of lower left arm. Sf 438.

Grave 345 (Figs 10.38, 10.97) ?M grown. 317°. Context 342. Plot S. 1.34m (min) x 0.90m (min) x 0.06m.
Cuts Grave 357; largely destroyed by modern terrace. Light-brown loam with frequent small and medium chalk. Fragmentary leg bones only.

a Cast copper alloy **buckle** with **fixed plate**. Oval loop, remains of iron tongue or anchorage on underside. Triangular plate with three lobes and rivet-holes. Decorated with a border of ?punched dots, linked by a dotted Y-shape in the centre of the plate. Amorphous organic remains under plate from possible leather strap. Remains of stitching thread in the two paired rivet-holes behind the loop. Width of loop: 12mm; width of plate: 12mm. Overall length: 26mm. South corner of grave. Sf 1050.

Grave 346 (Figs 10.38, 10.98) M 40+. 320°. Context 344. Phase 3. Plot S. 2.44m (min) x 0.80–0.95m x 0.35m.
Cuts Grave 237; relationship to Grave 353 (Phase 3a) unclear. Cream-brown loam with frequent small and medium chalk. Moderately well-preserved skeleton; skull half right.

a Iron **spearhead**. Long, lengthy narrow angular blade with a short shank finished by a long cleft socket containing beech wood (*Fagus sylvatica*) fragments. Length: 465mm. Right of skull. Sf 424.

b Iron **sword**. No pommel; traces of organic upper guard, grip and scabbard, on which the fleece has been cut short of the mouth on both sides. Traces of mineral-preserved ash wood (*Fraxinus excelsior*), ?wool fibres and calfskin leather are present, probably from scabbard. Traces of horn hilt are present. Length: 870 x 52mm. (42); grip length: 90mm (approx.). Over left arm, upper end by neck. Sf 499 (SN 1021; pp 246–9).

c Iron **knife**, lacking most of tang. Back straight, slight curve to tip. Cutting-edge sinuous. Length: 88mm. Left of lower spine. Sf 520.

d Fragment of iron **rod** looped at one end. Mineral-preserved hazel wood (*Corylus avellana*). Length: 54mm. Above left pelvis. Sf 521.

e Iron T-shaped **axehead**. T-shaped or axe-hammer type, symmetrical cutting-edge, square to trapezoidal heel. Mineral-preserved wood in socket. Length: 119mm. Width: 107mm (cutting-edge). Right of right foot. Sf 519.

f Iron **buckle**. Oval, highly corroded. Mineral-preserved textile on back. Right of right foot, under axehead (e). Sf 1265.

Grave 347 (Figs 10.39, 10.82, 10.121) ?F 14–16. 313°. Context 346. Phase 2a. Plot S. 2.26m (min) x 0.63m (min) x 0.48m.
Cut by Grave 264 (Phase 3). Brown loam with frequent small and medium chalk. Flint packing stones along north-east side of grave indicate a coffin. Well preserved but damaged skeleton; skull left; arms bent across body.

a Gold **strip**, remains of the central ornamental brocading from a tablet-woven band: the brocaded area is 6mm wide and threads represent a band at least 50mm long. The strip is variable in width, 330–440 microns wide, and rectangular in cross-section, 30–40 microns thick. Right of skull. Sf 467.

b   Glass **cone beaker**. Fragment. Very light olive-green to colourless. The fragments are extensively decomposed. The rim is rolled inwards and everted. Just below the rim are the channels of lost, decomposed trails. The tip, diameter: 12mm, is flat and chipped. The fragments are severely attacked by iridescence and decomposition so that they are largely opaque, only the very tip showing a light olive colour. Mineralised, preserved thread wound round the object. The original height is estimated at 180mm. Diameter: *c* 78mm. Left of skull. Sf 678.

c   Copper alloy **wire** fragments. Mineral-preserved thread wound round one fragment. Length of pointed fragment: 33mm. Adjacent cone beaker, (b). Sf 439.

d   Scatter of 24 amber, one jet and 16 glass **beads**. Skull, neck and chest. Sf 466 (see below).

e   Cast silver-gilt whirl-shaped **openwork brooch** with discoloured and fragmented glass settings, originally red in colour, on hatched gold foil. Gilding remains only in crevices, central setting and rim worn. Cast spring-holder and pin-catch. Remains of iron spring. Mineral-preserved textile on front. Cordage on catch-plate and lug. Loop of reinforced cordage on pin. Max diameter: 22mm. Weight: 4.9g. Left shoulder. Sf 440.

f   Silver-gilt cast Kentish small **square-headed brooch**. Set with square garnets on head-plate and mushroom-shaped garnet on rounded foot-plate terminal. Garnets not set on hatched foil. Most ridges nicked. Inaccurate zigzag band created by double row of copper niello triangles. Bow worn, gilding on all ridges worn. Cast spring-holder and pin-catch; catch broken and repaired with copper alloy strip soldered on. Remains of iron spring with mineral-preserved textile and cordage and amber bead (see below). Length: 50mm. Weight: 11.5g. Left chest. Sf 468.

g   Fragments of iron **chain**. Rings made of iron wire fitted with iron rivets. Diameter of rings: *c* 7.5mm. Remains of mineral-preserved textile, cordage, ?shell and glass bead (see below). Weight: 20g. Left chest. Sf 441. (*Several fragments not drawn.*)

h   Silver **sheet** folded into a ring. Maximum diameter: 7mm. Weight: 0.4g. Over lower spine. Sf 442.

i   Iron **buckle** and **plate**. Oval loop with approximately square plate. Mineral-preserved leather between plates from strap. Textile remains adhering to the surface of the object. Width of loop: 34mm; width of plate: 24mm. Overall length: 39mm. Left waist. Sf 443.

j   Iron **châtelaine** fittings. Three **keys** with looped heads, one with remains of suspension ring (4mm thickness). All three have flattened rectangular shafts and two have large hooked, semi-circular 'wards' which face in the opposite direction to the loops of the heads. The third has a tiny hook facing forward from the front of the shaft. Mineral-replaced textile on all. Associated with a **lozenge**, pierced at centre, and an **iron ring** of circular section. Length of keys/girdle-hangers: 149mm, 139mm and 126mm. Length of lozenge: 30mm. Diameter of ring: 44mm. Left pelvis. Sf 444.

k   Silver-gilt cast **radiate-headed brooch**. Garnets lost; remains of niello inlay in punched ring-and-dot decoration on bow and foot-plate. Knobs, bow and tip of foot-plate worn; gilding

remains only in crevices. Cast pair of spring-holders and pin-catch. Remains of iron spring with mineral-preserved textile and cordage. The cord is wound round the bow and is visible on the front of the brooch. Length: 80mm. Weight: 16.3g. Pelvis. Sf 469.

l   Iron **ring** with four suspension loops hanging from it. Possible mineral-preserved suspension thong around the ring. Diameter: 38mm. Length of suspension loops: 36–40mm. By left femur. Sf 445.

m   Incomplete lead or lead-alloy **spindle-whorl**, probably originally shallow biconical shape. Possible mineral-preserved organic remains in spindle hole. Diameter: 38mm, height: 10mm. Spindle hole oval, from 6 x 8mm to 8 x 10mm. Weight: 14.5g; estimated original weight: *c* 20g. Left of skull. Sf 446.

Grave 347 beads

d

amber: 24 beads

1	very long, spindle-shaped, diam 6–10mm. Fig 4.26, Grave 347, Sf 466 (d25)	
2	medium, rounded, diam 11–15mm	
4	medium, rounded, diam 6–10mm	
1	medium, rounded, diam 2–5mm	
12	medium, facetted, diam 11–15mm	
4	medium to long, facetted, diam 6–10mm	

jet: 1 bead

1   short, cylindrical, diam 16–20mm. Fig 4.26, Grave 347, Sf 466 (d24)

glass: 16 glass

Constricted Segmented (no 5)

1   four segments, very long, diam 2–5mm

5   three segments, very long, diam 2–5mm

3   two segments, long to very long, diam 2–5mm. Fig 4.26, Grave 347, Sf 466 (d32)

1   medium, diam 2–5mm

Constricted Cylindrical (no 6)

2   very long, diam 2–5mm. Fig 4.26, Grave 347, Sf 466 (d28)

light Constricted Cylindrical (no 7)

2   very long, beaded, diam 2–5mm. Fig 4.26, Grave 347, Sf 466 (d30), (d31)

?green Cylindrical (no 48)

1   very long, asymmetrical cross-section, diam 2–5mm, bright green. Fig 4.26, Grave 347, Sf 466 (d27)

other melon (no 59)

1   medium, barrel-shaped, 5-ribbed cross-section, diam 11–15mm, opaque, red. Fig 4.26, Grave 347, Sf 466 (d26)

f

amber: 1 bead

1   medium, rounded, diam 2–5mm

g

glass: 1 bead

Constricted Cylindrical (no 6)

1   beaded, diam 2–5mm

Grave 348 (Figs 10.40, 10.98, 10.118) M 30–35. 327°. Context 348. Phase 1b–2a. Plot S. 2.55m x 1.05m x 0.70m.

Grave damaged by modern terrace. Brown loam with frequent small and medium chalk. Chalk packing around sides of grave indicate a coffin 1.98m x 0.50m. Moderately well-preserved skeleton with weapon wound to skull.

a   Iron **key** from a châtelaine. Shaft is circular in section and tapers to a narrow neck. No attachment point survives. Two of three flattened 'wards' survive. The single outer one has sloping shoulders similar to copper alloy examples. Mineral-preserved textile on surface. Length overall: 136mm, Length of 'wards': 26mm. Left of skull. Sf 487.

b   Copper alloy **base** and **side mount** from an organic container, perhaps a quiver. The base is made from a circular sheet with a single lug. It is pierced with eleven nails at irregular intervals; the lug carries two nails. These are dome-headed with tapering shanks and have an average length of 9mm. Thickness of sheet: 0.75mm. The mount is a strip of metal in the form of an elongated triangle with 4 pairs of nails and one terminal nail – only 3 remain *in situ* and are thinner than those in the base. Length of strip: 89mm; width: 11mm. Length of nails: 9mm. The strip is undecorated, and plain apart from a carination, 4mm wide, which lies 7mm below the top edge. One fragment of wood from the container survives. By right elbow. Sf 488.

c   Copper alloy and iron **buckle** and **plate**, inlaid with garnet and glass. D-shaped iron loop with an iron rim and framework into which garnets and two green glass slips are set. The tongue rest was left plain and remains of a copper alloy anchorage are visible around the narrowed axis. Either side of the anchorage, two thin metal strips are discernible. These are matched on the copper alloy back-plate of the now separate buckle-plate. Set onto this semi-circular back-plate is a kidney-shaped iron framework containing garnet and glass cloisonné around a central cell with a ?bone inset punched with three ring-and-dots. The upper edge of the cloisonné is neatly framed by a copper alloy strip, now missing in places, which is held down by knob-headed rivets. The garnets on both loop and plate are backed with cross-hatched gold foil. The iron outer faces of both loop and plate are inlaid with vertical wires. Width of loop: 36mm; width of plate: 37mm. Length of loop: 26mm; length of plate: 28mm. Above right waist. Sf 489.

d   Iron **knife**. Sharply tapering tang, back straight and curving to tip, cutting-edge similar. Mineral-preserved horn handle. Leather from sheath and associated textile on blade. Length: 162mm. Under left pelvis. Sf 490.

Grave 349 (Figs 10.40, 10.99, 10.121) ?F 50+. 320°. Context 350. Phase 1. Plot S. 2.36m x 0.89m (min) x 0.35m.
Cut by Graves 276 and 350. Cream-brown loam with frequent small and medium chalk. Poorly-preserved skeleton; legs crossed at ankle (left over right).

a   One fossil and fourteen glass **beads**. Neck area. Sf 451 (see below).

b   Cast copper alloy **ring**. Wear on inner edge. Diameter: 18mm. Weight: 3.1g. Neck. Sf 452.

c   Copper alloy **tweezers**. Plain, with narrow, lightly expanded arms leading to incurved terminals. Possible mineralised

leather suspension thong between arms. Length: 47mm. Chest. Sf 453.

Grave 349 beads
a
fossil: 1 unidentified
glass: 14 glass
blobby trail (no 64)
    2   short, globular, diam 11–15mm, lost circumferential blobby trail on dark body (one with red streak). Fig 4.24, Grave 349, Sf 451 (a2), (a3)
Blue (no 1)
    7   very short to short, annular, diam 6–15mm. Fig 4.24, Grave 349, Sf 451 (a12), (a6)
    1   medium, globular, diam 11–15mm
    2   medium, coiled globular, diam 6–10mm. Fig 4.24, Grave 349, Sf 451 (a14)
other globular (no 63)
    1   short, asymmetrically globular, diam 11–15mm, translucent, dark. Fig 4.24, Grave 349, Sf 451 (a5)
unidentified
    1   short, cylindrical, diam 11–15mm, lost ?spiral on white body?. Fig 4.24, Grave 349, Sf 451 (a4)

Grave 350 (Figs 10.40–1, 10.99, 10.121) 315°. Context: Sk A, 352; Sk B, 379. Plot S. 2.36m x 0.91–0.99m x 0.44m (min).
Cuts Graves 349 (Phase 1) and 351 (Phase 1–2). Cut by Grave 276. Brown loam with frequent small and medium chalk containing two residual Iron Age pot-sherds. Double-stacked grave (Sk A 0.22m above Sk B).

Sk 350A ? *c* 8. Skull and leg bone fragment only.

a   Iron **knife**. Back curves lightly to tip, cutting-edge similar, little wear. Mineral-preserved horn handle and textile remains on blade. Length: 117mm. Central part of grave. Sf 491.

b   Iron **buckle**. D-shaped loop and plain tongue. Mineral-preserved leather. Width of loop: 24mm. Central part of grave. Sf 492.

Sk 350B ?M 20–25. Moderately well-preserved skeleton; skull right; arms bent.

a   Scatter of 13 amber and 22 glass **beads**. Neck area. Sf 544 (see below).

b   Copper alloy **loop** hinged on very worn copper alloy suspension ring by means of iron rivet. Traces of mineral-preserved hazel wood (*Corylus avellana*) and wool fibres. Combined length: 59mm. Weight: 6.5g. Above left pelvis, under (d). Sf 545.

c   Cast high-tin copper alloy **buckle**. Heavy faceted loop, narrowed axis with remains of an iron tongue. Two lines are incised either side of the axis. Also, two cast high-tin **cone-headed studs** with narrow flange with notched edge. The remains of the attachment lugs appear to be copper alloy in one case and iron in the other. Mineral-preserved leather on buckle from strap. Width of loop: 39mm. Diameter of studs: 14mm. Above right pelvis. Sf 546.

d   Iron **ring**. Mineral-preserved textile; pupae cases. Diameter: *c* 50mm. Over suspension loop (b). Sf 547.

e   Antler burr **ring**. Central, oval part of burr removed, coronet remains. Length: 52mm. Width: 50mm. Thickness: 9mm. Pelvis area. Sf 548.

f   Three fragments of iron, forming:
(i) **nail** with discoidal head and bent shank. Length: 51mm;
(ii) fragment of second **nail**, including part of the head. Length: 24mm; not illustrated; (iii) rectangular **strip**. Length: 44mm; width: 9mm; not illustrated; Between femurs. Sf 549.

g   Cast copper alloy **shoe-shaped stud** with pierced attachment lug. The face of the stud is criss-crossed by an ?incised pattern, perhaps keying marks for the white metal coating, only traces of which remain. Plus an iron lump. Length of stud: 22mm. Between femurs. Sf 550.

h   Amber **bead**. Between femurs. Sf 551 (see below)

i   Fragment of **glass vessel**. Small naturally-coloured blue-green fragment, possibly from shoulder of Roman glass bottle. Length: 10mm; width: 13mm. Between femurs. Sf 552.

Grave 350 beads
a
amber: 13 beads

3	medium, globular, diam 6–10mm
1	medium, globular, diam 2–5mm
3	medium, rounded, diam 6–10mm
3	medium, rounded, diam 2–5mm
3	medium, facetted, diam 2–5mm

glass: 22 beads
Constricted Segmented (no 5)

4	two segments, very long, diam 2–5mm. Fig 4.25, Grave 350B, Sf 544 (a1)
18	short to medium, diam 2–5mm. Fig 4.25, Grave 350B, Sf 544 (a7)

h
amber: 1 bead

1	fragments. Fig **4.25**, Grave 350B, Sf 551 (h1)

Grave 351 (Figs 10.41–2, 10.99, 10.121) 312°. Context: Sk A, 381; Sk B, 382. Sk A, Phase 1–2. Sk B, Phase 1. Plot S. 2.50m x 1.00m (min) x 0.41m.
Cut by Grave 350. Orange-brown loam with frequent small and medium chalk. Double-stacked grave
(Sk A 0.10m above Sk B).

Sk 351A M grown. Poorly-preserved skeleton; skull and most of left side decayed.

a   Iron **knife**. Broad tang, back straight, cutting-edge slightly sinuous, curving to tip. Mineral-preserved horn handle and traces of leather and textile on blade. Length: 162mm. Above right pelvis, over coin (b). Sf 555.

b   Copper alloy Roman **coin**. Silvered bronze *nummus* of Magnentius (AD 350–353), FELICITAS REIPVBLICAE. RIC VIII, Lyon 112 (but possibly barbarous). Weight: 3.88g. Under knife (a). Sf 556.

c   Cast copper alloy **ear-ring** with polyhedral terminal. Diameter: 17mm. Weight: 0.7g. Above right pelvis. Sf 557.

d   Iron **pin**. Small, tapering, lacking any head. Mineral-preserved wood. Length: 30mm. Diameter: 3mm. Above right pelvis. Sf 558.

Sk 351B F 40–45. Moderately well-preserved skeleton; left arm bent across pelvis

a, d   Matched pair of cast copper alloy **small-long brooches**. Square head-plates and foot-plates. Punched ring-and-dot decoration. No obvious signs of wear. Cast spring-holder and pin-catch. Remains of iron spring on brooch (a). Mineral-preserved textile on lug and pin of (a). Length of (a): 44mm. Weight: 9.9g. Length of (b): 44mm. Weight: 10.0g. Upper chest and under right pelvis. Sf 574 and Sf 577.

b   Copper alloy **tweezers**. Plain with lightly expanded arms ending in incurved terminals. Length: 31mm. By right humerus. Sf 575.

c   Cast copper alloy **radiate-headed brooch**. Chased multiple ring-and-dot 'bulls-eye' decoration; dots on lower foot-plate piercing plate. Grooves on bow forming ribbed design; worn. Cast spring-holder and pin-catch. Iron remains of spring. Mineral-preserved textile on lug. Length: 53mm. Weight: 9.3g. Lower chest. Sf 576.

e   Copper alloy cast **cruciform brooch.** Animal head with half-round nostrils. Knobs cast with head-plate. Knobs and foot-plate terminal worn. Cast pair of spring-holders/lugs and pin-catch. Remains of iron pin. Mineral-preserved textile on back. Length: 91mm. Weight: 25.8g. By right pelvis. Sf 578.

Grave 352 (Fig 10.97) ? 7–9. 303°. Context 356. Plot S. 1.75m x 0.80m x 0.22m (min).
Cut by Grave 353 (Phase 3a). Cream loam with very frequent small and medium chalk. Poorly-preserved skeleton. No grave goods.

Grave 353 (Figs 10.42–3, 10.98) ?F 30–35. 320°. Context 358. Phase 3a. Plot S. 2.02m (min) x 0.93m x 0.49m.
Cuts Grave 352; relationship to Grave 346 unclear. Cream-brown loam with frequent small and medium chalk. Fragmentary skull and leg bones only.

a   Cluster of 11 amber and 95 glass **beads**. Chest area. Sf nos 411, 412 and 420 (see below).

b   Silver-gilt cast Kentish **disc brooch**. Central shell setting, key stone garnet settings on hatched foil (one design different to the others); egg-timer punch-marks on ridge surrounding animal style design; row of sulphide niello triangles pointing outwards. Gilding on cast animal style decoration not worn and well preserved on most of the rim. Cast spring-holder and pin-catch. Iron remains of spring. Mineral-preserved textile folds on pin and catch-plate. Cordage on hinge. Diameter: 22mm. Weight: 5.7g. Neck area. Sf 413.

c   Iron **knife**, lacking tip of blade. Narrow tang, back straight and curving to tip, cutting-edge slightly sinuous. Well-defined junction between organic handle and blade. Mineral-preserved horn handle and leather on blade from sheath. Length: 132mm. Beyond left femur. Sf 414.

d   Iron **rod** fragment. Mineral-preserved textile. Longest length: 60mm. Over left femur and (e). Sf 415.

e   Iron pierced **lozenge**; possible remnants of leather strip or thong passing through the central perforation. Mineral-preserved textile on one side. Length: 44mm. Under (d), partially on left femur. Sf 416.

f   Glass **claw beaker**. Broken and restored, with gaps. Blue, narrow stemmed beaker shape, folded foot pushed in deeply with a pointed tool, straight rim slightly thickened. Self-colour trail dropped on and turned upwards to the rim fifteen times; a second trail dropped on below this and turned downwards to the foot fourteen times. Two rows of four claws each, drawn close to the wall with deep drawing channels, the top row applied in the plain zone and fixed *c* 25mm above the foot, the lower row applied on the lower zone of trails, causing a ragged edge to the blob, and drawn down to be fixed on the foot. Striations, small bubbles, patches of iridescence. The vessel is stable. Ring punty scar diameter: 24mm. Height: 187mm. Diameter: 76mm. Left of left foot. Sf 664.

g   (1–10) Iron **fittings** for **wooden box** made of beech (*Fagus sylvatica*). These include the following:
    1, **drop handle** with curved terminals, held at each end within ring fittings with outward curved ends. Mineral-preserved wood.
    2–9, eight **corner-plates** formed of trapezoidal sheets of iron which splay out towards each end, and narrow at the centre. Single iron nails towards each end, clenched over, retaining wood of 12–13mm. Mineral-preserved wood with evidence of comb jointing. Textile remains adhering to the outside of three of the fittings.
    10, **spring mechanism**. Thin strip of iron that tapers towards one end, where it is bent over to a shaft of square section, leading to a hooked terminal. Traces of mineral-preserved wood. South-east end of grave. Sf 419.

h   Silver **rim-bindings** from wooden vessel. Mineral-preserved wood inside binding. Adjacent to claw beaker (f). Diameter of ring: 79mm. Sf 417.

i   Iron **pin**. Associated mineral-preserved textile. Length: 40mm. Under beads (a). Sf 418.

j   Silver-gilt beaded **open ring** and copper alloy ?**pin-catch**. Inner surface of ring plain; traces of a grey, granular deposit along one side, possibly a soft solder. Ring much worn on the outside, remains of gilding only in crevices of remaining beaded decoration. Fragments of copper alloy sheet folded into a hook with a base. Remains of ?solder on the base. Mineral-preserved textile on surface. Diameter of ring: 34mm. Weight: 1.5g. Height of hook: 7mm. Around disc brooch (b). Sf 613.

Grave 353 beads
amber: 11 beads
    1   medium, rounded, diam 11–15mm
    9   medium, faceted, diam 11–15mm
    1   fragments
glass: 95 beads
greenish Constricted Segmented (no 5)
    5   medium to long, diam 2–5mm
    4   short to medium, diam 6–10mm. Fig 4.30, Grave 353, Sf 411 (a62), (a65)
Mosaic (no 25)
    1   very long, biconical, diam 6–10mm, mirror stripes of translucent blue and white; small piece of

opaque red attached to surface. Fig 4.30, Grave 353, Sf 411 (a38)

Koch49/50 (no 19)
    1   medium, cylindrical, diam 6–10mm, opaque red trail combed in one (or both?) direction(s) on white body. Fig 4.30, Grave 353, Sf 411 (a37)
polychrome red (no 68)
    1   medium, barrel-shaped, diam 6–10mm, yellow spiral trail on red body. Fig 4.30, Grave 353, Sf 411 (a36)
Koch 20 (no 14)
    1   medium, barrel-shaped, diam 6–10mm, white wide crossing trails (no 65) and dots on dark body. Fig 4.30, Grave 353, Sf 411 (a35)
    1   long, barrel-shaped, diam 6–10mm, white wide crossing trails (no 65) and dots on red body. Fig 4.30, Grave 353, Sf 411 (a32)
    1   medium, globular, diam 6–10mm, white wide crossing trails (no 65) and dots on red body. Fig 4.30, Grave 353, Sf 411 (a29)
    2   medium, asymmetrically globular or barrel-shaped, diam 6–10mm, yellow wide crossing trails and dots on red body. Fig 4.30, Grave 353, Sf 411 (a25)
    4   medium, barrel-shaped, diam 6–10mm, yellow wide crossing trails (no 65) and dots on red body
    1   very long, barrel-shaped, diam 6–10mm, yellow wide crossing trails (no 65) and dots on red body. Fig 4.30, Grave 353, Sf 411 (a34)
    1   medium, barrel-shaped, diam 6–10mm, white wide crossing trails (no 65) on red body
    1   medium, barrel-shaped, diam 11–15mm, white wide crossing trails (no 65) and 3 white dots on red body
variation Koch 20 (no 14a)
    1   medium, barrel-shaped, diam 6–10mm, lost wide crossing trails (no 65) and red dots on white body. Fig 4.30, Grave 353, Sf 411 (a24)
Koch34 (no 15)
    1   short, globular, diam 6–10mm, white narrow crossing trails on red body. Fig 4.30, Grave 353, Sf 411(a22)
    5   short or medium, globular or barrel-shaped, diam 6–10mm, translucent blue narrow crossing trails on white body. Fig 4.30, Grave 353, Sf 411 (a20), (a19)
    3   two segments, medium or long, globular, diam 6–10mm, translucent blue narrow crossing trails on white body. Fig 4.30, Grave 353, Sf 411 (a16), (a15)
Dot34 (no 17)
    1   medium, barrel-shaped, diam 11–15mm, lost narrow crossing trails and red dots on white body. Fig 4.30, Grave 353, Sf 411 (a13)
variation Dot34 (no 18)
    1   very long, biconical, diam 6–10mm, greyish blue wide crossing trails and red dots on white body. Fig 4.30, Grave 353, Sf 411 (a23)
monochrome biconical (no 61)
    1   medium, diam 6–10mm, translucent, blue. Fig 4.30, Grave 353, Sf 411 (a40)
Cylindrical Pentagonal (no 10)
    1   very long, diam 6–10mm, opaque, greyish blue. Fig 4.30, Grave 353, Sf 411 (a39)
Cylindrical Round (no 12)
    2   medium, diam 6–10mm, opaque, white

3   medium to long, cylindrical, diam 6–10mm, opaque, yellow. Fig 4.30, Grave 353, Sf 411 (a44)

1   medium, diam 6–10mm, opaque, red

other cylindrical (no 56)

1   medium, diam 6–10mm, opaque, white

1   two segments, very long, diam 6–10mm, opaque, yellow

3   medium (one very long), diam 6–10mm, opaque, red

1   two segments, very long, diam 6–10mm, opaque, red. Fig 4.30, Grave 353, Sf 411 (a58)

3   medium to long, diam 6–10mm, semi-translucent, blue. Fig 4.30, Grave 353, Sf 411 (a47)

1   two segments, medium, diam 6–10mm, semi-translucent, blue. Fig 4.30, Grave 353, Sf 411 (a57)

sharp globular (no 62)

3   short to medium, globular, diam 2–5mm, opaque, yellow

Segmented Globular (no 39)

8   two segments, long, diam 2–5mm, opaque, yellow. Fig 4.30, Grave 353, Sf 411 (a100)

single Segmented Globular (no 40)

26   short to medium, globular, diam 2–5mm, opaque, yellow. Fig 4.30, Grave 353, Sf 411 (a74)

other globular (no 63)

1   short, diam 6–10mm, opaque, red

other barrel (no 57)

1   medium, diam 6–10mm, opaque, yellow. Fig 4.30, Grave 353, Sf 411 (a41)

1   medium, diam 6–10mm, discoloured

folded? (no 72)

1   very long, asymmetrically biconical, diam 6–10mm, translucent, blue. Fig 4.30, Grave 353, Sf 411 (a60)

Grave 354 (Figs 10.43, 10.98) ?F 25–30. 130°. Context 218. Phase 2b. Plot S. 1.95m (min) x 0.82m (min) x 0.06m.

Cuts Grave 361. Brown loam with frequent small and medium chalk. Fragmentary skull and lone bones only; head at south-east end.

a   Scatter of 57 amber and 13 glass **beads**, with fragments of an iron ?**ring**. Diameter of ring: *c* 15mm. Chest area. Sf 454 and Sf 455 (see below).

b   Silver-gilt cast Kentish **disc brooch**. Central inlay lost, all garnets cracked, on hatched foil. Rim decorated with two rows of niello triangles creating a zigzag pattern, worn especially in area of pin-catch. Gilding worn on ridges. Cast spring-holder, pin-catch lost; traces of lead-tin solder in that area. Little remains of iron ?spring. Diameter: *c* 26mm. Weight: 8.1g. Neck. Sf 456.

c   Copper alloy **chain** of folded double loops made of fused wire, worn thin. One loop separate, possibly originally joint by organic replacement not preserved. Length of single loop: 15mm. Weight: 1.3g. Chest area. Sf 457.

d   Cast copper alloy **buckle**. Oval, of rounded section, with three incised lines either side of the narrowed axis. Tongue, now separate, has approximately square tongue shield with two incised lines running parallel to notched rear edge. A large iron rivet-head, the last trace of the iron anchorage, sits on the tongue shield. Plus one **shoe-shaped stud** with a pierced attachment

lug on the back. Width of loop: 29mm. Length of stud: 19mm. By pelvis. Sf 458.

e   Gold **strip**, remains of the central ornamental brocading from a tablet-woven band: the brocaded area is 5–6mm wide and threads represent a band or bands totalling 30–40mm in length. The strip is very irregular in width, 450–700 microns, and thickness is 30–55 microns; rectangular in cross-section. Area of right shoulder and skull. Sf 459.

Grave 354 beads

a

amber: 57 beads

1   medium, rounded, diam 11–15mm

2   medium, rounded, diam 6–10mm

1   long, facetted, diam 11–15mm

17   medium, facetted, diam 11–15mm. Fig 4.27, Grave 354, Sf 455 (a71)

1   facetted, diam 21–25mm

1   facetted, diam 11–15mm

26   medium, facetted, diam 6–10mm

8   fragments.

glass: 13 beads

light Constricted Cylindrical (no 7)

1   very long, beaded, diam 2–5mm. Fig 4.27, Grave 354, Sf 454 (a1)

other opaque red (no 46)

1   short, globular?, diam 6–10mm. Fig 4.27, Grave 354, Sf 454 (a13)

Roman Polyhedral (no 37)

1   medium, polyhedral, diam 2–5mm, translucent, blue. Fig 4.27, Grave 354, Sf 454 (a12)

Melon (no 21)

2   short, barrel-shaped, 5–10 ribbed cross-section, diam 11–15mm, translucent, yellow. Fig 4.27, Grave 354, Sf 454 (a2), (a3)

1   medium, globular, 6-ribbed cross-section, diam 11–15mm, translucent, blue. Fig 4.27, Grave 354, Sf 454 (a4)

variation Melon (no 22)

2   short, globular, diam 11–15mm, translucent, blue. Fig 4.27, Grave 354, Sf 454 (a6)

other barrel (no 57)

1   short, diam 6–10mm, semi-translucent, white. Fig 4.27, Grave 354, Sf 454 (a10)

1   short, diam 11–15mm, translucent, blue with some white streaks. Fig 4.27, Grave 354, Sf 454 (a7)

folded? (no 72)

1   short, cylindrical, asymmetrical cross-section, diam 6–10mm, opaque, orange. Fig 4.27, Grave 354, Sf 454 (a9)

1   medium, globular, diam 6–10mm, semi-translucent, green (bluish). Fig 4.27, Grave 354, Sf 454 (a11)

1   short, asymmetrically barrel-shaped, diam 6–10mm, translucent, blue. Fig 4.27, Grave 354, Sf 454 (a8)

Grave 355 (Figs 10.43, 10.99) ?F 22–27. 311°. Context 362. Phase 1. Plot T. 2.25m x 1.02m x 0.30m.

Cream-brown loam with frequent small and medium chalk. Moderately well-preserved skeleton; skull half right; left arm bent across pelvis.

a   Glass **bowl**. Very light green, broken-off, cupped, unsmoothed rim, grazed for a stretch of 35mm. where there are two adjoining cracks. Base slightly raised. Many small bubbles, some inclusions, one nucleus of small cracks and one large bubble. A little discolouration and striation. Height: 52mm. Diameter: 117mm. Left of skull. Sf 470.

Grave 356 (Fig 10.99) No bone. 334°. Context 353. Plot S. 1.53m x 0.65–0.80m x 0.22m.

Cream-brown loam with frequent small and medium chalk. No bones survived; grave length suggests a child. No grave goods.

Grave 357 (Fig 10.97) ?M grown. 329°. Context 360. Plot S. 2.58m x 1.00m (min) x 0.32m.

Cut by Grave 345 and modern terrace. Cream-brown loam with frequent small and medium chalk. Long bones only. No grave goods.

Grave 358 (Fig 10.43) ? 3–5. 326°. Context 364. Plot S. 1.68m x 0.65m x 0.14m.

Cuts Grave 237. Grey-brown loam with frequent small chalk. Skull fragments only.

a   Iron **knife**. Fragmentary, lacking most of blade. Broad tang, back straight, cutting-edge sinuous and fragmentary. Length: 112mm. Central part of grave (left side). Sf 486.

Grave 359 (Fig 10.83) M 45–55. 309°. Context 366. Plot S. 2.59m x 0.65–0.82m x 0.14m.

Cut by Grave 265 (Phase 3a). Orange-brown clay with frequent small and medium chalk. Poorly-preserved skeleton; left arm bent across pelvis; right arm decayed. No grave goods.

Grave 360 (Figs 10.43, 10.101) ?F 30–40. 330°. Context 368. Phase 3b. Plot S. 1.95m x 0.69m x 0.06m.

Cuts Grave 361. Grey-brown loam with frequent small chalk. Poorly-preserved skeleton.

a   Scatter of 74 glass **beads**. Chest area. Sf 493 (see below).
b   Point of copper alloy ?**pin**. Length: 36mm. Weight: 0.3g. Neck. Sf 494.
c   Iron **knife**. Incomplete. Broad tang leading to back, curving to tip. Cutting-edge sinuous and worn. Well-defined junction of organic handle and blade. Length: 70mm. Above left pelvis. Sf 495.
d   Iron **nail**. Fragmentary. Discoidal head, shank of circular section. Length: 37mm from x ray. Under left pelvis. Sf 496.
e   Undecorated copper alloy **sword pommel**. Truncated pyramidal type, rectangular slot for tang in top. Width: 31mm. Left pelvis. Sf 497.
f   Iron **keys** (2) with rounded heads tightly looped over suspension **ring**. Short, square shafts with one hooked and

one rounded 'ward'. Mineral-preserved textile on one face. Lengths: both 86mm. Left pelvis. Sf 498.

Grave 360 beads
a
glass: 74 beads
Constricted Segmented (no 5)
  6   short to medium (on very long), globular, diam 2–5mm, light. Fig 4.30, Grave360, Sf 493 (a71)
green segmented (no 47)
  2   short to medium, globular, diam 2–5mm. Fig 4.30, Grave360, Sf 493 (a66)
turquoise cylindrical (no 50)
  1   three segments, very long, diam 2–5mm. Fig 4.30, Grave360, Sf 493 (a1)
  13   two segments, long to very long, diam 2–5mm
  49   short to long, diam 2–5mm. Fig 4.30, Grave360, Sf 493 (a34)
turquoise square cylindrical (no 51)
  2   medium, diam 2–5mm
Orange (no 33)
  1   medium, barrel-shaped/biconical, diam 6–10mm. Fig 4.30, Grave360, Sf 493 (a74)

Grave 361 (Fig 10.101) F 30–40. 311°. Context 370. Plot S. 2.11m x 1.01–1.05m x 0.24m.

Cut by Graves 354 (Phase 2b) and 360 (Phase 3b). Cream-brown loam with frequent small and medium chalk. Poorly-preserved skeleton; skull ?removed by Grave 360. No grave goods.

Grave 362 (Figs 10.43, 10.101) No bone. 299°. Context 372. Plot T. 0.85m x 0.49m x 0.17m.

Light-brown loam with frequent small and medium chalk. No bones survived; grave length suggests a child.

a   Fragmentary iron **nail**, including shank and part of discoidal head. Mineral-preserved wood on shank. Length: 25mm. South-east end of grave. Sf 476.
b   Two fragments of square-sectioned shank of an iron **nail**. Mineral-preserved wood on shank. Length: 30mm. South-east end of grave. Sf 477.

Grave 363 (Figs 10.44, 10.91) M 45–55. 310°. Context 374. Plot T. 2.47m x 0.88m x 0.45m.

Cuts Grave 311. Grey-brown loam with frequent small and medium chalk. Moderately well-preserved skeleton.

a   Iron **spearhead**. Angular blade, slightly concave edges, lozenge-section, long split socket. Willow wood (*Salix* sp) fragments in socket. Mineral-preserved textile on socket. Length: 375mm. Left of skull. Sf 522.
b   Iron **knife**. Broad tang, back straight and curving to tip, cutting-edge slightly sinuous. Well-defined junction between organic handle and blade. Mineral-preserved horn handle, leather on blade from sheath and traces of textile on tip. Length: 174mm. Above right pelvis. Sf 523.

c   Iron **buckle**. D-shaped loop, now broken, with plain tongue. Amorphous organic remains on bar. Width of loop: 27mm. Right of lower spine. Sf 524.

Grave 364 (Fig 10.99) M 30–40. 316°. Context 392. Plot T. 2.07m x 0.90–0.95m x 0.20m.
Brown loam with frequent small and medium chalk. Moderately well-preserved skeleton; skull left; legs crossed at ankle (left over right). No grave goods.

Grave 365 (Fig 10.101) ?M grown. 309°. Context 394. Plot T. 2.57m x 1.08m x 0.30m.
Cut by Grave 330. Brown loam with frequent small and medium chalk. Poorly-preserved skeleton. No grave goods.

Grave 366 (Figs 10.44, 10.102) ?F 20–25. 311°. Context 398. Phase 1b–2. Plot V. 2.15m x 0.96m x 0.28m.
Cream-brown loam with frequent small and medium chalk. Poorly-preserved skeleton; skull half left; right arm bent across pelvis.

a, b   Matching pair of cast copper alloy gilt **saucer brooches**. Garnet settings not on hatched foil. Gilding slightly worn on ridges of cast decoration. Cast spring-holder and pin-catch. Remains of iron spring of (a); very little remains of iron spring of (b). Mineral-preserved cordage and leather/skin product remains on pin of (a). Diameter of both (a) and (b): *c* 21mm., weight of both (a) and (b): 8.8g. Neck. Sf 636 and Sf 637.

c   Iron **knife**. Fragmentary section of blade, lightly curved back. Tip missing. Mineral-preserved horn (from handle?) and leather on blade from sheath. Length: 69mm. Above left pelvis. Sf 638.

Grave 367 (Fig 10.44) ?M 30–40. 321°. Context 400. Plot V. 1.95m x 0.88m x 0.17m.
Cuts Grave 378; cut by modern pit. Brown loam with frequent small and medium chalk. Poorly-preserved skeleton; skull half right; right arm bent across body; legs bent to left.

a   Iron **knife**. Fragmentary, lacking part of tang. Back straight and curving to tip, cutting-edge sinuous. Well-defined junction of handle and blade. Mineral-preserved horn handle and leather on blade from sheath. Length: 140mm. By left elbow. Sf 646.

b   Copper alloy **tweezers**. Broad arms lying touching each other for half the length of the tweezers then lightly splayed to rounded incurved terminals. Arms decorated with transverse incised lines and criss-cross pattern close to indented loop. Length: 56mm. By left elbow. Sf 647.

c   Fragment of **glass vessel**. Handle sherd from Roman bottle in naturally coloured blue green glass, folded on one side, with small section of rib extant. Length: 17mm. Width: 17mm. By left elbow. Sf 648.

d   Iron **buckle**. Oval loop with the remains of a plain tongue. Amorphous organic remains. Width of loop: 23mm. Waist area. Sf 649.

e   Small, indistinct iron **object**, fragmentary and unidentifiable. Longest length: 40mm. By left elbow. Sf 650.

f   Iron ?open **ring**. Associated textile remains. Two distinct areas of mineral-preserved cordage and third area of possible hide and hair/skin product binding around the ring. Diameter: *c* 47mm. By left pelvis. Sf 651.

g   Copper alloy cast **annular brooch** with remains of iron pin. Traces of two ?decorative traverse grooves on flat section of ring. Ring worn in area of absent pin point, broken at indention. Mineral-preserved woven textile on hinge and pin tip; also traces of possible leather. Diameter: *c* 37mm. Weight: 5.6g. Right shoulder. Sf 652.

Grave 368 (Figs 10.45, 10.100) M 30–35. 317°. Context 402. Plot V. 2.37m x 0.67–0.75m x 0.15m.
Light-brown loam with frequent small and medium chalk. Flint packing stones along north-east side of grave indicate a coffin. Moderately well-preserved skeleton; legs crossed at ankle (right over left).

a   Cast copper alloy **buckle**. D-shaped loop of approximately oval section with narrowed axis for attachment of a slender copper alloy tongue. Width of loop: 26mm. Area of lower spine. Sf 617.

Grave 369 (Fig 10.102) F 30–35. 321°. Context 404. Plot V. 2.38m x 0.93m x 0.30m.
Cream-brown silty loam with frequent small and medium chalk. Poorly-preserved skeleton; left arm bent across body. No grave goods.

Grave 370 (Fig 10.102) ? 6–8. 332°. Context 406. Plot X. 1.83m x 0.60–0.83m x 0.05m.
Light-brown loam with frequent small chalk containing a Roman pot-sherd. Fragmentary skull and long bones only. No grave goods.

Grave 371 (Figs 10.45, 10.102) ?M 20–25. 315°. Context 412. Plot X. 2.44m x 0.74m (min) x 0.31m.
Cut by modern terrace. Grey-brown loam with frequent small and medium chalk. Poorly-preserved skeleton; skull half right; right arm bent across pelvis; left leg bent.

a   **Ceramic vessel**. Rounded undecorated vessel with everted rim. Complete following reconstruction. Fabric visible only on an abraded break. This shows a fine, dense sandy fabric reduced throughout. Occasional quartz sand grains to up to 0.5mm on the surface as well as a few surface pin-prick leach holes. Occasional larger voids where larger inclusions have dropped out and others which appear to be seed impressions and other organic material. Coil-built with clear fingernail impressions on the interior where the rim and shoulder have been added to lower coils. Exterior surface well burnished and the interior wiped smooth. Rim diameter: 110mm; base diameter: 45mm. Height: 130mm. Right of skull. Sf 690.

Grave 372 (Figs 10.45, 10.103) F 30–35. 134°. Context 414. Phase 2a. Plot V. 2.29m x 0.86m x 0.56m.
Cream-brown loam with moderate small and medium chalk. Poorly-preserved skeleton; arms bent across pelvis; head at south-eastern end.

a Two collections of **sheep bones**. Nineteen bones come from the four feet of a single sheep. This includes left and right metacarpals and metatarsals, a left carpal (magnum), seven proximal phalanges, three medial phalanges and four distal phalanges. Seven right ribs are identified as probably sheep and are also consistent with deriving from a single animal (not necessarily the same animal as the feet bones). One rib has a small healed fracture. Over right femur. Sf 628.

b Copper alloy cast **annular brooch** with iron pin. X-ray shows slight indention for pin. One side of ring decorated with cross-shaped punch-marks. Decoration worn; ring worn especially around pin-point. Mineral-preserved textile and cordage on pin. Diameter: *c* 36mm. Weight: 7.2g. Right shoulder. Sf 629.

c Copper alloy cast **annular brooch** with remains of iron pin. Ring broken at indention; no obvious signs of wear. Wool fibres. Folds of mineral-preserved textile on pin and ring. Diameter: *c* 36mm. Weight: 4.3g. Left shoulder. Sf 630.

d Iron **knife**. Fragmentary, lacking part of tang. Back straight and curving to tip, cutting-edge slightly sinuous. Well-defined junction of handle and blade. Mineral-preserved horn handle and leather on blade from sheath. Length: 128mm. Above left pelvis. Sf 631.

e Silver-gilt cast great **square-headed brooch**. Copper niello zigzag on rounded foot-plate terminal, niello triangles pointing inwards on upper foot-plate and on head-plate, opposing triangles creating zigzag pattern on bow. Gilding worn on bow and ridges of cast decoration. Cast pair of spring-holders and pin-catch. Copper alloy pin. Mineral-preserved cordage. Length: 60mm. Weight: 13.5g. Under chin. Sf 632.

f Silver-sheeted iron inlaid **disc brooch**. Central white glass setting surrounded by eight keystone garnets on hatched foil. XRF-analysis showed traces of mercury gilding. Iron remains of spring with mineral-preserved textile and leather. Diameter: *c* 22mm. Weight: 7.0g. Under (e). Sf 633.

g One amber and 10 glass **beads**. Neck and shoulders. Sf 634 (see below).

h Glass **claw beaker**. Broken and restored with some gaps. Brown, basic shape of a stemmed beaker, tall with flaring, slightly thickened rim. The foot is irregularly folded, probably hollow at the edge, and is pushed in twice with a pointed tool. A very fine trail is dropped on 33mm below the rim and turned downwards five times. Another, slightly thicker trail is turned from the foot upwards ten times. Two rows of four claws each are applied in the intervening plain zone, the claws fully blown but shallow, the lower row drawn down to fasten on the foot. Two opposite claws in the top row are higher than the other two. The glass is iridescent, bubbly and streaky with a thickened flaw near the rim, and the wall is paper thin in the claw area. Traces of a ring punty. Height: 201mm. Diameter: 92–100mm; diameter of foot: 33mm. Thickness: 3mm at rim. Right of skull. Sf 665.

i Iron **buckle**. Oval loop and plain tongue. Mineral-preserved leather from strap. Textile remains on back. Width of loop: 26mm. Under right pelvis. Sf 635.

Grave 372 beads
g
amber: 1 bead
    1   medium, fragment, diam 6–10mm
glass: 10 beads
Roman Hexagonal Cylindrical (no 35)
    1   very long, diam 2–5mm, semi-translucent (orig. translucent?), green. Fig 4.26, Grave 372, Sf 634 (g6)
    2   long, diam 6–10mm, translucent, green. Fig 4.26, Grave 372, Sf 634 (g5), (g7)
translucent green cylindrical (no 53)
    1   short, cylindrical, diam 6–10mm, orig. translucent?, green
Miniature Dark (no 24)
    1   very long, coiled, diam 2–5mm. Fig 4.26, Grave 372, Sf 634 (g4)
Blue (no 1)
    1   short, annular, diam 6–10mm. Fig 4.26, Grave 372, Sf 634 (g3)
sharp globular (no 62)
    1   short, globular, diam 6–10mm, opaque, green. Fig 4.26, Grave 372, Sf 634 (g9)
other globular (no 63)
    1   short, irregularly globular, diam 6–10mm, opaque, green. Fig 4.26, Grave 372, Sf 634 (g10)
other barrel (no 57)
    1   short, asymmetrically barrel-shaped, diam 6–10mm, opaque, green
other melon (no 59)
    1   medium, barrel-shaped, 6-ribbed cross-section, diam 11–15mm, opaque, red. Fig 4.26, Grave 372, Sf 634 (g2)

Grave 373 (Figs 10.46, 10.102) ?M 35–40. 334°. Context 416. Phase 2b–3a. Plot V. 1.84m (min) x 0.82m (min) x 0.15m.
Cream-brown loam with frequent small and medium chalk. Fragmentary skull and long bones only.

a Scatter of 44 amber and 22 glass **beads**. Area of lower body. Sf 603 (see below).

b Cast copper alloy **strap-end**. Leaf-shaped, with one disc-headed rivet at split end and traces of white metal coating. Upper portion decorated with an incised diagonal cross with transverse lines above and below and with notched upper edge. The back is convex with a central ridge. The back is an imitation of a strap-end with a moveable bar. However, in this object the bar is part of the casting of the strap-end and non-functional. Damaged in two places. Mineral-preserved leather on underside. Length: 53mm. Outside left leg. Sf 604.

c Iron **lozenge**. One side slightly curved, central perforation. Traces of leather strap passing through centre. Mineral-preserved textile on edges. Length: 40mm. Left of upper left leg. Sf 605.

d Iron **shaft**. Small, thin iron rod, with point bent over. Mineral-preserved wood. Length: 28mm. Area of left pelvis. Sf 606.

e Copper alloy cast **ring**. Covered with mineral-preserved pseudomorphs of ?nematode worms. Diameter: *c* 55mm. Weight: 36.9g. Area of left pelvis, over (f). Sf 607.

f Iron **knife**. Fragmentary, lacking part of tang and end of blade. Broad tang, back curving to tip, cutting-edge sinuous. Mineral-preserved horn handle and leather on blade from sheath with possible wood/plant stem stiffener along one edge. Length: 100mm. Area of left pelvis, under (e) and (g). Sf 608.

g Iron **ring**. Extensive mineral-preserved textile some of which appears to be wrapped around the ring. Remains of a leather suspension thong wound around the ring. Diameter: 69mm. Area of left pelvis, over (f). Sf 609.

h Cast copper alloy **buckle**. D-shaped, faceted loop with narrowed axis for attachment of the shield-tongue. The tongue shield is notched around the rounded edge and has swallow-tailed lateral finials. A large iron rivet on the tongue shield is part of the now broken iron anchorage and the tongue itself is waisted. Also, two **shoe-shaped studs** with one pierced attachment lug each. Both buckle and studs have traces of a white metal plating, probably tinning. Mineral-preserved leather on the back of the loop and the underside of the rivets, from a strap. Mineral-preserved textile adhering to the top of the tongue shield. Width of loop: 29mm. Length of studs: 17–19mm. Right pelvic region. Sf 610.

i Copper alloy **pin**. Incomplete, point missing. Circular section shaft leading to flattened spatulate head, slightly bent. Associated mineral-preserved organic remains. Tip missing. Length: 79mm. Neck. Sf 611.

j Silver-gilt cast Kentish **disc brooch**. Central shell setting, key-stone garnets on hatched foil; ridge around animal style decoration nicked; opposing silver niello triangles on rim creating zigzag pattern. Gilding worn on frames of settings and cast ridges. Remains of iron spring with mineral-preserved cordage. Diameter: 24mm. Weight: 5.8g. Under chin. Sf 612.

Grave 373 beads

a

amber: 44 beads

2 medium, rounded, diam 6–10mm
4 medium, rounded, diam 11–15mm
6 medium, faceted, diam 16–20mm
30 medium, faceted, diam 11–15mm. Fig 4.29, Grave 373, Sf 603 (a54)
1 medium, faceted, diam 6–10mm
1 fragments

glass: 22 beads

Mosaic (no 25)
1 cylindrical, hexagonal cross-section, diam 6–10mm, 4-leafed petal in translucent glass; leaves in three layers: inner dark, central opaque red, outer white; semi-translucent yellow rim at perforation. Fig 4.27, Grave 373, Sf 603 (a4)

Reticella (no 28)
1 medium, biconical, diam 16–20mm, 3 translucent, opaque red and opaque yellow twisted trails. Fig 4.27, Grave 373, Sf 603 (a1)
1 short, barrel-shaped, diam 16–20mm, 3 translucent, opaque yellow and opaque red twisted trail. Fig 4.27, Grave 373, Sf 603 (a53)

Melon (no 21)
1 medium, globular, 12-ribbed cross-section, diam 6–10mm, translucent, blue. Fig 4.27, Grave 373, Sf 603 (a58)
4 medium, globular, 7–8 ribbed cross-section, diam 11–15mm, translucent, blue. Fig 4.27, Grave 373, Sf 603 (a63)
1 short, globular, 10-ribbed cross-section, diam 11–15mm, translucent, blue

variation Melon (no 22)
1 short, irregularly globular, diam 16–20mm, translucent, blue. Fig 4.27, Grave 373, Sf 603 (a61)
1 short, globular, diam 11–15mm, translucent, yellow (greenish)

polychrome Melon-related (no 23)
2 short, globular, diam 11–15mm, white circumferential zigzag trail on dark body (one translucent green). Fig 4.27, Grave 373, Sf 603 (a47)

Koch58 (no 20)
1 medium, barrel-shaped, diam 11–15mm, opaque, red, 3 opaque yellow circumferential trails on white zigzag trail. Fig 4.27, Grave 373, Sf 603 (a11)

polychrome red (no 68)
1 short, globular, diam 11–15mm, lost zigzag on red body. Fig 4.27, Grave 373, Sf 603 (a23)
1 medium, barrel-shaped, diam 11–15mm, opaque yellow zigzag on red body. Fig 4.27, Grave 373, Sf 603 (a25)

Blue (no 1)
1 short, annular, diam 11–15mm

other barrel (no 57)
1 short, diam 6–10mm, opaque, red. Fig 4.27, Grave 373, Sf 603 (a40)

other globular (no 63)
3 short, globular, diam 6–10mm, opaque, yellow. Fig 4.28, Grave 373, Sf 603 (a33), (a39)

unidentified
1 two segments, asymmetrically globular fragment, diam 11–15mm, translucent, blue

Grave 374 (Figs 10.46, 10.102) ? 14–16. 308°. Context 418. Plot X. 2.20m x 0.79–0.90m x 0.70m.
Cream-brown loam with frequent small and medium chalk. Fragmentary femurs only.

a Iron **spearhead**. Short leaf-shaped blade of lozenge to lentoid section with a medium split socket containing ash wood (*Fraxinus excelsior*) fragments. Length: 220mm. Right of skull. Sf 594.

b Iron **buckle**. Oval loop, now broken, tongue with curved tip. Width of loop: 24mm. Area of right pelvis. Sf 595.

c Iron **knife**. Incomplete, lacking tip of blade. Back straight and curving to tip, cutting-edge slightly sinuous. Well-defined junction of organic handle and blade. Mineral-preserved horn handle. Length: 116mm. Left side of waist. Sf 596.

Grave 375 (Figs 10.47, 10.103) M 25–30. 317°. Context 420. Phase 3b. Plot X. 2.65m x 1.04m x 0.74m.

Brown loam with frequent small and medium chalk. Well-preserved skeleton; skull half right; arms bent across pelvis. Radiocarbon date from bone, 1493±18 BP (UB-4958), cal AD 540–615 (95%).

a   Iron **spearhead**. Angular to straight-sided blade, lozenge-section, with a long split socket. May have a sort of ring/track around the neck, can only see it on the X-ray. Beech wood (*Fagus sylvatica*) remains in socket. Length: 360mm. Right of skull. Sf 761.

b   Iron **sword** with traces of a mineral-preserved ash wood (*Fraxinus excelsior*) scabbard with sheep's wool fibres from scabbard. More mineral-preserved ash wood (*Fraxinus excelsior*) is present in association with horn on the hilt. Truncated pyramidal iron pommel; slight double rib on both sides of tang between guards (see discussion of hilt construction); traces of organic guards, grip; one edge of point damaged. Length: 900 x 50mm (43); grip length: 94mm; thickness of upper and lower guards, 10mm. (approx.) and 12mm (approx.) respectively. Left of body, under lower arm, pommel below shoulder. Sf 740 (SN 1022; pp 249–51).

c   Iron **shield boss**. Incomplete, lacking head of apex. Small uncarinated convex cone with slight sloping wall (height: 10mm), narrow flange (width: 10mm) and three small knob-headed flange rivets (diameter: 7mm). A fourth (replacement?) flange rivet, small and disc-headed (diameter: 7mm), is associated with a small rectangular copper alloy plate (length: 20mm, width: 8mm) and tiny rivets. Mineral-preserved wood and leather remains indicate a covering of leather to the front and back of the wooden shield board. Diameter: 120mm. Height: 70mm. Over sword handle on left upper arm. Sf 762.
Iron **shield grip**. Straight, narrow strap grip attached to shield boss (c) by a small knob-headed flange rivet at each end. Mineral-preserved wood remains indicate a wooden handle with a lap joint construction. Length: 130mm. Width: 15–20mm. Over sword handle on left upper arm. Sf 762.

d   1, iron **buckle** and **plate**. Oval loop, now split. with short tongue. Only the short, rectangular back-plate is preserved, the upper-plate having broken off. Mineral-preserved leather from strap. Textile remains from garment adhering to surface. Width of loop: 32mm. Width of plate: 23mm. Overall length: 31mm. Excavated from above the left pelvis. Sf 763.
2, small iron **cleat** of oval shape, with curved profile and rounded ends. Pierced by two iron rivets; Oak wood (*Quercus* sp) remains accreted to one rivet. Length: 32mm. Width: 12mm. Excavated from above the left pelvis. Sf 763.

Grave 376 (Figs 10.48, 10.103) ? 7–8. 326°. Context 422. Phase 5–7. Plot X. 2.00m x 0.90m x 0.45m.
Light-brown loam with frequent small and medium chalk. Fragmentary skull and leg bones only. Body appears to be laid on a feather-filled mattress or bedding (see Table 5.7).

a   Iron **knife**. Fragmentary, lacking part of tang and most of blade. Back straight, cutting-edge sinuous. Mineral-preserved leather, textile, feathers and pupae cases. Length: 72mm. Left of left femur. Sf 618.

b   Iron and copper alloy, two matching **keys/girdle-hangers** corroded together, with square shafts and hooked 'wards', both heads are looped over a length of thin copper alloy wire. Mineral-replaced textile and feathers survive on both sides of the shafts and 'wards'. Length: 110mm; diameter of wire: 2mm. Left of left femur. Sf 619.

c   Iron and copper alloy **key/girdle-hanger** with T-shaped wards and z- and s-barley-twist shaft and head looped over a copper alloy suspension ring. Folds of mineral-replaced textile remain on the wards with patches on the head and shaft. Left of left femur. Length: 115mm. Sf 620.

d   Copper alloy and ivory/bone, **rods** (2), one with barley-twist shaft and large ring head enclosing remains of bone ring and small loop on other end; the other with looped head and section changing from square to flat, damaged end. Both are associated with a thong of mineralised leather, and are corroded together although they are not necessarily linked. Seventeen associated fragments of bone of varying sizes, presumably a **purse ring**, of which the largest is 105mm long and the smallest 8mm. ?Part of purse ring h, below? Length of rods: both 111mm. Left of left femur. Sf 621.

e   Iron **rods**, corroded to each other at right-angles, one with barley-twist shaft, the other with changing cross-section. Mineral-replaced textile and remains of a leather thong at point of contact and on both shafts. Lengths: 88mm and 69mm. Left of left femur. Sf 622.

f   Iron ?**key/girdle-hanger**, small, with looped 'ward' and double collar beneath loop at head. Length: 81mm. Left of left femur. Sf 623.

g   Two iron **keys/girdle-hangers** corroded together. Left of left femur. Sf 624.
1, iron **key/girdle-hanger** with barley-twist shaft and hooked 'ward', looped head with remains of iron suspension ring. Length: 111mm.
2, iron **key/girdle-hanger** with flattened rectangular shaft and hooked double 'ward'. Head looped over iron ring. Mineral-replaced textile on bottom of shaft and 'wards'. Length: 122mm.

h   Ivory **purse ring**. Fragmentary, now in seventeen pieces. Part of (e) passes through one of the ivory fragments. Width: 10mm. Left of left femur. Sf 625.

i   Copper alloy **pin**. Circular head, flat section with transverse ribbed moulding at neck. Upper portion of shaft of circular section, lower part of square section, tapering to a point. Length: 45mm. Neck. Sf 626.

j   Twelve glass **beads**. Chest area. Sf 627.

k   **Ceramic bottle**. Tall necked bottle form, 90 per cent complete following reconstruction. Decorated with continuous incised wavy line which starts just below the neck and encircles the neck and shoulder two, sometimes three times. Oxidised, dense sandy matrix with very occasional large (up to 10mm) pieces of unmixed clay or mudstones visible in broken section otherwise it is very fine and is visually identical to the fabric of the bottle from grave 251. Wheel-thrown with wire cutting marks clearly visible across the base. Lower body vertical burnished or shallow knife-trimmed on the lower body. The vessel is more hard-fired than the bottle from grave 251. Rim diameter: 50mm; base diameter: 65mm. Height: 223mm. Over right lower leg. Sf 687.

Grave 376 beads
glass: 12 beads
Constricted Segmented (no 5)
2　　medium, diam 2–5mm. Fig 4.30, Grave 376 Sf 627 (j2)
green Cylindrical (no 48)
2　　two segments, long, diam 2–5mm. Fig 4.30, Grave 376 Sf 627 (j5)
4　　short to medium, diam 2–5mm. Fig 4.30, Grave 376 Sf 627 (j3)
yellow cylindrical (no 49)
3　　very long, diam 2–5mm. Fig 4.30, Grave 376 Sf 627 (j12)
Orange (no 33)
1　　medium, barrel-shaped/biconical, diam 6–10mm. Fig 4.30, Grave 376 Sf 627 (j1)

Grave 377 (Figs 10.48–9, 10.103) No bone. 312°. Context 424. Phase 1–2. Plot X. 1.68m x 0.65m x 0.23m.
Cuts gully, F 529. Cream-brown loam with frequent small and medium chalk containing a Roman pot-sherd. No bones survived; grave length suggests a child.

a　　**Ceramic vessel**. Shouldered vessel with hollow neck and slightly everted rim. Complete following reconstruction with some infilling. Decoration comprises two broad shallow neck rings on lower neck, below which, at the widest point are broad grooves arranged as a continuous scheme and extending onto the lower body. Examination of a non-joining sherd shows a fine sandy matrix, reduced throughout with some large rounded quartz sand grits 1–2mm. Coil built. Surface once burnished but now spalled off in parts and abraded over much of the exterior; interior is wiped. Rim diameter: 98mm; base diameter: *c* 50mm. Height: 130mm. South-east end of grave. Sf 1039.
b　　Fragment of **window glass**. Naturally coloured green-blue rectangular fragment, fractured on all four edges. Sandy texture on reverse face. Length: 11mm. Width: 10mm. Central area of grave. Sf 810.
c　　Fragment of **glass vessel**. Body sherd of colourless glass, heavily streaked across outer surface. Length: 19mm. Width: 14mm. Central area of grave. Sf 811.
d　　Fragment of **glass vessel**. Naturally coloured base fragment fractured around circular raised moulding. Length: 29mm. Width: 27mm. Central area of grave, under (e). Sf 812.
e　　**Glass stirring rod**. Fragment of upper part of rod of naturally coloured blue-green glass. Includes globular head and part of spiralled stem. Length: 24mm. Diameter of head: 11mm. Central area of grave, over (d). Sf 813.
f　　Fragment of **vessel glass**. Body sherd of naturally coloured light green glass with two applied ribs. Length: 26mm. Width: 14mm. Central area of grave. Sf 814.
g　　Cast copper alloy **buckle**. Oval loop with narrowed axis with remains of iron tongue or anchorage. Mineral-preserved leather around bar from strap. Width of loop: 28mm. Central area of grave. Sf 815.
h　　Iron **ring**. Mineral-preserved leather suspension loop wound around ring. Associated textile remains. Diameter: *c* 32mm. Central area of grave. Sf 816.
i　　Iron pierced **lozenge**. Mineral-preserved textile. Length: 36mm. Central area of grave. Sf 817.

j　　Iron pierced **lozenge**. Length: 32mm. Central area of grave. Sf 818.
k　　Chalk **bead**. Short, cylindrical; diameter:16–20mm. Within copper alloy ring (l). Sf 819. Fig 4.26, Grave 377, Sf 819 (k1).
l　　Copper alloy cast **ring**. Bent. Inner rim worn. Mineral-preserved leather suspension loop wound around ring. Maximum diameter: 50mm. Weight: 34.1g. Central area of grave. Sf 820.
m　　Copper alloy Roman horse harness **pendant**. Rounded knop with transverse moulding below. Pear drop form with abstract patterning in light relief, based on four lozenge patterns with curved sides. Circular opening with oval extension above, small circular perforation just below this. Rounded terminal at lower end. Length: 61mm. Width: 45mm. Central area of grave. Sf 821.
n　　Copper alloy cast **ring**. Mineral-preserved leather thong and additional cordage wound around the ring. Maximum diameter: 39mm. Weight: 8.2g. Central area of grave. Sf 822.
o　　Copper alloy wire spiral **ring**. One terminal expanded, other narrowed and cut off; section facetted. Iron corrosion products on small area of ring. Diameter: *c* 26mm. Weight: 6.4g. Central area of grave. Sf 823.
p　　Copper alloy **ring**. Iron corrosion in some areas. Diameter: *c* 23mm. Weight: 1.2g. Central area of grave. Sf 824.
q　　Copper alloy wire spiral **ring**. Wire twisted or decorated with grooves at one end, terminal flat, decorated with nicks; other end cut off. Mineral-preserved leather thong wound around the ring and textile adhering to the outside surface of the object. Diameter: *c* 22mm. Weight: 3.2g. Central area of grave. Sf 825.

Grave 378 (Fig 10.104) M 35–45? 318°. Context 426. Plot V. 2.50m x 0.78m x 0.20m.
Cut by Grave 367 and modern pit. Cream-brown loam with frequent small and medium chalk. Poorly-preserved skeleton; skull ?removed by Grave 367; right arm bent across pelvis. No grave goods.

Grave 379 (Figs 10.49, 10.103) M 30–35. 313°. Context 428. Plot X. 2.31m x 0.93m x 0.35m.
Light-brown loam with frequent small and medium chalk. Poorly-preserved skeleton.

a　　Iron **knife**. Fragmentary, part of blade and small section of tang. Straight back and cutting-edge. Mineral-preserved remains of leather from sheath in association with textile remains on blade. Length: 73mm. Area of body. Sf 757.

Grave 380 (Fig 2.2) No bone. 303°. Context 429. Plot X. 0.78m (min) x 0.55m x 0.37m.
Cut by Grave 404. Cream-brown loam with frequent small and medium chalk. No bones survived. No grave goods.

Grave 381 (Figs 10.49–50, 10.104, 10.120) ?M 30–40. 320°. Context 432. Phase 1b–2a. Plot X. 3.00m x 1.05m x 0.74m.

Cuts gully F 529; cut by Grave 406. Light cream-brown silty loam with frequent small and medium chalk. Chalk and flint packing along north-east side of grave indicates a coffin. Poorly-preserved skeleton; left arm bent across pelvis; legs crossed at ankle (right over left).

a   Iron **seax**. Incomplete, lacking tip of blade. Relatively short tang, with expanded ends. Straight back, edge slightly sinuous, curving to tip. Well-defined junction of organic handle and blade. Mineral-preserved horn handle and leather sheath; wood on blade from scabbard or edge stiffener. Length: 277mm; blade length: 205mm. Over left pelvis. Sf 913.

b   Cast copper alloy **buckle**. D-shaped loop with narrowed axis and club-shaped, waisted tongue. Cast and punched decoration along upper face of loop and back and ridge of tongue. Width of loop: 37mm. Above right pelvis. Sf 914.

c   Two copper alloy **heart-shaped studs** with silver sheet appliqués and one knob-headed rivet each. The rivet shank is of circular section and ends in a square sheet copper alloy washer. The appliqués were possibly attached using solder but the rivet shanks also hold them in position. The heart-shaped heads are also pierced by two holes, possibly for additional fastening. Width: 12 x 15mm. Depth of belt leather: 5mm. Near large buckle in pelvis area and above right femur. Sf 915.

d   Iron **nail**. Discoidal head, tapering shank of square section. Length: 95mm. By right humerus. Sf 916.

e   Cast copper alloy **buckle**. Oval loop of D-shaped section, with narrowed axis for attachment of the slightly waisted club-shaped tongue with curved tip. Traces of white metal on the surface. Width of loop: 19mm. By right femur. Sf 917.

f   Fragmentary iron **ring**. Diameter: 24mm. Right of right femur. Sf 918.

g   Series of objects (Sf 882 and Sf 883) found above left pelvis:
1, 2, incomplete iron and copper alloy **pursemount/firesteel** with attached buckle. one straight and two cureve copper alloy mounts with attached rivets. Straight mount originally set with four rivets. Decorated with sets of transverse punched lines either side of rivets. Curved mounts originally set with three rivets each (one riveted end missing), decorated with matching punched ring-and-dot decoration and punched lines. Mineral-preserved leather on back. Length of straight mount: 191mm; length of best preserved rivet: 6.5mm. Leather strap remnants on buckle. Extensive mineral-preserved leather, textile, *Quercus* sp, oak wood and vegetable fibres, perhaps straw. Length: 120mm.
3, iron **knife**. Incomplete, lacking tip of blade. Straight back, curving to tip, cutting-edge similar. Broad tang, slightly bent. Mineral-preserved horn handle and leather on blade from sheath. Length: 166mm; blade length: 106mm.
4, iron **spike** with rounded head, similar to (d); mineral-preserved leather on shaft and cordage wound in a spiral. The tip of angled bladed knife is corroded to it. Spike: length: 105mm. Blade: length: 40mm.
5, 7, iron ?**key** with loop head with curlicue terminal, the shaft circular and 'ward' missing. Mineral-preserved leather on shaft. Length: 136mm. Corroded to this is a round sectioned shaft ending in a serpentine ?ward with curlicue at end. Length: 150mm.

6, fragmentary iron **nail** with discoidal head and shank of round section.
8, numerous small indistinct **fragments** of iron, a copper alloy rivet and mineral-preserved organic material in association with pursemount. Found inside left upper arm.

h   Copper alloy, T-shaped **mount** from rim of vessel with slightly outflaring rim, thin sheet folded over and attached with two rivets. Both remain *in situ*. Mineral-preserved wood remains around rivets and inside mount. Width: 15mm; height: 19mm; length of rivets: 5mm. Left side of skull. Sf 885.

Grave 382 (Fig 10.104) ? 12–14. 309°. Context 434. Plot X. 2.13m x 0.87m x 0.74m.
Cuts gully F 529. Cream-brown silty loam with frequent small and medium chalk. Poorly-preserved skeleton. No grave goods.

Grave 383 (Fig 10.105) ?M 25–30. 313°. Context 436. Plot X. 1.98m x 0.84m x 0.47m.
Cuts Grave 384; cut by Grave 405. Brown loam with frequent small and medium chalk. Poorly-preserved skeleton; left arm bent across body.

a   Group of three amber **beads**. Left side of body. Sf 671.

Grave 383 beads
amber: 3 beads
1   very short, wedge-shaped, diam 11–15mm. Fig 4.23, Grave 383, Sf 671 (a2)
1   short, wedge-shaped, diam 11–15mm
1   medium, rounded, diam 6–10mm

Grave 384 (Fig 10.50, 10.105) No bone. 313°. (Context 438). Plot X. 1.62m x 0.87m (min) x 0.38m.
Cut by Grave 383. Cream silty loam with frequent small and medium chalk containing a lead alloy object (b). No bones survived; grave length suggests a child.

a   **Ceramic vessel**. Small undecorated wide-mouthed vessel. Fifty-five per cent complete but full profile reconstructed. Most of one half is missing which might or might not have included a handle. Fine dense, sandy fabric packed with sub-rounded quartz sand less than 0.5mm. Some pin-prick leach holes on surface where calcareous inclusions have leached out. Hand-made, probably coil built but with smooth rather than burnished surfaces. Rim diameter: 100mm; rounded base diameter: *c* 40mm. Height: 70mm. Towards south-east end of grave. Sf 692.

b   **Lead alloy model** for a button brooch. Spring-holder not perforated, pin-catch broken. Axis almost horizontal in relation to face decoration. Diameter: 20mm. Height of flange: *c* 3mm. Weight: 6.6g. General filling of grave. Sf 672.

Grave 385 (Fig 10.105) M 20–25. 326°. Context 440. Plot X. 2.35m x 0.92m x 0.78m.
Cream-grey silty loam with frequent small and medium chalk. Well-preserved skeleton lying on right side. No grave goods.

Grave 386 (Figs 10.50, 10.106) 323°. Context: Sk A, 550; Sk B, 442. Plot X. 2.50m x 0.96m x 0.68m.
Cuts gully F 529; cut by Graves 387 and 431. Cream-grey silty loam with frequent small and medium chalk. Flint packing stones along south-west and north-east sides of grave indicate a coffin. Double-stacked grave (Sk A 0.50m above Sk B).

Sk 386A ? grown. Lower arm bones only. No grave goods.

Sk 386B M 20–25. Poorly-preserved skeleton; left arm across pelvis.

a   Iron **knife**, lacking tip of blade. Back curves to tip, cutting-edge sinuous. Well-defined junction of organic handle and blade. Mineral-preserved horn handle and leather on blade from sheath. Length: 144mm. Left side of body. Sf 698.

Grave 387 (Figs 10.50, 10.106) ?F 20–25. 326°. Context 444. Plot X. 2.28m x 0.74m x 0.31m.
Cuts gully F 529 and Grave 386. Light-brown loam with frequent small and medium chalk. Fragmentary skull and long bones only.

a   **Ceramic vessel**. Wide-mouthed rounded asymmetrical vessel. Decorated with very simple shallow incised neck groove positioned just above the maximum diameter on the shoulder with simple vertical or angled incised grooves or slashes (*c*.29) on shoulder and lower body. Where abraded under burnish there is a reddish fabric packed with small quartz sand grains, less than 0.5mm with pin-prick leach holes from calcareous inclusions and voids (up to 8mm) from organic material (in some cases these are seeds) which burned out during firing. Coil built. Exterior smoothly burnished, interior wiped. Rim diameter: 115mm.; base diameter: 80mm. Height: 158–165mm. South-east end of grave. Sf 696.

b   Two iron **keys** and a **girdle-hanger**. Mineral-preserved textiles. Sf 733. Left side of decayed body.
     1, two **keys**, one with a flat straight-sided shaft and a pair of forward facing hooks, the other with flat expanding shaft with wards missing, both heads damaged. Lengths: 134mm. and 149mm.
     2, iron massive T-shaped **girdle-hanger** corroded to knife, head missing, shaft rectangular, 'wards' anchor-like and slightly tapering. Length: 176mm.

c   Cast copper alloy **shoe-shaped stud** with broken, pierced attachment lug on the back. White metal plating, possibly tin. Length: 20mm. Left side of decayed body. Sf 734.

Grave 388 (Figs 10.51, 10.107, 10.118) ? ½ – 1. 313°. Context 446. Plot X. 1.88m x 0.85m x 1.00m.
Brown loam with frequent small and medium chalk. Fragmentary femurs only.

a–h   **Angle-irons**. Eight angle-irons, all formed from broad, rectangular sheet, bent to provide a long and a short strip in each case. Single iron nails at each end, securing wood up to 38mm in width. Six angle-irons are bent to a 90 degree angle, two (c) and (g) to a deeper angle. Mineral-preserved oak wood (*Quercus* sp) inside all irons. Lengths: 75–90 and 45–55mm; widths: 38–45mm. Nail lengths: 23–51mm. North-west end of grave, 0.09–0.25m above base. See p 38. Sf nos 654–661.

i   **Ceramic vessel**. Undecorated rounded form with hollow neck, everted rim and hollow feeding spout. Scar on surface shows dense fine fabric with some organic matter, occasional quartz sand and flint particles 1–1.5mm, lots of surface pin-prick holes presumably from where calcareous inclusions have leached out. Hand-made, probably coil-built. Feeding spout is 300mm long and has been formed by pushing a tube of clay through the body wall and strengthening the attachment by adding clay to the exterior. A teat has been formed by an extra lump of clay being added to the end of the clay tube. Rim diameter: 96mm; base diameter: 73mm. Height: 114mm. North-west end of grave. Sf 688.

j   Copper alloy wire **slip-knot ring**. Maximum diameter: 42mm. Weight: 2.9g. Left side of body. Sf 662.

Grave 389 (Figs 10.52, 10.106) No bone. 301°. Context 448. Plot X. 0.96m x 0.43–0.48m x 0.20m.
Cream-brown silty loam with frequent small and medium chalk. No bones survived; grave length suggests a child.

a   **Ceramic vessel**. Small undecorated cup. No trace of a handle but the whole of one profile is missing. Dense fine-medium sandy fabric with some large quartz-sand grains (1mm) and some calcareous inclusions leached out of the vessel surface. Hand-made, surviving surface abraded. Wiping of the exterior surface has dragged grits across the surface leaving a scratched appearance. Rim 100mm. Height: *c* 90mm. Towards north-west end of grave. Sf 693.

b   Amber **bead**. Medium, globular, diam 11–15mm. Central part of grave. Sf 697.

Grave 390 (Fig 10.107) ?F 35–45. 319°. Context 450. Plot X. 2.09m x 0.60–0.85m x 0.52m.
Light-brown loam with moderate small chalk containing two Iron Age pot-sherds. Chalk and flint packing along north-east side of grave indicates a coffin. Poorly-preserved skeleton; partially decayed arms bent across pelvis. No grave goods.

Grave 391 (Figs 10.52–4, 10.107, 10.118) 312°. Context: Sk A, 452 ; Sk B, 548. Sk A, Phase 5–7. Sk B, Phase 2. Plot X. 2.38m x 1.05m x 0.75m.
Brown loam with frequent small and medium chalk containing an Iron Age pot-sherd. Chalk and flint packing around sides of grave indicates a coffin 2.05m x 0.55m Double-stacked grave (Sk A 0.35m above Sk B).

Sk 391A F 35–45. Poorly-preserved skeleton. Radiocarbon date from bone 1420±20 BP (UB-4959) cal AD 600–660 (95%).

a　(not allocated)

b　Iron **knife**. Fragmentary, lacking part of blade. Back straight, cutting-edge similar. Well-defined junction of organic handle and blade. Mineral-preserved wood handle (no evidence for sheath). Length: 104mm. Area of left pelvis, under (c). Sf 751.

c　Iron **hook** with looped head above shoulders of a tapering flat sectioned shaft with hook terminal covered with mineral-preserved textile. Length: 148mm. Associated with this is the curved 'ward' of a **key** with a terminal curlicue. Width: 39mm. Area of left pelvis, over (b). Sf 752.

d　Three **amethyst beads**. Neck area. Sf 753 (see below).

e　**Pendant** made of a single copper alloy sheet. Length: 16mm. Weight: 0.2g. Neck. Sf 754.

f　Two glass **beads**. Neck area. Sf 755 (see below).

Sk 391A beads

d

amethyst: 3 beads

> 2　almond-shaped, diam 11–15mm. Fig 4.30, Grave 391A, Sf 753 (d3)
>
> 1　almond-shaped, diam 16–20mm. Fig 4.30, Grave 391A, Sf 753 (d2)

f

glass: 2 beads

other globular (no 63)

> 1　two segments, medium, globular, diam 6–10mm, translucent, green. Fig 4.30, Grave 391A, Sf 755 (f3)

other cylindrical (no 56)

> 1　medium, diam 6–10mm, opaque, red (with dark streaks). Fig 4.30, Grave 391A, Sf 755 (f2)

Sk 391B F 20–25. Moderately well-preserved skeleton; legs crossed at ankle (left over right). Radiocarbon date from bone, 1611±18 BP, cal AD 405–535 (95%).

a　Stave-built wooden **bucket**, oak (*Quercus* sp) with copper alloy bindings and mounts. Four vertical struts attached to three horizontal bands by four copper alloy nails on sides where the handle would have been attached and three on opposite sides. Vertical struts edged with design of repoussé running dots. Vertical struts also decorated with pairs of repoussé imitation rivet-heads which do not appear to be functional. Top band wider than two lower bands and decorated on lower edge with repoussé line of running dots surmounted by hoops. Uppermost band curved over wood at top. Fragmentary iron handle attached to bucket by rivet passing through two oval escutcheon plates. Lower part of escutcheon riveted through bucket, top band and vertical strut. Escutcheon on handle side fits behind vertical strut. Mineral-preserved textile on handle and fitting. Left of skull. Sf 788

b　Clear **rock crystal ball** in silver-gilt **sling**. Sling made of four strips cut/cast from one sheet/mould, held by cap perforated to hold a slip-knot ring. Sling decorated with punched triangles and egg-timer pattern. Egg-timer punch marks and gilding worn especially at lower half of ball. Mineral-preserved textile on ribbed band. Diameter of ball with slings: 25mm. Weight: 28.9g. Right of right lower leg. Sf 850.

c　Gold **strip**, remains of the central ornamental brocading from a tablet-woven band: the brocaded area is 5–6mm. wide and threads represent a band 80–90mm long. Strip is of regular width, 320–325 microns wide, rectangular in cross-section, 40 microns thick. Around skull and neck. Sf 851 and Sf 1036.

d, e　Matching pair of silver-gilt **rosette brooches**. Centre set with a coil of gilt silver beaded wire; garnets on hatched foil; beaded rim part of back-plate, nicked, worn. X-ray suggests pin-catch and spring-holder made of separate folded silver sheets; remains of iron spring attached to ?cast spring-holder of (e). Pin-catch and spring-holder of (d) broken, base visible on X-ray; hole in back-plate shows white ?cement. Perhaps (s) is the repair for the missing pin-catch of brooch (d). Knotted cord on back of (e) near hinge. Diameter of (d) *c* 27mm. Weight: 7.4g. Diameter of (e) 27mm. Weight: 8.7g. Area of upper left chest. Sf 852 and Sf 853.

f　Roman **intaglio** set in silver-gilt **slings** suspended from copper alloy slip-knot ring. Crystal flattened on one side, convex on the other. Intaglio represents the Lydian queen Omphale, engraved on the flat face (*see* pp 83–8). Stone chipped, decoration largely covered by sling. Slings decorated with grooves and punched triangles, worn, very little remains of gilding. Originally two ends of the silver strips perforated to hold slip-knot ring, one preserved; all strips held in place by tube made of silver sheet. Slip-knot ring broken and repaired with thread fastening broken ends. Width of intaglio with slings: 29mm. Weight: 14.9g. Left side of body, amongst beads (cc). Sf 854.

g　Iron **pin**. Mineral-preserved textile on surface. Length: *c* 134mm. Chest area. Sf 855.

h　Gold **pendant**. Ribbed loop clamps beaded wire, both worn. Length: 16mm. Left side of chest, amongst beads (cc). Sf 856.

i　Silver **pendant** made of folded sheet lined by strip soldered on. Width: 11mm. Height: 13mm. Weight: 1.4g. Left side of chest, amongst beads (cc). Sf 857.

j　Silver wire slip-knot **ring** with the terminal of gold beaded wire wrapped around it. Diameter of silver ring: 20mm. Weight of both rings: 1.0g. Area of body, amongst beads (cc). Sf 858.

k　Large chalk **bead**. Pelvis area. Sf 859.

l　Silver-gilt cast Kentish **square-headed brooch** with garnet inlays on hatched foil. Some ridges nicked. Punched rings on plain borders. Single rows of niello triangles on border of bow and lower head-plate, double rows of opposing triangles on centre of bow and remainder of head-plate. Outline of bow, gilding and especially bow and nicked ridges on upper foot-plate worn. Cast spring-holder and pin-catch with ridge along the foot-plate. Remains of iron spring. Mineral-preserved textile on back. Length: 57mm. Weight: 13.6g. By right pelvis. Sf 860.

m　Silver-gilt cast Kentish **square-headed brooch** with garnet inlays on hatched foil. Single row of niello triangles pointing outwards on lower foot-plate, inwards on upper foot-plate, outwards on border of bow and lower head-plate, double row of opposing triangles on centre of bow and remaining head-plate. Gilding slightly worn on rim, preserved on cast decoration. Cast spring-holder and pin-catch with a slight ridge along the foot-plate. Remains of iron spring and pin. Mineral-preserved textile on back. Length: 58mm. Weight: 14.8g. By right femur. Sf 861.

n　Silver-gilt cast Kentish small **square-headed brooch**. Garnets set on hatched foil. Ridges nicked. Head-plate decorated with the halves of punched double rings and lines of dots. Rows of copper niello triangles, bordered by punched dots. Gilding hardly worn. Cast spring-holder and pin-catch. Remains of iron spring. Mineral-preserved textile on back. Length: 57mm. Weight: 16.0g. By right femur. Sf 862.

o   Cast high-tin copper alloy **buckle**. Heavy faceted loop with a shield-tongue with iron anchorage. Damaged. Leather belt is 21mm. wide, but tapers in to meet buckle. Plus three tinned copper alloy **shoe-shaped studs**, all without remains of their attachment lugs and cracked down the centre. Two layers of mineral-preserved textile on back. Width of loop: 31mm. Length of studs: 22 and 21mm. Inside of right femur. Sf 863.

p   Copper alloy Roman **coin**. Silvered bronze *radiate* of Tetricus I (AD 270–274). PAX AVG. cf RIC 100. Weight: 1.41g. Mineral-preserved textile on obverse. Left of left knee. Sf 864.

q   Copper alloy Roman **coin**. Silvered bronze *radiate* of Tetricus I (AD 270–274). PAX AVG. cf RIC 100. Weight: 2.15g. Left of left knee. Sf 865.

r   **Iron and lead fragments**. These consist of the following:
1, small fragment of lead **object**, flat on one face and roughly curved on the other. Purpose unclear. Length: 22mm. Width: 10mm. Thickness: 5mm.
2, iron **nail**. Fragment, curved shank only. Length: 62mm.
3, iron **nail**. Incomplete with discoidal head and shank of square section. Length: 34mm.
4, iron **nail**. Fragment, head only, possibly part of 2 above.
5, iron **nail**. Fragmentary, shank only, of square section. Length: 27mm.
Left of left knee. Sf 866.

s   Silver **hook** made of folded sheet. Missing pin-catch of brooch (d)? Width: 9mm. Weight: 0.4g. Area of body. Sf 867.

t   Iron **strip**. Curved iron strip with small iron ring accreted to one end. Mineral-preserved textile. Length: 76mm. Width: 6mm. Left of left femur. Sf 868.

u   Silver **rivet** with remains of silver washer. Diameter: 8mm. Weight: 0.4g. Left of left femur, over (z). Sf 870.

v   Iron **chain link**. Figure-of-eight chain link fragments, fused together. Left of left femur, over knife (w). Sf 871.

w   Iron **knife**. Long tang, back straight and curving to tip, cutting-edge similar. Well-defined junction of organic handle of beech wood (*Fagus sylvatica*) and blade. Copper alloy rivet passes through tang close to blade. Length: 184mm; blade length: 105mm. Left of left femur, under (x) and (v). Sf 869.

x   Iron **knife**. Back straight and curving to tip, cutting-edge similar. Well-defined junction of organic horn handle and blade with traces of ash wood (*Fraxinus excelsior*). Silver and niello chape at tip of blade. U-shaped binding with transverse marks to either side of rivets that fasten a leather sheath. Central bar on one side with stamped triangular patterns. Length: 196mm; blade length: 120mm. Left of left femur, over (w), under rings (aa). Sf 872.

y   Iron **strips**. Two thin iron strips, both bent over at one end. Mineral-preserved skin product/leather and textile. Length: 43 and 72mm. Left of left femur. Sf 873. *Not illus.*

z, aa   Pair of copper alloy **rings**. Show side fluted and gilt; back flat and plain. Gilding remains only in depressions. Diameter of (z): 42mm; weight: 2.9g. Diameter of (aa): 50mm; weight: 4.2g. Left of left femur, over (aa), under (u). Sf 874 and Sf 875.

bb   Iron **chain link** fragment. Single figure-of-eight link. Length: 18mm. Left of left femur. Sf 876.

cc   Scatter of 115 amber and 62 glass **beads**. Across chest and body. Sf 877.

Sk 391B beads

cc

amber: 115 beads

1	short, cylindrical, diam 6–10mm. Fig 4.25, Grave 391B, Sf 877 (cc64)
8	medium, globular, diam 6–10mm. Fig 4.25, Grave 391B, Sf 877 (173)
70	medium (one short), rounded, diam 6–10mm
5	medium (one long), rounded, diam 2–5mm
2	medium, barrel-shaped, diam 2–5mm
23	medium (one long), facetted, diam 6–10mm
3	fragments, diam 6–10mm
3	fragments

glass: 62 beads

Roman Polyhedral (no 37)

1	medium, diam 2–5mm, translucent, blue (dark). Fig 4.25, Grave 391B, Sf 877 (cc60)

Constricted Segmented (no 5)

12	three segments, very long, diam 2–5mm. Fig 4.25, Grave 391B, Sf 877 (cc4, 13, 21)
3	two segments, very long, diam 2–5mm
22	short to very long, diam 2–5mm

Constricted Cylindrical (no 6)

6	very long, diam 2–5mm. Fig 4.25, Grave 391B, Sf 877 (cc40)

light Constricted Cylindrical (no 7)

1	very long, beaded, diam 2–5mm. Fig 4.25, Grave 391B, Sf 877 (cc38)

Traffic Light Twisted Trail (no 29)

1	very long, cylindrical, diam 6–10mm, translucent green and opaque yellow twisted spiral trail on opaque red body. Fig 4.25, Grave 391B, Sf 877 (cc46)

Traffic Light Other (no 31)

1	medium, globular, diam 6–10mm, opaque red wide crossing trails and three opaque yellow dots on opaque green body

wide crossing trails (no 65)

2	short, asymmetrically barrel-shaped, diam 11–15mm, opaque red trails and three translucent blue dots on opaque white body. Fig 4.25, Grave 391B, (cc48), (cc49)

polychrome white (no 69)

1	short, globular, diam 6–10mm, red irregular trail on white body. Fig 4.25, Grave 391B, Sf 877 (cc50)

other cylindrical (no 56)

1	very long, asymmetrical cross-section, diam 2–5mm, opaque, green (light). Fig 4.25, Grave 391B, Sf 877 (cc56)

other globular (no 63)

2	short, diam 6–10mm, opaque, yellow (one bead has square perforation. Fig 4.25, Grave 391B, Sf 877 (cc52), (cc53)
2	short, diam 6–10mm, opaque, green. Fig 4.25, Grave 391B, Sf 877 (cc55)

white/yellow cylindrical (no 55)

2   long to very long, square cross-section, diam 2–5mm, translucent. Fig 4.25, Grave 391B, Sf 877 (cc57), (cc58)

turquoise cylindrical (no 50)

2   very long, square cross-section, diam 2–10mm. Fig 4.25, Grave 391B, Sf 877 (cc62), (cc61)

folded? (no 72)

1   medium, cylindrical, diam 2–5mm, opaque, green. Fig 4.25, Grave 391B, Sf 877 (cc59)

unidentified

1   short, globular, diam 6–10mm, discoloured

1   fragments, discoloured

Grave 392 (Figs 10.54, 10.107) ? 8–10. 318°. Context 454. Phase 2. Plot X. 1.74m x 0.80m x 0.67m.

Cream-brown silty loam with frequent small and medium chalk. Poorly-preserved skeleton; left arm bent across body.

a   Scatter of three amber and 42 glass **beads**. Neck. Sf 724 (see below).

b   Cast copper alloy **buckle**. D-shaped loop of approximately triangular section with cast decoration on the upper and outer faces and flanking the axis and tongue rest. The pin of the shield-tongue shows the same ridges and notched band. Ample gilding remains, particularly in the ridged areas. Traces of gilding are also found on the sides and underside of the shield-tongue. Width of loop: 30mm. Right waist area. Sf 666.

c   Iron **knife**. Broad tang, straight back curving to tip, cutting-edge sinuous. Well-defined junction of organic handle and blade. Mineral-preserved horn handle. Length: 149mm. Over left pelvis. Sf 667.

d   Two small iron **nail** shank fragments. Lengths: 16 and 18mm. Area of right pelvis. Sf 668.

e   Copper alloy **coin**. Silvered bronze *nummus* of AD 347–348. VICTORIAE DD AVGGQ NN. (Constans). RIC VIII, Arles 85. Weight: 1.14g. Between femurs. Sf 669.

f   Copper alloy rectangular **sheet**. Plain, with traces of gilding on surface. Length: 33mm. Width: 16mm. Between femurs. Sf 670.

g   **Ceramic vessel**. Wide-mouthed biconical vessel. Decorated with two horizontal neck grooves below which are 25 deep vertical grooves which form small bosses between the grooves arranged regularly all around the carination and extending onto the lower body. Worn patches on the exterior surface show where some calcareous inclusions have leached out. Some impressions of organic material, including seeds, visible on the surfaces together with occasional flint inclusions up to 4mm in size. Coil-built with clear fingernail impressions on the interior where the neck attaches to the lower coil. Well burnished exterior surface and inside the neck. Rest of the interior is wiped. Rim diameter: 112mm.; base diameter: 50mm. Height: 90mm. Over left ankle. Sf 686.

Grave 392 beads

a

amber: 3 beads

1   very short, wedge-shaped, diam 11–15mm. Fig 4.25, Grave 392, Sf 724 (a3)

1   short, globular, diam 11–15mm. Fig 4.25, Grave 392, Sf 724 (a2)

1   medium, rounded, diam 6–10mm

glass: 42 glass

Constricted Segmented (no 5)

5   three segments, very long, diam 2–5mm. Fig 4.25, Grave 392, Sf 724 (a7)

8   two segments, long to very long, diam 2–5mm

28   short to long, diam 2–5mm

Constricted Cylindrical (no 6)

1   very long, diam 2–5mm. Fig 4.25, Grave 392, Sf 724 (a4)

Grave 393 (Figs 10.54, 10.108, 10.119) 313°. Context: Sk A, 456; Sk B 538. Plot X. 2.44m x 1.03m x 1.03m.

Enclosed by ring-gully F 573. Brown loam with moderate small chalk containing one Roman pot-sherd. Double-stacked grave (Sk A 0.75m above Sk B).

Sk 393A M 25–30. Poorly-preserved skeleton; skull rolled backwards.

a   Iron **spearhead**. Angular blade curving towards the tip, lozenge-section, with a split socket. No shank. The socket is fragmentary, and may expand. Remains of straw (plant) on the socket and blade. Ash wood (*Fraxinus excelsior*) remains in socket. Length: 400mm. Left shoulder. Sf 771.

b   Iron **knife** (large). Broad tang, back straight and curving to tip, cutting-edge similar. Well-defined junction of organic handle and blade. Mineral-preserved horn handle and traces of wood. Length: 240mm. Blade length: 170mm. Above left pelvis. Sf 772.

Sk 393B M 35–45. Poorly-preserved skeleton; skull half left; right arm bent across pelvis. No grave goods.

Grave 394 (Figs 10.55, 10.108) M 40–50. 315°. Context 458. Plot X. 2.28m x 0.81m x 0.26m.

Brown loam with moderate small chalk and flint containing two Roman pot-sherds. Poorly-preserved skeleton; left arm bent across pelvis.

a   Iron **buckle**. Oval loop with the remains of a plain tongue with tip broken off. Mineral-preserved leather inside loop and on front of tongue from strap. Mineral-preserved textile on back. Width of loop: 36mm. Right waist area. Sf 756.

Grave 395 (Figs 10.55, 10.108) ?M 40–45. 310°. Context 460. Plot X. 2.30m x 0.81m x 0.14m.

Brown loam with moderate small chalk. Poorly-preserved skeleton; skull half left; left arm bent across body; legs crossed at ankle (left over right).

a   Iron **knife**. Long tang, back straight and curving to tip, cutting-edge similar. Well-defined junction between organic handle and blade. Mineral-preserved horn handle. Hide and hair remains on blade from a sheath; textile remains on blade. Length: 190mm. Above left pelvis. Sf 699.

b   Iron **buckle**. Circular loop of flat section with the remains
      of an incomplete plain tongue. Mineral-preserved leather on
      front and back of loop from strap. Mineral-preserved textile
      on back. Width of loop: 29mm. Above right hip. Sf 700.

Grave 396 (Fig 10.108) ? 35–45. 325°. Context 546. Plot U.
2.05m x 0.62–0.80m x 0.17m.
Grey-brown loam with frequent small and medium chalk.
Skull fragments only. No grave goods.

Grave 397 (Figs 10.55, 10.109) ? 35–45 143°. Context 464.
Plot S. 2.48m x 0.68m (min) x 0.22m.
Brown loam with frequent small and medium chalk.
Fragmentary skull and long bones only; head at south-east
end.

a   Iron **knife**. Incomplete, lacking tip of blade. Back straight and
      curving to tip, cutting-edge similar. Well-defined junction of
      organic handle and blade. Mineral-preserved horn handle.
      Length: 159mm. Left side of body. Sf 703.

Grave 398 (Figs 10.55, 10.109) ?F 30–40. 317°. Context
466. Phase 2b–3a. Plot S. 2.30m x 0.85m x 0.25m.
Cream-brown silty loam with frequent small and medium
chalk. Poorly-preserved skeleton.

a   Iron **knife**. Back curving to tip, cutting-edge similar. Well-
      defined junction of organic handle and blade. Mineral-
      preserved horn from handle; mineral-preserved textile and
      leather from sheath on blade. Length: 139mm. Between
      femurs, under (b). Sf 736.
b   Cast high-tin copper alloy **buckle**. Oval faceted loop with iron
      concretion on the narrowed axis for attachment of the tongue,
      which is missing. There is a marked dent on the tongue rest.
      Mineral-preserved leather on bar from strap and garment textile
      on front. Width of loop: 36mm. Left of left femur. Sf 737.
c   Cast copper alloy **buckle**. Oval loop of convex section with a
      narrowed axis for attachment of a shield-tongue. The tongue
      shield is recessed and decorated with seven punched ring-and-
      dots. Traces of a tin coating are found in several places on the
      loop. Width of loop: 33mm. Left of left femur. Sf 738.
d   Iron **implement** with closed loop leading to shaft of circular
      section. Mineral-preserved textile. Length: 56mm. Between
      femurs. Sf 739.

Grave 399 (Figs 10.55, 10.109) No bone. 315°. Context 468.
Plot S. 1.50m x 0.63m (min) x 0.10m.
Cream-brown silty loam with frequent small and medium
chalk. No bones survived; grave length suggests a child.

a   Iron **knife**. Small, with back straight and curving to tip,
      cutting-edge similar. Well-defined junction of organic handle
      and blade. Mineral-preserved leather on blade from sheath.
      Length: 104mm. Central part of grave. Sf 704.

Grave 400 (Figs 10.55, 10.109) No bone. 319°. Context 470.
Plot S. 1.74m x 0.83m x 0.20m.

Cut by plough-scores of Middle Terrace. Cream-brown silty
loam with frequent small and medium chalk. No bones
survived; grave length suggests a child. On evidence of grave
goods, skull at south-eastern end?

a   Silvered copper alloy **rivet**. Towards south-east end of grave.
      Length: 15mm. Sf 701.
b   Iron **spearhead**. Fragmentary. Angular blade, lozenge-section, with
      a short thin shank and a split socket containing ash wood (*Fraxinus
      excelsior*) fragments. Mineral-preserved textile on socket and blade.
      Length: 460mm. South corner of grave. Sf 735.
c   Iron **knife**. Back straight and curving to tip, cutting-edge similar.
      Well-defined junction of organic handle and blade. Mineral-
      preserved horn handle; mineral-preserved textile on blade.
      Length: 148mm. Towards south-east end of grave. Sf 702.

Grave 401 (Fig 10.109) ?M 50+. 303°. Context 472. Plot S.
2.50m x 0.75–1.05m x 0.13m.
Cream-brown silty loam with frequent small and medium
chalk. Poorly-preserved skeleton; skull right; right arm across
pelvis. No grave goods.

Grave 402 (Fig 10.109) M 28–33. 321°. Context 474. Plot
S. 2.55m x 0.96m x 0.94m.
Mattock marks on base. Cut by plough-scores of Middle
Terrace. Grey-brown loam with frequent small and medium
chalk. Chalk packing stones mostly along south-west side of
grave indicate a coffin. Well-preserved skeleton; skull right;
legs crossed at ankle (left over right). No grave goods.

Grave 403 (Fig 2.2) No bone. 318°. Context 475. Plot U.
1.15m x 0.45m x 0.16m.
Brown loam with frequent small and medium chalk. No bones
survived; grave length suggests a child. No grave goods.

Grave 404 (Fig 10.105) ? 13–15. 322°. Context 478. Plot X.
2.05m x 0.94m x 0.42m.
Cuts Grave 380. Cream-brown silty loam with frequent small
and medium chalk containing one Roman pot-sherd. Flint
packing stones indicate a coffin. Skull fragments only.

a   Group of four glass **beads**. Chest. Sf 758.

Grave 404 beads
glass
green Cylindrical (no 48)
      4   short to medium, diam 2–5mm, opaque Fig 4.30,
             Grave 404, Sf 758 (a4)

Grave 405 (Figs 10.56, 10.105) ?M 22–27. 134°. Context
480. Plot X. 2.31m x 0.81m x 0.67m.
Cuts Grave 383. Cream-brown silty loam with frequent small
and medium chalk. Chalk and flint packing along north-east
side of grave indicates a coffin. Moderately well-preserved
skeleton; skull left. Skull at south-eastern end.

a   Iron **knife**. Incomplete, lacking tip of blade. Long tang, straight back, cutting-edge sinuous and curving to tip. Well-defined junction of organic handle and blade. Mineral-preserved horn from handle and leather from sheath. Textile remains on blade. Length: 154mm. Above left pelvis. Sf 838.

Grave 406 (Figs 10.56, 10.104, 10.120) ?M grown. 324°. Context 482. Plot X. 1.66m x 0.62m x 0.12m
Cuts gully F 529 and Grave 381 (Phase 1b–2a). Cream-grey clay loam with frequent small and medium chalk. Poorly-preserved skeleton; left arm bent across pelvis.

a   Iron **knife**. Incomplete, lacking end of tang and tip of blade. Back straight and curving to tip, cutting-edge sinuous. Mineral-preserved horn handle and leather on blade from sheath. Length: 133mm. Above pelvis. Sf 675.
b   Iron **buckle**. Oval loop with remains of the tongue. Mineral-preserved leather inside loop from strap. Width of loop: 23mm. Above pelvis. Sf 676.

Grave 407 (Figs 10.56, 10.110) F 23–28. 322°. Context 484. Phase 2. Plot X. 2.38m x 1.10–1.20m x 0.75m.
Brown loam with frequent small and medium chalk. Moderately well-preserved skeleton; skull left; right arm bent across body; left arm bent across pelvis.

a   Group of 24 amber and 52 glass **beads**. Neck area. Sf 741 (see below).
b   Iron **knife**. Incomplete, lacking tip of blade. Tang ends in sharp point. Back straight and curving to tip, cutting-edge sinuous. Possible wood strip along back edge of blade associated with a sheath reinforcement. Length: 148mm. By left pelvis, under (c). Sf 742.
c   Copper alloy Iron Age **toggle**. Baluster-shaped hollow body with incised transverse lines and discoidal terminals. Square slot for suspension. Length: 17mm. By left pelvis, over (b). Sf 743.
d   Cast copper alloy **buckle** with faceted loop, narrowed axis and shield-tongue. Tongue shield and upper face are decorated with pairs of transverse lines and another two lines run around the outer face of the loop. Plus two copper alloy **shoe-shaped studs** of very different sizes, each with a pierced lug for attachment. Mineral-preserved textile and leather. Width of loop: 30mm. Length of studs: 16 and 24mm. Over right wrist. Sf 744.
e, f Matching pair of silver-gilt cast **bow brooches**. Copper niello opposing rows of triangles on foot-plate terminal and bow, single row on rim of foot-plate. Niello worn on bow and foot-plate, knobs on head-plate worn on top, ridges of cast decoration to lesser decoration to lesser extent. Cast pair of spring-holders and pin-catch. Iron spring. Extensive mineral-preserved textile. Length: of (e) 62mm, weight: 13.6g. Length of (f): 62mm, weight: 14.9g. Left side of body. Sf 745 and Sf 746.
g   Copper alloy Roman **coin**. Silvered bronze *nummus* of AD 323–324. CAESARVM NOSTRORVM (Crispus), mint illegible. Weight: 2.44g. By left pelvis, under (h). Sf 747.
h   Roman **intaglio**. Oval with bevelled edge. Over (g). Sf 748.

i   Copper alloy and iron: elements from a **châtelaine**. Complex of three copper alloy tubes separated by two iron lozenges. Each tube is different: one is seamless, with one flattened side, length: 37mm; width:13mm *and* contains a fragment of textile or a piece of flattened leather thong. At the centre of the group is a flattened tube made of folded copper alloy sheet with transverse hammered ribbing on the surface (length: 18mm; width: 16mm). The third element is a fully rounded tube also with transverse hammered ribbing (length: 25mm; diameter: 9mm). The iron lozenges are closely matched and their surface is covered with mineral-replaced textile (length: 46mm). Also associated with this complex is a length of iron strip with piercings at either end and two rivet-heads buried in the corrosion (length: 46mm; width: 13mm.). A copper alloy ?lace-tag was also found associated with this group. Extensive mineral-preserved textile on one side of lozenge. Remains of leather thong. By left pelvis. Sf 749.
j   Iron ?**pin shaft** (point appears to be missing) with a copper alloy ?cast ?head. Mineral-preserved textile. Diameter of head: 6mm. Length: 116mm. Left side of body. Sf 750.

Grave 407 beads
a
amber: 24 beads
18   medium (one short), rounded, diam 6–10mm. Fig 4.25, Grave 407, Sf 741 (a20)
1   medium, rounded, diam 2–5mm
3   medium, facetted, diam 6–10mm
1   medium, badly preserved, diam 6–10mm
1   fragments
glass: 52 beads
Constricted Segmented (no 5)
3   three segments, very long, diam 2–5mm
18   two segments, long to very long, diam 6–10mm. Fig 4.25, Grave 407, Sf 741 (a9)
23   short to medium, diam 2–5mm. Fig 4.25, Grave 407, Sf 741 (a46)
Constricted Cylindrical (no 6)
3   very long, diam 2–5mm. Fig 4.25, Grave 407, Sf 741 (a6)
Blue-green Spiral (no 2)
1   medium, globular, diam 6–10mm, translucent blue spiral on badly preserved (white) body. Fig 4.25, Grave 407, Sf 741 (a4)
polychrome blue (no 67)
1   short, barrel-shaped, diam 11–15mm, two lost circles and one open wave (probably intended circle) on semi-translucent blue body. Fig 4.25, Grave 407, Sf 741 (a1)
other globular (no 63)
1   short, globular, diam 6–10mm, badly preserved, blue. Fig 4.25, Grave 407, Sf 741 (a3)
other coiled (no 60)
1   short, diam 6–10mm, semi-translucent?, blue. Fig 4.25, Grave 407, Sf 471 (a2)
other cylindrical (no 56)
1   long, diam 6–10mm, opaque, yellow. Fig 4.25, Grave 407, Sf 741 (a5)

Grave 408 (Figs 10.57, 10.110, 10.119) ?F 30–40. 311°. Context 486. Phase 1b. Plot X. 2.29m x 1.09m x 0.87m.

Light-brown loam with frequent small and medium chalk. Chalk and flint packing along sides of grave indicates a coffin. Fragmentary skull and long bones only.

a   Iron **knife**. Slender blade, back straight and curving to tip, cutting-edge sinuous. Well-defined junction of organic handle and blade. Mineral-preserved horn handle. Organic remains on blade, possibly leather from sheath. Length: 160mm. By right femur. Sf 789.

b   Iron **pin** with globular head. Between femurs. Length: *c* 100mm. Sf 790.

c   Copper alloy gilt cast **miniature brooch**. Bow and triangular foot-plate decorated with double rows of punched dots or egg-timer punch marks worn away on top of ridge. Gilding remains only in crevices, bow worn. Cast spring-holder and pin-catch. Remains of iron spring with mineral-preserved textile. Length: 49mm. Weight: 7.0g. Area of left pelvis. Sf 791.

d   Copper alloy gilt cast **radiate-headed brooch** with garnet settings not on hatched foil. Some ridges nicked, centre of bow and foot-plate punched with rows of rings and two punch marks comprised of a ring and three triangles. Gilding on all ridges, garnet on bow and knobs on head-plate worn. Cast spring-holder and pin-catch. Remains of iron spring with mineral-preserved textile. Length: 59mm. Weight: 12.2g. Area of left pelvis. Sf 792.

e   Cast copper alloy **buckle** with remains of sheet silver plating which is now flaking off. Oval loop of D-shaped section, narrowed axis for attachment of the club-shaped tongue. The silver plating has groups of three grooves either side of the tongue rest and axis, which are also visible on the copper alloy buckle core. Detached mineral-preserved organic remains. Width of loop: 40mm. (see also (j) & (k), plate). Area of left pelvis. Sf 793.

f   Silver sheet spiral **finger ring**. Diameter: 21mm. Weight: 2.2g. With finger bones of left hand. Sf 794.

g   Copper alloy Roman **coin**. Brass *dupondius* of Marcus Aurelius (AD 161–180). Roma seated left. cf RIC 1040 or 1067. Weight: 11.94g. Between femurs. Sf 795.

h   Copper alloy Roman **coin**. Defaced brass *sestertius* (first–third century AD). Probably defaced by hammering (edges are also hammered up). Weight: 15.40g. Between femurs. Sf 796.

i   Fossil **bead**. Unidentified. Between femurs. Sf 797.

j, k   Iron **belt-plate**. High-rectangular with an applied repoussé copper alloy sheet. A central high-rectangular field with now indecipherable ornament is surrounded by a strand of tendrils. Four copper alloy corner **rivets** are held at the back by two transverse, rectangular copper alloy strips. Length: 44 x 26mm. (see also (e), buckle). Area of left pelvis. Sf 798 and Sf 799.

Grave 409 (Figs 10.57, 10.110) F 22–27. 310°. Context 488. Phase 1b. Plot X. 2.38m x 0.86m x 1.10m.
Grey-brown loam with frequent small and medium chalk. Well-preserved skeleton; right arm bent across pelvis.

a   Two iron linked **rings**, each fastened by an iron rivet. Mineral-preserved suspension thread. Diameter of single ring: *c* 12mm. Left of skull. Sf 732.

b   Group of nine amber and 56 glass **beads**. Neck area. Sf 725 (see below).

c   Iron **knife**. Back straight and curving to tip, cutting-edge sinuous. Mineral-preserved horn handle and organic remains on blade, mineral-preserved leather from sheath. Length: 157mm. Over left pelvis. Sf 726.

d   Cast copper alloy **buckle**. D-shaped loop of roughly circular section, narrowed axis for attachment of club-shaped, strongly waisted tongue. Mineral-preserved leather on loop, bar and tongue from strap. Width of loop: 34mm. Above right pelvis. Sf 727.

e   Copper alloy ?**finger ring.** Undecorated with white metal surface, high-tinned bronze or plated. Strip of fibrous matter on inside of band. Diameter: 23mm. Weight: 6.8g. Over left pelvis. Sf 728.

f   Iron pierced **lozenge**. Splayed central perforation. Mineral-preserved textile and thread through centre. Length: 23mm. Over left pelvis. Sf 729.

g   Pair of copper alloy **strap fittings**. Associated fibrous material. Length: 27mm and 28mm. Over left pelvis. Sf 730.

h   ?Point of an iron **pin**. Mineral-preserved textile and horn at one end. Length: 52mm and 36mm. Over left femur. Sf 731.

Grave 409 beads
b
amber: 9 beads

1   short, wedge-shaped, diam 11–15mm. Fig 4.26, Grave 409, Sf 725 (b57)

4   medium, rounded, diam 6–10mm

4   medium, facetted, diam 6–10mm

glass: 56 beads
Constricted Segmented (no 5)

3   four segments, very long, diam 2–5mm, light. Fig 4.26, Grave 409, Sf 725 (b1)

24   three segments, very long, diam 2–5mm, light

11   two segments, long to very long, diam 2–5mm, light

8   short to very long, diam 2–5mm, light

Constricted Cylindrical (no 6)

6   very long, diam 2–5mm. Fig 4.26, Grave 409, Sf 725 (b55), (b51)

light Constricted Cylindrical (no 7)

1   very long, diam 2–5mm

2   very long, beaded, diam 2–5mm. Fig 4.26, Grave 409, Sf 725 (b49)

Miniature Dark (no 24)

1   medium, coiled, diam 2–5mm. Fig 4.26, Grave 409, Sf 725 (b56)

Grave 410 (Fig 10.110) ? ? 312°. Context 490. Plot X. 1.51m x 0.56m x 0.57m.
Cream-brown silty loam with frequent small and medium chalk. A few tiny bone fragments only (not recovered); grave length suggests a child. No grave goods.

Grave 411 (Figs 10.58, 10.110, 10.119) ? 4–6. 313°. Context 492. Plot X. 1.75m x 0.75m x 0.68m.
Cream-brown silty loam with frequent small and medium chalk. Chalk and flint around sides of grave indicate a coffin. Fragmentary skull and leg bones only.

a　　Iron **spearhead**. Straight to slightly angular blade, lozenge-section, with a medium split socket. Ash wood (*Fraxinus excelsior*) fragment in socket. Length: 290mm. Left of skull. Sf 801.

b　　Iron **knife**. Fragmentary, lacking part of tang. Very broad tang, back curving to tip, cutting-edge similar. Well-defined junction of organic handle and blade. Mineral-preserved horn handle and leather on blade from sheath with stitching. Mineral-preserved textile and skin. Length: 117mm. Left side of body. Sf 802.

Grave 412 (Figs 10.58, 10.111) ?F 15–20. 313°. Context 494. Phase 2b–3a. Plot X. 2.48m x 0.91m x 0.47m.
Cuts Grave 430 and ring-gully F 571. Cream-brown silty loam with frequent small and medium chalk. Fragmentary skull and long bones only.

a　　Two cast copper alloy **shoe-shaped studs**, with traces of a white metal coating, possibly tinning, and pierced attachment lugs on the back. Mineral-preserved leather on lug. Length: *c* 23mm. Right side of body. Sf 803.

b　　Cast tinned copper alloy **buckle**. Faceted, convex D-shaped loop with narrowed axis for attachment of now separate shield-tongue. Extensive traces of white metal coating on both loop and tongue. Mineral-preserved leather on bar and tongue. Width of loop: 30mm. Right side of body. Sf 804.

c　　Iron **knife**. Incomplete, lacking tip of blade. Straight back, cutting-edge curving to tip. Well-defined junction of organic handle and blade. Mineral-preserved horn handle and leather from sheath. Length: 152mm. By left femur. Sf 805.

d　　Cast copper alloy **strap-end**. Leaf-shaped, split end with two rivets. Split ends are serrated and ridged front of strap-end is decorated with three ring-and-dots, while there are 12, including the decorated rivet stumps, on the flat back. Front tinned. Fine transverse lines originating along both front edges of strap-end may be keying marks to hold the tin in place. Length: 52mm. Between the femurs. Sf 806.

e　　Iron **pin** fragments with point. Mineral-preserved textile on shank. Length: *c* 80mm. Left side of knife (c). Sf 807.

f　　Copper alloy **ring** possibly with two broken terminals but more likely with a particularly worn part broken off. Diameter: 21mm. Weight: 2.1g. Chest area. Sf 808.

g　　Scatter of 30 amber and 45 glass **beads**. Chest area. Sf 809.

Grave 412 beads
g
amber: 30 beads
1　medium, rounded, diam 11–15mm
8　medium, rounded, diam 6–10mm
6　medium, facetted, diam 11–15mm
15　medium, facetted, diam 6–10mm
glass: 45 beads
red Constricted Segmented (no 43)
2　two segments, long, globular, diam 2–5mm, opaque
33　medium (2 short, 1 very long), globular, diam 2–5mm, opaque
Reticella (no 28)
2　medium, biconical, diam 11–15mm, 2 translucent, opaque yellow and opaque red twisted trails.

Fig 4.27, Grave 412, Sf 809 (g4), (g5)
variation Melon (no 22)
2　short, globular, diam 11–20mm, translucent, blue. Fig 4.27, Grave 412, Sf 809 (g2), (g1)
Koch49/50 (no 19)
2　very long, cylindrical, diam 6–10mm, opaque yellow spiral trail combed in one direction on opaque red body. Fig 4.27, Grave 412, Sf 809 (g9), (g10)
1　very long, cylindrical, diam 11–15mm, opaque yellow spiral trail combed in opposite directions on opaque red body. Fig 4.27, Grave 412, Sf 809 (g8)
poychrome biconical (no 66)
2　medium, diam 11–20mm, opaque yellow irregular wavy trail on opaque red body. Fig 4.27, Grave 412, Sf 809 (g7)
other globular (no 63)
1　short, diam 11–15mm, white. Fig 4.27, Grave 412, Sf 809 (g3)

Grave 413 (Figs 10.58–9, 10.111) F 22–27. 290°. Context 496. Phase 5–7. Plot X. 2.41m x 0.86m x 0.66m.
Cream-grey loam with frequent small and medium chalk containing one Iron Age pot-sherd. Poorly-preserved skeleton. Mineral-preserved textile may indicate the body was lain on bedding at burial.

a　　Iron **knife**. Incomplete, lacking tip of blade. Straight back, angled to tip, straight cutting-edge. Well-defined junction of organic handle and blade. Mineral-preserved horn handle and leather on blade from sheath. Length: 100mm; blade length: 80mm., By left foot. Sf 709.

b　　Silver and copper alloy **rim-bindings** from a wooden vessel. Includes six plain rim fragments and four others with ribbed rim clips. Mineral-preserved wood in clips. Mineral-preserved leather. Dimensions: 40mm, 37mm. By left foot. Sf 710.

c　　Iron **girdle-hanger**. Two iron rods without terminals. Looped ends over iron wire ring. Shafts appear to have possible twisting, circular section. Mineral-preserved textile on shafts; mineral-preserved plant fibres; mineral-preserved leather suspension thong. Length: 62mm. Between femurs. Sf 711 and Sf 723.

d　　Iron **rods** with looped heads, from girdle-hanger. Left side of body. Length: 64mm. Sf 714.

e　　Iron **pin** with a ?looped head and ?wire ?wrapped around it. Mineral-preserved textile on shaft and plant fibres. Length: *c* 7mm. Between femurs. Sf 712.

f　　Iron **pin** with a looped head or a hooked end with a ring. Mineral-preserved textile and plant fibres. Length: *c* 6mm. Area of left pelvis. Sf 713.

g　　Iron **knife**. Fragmentary, lacking part of tang and tip of blade. Broad tang, straight back, angled to tip. Straight cutting-edge. Well-defined junction of organic handle and blade. Mineral-preserved horn handle and leather on blade from sheath. Length: 134mm; blade length: 88mm. Left side of body. Sf 714.

h　　Three **amethyst beads**. Area of right chest. Sf 715 (see below).

i　　Silver wire **slip-knot ring**. Diameter: 21mm. Weight: 0.7g. Left of skull. Sf 716.

j   Fragment of a silver wire **slip-knot ring**. Length: 10mm. Weight: 0.1g. Left of skull. Sf 717.

k   Two glass **beads**. Neck area. Sf 718 (see below).

l   Copper alloy **pin** decorated with incised circumferential double lines. Length: 26mm. Weight: 0.2g. Chest area. Sf 719.

m   Silver wire **slip-knot ring**. Diameter: 21mm. Weight: 0.5g. Chest area. Sf 720.

n   Four silver sheet fragments from a **bead**. Chest area. Sf 721 (see below).

o   Silver-gilt **pendant** with opaque turquoise glass inlay. Silver back-plate set with frame made of silver strip, bordered by beaded wire rim. Ribbed loop set between frame and wire and soldered onto back-plate. Loop worn at back and top; beaded wire worn at border, remains of gilding in crevices of beaded wire and on frame. Length: 18mm. Weight: 1.1g. Neck. Sf 722.

Grave 413 beads

h

amethyst: 3 beads

     3   almond-shaped, diam 11–15mm. Fig 4.30, Grave 413, Sf 715 (h1) (h2)

k

glass: 2 beads

green segmented (no 47)

     2   short, globular, diam 6–10mm, semi-translucent. Fig 4.30, Grave 413, Sf 718 (k1)

n

silver: 1 bead

     1   almond-shaped, with decorative grooves

Grave 414 (Figs 10.59–60, 10.111) M 35–45. 142°. Context 498. Phase 2b–3a. Plot Y. 2.47m x 1.16m x 0.69m.

Cream-brown silty loam, with frequent small and medium chalk, containing two Iron Age pot-sherds. Flint packing stones indicate a coffin 2.23m x 0.67m Poorly-preserved skeleton; skull right; head at south-east end. Radiocarbon date: 1570 ± 20 BP (UB-6477) cal AD 425–545 (95%).

a   Iron **spearhead**. Very distinctive leaf-shaped blade of lozenge to lentoid section, with a short solid shank and a split socket containing ash wood (*Fraxinus excelsior*). Mineral-preserved animal fibres, possibly human hair. Length: 424mm. Left of skull. Sf 981.

b   Iron **sword** with mineral-preserved traces of ash (*Fraxinus excelsior*) scabbard wood on blade in association with sheep wool fibres and calfskin leather. Ash wood and horn were present on the hilt. No pommel, probably organic, possibly ivory; wood packing pieces; organic traces of upper guard and scabbard (traces of fleece on one side only); fullered. Length: 915 x 48mm (43); grip length: 95mm (approx.); thickness of upper and lower guards, 7 and 10mm (approx.) respectively. Left of body, top end by shoulder. Sf 920 and Sf 986.

c   Iron **knife**. Tang bent to one side in antiquity. Back straight and curving to tip, cutting-edge sinuous. Well-defined junction of handle. Traces of willow wood (*Salix* sp) on blade. Mineral-preserved horn handle and leather remains from sheath. Length: 166mm. Right side of body. Sf 987.

d   Iron **fiche à bélière** with rounded, looped head and shaft of

square section tapering to point. Mineral-preserved leather suspension thong on loop and on shaft. Length: 101mm. Right side of body, adjacent to knife (c). Sf 988.

e   Two iron **awl-like firesteels**. Sf 989.

     1, shaft of circular section tapering to sharp point. Handle of hazel wood (*Corylus avellana*) circular in section. Length: 65mm.

     2, shaft of circular section, tapering to blunt point. Mineral-preserved horn handle. Small fragment of hazel wood (*Corylus avellana*) at junction with handle. Length: 37mm. Right side of body, adjacent to (c).

f   Iron **buckle**. D-shaped loop and plain tongue. Mineral-preserved textile on back. Mineral-preserved leather on back and front. Width of loop: 36mm. Inside left forearm. Sf 990.

g   Iron **shield board mount**. Incomplete. Large disc mount with lozenge-shaped washer. Part of a set of four identical mounts arranged in pairs either side of boss (k). Mineral-preserved leather and wood. Diameter: 60mm. Over left ankle. Sf 991.

h   Iron **shield board mount**. Large disc mount with lozenge-shaped washer. Part of a set of four identical mounts arranged in pairs either side of boss (k). Mineral-preserved leather and wood. Diameter: 65mm. Over left ankle. Sf 992.

i   Iron **shield board mount**. Large disc mount with lozenge-shaped washer. Part of a set of four identical mounts arranged in pairs either side of boss (k). Mineral-preserved leather and wood. Diameter: 62mm. Over left ankle. Sf 993.

j   Iron **shield board mount**. Incomplete. Large disc mount with lozenge-shaped washer. Part of a set of four identical mounts arranged in pairs either side of boss (k). Mineral-preserved leather and wood. Diameter: 62mm. Over left ankle. Sf 994.

k   Iron **shield boss**. Incomplete, several pieces broken off flange. Slightly carinated convex cone with straight wall (height: 25mm), disc-headed apex (diameter: 20mm) and five disc-headed flange rivets (diameter: 20mm), each with plated disc and circular copper alloy washer. Mineralised wood and leather remains indicate a covering of leather to the front as well as the back of the wooden shield board. Diameter: 160mm. Height: 80mm. Over left ankle. Sf 983.

     Also, iron **shield grip**. Incomplete, lacking end of one terminal. Strap grip, narrow in the centre (width: 20mm) expanding towards its terminals (width: 60mm.). Fixed to shield board at each terminal by a disc-headed rivet, surviving *in situ* as one head with plated disc (diameter: 20mm) and one shank with copper alloy washer. No evidence of a wooden handle but possible handle of leather and textile. Length: 160mm. Over left ankle. Sf 983.

l   Iron **object**. Fragmentary, with suspension loop leading to shaft of square section, tapering to second fragmentary loop. Length: 85mm. Width: 8mm. Possible mineral-preserved leather suspension thong on loop. Right side of body, over spine. Sf 995.

Grave 415 (Fig 10.111) ? 1½–2½ 316°. Context 500. Plot Y. 0.95m x 0.41m x 0.18m.

Light-brown loam with frequent small and medium chalk. A few teeth only.

a   Amber **bead**. Central part of grave (lost).

b   Glass **bead**. Central part of grave. Sf 839.

Grave 415 bead
b
glass: 1 bead
other annular (no 58)
    1   very short, diam 11–15mm, opaque, yellow

Grave 416 (Figs 10.61, 10.112, 10.119) M 30–40. 310°. Context 502. Plot Y. 2.23m x 1.09m x 0.61m.
Light-brown loam with frequent small and medium chalk. Chalk and flint packing around sides of grave indicates a coffin 2.10m x 0.60m Moderately well-preserved skeleton; skull left; arms bent across body.

a   Iron **knife**. Back straight and curving to tip, edge slightly sinuous. Well-defined junction of organic handle and blade. Mineral-preserved horn handle and leather on blade from sheath. Length: 162mm. Above skull. Sf 937.

b   Iron **pin** with scrolled head. Mineral-preserved textile. Length: 123mm. Above skull. Sf 938.

Grave 417 (Figs 10.61–2, 10.112) F 40–50. 317°. Context 504. Phase 2a. Plot Y. 2.69m x 1.01m x 0.85m.
Cream-brown silty loam with frequent small and medium chalk. Chalk and flint packing around sides of grave indicates a coffin 2.30m x 0.58m Poorly-preserved skeleton; skull right; arms slightly bent.

a   Clear **quartz ball** set in silver sling. Sling made of four silver strips held by copper alloy rivets fastening opposing pairs and covered by silver sheet tube set with beaded wire rim. Double perforation of tube for suspension loop worn; beaded wire rim worn, silver strips worn especially at equator. Length: 36mm. Weight: 24.0g. Two incomplete silver slipknot rings. Diameter of larger fragment: 24mm; weight: 0.6g. Length of smaller fragment: 22mm, weight: 0.2g. Between knees. Sf 1019.

b   Pair of cast copper alloy **strap-ends**, corroded together. Narrow, tongue-shaped, with split ends and one rivet each. Both are decorated with a corroded incised cross between parallel transverse lines. Length: 54mm. Between knees. Sf 1020.

c   Silver-gilt cast openwork Kentish **square-headed brooch** with garnet settings on hatched foil. Faulty casting under right garnet head-plate patched with silver sheet ?under foil. Egg-timer punch marks on ridges; punched dotted lines on plain borders. Zigzag borders. Zigzag pattern created by double row of copper-nielloed triangles on foot-plate, bow and head-plate. Brooch rim, gilding and especially niello decoration on bow worn. Cast pair of spring-holders and pin-catch. Remains of iron pin. Mineral-preserved textile with stitching on back. Length: 76mm. Weight: 27.4g. Above right pelvis. Sf 1021.

d   Copper alloy gilt cast **radiate-headed brooch** with garnet settings not on hatched foil. Punched ring-and-dot decoration on bow, punched decoration on central ridges to both sides. Three garnets lost, left knob broken off. Break worn, outline of brooch (especially knobs on foot-plate) worn, top of bow worn, gilding on brooch remains only in crevices. Cast pair of spring-holders and pin-catch. Iron remains of spring. Mineral-preserved textile on back. Length: 91mm. Weight: 20.6g. Over lower spine. Sf 1022.

e   Cast copper alloy **buckle** and **plate**. Oval loop with hollow underside and club-shaped waisted tongue with ridged back. Square offset plate with three knob-headed rivets. Mineral-preserved leather between plate from strap. Width of loop: 37mm. Width of plate 20mm. Overall length: 43mm. By lower spine. Sf 1023.

f   Cast copper alloy **buckle**. Oval loop of semi-circular section, with narrowed axis for attachment of the waisted tongue. The tongue shield is trapezoid with a cast groove at the basal end. Mineral-preserved leather remains on surface. Width of loop: 29mm. By lower spine. Sf 1024.

g   Silver-gilt cast miniature **bow brooch** with garnets set on hatched foil. Four garnets lost, one shows remains of white cement under foil. Bow and outline of brooch worn, gilding remains only in crevices. Cast spring-holder and pin-catch (broken); iron remains of spring; X-ray suggests they include a straight copper alloy rod passed through the perforation of the spring-holder, possibly repair. Mineral-preserved textile on back with loop and knot. Length: 29mm. Weight: 3.5g. Neck. Sf 1025.

h   Iron **knife**. Poor condition. Sharply tapered tang, back straight and curving to tip, cutting-edge sinuous. Mineral-preserved horn handle. Well-defined junction between blade and handle. Traces of willow wood (*Salix* sp) on the blade. Length: 117mm. Above left pelvis, under ring (i). Sf 1026.

i   Cast copper alloy **ring**. Wear on inner edge. Mineral-preserved textile on surface. Diameter: *c* 46mm. Weight: 33.8g. Over knife (h). Sf 1027.

j   Two amber **beads**. Chest area. Sf 1028 (see below).

k   Scatter of 28 amber and 24 glass **beads**. Neck and chest. Sf 1029 (see below).

Grave 417 beads
j
amber: 2 beads
    1   short, cylindrical, diam 21–25mm. Fig 4.25, Grave 417, Sf 1028 (j1)
    1   medium, rounded, diam 6–10mm
k
amber: 28 beads
    2   medium, globular, diam 11–15mm
    1   medium, barrel-shaped, diam 6–10mm. Fig 4.25, Grave 417, Sf 1028 (k13)
    3   medium, rounded, diam 11–15mm
    14   medium, rounded, diam 6–10mm
    4   medium, rounded, diam 2–5mm
    2   medium, facetted, diam 6–10mm
    2   medium, facetted, diam 2–5mm

glass: 24 beads
Constricted Segmented (no 5)
    1   three segments, very long, diam 2–5mm. Fig 4.25, Grave 417, Sf 1029 (k33)
    10   two segments, long to very long, globular, diam 2–5mm
    13   short to medium, diam 2–5mm

Grave 418 (Figs 10.62, 10.112) ?F 16–18. 306°. Context 506. Phase 1–2. Plot Y. 1.85m x 0.74m x 0.49m.
Cream-brown silty loam with frequent small and medium chalk. Chalk and flint packing around sides of grave indicates

a coffin 1.46m x 0.46m Poorly-preserved skeleton; right; arms bent across pelvis.

a   **Ceramic vessel**. Biconical, 90 per cent complete with everted rim. Half of upper body has been reconstructed and parts of neck and rim are missing. Decorated with three very shallow broad neck grooves below which, on angle of carination, are shallow vertical grooves organised in bunches of three or five. Originally there were probably five–six bunches of which three bunches survive. These do not extend far onto the lower body. Under abraded burnish fabric has reddish sandy matrix. In fresh break on non-joining sherd dense scatter of rounded-sub-angular quartz sand grains (up to 1mm) and voids from leached calcareous inclusion (up to 1.5mm). Hand-made, probably coil built. Exterior surface was once well burnished but is now flaking and abraded, especially on one side. Interior is wiped smooth except where neck was once burnished. Rim diameter: 103mm; base diameter: 40mm. Height: 125mm. Left of skull. Sf 1041.

Grave 419 (Figs 10.62, 10.112, 10.119) F 30–35. 310°. Context 508. Phase 2a. Plot Y. 2.32m x 1.09m x 0.50m. Light-brown loam with frequent small and medium chalk containing three probably Roman pot-sherds. Chalk and flint packing around sides of grave indicate a coffin. Poorly-preserved skeleton.

a   Silver-gilt cast **bird brooch** with garnets not set on hatched foil. Some ridges nicked. Row of copper niello triangles pointing inwards. Gilding slightly worn. Cast spring-holder and pin-catch. Silver pin. Mineral-preserved cord or loop on back. Length: 38mm. Weight: 5.5g. Neck. Sf 1000.

b   Silver-gilt cast **disc brooch** with garnet not set on hatched foil. Egg-timer punch-marks on some ridges. Punched decoration on border almost worn away, gilding remains only in crevices of cast decoration. Cast spring-holder and pin-catch. Remains of iron pin. Mineral-preserved textile, cord and knots on back. Diameter: 22mm. Weight: 4.2g. Area of right chest. Sf 1001.

c   Scatter of five amber, one shell and 16 glass **beads**. Area of right chest. Sf 1002.

d   Ivory **purse ring**. Six small ivory fragments. Thickness: 12mm (sample drawn). Above left pelvis. Sf 1003.

e   Copper alloy **buckle**. D-shaped miniature loop, plain tongue, plus:
(i–ii) two **disc-headed studs** with sheet metal washers at base, (iii) another smaller **disc-headed stud**, and, (iv) a fourth **disc-headed stud** with curved shank. Mineral-preserved leather on rivet shafts and back of buckle ring. Width of loop: 12mm. Diameter of studs (i) and (ii): 6mm. Left of left femur, below purse ring (d). Sf 1004.

f   Cast high-tin copper alloy **buckle** with 3 **shoe-shaped studs**. Heavy buckle, D-shaped, faceted loop and narrowed axis for attachment of the now separate shield-tongue. This has swallow-tailed lateral finials and there are remains of an iron anchorage. Mineral-preserved leather from strap and textile. Width of loop: 37mm. Three cast copper alloy **shoe-shaped studs** with pierced lugs for attachment, one still attached to a fragment of leather belt at time of recording, now separated. Length of studs: *c* 18mm. Adjacent to right pelvis. Sf 1005.

g   Iron **chain** complex of at least four rings with two beads attached (see below), a single **ring** presumably related to the same complex, and iron ?**rod/pin**. Mineral-preserved suspension cord through centre of beads. Mineral-preserved textile remains. Diameter of single ring: *c* 14mm. Length: 9mm. Neck. Sf 1006.

h   Iron pierced **lozenge** with leather strap through central perforation. Mineral-preserved leather and textile on surface and leather thong through centre. Length: 23mm. Inside of left wrist. Sf 1007.

i   Copper alloy **mount**. Plain, sub-rectangular, with silver-headed rivets on obverse face. Rivets pass through segment of leather to plain rectangular mount on other side. Length: 23mm. Width: 9mm. By left wrist. Sf 1008.

j   Antler burr **pendant**. Incomplete, poor condition. Undecorated slice across naturally-shed burr. Fragmentary suspension hole. Undecorated and little modified. Length: 52mm. Width: 66mm. Thickness: 8mm. Within (d). Sf 1083.

Grave 419 beads

c

amber: 5 beads

    1   short, cylindrical, diam 21–25mm. Fig 4.24, Grave 419, Sf 1002 (c5)

    1   short, cylindrical, diam 16–20mm

    1   short, globular, diam 16–20mm

    1   short, globular, diam 11v15mm

    1   short, barrel-shaped, diam 11–15mm

shell?: 1 bead

    1   very long, cylindrical, square cross-section, diam 6–10mm. Sf 1002

glass: 16 beads

Constricted Segmented (no 5)

    1   two segments, very long, globular, diam 2–5mm. Fig 4.24, Grave 419, Sf 1002 (c22)

    1   medium, globular, diam 2–5mm

Constricted Cylindrical (no 6)

    4   very long, cylindrical, diam 2–5mm. Fig 4.24, Grave 419, Sf 1002 (c19)

Coiled Cylindrical (no 9)

    1   very long, cylindrical, diam 2–5mm. Fig 4.24, Grave 419, Sf 1002 (c17)

Miniature Dark (no 24)

    3   medium to long, coiled, diam 2–5mm. Fig 4.24, Grave 419, Sf 1002 (c14), (c15)

Traffic Light Twisted Trail (no 29)

    2   medium, globular, diam 6–15mm, opaque yellow and translucent green twisted trail on opaque red body. Fig 4.24, Grave 419, Sf 1002 (c10), (c9)

Traffic Light Imitation (no 30)

    1   medium, cylindrical, square cross-section, diam 6–10mm, opaque red frame on translucent green combed spiral on opaque yellow body. Fig 4.24, Grave 419, Sf 1002 (c8)

white/yellow cylindrical (no 55)

    3   long, square cross-section, diam 2–10mm, translucent, yellow (pale). Fig 4.24, Grave 419, Sf 1002 (c12)

glass?: 1 bead

    1   short, irregularly globular, diam 2–5mm, discoloured (dark?). Fig 4.24, Grave 419, (c6)

g
glass: 3 beads
Constricted Segmented (no 5)
  3 medium, diam 2–5mm

Grave 420 (Figs 10.63, 10.113) ?F 20–25. 324°. Context 510. Phase 2–3a. Plot Y. 2.31m x 1.05m x 0.98m.
Cream-brown silty loam with frequent small and medium chalk. Chalk packing along north-east side of grave indicates a coffin. Well-preserved skeleton; left arm bent across pelvis; right arm bent across body.

a Gold **strip**, remains of the central ornamental brocading from a tablet-woven band: the brocaded area is 5.5mm wide. Threads of Sf 1035 represent a band of about 290mm long and Sf 1279, 13mm long. The strip of Sf 1035 is 380–440 microns wide, rectangular in cross-section (thickness not recorded). The strip of Sf 1279 is 420–520 microns wide (mainly 450 microns), also rectangular in cross-section. By skull. Sf 1035 and Sf 1279.

b Iron **pin** with globular head. Mineral-preserved textile. Length: 108mm. Over right chest. Sf 1037.

c Glass **bell-beaker**. Light olive green, rim slightly thickened, cupped and everted; incurved wall, corded carination, convex base with point and a knob covered with white glass. Eight turns of fine white decomposed trail near the rim. Scar of ring punty round the knob. Diameter: 15mm. Bubbles, small, with a few large. Striations, patchy adhesions and iridescence. Height: 98mm. Diameter: 70–75mm. Thickness: 3mm at rim. By left foot. Sf 984.

d Single-sided antler composite **comb** and **case**. Comb consists of four tooth segments, and two end segments, attached to two antler connecting-plates by five iron rivets. Central tooth segment extends beyond line of back to form small handle. One connecting plate is decorated by double ring-and-dot patterns, confined within bands of quadruple diagonal lines. A similar pattern occurs on the connecting plates of the comb case. The other comb connecting-plate is undecorated except for two bounding lines below the back and two lines across the middle. Case includes two broad connecting-plates and two curved end plates, each of which is perforated, as is centre of connecting-plates, towards the base, above two projecting stubs. Comb length: 100mm. Case length: 122mm. By left ankle. Sf 922.

Sf 1284 Iron nail with associated mineral-preserved wood and an iron sheet fragment. Retrieved from the skeletal material Grave 420.

Grave 421 (Figs 10.63, 10.112) ? 3–4. 321°. Context 512. Plot Y. 1.69m x 0.85m x 0.81m.
Loose small chalk rubble. Skull fragments only.

a Iron **arrowhead**. Angular blade, solid split socket with rivet. Shape and size of object more reminiscent of an arrowhead than a spear. Willow wood (*Salix* sp) fragments in socket. Mineral-preserved textile on both sides of socket. Length: *c* 105mm. Above right side of skull. Sf 939.

b Iron **pin** with folded head. Mineral-preserved textile and wood on shaft. Length: 112mm. Right side of body. Sf 940.

c Iron **knife**. Back straight and curving to tip, cutting-edge

similar. Mineral-preserved horn handle and leather on blade from sheath. Length: 132mm. Right side of body. Sf 941.

Grave 422 (Figs 10.63, 10.113) ? 3–4. 321°. Context 514. Phase 1–2. Plot Y. 1.77m x 0.62–0.74m x 0.90m.
Light grey loam with frequent small and medium chalk. Skull and long bone fragments only.

a **Ceramic vessel**. Small well-made biconical vessel with hollow neck and slightly everted rim. Decoration in three zones. Zone of 21 paired stabs on neck, just below rim. Second zone is shallow broad horizontal neck groove just above carination, and below that is zone of short, broad, shallow vertical grooves arranged in nine bunches of three grooves. Pin-prick leach holes, some up to 1mm and some calcareous inclusions visible on the surface together with organic impressions of grass and occasionally seeds. Coil-built and exterior surface has been smoothly burnished a glossy black. Interior smoothed rather than burnished and there are clear fingernail marks where rim and neck have been added to the lower coil. Rim diameter: 75mm; rounded base diameter: *c* 40mm. Height: 69mm. Above skull. Sf 1049.

b Glass **bell beaker**. Complete, with one long crack starting at the rim. Very light green, the everted rim higher one side than the other, straight wall curving into a knob on the base. Empty channels of horizontal trails below the rim, nine turns. Empty channels of fourteen turns still containing white traces more widely-spaced from knob on base to mid wall. Striated surface with discoloured patches and iridescence. Few bubbles, some inclusions. Ring punty mark round knob: diameter: 17mm. Height: 92–95mm. Diameter: 70mm. Above skull. Sf 787.

c Iron **knife**. Incomplete, lacking tip of blade. Small, with tang running straight into blade. Back lightly curved to tip, cutting-edge curving to tip. Mineral-preserved horn handle and leather on blade from sheath. Length: 84mm. Left side of body. Sf 759.

Grave 423 (Figs 10.64, 10.113) M 40–50. 319°. Context 516. Phase 2–3a. Plot Y. 2.60m x 0.84m x 0.46m.
Brown loam with frequent small and medium chalk. Flint packing at north-west end of grave indicates a coffin. Poorly-preserved skeleton; skull half right; arms bent across pelvis.

a Iron **spearhead**. Broad, angular blade of lozenge-section. Distinction between socket and the shank is not obvious as the shank is very solid. Split socket. Two rivets. Ash wood (*Fraxinus excelsior*) remains. Length: 464mm. By left shoulder. Sf 982.

b Iron simple conical **ferrule**. Closed socket. Mineral-preserved wood in socket; mineral-preserved textile on surface. Length: 133mm. By left foot. Sf 959.

c Iron **?pin** fragment with folded ?head; pin missing. Mineral-preserved organic remains. Remaining length: 46mm. Under right femur. Sf 960.

d 1, iron **knife**. Fragmentary, lacking end of blade. Slender blade, back and cutting-edge straight. Well-defined junction of organic handle and blade. Mineral-preserved horn handle;

mineral-preserved leather from sheath with possible internal wood/plant stem stiffener on blade edge. Length: 92mm. Above left pelvis. Sf 961.

2, Iron **awl-like firesteel**. Small, with tang of circular section leading to blade of square section. Accreted to knife d1. Traces of mineral-preserved horn. Length: 45mm. Tang length: 15mm. Above left pelvis. Sf 961.

e   Copper alloy **tweezers**. Two raised ribs on loop (imitating swaged strip) resting on raised collar. Arms lightly splayed with incised zigzag pattern below collar, ending in terminals that are incurved at a virtual right-angle. Remains of copper alloy suspension **ring** in loop. Associated with two small knives. Length: 60mm. Above left pelvis. Sf 962.

f   Fragments of silver parcel-gilt sheet covers with remains of lead filling. The covers originally belonged to a D-shaped **buckle** with narrowed axis, shield-tongue and at least two shoe-shaped studs. Plain cover of underside of buckle loop is fully intact. Cover for upper face is in several fragments but retains its decoration in form of band made up from figure-of-eight-shaped punch marks. Inside this band, gilding is visible. There are matching cover fragments for a shield-tongue and for two shoe-shaped studs. Additionally, a plain copper alloy tongue of flat section was found. Silver cover for shield-tongue is somewhat wider than this tongue. Width of loop (based on silver cover for underside of buckle): 37mm. Lower chest area. Sf 963.

Grave 424 (Figs 10.64, 10.113) No bone. 327°. Context 518. Plot Y. 1.54m x 0.62m x 0.21m.

Cuts Grave 444 (Phase 1–2). Brown loam with moderate small chalk. No bones survived; grave length suggests a child.

a   Copper alloy **repair-staple** from wooden vessel. Length: 17mm. North corner of grave. Sf 887.

Grave 425 (Figs 10.64, 10.114, 10.120) ?F 20–25. 310°. Context 520. Phase 1b–2. Plot Y. 2.40m x 1.10m x 0.82m.

Cut by Grave 441 (Phase 1b–2). Cream-brown silty loam with frequent small and medium chalk. Chalk and flint packing around sides of grave indicate a coffin 2.00m (min) x 0.60m. Well-preserved skeleton; skull right.

a   Twelve amber and 15 glass **beads**. Right shoulder. Sf 953 (see below).
b   Copper alloy **spiral bead**. Diameter: 3–4mm. Right chest. Sf 954 (see below).
c   Iron **pin** with globular head. Mineral-preserved textile on surface. Length: *c* 105mm. Left chest. Sf 955.
d   Seven amber, one chalk and 16 glass **beads**. Left side of body. Sf 956.
a/d   Two amber beads and one glass bead. Location unclear, probably as (a). Sf 1278 and Sf 1288 (see below).

Grave 425 beads
a
amber: 12 beads
  1   medium, globular, diam 11–15mm
  2   medium, globular, diam 6–10mm
  4   medium, rounded, diam 6–10mm
  3   medium to long, facetted, diam 11–15mm
  2   medium, facetted, diam 6–10mm
glass: 15 beads
Constricted Segmented (no 5)
  6   short to medium, globular, diam 2–5mm
Constricted Cylindrical (no 6)
  4   very long, cylindrical, diam 2–5mm
discoloured Constricted Cylindrical (no 8)
  4   very long, one beaded, diam 2–5mm
Coiled Cylindrical (no 9)
  1   very long, cylindrical, diam 2–5mm
b
copper alloy: 1 bead
  1   wire spiral, diam 6–10mm
d
amber: 7 beads
  1   medium, rounded, diam 6–10mm
  2   medium, facetted, diam 16–20mm
  4   medium, facetted, diam 11–15mm
'chalk': 1 bead
  1   short, cylindrical, diam 16–20mm. Fig 4.26, Grave 425, Sf 956 (d8)
glass: 16 beads
Constricted Segmented (no 5)
  9   medium, diam 2–5mm. Fig 4.26, Grave 425, Sf 956 (d16)
Constricted Cylindrical (no 6)
  5   very long, cylindrical, diam 2–5mm. Fig 4.26, Grave 425, Sf 956 (d10)
discoloured Constricted Cylindrical (no 8)
  1   very long, diam 2–5mm
Miniature Dark (no 24)
  1   long, coiled, diam 2–5mm. Fig 4.26, Grave 425, Sf 956 (d9)

Sf 1278, Sf 1288
amber: 2 beads
  2   medium, rounded, diam 6–10mm
glass: 1 bead
Coiled Cylindrical (no 9)
  1   very long, cylindrical, diam 2–5mm

Grave 426 (Figs 10.64, 10.114) ?F 40–50. 303°. Context 522. Phase 2. Plot Y. 2.54m x 1.02m x 0.84m.

Grey-brown loam with frequent small and medium chalk. Chalk and flint packing around sides of grave indicates a coffin. Moderately well-preserved skeleton.

a   Iron **buckle**. D-shaped loop with an applied copper alloy sheet on upper face of loop and tongue. Now broken, copper alloy sheet seems to have been decorated with pair of grooves either side of axis. Originally, tongue may have been club-shaped. Mineral-preserved textile under loop. Width of loop: 36mm. Chest area. Sf 985.

Grave 427 (Figs 10.65, 10.115, 10.119) 316°. Context: Sk A, 524; Sk B, 580. Sk A, Phase 1b–2. Sk B, Phase 1–2. Plot X. 2.30m x 1.06m x 0.81m.

Enclosed by ring-gully F 571. Light-brown loam with frequent small and medium chalk. Flint packing around sides of grave indicates a coffin. Double-stacked grave (Sk A 0.50m above Sk B).

Sk 427A F 30–35. Poorly-preserved skeleton; skull right; left arm bent across body.

a Copper alloy Roman **coin**. Silvered bronze *radiate* of Tetricus I (AD 270–4). PRINC IVVENT. RIC 115. Weight: 2.03g. Over left humerus. Sf 1009.

b Copper alloy Roman **coin**. Silvered bronze *nummus* of AD 310–2. COMITI AVGG NN. (Constantine I). RIC VI, London 160. Weight: 4.05g. Over left humerus. Sf 1010.

c Copper alloy **pin**. Small oval head with transverse moulding at neck. Upper portion of shaft swollen, then of circular section tapering to point; tip missing. Length: 56mm Pelvis. Sf 1011.

d Iron **ring**. Mineral-preserved leather suspension thong. Mineral-preserved textile to both sides. Max external diameter: 67mm. By left elbow, under (e). Sf 1012.

e Fragments of iron **ring**. Mineral-preserved textile. Diameter: *c* 42mm. By left elbow, over (d). Sf 1013.

f Iron **knife**. Fragmentary. Short tang leading to thin blade with back curving to tip. Mineral-preserved horn handle and leather on blade from sheath. Length: *c* 133mm. Area of body. Sf 1014.

g Iron **buckle**. D-shaped loop with plain tongue which may have been club-shaped. Mineral-preserved leather remains on loop and tongue from strap. Width of loop: 36mm. Area of right hip. Sf 1015.

h Copper alloy **wire** of square section with pointed ends. Length of larger fragment: 11mm. Weight: 0.1g. By left elbow. Sf 1016.

i Copper alloy strip folded into oval **ring**. Diameter: 20mm. Weight: 1.6g. Area of left chest. Sf 1017.

j Copper alloy **wire** bent at one end, broken at other. Length: 17mm. Weight: 0.2g. Above right pelvis. Sf 1018.
Also six glass **beads**. Found in skull. Sf 1281.

Sk 427A beads
glass: 6 beads
Constricted Segmented (no 5)
  1 three segments, very long, diam 2–5mm. Fig 4.25, Grave 427A, Sf 1281 (1)
  2 two segments, long to very long, diam 2–5mm. Sf 1281
  3 short to medium, diam 2–5mm. Sf 1281

Sk 427B ? 20–25. Poorly-preserved skeleton; left arm bent across pelvis area.

a Copper alloy **repair-clip**. Grooved decoration on the outside. Remains of mineral-preserved wood indicating that the clip was part of a wooden vessel or object. Length: 12mm. Left of skull. Sf 1282.

Grave 428 (Fig 10.65) F 20–25. 314°. Context 526. Phase 2. Plot X. 2.41m x 0.97m x 0.83m.

Cream-brown silty loam with frequent small and medium chalk. Poorly-preserved skeleton; skull half right; arms bent across pelvis.

a, b Pair of matching copper alloy cast gilt **saucer brooches** with garnet inlay set on hatched foil. Some ridges nicked. Gilding worn only on flange and garnet setting. Spring-holder of (a) made of folded copper alloy sheet soldered onto back-plate, copper alloy spring ?held by iron ?rod ?through pierced copper alloy sheet of spring-holder. Under wire loop of pin-spring, a strip of leather folded lengthways, 4.5mm wide when folded, 15mm long. Mineral-preserved textile on back. (b) has cast spring-holder and remains of iron spring and pin. Leather suspension thong and mineral-preserved textile on back. Diameter of (a): 23mm, weight: 7.6g; Diameter of (b): 24mm, weight: 8.5g. Neck. Sf 894 and Sf 895.

c Cast copper alloy **buckle**. Oval loop of rounded section, with narrowed axis for attachment of tongue with square base and iron anchorage. Plus two copper alloy belt studs, sub-triangular with circular terminals and two shanks of circular section on back. Originally fixed by small rectangular copper alloy plate which is now separate. The front of each stud is decorated with three gilded leaf shapes. Mineral-preserved leather from strap and textile. Width of loop: 29mm. Right pelvic area. Sf 896.

d Copper alloy Roman **coin**. *Barbarous radiate* (AD 270s–280s). Divus Claudius type (Altar). Weight: 0.98g. Above left pelvis, over ring (o). Sf 897.

e Glass **bead**. Above left pelvis. Sf 898 (see below).

f Glass vessel fragment, used as a **bead**. Length: 12mm. Over left lower arm. Sf 899 (see below).

g Copper alloy **coin**. Silvered bronze ?*radiate*, late third century. Details illegible. Weight: 2.31g. (pierced). Under left lower arm. Sf 900.

h Iron **knife**. Fragmentary, lacking end of tang and part of blade. Long tang, back straight, cutting-edge sinuous. Well-defined junction of organic handle and blade. Mineral-preserved horn handle and leather on blade from sheath. Mineral-preserved textile on tang. Length: 165mm. Under left lower arm. Sf 901.
Leather. Several fragments of mineral-preserved leather with circular punched decoration and stitch marks along a seamed edge. Found in association with multiple smaller fragments. Longest piece: 11mm. Preserved beneath the knife (h), left lower arm. Sf 909.

i Iron pierced **lozenge**. Mineral-preserved textile. Length: 40mm. Over left lower arm. Sf 902.

j Eleven amber and nine glass **beads**. Neck area. Sf 903 (see below).

k Iron pierced **lozenge**. Incomplete. Central perforation set off-centre. Mineral-preserved textile. Length: 44mm. Above left pelvis. Sf 904.

l Copper alloy **binding** of oval section. Length: 21mm. Over left lower arm. Sf 905.

m Cast copper alloy **belt-plate**. Fragment. Openwork, one rivet shank on back. Length: 30mm. Roman. By left lower arm. Sf 906.

n Copper alloy Roman **coin**. Silvered bronze *nummus* of AD 330–335. GLORIA EXERCITVS. Details illegible. Diameter: 17mm. Weight: 2.35g. (two piercings). By left lower arm. Sf 907.

o ?Cast copper alloy **ring**. ?Wear on inner edge. Mineral-preserved textile and pupae cases. Max external diameter: 31mm. Weight: 3.0g. Under (d). Sf 908.

Grave 428 beads
e
glass: 1 bead
Traffic Light Twisted Trail (no 29)
1 short, barrel-shaped, diam 6–10mm, opaque yellow and translucent green twisted trail on opaque red body. Fig 4.23, Grave 428, Sf 898 (e1)

f
glass: 1 bead
rim fragment (no 34)
1 fragment of hollow vessel rim, diam 11–15mm, translucent, green-blue. Fig 4.23, Grave 428, Sf 899 (f1)

j
amber: 11 beads
8 medium (one long), rounded, diam 6–10mm
3 medium, facetted, diam 6–10mm
glass: 9 beads
Constricted Segmented (no 5)
3 medium, diam 2–5mm
green segmented (no 47)
2 short to medium, diam 2–5mm, opaque
Miniature Dark (no 24)
4 medium to very long, coiled, diam 2–5mm

Grave 429 (Fig 10.115) ? 20–25. 314°. Context 528. Plot Y. 2.62m x 0.66m x 0.31m.
Brown loam with frequent small and medium chalk. Skull fragments only. No grave goods.

Grave 430 (Fig 10.111) ? 6–9. 326°. Context 540. Plot X. 1.77m (min) x 0.27m (min) x 0.50m.
Cut by Grave 412 (Phase 2b–3a). Cream-brown silty loam with frequent small and medium chalk. One leg bone only survived. No grave goods.

Grave 431 (Figs 10.65, 10.106) ? 6–8. 327°. Context 542. Plot X. 1.82m x 0.64m x 0.25m.
Cuts gully F 529 and Grave 386. Light-brown loam with frequent small and medium chalk. Skull fragments only.

a Iron **knife**. Back straight and curving lightly to tip, cutting-edge curving to tip. Mineral-preserved horn handle and leather on blade from sheath in association with fine fibres, possibly the remnant of a hide and hair sheath. Length: 166mm. Area of left body. Sf 775.
b Iron **pin** with globular head, point missing. Length: 76mm. Area of left body. Sf 776.

Grave 432 (Figs 10.66, 10.116) F 20–25. 317°. Context 544. Phase 1b–2. Plot W. 2.25m x 0.97–1.14m x 0.23m.
Cream-brown silty loam with frequent small and medium chalk. Poorly-preserved skeleton; skull rolled forward; arms bent across pelvis.

a Cast copper alloy **pin**. Facetted oval head, decorative moulding at neck. Shaft of rounded then square section, tapering to point. Length: 129mm. Right of skull. Sf 842.
b Ivory **purse ring**. Incomplete and now in nine separate pieces. Heavily laminated; rounded square section. Width: 124mm. Under left elbow. Sf 843.
c Iron **knife**. Fragmentary, lacking tip of blade and part of tang. Back curving lightly to tip, cutting-edge similar. Well-defined junction of organic handle and blade. Mineral-preserved leather on blade from sheath or held in purse. Length: 78mm. Within ivory ring (b). Sf 844.
d Cast copper alloy **buckle**. D-shaped loop of D-shaped section with remains of a plain iron tongue and narrowed axis for its attachment. Mineral-preserved leather on bar and loop from strap. Mineral-preserved textile. Width of loop: 32mm. Excavated from above the left pelvis. Sf 845.
e Six glass **beads**. Area of pelvis. Sf 846 (see below).
f Glass **cone beaker**. Broken and restored with a few gaps. Light green-blue, slightly thickened and everted rim, straight sides ending in a pointed tip. A fine white trail turned about four times below the rim is overlaid by a thickened white trail turned twice. Seven white trails applied mid body were pulled downwards at seven points to form arcades and marvered. Traces of a ring punty, diameter: 13mm on tip. Many bubbles, some inclusions, striations. Height: 187mm. Diameter: 72mm. Thickness: 2mm at rim; 0.5mm in body. By left foot. Sf 847.
g Nine glass **beads**. By left foot. Sf 848 (see below).
h One glass **bead**. Within (b). Sf 849 (see below).
Also, three glass **beads**, location in grave unclear. Sf 1274.

Grave 432 beads
e
glass: 6 beads
Constricted Segmented (no 5)
5 two segments, long to very long, diam 2–5mm. Fig 4.26, Grave 432, Sf 846 (e2)
Coiled Cylindrical (no 9)
1 very long, cylindrical, diam 2–5mm. Fig 4.26, Grave 432, Sf 846 (e1)
g
glass: 9 beads
Constricted Segmented (no 5)
1 three segments, very long, diam 2–5mm. Fig 4.26, Grave 432, Sf 848 (g1)
6 two segments, long to very long, diam 2–5mm
1 medium, diam 2–5mm
Miniature Dark (no 24)
1 long, coiled, diam 2–5mm. Fig 4.26, Grave 432, Sf 848 (g9)
h
glass: 1 bead
discoloured Constricted Cylindrical (no 8)
1 very long, diam 2–5mm. Fig 4.26, Grave 432, Sf 849 (h1)
Sf 1274
glass: 3 beads
Constricted Segmented (no 5)
1 two segments, very long, globular, diam 2–5mm. Sf 1274
2 medium, globular, diam 2–5mm. Sf 1274

Grave 433 (Figs 10.66, 10.115) ? juvenile/grown. 315°. Context 552. Phase 1. Plot W. 2.01m x 1.02m x 0.26m.
Light-brown loam with frequent small and medium chalk. A few long bone fragments only.

a   Copper alloy gilt cast openwork **animal brooch**. Gilding hardly worn. Cast spring-holder and pin-catch. Remains of iron spring. Mineral-preserved textile and another organic material on pin. Length: 31mm. Weight: 5.1g. Towards north-west end of grave. Sf 910.
b   Copper alloy wire slip-knot ?**bracelet**. Incomplete. Remains of mineral-preserved leather ?thong. Diameter: 65mm. Weight: 6.9g. Towards north-west end of grave. Sf 911.
c   Iron **knife**. Very slender, tang leads directly to blade. Back straight and lightly curved to tip, cutting-edge sinuous. Mineral-preserved horn handle; leather and wood/plant stem stiffener on blade from sheath. Length: 140mm. Central area of grave. Sf 912.

Grave 434 (Figs 10.66, 10.115) ?M grown. 304°. Context 554. Plot Y. 1.75m (min) x 0.95m x 0.34m.
Cut by modern pit. Brown loam with frequent small and medium chalk. Damaged skeleton; skull and upper body removed; left arm slightly bent across pelvis.

a   Iron **knife**. Back straight and curving to tip, cutting-edge similar. Mineral-preserved horn handle and leather on blade from sheath. Length: 162mm. Above left pelvis. Sf 957.
b   Iron **pin**. Head bent into a loop. Mineral-preserved leather on shaft. Length: 109mm. Above left pelvis. Sf 958.

Grave 435 (Fig 10.66) ?M 30–40. 316°. Context 556. Phase 2–3a. Plot Y. 2.17m x 0.72m x 0.07m.
Brown loam with frequent small and medium chalk. Poorly-preserved skeleton; partially decayed right arm bent across pelvis.

a   Cast copper alloy **buckle**. Oval faceted loop with a narrowed axis for attachment of (now separate) shield-tongue which has remains of iron anchorage and visible mark where leather used to sit across it. Width: 32mm. Left pelvis area. Sf 888.

Grave 436 (Figs 10.67, 10.116) ? 35–45. 304°. Context 558. Phase 1b–2. Plot Y. 2.20m x 0.92–1.07m x 0.62m.
Light-brown loam with frequent small and medium chalk containing two Iron Age and one early Roman pot-sherd. Poorly-preserved skeleton.

a   Iron **knife**. Short tang leading to straight back, curved to tip. Cutting-edge similar, slightly worn. Traces of junction between organic handle and blade. Mineral-preserved horn handle, organic remains on blade. Length: 150mm. Left side of body. Sf 950.
b   Iron, silver, copper alloy, gilded, glass- and garnet-inlaid **buckle**. Rectangular iron loop with silver cloisons with traces of gilding. Seven garnets remain, only three of which appear to be set on cross-hatched silver-gilt foil. Additionally, there are two semi-circular glass slips. Waisted copper alloy tongue with remains of gilding and with rectangular box at base, which is now empty. Scientific examination showed that the silver cloisons were constructed as box frame into which the cross-walls were then slotted. Plus three dome-headed **studs**, copper alloy with ribbed dome and pierced lug for attachment. Folds of mineral-preserved textile on back of buckle. Width of loop: 43mm. Height of studs: 13mm. Area of waist. Sf 951.
c   Copper alloy **rim fragment** from a wooden vessel with two copper alloy **repair-clips**. Length: 23mm. Width: 11mm. Area of left shoulder. Sf 952.

Grave 437 (Figs 10.67–8, 10.116) M 35–40. 311°. Context 560. Phase 2. Plot Y. 2.50m x 0.90m x 0.30m.
Brown loam with frequent small and medium chalk. Poorly-preserved skeleton; left arm bent across pelvis.

a   Iron **sword** with traces of a mineral-preserved ash wood (*Fraxinus excelsior*) scabbard in association with sheep's wool fibres and calfskin leather. More mineral-preserved wood is present in association with horn on the hilt. Ovoid iron button pommel; hilt packing pieces and scabbard (fleece of long staple). Length: 880 x 45 (42)mm; grip length: 95mm (approx); thickness of upper and lower guards: 12 and 13mm respectively. On right of body, pommel by skull, over (i), (j) and (k). Sf 919 (SN 1023; pp 251–3).
b   Glass **bowl**. Complete except for one fragment restored. Light blue-green, straight-sided, thickened and everted rim, slightly pushed-in base. Seven turns of a white horizontal trail below the rim, and another zone of *c* nine turns at mid body. Below this a zone of eight turns is hooked downwards six times to form arcades which terminate in lumps in the wall of the vessel. Scar and metal remains of ring punty on base, diameter: 11 x 16mm. Small bubbles, striated surface, patches of discolouration. Height: 66mm. Diameter: 153mm. Thickness: 3mm at rim. Left side of skull. Sf 921.
c   Iron **fauchard**. Curving cutting-edge, straight back with an 'axe-like' addition, triangular section. Knife-like, split socket with mineral-preserved wood. Mineral-preserved textile on socket and blade. Length: 334mm. By left femur. Sf 973.
d   Iron **pin** with coiled head and unrelated curved iron fragment. Extensive mineral-preserved leather wound around pin with remains of stitching. Length of pin: 144mm; length of fragment: 25mm. By right knee. Sf 974.
e   Cast copper alloy **buckle**. Oval, of D-shaped section. Narrowed axis with iron concretion from the anchorage of the now separate tongue, which has a rectangular shield. Mineral-preserved leather on loop from strap. Width of loop: 34mm. Left side of body. Sf 975.
f   Copper alloy **tweezers** with narrow loop expanding to broad arms and incurved terminals. Extensively decorated, probably on both sides with circles and bands of linear patterning. Corroded to (g) and (h). Extensive mineral-preserved textile, cordage, leather thong and vegetable fibres. Length: 66mm. Width: 14mm. By right femur. Sf 976.
g   Copper alloy **slip-knot ring**. Part of tweezer and pin group. By right femur. Sf 1042.
h   Iron **pin** with looped head. Extensive mineral-preserved textile,

cordage, leather thong and vegetable fibres. Length: *c* 160mm. By right femur. Sf 1043.

i   Iron **knife**. Incomplete, lacking tip of blade. Short, broad tang. Back straight and curving to tip, cutting-edge similar. Well-defined junction of handle and blade. Mineral-preserved horn handle and organic remains on blade. Length: 178mm. Under sword (a). Sf 977.

j   Copper alloy **coin**. Silvered bronze *radiate* of Carausius (AD 286–293). Reverse illegible. Weight: 3.52g. Under sword (a). Sf 978.

k   Incomplete iron **pursemount/firesteel** with attached buckle. Found with a small flint. Extensive mineral-preserved leather, textile and wood. Leather strap remains on buckle. The iron pursemount has no rivet-holes present for attachment to the purse, but there is a piece of leather with a line of stitching along the loop of the central buckle. This may indicate the method in which the firesteel was attached to the pursemount, i.e. by stitching. Length: 108mm. Under sword (a). Sf 979.

Grave 438 (Figs 10.68, 10.117) M 15–17. 312°. Context 562. Plot Y. 2.58m x 0.91m 0.52m.
Cream-grey loam with frequent small and medium chalk containing one Iron Age pot-sherd. Poorly-preserved skeleton; right arm bent across pelvis area; legs crossed at ankle (right over left).

a   Iron **knife**. Back straight and curving to tip, cutting-edge similar. Well-defined junction of organic handle and blade. Mineral-preserved horn handle with leather on blade from a decorated sheath with a geometric stamped pattern of triangles and a single circle. Mineral-preserved textile. Length: 136mm. Chest area. Sf 886.

Grave 439 (Figs 10.68, 10.117) ? 12–14. 309°. Context 564. Plot Y. 1.60m x 0.65m x 0.12m.
Brown loam with frequent small and medium chalk. Poorly-preserved skeleton; left arm bent across body; legs bent to right.

a   Iron **knife**. Short tang and narrow blade. Back straight and curving to tip, cutting-edge similar. Well-defined junction of organic handle and blade. Mineral-preserved horn handle with leather on blade from sheath. Length: 134mm. Above left pelvis. Sf 1030.

Grave 440 (Figs 10.69, 10.117) ? 15–17 307°. Context 566. Phase 1b–2a. Plot Y. 2.14m x 0.83m x 0.22m.
Brown loam with moderate small chalk. Poorly-preserved skeleton; legs bent to left.

a   Copper alloy gilt cast **saucer brooch** with central garnet inlay not on hatched foil. Some ridges nicked. Gilding worn on all ridges, garnet setting and flange. Remains of iron spring with mineral-preserved textile on pin with loop. Diameter: 24mm. Weight: 8.9g. Neck. Sf 965.

b   Copper alloy gilt cast **saucer brooch** with a central and surrounding red enamel inlay. Some ridges nicked. Gilding

on ridges, enamel setting and flange worn. Remains of iron spring with mineral-preserved threads. Diameter: 24mm. Weight: 6.3g. Chest area. Sf 966.

c   Copper alloy Roman **coin**. Silvered bronze *nummus* of AD 330–335. CONSTANTINOPOLIS type. Mint illegible. Weight: 2.04g. Left of left femur. Sf 967.

d   Two amber and nine glass **beads**. Area of right chest. Sf 968 (see below).

e   Iron **knife**. Short tang leading to straight back, curving to tip. Cutting-edge little worn, straight and curving to tip. Abundant organic remains on mineral-preserved horn handle; trace of handle line; leather on blade from sheath. Length: 138mm. Left of pelvis. Sf 969.

Grave 440 beads
d
amber: 2 beads
    1   medium, facetted, diam 6–10mm
    1   short, cylindrical, diam 21–25mm. Fig 4.26, Grave 440, Sf 968 (d10)
glass: 9 beads
Constricted Segmented (no 5)
    1   four segments, very long, diam 2–5mm. Fig 4.26, Grave 440, Sf 968 (d1)
    2   two segments, long, diam 2–5mm
    4   short to long, globular, diam 2–5mm. Fig 4.26, Grave 440, Sf 968 (d5)
Constricted Cylindrical (no 6)
    2   very long, diam 2–5mm. Fig 4.26, Grave 440, Sf 968 (d3)

Grave 441 (Figs 10.69, 10.114, 10.120) ? 1½–2½. 316°. Context 568. Phase 1b–2. Plot Y. 1.14m x 0.75m x 0.67m.
Cuts Grave 425 (Phase 1b–2). Cream-brown silty loam with frequent small and medium chalk. Skull and long bone fragments only.

a   **Ceramic vessel**. Small well-made biconical vessel with hollow neck and slightly everted rim; complete following reconstruction. Decorated with three broad, very shallow neck grooves and broad, short, vertical grooves arranged in nine bunches of three around edge of the carination. Fabric visible on lower body where burnishing has spalled off. Dense reddish sandy matrix with occasional rounded and sub-rounded quartz sand grains of up to 1mm on surface. Occasional flecks of organic material on surface and occasional pieces of grog or un-worked clay 1–2mm diameter. Fabric is quite fine with occasional large chalk inclusions; the largest is 5mm others are 1–2mm. Coil-built, external surface burnished. Interior wiped by coil marks as well as fingernail impressions where upper coiled was added to that below. Rim diameter: 78mm; rounded base diameter: *c* 40mm. Height: 67mm. North-west (head) end of grave. Sf 1040.

b   Group of one amber and 21 glass **beads**. Right of pot (a). Sf 1038.

Grave 441 beads
b
amber: 1 bead
    1   medium, rounded, diam 6–10mm

glass: 21 beads
Constricted Segmented (no 5)
    6   three segments, long to very long, diam 2–5mm.
           Fig 4.26, Grave 441, Sf 1038 (b5)
    3   two segments, long to very long, diam 2–5mm
    5   short to very long, diam 2–5mm
Constricted Cylindrical (no 6)
    7   short to very long, diam 2–5mm. Fig 4.26, Grave
           441, Sf 1038 (b2), (b19)

Grave 442 (Figs 10.69, 10.113) ? 9–11. 311°. Context 578. Phase 1b–2. Plot Y. 1.87m x 0.66m x 0.47m.
Cuts Grave 444 (Phase 1–2). Cream-brown silty loam with frequent small and medium chalk. Skull and long bone fragments only.

a   Cast copper alloy **buckle**. Oval loop of D-shaped section with narrowed axis for attachment of the very thin, waisted tongue. Width of loop: 28mm. Area of right pelvis. Sf 1031.

b   Iron **knife**. Incomplete, lacking end of blade. Long tang, back straight and curving to tip, cutting-edge sinuous. Well-defined junction of handle and blade. Mineral-preserved horn handle with leather on blade from sheath. Length: 129mm. Left side of body. Sf 1032.

c   Iron **pin**. Scrolled head. Length: 86mm. Left side of body. Sf 1033.

d   Iron **firesteel** with copper alloy wire loop attached. Mineral-preserved woven textile and amorphous skin product. Length: 110mm. Left side of body. Sf 1034.

Grave 443 (Figs 10.69, 10.117) ?F 30–35. 310°. Context 584. Phase 1b–2. Plot Y. 2.16m x 0.70m x 0.44m.
Cream-brown silty loam with frequent small and medium chalk. Very large flint at south-east end could relate to packing around a coffin. Poorly-preserved skeleton.

a   Iron **knife**. Broad tang, bent upwards. Back straight and curving to tip, cutting-edge sinuous. Mineral-preserved horn handle with leather on blade from sheath. Length: 151mm. Left side of body. Sf 996.

b   Cast copper alloy **buckle**. D-shaped loop of D-section with narrowed axis for attachment of waisted shield-tongue with iron anchorage. Tongue shield is less well-defined than usual. Mineral-preserved leather on back from strap. Width: 29mm. Left pelvis area. Sf 997.

c   Iron **nail**. Incomplete with domed head and shank of square section. Lower part missing. Mineral-preserved textile. Length: 70mm. Above left pelvis. Sf 998.

d   Iron **pin** with two points. Mineral-preserved woven textile and leather. Length: 53mm. Above left pelvis. Sf 999.

Grave 444 (Figs 10.69, 10.113) ? 6–8. 129°. Context 586. Phase 1–2. Plot Y. 1.95m x 1.04m x 0.28m.
Cut by Graves 424 and 442 (Phase 1b–2). Cream-brown silty loam with frequent small and medium chalk. Skull and long bone fragments only; head at south-east.

a   Iron **nail**. Discoidal head, shank of circular section. Fragmentary. Mineral-preserved wood on shank. Length: 48mm. Along north-east side of grave. Sf 942.

b   Iron **nail**. Shank only, oak wood (*Quercus* sp) remains. Length: 36mm. Along north-east side of grave. Sf 943.

c   Iron **nail**. Discoidal head and shank of circular section. Mineral-preserved wood on shank. Length: 57mm. Along north-east side of grave. Sf 944.

d   Iron **nail**. Head only. Mineral-preserved wood on underside of head. Length: 13mm. Along north-east side of grave. Sf 945.

e   Iron **knife**. Broad, short tang. Back straight and curving to tip, cutting-edge similar. Traces of junction between organic handle and blade. Mineral-preserved leather on blade from sheath. Length: 135mm. Left side of body. Sf 946.

f   Iron ?**key** with rolled head and a flattened rectangular shaft which expands to break where it begins to flare. Mineral-preserved leather suspension thong. Mineral-preserved textile. Length overall: 72mm; width at break: 12mm. Area of left pelvis. Sf 947.

g   Copper alloy wire **ring** with pointed terminals. Diameter: 26mm. Weight: 3.3g. Area of left pelvis. Sf 948.

h   Copper alloy **mount**. Perforated circular head with splayed triangular plate below, also perforated. Plain, turquoise colour, heavy cast. Length: 53mm. Width: 23mm. Area of left pelvis. Sf 949.

Miscellaneous objects

Anglo-Saxon objects probably derived from specific graves

Sf 936   Tip of an iron **knife**. Rounded with a single sharpened cutting-edge. Mineral-preserved leather on blade from sheath. Filling of builder's trench cut through Graves 323 and Grave 342. Probably from Grave 323. Context 375. *Not illus.*

Sf 1280   Copper-gilt rectangular **mount**, pierced in two places. Remains of gilding in the grooved decoration. Traces of iron corrosion around the rivet-holes. Filling of builder's trench cut through Graves 323 and Grave 342. Probably from Grave 323. Context 375. Fig 10.70.

Objects from spoilheaps, context 37, etc

Sf 135   Illegible modern copper alloy coin – Georgian farthing? Unstratified, Context 37. *Not illus.*

Sf 305   Anglo-Saxon copper alloy **buckle** and separate fitting or plate. Cast, kidney-shaped loop with narrowed axis. The tongue base is decorated with two groups of transverse lines framing two notches reminiscent of early shield-tongue buckles. Separate sheet copper alloy plate and back-plate, linked by four corner rivets. Width of loop: 21mm. Plate 14 x 20mm. Unstratified, Context 37. Fig 10.70

Sf 409 Cast copper alloy **buckle**. D-shaped loop of D-shaped section with narrowed axis. Tongue missing. Width of loop: 25mm. Fig 10.70.

Sf 425 Copper alloy Roman **coin**. Silvered bronze *radiate* of Claudius II (AD 268–270). ANNONA AVG. cf RIC 18. Weight: 1.92g. Unstratified, Context 37. *Not illus*.

Sf 565 Model **spearhead,** Anglo-Saxon?, date uncertain. Unstratified, Context 37. *Not illus*.

Sf 566 Copper alloy **coin**. Cut medieval farthing, long cross class 3 (1248–1250). Moneyer Nicole, mint uncertain. Weight: 0.25g. *Not illus*.

Sf 568 Copper alloy **buckle** and plate. Medieval. D-shaped loop with narrowed axis. Partly gilded plate with four rivets and another rivet-hole and an incised line scalloped line with traces of gilding running parallel to the edge. Width of loop: 16mm. Width of plate: 12mm. Overall length: 36mm. Fig 10.70.

Sf 570 Two **buttons**: One copper alloy button. One copper alloy with decorated surface and white metal plating, ?silver. Unstratified, Context 37. *Not illus*.

Sf 571 Copper alloy **coin**. 1923 farthing. Unstratified, Context 37. *Not illus*.

Sf 572 Copper alloy **coin**. Illegible. Unstratified, Context 37. *Not illus*.

Sf 588 Lead or lead-alloy **spindle-whorl**, rounded conical with flanges from casting around top (widest) face and around spindle hole; the lower end of the spindle hole has been pinched in. Squared hole through centre. Diameter: 25mm tapering to 14mm. Height: 18mm. Spindle hole diameter: 7–8mm. Weight: 41.9g. Unstratified, Context 37. Fig 10.70.

Sf 590 Copper alloy **stud-head** with concentric ridged moulding. Remains of iron from shank on the underside. Unstratified, Context 37. Fig 10.70.

Sf 591 Copper alloy **ring** with inscription. Unstratified, Context 37. Fig 10.70.

Sf 677 Copper alloy disc-shaped fixing plate with numerous perforations and remains of hinge and pin. Gilded on one side. Unstratified, Context 37. Fig 10.70.

Sf 760 Iron **knife** with remains of mineral-preserved horn handle and mineral-preserved leather on the blade from the sheath. Unstratified, Context 37. Fig 10.70.

Sf 923 Cast copper alloy **buckle**. Elongated oval loop of D-shaped section, narrowed axis tongue missing. Width of loop: 35mm. Unstratified, Context 37. Fig 10.70.

Sf 1234 Cast copper alloy **ring** with opposite pairs of notches. Diameter: *c* 40mm. Weight: 19.2g. Fig 10.70.

Sf 1235 Silver spiral **ring**. Diameter: *c* 2mm. Weight: 1.5g. Fig 10.70.

Sf 1236 Anglo-Saxon cast, gilt copper alloy **buckle**. D-shaped loop of D-shaped section with club-shaped waisted tongue and narrowed axis. There are extensive remains of gilding on loop and tongue. Width of loop: 23mm. Fig 10.70.

Sf 1263 Iron **knife**. Fig 10.70.

Sf 1264 Iron **spear ferrule**. Mineral-preserved leather from a strap and textile. Wood in socket. Unstratified, Context 37. *Not illus*.

Sf 1265 Iron **buckle** with mineral-preserved leather from strap and traces of mineral-preserved textile from garment. Unstratified, Context 37. *Not illus*.

Sf 1285 Iron **knife/handle** fragment with remains of mineral-preserved horn. Unstratified, Context 37. Fig 10.70.

Grave 204

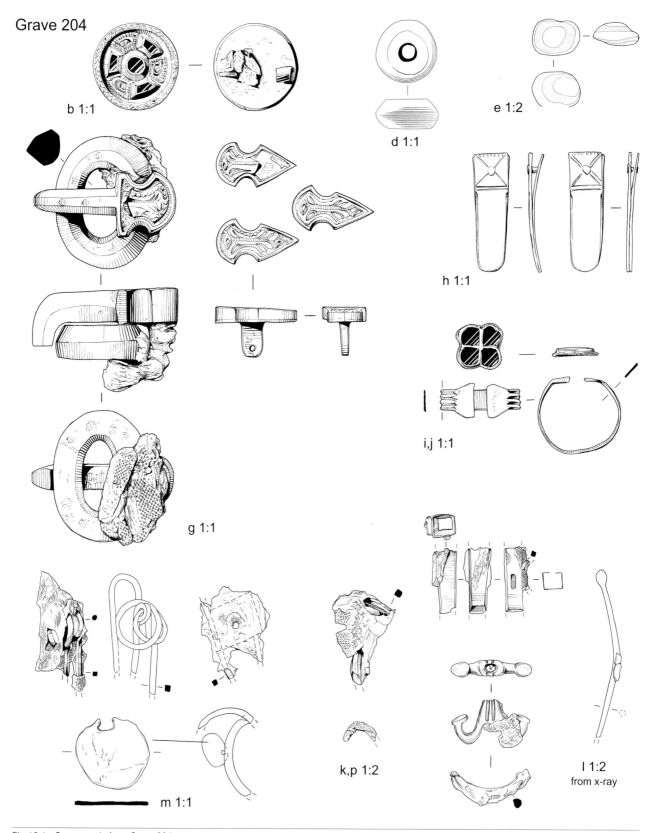

b 1:1

d 1:1

e 1:2

h 1:1

g 1:1

i,j 1:1

k,p 1:2

l 1:2
from x-ray

m 1:1

Fig 10.1. Grave goods from Grave 204.

Grave 204

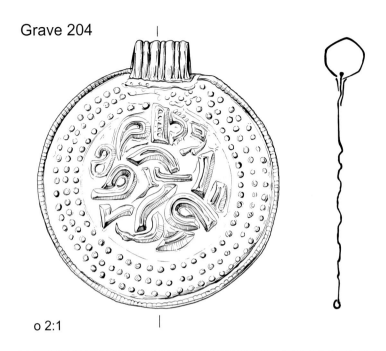

o 2:1

Grave 205

b 1:2

a 1:1

d 1:2

e 1:2

Grave 206

a 1:1

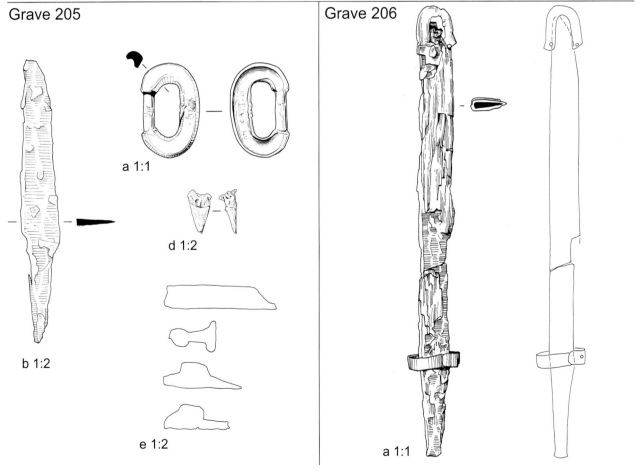

Fig 10.2. Grave goods from Graves 204, 205 and 206.

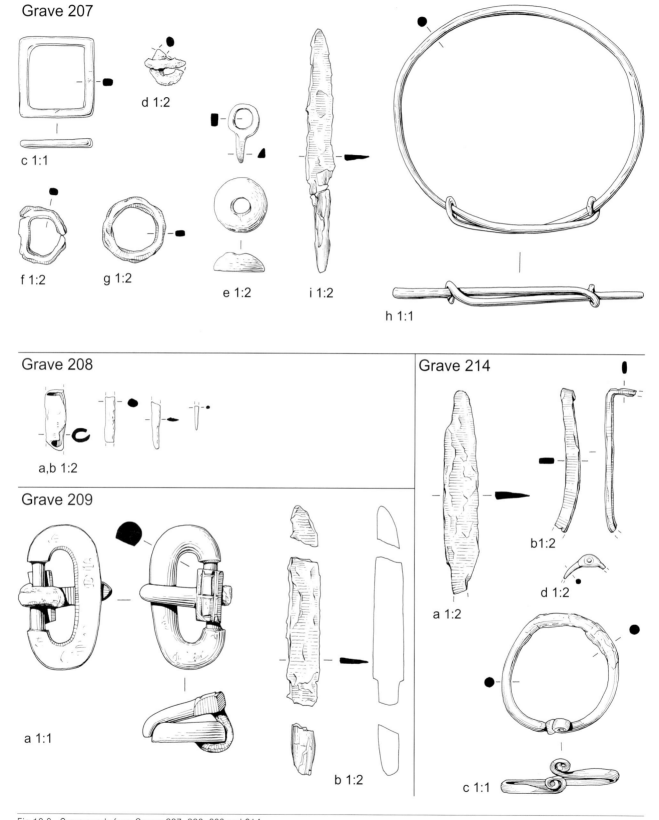

Fig 10.3. Grave goods from Graves 207, 208, 209 and 214.

456

Grave 215

b 1:2

c 1:2

d 1:2

a 1:2

e 1:2

Grave 217

k 1:1

l 1:2

m 1:2

Grave 218

a 1:2

b 1:2

c 1:2

r 1:2

g 1:2

f 1:1

d 1:2

e 1:2

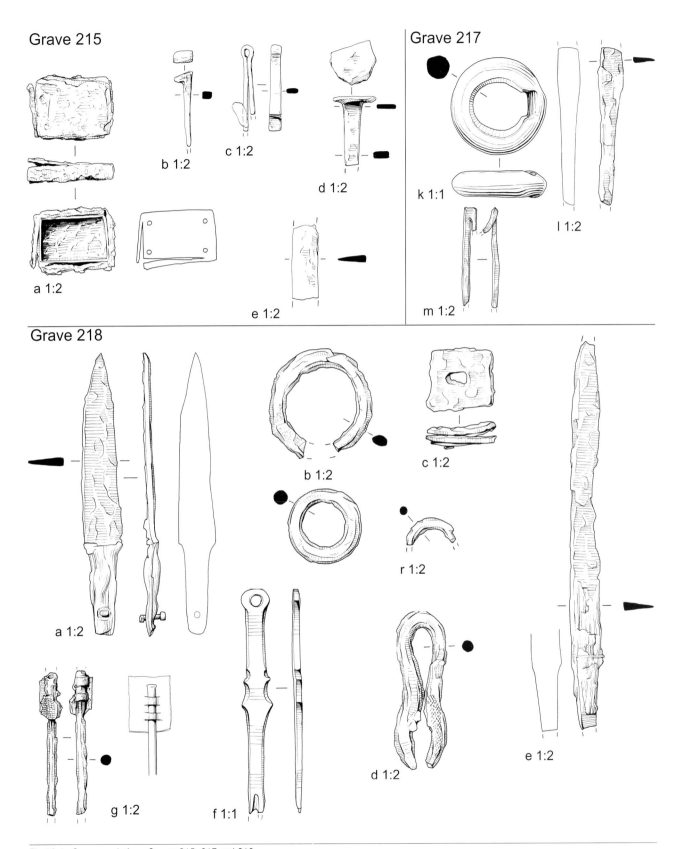

Fig 10.4. Grave goods from Graves 215, 217 and 218.

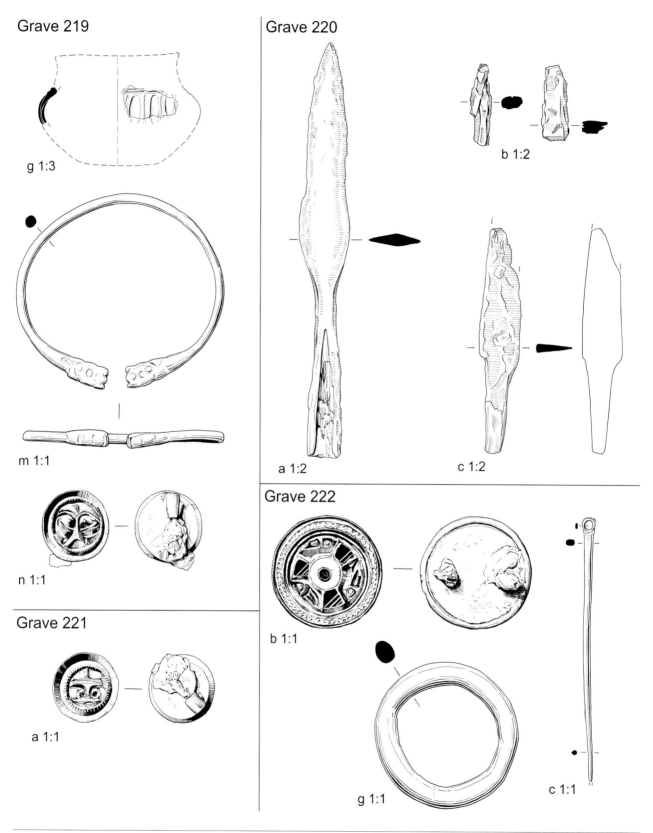

Grave 219

g 1:3

m 1:1

n 1:1

Grave 221

a 1:1

Grave 220

b 1:2

a 1:2

c 1:2

Grave 222

b 1:1

g 1:1

c 1:1

Fig 10.5. Grave goods from Graves 219, 220, 221 and 222.

Grave 222

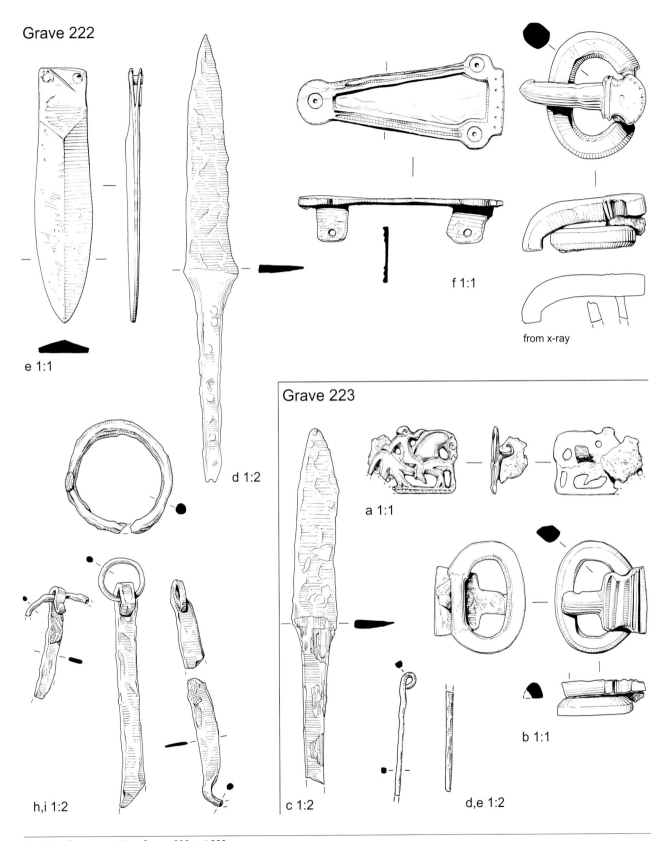

e 1:1

d 1:2

f 1:1

from x-ray

h,i 1:2

Grave 223

a 1:1

b 1:1

c 1:2

d,e 1:2

Fig 10.6. Grave goods from Graves 222 and 223.

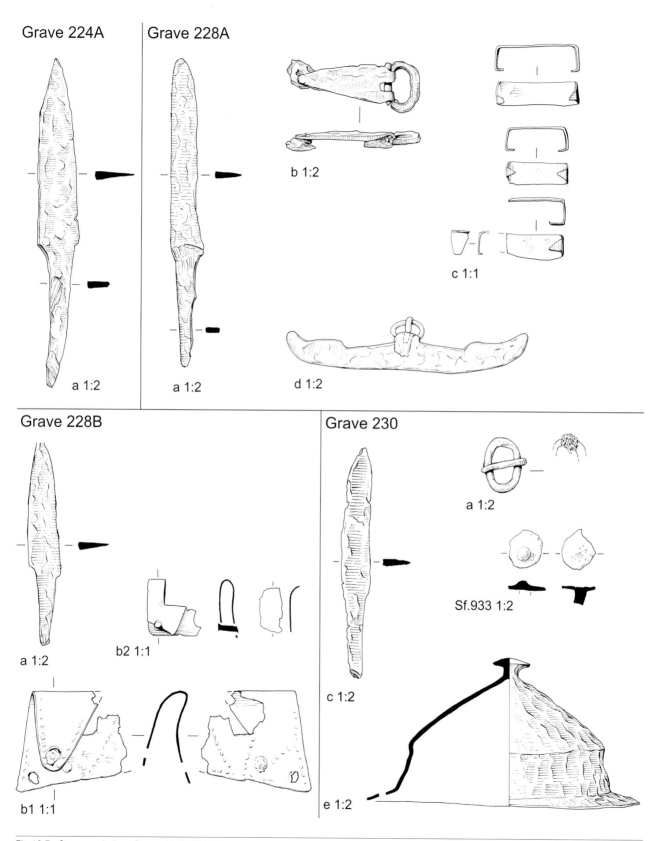

Grave 224A

a 1:2

Grave 228A

a 1:2

b 1:2

c 1:1

d 1:2

Grave 228B

a 1:2

b2 1:1

b1 1:1

Grave 230

a 1:2

Sf.933 1:2

c 1:2

e 1:2

Fig 10.7. Grave goods from Graves 224A, 228A, 228B and 230.

Grave 230

Grave 232

a 1:1　　　　　　c 1:2 from x-ray

Grave 233

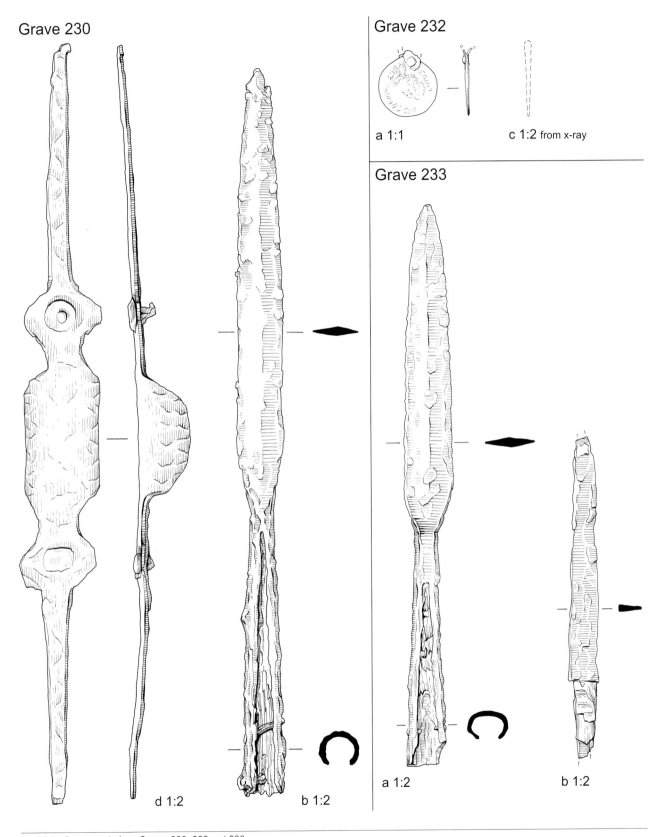

d 1:2　　　b 1:2　　　a 1:2　　　b 1:2

Fig 10.8. Grave goods from Graves 230, 232 and 233.

Grave 231

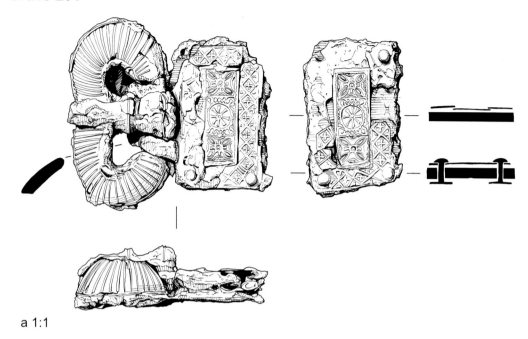

a 1:1

Grave 234

a 1:3

Grave 237

a 1:1

b 1:1

c 1:1

Grave 238

1:1

a 1:3

b 1:1

c 1:1

Fig 10.9. Grave goods from Graves 231, 234, 237 and 238.

Grave 239

a 1:2

b 1:1

c 1:1

d 1:1

e 1:1

f 1:1

Grave 240

a 1:2

b 1:2

c 1:2

d 1:2

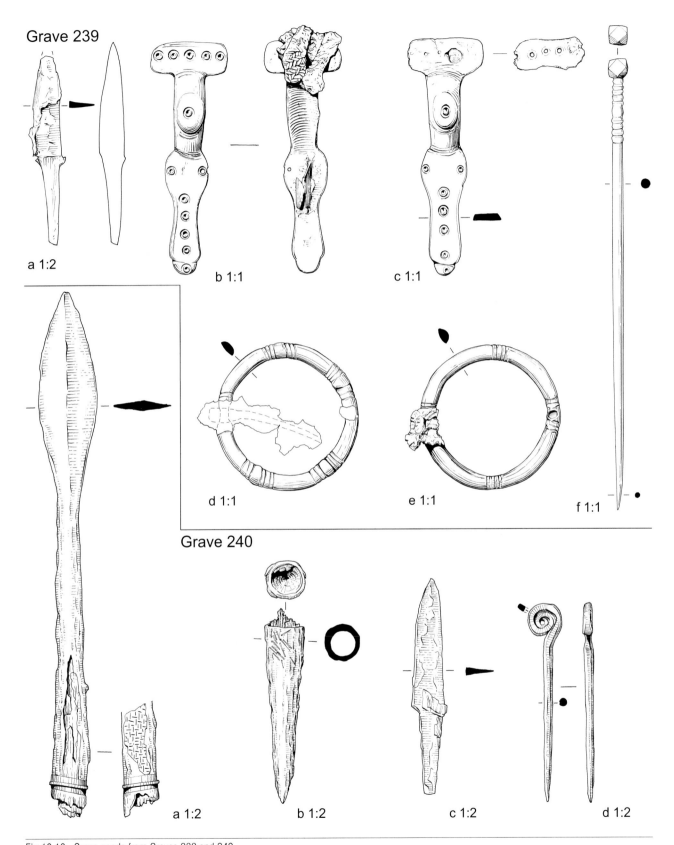

Fig 10.10. Grave goods from Graves 239 and 240.

Grave 245

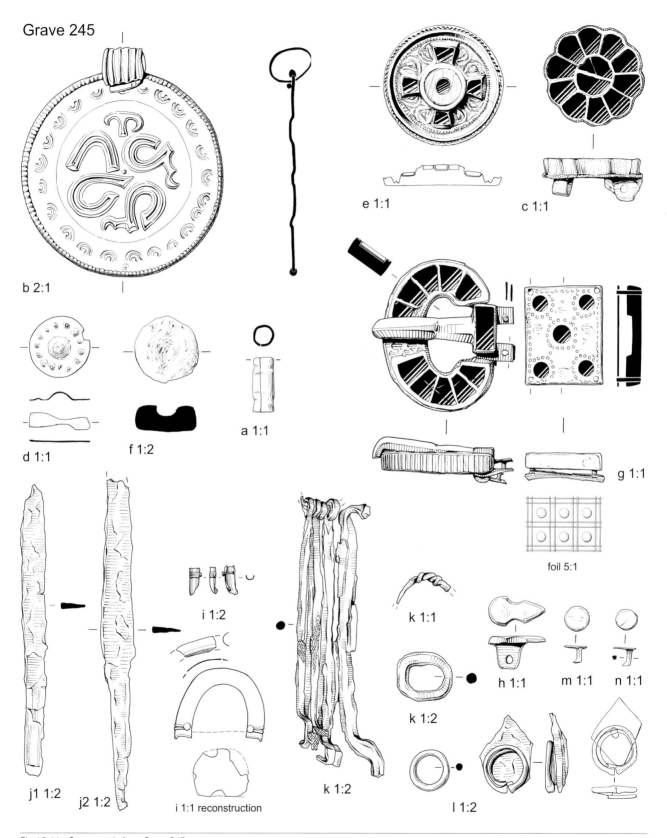

b 2:1

e 1:1

c 1:1

a 1:1

d 1:1

f 1:2

g 1:1

foil 5:1

j1 1:2   j2 1:2

i 1:2

i 1:1 reconstruction

k 1:1

k 1:2

k 1:2

h 1:1   m 1:1   n 1:1

l 1:2

Fig 10.11. Grave goods from Grave 245.

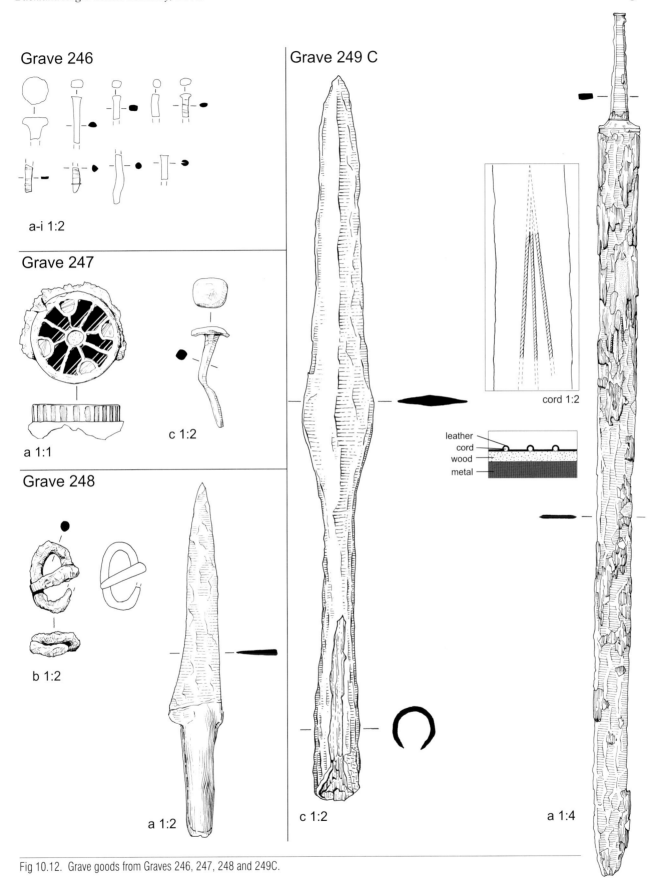

Grave 246

a-i 1:2

Grave 247

a 1:1

c 1:2

Grave 248

b 1:2

a 1:2

Grave 249 C

cord 1:2

leather
cord
wood
metal

c 1:2

a 1:4

Fig 10.12. Grave goods from Graves 246, 247, 248 and 249C.

Grave 249C

b 1:1

d 1:2

e 1:2

f 1:1

g 1:1

Grave 250

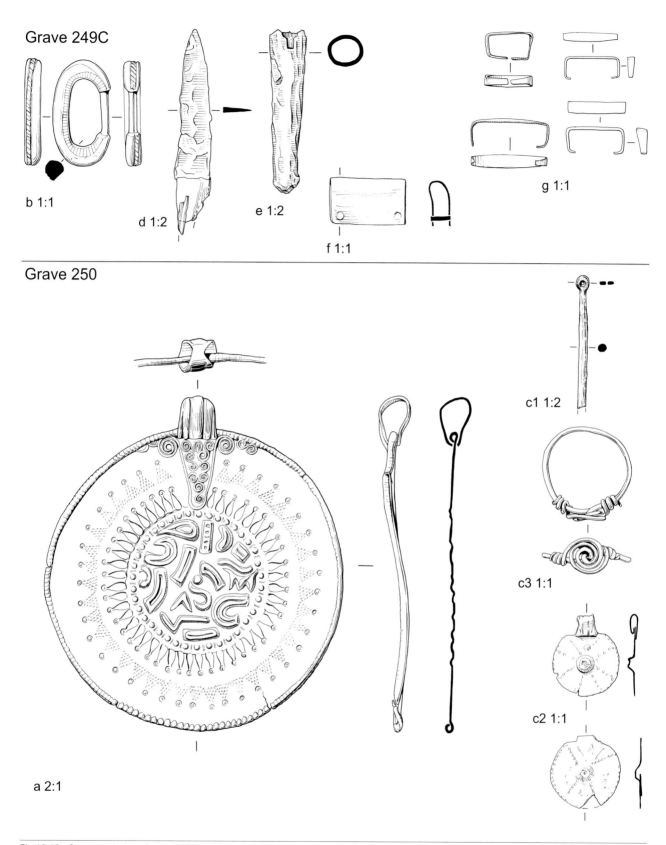

a 2:1

c1 1:2

c3 1:1

c2 1:1

Fig 10.13. Grave goods from Graves 249C and 250.

Grave 250

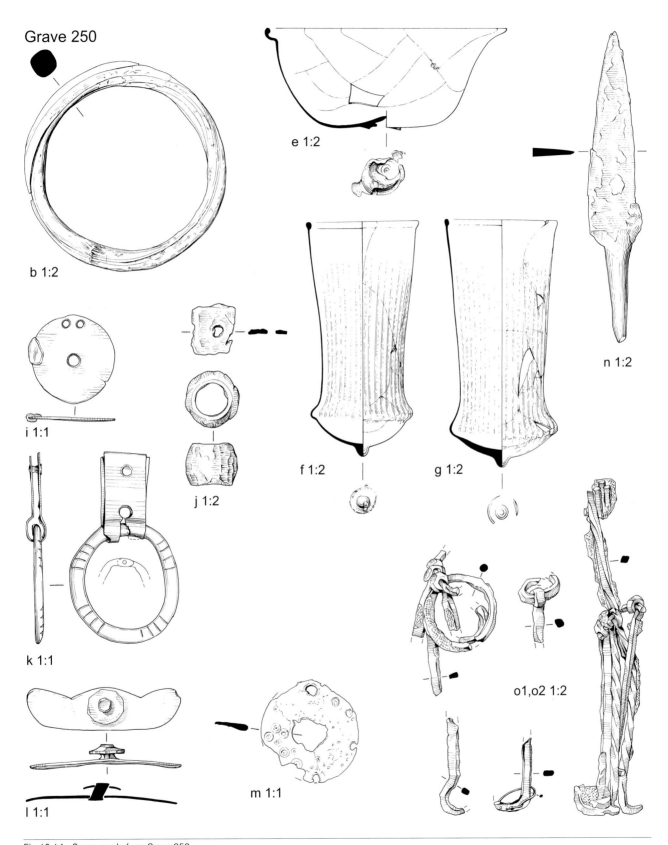

b 1:2

e 1:2

i 1:1

j 1:2

f 1:2

g 1:2

n 1:2

k 1:1

o1,o2 1:2

l 1:1

m 1:1

Fig 10.14. Grave goods from Grave 250.

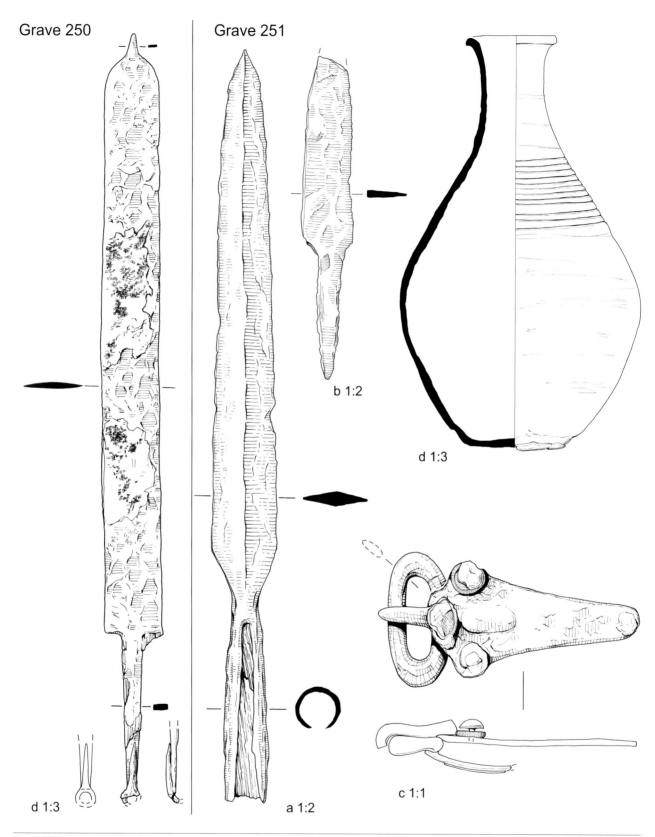

Fig 10.15. Grave goods from Graves 250 and 251.

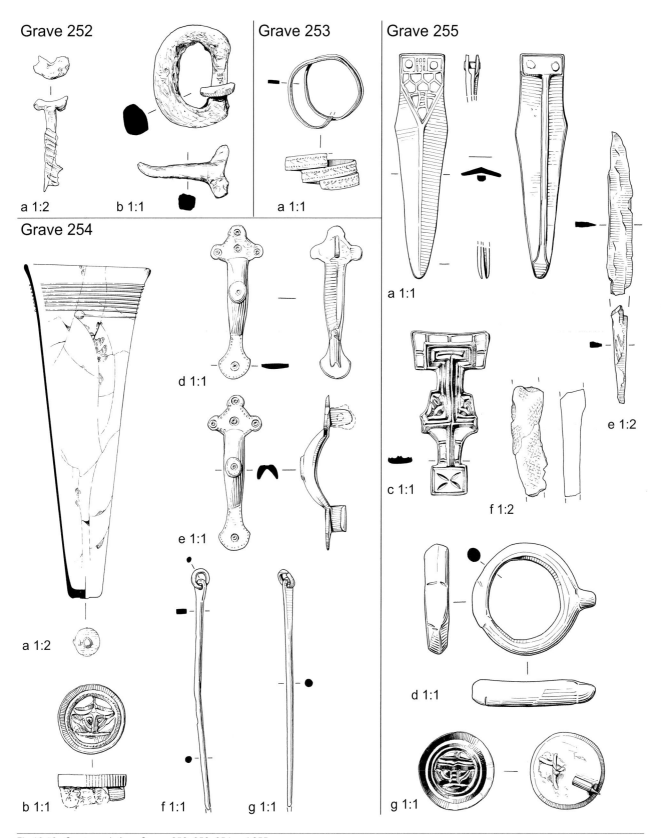

Grave 252

a 1:2   b 1:1

Grave 253

a 1:1

Grave 254

a 1:2   b 1:1   d 1:1   e 1:1   f 1:1   g 1:1

Grave 255

a 1:1   c 1:1   e 1:2   f 1:2   d 1:1   g 1:1

Fig 10.16. Grave goods from Graves 252, 253, 254 and 255.

Grave 255

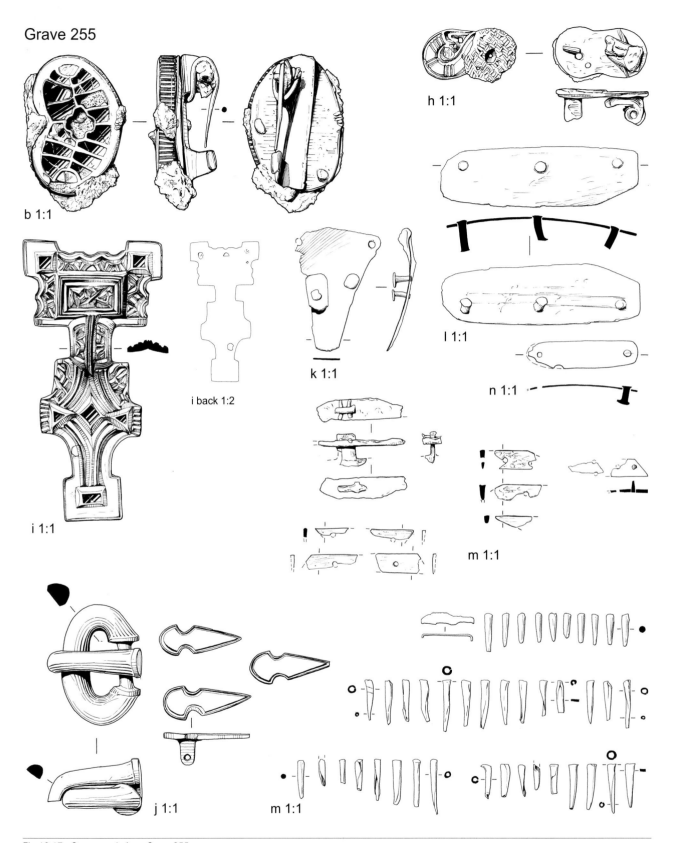

Fig 10.17. Grave goods from Grave 255.

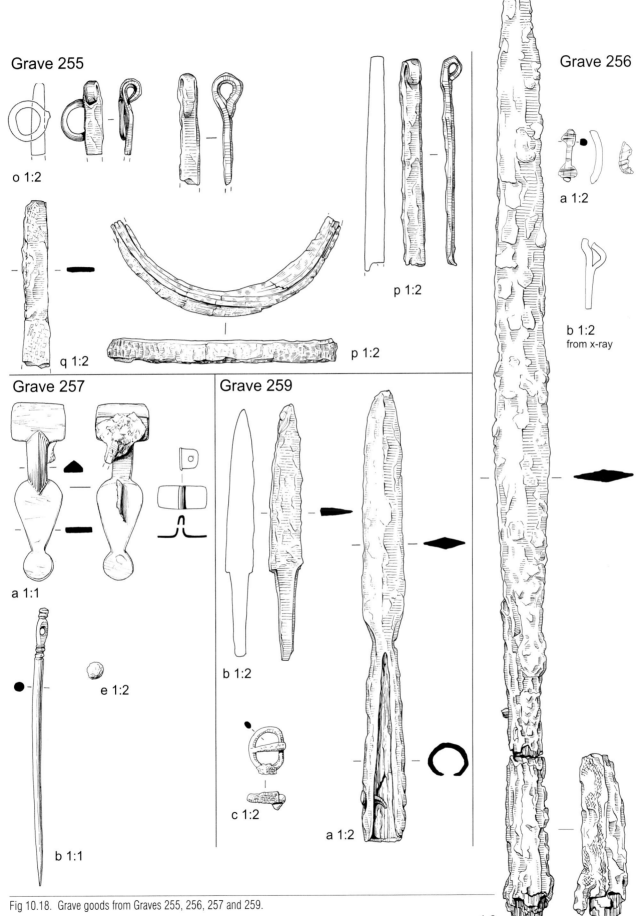

Grave 255

o 1:2

q 1:2

p 1:2

p 1:2

Grave 256

a 1:2

b 1:2
from x-ray

Grave 257

a 1:1

b 1:1

e 1:2

Grave 259

b 1:2

c 1:2

a 1:2

c 1:2

Fig 10.18. Grave goods from Graves 255, 256, 257 and 259.

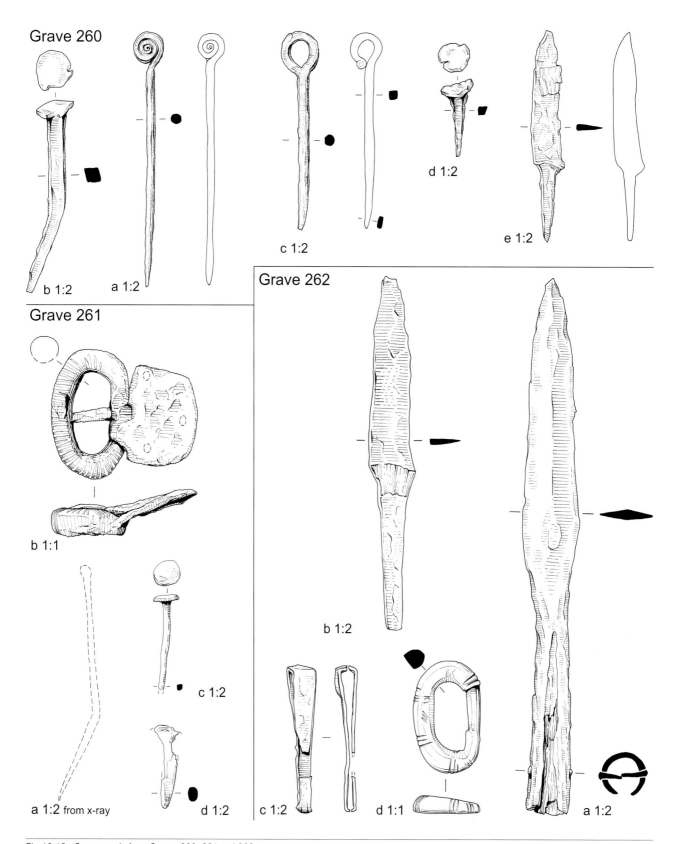

Grave 260

b 1:2   a 1:2   c 1:2   d 1:2   e 1:2

Grave 261

b 1:1

a 1:2 from x-ray   c 1:2   d 1:2

Grave 262

b 1:2   c 1:2   d 1:1   a 1:2

Fig 10.19. Grave goods from Graves 260, 261 and 262.

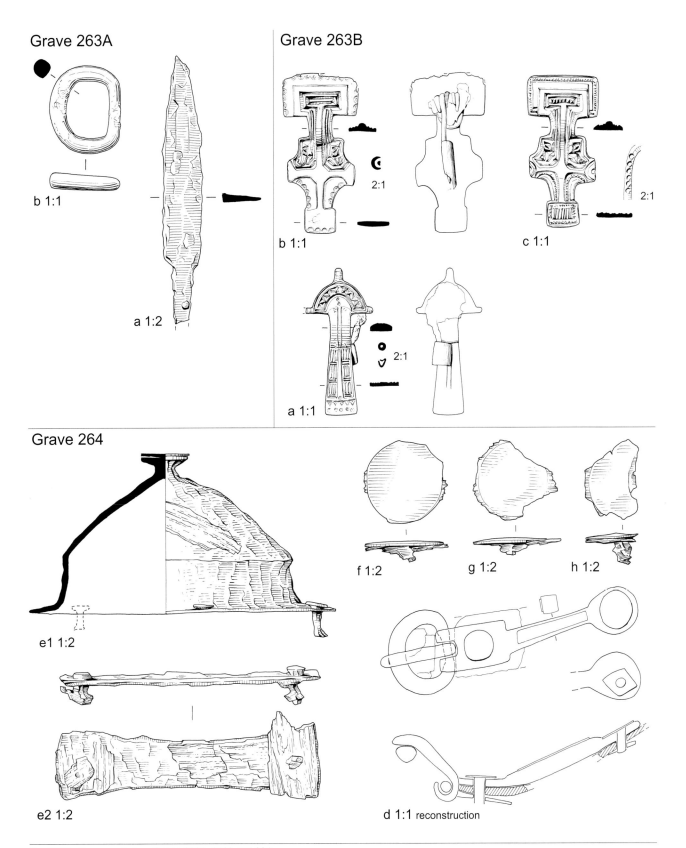

Grave 263A

b 1:1

a 1:2

Grave 263B

b 1:1

c 1:1

2:1

2:1

a 1:1

2:1

Grave 264

e1 1:2

e2 1:2

f 1:2

g 1:2

h 1:2

d 1:1 reconstruction

Fig 10.20. Grave goods from Graves 263A, 263B and 264.

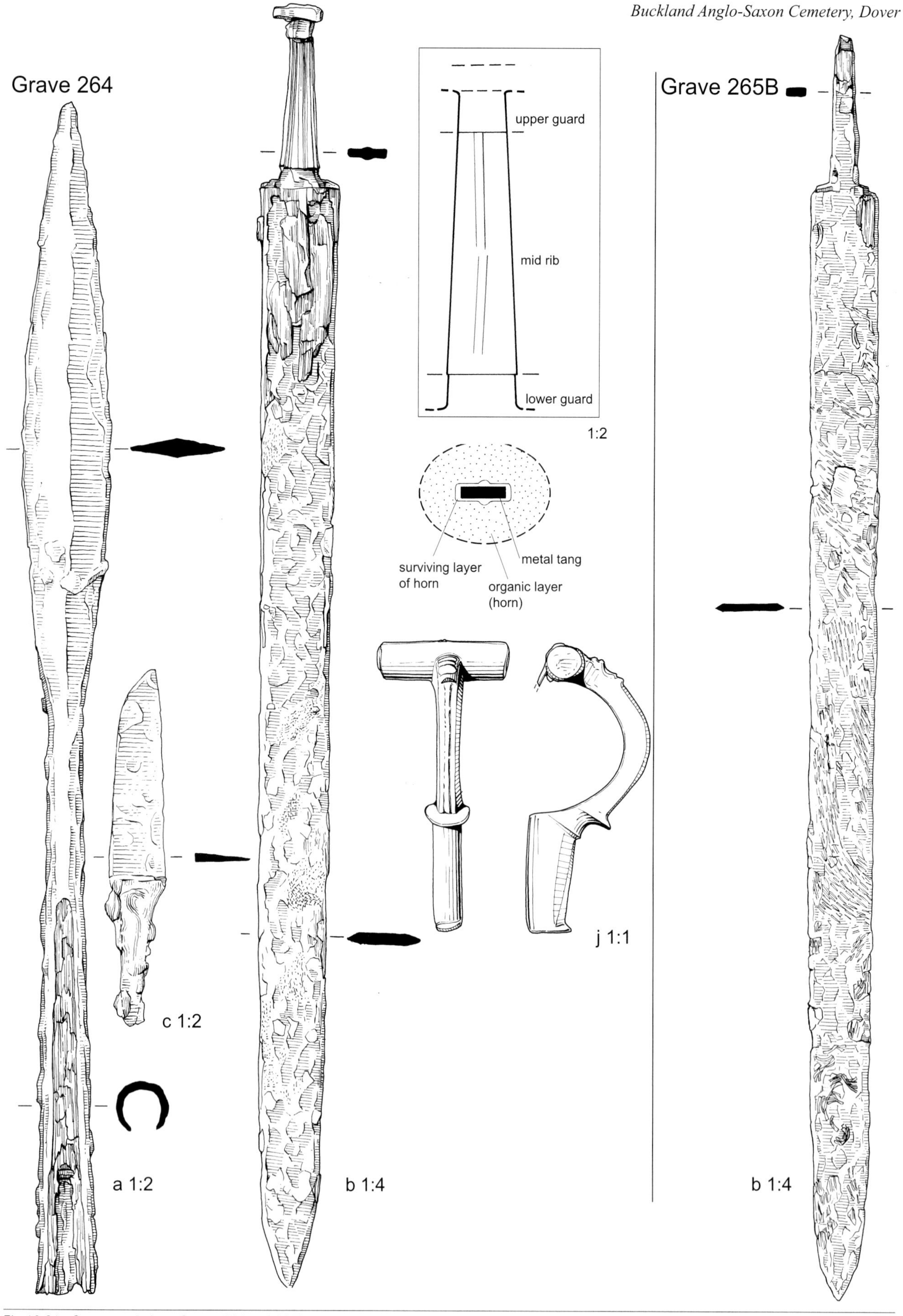

Grave 264

Grave 265B

upper guard

mid rib

lower guard

1:2

surviving layer
of horn

metal tang

organic layer
(horn)

j 1:1

c 1:2

a 1:2

b 1:4

b 1:4

Fig 10.21. Grave goods from Graves 264 and 265B.

Grave 265B

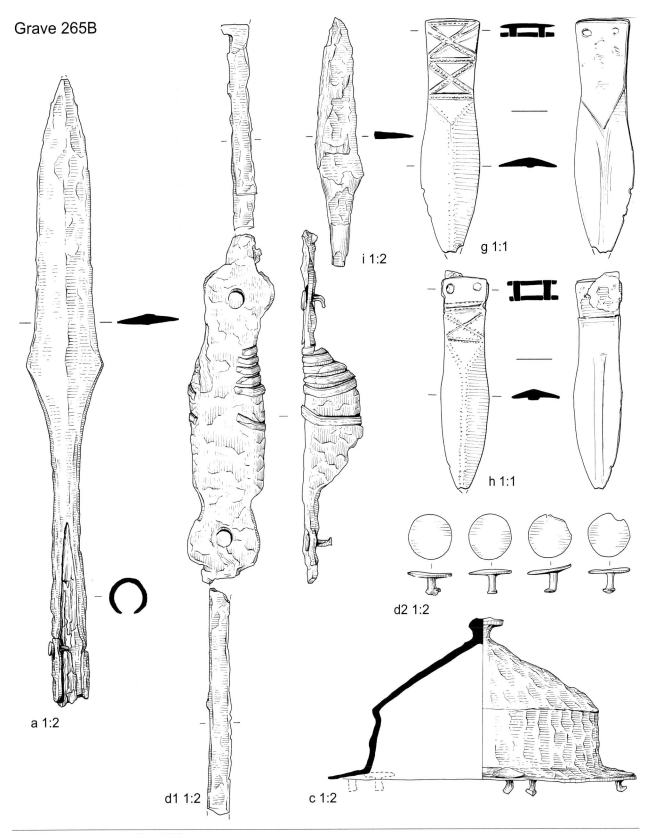

a 1:2

d1 1:2

c 1:2

i 1:2

g 1:1

h 1:1

d2 1:2

Fig 10.22. Grave goods from Grave 265B.

Grave 265B

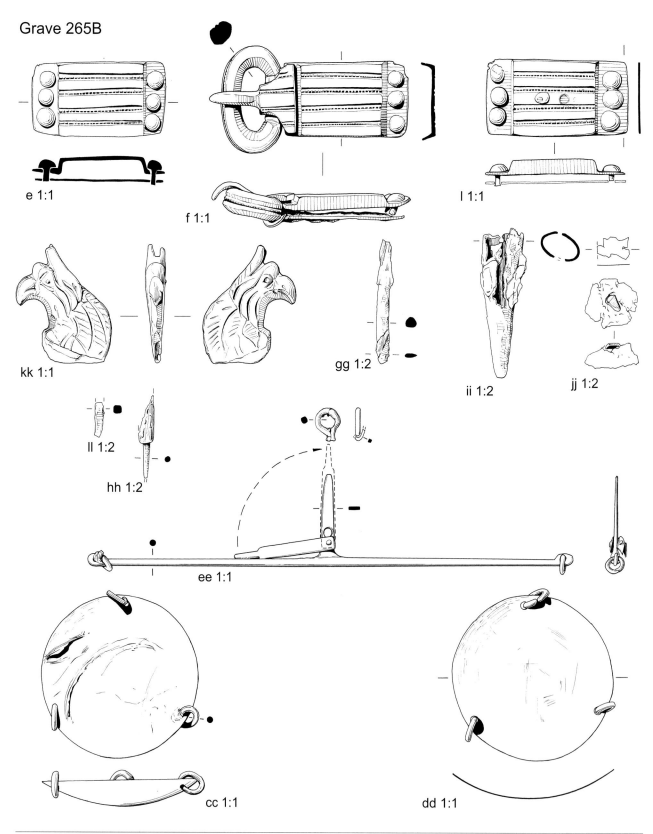

e 1:1

f 1:1

l 1:1

kk 1:1

gg 1:2

ii 1:2

jj 1:2

ll 1:2

hh 1:2

ee 1:1

cc 1:1

dd 1:1

Fig 10.23. Grave goods from Grave 265B.

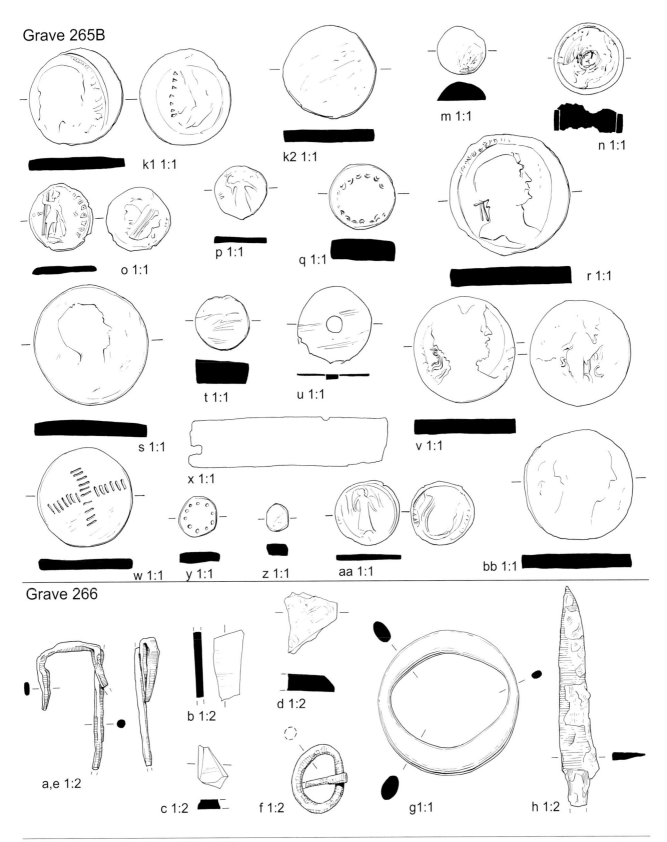

Fig 10.24. Grave goods from Graves 265B and 266.

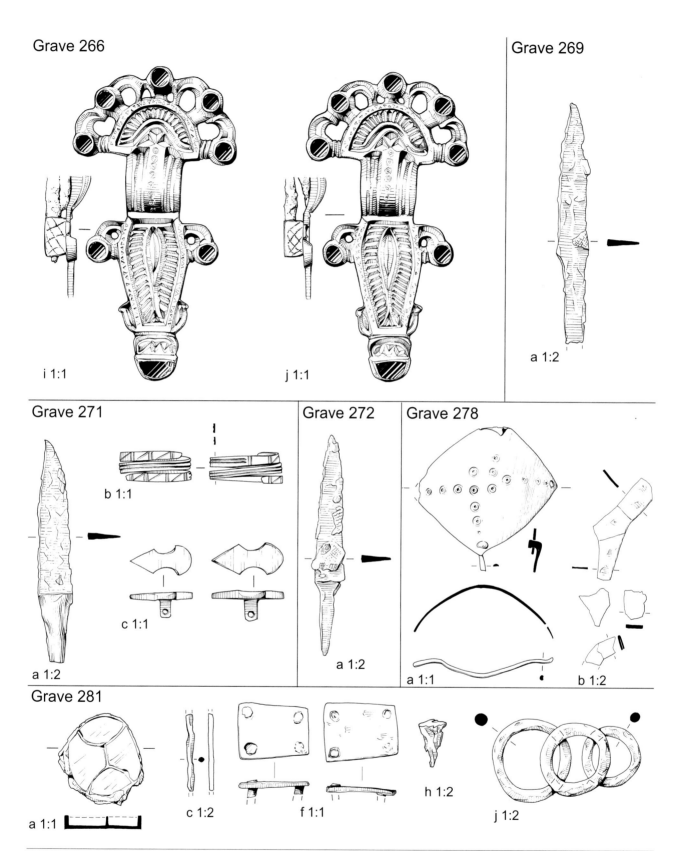

Fig 10.25. Grave goods from Graves 266, 269, 271, 272, 278 and 281.

Grave 281

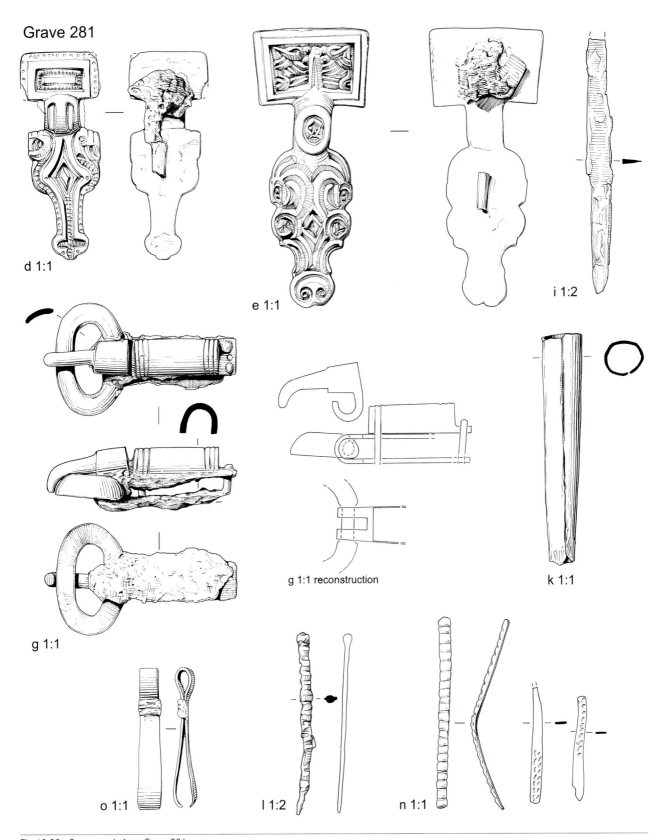

d 1:1

e 1:1

i 1:2

g 1:1 reconstruction

k 1:1

g 1:1

o 1:1

l 1:2

n 1:1

Fig 10.26. Grave goods from Grave 281.

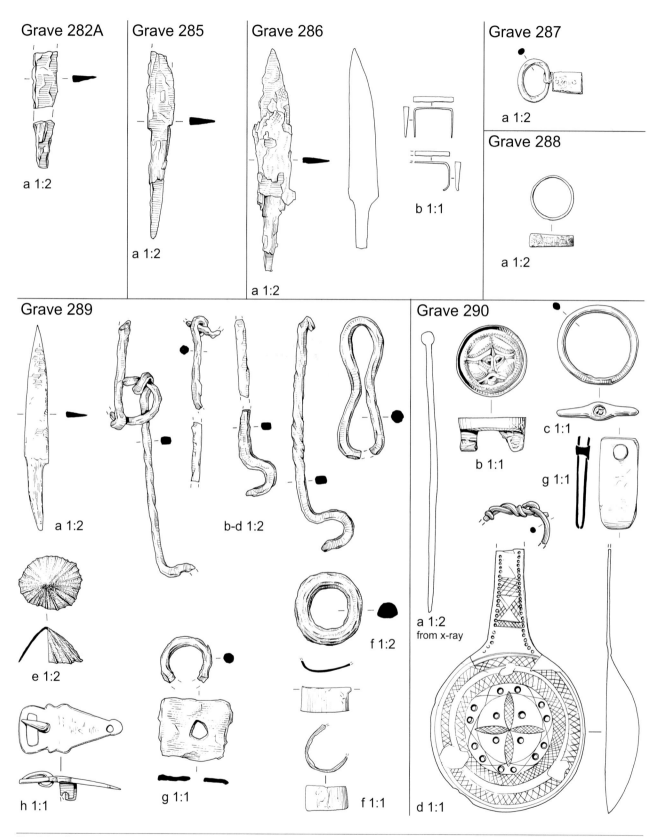

Fig 10.27. Grave goods from Graves 282A, 285, 286, 287, 288, 289 and 290.

Grave 292

a 1:1

Grave 293

a 1:2

b2 1:2

Grave 294

b 1:2

Grave 295

a 1:3

b 1:2

Grave 296

c 1:1

g 1:2

i 1:2

d 1:2

b 1:1

e 1:1

f 1:1

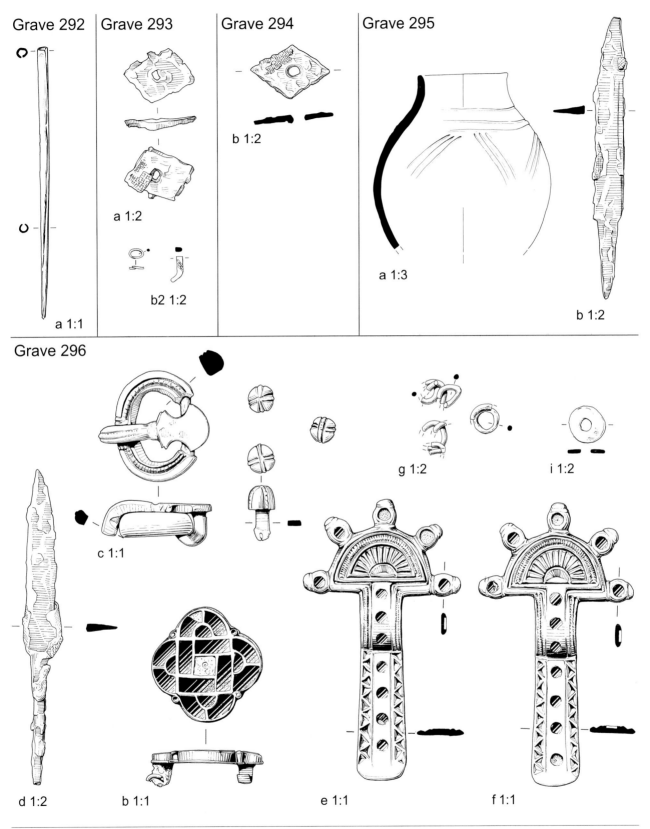

Fig 10.28. Grave goods from Graves 292, 293, 294, 295 and 296.

Grave 297

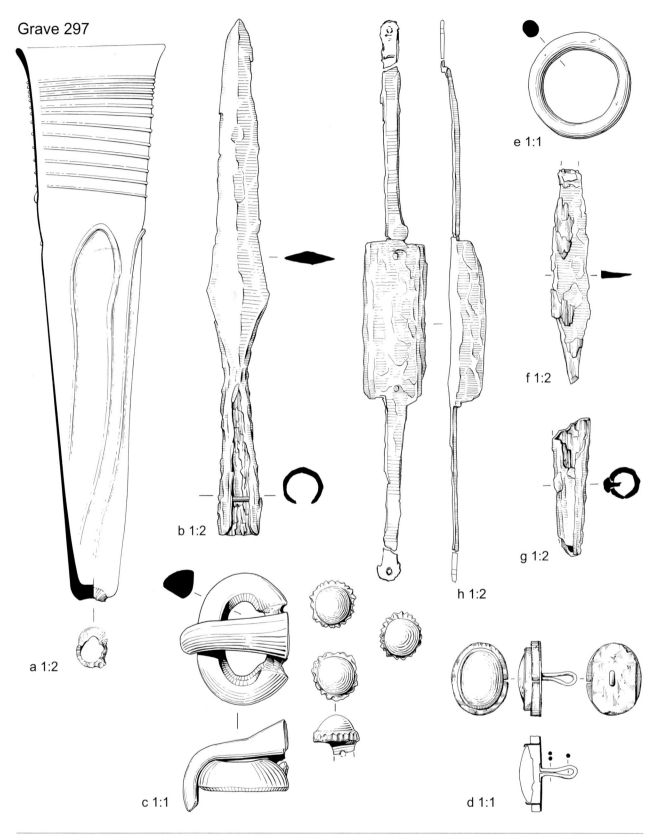

a 1:2

b 1:2

c 1:1

d 1:1

e 1:1

f 1:2

g 1:2

h 1:2

Fig 10.29. Grave goods from Grave 297.

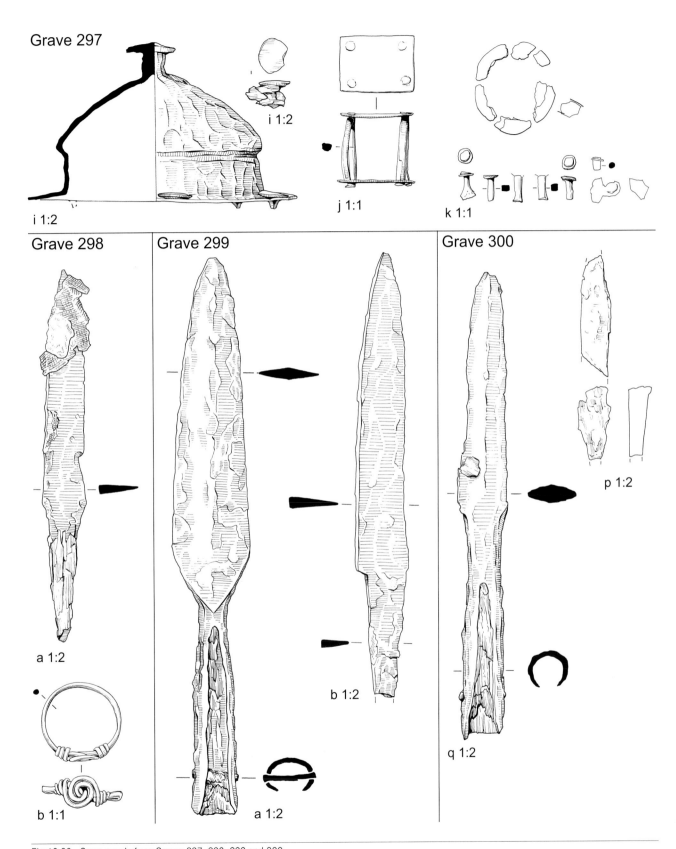

Grave 297

i 1:2

i 1:2

j 1:1

k 1:1

Grave 298

a 1:2

b 1:1

Grave 299

a 1:2

b 1:2

Grave 300

p 1:2

q 1:2

Fig 10.30. Grave goods from Graves 297, 298, 299 and 300.

Grave 300

Grave 301

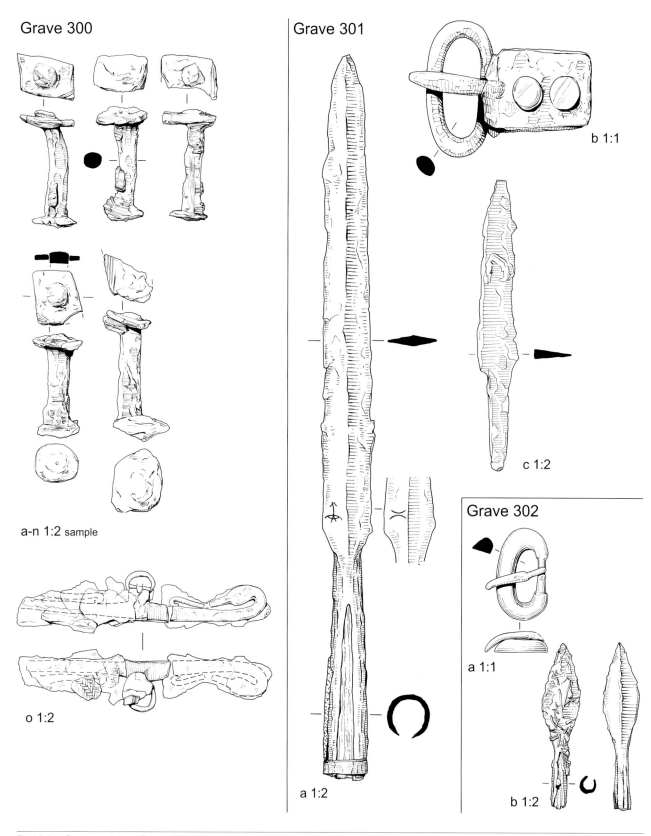

a-n 1:2 sample

o 1:2

b 1:1

c 1:2

Grave 302

a 1:1

b 1:2

a 1:2

Fig 10.31. Grave goods from Graves 300, 301 and 302.

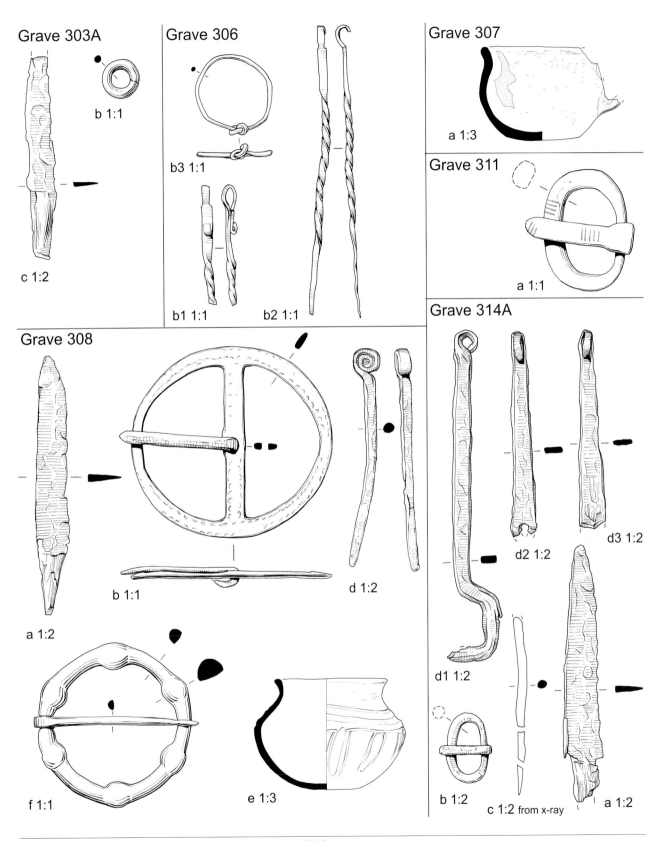

Fig 10.32. Grave goods from Graves 303A, 306, 307, 308, 311 and 314A.

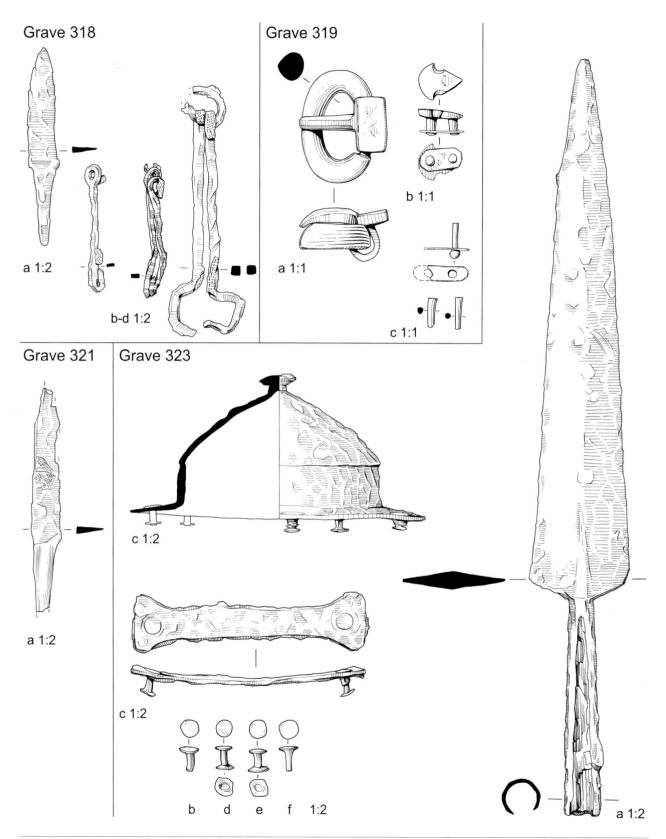

Grave 318

a 1:2

b-d 1:2

Grave 319

a 1:1

b 1:1

c 1:1

Grave 321

a 1:2

Grave 323

c 1:2

c 1:2

b   d   e   f   1:2

a 1:2

Fig 10.33. Grave goods from Graves 318, 319, 321 and 323.

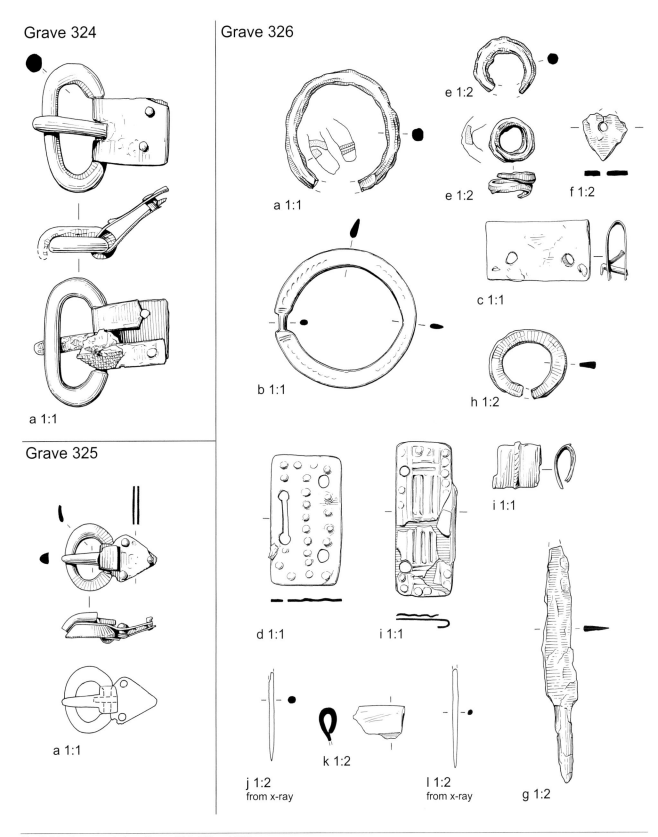

Fig 10.34. Grave goods from Graves 324, 325 and 326.

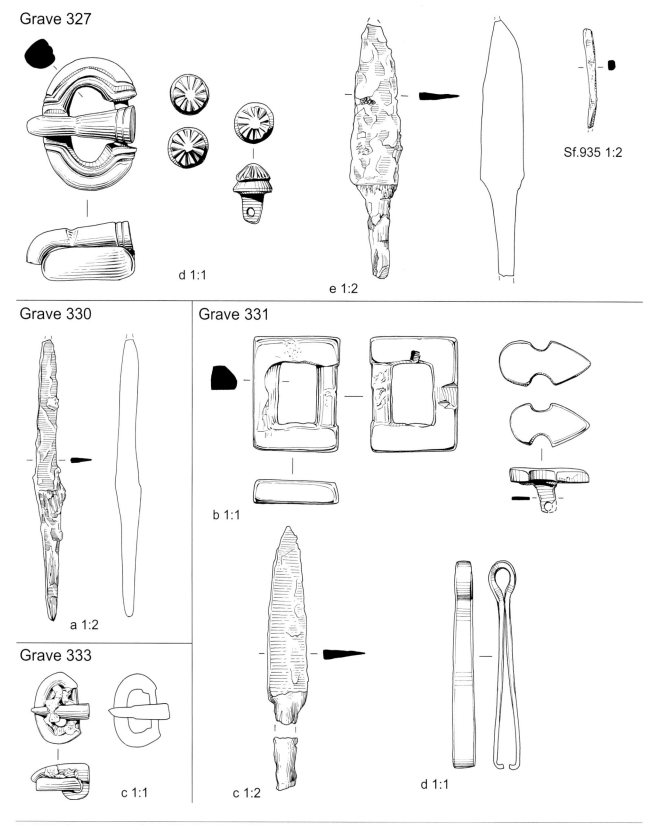

Fig 10.35. Grave goods from Graves 327, 330, 331 and 333.

Grave 334

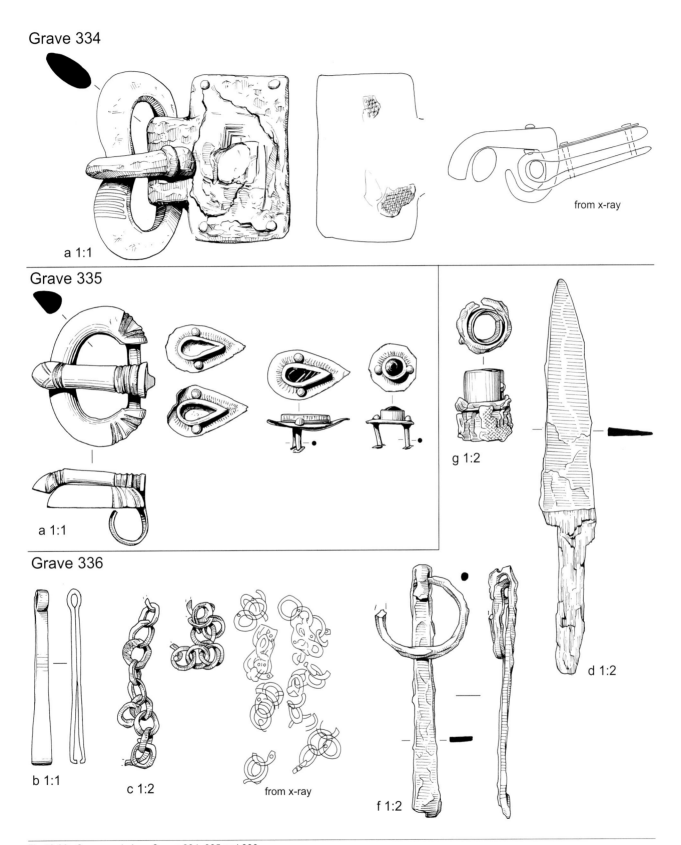

from x-ray

a 1:1

Grave 335

a 1:1

g 1:2

d 1:2

Grave 336

b 1:1

c 1:2

from x-ray

f 1:2

Fig 10.36. Grave goods from Graves 334, 335 and 336.

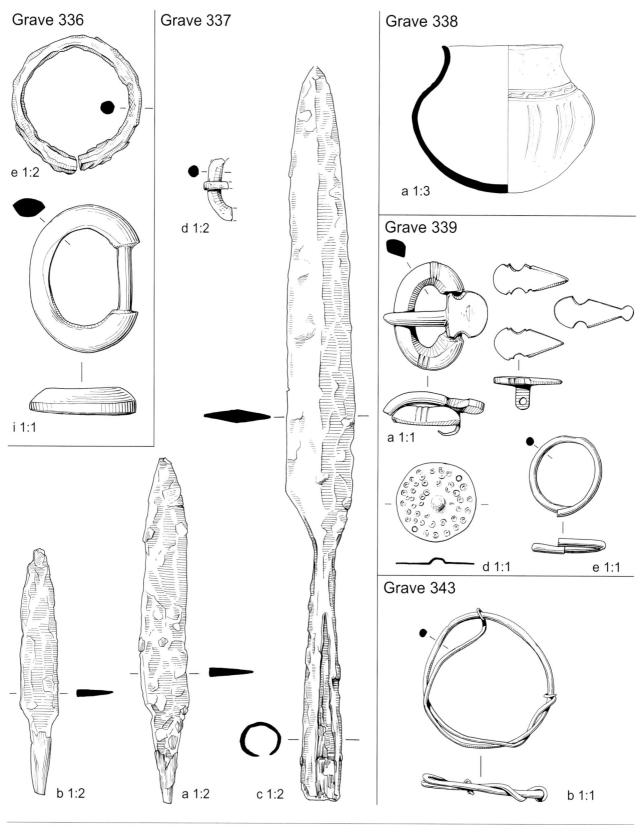

Fig 10.37. Grave goods from Graves 336, 337, 338, 339 and 343.

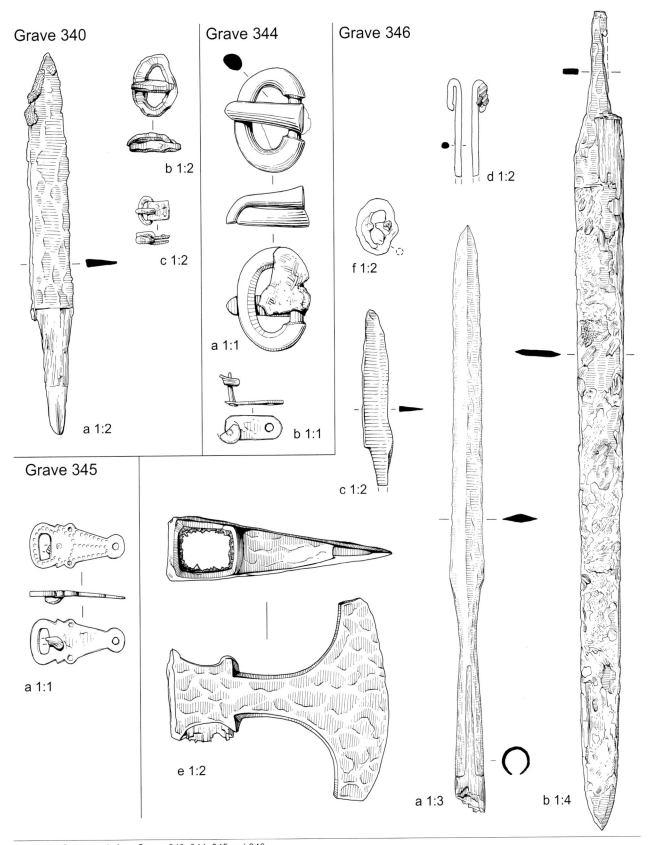

Grave 340

b 1:2

c 1:2

a 1:2

Grave 344

a 1:1

b 1:1

Grave 346

d 1:2

f 1:2

c 1:2

a 1:3

b 1:4

Grave 345

a 1:1

e 1:2

Fig 10.38. Grave goods from Graves 340, 344, 345 and 346.

Grave 347

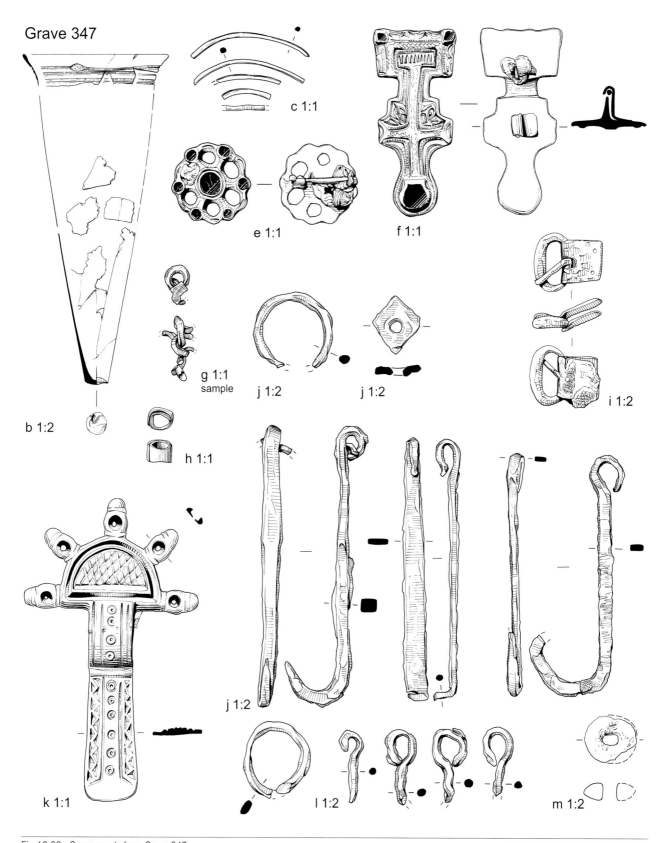

Fig 10.39. Grave goods from Grave 347.

Grave 348

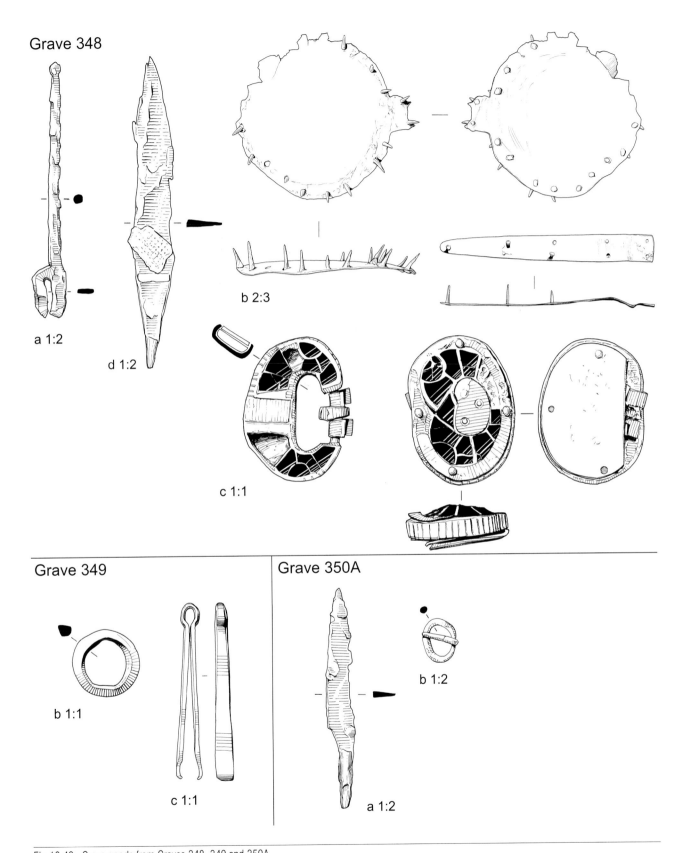

a 1:2

d 1:2

b 2:3

c 1:1

Grave 349

b 1:1

c 1:1

Grave 350A

a 1:2

b 1:2

Fig 10.40. Grave goods from Graves 348, 349 and 350A.

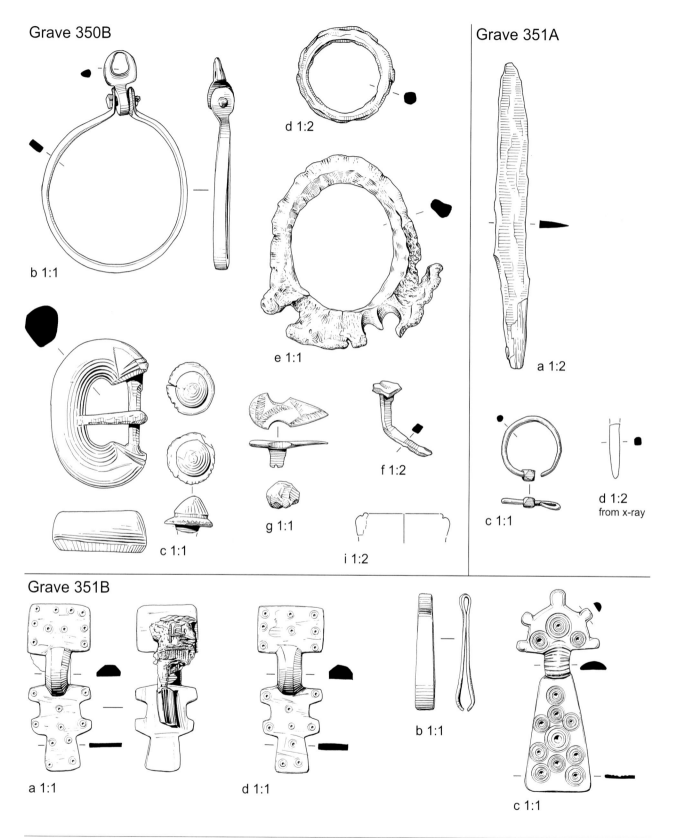

Fig 10.41. Grave goods from Graves 350B, 351A and 351B.

Grave 351B

Grave 353

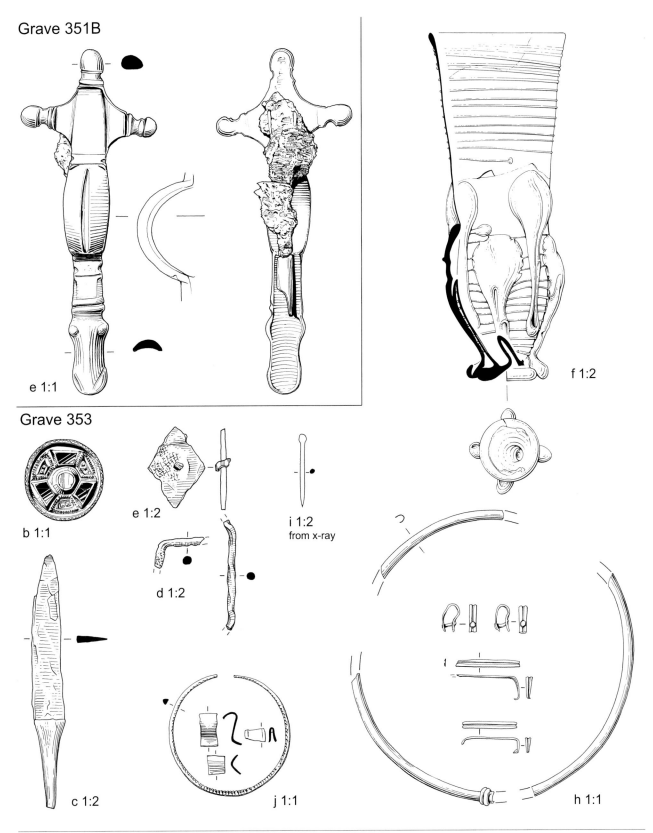

Fig 10.42. Grave goods from Graves 351B and 353.

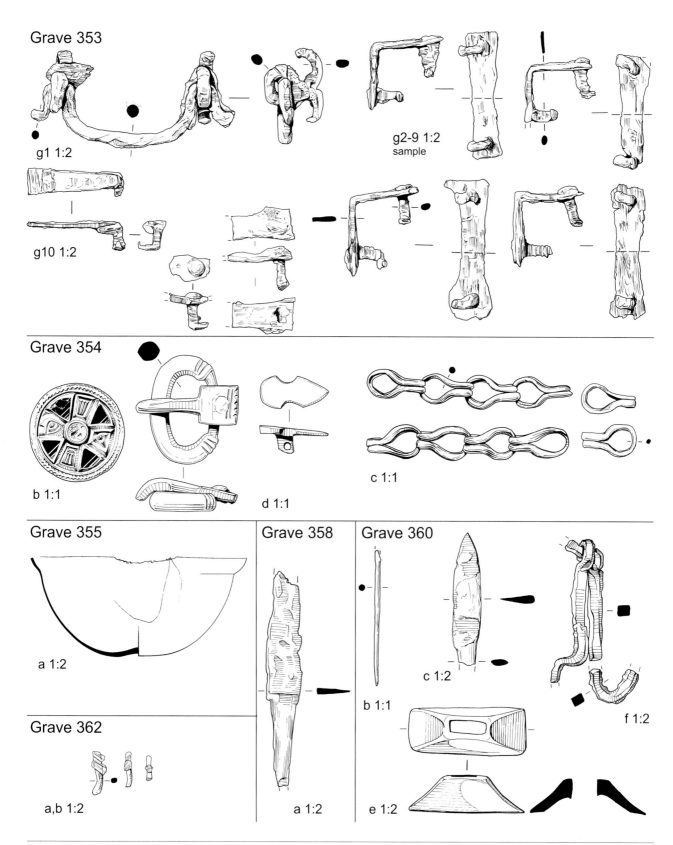

Grave 353

g1 1:2

g2-9 1:2
sample

g10 1:2

Grave 354

b 1:1

d 1:1

c 1:1

Grave 355

a 1:2

Grave 362

a,b 1:2

Grave 358

a 1:2

Grave 360

b 1:1

c 1:2

e 1:2

f 1:2

Fig 10.43. Grave goods from Graves 353, 354, 355, 358, 360 and 362.

Grave 363

Grave 367

Grave 366

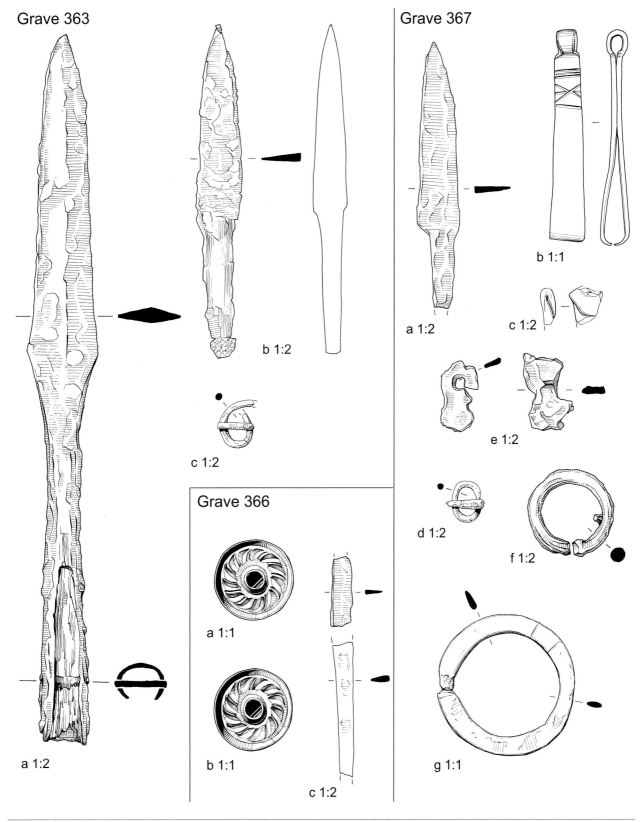

Fig 10.44. Grave goods from Graves 363, 366 and 367.

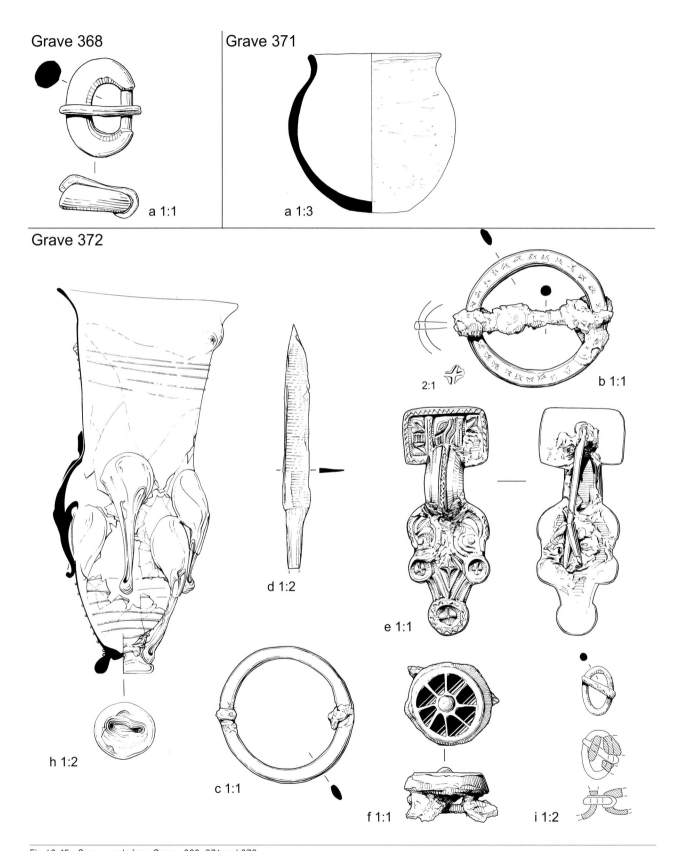

Grave 368

a 1:1

Grave 371

a 1:3

Grave 372

2:1

b 1:1

d 1:2

e 1:1

h 1:2

c 1:1

f 1:1

i 1:2

Fig 10.45. Grave goods from Graves 368, 371 and 372.

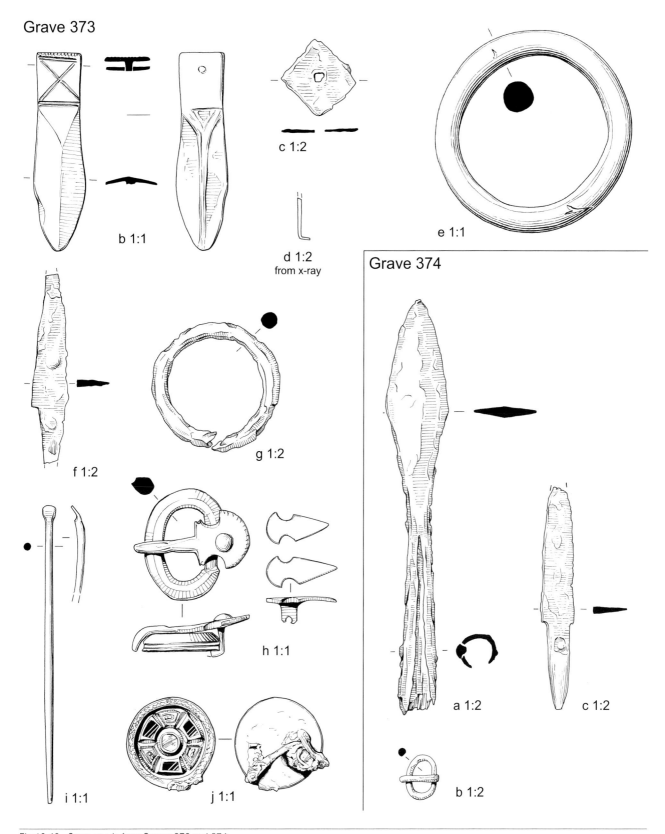

Fig 10.46. Grave goods from Graves 373 and 374.

Grave 375

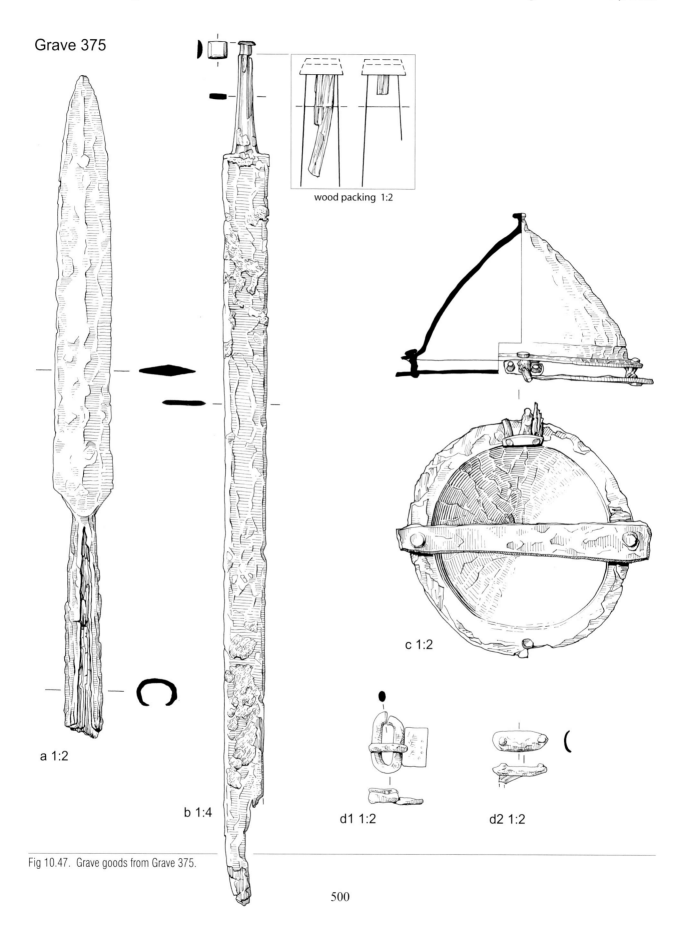

wood packing 1:2

a 1:2

b 1:4

c 1:2

d1 1:2

d2 1:2

Fig 10.47. Grave goods from Grave 375.

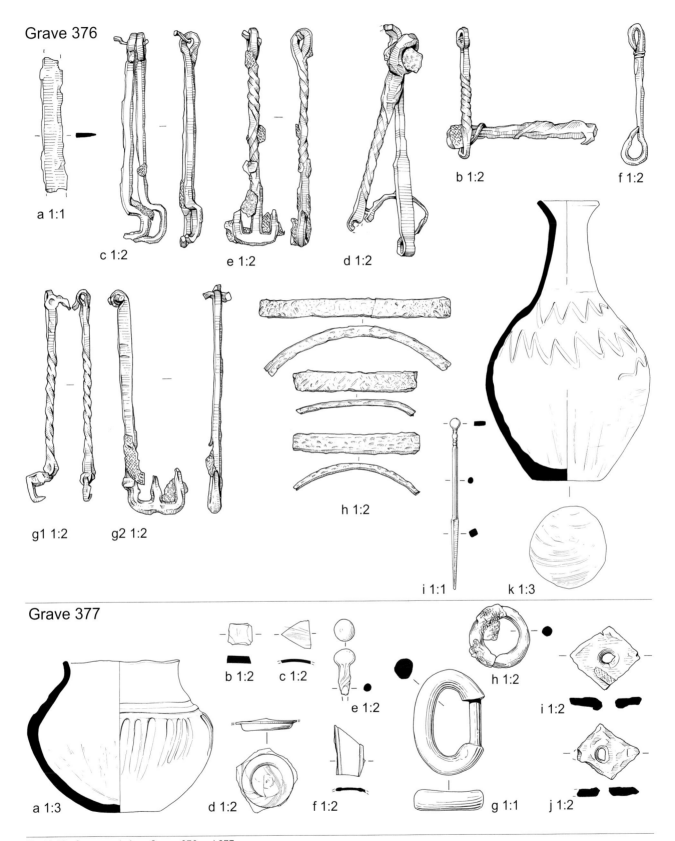

Grave 376

a 1:1

c 1:2

e 1:2

d 1:2

b 1:2

f 1:2

g1 1:2

g2 1:2

h 1:2

i 1:1

k 1:3

Grave 377

a 1:3

b 1:2

c 1:2

d 1:2

e 1:2

f 1:2

g 1:1

h 1:2

i 1:2

j 1:2

Fig 10.48. Grave goods from Graves 376 and 377.

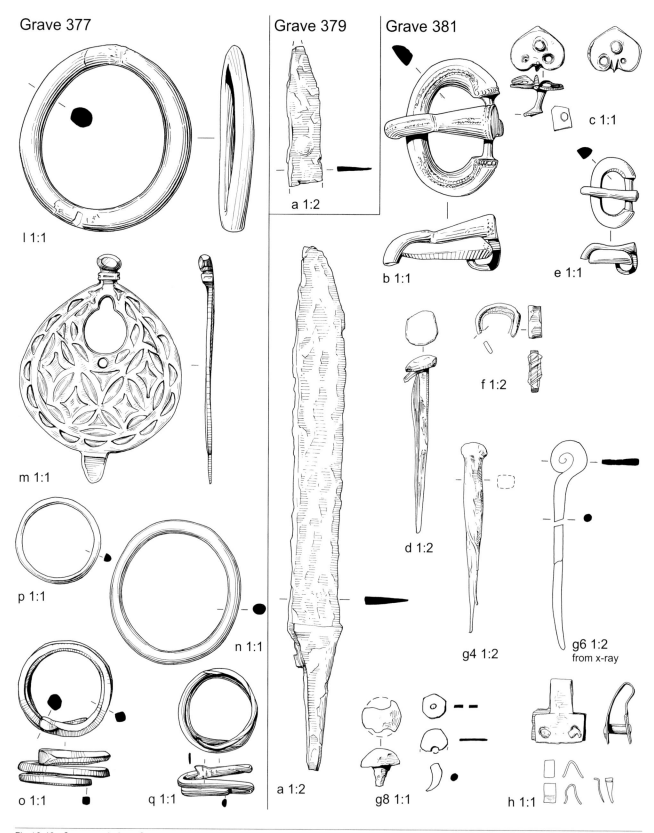

Fig 10.49. Grave goods from Graves 377, 379 and 381.

Grave 381

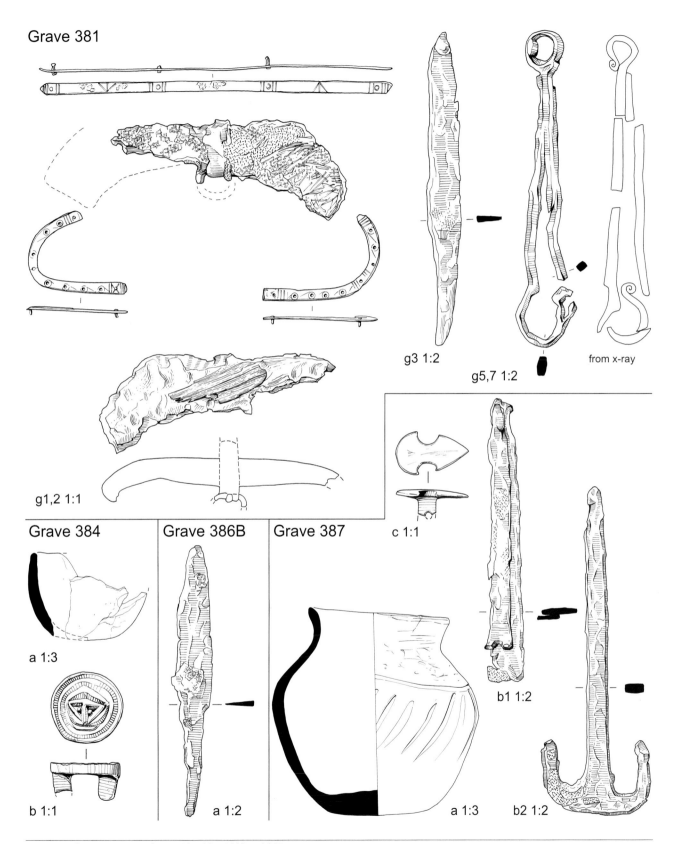

g3 1:2

g5,7 1:2

from x-ray

g1,2 1:1

c 1:1

b1 1:2

Grave 384

a 1:3

b 1:1

Grave 386B

a 1:2

Grave 387

a 1:3

b2 1:2

Fig 10.50. Grave goods from Graves 381, 384, 386B and 387.

Grave 388

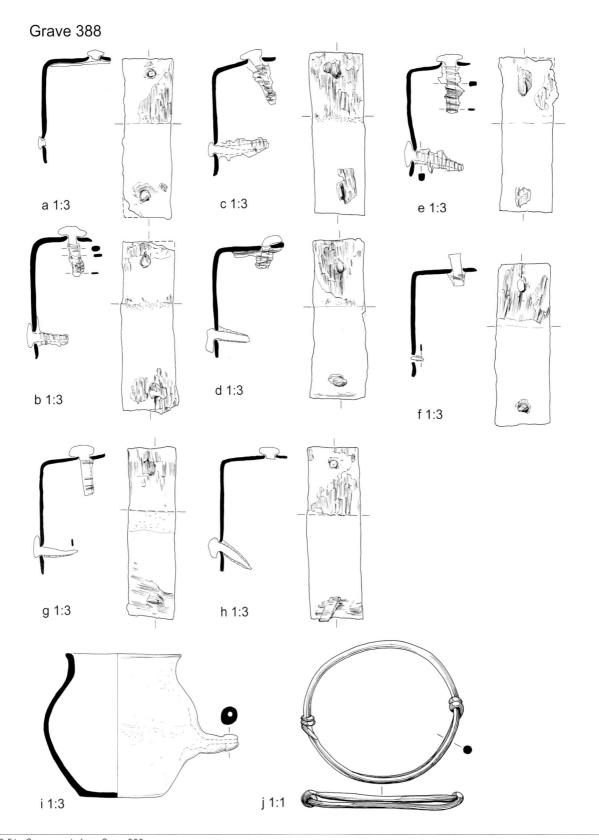

a 1:3

b 1:3

c 1:3

d 1:3

e 1:3

f 1:3

g 1:3

h 1:3

i 1:3

j 1:1

Fig 10.51. Grave goods from Grave 388.

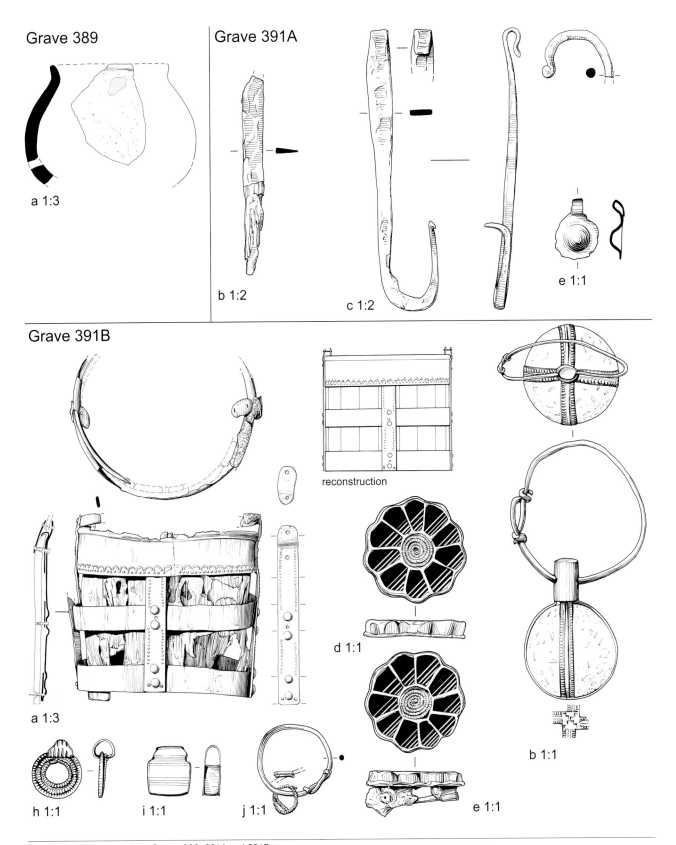

Grave 389

a 1:3

Grave 391A

b 1:2

c 1:2

e 1:1

Grave 391B

reconstruction

a 1:3

d 1:1

b 1:1

h 1:1

i 1:1

j 1:1

e 1:1

Fig 10.52. Grave goods from Graves 389, 391A and 391B.

Grave 391B

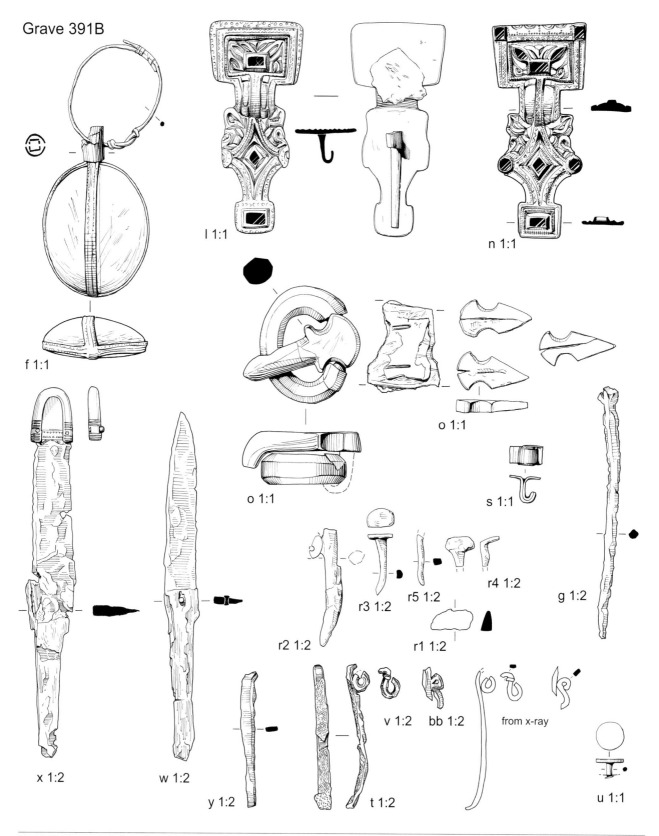

f 1:1

l 1:1

n 1:1

o 1:1

o 1:1

s 1:1

r2 1:2

r3 1:2

r5 1:2

r4 1:2

r1 1:2

g 1:2

x 1:2

w 1:2

y 1:2

t 1:2

v 1:2

bb 1:2

from x-ray

u 1:1

Fig 10.53. Grave goods from Grave 391B.

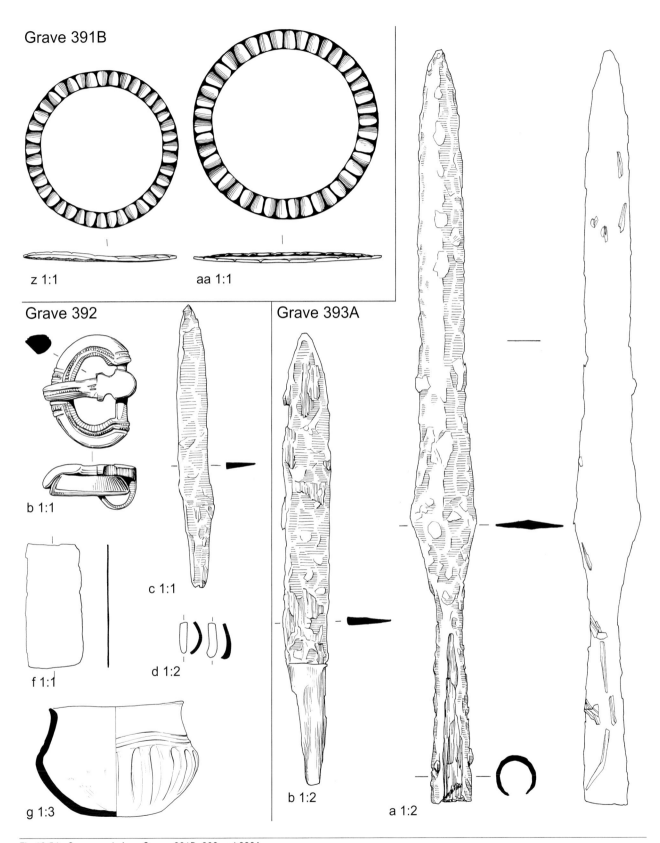

Fig 10.54. Grave goods from Graves 391B, 392 and 393A.

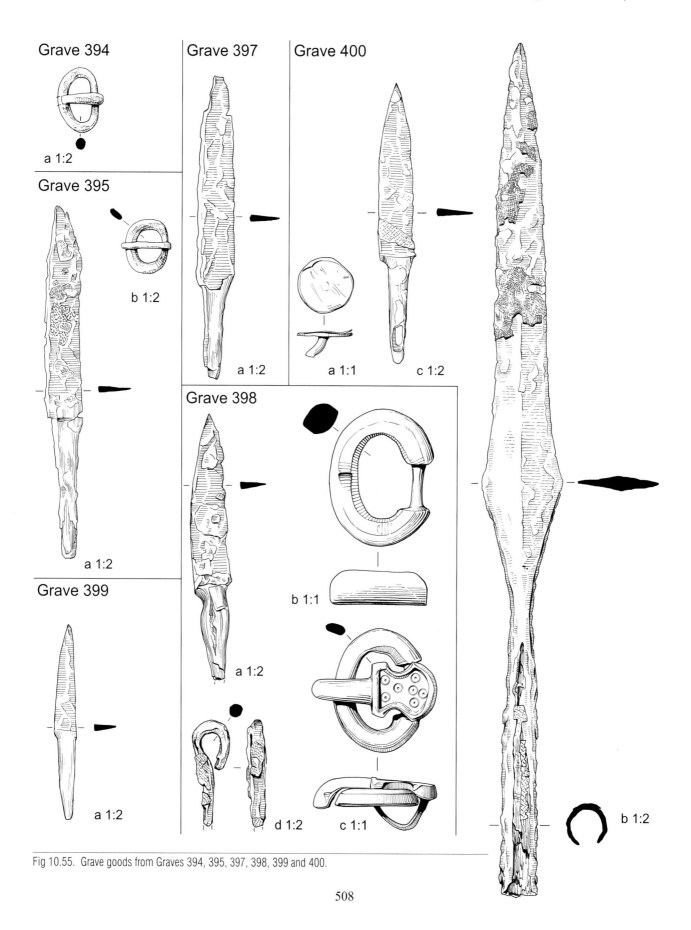

Fig 10.55. Grave goods from Graves 394, 395, 397, 398, 399 and 400.

Grave 405

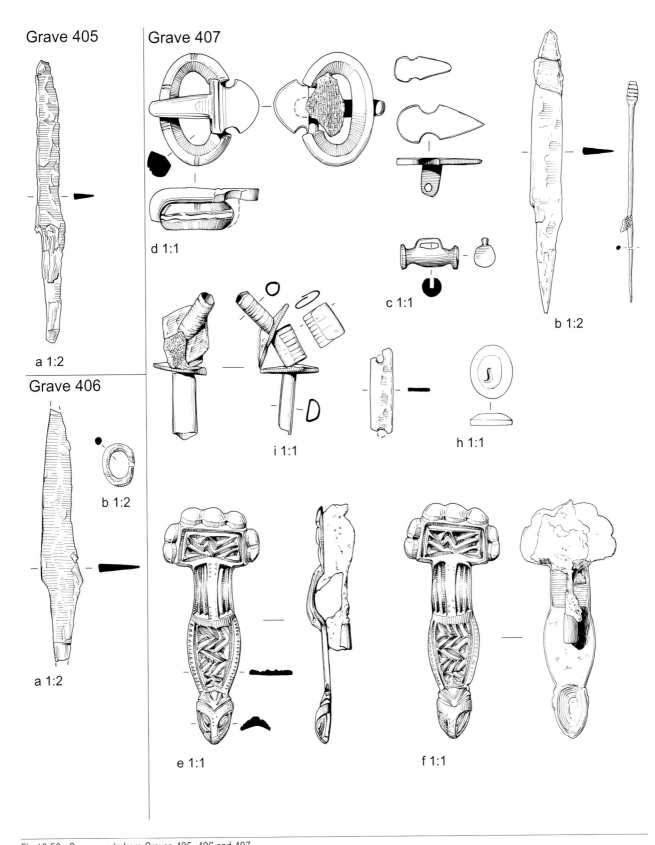

Grave 407

Grave 406

Fig 10.56. Grave goods from Graves 405, 406 and 407.

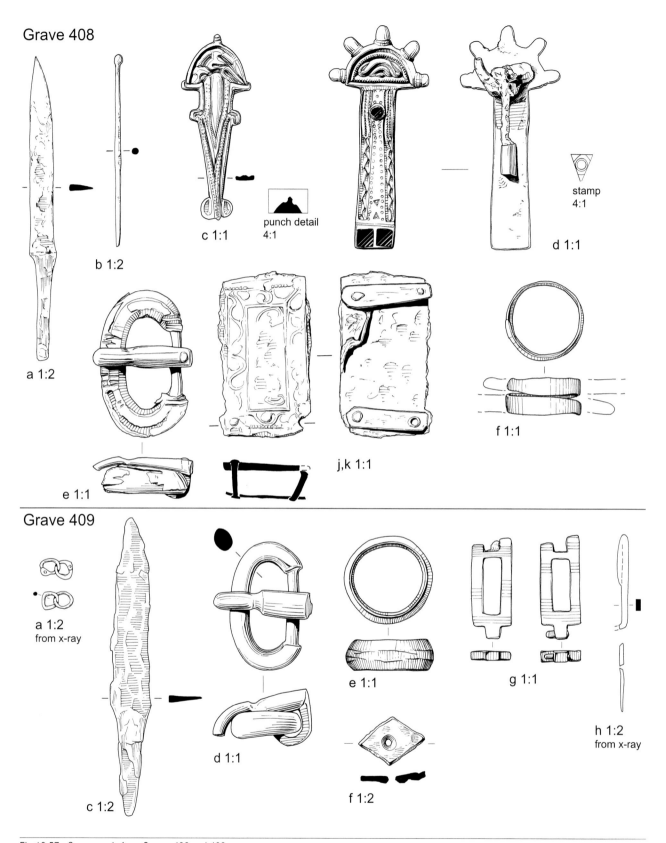

Fig 10.57. Grave goods from Graves 408 and 409.

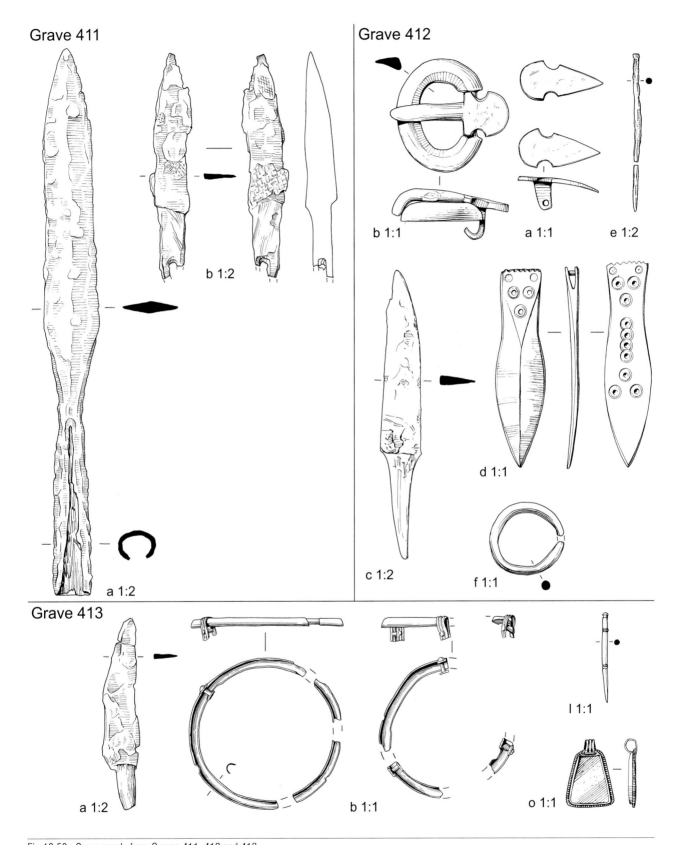

Grave 411

b 1:2

a 1:2

Grave 412

b 1:1

a 1:1

e 1:2

d 1:1

c 1:2

f 1:1

Grave 413

a 1:2

b 1:1

l 1:1

o 1:1

Fig 10.58. Grave goods from Graves 411, 412 and 413.

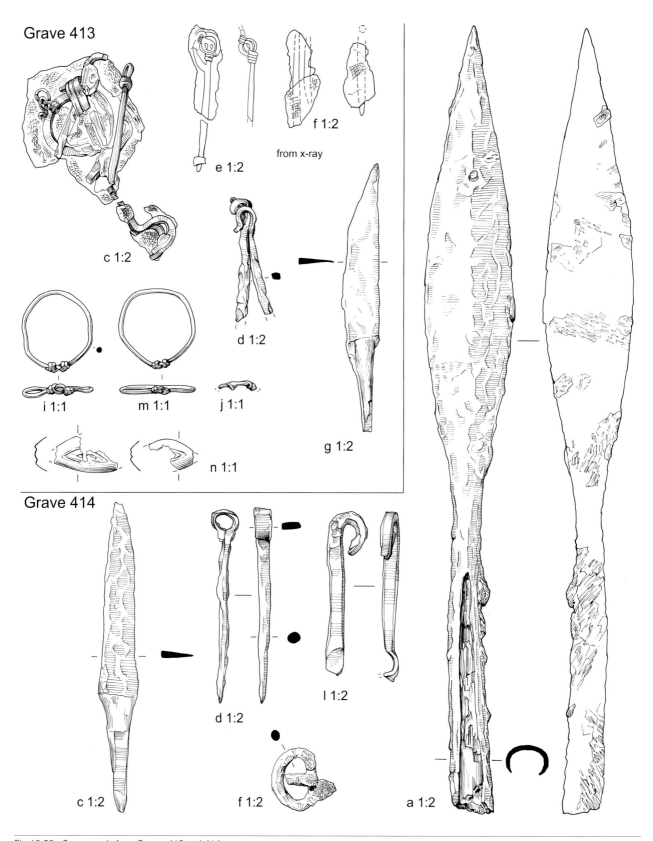

Grave 413

c 1:2

e 1:2

f 1:2

from x-ray

d 1:2

i 1:1   m 1:1   j 1:1

n 1:1

g 1:2

Grave 414

c 1:2

d 1:2

f 1:2

l 1:2

a 1:2

Fig 10.59. Grave goods from Graves 413 and 414.

Grave 414

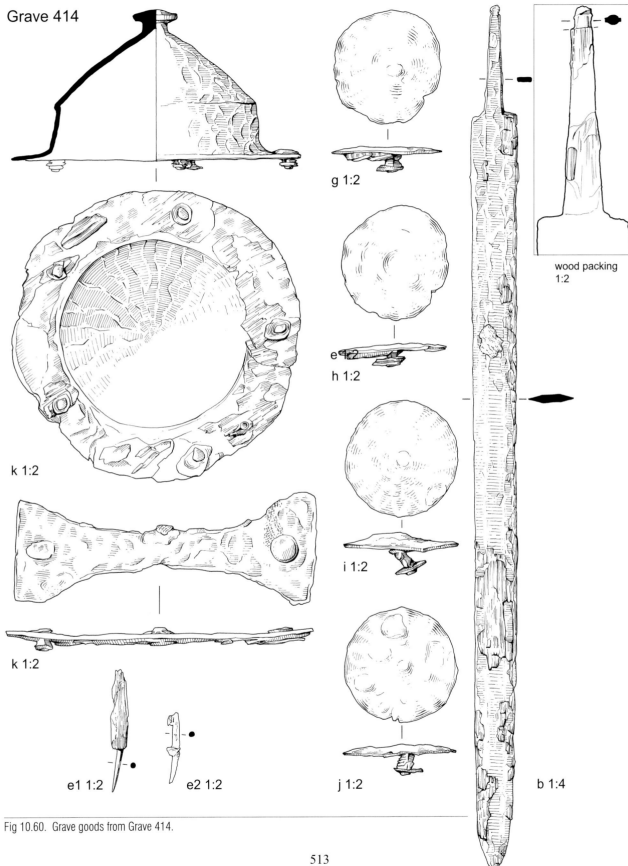

g 1:2

e
h 1:2

i 1:2

j 1:2

k 1:2

k 1:2

e1 1:2

e2 1:2

b 1:4

wood packing
1:2

Fig 10.60. Grave goods from Grave 414.

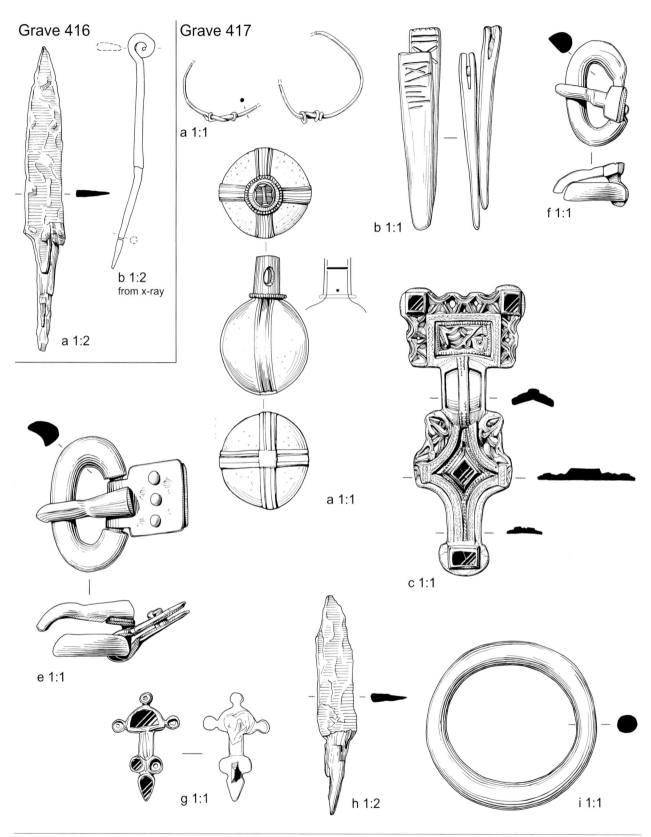

Fig 10.61. Grave goods from Graves 416 and 417.

Grave 417

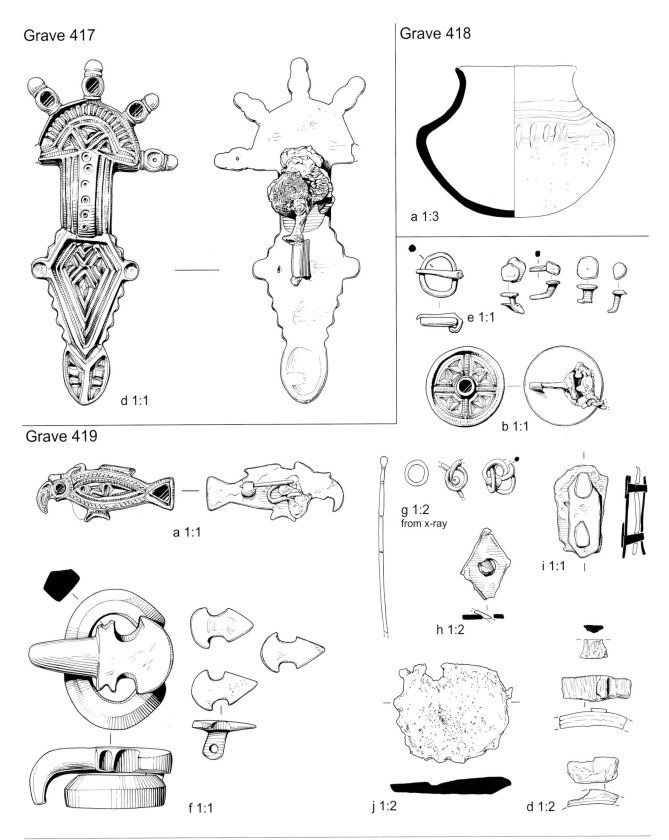

d 1:1

Grave 418

a 1:3

e 1:1

b 1:1

Grave 419

a 1:1

g 1:2
from x-ray

i 1:1

h 1:2

f 1:1

j 1:2

d 1:2

Fig 10.62. Grave goods from Graves 417, 418 and 419.

Grave 420

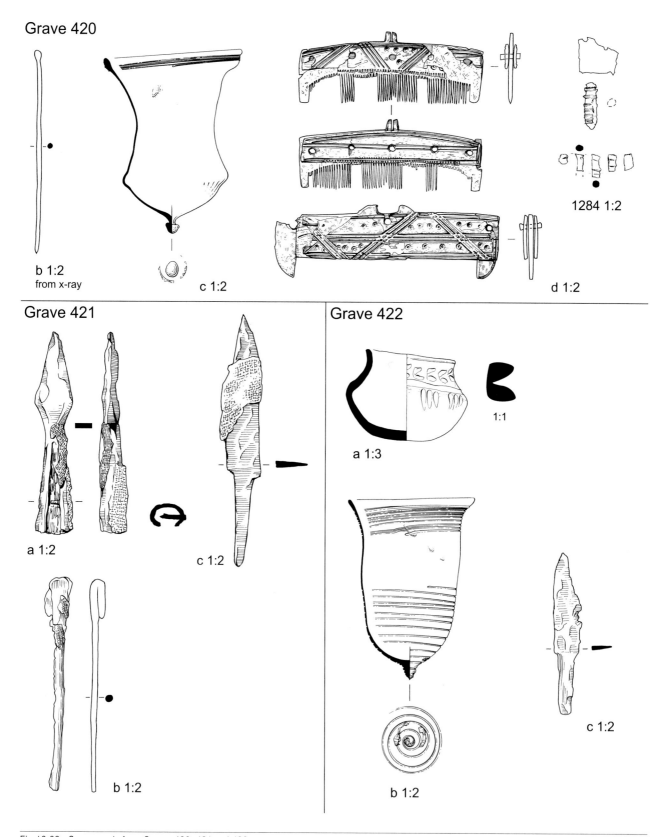

b 1:2
from x-ray

c 1:2

1284 1:2

d 1:2

Grave 421

a 1:2

c 1:2

b 1:2

Grave 422

a 1:3

1:1

b 1:2

c 1:2

Fig 10.63. Grave goods from Graves 420, 421 and 422.

Grave 423

b 1:2

c 1:2

d2 1:2

d1 1:2

e 1:1

a 1:2

f 1:1

Grave 424

a 1:1

Grave 425

b 1:1

c 1:2
from x-ray

Grave 426

a 1:1

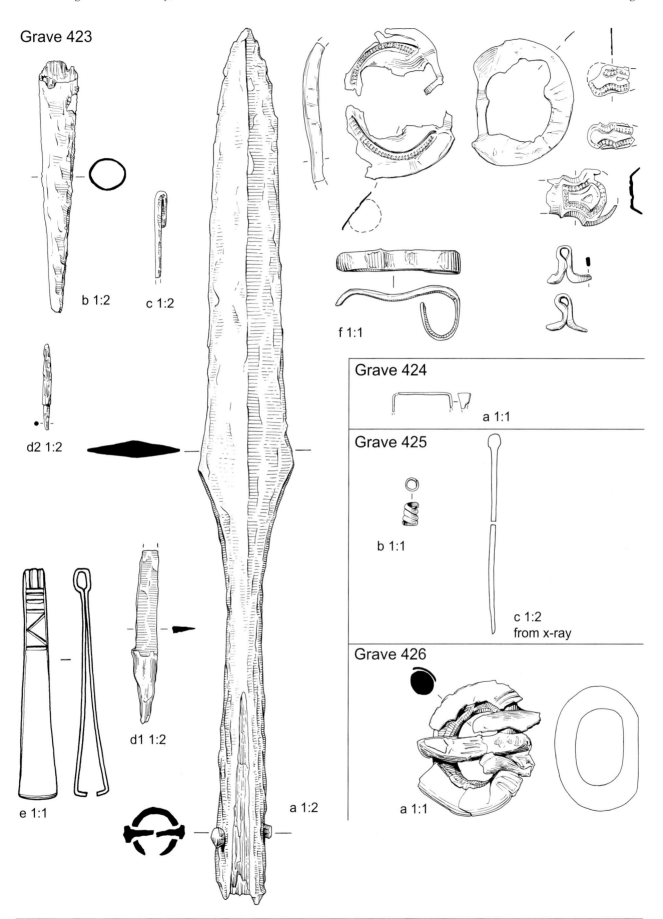

Fig 10.64. Grave goods from Graves 423, 424, 425 and 426.

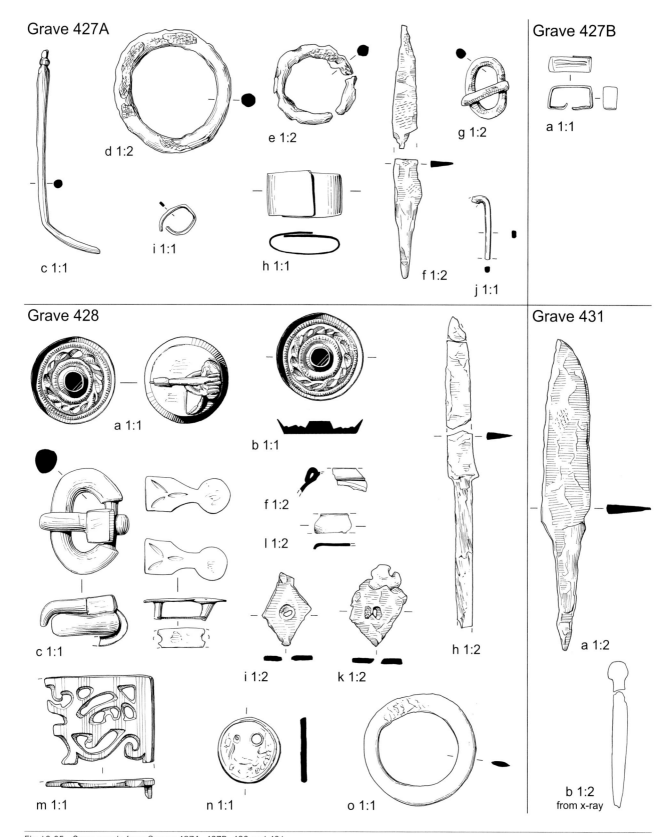

Fig 10.65. Grave goods from Graves 427A, 427B, 428 and 431.

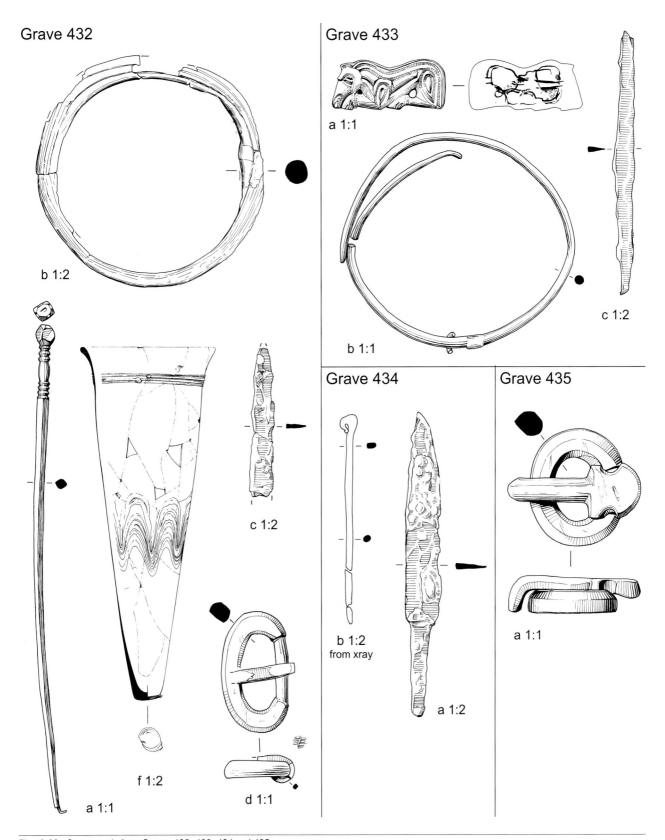

Grave 432

b 1:2

f 1:2

a 1:1

Grave 433

a 1:1

b 1:1

c 1:2

c 1:2

d 1:1

Grave 434

b 1:2
from xray

a 1:2

Grave 435

a 1:1

Fig 10.66. Grave goods from Graves 432, 433, 434 and 435.

Grave 436

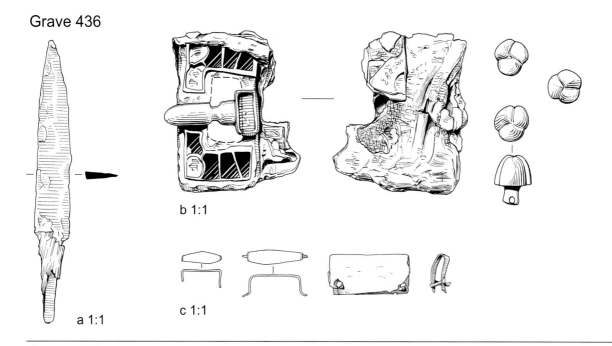

a 1:1

b 1:1

c 1:1

Grave 437

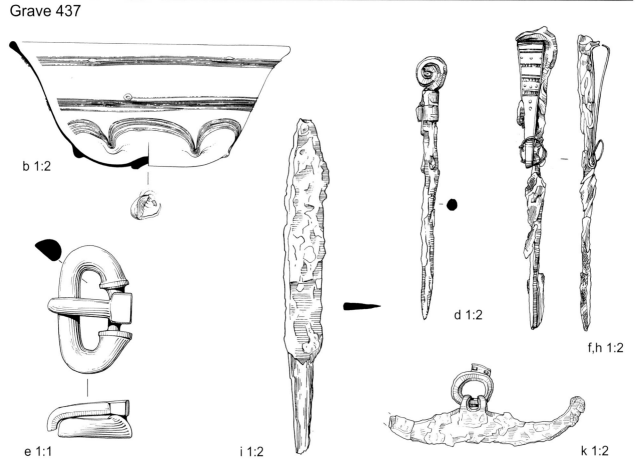

b 1:2

e 1:1

i 1:2

d 1:2

f,h 1:2

k 1:2

Fig 10.67. Grave goods from Graves 436 and 437.

Grave 437

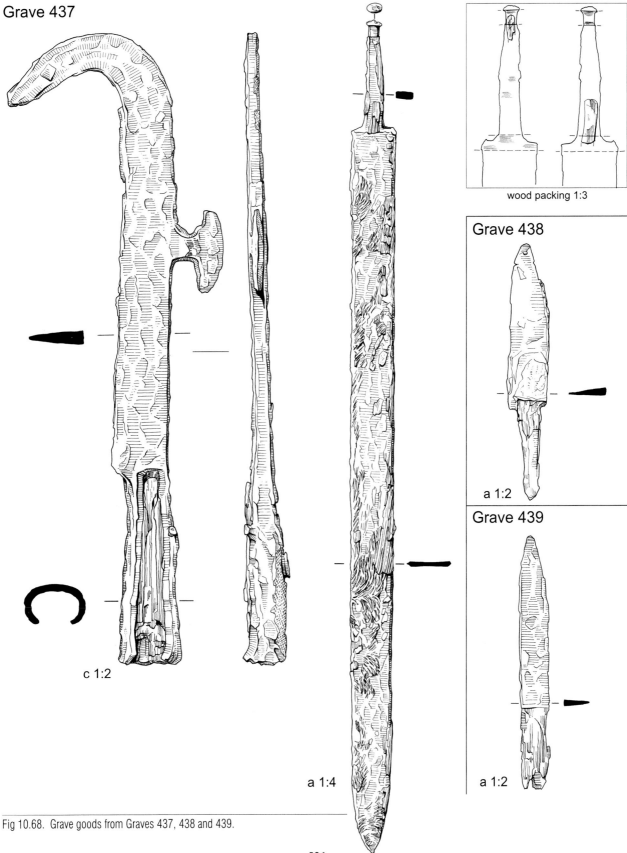

wood packing 1:3

c 1:2

a 1:4

Grave 438

a 1:2

Grave 439

a 1:2

Fig 10.68. Grave goods from Graves 437, 438 and 439.

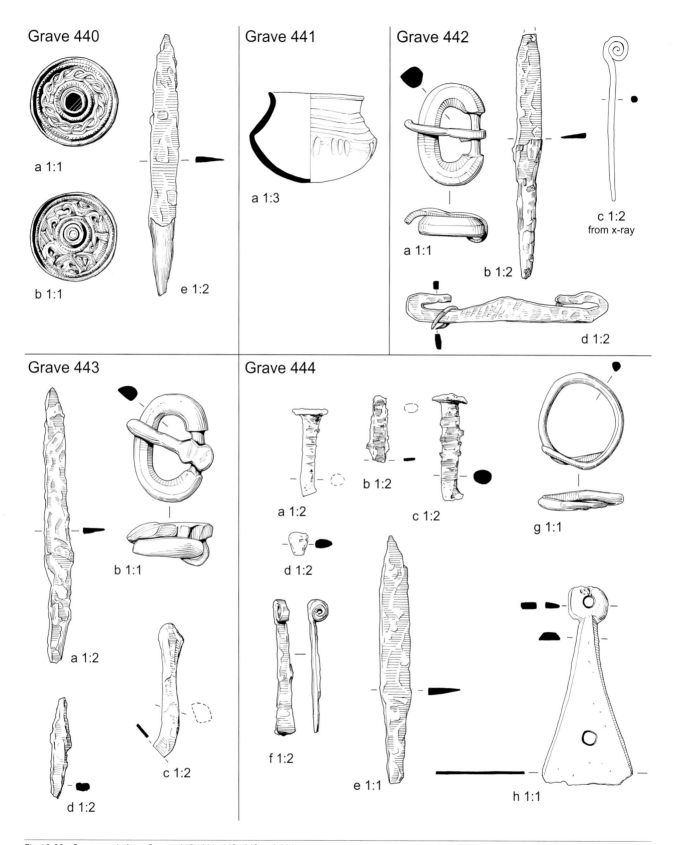

Fig 10.69. Grave goods from Graves 440, 441, 442, 443 and 444.

Unstratified

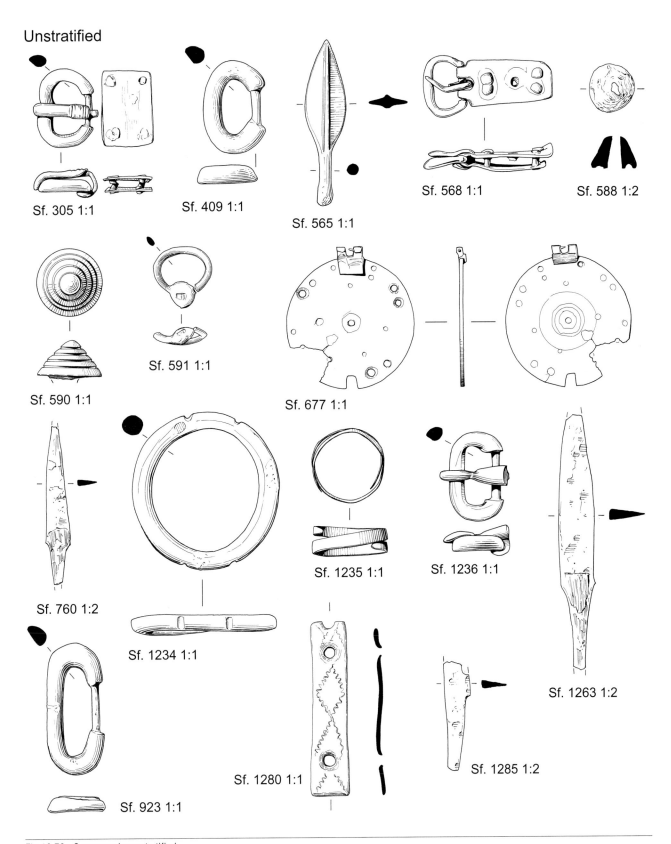

Sf. 305 1:1

Sf. 409 1:1

Sf. 565 1:1

Sf. 568 1:1

Sf. 588 1:2

Sf. 590 1:1

Sf. 591 1:1

Sf. 677 1:1

Sf. 760 1:2

Sf. 1234 1:1

Sf. 1235 1:1

Sf. 1236 1:1

Sf. 1263 1:2

Sf. 923 1:1

Sf. 1280 1:1

Sf. 1285 1:2

Fig 10.70. Grave goods: unstratified.

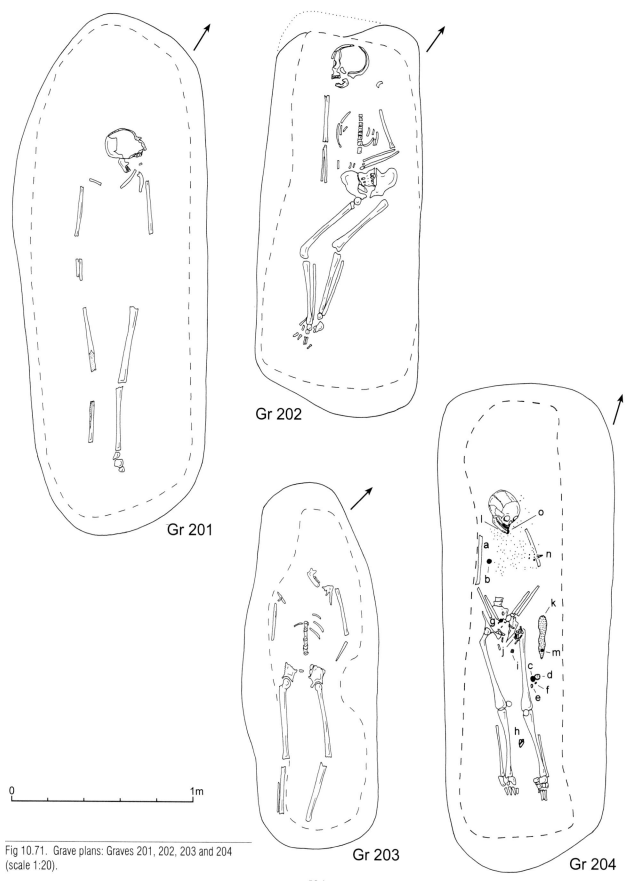

Gr 201

Gr 202

Gr 203

Gr 204

Fig 10.71. Grave plans: Graves 201, 202, 203 and 204 (scale 1:20).

0 _____ 1m

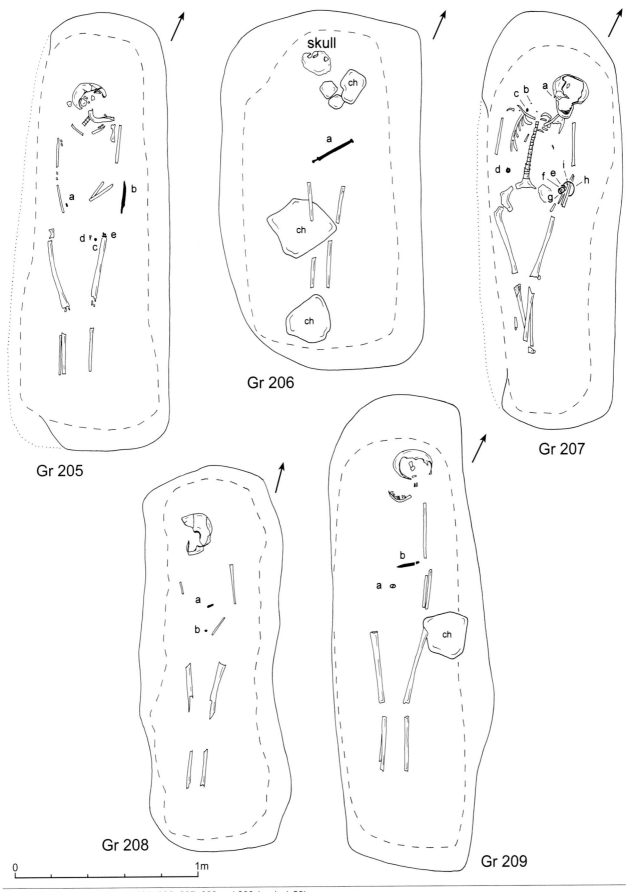

Gr 205

Gr 206

skull

Gr 207

Gr 208

Gr 209

0   1m

Fig 10.72. Grave plans: Graves 205, 206, 207, 208 and 209 (scale 1:20).

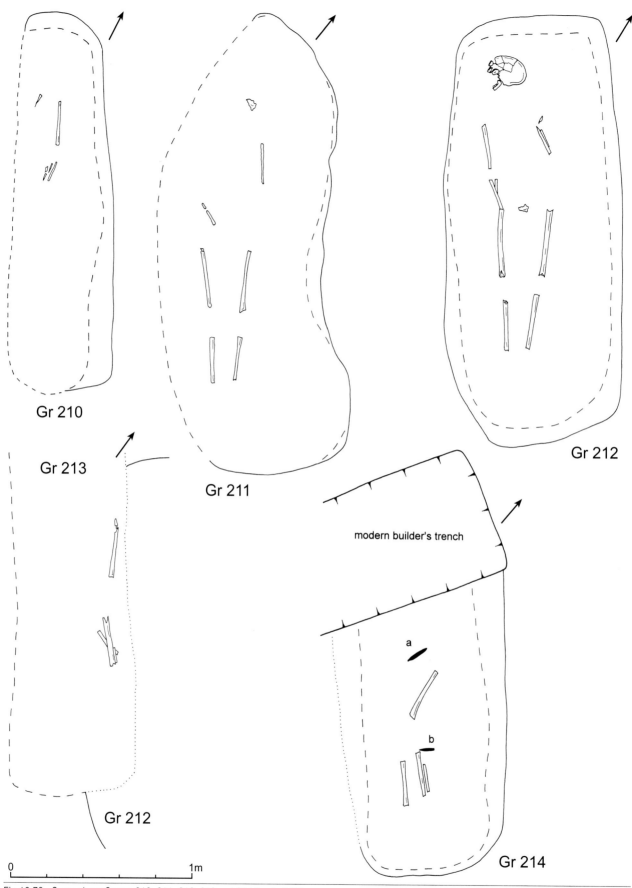

Gr 210

Gr 213

Gr 211

Gr 212

Gr 212

modern builder's trench

a

b

Gr 214

0   1m

Fig 10.73. Grave plans: Graves 210, 211, 212, 213 and 214 (scale 1:20).

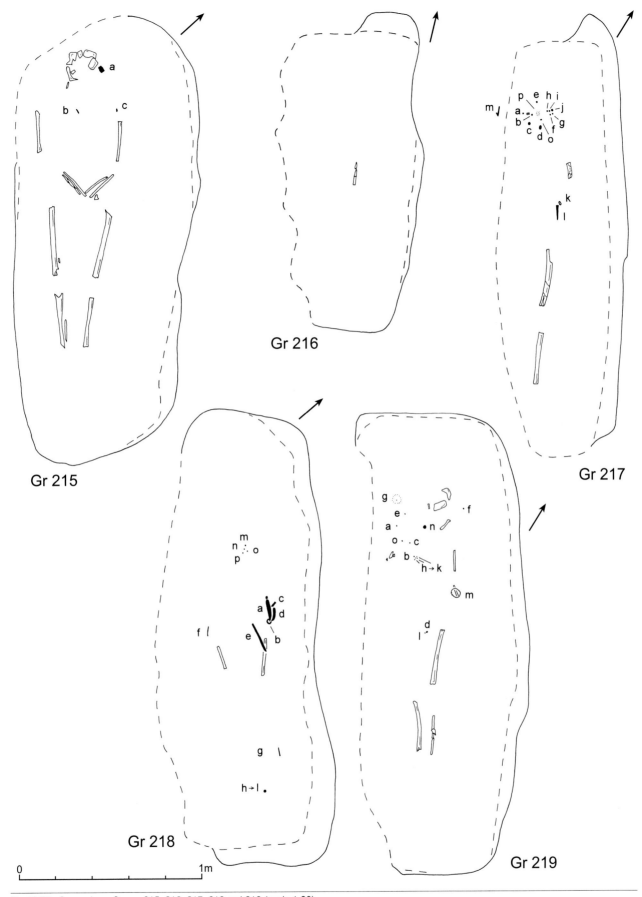

Fig 10.74. Grave plans: Graves 215, 216, 217, 218 and 219 (scale 1:20).

527

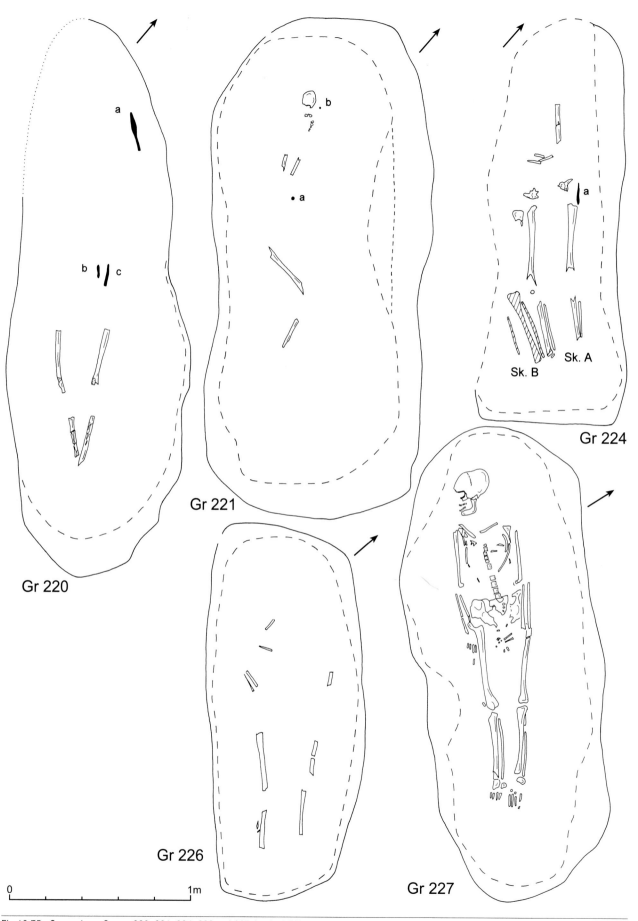

Gr 220

Gr 221

Gr 224

Sk. A

Sk. B

Gr 226

Gr 227

0   1m

Fig 10.75. Grave plans: Graves 220, 221, 224, 226 and 227 (scale 1:20).

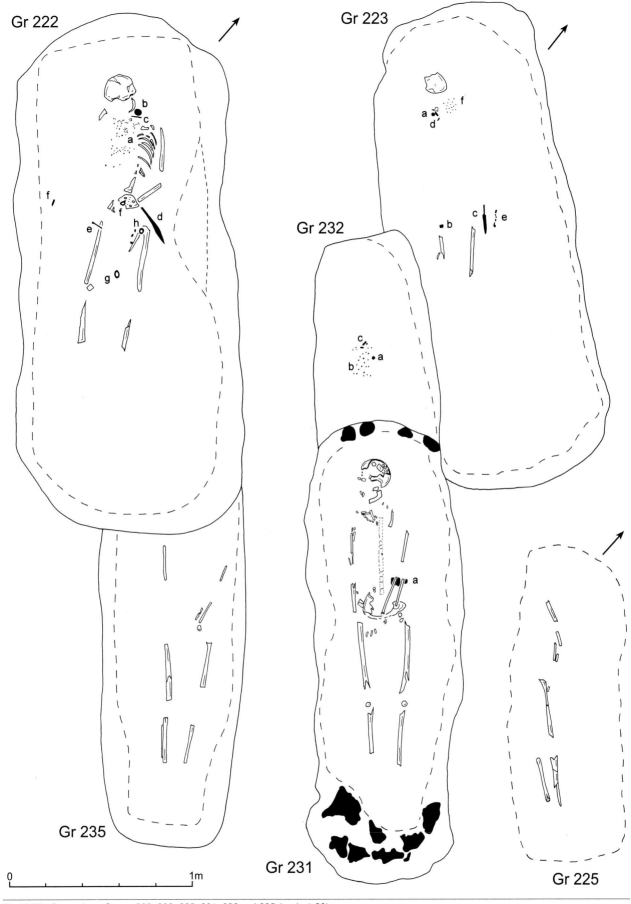

Gr 222

Gr 223

Gr 232

Gr 235

Gr 231

Gr 225

0   1m

Fig 10.76. Grave plans: Graves 222, 223, 225, 231, 232 and 235 (scale 1:20).

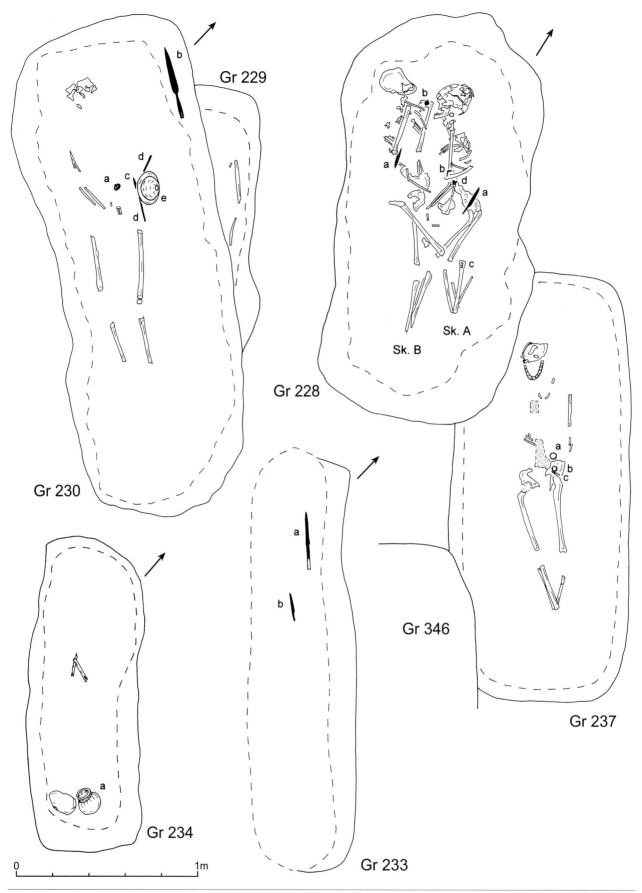

Gr 229

Gr 230

Gr 228

Sk. A

Sk. B

Gr 234

Gr 233

Gr 346

Gr 237

0   1m

Fig 10.77. Grave plans: Graves 228, 229, 230, 233, 234 and 237 (scale 1:20).

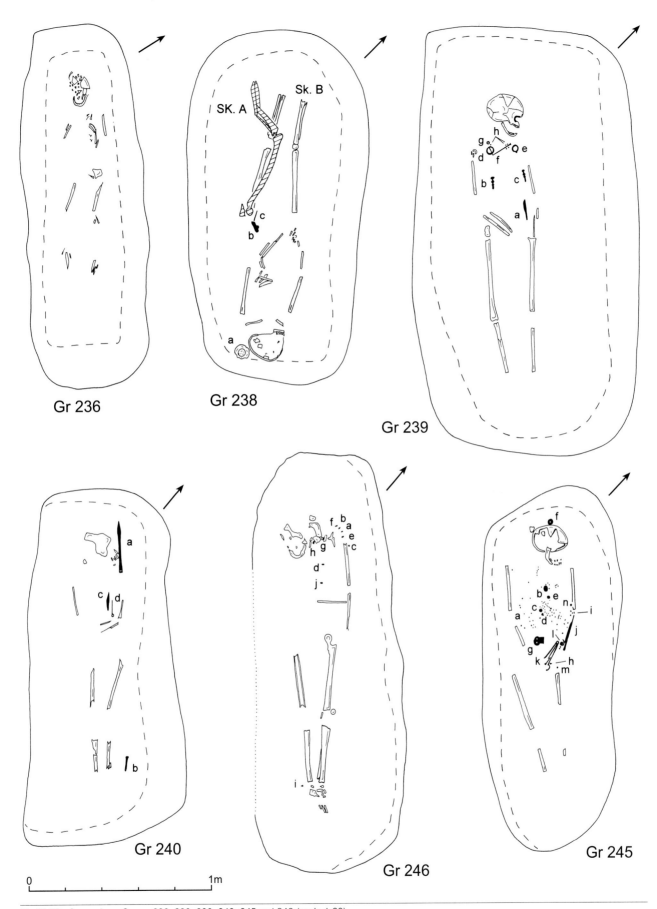

Fig 10.78. Grave plans: Graves 236, 238, 239, 240, 245 and 246 (scale 1:20).

531

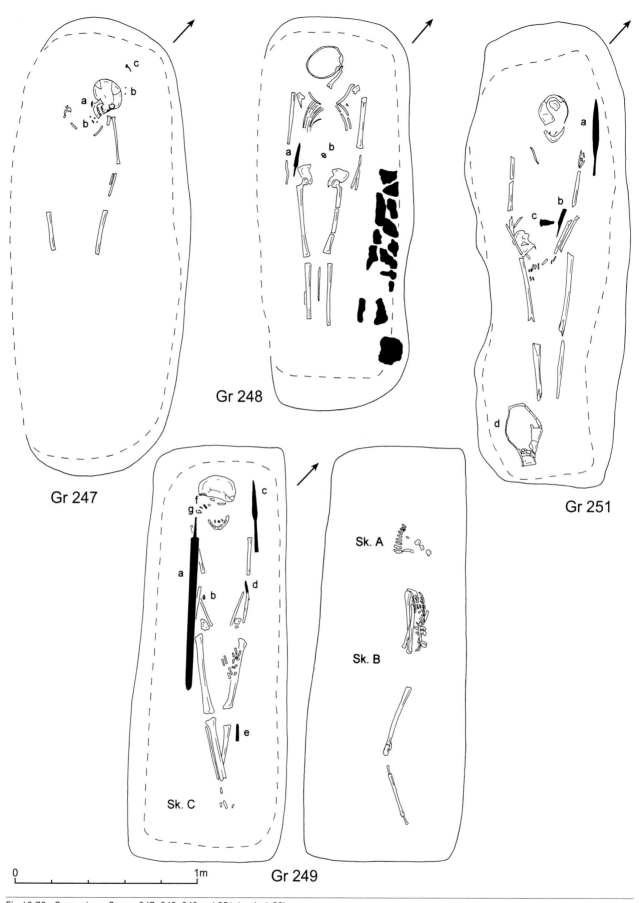

Gr 247

Gr 248

Gr 251

Gr 249

Sk. A

Sk. B

Sk. C

0   1m

Fig 10.79. Grave plans: Graves 247, 248, 249 and 251 (scale 1:20).

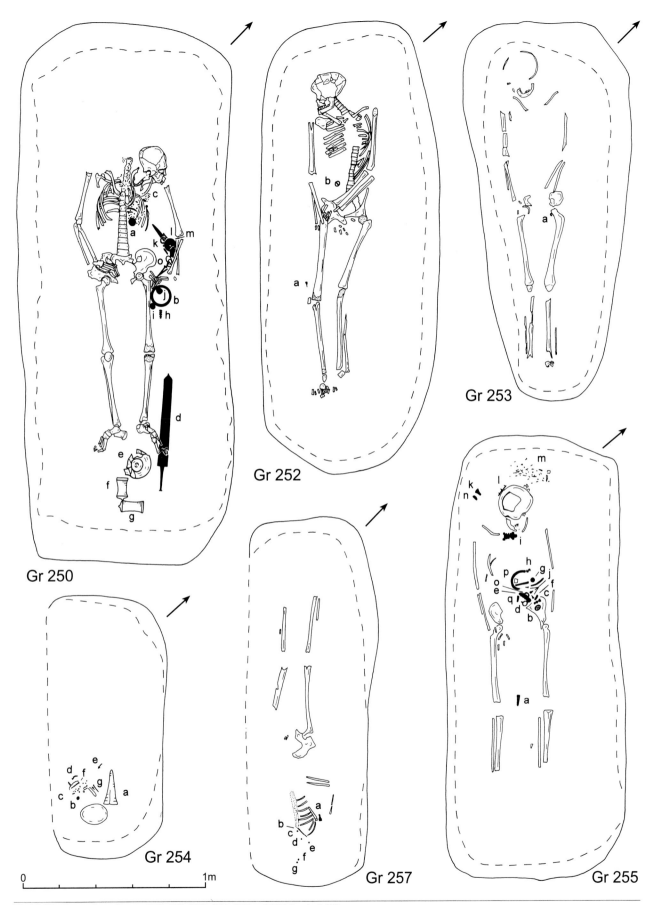

Gr 250

Gr 252

Gr 253

Gr 254

Gr 257

Gr 255

Fig 10.80. Grave plans: Graves 250, 252, 253, 254, 255 and 257 (scale 1:20).

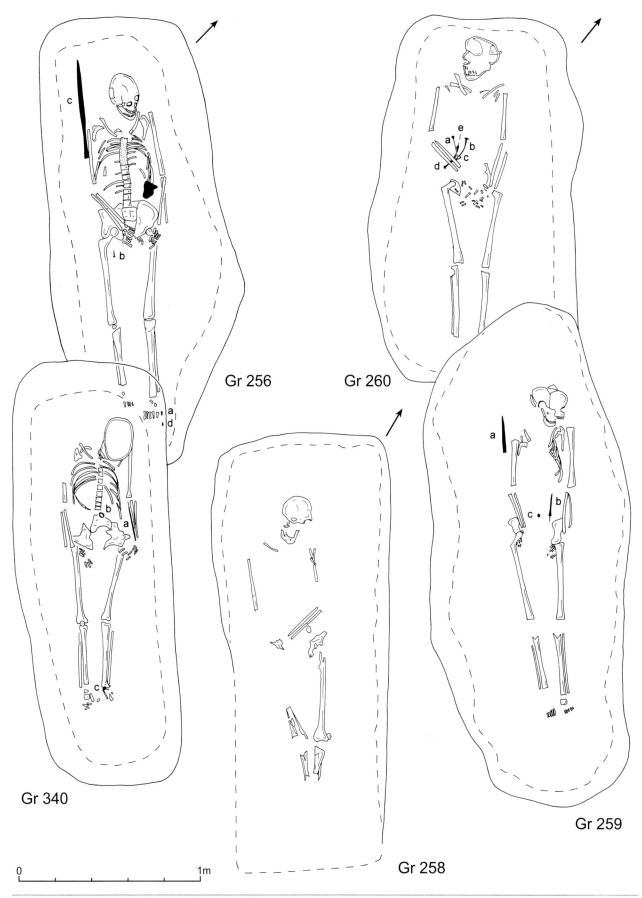

Gr 256

Gr 260

Gr 340

Gr 258

Gr 259

0   1m

Fig 10.81. Grave plans: Graves 256, 258, 259, 260 and 340 (scale 1:20).

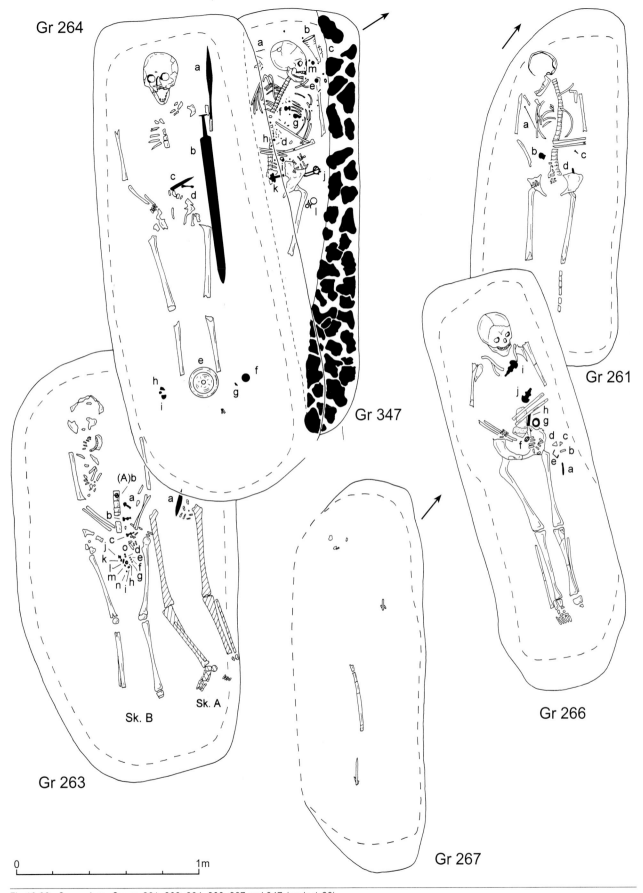

Fig 10.82. Grave plans: Graves 261, 263, 264, 266, 267 and 347 (scale 1:20).

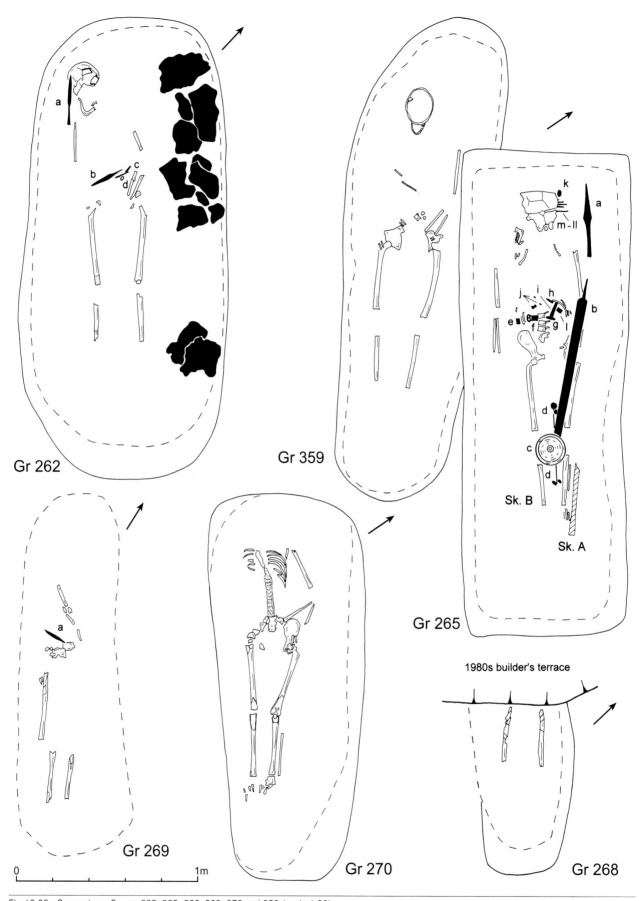

Gr 262

Gr 359

Gr 265

Sk. B

Sk. A

Gr 269

Gr 270

1980s builder's terrace

Gr 268

0   1m

Fig 10.83. Grave plans: Graves 262, 265, 268, 269, 270 and 359 (scale 1:20).

536

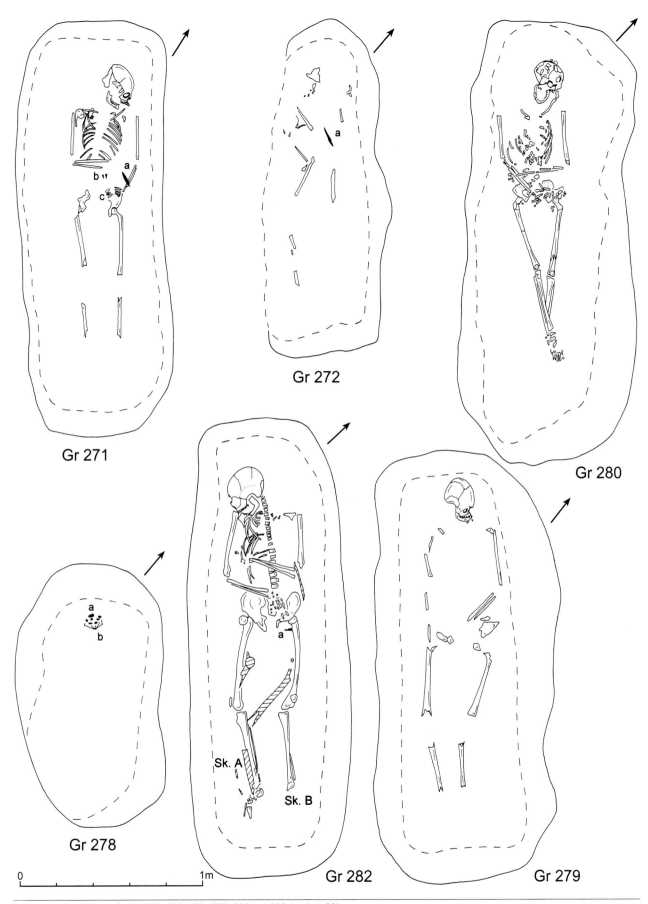

Gr 271

Gr 272

Gr 280

Gr 278

Sk. A

Sk. B

Gr 282

Gr 279

0   1m

Fig 10.84. Grave plans: Graves 271, 272, 278, 279, 280 and 282 (scale 1:20).

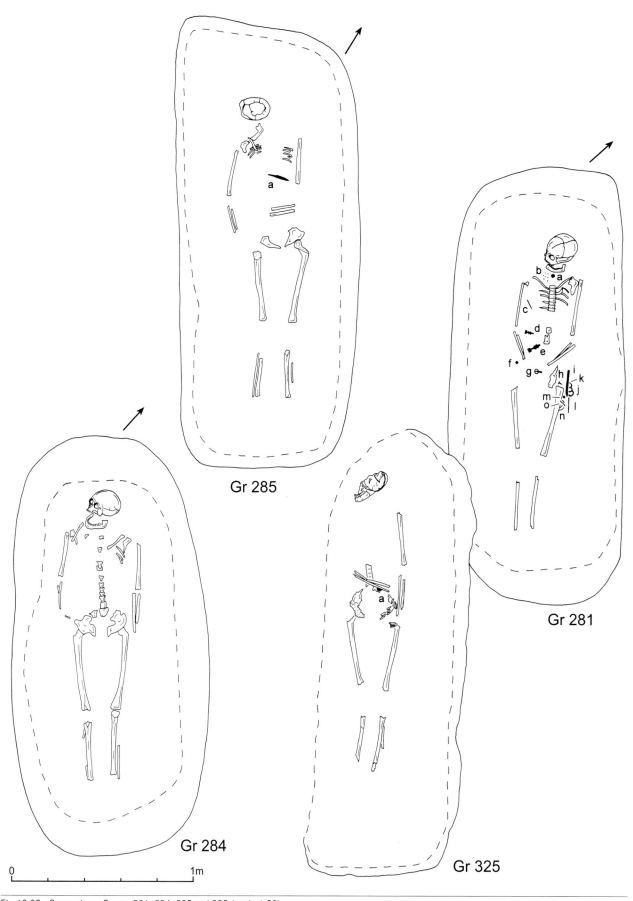

Gr 285

Gr 281

Gr 284

Gr 325

Fig 10.85. Grave plans: Graves 281, 284, 285 and 325 (scale 1:20).

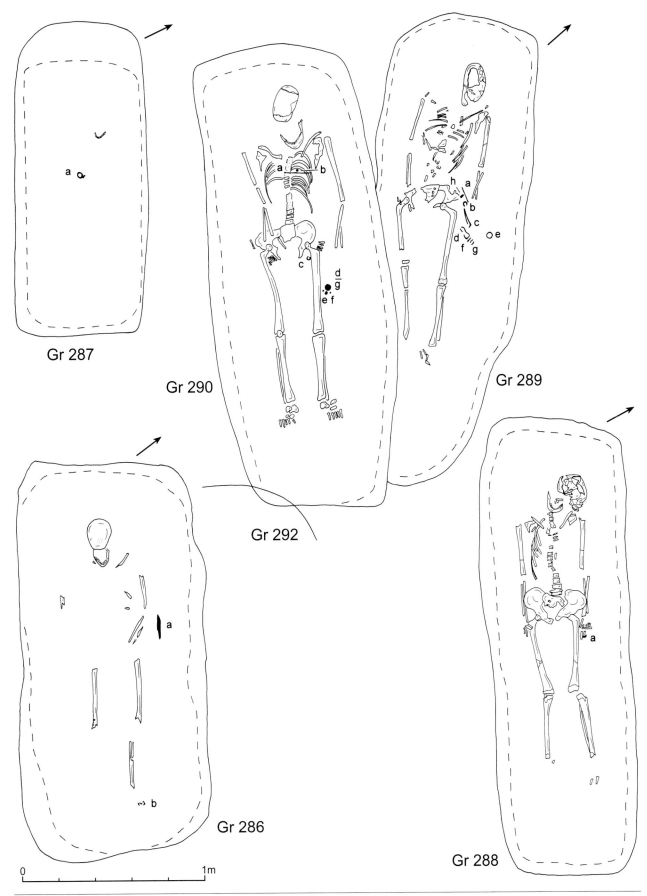

Gr 287

Gr 290

Gr 289

Gr 292

Gr 286

Gr 288

0   1m

Fig 10.86. Grave plans: Graves 286, 287, 288, 289 and 290 (scale 1:20).

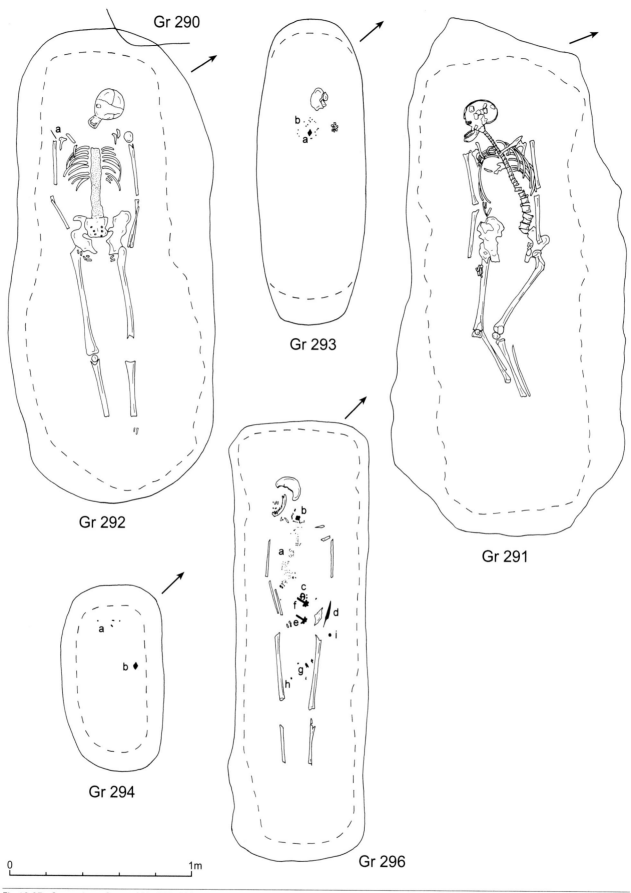

Gr 290

Gr 293

Gr 292

Gr 291

Gr 294

Gr 296

0   1m

Fig 10.87. Grave plans: Graves 291, 292, 293, 294 and 296 (scale 1:20).

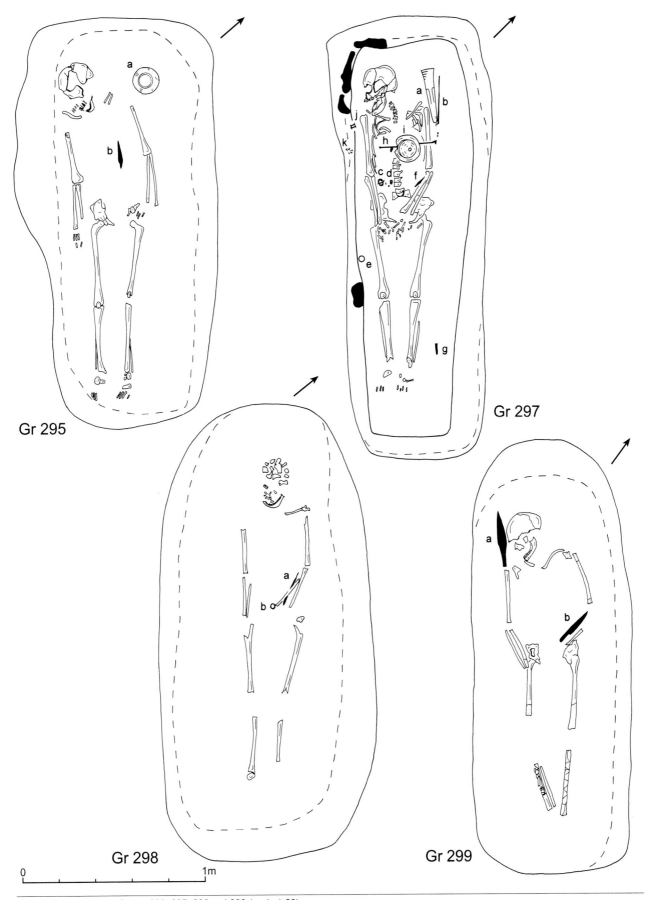

Gr 295

Gr 297

Gr 298

Gr 299

Fig 10.88. Grave plans: Graves 295, 297, 298 and 299 (scale 1:20).

0   1m

541

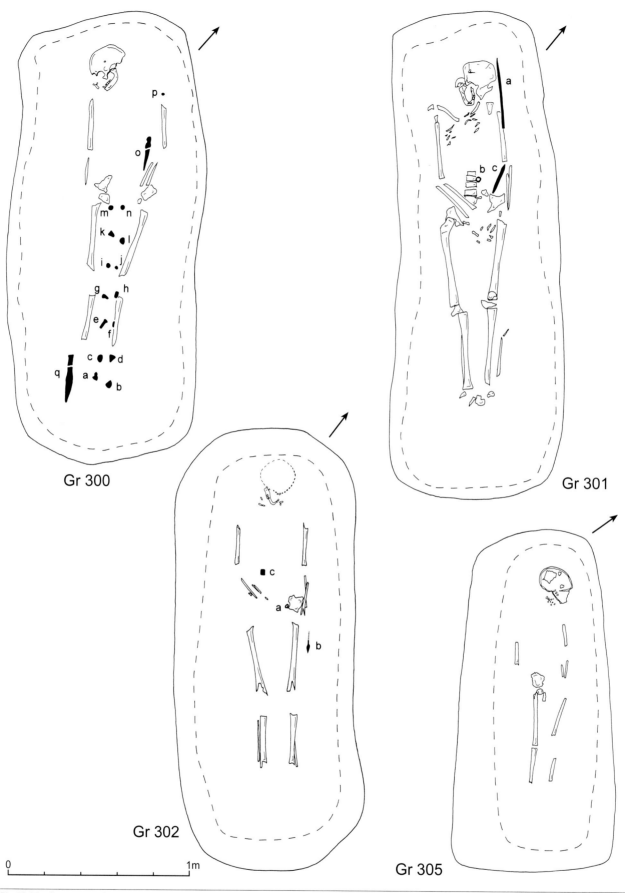

Gr 300

Gr 301

Gr 302

Gr 305

0   1m

Fig 10.89. Grave plans: Graves 300, 301, 302 and 305 (scale 1:20).

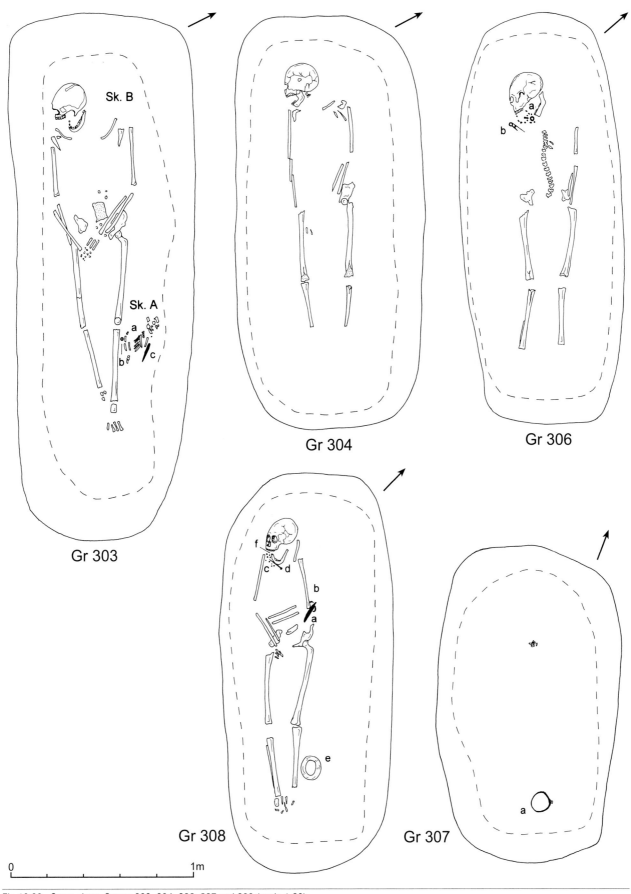

Fig 10.90. Grave plans: Graves 303, 304, 306, 307 and 308 (scale 1:20).

543

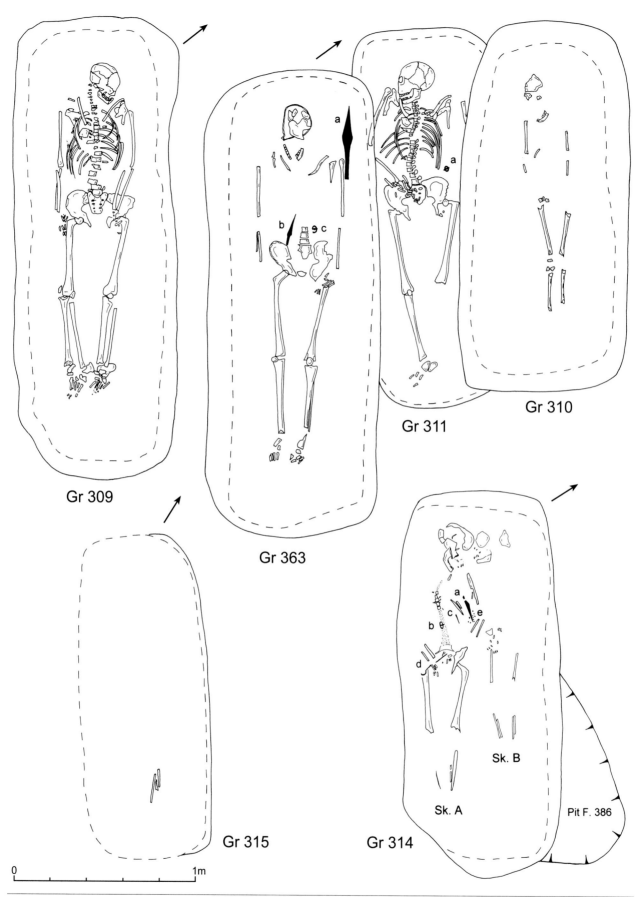

Gr 309

Gr 363

Gr 311

Gr 310

Gr 315

Gr 314

Sk. B

Sk. A

Pit F. 386

0   1m

Fig 10.91. Grave plans: Graves 309, 310, 311, 314, 315 and 363 (scale 1:20).

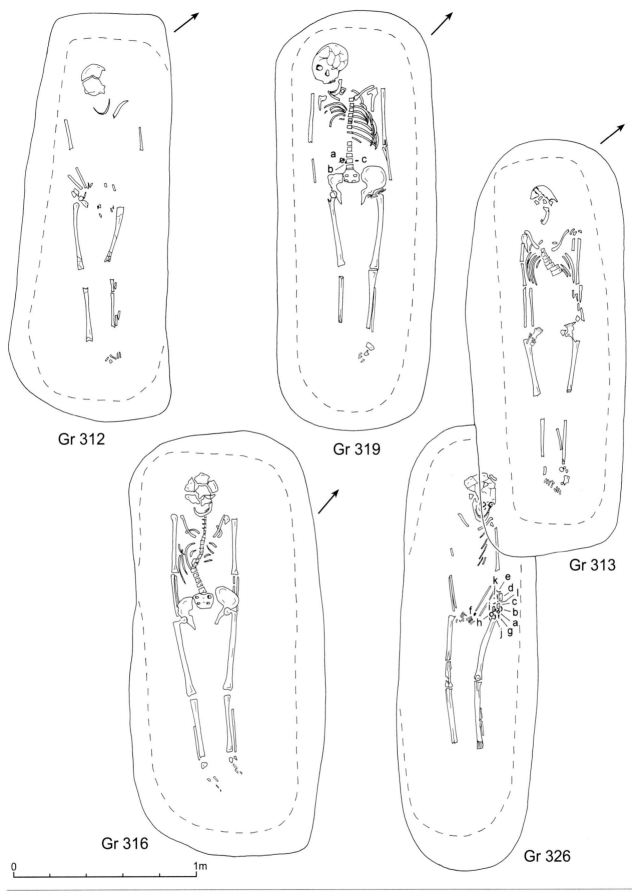

Gr 312

Gr 319

Gr 313

Gr 316

Gr 326

0 — — — — 1m

Fig 10.92. Grave plans: Graves 312, 313, 316, 319 and 326 (scale 1:20).

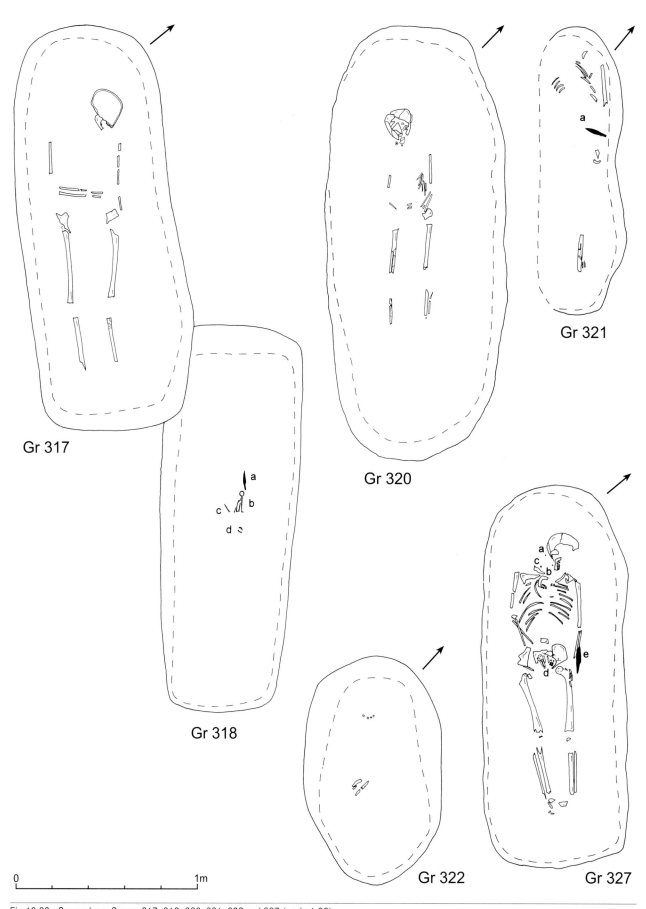

Gr 317

Gr 318

Gr 320

Gr 321

Gr 322

Gr 327

0   1m

Fig 10.93. Grave plans: Graves 317, 318, 320, 321, 322 and 327 (scale 1:20).

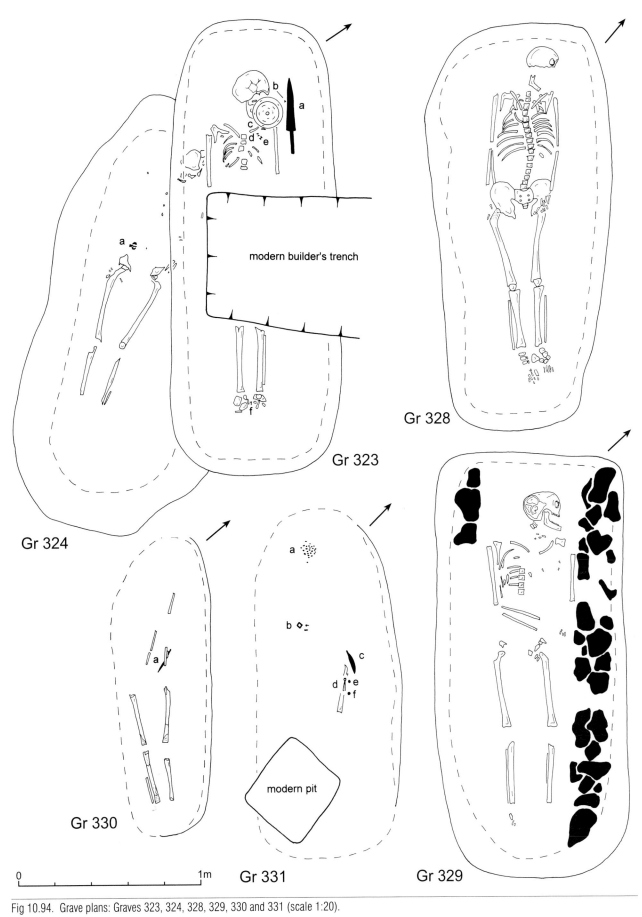

modern builder's trench

Gr 323

Gr 324

Gr 328

Gr 330

modern pit

Gr 331

Gr 329

0   1m

Fig 10.94. Grave plans: Graves 323, 324, 328, 329, 330 and 331 (scale 1:20).

547

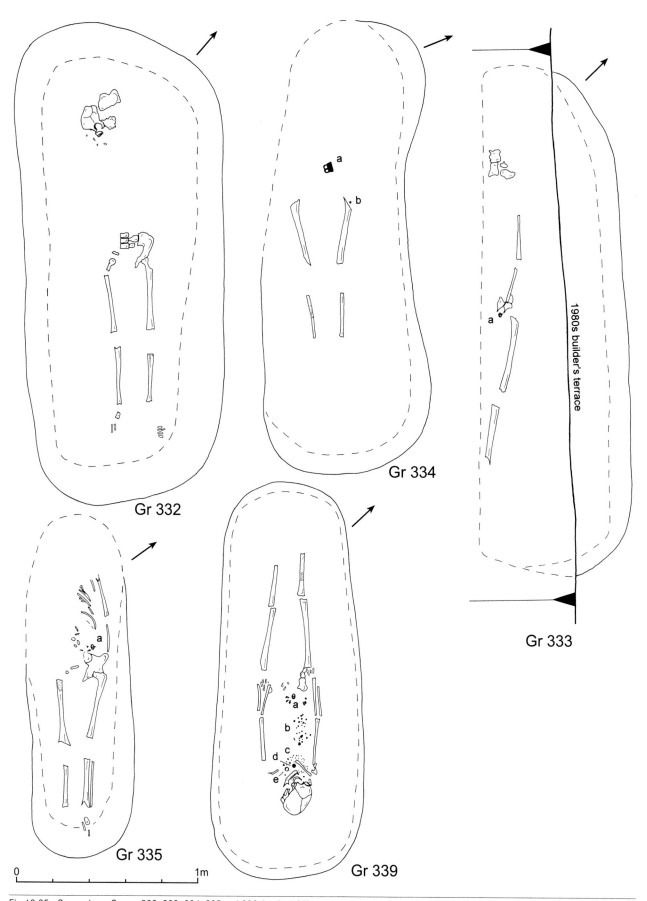

Fig 10.95. Grave plans: Graves 332, 333, 334, 335 and 339 (scale 1:20).

Gr 332

Gr 334

Gr 333

1980s builder's terrace

Gr 335

Gr 339

0   1m

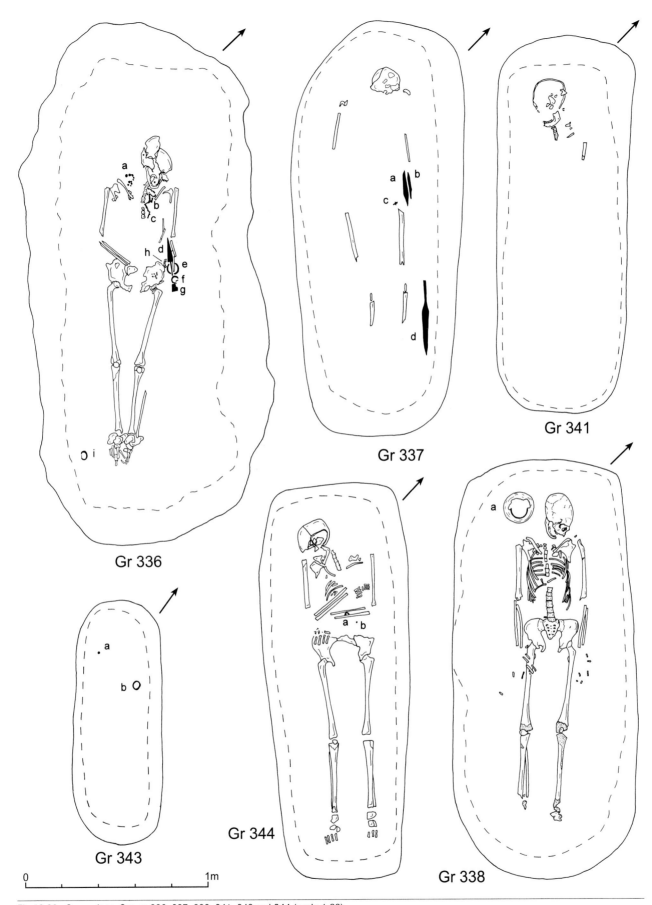

Gr 336

Gr 337

Gr 341

Gr 343

Gr 344

Gr 338

0   1m

Fig 10.96. Grave plans: Graves 336, 337, 338, 341, 343 and 344 (scale 1:20).

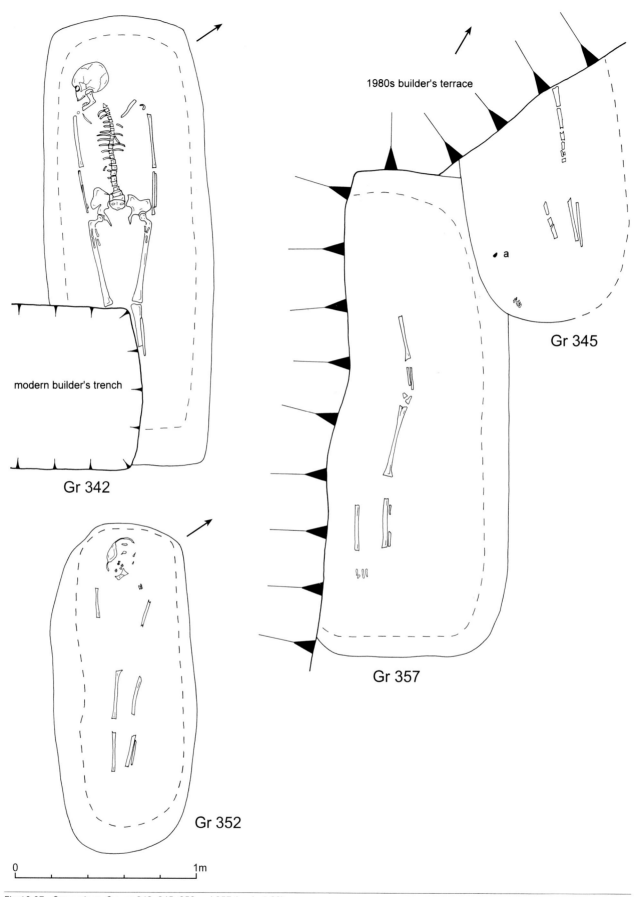

Gr 342

modern builder's trench

Gr 352

Gr 345

1980s builder's terrace

Gr 357

0   1m

Fig 10.97. Grave plans: Graves 342, 345, 352 and 357 (scale 1:20).

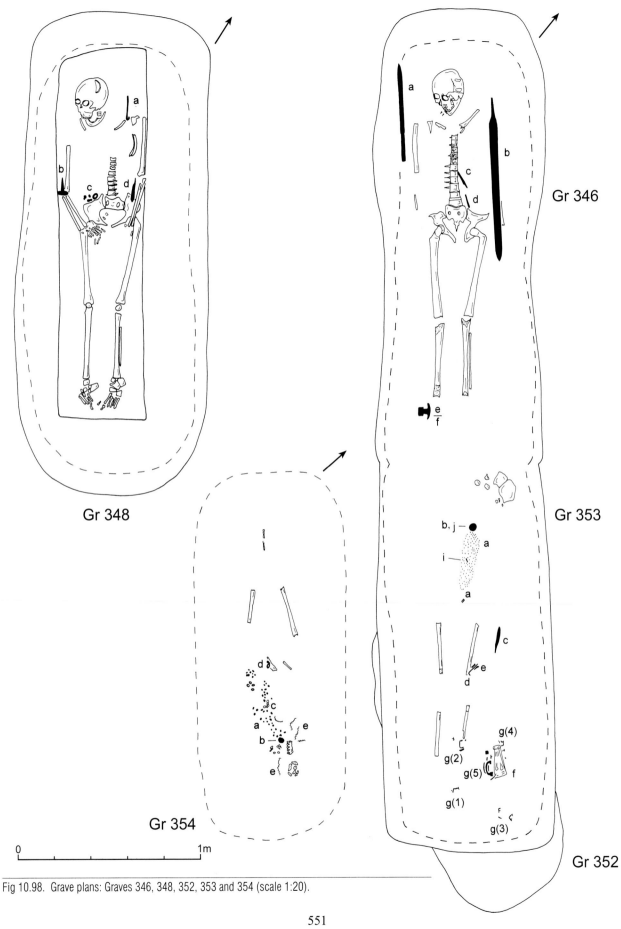

Gr 348

Gr 354

Gr 346

Gr 353

Gr 352

0   1m

Fig 10.98. Grave plans: Graves 346, 348, 352, 353 and 354 (scale 1:20).

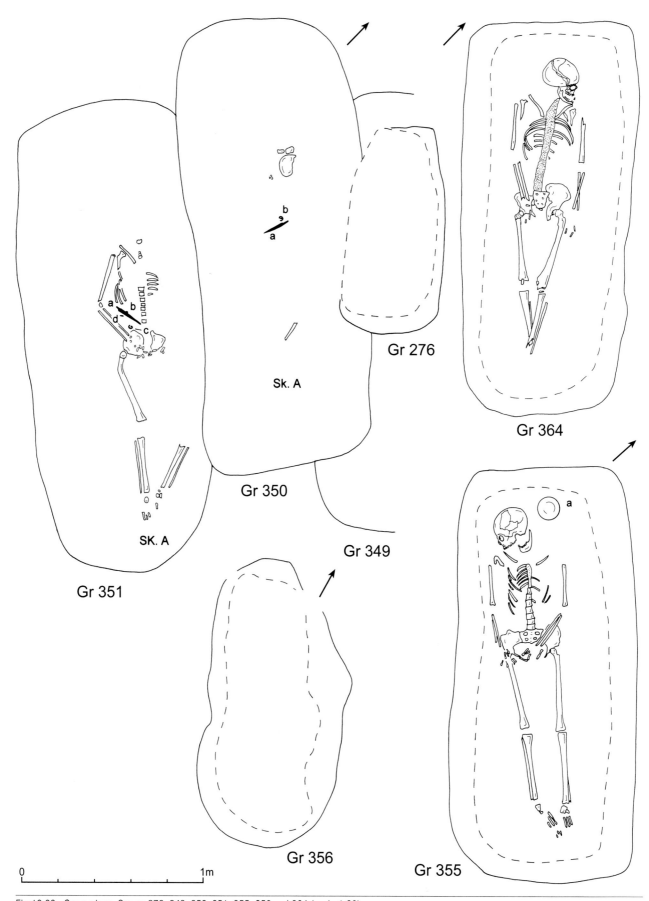

Gr 276

Gr 364

Sk. A

Gr 350

Gr 349

Gr 351

SK. A

Gr 356

Gr 355

0   1m

Fig 10.99. Grave plans: Graves 276, 349, 350, 351, 355, 356 and 364 (scale 1:20).

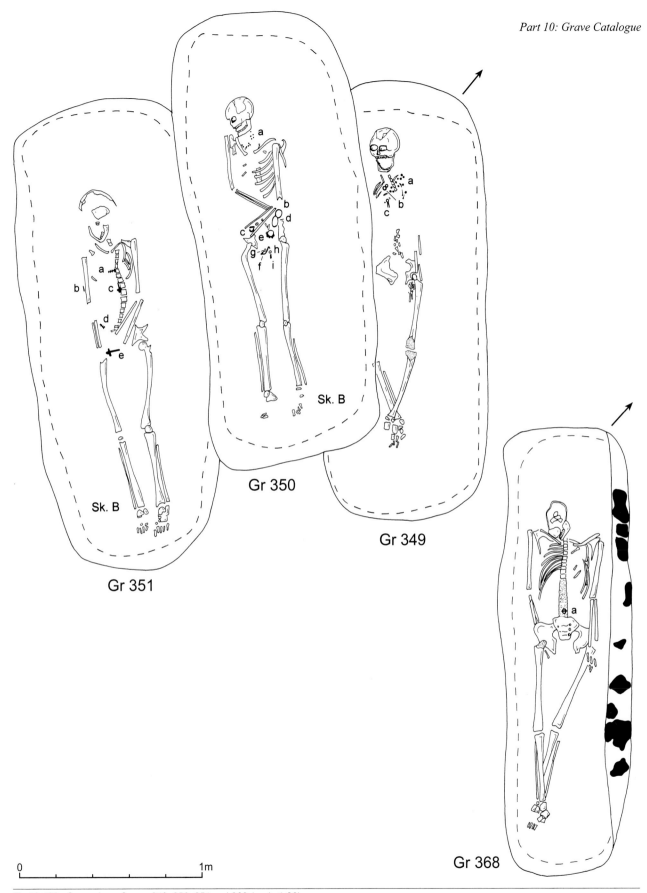

Fig 10.100. Grave plans: Graves 349, 350, 351 and 368 (scale 1:20).

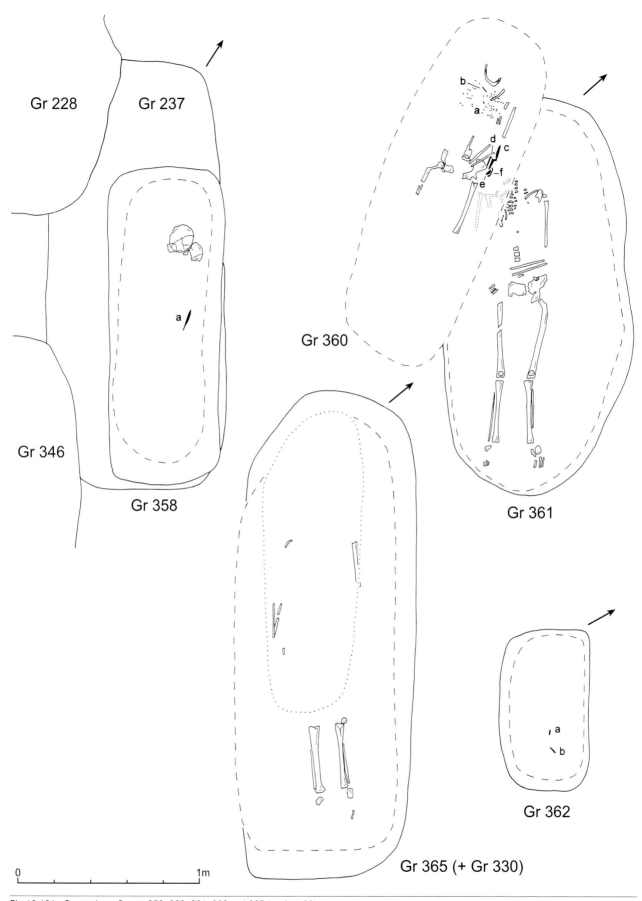

Gr 228

Gr 237

Gr 346

Gr 358

Gr 360

Gr 361

Gr 365 (+ Gr 330)

Gr 362

0   1m

Fig 10.101. Grave plans: Graves 358, 360, 361, 362 and 365 (scale 1:20).

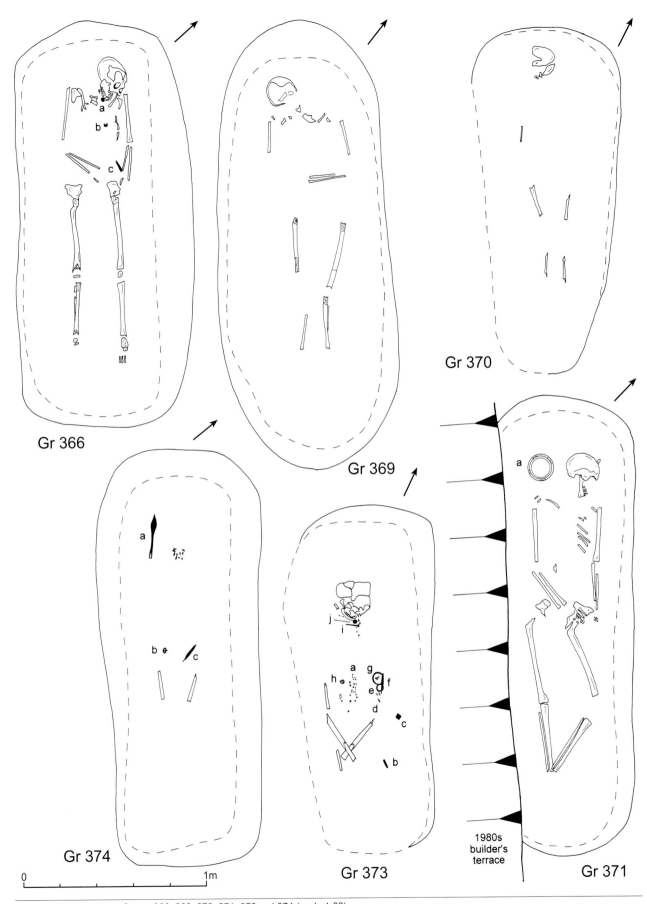

Gr 366

Gr 369

Gr 370

Gr 374

Gr 373

Gr 371

1980s
builder's
terrace

0   1m

Fig 10.102. Grave plans: Graves 366, 369, 370, 371, 373 and 374 (scale 1:20).

555

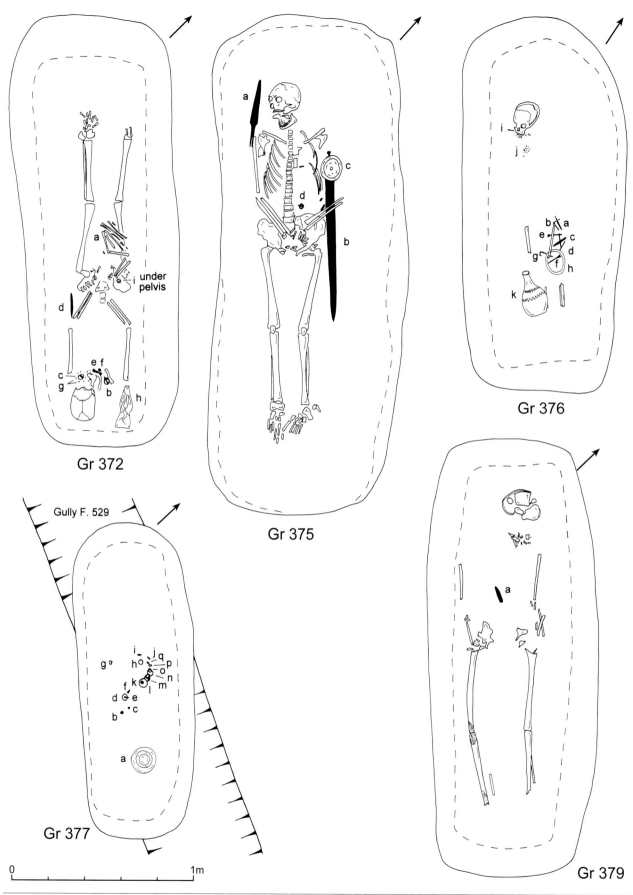

Gr 372

Gr 375

Gr 376

Gully F. 529

Gr 377

Gr 379

Fig 10.103. Grave plans: Graves 372, 375, 376, 377 and 379 (scale 1:20).

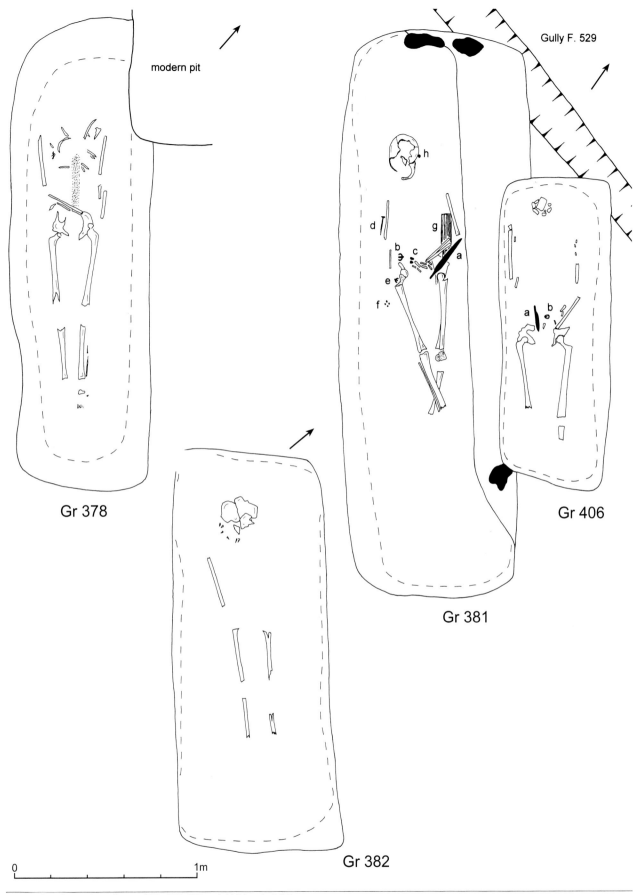

modern pit

Gully F. 529

Gr 378

Gr 381

Gr 382

Gr 406

0   1m

Fig 10.104. Grave plans: Graves 378, 381, 382 and 406 (scale 1:20).

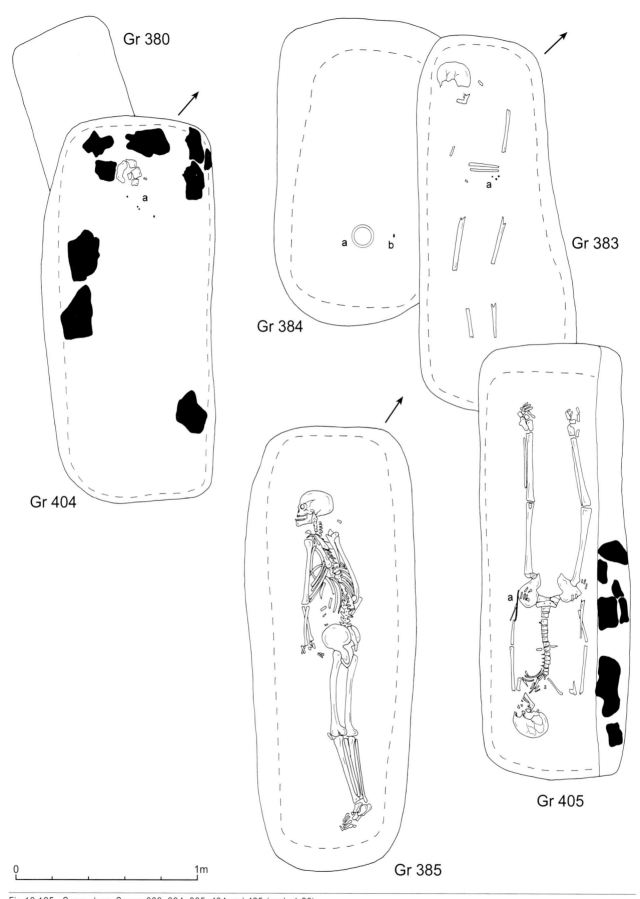

Gr 380

Gr 384

Gr 383

Gr 404

Gr 385

Gr 405

0   1m

Fig 10.105. Grave plans: Graves 383, 384, 385, 404 and 405 (scale 1:20).

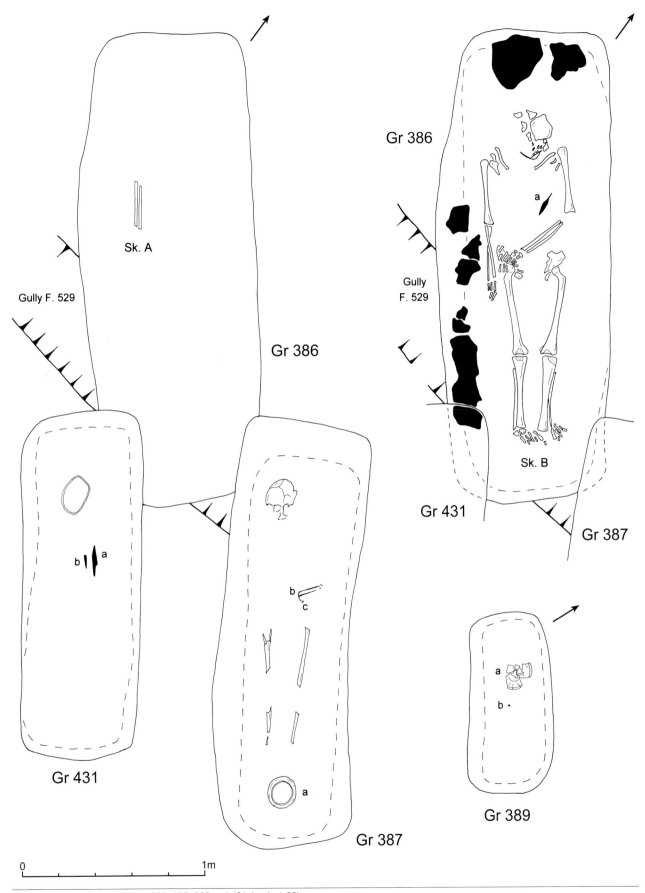

Sk. A

Gully F. 529

Gr 386

Gr 431

b a

Gr 386

Gully
F. 529

Sk. B

Gr 431

Gr 387

b
c

b

a

Gr 387

a

b

Gr 389

0　　　　　　　　　　　　　1m

Fig 10.106. Grave plans: Graves 386, 387, 389 and 431 (scale 1:20).

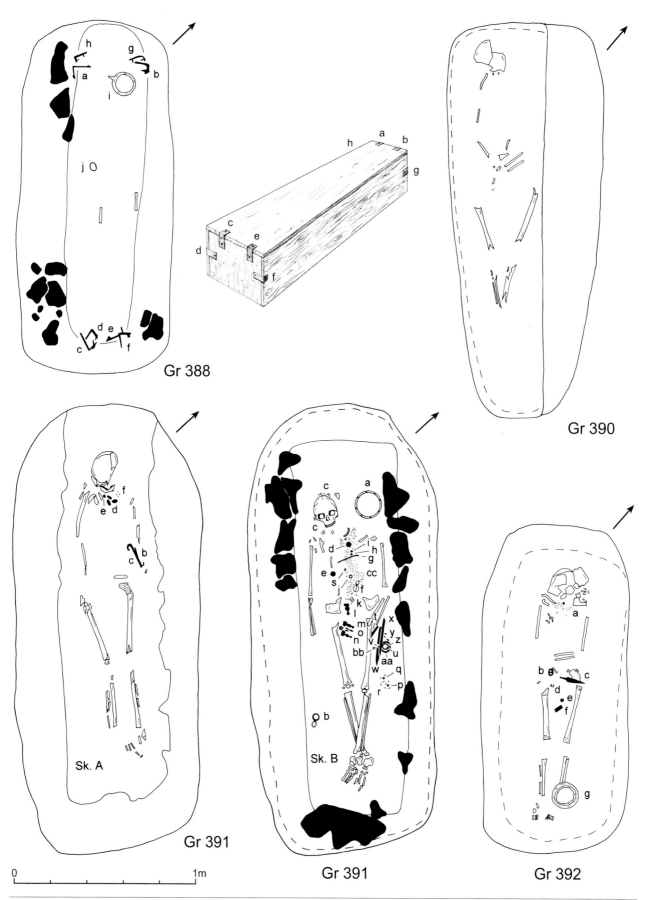

Gr 388

Gr 390

Gr 391

Sk. A

Gr 391

Sk. B

Gr 392

0   1m

Fig 10.107. Grave plans: Graves 388, 390, 391 and 392 (scale 1:20) and suggested reconstruction of a wooden coffin (*see* p 38).

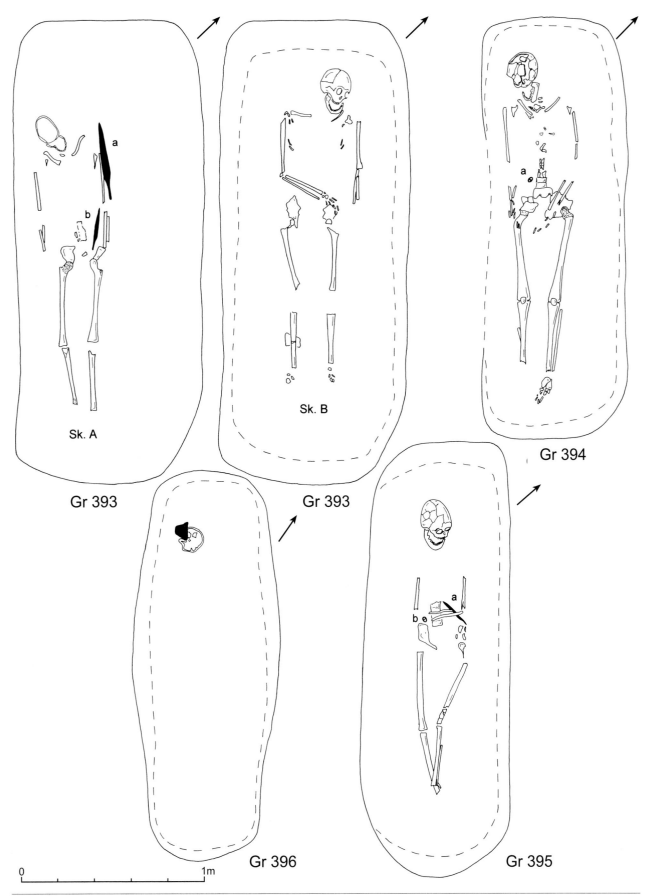

Sk. A

Gr 393

Sk. B

Gr 393

Gr 394

Gr 396

Gr 395

Fig 10.108. Grave plans: Graves 393, 394, 395 and 396 (scale 1:20).

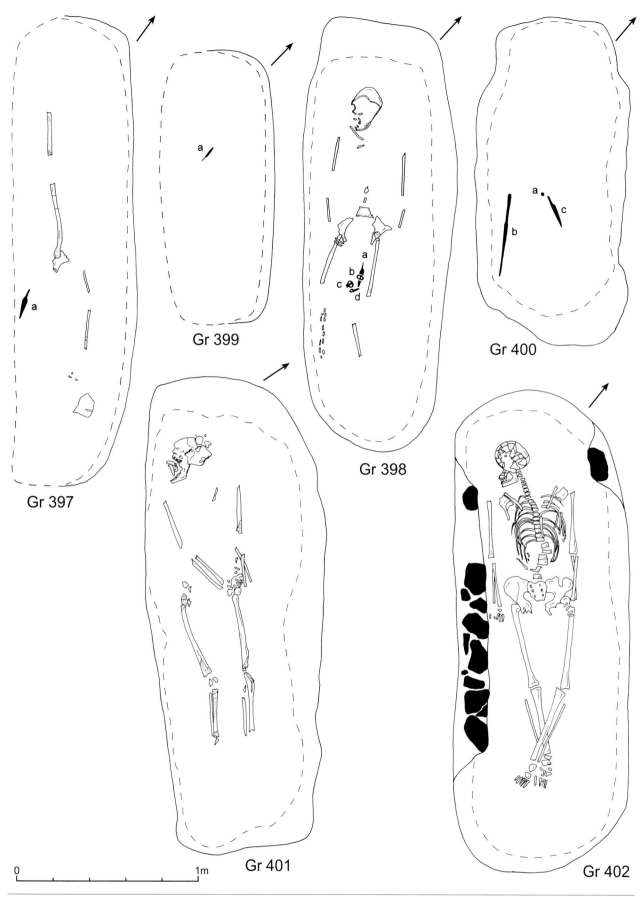

Gr 399

Gr 400

Gr 397

Gr 398

Gr 401

Gr 402

0   1m

Fig 10.109. Grave plans: Graves 397, 398, 399, 400, 401 and 402 (scale 1:20).

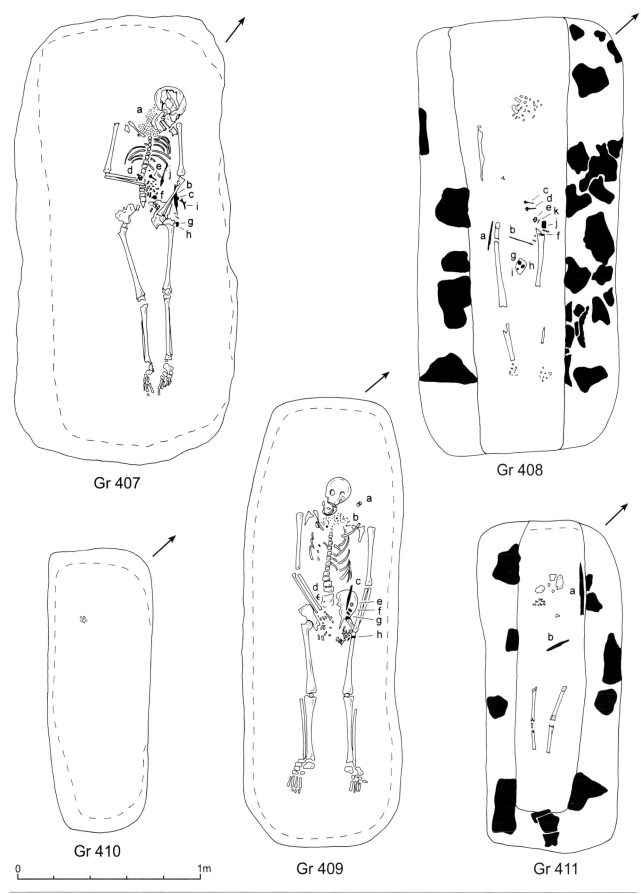

Fig 10.110. Grave plans: Graves 407, 408, 409, 410 and 411 (scale 1:20).

Gr 407

Gr 408

Gr 410

Gr 409

Gr 411

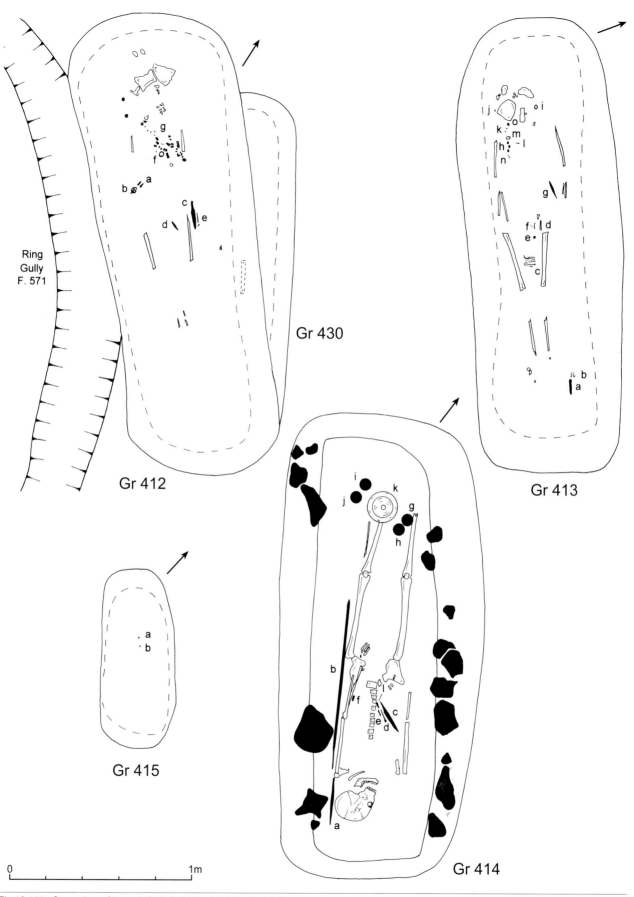

Ring
Gully
F. 571

Gr 412

Gr 430

Gr 413

Gr 415

Gr 414

0   1m

Fig 10.111. Grave plans: Graves 412, 413, 414 and 415 (scale 1:20).

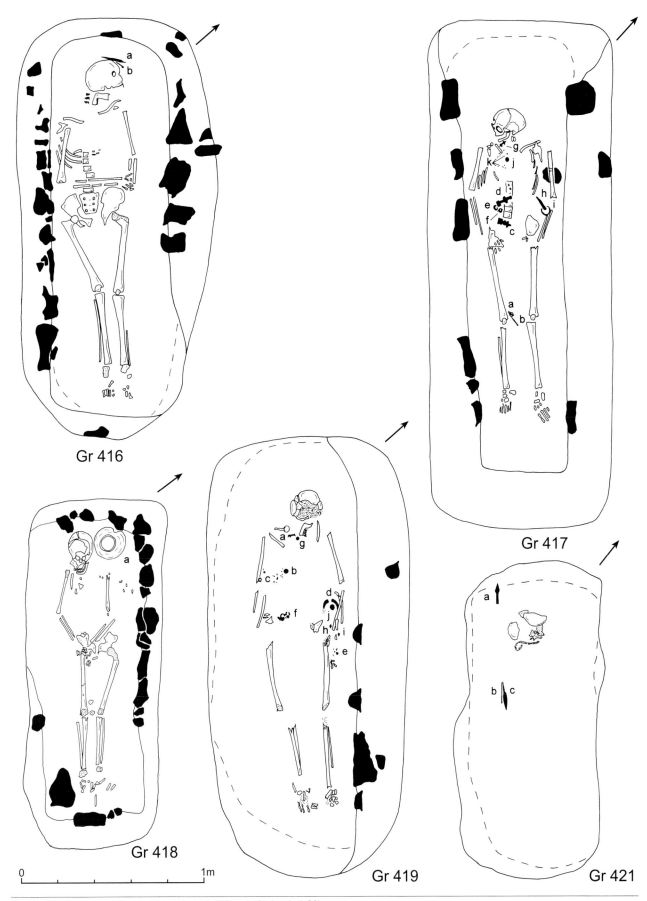

Gr 416

Gr 417

Gr 418

Gr 419

Gr 421

0   1m

Fig 10.112. Grave plans: Graves 416, 417, 418, 419 and 421 (scale 1:20).

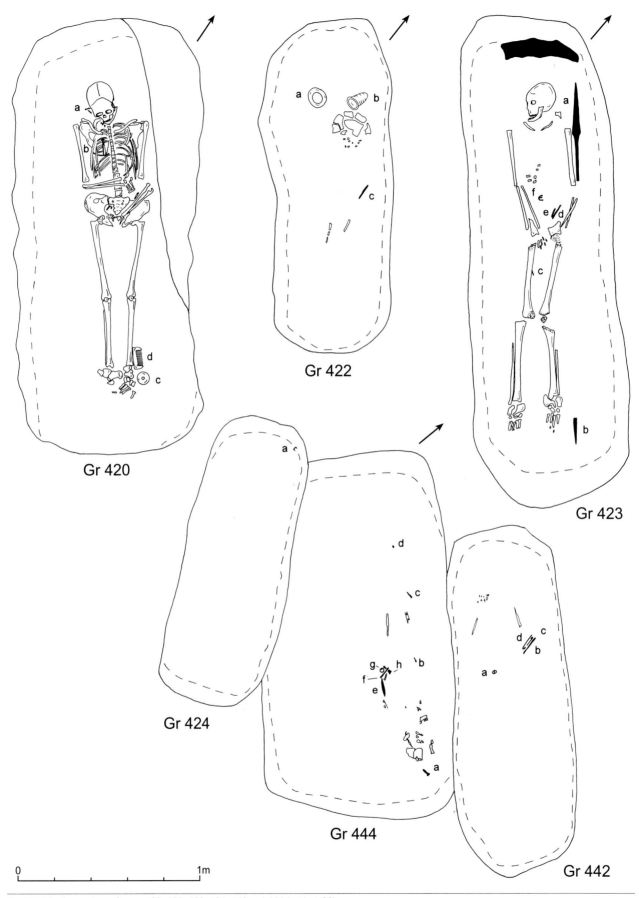

Gr 420

Gr 422

Gr 423

Gr 424

Gr 444

Gr 442

Fig 10.113. Grave plans: Graves 420, 422, 423, 424, 442 and 444 (scale 1:20).

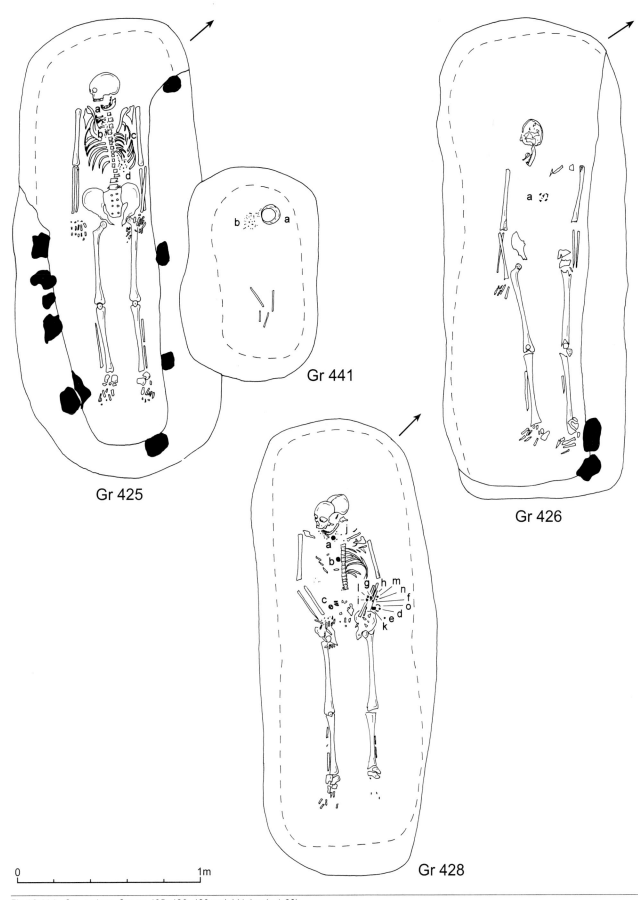

Gr 441

Gr 425

Gr 426

Gr 428

0   1m

Fig 10.114. Grave plans: Graves 425, 426, 428 and 441 (scale 1:20).

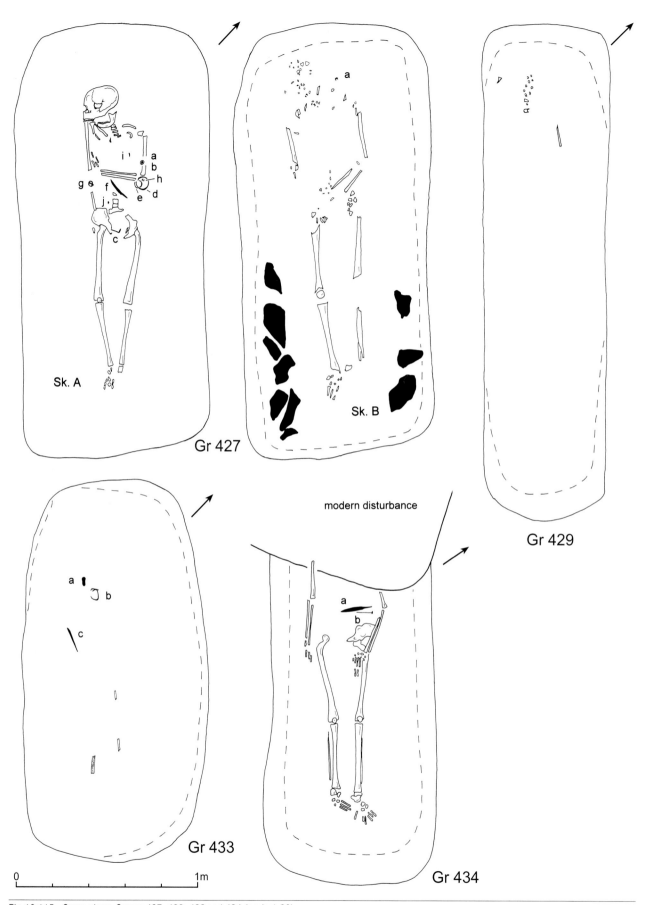

Sk. A

Gr 427

Sk. B

Gr 429

modern disturbance

Gr 433

Gr 434

0   1m

Fig 10.115. Grave plans: Graves 427, 429, 433 and 434 (scale 1:20).

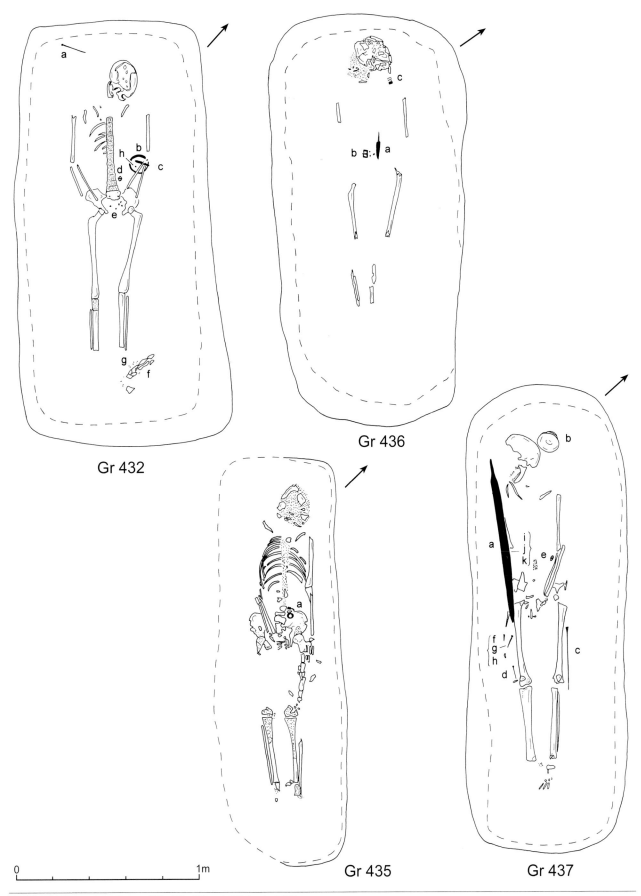

Gr 432

Gr 436

Gr 435

Gr 437

0   1m

Fig 10.116. Grave plans: Graves 432, 435, 436 and 437 (scale 1:20).

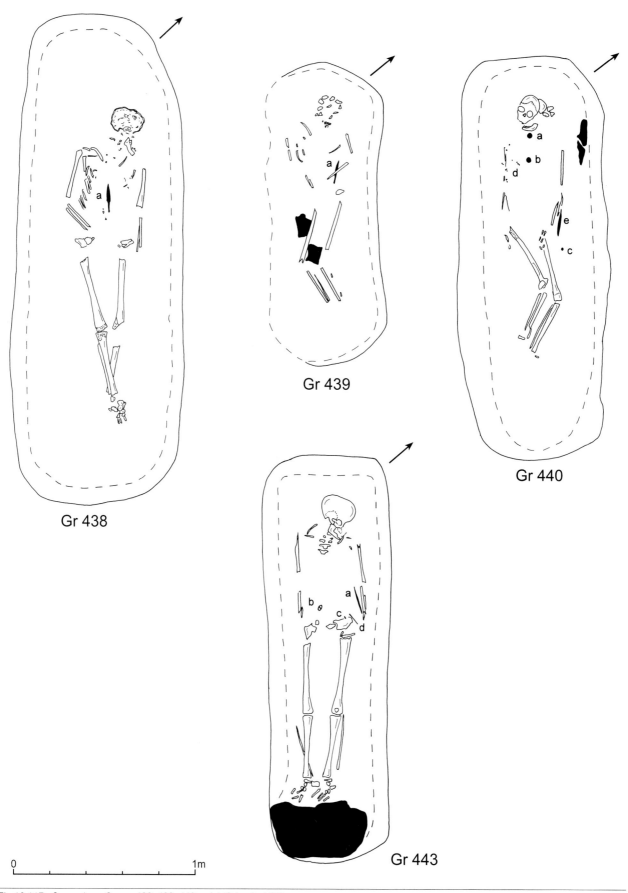

Gr 438

Gr 439

Gr 440

Gr 443

Fig 10.117. Grave plans: Graves 438, 439, 440 and 443 (scale 1:20).

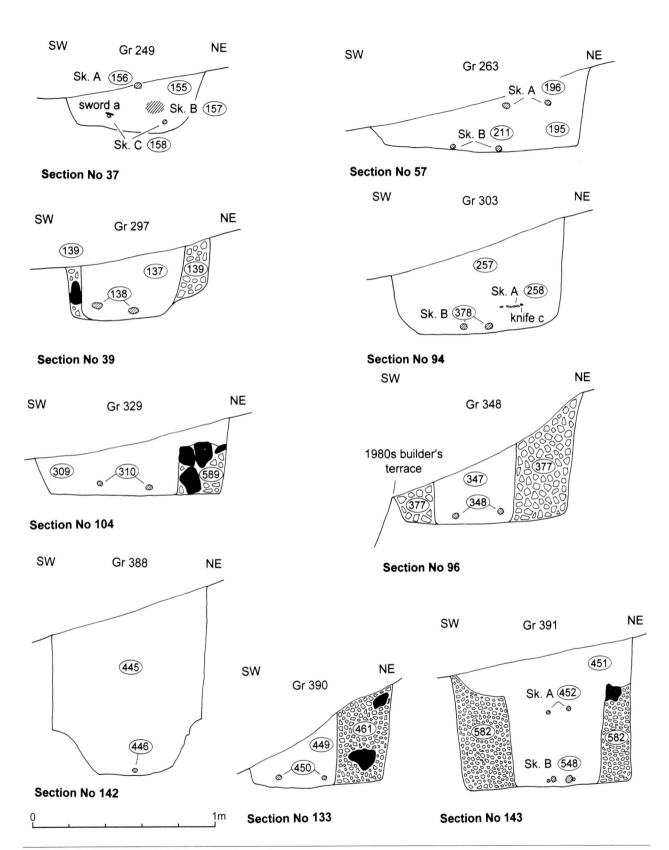

Fig 10.118. Sections across selected graves, 1994 excavation.

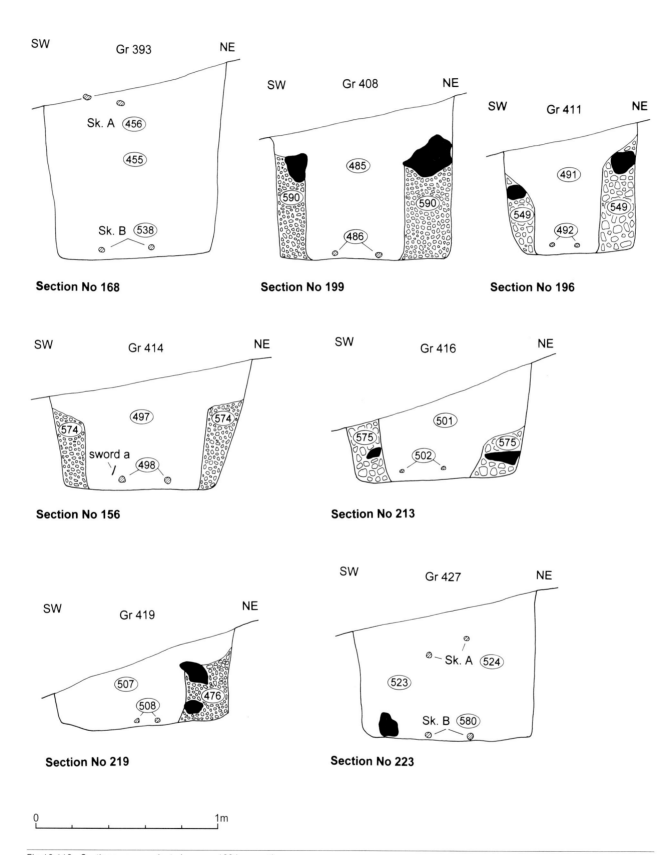

Fig 10.119. Sections across selected graves, 1994 excavation.

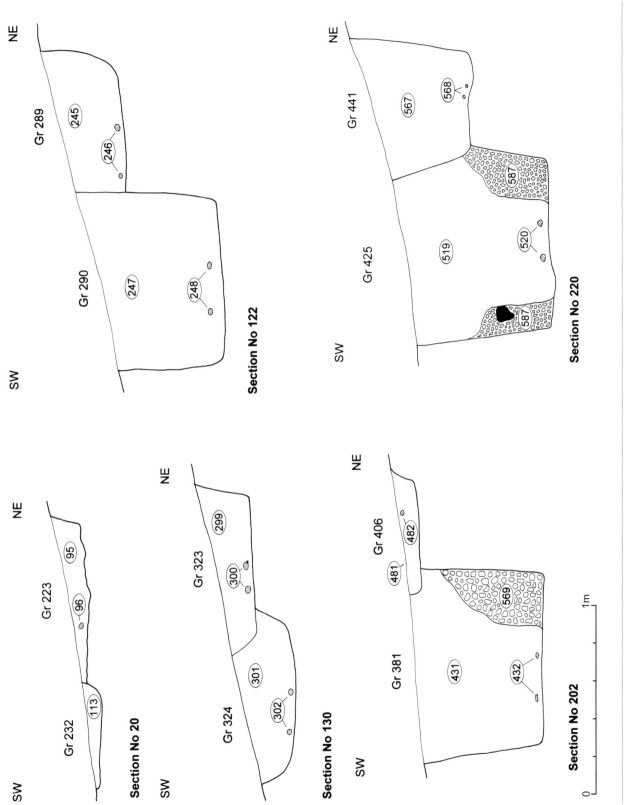

Fig 10.120. Sections across selected graves, 1994 excavation.

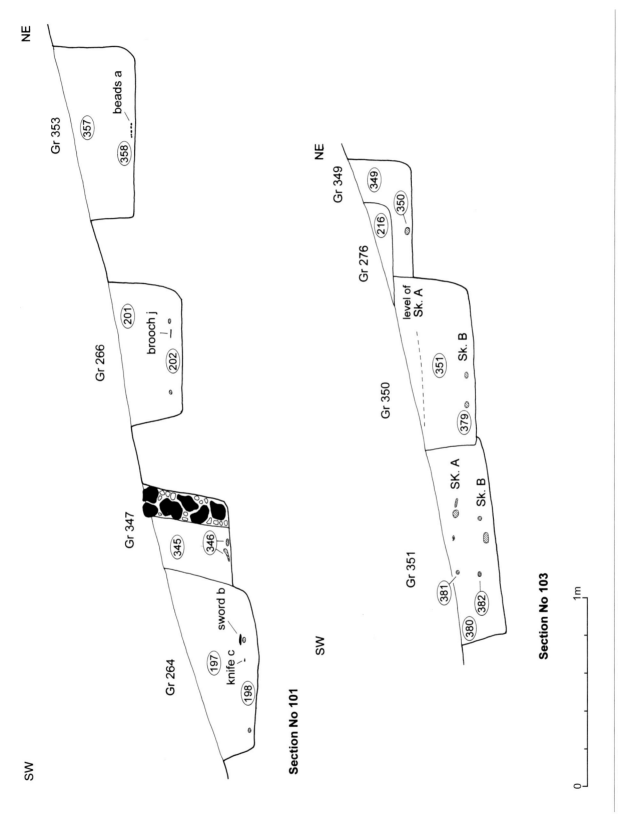

Fig 10.121. Sections across selected graves, 1994 excavation.

PART 11: SUMMARY

Summary

During the summer of 1994 the Canterbury Archaeological Trust conducted extensive excavations on the lower slopes of Long Hill, Buckland, on the outskirts of Dover in east Kent (NGR TR 3087 4291, centred). This revealed another large and hitherto unexpected portion of the early Anglo-Saxon inhumation cemetery already known from previous excavations carried out higher on the hill in 1951–3 (Evison 1987).

In 1994 evidence for both pre- and post-Anglo-Saxon agricultural terracing of the hillside was recorded. It seems probable that the cemetery had originally been established across an area of abandoned prehistoric fields. A substantial quantity of prehistoric flintwork was also recovered indicating activity in the area during the late Neolithic–Bronze Age period.

Nearly 250 new Anglo-Saxon graves were fully excavated. Fifteen contained more than one body. The remains of 233 individual skeletons, comprising men, women and children were recovered; many were associated with grave offerings. The graves were numbered from 201 to 444 in order not to duplicate numbers previously allocated in the 1951–3 excavations (Graves A–F, 1–165). Bone preservation was variable and although a number of moderately complete skeletons were recovered, a substantial group of graves contained very poorly preserved human remains, or no bone at all. There were no cremations. The distribution of graves across the site was uneven and various discrete groupings could be discerned (designated here Plots R–Z). All the burials were broadly aligned north-west by south-east, following the contours of the hill, with the head generally placed at the western end. Two graves were enclosed by small ring-gullies, implying that they had originally been covered by barrows and other mounds may have been destroyed without trace.

Most of the bodies had been interred fully clothed and just over two-thirds contained grave goods. Seven male graves contained a sword, which indicates that these were men of a high social status. Other men were provided with a spear and sometimes a shield. Women's graves included brooches and beads, together with a variety of other fittings and personal equipment. Poorer burials often contained just a small iron knife and a considerable number of people appeared to have been buried without anything. All the grave goods recovered are described and discussed in detail.

The dating evidence suggests that virtually all the 1994 graves fall within the period c AD 450–650 and most are earlier than those excavated in 1951–3. Some revision of the dating of graves excavated in the 1950s has been included. Buckland is now one of the most important Anglo-Saxon inhumation cemeteries to be excavated in southern Britain, although it is probable that not much more than 50 per cent of the total number of graves originally present have been recorded. Any general analysis of the composition and structure of the cemetery is therefore constrained by this factor.

The settlement associated with the cemetery probably lay in the valley below the site. There is now good evidence to show that Buckland was just one of a number of Anglo-Saxon cemeteries established on the hillsides around Dover. It would appear that several separate settlements had been founded within the Dour valley by the start of the seventh century AD.

Zusammenfassung

Im Sommer 1994 führte der *Canterbury Archaeological Trust* umfangreiche Ausgrabungen am unteren Teil des Hanges von Long Hill in Buckland am östlichen Rand von Dover in Kent aus (NGR TR 3087 4291, zentriert). Dabei wurde ein bis dahin unbekannter Teil eines frühmittelalterlichen Gräberfeldes entdeckt, das bis dahin vor allem durch Ausgrabungen oberhalb der Fundstelle in den Jahren 1951–3 bekannt geworden war (Evison 1987). Obwohl wahrscheinlich nicht mehr als die Hälfte der ursprünglich in Buckland angelegten Bestattungen ergraben sind, bilden die rund 400 Körpergräber einen der bedeutendsten Fundorte frühmittelalterlicher Bestattungen in Südengland.

Die Ausgrabungen von 1994 zeigten, dass der Hang sowohl vor als auch nach seiner Verwendung als Gräberfeld für landwirtschaftliche Zwecke terrassiert worden war. Erhebliche Mengen bearbeiteten Flints weisen auf Aktivitäten während des Spätneolithikums und der Bronzezeit hin. Wahrscheinlich wurden die Gräber angelegt, nachdem die Felder aufgelassen worden waren.

Im Jahr 1994 wurden fast 250 frühmittelalterliche Gräber vollständig ergegraben, von denen fünfzehn mehr als ein Skelett enthielten. Insgesamt wurden die Überreste von 233 Männern, Frauen und Kindern gefunden, überwiegend durch Beigaben datierbar. Um eine Duplizierung der 1951–3 vergebenen Buchstaben A–F und der Grabnummern 1 bis 165 zu vermeiden, erhielten die 1994 entdeckten Gräber die Nummern 201 bis 444. Während ein Teil der Gräber einigermaßen vollständige Skelette enthielt, waren die Knochen in vielen Grabgruben schlecht oder gar nicht erhalten. Brandgräber wurden nicht gefunden. Die Körpergräber verteilten sich unregelmäßig in Gruppen (R–Z) über den Hang. Die meisten Gräber hatten eine Ausrichtung nach NW-SO und folgten damit der Kontur des Hügels. Die Köpfe der Toten lagen in der Regel im Nordwesten. Kreisgräben deuten darauf hin, dass mindestens zwei der Gräber ursprünglich überhügelt waren.

Die Grabfunde, die in mehr als zwei Dritteln der Gräber gefunden wurden, weisen darauf hin, dass die Toten in der Regel bekleidet beigesetzt wurden. Die typische Waffenausstattung in Männergräbern besteht aus einem Speer, in manchen Gräbern ergänzt durch einen Schild, und in sieben Gräbern durch ein Schwert. In Frauengräbern sind Perlen die häufigste Beigabe, oft kombiniert mit Fibeln und anderen Tracht- und Gebrauchsgegenständen. Ärmere Bestattungen sind in vielen Fällen nur durch ein kleines Eisenmesser gekennzeichnet. In einem knappen Drittel der Gräber waren keine Beigaben erhalten. Sämtliche Grabfunde sind im Katalog ausführlich beschrieben und wurden einer antiquarischen Analyse unterzogen.

Den Beigaben zufolge wurde der 1994 ergrabene Abschnitt des Gräberfeldes im Wesentlichen von der Mitte des 5. Jahrhunderts bis zur Mitte des 7. Jahrhunderts belegt, mit einem zeitlichen Schwerpunkt, der vor dem 1951–3

ergrabenen Abschnitt liegt. Im Rahmen der chronologischen Analyse der Funde aus der neueren Grabung wurde die von Evison (1987) vorgelegte Gräberfeldchronologie teilweise überarbeitet.

Die zugehörige Siedlung lag wahrscheinlich unterhalb des Gräberfeldes im Tal. Seit der Publikation der älteren Grabung haben sich Hinweise darauf verdichtet, dass es sich bei Buckland um nur eines von mehreren frühmittelalterlichen Gräberfeldern an den Berghängen um Dover handelte. Es scheint, dass zu Beginn des 7. Jahrhunderts mehrere separate Siedlungen im Dour Tal existierten.

Résumé

Durant l'été 1994, le Canterbury Archaeological Trust a mené des fouilles extensives au pied du coteau de Long Hill, Buckland, dans les faubourgs de Douvres, East Kent (NGR TR 3087 42911, centré). Fait imprévu, elles ont révélé un nouveau grand secteur de la nécropole Anglo-Saxonne déjà connue par plusieurs fouilles réalisées plus haut sur le coteau, en 1951–53 (Evison 1987).

En 1994, des indices dévoilant l'existence de deux terrasses agricoles d'âge pré- et post-Anglo-Saxon ont été enregistrés sur ce coteau. Il semble probable que le cimetière ait été créé sur l'emplacement de champs préhistoriques abandonnés. Un important corpus de débitages préhistoriques a également été récupéré, indiquant une activité dans la région durant le Néolithique final et l'Âge du Bronze.

Près de 250 nouvelles tombes Anglo-Saxonnes ont été entièrement fouillées. Quinze contenaient plus d'un individu. Les restes osseux de 233 personnes, comprenant des hommes, des femmes et des enfants ont été récupérés; beaucoup étaient accompagnés d'offrandes funéraires. Les tombes ont été numérotées de 201 à 444 afin de ne pas dupliquer les numéros précédemment attribués durant les fouilles 1951–53 (tombes A à F, 1165). La préservation de l'os a été variable et bien qu'un certain nombre de squelettes quasi-complets aient été récupérés, un groupe important de tombes contenaient des restes humains très mal conservés, voire aucun reste osseux. Il n'y avait pas crémations. La répartition des tombes à travers le site était disparate et divers groupes discrets pourraient être discernés (désignés ici comme « locus R–Z »). Toutes les sépultures ont été globalement orientées nord-ouest/sud-est, suivant les contours de la colline, les têtes étant généralement placées à l'extrémité ouest. Deux tombes étaient entourées par de petits fossés circulaires, ce qui implique qu'elles ont été initialement couvertes par des tumulus ou autres monticules ; d'autres aménagements de ce type peuvent avoir été détruits sans laisser de trace.

La plupart des corps avaient été enterrés habillés et un peu plus des deux tiers contenaient des offrandes funéraires. Sept tombes masculines contenaient une épée indiquant que ces hommes étaient d'un statut social élevé. D'autres hommes étaient accompagnés d'une lance et parfois d'un bouclier. Les tombes des femmes comportaient des fibules et des perles, avec diverses pièces d'accessoires et d'équipement personnel. Les tombes les plus pauvres ne contenaient souvent qu'un petit couteau en fer et un nombre considérable de personne semble avoir été enterré sans rien. Tous les objets relevés sont décrits et discutés en détail.

Les datations suggèrent que presque toutes les tombes de 1994 se situent entre environ 450 et 650 AD et la plupart sont antérieures à celles fouillées en 1951–53. Une révision de la datation des tombes fouillées dans les années 1950 a été réalisée. Buckland est aujourd'hui l'un des plus importants cimetières d'inhumation Anglo-Saxons qui ait été fouillé dans le sud de la Grande-Bretagne, mais il est probable que seul 50 pour cent de l'effectif total des sépultures présentes à l'origine ait été enregistré. Toute analyse générale de la composition et de la structure du cimetière est donc limitée par ce facteur.

L'habitat associé à cette nécropole se situait probablement dans la vallée, en contrebas du site. Il y a maintenant des preuves suffisantes pour estimer que Buckland était seulement d'un des nombreux cimetières Anglo-Saxons établis sur les coteaux autour de Douvres. Il semblerait que plusieurs établissements distincts aient été fondés dans la vallée de la Dour au début du VIIe siècle après JC.

BIBLIOGRAPHY

Åberg, N 1926, *The Anglo-Saxons in England*, London

Adams, J C 1965, *Outline of fractures*, 4th edition, Edinburgh

Adams, N 2011, 'Earlier or later? The rectangular cloisonné buckle from Sutton Hoo Mound 1 in context' in S Brookes *et al*, 20–32

Adams, N 2012, *Bright Lights in the Dark Ages, The Eugene Thaw Collection*, New York

Affeldt, W (ed) 1990, *Frauen in Spätantike und Frühmittelalter. Lebensbedingungen - Lebensnormen – Lebensformen*, Sigmaringen

Ager, B M 1989, 'The Anglo-Saxon cemetery' in I M Stead and V Rigby, 219–39

Ager, B and Gilmour, B 1988, 'A pattern-welded Anglo-Saxon sword from Acklam Wold, North Yorkshire', *Yorkshire Archaeological Journal* 60, 13–23

Ahrens, C (ed) 1978, *Sachsen und Angelsachsen*, Helms Museum Publications 32, Hamburg, 231–43

Akerman, J Y 1853a, 'An account of excavations in an Anglo-Saxon burial ground at Harnham Hill, near Salisbury', *Archaeologia* 35, 259–78

Akerman, J Y 1853b, 'Note on some further discoveries in a cemetery of the Anglo-Saxon period at Harnham Hill, near Salisbury', *Archaeologia* 35, 475–9

Akerman, J Y 1857, 'Report of researches in a cemetery of the Anglo-Saxon period at Brighthampton, Oxon', *Archaeologia* 37, 391–8

Akerman, J Y 1860, 'Second report of researches in a cemetery of the Anglo-Saxon period at Brighthampton, Oxon', *Archaeologia* 38 (i), 84–97

Akerman, J Y 1862, 'Report of researches in an Anglo-Saxon cemetery at Long Wittenham, Berkshire, in 1859', *Archaeologia* 38 (ii), 327–52

Akerman, J Y 1863, 'Report on further researches in an Anglo-Saxon burial ground at Long Wittenham, Berkshire, in the summer of 1860', *Archaeologia* 39, 135–42

Aldsworth, F R 1978, 'Droxford Anglo-Saxon cemetery, Soberton, Hampshire', *Proceedings of the Hampshire Field Club and Archaeological Society* 35, 93–182

Alénus-Lecerf, J 1993, 'Le verre mérovingien dans les tombes de Walonie', *Trésors de Walonie. Les Verres Mérovingiens,* Musée Ourthe-Amblève, Comblain-au-Pont, 27–50

Alénus-Lecerf, J 1995, 'Contribution à l'étude des verres provenant des tombes mérovingiennes de Belgique' in D Foy (ed), 57–84

Allan, J P (ed) 1984, *Medieval and post-medieval finds from Exeter, 1971–1980*, Exeter Archaeological Reports 3, Exeter

Almgren, B 1982, 'Helmets, crowns and warrior's dress – from the Roman emperors to the chieftains of Uppland' in J P Lamm and H A Nordström, 11–16

Ament H 1970, *Fränkische Adelsgräber von Flonheim in Rheinhessen*, Germanische Denkmäler der Völkerwanderungszeit Serie B. Die fränkischen Altertümer des Rheinlandes 5, Berlin

Ament, H 1976, *Die fränkischen Grabfunde aus Mayen und der Pellenz*, Germanisches Denkmäler der Volkerwanderungszeit B9, Berlin

Ament, H 1977, 'Zur archäologischen Periodisierung der Merowingerzeit', *Germania* 55, 133–40

Ament, H 1991, 'Zur Wertshätzung antiker Gemmen in der Merowingerzeit', *Germania* 69/2, 401–24

Ament, H 1992, *Das alamannische Gräberfeld von Eschborn (Main-Taunus-Kreis)*, Wiesbaden

Anderson, S 1990, *The Human Skeletal Remains from Staunch Meadow, Brandon, Suffolk*, Ancient Monuments Laboratory Report 99/90

Anderson, S 1991, *The Human Skeletal Remains from Caister-on-Sea, Norfolk*, Ancient Monuments Laboratory Report 9/91

Anderson, S and Birkett, D 1989, *The Human Skeletal Remains from Burgh Castle, Norfolk*, Ancient Monuments Laboratory Report 27/89

Anderson, S, Bankier, A, Barrel, B, Debruijn, M, Coulson, A, Drouin, J, Eperon, I, Nierlich, D, Roe, B, Sanger, F, Schreier, P, Smith, A and Young, I 1981, 'Sequence and organization of the human mitochondrial genome', *Nature* 290, 457–65

Anderson, T 1987, 'Post-cranial non-metric variation: the examination of a neglected subject', MA thesis, Sheffield University

Anderson, T 1991, 'A medieval example of meningiomatous hyperostosis', *British Journal of Neurosurgery* 5, 499–504

Anderson, T 1992, 'An example of meningiomatous hyperostosis from medieval Rochester', *Medical History* 36, 207–13

Anderson, T 1993, 'A medieval example of meningiomatous hyperostosis', *Journal of Paleopathology* 4, 141–54

Anderson, T 1995, 'The human bones' in K Parfitt 1995c, 114–45

Anderson, T 1996a, 'Paracondylar process: manifestation of an occipital vertebra', *International Journal of Osteoarchaeology* 6, 195–201

Anderson, T 1996b, 'Cranial weapon injuries from Anglo-Saxon Dover', *International Journal of Osteoarchaeology* 6, 10–14

Anderson, T 2000a, 'A medieval Italian child with osteochondritis dissecans of the cuboid', *The Foot* 10, 216–18

Anderson, T 2000b, 'Congenital conditions and neoplastic disease' in M. Cox and S Mays (eds), 199–226

Anderson, T 2001a, 'An example of unhealed osteochondritis dissecans of the medial cuneiform', *International Journal of Osteoarchaeology* 11, 381–4

Anderson, T 2001b, 'An example of unhealed osteochondritis dissecans of the medial cuneiform', *The Foot* 11, 251–3

Anderson, T and Andrews, J 1997, 'The human bones' in K Parfitt and B Brugmann, Appendix II, 214–39

Appelton, A B 1922, 'On the hypotrochanteric fossa and accessory adductor groove of the primate femur', *Journal of Anatomy* 56, 295–306

Arrhenius, B 1985, *Merovingian Garnet Jewellery. Emergence and Social Implications*, Stockholm

Arnold, C J 1980, 'Wealth and social structure: a matter of life and death' in P Rahtz *et al* (eds), 81–142

Arnold, C J 1982, *The Anglo-Saxon Cemeteries of the Isle of Wight*, London

Arnold, C J 1988, *An Archaeology of the Early Anglo-Saxon Kingdoms*, London

Austin, W 1928, 'A Saxon cemetery at Luton, Beds', *Antiquaries Journal* viii, 177–92

Avent, R 1975, *Anglo-Saxon garnet inlaid disc and composite brooches*, British Archaeological Reports (British Series) 11, Oxford

Avent, R. and Evison, V I 1982, 'Anglo-Saxon button brooches', *Archaeologia* 107, 77–124

Axboe, M 1981, 'The Scandinavian gold bracteates: studies of their manufacture and regional variations. With a supplement to the catalogue of Mogens Mackeprang', *Acta Archaeologica* 52, 1–100

Axboe, M 1999, 'The chronology of the Scandinavian gold bracteates' in J Hines *et al* (eds), 126–47

Axboe, M 2011 (with C Behr and K Duwel), 'Katalog der Neufunde' in W Heizmann and M Axobe (eds), *Die Goldbrakteaten der Völkerwanderungszeit—Auswertung und Neufunde*. Ergänzungsbände zur Reallexikon der Germanischen Altertumskunde 40, Berlin, 893–999

Babb, L 1996, 'A corpus of Anglo-Saxon weapons and knives in Buckinghamshire County Museum', *Records of Buckinghamshire* 38, 139–52

Bach, S and Boudartchouk, J -L 1996, 'La nécrople franque du site de la Gravette à L'Isle-Jourdain (Gers)', *Aquitania* 14, 153–6

Bakka, E 1973, 'Goldbrakteaten in norwegischen Grabfunden: Datierungsfragen', *Frühmittelalterliche Studien* 7, 53–87

Bakka, E 1981, 'Scandinavian-type gold bracteates in Kentish and continental grave finds' in V I Evison (ed), 11–38

Balasubramaniam, G and R 2003, 'Alloy design of ductile phosphoric iron: Ideas from archaeometallurgy', *Bulletin of Materials Science* 26, 483–91

Baldwin Brown, G 1915a, *The Arts in Early England. Saxon Art and Industry in the Pagan Period* 3, London

Baldwin Brown, G 1915b, *The Arts in Early England. Saxon Art and Industry in the Pagan Period* 4, London

Banck-Burgess, J 1997, 'An Webstuhl und webrahmen: alamannisches Textilhandwerk', *Die Alamannen*, Baden-Württemberg, Theiss, 371–8

Barfod Carlsen, E 1997, 'En Stylistisk og Kronologisk Analyse af D-brakteaterne', unpublished hovedfag dissertation, Forhistorisk Arkæologi, Århus University

Barfod Carlsen, E 2002, 'Fabeldyr i udvikling: en analyse af D-brakteaterne', *Hikuin* 29, 119–42

Barham, A J and Bates, M R 1990, *The Holocene Prehistory Palaeoenvironments of the Dour Valley Catchment*, Geo-archaeological Service Facility, University College London, Technical Report 90/04

Barnes, E 1994, *Developmental Defects of the Axial Skeleton in Paleopathology*, Colorado

Barrie, H J 1987, 'Osteochondritis dissecans 1887–1987', *Journal of Bone and Joint Surgery* 69B, 693–5

Bartel, A and Knöchlein, R 1993, 'Zu einem Frauengrab des sechsten Jahrhunderts aus Waging am See, Lkr Traunstein, Oberbayern', *Germania* 71, 419–39

Bassett, S (ed) 1989, *The Origins of Anglo-Saxon Kingdoms*, London and New York

Batcheller, W 1828, *A New History of Dover and of Dover Castle*, first edition, Dover

Batchelor, D 1990, 'Darenth Park Anglo-Saxon cemetery, Dartford', *Archaeologia Cantiana* cviii, 35–72

Bates, M R, Barham, A J, Jones, S, Parfitt, K, Parfitt, S, Pedley, M, Preece, R C, Walker, M J C and Whittaker, J E 2008, 'Holocene sequences and archaeology from the Crabble Paper Mill site, Dover, UK and their regional significance', *Proceedings of the Geologists' Association* 119, 299–327

Bayliss, A, Scull, C, McCormac, F G, Bronk Ramsey, C and Athfield Beavan, N 2009, 'Radiocarbon dating' in C Scull, *Early Medieval (late 5th - early 8th centuries AD) Cemeteries at Boss Hall and Buttermarket, Ipswich, Suffolk*, Society of Medieval Archaeology Monograph 27, 261–7

Bayliss, A, Hines, J, Høilund Nielsen, K, McCormac, F G and Scull, C forthcoming a, *Anglo-Saxon Graves and Grave-goods of the Sixth and Seventh Centuries: A Chronological Framework*, Society of Medieval Archaeology Monograph

Bayliss, A, Hines, J, McCormac, F G and Thompson, M M forthcoming b, 'Chapter 2: Dating methods and their modelling' in A Bayliss *et al* forthcoming a

Bayliss, A, Hines, J and Høilund Nielsen, K forthcoming c, 'Chapter 6: Interpretative chronologies for the male graves' in A Bayliss *et al* forthcoming a

Bayliss, A, Hines, J and Høilund Nielsen, K forthcoming d, 'Chapter 7: Interpretative chronologies for the female graves' in A Bayliss *et al* forthcoming a

Bealer, A W 1995, *The Art of Blacksmithing*, Edison, New Jersey

Beals, K L 1972, 'Head form and climatic stress', *American Journal of Physical Anthropology* 37, 85–92

Beavan-Athfield, N R, McFadgen, B G and Sparks, R J 2001, 'Environmental influences on dietary carbon and ¹⁴C ages in modern rats and other species', *Radiocarbon* 43, 7–14

Beavan, N, Mays, S, Bayliss, A, Hines, J and McCormac, F G 2011, *Amino acid and stable isotope analysis of skeletons dated for the Anglo-Saxon chronology project*, Research Department Report Series 88/2011

Beavan, N and Mays, S forthcoming, 'Chapter 4: The human skeletons' in A Bayliss *et al* forthcoming a

Becatti, G 1955, *Oreficerie Antiche dale Minoiche alle Barbariche*, Rome

Beck, H, Jankkuhn, H, Ranke, K and Wenskus, R (eds) 1982–3, *Reallexikon der Germanische Altertumskunde*, Berlin

Behmer, E 1939, *Das Zweischneidige Schwert der germanischen Völkerwanderungszeit*, Stockholm

Behr, C 2010, 'New bracteate finds from Early Anglo-Saxon England', *Medieval Archaeology* 54, 34–88

Behrens, G 1947, *Merowingerzeit (Original-Altertümer des Zentralmuseums in Mainz)*, Römisch-Germanisches Zentralmuseum zu Mainz, Katalog 13, Mainz

Bender Jørgensen, L 1989, 'European textiles in later prehistory and early history: a research project', *Journal of Danish Archaeology* 8, 144–58

Bender Jørgensen, L 1992, *North European Textiles until AD 1000*, Aarhus

Bender Jørgensen, L and Wild, J P 1988, 'Clothes from the Roman Empire: barbarians or Romans?', *Achaeological Textiles*, Arkeologiske Skrifter 2, Copenhagen, 65–98

Bennett, P, Clark, P, Hicks, A, Rady, J and Riddler, I 2008, *At the Great Crossroads. Prehistoric, Roman and medieval discoveries on the Isle of Thanet 1994–95*, Canterbury Archaeological Trust Occasional Paper No 4, Canterbury

Berry, A C 1975, 'Factors affecting the incidence of non-metrical skeletal variants', *Journal of Anatomy* 101, 519–35

Berry, A C and Berry, R J 1967, 'Epigenetic variation in the human cranium', *Journal of Anatomy* 101, 361–79

Berthelier-Ajot, N, Oger, B and Vierck, H 1985, 'Tunique de la Reine Bathilde' in *La Neustrie* (Catalogue de l'Exposition), Rouen, Musée des Antiquités, 138–9

Bertram, M 1996, *Merowingerzeit. Die Altertümer in Museum für Vor- und Frühgeschichte*, Berlin

Bidder, H F and Morris, J 1959, 'The Anglo Saxon cemetery at Mitcham', *Surrey Archaeological Collections* 56, 51–131

Biddle, M 1990, *Object and Economy in Medieval Winchester*, Winchester Studies 7ii, Oxford

Bierbrauer, V 1974, *Die Ostgotischen Grab- und Schatzfunde aus Italien*, Spoleto

Birkett, D 1992, 'Skeletal pathology' in S J Sherlock and M G Welch, 118–19

Bishop, M C and Coulston, J C N 1993, *Roman Military Equipment from the Punic Wars to the fall of Rome*, London

Blakelock, E, Martinón-Torres, M, Veldhuijzen, H A and Young, T 2009, 'Slag inclusions in iron objects and the quest for provenance', *Journal of Archaeological Science* 36, 1745–57

Blockley, K, Blockley, M, Blockley, P, Frere, S S and Stow, S 1995, *Excavations in the Marlowe Car Park and Surrounding Areas Part II: The Finds*, The Archaeology of Canterbury V, Canterbury

Blunt, C E 1979, 'The Hougham hoard of sceattas *c.*1780', *Numismatic Chronicle* 19 (7th series), 108–10 and pl 15

Boardman, J 1994, 'Omphale', *Lexicon Iconographicum Mythologiae Classicae* VII, Zurich and Munich, 45–53

Boardman, J and Vollenweider, M-L 1978, *Catalogue of the Engraved Gems and Finger rings. I. Greek and Etruscan*, Ashmolean Museum, Oxford

Bode, M-J 1998, *Schmalstede. Ein Urnengräberfeld der Kaiser- und Völkerwanderungszeit*, Urnenfriedhöfe Schleswig-Holsteins 13, Offa-Bücher 78, Neumünster

Böhme, A 1972, 'Die Fibeln der Kastelle Saalburg und Zugmantel', *Saalburg Jahrbüch* xxix, 5–112

Böhme, H W 1974, *Germanische Grabfunde des 4.bis 5.Jahrhunderts zwischen unterer Elbe und Loire*, Münchner Beiträge zur Vor und Frühgeschichte 19, 2 vols, München

Böhme, H W 1988, 'Les Thuringiens dans le Nord du Royaume Franc', *Revue Archéologique de Picardie* 3/4, 57–69

Böhme, H W 1989, 'Eine elbgermanische Bügelfibel des 5. Jahrhunderts aus Limetz-Villez (Yvelines, Frankreich)', *Archäologisches Korrespondenzblatt* 19, 397–406

Böhme, H W 1994, 'Der Frankenkönig Childerich zwischen Attila und Aetius' in C Dobiat (ed), *Festschrift für Otto-Herman Frey zum 65. Geburtstag*, Marburger Studien zur Vor- und Frühgeschichte 16, Marburg, 69–110

Böhme, H W 2002, 'The cemetery of Aldaieta in Cantabria – evidence of a Frankish battlefield of the 6th century?', *Acta Praehistorica et Archaeologica* 34, 135–50

Böhner, K 1958, *Die Fränkischen Altertümer des Trierer Landes*, Germanische Denkmäler der Volkerwanderungszeit, Serie B 1,1 and 2, Berlin

Böhner, K 1959, *Das Grab eines frankischen Herren aus Morken im Rheinland, Kunst und Altertum am Rhein,* Führer des Rheinischen Landesmuseums in Bonn 4, Bonn

Bolk, L 1917, 'On metopism', *American Journal of Anatomy* 22, 27–47

Bóna, I 1976, *The Dawn of the Dark Ages: the Gepids and the Lombards in the Carpathian Basin*, Budapest

Bond, J 1994, 'An explanatory note on the identification of the ivory fragments' in C Hills *et al*, 35–6

Boulanger, C 1902–5, *Le Mobilier Funéraire Gallo-Romain et Franc en Picardie et en Artois,* Paris

Bowen, H C 1969, 'The Celtic background' in A L F Rivet, *The Roman Villa in Britain*, London, 1–48

Boyd, G I 1930, 'The emissary foramina of the cranium in man and the anthropoids', *Journal of Anatomy* 65, 108–21

Boyle, A, Dodd, A, Miles, D and Mudd, A 1995, *Two Oxfordshire Anglo-Saxon Cemeteries: Berinsfield and Didcot*, Thames Valley Landscapes Monograph 8, Oxford

Boyle, A, Jennings, D, Miles, D and Palmer, S 1998, *The Anglo-Saxon Cemetery at Butler's Field, Lechlade, Gloucestershire*, Oxford Archaeological Unit: Thames Valley Monograph No 10, 43–52

Boylston, A 2000, 'Evidence for weapon-related trauma in British archaeological samples' in M Cox and S Mays (eds), 357–80

Boylston, A, Wiggins, R and Roberts, C 1998, 'Human skeletal remains' in G Drinkall and M Foreman, 221–36

Boys, W 1792, *Collections for an History of Sandwich in Kent*, Canterbury

Brent, J 1862–3, 'Account of the society's researches in the Saxon cemetery at Sarr. Part I', *Archaeologia Cantiana* v, 305–22

Brent, J 1864–5, 'Account of the society's researches in the Saxon cemetery at Sarr. Part II', *Archaeologia Cantiana* vi, 157–85

Brent, J 1867, 'An account of researches in an Anglo Saxon cemetery at Stowting, in Kent', *Archaeologia* 41, 409–20

Brent, J 1868, 'Account of the society's researches in the Saxon cemetery at Sarr. Part III', *Archaeologia Cantiana* viii, 307–21

Breuer, J and Roosens, H 1957, 'Le cimetière franc de Haillot', *Archaeologia Belgica* 34, 320–37

Briscoe, T 1968, 'The Anglo-Saxon S-shaped brooch in England with special reference to one from Lakenheath, Suffolk', *Proceedings of the Cambridge Antiquarian Society* 61, 45–53

Bronk Ramsey, C 2009, 'Bayesian analysis of radiocarbon dates', *Radiocarbon* 51, 37–60

Brookes, S 2007, 'Boat-rivets in graves in pre-Viking Kent: Reassessing Anglo-Saxon boat-burial traditions', *Medieval Archaeology* 51, 1–18

Brookes, S and Harrington, S 2010, *The Kingdom and People of Kent AD 400–1066*, Stroud

Brookes, S, Harrington, S and Reynolds, A 2011, *Studies in Early Anglo-Saxon Art and Archaeology: Papers in Honour of Martin G Welch*, British Archaeological Reports (British Series) 527, Oxford

Brooks, N 1989, 'The creation and early structure of the Kingdom of Kent' in S Bassett (ed), 55–74

Brothwell, D R 1967, 'The human remains from Ports Down' in A Corney, P Ashbee, V I Evison and D R Brothwell, 'A prehistoric and Anglo-Saxon burial ground at Ports Down, Portsmouth', *Proceedings of the Hampshire Field Club and Archaeological Society* 24, 20–41

Brothwell, D R, Powers, R and Hirst, S M 2000, 'The pathology' in P Rahtz *et al*, 195–238

Brown, D 1977, 'Firesteels and pursemounts again', *Bonner Jahrbücher* 177, 451–77

Brown, K R, Kidd, D and Little, C T (eds) 2000, *From Attila to Charlemagne. Arts of the early Migration Period in the Metropolitan Museum of Art,* Yale

Brown, W M, George Jr, M and Wilson, A C 1979, 'Rapid evolution of animal mitochondrial DNA', *Proceedings of the National Academy of Sciences (USA)* 76, 1967–71

Bruce-Mitford, R 1978, *The Sutton Hoo Ship-burial*, vol 2, London

Bruce-Mitford, R 1983, *The Sutton Hoo Ship-burial*, vol 3: London

Brugmann, B 1999a, 'The role of continental artefact-types in sixth-century Kentish chronology' in J Hines *et al* (eds), 37–64

Brugmann, B 1999b, 'The bird mount' in K Parfitt, 394–6

Brugmann, B 2004, *Glass beads from Early Anglo-Saxon Graves. A study of the provenance and chronology of glass beads from Early Anglo-Saxon graves, based on visual examination*, Oxbow Books, Oxford

Brugmann, B 2011, 'Migration and endogenous change' in H Hamerow *et al* (eds), 30–45

Brynja, E 1997, 'Med Handtag och fodrol. Presentation av en folkvandringstida kemtyp från Mälarden' in S Åkerlund, S Bergh, J Nordblad and J Taffinder, *Till Gunborg, Arkeologiska samtal*, Stockholm Archaeological Reports 33, Stockholm, 105–17

Buchwald, V F 2005, *Iron and Steel in Ancient Times,* Historisk-fiflosofiske Skrifter 29, det Kongelige Danske Videnskabernes Selskab, 282–91

Buchwald, V F and Wivel, H 1998, 'Slag analysis as a method for the characterisation and provincing of ancient iron objects,' *Materials Characterization* 40, 73–96

Buck, C E, Cavanagh, W G and Litton, C D 1996, *The Bayesian Approach to Interpreting Archaeological Data*, Wiley, Chichester

Bühler H-E and Straßberger, C 1966, 'Werkstoffkundliche Untersuchungen an zwei fränkischen Schwerten aus dem 9, Jahrhundert', *Archiv für das Eisenhüttenwesen* 37(8), 613–9

Bullinger, H 1969, *Spätantike Gürtelbeschläge. Typen, Herstellung und Datierung*, Dissertationes Archaeologicae Gaudenses XII, Brugge

Bullough, P G and Boachie-Adjei, O 1988, *Atlas of Spinal Diseases*, Philadelphia

Bunning, P S C 1964, 'Some observations on the west African calcaneus and the associated talo-calcaneal interosseous ligamentous apparatus', *American Journal of Physical Anthropology* 22, 467–72

Burrows, V 2009, 'The Wolverton warrior, Alkham valley near Dover', *Kent Archaeological Society Newsletter* 81, 14–15

Burzler, A 2000, *Archäologische Beiträge zum Nobilifizierungsprozess in der jüngeren Merowingerzeit,* Materialhefte zur Bayrischen Vorgeschichte A77, Kallmünz

Busch, B W, Gustafsson, T and Uebing, C 1999, 'Competition of arsenic and sulphur segregation on Fe-9%W(100) single crystal surfaces', *Applied Physics Letters* 74, 23 3564–6

Bush H and Zvelebil, M (eds) 1991, *Health in Past Societies Biocultural interpretations of Human Skeletal Remains in Archaeological Contexts,* British Archaeological Reports (International Series) S567, Oxford

Butterworth, C A and Lobb, S J 1992, *Excavations in the Burghfield Area, Berkshire. Developments in the Bronze Age and Saxon Landscapes,* Wessex Archaeology Report 1, Salisbury

Cabart, H and Feyeux J-Y 1995, 'Verres en Champagne', *Bulletin de la Societé Archéologique Champenoise* 88, 1–180

Cahn, A and Kaufmann-Heinimann, A (eds) 1984, *Der spätrömische Silberschatz von Kaiseraugst*, Derendingen

Cameron, E 2000, *Sheaths and Scabbards in England AD 400 – 1100*, British Archaeological Reports (British Series) 301, Oxford

Cameron, E and Filmer-Sankey, W 1993, 'A sword hilt of horn from the Snape Anglo-Saxon cemetery, Suffolk', *Anglo-Saxon studies in Archaeology and History* 6, 103–5

Campbell, J (ed) 1982, *The Anglo-Saxons*, London

Capecchi, V and Rabino Massa, E (eds), *Proceedings of the 5th European Meeting of the Paleopathological Association, 1984*, Paleopathological Association, Siena

Cardy, A 1998, 'The human bones' in P Hill, 519–92

Carlson, D S G, Armelagos, G J and Van Gerven, D P 1974, 'Factors influencing the etiology of cribra orbitalia in prehistoric Nubia', *Journal of Human Evolution* 3, 405–10

Carver, M O H (ed) 1992, *The Age of Sutton Hoo. The Seventh Century in North-Western Europe*, Woodbridge

Carver, M O H 2005, *Sutton Hoo: a seventh-century princely burial ground and its context*. Society of Antiquaries Research Report 69, London

Catteddu, I 1992, 'L'habitat Mérovingien de Genlis (Côte-d'Or)', *Revue Archéologique de l'Est et du Centre-Est* 43, 39–98

Chabouillet, M 1858, *Des Camées et pierres Gravées de la Bibliothèque Impériale*, Paris

Chadour, A 1994, *Ringe. Rings. Die Alice und Louis Koch Sammlung. Vierzig Jahrhunderte durch vier Generationen gesehen, The Alice and Louis Koch Collection, Forty Years through four Generations*, Leeds

Chadwick, S 1958, 'The Anglo-Saxon cemetery at Finglesham, Kent: a reconsideration', *Medieval Archaeology* ii, 1–71

Chadwick Hawkes, S 1969, 'Early Anglo-Saxon Kent', *Archaeological Journal* cxxvi, 186–92

Chadwick Hawkes, S 1973, 'The dating and social significance of the burials in the Polhill cemetery' in B J Philp 1973a, 186–201

Chadwick Hawkes, S 1976, 'Orientation at Finglesham: sunrise dating of death and burial in an Anglo-Saxon cemetery in east Kent', *Archaeologia Cantiana* xcii, 33–51

Chadwick Hawkes, S 1982a, 'Anglo-Saxon Kent *c* 425–725' in P E Leach (ed), 64–78

Chadwick Hawkes, S 1982b, 'Finglesham: a cemetery in East Kent' in J Campbell (ed), 24–5

Chadwick Hawkes, S 1987, 'Some early Anglo-Saxon objects from east Kent', *Archaeologia Cantiana* civ, 1–7

Chadwick Hawkes, S 1989a, 'The south-east after the Romans: the Saxon settlement' in V Maxfield (ed), 78–95

Chadwick Hawkes, S (ed) 1989b, *Weapons and Warfare in Anglo-Saxon England*, Oxford University Committee for Archaeology Monograph No 21, Oxford

Chadwick Hawkes, S 2000, 'The Anglo-Saxon cemetery of Bifrons, in the parish of Patrixbourne, East Kent' in D Griffiths (ed), 1–94

Chadwick Hawkes, S and Grainger, G 2006, The Anglo-Saxon Cemetery at Finglesham, Kent, *Oxford University School of Archaeology: Monograph 64,* Oxford

Chadwick Hawkes, S and Hogarth, A C 1974, 'The Anglo-Saxon cemetery at Monkton, Thanet', *Archaeologia Cantiana* lxxxix, 49–89

Chadwick Hawkes, S and Pollard, M 1981, 'The gold bracteates from sixth-century Anglo-Saxon graves in Kent, in the light of a new finds from Finglesham', *Frühmittelalterliche Studien* 15, 316–70

Chadwick Hawkes, S and Wells, C 1975, 'Crime and punishment in an Anglo-Saxon cemetery?', *Antiquity* 49, 118–22

Chapman, H S 1921, *The Story of Dola*, London

Christlein, R 1979, *Die Alamannen, Archäologie eines lebendigen Volkes*, Stuttgart

Clason, A T (ed) 1975, *Archaeozoological studies*, Elsevier

Coatsworth, E and Pinder, M 2002, *The Art of the Anglo-Saxon Goldsmith. Fine Metalwork in Anglo-Saxon England: its Practice and Practitioners*, Woodbridge

Collingwood 1982, *The Techniques of Tablet-weaving*, London, Faber and Faber

Cook, A M and Dacre, M W 1985, *Excavations at Portway, Andover 1973–1975*, Oxford University Committee for Archaeology Monograph No 4, Oxford

Cook, J M 2004, *Early Anglo-Saxon Buckets. A Corpus of copper alloy and iron-bound, stave-built vessels*, Oxford School of Archaeology Monograph 60, Oxford

Corke, B and Parfitt, K 1997, 'Buckland valley, Dover', *Canterbury's Archaeology 1995–1996*, 39

Corney, A, Ashbee, P, Evison, V I and Brothwell, D R 1967, 'A prehistoric and Anglo-Saxon burial ground at Ports Down, Portsmouth', *Proceedings of the Hampshire Field Club and Archaeological Society* 24, 20–41

Cox, M 1990, *The Human Bones from West Heslerton, North Yorkshire*, Ancient Monuments Laboratory Report 112/90

Cox, M 1999, 'The human bones analysis and interpretation of the skeletal material' in C Haughton and D Powlesland, 172–88

Cox M and Mays S (eds) 2000, *Human Osteology in Archaeology and Forensic Science*, Greenwich Medical Media, London

Crabtree, P 1989, *West Stow, Suffolk: Early Anglo-Saxon Animal Husbandry*, East Anglian Archaeology Report No 47, Gressenhall

Craddock, P T 1995, *Early Metal Mining and Production,* Edinburgh

Cramp, R J 2006, *Wearmouth and Jarrow Monastic Sites* 2, English Heritage, Swindon

Crawford, S 1993, 'Children, death and the afterlife in Anglo-Saxon England' in W Filmer-Sankey (ed), 83–91

Crawford, S 1999, *Childhood in Anglo-Saxon England*, Stroud

Crew, P 1991, 'The experimental production of prehistoric bar iron', *Historical Metallurgy* 25(1), 21–36

Crew, P 1998, 'The influence of clay and charcoal ash on bloomery slags' in C C Tizzoni and M Tizzoni (eds), 1–12

Crew, P and Crew, S (eds) 1990, *Early Mining in the British Isles*, Plas Tan y Bwlch Snowdonia Study Centre, Maentwrog

Crew, P and Crew, S (eds) 1997, *Early Ironworking in Europe: archaeology and experiment*, Plas Tan y Bwlch Occasional Paper No 3, Maentwrog

Crew, P and Charlton, M 2007, 'The anatomy of a furnace ... and some of its ramifications' in S La Niece *et al* (eds) 219–25

Crew, P and Salter, C 1991, 'Comparative data from iron smelting and smithing experiments', *Materialy Archeologiczne*, 26, International Archaeometallurgy Conference, Krakow, 15–22

Crew, P and Salter, C 1993, 'Currency bars with welded tips' in A Esplund (ed), 11–30

Cronyn, J M 1990, *The Elements of Archaeological Conservation*, London

Cross, J F and Bruce, M F 1989, 'The skeletal remains' in J A Stones (ed), 119–41

Cross, R P and Parfitt, K 1999, *'Former Old Park Barracks, Whitfield, Dover Proposed Redevelopment. Archaeological Desk Study and Impact Assessment'*, unpublished Canterbury Archaeological Trust report prepared for Dover Harbour Board, May 1999

Crowfoot, E 1969, 'Textiles' in P J Tester, 'Excavations at Fordcroft, Orpington, Kent', *Archaeologia Cantiana* lxxxiv, 50–3

Crowfoot, E 1983, 'The textiles' in R Bruce-Mitford, 409–62

Crowfoot, E 1987, 'Textiles' in V I Evison, 190–5

Crowfoot, E 2008, 'Appendix II, The textiles from the graves excavated in 1976', pp 54–9 in M Welch, 'Report on excavations of the Anglo-Saxon cemetery at Updown, Eastry, Kent', *Anglo-Saxon Studies in Archaeology and History* 15, 1–69

Crowfoot, E and Chadwick Hawkes, S 1967, 'Early Anglo-Saxon gold braids', *Medieval Archaeology*, 11, 42–86; with addenda and corrigenda 209–10

Cuisinier, J 1988, *Un village au temps de Charlemagne. Moines et paysans de l'abbaye de Saint Denis du VIIe siècle à l'An Mil*, Paris

Cutler, D F 1987, 'Wood' in V I Evison, 195–6

Cybulski, J S 1977, 'Cribra orbitalia a possible sign of anemia in early historic native populations of the British Columbian coast', *American Journal of Physical Anthropology* 47, 31–40

Damm, I G 1988, 'Goldschmeidarbeiten der Völkerwanderungszeit aus des Nördlichen Schwarzmeetgebet. Katalog der Sammlung Diergardt 2', *Kölner Jarhbuch für Vor- und Frühgeschichte* 21, 65–210

Dannheimer, H 1998, *Das baiuwarische Reihengräberfeld von Aubing, Stadt München*, Monographien der Prähistorischen Staatssammlung München 1, Stuttgart

Darling, M J and Gurney, D 1993, *Caister-on-Sea. Excavations by Charles Green 1951–1955*, East Anglian Archaeology 60, Gressenhall

Dasen, V 2008, 'Le secret d'Omphale', *Revue archéologique* 2008/2, 265–81

Davidson, H E 1998, *The Sword in Anglo-Saxon England. Its Archaeology and Literature,* Woodbridge (corrected reprint of 1962 edition)

Davies, A 1932, 'A re-survey of the morphology of the nose in relation to climate', *Journal of the Royal Anthropological Institute* 62, 337–59

Davis, S J M 1992, *A rapid method for recording information about mammal bones from archaeological sites*, Ancient Monuments Laboratory Report 19/92

Davison, A, Green, B and Milligan, B 1993, *Illington: A Study of a Breckland Parish and its Anglo-Saxon Cemetery,* East Anglian Archaeology 63, Gressenhall

de Baye, J 1893, *The industrial arts of the Anglo-Saxons*, Lampeter, reprinted 1990

Dean, M J and Kinsley A G 1993, *Broughton Lodge*, Nottingham Archaeological Monographs 4, Nottingham

de Freitas, V, Madeira, M C, Toledo, J L and Chagas, C F 1979, 'Absence of the mental foramen in dry human mandibles', *Acta Anatomica* 104, 353–5

Delestre, X and Périn, P (eds) 1998, *La datation des structures et des objets du haut moyen âge: méthodes et résultats. Actes des Xve Journées internationales d'Archéologie mérovingienne. Rouen, Musée des Antiquités de la Seine-Maritime 4–6 février 1994*, Mémoires publiés par l'Association française archéologie Mérovingienne, Saint-Germain-en-Laye

Delestre, X, Kazanski M and Périn, P 2006, *De l'Âge du fer au haut Moyen Âge. Archéologie funéraire, princes et elites guerrières*, Mémoires publiés par l'Association française d'Archéologie mérovingienne XV, Saint Germain-en-Laye

DeNiro, M J 1985, 'Post-mortum preservation and alteration of *in vivo* bone collagen isotope ratios in relation to palaeodietary reconstruction', *Nature* 317, 806–9

Denston, C B 1974, 'Report on the skeletons' in S Chadwick Hawkes and A C Hogarth, 85–9

De Ricci, S 1912, *Catalogue of a Collection of Ancient Rings formed by the Late E Guilhou*, Paris

Desaulty, A-M, Mariet, C, Dillmann, P, Joron, J-L, Gratuze, B, Mahé-Le-Carlier, C and Fluzin, P 2009, 'Trace element behaviour in direct- and indirect-iron metallurgy: the case of Pays De Bray (France)', *Archaeometallurgy in Europe 2007*, Associazione Italiana di Metallurgia, Milan, 318–34

Deschler-Erb, E 1999, *Ad arma! Römisches Militär des 1.Jahrhunderts n. Chr. in Augusta Raurica,* Forschungen in Augst 28, Augst

Detsicas, A and Chadwick Hawkes, S 1973, 'Finds from the Anglo-Saxon cemetery in Eccles, Kent', *Antiquaries Journal* liii, 281–6

Dickinson, T M 1976, 'The Anglo-Saxon burial sites of the Upper Thames region and their bearing on the history of Wessex, *c* AD 400–700', unpublished D Phil thesis, University of Oxford

Dickinson, T M 1993, 'Early Anglo-Saxon saucer brooches: a preliminary overview' in W Filmer Sankey (ed), 11–44

Dickinson, T M and Härke, H 1992, *Early Anglo-Saxon shields*, (*Archaeologia* 110), London

Dickinson, T M and Speake, G 1992, 'The seventh-century cremation burial in Asthall Barrow, Oxfordshire: a reassessment' in M O H Carver (ed), 95–130

Didelot, C 1997, 'Memoire de Maitrise de Sciences et Techniques de conservation - Restauration des biens culturels', *Universite, Paris I*, Sorbonne

Dillmann, P and L'Héritier, M 2007, 'Slag inclusion analyses for studying ferrous alloys employed in French medieval buildings: supply of materials and diffusion of smelting processes', *Journal of Archaeological Science* 34, 1810–23

Dillmann, P, Bernardi, P and Fluzin, P 2003, 'Use of iron for building medieval monuments. The Palais de Papes in Avignon and other French buildings' in *Archaeometallurgy in Europe, 24-25-26 September 2003, Milan Italy,* 1, 199–208

Dobney, K and Goodman, A H 1991, 'Epidemiological studies of dental enamel hypoplasias in Mexico and Bradford: their relevance to archaeological skeletal studies' in H Bush and M Zvelebil (eds), 81–100

Dobney, K and Reilly, K 1988, 'A method for recording archaeological animal bones: the use of diagnostic zones', *Circaea* 5.1, 79–96

Doppelfeld, O 1960, 'Das fränkische Frauengrab unter dem Chor des Kölner Domes', *Germania* 38, 89–113

Doppelfeld, O 1964, 'Das fränkische Knabengrab unter dem Chor des Kölner Domes', *Germania* 42, 156–88

Doppelfeld, O and Pirling, R 1966, *Fränkische Fürsten im Rheinland. Die Gräber aus dem Kölner Dom, von Krefeld-Gellep und Morken.* Schriften des Rheinischen Landesmuseums Bonn 2, Düsseldorf

Douglas, J 1793, *Nenia Britannica. A Sepulchral History of Great Britain from the Earliest Period to its general conversion*, London

Down, A and Welch, M 1990, *Apple Down and The Mardens*, Chichester Excavations 7, Dorchester

Drancourt, M, Aboudharam, G, Signoli, M, Dutour, O and Raoult, D 1998, 'Detection of 400-year-old *Yersinia pestis* DNA in human dentai pulp: An approach to the diagnosis of ancient septicemia', *Proceedings of the National Academy of Sciences (USA)* 95 (21), 12637–40

Drinkall, G and Foreman, M 1998, *The Anglo-Saxon Cemetery at Castledyke South, Barton-on-Humber*, Sheffield Excavation Report No 6, Sheffield

Driver, J C, Rady, J and Sparks, M 1990, *Excavations in the Cathedral Precincts, 2. Linacre Garden, 'Meister Omers' and St Gabriel's Chapel*, The Archaeology of Canterbury IV, Maidstone

Duhig, C 1998, 'The human skeletal material' in T Malim and J Hines, 154–99

Dungworth, D 2011, 'The metalworking debris' in J A Nowakowski and H Quinnell, 220–44

Dunning, G and Wheeler, M 1931, 'A barrow at Dunstable, Bedfordshire', *Archaeological Journal* 88, 193–217

During, E M, Zimmerman, M R, Krikun, M E and Rydberg, I 1984, 'Helmsman's elbow: an occupational disease of the seventeenth century', *Journal of Paleopathology* 6, 19–27

Egan G and Pritchard F 1991, *Dress accessories c 1150 – c 1450*, Medieval Finds from Excavations in London 3, Museum of London, London

Ehrenreich, R 1986, 'Blacksmith technology in Iron Age Wessex', *Oxford Journal of Archaeology*, 5(2), 165–84

Elbern, V H 1972, 'Ein neuer Beitrag zur Ikonographie des Unfigurlichen. Über die bildliche Aussage beinerner Reliquienkastchen des frühen Mittelalters', *Munster Zeitschrift für Christliches Kunst und Kunstwissenschaft* 25, 313–24

El Eishi, H 1974, 'Variations in the talar articular facets in Egyptian calcanei', *Acta Anatomica (Basel)* 89, 134–8

Engstrom, R, Lankton, S M and Lesher-Engstrom, A 1989, *A Modern Replication based on the Pattern-welded Sword of Sutton Hoo,* Western Michigan University, Kalamazoo

Entwistle, C and Adams, N (eds) 2011, *Gems of Heaven': recent research on engraved gemstones in Late Antiquity, AD 200–600*, British Museum Publications 179, London

Esmonde Cleary, A S 1989, *The Ending of Roman Britain*, London

Esplund, A (ed) 1993, *Bloomery Ironmaking during 2000 years*, (3) Trondheim

Evans, A C 2000, 'Eriswell (RAF Lakenheath), Suffolk (1): Anglo-Saxon grave containing bridle fittings with appliqué silver mount' in R Bland (ed), *Treasure Annual Report 1998–1999,* London, 27–9

Evans, A C 2005, 'Seventh-century assemblages' in M O H Carver, 201–82

Evans, R T and Tylecote, R F 1967, 'Some vitrified products of non-metallurgical significance', *Historical Metallurgy,* 1(9), 22–3

Evenstad, O 1968, 'A treatise on the iron ores found in bogs and swamps of Norway and the process of turning into iron and steel', *Historical Metallurgy*, 2(2), 61

Everitt, A M 1986, *Continuity and Colonisation: the evolution of Kentish Settlement*, Leicester University Press

Evison, V I 1956, 'An Anglo-Saxon cemetery at Holborough, Kent', *Archaeologia Cantiana* lxx, 84–141

Evison, V I 1961, 'The Saxon Objects' in J G Hurst, 211–99

Evison, V I 1965, *The Fifth-Century Invasions South of the Thames*, London

Evison, V I 1967, 'The Dover ring-sword and other sword rings and beads', *Archaeologia* 101, 63–118

Evison, V I 1972, 'Glass cone beakers of the Kempston type', *Journal of Glass Studies* 14, 48–66

Evison, V I 1979, *A Corpus of Wheel-Thrown Pottery in Anglo-Saxon Graves*, Royal Archaeological Institute Monograph Series, London

Evison, V I 1980, 'Objects of Bronze and Iron' in J Haslam, 33–9

Evison, V I (ed) 1981, *Angles, Saxons and Jutes: Essays Presented to J N L Myres*, Oxford

Evison, V I 1982, 'Anglo-Saxon glass claw beakers', *Archaeologia* 107, 43–76

Evison, V I 1987, *Dover: Buckland Anglo-Saxon Cemetery*, Historic Buildings and Monuments Commission for England, Archaeological Report No 3, London

Evison, V I 1988, *An Anglo-Saxon Cemetery at Alton, Hampshire*, Hampshire Field Club and Archaeological Society Monograph 4, Winchester

Evison, V I 1989, 'The glass vessel' in P Rahtz and L Watts, 341–5

Evison, V I 1994a, *An Anglo-Saxon Cemetery at Great Chesterford, Essex*, Council for British Archaeology Research Report 91, London

Evison, V I 1994b, 'Anglo-Saxon glass from cremations' in C Hills *et al*, 23–46

Evison, V I 2000a, 'Bag beaker' in D A Hinton, 76–83

Evison, V I 2000b, 'Glass vessels in England AD 400–1100' in J Price (ed), 47–98

Evison, V I 2008, *Catalogue of Anglo-Saxon Glass in the British Museum*, British Museum Research Publication 167, London

Evison, V I forthcoming, 'Glass fragments' in D Hill, D Barrett and M Worthington, *Quentovic: an early medieval trading site: excavations 1984–1991*

Evison, V I and Hill, P 1996, *Two Anglo-Saxon Cemeteries at Beckford, Hereford and Worcester*, Council for British Archaeology Research Report 103, York

Färke, H 1991, 'Textile Reste an zwei Völkerwanderungszeitlichen Vogelfibeln', *Alt-Thüringen*, 26, 197–206

Farrell, R T (ed) 1982, *The Vikings*, London

Farwell, D E and Molleson, T I 1993, *Poundbury. Vol 2, The Cemeteries*, Dorset Natural History and Archaeological Society Monograph Series No 11, Dorchester

Faussett, B 1856, *Inventorium Sepulchrale*, (ed C Roach Smith), London

Fell, V 1997, 'Iron Age files from England', *Oxford Journal of Archaeology* 16(1), 79–98

Fell, V and Starley, D 1999, 'A technological study of ferrous blades from the Anglo-Saxon cemeteries at Boss Hall and St Stephen's Lane – Buttermarket, Ipswich, Suffolk', Ancient Monuments Laboratory Report 18/99

Feyeux, J-Y 1995, 'La Typologie de la verrerie mérovingienne du nord de la France' in D Foy (ed), 109–38

Filmer-Sankey, W 1989, *On the Function and Status of Prestige Finger-rings in the Early Medieval Germanic World, c 450–700*, PhD thesis Oxford

Filmer-Sankey, W (ed) 1993, *Anglo-Saxon Studies in Archaeology and History* 6, Oxford University Commitee for Archaeology, Oxford

Filmer-Sankey, W and Pestell, T 2001, *Snape Anglo-Saxon Cemetery: Excavations and Surveys 1824–1992,* East Anglian Archaeology 95, Gressenhall

Finnegan, M 1978, 'Non metric variations of the infra cranial skeleton', *Journal of Anatomy* 125, 23–37

Fingerlin, I 1971, 'Die Gürtel des hohen und späten Mittelalters', *Kulturwissenschaftliche Studien* 46, Munich

Fleury, M and France-Lanord, A 1998, *Les Trésors mérovingiens de la Basilique de Saint-Denis*, Luxemburg

Floud, R, Wachter, K and Gregory, A 1990, *Height, Health and History. Nutritional Status in the United Kingdom, 1750–1980*, Cambridge Studies in Population, Economy and Society in Past Time No 9, Cambridge University Press, Cambridge

Fluzin, P 1999, 'Ponte di Val Gabbia III: i reperti metallici dalla forgia. Primi risultati dello studi metallografico' in C Cuccini Tizzoni and M Tizzoni (eds), *La miniera perduta: Cinque anni di richerche archaeometallurgie nel territorio di Bienno*, Breno, 189–93

Foreman, S, Hiller, J and Petts, D 2002, *Gathering the People, Settling the Land. The Archaeology of a Middle Thames Landscape. Anglo-Saxon to Post-Medieval*, Thames Valley Landscapes Monograph 14, Oxford

Fortin, M 1999, *Syria. Land of Civilizations*, exhibition catalogue, Musée de la Civilisation, Quebec

Fornaciari, G, Mallegni, F, Bertini, D and Nuti, V 1982, 'Cribra orbitalia and elemental bone iron in the Punics of Carthage', *Ossa* 8, 63–77

Forriol Campos, F and Gomez Pellico, L 1989, 'Talar articular facets (facies articulares talares) in human calcanei', *Acta Anatomica* 134, Basel, 124–7

Fowler, P J 1983, *The Farming of Prehistoric Britain*, Cambridge

Foy, D (ed) 1995, *Le verre de l'antiquité tardive et du haut moyen âge*, Association Francaise pour l'archéologie du verre, Guiry en Vexin 15–19 Novembre 1992, Musée Archéologique Départemental du Val d'Oise

Frederickson, B E, Baker, D, McHolick, W J, Yuan, H A and Lubicky, J P 1984, 'The natural history of spondylolysis and spondylolisthesis', *Journal of Bone and Joint Surgery* 66A, 699–707

Freestone, I C, Hughes, M J and Stapleton, C P 2008, 'Composition and production of Anglo-Saxon glass' in V I Evison, 29–46

Fremersdorf, F 1955, *Das fränkische Reihengräberfeld Köln-Müngersdorf. Germanische Denkmäler der Völkerwanderungszeit A 6*, Berlin

Fuchs, K, Kempa, M, Redies, R, Theune-Grosskopf, B and Wais, A 1998, *Die Alamannen*, Stuttgart

Gale, D 1989, 'The Seax' in S Chadwick Hawkes (ed) 1989b, 71–83

Garbsch, J 1966, *Der Moosberg bei Murnau*, Veröffentlichungen der Kommission zur archäologischen Erforschung des spätrömischen Raetien 6, Munich

Gardiner, J (ed) 1993, *Flatlands and Wetlands: Current Themes in East Anglian Archaeology*, East Anglian Archaeology 50**,** Norwich

Gardiner, M, Cross, R, Macpherson-Grant, N and Riddler, I 2001, 'Continental trade and non-urban ports in mid-Anglo-Saxon England: excavations at *Sandtun*, West Hythe, Kent', *Archaeological Journal* 158, 161–290

Gassman, G 1998, 'New discoveries and excavations of early Celtic iron smelting furnaces (6th to 2nd century BC) in Germany', *The Beginnings of the Early Use of Metals and Alloys (BUMA) IV*, 59–63

Geake, H 1997, *The Use of Grave-Goods in Conversion-Period England, c.600 – c.850,* British Archaeological Reports (British Series) 261, Oxford

Geisler, H 1998, *Das frühbairische Gräberfeld Straubing-Bajuwarenstraße I, Katalog der archäologischen Befunde und Funde,* International Archäologie 30, Rahden

Giles, R E, Blanc, H, Cann, H M and Wallace, D C 1980, 'Maternal inheritance of human mitochondrial DNA', *Proceedings of the National Academy of Sciences* (USA) 77, 6715–19

Gilmour, B 1984, 'Appendix II: x-radiographs of two objects: the weaving batten (24/3) and the sword (40/5)' in C Hills *et al*, 160–1

Gilmour, B 1996, 'The patterned sword: its technology in medieval Europe and Southern Asia', *The Beginnings of the Early Use of Metals and Alloys* (*BUMA) IV,* Japan 1996, 113–31

Gilmour, B 2007, 'Swords, seaxes and Saxons: pattern-welding and edged weapon technology from Late Roman to Anglo-Saxon England' in M Henig and T J Smith, 91–109

Gilmour, B 2010, 'Ethnic identity and the origins, purpose and occurrence of pattern-welded swords in sixth-century Kent: the case of the Saltwood cemetery' in M Henig and N Ramsay, 59–70

Gilmour, B and Salter, C 1998, 'Detailed photographic and textual descriptions of thin-sectioned samples from 38 ferrous objects found at Edix Hill, 1989–91' in T Malim and J Hines, Appendix 1

Gingell, C J 1978, 'The excavation of an early Anglo-Saxon cemetery at Collingbourne Ducis', *Wiltshire Archaeological Magazine* 70–1, 61–98

Ginther, C, Isseltarver, L and King, M-C 1992, 'Identifying individuals by sequencing mitochondrial DNA from teeth', *Nature Genetics* 2, 135–8

Godfrey, E G, Van Nie, M and McDonnell, J G 2005, 'Phosphorus and carbon in ancient iron: analysis of artefacts from a 4th century AD Germanic iron-smelting site at Heeton, the Netherlands', *Geoarchaeological and Bioarchaeological Studies 3. Proceedings of the 33rd International Symposium on Archaeometry, 22-26 April 2002, Amsterdam,* 339–41

Godfrey-Faussett, T G 1876, 'The Anglo-Saxon cemetery at Bifrons', *Archaeologia Cantiana* x, 298–315

Godfrey-Faussett, T G 1880, 'The Saxon Cemetery at Bifrons', *Archaeologia Cantiana* xiii, 552–6

Goessler, P 1932, 'Das frühchristliche Beinkästchen von Heilbronn', *Germania* 16, 294–9

Goodall, A 1984, 'Objects of non-ferrous metal' in J P Allan (ed), 337–48

Goodway, M and Fisher, R M 1988, 'Phosphorus in low carbon iron: its beneficial properties', *Historical Metallurgy* 22 (1), 21–3

Gordon, R B 1984, 'The quality of wrought iron evaluated by microprobe analysis' in A D Romig and J I Goldstein (eds), *Microbeam Analysis,* San Francisco, 231–4

Gordon, R B 1997, 'Process deduced from iron making wastes and artifacts', *Journal of Archaeological Science,* 24, 9–18

Gräslund, A-S 1980, *Birka 4: The Burial Customs,* Uppsala

Green, B and Milligan, B 1993, 'Catalogue of cremations and inhumations' in A Davison *et al* (eds), 18–46

Green, B and Rogerson, A 1978, *The Anglo-Saxon Cemetery at Bergh Apton, Norfolk: Catalogue,* East Anglian Archaeology Report No 7, Norfolk

Green, B, Rogerson A and White, S G 1987, *The Anglo-Saxon Cemetery at Morning Thorpe, Norfolk,* East Anglian Archaeology Report No 36, Norfolk.

Green, C 1963, *Sutton Hoo. The Excavation of a Royal Ship Burial,* London

Greifenhagen, A 1970, *Schmuckarbeiten in Edelmetal, I,* Staatliche Museen Preußische Kulturbesitz Antikenabteilung, Berlin

Griffith, A F and Salzmann, L F 1914, 'An Anglo-Saxon cemetery at Alfriston, Sussex', *Sussex Archaeological Collections* 56, 16–51

Griffiths, D (ed) 2000, *Anglo-Saxon Studies in Archaeology and History* 11, Oxford University School of Archaeology, Oxford

Grinsell, L V 1992, 'The Bronze Age round barrows of Kent', *Proceedings of the Prehistoric Society* 58, 355–84

Gustafsson, A and Karlsson, H (eds) 1999, *Glyfer och arkeologiska rum – en vänbok till Jarl Nordbladh,* Göteborg University

Haas-Gebhard, B 1998, *Ein frühmittelalterliches Gräberfeld bei Dittenheim, (D),* Europe médiévale, Series 1, Montagnac

Haith, C 2008, 'Fiche à bélière' in P Bennett *et al*, 297

Hald, M 1980, *Ancient Danish Textiles from Bogs and Burials,* Archaeological-Historical Museum 21, The National Museum of Denmark, Copenhagen

Halsall, G 1995, *Settlement and social organization: The Merovingian region of Metz,* Cambridge

Hamdy, R C 1981, *Paget's Disease of Bone: Assessment and Management,* Armour Pharmaceutical, Eastbourne

Hamerow, H 1993, *Excavations at Mucking 2: The Anglo-Saxon settlement,* English Heritage Report 21, London

Hamerow, H and MacGregor, A 2001, *Image and Power in the Archaeology of Early Medieval Britain. Studies for Rosemary Cramp,* Oxford

Hamerow, H, Hinton, D and Crawford, S (eds) 2011, *The Oxford Handbook of Anglo-Saxon Archaeology,* Oxford

Hampel, A and Bannerjee, A 1995, 'Identifizierung und Differenzierung von Elfenbein am Beispiel des merowingerzeitlichen Grabfundes aus dem Frankfurter Dom', *Archäologisches Korrespondenzblatt* 25, 143–53

Hansen, E 1990, *Tablet Weaving: History, Techniques, Colours, Patterns,* Højbjerg (Denmark), Hovedland

Härke, H 1989a, 'Knives in early Saxon burials: blade length and age at death', *Medieval Archaeology* xxxiii, 144–8

Härke, H. 1989b, 'Early Saxon weapon burials: frequencies, distributions and weapon combinations' in S Chadwick Hawkes (ed), 49–61

Härke, H 1990, '"Warrior graves?", The background of the Anglo-Saxon weapon burial rite', *Past and Present* 126, 22–43

Härke, H 1992a, *Angelsächsische Waffengräber des 5 bis 7 Jahrhunderts.* Zeitschrift für Archäologie des Mittelalters Beiheft 6, Köln

Härke, H 1992b, 'Changing symbols in a changing society: the Anglo-Saxon weapon burial rite in the seventh century' in M O H Carver (ed), 149–66

Härke, H 1997, 'Early Anglo-Saxon social structure' in J Hines (ed) 1997b, 125–70

Härke, H and Salter, C 1984, 'A technical and metallurgical study of three Anglo-Saxon shield bosses', *Anglo-Saxon Studies in Archaeological History* 3, 55–66

Harman, M 1990, 'The human remains' in A Down and M Welch, 183–213

Harman, M 1993, 'The human burials: discussion' in M J Dean and A G Kinsley, 56–8; Table 9

Harman, M 1995, 'The human bones' in A Boyle *et al*, 106–8

Harman, M 1998, 'The human remains' in A Boyle *et al*, 43–52

Harman, M, Molleson, T and Price, J L 1981, 'Burials, bodies and beheadings in Romano-British and Anglo-Saxon cemeteries', *Bulletin of the British Museum, Natural History (Geology)* 35, 145–88

Haseloff, G 1974, 'Salin's Style I', *Medieval Archaeology* 18, 1–15

Haseloff, G 1981, *Die germanische Tierornamentik der Völkerwanderungszeit. Studien zu Salin's Stil I.* Vorgeschichtliche Forschungen 17, 1–3, Berlin, New York

Haslam, J 1980, 'A Middle Saxon Iron Smelting Site at Ramsbury, Wiltshire', *Medieval Archaeology* 24, 1–68

Hassall, M WC 1977, 'The historical background and military units of the Saxon Shore' in D E Johnston (ed), 7–10

Häßler, H-J 1985, 'Das sächsiche Gräberfeld bei Liebenau, Kr Nienburg (Weser). Teil 3', *Studien zur Sachsenforschung* 5.2, Neumünster

Hasted, E 1800, *The History and Topographical Survey of the County of Kent*, IX (second edition), Canterbury

Hauck, K, Axboe, M, Düwel, K, von Padberg, L, Smyra, U and Wypior, C 985, *Die Goldbrakteaten der Völkerwanderungszeit. Ikonographischer Katalog 1–3*, Münstersche Mittelalter-Schrifter 24, Munich, 3 volumes to date

Haughton, C and Powlesland, D 1999, *West Heslerton Anglian Cemetery,* Landscape Research Centre Archaeological Monograph Series 1, Nottingham

Hauser, G and de Stefano, G F 1989, *Epigenetic variants of the Human Skull*, Stuttgart

Hawkes, S C with Grainger, G 2003, *The Anglo-Saxon Cemetery at Worthy Park, Kingsworthy near Winchester, Hampshire*, Oxford University School of Archaeology Monograph 59, Oxford

Hawkes, S C and Grainger, G 2006, *The Anglo-Saxon Cemetery at Finglesham, Kent*, Oxford University School of Archaeology Monograph 64, Oxford

Heckett, E 1990, 'Some silk and wool head-coverings from Viking Dublin: uses and origins – an enquiry' in P Walton and J P Wild (eds), 85–96

Hedeager, L 1999, 'Sacred topography: depositions of wealth in the cultural landscape' in A Gustafsson and H Karlsson (eds), 229–51

Hedges, R E M and Salter, C J 1979, 'Source determination of iron currency bars through analysis of the slag inclusions', *Archaeometry* 21(2), 161–75

Heege, A 1987, *Grabfunde der Merowingerzeit aus Heidenheim-Großkuchen*, Materialheft zur Vor- und Frühgeschichte 9, Stuttgart

Hengen, P 1971, 'Cribra orbitalia: pathogenesis and probable etiology', *Homo* 22, 557–6

Henig, M 1978, *A Corpus of Roman Engraved Gemstones from British Sites*, British Archaeological Reports (British Series) 8, 2nd edition, Oxford

Henig, M and Smith, T J (eds) 2007, *Collectanea Antiqua: Essays in Memory of Sonia Chadwick Hawkes*, British Archaeological Reports (International Series) 1673, Oxford

Hensinger, R N 1989, 'Spondylolysis and spondylolisthesis in children and adolescents', *Journal of Bone and Joint Surgery* 71A, 1098–1107

Hermelin, E, Tholander, E and Blomgren, S 1979, 'A prehistoric nickel-alloyed iron axe', *Historical Metallurgy* 13(2), 69–94

Hill, P 1998, *Whithorn & St Ninian, The Excavation of a Monastic Town 1984–1991*, Stroud

Hills, C 1977, *The Anglo-Saxon Cemetery at Spong Hill, North Elmham; Part 1*, East Anglian Archaeology 6, Gressenhall

Hills, C 1981, 'Barred zoomorphic combs of the Migration Period' in V I Evison (ed), 126–67

Hills, C 1993, 'Who were the East Anglians?' in J Gardiner (ed), 14–23

Hills, C 2001, 'From Isidore to isotopes: ivory rings in early medieval graves' in H Hamerow and A MacGregor, 131–46

Hills, C 2003, *Origins of the English*

Hills, C and Hurst, H 1989, 'A Goth at Gloucester?', *Antiquaries Journal* lxix, 154–8

Hills, C and Penn, K 1981, *The Anglo-Saxon Cemetery at Spong Hill, North Elmham: Part 2*, East Anglian Archaeology 11, Gressenhall

Hills, C and Wade-Martins, P 1976, *The Anglo-Saxon Cemetery at the Paddocks, Swaffham*, East Anglian Archaeology Report No 2, Gressenhall, 1–44

Hills, C, Penn, K and Rickett, R 1984, *The Anglo-Saxon Cemetery at Spong Hill, North Elmham: Part 3: Catalogue of Inhumations* (East Anglian Archaeology Report 21, Gressenhall

Hills, C, Penn, K and Rickett, R 1987, *The Anglo-Saxon Cemetery at Spong Hill, North Elmham. Part 4: Catalogue of Cremations*, East Anglian Archaeology 34, Gressenhall

Hills, C, Penn, K and Rickett, R 1994, *The Anglo-Saxon Cemetery at Spong Hill, North Elmham. Part 5: Catalogue of Cremations*, East Anglian Archaeology 67, Gressenhall

Hines, J 1984, *The Scandinavian Character of Anglian England in the Pre-Viking Period*, British Archaeological Reports, (British Series) 124, Oxford

Hines, J 1989, 'Ritual hoarding in Migration-period Scandinavia: a review of recent interpretations', *Proceedings of the Prehistoric Society* 55, 193–205

Hines, J 1992, 'The seriation and chronology of Anglian English women's graves: a critical assessment' in L Jørgensen (ed), 81–93

Hines, J 1993, *Clasps, Hektespenner, Agraffen: Anglo-Scandinavian Clasps of Classes A–C of the 3rd to 6th Centuries A.D. Typology, Diffusion and Function*, Kungliga Vitterhets Historie och Antikvitets Akademien, Stockholm

Hines, J 1996, 'An early Anglo-Saxon wrist-clasp from the parish of Baydon', *Wiltshire Archaeology and Natural History Magazine* 89, 130–2

Hines, J 1997a, *A New Corpus of Anglo-Saxon Great Square-Headed Brooches*, Reports of the Research Committee of the Society of Antiquaries of London, LI, London

Hines J (ed) 1997b, *The Anglo-Saxons. From the Migration Period to the Eighth Century. An Ethnographic Perspective*, Studies in Historical Archaeology 2, Woodbridge

Hines, J 1999, 'Angelsächsische Chronologie: Probleme und Aussichten' in U von Freeden *et al* (eds), 19–30

Hines, J, Høilund Nielsen, K and Siegmund, F (eds) 1999, *The Pace of Change. Studies in Early Medieval Chronology*, Oxford

Hinton, D A 2000, *A Smith in Lindsey. The Anglo-Saxon Grave at Tattershall Thorpe, Lincolnshire*, Society for Medieval Archaeology Monograph 16, London

Hinton, D A and White, R 1993, 'A smith's hoard from Tattershall Thorpe, Lincolnshire', *Anglo-Saxon England* 22, 147–66

Hinz, H 1966, 'Am langen Band getragene Bergkristallanhänger der Merowingerzeit', Sonderdruck Jahrbuch des RZGM 13, 212–30

Hinz, H 1969, Die Ausgrabungen auf dem Kirchberg in Morken, Kreis Bergheim (Erft), *Rheinische Ausgrabungen* 7, 63–75

Hirst, S M 1985, *An Anglo-Saxon Inhumation Cemetery at Sewerby, East Yorkshire*, York University Archaeological Publications 4, York

Hobbs, R 1996, *British Iron Age Coins in the British Museum*, British Museum Press

Hoffmann, M 1974, *The Warp-weighted Loom*, Oslo-Bergen-Tromsø, Universitetsforlaget

Hofreiter, M, Jaenicke, V, Serre, D, von Haeseler, A and Pääbo, S 2001, 'DNA sequences from multiple amplifications reveal artefacts induced by cytosine deamination in ancient DNA', *Nucleic Acids Research* 29, 4793–9

Hogarth, C 1973, 'Structural features in Anglo-Saxon graves', *Archaeological Journal* 180, 104–19

Høilund Nielsen, K 1995, 'From artefact to interpretation using Correspondence Analysis', *Anglo-Saxon Studies in Archaeology and History* 8, 111–43

Høilund Nielsen, K 1997a, 'The Schism of Anglo-Saxon Chronology' in C K Jensen and K Høilund Nielsen (eds), 71–99

Høilund Nielsen, K 1997b, 'Die frühmittelalterlichen Perlen Skandinaviens. Chronologische Untersuchungen' in U von Freeden and A Wieczorek (eds), 187–96

Holck, P 1987, 'Scurvy a palaeopathological riddle' in V Capecchi and E Rabino Massa (eds), 163–71

Holden, E W 1969, 'Anglo-Saxon burials at Crane Down, Jevington', *Sussex Archaeological Collections* 107, 126–34

Holdsworth, P E 1980, *Excavations at Melbourne Street, Southampton, 1971–6*, Council for British Archaeology Research Report 33, London

Holman, D E 2000, 'Iron Age coinage in Kent: A review of current knowledge', *Archaeologia Cantiana* cxx, 205–33

Hooke, B G E 1926, 'A third study of the English skull with special reference to the Farringdon Street crania', *Biometrika* 18, 1–55

Hope-Taylor, B 1977, *Yeavering. An Anglo-British Centre of Early Northumbria*, London

Hopkins, B E and Tipler, H R 1958, 'The effect of phosphorus on the tensile and notch-impact properties of high-purity and iron-carbon alloys', *Journal of the Iron and Steel Institute* 188, 218–37

Howard, S 1994, 'Specification for works at Buckland, Dover', Kent County Council Heritage Conservation Group

Hrdlička, Ä 1934, 'The hypotrochanteric fossa of the femur', *Smithsonian Miscellaneous Collections* 92, 1–49

Huggett, J W 1988, 'Imported grave-goods and the early Anglo-Saxon economy', *Medieval Archaeology* xxxii, 63–96

Huggins, P J 1978, 'Excavation of Belgic and Romano-British farm with middle Saxon cemetery and churches at Nazeingbury, Essex', *Essex Archaeology and History* 10, 29–117

Humphreys, J, Ryland, J W, Barnard, E A B, Wellstood, F C and Barnett, T G 1925, 'An Anglo-Saxon cemetery at Bidford-on-Avon, Warwickshire: second report on the excavations', *Archaeologia* 74, 271–88

Hurst, J G 1961, 'The kitchen area of Northolt Manor, Middlesex', *Medieval Archaeology* v, 211–99

Hutchinson, P 1966, 'The Anglo-Saxon cemetery at Little Eriswell, Suffolk', *Proceedings of the Cambridge Antiquarian Society* LIX, 1–32

Hurd, H and Smith, R 1911, 'Notes on the discovery of an Anglo-Saxon burial ground at Broadstairs', *Proceedings of the Society of Antiquaries of London* 23, 272–82

Ierusalemskaja, A A and Borkopp, B 1996, *Von China nach Byzanz: Frühmittelalterliche Seiden aus der Staatlichen Ermitage Sankt Petersburg*, Munich: Bayerischen Nationalmuseum (and The Hermitage, St Petersburg)

Ilkjaer, J 1993, *Illerup Ådal 3. Gie Gürtel. Bestandteile und Zubehör*, Jutland Archaeological Society Publications xxv: 3, Aarhus

Isings, C 1957, *Roman Glass from dated Finds*, Archaeologica Traiectina Akademiae Rheno-Traiectinae Instituto Archaeologico, Groningen

Jakes, K A and Howard, J H 1986, 'Replacement of protein and cellulosic fibres with copper minerals and the formation of textile pseudomorphs' in H L Needles and S H Zeronian, *Historic Textile and Paper Materials* (Advances in Chemistry Series 212), Washington, 277–87

Jakes, K A and Sibley, L R 1983, 'Survival of cellulosic fibres in the archaeological context', *Science and Archaeology*, 25, 31–8

James, P M C and Miller, W A 1970, 'Dental conditions of medieval English children', *British Dental Journal* 128, 391–6

Janssens, P A 1981, 'Porotic hyperostosis and goat's milk anemia: a theory (more)', *Ossa* 8, 101–8

Jarcho, S (ed) 1966, *Human Paleopathology*, Yale University Press, New Haven

Jay, M and Richards, M P 2006, 'Diet in the Iron Age cemetery population at Wetwang Slack, East Yorkshire, UK: carbon and nitrogen stable isotope evidence', *Journal of Archaeological Science* 33, 653–62

Jenkins, F 1957, 'The Bekesbourne excavations', *Kent and Sussex Journal* 2, 11, 294f

Jensen, C K and Høilund Nielsen, K (eds) 1997, *Burial and Society. The Chronological and Social Analysis of Archaeological Burial Data*, Aarhus, Oxford, Oakville, Connecticut

Joffroy, R 1974, *Le Cimetière de Lavoye (Meuse). Nécropole Mérovingienne*, Paris

Johnson, S 1976, *The Roman Forts of the Saxon Shore*, London

Johnston, D E (ed) 1977, *The Saxon Shore*, Council for British Archaeology Research Report 18, London

Joosten, I, Jansen, B and Kars, H 1996, 'First witness of manganese-rich welding sand in an early medieval iron sax' in G Magnusson (ed), *The Importance of Ironmaking*, Norberg Conference, May 1995, 1, 65–72

Jørgensen, L (ed) 1992, *Chronological Studies of Anglo-Saxon England, Lombard Italy and Vendel Period in Sweden*, Arkeologiske Skrifter 5, København

Jørgensen, L and Nørgård Jørgensen, A 1997, *Nørre Sandegård Vest: A Cemetery from the 6th-8th centuries on Bornholm*, Nordiske Fortidsminder Serie B, Vol 14, København

Julien, S 1992, 'The Conservation of Mineral Preserved Organics', unpublished, undergraduate thesis for degree in Archaeological Conservation, Institute of Archaeology, University College London

K A R U 1989, 'Important Saxon discovery on Whitfield Hill, Dover', *Kent Archaeological Review* 96, 121

Kazanski, M 1994, 'Les plaques-boucles méditerranés des Ve - VIe siècles', *Archéologie Médiévale* xxiv, 137ff

Keller, P T 2003, 'The excavated objects' in B Philp, 73–7

Kendrick, T D 1937, 'Ivory mounts from a casket', *Antiquaries Journal* xxvii, 448

Kent, S 1987, 'The influence of sedentism and aggregation on porotic hyperostosis and anaemia: a case study', *Man* 21, 605–36

Kerep, A 2006, 'Les armes anglo–saxonnes du Ve au VIIe siècle' in X Delestre *et al*, 86–102

Kilbride-Jones, H E 1980, *Zoomorphic Penannular Brooches*, Reports of the Research Committee of the Society of Antiquaries of London 39, London

Kinsley, A G 1989, *The Anglo-Saxon Cemetery at Millgate, Newark-on-Trent, Nottinghamshire*, Nottingham Archaeological Monograph 2, Nottingham.

Kjølbye-Biddle, B 1995, 'Iron-bound Coffins and Coffin-Fittings from the pre-Norman Cemetery' in D Phillips and B Heywood, 489–521

Knight, B 1990, 'A review of the corrosion of iron from terrestrial sites and the problem of post-excavation corrosion', *The Conservator*, 14, 37–43

Knowles, A K 1983, 'Acute traumatic lesions' in G D Hart (ed), *Disease in Ancient Man*, Toronto, 61–83

Koch, A 1998, *Bügelfibeln der Merowingerzeit im westlichen Frankenreich*. Monographien Römisch-Germanisches Zentralmuseum Forschungsinstitut für Vor- und Frühgeschichte 41, Mainz

Koch, U 1977, *Das Reihengräberfeld bei Schretzheim*, Germanische Denkmäler der Völkerwanderungszeit A 13, Berlin

Koch, U 1987, *Der Runde Berg bei Urach IV. Die Glas- und Edelsteinfunde aus den Plangrabungen 1967–1983*, Heidelberger Akademie Wissenschaftliche Kommission Alamannische Altertumskunde 12, Sigmaringen

Koch, U 1990, *Das fränkische Gräberfeld von Klepsau im Hohenlohekreis*, Forschungen und Berichte zur Vor- und Frühgeschichte in Baden-Württemberg 38, Stuttgart

Koch, U 1993, *Alamannen in Heilbronn. Archäologische Funde des 4 und 5 Jahrhunderts*, Veröffentlichungen der Städtischen Museen Heilbronn, Heilbronn

Koch, U 1996, 'Glas -Luxus der Wohlhabenden' in A Wieczorek *et al* (eds), Teil II, 605–17

Koch, U 2001, *Das Alamannisch-Fränkische Gräberfeld bei Pleidelsheim*, Forschungen und Berichte zur Vor- und Frühgeschichte in Baden-Württemberg 60, Stuttgart

Konrad, M 1997, *Das römische Gräberfeld von Bregenz-Brigantium. I Körpergräber des 3–5 Jahrhunderts*, Veröffentlichungen der Kommission zur archäologischen Erforschung des spätrömischen Rätien der Bayrischen Akademie der Wissenschaften. Münchener Beträge zur Vor- und Frühgeschichte 51, München

Kornbluth, G 2011, 'Roman intaglios oddly set: the transformative power of the metalwork mount' in C Entwistle and N Adams (eds), 261–9

Kosec, L, Vodopicvec, F and Tixier, R 1969, *Metal Corrosion Industry* 525, 187–203

Kristoffersen, S and Magnus, B 2010, *Spannformete Kar: Utvikling og Variasjon*, AmS-Varia, 50, Arkeologisk museum, Universitet i Stavanger, Stavanger

Kronz, A 2003, 'Ancient iron production compared to medieval techniques in Germany: fayalitis slag and elemental mass balances', *Archaeometallurgy in Europe*, Milan vol 1, 555–64

Krug, A 1977, 'Die Gemme des Kleon', *Städel-Jahrbuch* 6, 19–26

Krug, A 1980, 'Antike Gemmen im Römisch-Germanischen Museum Köln', *Wissenschaftliche Kataloge des RGM Köln, Bd IV, Berichte RGK* 61, 153–260

Krug, A 1993, 'Antike Gemmen und das Zeitalter Bernwards' in M Brandt and A Eggebrecht (eds), *Bernward von Hildesheim und das Zeitalter der Ottonen, Band* 1, katalog der ausstellung Hildesheim, Mainz

Kruse, P 2007, 'Jutes in Kent? On the Jutish nature of Kent, southern Hampshire and the Isle of Wight', *Probleme der Küstenforschung im südlichen Nordseegebiet*, 31, 243–376

Kühn H 1974–7, 'Das Problem der S-Fibeln der Völkerwanderungszeit', *Ipek. Jahrbuch für Prähistorische und Ethnographische Kunst* 24, 124–35

Laidlaw, P P 1905, 'The oscalcis. Part II', *Journal of Anatomy* 39, 161–78

Lamm, J P and Nordström, H A 1982, *Vendel Period Studies*, The Museum of National Antiquities, Studies in Archaeology, 2, Stockholm, 11–16

Lang, J 1988, 'Study of the metallography of some Roman swords', *Britannia* xix, 199–216

Lang, J 1995, 'A metallographic examination of eight Roman daggers from Britain' in B Raftery, V Megaw and V Rigby (eds), *Sites and Sights of the Iron Age*, Oxbow Monograph, Oxford, 119–32

Lang, J (in press), 'The Celtic sword: a source of practical inspiration' in J Hošek, H Cleere and L Mihok, *The Archaeometallurgy of Iron: Recent developments in archaeological and scientific research*

Lang, J and Ager, B 1989, 'Swords of the Anglo-Saxon and Viking periods in the British Museum: a radiographic study' in S Chadwick Hawkes (ed) 1989b, 85–122

Lang, J and Price, J 1975, 'Iron tubes from a late Roman glassmaking site at Merida (Badajoz) in Spain', *Journal of Archaeological Science* 2, 289–96

Lang, J and Wang, Q forthcoming, 'The ironwork from the 1997 to 2000 excavations at Tranmer House, Sutton Hoo' in C Fern, *Before Sutton Hoo: the Prehistoric Landscape and Early Anglo-Saxon Cemetery at Tranmer House, Bromeswell, Suffolk*

La Niece, S, Hook, D and Craddock P (eds) 2007, *Metals and Mines. Studies in Archaeometry*, London

Laporte, J-P 1982, 'La chasuble de Chelles', *Bulletin du Groupement Archéologique de Seine-et-Marne* 23, 1–29

Lasker, G W 1946, 'Migration and physical differentiation', *American Journal of Physical Anthropology* 4, 273–300

Leach, P E (ed) 1982, *Archaeology in Kent to A.D. 1500*, Council for British Archaeology Research Report 48, London

Leeds, E T 1916–7, 'On an Anglo-Saxon cemetery at Wheatley, Oxfordshire', *Proceedings of the Society of Antiquaries* 29, 48–63

Leeds, E T 1923, 'A Saxon village near Sutton Courtenay, Berkshire', *Archaeologia* 72, 147–92

Leeds, E T 1924, 'An Anglo-Saxon cremation-burial of the seventh century in Asthall Barrow, Oxfordshire', *Antiquaries Journal* iv, 113–26

Leeds, E T 1936, *Early Anglo-Saxon Art and Archaeology*, Oxford

Leeds, E T 1945, 'The distribution of the Angles and Saxons archaeologically considered', *Archaeologia* 91, 1–106

Leeds, E T and Atkinson, R J C 1944, 'An Anglo-Saxon cemetery at Nassington, Northants', *Antiquaries Journal* xxiv, 100–28

Leeds, E T and Harden, D B 1936, *The Anglo-Saxon Cemetery at Abingdon, Berkshire*, Oxford Ashmolean Museum, Oxford

Leeds, E T and Shortt, H 1953, *An Anglo-Saxon cemetery at Petersfinger, near Salisbury, Wilts*, Salisbury

Legoux, R 1998, 'Le cadre chronologique de Picardie: son application aux autres régions en vue d'une chronologie unifiée et son extension vers le romain tardif' in X Delestre and P Périn (eds), 137–88

Leigh, D 1980, 'The square-headed brooches of sixth-century Kent', unpublished PhD thesis, Cardiff

Lethbridge, T C 1924/25, 'The Anglo-Saxon cemetery, Burwell, Cambs', *Proceedings of the Cambridge Antiquarian Society* 27, 72–9

Lethbridge, T C 1925/26, 'The Anglo-Saxon cemetery, Burwell, Cambs. Part II', *Proceedings of the Cambridge Antiquarian Society* 28, 116–23

Lethbridge, T C 1926/27, 'The Anglo-Saxon cemetery, Burwell, Cambs. Part III', *Proceedings of the Cambridge Antiquarian Society* 29, 84–94

Lethbridge, T C 1927, 'An Anglo-Saxon hut on the Car Dyke, at Waterbeach', *Antiquaries Journal* vii, 141–6

Lethbridge, T C 1927/28, 'The Anglo-Saxon cemetery, Burwell, Cambs. Part IV', *Proceedings of the Cambridge Antiquarian Society* 30, 97–109

Lethbridge, T C 1931, *Recent Excavations in Anglo-Saxon Cemeteries in Cambridgeshire and Suffolk*, Cambridge Antiquarian Society Quarto Publications, New Series 3, Cambridge

Lethbridge, T C and Carter, H G 1926/27, 'Excavation in the Anglo-Saxon cemetery at Little Wilbraham', *Proceedings of the Cambridge Antiquarian Society* 29, 95–104

Lewis, M, Macdonald, P and Smallwood, K 2002, 'An insular La Tène toggle: Wrotham', *Archaeologia Cantiana* cxxii, 399–401

Liddell, D M 1934, 'An Anglo-Saxon cemetery at Meon Hill, Hants', *Proceedings of the Hampshire Field Club and Archaeological Society* 12, 127–62

Lille, R D 1917, 'Variations of the canalis hypoglossali', *Anatomical Record* 13, 131–44

Lindahl, T 1993, 'Instability and decay of the primary structure of DNA', *Nature* 362, 709–15

Longin, R 1971, 'New method of collagen extraction for radiocarbon dating', *Nature* 230, 241–2

Lovejoy, C O, Burstein, A H and Heiple, K G 1976, 'The biochemical analysis of bone strength: a method and its application to platycnemia', *American Journal of Physical Anthropology* 44, 489–506

Lucy, S 2000, *The Anglo-Saxon Way of Death*, Stroud

Lucy, S and Reynolds, A (eds) 2002a, *Burial in Early Medieval England and Wales*, Society for Medieval Archaeology Monograph Series 17, Leeds

Lucy, S and Reynolds, A 2002b, 'Burial in early medieval England and Wales: past, present and future' in S Lucy and A Reynolds (eds), 1–23

Lüdemann, H 1994, 'Mehrfachbelegte Gräber im frühen Mittelalter', *Fundberichte aus Baden-Württemberg* 19.1, 421–589

MacGregor, A 1985, *Bone, Antler, Ivory and Horn. The technology of skeletal materials since the Roman period*, London

MacGregor, A and Bolick, E 1993, *A Summary Catalogue of the Anglo-Saxon Collections (Non-Ferrous Metals)*, British Archaeological Reports (British Series) 230, Oxford

Mack, I, McDonnell, G, Murphy, S, Andrews, P and Wardley, K 2000, 'Liquid steel in Anglo-Saxon England', *Historical Metallurgy* 34(2), 87–96

Mackeprang, M B 1952, *De Nordiske Guldbrakteater*, Jysk Arkæologisk Selskab Skrifter, II, Aarhus

Macpherson-Grant, N 1995a, 'Marlowe Theatre: Structure S30: S30/Frere Hut 1' in K Blockley *et al*, 857–60

Macpherson-Grant, N 1995b, 'The Marlowe I sequence: Periods 5–8' in K Blockley *et al*, 835–52

Madyda-Legutko, R 1987, *Die Gürtelschnallen der Römischen Kaiserzeit und der frühen Völkerwanderungszeit im mitteleuropäischen Barbaricum*, British Archaeological Reports (International Series) 360, Oxford

Magnus, B 1997, 'The firebed of the serpent: myth and religion in the Migration Period mirrored through some golden objects' in L Webster and M Brown, 194–202

Magnus, B forthcoming, 'Lux Scandza', *Fornvännen*

Malim, T and Hines, J 1998, *The Anglo-Saxon Cemetery at Edix Hill (Barrington A), Cambridgeshire*, Council for British Archaeology Research Report 112, York

Manchester, K 1982, 'Spondylolysis and spondylolisthesis in two Anglo-Saxon skeletons', *Palaeopathology Newsletter* 37, 9–12

Manchester, K unpublished, *Eccles Skeletal Report*, Bradford University, Calvin Wells Laboratory MS

Manchester, K and Elmhirst, O 1980, 'Forensic aspects of an Anglo-Saxon injury', *Ossa* 7, 179–88

Mandrioli Bizzarri, A R 1987, *La Collezione di Gemme del museo Civico Archeologico di Bologna*, Bologna

Mann, J 1989, 'The historical development of the Saxon Shore' in V Maxfield (ed), 1–11

Mannering, U 1997, 'The textiles from Nørre Sandegård Vest' in L Jørgensen and A Nørgård Jørgensen, 118–40

Manzanares, M C, Goret-Nicaise, M and Dhem, A 1988, 'Metopic sutural closure in the human skull', *Journal of Anatomy* 161, 203–15

Margary, I D 1967, *Roman Roads in Britain*, revised edition, London

Margeson, S 1993, *Norwich Households. Medieval and Post-Medieval Finds from Norwich Survey Excavations 1971–78*, East Anglian Archaeology 58, Gressenhall

Marlow, M 1992, 'The human remains' in S J Sherlock and M G Welch, 107–18

Marsh, B W, Bonfiglio, M, Brady, L P and Enneking, W F 1975, 'Benign osteoblastoma: range of manifestations', *Journal of Bone and Joint Surgery* 57A, 1–9

Marshall, P, Tipper, J, Bayliss, A, McCormac, F G, van der Plicht, J, Bronk Ramsey, C and Beavan-Athfield, N 2009, 'Absolute Dating' in S Lucy, J Tipper and A Dickens, *The Anglo-Saxon Settlement and*

Cemetery at Bloodmoor Hill, Carlton Colville, Suffolk, East Anglian Archaeology 131, 322–9

Marti, R 1990, *Das frühmittelalterliche Gräberfeld von St.-Sulpice VD*, Cahiers d'Archéologie Romande 52, Lausanne

Marti, R 1994, 'Die Burgunder: Minderheit mit Machtfunction', *Archäologie Deutschland* 4, 28–33

Martin, M 1976, *Das fränkische Gräberfeld von Basel-Bernerring*, Mainz

Martin, M 1984, 'Weinsiebchen und Toilettgerät' in A Cahn and A Kaufmann-Heinimann (eds), 97–132

Martin, M 1989, 'Bemerkungen zur chronologischen Gliederung der frühen Merowingerzeit', *Germania* 67 (1), 121–41

Martin, M 1991a, *Das spätrömisch-frühmittelalterliche Gräberfeld von Kaiseraugst, Kt Aargau*, Basler Beiträge zur Ur- und Frühgeschichte, Solothurn

Martin, M 1991b, 'Tradition und Wandel der Fibelschmŋkten Frühmittelalterlichen Frauenkleidung', *Jahrbuch des Romanisch-Germanischen Zentralmuseums*, 38, 629–80

Martin, M 1994, 'Fibel und Fibeltracht. K Späte Völkerwanderungszeit und Merowingerzeit auf dem Kontinent' in *Reallexikon der Germanischen Altertumskunde* 8, Berlin, New York, 541–82

Martin, M 1997, 'Die goldene Kette von Szilágysomlyó und das frühmerowingische Amulettgehänge der westgermanischen Frauentracht' in U von Freeden and A Wieczorek (eds), 349–72

Martin, M 1998, 'Kleide und Leute: Tracht und Bewaffnung in Fränkischer Zeit' in K Fuchs *et al*, 349–58

Maryon, H 1948, 'A sword of the Nydam type from Ely Fields Farm, near Ely', *Journal of the Cambridge Antiquarian Society* 41, 73–6

Marzinzik, S 2003, *Early Anglo-Saxon Belt Buckles (late 5th to early 8th centuries A D): Their classification and context*, British Archaeological Reports (British Series) 357, Oxford

Marzinzik, S 2010, 'Buckles and belt-fittings' in F K Annable and B N Eagles, *The Anglo-Saxon Cemetery at Blacknall Field, Pewsey, Wiltshire*, Wiltshire Archaeological and Natural History Society Monograph 4, Devizes, 53–5

Matthews, C L 1962, 'Saxon remains on Puddlehill, Dunstable', *Bedfordshire Archaeological Journal* 1, 48–57

Maxfield, V (ed) 1989, *The Saxon Shore*, Exeter

Mays, S 1990, *The Human Remains from Empingham II, Leicestershire*, Ancient Monuments Laboratory Report 61/90

Mays, S 1991, *The Medieval Burials from The Blackfriars Friary, School Street, Ipswich, Suffolk (excavated 1983–85)*, Ancient Monuments Laboratory Report 16/91

Mays, S and Turner-Walker, G 1999, 'A medieval case of Paget's disease of bone with complications', *Journal of Paleopathology* 11, 29–40

Mays, S and Beavan, N 2011, 'An investigation of diet in early Anglo-Saxon England using carbon and nitrogen stable isotope analysis of human bone collagen', *Journal of Archaeological Science,* doi:10.1016/jas.2011.10.013

McCormac, F G 1992, 'Liquid scintillation counter characterisation, optimisation and benzene purity correction', *Radiocarbon* 34, 37–45

McCormac, F G, Thompson, M and Brown, D 2001, 'Characterisation, optimisation and standard measurements for two small-sample high-precision radiocarbon counters', *Centre for Archaeology Report* 8/2001

McCormac, F G, Reimer, P J, Bayliss, A, Thompson, M M, Beavan, N, Brown, D and Hoper, S T 2011, *Laboratory and Quality Assurance Procedures at the Queen's University, Belfast Radiocarbon Dating Laboratory for Samples dated for the Anglo-Saxon Chronology Project*, Research Department Report Series, 89/2011

McDonnell, J G 1988, 'Ore to Artefact - a study of early ironworking technology' in E O Slater and J O Tate (eds), 238–93

McDonnell, J G 1989, 'Iron and its alloys in the fifth to eleventh centuries AD in England', *World Archaeology* 20(3), 373–82

McDonnell, J G 1991, 'A model for the formation of smithing slags', *Materialy Archeologiczne* 26, 23–6

McDonnell, J G 2000, 'Metallographic examination of 14 knives' in P Rahtz *et al*, 330–9

McKinley, J 1987, 'Report on the skeletal material' in B Green *et al*, 188–9

Meaney, A L 1964, *A Gazeteer of Early Anglo-Saxon Burial Sites,* London

Meaney, A L 1981, *Anglo-Saxon Amulets and Curing Stones*, British Archaeological Reports (British Series) 96, Oxford

Meaney, A L 1998, 'Girdle groups: reconstruction and comparative study' in T Malim and J Hines, 268–75

Meaney, A L and Chadwick Hawkes, S 1970, *Two Anglo-Saxon Cemeteries at Winnall*, Society for Medieval Archaeology Monograph Series No 4, London

Megow, W-R 1993, 'Gemmen und Cameen der Griechen, Etrusker, Römer und Byzantiner', *Aus den Schatzkammern Eurasiens, Meisterwerke Antike Kunst*, austellung, Kunsthaus Zurich, 29 Januar bis 2. Mai 1993

Menis, G C 1992, *I Longobardi*, Exhibition Catalogue, second edition, Milan

Menghin, W 1983, *Das Schwert im Frühen Mittelalter. Chronologisch-typologische Untersuchungen zu Langschwerten aus germanischen Gräbern des 5 bis 7 Jahrhunderts n Chr*, Germanisches Nationalmuseum, Stuttgart

Miki, Z 1990, 'Social stratification and the brachycranization process in the medieval period. The Stecci population of Yugoslavia', *Homo* 41, 136–45

Millard, L, Jarman, S and Hawkes, S C 1969, 'Anglo-Saxon burials near the Lord of the Manor, Ramsgate. New light on the site of Ozengell?', *Archaeologia Cantiana* lxxxiv, 9–30

Molleson, T I 1993, 'The human remains' in D E Farwell and T I Molleson, 142–214

Molleson, T, Cox, M, Waldron, A H and Whittaker, D K 1993, *The Spitalfields Project volume 2 - The Anthropology The Middling Sort*, Council for British Archaeology Research Report 86, London

Montelius, O 1869, *Från Jernaldern*, Häggström, Stockholm

Mook, W G 1986, 'Business meeting: Recommendations/Resolutions adopted by the Twelfth International Radiocarbon Conference', *Radiocarbon* 28, 799

Moosbrugger-Leu, R 1971, *Die Schweiz zur Merowingerzeit*, Bern

Mordvinceva V and Treisterm M 2007, *Toreutik und Schmuck im Nördlichen Schwarzmeergebiet, 2 Jh v Chr – 2 Jh n Chr*, Ancient Toreutics and Jewellery in Eastern Europe 2, 3 vols, Simferopol and Bonn

Morris, C A 1985, 'Anglo-Saxon and medieval woodworking crafts – the manufacture and use of utilitarian and domestic wooden artefacts in the British Isles, AD 400–1500', unpublished DPhil thesis, University of Cambridge

Mortimer, C 1990, 'Some aspects of early medieval copper-alloy technology, as illustrated by a study of the Anglian cruciform brooch', unpublished PhD thesis, Oxford

Mortimer, J M 1905, *Forty Years Researches in British and Saxon burial mounds of East Yorkshire*, London

Morton, G R and Wingrove, J 1969, 'Constitution of bloomery slags: part 1: Roman', *Journal of the Iron and Steel Institute* 207, 1556–64

Moseley, J E 1965, 'The palaeopathologic riddle of "symmetrical osteoporosis"', *American Journal of Roentgenology* 95, 135–42

Moseley, J E 1966, 'Radiographic studies in hematologic bone disease: Implications for paleopathology' in S Jarcho (ed), 121–30

Mourey, W and Robbiola, L (eds) 1998, *Metal 98, Proceedings of the International Conference on Metals Conservation,* London

Mullis, K and Faloona, F 1987, 'Specific synthesis of DNA in vitro via a polymerase-catalysed chain reaction', *Methods in Enzymology* 155, 335–50

Munksgaard, E 1984, 'A Viking Age smith, his tools and his stock-in-trade', *Offa* 41, 85–9

Munksgaard, E 1990, 'The costume depicted on gold-sheet figures (*guldgubbar*)' in P Walton and J P Wild (eds), 97–100

Musty, J 1969, 'The excavation of two barrows, one of Saxon date, at Ford, Laverstock, near Salisbury, Wiltshire', *Antiquaries Journal* xlix, 98–117

Myres, J N L 1977, *A Corpus of Anglo-Saxon Pottery of the Pagan Period*, Cambridge University Press

Myres, J N L and Green, B 1973, *The Anglo-Saxon Cemeteries of Caistor-by-Norwich and Markshall, Norfolk*, Reports of the Research Committee of the Society of Antiquaries of London No XXX, London

Näsman, U 1984, 'Zwei Relieffibeln von der Insel Öland', *Praehistorische Zeitschrift* 59, 48–80

Navasaitis, J, Selskienė, A and Žaldarys, G 2010, 'The study of trace elements in bloomery iron', *Materials Science* (Medžiagotyra) 16, (2) 113–18

Nerman, B 1969, *Die Vendelzeit Gotlands II Tafeln,* Stockholm

Neumann, B 1927–8, 'Romanische Damasstahl', *Archiv für das Eisenhüttenwesen*, Düsseldorf

Neverov, O 1976, *Antique Intaglios in the Hermitage Collection*, Leningrad [St Petersburg]

Neville, R C 1854, 'Anglo-Saxon cemetery excavated January 1853', *Archaeological Journal* 11, 95–115

Nicholson, R 1998, 'Animal bone from the graves' in G Drinkall and M Foreman, 236–40

Nielsen, J N 2000, *Sejlflod – ein eisenzeitliches Dorf in Nordjütland*, Katalog der Grabfunde. Bände 1: Text und Pläne, Bände 2: Abbildungen und Tafeln. Nordiske Fortidsminder Serie B, Bände 20:2, København

Nockert, M 1991, *The Høgom Find and Other Migration Period Textiles and Costumes in Scandinavia, Archaeology and Environment 9: Høgom part II*, University of Umeå/ Riksantikvarieämbetet, Umeå (Sweden)

Norgärd-Jorgensen, A 1999, *Waffen und Gräber. Skandinavische Waffengräber 530 – 900 n. Chr. Typologische und Chronologische Studien,* Nordiske Fortidsminder, Oslo

Nowakowski, J A and Quinnell, H 2011, *Trevelgue Head, Cornwall: The importance of CK Croft's 1939 excavations for prehistoric and Roman Cornwall*, Cornwall County Council

OAK 1898, Otcët (Imperatoskoj) Arheologičeskoj Kommissii, Moscow

Ogden, J 1982, *Jewellery of the Ancient World*, London

Oldenstein, J 1976, 'Zur Ausrustung römischer Auxiliarreinheiten', *Bericht der Römisch-Germanischen Kommission* 57, 49–284

Osborne, C unpublished, 'The human skeletal remains from Gunthorpe, 1987'

Osborne White, H J 1928, *The Geology of the Country near Ramsgate and Dover*, HMSO, London

Ottaway, P 1992, *Anglo-Scandinavian Ironwork from 16–22 Coppergate, The Archaeology of York, The Small Finds 17/6*, York Archaeological Trust, London

Owen-Crocker, G 2004, *Dress in Anglo-Saxon England*, Manchester

Padmanabhan, R 1986, 'The talar facets of the calcaneus - an anatomical note', *Anatomischer Anzeiger* 161, 389–92

Palm, M and Pind, J 1992, 'Anglian English women's graves in the fifth to seventh centuries AD - a chronological analysis' in L Jørgensen (ed), 50–80

Párducz, M 1935, *Die frühesten Funde der ersten Pontisch-Germanischen Denkmälergruppe in Ungarn*, Szeged

Parfitt, K 1994, 'Buckland Anglo-Saxon Cemetery, Dover: An Interim Report', *Archaeologia Cantiana* cxiv, 454–6

Parfitt, K 1995a, 'The Buckland Saxon Cemetery', *Current Archaeology* 144, 459–64

Parfitt, K 1995b, 'Royal Victoria Hospital, Dover', *Canterbury's Archaeology 1993–1994*, 20–1

Parfitt, K 1995c, *Iron Age Burials from St Richard's Road, Mill Hill, Deal*, London

Parfitt, K 1998, 'An unrecorded ?Anglo-Saxon cemetery at Water's End, near Dover', *Kent Archaeological Review* 134, 89–90

Parfitt, K 1999, 'A bird mount and other early Anglo-Saxon finds: Ripple/ Ringwould', *Archaeologia Cantiana* cxix, 394–8

Parfitt, K 2002, 'A prehistoric site off Green Lane, Whitfield, near Dover', *Archaeologia Cantiana* cxxii, 373–96

Parfitt, K 2003, 'Scientific examination of Anglo-Saxon grave-goods from Mill Hill, Deal', *Kent Archaeological Review* 154, 76–81

Parfitt, K forthcoming, 'Settlement at the Church Whitfield Crossroad' *in Excavations on the Whitfield-Eastry Bypass,* Canterbury Archaeological Trust Occasional Paper

Parfitt, K, Allen, T and Rady, J 1997, 'Whitfield–Eastry by-pass', *Canterbury's Archaeology 1995–1996*, 28–33

Parfitt, K and Brugmann, B 1997, *The Anglo-Saxon Cemetery on Mill Hill, Deal, Kent*, Society for Medieval Archaeology Monograph Series No 14, London

Parfitt, K and Dickinson, T M 2007, 'The Anglo-Saxon cemetery at Old Park, near Dover, revisited' in M Henig and T J Smith (eds), 111–26

Parfitt, K and Haith, C 1996, 'Buckland Anglo-Saxon Cemetery', *Canterbury's Archaeology 1994–1995*, 27–31

Parfitt, K, Corke, B and Cotter, J 2006, *Townwall Street, Dover, Excavations 1996,* Archaeology of Canterbury (New Series) III, Canterbury

Paroli, L 2000, 'The Langobardic finds and the archaeology of Central Italy' in K R Brown *et al* (eds), 140–63

Parsons, F G 1908, 'Report on the Hythe crania', *Journal of the Royal Anthropological Institute* 38, 419–50

Payne, G 1889, 'On a Roman statue and other remains in the Dover Museum', *Archaeologia Cantiana* xviii, 202–5

Paynter, S 2006, 'Regional variation in bloomery smelting slag of the Iron Age and Roman-British periods,' *Archaeometry* 48, 271–92

Paynter, S 2007, 'Innovations in bloomery smelting in Iron Age and Romano-British England' in S La Niece *et al* (eds), 202–18

Pearson, A 2002, *The Roman Shore Forts, Coastal Defences of Southern Britain*, Stroud

Pearson, G W 1983, *The development of high precision ^{14}C measurement and its application to archaeological time-scale problems*, unpublished PhD thesis, Queen's University Belfast

Pearson, K and Bell, J 1919, 'A study of the long bones of the English skeleton, I The femur', *Drapers Company Memoirs Biometrics Series* 10, 1–224

Penn, K 2000, *Excavations on the Norwich Southern Bypass, Part II: The Anglo-Saxon Cemetery at Harford Farm, Caistor St Edmund,* East Anglian Archaeology 92, Gressenhall

Penn, K 2011, *The Anglo-Saxon Cemetery at Shrubland Hall Quarry, Coddenham, Suffolk*, East Anglian Archaeology 139, Gressenhall

Penn, K and Brugmann B 2007, *Aspects of Anglo-Saxon Inhumation Burial: Morning Thorpe, Spong Hill, Bergh Apton and Westgarth Gardens*, East Anglian Archaeology 119, Gressenhall

Périn, P 1975, 'Ensembles archéologiques mérovingiens de la région ardennaise: 4. - Le cimetière de l'hôpital de Mézières (fouilles 1969–1971)', *Revue historique ardennaise* 10, 1–47

Périn, P 1980, *La datation des tombes mérovingiennes. Historique – Méthodes - Applications,* Centre de recherches d'historie et de philology de la IVe section de l'école pratique de des hautes études médievales et modernes 39, Geneva

Périn, P 1991, 'Pour une révision de la datation de la tombe d'Arégonde, épouse de Clotaire Ier, découverte en 1959 dans la basilique de Saint-Denis', *Archéologie Médiévale* 21, 21–55

Périn, P 1995, 'La datation des verres mérovingiennes du nord de la Agule' in D Foy (ed), 139–50

Périn, P 1998, 'La question des 'tombes-références' pour la datation absolue du mobilier funéraire mérovingien' in X Delestre and P Périn (eds), 189–206

Perkins, D R J 1985, 'The Monkton Gas Pipeline: Phases III and IV, 1983–84', *Archaeologia Cantiana* cii, 43–69

Perkins, D R J 1991, 'The Jutish Cemetery at Sarre revisited: a rescue evaluation', *Archaeologia Cantiana* cix, 139–66

Perkins, D R J 1992, 'The Jutish cemetery at Sarre revisited: Part II', *Archaeologia Cantiana* cx, 83–120

Perkins, D R J and Chadwick Hawkes, S 1984, 'The Thanet Gas Pipeline Phases I and II (Monkton Parish), 1982', *Archaeologia Cantiana* ci, 83–114

Pescheck, C 1996, *Das fränkische Reihengräberfeld von Kleinlangheim, Landkreis Kitzingen/Nordbayern*, Germanische Denkmäler der Völkerwanderungszeit A 17, Mainz

Petitjean, M 1995, 'Les peignes en os à l'époque mérovingienne: évolution depuis l'Antiquité tardive', *Antiquitiés Nationales* 27, 145–92

Phillips, A S 1964, Ordnance Survey Record card, TR 24 SE 13

Phillips, D and Heywood, B 1995, *Excavations at York Minster. Volume I. From Roman Fortress to Norman Cathedral,* London

Philp, B J 1973a, 'Site 24, The Anglo-Saxon Cemetery at Polhill, Dunton Green, Kent', *Excavations in West Kent 1960–1970,* Kent Archaeological Research Reports, Dover, 164–214

Philp, B J 1973b, 'Saxon gold ring found at Dover', *Kent Archaeological Review* 31, 10

Philp, B J 1981, *The Excavation of the Roman Forts of the Classis Britannica at Dover, 1970–1977,* Third Research Report in the Kent Monograph Series, Dover

Philp, B J 1989, *The Roman House with Bacchic Murals at Dover,* Fifth Research Report in the Kent Monograph series, Dover

Philp, B J 2003, *The Discovery and Excavation of Anglo-Saxon Dover,* Ninth Research Report in the Kent Monograph series, Dover

Philp, B J 2007, 'The Saxon Cemetery at Alkham, near Dover', *Kent Archaeological Review* 170, 213–4

Philpott, R 1991, *Burial Practices in Roman Britain. A survey of grave treatment and furnishing A D 43–410,* British Archaeological Reports (British Series) 219, Oxford

Piaskowski, J 1960, 'An interesting example of early technology', *Journal of the Iron and Steel Institute* 194, 336–40

Piaskowski, J 1961, 'Metallographic investigations of ancient iron objects from the territory between the Oder and the basin of the Vistula river', *Journal of the Iron and Steel Institute* 198(3), 263–82

Piaskowski, J 1989, 'Phosphorus in iron ore and slag and in bloomery iron', *Archaeomaterials* 3, 47–59

Pilet, C 1980, *La Nécropole de Frénouville. Étude d'une population de la fin du IIIe á la fin du VIIe siècle,* British Archaeological Reports (International Series) 83, Oxford

Pilet, C 1994, *La Nécropole de Saint-Martin-de-Fontenay (Calvados): recherches sur le peuplement de la plaine de Caen, du Ve s avant J-C au VIIe s après J-C,* Supplément à Gallia 54, Paris

Pilet, C, Alduc-le-Bagousse, A, Blondiaux, J, Buchet, L, Grévin, G and Pilet-Lemiere, J 1990, 'Les Nécropoles de Giberville (Calvados) fin du Vᵉ siècle – find du VIIᵉ siècle op J C', *Archéologie Médiévale* 20, 3–140

Pirling, R 1979, *Das römisch-fränkische Gräberfeld von Krefeld-Gellep 1964–1965,* Germanische Denkmäler der Völkerwanderungszeit Serie B, Band 10, 1

Piton, D 1985, *La nécropole de Nouvion-en-Ponthieu,* Berck-sur-Mer

Pitt Rivers, General A H L F 1898, *Excavations on Cranbourne Chase, 1887–1898,* Cranbourne

Place, C 1994, 'Castle View, Dover, Kent: Archaeological Evaluation Report', unpublished South-Eastern Archaeological Services report for Denne Builders, March 1994

Plantzos, D 1999, *Hellenistic Engraved Gems,* Oxford

Platz-Horster, G (ed) 1994, *Die antiken Gemmen aus Xanten. 2. Im Besitz des Archäologischen Parks, Regionalmuseum Xanten, der Katholischen Kirchengemeinde St Mariae Himmelfahrt Marienbaum sowie in Privatbesitz,* Koln and Bonn

Platz-Horster, G 1995, 'Königliche'Artemis? Eine neue Granatgemme im Kestner-Museum zu Hannover', *Niederdeutsche Beiträge zur Kunstgeschichte* 34, 9–26

Pleiner, R 1982, 'The Technology - the blacksmith' in M Richter (ed), 298–300

Pleiner, R 1993, *The Celtic Sword,* Oxford

Pleiner, R 2000, *Iron in Archaeology: the European Bloomery Smelters,* Archeologický Ústav AV ČR, Prague

Powell, F V H 1982, *Raunds: Human Skeletal Report,* unpublished manuscript, Calvin Wells Laboratory, Department of Archaeological Sciences, University of Bradford

Powers, R and Brothwell, D R 1988, 'Human bones - inhumations' in V I Evison, 59–64

Powers, R and Cullen, R 1987, 'The human skeletal remains' in V I Evison, 197–201

Price, J (ed) 2000, *Glass in Britain and Ireland AD 350–1100,* British Museum Occasional Paper 127, London

Prummel, W 2000, 'The significance of animals to the early medieval Frisians in the northern coastal area of the Netherlands: archaeozoological, iconographic, historical and literary evidence', *Environmental Archaeology* 6, 73–86

Quast, D 1993, Die merowingerzeitlichen Grabfunde aus Gültlingen (Stadt Wildberg, Kreis Calw), *Forschungen und Berichte zur Vor- und Frühgeschichte in Baden-Württemberg,* Bd 52, Stuttgart

Quast, D 2006, Die frühalamannische und merowingerzeitliche Besiedlung im Umland des Runden Berges bei Urach, *Forschungen und Berichte zur Vor- und Frühgeschichte in Baden-Württemberg,* Bd 84, Stuttgart

Rahtz, P and Hirst, S 1974, *Beckery Chapel, Glastonbury 1967–8,* Glastonbury Antiquarian Society, Glastonbury

Rahtz P and Watts, L 1989, 'Pagans Hill revisited', *Archaeological Journal* 146, 330–71

Rahtz, P, Dickinson T and Watts, L (eds) 1980, *Anglo-Saxon Cemeteries 1979,* British Archaeological Reports (British Series) 82, Oxford

Rahtz, P, Hirst S and Wright, S M 2000, *Cannington Cemetery,* Society for the Promotion of Roman Studies Britannia Monograph Series No17, London

Rau, A 2010, *Nydam Mose 1: Die peronengebundenen Gegenstände. Grabungen 1989–1999,* 2 vols, Jysk Arkæologisk Selskab: Jernalderen i Nordeuropa, Aarhus University Press, Aarhus

Read, C H 1895, 'On excavations in a cemetery of South Saxons on High Down, Sussex', *Archaeologia* 54, 369–82

Rehren, Th, Charlton, M, Chrikure, Sh, Hamphris, J, Ige, A and Veldhuijzen, A H 2007, 'Decisions set in slag - the human factor in African iron smelting' in S La Niece *et al* (eds), 211–18

Reimer, P J, Baillie, M G L, Bard, E, Bayliss, A, Beck, J W, Bertrand, C J H, Blackwell, P G, Bronk Ramsey, C, Buck, C E, Burr, Edwards, R L, Friedrich, M, Grootes, P M, Guilderson, T P, Hajdas, I, Heaton, T J, Hogg, A G, Hughen, K A, Kaiser, K F, Kromer, B, McCormac, F G, Manning, S W, Reimer, R W, Richards, D A, Southon, J R, Talamo, S, Turney, C S M, van der Plicht, J and Weyhenmeyer, C E 2009, 'IntCal09 and Marine09 radiocarbon age calibration curves, 0-50,000 years cal BP', *Radiocarbon* 51, 1111–50

Reiß, R 1994, *Der merowingerzeitliche Reihengräberfriedhof von Westheim (Kreis Weißenburg-Gunzenhausen),* Forschungen zur frühmittelalterlichen Landesgeschichte im südwestlichen Mittelfranken, Nuremburg

Renner, D 1970, *Die durchbrochenen Zierscheiben der Merowingerzeit,* Römisch-Germanisches Zentralmuseum zu Mainz, Katalogue Vor- und Frühgesechichtlicher Altertümer 18, Mainz

Resnick, D and Niwayama, G 1981, *Diagnosis of Bone and Joint Disorders,* Philadelphia

Reynolds, A 2009, *Anglo-Saxon Deviant Burial Customs,* Oxford

Richards, J D 1987, *The Significance of Form and Decoration of Anglo-Saxon Cremation Urns,* British Archaeological Reports (British Series) 166, Oxford

Richards, M P, Mays, S and Fuller, B 2002, 'Stable carbon and nitrogen isotope values of bone and teeth reflect weaning at the mediaeval Wharram Percy Site, Yorkshire, UK', *American Journal of Physical Anthropology* 199, 205–10

Richards, P 1980, 'Byzantine bronze vessels in England and Europe', unpublished PhD Dissertation, University of Cambridge

Richardson, A 2005, *The Anglo-Saxon Cemeteries of Kent,* British Archaeological Reports (British Series) 391, (two volumes), Oxford

Richardson, A 2011, 'The Third Way: thoughts on non-Saxon identity south of the Thames 450–600' in S Brookes *et al,* 72–81

Richter, G M A 1968, *Engraved Gems of the Greeks and the Etruscans, Part One,* London

Richter, M (ed) 1982, *Monumenta Archaeologica,* Prague, 20

Riddler, I D 2001, 'The small finds' in M Gardiner *et al,* 228–52

Riddler, I D 2006a, 'Social organisation and ethnicity in a small east Kent cemetery' in X Delestre *et al*, 69–78

Riddler, I D 2006b, 'Objects and waste of bone and antler' in R J Cramp, 267–81

Riddler, I D 2008, 'The Anglo-Saxon cemetery' in P Bennett *et al*, 279–305

Riesch, H 1999, Untersuchungen zur Effizienz und Verwendung alamannischer Pfeilspitzen. *Archäologisches Korrespondenzblatt* 29/4, 567–82

Rigold, S E and Webster, L E 1970, 'Three Anglo-Saxon disc brooches', *Archaeologia Cantiana* lxxxv, 1–18

Roach Smith, C 1854, 'Anglo-Saxon Remains discovered at Ozingell, Kent', *Collectanea Antiqua* 3, 1–18

Robin, E D and Wong, R 1988, 'Mitochondrial DNA molecules and virtual number of mitochondria per cell in mammalian cells', *Journal of Cellular Physiology,* 136, 507–13

Rodwell, K, 1993, 'Post-Roman burials' in M J Darling and D Gurney, 45–61 and 252–5

Rodwell, W J and Rodwell, K A 1982, 'St Peter's Church, Barton-upon-Humber: Excavation and Structural Study, 1978–81', *Antiquaries Journal* lxii, 283–315

Roes, A 1963, *Bone and Antler Objects from the Frisian Terp Mounds*, Haarlem

Roesdahl, E 1977, *Fyrkat. En jysk Vikingeborg II. Oldsagerne og Gravpladsen,* Nordiske Fortidsminder 4, Copenhagen

Rogers, N S H 1993, *Anglian and other Finds from Fishergate*, The Archaeology of York. The Small Finds 17/9, London

Rollason, E C 1973, *Engineering for metallurgists*, 170, Arnold, London

Rolleston, G 1870, 'Researches and excavations carried out in an ancient cemetery at Frilford, Abingdon, Berks in the years 1867–1868', *Archaeologia* xlii: 417–85

Rolsch, K and Kuhm, H H 1976, 'Synthetische Merstallung von Rennfeuereisen und dessen handwerkliche Verarbeitung', *Archiv für das Eisenhüttenwesen,* 47 (1), 5–8

Rosenqvist, A M 1968, 'Sverd med klinger ornert med figurer i kopperlegeringer fra eldre jernalder i Universitetets Oldsaksamling'. Svertrykk fra Universitetets Oldsakamlings Årbok 1967–1968, 143–200

Rösing, F W 1984, 'Discreta of the human skeleton: a critical review', *Journal of Human Evolution* 13, 319–23

Ross, S 1991, 'Dress pins from Anglo-Saxon England: their production and typo-chronolgical development', unpublished PhD thesis Oxford

Russell, D S and Rubenstein, L J 1989, *Pathology of Tumours of the Nervous System,* 5th edition, London

Sage, W 1984, *Das Reihengräberfeld von Altenerding in Oberbayern*, Germanische Denkmäler der Völkerwanderungszeit A 14, Berlin

Salter, C J 1999, 'The structure of welds in Iron Age ironwork (Abstracts)' in P Northover and C Salter (eds), *Founders, Smiths and Platers*, Oxford, 25

Salter, C J 2004, Lowbury Anglo-Saxon sword. http://users.ox.ac.uk/~salter2/Lowbury/Sword_Section.html

Salter, C J and Crew, P 2003, 'Early steel in Britain (Abstract)', *UK Archaeological Science 2003*, 60

Samuels, L E 1980, *Optical Microscopy of Carbon Steels*, American Society for Metals (ASM), Ohio, USA

Sanderson, D C W and Hunter, J R 1981, 'Composition variability in vegetable ash', *Science and Archaeology* 23, 27–30

Sarkar, G and Sommer, S S 1993, 'Removal of DNA contamination in polymerase chain reaction reagents by ultraviolet irradiation', *Methods in Enzymology* 218, 381–9

Sasse, B 2001, *Ein frühmittelalterliches Reihengräberfeld bei Eichstetten am Kaiserstuhl,* Forschungen und Berichte zur Vor- und Frühgeschichte in Baden-Württemberg 75, Stuttgart

Schajowicz, F 1981, *Tumors and Tumorlike Lesions of Bone and Joints*, New York

Schlitz, V (ed) 2001, *L'Or des Amazones, Peuples nomades entre Asie et Europe*, éxposition Musée Cernuschi, 16 mars – 15 juillet 2001, Paris

Schmerer, W, Hummel, S and Herrmann, B 1999, 'Optimized DNA extraction to improve reproducibility of short trandem repeat genotyping with highly degraded DNA as target', *Electrophoresis* 20, 1712–16

Schoppa, H 1953, 'Ein fränkisches Holzkästchen aus Weilbach', *Germania* 31, 44–9

Schultz, A M 1929, 'The metopic fontanelle, fissure and suture', *American Journal of Anatomy* 44, 475–99

Schulz, W 1933, 'Das Fürstengrab von Hassleben', *Römisch-germanische Forschungen* 7, Berlin

Schulze-Dörrlamm, M 1990, *Die spätrömischen und frühmittelalterlichen Gräberfelder von Gondorf, Gemeinde Kobern-Gondorf, Kreis Mayen-Koblenz*, Germanische Denkmäler Völkerwanderungszeit 14, Stuttgart

Schürmann, E 1959, 'Untersuchungen an Nydam-Schwerten', *Archiv für das Eisenhüttenwesen* 30(3), 121–6

Schuster, J 2006, 'Die Nuntmetallfunde der Grabung Feddersen Wierde. Chronologie - Technologie, in Feddersen Wierde. Die Ergebnisse die Ausgrabungen der vorgeschichtlichen Wurt Feddersen Wierde bei Bremerhaven in den Jahren 1955 bis 1963, Band 6', *Probleme der Küstenforschung im südlichen Nordeseegebiete* 30, Oldenburg (Isensee Verlag), 1–278

Schuster, J 2011, 'Saxon Objects' in P Andrews, L Mepham, J Schuster and C J Stevens, *Settling the Ebbsfleet Valley. High Speed I Excavations at Springhead and Northfleet, Kent. The Late Iron Age, Roman, Saxon and Medieval Landscape. Volume 4: Saxon and Later Finds and Environmental Reports*, Oxford, 23–37

Schweingruber, F H 1990, *Anatomy of European Woods*, Paul Haupt, Berne

Scull, C 1985, 'Further evidence from East Anglia for enamelling on early Anglo-Saxon metalwork', *Anglo-Saxon Studies in Archaeology and History* 4, Oxford University Commitee for Archaeology, Oxford, 117–24

Scull, C 1986, 'A sixth-century grave containing a balance and weights from Watchfield, Oxfordshire, England', *Germania* 64i, 105–38

Scull, C 1990, 'Scales and weights in early Anglo-Saxon England', *Archaeological Journal* 147, 183–215

Scull, C 1992, 'Excavation and survey at Watchfield, Oxfordshire, 1983–92', *Archaeological Journal* 149, 124–281

Scull, C 1993, 'Archaeology, early Anglo-Saxon society and the origins of Anglo-Saxon kingdoms' in W Filmer-Sankey (ed), 65–82

Sebesta, J L 1994, 'Symbolism in the costume of the Roman woman' in J L Sebesta and L Bonfante (eds), *The World of Roman Costume*, University of Wisconsin Press

Seeberger, F 1985, 'Zur Identifizierung von Feuerstählen', *Archäologisches Korrespondenzblatt* 15, 257–9

Segebade, C 1996, 'Remarks on European damascene steelware', *The Beginnings of the Early Use of Metals and Alloys (BUMA) IV*, Shimane, Japan, 133–49

Sena Chiesa, G 1966, *Gemme del Museo Nazionale de Aquileia*, Aquileia

Sena Chiesa, G 2011, 'Myth revisited: the reuse of mythological cameos and intaglios in late antiquity and the early Middle Ages' in C Entwistle and N Adams, 231–40

Serneels, V and Crew, P 1997, 'Ore-slag relationships from experimentally smelted bog-iron ore' in P Crew and S Crew (eds), 78–82

Sherlock, S J and Welch, M G 1992, *An Anglo-Saxon Cemetery at Norton, Cleveland*, Council for British Archaeology Research Report 82, London

Shinn, D L 1976, 'Congenitally missing third molars in a British population', *Journal of Dental Research* 4, 42–4

Sibley, L R and Jakes, K A 1984, 'Survival of protein fibres in archaeological contexts', *Science and Archaeology*, 26, 17–27

Siegmann, M 2001, *Bunte Pracht - die Perlen der frühmittelalterlichen Gräberfelder von Liebenau, Kreis Nienburg, Weser, und Dörverden,*

Kreis Verden, Aller: Chronologie der Gräber, Entwicklung und Trageweise des Perlenschmucks, Technik der Perlen, Beiträge zur Ur- und Frühgeschichte Mitteleuropas, Weißbach

Siegmund, F 1998, *Merowingerzeit am Niederrhein. Die frühmittelalterlichen Funde aus dem Regierungsbezirk Düsseldorf und dem Kreis Heinsberg*, Rheinische Ausgrabungen 34, Köln

Siegmund, F 2000, *Alamannen und Franken*. Ergänzungsbände zum Reallexikon der Germanischen Altertumskunde 23, Berlin, New York

Sim, D 1998, *Beyond the Bloom*, British Archaeological Reports (International Series) 725, Oxford

Slater, E O and Tate, J O (eds) 1988, *Science and Archaeology, Glasgow 1987*, British Archaeological Reports (British Series) 196 (i), Oxford

Smith, B C, Fisher, D L, Weedn, V W, Warnock, G R and Holland, M M 1993, 'A systematic approach to the sampling of dental DNA', *Journal of Forensic Science* 38, issue 5, 1194–1209

Smith, H E 1884, 'Notes on an ancient cemetery at Saffron Walden', *Transactions of the Essex Archaeological Society* 2, 284–7

Sørensen, P 1999, 'A reassessment of the Jutish nature of Kent, southern Hampshire and the Isle of Wight', unpublished D Phil thesis, Oxford University, 2 vols

Spain, S 2000, 'The shield in early Anglo-Saxon Kent: a computer-assisted analysis of shield bosses and an investigation into the use of the shield in the burial rite', unpublished MA dissertation, University of York

Speake, G 1980, *Anglo-Saxon Animal Art and its Germanic Background*, Oxford

Speake, G 1989, *A Saxon Bed Burial on Swallowcliffe Down*, English Heritage Archaeological Report 10, London

Spier, J 2007, *Late Antique and Early Christian Gems*, Wiesbaden

Starley, D 1999, 'Determining the technological origins of iron and steel', *Journal of Archaeological Science* 26, 1127–33

Stead, I M 2006, *British Iron Swords and Scabbards*. British Museum Press, London

Stead, I M and Rigby, V 1989, *Verulamium, The King Harry Lane Site*, London

Stevens, P M 1980, 'Ocklynge Hill Anglo-Saxon cemetery at Eastbourne', *Sussex Archaeological Collections* 118, 231–44

Stewart, J W, Charles, J A and Wallach, E R 2000, 'Iron-phosphorus-carbon system Part 3 - Metallography of low carbon iron-phosphorus alloys', *Materials Science and Technology* 16, 291–303

Stirland, A 1991, 'Paget's disease (osteitis deformans): a classic case?', *International Journal of Osteoarchaeology* 1, 173–7

Stones, H H 1957, *Oral and Dental Diseases*, Edinburgh

Stones, J A (ed) 1989, *Three Scottish Carmelite Friaries. Excavations at Aberdeen, Linlithgow and Perth 1980-86*, Society of Antiquaries of Scotland Monograph No 6, Edinburgh

Stoodley, N 1999, *The Spindle and the Spear. A Critical Enquiry into the Construction and Meaning of Gender in Early Anglo-Saxon Burial Rite*, British Archaeological Reports (British Series) 288, Oxford

Stoodley, N 2002, 'Multiple burials, multiple meanings? Interpreting the early Anglo-Saxon multiple interment' in S Lucy and A Reynolds (eds), 103–21

Storgaard, B 1990, 'Årslev-fundet-et fynsk gravfund fra slutningen af yngre romersk jernalder', *Aarbøger for nordisk Oldkyndighed og Histoire*, 23–58

Stow, S 1995, 'The Jutish pottery from East of the Marlowe Theatre' in K Blockley *et al*, 825–7

Stroud, G and Kemp, R L 1993, *Cemeteries of the Church and Priory of St Andrew, Fishergate*, York Archaeological Trust 12/2, York

Stuiver, M and Polach, H A 1977, 'Reporting of 14C data', *Radiocarbon* 19, 355–63

Stuiver, M and Reimer, P J 1993, ' Extended 14C data base and revised CALIB 3.0 14C age calibration program', *Radiocarbon* 35, 215–30

Stukeley, W 1776, *Itinerarium Curiosum,* 2nd edition, London

Sulava, N O 1996, Gornaya Kolkhida v Antichnuu Epoku, Tbilisi

Sutton, D 1975, *A Textbook of Radiology*, 2nd edition, Edinburgh

Suzuki, S 2008, *Anglo-Saxon Button Brooches. Typology, Genealogy, Chronology, Anglo-Saxon Studies 10*, Woodbridge

Suzuki, S and Yanagihara, K 2002, 'Nickel enrichment at the interface between oxide layer and matrix in iron-nickel alloys', *Journal of Surface Analysis* 9, 3, 384–7

Swanton, M J 1967, 'An early Alamannic brooch from Yorkshire', *The Antiquaries Journal* xlvii, 43–50

Swanton, M J 1973, *The Spearheads of the Anglo-Saxon Settlements*, Leeds

Swanton, M J 1974, *A Corpus of Pagan Anglo-Saxon Spear Types,* British Archaeological Reports (British Series) 7, Oxford

Sylvester, C 1984, 'Dental anomalies' in J B Woelfel, *Dental Anatomy*, Philadelphia

Thålin Bergman, L and Arrhenius, B 2005, *Excavations at Helgö XV,* Almqvist and Wiksell International, Sweden

Taylor, A, Duhig, C and Hines, J 1997, 'An Anglo-Saxon cemetery at Oakington, Cambridgeshire', *Proceedings of the Cambridge Antiquarian Society* lxxxvi, 57–90

Taylor, C 1975, *Fields in the English Landscape*, London

Teichert, M 1975, 'Osteometrische Untersuchungen zur Berechnung der Widerristhöhe bei Schafen' in A T Clason (ed), 51–71

Tester, P J 1968, 'An Anglo-Saxon Cemetery at Orpington: First Interim Report', *Archaeologia Cantiana* lxxxiii, 125–50

Theune, C 1999, *Archäologische Funde im Hegau*, Universitätsforschungen zur prähistorischen Archäologie 54, Bonn

Thomas, G W 1887, 'On excavations in an Anglo-Saxon cemetery at Sleaford, in Lincolnshire', *Archaeologia* 50, 383–406

Thomsen, R 1966, 'Metallographic studies of an axe from the Migration Age', *Journal of the Iron and Steel Institute* 204, 905–9

Thomsen, R 1989, 'Pattern-welded swords from Illerup and Nydam', *Archaeology of Iron, Symposium Liblice 1987*, 371–7

Thomsen, R 1994, 'Metallografiske undersøgelser af sværd og spydspidser fra mosfundene i Illerup og Nydam', *Aarbøger for nordisk Oldkyndighed og Historie*, København, 281–310

Thomson, A and Buxton, L H D 1923, 'Man's nasal index in relation to certain climatic conditions', *Journal of the Royal Anthropological Institute* 52, 92–122

Thorpe, L 1970 (trans), *The Life of Charlemagne*, Einhard the Frank

Timby, J 1993, 'Sancton I Anglo-Saxon cemetery. Excavations carried out between 1976 and 1980', *Archaeological Journal* 150, 243–365

Timby, J 1996, *The Anglo-Saxon Cemetery at Empingham II, Rutland. Excavations carried out between 1974 and 1975,* Oxbow Monograph 70, Oxford

Tizzoni, C C and Tizzoni, M (eds) 1998, *Iron in the Alps*, Conference, 2–4 October 1998, Bienno, 1–12

Todd, J A and Charles, J A 1977, 'The analysis of non-metallic inclusions in ancient iron', *Journal of the European Study Group on Physical, Chemical, Biological and Mathematical Techniques Applied in Archaeology* (*PACT)* 1, 204–2

Töpf, A 2003, 'Mitochondrial DNA diversity and origin of human communities from 4th–11th century Britain', doctoral dissertation, *School of Biological and Biomedical Sciences*, University of Durham

Torgersen, J 1951, 'Hereditary factors in sutural patterns of the skull', *Acta Radiologica Diagnostica* 36, 374–82

Trotter, M and Gleser, G C 1958, 'A re-evaluation of estimation of stature based on measurements of stature taken during life and long bones after death', *American Journal of Physical Anthropology* 16, 79–123

Trinkaus, E 1975, 'Squatting among Neanderthals: a problem in behavioural interpretation of skeletal morphology', *Journal of Archaeological Science* 2, 327–51

Tweddle, D 1992, *The Anglian Helmet from Coppergate*, The Archaeology of York 17/8, Council for British Archaeology, 882–8

Tylecote, R F 1962, *Metallurgy in Archaeology*, Arnold

Tylecote, R F 1976, *A History of Metallurgy*, Metals Society

Tylecote, R F 1986, *The Prehistory of Metallurgy in the British Isles*, The Institute of Metals, London

Tylecote, R F 1987, *The early history of metallurgy in Europe*, London

Tylecote, R F 1990, 'Oxidation enrichment bands in wrought iron', *Historical Metallurgy* 24(1), 33–8

Tylecote, R F and Clough, R E 1983, 'Recent bog iron ore analyses and the smelting of pyrite nodules', *Offa* 40, 115–18

Tylecote, R F and Gilmour, B 1986, *Metallography of Early Ferrous Edge Tools and Weapons*, British Archaeological Reports (British Series) 155, Oxford

Tylecote, R F and Thomsen, R 1973, 'The segregation and surface enrichment of arsenic and phosphorus in early iron objects', *Archaeometry* 15(2), 193–8

Ubl, H 1989, 'Was trug der Römische Soldat unter dem Cingulum?' in C van Driel-Murray (ed), 61–74

van Driel-Murray, C (ed) 1989, *Roman Military Equipment: the Sources of Evidence (Proceedings of the fifth Roman Military Equipment Conference)*, British Archaological Reports (International Series) 467, Oxford

Vanhaeke, L 1997, 'Le Coffret mérovingien des Maroeuil', *Histoire et Archéologie du Pas-de-Calais* 15, 59–92

Veeck, W 1931, *Die Alamannen in Württemberg*, Germanische Denkmäler der Völkerwanderungszeit 1, Berlin and Leipzig

Vierck, H 1978, 'Die anglische Frauentracht' in C Ahrens (ed), 245–53

Vizcaino, V, Budd, P and McDonnell, J G 1998, 'An experimental investigation of the behaviour of phosphorus in bloomery iron', *Bulletin of the Metals Museum* 29, 13–9

Vogt, E 1960, 'Interpretation und museale Auswertung alamannischer Grabfunde', *Zeitschrift für Schweizerische Archäologie und Kunstgeschichte* 20, 70–90

Vollenweider, M-L 1966, *Die Steinschneidekunst und ihre Künstler in Spätrepublikanischer und Augusteischer zeit*, Baden-Baden

Vollenweider, M-L 1995, *Camées et intailles, Tome I, Les Portraits grecs du Cabinet de médailles*, Paris

von den Driesch, A 1976, *A Guide to the Measurement of Animal Bones from Archaeological Sites*, Peabody Museum Bulletin 1, Harvard University Press

Von Endt, D W and Ortner, D J 1982, 'Amino acid analysis of bone form and possible case of prehistoric iron deficiency anemia from the American south west', *American Journal of Physical Anthropology* 59, 377–85

von Freeden, U 1979, 'Untersuchungen zu merowingerzeitlichen Ohrringen bei den Alamannen', Berichte der Römisch-Germanischen Kommission 60, 227ff

von Freeden, U and Wieczorek, A (eds) 1997, *Perlen: Archäologie, Technik und Statistik. Akten des Internationalen Perlensymposiums in Mannheim, vom 16–19.11.1994*, Kolloquien zur Vor- und Frühgeschichte 1, Bonn

von Freeden, U, Koch U and Wieczorek, A (eds) 1999, *Völker an Nord- und Ostsee und die Franken. Akten des 48. Sachsensymposiums in Mannheim vom 7. Bis 11. September 1997,* Kolloquien Vor- und Frühgeschichte 3, Bonn

Wade-Martins, P 1980, *Excavations in North Elmham Park,* East Anglian Archaeology Report No 9, Norfolk

Waldron, T 1991, 'Variations in the rates of spondylolysis in early populations', *International Journal of Osteoarchaeology* 1, 63–5

Waldron, T 1993, 'The health of the adults' in T Molleson *et al*, 67–89

Waldron, T 1994, 'The human remains' in V I Evison 1994a, 52–66

Walker, P L 1986, 'Porotic hyperostosis in a marine dependent Californian Indian population', *American Journal of Physical Anthropology* 69, 345–54

Wall, W R 1990, 'Anglo-Saxon Knives' in J C Driver *et al*, 199–206

Walsh, R M 1981, 'Darenth Park Anglo-Saxon cemetery, Dartford', *Archaeologia Cantiana* xcvi, 305–20

Walters, H B 1926, *Catalogue of Engraved Gems and Cameos, Greek, Etruscan and Roman in the British Museum*, London

Walton, P 1989, *Textiles, Cordage and Raw Fibre from 16–22 Coppergate,* The Archaeology of York 17/5, Council for British Archaeology, London

Walton P and Wild J P (eds) 1990, *NESAT III: Textiles in Northern Archaeology*, London

Walton Rogers, P 1992, 'The sword-beater' with contributions from J Jones and J G McDonnell in D Tweddle, 882–8

Walton Rogers, P 1995, 'The raw material of textiles from northern Germany and the Netherlands', *Probleme der Küstenforschung im südlichen Nordseegebiet* 23, 389–400

Walton Rogers, P 1997, *Textile Production at 16–22 Coppergate*, The Archaeology of York 17/11, Council for British Archaeology, York

Walton Rogers, P 1998, 'Textiles and Clothing' in G Drinkall and M Foreman, 274–9

Walton Rogers, P 1999, 'The textiles' in C Haughton and D Powlesland, 143–71

Walton Rogers, P 2001, 'The re-appearance of an old Roman loom in medieval England', in P Walton Rogers *et al* (eds), 158–71

Walton Rogers, P 2007, *Cloth and clothing in Early Anglo-Saxon England, AD 450–700*, Council for British Archaeology Research Report 145, York

Walton Rogers, P 2009, 'Textile production' in D H Evans and C Loveluck, *Life and Economy at Early Medieval Flixborough, c AD 600–1000: The Artefact Evidence (Excavations at Flixborough, Vol 2)*, Oxford and Oakville, 281–316

Walton Rogers, P, Bender Jørgensen, L and Rast-Eicher, A (eds) 2001, *The Roman Textile Industry and its Influence: a Birthday Tribute to John Peter Wild*, Oxford

Walton Rogers, P and Riddler, I 2006, 'Early Anglo-Saxon textile manufacturing implements from Saltwood Tunnel, Kent', CTRL Specialist Report Series, http://ads.ahds.ac.uk/catalogue/adsdata/ arch-335-1/dissemination/pdf/PT2_Spec_Reps/03_Small_finds/SFS_ research_reports_SmallFinds_Text/SFS_SAX_TextileImpl_SLT_text. pdf?CFID=573996&CFTOKEN=39545028

Ward, G K and Wilson, S R 1978, 'Procedures for comparing and combining radiocarbon age determinations: a critique', *Archaeometry* 20, 19–31

Warhurst, A 1955, 'The Jutish cemetery at Lyminge', *Archaeologia Cantiana* lxix, 1–40

Watkins, S, Shearman, F and Haith, C 1998, 'Conservation of metal artefacts from an Anglo-Saxon cemetery at Buckland, Kent, England' in W Mourey and L Robbiola (eds), 15–21

Watkinson, D 1987, *First Aid for Finds*, UKIC and Rescue, London

Watson, J 1987, 'Organic material associated with metal objects' in V I Evison, 196

Watson, J 1993, 'Carpentry details of mineral preserved wood on iron coffin fittings from Thwing, North Yorkshire', Ancient Monuments Laboratory Report 116/93

Watson, J 1994, 'Wood usage in Anglo-Saxon shields'. *Anglo-Saxon Studies in Archaeology and History* 7, 35–40

Watson-Jones, R 1943, *Fractures and Joint Injuries*, Edinburgh

Webster, L 1982, 'Stylistic aspects of the Franks Casket' in R T Farrell (ed), 20–31

Webster, L 1995, 'Anglo Saxon Brooches' in K Blockley *et al*, 1036–9

Webster, L and Backhouse, J 1991, *The Making of England. Anglo-Saxon Art and Culture AD 600–900*, British Museum, London

Webster, L and Brown, M 1997, *The Transformation of the Roman World, AD 400–900*, British Museum, London

Weimer, K 1996, 'Metallurgical analyses of iron knives' in J Timby, 76–85

Welch, M 1983, *Early Anglo-Saxon Sussex*, British Archaeological Report (British Series) 112, Oxford

Welch, M 1992, *Anglo-Saxon England*, London

Welch, M 2007, 'Anglo-Saxon Kent' in J H Williams (ed), 187–248

Wells, C 1966, 'Report on the human remains from Little Eriswell' in P Hutchinson, Appendix II

Wells, C 1967, 'Report on the human remains from Red Castle, Thetford', *Norfolk Archaeology* xxxiv (ii), 155–86

Wells, C 1974, 'Osteochondritis dissecans in Ancient British skeletal material', *Medical History* 18, 365–9

Wells, C 1980, 'Discussion of the human skeletal remains' in P Wade-Martins, 247–302

Wells, C and Woodhouse, N 1975, 'Paget's disease in an Anglo-Saxon', *Medical History* 19, 396–400

Wenham, J 1989, 'Anatomical interpretation of Anglo-Saxon weapon injuries' in S Chadwick Hawkes 1989b (ed), 123–39

Werner, J 1957, 'Annexe V: Les boucles de ceinture trouvées dans les tombes d'hommes VIII, XI, XIII, XVI et XVII' in J Breuer and H Roosens, 327ff

Werner, J 1962a, 'Ein reiches Leitengrab der Zeit um 400 n Chr aus Fécamp (Seine Maritime)', *Archaeologica Belgica* 61, 145–54

Werner, J 1962b, *Die Langobarden in Pannonien. Beiträge zur Kenntnis der langobardischen Bodenfunde vor 568*, Abhandlungen der Bayerischen Akademie der Wissenschaften Philologisch.-historische Klasse Neue Folge Heft 55A, München

Werner, J 1966, 'Zu den donauländischen Beziehungen des alamannischen Gräberfeldes am alten Gotterbarmweg in Basel' in R Degen, W Drack and R Wyss (eds), *Helvetia Antiqua. Festschrift für Emil Vogt*, Zurich, 283–92

Werner, J 1970, 'Zur Verbreitung frühgeschichtlicher Metallarbeiten, Antikvarisk Arkiv 38', *Early Medieval Studies* 1, 78–81

West, S E 1985, *West Stow. The Anglo-Saxon Village (2 Vols)*, East Anglian Archaeology Report No 24, Gressenhall

West, S E 1988, *The Anglo-Saxon Cemetery at Westgarth Gardens, Bury St Edmunds, Suffolk*, East Anglian Archaeology Report No 38, Gressenhall

West, S E 1998, *A Corpus of Anglo-Saxon Material from Suffolk*, East Anglian Archaeology Report 84, Suffolk

West, S E and Owles, E 1973, 'Anglo-Saxon cremation burials from Snape', *Proceedings of the Suffolk Institute of Archaeology* 33, 47–57

Wheeler, E A, Baas, P and Gasson, P (eds) 1989, 'IAWA list of microscopic features for hardwood identification', *IAWA Bulletin* 10, 219–332

Wheeler, E A, Pearson, R G, LaPasha, C A, Zack, T and Hatley, W 1986, *Computer-Aided Wood Identification,* North Carolina Agriculture Research Service Bulletin 474, North Carolina

White, R H 1988, *Roman and Celtic objects from Anglo-Saxon graves: a catalogue and an interpretation of their use*, British Archaeological Reports (British Series) 191, Oxford

White, W J 1988, *Skeletal Remains from the Cemetery of St Nicholas Shambles City of London*, London and Middlesex Archaeological Society, London

Whitehead, R 1996, *Buckles 1250–1800*, Chelmsford

Whiteman, J A and Okafor, E E 2003, 'Characterization of Nigerian bloomery iron smelting slags', *Historical Metallurgy* 37 (2) 71–84

Whiting, W 1929, 'Jutish cemetery near Faversham, Kent', *Archaeologia Cantiana* xli, 115–25

Wieczorek, A 1987, 'Die frühmerowingischen Phasen des Gräberfeldes von Rübenach', *Berichte der Römisch-Germanischen Kommission* 68, 353–492

Wieczorek, A, Périn, P, Welck, K von and Menghin W (eds) 1996, *Die Franken, Wegbereiter Europas*, Ausstellung Reiss Museum, Mannheim

Wild, J P 1968, 'Clothing in the north-west provinces of the Roman empire', *Bonner Jahrbuch* 168, 166–240

Wilkinson, D R P 1994, 'Excavations on the White Cliffs Experience Site, Dover 1988–91', *Archaeologia Cantiana* cxiv, 51–148

Williams, J H (ed) 2007, *The Archaeology of Kent to AD 800*, Kent County Council

Williams, H 1997, 'Ancient landscapes and the dead: The reuse of prehistoric and Roman monuments as early Anglo-Saxon burial sites, *Medieval Archaeology* 41, 1–131

Williams, H 1998, 'Monuments and the past in early Anglo-Saxon England', *World Archaeology* Vol 30, No 1, The Past in the Past: The Reuse of Ancient Monuments (June), 90–108

Williams, P W 1983, *An Anglo-Saxon Cemetery at Thurmaston, Leicestershire,* Leicestershire Museums, Art Galleries and Records Series Archaeology Report 8, Leicester

Williams, L and Warwick, R (eds) 1980, *Gray's Anatomy,* 36th edition, Edinburgh

Williams, S A and Curzon, M E J 1985, 'Dental caries in a Scottish medieval child population', *Caries Research* 19, 162 (abstract)

Willson, J 1987, 'A Saxon button-brooch from Dover', *Kent Archaeological Review* 87, 154

Willson, J 1988, 'Saxon burials from Priory Hill, Dover', *Kent Archaeological Review* 94, 81–92

Wilson, D M 1956, 'The initial excavation of an Anglo-Saxon cemetery at Melbourn, Cambridgeshire', *Proceedings of the Cambridge Antiquarian Society* xlix, 29–41

Wilson, D M 1992, *Anglo-Saxon Paganism*, London, New York

Wilson, J E, McCormac, F G and Hogg, A G 1995, 'Small sample high-precision ^{14}C dating: characterisation of vials and counter optimisation' in G T Cook, D D Harkness, A B MacKenzie, B F Miller and E M Scott (eds), *Liquid Scintillation Spectrometry 1994,* Tuscon, Arizona (Radiocarbon), 59–65

Wilson, K 1987, 'The wooden belt from grave 20' in V I Evison, 196–7

Wilson, M 1995, 'East of Marlowe Theatre' in K Blockley *et al*, 827–9

Windler R 1989, 'Ein frühmittelalterliches Männergrab aus Elgg (ZH)', Jahrbuch der Schweizerischen Gesellschaft für Ur- und Frühgeschichte 72, 181–200

Windler, R, Rast-Eicher, A and Mannering, U 1995, 'Nessel und Flachs – Textilefunde aus einem frühmittelalterlichen Mädchengrab in Flurlingen (Kanton Zürich), *Archäologie der Schweiz* 18, 155–61

Ypey, J 1982–3, 'Damaszierung' in H Beck *et al* (eds), 191–293

Zazoff, P (ed) 1975, *Antike Gemmen in Deutschen Sammlungen, Band IV, Hannover, Kestner-Museum, Hamburg, Museum für Kunst und Gewerbe*, Wiesbaden

Zeller, G 1996, 'Tracht der Frauen' in A Wieczorek, P Périn, K von Welck and W Menghin, *Die Franken: Wegbereiter Europas (5 bis 8 Jahrhundert n Chr)* von Zabern, vol 2, Mainz, 672–83

Zwierlein-Diehl, E 1969, *Antike Gemmen in Deutschen Sammlungen, Band II, Staatlich Museen Preußischer Kulturbesitz, Antikenabteilung, Berlin*, Munich

Zwierlein-Diehl, E 1973, *Die antiken Gemmen des Kunsthistorisches museums in Wien, Bd I, Die gemmen von der minoischen Zeit bis zur frühen römischen Kaiserzeit*, Munich

Zwierlein-Diehl, E 1986, *Glaspasten im Martin-von-Wagner-Museum der Universität Würzberg*, Munich

INDEX